Introduction

Roadbook Europe travels the fascinating and delightful routes of thirty five European countries, from Ireland in the west to the Caucasus in the east and from Sicily to the North Cape of Norway.

Rune Lagerqvist's experience of European travel, as the Swedish Touring Club's map and guidebook editor, has given him a unique knowledge of the Continent and motoring through it.

Country by country, the author takes you along its major routes, and with hand-drawn maps, pictures and information, helps you explore the villages, towns and beauty spots along the way, as well as those worth a detour. Special features – with colour town plans – are made of the larger and more interesting towns and cities. Knowledge gained over thirty years of travel writing is reflected in the introduction to each country, which describes the hotels, food and wine, the shopping, the people and their history.

The "before starting out" tour tips to help plan a journey and a twenty eight page road atlas of Europe, compiled by the Continent's major motoring clubs, complete this all-in-one guidebook to the pleasures of motoring in Europe.

AA

Roadbook Europe

RUNE LAGERQVIST

Contents

Translated by Richard B. Lane

Produced by Forum Publishers, Stockholm, Sweden, in co-operation with the Swedish Touring Club and the Automobile Association, England.

© Rune Lagerqvist 1984
© Forum Publishers Sweden
© Automobile Association 58052 English language edition worldwide

Cover photo (Hochalpenstrasse, Austria) Björn Nordien/Tiofoto
Cover design Paul Eklund

Most of the illustrations have been supplied by the Stockholm tourist offices of the countries included. Additional illustrations from the Automobile Association Picture Library, Icelandair, the Soviet Press Agency and the Swedish Tourist Council. Title page photo (Trollstigen, Norway) Kim Hart, p 295 Bo Dahlin/Bildhuset, p 315, 316 Mittet Foto A/S, p 356 Jan Rietz/Tiofoto.

© Map of Europe p 450-477 Servizio Cartografico del Touring Club Italiano, Milano.

The contents of this book are believed correct at the time of printing. Nevertheless, the Publisher cannot accept any responsibility for errors or omissions, or for changes in details given.

Typesetting Bokstaven/Reklam-Montage. Reproduction Offset-Kopio
Printed in Italy 1984 by New Interlitho SPA, Milano

ISBN 0 86145 169 4

Published by the Automobile Association, Fanum House, Basingstoke, Hampshire RG 21 2EA

The countries of Europe

The spelling of each place name has been determined by the country's own name of the locality. Sometimes the English name has been written in parentheses, e.g. FIRENZE (FLORENCE). This name form is also used in the text.
In some cases several name forms are given. This is meant to be of assistance when several names are found for the same community are found on direction signs, e.g. AACHEN (AKEN, AIX-LA-CHAPELLE).
In bi-lingual countries both names are given if they are officially recognized. e.g. HELSINKI/HELSINGFORS, BRUXELLES/BRUSSEL, BIEL/BIEN. If we have written MONS (Bergen), PORI (Björneborg), GENÈVE (Genf) the first name is the official one.
In countries that use the Cyrillic alphabet the English transcriptions of the names are given, e.g. Ushgorod and Chernovtsy. However, the spellings in the key map at the end of the book are those that are most common in maps from Continental publishers: Užgorod and Černovcy.
The road maps in this book do not have a common scale.

Legend to route maps

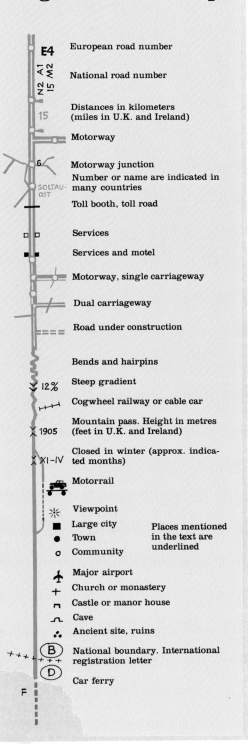

E4   European road number

N2 A1 / 15 M2   National road number

15   Distances in kilometers (miles in U.K. and Ireland)

Motorway

6   Motorway junction
Number or name are indicated in many countries
SOLTAU-OST

Toll booth, toll road

□ □   Services

■ ■   Services and motel

Motorway, single carriageway

Dual carriageway

Road under construction

Bends and hairpins

12%   Steep gradient

Cogwheel railway or cable car

1905   Mountain pass. Height in metres (feet in U.K. and Ireland)

XI–IV   Closed in winter (approx. indicated months)

Motorrail

Viewpoint

■   Large city

●   Town   Places mentioned in the text are underlined

○   Community

Major airport

Church or monastery

Castle or manor house

Cave

Ancient site, ruins

Ⓑ Ⓓ   National boundary. International registration letter

Car ferry

F

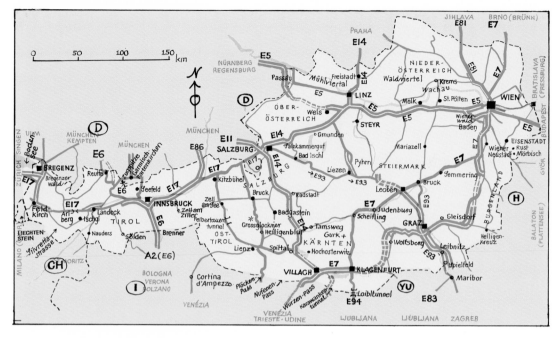

A · Austria

A·Österreich

Area: 83 850 km² (32 373 sq. miles).

Population: 7.5 million. 98 % of the population are German-speaking Austrians. 89 % of the population are Roman Catholics.

Major cities: Wien (Vienna) 1.6 million, Graz 250 000, Linz 207 000, Salzburg 139 000, Innsbruck 123 000, Klagenfurt 85 000, Wels 47 000, St. Polten 43 000, Steyr 42 000.

Government: Federal republic, made up of Wien (Vienna) and eight autonomous states (state capitals in parentheses): Voralberg (Bregenz). Tirol/Tyrol (Innsbruck), Salzburg (Salzburg), Steiermark/Styria (Graz), Oberösterreich/Upper Austria (Linz), Kärnten/Carinthia (Klagenfurt), Burgenland (Eisenstadt) and Niederösterreich/Lower Austria (Wien). There are two houses of parliament: Nationalrat and Bundesrat.

History:

976 The Emperor appoints a member of the House of Babenberger as Margrave of the eastern province of the Holy Roman Empire with the intention that this will protect the Empire from eastern invasion. The capital is Melk.

1270 The House of Habsburg become rulers of Austria and reign until 1918.

1493-1519 Reign of Maximilian I. His dynastic marriages bring him power over Franche-Compté (the area near Besançon in the county of Burgundy) and Flanders. His son acquires Spain through marriage and in turn, his son, Charles V, becomes "Emperor of the Holy Roman Empire of the German Nation" – and the ruler of Europe's mightiest realm. As the saying goes: "Let the others wage war – you, happy Austria, marry."

1529 The Turks lay siege to Vienna.

1683 The Turks are finally defeated in the Battle of Kahlenberg.

1740-1780 Austria flourishes under the rule of Maria Theresa.

1805-1813 Napoleonic Wars. Austria defeated.

1814-1815 The Congress of Vienna establishes new national boundaries in Europe.

1832 The Sachertorte is invented.

1848 Nationalistic uprisings are supressed in Prague, northern Italy and Hungary. March Revolution in Vienna.

1848-1916 Reign of Franz Josef.

1866 With the Battle of Königgrätz, Austria loses her position of superiority in the German states.

1867 Austro-Hungarian dual monarchy is established.

1914 Franz Ferdinand, heir to the throne, and his wife are assassinated in Sarajevo. The First World War breaks out.

1918 The defeated dual monarchy is dismantled. A republic is established in 1919.

1934 Civil war. Heavy fighting in Linz, Steyr and Vienna, the workers defeated by the forces of Chancellor Dollfuss' rightist dictatorship. Nazis murder Dollfuss.

1936 Hitler recognizes Austria's sovereignty.

1938 Hitler annexes Austria, the "Anschluss".

1939 The Second World War begins.

1945 The Russians occupy Vienna which is then divided between the Soviets, the Americans, the British and the French.

1955 Ratification of the peace treaty

Routes described:

E 5   Passau – Linz – Wien – Nickelsdorf

E 6   Garmisch – Innsbruck – Brenner

E 7   Drasenhofen – Wien – Klagenfurt – Villach – Tarvisio

E 14 Wullowitz – Linz – Salzburg – Villach – Tarvisio

E 17 Salzburg – Innsbruck – Arlberg – Bregenz

E 84 Klein Haugsdorf – Wien, see E 7

E 93 and A9 Salzburg – Graz – Maribor

Grossglockner Hochalpenstrasse and Felbertauernstrasse

Town plans: Graz, Innsbruck, Salzburg, Wien

makes Austria an independent neutral state.
1960 Austria becomes a member of the EFTA.

Currency: Austrian schillings (ATS). 1 schilling = 100 groschen

Business hours: Banks 8.00 a.m.–12.30 and 1.30–3 pm. Thursdays open till 5.30 p.m. Closed Saturdays. Post offices usually 8.00 a.m.–12.00 noon and 2.00 p.m.–6.00 p.m. Closed Saturdays. Shops 8.00 a.m.–6.00 p.m. Often closed at lunchtime. Saturdays open to 12.00 noon.

Holidays: New Year's Day, January 6, Easter Sunday, Easter Monday, May 1, Ascension Day, Whit Sunday, Whit Monday, Corpus Christi Day, August 15 (Assumption Day), October 26, November 1 (All Saints' Day), December 8, December 25 and 26.

Hotels

In smaller cities and in the country you can get good value in a Gasthof or a Gaststätte. Breakfast, which is generally included in the room price, is usually simple: coffee, two rolls, butter and jam. Lunch (Mittagessen) is served between 12 and 2, dinner (Abendessen) between 6 and 9. Many establishments have a "durchgehend warme Kuche" – hot prepared meals being available throughout the day. "Jausen", afternoon coffee, is served between 4 and 5. Austria has over 90 spas and climatic health resorts providing water and air cures. There are casinos in Vienna, Baden bei Wien, Bad Gastein, Bregenz, Kitzbühel, Kleinwalsertal, Salzburg, Seefeld, and Velden.

Camping

There are 400 camping sites. Most of them will charge a reduced fee if you present an AIT camping carnet.

Youth hostels

There are about 100 hostels. Motorists are accepted, but hikers and cyclists under 30 are given priority. Österreichischer Jugendherbergring, Schottenring 28, A-1010 Wien.

Food and drink

Austrian cooking is a combination of Eastern and Western European cuisines. Soups are popular. They are often rich and filling. Leberknödelsuppe is meat broth containing leverfilled dumplings. Serbian bean soup is heavily spiced.

Veal Cordon Bleu, i.e. cheese and ham rolled in a thin piece of veal and fried, is a favoured speciality.

Spanferkel is roast suckling pig: Wildschweinbraten is roast boar. Game is popular, especially during the autumn. Zwiebelrostbraten, thin slices of fried beef topped with onion rings, can be a memorable culinary experience. Backhendl, breaded and fried young chicken. Forelle blau is rainbow trout boiled in a court bouillion, as opposed to Forelle gelb, which is fried trout. Knödel are dumplings with sometimes surprising fillings. They often take the place of potatoes. Tafelspitz is boiled beef and Bauernschmaus is a hearty concoction of beef, dumplings, smoked ham and sauerkraut. Sometimes you can choose one of three portions of this substantial dish: "for a knight", "for a peasant" and "for a boy". But remember that even boys eat a lot in Austria. Desserts are important. Palatschinken are thin pancakes rolled around a sweet stuffing. Kaiserschmarren are shredded pancakes mixed and served with jam. Salzburger Nockerl is a soufflé. You can even have the beloved Knödel (dumplings) as a dessert – Marillenknödel have an apricot filling. The best known of all pastries,

The Tennengebirge along the E14 south of Salzburg

Apfelstrudel, is best when served warm. A vast selection of torte may be had as either a dessert or as an accompaniment to "Jausen", the afternoon coffee. Linzertorte is an almond cake with a jam filling. Sachertorte is a chocolate cake with an apricot jam filling. It is iced with additional chocolate (see Vienna). Often Schlag, i.e. whipped cream, accompanies the torte.

There are many varieties of coffee: Grosser Brauner is a large cup of coffee with a little milk. Kleiner Brauner is a small cup of the same combination. A Mokka is similar to espresso and a Schwarzer is even stronger. Kapuziner is also strong, while a Melange is half coffee and half milk. Einspänner is black coffee with one small portion of whipped cream. By the way, Einspänner is also the word for both hot dog and one-horse carriage. So be careful when ordering! Mineral water and Apfelsaft (apple juice) are favourite non-alcoholic beverages. Austrian beer is good, and the country produces such red wines as Vöslauer and Klosterneuburger. White wines, however, are perhaps more popular than the reds. Among the best known whites are Dürnsteiner, Gumpoldskirchner, Nussdorfer, Riesling, and Veltliner. Marillenweinbrand is an apricot brandy.

Shopping

Augarten porcelain, ceramics, wood carving, petit point.

Sachertorte packed for shipping can be bought at the Sacher shop in Vienna. Skis and other winter sports equipment can be worthwhile.

Speed limits. Traffic regulations

Autobahn (motorway) 130 kmh, with caravan 100 kmh, other roads 100 kmh, with caravan 80 kmh, built-up areas 50 kmh.

Smaller caravans that do not exceed a weight of 750 kg may be driven at a maximum speed of 100 kmh on secondary roads.

Roadsigns that state the name of a town or community also indicate the beginning of the built-up area (speed limit area). A sign with the text "Ortsende von" signals the end of the built-up area.

Children under the age of 12 are not allowed to travel in the front seat. An exception is made when an infant is seated in a special (rear-facing) baby seat.

If your car is fitted with seat belts it is compulsory to wear them. The car must be equipped with a first-aid box. Studded tyres are permitted during the period November 1–April 30. Minimum tread depth on all tyres: 1.6 mm.

Motorcycles and mopeds must have dipped headlights even during the daylight hours.

On Alpine roads, cars driving upwards always have the right-of-way.

Hitchhikers in Styria, Upper Austria and Vorarlberg must be at least 16

The Spanish Riding School in Vienna

years old. Female hitchhikers in Vorarlberg must be at least 18 years old.

Roads

Motorways have blue number signs, an "A" and the number. "S" indicates a Schnellstrasse (primary route). These also have special numbers. Other major roads (Bundesstrassen), with the right-of-way, have blue signs, while secondary roads, without the right-of-way, have yellow signs.

A road changes number when it becomes an Autobahn (motorway) or a Schnellstrasse (primary route). This can occur on short sections. Sometimes, rather than a number, the name of the community is indicated, and at other times, the name of the motorway or primary route is on the signs. A traffic sign may suddenly announce "Pyhrnautobahn" or "Westautobahn" or "Pinzgauer Strasse".

Some of the major routes are toll roads. This is true of the Grossglockner/Hochalpenstrasse, (toll 220 As), Felbertauernstrasse (toll 180 As), Brennerautobahn (toll 120 As), Tauernautobahn (toll 180 As). Many of the minor roads leading to beauty spots or places of particular interest are "Mautstrassen" = toll roads. As a rule, the roads are good. But even primary and major routes can be rather narrow and curves can be frequent. Heavy lorry traffic on the more impor-

tant routes can reduce speeds.

Alpine roads can be unnerving if you are not accustomed to mountain driving. Always try to avoid mountain driving when it is raining or when it is dark. Gradients are seldom excessive and hairpin bends can usually be easily negotiated. Precipitous sides are rarely if ever, totally unguarded; on the older roads stone pillars are placed at close intervals.

But, in general, the Alpine roads are in good condition and easily driven.

Road patrols

ÖAMTC road patrols operate 7 a.m.–7 p.m. on the West Motorway, the South Motorway, Grossglockner, Radstädter, Tauern, Katschberg, Arlberg, Flexenstrasse.

SOS telephones are placed along the motorways.

Breakdown-service is provided by the local service centres.

ÖAMTC (Österreichischer Automobil-, Motorrad- und Touring Club), 3 Schubertring, A-1010 Wien 1. Tel. 0222-729 90.

Austrian National Tourist office, 30 St George Street, London W1R 9FA. Tel. 01-629 0461.

E 5. Passau – Linz – Wien – Nickelsdorf

E 5 comes from London – Harwich – Ostende – Köln – Frankfurt – Nürnberg. This route follows the **Danube (Donau)**, Europe's longest river, 2 888 km from its source in Donaueschingen (southern Germany) to the Black Sea. North of the river is the beautiful Mühlviertel, see E 14.

LINZ, see E 14.

St. Florian. Baroque shrine-church. Anton Bruckner's organ and grave. Augustine abbey. Paintings by Albrecht Altdorfer (d. 1538).

Amstetten (12 000). St. Stephan's Church. The Kilian Fountain dates from 1644. Plague column.

STEYR (45 000) in an iron-ore district. Medieval and early-Renaissance Old Town in the centre of the city. Rococo town hall. Bummerlhaus, a Gothic private house. Dunkelhof with arcades. Stadtpfarrkirche and Dominikanerkirche. City Museum with Steyrer Krippel, a puppet theatre which gives performances only at Christmastime. During the 1920s and 1930s, "Steyr" was the name of a brand of well-known motorcars. Now the Steyr-Daimler-Puch concern manufacture lorries and mopeds.
A narrow-gauge railway runs through the Steyer Valley.

Ybbs was founded by the Romans. Remains of the original city wall and castle. Ybbs-Persenburg power station. From Ybbs you can drive north towards the rolling hills of Waldviertel. Extensive forests and winding roads. *Isperklamm* with a 300 m deep gorge.

Melk. The famous abbey, rising above this small town's solid houses, is one of the world's most beautiful Baroque buildings. 362 m long façade. Here the princes of the House of Babenberger established their residence in 984. It was given to the Benedictines in the 12th cent. Its present form dates from the 18th cent. In 1805 and 1809, Napoleon had his headquarters here. The abbey is open to the public and is one of Austria's major tourist attractions. The splendid church, with an interior dominated by masses of red marble and gold, has ceiling paintings and a 65 m high dome.

Schallaburg. Large Renaissance palace. Arcaded courtyard with beautiful terra-cotta friezes. Exhibitions. Major tourist attraction. Restaurant.

ST. PÖLTEN (41 000). Originally a Roman settlement. Superb Baroque houses. Cathedral with a 77 m high tower. Gothic town hall with octagonal tower.

Wienerwald. Large and beautiful area with wooded hills. A landscape that inspired Beethoven, Schubert and Strauss. Rolling vineyard-covered hills and wine-producing villages. Old, charming small towns.

From Ybbs or Melk, you can take the route through **Wachau**, one of Austria's loveliest areas. The Danube flows through a landscape of woods, cliffs, impressive heights and vineyards. Many castles crown the cliffs.

Willendorf. In 1908, a 25 000-year-old, 10 cm high chalk fertility goddess was discovered here. It is known as the *Venus from Willendorf* and is now in Vienna's Museum of Natural History.

Aggstein. The ruins of the castle are on a cliff, 300 m above the Danube. The castle was destroyed by the Turks in 1529.

Dürrnstein. Small city bearing the stamp of the Middle Ages. Fine riverside promenade. Richard the Lionheart was held prisoner after the Third Crusade (1192) in the castle (now in ruins). He heard his troubadour, Blondel, playing outside the walls, announced his presence, and was eventually ransomed. Inns are named after both "Löwenherz" and "Blondel".

Krems (24 000). Beautiful old houses, among them the exquisitely painted Passauerhof. *Wine museum* in the old Dominican abbey. There are lovely houses also in the suburb of Stein where you can visit the *Minoritetenkirche* (13th cent.), now a picture gallery with works by Martin Johann Schmidt (d. 1801) who is known as Kremser Schmidt. It was in Krems in 1130 that the first Austrian coins, the "Kremser Pfenning", were minted. Krems, Rust and Salzburg were Austria's choices during the European Architectural Heritage Year (1975).

Klosterneuburg, (Vienna), see E 7.

WIEN (Vienna), see town plans. *Schwechat.* Vienna's airport. Brewery. The countryside east of Vienna resembles the Hungarian puszta, but it is dotted with small oil rigs and giant oil refineries. Austria has large reserves of oil and natural gas and is able to fill a large part of her energy requirements.

Bruck resembles a Hungarian village with long rows of farms lining the main road. Baroque palace in lovely park.
The road goes through *Burgenland* which got its name from the many castles that were built here, in the border zone.

Neusiedler See, 320 km², Central Europe's only steppe lake. 36 km long, 4-12 km wide and about 1.5 m deep. Rich vegetation and bird life. The southern banks of the lake are part of Hungary.

Neusiedl, like most of the communities bordering the lake, has a little beach. Roman-built observation tower. Lake museum.

Petronell-Carnuntum has remnants from a pre-Roman settlement on the old Amber Route. It eventually became a Roman garrison, and was destroyed by Teutonic warriors in A.D. 400. Remains of a Roman amphitheatre with room for 8 000 spectators. Open-air museum in the castle. The park contains a new amphitheatre with room for 13 000 spectators.

Deutsch-Altenburg. Spa. Museum of African art in the 17th-cent. Ludwigstorff palace. Carnuntinum Museum with Roman finds.

Nickelsdorf, Austrian frontier post. E 5 continues via Budapest – Beograd – Sofia – Istanbul – Ankara – Antakya to the Syrian border.

Matzen Castle in a district of vineyards and oil rigs. Large wine cellar. Exhibitions from Vienna's Museum für Volkskunde (Ethnological Museum). **Gänserndorf.** Safari Park with a collection of more than 500 exotic animals.

Deutsch-Wagram, where Napoleon defeated the Austrian armies in 1809. Napoleon room in the local folklore museum. In 1867 Austria's first steam-drawn train travelled from here to the Spitz in Vienna-Floridsdorf.

E 6. Garmisch – Innsbruck – Brenner

Griessen, German frontier. E 6 starts from Nordkjosbotn (Tromsö) continuing via Narvik – Trondheim – Oslo – Göteborg – Trelleborg – Sassnitz – Berlin – München. E 6 follows the beautiful, but partially inferior, route through the Fern Pass. This has been a major trade route since the 15th cent. when it linked Augsburg and Venice. At present the routing from Garmisch to Innsbruck is via Mittenwald. The best route between Munich and Innsbruck is the autobahn (motorway) that goes via Kufstein. The shortest and most beautiful route goes through the Achenpass.

Lermoos. Winter resort with fine views of the Zugspitze.

The route from Lermoos to Reutte goes past **Ehrenberger Klause,** a 16th-cent. fortress that was destroyed by Napoleon's troops. **Reutte** is a tourist centre with many splendidly painted houses.

Ehrwald. Resort 10 km from the **Tiroler Zugspitzbahn,** a cable car that in 30 minutes takes the traveller up to Zugspitzkamm, 2 805 m above sea level. Extensive views. The line goes further to **Zugspitzgipfel,** 2 966 m. For further information on **Zugspitze,** see Germany E 6.

Fernpass (1 209 m). From a parking area 1 km north of the pass there are fine views of the Wetterstein mountains. A tower is all that remains of Fernstein Castle. The ruins of Sigmundsburg Castle lie on an island in the little Fernstein Lake. After the small resort of Nassereith the road climbs sharply to Holzleitensattel, 1 126 m.

Stams Abbey, see E 17. **INNSBRUCK,** see town plans.

Alternative route from Garmisch to Innsbruck via Mittenwald:

Scharnitz, frontier post. Ruins of Porta Claudia, a Roman fort.

Seefeld (2 000). One of Austria's major winter resorts. Cable car to Seefelderjoch, 2 054 m. Beautiful church dedicated to St. Oswald, an English missionary.

The road over Zirlerberg is straight and has a 19 % gradient. It is frighteningly steep. In the middle of the incline is a curve. Try to stop there as it provides a fine view and there is an excellent Gaststätte, 817 m above sea level. The road from Seefeld to Telfs is steep, narrow and winding.

Brennerstrasse, one of the oldest of the Alpine routes, used as early as the Roman period. Now a magnificent example of highway engineering, a memorable driving experience. In the Austrian sector there are 42 bridges.

Europabrücke, 820 m long and rising 190 m above the valley. Bergisel Tunnel at Innsbruck is 470 m long. The steepest climb is 6 %. Tolls.

Igls. Spa and winter resort. Now a part of Innsbruck. Cable car to Patscherkofel, 2 247 m. **Ellbögener Strasse** was used for salt transport. It is winding and steep but provides lovely views.

Stubaital is quiet and peaceful when compared to Silltal which is on the autobahn. Numerous small resorts: **Mieders, Fulpmes** (where mountaineering equipment is manufactured) and **Neustift** (where it is used).

The Brenner Pass (Passo di Brennero) is open all year. Heavy holiday and lorry traffic may cause queues at customs stations. E 6 continues to Bolzano (Bozen) – Trento – Verona – Bologna – Firenze – Roma.

E7. Drasenhofen– Wien – Klagenfurt – Villach – Tarvisio

Drasenhofen. Czechoslovakian border. E7 comes from Warszawa – Krakow – Brno.

Weinviertel (The Wine District) was named after the large vineyards in Lower Austria. Gaeras nature reserve.

Klosterneuburg (25 000). The abbey was founded in the 11th cent. The present building, dating from 1730, is quite large but Emperor Charles VI had planned that it should be four times its present size. The famous **Verduner Altar** by Niklaus von Verdun (1181) in the Leopold Chapel is an enamelled work depicting scenes from the life of Jesus.
Beautiful roads lead westward, traversing the *Leiser Berge* nature preserve. *Deutsch-Wagram* and *Matzen*, see E5.

WIEN (Vienna), see town plans.

Laxenburg. Nature reserve and gardens surrounding the romantic little Franzenburg, an imperial residence.

Baden bei Wien (30 000). Elegant spa in use as early as the Roman period. 16 sulphuric thermal baths with 36°C water temperature. Beautiful Kurpark. Casino. Trams (local trains) make the 26 km journey through the wine villages to the Opernplatz in the heart of Vienna in about an hour. The trip can be made in shorter time by bus or main line train.

Wienerwald, a large rolling wooded area with lovely valleys, vineyards. Idyllic towns and villages such as Mödling, Perchtoldsdorf, and Gumpoldskirchen. A landscape that inspired Beethoven, Schubert and Strauss. Sporach nature reserve with ruins of Johannstein fortress.

Helenental is one of the most beautiful valleys in the Wienerwald.

Heiligenkreuz, a Cisterician abbey founded in 1135, was destroyed by the Turks and then rebuilt in the Baroque style. Beautiful church and abbey gardens. The village of **Mayerling** was the scene of the Drama of Mayerling in which Emperor Franz Josef's only son, the Archduke Rudolf, successor to the throne, committed suicide together with his mistress, Maria Vetsera. The section of the hunting lodge in which the tragedy took place was razed on the orders of the emperor and a chapel put up in its place. The events surrounding the deaths are still clouded in mystery.

WIENER NEUSTADT (50 000), founded by the Princes of Babenberger in 1192. Their fortress still stands and Emperor Maximilian I is buried in its Georgskapelle (1519). His tomb is huge and well worth seeing – but it is in Innsbruck.

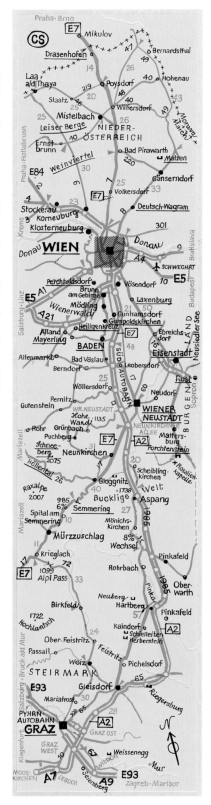

Eisenstadt (10 000). Capital of Burgenland. *Esterhazy Palace* (1672), a work of the Italian architect Carlone, is where Josef Haydn (1732-1809) was conductor and composer in service of the Esterhazy family. The palace ballroom is called the Haydn-Saal. It was in Eisenstadt that Haydn composed "The Seasons". Haydn's home is now a museum and his tomb is in Bergkirche on Kalvarienberg. *Burgenländisches Landesmuseum* (The Burgenland Folklore Museum) is located in the old ghetto, which, as late as 1938, was locked up on the sabbath.

Rust. Small town, wine centre. Almost every rooftop in the town has a frame that supports a stork's nest. Most of the nests are occupied. Unique architecture and views; carved doorways, picturesque courtyards and arcades, all contributed towards Rust's being chosen as a project city during the European Architectural Heritage Year 1975.

Mörbisch, close to the Hungarian frontier. Quaint town. White houses with flower-filled window boxes. Yellow husks of maize on the walls.
Burg Forchtenstein. Medieval fortress perched on a cliff. Enlarged during th 17th cent. by Prince Esterhazy. Armoury.

Gloggnitz (10 000). Tourist resort. The beautiful, deep *Höllental* (Hell Valley) leads up to Schneeberg, Puchberg and Reichenau. Schwarzau in Gebirge nature reserve.

Semmering. Large mountain resort (985 m above sea level). The Semmering railway line (1854) was Europe's first railway in a mountainous terrain.

Road 20, Aflenzer Seebergstrasse, goes from Kapfenberg past the ruins of Schachenstein Castle to the tourist resort of **Aflenz.** 20 % climb to the pass level (1 254 m). On to **Mariazell** where there is a large *shrine-church* (1709) in Gothic and Baroque, a work of Domenico Sciassia. The "Gnadenkapelle" with its simple wooden statue of the Virgin Mary is in the centre of the church. The statue, always decorated with flowers and gifts, is placed under a silver canopy that is supported by 12 pillars. Lavish treasury. Tomb of cardinal Josef Mindzenty (d. 1975). He spent 15 years in asylum in the American Embassy in Budapest.

Bruck a/d Mur (17 000). Traffic junction. Industrial town. Kornmesserhaus, a 15th-cent. dwelling built by the burgher Pankraz Kornmess, is on Hauptplatz. Exquisitely sculpted arcades and loggia. A text outside the house points out that, at times of war, the building is under international protection. The warning is in German, English, French and Russian. The Austrians are used to the ravages of war. Previously the notice would have needed a Turkish language warning too. The Eisener Brunnen is also in the square. It is a magnificent example of 17th-cent. wrought-iron work. Pfarrkirche with a beautiful door leading to the sacristy. A steep flight of stairs leads up to the Landskron fortress.

LEOBEN (40 000). Industrial town with mining engineering college. Town hall with five-sided tower (16th-cent). **Göss,** suburb with large brewery.

Österreich-Ring, motor racing track 6 km, average speed 200 kmh.

Judenburg (10 000) was a settlement inhabited by Jewish merchants as early as the 11th cent. Beautiful arcades and houses near the 16th-cent. town tower. 15th-cent. church.

St. Lambrecht. Benedictine abbey founded in the 12th cent. This huge construction was built in the 17th-cent. to the plans of Domenico Sciassia, the Mariazell architect. 126 m long gallery.

Friesach. Small town with partially preserved town wall, moats, three castles and six old cultures. As early as the 13th cent. the road from Vienna to Venice ran through this town and it was at this period that the Dominicans built their abbey and church.

Gurk with its enormous Romanesque cathedral was a bishopric until 1787. The abbey was founded in the 11th cent. The church was consecrated about 1200. Large 17th cent. altar with 72 statues and 82 angels' heads.

St. Veit an der Glan (15 000). Residence of the Dukes of Carinthia until 1518. Industrial town. Medieval buildings round Hauptplatz. Plague column and fountain with water receptacle said to have come from the Forum in the ancient Roman town of Virunum.

Burg Hochosterwitz. Castle perched on a 160 m high chalk cliff, reached by a winding lane with 14 tower gates. Walt Disney gathered inspiration here before making his "Snow White" film. Large armoury. The castle has been owned by the Khevenhüller family since 1571.

Maria-Saal. Large 15th-cent. shrine-church with ramparts, a necessity when this was a Christian outpost facing Magyars and Turks. Roman reliefs on the south wall depict a Roman post coach. Virunum, capital of the Roman province of Noricum, was near by.

Ossiacher See is beautiful and peaceful compared with the hectic tourist activity in and about Wörther See. Lovely church and abbey in Ossiach.

KLAGENFURT (85 000). Capital of Carinthia (Kärnten). Wide avenues and spacious squares contrast with ancient buildings and narrow alleys. Baroque houses on Alter Platz. *Landesmuseum,* exhibitions of art and technology. A 7 m long relief of the Grossglockner Range. Outdoor exhibitions of Roman antiquities. *Minimindus.* Park with miniature town similar to Madurodam on the Hague. Nature reserve with animals and hunting museum at *Kätner-Jägerhof.*

Wörthersee, 17 km long lake. Summer water temperature: 24-28° C. Numerous large resorts: **Velden** (with casino) and **Pörtschach** are the most fashionable. Perhaps the most beautiful place is at the shrine-church of *Maria-Wörth.* Good road up to the observation tower on Pyramidenkoge. *Wildpark Rosegg,* wildlife park.

VILLACH (34 000). Industrial town and railway junction. High Street lined with beautiful houses. Gothic church with frescoes depicting the legend of St. Christopher. Large relief map of Carinthia in the Schiller Park. Panoramic road goes from Villacher Warmbad (hot springs) to the *Alpine Gardens* (1 005 m above sea level) with 500 species of mountain flowers.

Unterhörl. Italian border. E 7 continues to Tarvisio – Udine – Mestre (Venezia) – Padua – Bologna – Cesena – Perugia – Roma.

Alternative route Wien – Klagenfurt via Graz:

Riegersburg. The fortress was built in the 13th cent. on a 200 m high basalt cliff. Often stormed by Magyars and Turks but never surrendered. In 1945 it was defended by the Germans against the Russians.

GRAZ, see town plans.

Piber. Lipizzaner stud farm. Horses bred here for Vienna's Spanish Riding School. Lovely road goes further by way of Stubalpe (Gaberlstrasse) to Judenburg (E 7). The route over the highest section is well constructed, but a shortish stretch on the southern side, which has a 20 % gradient, is winding, very narrow and badly gravelled.

Köflach. Large lignite (brown coal) mines. Good road over **Packsattel** (Vier Tore) past the artificial Packer Lake and Waldenstein Castle to the lovely little town of **Wolfsberg**.

E14. Wullowitz – Linz – Salzburg – Villach – Tarvisio

Wullowitz. Czech border. E 14 comes from Malmö – Swinoujscie – Szczecin – Jelénia Góra – Praha.

E 14 follows the old "Salt Road" from the salt mines in the Alps to Bohemia. It passes through *Mühlviertel and Waldviertel*, two beautiful regions with wooded heights reaching up to 600-700 m – in the Waldviertel up to 1 000 m. Many lovely and idyllic places off the beaten tourist track.

Freistadt. Small town built on a once fortified peak. Charming square. The narrow Schlossgasse with its flower-adorned balconies leads from one corner of the square to Alte Burg. Kefermarkt with St. Wolfgangskirche. Splendid 13 m high carved altar (15th cent.).

LINZ (207 000), capital of Upper Austria. The Federal Republic's third city. Steelworks and other major industries. The heart of Linz' beautiful Old Town is *Hauptplatz*, the main square, with its Dreifaltigkeitssäule, a column erected in 1773 in thanksgiving for deliverance from the plague. Martinskirche, built during the reign of Charlemagne in the 8th cent., is Austria's oldest church. Alter Dom, where Anton Bruckner was the organist. Neuer Dom, with a 130 m tower. Landesmuseum. 15th-cent. castle. Beautiful views from *Pöstlingberg*.

St. Florian. Baroque shrine-church. Anton Bruckner's organ and grave. Augustine abbey. Paintings by Albrecht Altdorfer (d. 1538).

WELS (47 000). Roman town. 1216 seat of the local prince. Industrial town. Internationl agricultural fair in even-numbered years; odd-numbered years the "Gastliches Österreich" tourism and travel fair. Beautiful Stadtplatz with flower-covered fountain and Baroque town hall. Lederer Tower. Beautiful windows in Stadtpfarrkirche St. Johann. Hans Sachs, inspiration for Wagner's "Meistersinger von Nürnberg", had his music school in Schloss Polheim. Emperor Maximilian I died 1519 in Kaiserburg.

Kremsmünster. Vast Benedictine abbey founded in the 8th cent. The present buildings are from the 17th and 18th cent. Stiftskirche, richly decorated with frescoes and plaster mouldings. "Kaisersaal" with portraits of the emperors. The *Tassilo Chalice*, beautifully wrought of gilded copper (8th cent.) donated by the founder of the abbey, the Bavarian Duke Tassilo III. Renaissance fountain which has been used as a fish basin. 60 m high mathematical tower with samples of the monks' scientific work.

Lambach was an important station for salt transports from Hallstadt. Large Benedicitine abbey founded in 1056.

Gmunden (12 500). Large resort, beautifully situated. Until 1850 a centre of the salt trade. Lovely old houses. View over the lake towards Traunstein. Orth Castle with 130 m long wooden bridge leading to Seeschloss.

Traunsee. This enchanting lake is 12 km long, up to 3 km wide and 191 m deep. Steamers connect the lakeside resorts.

Bad Ischl (16 000). Spa and resort. Centre of the Salzkammergut. The Lehár Museum and the Imperial villa bring to mind two of the many visitors who helped to spread the fame of Bad Ischl throughout Europe: Franz Lehár, the composer, and Emperor Franz Josef. A visit to the Konditorei Zauner in Pfarrgasse will bring to life Bad Ischl's Imperial past. Brine, mud and sulphur baths. The water's salt content is 27 %. *Salzbergwerk* in Perneck is open for inspection.

Attersee is the largest of Austria's Alpine lakes, 21 km long, 3 km wide and 171 m deep. *Mondsee.* Lively resort. Marktplatz with lovely old houses. Pfarrkirche and Benedictine abbey. Rauchhaus open-air museum. Big "Autobahnstation".

St. Wolfgang. The "Zum weissen Rössl", famed as Benatzky's White Horse Inn, attracts an overflow of tourists. Gothic shrine-church (15th cent.) with High Altar by Michael Pacher. Rack railway to *Schafberg*. The steam paddler Kaiser Franz Josef, plying the lake since 1873, is still in service on the Wolfgangsee.

SALZBURG, see town plans.

Hallein (15 000). Old salt centre. Gristor is one of the remnants of the original town wall. The folklore museum contains exhibits from the great salt mining period, and the original manuscript of "Silent Night".
This immortal Christmas song was composed by the priest Josef Mohr, who wrote the text, and Franz Xaver Gruber, who wrote the music. Gruber later became organist in Hallein Church. His grave and his house are within walking distance of St. Anton Church . Mohr is buried at Wagrein. "Silent Night" was first sung on Christmas morning, 1818, in Oberndorff Church, north of Salzburg. The church itself was destroyed in a flood in 1899. A "Silent Night Chapel" was consecrated in its place in 1937.

Dürrnberg. Here is one of Central Europe's oldest salt mines. Cable car to the summit, mining museum and subterranean lake, return trip by mine train to the valley station.

Gollinger Wasserfall. Magnificent 62 m high waterfalls.

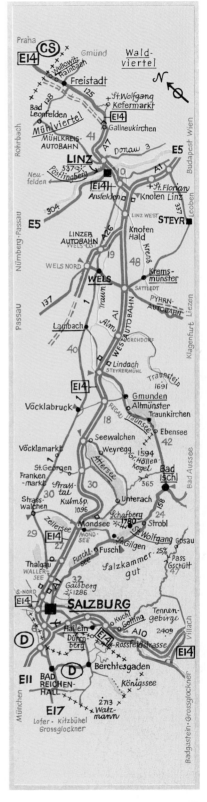

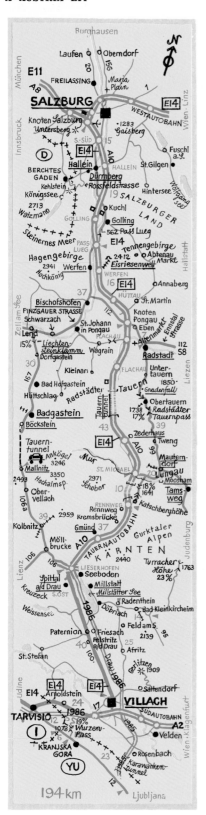

Werfen. Hohenwerfen Fortress was one of Salzburg's most important strongholds. Originally built 1077 and now a youth hostel.

Eisriesenwelt. The world's mightiest ice caverns, 1 656 m above sea level. A total of 50 km long trails lead through 25 m thick ice, built up during the ice age. The walk takes about two hours and warm clothes are a necessity. If you take into consideration the 6 km journey by taxi-bus and the walk back to the cable car, you must expect the return trip from Werfen to take at least four hours. The journey by cable car takes only four minutes.

The Tauern Autobahn passes through the untamed Hohe Tauern Range. Tolls. The *Tauern Tunnel* is 6.4 km long and the *Katschberg Tunnel* is 5.4 m. The highest point is at the southern entrance of the Tauern Tunnel, 1 340 m. The road's maximum gradient is 4.5 %. Inside the tunnels there is a constant 1.5 % gradient. The old road through the pass is narrow, has 317 bends, a 16 % gradient and rises to 1 738 m. Nevertheless, it is still quite busy as it leads to large winter resorts.

Radstadt. Medieval town (1289) with an almost completely preserved town wall and resort. A Roman road went here. There are a couple of Roman milestones along the road directly south of Untertauern.
Steep ascent past the delightful *Gnaden Falls* to the large winter resort of Obertauern just below the level of the pass.

Mauterndorf. Small resort with lovely views of **Lungau**, a mountain valley at an altitude of 1 000 m between Radstädter Tauern and Katschberg. Source of the River Mur. Mauterndorf Castle, originally completed in 1253, fell into ruin after 1809, and was restored in 1894. Lovely chapel.

Moosham. The castle was built in 1256. Known for its witch trials. Restored in the late 19th cent. The owner, Count Wilczek, has installed the *Lungauer Museum* in a number of rooms.

Tamsweg (4 000). Capital of the Lungau. Market town since 1296. Every year on the Sunday following Corpus Christi Day the "Samsonumzug" is celebrated: a 5 m high figure of "Samson", accompanied by two dwarfs, dances through the town. Beautiful Marktplatz. St. Leonard, a shrine-church.
You can return from Moosham by motorway, which takes just a few minutes, through tunnels to Rennweg. Or you can choose to follow the arduous road that within only a few kilometres climbs from 1 068 to 1 641 m with a 16 % gradient. Then it plunges, with a 20 % gradient, towards Rennweg.

Zederhaus. A little village, which, after hundreds of years of isolation in a mountain valley, has become linked to the outside world by the nearby motorway. On June 24 the inhabitants of the village celebrate Midsummer by carrying a maypole (Prangenstang) to the church.

Gmünd. Old town with partially preserved town wall and houses. It defended the old Nürnberg-to-Venice trade route.

Spittal an der Drau (14 000). Although founded during the 12th cent. it did not become a recognized town until 1930. Splendid 16th-cent. houses.

Porcia, owned by the Austrian State, is a Renaissance castle-palace with beautiful arcaded courtyard. Folklore museum. Library. Exhibitions.

The beautiful *Millstätter See* is 11 km long, 1 km wide, and 146 m deep. Many lakeside resorts. The largest of these is **Millstatt** (3 000). Climatic health resort. The abbey was founded in 1080 by the Benedictines. Since then it has also been owned by the Knights of St. George, and the Jesuits. The parish church has a splendid portal.

VILLACH, see E 7.

Karawankentunnel, 14 km long railway line. Passage time 15: minutes. Partially tunnelled from Rosenbach (601 m above sea level) to Jesenice (573 m above sea level) in Yugoslavia. Cars are transported on goods coaches, drivers and occupants in passenger carriages. Places should be booked at least one day in advance.

Bischofshofen. Industries. Beautiful Gothic church. During the summer, "Prangerstangen", flower-adorned maypoles, are carried in processions.

Liechtensteinklamm. 80 m high waterfall in an 1 800 m long gorge in Grossarlerache.

Badgastein (6 500). Large resort and spa with 18 hot springs in the heart of the town. They are directly linked to two large thermal baths. About 100 hotels and pensions with 6 700 beds. Fashionable during the 19th cent. when Franz Josef was a guest. Fine views from the Kaiser Wilhelm-Promenade. *Gasteiner Ache* waterfall.

Cars are put on trains for the 10 min. trip from *Böckstein* (1 131 m above sea level) to *Mallnitz* (1 190 m above sea level). The train goes through the Tauern Tunnel, and you may remain in your car during the journey.

E17. Salzburg – Innsbruck – Arlberg – Bregenz

SALZBURG, see town plans.

E17 passes through 20 km of Germany – a very beautiful section of Germany: Bad Reichenhall, Berchtesgaden, Königssee, Watzmann and Rossfeld Ringstrasse. See Germany, E11.

Steinpass, on the Austrian frontier, is only 615 m above sea level.

Lofer. Little town beautifully situated between mountains. Painted flower chains on house façades. Folk costumes often worn on Sundays.

Strub has traditional old Tyrolean houses.

St. Johann in Tirol. Large resort with splendid buildings. Cable car to Angerer Alm.

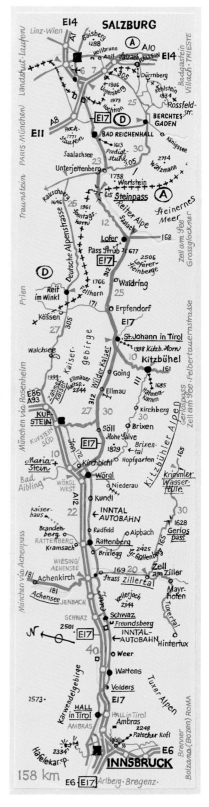

Here the road goes through the *Felbertauern Tunnel*, a good route from Munich to Yugoslavia. See also Grossglocknerstrasse.

Kitzbühel (8 000). One of Austria's oldest and largest resorts, especially popular for winter sports. Casino. Cable car to *Kitzbühler Horn* (1 996 m) and *Hahnenkamm* (1 650 m). The Baroque St. Andreas parish church was decorated by the local Faistenberger family of artists (17th and 18th cent.) who also created the works of art in Liebfrauenkirche. Folklore museums in the Gothic Katharinenkirche and Berggerichtshaus.

The Kitzbühel Alps rise 2 364 m. Beautiful and frequently visited Alpine range with gentle contours – a direct contrast to the wild and craggy cliffs of the Kaisergebirge Range to the north and the Hohe Tauern to the south. You can see the *Wilder Kaiser Range* from Kitzbühel.

The little resort of **Ellmau** with its beautiful church spire is marvellously set against this magnificent background. Further north lies Zahmer Kaiser. See also Germany, Deutsche Alpenstrasse.

Kufstein (1280) with solid *Geroldseck Fortress* was the scene of the century-long struggle between Bavaria and Tyrol. The present fortress dates from 1522. In the same year the Kaiserturm with its 7.5 m thick walls was completed. Folklore museum. *The Held Organ*, with nearly 2 000 pipes, the world's largest outdoor organ, was built into the wall in 1931. It was dedicated to the German and Austrian troops who were killed during the First World War. Organ concerts daily at 12 o'clock (also at 6 p.m. during the summer).

Wörgl, old settlement, town 1951. Baroque St. Lorenz Church. The monument in front of the church was raised in memory of the Tyroleans who fell in the battle against the Bavarians in 1809.

Rattenberg. Once a thriving mining town. When the mines were shut down during the 1500s, all growth stopped. No more houses were built. Thus Rattenberg became a well-preserved medieval town. The High Street is particulary interesting.

A scenic route leads north to Munich by way of the Achenpass. There are some loops up towards Achensee, but in general it is a very good road. Shortest route between Innsbruck and Munich. Small resorts line the lovely Achensee.

To the south the road runs through the beautiful *Zillertal* to the large resort of *Mayrhofen*. Onwards through the *Gerlos Pass* to Zell am See.

Krimmler Wasserfälle. Central Europe's highest waterfalls, over 400 m. Numerous vantage points overlooking the three falls. The most beautiful point is highest up and the excursion on foot takes two to three hours.

Schwaz (10 400) was a mountain town as long ago as the Bronze Age. Copper and silver mining during the 15th and 16th cent. made Schwaz the most important town in the Tyrol when it had 30 000 inhabitants. Fuggerhaus (15th cent.) is proof of the connection with the great trading house in Augsburg. But there are not many medieval houses left. In 1808, the Bavarians put it to the torch. *Pfarrkirche*, originally a 15th-cent. Gothic structure, was rebuilt in Baroque style during the 18th cent. and in 1910 returned to its original Gothic style. The roof is covered with 15 000 copper plates. Franziskanerkirche (16th cent.). Freundsberg Castle.

Volders. Red and white Servitenkirche.

Hall in Tirol (12 500), previously known as Solbad Hall. Once the Inn valley's major salt town with harbour and salt mines. Now an industrial town and spa. Houses from the Middle Ages line *Oberer Stadtplatz*. Beautiful town hall with magnificent councillors' room created in 1447. Mountain Museum in the old salt mine.

INNSBRUCK, see town plans. **Seefeld**, see E6.

Stams. Cistercian abbey (1272) founded by Elizabeth of Bavaria. Impressive Baroque decor. High Altar with the sculpted images of 84 saints.

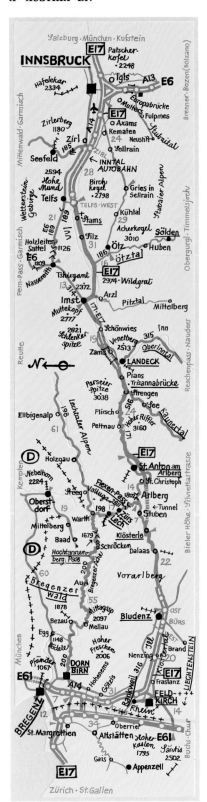

Very beautiful route leads through Ötztal to Obergurgl and over Timmelsjoch to Italy.

Sölden. Large spa and winter sports resort. Cable cars between Sölden Dorf (1 377 m) and Hochsölden (2 070 m) with many hotels.

Obergurgl (1 910 m). The highest village with parish church in Europe.

Timmelsjochstrasse, opened in 1969, is one of Europe's major tourist roads. Tunnels and enormous view out over the Alpine landscape. Tolls.

Landeck (7 500). Many beautifully painted houses. 13th-cent. castle.

Road through the heavily forested *Oberinntal* to Nauders and St. Moritz in Switzerland and through the *Reschen (Resia)* Pass to Italy. Directly to the south of the pass level, you can see the church spire in Graun sticking up out of Reschensee, a man-made lake.

The beautiful *Kaunertal* with waterfalls and glaciers.

Trisannabrücke, an often photographed 86 m high railway bridge over Wildbach near Wiesberg Castle.

Silvrettastrasse (toll) was completed in 1953. It is well constructed, but motorists using it should be adept at Alpine driving. From a 1 050 m height at Partenen, it rises to 2 036 m at Bielerhöhe.

The 95 km long road takes 4 hours to drive. At the level of the pass there is a hotel and an enormous view out over the Alpine landscape. Silvretta-Stausee at an altitude of 2 030 m has a 432 m long and 80 m high dam.

Ischgl. New winter resort.

St. Anton am Arlberg, one of Austria's oldest and largest winter resorts. The Arlberg railway route was opened as far back as 1884. It was here that Hannes Schneider established the world-famous Arlberger Ski School. Cable car up to *Vallugagipfel,* 2 811 m.

The railway tunnel is 10 250 m long. The new road tunnel (1979) is 14 km long. During a few months, until the opening of the Gotthard Tunnel, it was Europe's longest motor tunnel. However, the road over Arlberg, despite some loops, a 10 % gradient on the western approach and an even steeper incline on the eastern side, is well constructed and easily managed.

The road through the **Flexen Pass** is impressive as it skirts cliff edges and crosses the barren landscape well above the timberline. 600 m of tunnels and galleries. Easy driving. **Lech** and **Zürs**, winter resorts. From Warth you can take the lovely road through **Bregenzerwald** to Bregenz.

The Hochtannenberg Pass. Panoramic views. The road goes down into the wild valley near Bregenzer Ache. It is superseded by a wide landscape dotted with villages of typical shingled houses with broad gables and roofed-over windows.

Stuben, small village protected by an avalanche hinder.

Klösterle. Site of a Johannine hostel which gave Klostertal its name.

Bludenz (12 600). Town since 1295. The oldest house, Oberes Tor (with folklore museum) is from 1491. Beautiful Altstadt.

Feldkirch. The 12th- to 14th-cent. city centre is almost unchanged. Marktplatz has beautiful arcaded houses. During the Middle Ages Feldkirch was an important centre for trading, and for the training (through the Jesuits) of higher officials. *Schattenburg Castle* with restaurant and museum.

Liechtenstein, see Switzerland, E 61.

Rankweil. Liebfrauenkirche or Burgkirche shrine-church on a cliff overlooking the Rhine Valley orchards. Fine Alpine views from the castle.

Dornbirn (38 000). Largest town in Voralberg. The place has been known since 957, but did not become a town until 1901. Textile industry. Big annual textile trade fair. "Das rote Hous", a half-timbered house, completed in 1639, is on the main square. Stadtpfarrkirche St. Martin, a 19th-cent. church, may look familiar – it is a copy of the Madeleine Church in Paris.

E 17 passes over the Rhine to St. Gallen – Zürich – Basel – Belfort – Dijon – Beaune (connects to the Marseille – Paris motorway).

BREGENZ (25 000). Capital of Voralberg. Originally the fortified Roman post "Brigantium". The Old Town (Oberstadt) contains remnants of the medieval town wall with its Martinsturm. Modern Bregenz lies on the shores of Lake Constance with a view overlooking Lindau. Every August a music festival is held on a floating stage in the lake. A new Festspielhaus was built in 1979. *Vorarlberger Landesmuseum* (provincial museum) with exhibits from the Roman period and a collection of religious art.

Cable car to *Pfänder.* Panoramic views.

E 93 and A9. Salzburg – Graz – Maribor

SALZBURG, see town plans. St. Wolfgang and Bad Ischl, see E 14.

Hallstatt. Small resort and salt town with some of the most beautiful town architecture in Austria. The town, with its steep, narrow streets leading down to the Hallstätter Lake is surrounded by lofty mountains. The many prehistoric finds in the area have originated a scientific term: the Hallstatt Epoch (from 1 000 B.C. to 500 B.C.). Exhibits of mining equipment said to be 2 500 years old, and examples of Celtic pre-Christian culture in the museum. Church with a splendid altar-piece. The charnel house in St. Michael's Chapel contains an enormous number of human skulls – it is actually so crowded in the graveyard that graves are dug up after ten years.

Obertraun. Idyllic village. Cable car to Dachstein. 15 min. walk to Krippenstein, 2 109 m, with beautiful views. From the mid-point station, Schönbergalpe, a 15 min. walk to the large and beautiful *Dachstein-Rieseneishöhle* and Mammuthöhle ice caves. Enormous ice caverns, "ice chapel", frozen waterfalls and an underground glacier. The tour takes about an hour. From Obertraun, an hour's walk brings you to the Kopperbrüllenhöhle with impressive stalactites and stalagmites.

Bad Aussee. Spa where, in 1827, the Archduke Johann married the postmaster's daughter. Medallion portraying the romantic couple on the Erzherzog Johann-Brücke. Statue in the Kurpark. He was a popular prince interested in the natural sciences. *Alpine garden* containing 4 000 species of flowers.

The town centre is Chlumetskyplatz with Kamerhof, an old building, once the office for the salt mines, now a folklore museum. During the Second World War Austria's art treasures were hidden in the salt mines.

Liezen (6 700). Industrial town and winter resort.

This is where the mighty viaducts of the *Pyhrnautobahn* are being constructed. The Bosrück Tunnel should be completed by 1984. It will be 5 500 m long. As it will have a maximum gradient of 1 % and will be situated at just 742 m above sea level it will be of extreme importance for heavy commercial traffic. It will go close to the railway tunnel which was completed in 1905.

Beautiful road to *Hieflau* past *Admont* with large Benedictine abbey founded in the 11th cent. The buildings have been restored after a fire in 1865. The magnificent library with its 72 m long hall was saved. Over 1 000 manuscripts and 130 000 volumes.

Gesäuse is a beautiful gorge. The road follows the Enz for almost 20 km. The western approach near the steep cliff walls of Hochtor is the most dramatically beautiful section. From Hieflau you can drive over Eisenerzer Alpen (21 % gradient) to Leoben on E 7.

Leopoldsteiner See, a little lake nestled between high mountains. Cliff walls on the southern shore reach up 800 m.

Eisenerz (11 600 m). Old mountain town with gracious houses. The fortified church, Tabor, was built in 1532 to withstand the Turks. The characteristic profile of *Erzberg* with its over 30 terraces rises above the town. It was not until 1870 that open-face mining started. Then Erzberg was 1532 m high – now it is a mere 1 465 m. The ore has a high iron content (32 %) and has been an important factor in the economy of Austria. There has been mining activity here since the late Stone Age.

Rottenmann. Small mountain town with beautiful architecture. Known as early as 927, it has been a town since 1320.

Oberzeiring. Once one of Austria's most important towns as a result of the flourishing Schaubergwerk silver mines. The mines were flooded in 1361 and 1 300 miners lost their lives. Guided tours. Alte Knappenkirche, completed in 1111 (Knappen = miner). *Hanfelden Castle* where Emperor Maximilian I stayed in 1509 during an attempt to re-open the mine.

The Gleinalm Tunnel was opened in 1979. Length: 8.2 km.

Frohnleiten. Rabenstein Castle. Part of the town is very old.

Lurgrotte. Austria's deepest stalactite and stalagmite cave, located in the chalk cliffs east of Peggau. Guided tours. *Stübing.* The open-air museum of Austria.

GRAZ, see town plans.

Loibltunnel, 5.2 km long motor tunnel on E 94. Toll-free. Approach roads steep but in good condition. Open year-round.

Spielfeld, frontier post. E 93 goes to Maribor – Ljubljana – Trieste.

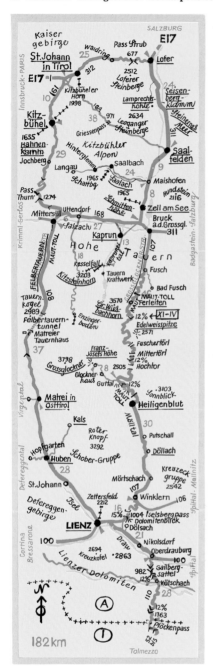

Grossglockner Hochalpenstrasse

After the road leaves E17 at Lofer it passes through the beautiful Saalach Valley. Subterranean river in *Lamprechtshöhle* cave. *Seisenbergklamm* waterfalls.

Saalfelden (11 000). Commercial town and winter resort.

Steinernes Meer is a massive chalk range. Felseneinsiedelei Chapel was hewn out of the cliff during the 18th cent. Alm shrine-church.

Saalbach. Major winter sports centre (1 003 m).

Zell am See (7 500). One of the country's major resorts. Internationally famous winter sports centre. One of Austria's oldest settlements, known as long ago as 740. Pfarrkirche St. Hippolyt. 15 min. cable car journey to *Schmittenhöhe* (1 968 m).

Kaprun. Enormous power stations. Artificial lakes. Austria's best summer skiing on Kitzstein Horn (3 027 m).

Grossglockner Hochalpenstrasse is one of Europe's most unforgettable tourist experiences. It is wide and easy to drive but has many loops. The steepest gradient is 14 %. Tolls. If you buy a ticket in advance from the Austrian Automobile Club (ÖAMTC), you will avoid queuing. Return tickets are also valid on Felbertauernstrasse. Not suitable for caravans.

Ferleiten (1 152 m). The road rises sharply. After the 15 km marker, the Schleier waterfall comes into view. Hairpin curves. The parking area provides spectacular views towards Grosses Wiesbachhorn (3 442 m). Remains of a Roman road after the 23 km marker.
Stupendous views from **Edelweisspitze.**

Franz-Josefs-Höhe. Beautiful views, but hordes of tourists, enormous enclosed car parks. Not recommended to nature lovers.

Grossglockner, 3 797 m, is the highest mountain in Austria. Glaciers cover Johannesberg, 3 460 m. The *Pasterze* is a glacial mass, 10 km long, as much as 5 km wide and 300 m thick.

Heiligenblut. Small village and resort. In the church (1483) there is a large altar and a sacramental casket that holds a bottle, which according to legend contains three drops of Christ's blood.

Döllach. Spa and winter resort. Picturesque houses. The folklore museum in Grosskirchheim Castle (1561) specializes in exhibits that recall the silver and gold mining that were once prevalent in the area.

LIENZ (12 000). Inhabited as early as the Hallstatt Epoch (1 000 B.C.). Since the 13th cent. it has been the seat of the powerful Counts of Görz (now Gorica). Their castle, Bruck, was given its present appearance in the 1500s. Now it houses the East Tyrolean folklore museum. The Church of St. Andreas contains the tombs of the Counts of Görz. Remains of the Roman town of Aguntum (destroyed about A.D. 600) lie east of Lienz.

Felbertauernstrasse (1967) is a fast route that goes from Munich to Lienz and on to Yugoslavia. The Munich-to-Trieste section is 100 km shorter than the alternative Brenner route. The road, open all-year-round, is 7 m wide and has a maximum gradient of 7 %.

Kitzbühel, see E17.

The Felbertauern Tunnel, 5.2 km long. The road's highest point (1 650 m above sea level) is reached in this tunnel. "Maut" = toll.

Matrei in Osttirol. Resort with beautiful churches. Road to the charming village of Virgen at 1 200 m above sea level. The resort of Prägraten is at the end of the road, and at the base of Grossvenediger, 3 674 m above sea level. From **Huben** road to **Kals** at the foot of the Grossglockner.

E 84. Klein Haugsdorf – Wien

Map, see E 7.

Klein Haugsdorf. Czechoslovakian border. E 84 comes from Praha – Jihlava – Znojmo.

Retz. Small town. Wine centre. Monumental square with two fountains. On the day of the wine festival, the last Sunday in September, one fountain spouts red wine, while the other spouts white wine.

Pulkau. Large wine town with two beautiful churches.

Eggenburg. Small town with town wall and tower. Medieval architecture. Lovely churches. Maypole, "Pranger", in the square.

Hollabrunn (10 400) in the Weinviertel at Manhardtsberg.

Stockerau (13 000) has some beautiful 15th-, 16th- and 17th-cent houses.

WIEN, (Vienna), see town plans.

TOWN PLANS

GRAZ (253 000).
Austria's second largest city. Capital of Steiermark (Styria). Commercial and industrial city. The Steyr-Daimler-Puch motor works manufacture mopeds. International trade fairs. University, technical college and state theatre. From the standpoint of tourism, Graz has been put into the background by larger tourist centres. But it is a charming town with a superb blend of impressive thoroughfares, picturesque alleys, beautiful parks, and interesting churches. "Das gemahlte Haus", a 17th-cent. building, is one of the many beautiful houses with Baroque façades. The Landhaus on Herrengasse is a Renaissance palace with fountains in a splendid arcaded courtyard.
Ständisches Zeughaus (The Styrian Armoury), built in the 17th cent., contains over 28 000 examples of weapons and armour that were used by the inhabitants of Graz during their many battles with the Turks. The town was seriously threatened by the Turks in 1480 and 1532. It was not until the 18th cent. that the risk of a Turkish invasion was eliminated. The city is beautifully situated on the banks of the Mur. Schlossberg towers 120 m above the town (473 m above sea level). Cable car to the summit. The fortress on top of the hill was destroyed by French troops in 1809. The 16th-cent. Uhrturm (clock tower) is all that remains of the original fortifications. Johanneum Landesmuseum is a religious art museum. Cathedral (15th cent.) with the mausoleum of Emperor Ferdinand II. *Steierisches*

Volkskundemuseum (Styrian Folklore Museum) in Stübing, with exhibits of everyday life. There are examples of arms from different parts of Austria. Typical handicrafts can be purchased in the "Heimatwerk" shop.
Eggenberg. 17th-cent. castle. Walled courtyard and corner tower. Jagdmuseum (Hunting Museum). City Museum, and Museum of Baroque Art.

INNSBRUCK (119 000).
Capital of the Tyrol. Since the 1200s the junction of many important trade routes. University. Site of 1964 and 1976 winter Olympic Games.
Maria Theresienstrasse. Beautiful old houses with the 2 334 m Nordkette Alpine mountain range as a backdrop. The St. Anne Column (Annasäule) in the middle of the avenue was raised in memory of the liberation of the Tyrol from the Bavarians in 1703. Two towers, Spitalkirche and Stadtturm. When you turn around, the harmony of the avenue disappears. The Triumphal Arch which has been standing in its present location since the wedding of Archduke Leopold in 1756, is now dwarfed by an elephantine Holiday Inn. The avenue leads down to ***Altstadt*** with its many fine old houses. The world-famous *Goldenes Dachl* (Golden Roof), a lavishly decorated stone balcony covered with 4 500 gilded copper plates. It was built by Emperor Maximilian in about 1500. Near by is the *Goldener Adler* (Golden Eagle), an inn and hotel that has been in service since 1390. Among the guests: Goethe, Gustav III of Sweden, Heine, Paganini, Metternich. All have probably eaten the speciality of the house, Tiroler Speckknödel. In 1809, the Tyrolean patriot Andreas Hofer made a fiery speech here just

after his army had routed the French troops and liberated the Tyrol at the Battle on Berg Isel. The following year he was executed in Merano on the personal order of Napoleon. The Dukes of the Tyrol had their residence in *Hofburg* Castle. In 1770, the long façade was given its typical ochre-coloured "Maria Theresa Yellow" hue. Riesensaal is 31 m long.
Hofkirche. Silberkapelle contains a silver madonna. The tomb of the Emperor Maximilian I has 28 enormous bronze statues (original plans called for 74 even larger and 100 minor statues). Most of the figures portray various Habsburgs and the emperor's ancestors, but other historical figures, such as the legendary King Arthur of England, are also depicted. Work on the monument lasted over a period of more than 100 years. The tomb itself is of black marble. Beautifully ornamented, it features a statue of the kneeling emperor. But the tomb is empty. Maximilian I was buried in Wiener Neustadt. By the time he died in Wels in 1519, the burghers of Innsbruck had long since tired of his lavish court and his enormous debts, so they refused to allow his remains to be buried in the tomb. The Tyrolean patriot, Andreas Hofer (1809), is buried in the church.
Tiroler Volkkunstmuseum displays beautiful chests from Zillertal, models of Tyrolean farm houses, peasant furniture, folk costumes, and much more.
Tiroler Landesmuseum Ferdinandeum. Art collection. *Stift Wilten.* An abbey founded in 1128 by the Premonstransian order. Abbey church and parish church in Baroque. *Kaiserjägermuseum* on top of Berg Isel. Here Tyrolean patriot Andreas Hofer defeated the troops of Napoleon in 1809, a

1 *Franziskanerkirche (Franciscan Church). 2 Landhaus. Weapons museum. 3 Cathedral. 3 Town hall.*

The Hauptplatz and the Clock Tower in Graz

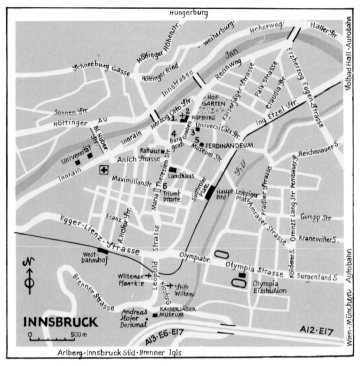

1 Goldenes Dachl (Golden Roof).
2 Hofburg and Hofkirche (Imperial Palace and Church).
3 Tiroler Volkkunstmuseum
4 City Tower. View.
5 Tiroler Landesmuseum Ferdinandeum (regional museum).
6 Triumphal arch.

of Europe's primary tourist attractions. The city of Mozart. St. Rupert founded the still existing convent in 1696. During the 8th cent. a bishopric, cathedral, school and library were all established in the town. About 1200 mining for salt, gold, silver and copper was started in Dürnburg. During the 17th cent. Fischer von Erlach built the Baroque town, parts of which still stand e.g. the narrow, winding and picturesque Judengasse, Getreidegasse and Pferdeschwemme. Fine old café, Tomaselli, first opened in 1703 at Alter Markt. Residenz (1595) with magnificent halls and picture gallery. Since 1705 carillon daily at 7 a.m., 11 a.m. and 6.00 p.m.

Domplatz Beautiful palaces. The *cathedral* (1655) in the Italian Renaissance style has two towers and is richly ornamented. "Jedermann" by Hugo von Hoffmansthal (his adaptation of the medieval English morality play "Everyman") is performed in the Domplatz. *Franziskanerkirche*, originally built in 1221, and *St. Peter's Basilica*, built in the 12th cent. but reconstructed in the Baroque style in the 18th cent., are close to the square. Lovely churchyard.

Hohensalzburg, castle of the prince-bishops on Mönchberg, 120 m above Salzach. Construction was begun in 1077, and continued for 600 years. The princes' chambers and the ramparts are open to the public. Organ

short-lived victory. His statue was cast with the metal from captured French cannon. After the First World War South Tyrol became a part of Italy, but many are still working (occasionally with bombs) for its reunification with the Austrian North Tyrol. Many Austrian cities have a Südtiroler Platz. The Battle on Berg Isel is depicted in the big painting *"Rundgemälde"* (Rennweg 13).

Schloss **Ambras** where Archduke Ferdinand of Tyrol laid the groundwork for the great collection of armour and curiosities.
Rack railway up **Hungerberg,** 860 m. Also motor road. Cable car further up to **Hafelekar,** 2 334 m.
Alpenzoo at Weiherburg.

SALZBURG (130 000)
Capital of the state of Salzburg and one

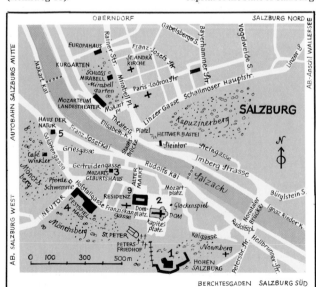

1 Hohensalzburg. 2 Residenzplatz. Cathedral. Carillon. 3 Mozart' birthplace. 4 Festspielhaus (New Festival Theatre). 5 Haus der Natur (Museum of natural science and biology). Photo: Getreidegasse, a winding street in old Salzburg

with 200 pipes. Access to the castle by cable car.

Wolfgang Amadeus Mozart was born in the house at Getreidegasse 9, now a *museum.* This musical prodigy quickly became famous throughout Europe. He started his triumphant procession through the continent at the age of six. Until the age of 20, he had an unbroken series of successes. Then he left Salzburg and his misfortunes began. He lived to be 35. No one followed him to his pauper's grave in St. Marxer Friedhof in Vienna. In 1842 his town of birth organized the first Mozart festival. Its present modern form dates from 1922. Every August there are concerts and performances in the old Festspielhaus which was once the Residenz's court riding school and stable, and in the new *Festspielhaus,* which was completed in 1960 and accommodates 2 340 spectators. There are also performances given in the *Mozarteum* musical academy, the Landestheater, Schloss Mirabell, and the Marionette Theatre. Chocolates and marzipans are sold in memory of Mozart all year round.

Schloss Mirabell, originally built in 1600, was restored after a fire in 1818. Beautiful garden by Fischer von Erlach. The witty sculptures of fairytale figures will certainly amuse the children.

Haus der Natur. Natural history and biological museum.

Hellbrunn. Castle with lovely gardens and amusing fountains, created by the prank-loving Bishop Marcus Sitticus (17th cent.), who liked to play jokes on his guests. Grottoes with hidden sculptures and fountains.

Tiergarten Hellbrunn. Alpine animals. Pelicans and storks are allowed to fly about freely.

Klessheim Castle, a Baroque structure with beautiful garden. Major political conferences have taken place here. Nixon, Brezhnev and Gerald Ford have all been guests.

Untersberg, 853 m. Cable car. Fine view. Nature reserve.

WIEN (Vienna, 1.6 million)
Capital of Austria and a federal state. The name "Vindobona" dates from the Celtic period. During the first century A.D. Vienna was a Roman stronghold at the crossing of the Danube and the Amber Route that led from the Baltic Sea to the Adriatic. In the 12th cent. it was the residence of the Dukes of Austria. Eventually it became the capital of the mighty Habsburg Empire. The imperial period ended in 1918.

Well-preserved architecture from the Habsburg period with palaces in the Renaissance, Baroque and rococo styles. In 1857 the city walls were razed and replaced with the monumental Ring – many broad avenues with different names that together form a circular avenue round the Inner City. Further away from the centre, there is another circular ring, the Gürtel. Vienna is divided into 26 districts, Bezirke, and their numbers

are often used when giving directions. District number 1 is the Inner City and lies within the Ring and the Danube Canal. The district between the Danube Canal and the Danube is number 2. Districts 3-9 are located between the Ring and the Gürtel. The major shopping streets in the Inner City are *Kärntnerstrasse* and *Graben,* now both pedestrian precincts. Lively and narrow streets of the Old Town, e.g. Domgasse (Mozart lived at No. 5, "Figarohaus"), Essiggasse and Backerstrasse. You can leave these streets for the quiet of the nearby Grasshofgasse and Heiligenkreuzer Hof. *Greichenbeisel,* an old inn with 15th-cent. walls, stands near the Fleischmarkt. Over the entrance is Augustin, a famous Viennese character in the song "Ach, du lieber Augustin, alles ist weg". On the Graben, and in front of St. Stephen's Cathedral, horse-drawn carriages, "Fiaker", wait for passengers.

St. Stephen's Cathedral is both the very heart of the city and its symbol. The tower is 137 m high. The great door, "Riesentor", and two towers, are all that remain of the original 12th-cent. church. It has been damaged and reconstructed after the city fire in 1258, the Turkish seige in 1683, and Allied bombing raids in 1945. The *Wiener Neustädter Altar* is in the left lateral aisle, the red marble tomb of Emperor Frederick III in the right. Gothic sandstone pulpit (16th cent.) by Anton Pilgram, who placed an image of himself near the organ under the stairs that lead up to the pulpit.

The Staatsoper is situated at the crossing of Kärntnerstrasse and the Ring. Opernpassage, an underground shopping centre. Splendid palaces line the Ring: the University (founded in 1365), the Parliament , Polizeipräsidium, the Burgtheater, etc. Many great parks and gardens: the Burggarten, Heldenplatz, Volksgarten. The famous monument to *Johann Strauss* (1825-99) stands in the Stadtpark. The *Rathaus* (Town Hall) is an enormous neo-Gothic building with a 104 m high tower.

Hofburg, the massive city palace of the Habsburgs, consists of several clusters of buildings constructed during different periods. The oldest palace in the group is Schweizerhof, originally from the 1200s. Magnificent and huge interior – 26 of the 2 600 rooms are open to the public. Exhibition of imperial china. The National Library (created during the 18th cent. by the famous architects Fischer von Erlach father and son). Treasure containing the regalia of the Holy Roman Empire: the royal crown used in the 10th cent. and the crown of the Austrian emperors. The *Albertina* Museum with a vast collection of aquarelles, drawings and engravings. *Kaisergruft* (Kapuzinerkirche) from 1632 with 140 Habsburg tombs. A dozen emperors including Franz Josef, and 16 empresses, among them Maria Theresa, are buried here. Their hearts are buried in the Augustinerkirche, and

The Graben, a shopping street in Vienna

their internal organs in the catacombs of St. Stephen's Cathedral.

The *Spanish Riding School* is also part of the Hofburg. Morning training exercises daily, performances on Sundays and Wednesdays, except during January, February and summer months.

Schönbrunn. A colossal Baroque palace with 1 441 rooms. Over 40 rooms, all in the period of Maria Theresa, are open to the public. Extensive parks, terraces and fountains bring to mind the glory of the Empire. The greatest artists, composers, architects, and inventors of their period appeared here. Emperor Franz Josef died here in the Schönbrunn in 1916. And it was here that the last Habsburg ruler abdicated on November 11, 1918. The line had reigned for 740 years. Mozart directed his first opera at the age of 9 in the *Palace Theatre. Wagenburg* has a collection of magnificent court carriages, among them Charles VI's coronation coach. *Tiergarten Schönbrunn* is a part of the palace park. Founded in 1752, it is thought to be one of the oldest zoos in the world. About 5 000 animals. Botanical gardens. Palm house.

Belvedere. Two Baroque palaces completed in the 18th cent. Built for Prince Eugen of Savoy, the conqueror of the Turks. 19th- and 20th-cent. Austrian art in *Oberes Belvedere,* medieval

View towards the Burgtheater from Vienna's 104 m high Town Hall Tower

Austrian and Baroque art in the *Unteres Belvedere.* Beautiful garden with fountains.

Alpengarten with 4 000 species of flowers. Alpine garden also in the Botanical Garden of the university.

Other museums:

Kunsthistorisches Museum (Museum of Fine Arts) contains one of Europe's foremost collections of paintings. Coins and medals. Europe's largest collection of buttons. Weapons and musical instruments are in the museum at the Hofburg. *Naturhistorisches Museum* (Museum of Natural History), prehistoric and geological finds, meteorites, botanical specimens. "Venus von Willendorf", a 10 cm high 25 000-year-old fertility goddess. Museum für Angewandte Kunst (Museum of Applied Arts), handicrafts, furniture, textiles, china. Museum des 20. Jahrhunderts (Museum of the 20th cent). Historisches Museum der Stadt Wien (Vienna City Museum). Uhrenmuseum (Clock Museum). Museum für Volkskunde (Ethnological Museum). *Technisches Museum* (Technical Museum) includes the Post and Railway Museum. *Heeresgeschichtliches Museum* (Army History Museum) has, among other exhibits, the Gräf und Stift motor car in which Franz Ferdinand was assassinated in Sarajevo in 1914. Many palaces are open to the public, among them *Schwarzenberg, Kinsky* and *Harrach.* There are many other museums that cater for a variety of tastes: Schubert Museum, Freud Museum, Esperanto Museum, Fire Brigade Museum, Jewish Museum, Blacksmith Museum, Tobacco Museum, Circus and Clown Museum, Burial Museum.

Churches:

The Baroque *Karlskirche* with a 72 m high dome inspired by St. Peter's in Rome (designed by Fischer von Erlach). Neo-Gothic *Votivkirche.* In 1683 Turkish gunfire shot away a section of the tower of the Gothic *Minoritetenkirche.* Gothic Maria am Gestade. Many well-known men are buried in *Zentralfriedhof* churchyard: Beethoven, Schubert, Brahms, Gluck, Millöcker, Johan Strauss the elder and, Johan Strauss the younger. Monument to Mozart. His actual burial place, in the St. Marxer Friedhof, is unknown.

Augarten. Large park with famous china factory. School for the Vienna Choir Boys. This famous boys' choir can be heard at Sunday morning mass at the Hofburg.

The Prater. Huge park with exhibition halls, stadium, race track. This is where, in the 19th cent, the Viennese waltz started out on its triumphant way. Here fashionable Vienna passed in elegant carriages. Simpler people amused themselves in the Volksprater or the Wurstelprater. The fun fair still stands. The 64 m high "Riesenrad" Ferris wheel can be seen from most parts of the city. A ride lasts for a single revolution. Fine views. It was in this wheel that Orson Welles travelled in "The Third Man".

Lobau, large wildlife reserve. *Lainzer*

Tiergarten, natural game park inside a 24 km long wall. Hiking paths and nature trails. Exhibitions in Hermesvilla, formerly the Imperial Hunting Lodge.

UNO-City with its enormous Donauhalle is Vienna's new international conference centre. Vienna is also the headquarters of the International Atomic Energy Commission, the Organization for Industrial Development, and OPEC, the oil producing nations' own organization.

Donau Park, site of the International Garden Show with the 250 m high *Donauturm* rotating restaurant.

Grinzing. Famous village at the northern edge of the city. You can taste and enjoy the new wines in one of the many wine taverns, "Heurigenschenke", in such places as **Nussdorf, Sievering,** or one of the wine villages in the Vienna Woods (Wienerwald).

Kahlenberg, 485 m, with panoramic view over Vienna. The Turkish armies were defeated here, and in the Vienna Woods, in 1683. Christianity had triumphed over Islam – at least until the oil crisis made its appearance. Supposedly the Turks received such a fright that they fled leaving a sack of coffee on the battlefield. This might have been the start of the Viennese café life. Here you sit with your coffee, a glass of water, and one of the café's newspapers. In the past it was common for the Viennese to make the café the centre of their social lives. Schwarzenberg, Hawelka, and Landtman, are three cafés that still provide the traditional atmosphere. The famous Viennese Konditoreien are flourishing. Here pastries play the leading role. At the Hotel Sacher, you are served the original (according to a decision of the Austrian Supreme Court) Sacher Torte. But a luscious Sacher Torte is also available at Demel's on the Kohlmarkt (Old Papa Demel was once the head pastry chef at Sacher's so who knows. . .). Over 100 varieties of tortes and pastries can be chosen in a magnificent setting of marble, mirrors, panelling, and gilt.

1 *St. Stephen's Cathedral.*
2 *Hofburg and Albertina (Imperial palace and museums).*
3 *Opera house.*
4 *Kunsthistorisches Museum (Museum of Fine Arts).*
5 *Naturhistorisches Museum (Museum of Natural History).*
6 *Museum für Angewandte Kunst (Museum of Applied Arts).*
7 *Historisches Museum der Stadt Wien (Vienna City Museum).*
8 *Museum des 20.Jahrhunderts (Museum of the 20th Century).*
9 *Heeresgeschichtliches Museum (Army History Museum).*
10 *Technisches Museum (Museum of Technology)*
11 *Schönbrunn Palace.*
12 *Volksprater amusement park with Ferris wheel.*

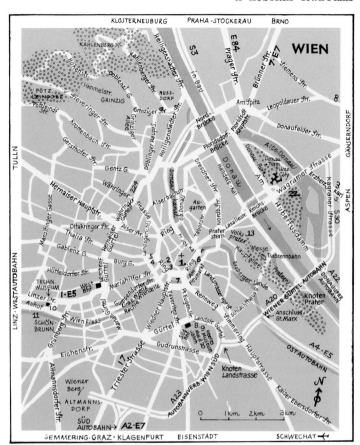

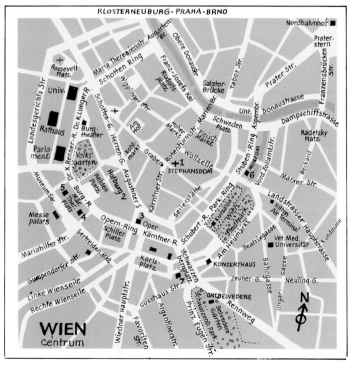

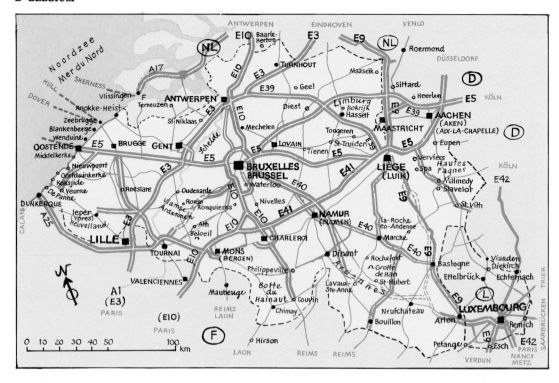

B · Belgium

B·Belgique/België

Area: 30 500 km² (11 275 sq. miles)

Population: 9.8 million. Belgium is one of Europe's most densely populated countries: 325 inh. per km². 85-90 % of the population are Roman Catholics.
The Belgian language frontier runs along the line Kortrijk – Ronse – Halle – Overijsel – Tirlemont – Sint Truiden – Tongeren – and the border north of Visé. Flemish, a form of Dutch, is spoken north of this boundary, while French is used in the south. German is the everyday language in some areas on the country's eastern frontier.

Major cities: Brussel/Bruxelles (Brussel) 1.1 million, Antwerpen/Anvers (Antwerp) 926 000, Liège 612 000, Charleroi 444 000, Gent (Gand) 486 000.

Government: Constitutional monarchy. Parliament consists of two houses, Senate and House of Representatives. There are nine provinces: Antwerpen, Brabant, Hainaut, Liège, Limbourg, Luxembourg, Namur, East Flanders and West Flanders.

History
57 B.C. The Romans conquer Belgium.
5th cent. The Franks conquer Belgium.
1515 The reign of Charles Quint begins.
1579 The Peace of Utrecht. The northern, Protestant provinces achieve independence from Spain. These United Provinces now form the Netherlands.
1714 Austria occupies Belgium.
1792 France occupies Belgium.
1814 The Kingdom of Belgium is proclaimed.

1815 Napoleon is defeated at Waterloo. The Belgian provinces are incorporated into the Netherlands.
1830 Revolution in Belgium. A provisional government with an elected National Congress is formed.
1914-1918 First World War. The Germans occupy Belgium.
1939-1945 Second World War. The Germans begin the occupation of Belgium in 1940.
1954 Belgium, the Netherlands and Luxembourg unite in economic partnership (Benelux).
1958 EEC (the Common Market) and Euroatom establish headquarters in Brussels.
1971 The French-speaking and Flemish-speaking areas are granted greater autonomy.

Currency: The Belgian franc (BEC). 1 franc = 100 centimes.

Business hours: Banks 9.00 a.m.-3.30 p.m. Occasionally the banks are closed at lunchtime (12.00-2.00 p.m.) Closed Saturdays. Currency exchange offices in the railway stations and at the Brussels airport are open Saturdays and Sundays. Shops open on weekdays 9.00 a.m.-6.00 p.m. and on Saturdays until 2.00 p.m. Often closed at lunchtime. Business hours can vary – the above are given as a guideline only.

Holidays: New Year's Day, Easter Sunday, Easter Monday, May 1, Ascension Day, Whit Sunday, Whit

Routes described:

E 3 Antwerpen – Gent – Lille
E 5 Oostende – Gent – Bruxelles/Brussel – Liège
E 9 Maastricht – Liège – Luxembourg
E 10 Breda – Antwerpen – Bruxelles/Brussel – Mons
E 39 Antwerpen – Maastricht – Aachen, see E 5
E 40 Brussel/Bruxelles – Namur – Luxembourg
E 41 Tournai – Mons – Charleroi – Namur – Liège

Town plans: Antwerpen, Bruxelles/Brussel, Liège

Monday, July 21 (National Holiday), August 15 (Assumption Day), November 1 (All Saint's Day), November 11 (Armistice Day), December 25 and 26.

Hotels

The hotels are rated – one to four "stars" – following a joint "Benelux classification ". The Commisariat Générale au Tourisme (The Belgian Tourist Authority) publish a list of hotels. If a hotel has been approved by the Commisariat it displays a special sign. Prices should be posted in the rooms. Breakfast is included in the room price.

Camping

More then 500 camping sites, divided into four categories.

Food and drink

Belgium is renowned for its cuisine. The restaurants near Brussels' Grand Place are among the finest in Europe. But even in less expensive eating places, the quality and standards remain quite high. Restaurants are required by law to display the menu outside the establishment. Some specialities: Carbonnades flamandes – a type of goulash, based on beef and onions. Minced meat with chicory (Chicorée de Bruxelles). Lapin (rabbit) is served with plums in Flanders, cherries in Tournai and Hainaut and raisins in Antwerp and Limbourg. Jambon d'Ardennes (smoked ham from the Ardennes). Hochepot Gantois (Gentse hutspot) is a beef, pork and vegetable stew. Boudin noir is a delicately spiced blood sausage. Boudin blanc is white sausage. Choesels au Madère is sliced meat served with a Madeira sauce and garnished with mushrooms. Volaille or Poulet is chicken. Poulet de Bruxelles is an exceptionally large and delicious chicken. Brussels kiekenwaterzooi is a stew that contains chicken breasts. Anguilles au vert (Paling in 't groen) is eel that has been sautéd in butter and is served with a vegetable sauce. Anguilles à l'escavèche is cold fried eel in aspic. Truite (trout) is prepared with vegetables, truite "Meunière" is fried and truite aux amandes is served with fried almonds. Mussels are available everywhere.

Oie à l'instar de Visé is a dish with a 2 000-year-old history. It consists of goose, first boiled with vegetables, then fried and served with a garlicky cream gravy. Beer is the national beverage. There are 300 kinds of beer. Some of the best known are Gueuze-Lambic, Krieken-Lambic, Trappist, and Diesters.

Belgian pastries, tortes and sweets are exceptionally good. Gaufres are sweet waffles. They are often sold in street stalls. They can be accompanied by butter, cream or preserves. Gaufres liègeoises contain caramel sugar.

Shopping

Lace from Brussels, Bruges, Binche and Mechelen. Copper and brass from Dinant. Crystal from Liège. Stoneware and crafts from the Ardennes.

Speed limits. Traffic regulations

Motorways 120 kmh, other roads 90

Bruges. The Procession of the Holy Blood takes place on the first Sunday in May

kmh, built-up areas 60 kmh.

On motorways the **minimum** speed is 70 kmh. During the period November 1-March 31 spiked tyres etc are permitted but vehicles using them are restricted to a speed of 90 kmh on motorways and 60 kmh on other roads. Children under the age of 12 are not allowed to travel in the front seat.

Roads

All of Belgium's motorways are illuminated, a road safety feature which is unique. However, in the interest of energy conservation, this lighting has been reduced on some stretches after midnight.

Direction signs can be confusing if the driver does not know that Belgian towns and cities can have two, or even three names. Usually just one of these names is posted. Some examples:

Aalst/Alost
Antwerpen/Anvers
Brugge/Bruges
Bruxelles/Brussel
De Haan/le Coq
Dendermonde/Termonde
de Panne/la Panne
Gent/Gand
Geraardsbergen/Grammont
Ieper/Ypres
Koksijde/Coxyde
Kortrijk/Courtrai
Leuven/Louvain
Liège/Luik/Lüttich
Lille/Rijsel
Mechelen/Malines
Mons/Bergen
Mouscron/Moeskroen
Namur/Namen
Nivelles/Nijvel
Oudenaarde/Audenarde
Roeselare/Roulers
Ronse/Renaix
Sint Truiden/Saint-Trond
Tienen/Tirlemont
Tournai/Doornik
Zoutleeuw/Léau

Road patrols

TCB, the Belgian Auto Club, has 350 patrol cars. They operate a regular service from 7 a.m. until 10.30 p.m. On the Brussels – Ostend and Antwerp – Liège stretches of the motorways, their cars are also on duty during the night. These yellow TCB patrol cars, easily identified by the sign "Touring Secours", provide free assistance to holders of AIT assistance booklets. The Auto Club of Flanders (VAB-VTB) and the Royal Automobile Club (RACB) both have patrol cars that carry the sign "Wacht op de Weg". These patrol cars do not accept AIT credit vouchers as payment.

Emergency telephones: 900 for fire brigade and ambulance, 901 for police.

TCB, Touring Club Royal de Belgique, 44 rue de la Loi, 1040 Bruxelles, tel. 02- 233 22 11.
Belgian National Tourist Office, 38 Dover Street, London W1X 3RB. Tel. 01-499 5379.

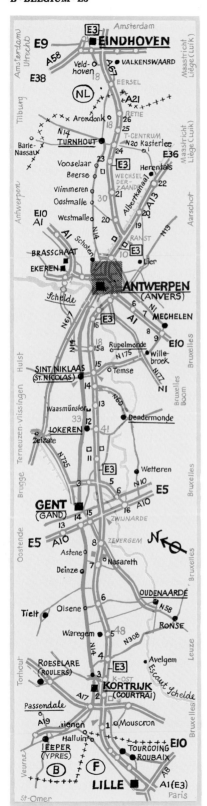

E 3. Antwerpen – Gent – Lille

Dutch border. E 3 comes from Helsinki – Stockholm – Fredrikshavn – Hamburg.

Turnhout (38 000). Industrial city. Beautiful castle with moat. Once owned by the Dukes of Brabant, it is now the Law Court. Musée national de la Carte à jouer/National Museum van de Speelkart are the imposing names for a museum of playing cards in Begijnhof. Musée Taxandria has exhibitions of archaeology and folklore.

ANTWERPEN (Anvers, Antwerp), see town plans.
The E 3 approach to the eastern opening of the Kennedy Tunnel goes by way of an intricate system of roads and flyovers. The motorist driving in the direction of Eindhoven should follow the direction signs to Turnhout. The signs reading "Nederland" indicate the way to Amsterdam.

Schelde (Escaut). The major river of Belgium, 430 km long.

Sint-Niklaas (50 000). The square is the largest in Belgium. A Thursday market has been held here since 1513. Museum of art, folklore and archaeology. One section is devoted to Mercator, who devised a method of map projection, probably the most widely used in the world, in which the globe is transformed into a rectangle, with America to the left and Asia to the right. Mercator was born in 1512 in **Rupelmonde** where a monument has been erected in his honour.

Dendermonde. Square with Renaissance town hall and old covered market. Museum of local folklore. **Lokeren.** Lovely square. Carillon. Zoo.

GENT (Gand, Ghent, 225 000). Belgium's fourth largest city and second largest port. Capital of East Flanders. During the Middle Ages this was one of Europe's most important trading centres. Many textile workshops. The brothers van Eyck and other Renaissance masters painted here. In parts the city preserves its medieval character and there are lovely views from St-Michielsbrug. The *Lakenhalle* (Cloth Hall) dates from the 14th cent. Stately town hall and the patrician mansions and guildhouses reflect the city's illustrious past. *Graslei*, a splendid array of buildings, guildhalls and warehouses, is an area near the old harbour. The Hôtel Court St-Georges is a fine hotel with an impressive history. It opened in 1228.
Sint-Bavo Cathedral (14th-16th cent.). Oldest sections date from the 10th cent. Simple exterior, magnificent interior. Baroque marble and wood pulpit (1745). Rubens' "The Conversion of Saint Bavo". The brothers van Eyck's *altar painting* "The Adoration of the Lamb". 95 m high belfry. Sint-Baafsabdij was founded in 631.
's-Gravensteen (1180). A grim castle where the Dukes of Flanders once ruled over their subjects. Extraordinary collection of torture instruments in the cellar.
Museum voor Volkskunde (Museum of Folklore), *Museum voor Schone Kunsten* (Museum of Fine Arts) and *Archaeological Museum* in the abbey at Bijloke.
Ghent is also called "the City of Flowers". During August and September begonias and roses fill the parks and fields in and around the town. Every fifth year an enormous flower show is held in the Floralia Palace in the Citadel Park. Ghent is the home of many industries.

Oudenaarde is well-known for its textile industry and its dark beer. During the 16th cent. it was the home of Charles Quint's daughter, Margaret of Parma, who ruled over the Spanish Netherlands. Her reign was followed by that of the notorious inquisitor, the Duke of Alba. Beautiful town hall.

Kortrijk (Courtrai, 45 000) was founded in 43 B.C. During the Middle Ages this town was famed for its skilled weavers. Now the centre of the linen industry, it is surrounded by fields of flax. *O.L. Vrouwkerk* (Church of Our Lady) contains Sir Anthony van Dyck's altar painting "The Elevation of the Cross". The *Begijnhof* (Almshouse) with 42 small Baroque houses, was founded in 1241. The bridge over the River *Leie* has two Broel towers which date from 1386 and 1413.

Ieper (Ypres.) The futile trench warfare in Flanders during the First World War caused the deaths of 300 000 Allied soldiers. 250 000 of these were from Britain and its Commonwealth. Numerous large war cemeteries, e.g. at **Passendale**. Every evening at 9 the last post is blown at the *Menin Gate* in memory of those who fell in both World Wars.
The *Lakenhalle* (Cloth Hall) is 132 m long and its tower is 70 m high. It was built during the 13th-14th-cent. when Ypres was an important trading centre with 200 000 inhabitants. The Hall was destroyed during the First World War but it has been faithfully restored. On the second Sunday in May a carnival (Kattenwoensdag – the Cats' Day) is celebrated with jesters, pranks and processions. The Museum of Art contains a collection of Expressionist paintings. Period furniture in the Museum Merghelynck.

Menen/Halluin on the French border. E 3 continues to Lille – Paris – Bordeaux – San Sebastián – Coimbra – Lisboa.

E 5. Oostende – Gent – Bruxelles/Brussel – Liège

The Oostende – Brussels route is known as the Autoroute du Littoral/Kustautoweg. E 5 comes from London – Dover. Ferries to Calais or Ostend.

Veurne (Furnes), the "Spanish City", with impressive *Grand Place* (Grote Markt). Renaissance town hall and the Church of St. Walburga (14th cent.). The Pavillon Espagnol, was, as late as the 18th cent., the headquarters of Spanish officers. Yearly *Procession of the Penitents,* said to have originated during a plague epidemic in 1644. Barefooted penitents, dressed in black robes and with covered faces bear crosses through the streets.

The entire Belgian sea coast, stretching from de Panne to Knokke is only about 70 km long, but it is the yearly host to over 9 million Belgian and foreign guests. Crowding is not unknown. It is advisable to avoid the motorway to Brussels on Sunday evenings.

De Panne (la Panne). Large resort popular with French visitors. On its broad beach it is possible to sail on land yachts – these wheeled vehicles can reach speeds up to 85 kmh.

Adinkerke. Inland sand dunes (Cabourg). Westhoek nature reserve. The Meli amusement park contains a zoo and a fairy-tale park.

Koksijde (Coxyde). Nature reserve with the Hoge Blekker sand dune. At 35 m, this is the highest dune on the Belgian coast. Ruins of the *Abbaye des Dunes,* an abbey founded in 1107. On the second Sunday in July there is a ceremonial blessing of the sea. Organ museum with over 80 mechanical organs.

Oostduinkerke. Resort. Mounted shrimp fishers. *Nieuwport.* Resort. Fishing port. The old town, completely destroyed during the First World War, has been reconstructed. During the German invasion in 1914, the sluice gates at Niewpoort were opened and the area was flooded. de Ilzermonding nature reserve. Witches' procession on the third Sunday in May.

OOSTENDE (Ostend, 75 000). Belgium's most distinguished health resort. Elegant promenade, casino and Kursaal. The lively and picturesque fishing harbour at Visserskai is the home of many excellent fish restaurants. The training ship *Mercator* now serves as a museum. The house that once belonged to James Ensor (1860-1949), the English painter who emigrated to Ostend, now features an exhibition of his works.

Road 72 continues to the little seaside resort of *Wenduine* and the larger, livelier *Blankenberge* (15 000). June 4-5 Harbour Festival, July 3 Blessing of the Sea. There is a parade of flowers on the last Sunday in August.

Zeebrugge. Belgium's sole deep water port. The harbour was completed in 1907. It is linked with Bruges by the Baudouin Canal. Seaside resort. Fishing port, open-air market, war museum. *Lissewege,* idyllic village with picturesque canal, 13th-cent. church and large Cistercian abbey. The Goedendag Inn dates back to the 15th cent. and still maintains a high standard.

Knokke-Heist (30 000) consists of the seaside resorts of Heist, Duinbergen, Albert Strand, Knokke, and Het Zoute. Greatest number of tourist beds in Belgium. Large variety of tourist services and sports. Notable among the many activities is the Festival of Humour held at the end of July. Zwin nature reserve.

The route continues to Breskens in Holland and the ferry to Vlissingen (Flushing).

BRUGGE (Bruges, 55 000). Old Hanseatic town. During the Middle Ages it had 200 000 inhabitants. The harbour silted up during the 16th cent. Bruges has preserved its medieval character. The buildings that face on to the *Grote Markt* have scarcely changed since the Middle Ages. The 83 m high *belfry* (13th cent.) houses a carillon with 47 chimes. Hour-long concerts are held once a week.

The *Chapel of the Holy Blood* (Heiligblutkapelle) houses a casket which is believed to contain a few drops of the blood of Christ. This holy relic was brought to Bruges by crusaders in the 12th cent. A Procession of the Holy Blood is held on the first Sunday in May and a Passion play is presented every fifth year (1987, 1992 etc.). Michelangelo's white marble "Madonna and Child" is in the *Church of Our Lady* (Onze-Lieve Vrouwkerk) (12th-15th cent.). The church tower is 130 m high. There is a museum in the St. Salvador Cathedral. *The Groening Museum* displays Flemish art. The exhibits include works of Jan van Eyck. Christopheros altar by Hans Memling. *The Palace of Justice* is one of Europe's most beautiful Baroque buildings. Lovely 15th-cent. Hotel Gruuthuse. Begijnhof (Almshouse) from the 13th cent. Boat excursions on the canals and in Minnewater, once a thriving harbour. The flood-lit buildings of night-time Bruges are an unforgettable sight.

Torhout. Town hall with pottery museum. *Tielt.* Centre of an agricultural district, whose small villages and hamlets seem to be lifted out of a painting by Breughel. A tourist route passes ten windmills. A Breughel festival is held in Wingere on the second Sunday in September in odd-numbered years (1985, 1987 etc.).

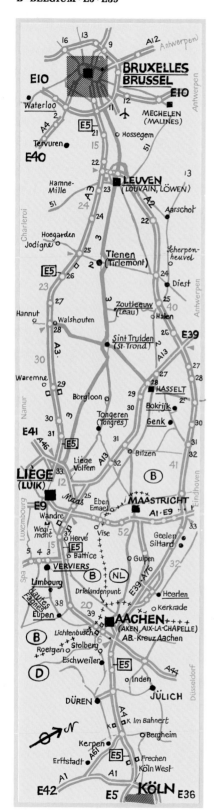

GENT, (Gand, Ghent), see route E3.

Aalst (Alost) has a famous pre-Lenten carnival. Impressive Grote Markt. St. Martin's Church. **Dendermonde,** see E3. **Gaasbeek.** A lovely park surrounds a medieval castle that is now a museum.

BRUXELLES/BRUSSEL (Brussels), see town plans.

Waterloo, see E40.

Leuven (Louvain, 30 000) was founded in the 10th cent. During the 14th cent. it became the residence of the Dukes of Brabant. Its famous university was founded in 1425. Textiles were Leuven's leading industry. Now they have been replaced in importance by breweries. The town was heavily damaged during the First World War. It suffered badly again during 1940 and 1944. *Grote Markt.* Splendid buildings line Naamsestraat. The town hall is richly ornamented and has lovely Renaissance rooms. St. Peter's Church (15th cent.) with examples of the work of Leuven artist Dierk Bouts (1415-1475). The Groot Begijnhof dates from the 13th cent. The Park Abbey was founded in 1129. Famous library.

Tienen (Tirlemont). Churches Onze-Lieve Vrouw ten Poel (Notre-Dame-au-Lac) and St. Germanus. *Zoutleeuw.* Lovely little walled town. St. Leonard Church (13th cent.).

Sint-Truiden (St-Trond). An important abbey once made this one of Limbourg's leading towns. There are three towers on the Grote Markt: the Abbey Tower, the Clock Tower and the Tower of Our Lady. Medieval Brustempoort. Astronomical compensation clock near the church in Begijnhof.

Tongeren (Tongres, 21 000). This town shares its ancient origins with Tournai. It was fortified by the Romans. Here the troops of Ambiorix overwhelmed the legions of Caesar in 59 B.C. There is a statue of Ambiorix in the main square. The early history of the province can be studied at the *Gallo-Roman Museum.* Medieval town hall with Moerenpoort. *Onze- Lieve Vrouwebasiliek,* a 12th-cent. cloister, has a rich treasury.

LIÈGE (Luik), see town plans.

Verviers (31 000). Textile-manufacturing town. Half-timbered houses. *Art museum* with pottery exhibition. *The Museum of Archaeology and Folklore* contains beautiful furniture and a special display of lace.

Limbourg. A small town which retains the imprint of the Middle Ages. Narrow alleys. Ramparts. A lovely road leads to Spa, see E9. *Hautes Fagnes* (the High Fenns), a beautiful undulating landscape. The Baraque-Michel plateau is about 600 m above sea level. Splendid views from *Le Signal de Botrange. Eupen* (15 000). Industrial town, famous for its pre-Lenten carnival.

E5 continues to Aachen – Köln – Frankfurt – Wien – Budapest – Beograd – Sofia – Istanbul – Ankara – Antakya.

E 39. Antwerpen—Heerleen – Aachen

See general map and maps of routes E3, E5, E9 and E10.

ANTWERPEN (Antvers, Antwerp), see town plans.

Lier (30 000) has beautiful houses round the town square. The imposing Church of St-Gommaire was under construction 1425—1540. The Zimmer Tower remains of the old fortifications. It was named after Louis Zimmer who constructed the astronomical clock.

Herentals. The town gates date from the 14th cent. Town hall with a beautiful "Lakenhalle" (Cloth Hall). The Church of St. Trudis (St-Waudry) is in the Gothic style. **Geel** (30 000) is known as the Town of Mercy. 3 000 mentally retarded people live with families of the town. this tradition dates back to the legend of Saint Dymphna, an Irish princess, who was raped by her father, the king, and later beheaded. This took place right here in Geel. Mentally retarded people are said to have been cured at her tomb in the Church of St-Dymphna.

Tongerloo. A local museum contains a replica of Leonardo's "The Last Supper". It was painted in 1545 by Solario, one of Leonardo's pupils, and retains its glowing colours. The original, in the monastery of Santa Maria delle Grazie in Milan, has faded and been damaged.

Hasselt (40 000). Capital of the province of Limbourg, famous for its Genever (gin). Interesting 17th-cent. half-timbered house, "Het Sweert" ("The Sword") faces the Grote Markt. There is a black madonna, "Virga Jesse", in the 18th-cent. Church of Our Lady (O.L. Vrouwkerk). Processions every seventh year.

Bokrijk. A large estate which has been transformed into a recreation area. Beautiful park with many small lakes, rose garden and arboretum. Open-air museum features a 13th-cent. church and old inn. There is an excellent restaurant in the castle. **Genk** (60 000). Industrial town.

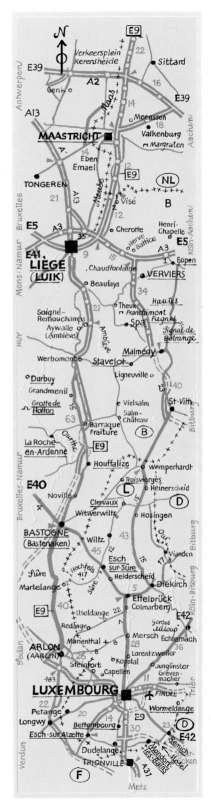

E 9. Maastricht – Liège – Luxembourg

Dutch border at *Visé*. E9 comes from Amsterdam.

The *Eben-Emael* fortress was thought to be impenetrable. It was a shock to the Allies in 1940 when it fell to the Germans after a two-hour battle.

LIÈGE (Luik), see town plans. *Verviers, Eupen, Limbourg,* see E5.

Spa. The original spa. Once Europe's most renowned thermal resort. A little town with lovely walks. Musée de la ville d'Eau contains the Musée du cheval (Museum of the Horse).

Hautes Fagnes (the High Fenns). A beautiful wooded high plateau. Observation point *Baraque-Michel*. At 694 m above sea level, *Le Signal de Botrange* is the highest point in Belgium.

The Ardennes. A woodland with deep valleys and heights that reach up to 500-600 m. Although the area is sparsely populated there are many fine inns where the visitor can eat very well indeed. Ardennes ham is justifiably world famous.

Malmédy. The beautiful centre of this old town was destroyed during the air raids in 1944. Its carnival is one of the largest in Belgium.

Stavelot (5 000). Lovely scenic location. Picturesque streets and alleys. Half-timbered houses. Luxurious inn, "Hostelier de Sanglier" (The Wild Boar). The Benedictine abbey was founded by St. Remacle in the 7th cent. A painting in the church shows him hunting. There is a yearly carnival on the third Monday after Easter.

Durbuy (320). Belgium's smallest town. Resort. Lovely church and palace. *Grotte de Hotton*, formed by the River Isbelle, is 300 m deep. A section of the cave is open to visitors and offers a beautiful display of colours. The cave was first discovered about 1960. The most famous cave, **Han-sur-Lesse,** a bit to the west, was discovered in 1819. Galleries, great halls, passageways. The "Cathedral Hall" is 129 m high. A tour of the cave in boats and on foot usually takes about two hours. Warm clothing is advisable. Safari park. There is a hunting museum in the Lavauz Ste-Anne castle.

La Roche-en-Ardennes. Small town but important tourist resort in the beautiful Ourthe Valley. Castle ruin.

Houffalize. Small town deep in the valley. 13th-cent. church.

Bastogne (7 000). St. Remacle Church. Trier gate and remains of a 14th-cent. fortification. Museum on *Mardasson Hill* next to an American monument. "Multivision" show describing the Battle of the Ardennes in 1944. Then, German troops under the leadership of General von Rundstedt started their last successful offensive and surrounded the American forces. Their advance was finally halted by the troops of the American general, Patton.

Saint Hubert, see E40.

Arlon (14 000). Capital of Luxembourg Belge (the Belgian province of Luxembourg) and a resort. Founded during the Roman occupation. Remains of a tower and a 3rd-4th-cent. basilica. *Musée Luxembourgeois,* an archaeological museum, contains artifacts that reflect the town's impressive history.

LUXEMBOURG, see page 295.

Alternative route:
A winding, beautiful road leads through the Vallée del'Our from Malmédy to Luxembourg.

Troisvierges (Three Virgins). Small resort. Church (1640) with splendid altar.

Clervaux. Small town situated in a deep narrow valley. The feudal castle was built in the 12th cent. Now a *museum* with displays of early monastery life, castles in Luxembourg and the Second World War. It also contains Edward Steichen's famed "Family of Man" photo exhibition.
The enormous St-Maurice et St-Maur Benedictine abbey, built at the turn of the century, was badly damaged during the Second World War.

Esch-sur-Sûre. Small town nestled between high mountains and bordered by the winding River Sûre. The houses hug a steep cliff. Ruins of a castle. The road approaching the town passes through two tunnels (1850 and 1954).

LUXEMBOURG, see page 295.

Bettembourg. Fairy-tale park *Parc Merveilleux*. Game preserve. *Esch- sur-Alzette.* Industrial town with beautiful surroundings. Fine views out over Luxembourg, Belgium, France and Germany from the Galgebierg nature reserve. *Museum* with displays from the Resistance Movement during the Second World War.

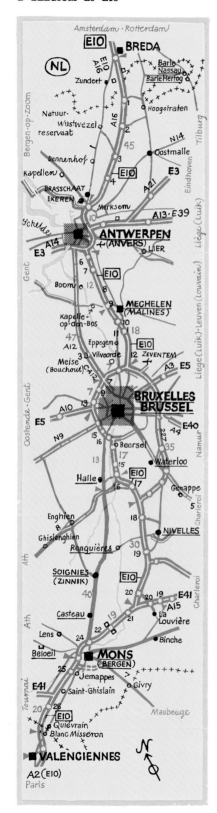

Dudelange (15 000) at the foot of Mont St-Jean. Industrial town. Paintings by Luxembourg artist Don Lang in the church. Radio Luxembourg TV transmitter on top of the Gintzebierg.

Mondorf-les-Bains. Large thermal spa with 24 warm springs. Splendid "Kurpark" with rose garden. Casino. **Remich.** Wine centre at the foot of steep, vineyard-covered hills. The St-Martin caves may be visited. Slightly to the north is **Wormeldange** with a cooperative wine factory which welcomes visitors. Special hall for wine-tasting.

E 9 continues to Metz – Strasbourg – Basel – Milano – Genova.

E 10. Breda – Antwerpen – Bruxelles/Brussel – Mons

Dutch border. E 10 comes from Groningen – Amsterdam.

Baarle-Nassau. Enclaves are not unusual in Europe, but Barle-Nassau is unique. There are no fewer than 30 small Belgian enclaves on Dutch soil – and in these there are five small Dutch enclaves. The Dutch enclaves are called **Baarle-Nassau** (5 000) and the Belgian **Baarle-Hertog** (Baerle-Duc) (2 500). National borders criss-cross the village and Dutch and Belgian shops stand side by side. Dutch florins and Belgian francs are universally accepted.

ANTWERPEN (Antwerp), see town plans.

MECHELEN (Malines) (65 000). Charles the Bold, Margaret of Austria and Charles Quint, each attended by learned men and artists, have all held court here. Now the town is famed for its lace and tapestries. Examples of these crafts are to be found in the City Museum. **Grote Markt** is one of the finest in Belgium. It is lined with the town hall and Baroque and Renaissance façades. **St. Rombaut's Cathedral** (13th cent.) has a 97 m high tower. The tower was originally planned to reach 167 m, 6 m higher than the tower in Ulm, West Germany. Carillon with 49 chimes. There is a school for carilloneurs in Mechelen. Many famous works of art, among them van Dyck's "Crucifixion". Rubens' triptych, "The Adoration of the Magi", in the Church of St. John (St-Janskerk).

BRUSSEL/BRUXELLES (Brussels), see town plans.

Waterloo, see E 40.

Nivelles (18 000). The town was largely destroyed in 1940, but the older houses have been reconstructed. The Reliquary of St. Gertrude (Collegiale Ste-Gertrude) was founded in 1046 but there have been many later additions. Its Gothic tower was destroyed in 1940. It was rebuilt, as a result of a referendum, in the original Romanesque style.

Halle (20 400). The Notre Dame basilica houses a statue of the madonna (La Vierge Noire) which was donated by Elizabeth of Austria in 1580. Procession September 1.

Soignies was founded in 640. Lovely old buildings. The St. Vincent Church was built in the 10th cent.

Ronquières on the Brussels-Charleroi Canal. At this point on the canal, boats of up to 1 350 tons are transported in an enormous lift up a 1 400 m long incline to a lock and connecting aqueduct. The process can be viewed from an observation tower.

Ath. Fortified town (Vauban) with 12th-cent. Tour de Burbant. Beautiful Grand-Place. Cortège des Géants festival held on the fourth Sunday in August. Giant-sized (4 m) figures are paraded through the streets. Goliath and Samson are followed by Ambiorix, who defeated the Romans at Tongeren (route E 5).

Casteau with SHAPE, the NATO headquarters.

Beloeil, the "Belgian Versailles", completed in 1699, was created by the architect Mansart for the Prince of Ligne. The château was rebuilt after a fire in 1900. Beautiful interior. Lovely park that retains the original 17th- and 18th-cent. atmosphere.

MONS (Bergen) (65 000). Capital of Hainaut. Industrial town. Famed as early as the Middle Ages for its cloth. St-Waudru, one of the most beautiful churches in Belgium, is on a hill. It is 108 m long. Lovely 17th-cent. belfry. Town hall (Hôtel de Ville) on the Grand-Place. To the left of the entrance is the statue of a crowned ape from the "Grand-Garde". Caresses of tourists have worn down the ape's crown. Trinity Sunday Procession (the Lumecon Festival) depicts the battle of St. George and the Dragon. Puissant Museum with religious and archaeological collections, war museum and displays of ceramics, industrial development and coal. Musée des Beaux-Arts (art museum).

Quiévrain/Blanc Misseron, French border.

E 10 continues to Valenciennes and Peronne. From there, together with E 3, the route leads to Paris.

E 40. Bruxelles/Brussel—Luxembourg

BRUXELLES/BRUSSEL, see town plans.

Forêt de Soignes. Large, beautiful forest, crisscrossed by roads and hiking trails.

Parc du Tervuren, to the northeast, contains an arboretum. *Central Africa Museum* in Tervuren is housed in Leopold II's large palace. Collections from the former Belgian Congo, present-day Zaire.

Waterloo. At the Battle of Waterloo (18 June 1815) Napoleon was defeated by the British under Wellington and the Prussians under Blücher. 65 000 lives were lost. "Waterloo" came to be synonymous with "definite defeat". *The Butte du Lion* offers a panoramic view of the battlefield. Large, cast-iron lion facing France. Panorama. Several museums and monuments.

Overijse. Small town with two beautiful churches, the Baroque Liebfrauenkirche and the Gothic Church of St-Martin.

Villers-le-Ville. Ruins of a Cistercian abbey, founded by St. Bernard in 1146. Abbey church dating from 1242. The buildings were destroyed in the French Revolution but have been reconstructed in the 20th cent. The restaurant in the former abbey mill serves beer and bakery goods prepared according the the monks' old recipes. Lovely surroundings.

NAMUR, see E41. The Meuse Valley is lovely. Marché-les-Dames got its name from a convent founded in the 12th century. The 70 m high cliffs are popular with mountaineering enthusiasts but are quite treacherous. King Albert perished here in 1934.

Annevoie-Rouillon Palace (17th—18th cent.). Lovely park with canals. **Bouvignes.** Small town dominated by the Crevecœur castle ruins. Interesting religious art in the Church of St-Lambert. *Leffe,* an abbey originally founded in 1152, contains an art museum.

Spontin. Beautiful medieval castle with pinnacles and turrets and a moat. Still used as a private residence. Mineral water springs.

Dinant (10 000). During the Middle Ages the town was an important commercial centre and a member of the Hanseatic League. Famous for its wrought-copper works. Beautifully set between steep mountains. Fine view from the Citadel, 100 m above the Meuse. Weapons museum. The original Church of Notre-Dame was destroyed by falling rocks in 1277. A Romanesque portico and a Madonna are preserved in the present 16th-cent. church. "La Merveilleuse" cave. Freyr Castle has a lovely park. 1.5 km south of Dinant is the legendary Bayard Rock.

Forneau St-Michel. Museum of ironworking and other Wallon trades. **Celles.** Village in the lovely setting. The Romanesque Church of St-Hadelin contains a crypt from the 9th cent. *Hastière-par-delà* also has an old Romanesque church.

Waha can boast Belgium's oldest church (1051). The interior has been totally refurbished. Waha is situated in Belgian Luxembourg which used to form part of the Grand Duchy.

Rochefort. Small town in the Lomme Valley. The river has created beautiful caves with stalactites and stalagmites. A tour takes 1 hour and 15 min. The most famous of the caves is *Han-sur-Lesse* which was discovered in 1819. Galleries, large halls and corridors. The "Cathedral" is a 129 m high cave. A tour takes about 2 hours. Warm clothing is advisable as the temperature is 12°C and the air is damp. Museum. Safari park. Hunting museum in *Lavaux Ste-Anne,* a castle. La Roche-en-Ardenne, see E9.

St-Hubert. Small town in the Ardennes Woods (see also E9). Beautiful church (mainly 16th cent.) dedicated to St. Hubert, patron saint of hunters. He was a nobleman who received his calling from God during a legendary stag hunt on Good Friday 683. The story is told in paintings in the church. Pilgrimages the first Sunday in September and on Hubertus Day, 3 November, which is celebrated with hunting on horseback in several countries.

Road N28 continues to the beautiful *Vallée de la Semois* with tobacco fields. The centre of the area is the little town of *Bouillon.* In 1095 Duke Godefroy of Bouillon became the leader of the first Crusade. After the conquest of Jerusalem he became governor of the town. He died in 1100. His enormous castle remains but has been rebuilt and added to several times. Superb views from the "Austrian Tower". Musée Ducal (the Duke's Museum) on the palace square contains folklore from the Ardennes. A large part of the museum is dedicated to the crusades.

Abbaye d'Orval. The monastery was founded in 1070 and soon became one of Europe's foremost and wealthiest. It was ravaged several times, finally in 1793, when it burned for six weeks. Ruins of the church. The new monastery was built in 1948. Tours. 4 km to the south is the little village of *Villers-devant-Orval.*

Bastogne and *Arlon,* see E 9.

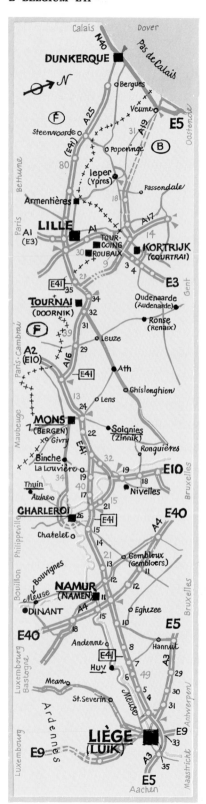

E 41. Tournai – Mons – Charleroi – Namur – Liège
Autoroute de Wallonie/Autoweg van Vallonie.

E 41 comes from Dunkerque.

TOURNAI (Doornik, 35 000). One of the oldest towns in Belgium. A Christian settlement as early as 200 B.C. During the Middle Ages, Tournai became one of the most important centres of art in Flanders. The French influence has always been very strong. Large numbers of old buildings were destroyed during an air raid in 1940. The *Cathedral of Notre Dame* (12th cent.) is one of Europe's most splendid churches. 134 m long, five towers, treasury, stained-glass windows, art treasures. "Souls in Purgatory" by Rubens. The 72 m high belfry, constructed in the 13th cent., is the oldest in Belgium. 256 steps, beautiful view. Carillon with 43 chimes. *Musée des Beaux-Arts,* art museum with works of Rubens, Breughel and Ensor. Musée de Folklore. *Musée d'Histoire,* art, mainly from the 18th cent., and porcelain from Tournai. The Hôtel de Ville is in a bishop's palace built in the 11th cent. but reconstructed in 1763. The *Pont des Trous* has two towers.
Festival of Military Music on June 11 and an historic festival, "La Peste", on the last Sunday in August and September 5.

MONS (Bergen), see E 10.

Soignies (Zinnik) with the Church of St. Vincent (10th-12th cent.). St. Vincent founded the town in 640.

Binche has an exquisite *Vieille Ville* (Old Town) and a well- preserved town wall with 27 towers. St-Ursmarus Church (12th cent.) has an organ which was brought from the Berlin synagogue in 1907. Beautiful town hall. The *Musée International du Carneval et du Masque* (1975) has exhibitions describing carnivals held all over the world. The Shrove Tuesday Carnival is one of the largest in Belgium. Its origins are said to date back to the 14th cent. Hundreds of costumed "fools" parade through the town.

Thuin. Medieval town with a "beffroi" (watch tower) that dates from 1628. The Marche militaire de Saint-Roch is a religious procession which is a reconstruction of the time when the Relics of St. Roch had to be guarded by an armed escort.

CHARLEROI (267000). The city was given its present name in 1666 in honour of Charles II of Spain. Heavy industry. The centre of an industrial and coal mining area. Modern industrial exhibition hall. Technical university. The *Musée du Verre* (glass museum). Musée archéologique.

The road leading south goes through a lovely wooded area dotted with small resort towns. *Philippeville,* the *Etang de Virelles* lakes and *Chimay* with a large château.

NAMUR (Namen, 32 000). Beautifully situated. From its promontory, the enormous citadel dominates the town. Aerial tramway. Lovely scenic motor tours on the *Circuit de la Citadelle.* Maison des Soeurs de Notre Dame (Sisters of Our Lady convent), completed in 1767, is mainly in the Italian Baroque style. *St. Loup,* also Baroque, is a Jesuit church. The belfry was originally a watch tower. Musée archéologique.
A beautiful road leads south through the *Meuse valley,* past the lovely town of *Bouvigne* to *Dinant* (10 000), which is dominated by the Citadelle, that looms 100 m above the river. Antique weapons museum. Impressive views. Cable car. La Merveilleuse caves.
An interesting, 40 km long, excursion can be made to Rocher Bayard, Foy-Notre- Dame, Celles, Vallée de la Lesse and Anseremme. Châteaux Spontin, Walzin, Feyr, Vèves and Annevoie. Furfooz nature reserve.

The road continues to *Bouillon* in the lovely Semois valley. The castle which has its origins in the 10th cent. was once the home of Gottfrid of Bouillon, the leader of the First Crusade. Beautiful views. A small museum has exhibits devoted to the First Crusade and life in the Ardennes.

The Ardennes is a wooded area with deep valleys and heights reaching 500-600 m. Sparsely populated, and relatively unspoiled landscape. Many picturesque inns serving superb food. Ardennes ham, slowly smoked over beech chippings, is served in paper-thin slices.

The **Han-sur-Lesse** caves, see E 9.

Huy (13 000). Picturesque old town. Notre Dame is one of the most beautiful Gothic churches in the country. Superb views from the citadel (cable car). The château was completed in 1818. During the Second World War it was transformed into a concentration camp. Huy is renowned for its pewter.

LIÈGE (Luik), see town plans.

E 42. Echternach – Luxembourg, see page 296.

TOWN PLANS

ANTWERPEN

(Anvers, Antwerp, 700 000)
One of the major ports of Europe, Belgium's largest harbour and second largest city. Diamond cutting. Old town with atmospheric streets and *Grote Markt* with picturesque old houses huddled around the *Onze-Lieve-Vrouwe Cathedral* (14th-16th cent.). Its 123 m tower is a symbol of the city. "The Descent from the Cross" by Rubens. Renaissance town hall and guildhouses line the Grote Markt. *Brabo fountain* (1887) in the centre of the Grote Markt has as its theme the legend of Brabo. He chopped off the hand of the giant Antigonus and hurled it into the Schelde with the cry "hand werpen" – this is said to be the origin of the city's name. The neighbouring Vleeshuis was built in 1503 by Waghemakere. *Museum of archaeology, history, handicrafts and musical instruments. Rubenshuis* (1610), the home and studio of Peter Paul Rubens. His tomb is in Sint-Jacob's (St. James') Church. A "Holy Family" is on the altar in the chapel. ***Plantin-Moretus Museum*** (16th cent.). Here the printer, Plantin, once worked. Manuscripts, first editions and museum of printing. ***Mayer van den Bergh-Museum*** with works by Breughel the Elder; ivories and gold. ***Koninklijk Museum van Schone Kunsten*** with rich collection of the works of Antwerp artists.

Antwerp's oldest building, Steen Castle, is now a maritime museum

Steen fortress was destroyed in 836. The present building dates from the 16th cent. Now it houses the *Maritime Museum.* Open-air museum of sculpture in Middleheim Park. Museum of folkore. Museum of handicrafts in Sterckshof. Smidt van Gelder. Museum with 18th-cent. French interiors.

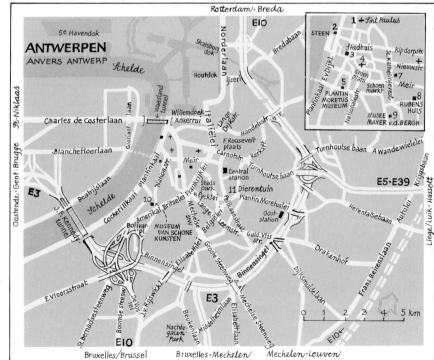

1 St. Paul's Church.
2 Steen Castle with Maritime Museum.
3 Grote Markt with town hall.
4 Cathedral.
5 Plantin-Moretus Museum.
6 St. James' Church.
7 Stock exchange.
8 Rubens' House.
9 Mayer van den Bergh Museum.
10 Koninklijk Museum van Schone Kunsten (art).
11 Zoo.

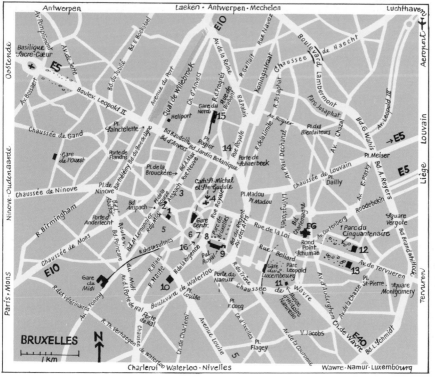

The Cathedral of St-Michel et Ste-Gudule in Brussels

1 Grand-Place.
2 Stock exchange.
3 Opera house.
4 Cathedral of St-Michel et Ste-Gudule.
5 Manneken pis.
6 Museum of Modern Art.
7 Albertina (National Library).
8 Place Royale with Musée d'Art and Palais des Beaux-Arts.
9 Royal Palace.
10 Palais de Justice.
11 Museum of Natural History.
12 Army History Museum.
13 Musées Royaux d'Art et d'Histoire.
14 Railway Museum.
15 Botanical gardens.
16 Musée d'Art ancien.

1 Royal Palace.
2 Art Museum.
3 Palais des Prince-Évêques (Prince-Bishops' Palace).
4 Place du Marché and town hall.
5 Musée de la Vie Wallonne (folklore).
6 Museum of Architecture.
7 Musée d'Ansembourg (furniture).
8 Musée Curtius (decorative art, glass, archaeology).
9 Arms Museum.
10 Palais des Congrès (Palace of Congress).
11 Musée d'Art wallon.
12 Museum of Iron and Coal.

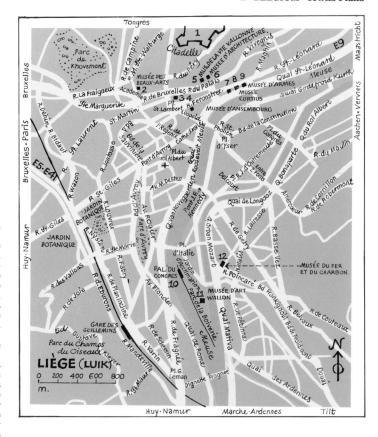

BRUXELLES/BRUSSEL

(Brussels, 1.1 million)
The bilingual capital of Belgium with its wide avenues, winding streets, splendid houses, monumental public buildings and magnificent squares in many ways resembles Paris. The approach from the north, past the Botanical Gardens and the Place Rogier with the Cinzano building, and with the Church of the Sacre Cœur as a backdrop, cannot fail to impress the visitor. The major shopping areas and traffic junctions are Place Rogier, Boulevard Adolphe Max and Place de la Bourse.
The **Grand-Place** is one of the most magnificent squares in Europe. It is lined with Baroque buildings that have replaced the earlier Gothic houses which were destroyed during the French bombardment in 1695. The Grand-Place must be seen both by day and at night when the ornate façades are illuminated (every evening until midnight).
The town hall (15th cent.) with its 90 m high tower dominates the south side of the square. It is topped by a statue of the Archangel Michael, the patron saint of Brussels.
A short walk from the Grand-Place is Manneken pis (1619), the famous statue by Jérôme Duquesnoy the Elder. He has become something of a symbol of Brussels and all of the nearby streets are crammed with shops selling replicas of the charming figure. On important holidays he is clothed in uniforms donated by his admirers. His complete wardrobe can be viewed in a museum. In the same area are many shops selling the well-known Brussels lace.
Many of the best (and most expensive) restaurants in Brussels are in this part of the city, among them L'auberge du Bon Vieux Temps.
The **Cathedral of Ste-Gudule,** also known as the Cathedral of St-Michel, built in the Gothic style (13th-15th cent.) has famous stained-glass windows and a pulpit carved in 1699 by Hendrik Verbruggen. Steep streets lead up from the old "lower city" to the newer "high city". The Parc de Bruxelles is lined by monumental buildings. Palais du Roi (Royal Palace). The enormous Palais de Justice (Law Courts), built in the Greco-Roman

style, is the largest 18th-cent. building in Europe.
Musée d'Art ancien is one of Europe's largest museums of fine art. Large collection of the works of Dutch and Flemish painters. The world's finest collection of musical instruments. Musée Royaux d'Art et d'Histoire (Museum of Art and History). Museum Wiertz with modern art, including the work of James Ensor.
Erasmus' house in Anderlecht where the great humanist Erasmus of Rotterdam lived in 1521. There is a Central Africa Museum in Tervuren (route E 5). Brussels has a total of 28 museums. The Royal Palace in Laeken is the location of the royal family's crypt. **Huizingen** is the site of a beautiful park and a small zoo.
The massive silver spheres of the Atomium are visible for miles. There is a restaurant in one of the spheres. The structure was the symbol of the Brussels World's Fair of 1958. Another reminder of the fair are the modern highways that circle the inner city. But boulevards in Brussels date back to the early 19th cent. when Napoleon had them constructed on the site of the 13th-cent. ramparts. The only remaining city gate is the Porte de Hal whith a weapons museum.
Brussels' earliest origins are in the 6th cent. Charles Quint transformed it into the capital of Europe. After the

Second World War it has regained this position for now it is the headquarters of EEC (the Common Market) whose mammoth office blocks dominate a part of the city. It is also the headquarters of the European Investment Bank and Euro-atom. Casteau, on the road to Mons, is the home of SHAPE, the NATO military headquarters.

LIÈGE (Luik, 450 000)

Belgium's third largest city. Heavy industry. University. The capital of Wallonia, a freedom-loving province, in constant struggle with would-be invaders. The Fontaine du Perron in the Place du Marché is the symbol of Walloon independence and justice.
St. Paul's Cathedral with exquisite stained-glass windows and a rich treasury. Palais des Prince-Évêques with splendid façade and an arcaded and galleried courtyard.
Musée de la Vie Wallonne is a folklore museum. Marionette collection and puppet theatre.
Musée Curtius in a 17th-cent. patrician house. Glass Museum. Musée d'Ansembourg with a furniture collection. Arms museum and a museum of iron and coal. The large aquarium is owned by the university.
Beautiful views out over Liège and the Meuse from the Citadelle. Access by car or on foot (stairs with 407 steps).

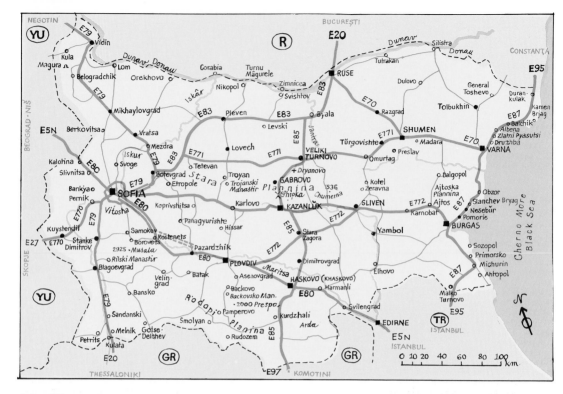

BG · Bulgaria

BG·Bâlgarija

Area: 111 000 km² (42 818 sq. miles)

Population: 9 million. Bulgarian is a South Slavic language similar to Serbo-Croatian and Russian. The Cyrillic alphabet is used. Most Bulgarians speak Russian. German, French and English are usually understood in the major tourist centres.

Major cities: Sofia 1 million, Plovdiv 309 000, Varna 250 000, Burgas 144 000, Ruse 160 000.

Government: People's republic with a National Assembly as the legislative power.

History
681-1018 First Bulgarian Kingdom.

863 The brothers Cyril and Methodius create the Cyrillic alphabet.
1187-1396 The Second Bulgarian Kingdom.
1396-1878 Bulgaria under Turkish rule.
1876 The April Uprising against the Turks.
1877-1878 Russo-Turkish War. Bulgaria gains independence.
1878-1944 Third Bulgarian Kingdom.
1914-1918 First World War.
1939-1945 Second World War. Bulgaria enters on the side of the Axis but after an armed uprising in 1944 joins the Allies.
1946 The People's Republic of Bulgaria is proclaimed.

Currency: Leva (BGL)
1 lev = 100 stotinki
The import and export of Bulgarian currency is strictly forbidden.

Business hours: Banks 8.30-11.45 a.m. Saturdays 8.00-11.00 a.m. In the major tourist centres it is possible to exchange money outside the regular banking hours. Post offices 8.00 a.m.-7.00 p.m. Saturdays in major towns 8.00 a.m.-1.00 or 2.00 p.m. Shops 9.00 a.m.-12.00 noon and 4.30-7.00 p.m.

Holidays: New Year's Day, May 1 and 2 (Labour Day), May 24 (Education Day) September 9 and 10 (National Holiday), November 7 (The Great October Revolution Day).

Hotels
The hotels are classified as de luxe, first class, second class and third class. The largest hotel chain is Balkantourist, a state-owned concern. Private rooms are also classified according to this system.

Camping
There are 130 camping sites divided into three categories: special, first and second. Most sites have chalets. Camping maps can be obtained from tourist offices. Camping is allowed only at officially recognized sites.

Food and drink
Succulent stews, fresh salads and yoghurt are all typical of Bulgarian

---

Routes described:

E 79   Vidin – Sofia – Thessaloniki (E 20)

E 80   Niš – Sofia – Plovdiv – Edirne (E 5N)

E 83   Ruse – Sofia (E 20)

E 85   Ruse – Stara Zagora – Kŭrdzhali

E 87   Constanţa – Varna – Burgas – Malko Tŭrnovo (E 95)

E 770   Sofia – Kyustendil – Skopje (E 27), see E 79

E 771   Sofia – Tŭrnovo – Varna (E 27)

Town plan: Sofia

N.B. The new European road numbers have recently been introduced in Bulgaria. As the old road numbers appear on most maps and are still used in the neighbouring countries, they are given here in parentheses.

The Rila Monastery, 1 147 m above sea level, was founded in 941

cuisine. Gyuvech is a meat and vegetable stew, baked in the oven. Kavarma kebab is a rich stew in which vegetables predominate. Kebabcheta is grilled minced beef, deliciously spiced. Moussaka is baked minced lamb, aubergines and spices. Tarator, based on yoghurt, includes thinly sliced cucumber and spices. Kisselo Mleko is Bulgarian yoghurt. Shopska salata is a tomato, pepper, onion and goat cheese salad.

Slivova is plum brandy. Mastika has a Pernod-like taste. Pliska is five-star brandy. Rosa is rose liqueur. Wines: Misket Karlovo, Riesling, Hemus (demi-sec), the white château wines of Euxinograd.

Shopping

Handicrafts, embroidery, handwoven rugs, jewellery, leather goods, pottery, woodcarvings, wrought iron, and copper. Keep the receipt if you pay with Western currency.

Petrol

Petrol stations are usually about 30-40 km apart. Petrol coupons are necessary to obtain fuel. They can be purchased at the border or through the Chipka (Union of Bulgarian Motorists) head office in Sofia. Balkantourist and Chipka sell special package tours to motorists that include a certain amount of free petrol.

Speed limits. Traffic regulations

Motorways 120 kmh, other roads 80 kmh, built-up areas 60 kmh. Cars towing caravans 100 kmh on motorways, 70 kmh on other roads and 50 kmh in built up areas. Persons who have been in possession of a driving licence for less than two years are not allowed to drive faster than 100 kmh on motorways and 70 kmh on other roads and

50 kmh in built up areas.
Children under the age of ten are not allowed to travel in the front seat. If your car is fitted with seat belts it is compulsory to wear them.
It is mandatory (even for foreign motorists) to see that the car is equipped with fire extinguisher and first-aid kit.

Roads

Main roads are usually good. Bulgaria has adopted the new European road numbering system. The previous numbers are also indicated, as they are shown on most maps and are still in use in neighbouring countries.

Road patrols

Yellow cars of the Bulgarian Motor Club provide free technical assistance. Some main roads are patrolled 6.00 a.m.-10.00 p.m. Some secondary roads are patrolled 10.00 a.m-7.00 p.m. Assistance can be summoned in most towns by dialling 146.

Union of Bulgarian Motorists, 6 Sveta Sofia, Sofia C. Tel. 87 88 01. Balkantourist, 1 Lenin Square, Sofia. Tel. 841 31. Tourist information, Bd Dondukov 37, Sofia.
Bulgarian National Tourist Office, 18 Princes Street, London W1. Tel. 01-499 6988.

Tourist resort on the Black Sea

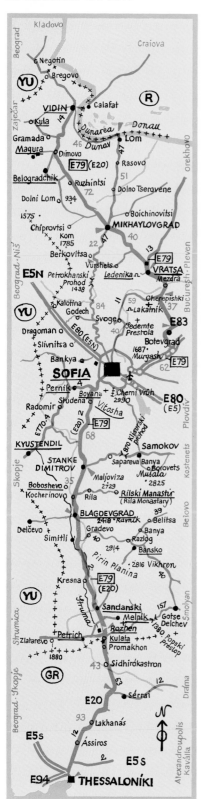

E 79. Vidin – Sofia – Thessaloníki

Previous number: E 20.

Vidin, a modern industrial town situated in a lovely bend of the Danube. The *Baba Vida Citadel* is the only completely preserved medieval fortress in Bulgaria. It was originally built in the 10th cent. on the site of Roman fortifications. Museum with medieval weapons, historical museum, mosque and two beautiful churches. House of Kossuth, the Hungarian patriot.

Kula, with ruins of a 3rd-cent. fortress.

The Magura Caves is a 3 km long labyrinth. Cave paintings from the 8th–9th cent. B.C. Animals, dancers, etc. The passages open up into gigantic halls of stalactites and stalagmites.

The Belogradchik Cliffs, an awe-inspiring landscape with up to 200 m high, strangely shaped chalk cliffs that have names associated with legends: Adam and Eve, the Sphinx, the Bear, the Monks, the Knights etc. Ethnological museum.

Vratsa. Resort associated with the poet Hristo Botev. Annual festival.

The Ledenika Caves with beautiful stalagmites and stalactites.

Iskur Gorge, 42 miles long. Very imposing cliffs, used as practice area for alpine climbers. *Lakatnik* with several caves. *Temnata Duopka* ("The Dark Hole") is more than two miles deep. *Kutino earth pyramids*—some are 100 ft high.

Cherepishki Monastary in beautiful surroundings. The road leading there runs through a canyon. *Sedemté Prestola Monastary* ("The Seven Thrones"). The chapel is a flat-roofed cruciform building. Six chapels have been added to the main altar—the "seven thrones".

SOFIA and the *Vitosha Mountain* with the Boyana Church, see town plans.

E 770 goes to Skopje in Yugoslavia by way of *PERNIK* (80 000) with coal mines and the Lenin Steel Works. House of Culture, theatre, symphony orchestra, museum. *Kyustendil.* Large spa with 40 mineral springs. *Gyueshevo.* Yugoslavian border. E 27 continues to Skopje.

Boboshevo. St. Dimiter Monastery. 15th-cent. frescoes. Church of the Virgin Mary. Contemporary frescoes by Stanislav Dospevski.

Rila Monastery (Rilski manastir), 1 147 m above sea level, was founded in 941 by Ivan Rilski and became the cultural centre of Bulgaria. A mighty construction in an untamed landscape. The present buildings were completed at the beginning of the 19th cent. The 23 m high Hrelyu Tower was completed in 1335. Wall paintings from the same period are still preserved. The main church is richly ornamented. Ikons, frescoes, woodcarvings, 300 monks' cells. Library with 20 000 volumes. Museum with the 14th-cent. wooden throne of Hrelyu. (He was a Bulgarian feudal lord.) Crucifix with 1 500 microscopic figures. Rafail, a monk, worked on it for 12 years. Strange cliff formations at Stob.

Blagoevgrad. Tobacco industry. The town was named in honour of Dimiter Blagoev, founder of the Bulgarian Socialist Party.

Bansko. Lovely location. Earlier an important centre of trade. Churches with beautiful interiors.

Sandanski. Small town with 6th-cent. church. Beautiful mosaics. Warm mineral springs which are used for heating the greenhouses where tomatoes and cucumbers are grown. Tobacco cultivation.

Melnik (600), Bulgaria's smallest town, has been proclaimed a national monument. The beautiful houses and churches date from the period when Melnik was an important centre of trade on the road leading from Greece to Vienna. In 1215 it became the seat of Alexi Slav, a feudal lord. Ruins of his fortress. The town flourished in the 18th and 19th cent. during the "Bulgarian Renaissance". Then there were 40 churches here. Parts of the town were destroyed by fire in 1912.

House of the Boyars (built between the 10th and 14th cent.) is the oldest house in Bulgaria. The Kordopoulo house has walls that are covered with paintings. This is where the famous Melnik wine was stored. Historical museum in the Pashova house. Ruins of the St. Nikola Monastery (13th cent.) and the fortress of Alexi Slav. *Rozhen Monastery* (6 km E). The abbey was built about 1600 and has fine ikons and woodcarvings.

Petrich. Resort. Mineral springs. Peach orchards. *Kulata* at the Greek frontier.

E 20 continues to Sidirókastron and Thessaloniki.

E 80. Niš – Sofia - Plovdiv – Edirne

Previous number: E 5N.

Kalotina. Yugoslavian border. E 5 comes from London – Bruxelles – Frankfurt – Wien – Budapest – Beograd – Niš.

Dragoman. Railway frontier station. Monastery and rock church. The village of **Berendé** has a church that is famous for its ikons.

The road goes through the lovely *Nishava valley.* **Bankya,** a modern thermal resort, 640 m above sea level. Mineral springs.

SOFIA, see town plans.

From Sofia it is possible to take the slightly longer (30 km) but beautiful route through the tourist resorts of **Samokov** and **Borovets,** both close to *Musala,* which at 2 925 m is the highest mountain in Bulgaria. **Rila Monastery,** is one of the major sights in Bulgaria. See E 79.

Kostenets with the **Momin Prohod** health resort. **Belovo.** Open-air pool with mineral waters. **Velingrad.** Spa.

Pazardzhik. *Sveta Bogoroditsa Church* with beautiful woodcarvings. The ornately decorated house of artist Stanislas Dospevski. The local art museum bears his name. The road going north leads to **Panagurishte,** where a large gold treasure, now in Plovdiv, was found. The Historical Museum has exhibitions related to the struggle for independence. In the museum garden there is a street with artisans' shops showing working conditions and equipment.

Road south to **Batak.** Its church was the scene of a terrible massacre in 1876 when the Turks slaughtered women and children who had sought sanctuary there.

PLOVDIV (300 000). Bulgaria's second largest city, founded by Alexander the Great in 273 B.C. Built on six hills. Originally called Philippopolis.

The old part of the city is protected by law. During the Roman period, when it was known as Trimontium (the Three Hills) it had a temple and an acropolis and was a centre of culture and learning. Now a charming *old town* with beautiful houses and picturesque cobbled streets. Remains of fortifications. In the *Museum of Archaeology* there is an impressive display of Thracian gold, including the Panagurishte Gold Treasure, nine golden ships weighing more than six kilogrammes.

The *Ethnographic Museum* is in a lovely fresco-façaded house built in 1847. Noteworthy examples of the goldsmith's art, handicrafts, folk costumes, weaving, musical instruments and architecture. Natural science museum. Independence museum. Art gallery with collections of Bulgarian art. The Lamartine Museum, where the French poet lived in 1883. Clock tower from the Ottoman period. Monuments on *Liberty Hill* dedicated to the Russian soldiers who liberated Bulgaria from the Turks in 1878 and to the Soviet army. Museum of the Revolution.

Plovdiv is a modern city with heavy industries, university, opera house, etc. A large international trade fair is held at the end of September.

Hissar. Spa known to the Thracians and Romans. Remains of a 2 km long Roman wall and a Roman bath. 16 mineral springs.

A road leads south through the *Rhodopean Hills.* **Asenovgrad** with an historical museum. *Assen Fortress,* high on a cliff, existed as long ago as the 9th cent. The present structure was completed in 1231 by Czar Ivan Assen. Beautiful church.

Bachkovo is an impressive monastery, founded in 1083. Museum with frescoes and manuscripts. **Pamporovo.** Tourist resort at over 1 600 m above sea level.

Road E 771 goes onward to **STARA ZAGORA** (115 000), a modern industrial town with remains of a Roman wall. Archaeological museum. The road continues to **Kazanlŭk** and the **Valley of Roses,** see E 85.

Haskovo (55 000). District capital, beautifully situated in the deep Caja River valley. **Dimitrovgrad.** Large industrial town. **Svilengrad** and Kapitan Andreevo at the Turkish frontier.

E 5 continues to Edirne – Istanbul – Ankara – Antakya.

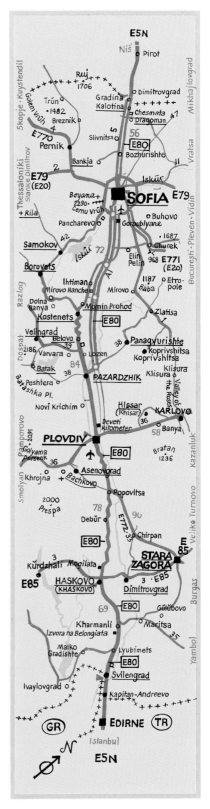

E 83. Ruse – Sofia

Previous number: E 20.

Roumanian border. E 20 comes from the Soviet Union and București. The long Friendship Bridge is also a very important rail link.

RUSE (Roussé, 160 000). Bulgaria's fourth largest city and major Danube port. Oil refineries and shipyards. National Transport Museum. Art museum. Museum in the house of Baba Tonka. Turkish fortifications with the Kjuntu Kapu Gate. Lipnik Park (10 km east), large recreation grounds.

Ivanovo. Close to the little village are remarkable churches, chapels and monks' cells, hewn out of the rocks in the canyon of the river Rusenski Lom. 14-th cent. frescoes. Proclaimed a "World Heritage" landmark by Unesco.

From **Byala** road E 83 continues to Pleven and Sofia. See maps E 79 and E 771.

PLEVEN (103 000). A modern industrial town which has been the victim of many wars during its long history. It was a settlement as long ago as the Stone Age. Thracian fortress from 200 B.C. Ruins of the Roman town of Storogosia. One hundred monuments tell of the joint struggles of Bulgarians and Russians against the Turks. The *Freedom Museum,* housed in the building where Czar Alexander II accepted the capitulation of Osman Pasha who surrendered with 40 000 troups. Diorama of the battle of Pleven 1878 completed in 1977. The District Museum has displays of archaeology, ethnology, natural history and the Revolution.

Vratsa, Ledenika, Iskur Gorge, see E 79. *Botevgrad,* see E 771.

SOFIA, see town plans.

E 85. Ruse – V. Tŭrnovo – Stara Zagora – Kŭrdzhali

Previous number: 3. *Ruse – Byala,* see above, E 83.

Veliko Tŭrnovo, Arbanasi and *Preobrazhenski Monastary,* see E 771.

Dryanovo Monastery in a narrow gorge was founded in the 13th cent. The Church of the Archangel Michael. Ossuary and museum devoted to the uprising in 1876. *Bacho Kiro Cave* with imposing rock formation is named after one of the leaders of the uprising.

Tryavna (Trjavna). Museum-town. Beautiful houses and churches with woodcarvings. Clock tower.

GABROVO (50 000). Industrial town. The Aprilov Fountain, built in 1762 and the clock-tower from 1835 are landmarks. Ethnographical museum. Efera Park, 8 km from the town. Gabrovo has a Museum of Humour and Satire and a Festival of Humour in May.

E 98 goes south through the **Shipka Pass** which has become well-known as a result of Verestyagin's painting of a frozen soldier with the communiqué reading "All Quiet in the Shipka Pass". Monument to the Russo-Bulgarian defence 1877-1878. Memorial church in the village of Shipka. Hotel on *Mount Stoletov.* National park.

View over the Valley of the Roses, where the air is filled with the scent of roses at the end of May and the beginning of June when millions of roses are transformed into perfume. 3 500 kilogrammes of roses are required for 1 kilogramme of perfume essence. The valley stretches to the west as far as the village of Rozino. The centre of the valley is **KAZANLŬK** (50 000) with the Rose Institute and Festival of Roses. There is a **Thracian grave** with unique murals in the northern part of the town. A large recreation area, adjacent to the Giorgi Dimitrov Dam, lies south of the town.

South of Omurtag are the two museum towns of Kotel and Zheravna.

STARA ZAGORA (115 000), a modern industrial town with remains of a Roman wall. Archaeological museum. Preserved old houses. Mosaic floors in ancient public building. **DIMITROVGRAD** (50 000), a young industrial town—14 000 young men and women started the construction on June 27, 1947.

HASKOVO (Khaskovo, 55 000). District capital, beautifully situated in the deep Caja River valley. Tobacco industry. Eski Dzumaja, an old mosque, national museum. Haskovo Mineral Baths (60°C), 6 km west.

Kŭrdzhali (35 000) in a wide valley in the Rodopi Mountains. Founded by a Turkish general, Kurdii Ali. Industrial centre with power plants and large dams. Many earth pyramids in the area—some shaped like rock mushrooms. **Momchilgrad** is a centre for tobacco growing.

No frontier passage to Greece.

E 87. Constanţa – Varna – Burgas – Malko Tŭrnovo

Previous number: E 95.

Dourankoulak. Roumanian border.

Rusalka. Seaside resort with holiday cottages. **Nos Kaliakra.** Peninsula with 70 m high cliff. Lovely views. Interesting rock formations. Seal colony. Museum and ruins.

Balchik This little town, founded in the 6th cent. B.C., is built on broad terraces. Royal Palace that once belonged to Queen Marie of Roumania. Botanical gardens and City Museum.

Tolbukhin (50 000). District capital named in honour of a Soviet war marshall.

Albena. One of the newer seaside resorts with many miles of beach and over 40 hotels. About 20 000 beds. Interesting examples of modern Bulgarian architecture.

Zlatni Pyasŭtsi (Golden Sands) with over 80 hotels and 18 000 beds. Druzhba (Friendship). One of the older resorts. Fine parks. Spa with two mineral springs, 18 hotels, 2 500 beds. Holiday cottages.

Aladzha Monastery, a two-story structure which has been hewn out of a chalk cliff. Beautiful frescoes, monks' cells, churches, chapels.

VARNA (250 000). Bulgaria's largest port. Large industries and shipyard. The city was founded in the 6th cent. by Greek colonists who called it Odessos (Odysseus). Sea Park with aquarium, naval museum, natural history museum, zoo. Nikolaus Copernicus Observatory, Palace of Sports and Culture with a memorial to the victims of capitalism and racism. Ikon museum in the St. Athanasius Church. *Sveta Bogoroditsa Cathedral* is in the centre of the city. Choir festival in May.

Bulgaria's largest summer resort is being constructed at the Kamachiya River. When completed in 1990, it will accommodate 40 000 visitors among many canals and little lakes. The beach is 9 km long and up to 250 m wide.

Slunchev bryag (Sunny Beach). One of the largest coastal resorts. Over 100 hotels provide 28 000 beds.

Nesebur. A small town on a small rocky peninsula. Cobbled streets and beautiful old houses with a ground-floor level of stone and upper stories of wood. Nesebur was founded in the 6th cent. B.C. and it became an important trading town, mentioned by the historian, Herodotus. In A.D. 72 it was occupied by the Romans and in 812 by the Bulgarians. During the Middle Ages it was famous for its 40 beautiful churches. Now it is a little fishing and museum town. Remains of ramparts and a city gate (5th-6th cent.). Eight ruined churches and three interesting museums. A few of the houses are open to visitors. A large resort has been built near by.

Pomorie. Spa and resort. Mudbath treatments. Vineyards. A grave from the Thracian period.

BURGAS (140 000). Founded towards the end of the 17th cent. Bulgaria's second largest port. Industrial town and cultural centre. City museum and art museum. Beautiful views from the Sea Park.

Sozopol. Little town, founded in the 9th cent. by Greeks from Miletus. It is the oldest settlement on the Bulgarian coast. It was an independent city-state, called Apollonia, with its own laws and fleet. Conquered and destroyed in A.D. 72 by the Romans. Large fishing harbour. Burgas is a picturesque and interesting town with lovely old wooden houses and winding streets.

The Ropotomo River with banks that are covered with luxuriant, jungle-like vegetation. Fishing. There are many smaller resorts along the coast to the south. The fishing towns of **Michurin** and **Akhtopol.** The largest tourist resort, **Primorsko** is the location of the large Georgi Dimitrov International Youth Centre.

Malko Tŭrnovo. Turkish frontier.

E 95 continues to Babeski on the E 5 N between Sofia and Istanbul.

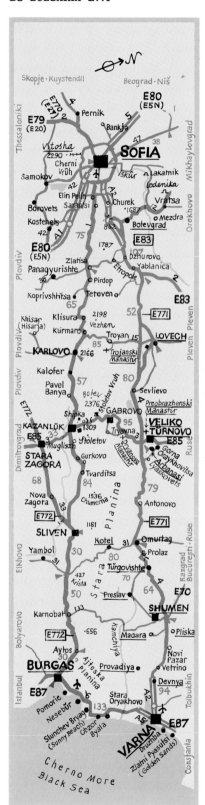

E 771. Sofia – Tŭrnovo – Varna

Previous number: E 27.

SOFIA and the **Vitosha Mountain,** see town plans.

Botevgrad. Fruit-growing centre with some industries. **Etropole.** Resort. Old monastery.

Koprivshtitsa. Situated in a valley at 1 060 m above sea level and surrounded by the highest mountains in the Sredna Gora Range, Koprivshtitsa is a typical Bulgarian town. It has been proclaimed a national monument. Two-story houses with spacious verandahs, stone walls with wooden gates, built in the 18th and 19th cent. During this period the town was three times ravaged by fire. Many of the houses are open to visitors. Ethnological museum. Monuments reflect the town's importance during the Bulgarian struggle for independence: the place where the first shots against the Turks were fired during the 1876 uprising and the mausoleum where the leaders of the uprising are buried. Church of the Holy Virgin (1817) with fine woodcarvings. 18 km SE the "Barricades", a memorial to the partisans who fought against the Nazis 1942-1944. Large hotel.

Lovech (30 000). Industrial town. Covered bridge where artisans and craftsmen have workshops in the Oriental manner. **The Troyan Monastery** (16th cent.) to the south is high up in the mountains. It is associated with the struggle for independence. The present buildings date from the 19th cent. Fine ikons, frescoes by Zachari Zograf and woodcarvings.

Veliko Tŭrnovo (50 000). The houses are perched high up on the cliffs along the banks of the River Yantra. The town has been proclaimed a national monument. Veliko Tŭrnovo is built on three hills. It was the capital of the Second Bulgarian Kingdom 1187-1393. In 1878 it regained its previous position, but only for a few months. Excavations on **Tsarevets Hill** have revealed the remains of the Royal Palace, a church, a bishop's palace, and King Ivan Alexander's grave (14th cent.). Ruins of 14 churches with rich mosaics, wall paintings, etc. on **Trapezitska Hill.** The uprising, which resulted in the establishment of the Second Bulgarian Kingdom, started in the St. Dimiter Church. The Church of the 40 Martyrs was built in 1230 as a memorial to the victory.

The **Preobrazhenski Monastery** with origins in the 14th cent. is situated in a deep gorge. Several churches with wall paintings and ikons. Opposite the monastery is the **Sveta Troitsa** (Holy Trinity) from the 12th cent. **Nikyup** with the ruins of the Roman town of Nicopolis ad Istrum.

Arbanasi (close to Veliko Tŭrnovo). A museum village with beautiful fortress-like houses, two monasteries, and five 18th- and 19th-cent. churches. Two museums. The **Dryanovo Monastery** in a narrow valley was founded in the 3rd cent. Imposing cliffs. Battles against the Turks in 1876.

Kotel was founded in 1545. Part of the town escaped a fire in 1894 and now shows what a town looked like during the 18th and 19th cent., the "Bulgarian Renaissance". The town was famous for its tapestries, and there are schools of handicrafts and music here. Ethnological and historical museums.

Zheravna, a village with large wooden houses with expansive overhanging roofs. Water runs along the steep cobble-stoned streets. Several houses are open to visitors. Fine woodcarvings. Museum.

Tŭrgovishte. Modern town with an old marketplace. **Razgrad.** Industrial town. The Ibrahim Pasha Masque. Ruins of the Roman town, Abrittus.

SHUMEN (77 000). Previously known as Kolarovgrad. Industrial town. Historical museum. Museum dedicated to the Communist leader Vassil Kolarov. **Lajos Kossuth House,** where the Hungarian patriot stayed in 1848. Toumboul Mosque (17th cent.) is the largest in Bulgaria. Turkish market.

Preslav, from 893 until 1072 the capital of the First Bulgarian Kingdom. Ruins of the original town. **Pliska** was the first capital (681- 893). Ruins of city wall, castle and churches.

The Horseman of Madara, a relief of a horseman, a dog and a lion, carved into the cliff. Its orgins are unknown. The Madara Caves were inhabited as early as 3000 B.C. Thracian and Roman remains. There was a monastery here during the 12th-14th cent. Hundreds of monks' cells and several churches have been hewn out of the rock.

Provadiya with salt mines. **Devnya** with chemical industries.

VARNA and **BURGAS,** see E 87.

TOWN PLANS

SOFIA (1 million)
Capital of Bulgaria. Situated at an altitude of 550 m, Sofia is, after Madrid, the second highest capital city in Europe. Excavations have shown that this location has been inhabited since about 3000 B.C. The Thracians founded a city called Serdica here about 400 B.C. It was ravaged by Attila. Justinian had it rebuilt. The Bulgarians called it Sredez ("in the middle"). In the 14th cent. it was given its present name. Sofia was occupied by the Turks in 1382 and their rule lasted until 1878 when it was taken by a Russian general, Gurko. At that time it was a sleepy little town with only 12 000 inhabitants. In the year that followed it was made the capital of Bulgaria and from then on it grew quickly and expanded until it became a stately city with broad boulevards and large parks. The Parisian influence is unmistakable.

Many museums, art galleries, opera and theatres. The city's oldest church is *Sveti Georgi* (5th cent.). It is now surrounded by the Balkan Hotel. Roman excavations beside the church. The *Church of St. Sofia* gave the city its name. The *Banya Bashi Mosque* is still in use. *Alexander Nevsky Cathedral* (1917) is one of the largest churches in th Balkans. Ikons and art treasures. *The Black Mosque* (Cherna Dyamia) was built in the 6th cent. to the plans of the famous architect, Sinan. The large *Büjük Dyamia* (15th cent.) is now an archaeological museum with ikons and gold treasures from the 10th cent. B.C.

Sofia. The Alexander Nevsky Cathedral and the Government Building

The *mausoleum* of the Bulgarian Communist leader Georgi Dimitrov is in the centre of the city. Dimitrov has been called the Father of Modern Bulgaria. He was one of those accused of the burning of the Reichstag in Berlin in 1933, and his arguments in his self-defence were shrewd and impressive. *Museum* in the house where he lived from 1888 to 1912. A long line of illustrious Bulgarians have been immortalized in museums in the houses where they once lived. The struggle for independence is the main subject of a number of museums. Ethnographic museum, natural history museum and art museum.

Sofia is also a spa with over 20 warm springs scattered about the city. In the centre of the city there is a large mineral bath in an ornate building dating from 1913. The water temperature is 46°C.

The **Vitosha Mountain** is just 8 km south of Sofia. It is the recreation area and national park for the capital's inhabitants. The highest point is *Cherni Vruh (Black Peak),* 2 290 m. Numerous hotels and restaurants. Extensive winter sports facilities. The lovely little **Boyana Church** lies at the foot of the mountain. Medieval art, frescoes from 1259, and other beautiful decorations.

1 Banya Bashi Mosque
2 Mineral baths
3 Lenin Square and Sveta Nedeliya Church
4 Sveti Georgi Church
5 Museum of Archaeology
6 9 September Square with Party House
7 Ethnographic museum and art museum
8 Mausoleum of Georgi Dimitrov
9 National Theatre
10 Opera house
11 Churches of St. Sofia and Alexander Nevsky
12 Parliament
13 University
14 Museum of the Revolution
15 Liberation Museum

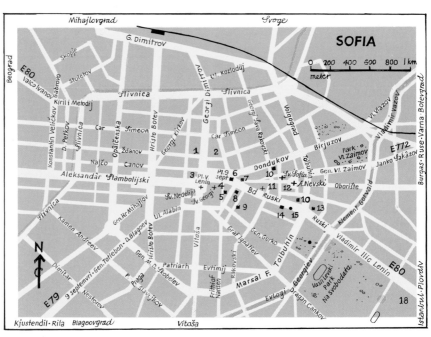

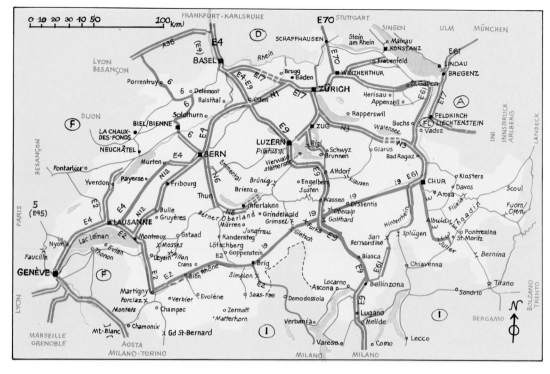

CH · Switzerland

CH·Schweiz Suisse Svizzera

Area: 41 000 km² (15 941 sq. miles)

Population: 6.3 million. 55% of the population are Protestants, 43 % Roman Catholics. Four official languages: German (65 %), French (18 %) Italian (12 %) and Romansh (1 %).

Major cities: Zürich 379 000, Basel 185 000, Genève 151 000, Bern 145 000.

Government: Federal republic made up of 23 cantons, each with its own government, capital and laws. The Federal Assembly has two chambers, the National Council and the States Council. The Federal Council consists of seven members who serve in office for four-year-periods. These members, in turn, act as President of the Council for one year. Plebiscites are held frequently. Most of them concern local matters which are directly decided on by the local voters. Switzerland can thus be said to be the only true democracy in Europe: here the voters not only choose candidates to represent them but also vote on and determine the issues that concern them. In the cantons of Appenzell, Glarus and Unterwalden, there is a unique form of democracy. On the final Sunday of April and the first Sunday in May, the voters gather in the main squares of the cantons' capitals, and by a show of hands vote on cantonal issues.

History

1291 The cantons of Uri, Schwyz and Unterwalden send representatives to the field of Rütli where they sign a pact that pledges eternal union.

1499 The Swiss free themselves from German domination.

1529-1712 Switzerland is torn by four religious wars all in some ways caused by the Reformation, led by Knox and Calvin.

1815 The Congress of Vienna declares that Swiss neutrality is a necessity for all of Europe.

1920 Switzerland enters the League of Nations. Swiss neutrality is respected during the Second World War.

1959 Switzerland joins EFTA and in 1963 becomes a member of the Council of Europe.

Currency: Swiss francs (CHF).
1 franc = 100 centimes (Rappen)

Business hours: Banks generally 8.30 a.m.-4.30 p.m. with lunchtime closing. Post offices 7.30 a.m.-12.00 noon and 1.45-6.30 p.m. Saturdays 7.30 a.m.-12.00 noon. Department stores and major shops are not closed during the lunch hour.

Holidays: New Year's Day, Good Friday (not a legal holiday in Tessin), Easter Sunday, Easter Monday, May 1

Routes described:

E 2 Vallorbe – Lausanne – Brig – Simplon

E 4 Basel – Bern – Lausanne – Genève

E 9 Basel – Luzern – Gotthard – Lugano

E 17 Bregenz – Zürich – Basel

E 21 A Martigny – St. Bernard – Aosta

E 61 Bregenz – Chur – S. Bernardino – Bellinzona

E 70 Donaueschingen – Schaffhausen – Zürich

N 3 Basel – Zürich – Chur – Julier – Chiavenna

N 6 Pourrentruy – Biel/Bienne – Bern – Interlaken – Gletsch

N 12 Bern – Fribourg – Vevey, see E 4

19 Chur – Oberalp – Andermatt – Furka – Brig

Town plans: Basel, Bern, Genève, Zürich

Weggis on the Vier-waldstättersee

(in some cantons), Ascension Day, Whit Sunday, Whit Monday, August 1 (National holiday; holiday in Freiburg, Genève, Schaffhausen, Tessin, Vaud, Zürich; half-day holiday in the remaining cantons), December 25 and 26. (Boxing Day is not a holiday in Geneva, Neuenburg, Vaud and Wallis).

Hotels
Hotels are classified. The Swiss Hotel Association publishes an annual guide, which can be obtained at Swiss tourist offices.

Camping
There are 600 camping sites, 80 of them run by TCS (Touring Club Suisse). Many sites rent out tents and camping huts. In the youth hostels guests up to 26 years of age are given priority.

Food and drink
Swiss cuisine is international in character and it is especially influenced by the cooking traditions of the neighbouring countries. The most specifically Swiss dish is probably cheese fondue – small bread squares on long forks are dipped into a mixture of melted Emmental and Gruyère cheese and a little white wine. Raclette is a combination of melted cheese, potatoes and pickled gherkins. Bündnerfleisch is an hors d'oeuvre of dried, paper- thin slivers of beef. Berner Platte is a dish consisting of beef, bacon, sausages, sauerkraut and beans. Rösti, a cheese and potato mixture, or Spätzli, often accompanies meat dishes. There are numerous local wines, most of them white. The large Mövenpick chain has many fine restaurants.

Shopping
Embroidery, handicrafts, cheese and other food stuffs.

Speed limits. Traffic regulations
Motorways 130 kmh, other roads 100 kmh, built-up areas 50 kmh.
Cars with caravans and other towing vehicles with a total weight of up to 1 000 kg 80 kmh, over 1 000 kg 60 kmh. Studded tyres are permitted during the period November 11-March 31, but never on motorways or major roads. The maximum speed limit when using this equipment is 80 kmh. Children under the age of 12 are not allowed to travel in the front seat – not even in specially constructed baby seats. If your car is fitted with seat belts it is compulsory to wear them.
It is compulsory to use dipped headlights at all times in tunnels.
On some roads the use of snow chains is mandatory. There are usually signboards located at the entrances to the Alpine passes. These inform drivers if the passes are open and if snow chains are required. On Alpine roads cars driving upwards always have the right-of-way. On Alpine postal roads, marked with signs showing a post-horn, the postal buses have priority over all other traffic. They have special horns with a distinctive three-note signal. If you hear this it is best to stop at the most convenient place on the road and let the bus pass. Occasionally more buses follow. Then all but the very last of them display a circular red sign that is crossed with a diagonal white line.

Roads
The network of national roads is being expanded. These roads are marked with N signs. Routes leading to the motorways are marked with green signs. All of the major Swiss roads are in good condition. The Alpine passes are traversed by tunnels or rail transport on the important north-south routes. Dipped headlights must be used in tunnels and when visibility is poor.

Road patrol
TCS (Touring Club der Schweiz) has road patrols which can be reached by telephoning 140. (Complete information is given in the AIT assistance and credit voucher.) There are local emergency centres – for their numbers refer to the local telephone directories.

Emergency telephones: 118 for fire brigade and 117 for police and ambulance.

By dialling 162 you can get weather reports in French, German or Italian, according to the canton where the call is made. Road conditions reports can be obtained by dialling 163.

TCS (Touring Club Suisse), 9, Rue Pierre Fatio, Genève. Tel. 022-37 12 12.
Swiss National Tourist Office, Swiss Centre, 1 New Coventry Street, London W1V 8EE. Tel. 01-734 1921.

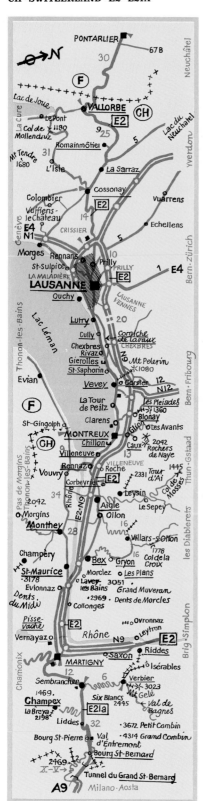

E 2. Vallorbe – Lausanne – Brig – Simplon

E 2 comes from London – Dover – Calais – Reims – Besançon. The motorway through France is not yet complete.

Vallorbe. Industrial town at the source of the River Orbe.

Romainmotier. Abbey church. The castle is now a museum. *La Sarraz* with chapel and castle. *Cossonay* with St. Peter and Paul Church (11th-13th cent.). Little museum. *Yverdon,* see E 4.

LAUSANNE (130 000). The capital of the canton of Vaud, Lausanne is built on a very hilly site. The narrow, sloping streets which often pass over each other on bridges make the city quite confusing for the foreign motorist. One solution to this problem is to leave your car at the charming former fishermen's hamlet of Ouchy. Many restaurants and car parks and a lovely view of the lake and the nearby mountains. Ouchy is linked with Lausanne's central railway station and Grand' Pont by a steep funicular that travels part of its short route underground. Lausanne is a delightful and lively tourist centre and a very popular centre of studies: university, language colleges, boarding-schools, and the well-known hotel school all attract students from many countries. Splendid Gothic cathedral. Palais de Rumine houses an impressive art collection.

Lutry (2 600). Castle (1642). The Gothic church has Romanesque origins. *Cully.* Lovely church with a unique belfry. Interesting 16th- cent. houses in the Bernese style.

The road passes the vineyard-covered *Mont de Lavaux. Rivaz* is a little wine producing village. Site of Glérolles Castle. *St-Saphorin* has picturesque houses and the popular "d l'Onde" inn.

Vevey. Resort and industrial town. St-Martin's Church (15th cent.). Jenisch Museum. At the end of the 19th cent. Heinrich Nestlé, a chemist, moved to Vevey from Frankfurt. He started to produce dry milk powder, and with this the mighty Nestlé concern was founded.
Charles Chaplin lived in Manoir de Bau until his death. He is buried in the cemetery at *Corsier-sur-Vevey.*
Magnificent surroundings. Superb views out over Lake Geneva from the N 9 (E 2) and N 12 motorways. Other beautiful views can be obtained from any of the many winding mountain roads, e.g. the *Corniche de Lavaux,* or from the rack railway train that goes from *Blonay* up to les Pléiades.

Montreux (20 000). Beautifully situated resort. Chatelard Castle and many fine observation points, such as Rocher de Naye. Annual international television festival with competition for the world's best entertainment programme.

Chillon. Famous castle (10th-12th cent.) beautifully situated, partially in Lake Geneva. Great hall and many exquisite interiors. Lord Byron wrote a poem about "The Prisoner of Chillon".

Caux. The castle is the headquarters of the Moral Re-Armament Movement.

Villeneuve. Old houses. *Rennaz.* Lovely 18th-cent. patrician houses.

Aigle (4 200) on the Grand-Eau, a tributary of the Rhone. The town is surrounded by famous vineyards. Imposing castle.

At *Corbeyrier* (7 km away), at a height of 986 m above sea level, there is a lovely view. Ruins of the 13th-cent. *St-Triphon Castle. Monthey* (5 000). Medieval castle.

Bex (4 800). Spa and bathing resort. The salt works have been in operation since the 17th cent. Vineyards. Beautiful surroundings: Les Plans and Gryon. *Rhône Bridge* from 1491. Lavez-les-Bains (3 km) and the Morcles look-out point.

Les Diablerets. A 5 km long cable car line goes from *Col de Pillon* to the mountain station of *Glacier des Diablerets* (3 000 m).

St-Maurice (2 500). Old fortress (the legendary massacre of St- Maurice and the 300 martyrs took place here in A.D. 285). The Augustinian abbey, consecrated in the 6th cent. has foundation walls and catacombs from the 11th cent. Lovely examples of the medieval goldsmith's art in the abbey church.

The Pissevache Waterfall is 65 m high and illuminated at night.

Martigny, an ancient Celtic town, is now a resort. The town is dominated by the ruins of the la Batiaz fortress. Remains of an amphitheatre. Very interesting museum of vintage cars (Fondation Pierre Gianadda)

E 21A. Martigny – St. Bernard – Aosta

Orsières. Village with gaily painted houses placed in a lovely setting.

Champex-Lac has a unique *Alpine botanical garden,* 1 500 m above sea level, with a collection of over 4 000 different plants brought from all over the world.

Champex. Resort at an altitude of 1 500 m. Chair-lift to la Breya (2 198 m).

Bourg-Saint-Pierre has a 12th-cent. church. "Napoleon's armchair" is in the village inn. The "La Linnea" *Alpine botanical garden* is at the top of a small hill.

Bourg-Saint-Bernard. From this point, a cable car goes to Super-St-Bernard and the Menouve Pass (2 800 m).

Grand St. Bernard (St. Bernard) is the vital trans-Alpine pass where the monks of St. Bernard established a hospice to assist travellers. It was reviewed in 1225 in a guidebook for pilgrims.

The *Grand St. Bernard tunnel*, completed in 1964 (5.8 km long) is open all year. The access roads are for the most part covered. A pair of air ducts extend up to the summit of the mountain (2 200 m above sea level). Tolls. Both Swiss and Italian customs stations have been placed at the northern entrance. The roads leading into the tunnel are more winding and narrower than the roads that enter the Mont Blanc tunnel but they have the advantage of being more interesting and less busy. Since the opening of the tunnel, the old route that goes over the pass, previously a source of exasperation, has become a pleasant tourist route. On this road points of interest include the High Alpine Observatory (1827) and the 18th-cent. Hospice of Bernard van Menthen. Interesting museum, library and the kennels where the famous St. Bernard Alpine rescue dogs are raised. The dogs no longer wander around alone with a keg of brandy around their necks, as was commonly thought. A bronze statue of St. Bernard is in the Plan de Jupiter. Chair-lift to Chenalette, 2 800 m above sea level.

From **Chamonix** (see France, route A 41) a lovely Alpine road leads via *Col des Montets* and *Col de la Forclaz* to Martigny. At **Vallorcine** it is possible to inspect kennels where St. Bernard dogs are raised and trained. *Emosson* is an artificial lake in a magnificent setting. The dam itself is 180 m high. It is possible to reach this point by travelling first from Martigny to le Chatelard by rack railway, then by funicular and finally by narrow-gauge (600 mm) railway.

From the area above Martigny there are magnificent views out over the *Rhône Valley*.

The River **Rhône** has its source in the Rhône Glacier. It flows through Lake Geneva and empties into the Mediterranean near Marseille. It is 810 km long.

Verbier. Large resort.

Riddes. Starting point of the cable car line to Isérables, a picturesque village and observation point.

St-Pierre de Clages has a 12th-cent. church.

Sion (German: Sittens, 20 000). Two cliffs dominate the town. One of them is crowned by a medieval bishop's castle, the other by the Valère *fortress church* which is now a museum containing medieval art treasures and Europe's oldest functioning organ (14th cent.). The *cathedral* houses valuable religious treasures. The town hall has an interesting astronomical clock (17th cent.) and Switzerland's oldest inscription (A.D. 377).

Val d'Herens with the intriguing earth and rock "pyramids". Similar strange natural formations can be found near Bolzano (see Italy, E 6). *Evolène* is a lovely little Alpine village with ancient traditions. Folk costumes are still in everyday use. Numerous beautiful hiking trails.

Once you have travelled through the **Val d'Herémence** you come to the 285 m high *Grande Dixence Dam*. A cable car goes up to the dam's edge.

St-Leonard. Vineyards. Europe's largest underwater lake, 300 m long, 25 m wide and 20 m deep. Rowing-boat tours.

Sierre has splendid remains from its former days of glory. Witztume Castle was built in the 16th cent. and the Goubin tower dates from the 13th cent.

Roads lead from Sierre to the fashionable resorts of **Crans, Vermala** and **Montana.** Cable car to *Bella Lui*. The route leading south goes through the lovely *Val d'Anniviers*. Charming brown wooden houses covered with painted flowers in **Grimentz.**

Susten is the site of the Leuk fortress. **Leukerbad** is a popular spa. Cars are transported by rail through a tunnel from **Goppenstein** to **Kandersteg** for the journey onwards to Thun and Bern.

Raron. Little town with old houses and a fortress.

Visp has an imposing fortress.

Road to the tourist resorts of **Saas-Fee, Stalden** and **St-Niklaus.** A narrow-gauge railway goes from Täsch to **Zermatt**, 1 608 m, at the foot of the **Matterhorn**, one of the world's most beautiful and best-known mountains, famous for its distinctive profile. There are over 30 different cable car lines, chair-lifts and ski-hoists. One of the most beautiful is a rack railway line that goes over the Gornergletscher. The Matterhorn has attracted many alpinists. Over a hundred who fell to their deaths are buried in a special cemetery in Zermatt.

Brig (15 000). During the 17th cent. this town was known as "rich Brig". Trade flourished, and the town's most prosperous citizen, Kasper von Stockalper, was known throughout Europe. His enormous mansion (17th cent.) still stands in the well-preserved medieval heart of the town. It has three towers and an arcaded courtyard.

The *Ganter Bridge* (1980) is one of the most beautiful modern structures in the Alps. It is 174 m long and rests on 150 m high columns. The bridge is 1 450 m above sea level.

Simplon, 2 005 m above sea level.

E 2 continues to Milano – Bologna – Rimini – Ancona – Bari – Brindisi.

E 4. Basel – Bern – Lausanne – Genève

E 4 comes from Helsinki – Haparanda – Stockholm – København – Hamburg – Frankfurt – Karlsruhe.

BASEL, see town plans.

A motorway (1980) crosses the Rhine and links the German A 5 with the Swiss N 2. In 1225 Bishop Heinrich of Thun opened a bridge over the Rhine at the same place. It served as a link with the then new Gotthard route.

Arlesheim. Splendid Baroque cathedral. **Augst** has the remains of a Roman encampment, theatre and temple. From 44 B.C. until A.D. 260, this was the site of a thriving city. The silver treasure from Kaiseraugst (4th cent.) was recovered in 1962. Römerhaus is a reconstruction of a Roman dwelling and shop.

Rheinfelden has a medieval watchtower. Impressive town hall.

The motorway passes *Sissach* with Eberain-hof from 1776, and continues on through the 3 km long *Belchen Tunnel*. *Olten,* see E 9.

Liestal. Founded in the 13th cent., capital of the canton of Basel-Land. Obertor Tower. From here it is possible to take the major road that connects with the E 4. However, the road that goes via *Waldenburg* (Revue watch factory) is beautiful and varied. But mind the high and unprotected boundary to the narrow-gauge railway. There are pleasant inns on the square in *Balsthal.*

Klus. Small village. During the Middle Ages this was one of the fortified towns in the beautiful Jura Valley. Folklore museum in *Alt Falkenstein Castle.*

Murgenthal. Industrial town with the handsome St-Urban Church, one of the most beautiful Baroque churches in Switzerland. Exquisitely carved pulpit. *Langenthal.* Porcelain is produced here. Large covered market. *Wangen a/d Aare* is a lovely town with old fortification walls.

Solothurn (16 000). Capital of the canton. Beautiful houses in the Altstadt (Old Town). The medieval town hall, in the Gothic style, is on the Marktplatz. Zeitglockenturm also dates from the Middle Ages. Its astronomical clock was placed on the tower in 1547. Weapons collection in the Old Arsenal. The Cathedral of *St. Ursen,* with its distinctive broad façade, was designed by Italian architects and completed in 1773.

Burgdorf. Enormous 13th-cent. castle. In 1800 Pestalozzi started his famous school here. Burgdorf is at the entrance to the Valley of the Emme, the *Emmental,* which is world-famous for its "Swiss Cheese". Idyllic area with beautiful views of the Alps. Hundreds of hiking trails. Beautiful houses that have been darkened by the sun. The nearly black houses are the oldest. The major town is *Langnau.*

BERN, see town plans. *Biel/Bienne,* see 6.

A lovely road skirts the shores of *Bieler See* on its way to *Neuchâtel.* This modern industrial town has a picturesque Old Town, a castle and an abbey church. Museum of Art and History (Musée d'Art et d'Histoire). The mechanical figures of Jacquet-Droz can write, draw and play musical instruments. High up in the majestic Jura Mountains is *La Chaux-de-Fonds,* a large industrial town with modern buildings that have replaced older structures which were destroyed in a fire. Clock, art, ethnological and natural history museums. Small zoo.

Murten (Morat). Situated astride the French-German language boundary, this is one of the best-preserved medieval towns in Switzerland. The city wall has many handsome towers. Visitors can go up on the ramparts. Zeitglockenturm (1778). Murten was one of Switzerland's project cities during the European Architectural Heritage Year (1975).

Avenches. The Roman town of Aventicum was destroyed in A.D. 260. Remains of a 5.5 km city wall, temple and amphitheatre with room for 8 000 spectators. 16th-cent. castle. *Estavayer-le-Lac.* Charming little town and site of Chenaux Castle.

Payerne. The 11th-cent. abbey church is one of the most exquisite Romanesque structures in Switzerland. Many houses with arcades. Hennies. Spa. Surpierre Castle.

Lucens. Sherlock Holmes Museum in the castle. *Moudon.* Picturesque old town. The Moses Fountain was completed in 1557. Church of St-Etienne. Imposing belfry.

Yverdon. There is a magnificent rococo town hall in the old town. 13th-cent. castle. During the 19th cent. this was the headquarters of Pestalozzi's school.

Grandson. Lovely old town. Church of St-Jean-Baptiste. The huge castle (13th-15th cent.) has an interesting armoury and a great hall. Motor museum.

Romainmoutier. Location of the oldest abbey church in Switzerland, constructed in the 11th cent. Some parts of the building date from the 7th cent. *La Sarraz* with a mighty fortress, destroyed in 1475 but reconstructed.

LAUSANNE, see E 2.

Vufflens-le-Chateau. The splendid fairy-tale castle was built about 1400. Morgens. Lovely little town with castle and Baroque church. Nyon was founded by Julius Caesar. Charming streets and buildings. It is both a mountain village and a port. Fine views from the city walls. The Historical Museum has a noteworthy collection of ceramics.

E 45 goes by way of *Col de St-Cergue* and *Col de la Givrine* to la Cure, Dijon and Paris.

Coppet has many very old buildings. Madame de Staël, the famous French woman of letters, who was exiled by Napoleon, lived in the castle. *Cointrin,* Geneva's international airport, is actually situated in France, in a tax-free zone.

GENÈVE, see town plans.

Lac Léman is the largest lake in the Alps: 581 km², 375 m above sea level, greatest depth 310 m. The Rhône flows through this lake which is famous for its blue water and great beauty. It is lined with tourist resorts and is best known outside of Switzerland as Lake Geneva.

E 4 continues to Chambéry – Grenoble – Valence – Barcelona – Madrid – Lisboa.

N12. Bern – Fribourg – Vevey

This motorway was opened in 1981. It provides a rapid link between Bern and Geneva and on to Simplon and St. Bernard.

Originally motorway N 1 was to have been completed first, but clever politicians in Fribourg saw to it that N 12 was given priority. The N 1 route, which is to connect Bern – Yverdon – Lausanne, is estimated to be in operation in 1992 – if it is built at all.

Fribourg (40 000). Capital of the canton. Founded in 1157, it is considered to be a "museum of the art of Swiss town architecture", as it has many buildings that reflect the changing styles of different eras. The oldest part of the town is situated on a peninsula and is surrounded by a city wall. The imposing *Gotteron Bridge* was constructed in the 13th cent. over a deep gorge. The *Eglise des Cordeliers* (Franziskanerkirche) has a stately Baroque façade and architectural details from other periods. The *Cathedral of St-Nicolas* contains a famous organ (concerts daily). Many other beautiful churches. Impressive town hall. The Samaritan Fountain dates from 1550.

Hauterive. Cistercian abbey (12th cent.). *Romont.* Picturesque medieval town. Castle.

Gruyères (Greyerz). Situated on the crown of a hill, this is a picturesque medieval town. The castle, now a museum, has beautiful halls and paintings by Corot. Though its massive tower was built in the 12th cent., the remainder of the castle was not completed until the early 16th cent. The dairy which produces the world-famous Gruyère cheese is on the outskirts of the town.

N 12 goes over the 2 km long Greyerzer Viaduct. A few kilometres north of Vevey, the road reaches an altitude of 864 m (beware of icy stretches in the winter). 6% gradient over a distance of 6 km – this is unusual for a motorway and can seem unpleasant. But the views of Lac Léman are fantastic. The connection to N 9 is at an altitude of 500 m.

Vevey, see E 2.

E 9. Basel – Luzern – Gotthard – Lugano

E 9 comes from Amsterdam – Liège – Luxembourg – Strasbourg.

BASEL, see town plans. Basel-Olten, see E 4

Olten. Charming streets and houses in the older part of the town. Castle and churches. Museums of history and art.

Zofingen. Splendid 18th-cent. town hall. Exquisite medieval stained-glass windows in the chancel of the town church. The former Cistercian abbey contains one of the most beautiful Baroque churches in Switzerland. Superbly carved chancel stalls. Remains of Roman baths.

Sursee. Baroque church and lovely 18th-cent. houses.

Beromünster. The Church of St-Michael, with origins in the 11th cent. was remodelled in the Baroque style. Beautiful interior. Gilded copper reliquary of Warnebert (7th cent.) *Werthenstein* has a 17th-cent. monastery high on a promontory overlooking the River Emme.

LUZERN (Lucerne 65 000), was an important town during the 13th cent. when the St. Gotthard Pass was opened. *Kapellbrücke,* a covered, wooden bridge (1333) has 112 7th-cent. ceiling paintings. The octagonal *Wasserturm* (water tower) has become the symbol of the town. *Spreuerbrücke* has paintings of the Dance of Death. Old part of town with charmingly painted houses. Late-Renaissance *Hofkirche* (1639). Town wall with the Musegg Tower (1408). The *Löwendenkmal* (Lion Monument) is dedicated to the memory of the Swiss Guard who fell at the Tuileries in Paris in 1792. *Gletschergarten,* Ice-Age rock formations.

Verkehrshaus der Schweiz is Europe's largest transport museum. Animated models, trains, boats, post coaches, cars, rack railway, aircraft and space ships. Bread museum. Museum of local folklore and folk dress. Richard Wagner Museum. Works of Picasso in the Am Rhyn art museum. Miniature railway on the Dietschiberg which also offers superb views. Lake excursions on many boat lines.

Mount *Pilatus* rises to 2 129 m. Visitors who make the trip up the mountain will be rewarded with magnificent views of Vierwaldstätter See and the surrounding Alps. The journey can be made in 40 min. by cable car from *Kriens* or in 30 min. by rack railway from *Alpnachstad.* This railway is the steepest of its kind in the world.

Stans has a beautiful town hall and lovely St. Peter's Church. The road to Interlaken passes Sarnen which has charming houses and churches. A road leads to the popular resort of *Engelberg.*

The new motorway that goes west of *Vierwaldstätter See* passes through a thrilling landscape and provides superb views of the *Rigi.* The roads that lie to the east of the lake are also beautiful and interesting.

Küssnacht am Rigi. Large tourist resort with superbly painted houses. In 1552 Goethe was a guest at the Hotel Engel. The *Astrid Chapel* (Astridkapelle) marks the place where Astrid, Queen of the Belgians, was killed in a motor accident in 1935.

Arth. 17th-cent. Capucine monastery. St. George's Church. *Schwyz* (10 000). Capital of the canton of the same name. The original document of the 1291 Pact which was the foundation of the modern state of Switzerland, is preserved here.

Hölloch. The world's largest explored grotto. About 2 km of the galleries (out of a total of about 93 km) are open to the public.

Scenic route from Küssnacht to *Brunnen.* It passes the many resorts and numerous hotels that line the lake. Some sections of the road are narrow and winding.

A rack railway goes from *Vitznau* to an observation area on *Mount Rigi* (Rigi-Kulm). This was Europe's first true mountain railway. In 1871 its first trains operated to Staffel and in 1873 the line was extended to Rigi-Kulm. In 1875 a branch linked it to Arth. It is also possible to travel from *Weggis.* The views from Rigi are splendid. Beautiful hiking trails.

Axenstrasse is an impressive and magnificent motor route that follows a system of galleries and corniches. *Tellskapelle* (the Tell Chapel), situated near the lake, is adorned with frescoes dating from 1879, depicting the legend of the Swiss national hero, William Tell. He was forced to show his skill with bow and arrow by shooting an apple from his son's head.

Altdorf. Capital of the canton of Uri. A medieval tower and William Tell monument (1895) face the town hall. Summer performances of the Schiller drama based on the William Tell legend. The Swiss hero is said to have lived in the nearby village of *Bürglen.*

Schattdorf is the oldest village in the canton. Magnificent views from the shrine-church. Silenen is a typical Uri village. Chapel and 12th-cent. castle ruins (Zwing-Uri). *Amsteg,* in the lovely Maderaner Valley, has many beautiful houses.

Wassen. A resort, beautifully situated at a place where the valley becomes more and more narrow and wild. According to the legend, the Devil was once tricked into helping to build the so-called *Devil's Bridge* (Teufelsbrücke). He hurled a gigantic bit of rock which still lies to the east of the road at the entrance to the St. Gotthard tunnel. Nowadays the rock is topped by a waving Swiss flag.

The *St. Gotthard tunnel*, the longest in Europe (16.3 km), was under construction from 1970 until 1980. The northern entrance is situated at 1 080 m above sea level, the southern entrance is at 1 145 m. Two ventilation shafts extend 522 and 896 m upward. The mid-point is the highest place in the tunnel (1 170 m above sea level). Air is blown into the tunnel in a north-to-south direction at about 3 m per second. But when there is a foehn, the wind enters the tunnel from the south. Speed limits are posted on signs placed 250 m apart. SOS telephones are at 125 m intervals. Entrances to a special emergency tunnel are 250 m apart. The tunnel can accommodate as many as 1800 vehicles per hour in each direction. This is an extraordinary development. The pass was first crossed by motor cars in 1902.

The *St. Gotthard railway tunnel* (14.9 km) was opened as early as 1882. It had taken seven years to build and is as impressive an engineering achievement as the more recent motor tunnel. Of the 2 000 workers who constructed the earlier tunnel, 177 were killed, among them their leader, Luis Favre. They are all buried in the St- Gotthard cemetery.

It is more rewarding to drive over the pass. The road is in excellent condition. In 1967 the 24 hairpin bends in the **Tremola Pass** were replaced by two sweeping curves that have a mere 5% gradient. On the southern side of the pass the road is steeper and winding but well built, and it provides a fantastic view out over the *Leventina Valley.*

The even older road through the pass, however, is a bit more difficult to drive. But the motorist who chooses this route should think of the problems of the Russian general, Suvorov, who, in 1799, led an army of 22 000 men through the pass during the war against the French. The 12th-cent. Gotthard Hospitz was destroyed during the struggles.

Andermatt. Resort situated where the Gotthard, Oberalp and Furka Passes meet. Its houses are built to withstand the harsh winter climate.

Hospental has a 13th-cent. watchtower. Old cart sheds remind the visitor of the once important traffic that flowed through the area.

Airolo, 1 154 m, at the southern entrance to the Gotthard tunnel. The road plunges into the *Leventina Valley*. It passes through the Piottino Gorge to **Faido** (711 m), the principal town in the valley. The town, surrounded by lush semi-tropical vegetation, has old wooden houses (some dating from the 16th cent.), mixed in with typical, southern-European stone houses. **Giornico.** Charming village with two large churches. The first vineyards appear at **Bodio. Biasca.** Pleasant resort with semi-tropical vegetation.

Bellinzona (20 000). Capital of the canton of Ticion (Tessin). The town has been fortified since the Roman era. There are three large castles. Castello di Sasso Corbaro was built in 1479 by the Milanese as a part of their defences against the Swiss. It contains a folklore museum.

Locarno (15 000). Large resort with an Italian flavour. Charming cafés line Lago Maggiore and Piazza Grande. Beautiful mansions and churches. The Locarno Pact of 1925 ratified the Treaty of Versailles. **Ascona.** Another popular resort with many beautiful churches.

The road climbs steeply offering a splendid panorama out over the valley. It traverses the **Monte Ceneri Pass** (550 m) and continues to Lugano, providing impressive views of Monte San Salvatore and Monte Bré.

Road to *Val Maggia*, a lovely valley with picturesque villages. They line a green-watered river that flows over a bed of white granite.

LUGANO (25 000). The largest town in the canton of Ticino. Internationally famous tourist resort with palm trees, lovely promenades and old mansions. On summer evenings lakeside concerts are given in the Parco Civico. Views over the many-coloured waters of the lovely fountain. Steamer services on Lago di Lugano. Water-cycles are available for hire. San Lorenzo Cathedral was rebuilt after having been badly damaged by a 13th-cent. earthquake. Its interior was reconstructed in the 18th cent. Santa Maria degli Angioli, originally a Franciscan church, was completed in 1500. *Villa Favorita* contains an impressive art collection that includes works by Holbein, Dürer, van Dyck, Rubens, Rembrandt, El Greco, Titian, Tintoretto, and many others.

Carona. Mountain village that has retained its old picturesque character. **Morcote.** Pretty fishermen's hamlet. *Madonna del Sasso*, a shrine-church, was built in 1200 but has undergone many alterations since then. Interesting frescoes. **Mendrisio** has a Baroque church and Palazzo Torriani-Fontana.

The Italian border at **Chiasso.** E 9 continues to Milano and Genova.

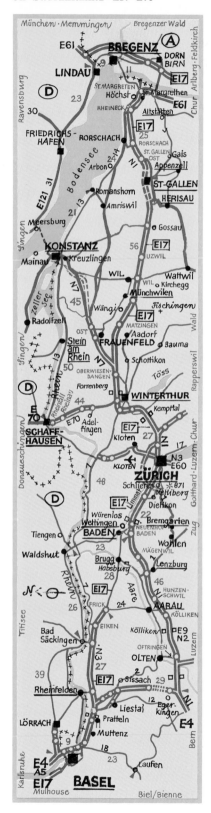

E17. Bregenz – Zürich – Basel

E 17 comes from Salzburg – Innsbruck – Arlberg.

St. Margrethen. Small town. A chapel with the same name has been built high above the River Rhine.

ST. GALLEN (74 000). Capital of the canton. The lovely Altstadt (Old Town) has many picturesque 17th- and 18th-cent. buildings. The town grew up during the 9th cent. around one of Europe's most important abbeys. The cathedral as well as the beautiful abbey church are in the Baroque style. The Othmar Crypt was completed prior to the year 1 000. The Abbey Library has a magnificent rococo hall. Interesting examples of local handicrafts in the Industrie- und Gewerbemuseum. St. Gallen is famous for its production of textiles and embroidery. Among the animals in the *Peter und Paul Wildpark* are steenbocks.

Appenzell. The centre of a lovely farming area. Woodcarvings and cowbells are favourite souvenirs. The "Alpenhorn" is a unique musical instrument native to Alpenzell. It is so long that it must be rested on the ground. Old customs and traditions have been kept alive in this canton and folk costumes are often seen. Magnificent panorama from the road between Gais and Altstätten.

Lovely houses in *Herisau* which also has an interesting folklore museum in its town hall.

Konstanz and *Mainau,* see Germany, E 70.

Bischofszell has a town hall with a rococo façade and intricate wrought-iron decorations, a belfry (Binnentor), a bridge, from 1487, and the handsome Church of St. Pelagius.

Wil. Picturesque old town with graceful arcades. The Barons' House was built in 1795. *Münchwilen* in the Murg Valley. *Fischingen abbey* (12th cent.).

Frauenfeld. Capital of the canton of Thurgau. The town was founded in the 13th cent. The Canton Museum is housed in the mighty castle.

WINTERTHUR (80 000). Centre of trade and industry. Headquarters of the Winterthur insurance company. Splendid patrician houses line the Marktgasse (18th cent.). Rathaus (town hall). The art museum specializes in examples of Swiss art. The Oskar-Reinhart Foundation (Stiftung Oskar-Reinhart) displays works by Swiss, German and Austrian artists.

ZÜRICH, see town plans.

Wettingen. The best-preserved Cistercian abbey in Switzerland, founded in the 13th cent.

Bremgarten. Charming and picturesque old town with parts of a mediaval city wall. The symbol of Bremgarten is its Spiral Tower (1559) with an interesting astronomical clock. Hexenturm (Witches' Tower), Cat Tower and Herrmann Tower are other noteworthy towers in the town. *Lenzburg* has a large castle, an interesting town hall and the 18th-cent. Gasthaus Krone.

Baden. The old town is high above the banks of the river. The spa, *Bäderstadt,* with 20 sulphur springs, lies below it. The baths have been in use since the Roman period. Picturesque covered wooden bridge (1810) over the Limmat.

Brugg. Schwarzer Turm (Black Tower) was built in the 11th cent. *Aarau.* Capital of the canton. Industrial town with a uniform and lovely Altstadt (Old Town). Several fortification towers have been preserved. Beautiful glass objects in the Museum of Arts and Crafts.

Rheinfelden. An idyllic small town with a medieval fortification tower.

BASEL, see town plans. French border.

E 17 continues to Belfort – Dijon – Tours – Nantes – Brest.

E70. Donaueschingen – Schaffhausen – Zürich

Donaueschingen, see Germany. E 70 comes from Autobahndreieck Hattenheim (E 4) near Bad Hersfeld – Fulda – Würzburg – Stuttgart.

SCHAFFHAUSEN (32 000). Capital of the canton of the same name. Extremely picturesque town with many fine patrician houses. The best known are the Zeughaus, the Haus zum Ritter and the Goldener Ochsen. The huge Munot fortress was completed in 1585. You can ride on horseback all the way to the top of the round tower.

Rheinfall (the Rhine Falls). These mighty falls should, if possible, be viewed early in the morning. Later on in the day the area is packed with tourists. The falls are 21 m high and 160 m wide.

Stein am Rhein is the best-preserved medieval small town in Switzerland. Wonderful square. Beautifully and intricately painted houses and flower-decked fountains. Some particularly beautiful and noteworthy houses are the Vordere Krone, the Weisser Adler, the Gasthaus (inn) Roter Ochsen and the town hall which has a mural (1900) depicting the history of the area.

E 61. Bregenz – Chur – S. Bernardino – Bellinzona

E 61 comes from München.

BREGENZ, see Austria, E 17.

Appenzell, see E 17. ***Altstätten.*** Old market town with a preserved city gate. Magnificent panoramas on the road to Gais and Appenzell.

Werdenberg is an idyllic town with some charming half-timbered houses and many picturesque wooden houses built during the 15th-17th cent.

Säntis, 2 504 m, is the highest peak in the Alpsteingebirge (Alpstein Massif). It can be reached by cable car. Magnificent views over the Alps and Bodensee (Lake Constance).

LIECHTENSTEIN, see town plans.

St. Luzisteig. The old fortress is placed at a strategic point where fortifications once existed as long ago as the Roman era. Small abbey with Gothic church. The entrance through the gates is quite narrow.

Heidibrunnen (the Heidi Fountain) is situated in majestic surroundings. Johanna Spyri was the authoress of the popular Heidi books.

Maienfeld. Beautiful square and the house where Johanna Spyri lived. Traffic must pass through very narrow streets.

Sargans. The folklore museum is housed in a mighty 12th-cent. castle. Bad Ragaz, a popular spa, has radioactive thermal baths with waters from the Pfäfer Springs.

Pfäfers has an 8th-cent. Benedictine abbey that was completely remodelled in the 17th cent.

A road goes from the industrial town of ***Landquart*** to ***Davos,*** Switzerland's largest winter resort.

CHUR (32 000). Major town in the canton of Graubünden. First mentioned in 452 as the seat of a bishop. The Roman citadel was replaced by the 18th-cent. *bishop's palace,* which still stands on a hill high above the medieval Altstadt (Old Town). 12th-cent. cathedral with a treasury. Despite Chur's lofty position (587 m above sea level) it is filled with semi-tropical vegetation.

From Chur it is possible to take the little narrow-gauge railway through a magnificent landscape to the large resort of ***Arosa*** (60 min.). The *Rhaetian Railways* (Rhätische Bahn), a metre-gauge private railway, also has lines that stretch to St. Moritz, Klosters, Davos, Landquart, etc. Travelling on this railway is a wonderful experience for nature lovers and rail buffs alike.

Rhäzüns. Castle and the Church of St. George with lovely 14th-cent. frescoes. ***Thusis*** is a resort and the major town in the *Domleschg,* an untamed landscape dotted with castles and rocky heights. The narrow *Hinterrhein* flows through deep gorges. It is still clear and clean at this point of its 1 320 km journey from Gotthard to Rotterdam. The motorist may prefer to choose the old road rather than Autostrasse N 13. Although the older route is narrow and winding it has nevertheless been improved since the Romans called it the *"Via Mala"* – the Bad Road. Via Mala is now the name for a wild and romantic gorge. A staircase with 250 steps leads directly from the road. A beautiful road passes through the exciting *Albula Valley* on the way to Tiefencastel.

The *Church of St. Martin* in *Zillis* was built in the 12th cent. Painted ceiling, that depicts scenes from the Old Testament and the Life of Christ. (12th cent.) ***Andeer.*** Climatic health resort with thermal baths.

The road follows the shore of a series of artificial lakes. At *Rofflaschlucht* there is a promenade that includes a tunnel under the Rhine.

Splügen. Resort with sturdy old houses. The view from the ruined Zur Burg tower is towards Tombohorn on the Italian border. *Hinterrhein* has a partially Italian atmosphere. An old stone bridge crosses the Rhine.

The *San Bernardino tunnel* was opened in 1969 and N 19 is one of the easiest trans-Alpine routes. However, there are some sharp curves on the southern section. The village of ***San Bernardino*** is a climatic health resort and a centre for winter sports.

Mesocco has white stone houses and an impressive ruined castle. Beautiful frescoes in the Church of Santa Maria del Castello. ***Soazza.*** Charming village and the lowland boundary for mulberry trees. ***Buffalora.*** Beautiful waterfall. The boundary for grapevines is in ***Lostallo.***

Grono has the Fiorenzana Tower which protected the road during the Middle Ages. ***Roveredo.*** Splendid frescoes in the Church of San Giulio. The 17th-cent. Madonna del Ponte Chiuso is at the entrance to the Traversagna Valley.

Bellinzona – Lugano – Como, see E 9.

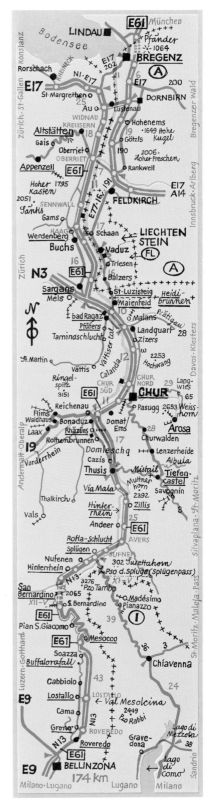

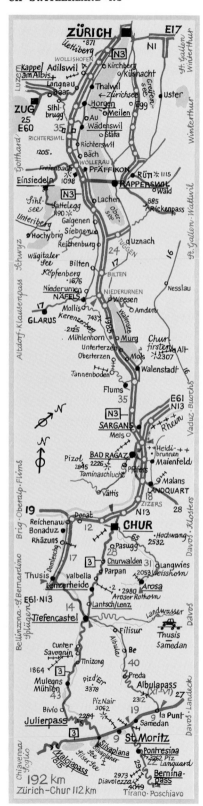

192 km
Zürich–Chur 112 km

N 3. Basel – Zürich – Chur – Julier – Chiavenna

Basel – Zürich, see E 17.

ZÜRICH, see town plans.

A very scenic route with superb views of Lake Zürich. Alternatively, it is possible to drive along the roads that follow the lake shore, passing through a series of towns. It is also possible to use the route that passes Egg on the way to Rapperswil.

Horgen. Large industrial town. The home of a branch of the American Dow Chemicals Corp. A ferry takes visitors to *Meilen* where Richard Wagner once lived.

Route 4 (E 60) goes to Lucerne (Luzern) and Arth.

At *Kappel am Albis* there is an abbey with a church, built in 1305.

Zug (21 000). Capital of the canton of the same name. Several fortification towers. Astronomical clock in the Zeitturm (Zytturm). Liebfrauenkirche, in Gothic and Baroque, is built into the town wall.

Wädenswil has a ruined castle. *Pfäffikon.* Beautiful Baroque chapel.

Rapperswil is built on a peninsula. Its medieval character and houses make it one of the loveliest towns in the country. Arcaded patrician houses. The castle dates from the 13th cent.

Einsiedeln. Meinrad the Hermit settled here in 861. (Hermit = Einsiedler). This was the origin of one of Europe's most influential abbeys. The mighty building measures 130 × 150 m and its total area includes four courtyards. Switzerland's most renowned *Baroque church*, decorated by the brothers Asam (see Munich).

Unteriberg. Large recreation area with the new Hoch-Ybrig winter sports centre, situated by the shores of an Alpine lake, 2 000 m above sea level.

Niederurnen with the ruins of Oberwindeck Castle. *Näfels.* Freulerpalast was completed in 1647 and now houses the Glarus regional museum. Splendid interior.

Scenic route along the shores of *Walensee.* It goes through a series of galleries and one tunnel (1.5 km long) and provides beautiful views of the *Churfirsten.* *Murg* is a resort with charming houses. *Walenstadt.* Resort. When the motorway now under construction is completed in 1985, it will include a 5.7 km long tunnel under *Kerenzerberg.* *Sargans, Bad Ragaz, Davos, Chur, Arosa,* see E 61.

Churwalden. Resort. The church was built in 1477. Nowadays Protestant church services are held in the nave and Roman Catholic services in the chancel.

Lenzerheide. Large resort. *Lantsch.* Village well-known for the handsome Haus Amilcar from 1694. *Tiefencastel.* Spa.

The *Julier Pass* (2 284 m above sea level) has a maximum gradient of 10%. Open all year and suitable for caravans. At its highest point, there are two pylons said to be remains of a temple dedicated to the Celtic Sun God, Jul.

Silvaplana. One of many resorts on the beautiful Oberngadiner Lakes. Numerous excellent hiking trails.

The *Maloja Pass* (1 815 m above sea level). 10% gradient. It is possible to drive with caravans through this pass.

Soglio is on a narrow and extremely steep by-road. Lovely views. Partially encircled by beautiful chestnut woods.

Italian border. The road continues to Chiavenna, Lugano and Milano.

Route 27 goes through the *Engadine Valley* to Nauders and Landeck in Austria.

St. Moritz. One of Switzerland's oldest and most exclusive resorts. This was the site of the Winter Olympic Games in 1928 and 1948. *Engadiner Museum.* Leaning tower in front of the church. Summer skiing is possible on the nearby Corvatsch Glacier.

From *Celerina* the road goes through the Bernina Pass to Tirano in Italy. The road passes *Pontresina,* a resort which has a mountaineering school. The *Bernina Pass* (2 323 m). 10% gradient. It is possible to drive with a caravan in tow. 15 min. after leaving the ice and snow in the pass, you are down in a flower-filled valley that is almost Italianate in character. The major town, *Poschiavo* (Puschlav) has Mediterranean vegetation and picturesque pavement cafés.

6. Porrentruy – Biel/Bienne – Bern – Interlaken – Gletsch

Boncourt. Frontier town with charming half-timbered houses. Tobacco industry. *Grottes de Milandre.* Stalactite and stalagmite caves of Jura chalk. The grottoes are open to tourists.

Porrentruy-Pruntrut is the picturesque major town in the Ajoie country. The mighty castle was once the residence of the prince-bishops of Basel. Many churches from different periods.

The road goes over *Les Rangiers* (856 m), a natural divide between the Rhône and the Rhine. *St-Ursanne* is a lovely old abbey town. Three town gates and a stone bridge (1728) over the Doubs Valley.

Delémont is the major town in the Jura. The Old Town is above the rest of the town, at the same level as the bishops' palace and the churches. *Jurassisches Museum.* Route 18 continues to Bern/Berne.

BIEL/BIENNE: A bi-lingual town – the only place in Switzerland where the street signs are in two languages. It is a large and modern industrial town. (Omega watch factory). Charming Altstadt (Old Town). The Schwab Museum contains an impressive archaeological collection.

To the east lies *Grenchen* (Certina watch factory.)

Solothurn, see E 4. *BERN,* see town plans.

Münsingen has a medieval castle. *Riggisberg* is the site of the Abegg Foundation, which includes a museum and an art sciences institute.

THUN (35 000) is an industrial town with a beautiful Altstadt (Old Town). The *castle,* which has four distinctive towers, was built to the plans of Berchthold von Zähringen (see Bern) in about 1190. Now an historical museum. Art museum. The Gesslerschiessen Festival is held on the last Sunday – Tuesday in September. Gessler was the bailiff who ordered William Tell to shoot the apple from his son's head.

Spiez. Large and lovely resort on the shores of Thuner See. The medieval castle is now a museum. 11th-cent. church. An exceptionally beautiful road leads through the Simme Valley to the *Jaun Pass* and on to Lake Geneva. From Spiez the road goes to *Kandersteg* where there are auto-rail facilities through the Lötschberg tunnel to Goppenstein .

Beatenberg. Fine views: Blümlisalp. Holiday apartment blocks. The area is swarming with tourists, most of them from Germany. The stalactite and stalagmite *Beatushöhlen grotto* has an 800 m long cavern.

INTERLAKEN (15 000). One of Switzerland's earliest major tourist resorts, beautifully set between the lakes, "inter-laken". Imposing turn-of-the-century hotels. Casino. Flower clock in the park. From the Höhematte there are superb views of the Jungfrau. The castle was once an abbey. *Alpenwildpark* (Alpine botanical garden). Schiller's "William Tell" is presented during the summer in the Rugen Park.

Schynige Platte is a look-out mountain (2 101 m) situated between Bödeli and the Grindelwald Valley. *Grindelwald* is a large touring centre.

Road to *Lauterbrunnen* (1 800 m). From here it is only 9 km as the crow flies to the top of the *Jungfrau* (3 358 m). Cable cars to Wengen – Kleine Scheidegg and to Grütschalp – Mürren.

From the tourist resort of *Mürren* (1 645 m), a cable car goes to Schilthorn (2 970 m). Magnificent views. The revolving restaurant atop the Piz Gloria may look familiar to you – it was featured in a James Bond film.

A rack railway line runs from the popular resort of *Wengen* to *Kleine Scheidegg.* From here, connecting trains travel to *Jungfraujoch.* This railway station, adjacent to the glacier, at 3 454 m, is the highest in Europe. Cable car to the summit where there is a meteorological observatory and an Alpine research institute with interesting exhibitions. Visitors can also inspect ice grottoes, ride in sleighs pulled by huskies or do some summer skiing. Trains continue to Grindelwald. The station at *Eigerwand* (2 864 m) is in a tunnel. Observation windows are built into the tunnel wall.

Brienz, a picturesque and lovely town, has a school for woodcarving, but it is primarily a Mecca for railway buffs: the *Brienz-Rothorn Bahn* (8 km) has regular steam-train services. The small locomotives are rather grotesque in appearance as they seem to lean strangely forward. But out on the line, which has a 20-25% gradient, they look quite normal. *Brienzer Rothorn* (2 350 m). Magnificent views. The *Swiss Open-Air Museum* (Schweizerisches Freilichtmuseum) is in *Ballenberg.* Houses typical of different parts of Switzerland have been transported here.

Meiringen. Folklore museum. Road to the lovely valley of *Rosenlaui* in a beautiful valley lined with cliffs and glaciers.

Road 11 runs through the *Susten Pass* (2 224 m) to *Wassen.* Maximum 9% gradient. The road is easy to drive and suitable for caravans.

The *Grimsel Pass* ((2 165 m). Maximum 9% gradient. Rather difficult road, long incline and then a series of curves. After leaving the pass, six curves lead down to Gletsch (see road 19).

Gletsch, see route 19.

19. Chur – Oberalp – Andermatt – Furka – Brig

CHUR, and **Arosa,** see E 61. Road to **Klosters,** a lovely resort town. Its church has a Romanesque tower.

Davos (10 600). One of Switzerland's best-known resorts, consisting of the village of Davos, to the north, at the foot of the Schiahorn, and Davos Platz.

Flims, Laax and **Falera** are all winter resorts. Cable car to the summit of Crap Sogn Gion (2 228 m). The journey takes 10 min.

Ilanz is an old trading town. When written about in 766, it was called "the most important town on the Rhine". Remains of a town wall. Picturesque Gothic church, Baroque Obertor tower and Rotes Tor.

Breil. Tourist resort. Baroque Church of Santa Maria. The Church of St. Martin has an altar, carved in 1518.

Somvix, situated high above the valley, has a magnificent view. Above the village there is a Gothic chapel with interesting paintings. The road continues over a wooden bridge with intricate lattice work.

Disentis/Muster. The Benedictine abbey was founded in the 8th cent. The present buildings are Baroque. St. Martin, an abbey church (1712) designed by Kaspar Moosbrugger, who also designed Einsiedeln.

The **Lukmanier Pass** (Passo Lucomagno). From Disentis, a maximum 3% gradient rising up to 1 916 m. From **Biasca,** the gradient increases to a maximum of 9%. The route is rather difficult and not quite suitable for caravans. Open May-October.

Sedrun. Resort with lovely wooden houses and a church with a Romanesque clock tower. **Tschamut.** Tourist resort.

The **Oberalp Pass.** From Disentis, a maximum 10% gradient up to a height of 2 044 m. From Andermatt the gradient is the same. The route is rather difficult and not suitable for caravans. Open June-October.

Andermatt. Old fortification built at the meeting place of Alpine passes. Even today it is a garrison town. Andermatt is a large resort with sturdy houses, built to withstand the severe winter climate.

The **Furka Pass.** From Realp there is a maximum 10% gradient to the pass height (2 431 m). From Gletsch the gradient is the same. The route through the pass is well planned and constructed. Rather difficult and not suitable for caravans.

Gletsch. Tourist resort situated at 1 759 m. During the 1860s the Rhône Glacier (Rhônegletscher) extended as far as the present town, but it has receded. Warm clothing is advisable if you visit the Gletscher ice caves. This is where the River Rhône rises to flow through the Lake of Geneva, to Lyon in France, eventually to enter the Mediterranean just west of Marseille.

Oberwald. The highest village in the Goms Valley which in turn is the highest section of the Rhône Valley. **Münster.** The wooden houses, darked by the sun, are typical of the area.

Niederwald has a Baroque church and many picturesque houses. Birthplace (1850) of Cesar Ritz, the hotel king. **Beilwald.** Tourist resort. **Ernen.** Beautiful houses line the square. The legend of William Tell is painted on the façade of the Tellenhaus.

Eggishorn. Here, at 2 927 m, there are magnificent views of the Aletschgletscher, the Berner Alps and the Jungfrau. See also road 6.

Binntal is undisturbed by tourism. Nature preserve at Riederfurka. **Mörel** has a holiday centre and the 1730 Hohenflühen shrine-church.

BRIG, see E 2.

TOWN PLANS

BASEL (Basle, Bâle, 181 000)

Large junction where railways and motorways meet the enormous Rhine transport system. Here France, Germany and Switzerland have common boundaries, and here, as early as the Middle Ages, a wooden bridge, the Mittlere Brücke, was constructed. In 1905, it was replaced by a modern structure. The newest bridge over the Rhine is the motorway bridge which has visibly eased the former traffic problems. The German Federal Railways have their terminus here, the Badischer Bahnhof, situated on Swiss territory. The Basel airport is situated on French territory. The SBB railway station is an impressive iron structure with lovely landscapes painted over the booking offices.

The university was founded in 1460. It is associated with a long line of famous men, from Erasmus to Nietzsche. The *cathedral* (11th-15th cent.), built of red sandstone from the Vosges, has two slender towers. The *town hall* (1521) on the Marktplatz, has an ornately painted façade. Spaltentor (1370) is one of the country's most beautiful city gates. The old parts of the town near the cathedral are picturesque and interesting. The Hotell Drei Könige/Hotel des trois

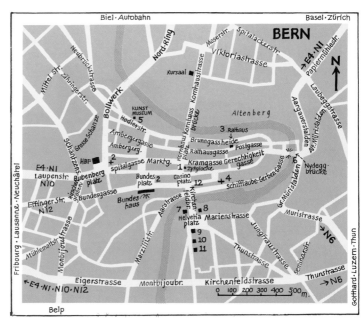

1 Zeitglockenturm. Zähringerbrunnen. Kramgasse.
2 Bundeshaus (House of Parliament).
3 Town hall.
4 Cathedral.
5 Kunstmuseum (Art Museum).
6 Bear pit.
7 Alpine Museum with Post Museum.
8 Kunsthalle (Art Gallery).
9 Historical Museum.
10 Weapons Museum.
11 Natural History Museum.
12 Casino.

The Basel Cathedral and the River Rhine

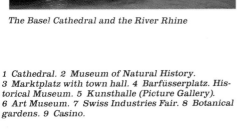

1 Cathedral. 2 Museum of Natural History. 3 Marktplatz with town hall. 4 Barfüsserplatz. Historical Museum. 5 Kunsthalle (Picture Gallery). 6 Art Museum. 7 Swiss Industries Fair. 8 Botanical gardens. 9 Casino.

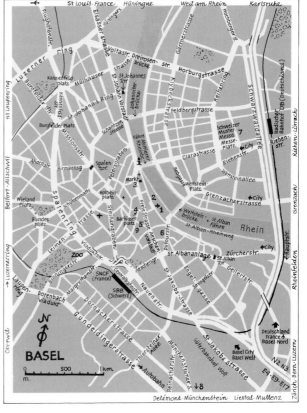

Geneva. The River Rhone flows into the Lake of Geneva

Rois (The Three Kings) is one of the most outstanding hotels in Europe, with traditions that stretch back to the 11th cent.

The *Kunsthalle* (Picture Gallery) exhibits paintings by Hans Holbein the Younger and Arnold Böcklin, two artists who worked in Basel. There are 23 museums in Basel. Among the more noteworthy are the Museum of Natural History, the Ethnological Museum, and the Swiss Pharmacy Museum.

Basel is the site of the largest *zoo* in Switzerland. *Botanical gardens.*

Basel is an important industrial city and the pharmaceutical industry is especially prominent: Hoffman la Roche, Sandoz and Ciba Geigy are all situated here. Annual trade fair.

BERN (Berne, 141 000)

The city was founded in 1191 and became the capital in 1848. The picturesque old part of the town lies high on a sandstone peninsula, overlooking the River Aare. Five high bridges, soaring about 40 m above the water, lead to the newer sections of the city. Kramgasse has the *Lauben,* an arcaded pedestrian precinct, and *Zeitglockenturm* (clock tower), or, as it is known in the Bernese dialect, the "Zytglocke". Every hour on the hour mechanical figures "perform" on this 16th-cent. clock. Just beneath them is an astronomical clock. In the middle of the street stands an armoured bear holding the Zähringen flag – the Count of Zähringen was the founder of Bern and the bear has a prominent place on the city's coat of arms. Live bears, the mascots of Bern, can be found in the Bärengraben. Many beautiful fountains.

The late-Gothic cathedral was built in the 13th cent. and the Käfigturm (Prison Tower) dates from the same period. The Church of the Holy Ghost (Heiliggeistkirche) and the Federal Houses of Parliament (Bundeshaus) are in Baroque. Impressive view from the *Kleine Schanze* which has the Oskar-Bider-Denkmal, dedicated to the memory of the man who made the first trans-Alpine flight in 1913. University.

The railway station is extremely modern. In the pedestrian tunnel leading to the underground station is a statue of St. Christopher, a copy of a mighty statue that once adorned one of the city gates from medieval times. It was removed and destroyed in the 19th cent. on orders of the city fathers. Its head and a hand are in the *Historical Museum,* situated on Helvetiaplatz. Here, the visitor can also see a burlesque carving of William Tell and his son. The *Art Gallery* (Kunsthalle) has an impressive collection of works by Paul Klee. Among the city's other museums are the Alpine Museum (with Postmuseum), and the Natural History Museum. Botanical Institute and Gardens and a zoo at Dahlhölzli.

GENÈVE

(Geneva, Genf, Ginivra, 151 000).

The city is beautifully situated at the point where the River Rhône enters the Lake of Geneva (Lac Léman). There is a particularly lovely view from the *Quai du Mont-Blanc.* Here, the visitor can see the bustling lake traffic, the 145 m high *Jet d'eau* fountain, and in the background, the *Salève Mountain.* Splendid views also from *Pont du Mont-Blanc,* the busiest street in Switzerland. In the middle of the river is the little *Rousseau Island* with a statue of the writer and philosopher Jean-Jacques Rousseau (1712–1778). Picturesque medieval streets and houses in the older sections of the city which are built on a higher level than the newer areas. Every visitor should take a walk along the Grand' Rue. The *Cathedral of St. Pierre* was built in the 13th cent. and there are magnificent

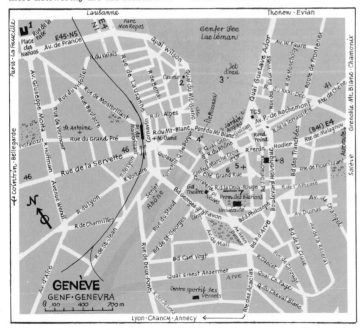

1 Palais des Nations (U.N. headquarters). 2 Casino. 3 Jet d'eau. 4 Rousseau Island. 5 Cathedral. 6 Town hall. 7 Reformation Monument. 8 Musée d'Art et d'Histoire.

Zürich's Old Town is situated along the River Limmat

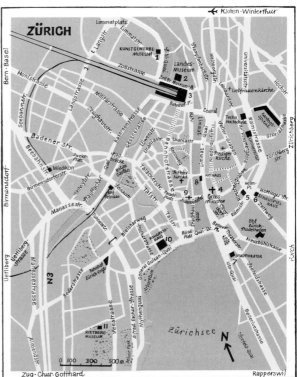

1 Arts and Crafts Museum. 2 Landesmuseum.
3 Cathedral. Altstadt. 4 Art Museum. 5 Town hall.
6 Fraumünsterkirche. 7 Convention hall and concert hall. 8 Rietberg Museum (ethnography).
9 Botanical gardens. 10 Zoo.

views from its tower. The Temple de l'Auditoire is close to the cathedral. It was here that the religious reformers Calvin and Knox preached. Their work has been immortalized in the mighty *Reformation Monument*. The Museum of the City of Geneva is housed in the 13th-cent. Maison Tavel. Voltaire Museum. Musée d'Art et d'Histoire has archaeological finds, crafts, and a fine collection of Impressionist paintings. Monument dedicated to l'Escalade. On December 12, 1602, the citizens of Geneva repelled a night-time attack (l'Escalade) of the soldiers of the Duke of Savoy. Annual celebrations of the victory.

Geneva is the European headquarters of the United Nations, which occupy the splendid buildings that were used by the League of Nations from 1919 until 1946. Geneva is also the headquarters for over 200 international organizations such as the Red Cross, the International Labour Office and the AIT, the International Tourist Alliance.

Nine-tenths of Geneva's boundaries are also the boundary to France. The "City Mountain" of Salève is actually on French territory as is part of the *Cointrin airport*. Close to the city is *Cern*, headquarters for the European Atomic Energy Commission. Large Cyclotron.

ZÜRICH (375 000)

The largest city in Switzerland. The beautiful older sections of Zürich are on the banks of the *River Limmat*.

This is an important centre of industry, trade and particularly banking: it is the home of the "gnomes of Zürich". It is also a centre of education with university, Federal Institute of Technology and many colleges.

The picturesque winding streets in the *Altstadt* are lined with colourfully painted houses, charming restaurants and lively places of entertainment. The lovely Zur Meisen guildhouse (1737) has an outstanding collection of porcelain and ceramics. Fraumünsterkirche (13th-15th cent.) and Grossmünster Cathedral (11th-13th cent.).

Zwingli started the Swiss Reformation (1519) in Kirchgasse 13. His statue is at the Wasserkirche. Town hall in Renaissance style. Beautiful view over the Lake of Zürich from *Bürkliplatz*. This square marks the beginning of *Bahnhofstrasse*, that leads to the central railway station (Hauptbahnhof). It is one of the most elegant shopping streets in Europe. Sprüngli, one of the finest pastry shops in Europe, is situated on Paradeplatz. Many visitors also patronize the well-known Globus department store. The *Schweizerisches Landesmuseum* (Swiss National Museum) has exhibitions devoted to the development, culture and art history of the country. Art museum. Museum Rietberg specializes in primitive and Asian art.

FL · Liechtenstein

A principality with a population of 15 000. Area: 158 km² (62 sq. miles). The overwhelming majority of the inhabitants are German-speaking Roman Catholics. In 1719, Liechtenstein was created as a principality within the Holy Roman Empire and in 1866 it became an independent state. After the First World War it joined in a customs, currency and postal union with Switzerland. Tourism and postage stamps play a vital role in the country's economy.

The capital, *Vaduz* (3 000), is usually swarming with tourists. The town is dominated by the medieval castle, which was once the residence of Emperor Franz-Joseph of Austria. It is not open to visitors. Now it is the residence of the prince who governs the country with the aid of a parliament made up of 15 members.

The *National Museum* (Liechtensteinische Gemäldesammlung), housed in the same building as the tourist office, has an impressive collection of art that includes works of such masters as Rubens, Breughel and Frans Hals. Postal museum in Engländerstrasse.

Triesen. Old chapel. Balzers with the medieval Gatenberg Castle.

St. Katerinabrun Chapel and a 1592 frontier stone are situated together on the Liechtenstein-Swiss boundary.

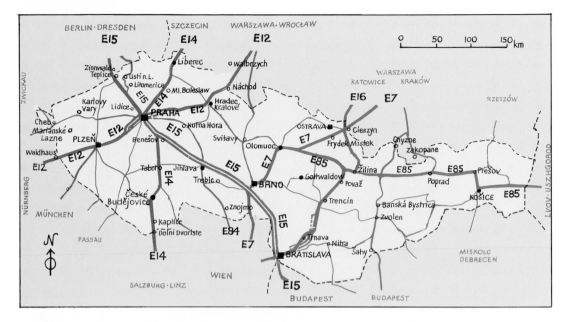

CS · Czechoslovakia

CS·Československo

Area: 127 800 km² (49 366 sq. miles)

Population: 15 million. 65% of the population are Czechs, 29% Slovaks and 4% Hungarians. The remaining 2% is made up of Polish, German and Ukrainian minorities. Languages: Czech and Slovak.

Major cities: Praha (Prague) 1.2 million, Brno 370 000, Bratislava 380 000, Ostrava 310 000, Plzeň (Pilsen) 167 000, Košice 210 000.

Government: The Czechoslovakian Socialist Republic is a federation of two republics: the Czech Socialist Republic, which takes up 62% of the nation, and consists of Bohemia and Moravia, and the Slovakian Socialist Republic which takes up 38% of the national territory. There are 10 administrative regions (corresponding to the former provinces), 100 administrative districts, and about 10 000 communities.

History

800 The Great Moravian Empire.
900 The Premyslid dynasty gains power. Prague becomes the capital.

1355 Karel IV (Charles IV) is crowned Holy Roman Emperor.
1415 Jan Hus (John Huss) is burned at the stake. Growth of the Hussite movement.
1500 Habsburg rule begins.
1618 The Emperor's Czech Catholic counsellors are defenestrated at Hradčany Palace. The Thirty Years' War begins.
1620 The Battle of White Mountain. The Czechs are defeated.
1848 Unsuccessful uprising against the Austrians.
1918 The First World War ends. Fall of the Austro-Hungarian Empire. The Republic of Czechoslovakia is proclaimed and recognized.
1938 The Czechoslovakian government is forced by the Munich Pact agreement to relinquish one-fourth of the national territory to Germany.
1939 Hitler's troops occupy Bohemia and Moravia, and Czechoslovakia is proclaimed an "independent nation".
1945 Liberation of Czechoslovakia.
1948 Czechoslovakia becomes a People's Democracy.

Currency: Czechoslovakian crowns,

Koruna (CSK)
1 koruna = 100 hellers (Haléř).
The import and export of Czechoslovakian currency is strictly forbidden. Local currency can be purchased at officially recognized banks. There is a special rate of exchange for foreign tourists. Visitors to Czechoslovakia are required to exchange an amount that corresponds to a prorated cost of their daily living expenses.
Citizens of non-Socialist nations must have a valid visa to Czechoslovakia. (Transit visas are obligatory.)

Business hours: Banks 8.00 a.m.-3.00 p.m. In major tourist centres currency exchange offices are open on Saturdays. Post offices 8.00 a.m.- 6.00 p.m. Closed Saturdays. Central offices in major cities 8.00 a.m.-12.00 midnight. Saturdays 8.00 a.m.-12.00 noon. Shops 9.00 a.m.-6.00 p.m. Saturdays 9.00 a.m.-12.00 noon.

Holidays: New Year's Day, May 1, May 9 (National Liberation Day), Easter Monday, December 25 and 26.

Hotels
Hotels are divided into four categories.

Camping
The camping sites are divided into two categories, A and B. All ČEDOK-camping sites are category A.

Food and drink
The Czech cuisine, like its German counterpart, is rather substantial. You usually begin with a hearty soup – potato soup, goulash soup, and mushroom soup are among the most popular. Sausages in different forms are often served. Dumplings are often

Kolonáda, a promenade in Karlovy Vary

served with meat, but might appear as a main course. Dumplings with a fruit filling have a thin covering and are a delicious dessert. Vepřová is roast pork. Pečená husa is roast goose. Both are usually accompanied by dumplings and sauerkraut. Prague ham is world famous.

Czech beer is famous – and strong: Pilsner Urquell, Budvar (Budweiser), Staropramen.

Slivovice is plum brandy. Becherovka is a liqueur from Karlovy Vary (Karlsbad). Hanácká Řezná is a type of rye vodka.

The mineral water is exceptionally good.

Shopping
Bohemian glass, crystal, leather goods, embroidered blouses, costume jewellery, handwoven tablecloths, woodcarvings.

Petrol
Holders of petrol coupons are entitled to reductions. They can be purchased at ČEDOK offices. Diesel oil is sold only to holders of special coupons.

Speed limits. Traffic regulations
Motorways 110 kmh, other roads 90 kmh, built-up areas 60 kmh.

Children under the age of 12 are not allowed to travel in the front seat.

If your car is fitted with seat belts it is compulsory to wear them.

All motorists must carry a first-aid kit nad a replacement set of light bulbs.

If a vehicle is damaged within the country a report must be produced at the frontier when leaving.

Roads
The roads are fairly good, but within towns they can be narrow. The newer roads often go outside the towns.

Road patrols
The Czechoslovakian Motor Club has road patrols which provide assistance. They can be reached by local emergency telephones. In Prague the number is 22 49 06.

UAMK, Ústřední Automotoklub ČSSR, 29 Opletalova, Praha.
ČEDOK, Příkopy 18, Praha. Offices in all major cities.
Czechoslovak Travel Bureau (ČEDOK), 17/18 Old Bond Street, London W1X 3DA. Tel 01-629 6058.

The High Tatras

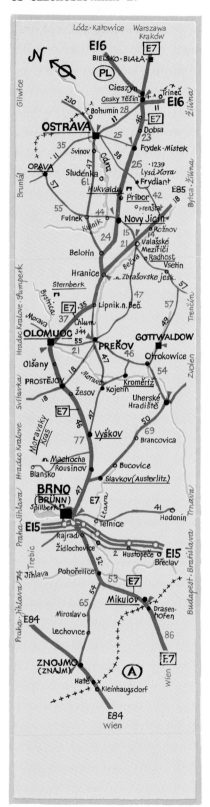

E 7. Český Těšín – Brno – Mikulov – Wien

Cieszyn/Český Těšín. Polish frontier. E 7 comes from Warszawa–Krakow. The town, divided by the River Olza, is part Polish and part Czech.

OSTRAVA (85 000). Capital of North Moravia. Steel industry and the centre of a large coal-mining area. College of mining. Václav Church and lovely town hall. Zoo.

Opava. Once the capital of Silesia. Several monuments. The royal castle of Hradec nad Moravicí is near by. Rooms dedicated to Beethoven, Liszt and Paganini who were all guests here.

Příbor. Birthplace of Siegmund Freud, the father of psychoanalysis (1856-1939). Museum in the house where he was born. **Kopřivnice**. The Tatra car factory has been in operation here since 1901. Interesting motor museum. **Hukvaldy**. Village at the foot of a large ruined castle. Birthplace of the composer, Leo Janáček. The house is now a museum.

Novy Jičín (22 000). Beautiful 16th-cent. houses, especially on the imposing main square. 18th-cent. castle with ethnological and hatters' museums.

OLOMOUC (82 000). Remains of a Přemyslide fortress. Bishopric since the 11th cent. The city was conquered by the Swedes in 1642, during the Thirty Years' War, and Brno replaced it as capital of Moravia. Picturesque streets and houses. Václav Cathedral and the Baroque Marie Snězna Church. Annual "Flora" flower show.

Radhost. Large open-air museum.

Přerov. Square lined with beautiful buildings. Castle with museum of archaeology and display of optical instruments.

Kroměříž is a beautiful town. Houses in Gothic, Renaissance and Baroque styles. Art gallery in the castle.

Vyškov. Birthplace of Klement Gottwald (1896-1953) in Dedice. He was the first president of the People's Democracy of Czechoslovakia. Castle with ceramics exhibition.

Slavkov (Austerlitz). Here, in 1805, the troops of Napoleon defeated the armies of Russia, Austria and Hungary during the "Battle of the Three Emperors". Small museum. Monument. 5 km away is the hill where Napoleon declared, "Proudly, you will declare that you took part in the Battle of Austerlitz". About 32 000 of the soldiers who heard his cry never lived to express their pride. Peace memorial. Museum in the Baroque Slavkov Castle.

Moravský Kras. Underground rivers and large stalactite caves. Four of the caves are open to tourists.

BRNO (Brünn, 370 000). The major city of South Moravia and Czechoslovakia's second largest city. Industries and trade fairs. **Špilberk Castle** on its hill looms over the city. During the Nazi occupation it was used as a prison. Now the castle is a national monument. Svoboda Square is dominated by a beautiful Baroque palace that contains the **Moravian Museum**, a folklore museum, an art museum, etc. The old town hall dates from 1311. Augustinian church and the Church of St. James. The church of the Capucines contains the mummies of monks and the legendary Hungarian colonel, Trenck. The father of the science of genetics, G. Mendel, was a monk in the Staré Brno monastery. Museum and experimental gardens. The Pisarky park has extensive fair grounds. The Anthropos Museum specializes in prehistorical artifacts.

Mikulov is on the old "Emperors' Road" from Brno to Prague. Medieval fortress, often reconstructed. The enormous collection of art was damaged in 1945, but the treasures that survived are quite impressive. The Mikulov wine is famous. The castle's cellar contains a barrel, stored there in 1643. It holds over 100 000 (22 000 gallons) of wine.

Austrian border. E 7 continues to Wien – Klagenfurt – Mestre (Venezia) – Bologna – Perugia – Roma.

E 12. Hradec Králové – Praha – Plzeň – Nürnberg.

Běloves. Polish frontier. E 12 comes from Białystok – Warszawa – Wrocław.

Náchod (20 000). Textile industry. Castle with Baroque and Empire furniture and Dutch tapestries. Road to **Trutnov**. Lovely square with arcades. Folklore museum with exhibits from the **Krkonoše area** (Riesengebirge, "The Giants' Mountain"). **Dvůr Králové nad Labem**. Square with beautiful houses and arcades. Textile museum and safari park. **Kuks** with an enormous Baroque building (1724) which spans both banks of the Elbe. Castle, church, open-air bathing and hospital.

HRADEC KRÁLOVÉ (87 000). Centre of East Bohemia. Modern town with old centre (national monument). Gothic brick church (14th cent.). Provincial museum (1912). The German name for the town is Königgrätz. The Prussians won a great battle here in 1866. By defeating the Austrians they achieved the unification of Germany.

Route 37 goes to **Pardubice** whose Old Town has been proclaimed a national monument. Castle with art museum that specializes in the work of North Italian artists. **Zámeček.** (the Small Castle). Memorial to the Resistance movement. Here the Gestapo had its execution grounds. The town is famed for its equestrian and motorcycle competitions. **Kutná Hora**, see E 15.

Chlumec nad Cidlinou. The Baroque Karlova Koruna (Charles' Crown) Palace has collections of sculpture, paintings and handicrafts. **Poděbrady.** Spa. Square with Renaissance palace. **Nymburk**. Industrial town. Preserved ramparts. Průhonice, see Praha, town plans.

PRAHA (PRAGUE), see town plans.

Karlštejn. Magnificent castle, built in the 14th cent. for Emperor Charles IV as a repository for his crown jewels. The Chapel of the Holy Cross is decorated with 3 000 precious stones. Beautiful frescoes.

Beroun. Splendid square lined with Renaissance and Baroque buildings. Jenštejn House with geological museum. Partially preserved fortifications with two 14th-cent. town gates. Ruined castle in **Žebrák. Křivoklát** has a large castle. Construction on it started in the 13th cent. and continued into the 17th cent.

Rokycany (13 000). One of the oldest Czech towns. Remains of town fortifications. Baroque and Renaissance houses, museum.

Příbram. Once the site of silver mines. Now uranium is mined here. Modern town with older buildings in the centre. There is a museum in Ernestinum, a Gothic castle. Old miners' houses on Havířská ulice (Miners' Street).

PLZEŇ (Pilsen, 159 000). Capital of West Bohemia. Large industrial town with Škoda factory and breweries. Picturesque town centre. Gothic church in the middle of the square. Renaissance town hall. Museums, zoo, planetarium, marionette theatre. The town gave its name to the world famous beer. The only true (and strong) Pilsen beer is called Prazdroj-Urquell (the original spring).

Route 26 goes southwards through the lovely old towns of **Horšovský Týn** and **Domažlice** with fine folklore museums in the Chodský hrad castle and Jindřich. Many beautiful and picturesque streets.

Rozvadov. West German frontier. E 12 continues to Nürnberg – Mannheim – Saarbrücken – Metz – Paris.

Alternative route via Karlovy Vary (Karlsbad).

KARLOVY VARY (Karlsbad, 44 000). One of the large old European spas, Karlovy Vary has retained the atmosphere that it had when emperors and kings were frequent visitors. The large Moskva-Pupp hotel is typical of that era. It was founded by a confectioner named Pupp, who came to Karlsbad in 1782 and opened the hotel at the end of the 18th cent. Goethe once declared that there were only three cities in which he would want to live: Weimar, Rome and Karlsbad. Film festivals. Beautiful walks, surrounding woods. To the north lies **Krušné Hory** (Erzgebirge, "the Ore Mountains"), a 130 km long mountain range on the East German frontier. Beech woods and pine forests. Winter sports.

Klínovec (1 244 m) is the highest mountain. Cable car from Jáchymov, a spa with buildings from the 16th- cent. mining era.

Loket. Lovely houses. Gothic castle, museum.

Mariánske Lázně (Marienbad). Spa with old traditions. Buildings from the late 19th cent. Music festival.

Cheb (Eger). One of the oldest towns in Bohemia. Restored town centre. The St. Bartholomew Church has Gothic sculptures. Museums. The house where Wallenstein, the general, was murdered in 1634.

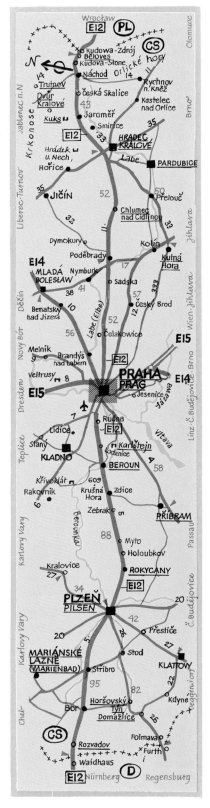

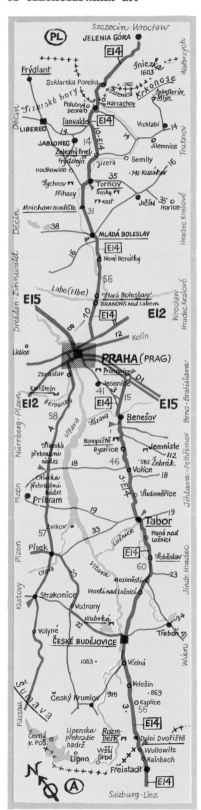

E14. Jelenia Góra – Praha – České Budějovice – Linz

Polish frontier at Jakozyce/Harrachov. E14 comes from Malmö – Trelleborg – Szczecin – Jelenia Góra. Polish roads 10 and 3.

Harrachov. Lovely location. Glass works. Winter sports centre on Mount Krkonoše (Riesengebirge, "the Giants' Mountain"). *Tanvald.* Lovely little tourist resort. *Špindlerův Mlýn* (Spindlermühle). Climatic health resort and winter sports resort.

Jablonec nad Nisou. Centre of the jewellery industry. Permanent exhibition in the town museum. *Liberec* (65 000) in the Nisa Valley. Founded in the 13th cent. Partially preserved old streets with 18th-cent. patrician houses. Renaissance chapel in the palace garden. The art gallery specializes in Czech art. The Bezruč Park has an open-air theatre that seats 30 000, a botanical garden famous for its orchids, and a zoo. The town's German name was Reichenberg.

Frýdlant. Lovely square with gabled houses. Fine views from the castle where Wallenstein once lived. Collections of glass, weapons, ceramics and art. The town's German name was Friedland.

Železný Brod. Famous for its Bohemian glass. Location of Czechoslovakia's sole school of glass. Permanent exhibition. Picturesque town with many wooden buildings. The 13th-cent. church, originally Gothic, has been renovated in the Baroque style.

Turnov. Jewellery industry. Semi-precious stones are obtained from the nearby Mount Kozákov (1 743 m). Dvořák was a frequent guest at Sychrov Palace. During the summer, concerts are held in the Memorial Hall. Beautiful park. *Mnichovo Hradiště.* Lorry factory. Lovely château (1694) in an English park. Museum with displays of art, weapons and archaeology.

Mladá Boleslav (37 000). Industrial town. Car factories (Škoda). Old town centre. Castle, built for Prince Boleslav II.

Stará Boleslav. Old town. Once the royal residence. *St. Wenceslas Church,* where the saint was murdered in 929. *Houštka,* a spa, is near by.

PRAHA (PRAGUE), see town plans.

Pruhonice. Renaissance mansion, reconstructed 1889. Now a botanical institute. One of the loveliest natural parks in Europa.

Konopiště. The castle was built for Charles IV during the 14th cent. King Václav was once held prisoner in the round tower during a nobles' rebellion. The 82 rooms contain rich collections of paintings, statues and weapons. Large park and game preserve. *Jemniště.* Baroque palace with ornate plaster work and wall paintings. Museum devoted to the history of clothing.

Tábor (28 000) was founded in the 15th cent. by the followers of Jan Hus (John Huss). The Reformer fled here after he had been banished from Prague in 1412. Underneath the town centre is a network of tunnels and cellars that have been hewn out of the cliff. A museum in the town hall is devoted to the Hussite period. The oldest section of the town, with narrow winding streets and picturesque houses, retains its original atmosphere.

Jindřichův Hradec. Lovely little town (urban reservation) with patrician houses and mansions from the 15th cent. Large palace. Museum with tapestries, embroidery and musical instruments. *Třeboň.* Lovely square with Baroque gables.

This district is filled with fishponds. There are about 5 000 of them (in the whole country about 22 000). Many of them are connected by canals. The largest pond is Rožmberk (489 hectares). The building of the ponds began in the 16th cent.

Soběslav. Historical town and resort. Smrček's house (1504). Folklore museum in Petr Vok's house.

Hluboká nad Vltavou. Large 13th-cent. castle built on an 83 m high promontory. Rebuilt in 1871 to resemble Windsor Castle. 140 rooms with rich art collections: weapons, porcelain, glass, etc. Large park.

ČESKÉ BUDĚJOVICE (Budweis, 81 000). Industrial town, founded in 1265. Famous brewery. Square with Baroque fountain and arcades. The 68 m high tower was built in 1553. The town hall was remodelled in the Baroque style in 1730. Many beautiful houses and churches. The railway station in Karel Čapek Street is the oldest in Europe (1832). It is on the line to Linz. Once the carriages were drawn by horses. *Dolní Dvořiště* (border crossing) has a lovely square. *Šumava* (Böhmerwald) is a popular summer and winter tourist area.

Austrian border. E14 continues to Linz – Salzburg – Tauern – Trieste.

E15. Dresden – Praha – Brno – Bratislava

Cinovec. DDR (East German) frontier. E 15 comes from Hamburg – Berlin – Dresden.

The road goes through *Krušné hory* ("the Iron Mountains"), a beautiful mountainous landscape with woodlands, lakes and meadows. *Dubí.* Little spa town. *Teplice.* Industrial town with mineral springs that were known to the Romans. A monastery was founded in 1158. Theatre, symphony orchestra, ethnographic museum. 12th-cent. church.

Lovosice. Large chemical industry. 16th-cent. castle and church from 1733. *Litoměřice.* Lovely town at the confluence of the Rivers Eger and Elbe. Town wall. 13th-cent. fortification tower. Cathedral with beautiful paintings. 17th-cent. Dominican monastery. Ethnographic museum.

Terezín (Theresienstadt). During the Second World War the 18th-cent. fortress was used as a concentration camp. 52 000 died here. Museum and large cemetery with monument.

It is also possible to enter Czechoslovakia at *Hřensko.*

Děčín. Old Slav settlement. Modern industrial town. Fine Baroque and Renaissance houses in the older parts of the town. Church (1691) with wall paintings. The town is dominated by a Baroque palace, built on a 50 m promontory.

Ústí nad Labem has two lovely churches. *Střecov Castle* on a mountain top. The castle was first written about in 1319. Its present appearance dates from 1912. Museum. *Krásné Březno,* a Renaissance palace, was remodelled in the Baroque style in 1750.

Dokšany. A picturesque town imprinted with the styles of the 17th and 18th cent. The abbey was completed in 1144. From the road you can see *Mount Rip,* a 459 m high basalt rock mountain. At its summit is the Church of St. George (12th cent.).

Veltrusy. Lovely Baroque castle. Fine park with 13th-cent. church.

Mělník. Beautiful town at the confluence of the *Vltava* (Moldau) and *Labe* (Elbe) rivers. Charles IV imported Burgundian vines to Mělník during the 14th cent. and it is still the centre of a wine district. Renaissance castle.

Lidice. In June, 1942, the town was razed to the ground and its inhabitants were shot by the Nazis. A monument has been erected in their memory, and there is a rose garden with bushes, donated by 36 nations.

PRAHA (Prague), see town plans. *Karlštejn,* see E 12. *Pruhonice* and *Konopiště,* see E 14.

Český Brod with few reminders of its long history. Church, abbey and clock tower from 1585. *Kolín.* One of the oldest towns in Bohemia (1237). The sacristy of the *St. Bartholomew Cathedral* was reconstructed during the 14th cent. by Peter Parler (the master who helped create the St. Vitus Cathedral in Prague).

Kutná Hora. As early as the 14th cent., this was an important town. Considerable silver deposits. Royal Mint. Vlašský dvůr ("the Italian Garden") was built for the Florentine silver craftsmen who worked at the mint. *Hrádek* (the Castle) was constructed for King Wenceslas IV. Construction work on the *St. Barbara Cathedral* started in the 14th cent. One hundred years later it was completed by Matthias Rejsek (who also built the Powder Tower in Prague). Many art treasures. In the 16th cent. the silver mines were closed down and Kutná Hora lived on in the shade of its former greatness. Now it is preserved as an historic town but it has been given new economic life.

Sedlec. The Kostnice Church (Charnel House). Its interior is decorated with human bones and skeletons gathered from plague cemeteries and battlefields.

Čáslav. Gothic cathedral, originally from the 10th cent. Žižka Gate. Baroque town hall. *Havlíčkův Brod.* Gothic and Renaissance houses with Baroque façades on the square. Gothic church. Views of the town from the gallery at the summit of the 51 m high tower.

JIHLAVA (45 000). Centre of the Českomoravská vysočina, the Bohemian-Moravian Highlands, one of the country's most beautiful areas, with many historic towns that grew up and flourished during the silver mining era (13th-14th cent.). When the silver deposits were depleted, mining was replaced by textile handicrafts and industry.
Jihlava is a protected urban reservation with over 60 registered Gothic and Baroque buildings. The town hall has a late-Gothic Counsellors' Hall. Jesuit church with beautiful ceiling paintings. A network of underground tunnels and cellars were originally intended for the storage of wine, but were later used in the defence of the town. The *Muzeum Vysočiny,* a folklore museum, is on the square.

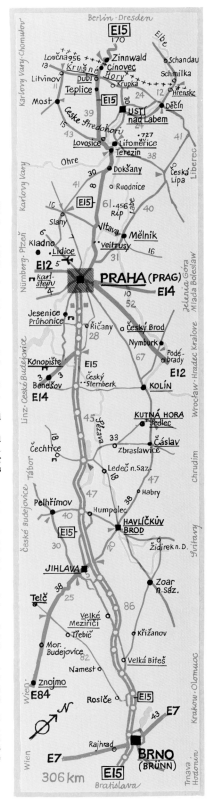

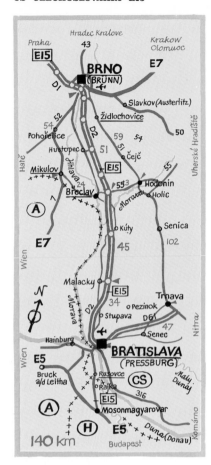

From Jihlava, E 84 continues to Wien (Vienna).

Telč. Protected urban reservation. Beautiful, picturesque streets. Rectangular square. Palace and park. *Slavonice.* Splendid old town with late-Gothic and Renaissance houses.

Znojmo is a protected urban area with picturesque old streets. Romanesque rotunda (11th cent.) at the castle whose present appearance dates from the 18th cent. South Moravian museum.

Hatě. Austrian border. E 84 continues to Hollabrun and Wien (Vienna).

Velké Meziříčí. Historic town. Beautifully ornamented houses on the square. Remains of the town wall and three town gates. High on a promontory is a castle containing a folklore museum. Velká Biteš with old fortifications.

BRNO, see E 7.

Židlochovice. Centre of a hunting district. *Mikulov.* Old town with beautiful Baroque town centre. The enormous castle (origins from the 13th cent.) looms over the town. Now it houses an archaeological and natural science museum and library. The town's German name was Nikolsburg. *Břeclav* with Renaissance palace. *Pohansko.* Excavations of an early Slav settlement. Walls with remains of wall paintings. Foundations of a 9th-cent. church.

BRATISLAVA (Pressburg, 353 000). Capital of the Slovakian Republic. Originally a Roman encampment where the Danube and the Morava Rivers met. The town centre is filled with buildings that are well worth seeing. 14th- cent. *Michalská brána* ("Michael's Gate") is a preserved part of the town wall. It contains a museum. The town hall in the Gothic and Renaissance styles has a tower that was reconstructed in the Baroque style. Close by is the *Primatial Palace* (Archbishop's Palace) which houses an art museum and a city museum. *St. Martin's Cathedral* dates from the 13th cent. and has a magnificent interior. From the 16th cent. until the 18th cent. the Hungarian kings were crowned here.

The *castle* (Bratislavský hrad) was written about as early as the 10th cent. It was destroyed by fire in 1911 and reconstructed in the 1960s in the manner of the 17th cent. During the reconstructions, workers discovered walls from the Greater Moravian period (9th cent.). Viticulture museum. Watchmaking museum. Slovakian museum, Lenin museum, Academia istropolitana, a university founded in 1466. Slavin. Monument to the over 6 000 Russian troops who fell here during the Battle of Bratislava.

Rusovce at the Hungarian frontier. E 15 goes from Mosonmagyaróvár together with E 5 to Budapest.

E16. Katowice – Český Těšin – Žilina – Trenčin – Bratislava

Cieszyn / Český Těšín. Polish frontier. E16 comes from Gdansk – Torun – Katowice. The town is divided by the River Olza into two sections, one Polish and one Czech. Těšin Museum. Třinec with large steel works. Chair lift to Javorovy peak (1 032 m). Jablunkov become an important trading centre during the 16th cent. *Čadca* with textile industry.

Kysucké Nové Mesto. Industrial town in beautiful surroundings. Picturesque old cottages in the two villages of Stará and Nová Bystrica.

Žilina. Historic town centre. Arcaded square. St. Stephen's Church (13th cent.) on the outskirts of the town has beautiful frescoes. Budatin Castle with museum. Ruins of *Hričov Castle* can be seen from the E16.

Bytča. A town as early as 1248. Large Renaissance palace with ornately decorated Dom snúbencov (the Wedding Palace). Bytča is the starting point for excursions to the Súlovske skaly nature preserve, with its fantastic rock and cliff formations. Ruins of the 12th-cent. Súlov Castle.

Podhradie, with ruins of a castle and impressive views over the Váh Valley. Also a Renaissance castle (1631) and a rococo palace (1775). Manínska nature reserve is popular with alpinists. Gigantic Havania rocks. *Považská Bystrica.* Industries (motorcycles). The "Lake of Youth" is an artificial lake. Water sports. Ilava has a castle and a castle ruin.

Trenčianske Teplice in a lovely valley 272 m above sea level. Large spa with beautiful park. The large Hamman Hall, built in Morish style 1888. Music festival. The mineral springs were well known as early as the Roman period.

Trenčin. There is a Roman inscription just below the castle proclaiming the victory, in A.D. 179, of Emperor Marcus Aurelius, his son Commodius, and their 855 legionaries over the Germanic tribes. This is the oldest inscription in Czechoslovakia. The name Trenčin was first mentioned in 1069. The castle has been rebuilt several times and it has withstood Turkish attacks. In 1790 both the castle and the town were severely damaged by fire. Beautiful houses and city gate from 1534. District museum.

Nové mesto nad Váhom. Although the 13th-cent. church has been rebuilt several times, it has retained its Romanesque tower. *Beckov* is a lovely little place with a ruined castle. SW is the *Čachtice Castle* where the evil Countess Báthory murdered dozens of young maidens so that she could bathe in their blood.

Piešťany. One of the most famous spas. The Romans knew about its waters and it was established as a spa as early as 1571. It was destroyed during the Turkish occupation but was in use again in 1721 and completely rebuilt during the 19th cent. The water rises from a depth of 2 000 m and has a temperature of 67-69 degrees centigrade. Many cultural activities. Beautiful parks.

Trnava on the fertile Trnava Plain. Founded in 1238. During the 16th cent. it became one of the most important commercial centres in the then kingdom of Hungary. Until 1820 it was the seat of the Archbishop of Esztergom (which the Turks occupied). *St. Nicholas Church* (14th cent.) has a splendid High Altar. There was a university here from 1635 until 1777 and its fine Baroque buildings are still standing. The town is dotted with churches, abbeys and beautiful old buildings. The town museum is housed in a 17th-cent. monastery. Large memorial dedicated to the Red Army.

Route 51 goes to *Nitra,* a town settled during the 9th cent. Large castle (2nd-15th cent.). Baroque bishop's palace and cathedral. Romanesque church which probably dates from the 10th cent.

BRATISLAVA, see E15.

E85. Hranice – Žilina – Prešov – Košice – Užgorod
Map on next page.

Valašské Meziřiči is in the province of Valašsko (Wallachia). It is an area that has managed to retain much of its former character. The *Vsetín Hills* is a beautiful recreation area. Open-air museum in *Rožnov Pod Radhoštěm.*

Bytča and *Žilina,* see E16.

Strečno. Ruins of a once magnificent castle on a promontory at the River *Váh.* Violent battles took place here in 1944. On Zvonica Hill there is a monument to the French partisans who took part in the struggle. The village of *U Jánošov* has a museum dedicated to Juraj Jánošik, a Slovak Robin Hood, who was born here in 1688. *Čičmany,* a village containing lovely examples of picturesque houses, built and decorated in the local style.

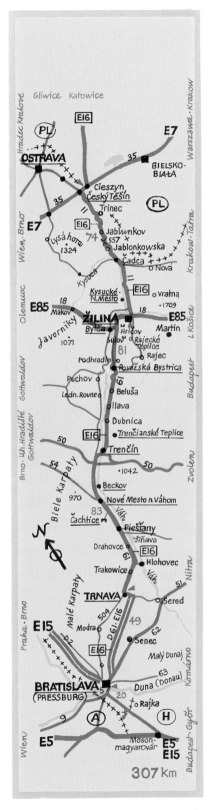

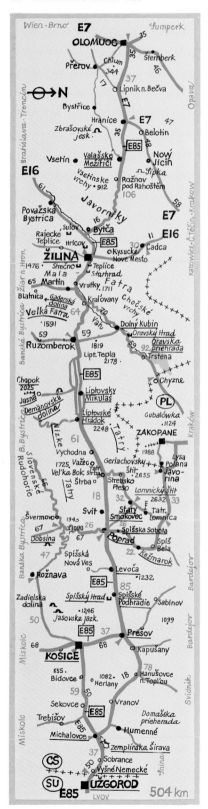

Martin. Once a centre of Slovak culture. Slovakian college, newspaper and the Matica Slovenská publishing house. Modern museum with examples of picturesque local architecture. **Vrútky** was once the centre of political activity. It was here that Klement Gottwald (who later went on to become president of Czechoslovakia) was editor of a Communist newspaper. The printing office and editorial offices are now a national monument.

Ružomberok with memories of the Slovak uprising. Museum. Starting point for excursions to the *Velká Fatra* (Great Fatra) mountain range, and to one of its beauty spots, the *Gaderská Dolina*, a narrow canyon lined with high karst cliffs.

Road southwards to **Banská Bystrica**, heart of Central Slovakia, and centre of a national uprising that took place in 1944. Many memorials from that period. The old centre of this former mining town is well preserved and lovely.

Road leading north to **Dolný Kubín** and *Oravská Priehrada*, the largest artificial lake in Slovakia. Water sports. There is a museum in the medieval *Oravský Hrad* fortress.

Liptovský Mikuláš. Major town in the province of Liptov. Beautiful location near the Low Tatras. *Museum* with exhibits from the Slovak karst caves. Museum devoted to Janko Kráľ, the poet. Memorial to a May Day meeting in 1918 when it was proclaimed that the Slovaks were willing to help form the new state of Czechoslovakia. Slightly to the east is the Liptovský Hrádok fortress with an ethnographic museum.

Nízke Tatry (the Low Tatras) is the largest mountain range in the Central Carpathians. Interesting and unique wild life and flora. Lovely towns and mountain villages. Museums and monuments dedicated to the partisan battles during the Second World War. A 105 km long hiking trail traverses the entire area. There is a cable car from Jasná to *Chopok*, at 2 024 m.

The resort of **Demänovská Dolina** is well known for its extremely beautiful blue-grey chalkstone caves. The Freedom Cave is 1 600 m long and the Ice Cave is 600 m.

The **Tatra National Park** (Tatranský národný park, TANAB), nearly 120 000 hectares large, has unique animal and plant life. The highest peak is Lomnický štít, 2 632 m. Many tourist resorts, particularly in the High Tatras.

Poprad. Starting point for the railway that leads to the tourist resorts in the Tatras and for the road to Zakopane. *Spišská Sobota*, a national monument, has beautiful Gothic, Renaissance and Baroque buildings. There are also lovely old buildings in *Kežmarok*. Museum in the fortress. Wooden church from 1717. The reconstructed abbey (1319) is now a hotel. *Pieniny National Park.*

Starý Smokovec is one of the largest resort towns.

Tatranská Lomnica, another large resort, contains the *Tatra National Park Museum* and is the starting point for a cable car route to *Lomnický Štít* (2 632 m), the highest inhabited place in Czechoslovakia.

South of Poprad is the *Dobšiná* ice cave.

Levoča. Old trading town with lovely old streets and houses, surrounded by a well-preserved fortification wall. The Gothic church on the square has a famous altar, created by Pavol. Road to *Spišská Nová Ves* and the nature preserve around the waterfalls of the River *Hornád*. Hiking trails and tourist resorts.

Spišské Podhradie, protected urban reservation. Rising above the town are the ruins of *Spišský Hrad*. The magnificent castle was built in the 12th cent. and destroyed by fire 1870.

Prešov. The centre of the old town, with its beautiful old churches and houses is an official national monument. In 1919, the Slovak Soviet Republic was proclaimed in Prešov.

Road north to **Bardejov** which has a lovely Old Town. Renaissance town hall directly on the square. Gothic St. Aegedius Church. Open-air museum in *Bardejovské Kúpele*. In the area around Bardejov and Svidnik there are 25 splendid old wooden churches (Orthodox). They are protected by law and have been proclaimed national monuments.

Svidnik at the Dukla Pass. What was in 1944 a battlefield is now an open-air military museum where the battle is depicted. Monument. During the fighting 80 000 Russian and 6 000 Czechoslovakian soldiers were killed.

KOŠICE. Capital of East Slovakia. Important heavy industries. The modern city surrounds an old town centre. Museum with gold treasure. Cathedral (12th-16th cent.). In *Herlany* there is a geyser that erupts at intervals of 32-36 hours. The water surges up to a height of 40 m.

Michalovce. The large Zemplínska Šírava Lake has sandy beaches, tourist resorts, facilities for water sports and boat services.

Vyšné Nemecké. USSR (Soviet Union) frontier. Road to Užgorod and Lvov.

TOWN PLANS

PRAHA (Prague, 1.2 million)
Capital of Czechoslovakia. Its roofs
and spires have caused it to be known
as "the Golden City". Prague, one of
Europe's most beautiful cities, has
emerged unscarred from many wars.
It follows the banks of the River Vltava
(Moldau). 12 bridges span the river.
Prague was founded in the 7th cent. at
a junction of important trading
routes. **Hradčany.** The Prague Castle
on the left bank of the Vltava dominates the city. It is a complete quarter
of the town and has churches,
squares, streets and a palace. Begun
in the 9th cent., the castle has been
rebuilt many times, and its original
character has been lost. Charles IV
transformed the castle during the
14th cent. into the seat of the German-
Roman Empire. He also had the Royal
Palace restored. Later, after his reign
in the 15th cent., the palace was
enlarged with the addition of the
Vladislav Hall, 62 m long, 16 m wide
and 13 m high. It has been used as a
throne room, as a chamber for parliament, even tournaments have taken
place here. Since 1918 it has been the
site of the election of the Czechoslovakian presidents. Near by is the
famous window from which the
Hussites hurled the King's emiss-
aries. This was repeated in 1618 when
two of the Emperor's representatives
(and a scribe) were hurled out of the
window. They survived but it was the

*Stare Mesto, Prague's
Old Town*

1 Strahov Monaste-
ry. Library
2 Czernin Palace
3 Castle and St.
Vitus Cathedral
4 Wallenstein Palace
5 Church of St. Nic-
holas
6 Charles Bridge
7 Clementinum. Na-
tional Library
8 Synagogue
9 Jewish cemetery
10 Old Town Square.
Old Town Hall.
Týn Church
11 Charles University
12 Powder Tower
13 National Museum
14 U Kalicha
15 National Theatre

spark that set off the Thirty Years' War. Throwing a person out of a window is called defenestration.

St. Vitus Cathedral (Chrám sv. Vita). Construction was begun in 1344. When the famous French architect, Matthias of Arras, died in 1352, Emperor Charles IV called in the young, unknown Peter Parler from South Germany. The structure was finally completed in 1929. Airy, beautiful interior with vaults in Parler's original network. The church is 124 m long, 60 m wide and 38 m high. Beautiful stained-glass windows. Royal Mausoleum. The collection that makes up the Bohemian crown jewels includes the famous 2.5 kilo *St. Wenceslas gold crown* which is studded with 91 precious stones and 20 pearls. (Seldom on display.). No unworthy person may place the crown on his head. Richard Heydrich, the Nazi Protector of Bohemia, and his two sons tried it on. They all met sudden and violent deaths. Heydrich was assassinated by two Czech officers.

The *Bishop's Palace* (Arcibiskupský palác) is also in Hradčany. It is a Baroque building with a rococo façade. Rich interior with exquisite tapestries. The *Sternberg Palace* contains the collection of the National Gallery (El Greco, Dürer, Cranach, Breughel, Rembrandt, Rubens). The *Czernin Palace*, now the Foreign Office, and the *Loretto Church* with a carillon are on Loretto Square. The *Strahov Monastery* is a beautiful building that now houses the National Library. The visitor to its garden will be rewarded with a fine view over Prague.

Zlatá ulica, the goldmakers' street. A picturesque street lined with the small houses where Rudolf II's alchemists once lived. The *Belvedere* Royal Summer Residence is a beautiful Renaissance building. The "Singing Fountain" is in its park. *Malá Strana* ("the Lesser Side") is situated below the castle mountain. Airy Baroque quarters with splendid palaces (many of them now embassies), and parks around one of the world's most beautiful Baroque churches, *St. Nicholas* (sv. Mikuláše). Built in the 18th cent. and mainly created by Dienzenhofer, it has a 75 m high dome and belfry. Its interior is enhanced by the frescoes of Jan Lukas Kracker. The *Wallenstein Palace* was once the residence of the mighty German general during the Thirty Years' War.

The *Charles Bridge* (Karlův most) was designed and built by Peter Parler in the 14th cent. 30 statues of saints line the 520 m long bridge which is limited to pedestrians. Křižovnické náměsti (Square of the Knights of the Cross) with statue of Charles IV.

The *Old Town* (Staré Mešto) is a well-preserved medieval town with narrow streets that during the daylight hours are filled with people and activity.

An evening walk through the sparsely lit alleyways will give a memorable impression of this old quarter where once Faust signed his pact with the devil, where the Rabbi once created a

CY · Cyprus

Cy · Kypros/Kibris

Area: 9 251 km (3 572 sq. miles).

Population: 640 000.

Cyprus is situated 400 km from the Greek mainland, 65 km from Turkey.

A wealth of ancient monuments testify to Cyprus's former glory. Particularly during the Bronze Age it was a great trading power. Several conquerors have ruled Cyprus, which only became an independent republic in 1960 after a period as a British crown colony. 80% of the inhabitants are Greeks, about 19% Turks. Conflicts between them led, in 1974, to a Turkish invasion and a partition of the island. The Turkish part is made up of 40% of the area and was proclaimed a separate state in 1983. U.N. troops keep watch over the truce and the border.

Tourists have started coming to Cyprus again but now mainly to the Greek part.

Nicosia (Gr. Levkosia, Turk. Lefkoscha, 45 000) is the chief town of the island. The Selimiye Mosque was once the Cathedral of St. Sophia. Bedesten (which means "covered market-place") is a former Gothic

KYPROS (CYPERN, CYPRUS)

14th-cent. church. Museum of archaelogy.

Larnaca. Port town. Museum of archaeology.

Limassol. Centre of the wine trade. Ruined city at Salamis. Excavations at Engomi and Paphos. Antique centre at Soli.

Famagusta (in the Turkish part) is the largest town and resort. Mustapha Pasha's Mosque was once the Cathedral of St. Nicholas. The Citadel, site of Shakespeare's Othello.

mechanical man, the Golem, and where Kafka experienced the anguish of isolation.

The *Jewish Cemetery*, tightly packed with about 12 000 tombstones, and the Staronová Synagogue, Europe's oldest temple (1270). The *Old Town Square* (Staroměstké nám) has a monument to Jan Hus (John Huss), the religious reformer who was burned at the stake for heresy in 1415. 27 Bohemian noblemen were beheaded here in 1621. The *Týn Church* has two characteristic towers. The Danish astronomer, Tycho Brahe (d. 1601), is buried here.

Astronomical clock (15th cent.) on the Old Town Hall. Every hour on the hour a procession passes before the small opening above the face of the clock. First the apostles appear, and then the figure of Death reminds us of the shortness of life. But the other figures shake their heads in disbelief – even the little rich man who is Prague's last official capitalist. The *Kinský Palace* is a splendid Baroque building.

Carolinum, the oldest building belonging to the university, was built in 1370. The university itself was founded in 1348. There is a library in the *Clementinum* (17th-18th cent.) which was originally a Jesuit school and is still the second largest building in Prague. (Only the castle is larger.) The *Tyl Theatre* where Mozart's Don Giovanni had its première in 1787. The *Powder Tower*, from 1475, received its present appearance in the 19th cent. It stands on the boundary between the

New Town and the Old Town.

The *New Town* (Nové Město) was founded as long ago as 1348 by Charles IV. He planned for it to be the very heart of European administrative, cultural and economic life. Prague's present-day commercial centre is in the New Town. Two of the major streets are Příkopy and nám Republiky, with the large Prior department store. The splendid *Václavské náměsti* (Wenceslas Square) contains an equestrian statue of the saint. The *National Museum* (Národní muzeum) has a noteworthy collection of coins, and permanent natural history and archaeological exhibitions.

Not far from the National Museum, at Bojišti 12, is the famous beer hall and restaurant *U Kalicha*. Here Hašek's Good Soldier Švejk once whiled away the hours. *U Fleku*, at Kremencova ul 11, is a veritable temple of beer. It alone has the right to sell the renowned Flekovska 13 beer.

To the south, perched high on a cliff, is *Vyšehrad Castle*. This was the residence of the first Czech princes. The Sv. Martina Rotunda was built in the 11th cent. Later the area was transformed into a Baroque fortress. Opposite Vysehrad, on the other side of the Vltava (Moldau), lies a part of the city called *Smíchov*. Here is the Strahov Stadium which accommodates 200 000 spectators. The Spartakiade, a mass-participation sporting event, is held here. The first Russian tank that managed to force its way into Prague in May, 1945, is in one of the squares of Smíchov.

D · Federal Republic of Germany

D·Bundesrepublik Deutschland

Area: 248 500 km² (95 908 sq. miles)

Population: 61.3 million. 49 % of the population belong to the Protestant Evangelical Church, 44 % are Roman Catholics and 7 % belong to other faiths.

Major cities: West Berlin 2.2 million, Hamburg 1.8 million, München (Munich) 1.3 million, Köln (Cologne) 990 000, Frankfurt am Main 680 000, Essen 670 000, Dortmund 625 000, Düsseldorf 620 000, Duisburg 602 000, Stuttgart 600 000, Hannover 560 000, Bremen 560 000, Bonn, capital of the Federal Republic, 300 000.

Government: The Federal Republic is made up of the following states (state capitals in parentheses): Schleswig-Holstein (Kiel), Niedersachsen/Lower Saxony (Hannover), Nordrhein-Westfalen/North Rhine- Westphalia (Düsseldorf), Hessen/Hesse (Wiesbaden), Rheinland-Pfalz/Rhineland-Palatinate (Mainz), Saarland (Saarbrücken), Baden-Württemberg (Stuttgart), Bayern/Bavaria (München/Munich), West Berlin and the free Hanseatic cities of Hamburg and Bremen. The National Assembly (518 seats) is elected every four years. The Federal President is the head of state and the Federal Chancellor is the head of government.

History

800 Charlemagne is crowned Emperor of the Holy Roman Empire.
1200 Collapse of the Holy Roman Empire of German States.

1273 The House of Habsburg attains the imperial throne.
1517 Martin Luther initiates the Reformation.
1618-1648 Thirty Years' War. The powers of the Emperor gradually diminish.
1701 Brandenburg becomes the Kingdom of Prussia which flourishes during the reign of Frederick the Great (1740-1766).
1806 Napoleon forces the Habsburg Franz II of Austria to renounce his claim to the Imperial German throne.
1854 Prussia and Austria conquer Schleswig-Holstein and wrench it from Denmark.
1866 Austria is defeated. The North German Alliance is created.
1871 France is defeated. The German Federal Empire is proclaimed. Wilhelm I of Prussia (Hohenzollern) becomes Emperor of Germany.
1914-1918 First World War. Germany is defeated. Emperor Wilhelm II abdicates. The Weimar Republic is founded. Germany suffers from inflation and economic depression.
1933 The Parliament (Reichstag) burns. Hitler gains power.
1936-1939 Hitler incorporates the Rhineland, Austria, and Czechoslovakia into Greater Germany.
1939-1945 Second World War. In 1940 German troops occupy Norway, Denmark, the Netherlands, Belgium, Luxembourg and a part of France. Enormous German military victories are followed by defeat. Germany is reduced to ruins by Allied bombing raids and is occupied by the four Allied

powers: the U.S.A., Britain, France and the USSR.
1948 The West German Federal Republic is established. Berlin is blockaded by the Soviets.
1949 The blockade is ended. The German Democratic Republic (DDR) is established.
1961 The Berlin Wall is constructed. A treaty leads to a lessening of tension between the two German states.

Currency: German marks (DEM).
1 Mark = 100 Pfennig

Business hours: Banks 8.30 a.m.-12.00 p.m., 2.00-4.00 p.m. Thursdays or Fridays open until 5.30 p.m. Closed Saturdays. Post offices (usually) 8.00 a.m.-12.00 noon and 2.00-6.00 p.m. Saturdays 8.00 a.m.-12.00 noon. Shops 9.00 a.m.-6.30 p.m. Saturdays open until 2.00 p.m. On the first Saturday of the month shops are usually open until 6.00 p.m.

Holidays: New Year's Day, Good Friday, Easter Sunday, Easter Monday, May 1, Ascension Day, Whit Sunday, Whit Monday, June 17 (Tag der Deutschen Einheit/Unity Day, the National Holiday), November 21 (Buss-und Bettag/Prayer and Repentance Day – not a holiday in Bavaria), December 25 and 26.

January 6 (Epiphany) is a holiday only in Baden-Württemberg and Bavaria. June 14 (Fronleichnam/Corpus Christi) is a holiday in Baden-Württemberg, Bavaria, Hesse, North Rhine-Westphalia, Rhineland-Palatinate and Saarland. August 15 (Assumption Day) is a holiday in Bavaria and Saarland, and November 1 (All Saints' Day) is a holiday in Baden-Württemberg, Bavaria, North Rhine-Westphalia and Saarland.

Hotels
Hotel rooms can be obtained through the local tourist office (often found in the railway station). There is a nominal fee for this service. Breakfast, which is usually included in the price of the room, consists of coffee or tea, different sorts of excellent German bread, butter, two or three types of marmalade or jam, cheese and cold cuts, such as ham or sausage. Inexpensive accommodations in a Gasthof (inn) are often supplemented by hearty breakfasts.
The service charges are included on the bill, but it is common practice to round off the final sum. Castle hotels are sometimes rather expensive but they give good value for the money charged. The accommodation, food and service are all of high quality, and they have a memorable and charming atmosphere. "Romantik" hotels are privately owned establishments that maintain high standards. They are housed in historical or authentic period buildings. There are over 250 recognized spas and medicinal baths. Many of these towns have casinos.
The German Tourist Association

Routes described:

E 3   Flensburg – Hamburg – Bremen – Ruhr – Venlo

E 4   Puttgarden – Hamburg – Frankfurt – Karlsruhe – Basel

E 5   Aachen – Köln – Frankfurt – Nürnberg – Passau

E 6   Hof – Nürnberg – München – Garmisch

E 8   Helmstedt – Hannover – Osnabrück – Oldenzaal

E 11 Salzburg – München – Stuttgart – Karlsruhe – Strasbourg

E 12 Plzeň – Nürnberg – Mannheim – Saarbrücken

E 36 Arnhem – Oberhausen – Köln

E 42 Köln – Luxembourg – Saarbrücken

E 61 München – Kempten – Lindau

E 70 Bad Hersfeld – Würzburg – Stuttgart – Donaueschingen – Schaffhausen

E 75 Hannover – Kamen – Köln

B 22, B 85 Bayreuth – Cham – Passau – Ostmarkstrasse

A 48, B 49 Koblenz – Trier. The Mosel Valley and the Eifel

A 61 Köln – Koblenz – Bingen – Mannheim – Walldorf

B 9   Köln – Bonn – Koblenz – Bingen

B 42 Köln – Königswinter – Koblenz – Wiesbaden. Romantische Strasse (The Romantic Road)

Town plans: Berlin, Bonn, Bremen, Düsseldorf, Frankfurt, Hamburg, Köln, Lübeck, München, Nürnberg, Stuttgart

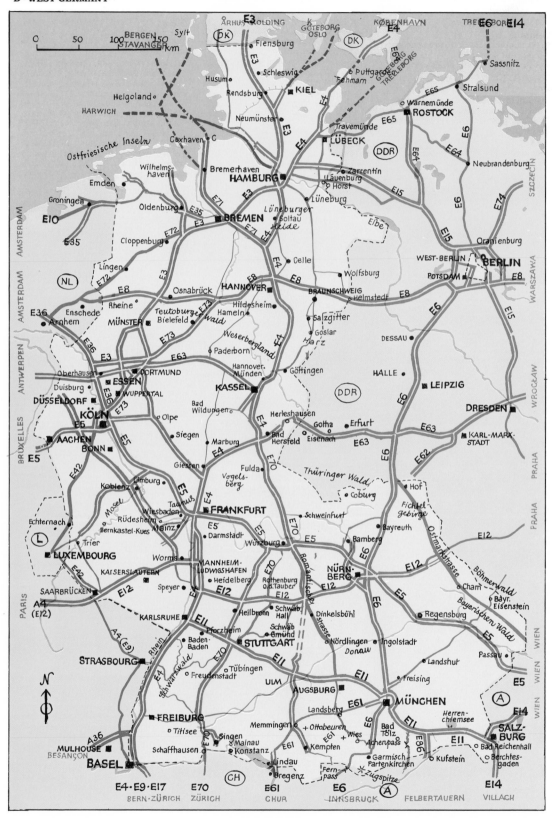

publishes lists of hotels.

Camping
2 100 camping sites. 350 are open also during the winter.

Youth hostels
There are 700 youth hostels. In Bavaria the maximum age is 27.

Food and drink
West Germany has a great variety of local specialities and traditions. In general one eats heartily and well in Germany. In addition to the regular meals, many people also stop at pavement kiosks, "Imbiss-stuben" for extra snacks.
German meals often begin with a rich soup. Sausages in all forms are extremely popular and Bockwurst accompanied by potato salad is a favourite dish. The exquisitely spiced Knobländer is another very popular sausage type. The world-famous Frankfurter sausage from Hesse has its origins in the late 13th cent. A speciality of Munich is the Weisswurst, a white sausage associated with the festivals held in the Bavarian capital.
Eisbein mit Sauerkraut is a typical German dish: boiled salted pig's trotters on a bed of sauerkraut. Kalbshaxen is grilled leg of veal. Sauerbraten is roast marinated pork. Gefüllte Schweinerippchen is stuffed ribs of pork. Favourite Berlin dishes are leg of pork accompanied by green pea and potato purée, and eel in green sauce. Universally popular dishes are Schweinebraten, a thin slice of breaded and fried pork, and Kassler, smoked and salted pork.
On the North Sea coast the visitor can gorge himself with freshly caught flounder and eel. Every German city has a "Wienerwald" – a chain of restaurants that have extensive menues and specialize in chicken dishes. Although delicious and delicate desserts do exist, after a typically hearty German meal not many restaurant patrons, unlike their Austrian neighbours, seem to have the capacity for them. However, pastries and cakes often accompany the afternoon coffee.
Beer is the most popular mealtime beverage. It is produced by innumerable local breweries, each one claiming that its beer is the best in the land. The major brands are Munich's Löwenbräu, Becks from Bremen and Dortmunder Actien. A Berlin speciality is Berliner Weisse, a rather weak beer, often served "mit Schuss", flavoured with raspberry syrup.
The wines from the Rhine and Mosel areas and the German schnapps are world famous. In Hannover one drinks a "Lütje Lage", (a glass of schnapps with a beer chaser). In Hamburg, the same combination is called "Lütt un Lütt". On the North Sea coast, the local drink is a concoction made of Jamaica rum, sugar and hot water.
Kirschwasser is black cherry brandy. Kölnisch Wasser is eau de cologne and should only be used externally. Apfelsaft (apple juice) is popular, good and non-alcoholic.

Shopping
Cameras and photographic equipment are reasonably and often advantageously priced. Other worthwhile and typically German products are leathergoods, toys, electric trains, porcelain (Rosenthal, Nymphenburg), earthenware, woodcarvings from Oberammergau, gold articles from Hanau and Pforzheim, costume jewellery from Offenbach and cuckoo clocks from the Black Forest.
Aachener Printen and Nürnberger Lebkuchen are two well-known types of gingerbread. Among other recommended culinary souvenirs are pumpernickel bread, jams and ham from Holstein, the Black Forest and Westphalia.

Petrol
There are over 250 petrol stations along the motorways. Most of them are open 24 hours a day and have attendants. At petrol stations on the adjacent byways prices are lower, especially at SB stations (SB = Selbstbedienung = Self Service). After filling the tank you get a slip with the price from an opening in the petrol pump. You just take the slip to the cashier and pay there.

Speed limits. Traffic regulations
The highest recommended speed on the Autobahn (motorway) is 130 kmh. When towing a caravan 80 kmh. On other roads the limit is 100 kmh and when towing a caravan 80 kmh. A yellow sign with a place name in black indicates the beginning of the 50 kmh speed limit. The end of the built-up area is indicated by a sign reading "Ortsende". This sign includes information about the distance to the next built-up area.
Recommended speeds are posted on blue rectangular signs with white figures.
Children under the age of 12 are not allowed to travel in the front seat. Rear-facing baby seats are allowed, but local police may object to them. If your car is fitted with seat belts it is compulsory to wear them.
Dipped headlights should be used when visibility is poor, in heavy rain or in snow storms. The use of studded tyres is prohibited. Snow chains may be necessary for Alpine driving. They can be hired from ADAC offices.

Roads
The West German Autobahn (motorway) network (total length: over 7 800 km) is Europe's most efficient road system. Providing fast and safe routes for mass motor traffic, it serves as the main arteries of the West German economic system.
Statistics lead one to believe that the Autobahns are exceptionally safe motor routes. However, as the statistics also reflect the tremendous volume of traffic that uses these roads, it is best to be cautious while driving the Autobahn, and to be particularly careful when overtaking.
Leave enough space between you and the vehicle in front. A gap of 1.5 seconds is the rule. At 120 kmh this means at least 60 m. Police keep watch from Autobahn crossovers. On-the-

Gutenfels Castle on the River Rhine in the Palatinate

spot fines of up to DM 1 000 are imposed. Foreigners are not exempt.

Long, uninterrupted Autobahn journeys are best avoided. Take short, frequent pauses at some of the many rest stops. There are about 170 of these Raststätte, each with a restaurant or buffet, toilets and wash rooms and an information desk, where you can find copies of "Autobahn Service", a brochure available in English and several other languages. It contains information about the proper wavelengths for the traffic information programme that is broadcast hourly on Programme 3. This programme gives the latest reports on such things as traffic diversions, "Umleitung", and traffic queues, "Stau". The appropriate wavelengths for the traffic programmes are also posted on special signs along the Autobahn. Blue signs with a "U" and a number indicate a diversion (Umleitung). You leave the Autobahn and follow the road which has its number posted. Eventually the diversionary route will return to an Autobahn entrance. Although there may not be a traffic problem that requires you to leave the Autobahn, it can be a good idea to occasionally leave the fast tempoed motorways in favour of the more interesting and leisurely secondary roads.

The Autobahns are numbered from A 1 to A 995. The numbers are white and the sign is blue. Signs that indicate the nearest Autobahn entrance are also blue. Other roads have yellow and black number signs and direction signs. Note that 'Autobahndreieck' is a motorway fork, an 'Autobahnkreuz' is a motorway interchange, and 'Ausfahrt' is signposted at every motorway exit.

Tourist routes

Many roads in Germany have been given special names, and often these routes are signposted with distinctive signs. Some of the most popular roads:

Grüne Küstenstrasse Tønder (Denmark) – Husum – Cuxhaven – Wilhelmshaven – Emden – Nieuweschans (Netherlands).

Alte Salzstrasse Lübeck – Lauenburg – Lüneburg.

Wesertalstrasse Bremen – Minden – Höxter – Münden.

Deutsche Ferienstrasse Ostsee – Alpen Puttgarden – Plön – Lübeck – Celle – Harz – Vogelsberg – Spessart – Odenwald – Dinkelsbühl – Landshut – Berchtesgaden.

Deutsche Weinstrasse Bockenheim/Worms – Neustadt – Schweigen.

Bergstrasse Darmstadt – Heidelberg/Wiesloch.

Nibelungenstrasse Worms – Miltenberg – Würzburg.

Romantische Strasse Würzburg – Rothenburg – Augsburg – Füssen.

Bayerische Ostmarkstrasse Bayreuth – Cham – Passau.

Schwarzwald-Hochstrasse Baden-Baden – Freudenstadt.

Oberschwäbische Barockstrasse Ulm

Holstentor in Lübeck

– Zwiefalten – Friedrichshafen – Ottobeuren – Ulm.

Deutsche Alpenstrasse Berchtesgaden – Reit im Winkel – Garmisch – Füssen – Sonthofen – Lindau.

Road patrols

The yellow assistance-service cars of the ADAC patrol the Autobahn and the major secondary roads. Assistance is given free of charge, but any materials provided and any car-towing that is necessary must be paid for, most conveniently with the AIT credit voucher. Emergency telephones are placed at every other kilometre along the Autobahn. Arrows on road-side posts indicate the direction of the nearest telephone. Ask for road service assistance or "Strassenwachthilfe". English-speaking assistance is available. Remember that a disabled car should be parked as far away from the traffic lanes as possible and that a red warning triangle must be placed 150 m behind the vehicle.

ADAC breakdown service, tel. 19211.

In case of accident, the same procedure should be carried out – the warning triangle must be put up as soon as possible and passengers and driver must leave the vehicle. Many minor accidents have turned into ma-

jor tragedies because people have remained in the car.

Emergency telephones: Police (Polizei) and ambulance (Krankenwagen) 110, fire brigade (Feuerwehr) 112.

ADAC (Allgemeiner Deutscher Automobil Club), Am Westpark 8, D-8000 München, has about 150 offices throughout the country. With 6 million members it is the largest motoring organization in the country. In cases of emergency, telegrams can be sent to motorists through the ADAC-Reiseruf. The nearest ADAC office and the police can give you further details.

AvD (Automobilclub von Deutschland), Lyoner Strasse 16, D-6000 Frankfurt/Main - Niederrad.

DTC (Deutscher Touring Automobil Club), Amalienburgstrasse 23, D-8000 München 60.

Deutsche Zentrale für Fremdenverkehr (German National Tourist Board), Beethovenstrasse 69, D-6000 Frankfurt/Main.

German National Tourist Office, 61, Conduit Street, London W1R 0EN. Tel. 01-734 2600.

E3. Flensburg – Hamburg – Bremen – Ruhr – Venlo

E3 comes from Viborg – Helsinki – Turku – Stockholm – Göteborg – Fredrikshavn – Århus – Ålborg – Kolding to the border at Flensburg.

FLENSBURG (100 000). The northernmost town in West Germany. Large harbour and shipyards. Parts of the city are picturesque and charming with delightful old houses in different styles. Gabled Nordertor (1565). Two Gothic churches. *Städtisches Museum* contains room interiors which show how burghers, fishermen and peasants once lived. The *Rathsapothek* has an 18th-cent. façade. Gastronomic specialities of Flensburg are rum and smoked eel. The city's proximity to Denmark is noticeable in many ways. The local newspaper has a Danish language edition. Yacht harbour with sailing school in the Flensburg Fjord.

Glücksburg. Little town in the densely wooded Rüder Au Valley. Wasserschloss, a castle surrounded by water, was built in 1587, apparently inspired by the Château Chambord (E3 south of Paris). Interesting interiors and a noteworthy collection of tapestries.

Oeversee. 12th-cent. church with a round tower. Monument to the battles of 1864. *Idstedt.* Memorial church and a monument dedicated to the Danish victory of 1850.

Schleswig (40 000). Beautiful Altstadt (Old Town) and a view out over the Bay of Schlei. The Gothic St. Peter's Cathedral has a 110 m high tower. Statue of St. Christopher. The wooden *Bordesholm Altar* was carved in 1521 by Hans Brüggemann. It consists of 392 figures. *Schloss Gottorf,* once the residence of the Dukes of Schleswig-Holstein, houses two museums: Schleswig-Holstein Landesmuseum with a collection of ecclesiastical art and beautiful furniture, and the Castle Chapel with a "Golden Hall" from Bergen in Norway. The *Nydam Boat,* which was probably built in the 4th cent., is a wooden boat, 23 m long and 3 m wide, with places for 36 oarsmen. It was discovered in 1863 in a peat bog in Nydam (now in Denmark) together with other important archaeological finds.

Haithabu (Hedeby, Haddeby). During the Viking Age, this was one of northern Europe's most important trading towns. In a history of the life of Ansgar, written in 870, the towns of Hedeby, Ribe and Birka are mentioned. Dannewerk fortifications. The *Busdorfer Rune Stone* is the only one of its kind in Germany. Its inscription tells of a battle in 995 when Sven Forkbeard, the Danish king, conquered the town. Then the town was moved to the present location of Schleswig Altstadt.

Damp 2 000. Holiday centre with 1 000 apartments in 12-storey buildings and chalets. Shops, restaurants, cafés, etc. Golf course. Several holiday resorts line the Kieler Fjord.

RENDSBURG (40 000) has a lovely Altstadt (Old Town) on an island in the Eider. The "Zum Landknecht" inn (1541) is one of many picturesque half-timbered houses. The town hall is another. Several industries. Nord-Ostsee (Kiel) Canal. Rendsburger Hochbrücke is one of the largest railway bridges in Europe. On the south side of the canal, the rail lines go in a circle so that the trains can attain the 42 m height of the bridge. A 640 m long, 20 m deep, motor tunnel was opened in 1961. A pedestrian tunnel has escalators of a total length of 1 278 m.

KIEL (270 000). Capital of Schleswig-Holstein. Port. University. Earlier this was an important naval base. Kieler Hohwaldtswerke is one of Europe's major shipyards. Impressive views from the 106 m high tower of the stately town hall (1911). Hindenburgufer is a lovely water-edge promenade, almost 3 km in length. *Laboe Marine-Ehrenmal* is an 85 m high monument that resembles the prow of a ship. Fine views from its top. Constructed in memory of the seamen who lost their lives during the First World War. Maritime museum. The "Kieler Woche" is an annual June sailing regatta.

Holm. Modern seaside resort with restaurants, beer halls, bowling facilities, supermarkets and winter garden. Marina. This sports and sailing centre played host to the boating events of the 1972 Olympic Games.

Bordesholm. The Augustinian Order had a university here that was moved to Kiel in 1665. The Bordesholm Altar is now in Schleswig.

Neumünster (90 000). Industrial town. Textile museum. *Bad Bramstedt.* Spa. Lovely park.

404. Kiel – Bargteheide – Hamburg. 404 to E4 (A1) at Bargteheide. In Bad Segeberg plays based on the writings of Karl May are presented every summer in an outdoor theatre. Marienkirche (12th cent.) Motor car museum in Tremsbüttel.

Bargteheide – Hamburg, see E4.

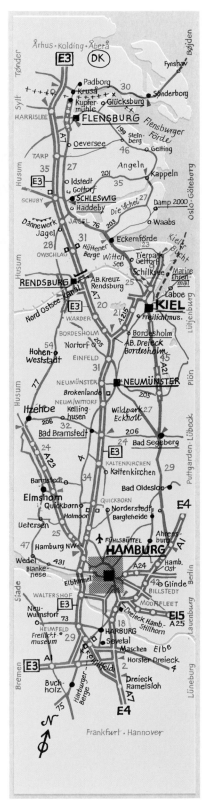

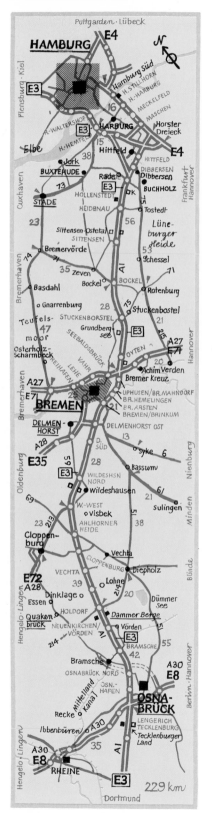

HAMBURG, see town plans. E3 goes through a 3.3 km long tunnel, 29 m under the River Elbe, and then passes through Hamburg's enormous dock area, which is dominated by the huge *Köhlbrandsbrücke*, a suspension bridge. Its pylons are 130 m high. **Hamburg-Harburg,** large industrial town. **Horster Dreieck.** On to A1.

Hittfeld has a 9th-cent. church.

Route 73. Hamburg-Cuxhaven

Buxtehude. Once a Hanseatic town. Splendid patrician houses, built in the 16th-18th cent. **Jork.** Picturesque town with half-timbered houses. **Stade** (50 000). A former Hanseatic town. Town hall (1667). St. Cosmae and Damiani churches.

CUXHAVEN (62 000). Industrial town and one of West Germany's major fishing ports. (Fish auctions are held at 7.00 a.m.). The Alte Liebe (Old Love) Quay is the departure point for boats to Helgoland. *Ritzebüttel Castle* now houses a folklore museum. Sea bathing at *Duhnen*.

BREMEN, see town plans.

Delmenhorst (60 000). Industrial town.

Wildeshausen has a 13th-cent. church. The road goes over a heath with many Stone Age graves. *Visbeker Braut*, 82 m long grave. Another grave, the *Visbeker Bräutigam*, is 108 m long.

Cloppenburg (20 000). *Niedersächsisches Freilichtsmuseum* is an open-air museum, containing over 50 farmhouses and workshops. Windmills. The oldest houses in the collection date from the 16th cent.

E72 continues to Oldenzaal in Holland (E8).

Quakenbrück with splendid half-timbered houses.

Vechta has a Baroque church. **Dammer Berge** is the location of a "Raststätte" built over the road.

OSNABRÜCK (176 000). A former Hanseatic town, founded in 765 by Charlemagne. St. Peter *Cathedral* was built during the 11th- 16th cent. The statues of the apostles are of sandstone. The Antwerp Passion Altar (16th cent.) is in the Marienkirche. The *town hall* contains the Friedenssaal, where the Treaty of Westphalia (1648), which ended the Thirty Years' War, was signed by the Emperor, the Protestant Estates and the Swedes. *Krahnstrasse*, lined with many fine old buildings, leads from the town hall to the shopping and business centre.

MÜNSTER (200 000). Major town of Westphalia. The medieval heart of the city has been reconstructed after wartime destruction. The Gothic *town hall* has also been reconstructed but has retained its original furnishings. The peace treaty between Spain and the Netherlands was signed here in 1648. Lovely patrician houses and mansions, once occupied by Westphalian noble families. The Prince-Bishop's Palace is now the centre of the University of Westphalia. Many splendid churches. *Ludgerikirche* (13th cent.) is named Saint Ludger who founded an abbey on this site in the year 800. In 1562 Anabaptists were hanged in the tower of the Lambertikirche. They belonged to a religious sect that had held a reign of terror in the city.

Warendorf with the impressive Freckenhorst abbey church. Nordkirchen. This large palace (1705) is the "Versailles of Westphalia". 17th-cent. palace in **Westerwinkel. Selm.** Prämonstratenserkirche contains the 12th-cent. Cappenberger Crucifix.

The motorway enters the **Ruhr,** West Germany's most important industrial area. It is about 110 km (66 miles) long and about 30 km (18 miles) wide and is inhabited by almost 6 million people. With 1 500 inhabitants per km², it is Europe's most densely populated area. Coal mining was begun in the middle of the 19th cent. In about 1970 coal production was greatly reduced. The iron, steel and chemical industries which had been severely damaged during the war, were dismantled by the victorious Allies so that the weapon- might of Germany would be permanently crushed. The result of these actions were that ten years later, with ultra-modern equipment, these factories were once again in a competitive situation. The enormous supply of coal has, as a result of the oil crisis, gained a new significance. When seen from the Autobahn, the mighty industrial complexes, spewing smoke out over tightly packed grimy houses give the traveller an extremely negative impression. But once off the Autobahn the outlook changes: beautiful parks, green belts, recreational facilities and cultural institutions.

DORTMUND (650 000). Industrial town (Hoesch), once a Hanseatic city. Iron, coal, beer. *Marienkirche* (12th cent.) has an altar by Konrad von Soest (1420). Petrikirche has a 7 m wide altar, carved by Gillis of Antwerp. The *Museum am Ostwall* has a collection of Expressionist art. Botanical gardens and zoo. Westfalenhalle is a large indoor arena.

BOCHUM (450 000). Mines and industries. The Opel factories are open to visitors. University. *Bergbau-Museum* (mining museum). Geological museum. Planetarium.

GELSENKIRCHEN (320 000). Industrial town with harbour on the Rhein-Herne Canal. Hans-Sachs-Haus, concert hall for 2 000 people. The Buerscher Grüngürtel is an attractive park. *Ruhr Zoo.* The moated Horst Castle is in the Renaissance style. Westerholt Lion Park.

ESSEN (700 000) is the major city of the Ruhr. Heavy industry (Krupp). University. The Folkwang College of Music, Theatre and Dance. The *cathedral* has ecclesiastical treasures in the Goldene Kammer, and a Golden Madonna from 980. Werden abbey church. *Museum Folkwang.* (modern art). *Ruhrland Museum. Villa Hügel,* once the home of the Krupp dynasty, is now a cultural centre in a lovely park. The *Gruga Park* has a botanical garden, aquarium and terrarium.

OBERHAUSEN (260 000). Industrial city. The Gutehoffnungshütte in Sterkrade is one of the oldest and largest steel works in the Ruhr. Annual international short film festival. **Moers** (60 000) has a medieval town centre. Folklore museum in the castle.

DUISBURG (602 000) is situated at the point where the waters of the River Ruhr empty into the Rhine. As early as the Roman era, this was an important port. Later it became a Hanseatic town. University. Opera. Duisburg has the largest inland harbour in Europe and is Europe's greatest producer of steel. Harbour tours. The grave of the Dutch cartographer, Mercator (d. 1548) is in the Salvatorkirche. See also Sint Niklaas, Belgium, E 3. Lembruck Museum has works of Wilhelm Lembruck, a Duisburg sculptor. Niederrheinisches Museum. The zoo on Kaiserberg has an aquarium and a dolphinarium.

KREFELD (250 000). Centre of the silk and velvet industries. Steel industry. Museums. Zoo and botanical gardens. See E 36.

Dutch border. E 3 continues to Antwerpen – Lille – Paris – Bordeaux – Madrid – Lisboa.

E 4. Puttgarden – Hamburg – Frankfurt – Karlsruhe – Basel

E4 comes from Helsinki – Haparanda – Stockholm – Helsingborg – Helsingør – København – Rødby.

Puttgarden is on the flat, fertile island of Fehmarn. There are frequent train and car ferries to Denmark. Duration of journey: 50 minutes. Earlier the little fishing village of Grossenbrode was the terminus of the ferry traffic. 13th-cent. church. **Burg auf Fehmarn** is now a large seaside resort with holiday apartment blocks. A five-storey high *windmill* with enormous sails is situated north of Lemkenhafen. It is now a museum.

Fehmarn is connected to the mainland by a bridge that has original and unique contours. But be careful! The winds that buffet the bridge can be extremely forceful.

Heiligenhafen, Weissenhäuser Strand and other large resorts line the coast to the west. In *Lütjenburg* there is a little stone 13th-church that has a splendidly carved altar (1467).

Oldenburg. An old town situated in the Oldenburger Graben, once a waterway that connected Kiel with the bays of Lübeck.

Holsteinische Schweiz (the Holstein Switzerland) is a lovely, hilly area with many lakes. Large castle (1636) at **Plön**. Views out over the Plöner Lake from its terrace. *Eutin.* Lovely half-timbered houses. One of them is the pharmacy. Empire-style railway station. Large Renaissance castle in a lovely park, where operas by Carl Maria von Weber (1786-1826) are performed. The composer was born at Lübecker Strasse No. 48.

Neustadt. Port town. Folklore museum in the Kremper Tor, a town gate. **Hansaland**, large amusement park.

Bäderstrasse goes to Travemünde, past a series of seaside resorts that have erupted along the Baltic coast in a period of a few years. The old fishing villages are now overwhelmed by concrete tower blocks. Between Kiel and Travemünde there are accommodations for over 200 000 visitors.

Travemünde is a classic old resort, famous for its beaches and casino. It is also the terminus for ferry traffic to Sweden and Finland – in the morning the harbour is a hive of activity.

LÜBECK, see town plans. **Bad Schwartau.** Marmalade and jam factories.

To the west of the motorway lies the area of **Stormarn** with idyllic roads, woods and lakes. The major town, **Bad Oldesloe**, was once a spa.

Bad Segeberg, small town with a Romanesque brick church. A 91 m high, naked rock with grottoes and an open-air theatre. Karl May festival. Karl May was a German author who wrote Westerns – among his famous characters are Old Shatterhand and Winnitou. *Tremsbüttel Castle Hotel* is in Bargteheide. *Ahrensburg Castle Hotel* with four towers. *Reinbek Castle,* built in 1570 in the Dutch style, is now a forestry institute.

HAMBURG, see town plans.

The **Alte Salzstrasse** goes from Lübeck to Lüneburg. This important trade route was the base of Lübeck's prosperity. Now it is a good alternative to the busy Autobahn. Idyllic scenery and pleasant small towns.

Ratzeburg is on an island. The large 13th-cent. church was built for Henry "the Lion". The German rowing teams train for the Olympic Games on the lake. *Mölln* has a little medieval square with houses that lean haphazardly. In the square is the Eulenspiegel Fountain (1951), named after a famous prankster who died in 1350. His tomb is in the church. The little bronze statue on the fountain has a worn thumb and toes. The legend is that if you hold on to the toes, your wish will come true, and if you hold on to the thumb, then you will have many children. It is best if you hold on to both simultaneously. Scenic route from Mölln through the *Lauenburgische Seen* nature preserve to Güdow.

Lauenburg. Beautiful half-timbered houses. The old town hall houses a folklore museum.

LÜNEBURG (70 000). Old Hanseatic town and salt trading centre. One of the most beautiful towns in northern Germany. Renaissance and Gothic patrician houses. The long **Am Sande** square is lined with lovely gabled houses. The 14th-cent. *Church of St. John* has a 106 m high tower and a splendid altar. The architectural details of the **town hall** (13th-18th cent.) reflect different periods. Baroque façade. Silver treasure. The former *Lüne abbey*, northeast of the town, contains a valuable collection of embroidered tapestries and weavings. Lüneburg Museum and East Prussian Hunting Museum.

Scharnebeck (east of Lüneburg). Schiffshebewerk is one of the largest locks in Europe. Vessels are raised and lowered 38 m. Lüneburg will become an important port with the completion of the new canal that will link the Elbe (Hamburg-Berlin) with the Mittelland Canal and the Europa Canal from the Netherlands to the Black Sea. The canal is 4.5 m deep.

HAFRABA Autobahn is the name given to the motorway that runs from Hamburg via Frankfurt to Basel. It has several numbers: A 7, A 48 and A 5. It takes about the same time to drive the E 3 (A 1) via Bremen to Kamener Kreuz and A 45 to Gembacher Dreieck on the E 4 near Giessen, as to take one of the motorways from the Cologne area (A 3 or A 61) back to E 4.

The motorway goes over the **Lüneburg Heath** (Lüneburger Heide), a softly undulating landscape, dotted with juniper bushes, heaths, bogs, bee hives, and "Heidschnucken" sheep. Park the car in Undeloh and walk through the park to Wilsede where there is a Heath Museum. *Wilseder Berg* is 169 m high. **Fallingbostel.** Monument on the 102 m high *Witzer Berg.*

Schneverdingen. Lovely town. Spa. *Sieben Steinhäuser* are well-preserved Stone Age tombs. Although situated in a military area, as a general rule they can be inspected on weekends. The Germans surrendered to Field Marshal Montgomery on Lüneburg Heath in May, 1945.

Soltau. The town was founded by Emperor Otto in 930. Lovely half- timbered houses. Wall paintings in the Church of St. John. **Walsrode.** Abbey church with beautiful 15th-cent. stained glass. Folklore museum with exhibits related to Hermann Löns. *Bird park* 2 km north. 600 species. The Serengeti Grosswild safari park is at Hodenhagen.

Bergen-Belsen. A beautiful and peaceful place despite the gruesome memories. Museum and memorial to the people who perished in the concentration camp. Anne Frank was one of them.

CELLE (80 000). A homogeneous old town with half-timbered houses, particularly in the *Neue Strasse.* The *castle* (now an administrative building) was from 1292 until 1866 the residence of the Dukes of Lüneburg and Braunschweig. Chapel and beautiful little theatre (1674) with seats for 300. Large castle park. *Bomann Museum* is a folklore museum. Stallion breeding and (since 1912) annual parade of stallions in the autumn. A show of manège riding, drills, four-in-hand, a post coach drawn by 10 horses and Roman war chariots in violent races. It is difficult to obtain tickets.

Wienhausen. Cistercian *abbey* (14th cent.) with art treasures. The *Wienhäuser Tapestry* (1300-1500) is fragile and is displayed only a few days each year.

HANNOVER (560 000). Capital of Lower Saxony, founded in about 900. Hanseatic city. University of technology, several colleges. In 1714, Georg Ludwig, elector of Hanover, became King George I of England. The personal union between Hanover and the British Crown lasted until 1837. The city was heavily damaged during the Second World War. The modern city centre has been constructed around the old central point, am *Kröpcke.* The Old Town Hall (Altes Rathaus) and Marktkirche are on *Marktplatz.* Some old half-timbered houses on *Kramerstrasse* have survived. The present town hall was built in 1913. Ballhof, a half-timbered house, is a theatre. Historisches Museum. Kestnermuseum (arts and crafts), Landesmuseum, Kunstmuseum. To the east are the Eilenriede Woods and a zoo, Stadthalle (convention centre) and Niedersachsenhalle. South of these is the *Hannover Messe* (Fair) with the 83 m high Hermesturm. The Hannover Fair is one of the largest in Germany.

Herrenhausen Gardens is a beautiful park. Herrenhausen Castle was destroyed during the war, but one building, the 1698 *Gallerigebäude* survived. *Grosser Garten* is a Baroque park with fountains, an orangery and an open-air theatre. There are orchids in Berggarten. Mausoleum with the grave of the English king, George I.

HILDESHEIM (100 000) was once one of Germany's loveliest half- timbered cities. It was laid waste during a bombing raid, shortly before the end of the war. Now it has a modern city centre. Some of the old buildings in Brühl, the southern section of the Altstadt, survived the war as did the Kehrwiederturm (1465) on the Lappenberg. It is the city's only preserved fortification tower. Godehardkirche (1172) was unharmed. Romanesque cathedral.

Michaeliskirche is a magnificent 12th-cent. Romanesque basilica with a wooden ceiling on which is painted the "Jessebom", the Tree of Jesus, i.e. his family tree. *Pelizaeus Museum* with an exceptionally fine Egyptian collection.

At Hildesheim the motorway crosses the nowadays humble Bundesstrasse 1. This was a road that went across the entire German nation from Aachen to Königsberg (now Kaliningrad in the USSR), a distance of 1 100 km.

Hameln, see E 71. **Braunschweig,** see E 8. **Salzgitter,** an industrial area with 120 000 inhabitants, formed in 1942 when 29 villages were merged.

The **Harz** is one of Germany's most popular recreation areas with spruce forests, rocky landscapes, bogs, dams, small idyllic resorts and enormous holiday centres. **Hahnenklee** and **Altenau** are the largest resorts. Hahnenklee-Bockswiese has a *stave church*, built in 1908 in the style of the famous Borgund stave church in Norway.

Goslar (45 000). Exceptionally handsome town with half-timbered houses. The 15th-cent. town hall on *Marktplatz* has paintings in the "Huldigungssaal". Carillon with figures representing miners working in the 1 000-year-old silver mines in Ramelsberg. Also on the square is the *Kaiserworth*, now a member of the "Romantik" hotel chain. The carved "Dukatenmännchen" figures are on one of its brackets. Several notable churches. *Kaiserpfalz*, the Emperors' House, is the largest Romanesque palace in Germany. It was originally built for Heinrich III, whose heart is buried in St. Ulrichskapelle. The silver and gold mines in *Ramelsberg* (636 m) started operation in 968 and eventually yielded lead, copper and zinc.

Braunlage. Resort and spa. **Clausthal-Zellerfeld** is a resort with mining activity (lead, zinc, and copper) dating back to the 16th cent. The Bergakademi (university of technology) was founded in 1775. Pharmacy from 1674. Oberharzer Museum.

Einbeck has splendid half-timbered houses. Its brewery was started in 1378 (beer museum). The term "Bockbier" comes from Einbeck. **Northeim**. Hanseatic town. Half-timbered houses. **Nörten** with the Hardenburg Castle ruins.

Duderstadt was founded in 927. Lovely town with 400 half-timbered buildings. One of them, the imposing *town hall*, is the oldest in Germany (1229). The town is close to the East German frontier.

GÖTTINGEN (125 000). According to Goethe, this city is known for two things: its sausages and its university. The university was founded in 1737 and gained importance in the 19th cent. especially within the area of natural sciences. It possesses the largest scientific library in the land. Narrow, winding streets and half-timbered houses, for example the pharmacy on the square. Gänselieselbrunnen – the little goose-girl is the most kissed girl in Germany (a student tradition). Massive 15th-cent. town hall.

Uslar. Pretty little town with half-timbered buildings, town hall, castle and St. Johanniskirche.

Hannoversch Münden (30 000). Handsome uniform town with many half-timbered buildings. It is situated on the triangle of land between the Fulda and the Werra which merge here to form the Weser. The Werrabrücke was built in the 14th cent.

Route 80 goes through *Weserbergland* to *Höxter*. Picturesque town with half-timbered buildings, among them the Dechanei, from 1561. The Benedictine Corvey abbey was founded in 822. **Hameln**, see E 71.

Sababurg. The little castle in the Reinhardswald (14th-16th cent.) is now a castle hotel. It is said to have provided the Brothers Grimm with inspiration for Sleeping Beauty's castle. Large park with game.

KASSEL (210 000). Industrial and administrative centre. The main shopping street, Obere Königsstrasse, was named for Landgrave Friedrich, who was married to Ulrika Eleonora, sister of Charles XII of Sweden, and who eventually became King of Sweden. *Hessisches Landesmuseum* has a splendid art gallery (several Rembrandts). The collection of antiquities includes a famous statue of Apollo. Natural history museum in Ottoneum, Germany's oldest preserved theatre (1605). *Brüder Grimm Museum*. Jacob and Wilhelm Grimm were professors in Göttingen and famous for their fairy-tales. Fridericianum: Landgrave Friedrich II's art collection and library.

The **Wilhelmshöhe** palace was built in the 18th cent. German wallpaper museum. Magnificent Baroque mountain park with fountains, the tallest 53 m high. 32 m high column with an 8 m high Hercules statue. Emperor Napoleon III lived in the palace after his defeat at Sedan. *Löwenburg*, situated in the park, is an enormous English-inspired knight's castle. It was built as a folly for William I in the 1790s. His mistresses resided here.

Fritzlar. Handsome half-timbered houses on the Marktplatz which is also the site of the Roland Fountain (1564). The town's museum is in the *Hochzeitshaus*. Cathedral with 11th-cent. crypt. 12 fortified towers.

Melsungen. Half-timbered town hall. Castle and bridge from the 16th cent.

Bad Wildungen. Large spa. Lovely park. Friedrichstein Castle. The *Wildungen Altar* (1403) by Konrad von Soest is in the 14th-cent. church.

Bad Hersfeld has been a town since 1170. "Official Hessian State Spa". Picturesque medieval town with many half-timbered houses. Ruins of a large medieval church.

Autobahn-Dreieck *Kirchheim* and *Hattenbach*. Large motel. The E 4 continues along the A 48 to *Gambacher Dreieck* at Giessen. A 7 (E 70) goes on to Würzburg.

Alsfeld. The *town hall* is one of the town's many half-timbered structures. Interesting market square. Folklore museum in the Hochzeitshaus. Walpurgiskirche. Alsfeld was one of Germany's project towns during the European Architectural Heritage Year 1975.

Vogelsberg. Large forest area with resorts, spas and castles. Lovely views from the flat summit, the crater of an extinct volcano. *Schottenring,* a motor racing circuit.

MARBURG (75 000). Old cultural centre with university, founded in 1527. Beautiful *Altstadt* with half-timbered houses, particularly near the Obermarkt. Narrow, terraced streets. 16th-cent. town hall with interesting clock. University Museum (art and cultural history). The Gothic *Elisabethkirche* was the church of the Teutonic Knights. It was built in 1235 in dedication to the canonized Elisabeth von Thüringen, 24-year-old daughter of the King of Hungary. The golden Elisabeth shrine is in the sacristy. This was once a pilgrimage church. Modern church of Saints Peter and Paul.

GIESSEN (80 000). Industrial and garrison town. University. The old castle dates from the 14th cent., the later, half-timbered, castle, from the 16th cent. Liebig Museum (Baron Justus von Liebig, 1803-1873, was a famed German chemist.).

Wetzlar is the home of Leitz, manufacturers of camera lenses. 13th- cent. cathedral. *Altstadt.* It was here in Wetzlar that Goethe wrote "Die Leiden des jungen Werther". Museum in Haus von Lottchen. *Butzbach* has picturesque streets and houses. Town wall. Folklore museum in the Michael Chapel. Impressive ruined castle in *Münzenberg*.

Taunus, a 70 km long, hilly region. Forests, many small resorts. The highest peak is the *Feldberg.* The largest spa is **Bad Homburg** (55 000). Castle with park. Kurpark with Kaiser-Wilhelm-Bad. Casino. Roulette was invented here in 1841. Siamese temple and Russian chapel. *Saalburg.* Roman fort, reconstructed to look as it did in the 1st and 2nd cent. A.D. Museum. *Königstein,* zoo.

FRANKFURT am Main, see town plans. *Frankfurter Kreuz.* One of Europe's busiest motorway junctions. Prepare to be on the look-out for direction signs. Although the area is now filled with a network of motorways that offer a variety of driving alternatives, traffic jams are not unusual.

DARMSTADT (150 000). Chemical industry and university of technology. Headquarters of the PEN Club. At the turn of the century, there was an artists' colony on the *Mathildenhöhe* that turned Darmstadt into the centre of the German "Jugend" (Art Nouveau) style of architecture and design. The *Hochzeitsturm* is a typical Jugend building. Examples are further displayed in *Hessisches Landesmuseum.* Castle and garden with the *Porzellanschlösschen* (Porcelain Castle) with a rich collection of porcelain. Hunting museum in *Kranichstein Castle.*

Bergstrasse is extremely lovely during blossom time. There are large vineyards on the slopes of the Odenwald facing the Rhine Valley. *Heppenheim* has a beautiful square, town hall and many half-timbered buildings.

Nibelungenstrasse goes from Bensheim and *Siegfriedstrasse* goes from Heppenheim to Michelstadt. The saga of the Nibelungen was made into opera by Wagner. At either *Gras-Ellenbach* or *Hüttental,* the noble Siegfried was killed by the swarthy Hagen. Here are the Siegfriedsbrunnen Hotel and the simpler Gasthaus Hagen. *Lindenfels* is a lovely little town on a mountain.

Lorsch has the ruins of an abbey built in 764. The Karolingische Königshalle and a large section of the wall remain.

WORMS, see E 12. Katharinenkirche and the Landskron ruin.

MANNHEIM (330 000). Industrial city. Europe's second largest inland harbour. University. College of drama and music. The city is built to a square plan with 136 blocks. Letters of the alphabet and numbers are used instead of street names. Schiller's "Die Räuber" was first performed at the National Theatre (reconstructed) in 1782. The symbol of the city is the Wasserturm (1888) on Friedrichsplatz. The Baroque Electors' Palace was destroyed during the war but has been reconstructed. The Old Town Hall (1711) is the oldest building in the city. Reismuseum (City history).

LUDWIGSHAFEN (180 000). Large harbour. Chemical industries.

HEIDELBERG (130 000). Oldest university in Germany (1386). Beer halls and wine taverns line the long and lively *Hauptstrasse.* College of music and drama. The castle is an enormous building complex with fine views out over the **Neckar Valley.** Built during the 16th and 17th cent., it bears the imprint of the Renaissance. The castle was largely destroyed, first during 17th-cent. wars, and later by lightning in 1764. A famous wine barrel (1751) measuring 9×8 m and capable of holding 221 000 litres, is in the cellar. A cable railway leads up to the castle (2 minutes). The path up is not long but extremely steep (steps). *Kurpfälzisches Museum* contains

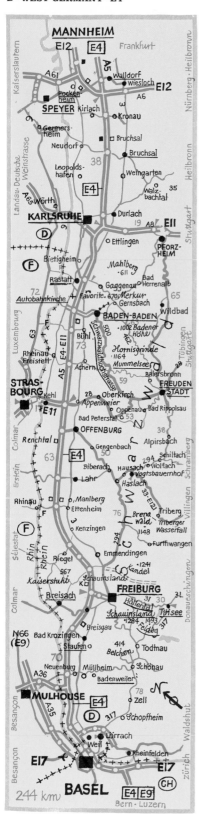

Riemenschneider's *Windsheimer Altar* (the 12 apostles). A road leads from the castle to *Molkenkur* (301 m above sea level) and *Königsstuhl* (568 m). Superb views. Cable car. There are lovely views also from *Heiligenberg*. Ruins of the Stefan abbey and the Michael abbey from the 11th cent. This area has been inhabited since the 5th cent. B.C. A jawbone of the Heidelberg Man is reckoned to be 500 000 years old.

Schwetzingen. Castle with splendid French gardens and an 18th-cent. theatre. *Walldorf,* original home town of the Astor family (who built the Waldorf Astoria hotel in New York). *Hockenheim.* Motor racing circuit.

SPEYER (50 000). Bishopric in the 7th cent. Construction work on the cathedral, Kaiserdom, started in 1030. Crypt with the tombs of eight emperors. Some of the treasures found in them are now in the Pfalz *Historical Museum.* Over 50 parliaments have been held in Speyer. The beautiful Altpörtel is a part of the town wall. Judenbad (12th cent.) The Pfalz *Historical Museum* contains the previously mentioned emperors' grave treasures. Wine museum with the world's oldest wine (4th cent.).

Bruchsal. The Baroque palace (1772) has an exquisite *staircase*, designed by Balthasar Neumann.

KARLSRUHE (290 000). Founded in 1715 as capital of the Duchy of Baden. The enormous palace contains the *Landesmuseum.* Seat of the Supreme Constitutional Court of the Federal Republic. University. *Marktplatz* with the "Pyramid" where the founder of the city, Margrave Karl Wilhelm, is buried. Kunsthalle with the *Hans Thoma Museum* (German art of the 19th and 20th cent.). Stadtgarten with zoo. Rack railway to the summit of *Turmberg*, 255 m. Magnificent view.

Rastatt. Castle with army and folklore museums. Baroque churches.

BADEN-BADEN (50 000). Spa. Casino. The over 20 hot springs with water temperatures as high as 70° were known to the Romans. (Emperor Caracalla was here.) During the 19th cent. it became Europe's perhaps most distinguished spa. Royalty and other well-born people strolled along the lovely Lichtentaler Allee. Many different species of trees. The Zähringer Museum, which has displays of porcelain and the goldsmith's art, is housed in *Neues Schloss*, a Renaissance palace. *Autobahnkirche Baden-Baden* is an interesting modern church.

Schwarzwald (the Black Forest), the 170 km long forest between Karlsruhe and Basel, has become an enormous recreation area. The Rhine separates the Schwarzwald from the Voges in France. The highest peak is *Feldberg* (1 493 m). Innumerable hotels and resorts. *Schwarzwald-Hochstrasse* goes to Freudenstadt via Allerheiligen, with a 13th-cent. church and a beautiful waterfall. The *Mummelsee* is a small, circular, legendary lake, situated at 1 030 m above sea level. The Berghotel Mummelsee is the perfect place to enjoy a thoroughly authentic Black Forest gateau. *Freudenstadt,* see E 70.

FREIBURG (im Breisgau) (180 000) was founded in 1120 by Duke Konrad von Zähringen. From 1368 until 1806 the city belonged to Austria. During the Thirty Years' War, it was conquered by German, Swedish, Spanish and French troops. The greater part of the city was destroyed in 1944.

Work on the *cathedral* started in 1124 and continued until the 16th cent. Extraordinary and beautiful tower. Fine view (328 steps). Splendid Gothic choir. *Oberried Altar* by Holbein the Younger. Lovely buildings on Münsterplatz and Rathausplatz. The red 16th-cent. Kaufhaus has sculptures of four Habsburg emperors. Haus zum Walfisch. Splendid old university buildings. The Gasthof zum Bären near the Schwabentor has served as an inn since the 13th cent. Cable car (6 min.) to *Schlossberg*. A great number of streams flow from this mountain down through the city's streets in deep gutters along the kerbs. Drive carefully and park with great care! *Schauinsland* lookout point (1 286 m above sea level). Road and cable car (15 min.). To the east of Freiburg, a scenic route goes through *Höllental* (the Valley of Hell). The meaning of its name can be understood at the extremely wild and narrow Hirschsprung. A railway station in the Valley of Hell is called Himmelreich (the Kingdom of Heaven). The road continues to the large resort of *Titisee*.

Breisach am Rhein with St. Stephan's Cathedral.

Staufen was founded in 1250. Renaissance buildings on the Marktplatz.

Badenweiler has the ruins of baths, founded in 331 B.C.

Swiss border at Basel. E 4 continues to Bern – Genève – Grenoble – Avignon – Barcelona – Madrid – Lisboa.

E 5. Aachen – Köln – Frankfurt – Nürnberg – Passau

AACHEN (Aken, Aix-la-Chapelle, 245 000) Charlemagne's city. The sulphur springs (with temperatures as high as 74°C, the hottest in Central Europe) were known as early as the Roman period. The **Kaiserdom** has a octagonal dome. Construction was begun in the 15th cent. The Gothic choir was added in the 15th cent. Charlemagne's marble throne and the Karlschrein, containing his remains (he died in 814). Sumptuous ecclesiastical treasures. From 936 until 1531 the German kings were crowned in the Cathedral of Aachen. **Rathaus** (town hall) from the 14th cent. with sections of Charlemagne's fortress. Coronation Hall with frescoes. Ponttor is one of the few remaining parts of the once mighty town wall. *Suermondt-Museum* (art). *Couven-Museum* (18th-cent. furniture). Kurhaus with casino. Elisenbrunnen and Pump Room. Fountains on the large Europaplatz. Kornelimünster, a massive Baroque abbey, now serves as a national archive. Lovely 10th-cent. church with interesting additions from different periods.

Düren (90 000). Industrial town.

KÖLN (Cologne, Keulen), see town plans.

Siegburg (35 000). Industrial town. The 17th-cent. Church of St. Michael has an older crypt. Siegenthal abbey and the Church of St. Servatius with many superb works in gold.

BONN, see town plans

Bad Honnef. Spa with hot springs, known as early as the 8th cent.

Drachenfels. Castle ruins with beautiful view. One of the first Roman citadels. **Kannenbäckerland,** famous for its ceramics.

KOBLENZ and the **Rhine Valley,** see A 61.

Montabaur. Church with four towers (16th cent.).

Weilburg. Beautiful Altstadt (Old Town). 18th-cent. patrician houses. Remains of the town wall. Renaissance palace with orangery and French gardens.

LIMBURG an der Lahn (30 000). The old town flourished during the 13th cent. Picturesque old streets with half-timbered houses, among them the oldest of this type in Germany (1296). High on a promontory, overlooking the River *Lahn*, rise the four towers of the *cathedral*. Gold treasure (13th cent.). *Runkel*. Castle ruins with weapon collection.

Idstein. Handsome town with many half-timbered houses. In 1680 the first official post office in Germany was opened here. Remains of a medieval fortress. Renaissance palace.

WIESBADEN (270 000). Capital of Hesse. Famous spa between the Taunus and the Rhine. 27 hot springs. Kurhaus with casino and park. Rhein-Main-Halle, a convention and conference centre. Wilhelmstrasse, the main shopping street, is called *"the Rue"*. The Baroque Biebrich Palace dates from the 19th cent. Splendid views from *Neroberg* (245 m). It is topped with a chapel, built in the Greek style.

MAINZ (190 000). The capital of the Rhineland-Palatinate, founded 2 000 years ago as a Roman encampment. During the Middle Ages it was a major trading centre, specializing in wine. In 1450 the art of printing (with loose type) was invented by Johann Gutenberg, a goldsmith. A statue of him (by Thorvaldsen, a Danish sculptor) is near the theatre. A Latin bible, printed in 1445, is on display in the *Gutenberg Museum*. The university (1477) bears his name. Romanesque *cathedral* (12th-13th cent.). Magnificently adorned interior and Cathedral Museum. The *palace* (17th cent.) is one of Germany's last authentic and most beautiful Renaissance buildings. It now houses the Römisch-Germanisches Zentralmuseum (ancient history). Mittelrheinisches Landesmuseum (prehistoric finds and examples of the goldsmith's and silversmith's art). The Gothic *St. Stephan's Church* has a stained-glass window by Marc Chagall. Christus-Kirche with its large dome is the symbol of the city. Mainz is one of the capitals of German carnival festivities. The Mainzer Fassennacht with the Rosenmontagzug is one of the major festivals. Wine market in September.

FRANKFURT, see town plans.

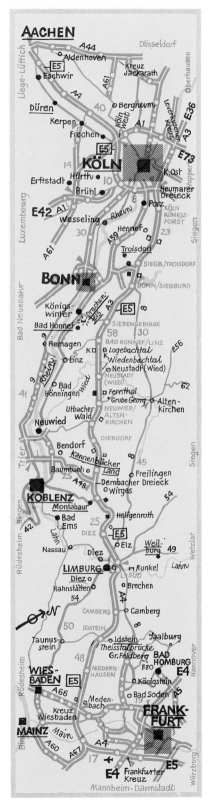

OFFENBACH (125 000). Leather industry. German Leather Museum. German Shoe Museum. The Renaissance Isenburger Castle.

HANAU (90 000). Industrial town. The folklore museum is housed in *Philippsruhe Palace*. Hannau faience. Niederländische Wallonische Kirche was built in 1608 for Dutch immigrants. Monuments to the Brothers Grimm. Deutsches Goldsmiedehaus (Goldsmiths' House) with exhibitions.

Aschaffenburg (55 000). During the 10th cent. it was the residence of the bishops of Mainz. Mighty *Renaissance castle* (17th cent.). Art collection (Rubens, van Dyck, Cranach), crafts, ecclesiastical art, etc. In the castle garden is a reproduction of a Pompeian house. *Schönbuch Palace* (18th cent.) is in a setting of canals, islands and pavilions.

Spessart. An undulating area of leafy woods, lovely valleys. The highest point is *Geyersberg*, 585 m. One of the loveliest sights is the little *Mespelbrunn Castle* and its reflection in the woodland lake. Its tower dates from 1430. Pilgrimage church in **Hessenthal**. Sculpture by Tilman Riemenschneider. **Wertheim** with castle, fountains, half-timbered houses, Marktplatz and the Engelsbrunnen is a beautiful little town. So is **Michelstad** with its Einhardt Basilica from 827, a half-timbered town hall and Fürstenau Castle. Romantic Eulbacher Park. **Miltenberg**. Half-timbered houses line the *Marktplatz*, among them the *Gasthaus zum Riesen*, Germany's oldest building.

WÜRZBURG (126 000). The major town in Unterfranken (Lower Franconia). The prince-bishops gave this city its unique Baroque appearance. University. Wine trade. *"Residenz"* (the palace), has 360 rooms. There are frescoes by Tiepolo in the Emperors' Room. One of them depicts the wedding of Emperor Barbarossa in 1156. Museum of antiquities. *St. Kilian's Cathedral* (1188) has sepulchral monuments dedicated to the bishops. Some of these stone works have been created by Tilman Riemenschneider, "the Master from Würzburg". His Madonna and a crucifix are in *Neumünster Kirche*, opposite the cathedral. Marienkapelle and the rococo *Haus zum Falken* are on the Marktplatz. *Alte Mainbrücke* (1543) is decorated with the statues of 12 saints. It is similar to the Charles Bridge in Prague. High above the city sits the Festung (Fortress) *Marieberg*. It was the bishops' residence from the 13th cent. until the 18th cent. There are several buildings within the encircling wall. Fine views. *Mainfränkisches Museum* contains works by Riemenschneider. The rococo **Käppele** pilgrimage church (18th cent.) was designed by Balthasar Neuman. Road with steps. Beautiful views. The tomb of the poet and singer, Walter von der Vogelweide (d. 1231) is in the *Lusamgärtlein* of Neumünster Kirche. The *summer palace* of the prince-bishops is in *Veitshöchheim* (7 km NW). The 18th-cent. garden is one of the most magnificent rococo gardens in Germany.

To the east of Würzburg lies a lovely area with many vineyard slopes near the Main, and idyllic towns and wine-producing villages: **Sommerhausen**, **Ochsenfurt** with well-preserved town wall. **Dettelbach**. Town wall with 32 towers and the *Maria am Sande* pilgrimage church. Half-timbered houses line the Hauptstrasse in **Prichsenstadt**.

Ebrach. Large Baroque abbey (1730). Beautiful church. **Pommersfelden**. Schloss Weissenstein (1718) was the summer palace of the prince-bishops. Famous staircase.

BAMBERG (80 000) was founded in 1007. The city survived the ravages of the Thirty Years' War and the Second World War without serious damage. *Kaiserdom* (Emperor's Cathedral), founded in 1004, contains the famous *Bamberger Reiter* (1240). The emperor's tomb was created by Tilman Riemenschneider. Altar by Veit Stoss (1523). Ecclesiastical treasures in the *Diözesan Museum*. *Domplatz* is considered by many to be one of the most beautiful squares in Germany. This is the location of the *Alte Hofhaltung*, the residence of the emperors and prince-bishops. The façade is in the Renaissance style while the sections facing the courtyard are half-timbered. Folklore museum. Neue Residenz (1704) consists of four massive buildings. Rose garden. Old town hall on the island of Regnitz.

ERLANGEN (100 000). University (1743), where Georg Ohm, the physicist, established the relation between electrical current, resistance and electromotive force (19th cent.). During the 17th cent. Protestant French Huguenots fled to Erlangen. Their *Reform Church* on Hugenottenplatz has an interior that lacks all decorations and adornment. The Huguenot Fountain in the palace park. Palace (18th cent.). The Markgrafentheater (1718) is the oldest Baroque theatre in Bavaria (1719). The Erlanger Bergkirchweih fair has been held every Whitsun since 1755. Altstadt with Altstädter Rathaus, now the City Museum.

NÜRNBERG, see town plans.

Neumarkt (30 000) was founded in 1 000. Baroque church. Castle. Ruin of Wolfstein Castle and the Mariahilf pilgrimage church.

AMBERG (50 000) preceded Regensburg as capital of Oberpfalz. Ancient and picturesque town. Town wall. Splendid *Marktplatz* and town hall. The part of the town wall that spans the River Vils is called the *"Stadtbrille"*. Here two of the wall's arches are reflected in the water so that one gets the impression of a pair of eyeglasses (Brille).

REGENSBURG (135 000). Roman fort. The city was founded in A.D. 179. From the 9th cent., Regensburg was one of Europe's most important cities. Medieval *Altstadt*. Lovely views from the 300 m long *Steinerne Brücke* (1145). The tower of *St. Peter's Cathedral* is 105 m high (19th cent.). The western façade was completed in the 15th cent. 14th- cent. stained-glass windows. Rococo Alte Kapelle. Alter Kornmarkt with Römer Tower. St. Emmeran's Church (8th cent.). Weltenburg. The Asam brothers designed the Baroque *abbey church* (1730). Gothic Altes Rathaus (Old Town Hall) (1360). The first parliament in Germany, the "immerwährender Reichstag", assembled here. It was in permanent session from 1663 until 1806. Medieval torture chamber in the cellar. *Keplergedächtnishaus*, where Johannes Kepler, the astronomer, died in 1630. Museum. City museum. Porta Praetoria has its origins in the Roman fortifications from about A.D. 100. *Marstallmuseum* in the Palace of the Princes of Thurn and Taxis. The family had the post monopoly in Germany until 1867. At the beginning of the 16th cent., they inaugurated the first post service between Brussels and Vienna. *Walhalla* (11 km to the east) is a memorial temple, in the ancient Greek style and with a Nordic name. It was built for King Ludwig I of Bavaria in 1842. 118 marble busts and 64 memorial plaques of "prominent Germans".

Straubing (45 000). Spitaltor is one of the remaining parts of the old city defence system. Some sections left are a bit of the wall and the Pulverturm (Powder Tower). Lovely elongated *Stadtplatz* with the 13th- cent. *Stadtturm* (68 m) which has five spires. Houses with high stepped gables over Baroque façades. The square looks rather Austrian. *St. Jakob*, a Gothic church with a beautiful altar painting. *Gäuboden-Museum* with Roman exhibits. *St. Peter-Kirche*, begun in the 12th cent., was completed in 1888. In the graveyard is the Agnes-Bernauer-Kapelle (1436) with the tombstone of Agnes Bernauer, a beautiful commoner who was married to the son of Duke Albrecht II, accused of sorcery by her stepfather and hurled into the Danube.

Aldersbach. Mariä Himmelfahrt (The Assumption of Mary) abbey church (17th-18th cent.). Plaster work by one of the Asam brothers.

PASSAU (50 000). Once a Roman encampment. It was founded as a bishopric in the 8th cent. by St. Bonifacius, the apostle of the Germans. Important trading centre with closely-packed houses in the *Altstadt,* situated on a small peninsula. *Rathausplatz* is one of the most beautiful in Germany. At the *Dreiflusseck*, you can see how the yellow-green waters of the Danube, the grey waters of the Inn and the brown waters of the Ilz blend together. *St. Stephan's Cathedral* (17th cent.) was created by an Italian, Carlo Lurago. The Italian influence is apparent in the plaster work. The organ has 17 000 pipes and is said to be the largest in the world. *Festes Oberhaus*. Fortress of the prince-bishops, built on a promontory between the Ilz and the Danube (1219). Octagonal powder tower, fine view. Museum (art and folklore).

Fürstenzell with beautiful abbey church (1745).

Austrian border at *Schärding*. E 5 continues to Linz – Wien – Budapest – Beograd – Niš – Sofia – Istanbul – Ankara – Antakya.

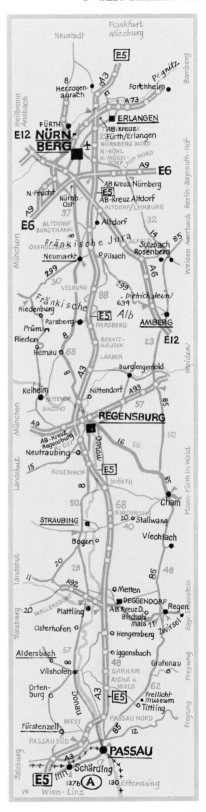

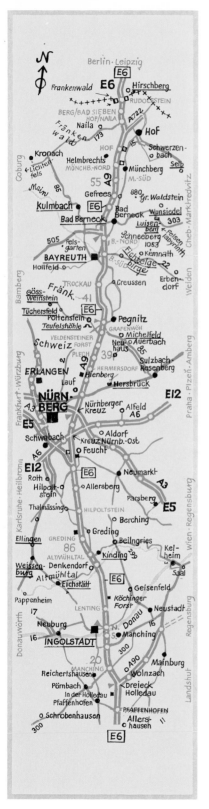

E 6. Hof – Nürnberg – München – Garmisch

Hirschberg. DDR (East German) frontier. *Hof* (55 000). Industrial town on the Saale. Beautiful altar in Lorenzkirche. Stadtmuseum.

Kulmbach. Industrial town. Breweries. The Renaissance *Plassenburg* fortress (1569) has a beautiful courtyard, the "Schöner Hof". Zinnfiguren-sammlung (tin figures' museum). Road to Lichtenfels, see "Ostmarkstrasse".

Bad Berneck. Spa in beautiful setting. Two castle ruins. Route 303 goes through *Fichtelgebirge,* a splendid area with lovely valleys and wooded mountains, with weathered cliffs, as at *Luisenberg,* or with a "rocky sea" as at *Wunsiedel.* Open-air theatre. *Selb* in eastern Fichtelgebirge is a centre of the porcelain industry. *Waldsassen.* Cistercian abbey (1131) reconstructed in the Baroque style by Georg Dientzenhofer. Imposing library.

BAYREUTH (70 000). The Richard Wagner Festival takes place in July and August in the *Festspielhaus* (1876) which accommodates an audience of 1 800. Wagner (1813-1883) lived in Haus Wahnfried. He and his wife, Cosima (daughter of Franz Liszt), are buried in the park. Baroque opera house. *Altes Schloss,* from the 17th cent., was rebuilt after a fire in 1945. *Neues Schloss* (1759). Art museum and ceramics museum. The rococo *Eremitage palace* is east of the town.

Fränkische Schweiz (Franconian Switzerland) is a mountain area (national park), for the most part 500-600 m above sea level. Deep, narrow valleys and fantastic stone formations, e.g. at the village of *Tüchersfeld.* *Teufelshöhle* is one of the largest and most beautiful stalactite and stalagmite caves in Germany.

Gössweinstein has a pilgrimage church.

Michelfeld. The abbey church was one of the first creations of the Asam brothers. Hersbrück. Old, fortified town in beautiful surroundings.

NÜRNBERG, see town plans.

Kinding. Lovely town in the Altmühl Valley. Fortified church. Hirschberg Castle.

Alternative routes B 2 and B 13 can be recommended.
Weissenburg. 14th-cent. town wall with town gates. 31 towers. Town hall from 1476. Recently discovered remains of Roman baths. *Ellingen.* Picturesque sections of the town date from the 18th and 19th cent. Splendid palace (1724) with beautiful church. *Eichstätt,* where Willibald served as bishop during the 8th cent. Uniformly built Baroque town. Town wall. Richly adorned cathedral (13th cent.) with the Pappenheimer Altar (1495). St. Walburg (d.779) is buried in the church that bears her name. Historical museum in the *Willibaldsburg* fortress.

INGOLSTADT (90 000). The fortress was built as early as the 9th cent. and expanded in the 15th cent. Beautiful Altstadt, town wall and Kreuztor (a tower). The rococo *Maria de Victoria Church* was designed by the Asam brothers. Liebfrauenmünster (15th-17th cent.). Neues Schloss from 1430. Important industries. Large oil refineries. Pipelines from Marseille. Audi (formerly DKW) car factories. Neuburg an der Donau is situated high above the river. Picturesque streets near the Karlsplatz. 16th-cent. castle.

LANDSHUT (58 000). Medieval Altstadt (Old Town) with beautiful houses. Burg *Trausnitz* was once the residence of the Dukes of Wittelsbach. *Martinskirche* has a 133 m high tower. The Stadtresidenz has a superb interior and houses a folklore museum. In July every third year (1986, 1989 etc.) an impressive festival, recreating the wedding of a German duke and a Polish princess is held in the town.

Freising. Magnificent 17th- and 18th-cent. façades. 19th-cent. cathedral with older (1210) crypt.

MÜNCHEN (Munich), see town plans.

Exit road leads through the *Forstenrieder Wald.* Bundesstrasse 2 is also known as Olympiastrasse (it was constructed for the Olympic Winter Sports in Garmisch in 1936). A beautiful alternative route.

Schäftlarn. Benedictine abbey founded in 1762. Church with decorations by Zimmermann. *Starnberg,* little town on the *Starnberger See* (lake that is 2 km long, 2-5 km wide and 123 m deep). Ludwig II, King of Bavaria, drowned in the lake at Schloss Burg, in 1886, together with his doctor. He had already been dethroned (see Romantische Strasse).

Murnau. Resort on the *Staffelsee.* A plastic plank, 1.5 km long and a mere 30 cm high, lines the Autobahn. It is an adequate protection from an invasion of frogs. They were once a traffic problem, but now they have their own tunnel under the motorway.

Bad Tölz. Large spa. The waters have a high iodine content. Picturesque area at Marktstrasse. Views from *Kalvarienberg* with Leonardkapelle, a pilgrimage church. On November 9 St. Leonard, patron saint of horses, is celebrated here. *Kochel.* Resort.

Oberammergau. Lovely little town, made famous by its Passion Play. The tradition was started in 1634 when the inhabitants of the town presented the play as thanks for the town's surviving the Black Plague. The play, presented every ten years, is about the sufferings of Christ. It takes a full day to perform and is presented about 100 times throughout the summer. The next performances will be in 1990. Numerous woodcarvings and a national woodcarving school. Cable cars to *Lauser,* 1 684 m.

Echelsbacher Brücke, 70 m above the Ammer Valley. **Wieskirche, Königsschlösser,** see Romantische Strasse.

Ettal. In 1330 a Benedictine abbey was founded on the old road to Brenner and Italy. The mighty structure was recreated in the Baroque style during the 18th cent.

Linderhof. Rococo castle (1879) in a lonely mountainous area, built for King Ludwig of Bavaria. Lovely gardens with fountains. Grotto with il-luminated lake – a scene out of Tannhäuser by Wagner.

Garmisch-Partenkirchen (828 000). Two villages that together form one of Germany's largest spas and resorts. Beautifully set at the foot of *Wettersteingebirge,* the northernmost of the Alps. Winter Olympic Games 1936. *Kurpark,* theatre, conference hall and a church from 1733 are in Garmisch. Town hall, folklore museum and St. Anton pilgrimage church (1704) in Partenkirchen. Cable car to *Wank* (10 min.) and to *Eckbauer* (14 min.).

Zugspitze (2 966 m) is the highest peak in Germany. From Garmisch, the Bayerische Zugspitzbahn goes to *Eibsee* (about 10 km from Garmisch by road). Then there is a 25% gradient and a 4 km tunnel that leads to *Schneefernerhaus.* Lift in the hotel ascends to the station for the cable car up to Zugspitzkamm. A cable car goes direct from Eibsee up to the summit. From *Ehrwald* in Austria a cable car line goes to the Zugspitzkamm and another line goes up to the summit. A pedestrian tunnel leads from the Zugspitzkamm to Schneefernerhaus. *Zugspitzgipfel* is usually swarming with tourists.

E 6 follows the rather poor route through the *Fern Pass.* Passing the Austrian border, E 6 continues to Innsbruck – Brenner – Verona – Firenze – Roma.

The best route from Garmisch to Innsbruck goes by way of **Mittenwald,** using the old trade route that linked Augsburg with Verona. Exquisite town with ornately painted buildings along the High Street and at the Obermarkt. The Church of St. Peter and Paul (1749) also has a richly painted steeple. Mittenwald is famed for its violin-makers. School of violin-making. *Geigenbau- und Heimatmuseum* (museum of violin-making and local folklore).

The road continues to the Austrian border at Scharnitz and on, via Seefeld, to Innsbruck.

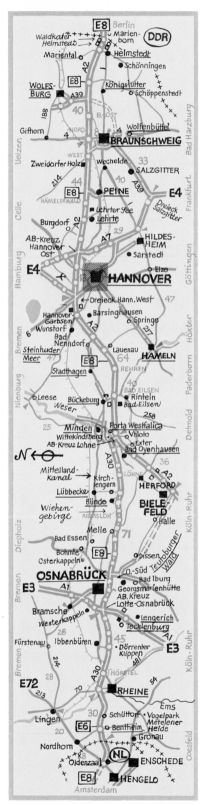

E 8. Helmstedt – Hannover – Osnabrück – Oldenzaal

E 8 comes from the Soviet frontier at Brest – Warszawa – Berlin. In the German Federal Republic it follows routes A 2 and A 30.

Helmstedt (28 000) was founded in the 8th cent. Very old and picturesque town with half-timbered houses. Parts of the St. Ludgeri abbey church date from the 11th cent. In 1576, a university was founded here. The Juleum, a 50 m high tower, remains. To the west are the Lubben Stones, two megalithic tombs. The Hausmann Tower, an old town gate.

Königslutter am Elm. Idyllic town. 16th-cent. wooden houses with carved figures. Abbey church (1135) with the grave of Emperor Lothar.

WOLFSBURG (135 000). Volkswagen factories. Castle. Folklore museum.

BRAUNSCHWEIG (Brunswick, 270 000). Old Hanseatic town that was ruled by the Welfen family, whose best-known member was Henry "the Lion". He died in 1195 and is buried in the Cathedral of *St. Blasius* which has a splendid late-Gothic interior. Wooden crucifix from 1160. Beautiful *Burgplatz* with cathedral, Dankwarderode Castle, built at the same time, and half-timbered houses. A bronze lion is a reminder of the founder of the city. Late-Gothic town hall on *Altstadtmarkt*. Dreischalen Fountain (1408). Martinekirche and Gewandhaus with Renaissance gable.

Wolfenbüttel (55 000). Stadtmarkt with lovely half-timbered houses. Old streets and houses with beautiful churches. The folklore museum is in a 13th-cent. castle. Lessinghaus, where the poet, G.E. Lessing (1729- 1781), lived. Another of Wolfenbüttel's renowned sons was the courtier, J.G. Schottelius, the "father of German grammar", who invented the semicolon.

Peine (30 000). Iron industry. The Peiner Freischiessen, a marksmanship competition and general fair, is held on the first Sunday in July.

Lehrte. Industrial town.

HANNOVER, see E 4.

The *Steinhuder Meer* (3 000 hectares). At its deepest, the lake is 3 m. A favourite of yachtsmen and lovers of succulent eels. The man-made island in the middle of the lake is the site of *Wilhelmstein Castle,* which, during the 19th cent., housed a Prussian military school.

HAMELN (Hamelin, 60 000). Splendid *Altstadt* with patrician houses in the "Weser Renaissance" style. Goethe wrote the famous story about the Pied Piper of Hamelin who played a melody on his flute and lured all of the rats in the town to the River Weser, where they drowned. *Rattenfängerhaus* (the Pied Piper's house) is richly adorned (1603). *Hämelschenburg* is a splendid castle.

Stadthagen. The Alte Amtspforte is an ornately half-timbered house from 1553. Martinekirche. Beautiful town hall and castle. *Bückeburg* Castle with sculptures by Adrian de Vries (1620). Church with Baroque façade (1620). The castle chapel is exquisitely decorated.

Minden was founded by Charlemagne about 800. It belonged to the Hanseatic League. Handsome *Altstadt* surrounds the Gothic St. Peter's Cathedral (11th cent.). Bronze crucifix from the same period. 375 m long bridge over the Mittelland Canal. Schachtschleuse, an 8.5 m long and 10 m wide lock. It takes 10 minutes for a vessel to pass through the lock. The Coeln-Mindener Railway was inaugurated in 1850. As early as 1855 it had carriages that accommodated horse-drawn coaches – predecessors of the present-day auto-rail.

Porta Westfalica, where the River Weser breaks through the mountains. The mighty Kaiser-Wilhelm-Denkmal on Wittekindsberg (280 m). Telephone tower atop Jakobsberg (238 m).

Bad Oyenhausen. Spa. Bugatti Automobile Museum. *Deutsches Märchenmuseum* (German Fairy-tale Museum).

Bünde. Tobacco factory. Tobacco museum with the largest cigar in the world: 1.70 m long and weighing 9 kg. *Lübbecke.* Little town with half-timbered houses, watermill.

OSNABRÜCK, see E 3.

Teutoburger Wald, a mountainous, forested area with heights reaching from about 190 m to over 400 m. The area is about 100 km long and 8-15 km wide. It boasts fine hiking trails and many idyllic towns. e.g. Ibberbüren with summer rodel track. The sandstone Dörenther Cliffs are used as a training ground for alpinists. *Tecklenburg* with picturesque castle ruins. Summer theatre in the courtyard. *Lengerich* with cement factory.

RHEINE (50 000). Industrial town. Wool spinning was started here in 1835. The Antonius Church has a 116 m high tower. Bentlage Castle with zoo.

Bad Bentheim. Sulphur baths, in use since the 11th cent. Casino. Spa.

Dutch border. E 8 continues to Oldenzaal – Hengelo – Utrecht – den Haag – Hoek van Holland – London.

E11 Strasbourg – Karlsruhe – Stuttgart – München – Salzburg

E11 comes from Paris – Nancy – Strasbourg. Kehl – Karlsruhe, see E 4.

Kehl (30 000). Industrial town and port. The "Europabrücke" crosses the Rhine to Strasbourg in France.

PFORZHEIM (110 000). Centre of the goldsmithing and jewellery industries. *Schmuckmuseum* (Jewellery Museum).

Maulbronn. Cistercian abbey 1178-1556. The only completely authentic abbey in Germany from that period – all of the others were remodelled in the Baroque style. A complete abbey town with 30 buildings and three defence towers. Beautiful courtyard with cloister. Marienkirche with Paradies entrance hall. Half-timbered farm buildings.

Tiefenbronn. Gothic church with impressive treasures. Altar by Lucas Moser. *Calw-Hirsau.* Aureliuskirche with the remains of an 11th-cent. basilica. St. Peter und Paul from the same period is now a ruin. *Hirsau* was one of the most important monasteries in Germany but in 1692 it was destroyed during a war.

STUTTGART, see town plans.

Esslingen am Neckar became a town in 866. Beautiful Marktplatz with half-timbered houses. Old town hall (1439). Stadtkirche St. Dionysius and Frauenkirche.

Schwäbisch Gmünd (60 000). Founded in the 12th cent. Splendid medieval half-timbered houses line the long *square*. Heiligenkreuzmünster (1380). Six towers remain of the town wall. In 1352, Peter Parler, a young master builder from this town, was called to Prague by Emperor Charles IV and commanded to complete the Cathedral of St. Vitus. The town was founded by the Hohenstaufs, a powerful line of princes, who, during the 12th and 13th cent., were German kings and ruled southern Italy. There are no traces of their fortress, Hohenstaufen, but the view from its former site is superb.

Blaubeuren. Benedictine abbey founded in the 12th cent. Abbey church (1499) by Peter von Koblenz. The High Altar was carved by Jörg Syrlin the Younger. **Urach** with fine half-timbered houses on the Marktplatz. **Reusslingen** and **Teck,** castle ruins with lovely views.

ULM (100 000). Old trading town. University of medicine and natural science. *Münster* (Cathedral), under construction from 1377 until 1529, and expanded during the 19th cent. After the cathedral in Cologne, this is the largest Gothic church in Germany. Reaching a height of 161 m, its tower is the highest in the world. (The tower in Cologne's cathedral is 157 m high.) After climbing 768 steps, the visitor is rewarded with a beautiful view. The interior of the church is superbly decorated. The choir with woodcarvings by Jörg Syrlin the Elder, is particularly noteworthy. Splendid patrician houses. Half-timbered houses, including the Schiefes Haus (1482) in Fischerviertel. Many lovely fountains: Jörg Syrlin designed the Fischkasten (1482) in the Markt. Ulmer Museum with art from Ulm. Town hall. A bit of the town wall, Metzgerturm, and *Deutsches Brotmuseum* (German Bread Museum) are on the banks of the Danube. There have been many jokes about the inhabitants of Ulm, for instance the one about the Ulmer Spatz, the sparrow, who was cleverer than the natives. They are considered to be a bit less than bright. But then, Albert Einstein was born in Ulm, in 1879.

Charlottenhöhle, a more than 500 m deep cave – the result of erosion.

Dillingen. Once a university town. Rich cultural life during the 16th cent. Large castle and church.

AUGSBURG (250 000). Founded by the Romans. During the Middle Ages one of the richest and most powerful cities in Europe, dominated by the Fugger family of businessmen. In 1530 the Augsburg Confession was signed here. The Thirty Years' War ended the town's prosperity and influence. Previously a part of Swabia, Augsburg was granted to Bavaria in 1806.

The *town hall* (1615) was designed by Elias Holl. Magnificent, 57 m high, Renaissance façade. Augustus Fountain and Perlach Tower (1616), 78 m high *carillon* and view that even includes the Alps (when the yellow flag is hoisted). The *cathedral,* with 9th-cent. origins, has been rebuilt in the Gothic style. The 11th-cent. stained-glass windows are believed to be the oldest in the world. Splendid bronze doors.

Maximilianstrasse has a uniform Renaissance character. Münster St. Ulrich und Afra (origins in the 15th cent.). *Fuggerei* (1519), the world's first social settlement: 66 small houses set in their own little town with four town gates. The houses are let to the indigent for a symbolic sum. Zeughaus. Germany's first Renaissance house was designed by Elias Holl after his return from a tour of Italy. Roman museum in a church. Staatsgalerie with the works of old German masters. Birthplace of Bertholt Brecht and Rudolf Diesel.

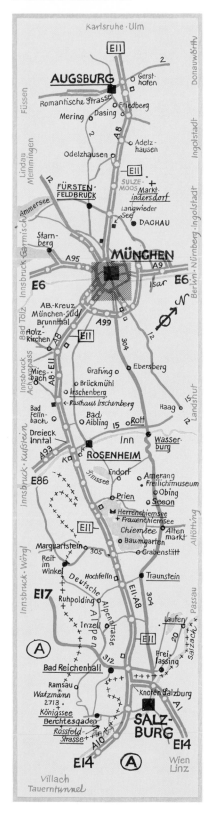

Markt Indersdorf. Church with huge, ornate altar (1690).

Fürstenfeldbruck. Enormous monastery, originally from the 13th cent. Elaborate plaster and marble decorations by the Asam brothers. A tragic drama took place at the military airbase during the 1972 Olympic Games. 14 Israeli athletes, who had been kidnapped by terrorists, were killed. **Dachau.** Site of the former concentration camp. Museum. Memorial.

MÜNCHEN (Munich), see town plans.

The beautiful road Füssen (Romantische Strasse) – Bad Tölz – Reit im Winkel – Berchtesgaden – Salzburg is called the **Deutsche Alpenstrasse.**

Irschenberg. The highest point on the Munich-to-Salzburg route (717 m). Views. Weyern monastery with church from 1687. Beautiful road via Achensee to Innsbruck. **Bad Tölz,** see E 6.

E 85 (A 93) Rosenheim – Wörgl is the fastest route from Munich to Innsbruck. It makes it possible to drive on motorways all the way from the Baltic Sea to the Adriatic Sea.

Rosenheim (40 000). Industrial town. Beautiful Altstadt (Old Town). Städtische Kunstsammlung (art gallery). Folklore museum.

Seeon with 12th-cent. Benedictine abbey. Rococo chapel. **Wasserburg.** Beautiful old town with arcades. Frauenkirche. Heimatmuseum (folklore museum) with Bavarian peasant furniture. **Rott am Inn.** The church (11th cent.) was once part of an abbey. Rebuilt in the Baroque style by Johann Michael Fischer, Fichtmayer, the plaster artist, and Günther, the painter.

Prien. Spa. The railway with its steam locomotives is not part of a museum – it provides regularly scheduled service to the harbour of Prien- Stock and the boat to Herrenchiemsee. A once royal carriage is for first-class passengers.

Chiemsee, the largest lake in Bavaria. Island with the Versailles-like **Herrenchiemsee Palace** (1885), built for King Ludwig II (see Romantische Strasse). Only one section was built, but that is imposing enough. Spectacular Hall of Mirrors. Beautiful gardens with fountains. Altes Schloss (Old Castle) was a monastery. Convent on the island of Fraueninsel. Chiemsee is best seen from the northern banks with the Alps in the background.

Reit im Winkel. Large resort on the Deutsche Alpenstrasse.

Laufen an der Salach. Handsome old salt town. Arcaded patrician houses. St. Mariä Himmelfahrt abbey church (1338).

Königssee. Lovely Alpine lake, 8 km long, 1 km wide, and 180 m deep. Boat service to the beautifully situated **St. Bartolomä pilgrimage chapel.** "Eiskapelle", the remains of an avalanche.

Rossfeldstrasse with superb views. 16 km, 13% gradient.

Berchtesgaden. Large resort between two mighty peaks in a lovely Alpine setting. Splendid Kurgarten. Castle with "Wittelsbacker Hausmuseum". Salzbergwerk. Cable car and road to Obersalzberg (1 000 m). Road (for buses) to **Kehlstein** (1 834 m) where Hitler had his "eagle's nest".

Bad Reichenhall. One of the largest spas in Germany, on the northern slope of the Berchtesgadener Alps. Kurhaus and park. Casino. St. Zenokirche. Cable car (10 min.) to **Predigtstuhl** (1 613 m) with fine view.

SALZBURG, see Austria, town plans.

Austrian frontier.

E12. Plzeň – Nürnberg – Mannheim – Saarbrücken

Waidhaus. Czech frontier. E12 comes from Białystok – Warszawa – Łodz – Praha.

Vohenstrauss. *Friedrichsburg Castle* (1590) with six towers. Hochspiecher Rabenleite, artificial lake. **Leuchtenberg** with castle ruin. **Weiden** (45 000). Industrial town. Lovely Marktplatz in the picturesque Altstadt (Old Town). Max-Reger-Haus with memorial tablet dedicated to the composer (1873-1916).

Wernberg. 14th-cent. castle. Hahnback with rococo church. **Sulzbach-Rosenberg.** Iron industry. Folklore museum in the castle.

AMBERG (50 000). Old cultural centre. Picturesque old town. St. Martin's Church (15th cent.) and one of the most beautiful town halls in Germany (14th-16th cent.) are on the Marktplatz. Town wall with Nabburger Tor. Alte Veste, the castle of the Counts Palatine houses a folklore museum. The Electors' Palace is now an administrative building. The *Maria-Hilf* pilgrimage church (1702) is richly adorned.

Hersbruck at the foot of Michelsberg. Castle. Abbey church decorated by the Asam brothers. **Lauf.** Charming old town. Castle on an island in Lake Pregnitz.

NÜRNBERG and **Fürth,** see town plans.

Schwabach. Old town. Church and town hall with museum.

Heilsbronn. Sections of the abbey church date from 1132. Splendid altars and burial vaults of the Hohenzollerns, the German dynasty of electors, kings and emperors.

Ansbach. For the most part the town has the stamp of the Baroque period. Residenz (12th cent.) created by Gabrieli and Retti. Mirrored boudoir. Beautiful ceramics from the Ansbacher Fayancen Manufaktur. Orangery. St. Gumpertkirche. *Rothenburg, Feuchtwangen* and *Dinkelsbühls,* see Romantische Strasse.

Langenburg. Castle (15th-18th cent.) with motor car museum. The vehicles have been collected by Von Frankenberg, the racing driver.

Schwäbisch Hall. Even the Celts were familiar with the salt deposits. Town privileges were granted in 1156 by Frederick Barbarossa. Lovely, picturesque town. *Marktplatz* with Baroque town hall and splendid half- timbered houses that survived the great fire of 1728. Lovely fountain and famous staircase (1507) whose 53 steps lead up to Michaelskirche. During the festival, the stairs are transformed into an open-air stage where "Jederman", Hofmannsthal's version of the English morality play, "Everyman", is performed. St. Katharinenkirche. Keckenburg-Museum, the town museum, housed in a 10-storey residential tower. During the Middle Ages the town was the site of a famous mint. The "Kuchenfest" is a large, annual Whitsun festival. *Grosscomburg,* a mighty, fortified abbey with buildings that date from different periods. Abbey church with three towers. Famous antependium and chandelier (1130).

Waldenburg. Fortified, highly situated town. The three town centres are separated by moats. **Neuenstein.** Impressive Renaissance castle with interesting interior. The Hohenlohe princes held court here. **Öhringen.** Church with Hohenlohe burial vaults (16th cent.) and the Margareten-Altar.

Jagsthausen, see E 70.

Beautiful monastery in **Schöntal.** Church with 17th-cent. alabaster altar.

HEILBRONN (115 000). Industrial city and port on the River Neckar. Marktplatz, restored after severe wartime damage, is the site of *Kilianskirche* (1529). Its tower is the symbol of the city. It is said that Götz was imprisoned for one night in the Götzenturm, but in reality, he was incarcerated in the Bollwerksturm. Kätchenhaus, home of Lisette Kornacher. She inspired Heinrich von Kleist (1777-1811), the early Romantic poet.

Neckarsulm. NSU factories. *Deutsches Zweiradmuseum* (bicycles and motorcycles) in the castle.

Bad Wimpfen. Salt town, founded by the Romans. Picturesque town and large resort. Winding streets and lovely half-timbered houses, particularly in Klostergasse. Kaiserpfalz, now a ruin, was built about 1200. Blauer Turm and Roter Turm. Splendid churches.

The road that follows the Neckar to Heidelberg is recommended. Romantic castles and ruins on the vineyard-covered mountains that slope down to the winding river, bustling with intensive boat traffic.

Guttenberg Castle with library and art collection. *Burg Hornberg* where Götz von Berlichingen died in 1562. His armour is on display in the museum. One of the most beautiful castles is *Burg Zwingenberg*. Superb views from *Burg Hirschhorn*. And if you have not had enough there are four more castles in *Neckarsteinach* and one more in *Dilsberg*.

The motorway goes over the hills of *Kreichgau* between Odenwald and Schwarzwald (the Black Forest). *Sinsheim* with lovely half-timbered houses. *Walldorf.* Original home of the Astor family who went on to build the Waldorf-Astoria Hotel in New York. *Hockenheimer Ring.*

Schwetzingen. Castle with 18th-cent. *French garden.* Theatre (1752). Summer performances. Fountains, artificial ruins, temples.

SPEYER, see E 4.

MANNHEIM and *LUDWIGSHAFEN,* see E 4.

WORMS (80 000). One of the oldest Roman towns in Germany. Capital of the Kingdom of Burgundy, which was extirpated by the Huns in 437. Its destruction was the basis of the saga of the Nibelungen. Many parliaments (diets) during the Middle Ages. In 1521, Martin Luther had to defend himself before Charles Quint. The Lutherdenkmal (Luther Memorial) was erected in memory of this event. Much of the town's elegance was destroyed during the Thirty Years' War and the Second World War. *St. Peter's Cathedral* was consecrated in 1018. High Altar by Balthasar Neumann. Paulskirche with a tower in the Byzantine style. Museum in the Andreas abbey (ceramics, glass, weapons, jewellery). *Kunsthaus Heylshof* (art, ecclesiastical art, ceramics and porcelain). Synagogue and Europe's oldest Jewish cemetery. Worms is a wine centre – there are vineyards within the town limits. Liebfrauenkirche (14th-15th cent.) is in one of the vineyards. It gave its name to Liebfraumilch.

NEUSTADT an der Weinstrasse (56 000). Capital of the Palatinate. Wine centre. Old town, beautifully situated. *Bad Dürkheim.* Wine town and spa. Kurhaus and casino. The Dürkheimer Fass is a unique wine tavern.

KAISERSLAUTERN (105 000). Industrial city. University of technology. American military base. Town hall (1968) with an 84 m high tower. Pfalzgalerie (art). Abbey church (1250). *Barbarossaburg,* the remains of Frederick Barbarossa's castle (1158).

Landstuhl. Spa. Ruins of Nannstein Castle.

Homburg (43 000). University of medicine. Schloss Mountain (Schlossberg) with Hohenburg (1152). The interior of the mountain is a labyrinth of caves and tunnels. *Zweibrücken* (40 000). Industrial town. The 18th-cent. palace has been restored (now an administrative building). Rose garden.

Alternative routes: B9 and B272 Speyer – Landau – Saarbrücken
See also A61. *Speyer.* See E 4

Landau (40 000). Wine town. Between 1697 and 1816 the town belonged to France. The Deutsches Tor (German Gate) remains from the original fortifications. Splendid churches. The road crosses the *Deutsche Weinstrasse* (German Wine Road) which goes from Worms to the "Wine Gate" at *Schweigen.*

The road goes through the *Pfälzer Wald nature park,* a wooded area with many ruined castles. The highest area is *Hardtgebirge* (673 m). *Trifels Castle* (497 m) was a favourite of Emperor Frederick Barbarossa. In 1193, the English king, Richard the Lionheart, was imprisoned here. Königskapelle (where the crown jewels were kept during the Middle Ages). Visitors can still view the Kaisersaal, etc. The road up is steep (18% gradient).

Pirmasens (60 000). Shoe industry and shoemakers' trade school.

Kirkel. A ruined castle (11th cent.) rests on the remains of a Roman watch tower. *St. Ingbert* with the odd *Grosser Stiefel* (Big Boot) cliff. Near by is *Hänsel und Gretel,* a stone relief from the Roman period.

French border. E 12 continues to Metz – Paris.

E 36. Arnhem – Oberhausen – Köln

E 36 comes from Hoek van Holland – Rotterdam – Utrecht. German route A 3. Dutch border.

Emmerich (25 000). Hanseatic town. Customs station for Rhine traffic. Parts of St. Martini Church have twice been swept away by the river. The crypt and 12th-cent. choir remain, as does the wooden crucifix from 1170. St. Aldegundis Church (16th cent.). Modern Heilig-Geist-Kirche. Rheinmuseum. 1 228 m long Rhine Bridge. Lovely promenade.

Kleve (50 000). Spa and industrial town. Schwanenburg Castle, home of Anne of Cleves, fourth wife of Henry VIII.

Kalkar. Beautiful Gothic gabled houses. Städtisches Museum (16th cent.) St. Nikolai Church is richly adorned.

Bocholt (50 000). Industrial town. Renaissance town hall. *Gemen* and Raesfeld, moated castles.

Xanten was originally a Roman outpost, referred to in the Nibelungen sagas as the home of Siegfried. It became a town in 1228. One of Germany's project cities during the European Architectural Heritage Year 1975 as an "example of urban renewal in a highly developed industrial area". Remnants of a Roman amphitheatre (A.D. 15). Roman museum in *Klever Tor* (1393). The cathedral was built between 1190 and 1530. Marienaltar.

Wesel (50 000) . Gothic Willibrordi Cathedral. Baroque Berliner Tor.

From the rather isolated woodlands and bogs of Nordrhein-Westfalen, the motorway suddenly plunges into the heavily industrialized, crowded, smoky and road- crossed Ruhr area.

OBERHAUSEN and **DUISBURG,** see E 3.

KREFELD (240 000). Steel industry. Centre of German silk and velvet industry. Textile museum. Large Rhine port. *Burg Linn*, a museum with Roman and Frankish relics and items of local interest. The original castle was destroyed in 1704 during the War of the Spanish Succession. Zoo and botanical garden. Haus Lange with modern art. Kaiser-Wilhelm-Museum.

Ratingen and **Mettman** with old town centres. Neanderthal nature preserve, where, in 1856, the skeleton of the "Neanderthal Man" was discovered. He dated from the late Stone Age and had lived in the Neanderthal Valley about 175 000 years ago. Small museum. Park with buffalo, bison and wild horses.

Solingen (180 000). *Deutsches Klingenmuseum* with examples of the famous knives that are produced in the city. 506 m long and 107 m high, the Müngstener Brücke is the highest railway bridge in Germany.

DÜSSELDORF and **Neuss,** see town plans.

Zons. Lovely little medieval town with old fortified customs house.

Altenberger Dom (1379) in the heavily wooded Dünnthal. Stately Gothic abbey church. "Bergischer Dom". **Leverkusen** with chemical industry (Bayer). Köln-Niehl with Ford factories.

KÖLN (Cologne), see town plans.

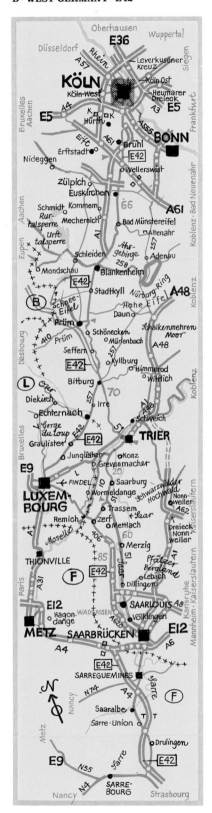

E 42. Köln – Luxembourg – Saarbrücken

KÖLN (Cologne) and **BONN,** see town plans.

Brühl (50 000). Augustenburg Castle (16th cent.), in the Regency and early rococo styles, was created by François de Cuvilliés the Elder. Magnificent staircase by Balthasar Neumann. *Falkenlust Hunting Castle* designed by de Cuvilliés. The chapel in the park is decorated with mussel shells, lava, mountain crystal and glass. "Phantasieland", an amusement park with dolphinarium.

Erftstadt with the beautiful Baroque Gymnich Church. The moated castle now accommodates guests of the government.

Niedeggen. Romantic fortress (1180), built on a promontory high over the River Ruhr. *Burgenmuseum der Eifel* is housed in the tower.

Euskirchen. Industrial town. Remains of fortifications. The road that goes east traverses the lovely Ahr Valley and passes through the spa of **Altenahr,** the centre of German red wine production.

Kommern. Lovely half-timbered houses. **Rheinisches Freilichtsmuseum.** Windmills and farmhouses. A complete Eifel village.

Schleiden. Late-Gothic castle church (1525) with original stained-glass windows. Fine organ.

Bad Münstereifel. Spa. Well-preserved town wall. Romanisches Haus (1166) on the Klosterplatz is a stone house in excellent condition. Town hall with folklore museum. St. Chrysanthus und Daria abbey church with carved 14th-cent. Madonna. Radio telescope in Stockert.

Eifel. A 70 km long and 30 km wide mountainous area, bounded by the Rhine, the Mosel and the Ruhr rivers. Over 200 extinct volcanoes. Lava can be seen at the over 52 m deep *Laacher See.* Numerous dams, "valley dividers", which have created artificial lakes. The Eifel is a wonderful area for motorists. The *Nürburgring,* see A 48.

Stadtkyll. Superb location. Remains of fortifications. **Prüm** with an old abbey on Kalvarienberg. **Bitburg** with the remains of a Roman fortress. Large breweries, famous beer.

Luxembourg border. E 42 goes via Luxembourg to the German border at Remich and then to Saarbrücken and Strasbourg. From Bitburg you can take B 51 via Trier. **TRIER,** see A48. The road goes over an extension of the *Hunsrück,* a mountain area that rises near the Rhine.

Merzig. Little industrial town. St. Peter's abbey church (13th cent.) **Dillingen.** Industrial town with iron works.

Saarlouis. Modern industrial town. The motorway winds its way through a highly industrialized area.

SAARBRÜCKEN (210 000). Major city in the coal-rich Saar area. University. *Saarlandsmuseum* (art and furniture). The modern part of the city, including the major shopping area, is on the right bank of the river. Alt-Saarbrücken with the palace (reconstructed in the 19th cent.) is on the left bank. Splendid views from its garden. Exquisite stained-glass windows in the palace church. *Ludwigsplatz* with lovely Baroque buildings. The 18th-cent. Ludwigskirche is now a museum. Museums. Zoo.

French border. E 42 continues to Strasbourg.

E 61. München – Kempten – Lindau

MÜNCHEN (Munich), see town plans. *Fürstenfeldbruck*, see E 11.

Diessen and *Herrsching* are two of the small resorts on the shores of the lovely Ammersee. Andechs Benedictine monastery is set 200 m above the surface of the lake. Beautiful 18th-cent. abbey church.

Landsberg was an important trading centre during the Middle Ages. Town wall (13th-15th cent.) with Bayer Gate (1425). Picturesque houses line the *square* (Hauptplatz). *Town hall* with splendid plaster work by Domenikus Zimmermann who was mayor of the town 1759-1764. He also decorated the Ignatius Chapel in the Heiligenkreuzkirche.

Kaufbeuren (46 000). St. Blasius' Chapel is a part of the old town wall. Irsee. The Benedictine Mariä Himmelfahrt abbey church is in the Baroque style.

KEMPTEN (60 000). The "Capital of the Allgäu", the lovely and colourful mountain area "in front of" the Alps. Roman strong-hold. Archaeological finds in the Zumsteinhaus. Beautiful *Altstadt* with town hall and fountain. Baroque St. Mangkirche.

There are large resorts south of Kempten. The most prominent is *Oberstdorf* (843 m) which is surrounded by lofty peaks. Cable car to Nebelhorn, 2 224 m. Stupendous views. Another sight is the Breitachklamm, a gorge with waterfalls. Road to Kleinwalsertal which belongs to Austria but is under the jurisdiction of the German customs authorities.

From *Immenstadt* it is possible to drive the westernmost section of the Deutsche Alpenstrasse to *Wangen*. Streets lead from four town gates to the handsome Marktplatz. Town hall with richly adorned gable.

Lindau (27 000). Beautifully situated. The oldest section of the town is on an island in the Bodensee (Lake Constance). The view from the harbour out towards the breakwater, adorned with a 6 m high stone Bavarian lion, and two lighthouses, is world famous. The city museum is housed in the Zum Cavazzen, a Baroque structure on the Marktplatz.

The *Bodensee* (Lake Constance) is about 64 km long and as much as 14 km wide. Several resorts. The major tourist attraction is *Mainau* near Konstanz. See E 70.

Austrian frontier. E 61 continues to Bregenz – Chur – S. Bernardino – Milano.

Alternative route: 13 Landsberg – Memmingen – Lindau is faster than E 61.

Bad Wörishofen became a spa as a result of the ministrations of the parish priest, Sebastian Kneipp (1821-1897), who prescribed a diet of water and vegetables. He was naturally thought a quack by doctors, but now there are many spas in Germany that abide by his dietary rules. *Mindelheim*. Picturesque little town.

MEMMINGEN (40 000). Remains of the town wall and a handsome square. Museum in the beautiful Herrmansbau mansion.

Ottobeuren. In 764 Charlemagne founded the Benedictine abbey which became an important cultural centre. The building is 480 m long and has two 82 m high towers. The abbey church was transformed in the 18th cent. by Johann Michael Fischer and became one of the most beautiful Baroque churches in the country.

Bad Wurzach with beautiful church. *Kisslegg*. Castle and splendid rococo church. *Wolfegg*. 16th-cent. castle with magnificent Knights' Hall.

Ravensburg (45 000). Medieval walls and tower. Superb buildings from the time when the guilds flourished. Mehlsack, a 50 m high watch tower with fine views (240 steps up to the top). *Liebfrauenkirche* with a copy of the Ravensburger Schutzmantelmadonna (15th cent.). The original is in the Dahlem-Museum in Berlin. *Weingarten*. Benedictine abbey, founded in 1050. Ornately decorated Baroque basilica (1724) by Kaspar Moosbrugger.

FRIEDRICHSHAFEN (55 000). Restored after wartime damage. Magnificent views from the Stadtgarten out over Lake Constance towards the Alps. The castle church with its two towers (1701) is the symbol of the town. *Bodensee-Museum* (art, archaeology, Zeppelin museum). Count Ferdinand von Zeppelin (1838-1917) had many airships constructed here. The age of the airship ended on May 6, 1937, when the "Hindenburg" exploded in Lakehurst, New Jersey, U.S.A., and 36 people died.

E 70. Bad Hersfeld – Würzburg – Stuttgart – Schaffhausen

Bad Hersfeld (30 000). Spa. Beautiful *Altstadt* (Old Town) with half-timbered houses. Ruin of the large 10th cent. monastery church, destroyed in 1761. Germany's oldest church bell (11th cent.). Drama festival. E 63 crosses the DDR (East German) frontier and continues to Erfurt – Karl-Marx-Stadt – Dresden.

Schlitz. Romantic old town. Five castles. Hinterburg (13th cent.), partially in ruins, Vorderburg (Renaissance), Schlachterburg (half-timbered, 16th cent.), Ottoburg (Baroque), now a youth hostel, and Hallenburg (18th cent.), now a school.

FULDA (60 000). St. Boniface, the English monk and missionary, and the "Apostle of Germany", founded a monastery here in the 8th cent. His grave is under the High Altar of the cathedral, built in 1712 to the plans of Johann Dientzenhofer. Ecclesiastical treasures. *Michaelskirche* (822) is one of the oldest churches in Germany. It is a reproduction of the Church of the Holy Sepulchre in Jerusalem. Medieval town wall, Baroque town centre. *Palace* with orangery. *Fasanerie Palace* (also known as Adolfseck, 1756) with splendid rooms and park.

Rhön. Mountainous area and nature park that extends into East Germany (DDR). Many bare peaks of what were once volcanoes. *Wasserkuppe* (950 m) is the highest. Popular with sail-plane and gliding enthusiasts. The area around *Kreuzburg* (932 m) is more heavily wooded. Several spas. **Gersfeld.** Kneipp cures and climatic cures. **Bischofsheim** and **Bad Neustadt. Bad Brückenau** and Staatsbad Brückenau with mineral springs. **Tann**, close to the East German (DDR) frontier, has lovely half-timbered houses, town gate (1557) and three 17th-cent. castles.

Bad Kissingen (23 000) is one of the largest spas. Beautiful parks. Half-timbered houses. *Münnerstadt.* Medieval buildings on the Marktplatz. Half-timbered houses and late-Gothic town hall. Town wall from 1251. Church with reliefs by Riemenschneider and paintings (the only known surviving ones) by Veit Stoss.

SCHWEINFURT (56 000). Industrial town. Renaissance town hall.

Hammelburg. Old town and castle. *Karlstadt* with the Maintor town gate.

WÜRZBURG and **Veitshöchheim,** see E 5. Autobahndreieck Biebelried is one of Germany's busiest motorway junctions.

Sommerhausen. Handsome gate tower, the site of the smallest theatre in Germany. The stage is 3×5 m and the auditorium seats 54 spectators. **Ochsenfurt** with imposing town hall.

Tauberbischofsheim. Wine trade. Beautiful town with half-timbered houses. The 16th-cent. castle houses a folklore museum. Church with Riemenschneider altar from 1500. *Weikersheim Castle* (15th cent.) with Knights' Hall and Baroque garden.

Bad Mergentheim. Spa. Folklore museum in the castle, which from 1500 until 1809 served as the seat of the Grand Master of the Order of the Teutonic Knights.

Creglingen. Herrgottkirche (1396) with the *Marienaltar* by Tilman Riemenschneider. **Stuppach.** Church with the *Stuppach Madonna* by Matthias Grünewald. **Künzelsau.** Picturesque old town with castle.

Jagsthausen. Götz von Berlichingen, the knight who is a leading character in a play by Goethe, was born in 1480 in Götzenburg (now a hotel). He was called the "Man with the Iron Hand", and his artificial hand is on display in the castle museum. Drama festival in the castle courtyard. Preserved steam railway.

Neckarsulm, Bad Wimpfen, Heilbronn and **Schwäbisch Hall,** see E 12. **Maulbronn,** see E 11.

Lauffen. Charming old town. Gothic Rigiswindiskirche. *Tripsdrill.* Game preserve, mills, preserved steam railway. **Besigheim** with town wall, half-timbered houses and town hall (1459). Engbrücke (1581). **Bietigheim.** Industrial town.

LUDWIGSBURG (85 000). Marktplatz with two churches, arcaded houses and a splendid fountain. The largest *Baroque palace* in Germany (1704), inspired by Versailles. Hoftheater with 18th-cent. machinery and stage sets. Impressive park. Fairy-tale park with figures from the tales of the Brothers Grimm. The little Favorite Palace. *Monrepos Palace* (1767) is near the idyllic half-timbered town of **Markgröningen.**

Marbach. Charming old town. Birthplace of Friedrich Schiller (1759-1805). Schiller-Nationalmuseum.

STUTTGART, see town plans. **Esslingen,** see E 11.

Leonberg. Half-timbered houses, church, castle.

Bebenhausen. Cistercian monastery, founded in the 12th cent. *Würtembergisches Landesmuseum* and Hölderlin-Museum (art).

TÜBINGEN (75 000). Picturesque old town, dominated by the Renaissance Hochtübingen Castle. University (1477). The town hall (1477) with an astronomical clock (1511) is on the lovely *Marktplatz.* Splendid views from the *Eberhardsbrücke.* Famous avenue of plane trees on an island in the Neckar. Hölderlinturm where the poet, Friedrich Hölderlin (1807-1843) spent his last years. Stiftskirche (1470) with stained-glass windows.

REUTLINGEN (100 000). Textile industry. The Gothic Marienkirche. Spendhaus with folklore museum in one of the half-timbered 15th-cent. houses. *Nebelhöhlen*, stalactite and stalagmite cave. *Lichtenstein Castle* (1841) is set 200 m above the valley.

Heigerloch between two rocky hills. Castle with church. St. Anna pilgrimage church (1755). Burg *Hohenzollern,* a romantic knights' castle with turrets and pinnacles, built high on a promontory on the site of an earlier castle. Friedrich Wilhelm I and Friedrich (Frederick) the Great are buried in the chapel. The latter's snuffbox and the Prussian royal crown are on display. The famed noble dynasty received the Imperial German crown in 1871. The last emperor of Germany was Kaiser Wilhelm II, who abdicated in 1918, and died in 1941.

Sigmaringen with the *Hohenzollern-Museum* (paintings, sculpture, arms, tapestries and postage stamps).

Road east to *Zwiefalten.* Benedictine monastery since 1089. Johann Michael Fischer designed the Baroque church (1739). The interior decorations are by Michael Feuchtmayer. *Heiligkreuztal.* Abbey church, dating from 1256. Sculptures and paintings.

West of the motorway on the Schwarzwalder Hochstrasse from Baden-Baden lies the little spa of *Freudenstadt.* It was largely destroyed during the war. Large arcaded Marktplatz. Kurgarten with Kurhaus. *Alpirsbach.* Little spa with lovely abbey church. Summertime chamber music concerts.

Rottweil. Roman settlement from A.D. 74. Medieval walls and towers. Beautifully situated above the Neckar. Handsome patrician houses on the High Street which leads to the Schwarzer Tor (Black Gate). *Heiligen-Kreuz-Münster* (15th cent.) with a crucifix, probably by Veit Stoss. Medieval sculpture in the St. Lorenzkapelle. Large pre-Lenten carnival with masks, "Fasnet", and "Narrensprung". *Schramberg.* Watch factories (Junghans).

VILLINGEN-SCHWENNINGEN (85 000). Climatic health resort. Kneipp baths. Computer and watch factories (Kienzle). *Trossingen.* The Hohner company (founded in 1857) manufactures accordions and harmonicas.

Donaueschingen. Little town on the River Brigach. The *Donauquelle* at the castle, surrounded by balustrades and sculptures, is thought to be the source of the *Danube.* The road east of the town passes over the small river with the sign "Donau" (Danube). The river is considerably wider and much more impressive in Regensburg, Linz, Vienna, Budapest and Belgrade. It extends 2 888 km to its mouth at the Black Sea.

Road 31 to *Löffingen.* Beautiful and picturesque 18th-cent. town centre on the Marktplatz. Splendidly painted houses. Town hall. Maienländer Tor. Onward to *Titisee,* a large climatic health, summer and winter resort on the shores of the lovely little Titisee, which is about 2 km long and 500 m wide. The road continues to Freiburg (see E 4).

Swiss border at *Neuhaus.* E 70 continues to Schaffhausen, Winterthur and Zürich.

E 121 (A 81) goes on to *SINGEN* (50 000). Industrial town. Atop the cone of an extinct volcano rise the mighty ruins of *Hohentwiel Castle.* Expansive views. The castle was destroyed during the Napoleonic Wars. Road 33 goes to *Radolfzell.* The church (1436) contains the gräve of Saint Radolf (d. 874).

KONSTANZ (70 000), beautifully situated on the shores of the Bodensee (Lake Constance). The Council of Konstanz (1414-1418) met to settle religious conflicts. They also managed to elect a new pope instead of the three who were competing against each other. Large-scale conferences are not a new phenomenon – it is said that 7 200 delegates met at the council. (At the time, Konstanz had a population of 10 000.) The Emperor, Sigismund granted the Czech religious reformer, Jan Hus (John Huss), safe conduct at the Council. He was seized, condemned and burned at the stake in 1415 (memorial stone). His ashes were strewn in the Danube.

The *cathedral* was under construction from the 11th to the 17th cent. Stately Renaissance town hall. The *Konzilgebäude* (Hall of the Council), where Pope Martin V was elected in 1417. Memorial to Count Zeppelin (1838-1917) near the harbour. He was born in Konstanz. A memorial in the park recalls the opening of the first large-scale European hiking trails that meet here.

Mainau. A footbridge connects the island with the mainland. A fantastic park with magnificent flower beds. Orange and lemon trees, palms, magnolias and a rose garden. The park was created by the Grand Dukes of Baden. The present owner is Count Lennart Bernadotte of Sweden.

99

E 73. Hannover – Kamen – Köln

Hannover – Autobahnkreuz Löhne, see E 8.

Herford (70 000). Hanseatic town. Many half-timbered houses. Mayor's house with stepped gable (1538).

Bad Salzuflen. Spa. *Lemgo.* Once an important Hanseatic town. Splendid stone and half-timbered houses. One of the most superb dwellings is *Hexenbürgermeisterhaus* (1571). During the 16th cent., Cothmann, the mayor of the town, lived here. Under his jurisdiction, 90 women were executed for witchcraft. The town hall consists of eight different buildings. The town hall *pharmacy* is one of the oldest in Germany.

Detmold (65 000). Altstadt (Old Town) with half-timbered houses. 16th-cent. castle. *Lippisches Landesmuseum* with examples of half-timbered houses, historical exhibitions, arts and crafts, natural history and weapons. *Westfälisches Freilichtsmuseum*, open-air museum.

BIELEFELD (320 000). Industrial town. Linen-weaving factories. Linen-weavers' Fountain (Leinenweberbrunnen). *Playing card museum* in Sparrenburg Castle. The **Sennestadt** section of the city (24 000) presents an interesting solution to a common traffic problem. Pedestrians and motor traffic are well segregated. Excellent access to car parks transforms motorists into contented pedestrians.

Teutoburger Wald, an undulating wooded area, for the most part 100-200 m above sea level. The highest point is Velmerstot, 468 m. *Herrmannsdenk-mal* on Grotenburg, 368 m, brings to mind the Battle of the Teutoburger Woods in 9 B.C., when troops led by Herrmann (Armin), the Germanic chieftain, annihilated the Roman armies. Ernst von Bandels took 38 years to complete the 26 m high statue which has a 56 m high pedestal.

Externsteine. Five sandstone cliffs, 30-38 m high. During the 12th cent. a grotto was carved out of the cliff, a chapel was formed, and a relief of the descent of Christ from the cross was carved into the wall.

GÜTERSLOH (80 000). Heavy industries and food processing industries (pumpernickel bread, macaroni, Westphalian ham). Vineyards. Half- timbered houses. Town park with botanical gardens.

Wiedenbrück, founded in the 10th cent. Picturesque old town with half-timbered houses.

The **Ruhr area** and **Dortmund,** see E 3.

ISERLOHN (100 000). Industrial city. Bauernkirche. St. Pankratius, a 15th-cent. church with carved altar. Obere Stadtkirche St. Marien. *Dechenhöhle,* 300 m deep stalactite and stalagmite caves. Lovely road south to *Altena Castle* with smithery museum and the world's first youth hostel, opened 1912.

HAGEN (225 000). Industrial city. Art museum. Museum of technology. *Westfälisches Freilichtsmuseum,* an open-air museum with artisans' village. Beautiful road south in the Volme Valley traverses the **Sauerland.** *Kluterhöhle* in Ennepetal, the largest natural cave in Germany with hundreds of tunnels, in all over 5 km long. Treatments for asthma.

WUPPERTAL (410 000). A number of minor industrial towns joined to form the city of Wuppertal in 1930. Construction of the 14 km **Schwebebahn,** an elevated iron monorail system, was begun as early as 1900. Although the trains seem to hang precariously from their overhead tracks, the line has proved to be a safe and effective means of transport. Von der Heydt-museum with 20th-cent. art. Watch museum. Zoo. Schauspielhaus (a theatre) from 1967.

REMSCHEID (140 000). Tool manufacturing. Röntgen-Museum. **Burg.** Little town with castle which once belonged to the Counts of Berg. Museum and Gasthof (inn). Müngsteiner Brücke is the highest railway bridge in Germany. It is 107 m high and 506 m long.

SOLINGEN (180 000). World-famous for its production of knives, scissors and surgical instruments, etc. "Klingen-Museum". Idyllic *Odenthal* with the **Altenberger Dom,** "Bergischer Dom", a highly impressive early-Gothic church (14th cent.) with exquisite stained-glass windows above the west portal.

LEVERKUSEN (170 000). Ford factories. Pharmaceutical and chemical products (Bayer). The Bayer company have a beautiful Japanese garden with lovely bridges, Japanese houses, and an image of Daikoku, the God of Wealth, all under the shadows of Bayer's looming 33-storey office tower. The factory and the garden (originally laid out in the English manner) were once created by the wealthy Herr Leverkus.

KÖLN (Cologne), see town plans.

B 22. Bayreuth – Cham. B 85. Cham – Passau
Ostmarkstrasse

BAMBERG, see E 5.

COBURG (48 000). Residence of the Dukes of Saxe-Coburg-Gotha. One of the major exports of the area were members of this family; Saxe-Coburg's are numerous among present-day European royals. Duke Johann Casimir (17th cent.) gave the town its Renaissance atmosphere. One of the most beautiful buildings is *Gymnasium Casimirianum*. Large *Marktplatz*. 16th-cent. town hall. **Veste** is one of the largest castles in Germany. The oldest parts date from the 12th cent. Enormous collection of art, antiques, weapons, glass, etc. Many works by Lucas Cranach the Elder. Carriage museum. In 1530 Martin Luther lived at Veste. The Renaissance *Ehrenburg Castle* is open to visitors. This was where Prince Albert, Queen Victoria's consort, came of age. *Hofgarten*, with natural science museum, is situated between the two castles.

Vierzehnheiligen. The Baroque pilgrimage church, built between 1743 and 1772 to the plans of Balthasar Neumann, is one of the most beautiful in Germany. A rococo altar portrays the "vierzehn Heiligen", the 14 patron saints. One of them is St. Christopher, who has been adopted by contemporary motorists.

The **Banz** monastery is on the opposite side of the Main Valley. In 1120 it was placed under the protection of **St. Dionysius**. The enormous Baroque abbey was constructed in the 18th cent., as was the beautiful abbey church by Johann Dientzerhofer.

BAYREUTH and **Kulmbach,** see E 6.

Speinshart. Beautiful abbey church by Wolfgang *Dientzenhofer.* The road passes through the *Hessenreuther* and *Mantler Wald* nature park.
Weiden (45 000). is an industrial town with a handsome Marktplatz. Venerable *Altstadt* (Old Town) with delightful square. *Flossenburg* (1105). Castle ruin on a granite cliff. Road 15 north to **Tirschenreuth** with lovely church and **Waldsassen** with abbey church and chapel by Georg Dientzenhofer. Splendid library.

Vohenstrauss. *Friedrichsburg* Castle (1590) has six towers. **Oberviechtach** with rococo church. **Cham** with beautiful Marktplatz. 13th-cent. church of St. Jakob. Biertor town gate.

Bayrischer Wald. Nature park, a part of the Böhmerwald (Bohemian Forest) that extends into Czechoslovakia. A softly undulating wooded area, relatively unscathed by tourism. Several pretty towns. The highest peak in the area is **Grosser Arber** (1 457 m). Cable car terminus almost at the summit.
Bodenmais. Resort. Guided tours of mines in the 955 m high Silberberg.
Bayer Eisenstein (724 m) is one of the largest resorts.

Zwiesel. Bergkirche with beautiful paintings. Glass blowing workshops. Museum of forestry in the town hall. **Regen.** Ruins of Weissenstein Castle (11th cent).

PASSAU, see E 5.

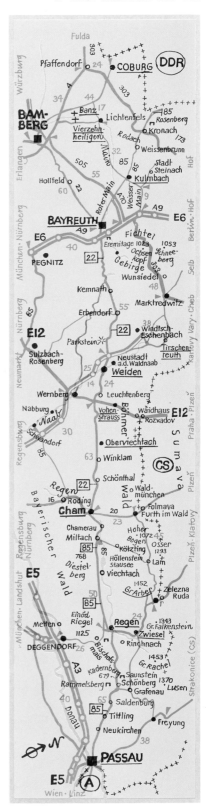

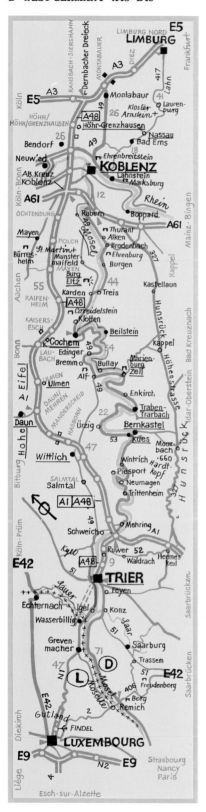

A 48 and B 49. Koblenz – Trier
The Mosel Valley and The Eifel

Autobahn A 48 comes from the Dernbacher Dreieck on E 5 (A 3). **Höhr-Grenzhausen** with the ruins of Grenzau Castle. Unique triangular tower.

KOBLENZ, see A 61.

Laurenburg. Half-timbered houses. Town hall with folklore museum.

Nassau. Half-timbered town hall. 17th-cent. castle.

A 48, the *"Eifel-Autobahn"*, completed in 1975, is a fast and beautiful road in an area where the majority of roads are winding and time-consuming. A 49, which follows the banks of the **Mosel**, is one of the most beautiful tourist routes in Germany. It passes innumerable exquisite old towns and wine villages. The road distance between Koblenz and Bernkastel is 75 km. As the crow flies, the distance is a mere 27 km.

A 48 follows the southern sections of the **Eifel**, a magnificent wooded highland area (about 70×30 km) with volcanic origins. The average altitude is 600 m. *Hoher Acht* is 747 m. Old fortresses, castles and idyllic resort-towns. Excellent hiking trails.

Mayen. Old town. Eifel-Museum in Genovevaburg. *Bürresheim Castle* (14th-17th cent.).

Nürburgring. Motor racing circuit, used for races as well as for the testing of cars. A 23 km northerly loop and an 8 km southerly loop. 8 m wide road with 172 curves and a height differentiation of about 300 m. Gradients up to 17%. (One special track has a 27% gradient.) The facilities are usually open to the public on week-days, so it is possible to put your own car to the test. But do not attempt to break the record as it stands – about 7 minutes on the northerly loop, an average speed of 193 kmh!

The Autobahn passes the idyllic towns of **Ulmen, Daun** and **Wittlich**.

The routes round the Mosel: It is impossible to mention all of the beautiful castle ruins and wine villages in this text. Please refer to the map! One of the most beautiful castles is **Burg Eltz**, 184 m above the Mosel. It was built in the 13th cent. All of the successive 14th-, 15th- and 16th-cent. owners made their own unique additions. Nothing has been destroyed – it remains a fantastic and lovely confusion of building forms. The castle is still owned by the Counts of Eltz.

Cochem. One of the largest resorts and wine towns in the Mosel Valley. Famed for its beauty, castle and nearby vineyard slopes. The castle was destroyed by French troops in 1689, but the foundation walls and the tower remain. It was restored in the 19th cent. and now, with its turrets and pinnacles, it looks more medieval than it ever did.

Beilstein. One of the best-preserved half-timbered towns in Germany. Picturesque, narrow streets and wine cellars. Ruined castle. The town at one time belonged to Chancellor Metternich.

Marienburg was once a monastery. Superb views from the terrace of the restaurant. **Zell** with a long and narrow street. The town's famous cat, arching its back, on a wine barrel, is on the fountain. "Zeller Schwarzer Katz" (the Black Cat of Zell), is a well-known Mosel wine. The symbol of the town is Runder Turm (the Round Tower). Art treasures in the Electors' Palace. **Traben-Trarbach** with the ruins of Crevenburg Castle (14th cent.).

Bernkastel-Kues. Venerable town with half-timbered houses and town hall (1608) on the little Marktplatz. Resort and wine industry ("Bernkasteler Doktor"). St. Michael's Fountain (17th cent.). In September there is a wine festival and wine is served from the fountain. Several wine taverns in the narrow streets. The archbishops of Trier once owned the Landshut fortress. It has been in ruins since 1692. Superb views.

TRIER (110 000). The oldest town in Germany, founded by the Romans in 15 B.C. In the 3rd cent. Trier became the capital of the West Roman Empire. Six Roman emperors reigned over Trier. In A.D. 314, during the reign of Constantine the Great, Trier became the first bishopric in Germany. **Porta Nigra** (The Black Gate) is the largest Roman structure in Germany (2nd cent.). When it was erected, the stones were light in colour. The **Kaiserthermen** (4th cent.) are the massive remains of Roman baths (in all probability they were never used). The *Barbarathermen* are older, but only foundations remain. 30 000 spectators could watch the gladiators battle in the 2nd-cent. amphitheatre. Roman finds in the **Rheinisches Landesmuseum**. Bischöfliches Museum (ceiling paintings from the palace of Emperor Constantine) and Städtisches Museum.

Liebfrauenkirche (1260). Although the earliest parts of the cathedral date from the 4th cent., most of the structure was built in the 11th cent. Several other beautiful churches. **Hauptmarkt** with a cross, erected in 958. **Steipe** (15th cent.), the house where the town council met. Legend has it that the town was founded by Trebeta in 2 000 B.C. Trebeta was the son-in-law of Semiramis, the Queen of Babylon (she was the one who ordered the famed hanging gardens of Babylon – one of the seven wonders of the ancient world).

There is a *museum* at Brückenstrasse 10, in the house where Karl Marx (1818-1883) was born.

A 61. Köln – Koblenz – Bingen – Mannheim – Walldorf
B 9. Köln – Bonn – Koblenz – Bingen
B 42. Köln – Königswinter – Koblenz – Wiesbaden

Fast, recently constructed motorway. Beautiful views but some long sections pass through a forest. The road that follows the banks of the River Rhine is naturally of greater interest to the tourist. Several connecting roads and car ferries make route variations possible.

KÖLN (Cologne) see town plans. *Brühl*, see E 42. *BONN*, see town plans.

Bad Godesberg. Old spa, now a part of Bonn. Many foreign embassies. The venerable Zur Lindenwirtin Ännchen Inn is associated with Heinrich Heine. *Königswinter.* Resort. Ruins of *Drachenfels* (Dragon Cliffs) Castle. *Drachenburg* (Dragon Fortress), 19th cent., is a copy of a castle and the interior is filled with all sorts of copies. *Rhöndorf,* once the home of Chancellor Konrad Adenauer (1876-1967), and the location of his grave. *Bad Honnef.* Spa. Half-timbered houses. Beautifully situated at the foot of the Siebengebirge and opposite Rolandsbogen, an observation point.

Remagen. The railway bridge once situated here was seized, unscathed, by American troops in 1945. Its capture is said to have shortened the Second World War.

Bad Neuenahr-Ahrweiler (30 000). Spa with beautiful Kurpark. Casino. Hot springs (36°C). Half-timbered houses. 13th-cent. town hall. St. Peter's Church in the Waalporzheim section of the town (1246). *Sinzig.* St. Peter's Church has 13th-cent. wall paintings. *Burg Reineck* with superb views out over the valley. Cable car.

Linz. Lovely little town with half-timbered houses. 13th-cent. wall paintings in St. Martinskirche.

Maria Laach. Benedictine monastery on the shores of the little Laacher See. Romanesque abbey church, with some sections dating from the 12th cent. Paradies entrance hall (1220) with sculpture and arcades. Stained-glass windows from 1956.

Andernach. Picturesque, medieval Altstadt (Old Town). Remains of the town wall with the 12th-cent. Rheintor. Romanesque Liebfrauenkirche. *Neuwied* (70 000) with lovely riverside promenade.

KOBLENZ (120 000) was founded by the Romans in about A.D. 15. Wine centre. *Altstadt* (Old Town) with the Church of St. Kastor, where the Empire of Charlemagne was divided up in 836. Balduinbrücke (1420). Alte Burg (1280). *Deutsches Eck* where the Rhine and the Mosel join. Kaiser Wilhelm I had a colossal monument, symbolizing German unity, raised at this spot. His own equestrian statue has been removed.

The mighty *Ehrenbreitstein* fortress, on the opposite bank of the Rhine, was completed in 950. It was destroyed in 1801 by French troops. Now the site of the *Landesmuseum* (one of its sections deals with technical history). Rheinmuseum and youth hostel. In June of every third year (1986, 1989, etc.) enormous fireworks display, the "Rhein in Flammen" (the Rhine in Flames). Some smaller-scale annual fireworks in August.

Stolzenfels Castle, on the left bank, was restored in 1836. Museum and lovely views. Rhens with half-timbered houses. View from Gedonseck. *Boppard.* Lovely little town. Burg *Laneck,* restored in the 19th cent. Open to the public. Views.

The romantic *Lahntal* and road 260 leads to *Limburg an der Lahn* (see E 5) and *Bad Ems,* a spa known for its waters, "Emser Water". *Nassau.* Half-timbered town hall and 17th-cent. castle. The Nassaus are on the throne of Luxembourg, and the Orange-Nassau branch of the family is the reigning family of the Netherlands. The lovely *Arnstein monastery* is on a wooded cliff. See also E 5.

Marksburg is the only castle on the Rhine that has never been damaged. The German Federation of Castles has a *museum* here. Fine herb garden.

St. Goarshausen. Old town with *Katz* Castle (named for Count von Kaatzenbogen). It was erected as a "Trutzburg" (defiance castle) against the *Maus* Castle. This arrangement where two or more castles were built in defiance of each other was a common phenomenon during the age of competing feudal lords.

Lorelei. The world-famous rock (132 m above the Rhine) extends out into the river and creates the currents that once endangered the simple vessels that plied the Rhine. Legend has it that Lorelei, a beautiful siren, sat on the rock, singing a lovely song and combing her golden hair. Her song and her beauty were so extraordinary that she enchanted passing captains to such an extent that their boats foundered and the crews were drowned. Nowadays, the river traffic is mainly made up of large and powerful motorized barges, that can resist her charms. The Rhine cruise ships usually arrange for the passengers to hear the famous song of the Lorelei by Heinrich Heine.

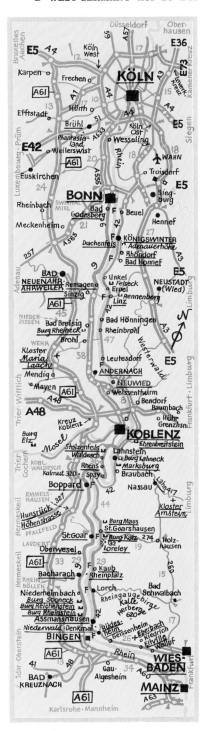

View towards **Oberwesel.** Lovely town with many towers. **Kaub.** Old wine town with town wall. *Pfalz,* a castle, built in the 14th- 17th cent., is on an island in the middle of the Rhine. It was a customs station.

Bacharach. Little, lovely town with town wall. The southernmost castles on this stretch of the Rhine are *Sooneck, Reichenstein* and *Rheinstein.*

Bingen. Wine-trading town. Folklore museum in *Burg Klopp. Mäuseturm* (Mouse Tower), on an island, was once a customs station for river traffic. Legend has it that it was here that Archbishop Hatto of Mainz was devoured by rats in punishment for having had poor people killed.

Assmanshausen. Handsome resort. Wine trade. Hotel Krone is 400 years old. Half-timbered houses and a terrace restaurant.

Niederwaldendenkmal with a 10 m high statue of Germania, symbol of Germany's unification in 1871. She is a rather stout lady, 13 m high and set on a 24 m high pedestal. Fine views, 225 m above the Rhine.

Rüdesheim. Large and lovely resort with an abundance of hotels, wine taverns and tourists. Most of the action is in the narrow *Drosselgasse. Brömserburg* (10th cent.), once the archbishop's castle, now houses museums of folklore and wine. *Boosenberg* (1868) with a museum dedicated to mechanical musical instruments.

Eberbach, a well-preserved medieval Cistercian abbey. Church from 1186 and monastery from the 13th cent. The monks' dormitory is 72 m long. **Eltville** with a 7 km long promenade on the bank of the Rhine. In the tower there is a small museum dedicated to Gutenberg (the father of printing) who at one point resided here. **Kiedrich.** Church chapel and half-timbered vicarage, enclosed by a high wall. 14th-cent. Kiedricher Madonna.

MAINZ and **WIESBADEN,** see E 5.

Autobahn A 61 goes on to Speyer. *Hunsrück-Höhenstrasse* goes west through one of Germany's largest pine forests. Extensive mountain ridges, 400-500 m high. The highest peak is *Erbeskopf,* 816 m. Several spas. *Ingelheim* with the remains of Charlemagne's castle.

Bad Kreuznach. Spa with vineyards around the castles near the town. Alte Nahebrücke, with 15th-cent. houses built on it, leads to the island of Badewörth. Folklore museum. **Bad Münster** am Stein. Spa. Rock formations at Rheingrafenstein. **Alzay** was founded by the Romans. Castle. Road to **Kirchheimbolanden,** a small picturesque town with lovely churches, town wall and town gates.

WORMS, see E 12. **MANNHEIM and Ludwigshafen,** see E 4.

The **Deutsche Weinstrasse** (German Wine Road) goes south from Bockenheim, passing through the Pfälzer Bergland with woods and sandstone heights. The *Pfälzer Wald* (175 000 hectares) is the largest nature park in Germany.

Freinsheim, large wine town, encircled by a wall. **Bad Dürkheim,** spa with lovely park. One of the largest wine centres in the country, it is famed for its annual Wurstmarkt wine festival, held on the second and third Sundays in September. *Limburg.* Abbey ruins with splendid views. *Deidesheim.* Lovely wine town. Stupendous views from *Kalmit* (673 m). *Ludwigshöhe* Castle was built in 1850 for King Ludwig I of Bavaria. *Trifels* (497 m). The entire area is lavishly dotted with castle ruins, often set high up on cliff tops.

The German Wine Road ends at the massive Weintor (Wine Gate 1936) in **Schweigen,** close to the French border.

B 42. Köln – Köningswinter – Koblenz – Wiesbaden
Romantische Strasse

Map on next page.

WÜRZBURG and **Wertheim,** see E 5.

Tauberbischofsheim. Wine trade. Beautiful old town with half-timbered houses. Folklore museum in the 16th-cent. castle. Church with Riemenschneider altar (1500). **Bad Mergentheim.** Spa. The castle, which from about 1500 until 1809 was the seat of the Grand Masters of the Order of the Teutonic Knights, now houses a folklore museum. **Stuppach.** Church with the *Stuppach Madonna* (1519) by Matthias Grünewald. **Weikersheim.** The castle (15th cent.) was once owned by the Hohenlohes. Knights' Hall and Baroque garden.

Creglingen. Herrgottkirche with the *Marienaltar* (1505), the most famous work of wood sculptor Tilman Riemenschneider. The crucifix is assumed to have been a creation of Veit Stoss.

Rothenburg ob der Tauber. A well-preserved medieval town with town walls, moats, pinnacles and turrets, town gates, narrow streets and exquisite buildings – and enormous hordes of tourists. *Plönlein* is one of the best-known parts of this fairy-tale town. Frederick Barbarossa granted the town its charter in 1172. The *Marksturm* and the *Weisser Turm* remain from Rothenburg's oldest fortification system. During the Thirty Years' War, the town suffered badly and was almost completely deserted. The inhabitants were so poor that they could not afford serious repairs or reconstructions. As a result the medieval character of the town survived. Count Tilly, general of the Catholic League during the Thirty Years' War, threatened to put the town to the torch, but showed compassion when Nusch, the burgomaster, managed to empty a large, 3 litre, mug of wine in one swallow. This was the famous "Meistertrunk". It is repeated every year during the Whitsun celebrations. The role of the 17th-cent. burgomaster is played by the present mayor. The event took place in the Kaisersaal of the impressive *town hall* on the *Marktplatz*. The original drinking vessel is on display in the Reichstadtmuseum.

Feuchtwangen. Large *Marktplatz* with Baroque town hall and half-timbered houses. Famous Romanesque cloister (arcades lining the church courtyard). Folklore museum.

Dinkelsbühl. Resort. Medieval atmosphere with town wall and four town gates. Sections of the Wörnitztor date from the 13th cent. *Deutsches Haus*, a half-timbered structure with Renaissance paintings. St. Georgskirche from 1492. Views from the tower. The Kinderzeche festival is held every third Monday of July, in memory of an event that took place in 1632. The children of the town successfully beseeched the Swedish troops to spare Dinkelsbühl from plundering.

Ellwangen. Lovely town with splendid houses on the Marktplatz. Stiftkirche St. Veit (1233). Schönenberg pilgrimage church (1682).

Nördlingen. The third large resort and medieval town on the Romantische Strasse. The town, protected by a perfectly preserved town wall, is circular in form. The town gates and towers are also in excellent condition. St. Georgskirche (15th cent.) with "Daniel", a 90 m high tower. Städtisches Museum.

Donauwörth. Lovely streets and houses. Partially preserved town wall with Riedertor and Färbertor. Many splendid buildings. Town hall, House of the Order of the Teutonic Knights, and 16th-cent. Fuggerhaus. Folklore museum in a red 15th-cent. half-timbered house in Ried. *Heiligkreuz abbey church.*

AUGSBURG, see E 11. **Landsberg**, see E 61.

Kloster Lechfeld with the Mariahilf pilgrimage church (17th cent.) **Diessen** am Ammersee. The Church of St. Maria was designed by J. M. Fischer.

Wessobrunn. Once an abbey with a beautiful interior. St. Johannes' Church (1759). The Wessobrunner Gebet (a book of prayer) is one of the oldest German texts (9th cent.).

Schongau. Old town with partially preserved town wall. **Rottenbuch.** Augustinian abbey with Baroque church. *Echelsbacher Brücke*, 76 m above the Ammer Valley. **Steingaden** with Baroque church.

Wieskirche. One of the most splendid rococo churches, the greatest achievement of the Zimmermann brothers. Simple exterior, magnificently decorated interior. Touchingly naive paintings depict thanksgiving for the delivery from plagues and catastrophes.

Oberammergau, Linderhof and **Garmisch-Partenkirchen,** see E 6.

Neuschwanstein with its overpowering pinnacles and turrets in a romantic Alpine setting is the archetypal German castle of one's dreams. It brings to mind the romance of the Middle Ages, but in reality, it was built between 1869 and 1886 for King Ludwig II of Bavaria. The same year that the castle was completed, King Ludwig learned from a government commission that he had been removed from the throne. A few days later, he drowned in the Starnberger See (see E 6). The unbelievable décor gives an indication of the king's mental state. The interior's fantasies culminate in the third floor's artificial stalagmite and stalactite cave and winter garden with Tannhäuser's cave, and the fourth floor's "Meistersänger Hall", a copy of the one at Wartburg. The king's admiration for Wagner was boundless, and in all probability was too overwhelming for the composer. Although Wagner lived for a while in Hohenschwangau, he never set foot in Neuschwanstein.

Hohenschwangau was completed in 1836 and is not quite as exaggerated as Neuschwanstein. Art, furniture and a music salon. Ludwig II grew up here, and with binoculars he could watch the construction of Neuschwanstein.

Füssen. Old trading town. Beautiful Altstadt (Old Town). The former St. Magnus abbey, a Benedictine monastery, is affiliated with the one at St. Gallen. St. Magnus, the apostle of the Swabians, was buried here in 750. Michaelskirche from 820. *Hohes Schloss* with museum.

TOWN PLANS

BERLIN (West Berlin, 2.2 million)
Berlin came into existence during the 13th cent. and became the residence of the electors in the 14th cent. Capital of Prussia 1848-1871, capital of the German Reich until 1945. Berlin had already suffered over 300 bombing raids when, in April 1945, the Russians mounted an artillery offensive against the city. The destruction was incredible, as is the fact that just a few decades later, a thriving modern city had risen from the ruins.
Berlin was jointly administered by the victors until 1948, when the Soviet sector was transformed into Berlin, Hauptstadt der DDR (East Berlin), the seat of the government of the German Democratic Republic. The other sectors formed West Berlin. From June 1948 until May 1949, West Berlin was subjected to a Soviet blockade. But the Western occupation forces succeeded in creating an "airlift" from West Germany to the isolated city. On August 13, 1961, the East-West borders were sealed and the Berlin Wall was raised, primarily to staunch the flow of East-to-West refugees. It is possible to cross into the Eastern section of the city at "Checkpoint Charlie", and at the Friedrichstrasse stations of the U-Bahn and the S-Bahn. Some U-Bahn lines travel under East Berlin, but the trains do not stop at the blockaded and patrolled stations, that give an unreal and spooky impression.
The centre of West Berlin is the area around the Bahnhof am Zoo and **Kurfürstendamm** (popularly called "Kudamm"), a splendid shopping avenue, lined with department stores, large hotels, restaurants and cafés. The famous Kafé Kranzler, one of the most popular meeting places, is at the corner of Joachimstaler Strasse. Guests who sit on its terrace can drink in the authentic "Berliner Luft" (Berlin air). In the background is *Kaiser-Wilhelm-Gedächtniskirche,* whose shell-scarred tower remains as a memorial to the insanity of modern warfare. A modern, colourful glass cathedral was added in 1961. Near by is the newly built *Europa-Center,* a skyscraper and shopping complex with artificial ice-skating rink and planetarium. The **zoo** is one of the oldest in Europe. It was reconstructed after almost complete wartime destruction. Terrarium and aquarium.

Tiergarten was formerly the most popular park in Berlin. During the last wartime winter, its trees were chopped down and used as firewood. Large and beautiful flower beds. Impressive porcelain factory, founded in 1751. The *Siegessäule* (1870), 67 m high, is decorated with a gilded statue of Victoria, Goddess of Victory. *Kongresshalle* (by H.A. Stubbings), was the United States' contribution to an architectural exhibition in 1957. Philharmonie Concert Hall (1963). The broad avenue that goes through Tiergarten is now named Strasse des 17. Juni in memory of the East Berlin uprising of 1953. It passes the *Soviet Victory Monument* and leads to the *Brandenburger Tor* which is now next to the Berlin Wall. The neo-Renaissance Reichstag building has been restored, The burning of the Reichstag in 1933 created the spark that allowed for the Nazi take-over. Further destruction in 1945. When a Russian flag was raised from its roof it became the symbol of the defeat of Nazism. *Hansaviertel.* A housing area created by 48 international architects – among them Aalto (Finland), Gropius (Germany/USA), and Niemeyer (Brazil). Fair grounds with the Funkturm, 138 m high – the symbol of West Berlin. The large Deutschlandhalle. Restaurant and observation terrace.
Schöneberg and *Steglitz* with the lively Hauptstrasse and Schlosstrasse shopping streets. The *town hall* in Schöneberg is the seat of the Senate of West Berlin. The *Liberty Bell,* in the 71 m high tower, is a copy of the bell in

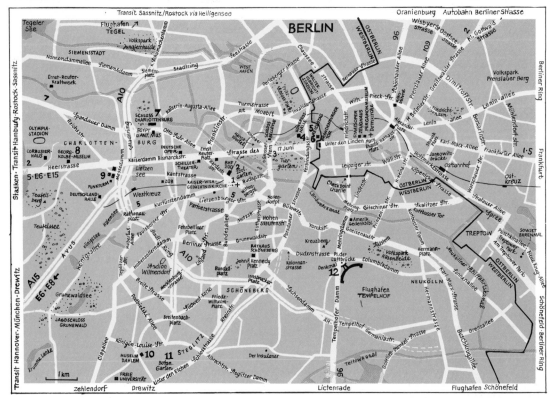

1 *Kaiser-Wilhelm-Gedächtniskirche (Kaiser Wilhelm Memorial Church). 2 Zoo. 3 Siegessäule (Victory Column).*
4 *Congress Hall. 5 Reichstag building. 6 Soviet Victory Monument. 7 Charlottenburg Palace. 8 Georg Kolbe Museum.*
9 *Exhibition grounds. Congress Centre. Radio tower. 10 Museum Dahlem. 11 Botanical Gardens. 12 Airlift Monument.*

Philadelphia. There is a monument to the "airlift" during the blockade of Berlin at the former Tempelhof airport. *Charlottenburg Palace* was built in 1695 as a summer residence for Sophie Charlotte, who became the first Queen of Prussia. The east wing by G. von Knobelsdorff was completed in 1743. Now it is an art museum. Other buildings contain an archaeological and antiquities museum. The famous bust of Queen Nefertiti of Egypt (14th cent. B.C.) is in the *Egyptian Museum.* Equestrian statue of the elector, Friedrich Wilhelm. There is a mausoleum in the park.

Other Berlin museums are the Neue Nationalgalerie (1968, art), National Museum (in Dahlem, art, sculpture, ethnography, Asian art), Georg-Kolbe-Museum, Berlin-Museum, Brücke-Museum, Humboldt Palace Post, Telephone and Traffic Museum.

The Gedenkstätte Plötzensee is a memorial dedicated to the revolutionaries involved in the assassination attempt on Hitler in 1944. Maria Regina Martyrum, a contemporary Roman Catholic church, dedicated to the victims of Nazism.

The Olympia Stadium with places for 100 000 spectators, was built for the Olympic Games of 1936. Berlin is a major industrial city and river port. Siemens, AEG-Telefunken. Ullstein and Springer publishing houses. University and colleges.

The population of West Berlin, which in itself is a small enclave in East Germany, do not have access to large recreation areas, but they can go to the *Grünewald,* an area with lakes that sailors and swimmers alike can enjoy. The beaches of the Wannsee (several kilometres long) are sometimes the goal for as many as 30 000 bathers. And it is possible to stroll through the Tegel Woods or in the Klein-Glienicke nature park. Lubärs is the final rural village in the West Berlin area.

Macabre as it seems, it must be admitted that the *Berlin Wall* is a very unique "sight". To see it at its most frightening, the visitor should go to Bernauerstrasse. Here, all of the windows in the Eastern sector, facing West Berlin, have been bricked up, and most of the houses have been torn down. Or, go to *Potsdamer Platz,* once one of Europe's liveliest squares, now almost completely deserted.

Berlin, Hauptstadt der DDR (East Berlin), see the German Democratic Republic.

BONN (300 000).

Originally a Roman fort, it became a city ruled and dominated by bishops, electors and kings. In 1949, Bonn became the provisional capital of the Federal Republic – an eventual reestablishment of the government in Berlin was planned. Konrad Adenauer lived in nearby Rhöndorf, so the "temporary" solution suited him perfectly. When the return to Berlin was cancelled, vast government office buildings were constructed along the Adenauer Allee. The Federal President

Berlin. Kurfürstendamm and the Kaiser-Wilhelm-Gedächtniskirche

resides in the Villa Hammerschmidt and the Chancellor in the Palais Schaumburg. *Beethovenhaus* is in Bonngasse in the lovely *Altstadt* (Old Town). Ludwig van Beethoven was born here in 1770. Museum. There is a festival of his work every third year in the enormous Beethovenhalle convention centre and concert house. The stately 18th-cent. town hall and Romanesque cathedral (11th-13th cent.) are on *Marktplatz.* Two German kings were crowned in the cathedral. The university was originally the residence of the electors. *Poppelsdorfer Schloss,* built in the French Baroque style, is set in a botanical garden. *Rheinisches Landesmuseum.* The skull of the Neanderthal Man is on display in the archaeology section. Zoological research institute and Alexander Koenig museum. Splendid

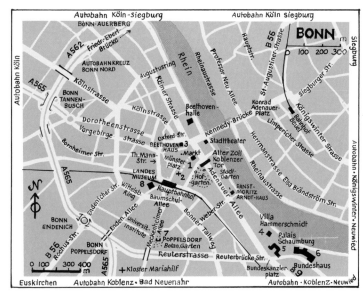

1 Town hall. 2 Cathedral. 3 Beethovenhaus. 4 Residence of the Federal President. 5 Residence of the Federal Chancellor. 6 Parliament Building. 7 Poppersdorfer Schloss. Botanical gardens. 8 Landesmuseum.

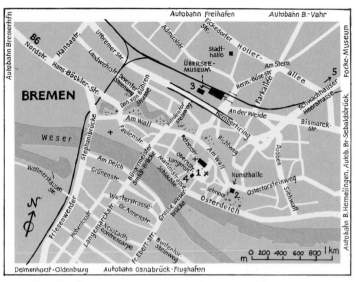

1 Markt with cathedral, town hall and Schütting. 2 Art gallery.
3 Überseemuseum. 4 Böttcherstrasse. 5 Focke-Museum.

Harbour. Sightseeing tours by boat from Martine-Kirche.

Neues Wahr, a new section of the city, is the site of the Berliner Freiheit shopping centre.

Vegesack where you can watch the harbour traffic from the Utkiek am alten Hafen.

DÜSSELDORF (620 000. 9 million people live within a radius of 50 km). Capital of the State of North Rhine-Westphalia. The little fishing village (dorf = village) on the Düssel has become one of the most important industrial cities in Germany. Many concerns have their headquarters here. Their skyscrapers dominate the skyline: the Mannesmann-Haus, the 98 m high Thyssen-Haus. The tallest is the LVA (insurance) building, 125 m. In contrast, the houses in the *Altstadt* (Old Town) are beautiful. Düsseldorf's Altstadt is one of the most concentrated amusement centres in the country. This is where rivers of the city's speciality, the rich Altbier, flow. The carnival begins here on November 11 (Düsseldorf, Cologne and Mainz are the major carnival cities of Germany.) It starts again at the beginning of January. Heinrich Heine was born at Bolkerstrasse No 53 in 1797. A statue of the popular elector, Johann Wilhelm II, often called simply *Jan Wellem*, is in front of the old town hall on the Markt. Annual torchlight procession of children to the statue on November 10.

"*Kö*", the popular name for Königs-

views from the Rheinpromenade, Venusberg and Alter Zoll. Many embassies are situated in the elegant **Bad Godesberg** district of the city.

BREMEN (560 000)

Charlemagne created the Bishopric of Bremen in 787. Major Hanseatic town and the second largest port (including Bremerhaven) in Germany. Bremen has long been an important centre for wool, coffee, fruit, wine and tobacco imports. Industries flourished after the start of direct trade with the U.S.A. in 1783. The Überseehafen is almost 2 km long. Large industries, shipping, university.

Picturesque area around the **Markt** in the Altstadt (Old Town). The square is dominated by the *town hall* (1409), which has a Renaissance façade from 1612. Splendid banqueting Hall. 600 German wines are available in the vaults (1409) of the *Ratskeller*. The town hall is in the vicinity of the *cathedral* and the 13th-cent. *Liebfrauenkirche*. Construction of St. Petri Cathedral began in 1042. There are nine mummies in the lead cellar. One of the corpses is of a roofer who tumbled to his death from the cathedral's roof in 1450. Schütting (1538), the merchants' old guildhall, is now the site of the Chamber of Commerce. The 4.2 m high statue of *Roland* (1404), on the Markt, is the symbol of the city's independence. On the west side are the Bremer Stadtmusikanten (the Brothers Grimm's Bremen Town Musicians), with a cock, a cat and an ass, standing atop each other. The narrow **Böttercherstrasse**, an old artisans' street that leads from the Marktplatz, was remodelled in 1930. Interesting atmosphere and shops. Roseliushaus from 1588. **Schnoorviertel,** a lovely and lively part of Bremen, filled with

shops, artists, artisans' workshops and restaurants, Renovated 17th- and 18th-cent. houses.

Überseemuseum with aquarium and terrarium. *Focke-Museum* (art, cultural history, and maritime history). Rhododendron Park and botanical gardens. Daringly modern Stadthalle with places for an audience of 6 500.

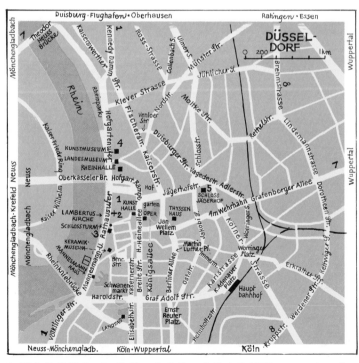

1 Altstadt. 2 St. Lambert's Church. 3 Town hall. 4 Exhibition grounds and museums. 5 Jägerhof.

allée, is one of the most elegant streets in Germany. 1 km long, 82 m wide and with the Stadtgraben in the centre (swans, chestnut and plane trees). The elegant shops bear evidence that Düsseldorf is the centre of German fashion industry. The Rhine bridges are also elegant. One of them, the *Kniebrücke,* rests on 130 m high pylons.

The Academy of Art was opened in 1787, the university in 1965. Opera house and theatres. During the 19th cent., a group of artists formed the Düsseldorf School.

Schlossturm remains of a castle that was destroyed by fire in 1872. The Ratinger Tor (1812), at the entrance to the *Hofgarten,* and *Jägerhof Castle* (18th cent.), museum with art (Paul Klee, etc.) and Meissen porcelain. Art museum in Ehrenhof, Hejens-Museum (ceramics), Löbbecke-Museum in the Benrath Palace (1768). Miniature city Minidomm. The Rhein Stadium in the fair grounds accommodates 70 000 spectators.

FRANKFURT/M (680 000)

In Frankfurt am Main the visitor comes face to face with the "German Miracle", the impressive post-war prosperity that replaced wartime destruction. Frankfurt's beautiful half-timbered Old Town escaped destruction up until March 22, 1944, when 100 English bombers flattened the city in a mere 40 minutes. From the ruins has risen a skyline of skyscrapers, housing industrial concerns, banking offices, and insurance companies. Frankfurt is the commercial capital of West Germany and its airport is the most important in the country. The centre is the Altstadt (Old Town) with *Hauptwache* (1730), a lovely little guard's house and *Römer,* the old town hall with three medieval gables. Coronations were held in the Kaisersaal. The *cathedral* (14th cent.) was the coronation church from 1562 until 1809, but as early as 1152 Frederick Barbarossa was crowned king here in Frankfurt. *Goethehaus,* where Johann Wolfgang von Goethe was born on August 28, 1749. He lived here during his childhood and from 1772 until 1775. The house was totally demolished during the war but has been restored. Original 18th-cent. furnishings. The *Goethe-Museum* is in the house next door.

Numerous beautiful churches. **Städelsches Kunstinstitut** has a large collection of paintings by 16th-cent. Dutch and German masters. *Liebighaus* with antique, medieval, Renaissance, Baroque and Asian sculpture. The collection includes a stone madonna by Riemenschneider. *Bundespostmuseum.* Botanical gardens with Palmengarten. *Zoo.*

Enormous *exhibition halls* where every autumn, a large international book fair is held. Frankfurt is the West German centre of printing and publishing.

The *Sachsenhausen* section of the city, south of the Main, is famous for its wine taverns serving Appelwoi, apple wine.

HAMBURG (1.8 million)

Hamburg is the second largest city in the German Federal Republic. (West Berlin has the largest population.) It was founded in 811 by Charlemagne. Important Hanseatic city. Largest harbour in West Germany. Heavy industries, shipyards, shipping companies. University and colleges. Modern opera house.

A severe fire and heavy wartime damage during the period 1943-1945, when 55 000 inhabitants were killed, have left few traces of the old Hamburg. No Altstadt (Old Town) remains. Instead there are stately buildings grouped about the lakes. *Binnenalster* with *Ballindamm* and *Jungfernstieg,* two elegant streets. The famous Alsterpavillion, a café-restaurant. *Aussenalster* with parks and sailing-boats.

The area south of the Alster Lakes is the heart of Hamburg. *Mönckebergstrasse,* the major shopping street, with department stores and pedestrian precincts, starts at the Hauptbahnhof and leads to the *Rathausmarkt* with a Renaissance town hall (1897). St. Petri Church has a 133 m high tower. *St. Michaelis* is the symbol of the city. This Baroque church was completed in 1762. Fine views from its 132 m high tower ("Michel"). Lift or a climb of 450 steps. In addition to the previously mentioned towers, the Hamburg skyline is also graced by the towers of St. Jakobi, 124 m, St. Katharinen, 112 m (the same height as the town hall tower), and St. Nikolai, 147 m and the third highest in Ger-

1 *Römer.*
2 *Hauptwache.*
3 *Goethehaus.*
4 *Exhibition and festival halls.*
5 *Naturmuseum Senckenberg.*
6 *Museum of History.*
7 *Arts and crafts Museum.*
8 *Ethnographical Museum.*
9 *Post Museum.*
10 *Art gallery.*
11 *Liebighaus (art museum).*

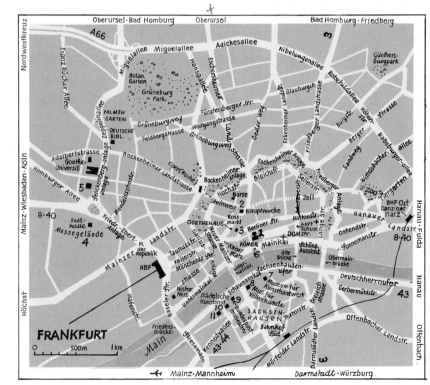

FRANKFURT

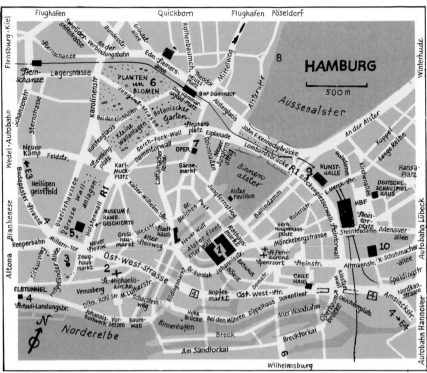

1 Town hall.
2 St. Michaelis Church.
3 Bismarck Monument.
4 Tours of the harbour.
5 Museum für Hamburgische Geschichte (Museum of Hamburg History).
6 Planten un Blomen. Congress centre. Exhibition grounds. Botanical gardens.
7 Opera house.
8 Tours on the Alster.
9 Art Gallery.
10 Museum of Arts and Crafts.
11 Hagenbeck Zoo.

many (only the cathedral towers of Ulm and Cologne are taller). Near by is the impressive Chilehaus office block, which resembles the prow of a ship, and the Sprinkenhof. Both buildings, by Fritz Häger, were built in the 1920s.

Hagenbeck Zoo with animals from all over the world. Dolphinarium and Troparium.

Planten un Blumen. Beautiful gardens, exhibition halls and restaurants. Near by is the "CCH", Hamburg's convention centre with enormous exhibition halls, used for the Hamburg Fair. The CP Hamburg Plaza Hotel is 118 m high. Planetarium in the Stadtpark.

St. Pauli. An amusement centre whose major streets are *Reeperbahn* and Grosse Freiheit (Great Freedom). The former sailors' pleasure centre has become extremely commercialized and vulgar. Countless night clubs, dance halls, beer halls, bars, sex-shows and hyperactive touts. Prostitution at the Eros Centre, and on Herbertstrasse. Germany's sole waxworks museum is in Reperbahn.

Altona has a few old houses left in the formerly uniform Palmaille street. The *Fish Market* in Altona, a 270-year-old institution, is well worth visiting on a Sunday morning.

Museums: *Museum für Kunst und Gewerbe* (handicrafts, ceramics, porcelain, examples of the "Jugend" style). *Kunsthalle* (art museum). *Museum für Hamburgische Geschichte* (the city's history, ships' models, model railways). Museum für Völkerkunde (archaeology and folk-

lore). Jenisch-Haus (urban middle-class interiors), *Altonaer Museum* (fishing, maritime history, ships' figure-heads, history, toys). Ernst-Barlach-Haus (sculpture, drawings), Hillers Automuseum. Three open-air museums: *Klekeberg* at Ehestorf (examples of peasant life on the Lüneburg Heath 300 years ago), Museumsdorf *Volksdorf, Vierländer Freilichtsmuseum* in Curslack (27 km to the south).

Pöseldorf, art, handicrafts, boutiques; a newly fashionable area of the city as is Eppendorf.

Planetarium in the Winterhude Stadtpark. Germany's only variety theatre is the Hansa-Varieté near the Hauptbahnhof (central railway station). Pop, rock and jazz in many famous places: Fabrik, Markthalle and Onkel Pö's Carnegie Hall. Sachenwald with boars and the Bismarck Museum.

There are three large railway stations: Hauptbahnhof, Dammtor and Altona (with motor-rail terminal and facilities). The *new Elbtunnel*, 3.3 km long under the Elbe, is a section of the E 3 (A 7). The large *Elbbrücken* east of the centre, handle the heavy E 4 (A 1) traffic. The *old Elbtunnel* which serves both pedestrians and motor traffic starts from the Landungsbrücke in the St. Pauli district. Motor vehicles must ascend and descend on special lifts. The beautiful *Köhlbrandsbrücke* is 4 km long, 53 m above the water, 130 m high pylons. It goes to the freeport, so do not have dutiable goods in your car.

KÖLN (Cologne, 990 000)
The city was founded by the Romans in about A.D. 50. The two beautifully formed round towers, which are still well preserved, were built at that time. The remainder of the town, created during the following 2 000 years, has, for the most part, vanished.

The **Kölnerdom,** one of the largest churches in Europe, has survived almost unscathed. The structure was started in 1282, but the cathedral was not consecrated until 1842. Construction was completely suspended from 1560 until 1842. The tower is 157 m high (500 steps). Rich ecclesiastical treasures and decorations. The shrine of the Three Holy Kings was brought from Milan in 1164, and has attracted pilgrims ever since. Their three crowns are included in Cologne's coat of arms. Organ concerts.

Römisch-Germanisches Museum has displays of Roman antiques, glass and a Roman tomb. The *Dionysos Mosaic,* 10 × 7 m, was a section of the floor of a 1st-cent. Roman banqueting hall, discovered in 1941. **Willraf-Richartz-Museum** has artwork from the Cologne School (14th-15th cent.) and modern art: "The Bridge at Arles" by van Gogh. **Schnütgen-Museum** in Cäcilienkirche displays medieval ecclesiastical art. Eigelstein-Tor with handicrafts. Deutsches Gesundheitsmuseum (museum of health).

Hohe Strasse, a shopping street, now free from motor traffic, still follows the same route as it did during the Roman era. Winding pedestrians-only streets pass through the *Altstadt* (Old Town), a 3 km semi-circle between the

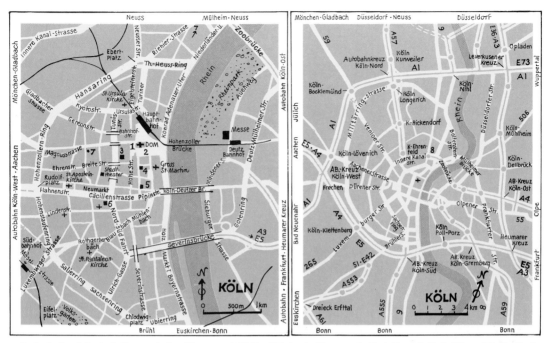

1 Cathedral. 2 Römisch-Germanisches Museum. 3 Wallraf-Richartz-Museum (art). 4 Town hall. 5 Gürzenich (festival hall). 6 Schnütgen Museum (religious art). 7 Römerturm. 8 Botanical gardens.

Rhine and the ring roads. Countless taverns where Kölsch, a mild, almost white beer, is served. Kölnisch Wasser, however, is only for external use. In 1709, Farina, an Italian, came to Cologne and started production of this "water from Cologne" (eau de Cologne), also known as 4711. The ring roads, outside the Altstadt, are large shopping streets. Further out is an additional ring road: the Gürtel.

Botanical garden. Zoo in a park. Cable car over the Rhine to the *Rheinpark* with Tanz Fountain.

Cologne is a major centre of transport. Heavy rail traffic at the Hauptbahnhof (central railway station) which has a glass façade facing the cathedral. Intensive river traffic on the Rhine and a flood of motor traffic on the motorways that encircle the city. These are the first of their type to be completed in Europe. The *carnival*, on the Thursday before Lent, is one of the largest and most popular in Germany.

LÜBECK (230 000)
Founded in 1143. One of the most important Hanseatic towns. Partially well- preserved streets and buildings from that period. **Holstentor** (1477) to the west, and *Burgtor*, to the north, both lead into the heart of the city, which is surrounded by water. Holstenstrasse, a shopping street, goes to the *Rathaus* (13th-15th cent.), the most elegant in Germany. Imposing halls and an exquisite external staircase facing the Breite Strasse, the major street in the city. Splendid vaults in the old *Ratskeller* restaurant.

The *Haus der Schiffergesellschaft*, a lovely house with stepped gables, contains a restaurant (1535). The interior has not been much altered since seafarers met here before voyages to Visby, Bergen or Novgorod. Ships' models hang from the ceiling, display of silver treasures at the entrance. The *Schabbelhaus* is another famous inn.

Marienkirche (1350) with altar from 1518. The Buxtehude Organ. The composer Buxtehude (1637-1707) was organist in this church. Bronze baptismal font from 1137. The church was consecrated in 1173 by Henry the Lion. Triumphal cross by Bernt Notke. *Heiligen-Geist-Hospital* (1280) is one of the world's oldest homes for old people.

St. Annen-Museum (1515) was once an abbey. Sculpture and paintings from

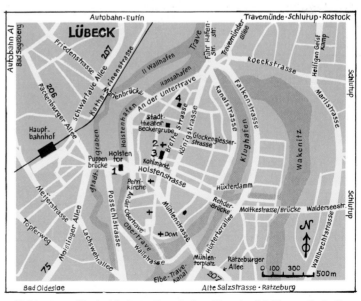

1 Holstentor. 2 Marienkirche. 3 Town hall. 4 Haus der Schiffergesellschaft. 5 St. Annen-Museum (religious art).

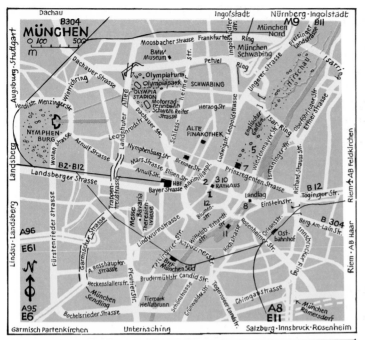

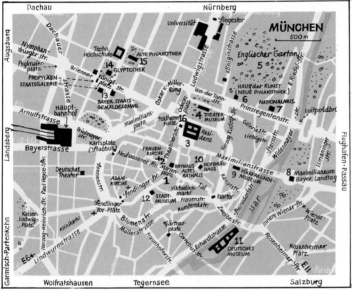

1 *Marienplatz* with town hall. 2 *Frauenkirche (cathedral)*. 3 *Residenz*.
4 *Theatre Museum*. 5 *Englischer Garten*. 6 *Neue Pinakothek*. 7 *National
Museum*. 8 *Bavarian State Parliament*. 9 *Ethnographical Museum*. 10 *Hofbräuhaus*. 11 *Deutsches Museum*. 12 *City Museum*. 13 *Art museums*.
14 *Glyptothek*. 15 *Alte Pinakothek*. 16 *Feldherrnhalle*. 17 *Nymphenburg*.

activity. Its university is the largest in Germany. Numerous museums, art galleries and drama and music festivals. 30 theatres, a symphony orchestra and the Bavarian State Opera.

The centre of the city is the **Marienplatz,** where the major streets meet. For the most part, this is a pedestrian precinct and motor traffic travels on the ring roads which follow the old fortification walls that encircle the city centre. *Neues Rathaus* (1908) with carillon on the north side of the square. *Peterskirche* with the Alter Peter tower is on the south side. On the east side is the *Altes Rathaus* (15th cent.). The street passes under the vault of the house, and here stands a little statue of Juliet, donated by the citizens of Verona, Munich's sister city. Above the houses rises the symbol of Munich, the copper cupolas that top the two towers of the Frauenkirche.

The lively (even in the evenings) traffic-free Kaufinger Strasse and Neuhauser Strasse lead west to Karlstor and *Karlsplatz* (Stachus). The Hauptbahnhof (central railway station) is slightly beyond the square. Sendlinger Strasse goes south-west from Marienplatz to Sendlinger Tor. *Viktualienmarkt* with colourful open-air food market. Alpinists and other sports enthusiasts will delight in the famous Sporthaus-Schuster. Tal goes to the Isartor (1314). Weinstrasse and Theatinerstrasse go north to *Odeonsplatz* which bears the stamp of Ludwig I's grand 19th-cent. city planning principles. The Baroque *Theatinerkirche* has a 71 m high dome. *Feldherrnhalle*, patterned after the Loggia dei Lanzi in Florence, contains portraits of great warriors. At the far right is Tilly, hero of the Thirty Years' War. The long Ludwigstrasse goes north through the *Siegestor* towards Nürnberg. The university was founded in 1472 in Ingolstadt. It was moved in 1800 to Landshut, and in 1826 to Munich. Ludwigstrasse goes to **Schwabing,** a lively section of the city, popular with artists and students. Shops, restaurants, night clubs, etc. To the west of Odeonsplatz lies Königsplatz with the *Propyläen* (1862), a magnificent gate in pseudo-antique style, as is the *Glyptothek*.

Asamkirche is the highpoint of the work of the Asam brothers. This Baroque church (1733) was built next to their home. Museums: The Bavarian State's art collection is in the **Alte Pinakothek** (one of the world's largest art museums). Haus der Kunst and Schackgalerie. The Bavarian National Museum (art and handicrafts, furniture, carpets, porcelain). Opposite is the *Neue Pinakothek*, a modern mass of concrete and steel with displays of 20th-cent. art. *Glyptothek* (museum of antiques). Ethnographical museum. *Residenz* with interesting interiors, furniture, porcelain. Treasury with world-famous gold and silver masterpieces. Rococo Cuvilliés Theatre. Lenbach-Haus with the works of Munich pain-

the city's past. The Memling Altar (1491) was rescued from the cathedral in 1942. Museum of Lübeck history in Holstentor. Bahnhaus (1783) with native art. *Buddenbrockhaus*, made famous by Thomas Mann's novel, is a reconstruction.

Lübeck is a lively port and industrial city. It is world-famous for its

Niederegger marzipan which can be bought in their excellent pastry shop near the town hall.

MÜNCHEN (Munich, 1.3 million) Capital of Bavaria, Germany's third largest city, founded in 1158. A lively and merry city distinguished by splendid buildings, art and cultural ters. *City museum* (city history, photography, film, musical instruments and puppetry).

Nymphenburg. Delightful summer palace of the Kings of Bavaria (17th-18th cent.). Ludwig I's portrait gallery in the main building with portraits of Munich ladies. It was for these beauties that the palace was named. Splendid park. The state-owned porcelain factory was founded in 1747. *Marstallmuseum* with carriages, coaches and Ludwig II's sleigh. The park is extremely lovely. *Amalienburg* Hunting Palace (1739) and other pavilions. Botanical gardens. **Deutsches Museum** (under construction from 1906 until 1935): science and technology, the world's largest technical museum. Examples of motor cars, steam locomotives, mines, water wheels, space ships, submarines, alchemists' workshops, oil rigs and Galileo's work room. If you cannot spend at least a week, and investigate all the exhibits, it is probably best to concentrate on just a couple of the sections.

The *Englischer Garten*, beautiful park with *Chinese tower* (at Theresienwiese), a symbol of the land, is a 30 m high female figure. Fine views from her head. Maximilianeum (1874), seat of the Bavarian parliament. *Hellabrunn Zoo. Schleissheim Palace* (1777), 330 m long. Magnificent interiors containing art collections. *Olympia Stadium*, with unique "tent roof", built for the Olympic Games of 1972, and the Olympia tower with rotating restaurant at a height of 100 m. Near by is the elegant BMW skyscraper (BMW = Bayrische Motoren Werke = the Bavarian Motor Works).

The carnivals and beer of Munich are world famous. The *Fasching*, at the start of the year, is a 600-year-old tradition: masquerades and carnivals. When it ends, participants seek solace in Starkbier, a strong beer with names that end in "-ator", e.g. "Salvator". As early as September, celebrants begin the *Oktoberfest* in enormous beer tents and in the Theresienwiese amusement grounds. It is celebrated in memory of the 1810 wedding of the Crown Prince. But beer flows the year round in Munich's mammoth beer halls. The biggest in the world is *Mathäser* near Stachus. The most famous is the **Hofbräuhaus,** originally from 1589. In the huge vaults on the ground floor (Schwemme), earsplitting sing-alongs and Bavarian bands. It is a bit quieter on the upper floor. Traditionally, white sausage (Weisswurst) or Leberkäs, accompany the beer. The shady garden is also worth seeing.

Biergärten (beer gardens), often enormous, can be found all over the city.

It was in the Hofbräuhaus that Hitler proclaimed the establishment of the Nazi party (1920). His 1923 putsch failed. In 1938, Hitler, Mussolini, Chamberlain and Daladier, signed the Munich Pact, when Czechoslovakia was sacrificed for "peace in our time".

Marienplatz in Munich

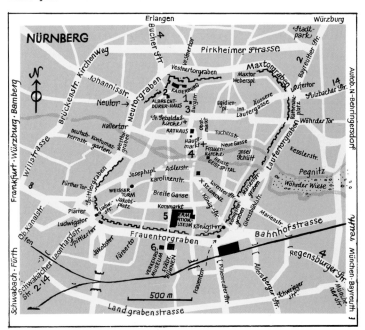

1 *Kaiserburg (castle).* 2 *Albrecht Dürer-Haus.* 3 *Fembohaus.* 4 *Hauptmarkt. Frauenkirche. Town hall. Schöner Brunnen.* 5 *Germanisches Nationalmuseum.* 6 *Verkehrsmuseum (traffic museum).*

1 *Altes Schloss (the Old Castle).*
2 *Neues Schloss (the New Castle).*
3 *Town hall.*
4 *Landesmuseum.*
5 *Television tower.*
6 *Daimler-Benz Motor Museum.*

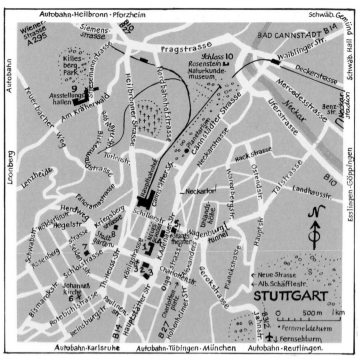

NÜRNBERG (490 000)

The best-preserved medieval city in Germany was reduced to ruins during the Second World War. But the surviving buildings and the reconstruction work have contributed to at least a partial retention of Nürnberg's unique atmosphere. The stout town wall (1452) with 128 towers is well preserved. It includes the 12th-cent. Kaiserburg. Mighty tower and Pfalzkapelle.

Altstadt (Old Town) with winding streets near the *Hauptmarkt,* which is dominated by the eccentric gable of the Frauenkirche (1335). Every day at 12 o'clock, the "Männleinlauten" figures appear on the church's silhouette. They depict six electors who praise the emperor, Charles IV. *Schöner Brunnen* (the Beautiful Fountain) in the Hauptmarkt is octagonal, 19 m high and adorned with 40 biblical figures. Several other beautiful fountains in the city.

Splendid view from Maxbrücke, which spans the River Pegnitz. Lovely half-timbered houses and Wasserturm. *Dürerhaus,* a beautiful half-timbered house, where Albrecht Dürer lived from 1509 until his death in 1528. It has been furnished as an example of a typical medieval dwelling. Waffenhof is an artisans' area with old workshops: goldsmithing, wrought iron work, basket weaving, doll making, watch making, and bakeries. *Sebalduskirche* (1379). Tomb of Sebaldus by Peter Fischer and sculptures by Veit Stoss (16th cent.). *Lorenzkirche* with Engelsgruss by Veit Stoss.

Germanisches Nationalmuseum with 100 rooms filled with paintings

Christmas fair in Nürnberg

and works of art from different periods. Many works by Albrecht Dürer. *Fembohaus,* the city museum, display period house furnishings (16th-19th cent.).

Verkehrsmuseum, a splendid railway and post museum with a myriad of exhibits. Large model railway. Reconstruction of the first German railway (1835) that ran between Nürnberg and Fürth. Copy of the Adler, Germany's first locomotive. Toy museum. Nürnberg has always been a toy manufacturing centre.

Two of Nürnberg's culinary specialities are Lebkuchen, a gingerbread cake, and Nürnberger Bratwurst. This famous white sausage is served in special eating places. The city has always had a rich cultural life. During the 15th and 16th cent., it was one of the cultural centres of Europe. *Meistersingerhalle* brings to mind the flourishing Nürnberg music and poetry guilds of that period.

The name, Nürnberg, is also associated with the enormous Nazi party gatherings that took place in the city. The Nürnberg Laws of 1935, restricting the freedom of Jews, were an introduction to the holocaust. The 1945-1946 Nürnberg Trials against Nazi war criminals.

STUTTGART (600 000).

Capital of Baden-Württemberg. Originally the site of a stud farm ("Stuttgarten"), established in 950. Now it is a large and modern industrial city with over 160 publishing houses. Lovely surroundings: vineyard slopes come down to just a couple of hundred metres from the central railway sta-

tion *Marktplatz* with modern town hall, restored in 1958. 68 m high tower with carillon. A statue of the poet Schiller is in *Schillerplatz,* centre of the Altstadt (Old Town). The abbey church originally dates from the 12th cent. *Altes Schloss,* reconstructed in the 16th cent., now contains *Württembergisches Landesmuseum* with archaeological finds, medieval art, handicrafts, musical instruments and watches. Neues Schloss (1807) contains administrative offices and halls for official receptions. The *castle gardens* extend 3 km to the banks of the Neckar. Famous opera house, city theatre, ballet and chamber orchestra. Stuttgarter Liedenhalle, a concert hall, was opened in 1956. *Linden Museum* of Ethnology, Zoological-Botanical Gardens Wilhelma. *Solitude Palace* (1769) has a large dome. Natural history museum in *Rosenstein Castle.* TV tower, 217 m high. The observation terrace (with restaurant) is 150 m high, but the visitor is 400 m above Stuttgart's centre. The *Weissenhof* complex was completed in 1927. Le Corbusier and Walter Gropius worked here.

The *Bad Cannstatt* section of the city is a venerable spa with Kursaal and park. The Cannstätter Volksfest (Cannstatt Festival) is an extremely popular carnival. The *Daimler-Benz* factories, which produce Mercedes cars, are in Undertürkhem. *Motor car museum.* One section is devoted to racing cars. The engineers Gottlieb Daimler and Carl Benz worked separately in Stuttgart until their companies merged in 1926.

DDR · German Democratic Republic

DDR·Deutsche Demokratische Republik

Area: 108 333 km² (41 802 sq. miles)

Population: 17 million. The language is German. Sorbian is spoken in small areas in and near Cottbus and Dresden.

Major cities: Berlin, Hauptstadt der DDR, 1.1 million, Leipzig 563 000, Dresden 516 000.

Government: The GDR is a people's democracy. A People's Chamber is elected every five years with representatives from all political parties and from the trade unions. The Council of Ministers governs.

History
May 1945 Collapse of Nazi Germany. The Potsdam Conference's decision to form four zones of occupation.
July 1949 The Federal Republic of Germany is created.
October 1949 Founding of the German Democratic Republic.
1950 A treaty with Poland determines the Oder-Neisse border.
1955 Signing of the Warsaw Pact. Treaty with the Soviet Union.
1973 The GDR becomes a member of the United Nations.

Currency: Mark der DDR (DDM).
1 Mark = 100 Pfenning
The import and export of banknotes and coins of the GDR is not permitted. Foreign currency must be declared. Currency declaration, exchange receipts and receipts for larger purchases must be saved and shown when leaving the country.
A certain amount of money must be changed even for one-day excursions to Berlin from West-Berlin. Visas are obligatory for visitors from non-Socialist countries. Special transit visas are issued for direct transit (or transit with one night in a hotel room booked in advance).
Please note: Many of the places described can only be visited by tourists with visas to the German Democratic Republic. Motorists with transit visas are restricted to the transit routes.
It is advisable to contact the local office of the Travel Representation of the German Democratic Republic before departure for information about the latest rules and regulations.
A special Road Users' Tax must be paid. The green insurance card should be brought along.

Business hours: Banks 8.00-11.30 a.m. Tuesdays and Thursdays also 2.30 – 5.30 pm. Closed Saturdays. Post offices 9.00 a.m.-6.00 p.m. Saturdays 9.00-11.00 a.m. or closed. Shops 10.00 a.m.-7.00 p.m. Small shops are often closed on Saturdays but department stores and some food shops are open.

Holidays: New Year's Day, Good Friday, Easter Sunday, May 1, Whit Sunday, Whit Monday, October 7, December 25 and 26.

Hotels
The largest chain is Interhotel with about 30 hotels in 14 cities. Rooms must be booked and paid for in advance. The hotel vouchers must be presented when applying for a visa.

Camping
Camping vouchers must be purchased in advance from your motoring organization, at road crossing points with service bureaus or on the car ferry. On presentation of camping vouchers a

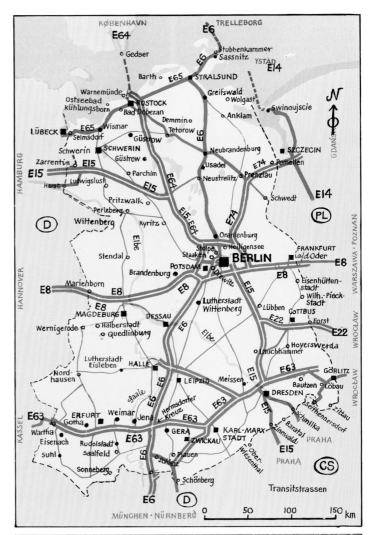

Routes described:

E 6 Sassnitz – Berlin – Leipzig – Hof

E 8 Frankfurt an der Oder – Berliner Ring – Magdeburg – Braunschweig

E 15 Hamburg – Berlin – Dresden – Praha

E 63 Görlitz – Dresden – Karl-Marx-Stadt – Eisenach

E 64 Warnemünde – Rostock – Berlin, see E 6

E 65 Stralsund – Rostock – Lübeck, see E 6

Town plans: Berlin, Dresden, Leipzig

View from Königstein

visa for the equivalent number of days is obtained and currency can be exchanged.

Youth hostels
Youth hostels are open only to youth groups and are not affiliated with the International Youth Hostel Organization.

Food and drink
East German cooking is very similar to West German cuisine. Sausages come in all shapes and forms, e.g. Thüringer Rostbratwurst mit Klös-sen (a kind of dumpling). Halber-städter Würtchen is another variety. Entenbraten (roast duck) mit grünen Klössen. Eisbein mit Sauerkraut (knuckle of pork with pickled cabbage). Radeberger is the best-known East German beer. Czech beer is often served. A Berlin speciality is Weisse mit Schuss, a light beer to which black currant or raspberry syrup has been added. It is served in a large bowl-shaped glass.

Shopping
Porcelain from Meissen – although it may be difficult to obtain. Gramophone records, books, musical instruments, printed music, chess sets, art reproductions.

Petrol
Petrol coupons should be bought in advance. However, the Intertank petrol stations also accept payment in foreign currency.

Speed limits. Traffic regulations
Motorways 100 kmh, other roads 80 kmh, built-up areas 50 kmh. Certain "Schnellstrassen" 60 kmh. Speed limits should of course be adhered to in all countries, but it should be pointed out that traffic supervision is most meticulous in East Germany.
Children under the age of seven are not allowed to travel in the front seat. If your car is fitted with seat belts it is compulsory to wear them.
It is compulsory for all motorists to carry a spare set of light bulbs, a first-aid kit and a fire extinguisher.

Roads
Be careful when reading the direction signs, especially if you have a transit visa. Motorists heading for West Berlin must follow signs reading "Transit", not "Berlin, Hauptstadt der DDR".

Road patrols
Signs along the motorways contain information about emergency telephones. Police stations and petrol stations offer assistance.

Emergency telephones: police 110, ambulance 115.
Berolina Travel Ltd, 20 Conduit Street, London W1R 9TD. Tel. 01-629 1664.

A beach on the Baltic coast

E 6. Sassnitz – Berlin – Leipzig – Hof

Sassnitz. E 6 comes from northern Norway by way of Trondheim – Oslo – Göteborg – Malmö – Trelleborg. Large goods traffic by train and car ferry (five times daily) from Trelleborg in Sweden. Fishing port. Enormous chalk cliffs. On the island of *Rügen* are several seaside resorts, e.g. *Binz* and *Sellin. Bergen* with Marienkirche, founded in 1180 by the Danish king, Valdemar I. *Granitz.* Hunting castle with the *Rügen Museum.*

STRALSUND (68 000). One of the most important Hanseatic towns. During most of the period 1648-1815 the town belonged to Sweden. The Gothic *Marienkirche* (14th-15th cent.) has a 108 m high tower. *Alter Markt* (the Old Square) is very beautiful. Town hall with stately brick façade (15th cent.). Beautiful old churches. Museum of oceanography. Museum of cultural history in St. Katharinen Dominican abbey. Nikolaikirche with art treasures

GREIFSWALD (50 000). Hanseatic town. Beautiful, old patrician houses in the *Altstadt* (Old Town) and fishermen's houses in the village of *Wieck.* Famous university, founded in 1456, with Baroque buildings from 1750. Remains of the town wall. Folklore museum in the former Franciscan abbey. Paintings by C.D. Friedrich, born 1774 in Greifswald. Room dedicated to E.M. Arndt, the German poet and historian who lived here. *Eldena,* ruins of an abbey, founded in 1199. Long red-brick town hall.

Neubrandenburg (50 000). Founded in 1248. Beautiful centre which was razed during the war. Partially reconstructed. Remains of the medieval city wall stretching over a distance of 2300 metres. Stargarder, Friedländer, Treptower Tor and Neues Tor, town gates built in the 14th-15th cent.

Neustrelitz (30 000). Town hall from 1841. Fine gardens with "Orangerie".

Fürstenberg. Baroque château (1752). During the war there was a concentration camp at Ravensbrück, where over 90 000 perished. *Himmelpfort* with a Gothic abbey in red brick. *Zehdenick,* formerly a convent.

Oranienburg, 18th-cent. château. Baroque portal at the entrance to the park. Memorial on the site of the concentration camp of *Sachsenhausen.*

Watch out for the direction signs. Motorists with transit visas for West Berlin must take the road marked Transit. To enter East Berlin it is necessary to have a visa to the German Democratic Republic. Tourists with such visas should follow signs reading "Berlin, Hauptstadt der DDR".

E 64. Warnemünde – Rostock – Berlin

E 64 goes from København (Copenhagen) to Gedser. Train and car ferries to Warnemünde. The E 65 Stralsund – Rostock and E 64 to Berlin is a faster route to E 6.

Warnemünde and *Kühlungsborn,* large seaside resorts. Baroque church.

ROSTOCK (200 000). The town was founded in 1265. University from 1419. Industries, large harbour and shipyards. The *town hall* has a yellow and white Baroque façade and seven small towers. Beautiful gabled houses on Ernst-Thälmann-Platz. *Lange Strasse* is a wide, modern shopping street. Remains of the city wall with the 54 m high *Kröpeliner Tor,* now the city museum. The Gothic *St. Peter's Church* used to be a landmark for seafarers. *Marine museum.* In July the Ostseewoche (Baltic Week) is celebrated. Zoo and botanical gardens.

Güstrow. Construction work on the *cathedral* started in 1206. Large altar and 16th-cent. sculptures of the apostles. Beautiful woodcarvings also in St. Martin's Church. Large *Renaissance palace,* now a cultural centre. Ernst Barlach, the sculptor and poet, worked in Güstrov 1910-1938. His works can be seen in his old studio and in Gertrudenkirche.

Wittstock. Ruined castle with folklore museum.

Rheinsberg with the palace of Frederick the Great (1734).

Potsdam, see E 8.

E 65. Stralsund – Rostock – Lübeck

STRALSUND, see E 6. *Barth,* Gothic church. Dammtor (15th cent.), remains of fortifications. *Ribnitz-Dammgarten.* 19th-cent. town hall. Abbey with folklore museum.

ROSTOCK, see E 64. *Bad Doberan.* Gothic abbey church (13th cent.). *Kühlungsborn,* large seaside resort. *Rerik* on a narrow peninsula. 13th-cent. church with Baroque interior.

WISMAR (56 000), see general map. Beautiful *Marktplatz* with 17th-cent. town hall and old fountain. *Nikolaikirche* (14th-15th cent.). Old Hanseatic town, which became a Danish possession in 1511 and belonged to Sweden from 1648 until 1803 (formally until 1903).

Schabbelthaus (1571) with folklore museum.

Selmsdorf. West German border. E 65 continues to Lübeck.

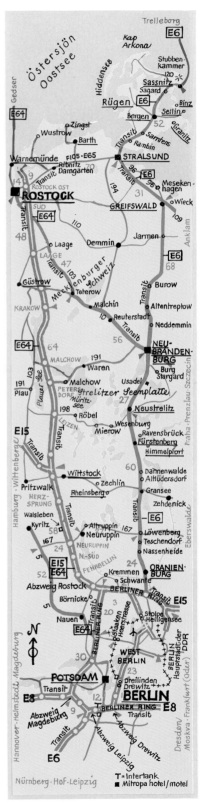

BERLIN, see town plans. Motorists with transit visas leave West Berlin by way of the Avus, one of the first German motorways, once used for motor races. Frontier crossing point at Zehlendorf. Figures on signs often indicate number of kilometres to the motorway ring around Berlin.

WITTENBERG (50 000). It was here, in 1517, that Martin Luther nailed his 95 theses to the door of the Castle Church. This marked the beginning of the Reformation. Luther's residence in the *Augusteum* is open to visitors. Near by is an oak, which marks the place where he burned the papal bull. The *Castle Church* was destroyed in 1760 during the Seven Years' War and was rebuilt in the neo-Gothic style in the 19th cent. Tombs of Luther and Melanchton. Their statues at the 16th-cent. town hall. *Melanchton-Haus* where the humanist lived, is now a museum. *Marienkirche* on Marktplatz. Baptismal font by the Nurenberg master, Vischer, and altarpiece by Lucas Cranach the Elder.

Wörlitz. Castle (1773) and very large park. Temples of Vesta and Venus, amphitheatre – all built at the end of the 18th cent. Art collection in Gotisches Haus (1810).

DESSAU (100 000) was founded in the 12th-cent. by immigrants from Flanders. Industrial town. Marienkirche (1526) is now in ruins. The altar (1565), by Lucas Cranach the Younger, is now in the church at Pötnitz. The Georgium castle, with a collection of art, was built to the plans of Dessau architect Erdmannsdorf, who also designed the little castle in Luisium and the palace in Wörlitz. Bauhaus, the world-famous art school, was situated in Dessau during the years 1925–33, under the leader-ship of W. Gropius (Before this school was in Weimar). The style of architecture, crafts and art brought forth at the Bauhaus marked the beginnings of functionalism. *Bernburg* with an imposing castle. Roter Turm from the 12th cent. Marienkirche.

HALLE (260 000) was known as a trading centre in the 9th cent. The university was founded in 1694. In 1520 a bishopric was founded in opposition to the Lutheran Wittenberg and a Dominican church was elevated to *cathedral* (1520). Händel, born in Halle in 1685, was organist here. Impressive *Marktplatz* with medieval houses, Roter Turm (15th cent.) and *Marktkirche,* where Luther preached. It is the symbol of the city. Its appearance – it has four towers – is due to the fact that the church is made up of two churches, joined into one in the 14th cent. *Moritzkirche* (about 1400), decorated by the sculptor, Konrad of Einbeck, who has left his self-portrait in the form of one of the figures in the choir. In *Moritzburg* (1503), the archbishop's palace, is an art gallery. Annual festival in memory of George Friedrich Händel, who was born here in 1685. The house in Nikolaistrasse where he was born, is now a museum. Halle is the centre of an industrial area with mostly chemical industries. Large lignite deposits.

Road 80 west to *Eisleben.* Old mountain town. Museum in the house where Martin Luther was born (1483) and died (1546). There is a statue of him in front of the town hall in the Old Town. *Annenkirche.* In the choir is the Eislebener Steinbilder Bible (1585) with scenes from the Bible.

Merseburg. One-thousand-year-old town with old churches. Castle with summer festivals.

LEIPZIG, see town plans.

Naumburg (38 000). Town privileges in 1030. Remains of city fortifications. Beautiful houses on *Marktplatz.* Impressive 16th-cent. town hall. *Peter-Pauls-Dom* with four towers and famous sculptures by an unknown master. The watchman still has his home high up in the tower of the 15th-cent. St. Wenzel-Kirche. Dornburg with three castles. Goethe once lived in one of them – his room has been preserved.

GERA and **JENA,** see E 63.

PLAUEN (80 000) is famous for its lace. Town as early as the 11th cent. Textile industries and tanneries. Dutch weavers, Protestants seeking refuge, came here in the 16th cent.

The Autobahn continues through the *Schleizer Seenplatte* lake district, with artificial lakes, and across the *Saale.* The motorway bridge was destroyed in the war and was not reopened until 1966.

West German border at *Hirschberg.* E 6 continues to Nürnberg – München – Innsbruck – Verona – Bologna – Firenze – Roma.

E 8. Frankfurt an der Oder – Berliner Ring – Magdeburg – Braunschweig

Polish frontier. E 8 comes from Brest – Warszawa – Poznan.

FRANKFURT (Oder) (60 000). Industrial town. Gothic *town hall* with richly ornamented southern façade. The 16th-cent. Marienkirche was almost totally destroyed in 1945. Two beautiful sandstone portals remain, as does a bronze baptismal font. Friedenskirche – construction started in 1230.

A road goes south to *Eisenhüttenstadt* (45 000), a completely new, post-war town.

Berliner Ring. The southern part of the motorway ring around Berlin. Transit visa to West Berlin entitles the motorist to entry at the Drewitz/ Dreilinden check-point. Transit visa does not give access to *Berlin, Hauptstadt der DDR* (East Berlin).

BERLIN see town plans.

POTSDAM (120 000) Sans-Souci Castle (1747) was built by von Knobelsdorff in the rococo style to the designs of Frederick the Great. He also designed the *Marmorpalais* (the Marble Palace) in Neuer Garten, now a military museum. *Neues Palais* was built in 1769. Chinese teahouse with porcelain. Art gallery with Flemish and Italian Baroque art. *Charlottenburg Castle* was built in 1829 by Schinkel. *Kolonie Alexandrowka* with a Greek-Orthodox chapel and blockhouse, built in 1829 for Russian military musicians. *Cecilienhof Castle,* where the Potsdam Conference between the victorious powers was held in 1945.

BRANDENBURG (95 000) was founded in 948 by Otto the Great. Altstadt (Old Town) with Dominsel, an island in the River Havel. The *Cathedral of St. Peter and Paul* was begun in 1165. Late-Gothic town hall (16th cent.). Fine red-brick *Katharinenkirche* with an impressive High Altar from 1474. Two city gates from the 15th cent.

NW to *Jerichow* with a Romanesque abbey church from 1148.

MAGDEBURG (270 000). Mentioned 805, town 937. Severely damaged during the war. Industrial town and the largest inland port in the GDR. The cathedral, *St. Mauritius und Katharina* (13th cent.) was the first Gothic cathedral to be built in Germany. Famous sculptures and several tombs from the same period. The oldest parts of the Abbey of Our Lady are from the 11th cent. In the *Museum of Cultural History* is the *Magdeburger Reiter* (1240). A copy of the statue is in front of the Baroque town hall.

Marienborn. West German border. E 8 continues to Braunschweig – Hannover – Utrecht – Hoek van Holland – London.

From Magdeburg road 189 goes north to *Stendal.* Once an important Hanseatic town. *Uenglinger Tor* is one of Germany's most beautiful city gates. *Markt* with an impressive town hall. Red-brick *cathedral* with fine stained-glass windows.

South to *Werningerode,* a charming little town with half-timbered houses, very similar to Goslar, its close neighbour. But the towns are far apart now, separated by the frontier. On the square is the half-timbered *town hall,* one of the most beautiful in Germany. Next to it is an historic inn, Hotel Gothisches Haus (1480).

Halberstadt (50 000). Bishopric 827. Gothic cathedral (13th cent.).

Quedlinburg. Old town with fine half-timbered houses. Town walls and 12 towers. Town hall (1615) with a Roland statue. Several fine churches. *Wipertikirche* with a crypt from 966. *Stiftskirche* (1129) with tombs of Heinrich I and Queen Mathilde (10th cent.). Very rich treasury. Castle (17th cent.). Finkenherd, a small half-timbered house. Klopstock-Museum (the poet Klopstock was born here in 1724).

E 15. Hamburg – Berlin – Dresden – Praha

West German border at **Lauenburg/Horst** and **Zarrentin** (motorway).

Ludwigslust. Baroque castle (1776) and beautiful park.

Road north to **SCHWERIN** (108 000). Palace (1875) with art museum and Baroque garden. Fine Gothic Cathedral. Open-air museum with half-timbered houses. **Neustadt-Giewe** with castle in Dutch Renaissance style. **Parchim.** Red-brick town hall and Church of St. Maria (14th cent.).

Perleberg with lovely old houses. Town hall, church and Roland statue in the square. **Bad Wilsnack.** Church of St. Nicholas (1430), a pilgrimage church. **Havelberg** with impressive 14th-cent. cathedral.

BERLIN, see town plans. **Potsdam,** see E 8.

Luckau with city wall. **Lübben.** Paul-Gerhardt-Kirche, late-Gothic red-brick church. **Lübbenau.** The centre of **Spreewald,** an area where rivers and canals run criss-cross and where you transport yourself in small punt-like boats, "Spreewaldkähne". Each boat takes 5-25 passengers and is propelled with long wooden poles. Excursions from Lübbenau. **Lehde,** a village with thatched houses and an open-air museum.

From Abzweig Lübbenau the E 22 motorway goes to **COTTBUS** (65 000). It was a textile-manufacturing town as early as the 16th cent. In 1817 the first steam spinning mill was established by a Belgian, named Cockrill. Beautiful **Altstadt** (Old Town) and city fortifications. Münzturm and Sprengberger Torturm. Lovely Baroque guildhouses. Franciscan abbey church (Wendische Kirche). The Wends, a West Slavic people, on the whole became extinct during the Middle Ages. The Swedish king, Gustav Vasa, proclaimed himself their king, in order to annoy the Danes. The Swedish kings were called King of the Wends until 1973.

Moritzburg Castle. Hunting castle from 1500, enlarged 1736 by Pöppelmann. Baroque museum with Saxon crafts. The **Fasanerie** miniature castle (13 m wide), was built in 1782. Museum (birds and bird protection).

Radebeul. Beautiful little wine château's from the 17th cent. Villa Shatterhand (18th cent.), where Karl May wrote his books about Indians. American Indian museum.

Meissen (45 000). The cathedral was founded in the 13th cent. and was adorned with famous stone figures. Electors and margraves resided here and built the enormous **Albrechtsburg Castle.** In 1710, the first European porcelain factory was established in the town. In 1863 the factory moved to a building of its own. There is a **porcelain museum** in Albrechtsburg and an exhibition hall in the Porzellanmanufaktur. The cathedral has a carillon made out of Meissen porcelain. A small, beautiful market-place. Vineyards in the Elbe valley.

DRESDEN, see town plans.

Route E 15 (120) meanders upwards with beautiful views back towards Dresden. **Erzgebirge** (Ore Mountain) is one of the Bohemian mountain ranges on the Czechoslovakian border. The highest peak is **Keilberg,** 1 244 m. To the east of Dresden is **Elbsandsteingebirge** with steep cliffs and gorges, among them the high **Bastei** cliff, 149 m. Fine rock climbing area. The fortress of **Königstein** (1241).

Bad Schandau. Spa. Lichtenhainer Waterfall, **Kuhstall,** Schrammenstein's cliff labyrinth. **Pirna** with beautiful **Altstadt** (Old Town). Marienkirche (1470) with a 12-sided Gothic choir.

Frauenstein. Birthplace of the famous organ-builder G. Silbermann. Folklore museum in the Renaissance castle (1588). Ruined castle.

Zinnwald. Czechoslovakian border. E 15 continues to Praha – Budapest – Bucureşti – Constanţa.

E 63. Görlitz – Dresden – Karl-Marx-Stadt – Eisenach – Bad Hersfeld.

GÖRLITZ (87 000). Beautiful town with Renaissance and Baroque houses. 16th-cent. town hall with outside staircase. The Neptune Fountain from 1756. Remains of the town wall.

To the south is *Zittau* with a beautiful town hall and Petri-Pauli- Kirche. Car factories. The spas of *Jonsdorf* and *Oybin*, old villages with half-timbered houses.

Reichenbach with a 15th-cent. church. *BAUTZEN* (45 000). The Gothic Cathedral of St. Peter and Ortenburg Castle. Cultural centre of the Sorbian area, where about 70 000 Sorbs live.

DRESDEN see town plans.

Meissen, see E 15.

Freiberg. Cathedral with a golden door from 1230. Beautiful pulpit and organ by Silbermann.

KARL-MARX-STADT (300 000). Large industrial city – tools and textile industry. It was formerly called Chemnitz. Beautiful *old town hall* (1498) in the Renaissance style. The Roter Turm, a fortified tower (16th cent.), is now a museum. The late-Gothic St. Maria abbey church. The *"Versteinerter Wald"* (Petrified Forest) with tree trunks that turned into silicon about 200 million years ago, is a unique sight. The major part of the city is modern. Palace of Culture. The puppet theatre is famous.
The 800-year-old *Rabenstein Castle. Rabensteiner Felsendome,* a limestone quarry formed like a rock castle. *Augustusburg Castle* (1573). Interesting interiors. Folklore museum and motorcycle museum. Castle chapel with works by Lucas Cranach the Younger (1571). *Forchheim.* Beautiful and original 18th-cent. church by Georg Bähr. Organ by Silbermann.

To the south lies the *Erzgebirge* (Ore Mountain) on the Czechoslovakian border. *Fichtelberg,* 1 214 m, is the highest mountain in East Germany. *Oberwiesenthal* is the largest winter resort in the country. Numerous small villages with woodcarvers and masters of other old crafts. *Annaberg-Buchholz.* The Gothic Annenkirche has a beautiful altar and baptismal font. *Schwarzenberg* with castle and fine church.

Route 62 continues to Zwickau and Plauen. No crossing-points to West Germany. *ZWICKAU* (127 000) has coal mines and industries. Katharinenkirche (13th cent.) with altarpiece by Lucas Cranach the Elder. Robert Schumann, the composer, was born in Zwickau.

PLAUEN, see E 6.

GERA (111 000). Industrial town. Stadtapotheke (town pharmacy), with bay windows, and other beautiful Baroque buildings.
Beautiful town hall. Marienkirche (12th cent.) with a carved altar. Trinitatskirche with an outside pulpit. Osterstein Castle with a museum dedicated to the workers' movement.

JENA (105 000). The famous university was founded in 1558. Goethe, Schiller, Fichte and Schelling all studied here. Johannistor, Roter Turm and Pulverturm are among the remains of the city wall. 14th-cent. town hall. The Zeiss Works, an optical factory, was founded here in 1846. Zeiss-Planetarium. Botanical gardens. Splendid views from Jenzig, a chalk cliff. *Thüringer Wald* is a beautiful, hilly area.

WEIMAR (650 000). In the 18th and 19th cent. Weimar was the centre of German culture. This was where artists, poets and musicians gathered. *Goethe's home* on Frauenplan (where he died in 1805) is now a museum as is his little *garden house* and *Schiller's home.* Liszt lived here at the end of the 19th cent. and his home is a museum. Statues of Goethe and Schiller can be found outside the Deutsches Nationaltheater. The Gasthaus zum Weissen Schwan, where all the great men met, is still a meeting- place in Weimar and almost unchanged since it first opened 400 years ago. The Elephant Hotel (from 1521) where they also liked to gather, is now a state-run Interhotel.
The *castle* has collections of German art. On the opposite bank of the River Ilm is a palace in the Italian Renaissance style with the Goethe- Schiller Archives. Both men are buried in the cemetery south of the town centre. *Herderkirche* (1500), with an altar created by Cranach Father and Son. Lucas Cranach the Elder came to Weimar in 1552. *Lucas-Cranach-Haus* has a beautiful green stepped gable. Tiefurt Palace and Belvedere Palace in rococo style.
In 1919 the "Weimar Republic" was founded through a national assembly which decided to sign the Treaty of Versailles and adopted a new constitution. It was crushed by Hitler in 1933. The *Buchenwald* concentration camp was situated on Ettersberg. A memorial, the "Oath of Buchenwald" reminds us of the 56 000 who died here.
Ettersburg Castle (18th cent.) with a beautiful park.

ERFURT (200 000). Bishopric since 743. University (1392) where Martin Luther studied. Beautiful *Altstadt* (Old Town) with patrician houses in Baroque and Renaissance styles. *Kräumerbrücke* (1325), a stone bridge

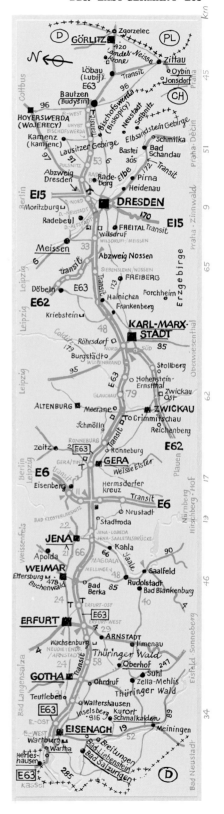

East Berlin by night with the impressive TV tower

with 33 houses built on it. *Angermuseum* with medieval art. The Neuwerk Madonna and Erfurter faience (glazed pottery). *Marienkirche* (Erfurter Dom) with a 25 m high High-Gothic choir (1372) with beautiful stained-glass windows. *Severikirche* (1278-1400), next to the cathedral, is one of the most handsome hall churches in the country. Erfurt is by tradition a flower-growing city. "Iga" is the name of the international garden fair.

GOTHA (57 000). Founded 1180. Beautiful, well-preserved *Altstadt*. **Friedenstein Castle** is now a museum with art, faience, furniture, and a large collection of Chinese porcelain. *Castle church* in Baroque and the *Eckhoff-Theater* with stage equipment from 1683. Beautiful park. Remains of Grimmenstein Castle. *Lucas-Cranach-Haus* is half-timbered. Gothaer Lateinschule was founded in 1292. The first "Realgymnasium" (upper secondary school) was established in 1837 in what is now the Geschwister-Scholl-Haus (named after the three siblings who opposed the Nazis and were executed).

EISENACH (50 000). Martin Luther went to school here (1497-1501). Johann Sebastian Bach was born here (1685). His house is now a *museum* of musical history. The *Reuter-Wagner Museum* is dedicated to Fritz Reuter, the writer, and Richard Wagner, the composer. The Social Democratic Party was founded here in 1869 by August Bebel and

Wilhelm Liebknecht. Centre of the Old Town is *Marktplatz* with many lovely half-timbered houses, a pharmacy, the old town hall (1638) and the town castle (1752) with *Thüringer Museum* and an impressive Baroque ballroom, now used for official receptions.

Wartburg Castle is 400 m above the city. It became the residence of the counts of Thuringia in the 12th cent. This is where the "singing battle" took place in 1207 between the two minstrels Walter von der Vogelweide and Wolfram von Eschenbach. Wagner has included it in "Tannhäuser". *Lutherstube* is the room in which Luther translated the New Testament into German and threw an ink-pot at the devil. The ink must have been of good quality – the stain can still be seen.

Wartha/Herleshausen. West German border. E 63 continues to Kassel – Dortmund.

Bad Liebenstein and *Bad Salzungen*. Spas. Beautiful roads south through the *Werra Valley* and the *Thüringer Forest*. *Oberhof* and other winter sport resorts. *Schmalkalden* with fine half-timbered houses. Hessenhof from 1555. Georgenkirche, where Luther preached. Wilhelmsburg Castle (1585). In 1531 a league to defend Protestantism was formed here. It was a step towards the Thirty Years' War.

TOWN PLANS

BERLIN, Hauptstadt der DDR (Capital of the German Democratic Republic, East Berlin, 1.1 million).

For the history of Berlin and its division, see West Germany.

East Berlin can be reached from West Berlin at Friedrichsstrasse (Checkpoint Charlie). It is also possible to enter East Berlin by S-Bahn or U-Bahn at Friedrichsstrasse.

East Berlin consists of the older parts of the Berlin city centre. **Unter den Linden** was laid out in the 17th cent. It starts at the **Brandenburger Tor,** built in 1791 by Langhans on what was then the city boundary. The gate is crowned by the Goddess of Victory, "Quadriga" (four-in-hand) by Gottfried Schadow. Napoleon took it to Paris in 1806, but it was brought back in 1814.

In Unter den Linden is the *Humboldt University,* founded in 1810 and *Deutsche Staatsoper* (1743) with the Operncafé in the Baroque style. *Zeughaus* (1700), the former arsenal is now a museum of German history, devoted to social progress. *The Neue Wache* (Schinkel, 1818) is now a monument to the victims of Fascism. A guard of honour, always on duty, parades Wednesdays at 2.30 p.m. Not far from here was the bunker, where Hitler committed suicide in 1945.

Unter den Linden leads up to the **Museuminsel** (Museum Island) in the River Spree. The *Virgin Bridge,* the old drawbridge from 1798, still stands. This was the site of Cölln, one of the original villages from which the city of Berlin was formed. The enormous *Marx-Engels-Platz* for parades and mass meetings. The Foreign Ministry of the German Democratic Republic is in the Palast der Republik. Oldest of the museums is **Altes Museum** (1828) with copperplate engravings, etc. **Nationalgalerie** contains paintings and drawings from the 19th and 20th cent. **Pergamonmuseum** with the enormous Pergamon Altar, Islamic museum and objects from Babylon with a reconstructed procession street. **Bodemuseum** with Egyptian museum, archaeology, coins and art.

Not far from the Museum Island is **Märkisches Museum,** the Berlin city museum. The nearly 4 m long altarcloth (15th cent.) from Zehdenick Abbey depicts scenes from the life of Christ. Circus museum. Several other museums, among them the Museum of Natural History, and the Postal Museum.

Marienkirche. Gothic red-brick church (1260), the Berlin cathedral. The "Death Dance" is a 22 m long fresco painting. The church tower was reconstructed in 1790 by Langhans.

Alexanderplatz, the centre of the city. An enormous expanse dominated by the 365 m high *TV tower* (65 m higher than the Eiffel Tower). The café at 207 m rotates at a speed of one full turn per hour. The 123 m high Interhotel Stadt

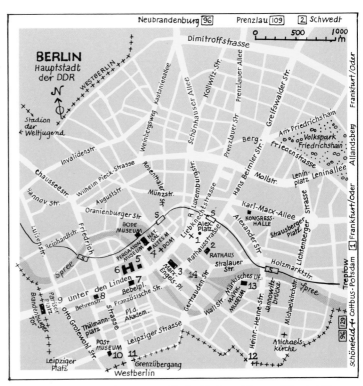

1 Town hall and television tower. 2 Marienkirche. 3 Museum Island. 4 Museum of German History. 5 Neue Wache. 6 Opera house. 7 Komische Oper. 8 Brandenburger Tor. 9 Postal museum. 10 Märkisches Museum. 11 Friedrichsfelde Zoo. 12 Treptower Park.

Berlin has 39 storeys and 2 000 beds. The World Clock and Brunnen der Völkerfreundschaft (the Fountain of Friendship between All Peoples), also referred to as Alexstrudel. The "Red" Town Hall in neo-Renaissance (1868). The name is due to its red brick façade. The *town hall* is the only building that remains of the old, pre-war Alexanderplatz, depicted in Döblin's novel and Fassbinder's television series. A few old houses still stand in the area just behind the square; e.g. Berlin's oldest inn, "Zur letzten Instanz". The pre-war continental hotel atmosphere can be found at the Adlon Hotel, the setting for Vicki Baum's "Grand Hotel".

Karl-Marx-Allée was built in the 1950s in the East European style popular at the time. At first it was known as the Stalin-Allée.

Several **theatres:** the Staatsoper, Komische Oper, Berliner Ensemble (where Bertholt Brecht worked), the Maxim Gorkij Theatre and others.

Zoo. Friedrichsfelde, built in 1955 with Alfred Brehm's "Tropenhalle". People's Park in Friedrichshain. Müggelbergen recreation area with observation tower.

Treptower Park with a large war cemetery and an enormous **monument** to the Russian soldiers who fell here. *Köpenick Castle* with museum containing crafts, furniture, ceramics, goldsmith's works from the Middle Ages to the 18th cent. "The Shoemaker from Köpenick", Wilhelm Voigt, put on a captain's uniform (1906) and requisitioned the state's treasury. The world laughed at Prussian discipline and militarism and the word "Köpenickiade" was coined.

DRESDEN (500 000). The town, over 700 years old, with its enormous art treasures, and one of Germany's most beautiful cities, was spared until the very end of the Second World War. Then, in February 1945, the bombers attacked, laying the entire city waste and killing 130 000 of its inhabitants. Many of its treasures survived, however, and parts of the town have been rebuilt in the former styles.

Zwinger (1725) is the late-Baroque masterpiece by Pöppelmann and Permoser. Impressive art treasures. Art museum with works from the 15th-18th cent. Raphael's Sistine Madonna. Porcelain collection. Concerts in the Zwingerhof, often by the world-famous Dresdner Kreuzchor (a boys' choir) from *Kreuzkirche.*

Albertinum (Zeughaus) was built in the 16th cent. as the elector's treasury. Art (contemporary), collections of antiquities and sculptures. Objects from the "Grünes Gewölbe" (Green Vault). **Altmarkt** with Kreuzkirche. The new town hall (1912) has a 100 m high tower. Modern Prager Strasse. Opera house (1878) by G. Semper.

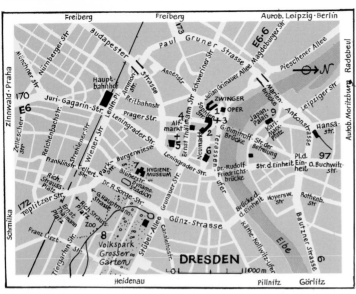

1 Zwinger and opera house. 2 Residenzschloss and museums. 3 Hofkirche. 4 Altmarkt, Palace of Culture, Kreuzkirche. 5 New town hall. 6 Albertinum. 7 Hygiene-Museum. 8 Grosser Garten with Pioneer railway, zoo and botanical gardens. 9 Japanisches Palais. 10 Museum für Volkskunst. (Museum of Folk Art).

Kathedrale (Hofkirche) in the Baroque style with an organ by Silbermann. The large Frauenkirche was totally destroyed in 1945.
Rezidenzschloss, mainly from the 16th cent. Castle chapel with the "Schönes Tor" (Beautiful Gate). The treasury was called the "Grünes Gewölbe" (Green Vault).
Trafikmuseum and Deutsches Hygiene-Museum (German Hygiene Museum) with the talking glass woman (Gläserne Frau). There is also a glass man and a glass cow, but they do not say anything. Zoo. Memorial to Martin-Andersen-Nexö. In Wachwitz, a television tower with observation deck.
Pillnitz Castle, in the Chinese style, was designed by Pöppelmann for August the Strong. Boat trips on the Elbe into the "Saxon Switzerland".

LEIPZIG (600 000).
Founded 1170. Large industrial town. Trade fair in spring and autumn. Centre of the printing and book trade. University founded in 1409, the second oldest in Germany, after Heidelberg. Now called the Karl Marx University. Several other colleges and institutions of learning.
The Old Town has been largely rebuilt since the war. Marktplatz with the Old Town Hall, a 90 m long façade. City museum. Near by is Auerbach's Keller, a restaurant which first opened in 1525 and is the site of one of the scenes in Goethe's Faust. The Zum Kaffeebaum restaurant is associated with Lessing and Robert Schumann. The new town hall (1907) has a fortress-like tower. Wagner and Leibnitz were born in Leipzig and Johann Sebastian Bach was precentor at the Thomaskirche. His grave was moved here in 1950. In 1212 the Thomas School was established here with its famous boys' choir, the Thomaner Knabenchor. In Gohliser Castle are the Bach Archives.
Museum der Bildenden Künsten forms a part of the Georgi-Dimitroff-Museum, which also contains exhibitions concerning the history of the German workers' movement. Dimitroff, who gave his name to the museum, was a Bulgarian Communist leader, and one of those prosecuted for the fire at the Reichtag in 1933. The present museum was then the German Supreme Court. Grassimuseum (crafts and musical instruments). Deutsche Bücherei collects examples of everything printed in Germany and has 5 million books. One of the oldest railway stations in Europe, the Bayrischer Bahnhof (Bavarian station), built in 1842. The Leipzig-Dresden railway was opened in 1831. Large zoo. Botanical gardens. Zentralstadion (Stadium) has room for 100 000 spectators.
Völkerschlachtsdenkmal, an enormous monument, erected in 1913 in memory of the "Battle of the Nations" in 1813 when Napoleon's army was defeated. Among the fallen soldiers were 22 000 Russians. A Russian church was built in their memory in 1913. With its golden cupola it looks like a Novgorod church.

Lützen. This is the place where Gustavus Adolphus, the Swedish king, fell on November 6, 1632. Memorial chapel.

1 Thomaskirche (Church of St. Thomas). 2 Marktplatz with the old town hall. 3 Alte Waage (Old Weigh House). 4 New town hall. 5 Georgi-Dimitroff-Museum. 6 Nikolkirche (Church of St. Nicholas). 7 Karl Marx University. 8 New opera house. 9 Grassi-Museum. 10 Deutsche Bücherei (library). 11 Exhibition grounds.

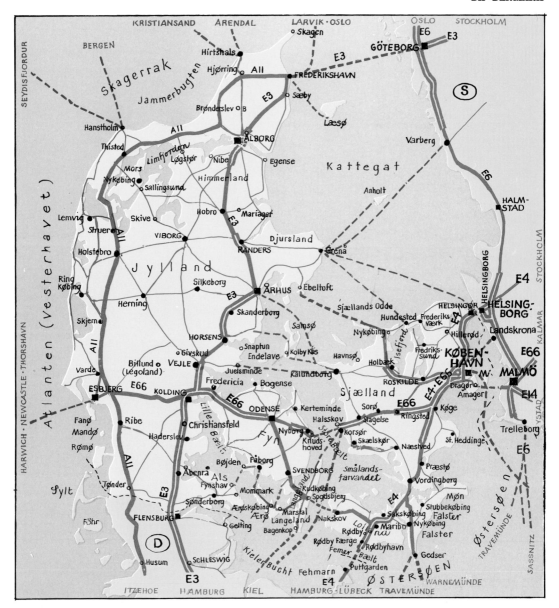

DK · Denmark

DK·Denmark

Area: 43 000 km² (16 650 sq. miles) The country consists of the peninsula of Jylland (Jutland) and 500 islands of which 100 are inhabited. The Faroe Islands, 1 400 km² (540 sq. miles), and Greenland, 2 000 000 km² (639 800 sq. miles) also belong to Denmark.

Population: 5.2 million. 97% belong to the Lutheran State Church. The Faroe Islands have 42 000 inhabitants and Greenland 50 000, 10 000 of whom have moved there from Denmark.

Major cities: København (Copenhagen) 1.4 million (with suburbs), Århus 245 000, Aalborg 153 000, Odense 170 000, Thorshavn on the Faroe Islands 13 000, Godthåb on Greenland 10 000.

Government: Constitutional monarchy. Europe's oldest kingdom. The one-chamber parliament is called Folketing. It has 179 members, including two from the Faroe Islands and two from Greenland. Greenland is part of Denmark but the Faroe Islands enjoy a certain amount of autonomy.

History

983 King Harald Bluetooth unites Norway and Denmark to form the Kingdom of Denmark.

1013-1042 England is part of the Danish Kingdom.

1397 Queen Margaret of Denmark unites the Scandinavian countries through the Union of Kalmar.

1521 The union with Sweden is dissolved. Until the 18th cent. many wars with Sweden.

1645 Denmark cedes Gotland, Jämtland and Härjedalen to Sweden.

Gudhjem, Bornholm

Løkken on the west coast of Jutland

Routes described:

E 3 Frederikshavn – Ålborg – Århus – Vejle – Flensburg

E 4 Helsingør – København – Rødby færge

E 64 Vordingborg – Gedser

E 66 København – Store Bælt – Odense – Esbjerg

A 8 Nyborg – Bøjden – Sønderborg – Kruså, see E 66

A 9 Odense – Svendborg – Spodsbjerg, see E 66

A 11 Fredrikshavn – Holstebro – Esbjerg – Tønder

A 15 Århus – Grenå, see E 3

A 16 Randers – Grenå, see E 3

Special map: Bornholm

Town plans: København, Odense, Århus

1658 Denmark cedes Skåne (Scania), Halland, Blekinge and Bohuslän to Sweden.
1807 The British navy bombard Copenhagen.
1814 Norway is ceded to Sweden.
1864 Prussia and Austria unite to occupy Schleswig-Holstein.
1920 Schleswig and Sønderjylland (Southern Jutland) are returned to Denmark.
1940 Germans occupy Denmark after brief struggles. Towards the end of the war Danish resistance against the Germans hardens.
1944 Iceland dissolves the personal union with Denmark.
1945 Denmark is liberated.
1947 Denmark joins NATO.
1973 Denmark joins the Common Market (EEC).

Currency: Danish crowns (kroner) (DKK).
1 krone = 100 øre

Business hours: Banks 9.30 a.m.-4.00 p.m. Thursdays open until 6.00 p.m. Closed Saturdays. Outside the big cities opening times may vary. Post offices 9.00 or 10.00 a.m.-5.00 or 5.30 p.m. Saturdays 9.00 or 10.00 a.m.-12.00 noon. Shops 9.00 a.m.-5.30 p.m. Fridays until 7.00 or 8.00 p.m. Saturdays until 12.00 noon or 2.00 p.m. Business hours can vary – the above are given as a guideline only.

Holidays: New Year's Day, Maundy Thursday, Good Friday, Easter Sunday, Easter Monday, Store Bededag (The Great Prayer Day, the fourth Friday after Easter), Ascension Day, Whit Sunday and Whit Monday, June 5 from 12 noon, (Grundlovsdagen, Constitution Day) December 25 and 26.

Hotels
The Danish Tourist Association publish a list of hotels. There is no official classification. Prices include VAT and service charges, often also breakfast. The Mission hotels, which are found all over the country, are particularly good value.
Most local tourist offices will assist tourists in finding accommodation. In Copenhagen there is a special Accommodation Service at the Hovedbangården (Central Railway Station). The "kroer" are unique to Denmark. They are little inns that can be found all over the country. They offer good food and comfortable accommodation at reasonable prices. Some "kroer", however, are among Europe's best eating-places, and naturally prices have been adjusted to fit the standard of the food.

Camping
525 camping sites. Many have cottages for self-catering, but this feature is not as widespread as in the other Scandinavian countries. FDM (Forenede Danske Motorejere, the Danish Automobile Club) operate 26 camping sites where members of other AIT clubs are welcome.

Youth hostels
Herbergs-Ringen runs about 90 youth hostels all over Denmark. Many have family rooms.

Legoland version of Amalienborg, the Copenhagen Royal Palace

Youth hostels

Herbergs-Ringen runs about 90 youth hostels all over Denmark. Many have family rooms.

Food and drink

"Morgenmad", breakfast, is usually "continental" but often coldcuts, cheese and a Danish pastry are also included. "Frokost" means lunch. This often consists of "smørrebrød", open-faced sandwiches, made of a thin, often dark, piece of bread, and a pile of coldcuts, vegetables etc. on top. The longest list of "smørrebrød" can be found at Davidsens in Copenhagen.

Another popular lunch dish is "platte", consisting of pickled herring, hot filet of fish, a meat ball, sausage slices, liver paste, cheese etc. Sometimes this is referred to as "kroplatte", sometimes – if it is a fancier variety (with shrimp, salmon, smoked eel etc.) – as "luksusplatte".

Dinner is eaten in the evening, between 6.00 p.m. and 8.00 p.m. and is the main meal of the day. Often a soup is served first – a clear bouillon with "klimp", a kind of dumpling, or asparagus or cauliflower soup. Frikadeller are minced pork or veal patties. Dansk bøf is minced beef, often accompanied by fried eggs and onions. Popular fish dishes include fried plaice, boiled cod and fried eel.

The national beverage is beer and it is superb – Tuborg and Carlsberg are world famous. Aalborg aquavit is the best-known snaps.

"Pølsevogne", hot dog stands, are a common sight in Danish towns.

Shopping

Danish handicrafts and porcelain (Bing & Grøndahl, Den Kongelige). Silver. Antiques. Food stuffs.

Speed limits. Traffic regulations

Motorways 100 kmh, other roads 80 kmh, built-up areas 60 kmh. Cars towing caravans 70 kmh, in built-up areas 60 kmh.

Road controls are frequent and fines for speeding are high.

If your car is fitted with seat belts it is compulsory to wear them.

Be careful on the motorways. Danish drivers entering these roads seldom take notice of approaching vehicles. And watch out for the cyclists. In some countries cyclists ignore the traffic rules. This is not the case in Denmark. Cyclists here obey the regulations and expect motorists to do the same, for example with regard to the right of way.

Parking

It is permitted to park outside a building with an evennumber on evennumbered days and outside an oddnum-bered building on oddnumbered days. Standing for up to three minutes or loading or unloading goods is not considered to be parking. If there is a limited-time parking, this is indicated by a sign. Black numbers = Monday to Friday, black numbers in parentheses = Friday, red numbers = Sunday and holidays. Parking discs are required in time-limited zones. These can be obtained at police stations, tourist offices, post offices, petrol stations and at some banks.

Roads

The roads in Denmark are generally of a very high standard and well signposted.

Road patrols

The Falck rescue service provides towing to garages (payment required). AIT credit vouchers are not accepted. Local emergency centres are open 24 hours. The FDM automobile club has no patrol cars.

Emergency telephone: To police, ambulance, fire brigade: 000.

FDM, Forenede Danske Motorejere, Blegdamsvej 124, DK-2100 København. Tel. 01-38 21 21.

Danish Tourist Board, Sceptre House, 169/173 Regent Street (entrance New Burlington Street), London W1R 8PY. Tel. 01- 734 2637/8.

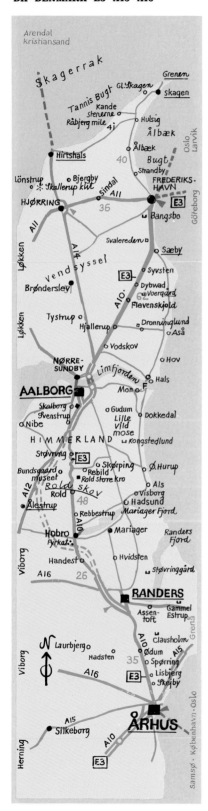

E 3. Frederikshavn – Ålborg – Århus – Vejle – Flensburg

FREDERIKSHAVN (33 000)was granted its charter in 1818. Fishing and ferry port. *Krudttårnet* (the Powder Tower) remains of a fortress. Museum and weapons collection. Fine views of sea and land from the 58 m high Cloos Tower. *Fiskerklyngen,* the oldest part of the town, has small, picturesque fishermen's houses and winding streets. A culinary speciality of Frederikshavn is large plaice. *Bangsbo Museum* in a 19th-cent. manor house. Town history, shipping and figure heads. Views from Pikkerbakken.

Road north to **Skagen**. Modern fishing port with daily fish auctions. At the end of the 19th cent. many painters and poets lived here. *"Den Tilsandede Kirke"* (the Sanded-up Church). Only the tower remains.
Grenen, the northern tip of Jutland. The changing shape of the land is determined by the powerful currents. Special "Sandormen" (Sandworm) vehicles transport tourists over the sand. Skagen's lighthouse (1858), 50 m high, is the tallest in Denmark.

Sæby with abbey church. 16th-cent. wall paintings.Folklore. *Hammer Bakker.* Nature preserve with heather-covered heaths. Hiking trails. *Voergård Castle* (1591). One of the most beautiful Renaissance buildings in Denmark. Art collection.

Lindholm Høje, Denmark's largest Viking Age burial ground.

Rebild Bakker. National park with lovely heather-covered slopes. It was donated by Danish-Americans in 1912. Annual Fourth of July (American National Holiday) celebrations. The Danish Emigration Museum is in the *Lincoln Log Cabin,* a replica of Abraham Lincoln's childhood home. *Bundgaard Museum* is located in the abandoned Tingbæk chalk mines. Models of several of Bundgaard's works.

Rold skov, largest forest in Denmark, 10 x 20 km. Mainly pine trees.

Ålestrup, site of the *Jutlandian Rose Gardens.*

Hobro. Little town founded in the 12th cent. Beautifully situated. The Hobro Museum has displays of silver and porcelain. Finds from the *Fyrkat* Viking fortress from about A.D. 1000. Circular ramparts.

Mariager (1 000). One of the smallest and most idyllic towns in Denmark. Half-timbered houses. 300-year-old oak in the Egepladsen. Once this town lived up to being called "The Town of Roses". Only one building remains from the 14th cent. Birgittine abbey. Remains of abbey church (1470).

Lille Vildmose is Denmark's largest bog. *Kongstedlund* (1592) is a handsome Renaissance manor house.

RANDERS (66 000) was mentioned as early as 1086. Town since 1302. During the Middle Ages, there were three abbeys and three churches here. A few old buildings remain. *Skt. Mortens Kirke* (1340) was built by the monks of the Helligånd abbey (1490) which has galleries and a stork's nest. The **Kulturhus** contains a cultural and historical museum and an art museum. Half-timbered Niels Ebbesen's manor house. A third-floor window is always open to allow the ghost of the count to move in or out at will. Lovely Skovbakken and Tøjhushaven parks. *Hornslet Church* (12th cent.) with wall paintings depicting the capture of a city.

A 15. Århus – Grenå. A 16. Randers – Grenå

Gl. Estrup, manor house from about 1500. Jutland's Manor House Museum. Danish Agricultural Museum.

Djurs Sommerland, a playground for the entire family. The entrance fee covers the use of all attractions.

Rosenholm Castle (1559) with fine interiors and park.
Thorsager Church (1200). The only round church on Jutland. **Grenå.** Town since 1445. Delightful streets and houses. Djursland's Museum. Folklore.

Ebeltoft. Idyllic town with lovely houses. Lille rådhus (Little Town Hall) from 1576, museum. Farvergården, a 17th-cent. dyer's home with original tools and furnishings. The old Postgård now houses a museum with Far Eastern ethnographical collections. The frigate "Jylland" is the Royal Danish Navy's last surviving full-rigged ship.

ÅRHUS, see town plans.

Silkeborg (25 000), beautifully situated on the Silkeborg Langsø. Ruins of an old royal castle. Town since 1900, when the paper industry developed. Lovely promenades along the River Gudenåen. Museum with art and ceramics. Museum with the 2000-year-old *Tollund Man,* who was discovered in a peat bog.

From Silkeborg it is possible to travel on the paddle steamer "Hjejlen" to the foot of **Himmelbjerget** (147 m). From its summit magnificent views out over lakes and forests. Observation tower, restaurant and hotel. Ruins of the Om Cistercian abbey (12th cent.). 10 km W of Silkeborg is a memorial cross on the site where Kaj Munk, writer, resistance leader and pastor of Vedersø parish, was murdered by Germans in 1944.

Yding Skovhøj, 173 m. Denmark's highest point. Lovely view from here and from *Ejer Bavnehøj*, which is a bit lower. Its official height is 171 m. The observation tower adds another 13 m to its height.

HORSENS (40 000). Industrial and commercial town with beautiful views out over Horsens Fjord. It became a town in 1442, when it was an important trading centre with an abbey and fortifications. Handsome 18th-cent. houses. Delightful castle with charming park (1775).

Preserved steam railway Vrads – Byrub, 5 km, 15 minutes. Locomotive from 1918. Sundays only. Little car ferry from Snaptun to the lovely islands of **Endelave** and **Hjarnø.**

VEJLE (40 000) has been a town since 1327. Beautifully situated. 13th-cent. Skt. Nikolaj Church is the town's oldest building. Vejle Museum (graphic art and drawings). Vejle Nørreskov with zoo.

Alternative route from Ålborg to Vejle via Viborg.

Viborg (28 000). Old capital where once the kings of Denmark were chosen. Bishopric during the 11th cent. Town charter 1150. In about 1500, the town is said to have had six abbeys and 12 churches. Starting point for the "gamle Haervej" (Old Army Road) that went south to the German frontier. Vor Frue Cathedral (12th cent.) was given its present appearance in 1876. Biblical frescoes by Joakim Skovgaard.

Løvepark/Safariland in *Givskud*, on A 18 between Vejle and Brande. A Jutlandian heath (75 hectares) with over 40 lions. You can drive along one winding road through the lion park, and along another through Safariland with deer, donkeys, zebras, ostriches, boar and antelopes. Zoo.

Jelling. "Gorm the Old", the first king of Denmark, was in residence here about 950. He was the first to unite Denmark. In 1978 his skull was discovered under the floor of the church (1100) that had been built on the site of Harald Bluetooth's stave church, which itself had been built on the site of a pagan sacrificial altar. Two large rune stones. Two burial mounds – Gorm's and his wife Thyra's. But it had long been known that the grave in Gorm's mound was empty. **Legoland** and **Billund,** see E 66.

KOLDING (40 000). Koldinghus Fortress (1208), partially restored after a fire in 1808, set by resident Spanish troops who had been sent to Denmark by Napoleon. Museum with art and displays concerning the war for Schleswig. *Koldings Geografiske Have,* a park with about 2 000 exotic plants, arranged in geographical groups. Large bamboo grove.

Fredericia, see E 66.

Christiansfeld. The town was founded in 1773 by members of the Moravian Church, a revival of the teachings of the Bohemian reformer Jan Hus (John Huss). Of their original industries, only the production of honey comb remains. They can be bought everywhere. *Museum for Brødremenigheden (Museum of the Brothers in Faith),* church and original churchyard. Yellow, two-storey buildings for the sect's brothers, sisters and widows. Christiansfeld was one of Denmark's project cities during the European Architectural Heritage Year 1975.

Haderslev (25 000). Idyllic town clustered about the Vor Frue Church (13th-15th cent.). *Haderslev Museum,* an archaeological museum with the Skrydstrup Girl (from about 1300 B.C.), the corpse of an early-Bronze Age woman, found in a peat bog. *Open-air museum* with old farm buildings.

Åbenrå. Town with many lovely buildings. Slotsgade has a uniform 18th-cent. appearance with tapered, gabled houses. The *Åbenrå Museum* has displays about commerce, fishing, industry, organ-building, the town's maritime history and the Nybøl Man. His corpse was discovered in a peat bog. Skt. Nikolaj Church.

Kruså. West German border. Shops, currency exchange, etc. Nowadays the heavy traffic is on the motorway, a bit to the west.

E 3 continues to Hamburg – Bremen – Antwerpen – Paris – Lisboa.

Roads east to **Als** and **Sønderborg.**

Gråsten Palace · is Queen Ingrid's summer residence. Lovely park.

Dybbøl redoubts with the Dybbøl Mill, a national monument for the Danes, because of its heroic defence against the Germans. It withstood a month-long siege and was finally surrendered on April 4, 1864.

Sønderborg (25 000). Sønderborg Castle (13th cent.) houses the *Amt (County) Museum* with exhibits concerning the history of Southern Jutland, the Schleswig wars and the Occupation during the Second World War.

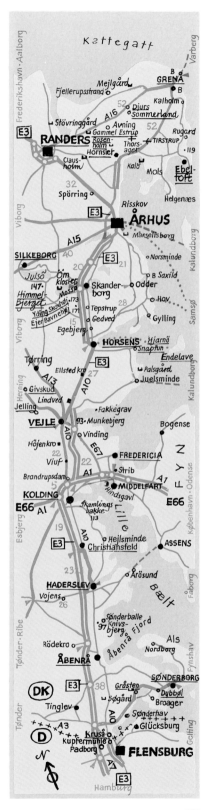

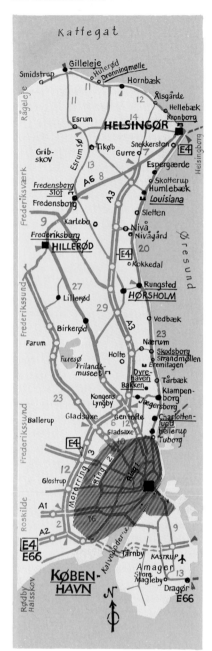

E 4. Helsingør – København – Rødby færge

E 4 comes from Helsinki – Torneå – Haparanda – Stockholm – Helsingborg.
The ferry link between Helsingborg (Sweden) and Helsingør is one of the
most travelled in the world: about 24 million passengers annually. SJ/DSB
ferries every 15 minutes. Linjebuss ferries every 30 minutes.

HELSINGØR (Elsinore, 55 000). Reverently preserved town centre with
handsome 16th- to 18th-cent. buildings. A second modern town centre has
been constructed 3 km W. Sct. Olai Kirke (the cathedral), with origins in
the 13th cent., has been remodelled. Renaissance interior. The Carmelite
abbey with wall paintings is well preserved.

Kronborg Castle (16th-cent.). This Dutch Renaissance building with an
verdigris green copper roof, lies near the Sound. During the Middle Ages,
Eric of Pomerania had a castle built at this strategic point, where customs
duties could be demanded. The present castle was built 1574-1584. It was
rebuilt after a severe fire in 1629. Splendid interior with 63 m long Knight's
Hall and charming little castle church. Shakespeare placed the action of "Hamlet" here at the castle of Elsinore.

Marienlyst Castle received its present appearance in 1760. It houses the
town museum. **The Danish Technical Museum** has a wide range of exhibits. Large motor car section. Model railway. There is another motor car
museum in *Rågleje Egemosegård.* 24 km long preserved *steam railway*
from Elsinore to Gilleleje.

Fine road north along the coast. *Dronningmølle.* The lovely little palace is
now a distinguished hotel (apartments) and restaurant. *Gilleleje,* large
seaside resort and fishing port. Daily fish auctions.

Hillerød (22 000) with *Frederiksborg Castle,* a mighty Dutch Renaissance (1620) structure. Destroyed by fire in 1859, it was restored in 1878 as
a *National Historical Museum,* with money donated from the Carlsberg
(breweries) Foundation. Knight's Hall with magnificent ceiling. Castle
church with ivory and silver pulpit and altar. Compenius organ from 1610.
Baroque park. Badestuen pleasure palace (1580). Box-hedges and linden
avenues. Canals, carp ponds. *Nordsjællands Folkemuseum* (folklore).

Fredensborg Palace, built in 1722 in the Italian style, is the residence of
the Danish royal family during spring and autumn. Open to the public in
July. The large and lovely palace park was obviously inspired by the
gardens at Versailles. 69 sandstone statues of peasants and fishermen.

Strandvejen (the road that follows the coast) goes through lovely little
seaside resorts and offers fine views of the Sound.

Louisiana in Humlebæk is an interesting and attractive art gallery. Formerly a private home, it has been expanded and long glass-walled exten-
sions facing the park have been added. Concert hall and theatre.
Restaurant. The present gatehouse was built at the end of the 19th cent. by
Brun, the Royal Forester. He was married three times and all of his wives
were named Louise.

Hørsholm. Jakt- og Skovbrugsmuseet (the Hunting and Forestry
Museum) in the farm buildings of a castle that was demolished in 1810.
Rungsted. Home of the writer Isak Dinesen (Karen Blixen). Her grave is in
the park. *Skodsborg.* Spa that pioneered in vegetarian treatments.

Dyrehaven. Lovely forest and wild life park. The little rococo *Eremitage*
hunting palace (1736) is set in an open plain. Dyrenhaven provides a
wonderful frame for the popular *Bakken* (Dyrehavsbakken) amusement
park, which is perhaps the most truly Danish place in all of Denmark. You
can take a horse and carriage from Klampenborg's S-train station. Bakken
is open from mid-April until the end of September. Near by is the *Ordrup-
gård Collection,* a private collection of 19th-cent. Danish and French art,
furniture and handicrafts.

Charlottenlund and Denmark's Aquarium, see *København.*

KØBENHAVN (Copenhagen), see town plans.

KØGE (35 000). Town since 1288. Many beautiful half-timbered houses
along the Kirkestræde, in a 17th- cent. building. *Skt.
Nikolaj Church* (12th-13th cent.), with a large tower that has served as a
lighthouse, is dedicated to the patron saint of mariners.

Vallø Castle (1586) with beautiful park. Flower shows. *Gjorslev Castle*
(14th cent.). Visitors may enter the park. *Store Heddinge.* Little town with
fortified medieval church. *Stevns Klint,* 40 m high limestone and chalk
coastal cliffs. 40 m high Stevns lighthouse. *Højerup Church,* at the edge of
the cliff, was last used in 1910. In 1928 the chancel tumbled into the sea.
The remains are now supported with concrete. *Stevns Museum* with folk
costumes and crafts.

Fakse. Little town with limestone mines, in operation since the Middle Ages. Originally this was a coral reef, created about 70 million years ago.

Bregentved. Rococo mansion (1887) with large park and linden avenues. Open Wednesdays and Sundays. The Holmegård glass works, in Fensmark, was founded in 1825. Open to the public.

NÆSTVED (46 000). Founded in the 12th cent., near the Sct. Peder Benedictine monastery. During the Hanseatic period, this was one of Denmark's most important towns. *Sct. Peder's Church* (13th-14th cent.) is the largest Gothic church in the country. Frescoes. Famous painting of Valdemar Atterdag and Queen Hellvig. *Sct. Morten's Church* with carved altarpiece. *Helligåndshuset* (1420), remnant of a medieval hospital, now houses a folklore museum. A special section deals with leprosy. Annexe in Boderne with silver, glass and ceramics. Henrik Gottschalk's House (15th cent.). Many half-timbered houses.

Gavnø. Tulip and rose gardens around a rococo palace (1758). Art museum. Palace church, Queen Margaret's abbey church.

Praestø. Town since 1403. Idyllic atmosphere. 15th-cent. church. Fire brigade museum. *Nysø Castle* (1673) with memorabilia of Thorvaldsen, the sculptor.

Stege is the only town on Møn. The Mølleporten town gate remains of the Stegeborg fortress. *Møn's Museum* in the *Empiregården (1813)*. Folk costumes, furniture, etc. *Møns klint* consists of 7 km of up to 130 m high chalk cliffs. Beautiful views and lovely shifting of colour and light across the cliffs. Three hiking trails, 6, 8 and 10 km long. Bridle path, 12 km. Birdwatchers' tower (80 species). Denmark's only ski-lift. Recreation area. *Liselund*, a charming little pleasure palace (1792) with a thatched roof.

Vordingborg (12 000). Industrial and garrison town. Large area of ruins from Valdemar the Great's 12th-cent. castle and ring-wall. *Gåsetårnet* (the Goose Tower) got its name from the gilt goose that King Valdemar Atterdag put on top of the tower to annoy passing enemies in the Hanseatic League. Historical-botanical gardens in the ruin area. Reconstructed 16th-cent. castle garden. Beautiful church with frescoes.

Udby Church with fine frescoes. Memorial room in the rectory dedicated to Bishop N.F.S Grundtvig (1783-1872), father of the Danish folk high schools.

Sakskøbing. Little town, centre of fruit-growing and sugar industry. 14th- cent. church with gilded altarpiece.

Maribo. Little town built around an abbey. The cathedral (1470) is a part of the abbey. Abbey museum, folklore and art. *Friland Museum* with farmhouses from Lolland. The Maribo Lakes are in a lovely recreation area. Preserved *steam railway* Maribo-Bandholm (7 km, 30 minutes). Denmark's oldest preserved locomotive (1879).

Knuthenborg Park was laid out at the end of the 19th cent. It takes in 600 hectares – its wall is 8 km long. 500 species of deciduous and coniferous trees. Rhododendron garden. Safari Park with 700 animals. Giraffes, zebras, elephants, camels. You can drive the 16 km long road that traverses the park. Enclosed areas with baboons and open areas for tigers. Lovely park around a lake with swans, wild ducks, flamingos. Nice spot for a picnic, but there are good restaurants in the area.

A 7 west to **Nakskov** (17 000) with medieval town plan and old houses in Søndergade and Axeltorv. Pederstrup manor house (1822) with the *Reventlow Museum* (displays concerning 18th-cent. agricultural reforms). Kong Svends Høj with a 12 m long tomb.

Car ferry from Tårs to Spodsbjerg on Langeland. A 9 to Svendborg and Odense, see E 66.

Rødby. Old port town. Rødbyhavn (Rødby færge) with "Fugleflugt Line" services to Puttgarden. About 35 daily sailings (50 minutes). E 4 continues to Lübeck – Hamburg – Basel – Genève – Barcelona – Madrid – Lisboa.

E 64. Vordingborg – Gedser

Stubbekøbing. Little town, the oldest on Falster. 13th-cent. Romanesque church. *Museum* with motorcycles and mopeds.

Nykøbing Falster (26 000) was founded in the 13th cent. Industrial town. Lovely old buildings in St. Kirkestræde. Czar Peter's House, a beautiful half-timbered structure, now houses a folklore museum. Peter the Great stayed here during a visit in 1716. The church is a part of what was once a Franciscan monastery. *Marielyst* has a fine beach that extends all the way to **Gedser**, at the southernmost tip of Denmark. Car and train ferries to Warnemünde in the DDR (East Germany). E 64 continues to Berlin.

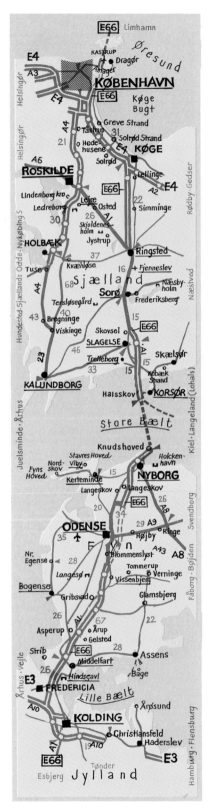

E 66. København – Store Bælt – Odense – Esbjerg

E 66 comes from Norrköping – Kalmar – Karlskrona – Malmö.

KØBENHAVN (Copenhagen), see town plans.

Alternative route via Roskilde.

ROSKILDE (50 000). Harald Bluetooth, who converted the Danes to Christianity, had a stave church erected here in 960. The *cathedral* in Romanesque and Gothic styles was built on the same site in about 1170. Two slender towers. Burial church of the Danish kings. Queen Margaret's sarcophagus with her effigy. Splendid interior with wall paintings, etc. The height of visiting monarchs has been recorded on one of the pillars. Absalonsbuen leads to the former Royal Palace (1733). *Vikingeskibshallen* contains five 11th- cent. Viking ships, recovered in 1957. They were sunk in the fjord as an obstruction for attacking enemy ships. Two of the five are war ships. One is 30 m long. As a result of the 1658 Peace of Roskilde, Denmark lost her provinces of Scania, Halland and Blekinge to Sweden. *Gyldenløves høj*, 126 m, is the highest point on Zealand.

Lejre. A reconstructed Iron Age village inhabited during Summer months.

Ringsted (25 000). An ancient place of sacrifice. Later the place where the "Ting" (Council) met. The Ting stones remain in the square. *Sct. Berndt's Church* was founded in the 12th cent. as part of a Benedictine monastery. 12 medieval Danish kings are buried here. Splendid furnishings.

Fjenneslev Church is Zealand's sole round church (1170). It is a defence-church with 2 m thick walls.

Sorø. Denmark's largest *abbey* was erected here in the 12th cent. The old abbey buildings were gutted by fire in 1247, but the abbey church (1160) survives. 8 m high Triumphal Cross by Claus Berg (1527). Tombs of Danish kings. Grave of Ludvig Holberg, the writer. *Sorø Academy*, a boarding-school, started in 1586. Akademihaven, lovely gardens down by the water.

Slagelse (33 000). Medieval town. Skt. Mikkel's Church (1333). Ruins of the Antvorskov abbey, founded in 1165.

Trelleborg. Viking Age fortifications (11th cent.). The fortress was manned by 1 500 warriors. Reconstruction of one of the 16 buildings.

Korsør (15 500). Since the 11th cent. this has been a port for the journey to Fyn (Fünen). Kings of Denmark waited out bad weather in the Kongegård. The Korsør Tower is what is left of an old fort. The *Store Bælt* is one of the busiest ferry routes in the world. About 35 daily sailings.

Kalundborg (12 000), further north, with ferry service to Samsø, Århus and Juelsminde. King Valdemar Atterdag had a castle built here, but the Swedes demolished it. Picturesque streets and houses. *Church* with centre tower and four corner towers. The church was originally built in 1170, but the centre tower collapsed in 1827, so reconstruction was necessary on a large scale. *Museum* with prehistoric finds and town history. *Lerchenborg manor house* (1753) in the Baroque style. French and English gardens. Room dedicated to Hans Christian Andersen.

Holbæk (24 000) with museum in old merchants' houses.

Nykøbing S (Sjælland, Zealand). Little, old town. *Odsherreds Museum* has a copy of the *Sun Chariot*, which was discovered in the Trundholm peat bog. Bakery museum. Anneberg-Samlingerne, large, private collection of antique glass. *Jaegerspris*, a 13th- cent. castle.

Nyborg (14 000) at the narrowest part of the Store Bælt. The town got its name from a "borg" (castle) that was built here in 1170. Medieval kings, nobility and priests gathered in the castle for meetings of the "dannehof", a form of parliament. Some of the buildings were pulled down during the 19th cent. The main building, a fortified tower and a large gate, the Landport, survive. *Vor Frue Church* was founded by Queen Margaret in 1388. Museum in Mads Lerche's half-timbered manor house.

Kerteminde. Little town and fishing port. Half-timbered houses. Museum in Farvergården (the Dyer's House). *Ladbyskibet,* grave of a Viking chieftain and a 10th-cent. Viking ship. It has been preserved here, where it was discovered. **Viby.** Charming little village with windmill.

A 9. Odense – Svendborg – Spodsbjerg

Svendborg (25 000). 700-year-old trading centre. Museum in Anne Hvide's House (1570) facing the square. Skt. Nikolai Church from 1220. The Svendborg Bridge (1966), a 33 m high pillar bridge to the idyllic island of **Tåsinge.** *Troense,* fishing port with half-timbered farm houses and gardens. Valdemar Castle, originally built in 1664 and remodelled in the Baroque style in 1754, is now a *naval museum* dedicated to Niels Juel. *Bregninge* Church has a 13th-cent. Christ's head. Fine views from the tower. 1 700 m long bridge to the island of *Siø* and onward over a causeway to **Langeland** (the "Long Land"). *Rudkøbing.* Charming old town. Museum. Bymøllen, a Dutch windmill from 1826. *Tranekær,* manor house with moat. Park and walking paths round the little Borresø lake. Road continues north to *Egelykke*, 19th-cent. manor house with park, then on to **Lohals** with Tom Knudsen's Safari Museum. Trophies from wild game hunting.

From Svendborg car ferries travel to *Ærø* and *Ærøskøbing*. Bearing the stamp of the 18th cent., this is one of the loveliest small towns in Denmark. Folklore museum with pharmacy museum, pipes and 400 ships in bottles. Hammerich's House with furniture and splendid interiors. **Marstal** (5 000) is the largest town on the island. Fishing port with idyllic streets. Shipyard, seamen's school, maritime museum. Church (1737) with ships' models. Car ferries to Rudkøbing (Langeland).

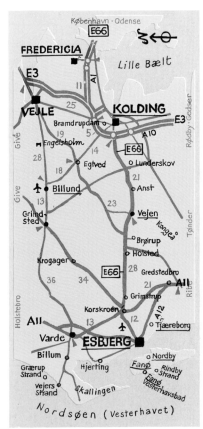

ODENSE, see town plans.

Frøbjerg Bavnehøj, 131 m, is the highest point on Fyn. *Vissenbjerg*. Large terrarium and aquarium. 500 specimens.

Bogense. Old houses and the North Fünen Museum. Square with beautiful linden trees and a copy of "Mannekin pis", the famous Brussels statue.

Middelfart (13 500). *Museum* in a half-timbered building. Exhibitions concerning ferry-traffic, shipping and the fishing and hunting of porpoises in the Lille Bælt. Collection of women's hats from 1870 to 1930. *Hindgavl Castle* from 1784.

Two bridges across **Lille Bælt**. A car and railway bridge, 1 170 m long and 33 m above the water, was inaugurated in 1935. In 1970 the suspension bridge was built. It is 1 080 m long and 32 m above the water.

Fredericia (36 000) was founded in 1650 as a fortress, built for the defence of Jutland. The fort was dismantled in 1909. Charming old part of the town. "Den tapre Landsoldat" (the Brave Soldier) monument. It is possible to stroll on the ramparts. Museum in an 18th-cent. building.

Kolding, see E 3.

Vejen (7 500). Art museum. *Billingland* amusement park. Naval history. Remote-control boats. *Skodborghus*. A royal castle once stood here, where the Old Army Road crossed over the River Kongeå, the natural and political boundary between Denmark and Germany. *Tjæreborg*. After the Second World War the local pastor started organizing tours for his parishioners. This has developed into the large Tjæreborg Travel Organization.

Billund. Airport. **Legoland.** Wonderful amusement park for young and old alike, at the same time an effective and impressive advertising and publicity gimmick for the Lego factory which manufactures the world-famous toy building-blocks. Beautiful park with Lego models of castles, palaces, towns, harbours, airports, and railways. Dutch canals. Medieval German town. Norwegian stave church, Cape Kennedy, etc. Splendid night-time illumination. Doll museum with dolls from 1580 to 1900. Titania's Palace, an English dolls' house, built by Sir Neville Wilkinson, was bought in 1977 for 1.6 million kroner. Traffic school where children get a "driving licence" after passing a driving test. Wild West town.

Løvepark/Safariland in Givskud, see E 3.

ESBJERG (72 000) has grown up around the large harbour, built in 1868, after Denmark had lost southern Jutland to the Germans and needed a large export harbour that could handle the vital transport of dairy and agricultural products (especially eggs and bacon) to Great Britain. Denmark's largest fishing port. Shipyards. *Fishing and maritime museum* with collections of fishing equipment and ships' models. Aquarium. Sharks and seals. The *Fish Auction Hall* is 225 m long. Daily auctions from 7.00 a.m. Esbjerg *Art Museum* with contemporary Danish art.

Fanø (3 000), 56 km flat island. The highest point, Perlebjerg, 21 m, is situated on the 17 km long stationary sandy beach. Fanø Vesterhavsbad is a large seaside resort. The small, wheeled bathing huts are towed out onto the beach at low tide. Interesting birds on the east coast. *Nordby*, with 2 000 inhabitants, is the largest town on Fanø. School for mariners. *Fanø Museum* with interiors of 18th-cent. homes. *Sønderho* with low, preserved and state-protected shipmasters' houses. Their building style reflects a relationship with houses on the Frisian Islands, off the Dutch coast.

A 8. Nyborg – Bøjden – Sønderborg – Kruså

South of Nyborg lies **Hesselagergård** manor house from 1583. Moat. The Dame Stone, the largest erratic block remaining in Denmark after the Ice Age glaciers receded. *Egeskov*. Large castle in an artificial lake. Summer concerts in the Knight's Hall. Castle park. Oak-hedge maze. *Museum* with vintage aircraft, motor cars, motorcycles, etc. in an 18th-cent. barn.

Fåborg with old streets and houses. Museum with paintings by Fünen artists. Clock tower and town gate. *Svanninge Bakker* are known as "the Fünen Alps". **Assens**. Small industrial town. Vor Frue Church (1488). *Willemoesgården* (1675) is a local history museum.

Car ferry Bøjden-Fynshav. A 8 to Sønderborg and Kruså, see E 3.

A11. Frederikshavn – Holstebro – Esbjerg – Tønder

Frederikshavn and *Skagen,* see E 3.

Kandestederne. Seaside resort with high sand dunes. *Råbjerg Mile,* a drifting sand dune that moves 8 – 10 m east every year.

Hirtshals. Ferry and fishing port. The town was built 1919-1930. Fyrklit. *Hjørring* (32 000). Chief town of Vendsyssel. Town since 1243. A few idyllic streets remain, e.g. Østergade. *Historical museum* housed in six old buildings. Art museum. Skt. Catherine Church. Lønstrup with the Skallerup Klit holiday resort. Rudbjerg Knude, a 74 m high clay cliff, covered with sand dunes, that eventually obstructed the light from the *Rudbjerg Lighthouse,* which had to be closed down in 1967. Now a little museum with exhibits about the drifting sand dunes. *Børglumkloster.* Manor house restored during the mid 18th cent. Admission to the castle courtyard and the church. Abbey 1150-1536.

Løkken. Large seaside resort. During the summer, motorists can drive on the broad sandy beach 16 km south to the seaside resort of *Blokhus.* Strandningskroen (an inn) housed in an 18th-cent. ship- outfitter's shop. *Fårup Sommerland,* a playground for the entire family. The entrance fee covers the use of all attractions. *Store Vildmose* (a peat bog) has been partially cultivated but some unspoiled areas remain.

Fjerritslev. Brewery and folklore museums in "Den Gamle Bryggergård" (the Old Brewer's House). *Løgstør,* to the south, is an old fishing town on the Limfjord. *Limfjord Museum.*

Svinklev. Enormous chalk cliffs. *Bulbjerg,* a 47 m high limestone cliff, once united with Skarreklit, another cliff, that tumbled into the sea in 1978.

Hanstholm, fishing and commercial port, opened in 1967. Daily *fish auctions.* The light from Hanstholm Lighthouse, the most powerful in Denmark. Museum devoted to the sea- rescue service.

Thisted. Museum with room dedicated to the poet J.P. Jacobsen. Lundehøj. Large passage grave. *Vestervig* Church, thought to be the largest rural church in *Scandinavia. Ydby* with about 200 burial mounds.

Mors is the largest island in the Limfjord. *Hanklit,* a 65 m high clay cliff with black stripes, remains of ashes from a volcano eruption in the Skagerak.

Nykøbing M (Mors). The town prospered during the 15th-17th cent. when the Limfjord was rich in herring. Extensive oyster beds. *Dueholm abbey* with Morsland's Historical Museum. *Legind Bjerge.* Forests on gentle hills. Arboretum. *Jespershus.* Flower park, fresh water aquarium and hot houses.

Spøttrup, medieval moated castle. *Herb garden* and *rose garden. Lihme* Church from the 12th cent.

Skive (27 000). Town charter 1326. *Skive Museum* has a large amber collection and Greenland exhibits. Contemporary Danish art. Old church with frescoes from 1522. Folk high school in the *Krabbeslund* mansion (16th-18th cent.). Sahl Church. Romanesque church with a "golden altar" from the 13th cent.

Hjerl Hede. "Den Gamle Landsby" *open-air museum* on a large heath (nature reserve). Over 40 buildings, including workshops. During July, on the site of a Stone Age settlement, visitors can get a glimpse of what life was like in Denmark 5 000 years ago. Sevel, with ruins of 12th-cent. abbey.

Daugsbjerg. 71 m high ridge. Medieval limestone mine, discovered in 1922. Visitors may go down 70 m in one of the tunnels. *Kongenshus Mindepark,* state-protected heath area with little heath museum.

Herning (33 000). Herning Museum recounts the history of the farmers on the heath. Carl-Henning Pedersen and Else Ahlefeldt's Museum is a remarkable circular, splendidly decorated building. Park with modern iron sculptures. Brande. 23 houses with paintings on the gables. They were completed in 1968.

Løveparken/Safariland Givskud, see E 3. *Billund* with *Legoland,* see E 66.

Struer (18 500). Museum and maritime collection.

Holstebro (25 000). Industrial town. Art museum with Danish and African art. *Museum* with pipe collection and other items of cultural- historical interest. Jens Nielsen's *Art Museum* with ecclesiastical art. Old post office, with authentic period furnishings.

Skjern. Little town with Romanesque church. Beautiful surroundings.

Varde (11 500). Folklore museum with furniture and handicrafts. A miniature village in the Arnbjerg Park shows what Varde looked like during the 1830s. Sct. Jacobi Church (12th-13th cent.).

ESBJERG, see E 66.

Road west from Holstebro through the *Klosterhede Plantage,* 6 000 hectares of fine countryside with hiking trails and many species of game.

Lemvig. Port town in the undulating Limfjord landscape. 13th-cent. church with onion-shaped copper spire from a later period. *Museum* dealing with the history of the sea-rescue service and displaying the works of west coast artists.

Bovbjerg Klint, 43 m, lighthouse. Jens Søndergård's Museum. **Vedersø,** where Kaj Munk, the writer, was parish pastor. He encouraged and rallied the Danes during the German occupation, was carried away and murdered by Nazis near Silkeborg. His grave is in the churchyard.

Søndervig. Seaside resort. **Ringkøbing.** Old houses and medieval church. *Museum* with folklore and a special section devoted to Greenland. Hee zoo. Wildlife park and children's amusement area.

Holmsland Klit, a 35 m long peninsula. Heaths and sand dunes. *Hvide Sande.* Fishing port near the lock which regulates the water level in Ringkjøbing Fjord. *Blåbjerg,* a 64 m high drifting sand dune. *Blåvands Huk* is Denmark's western-most point. 39 m high lighthouse. Horn's Reef extends 40 km out into the North Sea and has caused countless shipwrecks.

Ribe (8 000). One of the oldest towns in Denmark. Picturesque streets and delightful buildings, some open to visitors. During the 9th cent., Ansgar, apostle of the Swedes, had a church built here. Ribe became a bishopric in 948, and until the Reformation it was an important commercial centre. Large 12th-cent. cathedral. Dominican monastery with origins in the 13th cent. Sct. Catherinae Church (15th cent.) was once the abbey church. Art museum with Danish paintings. Johanne Dame, a flat-bottomed boat, is now a museum. Folklore museum in three old houses.

Mandø. Island in the marshes. Excursions by tractor bus at low tide from V. Vedsted. Museumshuset, a reconstructed ship captain's house.

Brøns. One of the largest rural churches in Denmark. Interesting wooden ceiling and frescoes.

West to *Rømø,* the largest of the Danish islands in the North Sea. Since 1948, it has been linked to the mainland by a 10 km long causeway. Drainage work has resulted in newly recovered fertile farmland. Very broad sandy beach. Large protected area teeming with bird life. The highest point is Høstbjerg (19 m). Folklore museum in the *Kommandørgården,* a farm from 1746. "Kommandører" were the captains of whaling ships during the 18th cent. when Rømø was at the peak of its prosperity. *Rømø Church* (Skt. Clemens). Low ceiling. Ships' models and hat pegs above the pews.

Tønder. Little town with lovely 17th- and 18th-cent. houses. Tønder Museum and Sønderjyllands Kunstmuseum with examples of the highly developed handicrafts typical of the area. Kristkirke (1592). Latin School from 1612.

The *Green Coast Road* (Grüne Küstenstrasse) continues from Tønder through northern Germany to Holland.

Road west to the delightful town of **Møgeltønder.** Linden trees and thatched houses in Slotsgade. Baroque *Schackenborg Castle.* Church with medieval frescoes. Denmark's oldest, still functioning organ (1679).

Rudbøl. The German border runs through the village's High Street. The houses on its east side are in Germany.

Højer. Little town in a marshland. Old buildings and windmill. Højer Sluse (lock) regulates the 2 m change of water level between high and low tide. Special pillars recount the height of previous flood waters. Abundant bird life. South of Højer, the farm buildings on the marshes are situated on mounds to avoid flood damage.

Løgumkloster. Idyllic small town. Beautiful abbey church to which a ducal castle was joined in 1614. Holmen museum of art.

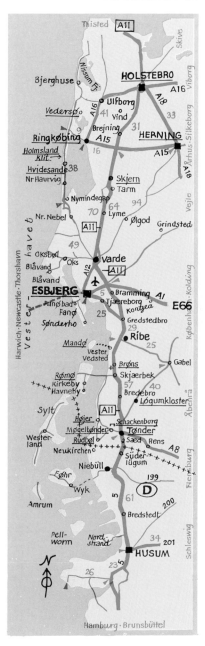

TOWN PLANS

AALBORG, Ålborg (145 000)
Cement factories, shipyards, aquavit.
Large port. Busy centre with
pedestrian precincts. Although not a
large city, Ålborg boasts 170
restaurants and seven nightclubs.
Jens Bang's House (1624) is a mansion in the Dutch Renaissance style,
built for the merchant Jens Bang. It
now houses the Duus vinkjelder (wine
cellar). Town hall (1782). Castle
(1557). The medieval *Skt. Budolfi
Cathedral* was named for the English
saint, Botolph. Remodelled in 1943.
Carillon with 48 bells played every
third hour 9.00 a.m. – 10.00 p.m. Vor
Frue Kirke (Church of Our Lady).
Helligånd Monastery with well-
preserved 15th-cent. buildings.
Ålborg *Historical Museum.* The North
Jutland *Art Museum,* designed by
Aalto and Barüel in Carrara marble,
glass and cement. 20th-cent. Danish
and international art, especially by
members of the COBRA group.
Ålborghallen. Largest cultural centre
in Scandinavia. Concerts, theatre,
conferences, art exhibitions, etc. The
main hall accommodates 3 400. Splendid swimming baths, donated by
Jensen, the aquavit king. *Ålborg's zoo*
and the Ålborg Tower with
restaurants and fine view.

ÅRHUS (245 000)
Second largest city in Denmark. Major industries, large port. 10th-cent.
bishopric. Town charter 1441. University 1928. Århus Festival Week at the
beginning of September.
Den Gamle By, an open-air museum,
with over 50 old buildings, gives a
glimpse of Danish urban life and
crafts during the period 1500-1850.
Burgomaster's house from 1597 on
the square. Helsingør Theatre, the
oldest provincial theatre in Denmark.
Summer opera and drama performances. Other museums: Århus Museum,
press museum (a part of the Danish
Journalists' Collage), Viking museum, natural history museum. Danish
fire-fighting museum, with over 60
fire-extinguishers. South of Århus is
the *Moesgård* manor house (1748)
with extensive modern exhibitions
relating the history of Denmark from
the Stone Age to the Viking era. Large
displays of Iron Age weapons. The
Grauballe Man, the corpse of a man
who lived about 2 000 years ago,
discovered in a peat bog. In the park is
a path which goes past several reconstructed prehistoric dwellings.
Rådhuset (the town hall, 1941), a
splendid example of modern Danish
architecture. Interesting decorations.
60 m high tower with carillon.
Modern university.
Skt. Clemens Cathedral (13th-cent.) is
the longest church in Denmark, 93 m
Altarpiece (1479) by Bernt Notke of
Lübeck. Exquisite baptismal font and
pulpit. Denmark's largest church
organ. *Vor Frue Church* and 12th-
cent. abbey. Altarpiece from 1525 was
carved by Claus Berg. In 1956, the
crypt from about 1060 was re-opened.
This is the oldest church in Scandinavia. *Marselisborg* Palace, Queen
Margarethe's summer residence with
park and rose garden. Forst-botanisk
have. Mindeparken, a 25-hectare park
surrounded by beech woods, near the
water. Monument to the 4 000 Danes
from North Schleswig who were killed
during the First World War.
Tivoli-Friheden, amusement park,
open May – September.

KØBENHAVN
(Copenhagen 650 000)
1.4 million people live in the 22 inde-
pendent communities that make up
Greater Copenhagen. Bishop Absolon
founded the city in 1167. The centre of
Copenhagen is *Rådhuspladsen*
(Town Hall Square). Enclosed by busy
streets with heavy motor traffic it
nevertheless has ample space for its
milling crowds and its many pigeons.
The square is dominated by the *Town
Hall* (rådhuset) built in 1905 in the
Italian Renaissance style. 105 m high
tower. *Astronomical world clock* by
Jens Olsen.
Strøget, the main shopping street of
Copenhagen, starts at Rådhuspladsen. It consists of several streets:
Nygade, Vimmelskaftet, Amagertorv
and østergade. Here are the Illum
department store, Bing & Grøndahl
(porcelain) and Den Kongelige Por-
celainsfabrik with a pastry shop
decorated in the manner of the 18th
cent.: gold and white, with palm trees
and plaster busts.
Strøget ends at *Kongens Nytorv.* Here
are the large equestrian statue of
Christian X (popularly known as
"Hesten", the Horse), the large
Magasin du Nord department store,
the Hotel d'Angleterre (one of the most
distinguished hotels in Europe), and
the Royal Danish Theatre (opera,
drama and ballet). Adjoining these
dignified surroundings is *Nyhavn*
where small sailors' taverns are in full
swing 24 hours a day. Nyhavn is the
place to go if you want a tattoo for your
holiday souvenir. There are several expert tattoo-artists to choose from. *Vor
Frue Church* (the cathedral) is near
Strøget. The original 12th-cent.
church on this site was destroyed during the English bombardment of
Copenhagen in 1807. It was rebuilt in

Bornholm

The island of Bornholm (588 km²) is
in the Baltic Sea, about 150 km north-
east of Copenhagen and 37 km east of
the Swedish coast.
Rønne (14 700). Chief town of
Bornholm and the island's major port.
Museum (geology, history, shipping
and local art). Visitors are welcome in
the 19th-cent. Ericsen's House. Citadel
from 1650. Well-preserved round
church in Nylars (1335).
Hasle. Little town with delightful
half-timbered houses; even the spire
(40 m high) of the medieval church is
half-timbered. Interesting cliffs at
"Jon's Chapel", where Jon, a monk, is
said to have preached from one of the
ledges. 108 steps lead down to the
beach. **Hammerhus.** Denmark's
largest castle ruin, 74 above the sea. It
was founded in 1258 by the Archbishop of Lund. Partially dismantled.
The six-storey high Mantel Tower remains. Caves and cliffs.
Sandvig-Allinge. Two villages that
have become a town. Large resort.
Bronze Age rock carvings. Ols Kirke,
the highest round church on the island, is dedicated to Saint Olaf (12th-
cent.). Loop-holes.
Gudhjem. Idyllic fishing village with
lovely houses and steep streets. Her-
ring-smoking and tourist-resort. 22
m high Helligdomen Cliffs overlooking the Baltic at Rø. 50 m deep stalic-
tite and stalagmite Sorte Gryde (Big
Stew Pot) Cave. Two Dutch windmills.
Views from Bokul Cliff. Skt. Lauren-
tiuskirke in Østerlars (11th-cent.) is
the largest round church on Bornholm, with a diameter of 18 m.
Boat service from Gudhjem to **Chris-
tiansø,** the largest of the Ertholmene
Islands. Semi-tropical vegetation. The
fortifications here were built in 1684
and abondoned in 1855. Museum with
military and folkloric artifacts.
Fredriksø was once a prison island.
Svaneke. Delightful town. Fishing
port, herring smoking and tourists.
Brændesgårdshavn amusement park.
Paradisbakkerne, beautiful area (partially nature reserve) with unique
vegetation.
Neksø (3 500). Museum in the old
town hall (1796). Shipping and fishing. The writer Martin Andersen
Nexø's childhood home. *Dueodde,* at
the southernmost tip of the island, has
splendid white sandy beaches and a 48
m high lighthouse.
Åkirkeby (2 000). The sole inland
town on Bornholm. Church from 1150
with sturdy defence-walls and tower.
Gotlandian sandstone baptismal font
with reliefs and rune carvings.
Almindingen is a woods, planted in
the 19th-cent. Cliffs, lakes, castle
ruins. Ekko Valley divides the steep
cliffs. *Rytterknægten,* 162 m, is the
highest point on Bornholm.

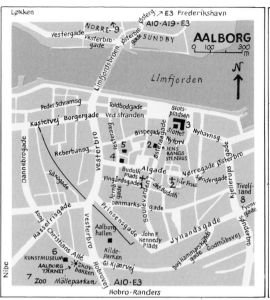

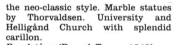

1 St. Budolfi Cathedral.
2 Jens Bang's Stonehouse.
3 Aalborg Castle.
4 Monastery of the Holy
  Ghost.
5 Historical museum.

6 North Jutland Museum
  of Art.
7 Zoo.
8 Tivoliland.
9 Lindholm Høje (hills).

1 Cathedral.
2 Vor Frue Kirke (Church
  of Our Lady).
3 Den Gamle By (open-air
  museum).
4 Museum of art.

5 University.
6 Mindeparken (Remem-
  brance Park), Marselis-
  borg Palace and Tivoli-
  Friheden.

the neo-classic style. Marble statues by Thorvaldsen. University and Helligånd Church with splendid carillon.

Rundetårn (Round Tower, 1642), an astronomical observatory whose spacious interior was once mounted by Peter the Great on horseback. He returned down its 209 m long spiral ramp in the same manner. Many of the winding streets in the immediate neighbourhood are well worth a visit. One of them, Fiolstræde, is of particular interest for antiques enthusiasts. Several shops selling old books and antiques. Gråbrødre torv (Grey Friars' Square) with splendidly painted old houses and several small restaurants. North of Kongens Nytorv is *Amalienborg*, the Royal Palace. Four impressive buildings grouped around an open square. The vast *Marmorkirken* (Marble Church) has a 45 m high dome. Work on the church began in 1746, was interrupted in 1770, and completed in 1894. The *Gefion Fountain* and the *Liberation Museum* (Frihedsmuseum) which gives a worthwhile insight into the resistance movement during the 1940-1945 German occupation of Denmark. Langelinie is a long and lovely esplanade that skirts the harbour entrance. On a rock sits the **Little Mermaid** (Den lille Havfrue), Copenhagen's most famous statue. Vesterbrogade, the shopping street south of Rådhuspladsen, passes the **Tivoli Gardens** (open from May 1 until the middle of September). Amusement park, restaurants, concert hall, Peacock Theatre with pantomime,

Den Gamle By, Århus

open-air theatre, children's playgrounds, etc. All of these – and more – comprise an extraordinary park that is unique in Europe, if not the world. Fireworks on Wednesdays, Saturdays and Sundays.

Vesterbrogade continues past the Central Railway Station and Den Permanente, an exhibition hall where examples of contemporary Danish handicrafts are displayed and sold.

The permanent circus arena is near by. Københavns *bymuseum* (city museum) which, in the summer, has an outdoor model of Copenhagen as it looked in 1536. Vesterbrogade goes on to the independent borough of Fredriksberg. *Zoologiske Have,* founded in 1859, is one of the largest zoos in Europe. 43 m high observation tower.

Dutch Renaissance *Rosenborg Castle* (1617). Splendid interiors. Since 1833 the Royal Family Museum. Impressive collections of furniture, paintings, porcelain, silver. The *Thorvaldsen Museum* with the sculptor's grave in the courtyard. Thorvaldsen (1770-1844) was one of the most renowned artists of his age. Active all over Europe, he had a studio in Rome where he was in charge of over 40 pupils. *Glyptoteket* (Ny Carlsberg Glyptotek) with prehistoric art (its Etruscan collection is the largest outside of Italy) and French and Danish art: Monet, Gaugin, Toulouse-Lautrec, Degas. The museum was founded by the Carlsberg (brewery) Foundation.

National Museum in an 18th-cent. rococo palace. Historical and ethno-graphical exhibits. The Bronze Age *"Sun Chariot"* discovered in the Trundholm peat bog. *Open-air museum in Lyngby* with farms from Denmark and Scania (now a part of Sweden) and workshops. Charlottenlund *Aquarium.* Museum of industrial arts, toy museum, the Tussaud Waxworks Museum, zoological museum (the most modern in Europe), the Hirschsprung Collection (Danish art), military museum in the 1605 Tøjhus (arsenal).

Børsen (the Stock Exchange, 1640) has a long Renaissance façade and a spire of dragons' tails. *Christiansborg Palace,* an impressive building from 1928, is the third palace to be built on this site. It houses Folketinget (the Danish parliament), the Foreign Ministry, and the royal banqueting

Central Copenhagen. Knippelsbro

halls. In the cellar are remains of the first castle, from 1167. Palace church (1826), built at the same time as the second palace. Riding academy from the first castle. *The Royal Theatre* (1766) is now a theatre museum.

Italian Baroque *Vor Frelsers Kirke* (Church of Our Saviour, 17th- cent.) with interesting tower. *Grundtvigs-kirken* (1921-1940) resembles a late-Gothic rural church but is as large as a cathedral. It is dedicated to the educator Grundtvig who founded the Danish folk high schools. Nyboder is a charming, uniform 17th-cent. quarter of the town, built to house naval personnel. *Kødbyen.* Square and market halls. In addition to its many places of cultural, historical and architectural interest, Copenhagen is a truly merry city with many enjoyable amusement areas and exceptional restaurants.

Copenhagen is an excellent starting point for excursions. All of Zealand is within easy reach **Strandvejen,** and **Dyreshavsbakken** amusement park, see E 4.

ODENSE (170 000)

Third largest city and second most important industrial centre (shipyard and brewery). Large port with an 8 km long canal (1804) that links it with Odense Fjord. One of the oldest cities in Scandinavia. Bishopric since 1020. After St. Knut (Canute) was murdered in the Skt. Albani Church in 1086, Odense became a pilgrimage place with many churches and abbeys.

The childhood home of Hans Christian Andersen is now a **museum.** It is a little house in the centre of the town that is marked by charming, winding streets and half-timbered houses. Hans Christian Andersen's House has a special room dedicated to the famous writer. Books, letters, drawings and some of the writer's possessions. Andersen (1805-1875) created "The Ugly Duckling", "The Emperor's New Clothes", "The Little Match Girl", "The Princess and the Pea" and many more familiar fairy-tales.

Møntestræde. Folklore museum in 16th to 17th-cent. houses, e.g. Møntergården. Art museum with Danish art. **Den fynske landsby,** an open-air museum with over 20 buildings: farmhouses, smithy workshops, mills, brick works, and the Sortebro Kro (inn). In July performances of the works of Hans Christian Andersen. **DSB** (Danish State Railways) **Museum** with seven steam locomotives (1869-1910). *Falck Museum* with collections of fire- fighting and life-saving equipment. The Falck Rescue Service, a unique Danish phenomenon, was founded in 1906 by Sophus Falck. *Skt. Knuds Church* (the cathedral) was consecrated in 1101, but only a part of the crypt remains of the original church. It was discovered in 1872. The present church (13th-15th-cent.) is one of Denmark's most impressive Gothic churches. 5 m long altarpiece with 300 figures by the sculptor Claus Berg from Lübeck (16th-cent.) Zoo. Amusement park.

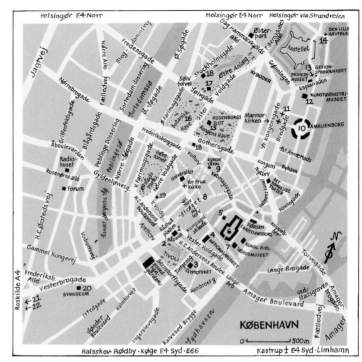

1 *Rådhuset (town hall) and Rådhuspladsen (Town Hall Square). 2 Tivoli and the Tussaud Waxworks Museum. 3 Ny Carlsberg Glyptotek. 4 National Museum. 5 Thorvaldsens Museum. 6 Christiansborg Palace and theatre museum. 7 Arsenal (military museum). 8 Strøget. 9 Round Tower. 10 Amalienborg Palace. 11 Marble Church. 12 Museum of Industrial Arts. 13 Gefion Fountain and Freedom Museum. 14 The Little Mermaid. 15 Rosenborg Castle. 16 Botanical garden. 17 Royal Museum of Fine Arts. 18 Hirschsprung Collection. 19 Toy museum. 20 City museum. 21 Zoo. 22 Mechanical music museum.*

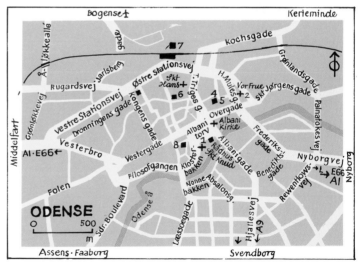

1 *Cathedral. 2 Vor Frue Kirke (Church of Our Lady). 3 St. Hans Church. 4 H.C. Andersen's House. 5 Møntestræde. 6 Museum. 7 DSB (railway) Museum. 8 Birthplace of H.C. Andersen. 9 Den fynske Landsby (open-air museum).*

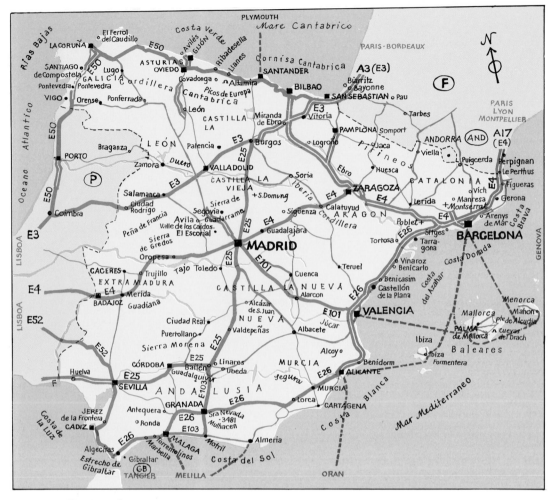

E · Spain

E·España

Area: 504 750 km² (196 700 sq. miles).
This includes the Canary Islands and the Balearic Islands (Majorca, Menorca and Ibiza).

Population: 37.5 million. The majority of the population are Roman Catholics. The national language, Spanish (Castilian/castellano), is universally spoken. Catalan is spoken by 6 million people, Basque by 1.1. million and Galician (gallego) by 1.8 million.

Major cities: Madrid 3 million, Barcelona 1.8 million, Valencia 770 000, Sevilla 600 000, Zaragoza 550 000, Bilbao 500 000, Málaga 500 000.

Government: Constitutional monarchy. Parliament consists of two houses, the Senate and the Congress. Recently a degree of independence has been granted to the Basque provinces and Catalonia. Spain is divided into 50 provinces.

History
226-219 B.C. The Romans conquer the Iberian peninsula.
2nd cent. Christianity adopted in Spain.
6th cent. Visigoth kingdom established.

Routes described:

E 3	Irún – Burgos – Valladolid – Vilar Formoso
E 4	Perpignan – Barcelona – Zaragoza – Madrid – Badajoz
E 25	Burgos – Madrid – Sevilla – Algeciras
E 26	Barcelona – Valencia – Granada – Algeciras
E 50	San Sebastián – La Coruña – Vigo
E 101	Madrid – Valencia
E 102	Mérida – Sevilla, see E 4 and E 25
E 103	Bailén – Motril – Málaga
N 623	Santander – Burgos, see E 25

Special map: Balearic Islands

Town plans: Barcelona, Córdoba, Granada, Madrid, Sevilla, Toledo, Valencia

Manzanares El Real, a castle outside Madrid

711 The Moors conquer Spain. Resistance to their rule begins in the 11th cent. (El Cid is one of the best-known heroes of this struggle) and Christian kingdoms are proclaimed. La Reconquista, the re-conquest, begins.

1469 Ferdinand of Aragon marries Isabella of Castile.

1492 Granada, the final stronghold of the Moors, falls. Columbus discovers America.

1516 Spain is formally united when Charles I, a Habsburg, becomes king. (The same monarch, as Charles Quint, is Emperor of the Holy Roman Empire.)

1571 Spain defeats the Turks at the Battle of Lepanto.

1588 The English destroy the "Great Armada".

1648 The Netherlands achieve independence from Spain.

1714 The Treaty of Utrecht follows the War of the Spanish Succession. Philip V becomes the first Bourbon king.

1805 The Spanish fleet is defeated by the British fleet under Nelson at the Battle of Trafalgar.

1813 With British support, and under the leadership of Wellington, French troops are expelled from Spain.

1819 Spain sells Florida to the U.S.A. Mexico achieves independence. California is lost in 1823.

1898 The Spanish-American War. Spain loses its Pacific (Philippines) and West Indian (Cuba, Puerto Rico, Hispañola) possessions.

1923 Dictatorship of Primo de Rivera.

1931 Democracy.

1936-1939 Civil War. General Franco seizes power.

1975 Franco dies. Juan Carlos becomes king. Democratization begins.

1977 Free parliamentary elections.

Currency: Peseta (ESP).
1 peseta = 100 céntimos

Business hours: Banks 9.00 a.m.-2.00 p.m. Some banks in major tourist centres are open 9.00 a.m.-1.00 p.m. Post offices 9.00 a.m.-1.00 p.m. and 5.00-7.00 p.m. Saturdays 9.00 a.m.-1.00 p.m. or closed. Shops 9.00 a.m.-1.00 or 2.00 p.m. and 4.00 or 5.00 p.m. to 7.00 or 8.00 p.m.

Holidays: New Year's Day, Epiphany, March 19, Maundy Thursday, Good Friday, May 1, May 15 (only in Madrid), July 25, August 15 (Assumption Day), October 12, November 1, December 8, December 25. In addition to these, there are some purely local holidays.

The cathedral, Cadiz

Avila's turreted, granite town wall is 2 400 m long

Hotels
The hotels are officially classified with a 1-5 star rating. The classification should be posted outside the hotel. Country inns and hotels are usually quite simple. Lunch is served 1.00-3.00 p.m. and dinner 8.00-10.00 p.m. *Paradores* are tourist hotels, sometimes situated in old castles, palaces and abbeys. During the high tourist season, guests may stay for no longer than ten days.
Major Spanish hotel chains: Entursa, Horesa, Hotel Agrupados, Hoteles Mallorquines, Melia, Husa, Interhotel.
There are many spas and health resorts in Spain.

Camping
About 500 camping sites, divided into four categories. More than 100 are situated along the Costa Brava.

Youth hostels
Priority is given to travellers up to 25 years of age.

Food and drink
Restaurants are classified: Deluxe, 1A, 2A, 3A and 4A. Restaurants serving typical local provincial cuisine in authentic settings are called hostelerías. Some Spanish specialities: Paella, the internationally best-known dish, is a combination of rice, chicken, meat and shellfish. Zarzuela de mariscos, shellfish. Calamares á la romana, fried squid. Squid is also served "en su tinta ", in its own ink. Parrilla de pescado is a mixed grill of fish, while parrilla de carne is a mixed grill of meat cuts. Escalope de ternera is a thin slice of fried veal. Chuletas de cordero are lamb chops, and pollo is chicken. Northern specialities include bacalao "al pil-pil", dried cod; conchas (conch), a shellfish; fabada, a bean soup. Catalonian dishes include lobs-

ter a la Catalana, and butifarra con judías, sausage and beans. Cocido, a meat, sausage and vegetable stew, is typical of Castile, and gazpacho, a chilled vegetable soup, and pescadilla, diminutive fried fish, are favourites of Andalusia.
Wines: Among the most popular are Manzanilla, from Cordova, sherry from Jerez and Cádiz, white, red and rosé wines from Rioja, Valdepeñas, Panadés and Priorato.

Shopping
Ceramics, leather goods, costume jewellery and knives from Toledo, wrought-ironwork, lace, mantillas from Seville, castanets, chocolates and nougats.

Speed limits. Traffic regulations.
Motorways 120 kmh, dual carriageways 100 kmh, other roads 90 kmh, built-up areas 60 kmh (but often no restrictions). Cars towing caravans 80 kmh, in built-up areas 50 kmh.
It is recommended that children under the age of 14 do not travel in the front seat.
If your car is fitted with seat belts it is compulsory to wear them outside built-up areas.
It is compulsory for all motorists to carry a set of replacement light bulbs. It is still advisable for motorists in Spain to carry an international driving licence and a green insurance card. A motor accident in Spain can have unpleasent consequences, for both car and driver can be taken into custody if valid credentials are not presented. The police are extremely conscientious when it comes to upholding local traffic regulations, and they are enpowered to fine lawbreakers on the spot. (Traffic fines can be as much as 5 000 pesetas.) A bail bond can be obtained from your motoring club.

Parking
Several cities have a "blue zone", where parking discs must be used. These can be obtained at the town hall, from tourist offices and in the major hotels. In general, there is a 2 1/2 hour parking limit. As a rule, free parking is available from 9.00 p.m. until 8.00 a.m., and occasionally this is extended to 10.00 a.m.

Roads
All major roads have numbers preceded by the letter N. Six roads, all starting from Madrid, have an N and a Roman number. The motorways, which are all toll roads, have A (Autopista) numbers. Many roads over the Pyrenees are closed during January and February. Other roads may also be closed by snow.
Some major roads are narrow and winding. Do not count on fast driving. Secondary roads are often in poor condition.

Road patrols
Some of the major roads are equipped with SOS telephones for emergency telephone calls. If you need towing, request "auxilio en carretera". In case of physical injury, request "accidente". Blue and yellow cars, identified by the sign "Ayuda automobilistica" patrol some of the major roads near the larger cities. They are operated by RACE, the Spanish Automobile Club.
Police: In Barcelona and Madrid, dial 091.

RACE Real Automóvil Club de España, calle José Abascal 10, Madrid 3. Tel. 44 73 200.
Spanish National Tourist Office, 57/8 St James's Street, London SW1A 1LD. Tel. 01-499 0901.

E 3. Irún – Burgos – Valladolid – Vilar Formoso

French frontier. E 3 comes from Helsinki – Stockholm – Hamburg – Antwerpen – Paris – Bordeaux – Irún.

IRÚN (45 000). Modern town with lovely views, particularly from Cabo Higuer. **Fuenterrabía.** Walled town which has been the object of many battles between the French and the Spanish. Calle Mayor is the High Street. Fiesta June 29-30.

SAN SEBASTIÁN (160 000). Capital of the Basque province of Guipúzcoa. Elegant seaside resort with dignified older sections. The Santa María Church has an exquisite rococo façade. *Museo Municipal de San Telmo*, in a former 16th-cent. monastery, has collections of Basque ethnological exhibits and an art gallery with works by El Greco. Beautiful views from the road below the Urgull mountain and from the summit of the Igueldo.

Loyola. Monastery by the Italian, Carlo Fontana, built at the end of the 17th cent. Broad staircase leads up to the semi-circular façade. 56 m high dome. The monastery is built around the castle where Ignatius Loyola, the founder of the Society of Jesus (Jesuits), was born. *Oñate.* Baroque town hall. San Miguel Church. University, founded in 1542.

BILBAO, see E 50.

The alternative route via Pamplona to Burgos is 300 km long, while the E 4 routing is 240 km.

PAMPLONA (100 000). Once the capital of the kingdom of Navarre. The city was founded in 75 B.C. by Pompeius. This was a stop for pilgrims on their way to the shrine at Santiago de Compostela. *Cathedral* (15th cent.) with the tomb of Charles III. *Museo de Navarra* with prehistoric finds. Splendid Baroque buildings on the Plaza del Castillo. University. One of the city's best-known sons is the violinist, Pablo Sarasate. During the annual *Fiesta de San Fermín,* July 6, there is a "running of bulls" through the streets of the city from the railway station to the arena.

LOGROÑO (60 000). One of the oldest towns in Spain. Beautiful churches. Vineyards and famed wines.

Soria in beautiful mountain surroundings. San Pedro Church. Near by are the remains of Numancia, see E 4.

VITORIA (75 000). The oldest part of Vitoria is atop a hill overlooking the modern town. *Santa María Cathedral* (14th cent.). Typical of the town are the *"miradores",* balconies with panels of plate glass. Archaeological museum with weapons collection. Provincial museum with art collection. Here, in 1813, the French were defeated by Wellington's English troops.

Ruins of a Roman town at *Zadorra.* The Armiñón is a beautiful bridge over the river.

Miranda de Ebro (40 000) with the Romanesque San Nicolas Church, which was rebuilt as a mosque. *Pancorbo,* where the soldiers of Wellington battled the French in 1813. Ruins of a Moorish castle and a Spanish fortress. *Briviesca.* Little fortified town. *Rodilla.* Monastery with Romanesque church.

BURGOS (85 000). Founded in the 9th cent., Burgos preceded Valladolid as the capital of Castile. The white marble **cathedral** is one of the finest examples of Gothic church architecture. Construction was started in 1221 and lasted 300 years. The lantern and the western spires by Hans of Cologne were completed in 1458. Tomb of El Cid. This legendary warrior, who led the struggle against the Moors, was probably born in Burgos, about 1026. Capilla del Condestable is one of the lovely chapels. Clock with "Papamoscas"(Fly-Eater), a fairy-tale figure who opens his mouth at the stroke of the hour.

Las Huelgas monastery (1187) has beautiful buildings and contains a museum. The *Cartuja de Miraflores Church* was reconstructed in the 15th cent. by Hans of Cologne, and his son, Simon. Sculptures by Gil de Siloé (15th cent.). Archaeological museum in *Casa de Miranda,* a 16th-cent. palace. The citadel is situated 80 m above the city.

Quintanilla de las Viñas. The oldest sections of the Ermita de Santa María Church date from the 7th cent. *Covarrubias* with Romanesque church from the 10th-12th cent. *Quintana del Puente,* an old bridge over the Arlanzón.

Torquemada, birthplace of the feared Grand Inquisitor of the same name. Famous local wine.

Palencia (42 000) has the oldest university in Spain (1208). Gothic cathedral (14th-16th cent.) with exquisite altar by Jan Joest van Haarlem. Archaeological museum with coin collection.

VALLADOLID (212 000). One of the old capitals of Castile. University city. Ferdinand and Isabella were married here in 1469. Christopher Columbus lived in *Casa de los Viveros* until his death in 1509. The House of Cervantes is also open to visitors. Work on the *cathedral* (by Juan de Herrera) started

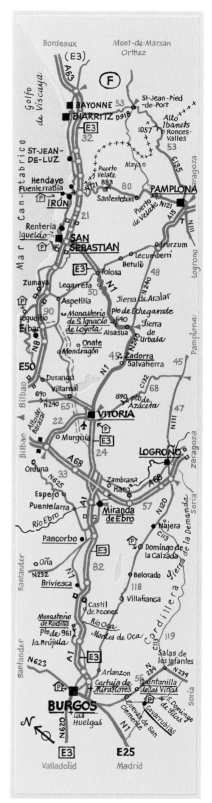

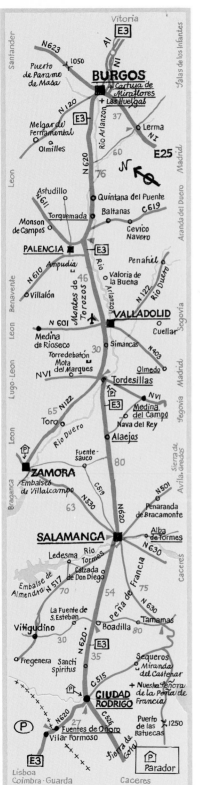

in 1585 and continued up until the 18th cent. (Herrera was also responsible for the Escorial.) The Colegio de San Gregorio is a splendidly adorned 15th-cent. building. Museo Arqueológico Provincial. The *Campo Grande* park has fountains and a little lake. Annual fiesta the second week in September.

Tordesillas. Little town with handsome Plaza Mayor (main square). A bridge with ten arches over the Duero leads to the *Santa Clara monastery*, originally a 14th-cent. royal palace, built for Alfonso XI. It is built in the Mudéjar style, an amalgamation of Oriental and West European styles. Moorish artists and craftsmen joined forces with the Spaniards. The throne room became an abbey church. Well-preserved Moorish baths.

Medina del Campo with the huge La Mota Castle (15th cent.). *Olmedo.* San Miguel Church in the Mudéjar style (13th cent.) has tombs with plaster decorations. *Alaejos* with Santa María Church.

SALAMANCA (120 000). Situated at 800 m above sea level, Salamanca is the site of one of the world's oldest universities (1250s). Alfonso VI liberated the city from the Moors in 1085. Uniform houses on the Plaza Mayor (main square). *Catedral Vieja* (Old Cathedral), from the 15th cent., has the stately, octagonal Torre del Gallo (Cock's Tower). Richly adorned interior. Altar by Nicolo Florentino. Capilla de San Martín with 14th-cent. wall paintings. Capilla Talavera with Moorish arches. 15th-cent. *Catedral Nueva* (New Cathedral). The Augustinian monastery (16th cent.), with an enormous dome, was created by Domenico Fontana, who was also responsible for the royal palace in Naples. *Casa de las Conchas,* a work of Juan de Talavera, (1495), has an exterior decorated with shell (conch) reliefs. The university, founded in the 13th cent., was during the following centuries one of the most renowned in all of Europe. 16th-cent. buildings and magnificent library. Goya's portrait of Charles IV in the main hall.

Road to *Ávila* and the *Sierra de Gredos* winter resorts. See also E 4.

Alba de Tormes. Roman Catholic pilgrimage place. In 1571, an abbey was founded here by Santa Teresa of Ávila. Her relics are in a black marble casket on the high altar. Four churches, all in the Mudéjar style, combine to form the Church of San Juan.

Nuestra Señora de la Peña de Francia abbey, 1 723 m, with an inn and lovely views. **Tamames,** famed for its breeding of bulls.

Ciudad Rodrigo. Imposing 14th-cent. cathedral. Magnificent west façade with figures of the apostles. Castle and town hall, which has its origins in the Roman period. Troops under Wellington defeated the French here during the Napoleonic Wars. He was granted the title "Duke of Ciudad Rodrigo".

Fuentes de Oñoro. Portuguese border. E 3 continues to Guarda – Lisboa (Lisbon).

E 4. Perpignan – Barcelona – Zaragoza – Madrid – Badajoz

Map on next page.

French border. E 4 comes from Helsinki – Stockholm – København – Hamburg – Basel – Bern – Genève – Montpellier.

Le Perthus. The town is half French, half Spanish.

Figueras. Fortified town, famous for its wine. Ampurias was founded in the 6th cent. B.C. by Greeks. Later, another ancient town, "Neapolis", surrounded by a town wall, grew up near by. Between the two towns lay an important harbour, which has silted up. In 49 B.C. Caesar founded a Roman town on this site. Many mosaics and some antique palaces have been discovered. They are similar to the finds at Pompeii. Museum. A large number of the archaeological finds have been removed to museums in Gerona and Barcelona.

Gerona (35 000). One of the most ancient cities in Catalonia. Beautiful old section of the city with 16th-cent. *cathedral.* Earlier, this was the location of a mosque, and before that, it was the site of an early Christian church. Staircase with 90 steps leading up to the ornate Baroque façade. The altar is adorned with silver, gold and precious stones. Museum with the 11th-cent. Tapiz de la Creación, depicting the creation of the world. Remains of Moorish baths. San Feliu Church. There is an archaeological museum in the San Pedro Galligans Church.

Costa Brava, the "Wild Coast", is a beautiful coastal area that stretches from the French border south to Blanes. Here, the shores of the Mediterranean are lined with fishing villages and resorts, and, surprisingly, many areas are still unscathed by mass-tourism.

Bagur, 2 km from the sea. Narrow streets, splendid buildings, and several towers. National monument.

Palafrugell (8 000). Large resort. Three long sandy beaches.

Palamós (6 000). Fishing port. Excellent beach. Museum with collection of shells, pre-Christian ceramics and modern art. *Playa de Aro.* Lively seaside resort. *S'Agaró.* Modern seaside resort. Music and art festival.

San Feliu de Guíxols (9 000). Chief town of the Costa Brava. Beach adjacent to the fishing harbour. Bull-fight arena. Cork industry. *Tossa de Mar* (1 300). 11th-cent. town wall and lovely old streets and houses. Canning industry.

Lloret de Mar (3 000). Well-known resort with over 100 hotels. *Blanes.* Little town with white houses. Here begins the *Costa Dorada,* the "Golden Coast", which extends south as far as Tortosa. In general, the beaches here have coarser sand than those on the Costa Brava.

Tordera. Roman Catholic pilgrimage place, famous for its lace. *Arenys de Mar.* Large resort.

BARCELONA, see town plans.

Road N 152 comes from Andorra (see France, N 20,) via Puerto de Tosas, a memorable journey through a pass with exceptional views. *Ripoll,* where a Benedictine abbey was founded in the 10th cent., severely damaged in the 15th cent., destroyed by fire in 1835, and subsequently restored in an ornate style. *Vich* (20 000). Lovely old town with narrow streets. The town is famous for its sausages. The cathedral (1803) contains the fittings from earlier churches. Medieval ecclesiastical treasures in the Museo Episcopal.

TARRASA (95 000). Three churches on a hill: San Miguel, San Pedro and Santa María. The murder of St. Thomas à Becket in Canterbury Cathedral is depicted on a wall.

The monastery of *Montserrat* lies high in a wild and narrow cleft, 725 m above sea level, in a weird, pinnacled, mountainscape, formed by the process of erosion. The monastery was founded in the 10th cent. and destroyed in 1812 by French troops. The present buildings date from the 19th cent. A 12th- cent. Black Virgin, patron saint of Catalonia, is in the basilica.

Manresa (50 000). Textile industry. Splendid Gothic church. *Cervera* is high atop a hill. Lovely old buildings. Old university. Grotesque figures adorn the town hall (1679). Circular San Pere Church (11th cent). *Tárrega.* Castle with marvellous views out over the fertile Urgel area.

The new motorway goes near the *Santes Creus monastery,* founded in 1169 by Cistercian monks. Tombs of the princes of Aragon.

The monastery of *Poblet,* founded in the 12th cent., flourished during the 14th cent. It was a major religious centre, encircled by three walls. The kings of Aragon have been entombed here since the 12th cent. *Tarragona.* see E 26.

LÉRIDA (65 000) has a splendid Old Town. The *Catedral Vieja* (Old Cathedral) was consecrated in the 13th cent. From the 19th cent., and up until 1926, it served as a barracks. It has since been restored and is now richly adorned. The *Catedral Nueva* (New Cathedral) dates from the 18th cent. Museum with displays of Flemish weaving. Zuda Castle was originally a Moorish fortress. Archaeological museum. *Cogull* with prehistoric cliff carvings in the *Cuevas des Morros* (8000-4000 B.C.).

Fraga. Charming old town with colourfully painted houses, clustered on a cliff. Fig export. *Castejón de Monegros* with castle and lovely church.

ZARAGOZA (Saragossa, 350 000). A town existed on this site even prior to the Roman invasion. Famous university and beautiful sections. The modern parts of the city are marked by splendid and broad avenues. *Aljafería,* the summer palace of the Moorish kings (11th cent.), became the residence of the kings of Aragon. Magnificent Mudéjar (a combination of West European and Oriental styles) ceiling. The Gothic El Salvador Cathedral, *La Seo,* has been marked by different periods, but in general it is dominated by the medieval period. Museum with French and Flemish tapestries. The *Church of Nuestra Señora del Pilar* was built in the 17th cent. Paintings by Goya and Velásquez.

Route 123 to *Huesca* (25 000), once one of the major Moorish strongholds. The *cathedral* (1273-1515) was built on the site of what had been a Roman temple, a Visigoth church and a Moorish mosque. Interesting provincial museum.

The new motorway passes *Tudela* with its imposing cathedral and continues on to Pamplona and Bilbao (see E 50). *Veruela* has a Romanesque abbey church. The monastery was founded in 1146 by the Cistercians. Now it is owned by the Jesuits.

Calatayud (18 000). Ruins of a Moorish castle, Kalat Ayud, the "Castle of Ayud", high atop a hill. Mudéjar church of Santa María la Mayor (13th cent.). *Piedra* monastery was founded in 1195 by Cistercian monks from

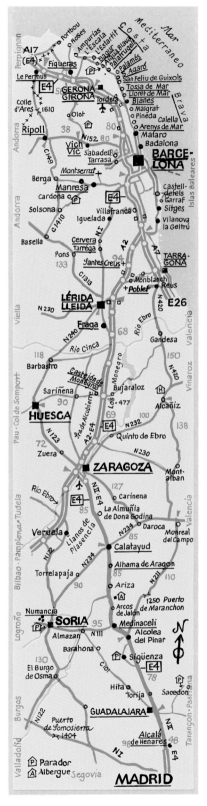

145

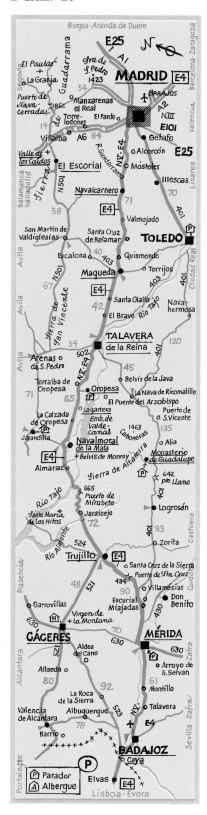

Poblet. One section has been transformed into a hotel. Splendid park with grottoes, lakes and fountains, a contrast to the dry Aragon landscape.

Alhama de Aragón. Climatic health resort. Santa María de Huerta, a Cistercian monastery (except the period 1835-1930). Los Caballeros cloister. Gothic refectory, 35 m long and 15 m high. Magnificent gardens. Archaeological collection.

Medinaceli. Situated at 1 201 m on a summit, with a splendid view out over the bare mountain peaks. Remains of Roman fortification walls. Roman triumphal arch. Church with the tombs of the counts of Medinaceli.

Road north to **Soria** (20 000), at 1 050 m, capital of the province of the same name. San Pedro Cathedral and San Domingo Church with a splendid, broad, façade. San Juan de Duero has an exquisite cloister. Near by are the ruins of **Numancia,** the capital of a Carthaginian republic (4th cent. B.C.). The Roman general, Scipio, scourge of the Carthaginians, destroyed the city in 134 B.C. Most of the population committed suicide, the remainder were carried away to slavery.

Sigüenza. 1 070 m above sea level. Founded in the 4th cent. B.C. Beautiful town with stately poplar trees lining the Alameda. The fortress-like cathedral was built between 1140 and 1495. Magnificent sacristy, cross-aisle and chapels. Museum with paintings by El Greco, etc.

Guadalajara (22 000). The name of the town, which means "the stone-filled river", comes from the Moors. The Dukes of Mendoza once reigned here. The Princes' Palace, *Palacio del Infantado,* has a splendid façade and a magnificent courtyard. Here Philip II wedded Isabella. *Santa María* Church has minaret-like towers that recall the time when it served as a mosque. Guadalajara became world-famous when, during the 1930s, it became the centre of a battle between the Falangists and the Republicans. Excursions south to El Mar de Castilla, beautiful artificial lakes. 16th-cent. castle in **Pastrana.** It was once the residence of Princess Éboli, a character in Schiller's "Don Carlos".

Alcalá de Henares (25 000). University founded in 1498. *The House of Cervantes* on the site of the house where the great author was born. Cervantes (1547-1616) is best known for his "Don Quixote". The old university building has an interesting façade (1543), adorned with the emperor's two-headed eagle. Stately Archbishops' Palace (14th cent.). Remains of a town wall with ten defence towers.

MADRID and *Toledo,* see town plans. *El Escorial,* see E 25.

Navalcarnero with a typical Castilian square.

Maqueda with remains of a Moorish castle. **Torrijos.** Picturesque old town. Altamira Palace was designed by the architect, Juan de Herrera.

Talavera de la Reina (32 000). The Ruiz de Luna *Ceramics Museum* exhibits the famous blue-white ceramics that are a speciality of the area. Blue and white tiles also adorn the Church of the Virgen del Prado.

Oropesa. Old town with medieval castle that in part serves as a parador (state-owned country hotel). Picturesque **Lagertera**, where the women of the village sit in front of their houses embroidering, just as their foresisters have done for hundreds of years.

Navalmoral de la Mata. Tobacco centre. After his abdication in 1557, Charles Quint withdrew to the San Jerónimo monastery. Road to **Guadalupe.** Monastery with handsome Gothic façade on the Plaza Mayor. Its 14th-cent. bronze doors depict the life of Jesus. The head of the Black Virgin is adorned with 30 000 precious stones.

Trujillo. Birthplace of Pizarro (1475-1541), the conquistador who became the ruler of Peru. Plaza Mayor with splendid houses that reflect the wealth taken from Spain's South American colonies. Town wall and castle partially date from the Moorish period. Trujillo was one of Spain's project cities during the European Architectural Heritage Year 1975.

CÁCERES (50 000). Capital of Estremadura. Founded by the Roman general, Metellus. The entire old town has maintained its medieval character. Two splendid squares: San Mateo and Santa María. The provincial museum is housed in Casa de las Veletas.

Mérida was founded in 25 B.C. by the Romans. *Amphitheatre* with places for 15 000 spectators and *Roman theatre,* accommodating 6 000. Los Milagros, a Roman aqueduct. The *Roman bridge* that spans the Guadiana is 782 m long and has 60 arches. Several Roman temples. Archaeological museum in the Santa Clara abbey. The *Alcazaba,* a Moorish fortress, was completed in 835. The tower and other additions were constructed during the Christian era. Hornito de Santa Eulalia on the site where the saint was roasted in an oven in 292.

BADAJOZ (100 000). Built on a hill above the Guadiana. Remains of the *Alcazaba,* a Moorish fortress. Fortress-like San Juan Bautista Cathedral. Octagonal Espantaperros tower. *Puente de las Palmas* (16th cent.), stone bridge with 32 arches.

Caya. Portuguese border. E 4 continues to Lisboa.

E 25. Burgos – Madrid – Sevilla – Algeciras
N 623. Santander – Burgos

SANTANDER, see E 50. *BURGOS,* see E 3.

Quintanilla de las Viñas. Sections of the Santa María Church remain from a 7th-cent. Visigoth church. Stone reliefs. *Covarrubias* with lovely old alleys and exquisite buildings. Romanesque church with carved altar by Gil de Siloé (16th cent.). Museum. *Santo Domingo de Silos* with remains of the original abbey, founded in 919. Magnificent 11th-cent. cloister. Art treasures in the museum. Old pharmacy with ceramic vessels from Talavera. Laboratory and library.

Aranda de Duero (14 000). Wine centre. The Church of Santa María la Real was designed by Simon of Cologne. Beautiful façade. *Sepúlveda.* Lovely old town.

From the almost completely desolate Old Castilian Plain – all of the villages are in the valleys – the road ascends up to *Puerto de Somosierra,* where Napoleon won the important battle that cleared the way to Madrid. *Buitrago del Lozoya.* Fortified town with Roman origins. Medieval atmosphere. Wild landscape of strange rock formations.

Route N 110 goes to Segovia. From there it is possible to drive via Puerto de Navacerrada or Guadarrama to Madrid.

Pedraza is said to have been the birthplace of Trajan (Marcus Ulpius Trajanus), Roman emperor A.D. 98-117. Beautifully decorated houses and medieval castle. *Turégano.* A typical Castilian village with lovely buildings and arcades on the Plaza Mayor, which is dominated by a palace.

Segovia (35 000) is situated 1 000 m above sea level. The town's beautiful houses and churches are set on a hill which is crowned by the *Alcázar* (14th cent.), a large castle. The Patio de las Doncellas, a lovely courtyard, is in the Mudéjar style. View. Gothic *Santa María Cathedral* (16th cent.). Tapestries. Cathedral museum with paintings by Van Eyck and Ribera. 15th-cent. del Parral monastery (Hieronymite order). Several other splendid churches. The dual-levelled *Roman aqueduct,* 813 m long and with 163 arches, was in use until 1974. Segovia was one of Spain's project cities during the European Architectural Heritage Year 1975.

11 km south lies *La Granja* (San Ildefonso), a palace inspired by Versailles and built for Philip V in the 18th cent. Exquisite furniture, ceiling paintings and frescoes. The beautiful Patio de la Herradura. Exquisitely adorned throne room with frescoes. Tapestry museum. Large park with fountains and sculptures. Fiesta June 23 and 30.

Puerto de Navacerrada, at 1 860 m, with impressive views. Winter resort. *Manzanares el Real* with magnificent 15th-cent. castle. Several kilometres of peculiar rock formations.

Valle de los Caídos, the "Valley of the Fallen ". Benedictine abbey and monument to those who fell during the 1936-1939 Civil War. 125 m high cross. Basilica with enormous dome. The nave is 260 m long. (The nave of St. Peter's Cathedral in Rome is 186 m long.)

El Escorial, under construction 1563-1584, was built for Philip II by Juan de Herrera. This enormous monastery (206×106 m) is in the form of a grid-iron, the symbol of St. Lawrence. (He was martyred on a grid-iron in A.D. 258.) The complex includes an Augustinian monastery, the royal palace, a domed church with the tombs of the kings of Spain. Architectural museum and one of the largest libraries in the world: 40 000 folios rest in the bookcases, designed by Juan de Herrera. Salas de Pintura, an art museum with masterpieces by Bosch, El Greco, Ribera, Rubens, Tintoretto, Titian, Velásquez, etc. Beautiful park with the little 18th-cent. Casita del Príncipe (a palace). 6 km to the west is the Silla de Felipe II, "Philip II's chair", a rock where the king used to sit and watch the builders' progress. Such a distance was necessary to gain perspective of the mighty edifice.

MADRID, see town plans.

Cerro de los Ángeles is the geographic mid-point of Spain. Monument. *Valdemoro.* 16th-cent. church with paintings by Goya. In *Ciempozuelos* Bronze Age ceramics have been discovered.

Aranjuez (30 000) in a fertile area that lies like an oasis in an otherwise barren tract. The town is distinguished by many beautiful Baroque palaces.

Illescas. Sculptures, paintings and examples of the goldsmith's art in the Hospital Santuario de la Virgen de la Caridad. Paintings by El Greco.

TOLEDO, see town plans.

Manzanares. Even early Roman colonists were familiar with the copper mines here. Medieval fortress. Orchards. *Valdepeñas* (25 000). Famed for its wine.

Ciudad Real (40 000) was founded in the 13th cent. by Alfonso X on the ruins of Alarcos. Puerta de Toledo is all that remains of the mighty town fortifications that once boasted 130 towers. 16th-cent. cathedral. *Almagro*

with *La Asunción monastery* (16th cent.). Courtyard with double arcades. Corral de Comedias is a reconstruction of a 16th-cent. theatre.

Almuradiel, or El Visollo. Village, founded by Charles II in an attempt to colonize the *Sierra Morena,* the mountain ridge that is the natural boundary between Andalusia and New Castile.

Bailén. Site of a famous battle in 1808, where the French forces capitulated to Spanish guerillas.

Úbeda (30 000). Olive-growing centre. Exquisite Renaissance buildings and atmosphere. Winding streets round the Plaza de Vázquez de Molina, which is lined with handsome palaces and churches. *Santa María,* built over a mosque. The minaret has been transformed into a steeple. Side chapel with filigree decorations in the Mudéjar style. *El Salvador Church,* designed by Diego de Siloé, and decorated by Andrés de Vandelvira, was completed in 1536. Baeza also has splendid Renaissance houses close to the cathedral. Exquisite doors and chapels. Town hall and former university. The twin cities of Úbeda-Baeza were one of Spain's project cities during the European Architectural Heritage Year 1975.

Andújar (32 000). Olive-growing centre. Remains of Roman walls. Romans built the original *bridge,* with 13 arches, over the Guadalquivir, 15th-cent. Church of Santa María. El Greco's "Jesus on the Mount of Olives". 32 km from Andújar, in lovely surrounding, is *Virgen de la Cabeza* with shrine church. Pilgrimages have been made here since an alleged appearance of the Virgin Mary in 1127. It was destroyed during the Civil War.

Marmolejo. Health resort. Roman bridge over the river.

CÓRDOBA (CORDOVA), see town plans.

Ecija (50 000) with splendid churches, Moorish gateway and remains of the town wall. Las Teresas abbey is housed in a former Moorish palace. *Carmona* (27 000), Moorish town with lovely buildings, monastery and Santa Clara Church. Roman town gate and necrópolis. *Alcalá de Guadaira.* Remains of Roman fortifications.

SEVILLA, see town plans.

JEREZ de la Frontera (130 000). Famous for its wine, wine cellars and bodegas (wine taverns). Centre of sherry production. 11th-cent. fort. Magnificent palaces and churches. Archaeological museum. Annual Horse Festival May 2-9.

Arcos de la Frontera (25 000). One of Spain's project cities during the European Architectural Heritage Year 1975. Delightful white houses in a lovely setting. Plaza de España. Gothic Church of Santa María .

Puerto de Santa María (35 000) was founded by the Romans. Beautiful view from the San Marco Castle. *Rota.* American naval base.

CÁDIZ (120 000). The city was founded by Phoenicians in about 1100 B.C. The Romans expanded the city, which was destroyed by the Visigoths during the 4th cent. It prospered again after the discovery of America. The city is distinguished by its white, balconied houses. It is situated on an island-like peninsula, and there are superb views from the Alameda. Fine views also from the Avenida de Primo de Rivera. The cathedral was completed in 1838. *Iglesia de Capuchinos* contains the last work of Murillo. He fell to his death from a scaffolding while the work was in progress. 4 km long 17th-cent. city wall.

Cabo Trafalgar, where the British fleet under the leadership of Lord Nelson defeated the combined fleets of France and Spain on October 21, 1805. Nelson was killed during the battle.

Vejer de la Frontera. Picturesque town with white houses. *Benalup de Sidonia.* Caves decorated with prehistoric paintings. *Zahara de los Atunes.* Fishing port (tuna). *Punta de Tarifa,* Europe's southernmost point.

ALGECIRAS (70 000). Port city with beautiful views towards the Rock of Gibraltar and the Strait of Gibraltar that separates Europe from Africa.

GIBRALTAR (25 000) has been in British ownership since 1704. It was granted to Britain by the 1713 Treaty of Utrecht. Since 1970, Spain has contested Britain's right to the Crown Colony and has made it impossible to travel directly to or from Gibraltar from Spain. The Rock of Gibraltar, one of the "Pillars of Hercules," has a steep eastern elevation, and a terraced western incline. The highest summit is the Pau de Azúcar (Sugarloaf), 400 m above sea level. The Punta de Europa (Europe Point) stretches furthest out into the sea. Ruins of a Moorish castle. Tropical vegetation in the Alameda Gardens. Lovely views from the Upper Galleries. St. Michael's Cave with stalactites and stalagmites. Legend has it that as long as the famous Barbary apes remain, Britain will continue to own the Rock.

E 26. Barcelona – Valencia – Granada – Algeciras

BARCELONA, see town plans.

Sitges. Little town with narrow streets and delightful houses. Popular seaside resort with a 4 km long sandy beach. Museo *Cau Ferrat* (art) and Museo *Hogar Ochocentista* (19th-cent. home interiors). **Vilanova i la Geltrú** (26 000). Industrial town and coastal resort. Museo *Víctor Balaguer* (art and coins). **Cubellas.** 3 km long sandy beach. **Calafell.** Resort with long sandy beach.

Costa Dorada, the "Golden Coast", with its centre, Tarragona, is lined with seaside resorts.

Torredembarra, fishing village. **Santes Creus** and **Poblet,** see E 4.

TARRAGONA (50 000) was founded 3 000 years ago. It became the Romans' most important town in Spain. Severely damaged during the 5th cent. and laid waste again in the 8th cent. The Murallas Ciclópeas are the remains of 3 000-year-old fortifications. On these, the Romans built their town wall which was probably 4 km long. Slightly more than 1 km of this wall is in good state of preservation. Stroll along the Paseo Arqueológico, a lovely avenue. *Archaeological museum* with a mosaic of the head of Medusa. *Pretorio Romano,* next to the museum, also known as the Palace of Augustus, or the Palace of Pilate, has been used as a royal castle. *Necrópolis Paleocristiana,* a Roman burial place (3rd-4th cent.). 13th-cent. *cathedral* with Museo Diocesano (antiquities, gold, silver, pottery). Magnificent processions during Holy Week. Torre de los Escipiones, a Roman tower, is 5 km away. A Roman aqueduct, *Las Ferreras,* is 4 km outside the town. It is 217 m long and 26 m high. Tarragona is a large seaside resort.

Reus (40 000). Industrial town in the centre of a fertile area with orange and olive groves. **Salou,** its harbour, was of great importance during the Middle Ages. Hospitalet del Infante, founded in 1314, was once a Pilgrims' hostel. **Ametlia de Mar.** Picturesque fishing port.

Tortosa (45 000). 14th-cent. cathedral. Colegio San Luis de Gonzaga was founded by Charles Quint. Beautiful arcaded buildings.

The coastline between Vinaroz and Valencia is known as the **Costa del Azahar,** "Orange Blossom Coast". Vinaroz. **Peñíscola** is a lovely old town with splendid views from the castle. Fiesta September 8-9 commemorating the town's liberation in 1214. Fishing port (spiny lobsters).

Benicasim. Picturesque fishing village and popular resort.

CASTELLÓN DE LA PLANA (65 000). Modern town. Wine centre and orange orchards. *Palacio de la Diputación Provincial,* a museum with art, tools, weapons and ceramics. Santa María Cathedral was restored after Civil War damage. Fiesta March 13-21. Villareal with extensive orange orchards.

Sagunto (40 000) Important town during antiquity. In 219 B.C., during the Punic Wars, Hannibal finally destroyed the town after a 17-year-long siege. It was later reconstructed by Scipio. Fortification walls and remains of a Roman amphitheatre.

VALENCIA, see town plans.

Costa Blanca, the "White Coast ", extends from Denia to Torrevieja. Numerous enormous concrete-dominated resorts. But there are still some quiet enclaves on this 210 km coastline. On June 24 (the Feast of San Juan) celebrations are held along the entire coast.

La Albufera is a lagoon with eel-fishing and duck-hunting. Rice fields, gardens and small villages line the shores of the lagoon. **Gandía.** Orange-growing centre. The *Palacio del Santo Duque* was named after Duke Francisco de Borja (Borgia) who owned the palace in the 17th cent. Now it belongs to the Jesuits. Beautiful interiors and museum. The Borja family originally came from **Játiva,** a little town with splendid churches. Birthplace of the painter, José (called Spagnoletto) Ribera (1588-1652).

Benidorm (6 000). This little fishing village has been transformed into one of the great cosmopolitan Mediterranean resorts. Beaches on both sides of the town, the Levante (east) and the Poniente (west). Over 50 hotels. Beautiful views on the road from Calpe, past the steep, 328 m high, Peñon de Ifach cliff.

Alcoy. Industrial town. Fiesta April 20-24 to commemorate the town's liberation from the Moors.

Christmas nougat (turrón) is manufactured in **Jijona.**

ALICANTE (120 000). Founded by the Carthaginians. Romans built the Castrum Album (White Fortress). Chief city of the Costa Brava. Major resort. Harbour. Export of wine, raisins and almonds. Fine view from the Castillo de Santa Bárbara. Baroque town hall. Beautiful churches. Fiesta June 21-19.

ELCHE (75 000) with large palm gardens criss-crossed by irrigation canals. There is a large palm grove, with some trees as high as 40 m, in the *Parque Municipal.* The town is old and has a distinctive Oriental flavour.

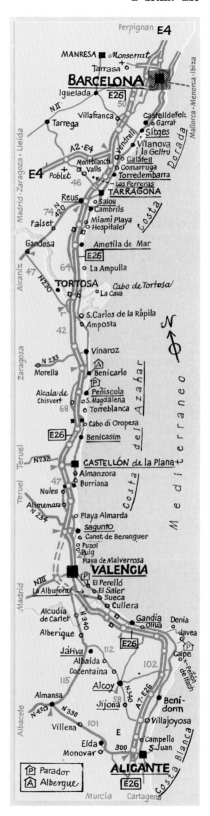

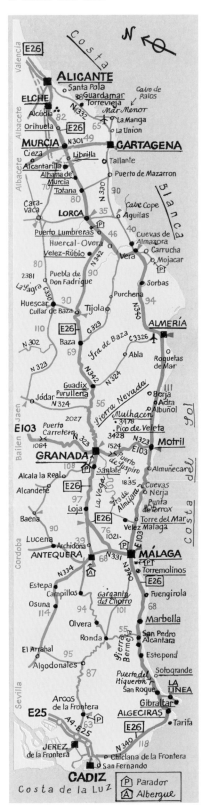

Baroque Santa María Church. Performances of *"The Mystery of Elche"* August 13-15. This religious play traditionally has an all-male cast. Costumes, sets and music are passed on from father to son. *La Alcudia* with excavations of a nearly 4 000-year-old village. This was where the famous *Dama de Elche* was found, a sculpture that is now in the Archaeological Museum in Madrid.

Guardamar. Fishing village, resort. Woods with pine, eucalyptus and palm trees.

Orihuela. Centre of an orange-growing area. Work on the Gothic Cathedral del Salvador was begun in the 14th cent. Museum with sculpture, paintings and examples of the goldsmith's art.

MURCIA (84 000). Provincial capital in a fertile area. Gothic cathedral with Baroque façade and beautiful view from the tower. Archaeological museum. Fiesta April 12-20. "War of the Flowers."

CARTAGENA (42 000). Founded by Carthaginians. Badly damaged during the Civil War. Archaeological museum. Roman Torre Ciega (a tower).

Alcantarilla. Industrial town. *Librilla.* Beautiful castle at the edge of a deep ravine. Remains of Moorish walls. *Alhama de Murcia.* Health resort. Ruins of a Moorish fortress. *Totana* with Baroque fountain in the Plaza Mayor. *Lorca* (60 000). Baroque buildings. *Puerto Lumbreras* with Moorish Torrecilla tower.

Route N 340 goes to *ALMERÍA* (90 000). Founded by the Phoenicians, it became one of the Moors' most important cities. Large fruit-exporting harbour. Triple fortification walls encircle the *Alcazaba,* an 8th-cent. Moorish castle. *Cathedral* with four circular fortification towers. Construction, led by Diego de Siloé, started in 1524. Lovely views from the Castillo de San Cristóbal.

Vélez Rubio with Renaissance castle. Caves with prehistoric paintings. *Cullar de Baza* at the foot of the Sierra de las Estancias. Galería with the Necrópolis (Roman burial ground) *Tutugi* (800-700 B.C.) Baza retains its Moorish flavour. Castle ruins. The town in famed for its exquisite cloth.

Guadix (25 000). Ancient town, once inhabited by Romans, Visigoths and Moors. The Oriental *Barrio de Santiago* section of the town is particularly noteworthy. Cathedral, built 1510-1796. *Purullena,* where many people live in caves, carved out of the mountain.

GRANADA (160 000), see town plans.

Sierra Nevada, the "Snow-Covered Mountains", is a 90 km long mountain range. The highest summit, the snow-capped *Cerro de Mulhacén* (3 478 m) is the loftiest peak on the Iberian peninsula. The highest mountain road in Europe leads to *Pico de la Veleta* (3 428 m).

E 103. Bailén – Motril – Málaga

For Bailén – Motril section, see E 25.

Motril. Port. Resort. Luxuriant vegetation and semi-tropical fruits. Nerja in an area of sugar-cane fields. Beautiful views from the *Balcón de Europa* and the corniche road to Salobreña. Prehistoric caves extend 200 m into the mountain. The largest grotto is 70 m high. *Punta de Torrox.* Picturesque mountain village. *Torre del Mar* and other fishing ports with fine sandy beaches.

Santa Fé. Famed for its manufacture of embroidered mantillas. Beautiful stretch of road along the Genil. *Lojas los Infiernos,* the "Devil's Gorge". *Loja* (30 000). Old houses. Pottery workshops.

MÁLAGA (300 000). Beautiful town in a magnificent setting. Port and resort. Chief town of the Costa del Sol. Splendid view from the Gibralfaro. Parador. The *Alcazaba,* originally one of the mightiest Moorish fortresses (11th cent.) was expanded during the 14th cent. Archaeological museum. The cathedral was completed in the 18th cent. *Art museum* with works of Murillo, Zurbarán, Picasso. Fiestas during Holy Week and early August.

Antequera. Inhabited as early as the Stone Age. Archaeological museum in the Palacio Nájera. Cueva del Romeral, a Roman tomb. Roman burial place. Remains of Moorish fortifications. 16th-cent. Papabellotas tower.

Garganta del Chorro, a 400 m deep gorge. Dammed lakes.

The road follows the *Costa del Sol,* "Sun Coast", now heavily commercialized and bursting with tourists. One of the centres of mass-tourism is *Torremolinos,* with the large Costa del Sol amusement park. Numerous large resorts. *Marbella* is one of the largest. The *Sotogrande golf course* is one of the most distinguished in Europe. Fiesta June 10-15.

Algeciras, Gibraltar and *Cádiz,* see E 25.

E 50. San Sebastián – La Coruña – Vigo

SAN SEBASTIÁN, see E 3.

Zumaya. Seaside resort and fishing village with delightful houses and churches. *Eibar* (30 000), famous for its Damascus steel workshops and sword-making. Damascus steel is created by forging together steel and iron, and etching into the surface. The result is a wavy pattern.

The motorway provides fast travel to Bilbao. The coastal route is extremely picturesque. Corniche roads lead out to the lovely, rocky coast. The *Cornisa Cantábrica* is particularly beautiful between the fishing villages and resorts of Ondárroa and Lequeitio, and further on to Arteaga.

Guernica is the Basques' holy town. Ancient oak where fealty to the Basque nation and traditions is sworn. On April 27, 1937, during the Civil War, Guernica suffered a destructive bombing attack. This inspired Picasso, who created the famed work that testified to the madness of warfare. Picasso's "Guernica" is now in a museum close to the Prado in Madrid.

BILBAO (470 000). The second largest port in Spain. (Only Barcelona is larger.) Metal-working industry. *Santiago Cathedral* was rebuilt after a severe fire in 1571. *Museo de Bellas Artes* and *Museo de Arte Moderno* contain works of famous masters. Historical museum.

Castro Urdiales. Resort. Oldest town on the Cantabrian coast. Gothic (13th-15th cent.) Church of Santa María. *Laredo.* Beautifully situated resort.

SANTANDER (120 000). Fashionable resort with elegant beaches and dignified Sardinero (one of the sections of the city). The cathedral was damaged, and the oldest parts of the city were completely destroyed, during a tornado in 1941. The *cathedral*, with 12th-cent. crypt, has since been restored. Archaeological and art museums.

Santillana del Mar. Little town, one of the most beautiful in Spain. In the 6th cent., an abbey was founded here, devoted to Santa Iliana. Lovely streets and palaces, one of them now housing the Gil Blas Parador, named after the legendary hero. *Regina Coeli,* once a monastery, now a museum. Church with splendid façade.

Cuevas de Altamira. Caves with 15 000-20 000-year-old, vividly coloured, paintings of prehistoric animals. The caves reach a total length of 160 m. One grotto was found to contain skeletal remains.

Cabezón de la Sal. Salt mines. *San Vicente de la Barquera.* Port town, dominated by the ruins of the Santa Cruz fortress.

Llanes (20 000) with picturesque streets and houses. Fishing port and the de Barro beach. *Ribadesella.* Fishing port and resort. Famed for canoe competitions held on the Río Sella on the first Saturday in August. *Cuevona* stalactite and stalagmite cave.

Covadonga in a wild, forested mountain area. National park and nature reserve. Two beautiful roads: the Route de Panes and the Route de lac Enol. Here in the mountains of Asturias, resistance to the Moorish occupation grew and flourished. It was here that the soldiers of Prince Pelayo triumphed over the troops of the Caliph in 718, at the Battle of Covadonga. The Blessed Virgin was his protectress, and her image adorns the cave where Pelayo is entombed. Many beautiful mountain roads in the *Picos de Europa* (a part of the Cantabrian mountains). Mighty gorges, "desfiladeros". The *Desfiladero del Sella* is one of the magnificent canyons. It is 20 km long and the site of the *Virgen de la Cueva* pilgrimage church. Valldediós with the Santa María abbey church, begun in 1218. The Church of San Salvador dates from 893.

GIJÓN (130 000). Industrial city. Spain's third largest harbour (El Musel, 8 km to the west). Coal export. Modern university. Large seaside resort. Fiesta August 9-15.

OVIEDO (130 000). Chief city of Asturias. Mild and rainy climate. From the 9th cent. the seat of the kings of Asturias who started the struggle against the Moorish invaders. The city was severely damaged during the Civil War. Gothic cathedral (14th-16th cent.) with 80 m high spire and magnificently sculptured portal. The *Cámara Santa* (Chapel of San Miguel) is what remains of a church erected for King Fruela in the 8th cent. Exquisite examples of the goldsmith's art are included in the church's treasures. Archaeological museum in the former San Vicente monastery, founded in 781. 16th-18th cent. buildings. *Avilés* (50 000). Picturesque town with arcades and Gothic churches.

Route N 630 goes to *LEÓN* (75 000), situated 820 m above sea level. Founded by the Romans, it became an independent kingdom in the 10th cent. A stopping place for pilgrims on their way to Santiago de Compostela. The *cathedral*, inspired by he cathedrals in Reims and Chartres, was under construction 1252-1300. It is, together with the cathedrals of Burgos, Toledo and Seville, one of the most magnificent ecclesiastical structures in Spain. The Romanesque church of *San Isidoro* (11th-12th cent.) contains a royal mausoleum and interesting frescoes.

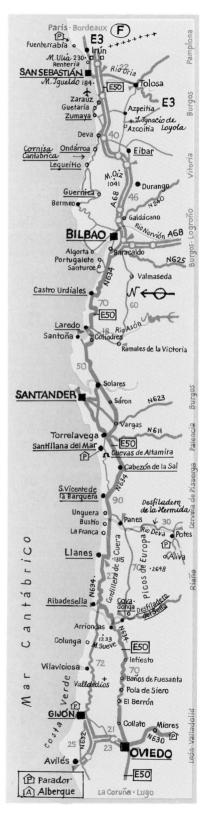

Cornellana and *Salas*. Delightful villages. *Río Narcea,* a fisherman's paradise. *Luarca* (25 000). Lovely beaches interrupted by dramatic cliffs. Atalaya castle ruins. *Navia.* Beautifully situated. Remains of an encircling wall. *Ribadeo.* Port for iron ore. Salmon fishing. Beautiful views from the Albergue Ribadeo. *Lorenzana* with the San Salvador monastery. *Mondoñedo.* Interesting Romanesque-Gothic cathedral. *Villalba* with medieval castle. One of its towers now houses a fine restaurant.

LUGO (60 000). Provincial capital. During the Middle Ages this was a fortified town. Centre of an agricultural area. Remains of Roman baths and town walls (2nd cent.) with 50 towers and 10 gates. Work on the cathedral started in 1129, and work on the new sections continued up until the 18th cent. Provincial museum.

Betanzos. Old town in a lovely valley. Splendid churches. *El Ferrol.* Naval base. General Franco was born here in 1892.

LA CORUÑA (180 000). Chief town of Galicia. Harbour and canning industry. The oldest section of the city huddles on a narrow peninsula. Farthest out is the Roman Torre de Hércules, a tower with beautiful views. Several interesting churches. Exceptional *art museum* with an abundance of masterpieces. The 11th-cent. Santa Barbara abbey was once a synagogue. Exquisite reliefs above the portal. Romanesque 12th-cent. Santa María del Campo Church. The Great Armada set forth from La Coruña in 1588. Its destruction, a result of storm and the opposing fleet of Sir Frances Drake, took place off the English coast. Fiesta August 2-9.

To the west are the little fishing ports of *Corcubión* and *Cabo Finisterre* (the "End of the World").

SANTIAGO DE COMPOSTELA (60 000) equalled Rome and Jerusalem as a major pilgrimage place. Hundreds of thousands followed the pilgrimage route from Arles, Le Puy, Autun, Vezelay, Paris and Chartres to the shrine of St. James. Pilgrims from Britain, Brittany and Normandy started their journey at Soulac, north of Bordeaux. The routes traversed the Pyrenees where the pilgrims were exploited by the local population. An early guide book for pilgrims warns of avaricious Basque inn-keepers and bandits. Legend has it that St. James, the apostle, is entombed here. St. James became the patron saint of the "Reconquista", the struggle against the Moors, and the "conquistadores", who defeated the Incas, Mayas and Aztecs in the New World.

The *cathedral*, raised above the apostle's grave, was originally built during the 11th and 12th cent. and was expanded and adorned during the 17th and 18th cent. Romanesque style with the western façade in ornately decorated Churrigueresque style (an exhuberant style named for the architect, Juan Churriguera, 1665-1723). One of the largest church bells in the world hangs in the Torre del Reloj, a 72 m high belfry. The cathedral is 94 m long. 13th-cent. statue of St. James.

Silver casket containing the relics of St. James in the 12th-cent. crypt. During the 16th cent. an archbishop hid this from English pirates and it was not rediscovered until 1879.

The cathedral, on the Plaza de España, is neighboured by magnificent palaces. The old pilgrims' hostel, Hostal de los Reyes Católicos, has a magnificent façade. It was founded by Ferdinand and Isabella. Now it is a distinguished tourist hotel. Paseo de la Herradura with lovely views.

Caldas de Reyes. Spa with sulphur baths. *Pontevedra* (50 000) with picturesque Old Town. Splendid façade on Santa María la Mayor. The corniche road follows the bank of the river to *Sangenjo,* a little fishing port, and continues on to Toja, an island that has become a tourist resort.

VIGO (150 000) is dominated by the Castillo del Castro. Beautifully situated. Large harbour and fishing port. Canning industry (sardines).

Tuy. Picturesque town with fortress-like cathedral. Portuguese border. E50 continues to Porto (Oporto) and Madrid.

E101. Madrid—Valencia

MADRID, see town plans.

Arganda del Rey. Casa del Rey, a lovely house, once belonged to the royal family. Beautiful churches and a palace. The road continues with impressive changes in height, and splendid views.

Tarancón. Small town with a Gothic church.

Saelices. Excavations of a Roman town from the 2nd cent. and remains of a Roman aqueduct.

Uclés has an enormous monastery, reminiscent of Escorial.

Àlarcón is beautifully set on a cliff by the River Júcar. Castle with Parador. Embalse d'Alarcón is a 25 km long artificial lake formed by the River Júcar.

An alternative route (road 400) runs from Tarancón via the Puerto de Cabrejas Pass (1 150 m) past ruined castles and churches.

Cuenca (36 000). Provincial capital with a medieval flavour, situated on a cliff high above the River Huecár. Eight bridges. Some houses, "Casas Colgadas", are suspended above the abyss. Gothic cathedral with paintings by El Greco.

Ciudad Encantada, an area with rock formations that looks like a town.

Puerto de Contreras (890 m) on the border between the provinces of Cuenca and Valencia. **Utiel** is a small, lovely, venerable town. **Requena** is beautifully set on two hills. Churches. Castle with wine museum, Museo del Vino. Remains of Moorish castles in *Chiva* and in the little resort town of Buñol.

Huerta de Valencia is the name of the fertile plains whose irrigation system was created by the Romans and improved on by the Moors. The white farmhouses, "barracas", stand out against the green fields.

VALENCIA, see town plans.

Alternative route: N 301 Madrid—Albacete. N 430 Albacete—Valencia

Aranjuez, see E 25. **Quintanar de la Orden.** This area, La Mancha, is the setting for Don Quixote. Cervantes was a prisoner in Argamasilla de Alba when he started work on the novel.

Mota del Cuervo with the windmills which Don Quixote fought against. Belmonte is an impressive castle high on a hill.

ALBACETE (85 000). Provincial capital. Gothic cathedral. Museum of archaeology with pottery in the new part of town. The old speciality of the town, knives and daggers, has been turned into a tourist industry.

The road continues through the mountains of **Chinchilla. Chinchilla de Monte Aragón** was once the provincial capital and contains old palaces in the Mudéjar style.

TOWN PLANS

Barcelona

BARCELONA (2.2 million)
Spain's second largest city and largest
sea port. Capital of Catalonia. Plaza
Puerto de la Paz, near the harbour, is
dominated by the 60 m high *Columbus
Monument.* (Lift to observation platform.) A copy of Columbus' flagship,
the Santa María. The *Maritime
Museum* has displays that recall Barcelona's seafaring traditions. The
museum includes Europe's only surviving medieval shipyard. **Las
Ramblas** goes through a tangle of
streets and alleys to the splendid Plaza
de Cataluña. With its flower-beds and
lawns it is a popular Barcelona promenade. Bird market. The Black
Madonna, patron saint of Catalonia, is
in a monastery on the Plaza de
Cataluña. *Rondas,* following the old
town wall, encircles the Old Town. Remains of the Roman town wall. A
Gothic town, *Barrio Gótico,* now a part
of Barcelona, was built on the ruins of
the Roman city. The *cathedral,* begun
in 1298, has a façade from 1892. Crypt
with Saint Eulalia's alabaster sarcophagus. Cathedral museum. Santa
María del Mar (14th cent.).
The **Sagrada Familia**, Antonio
Gaudí's unfinished cathedral (under
construction from 1884 to 1926) is a
bizarre structure, a surrealistic combination of Gothic and Art Nouveau.
Four high spires were constructed –
the original plans called for 12 representing the 12 apostles. Another work
by Gaudí is the fantastic *Casa Milá.*
Archaeological museum with finds
from Ampurias (see E 4). *Museum of
Catalonian art* (in the Palacio Nacional de Montjuich). *Picasso Museum.*
Museum of Modern Art and another
20 museums.
The Montjuich Park, 213 m, with
museums, stadium, amusement park
and open-air museum. Views from
Mount Tibidabo. Montserrat, see E 4.

CÓRDOBA (Cordova, 200 000)
Moorish capital and seat of the Caliphs
from 711. An independent kingdom
during the 11th cent., Cordova was
later incorporated into the Kingdom
of Seville. Reconquered by Christian
armies in 1236. *La Mezquita* (the Mosque), built 781-1009 on the site of what
was once a Visigoth church and
earlier a Roman temple. It is an enormous edifice, 130×180 m, facing Mecca. Splendid forecourt with orange
trees and magnificent bronze doors.
The mosque's interior is adorned with
pillars of marble, jasper and porphyry. Over 200 of these unique pillars
were removed during the 15th cent. so
that Christians could erect a cathedral, in the Renaissance style, within
the mosque. Beautiful mosaics and inscriptions in Mihrad, a small, octagonal prayer room. Exquisite mosaics
also in the Capilla de Villaviciosa.
The *Barrio de la Judería* (Jewish Quarter) consists of narrow alleys and

1 *Ramblas.*
2 *Barrio Gótico (Gothic Quarter).
Cathedral. Casa de la Disputación.
City museum.*
3 *Museum (fine arts and applied
arts). Market hall.*
4 *Columbus Monument. Santa
María (replica of Columbus' ship).
Paseo de Colón.*
5 *Museo Marítimo.*
6 *Church of Santa María del Mar.*
7 *Picasso Museum.*
8 *Municipal park. Zoo. Zoological*

*museum. Geological museum.
Museum of modern art.*
9 *The Church of Sagrada Familia.*
10 *Tibidabo.*
11 *Markets.*
12 *Museum of Catalan arts.*
13 *The Spanish Village (open-air
museum).*
14 *Museum of ethnology. Archaeological museum.*
15 *Montjuich Hill. Military museum.
Amusement park.*
16 *Cableway.*

flower-adorned white houses. 14th-cent. synagogue. 240 m long Roman bridge, with 16 arches, over the Guadalquivir. *Archaeological museum.* Plaza del Potro, a delightful little square with a fountain crowned with a cock. It is mentioned in Don Quixote. Art museum near by.

The *Alcázar,* a mighty 14th-cent. fortress. Remains of Roman walls. Fiesta May 25-31.

GRANADA (160 000)

The city was founded in the 5th cent. B.C. It was the capital of the Moors and was reconquered by Christian armies in 1492.

The **Alhambra** was the residence of the Moorish king of Spain. It consists of a fortress (Alcazaba) and a palace (Alcázar). The fortress was originally constructed in the 9th cent. The towers are from the 13th cent. Fine view out over the palace, the city and the Sierra Nevada. The Alcázar, built in the 14th cent., has an abundance of exquisite halls and courtyards, lavishly decorated with ornaments and arabesques. The Patio de los Mirtos (Court of the Myrtles) and the Patio de los Leones (Court of the Lions) are two of the loveliest courtyards. Patio de los Leones has arcades with 124 slender pillars. In its centre is the famed Lion Fountain, with 12 lions. Charles Quint had a Renaissance palace constructed next to the Alhambra.

Generalife. Summer residence of the kings of Granada. Beautiful gardens with fountains and canals. *Gothic cathedral* (1703) built to the plans of Diego de Siloé. Baroque façade. **Capilla Real** (Chapel Royal) with the Carrara marble tombs (by Domenico Fancelli) of the "Catholic Kings", Ferdinand and Isabella. They ruled from 1479 until 1516 and laid the groundwork for Spain's epoch as a Great Power. Here are also the tombs of their daughter, Juana la Loca (Joan the Mad) and her husband, Philip the Handsome of Burgundy.

Albaicín. Delightful part of the city, once the centre of the old Moorish town. *Sacro Monte,* near by, with a picturesque tangle of streets, is the Gypsy Quarter.

MADRID (3.4 million)

Capital of Spain, situated at the geographic centre of the country. High on a plain, this is Europe's loftiest capital (655 m). Philip II declared Madrid the nation's capital in 1561. Old Madrid had narrow, winding streets, but Napoleon had them replaced by broad avenues. Seven splendid avenues, among them the long *Alcalá,* extend outward from the *Puerta del Sol.* Another important intersection is the Plaza de la Cibeles with 18th-cent. fountain. Avenida José Antonio (or Gran Vía) is one of the major shopping streets. Paseo del Prado goes through the entire city. *Plaza Mayor* is surrounded by stately arcaded Baroque structures. In the centre is an equestrian statue of Philip

1 *Cathedral (Mezquita).*
2 *Alcázar.*
3 *Roman Bridge and Arab tower.*
4 *Old Town.*
5 *Bull-fighting museum.*
6 *Archaeological museum.*
7 *Plaza del Potro and Art museum.*
8 *Town walls.*

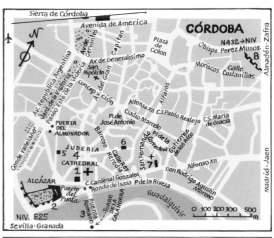

1 *Alhambra.*
2 *Generalife.*
3 *Town hall.*
4 *Cathedral. Capilla Real.*
5 *Albaicín (Gypsy quarters).*
6 *Sacro Monte Caves.*

Granada

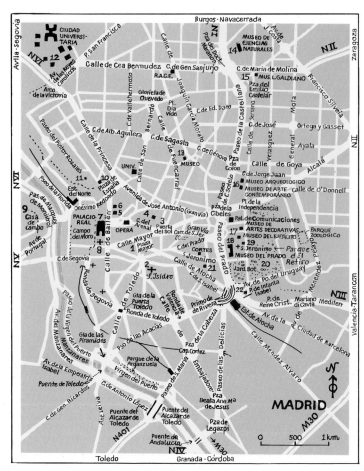

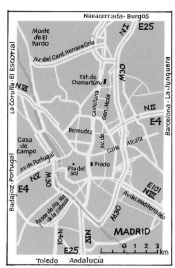

1 Plaza Mayor.
2 Cathedral of San Isidro.
3 Puerta del Sol.
4 Convento de las Descalzas Reales.
5 Convento de la Encarnación.
6 Museum of folk life traditions.
7 Royal Palace.
8 Cathedral de la Almudena.
9 Casa del Campo.
10 Plaza de España. Museo Corralbo.
11 Temple of Debod.
12 University town. Museum of
   America.
13 Theatre museum.
14 Museum of natural science.
15 Museo de Lázaro Galdiano.
16 Museum of archeology
   Museum of modern art.
17 Museum of applied arts.
18 Prado Museum.
19 Guernica (Picasso).
20 Parque del Retiro.
21 House of Lope de Vega.
22 Ethnological museum.

III. It is in the old section of the town which has narrow streets and alleys and lots of restaurants. Hemingway liked the "Botin". Several restaurants have flamenco shows. One of the best is Corral de la Moreira. Statue of Columbus in Plaza de Colón.

The **Prado Museum,** one of the most distinguished in the world, has lavish collections of Spanish, Flemish and Italian Renaissance art. Goya's famous paintings "Dos de Mayo"and "Tres de Mayo"(2nd and 3rd of May) illustrating the madness of war, depict the events when a Madrid crowd attacked French troops and started the War of Independence (the Peninsular War). Antique sculpture. In an annexe is Picasso's *"Guernica"*, inspired by a bombing raid on the Basque town of Guernica in 1937. The painting was

The Sabatini Gardens at the Palacio Real in Madrid

delivered to Spain, and donated to the Prado, in 1981.

Palacio Real. This vast royal palace, created by the Italian architects Juvara and Sanchetti, was begun in 1738 and finally completed in 1891. Magnificent interiors and works of art. Throne room with frescoes by Tiepolo. Carriage museum in the Campo del Moro. Amería (weapons museum).

Monasterio de las Descalzas Reales (1564). Magnificent art museum with sculpture, textiles and examples of the goldsmith's art. Museum Arqueológico Nacional. Iberian sculpture, including the Lady from Elche (2nd cent. B.C.). Ceramics. Copy of the Altamira Caves in the garden. Museo de América with pre-Columbian exhibits. In addition to these there are about 25 more museums in Madrid.

Work on the *Cathedral of Almudena* began in 1883, but as yet it is incomplete. Goya's tomb in the San Antonio de la Florida Church. The dead artist's head was misplaced while he was buried in Bordeaux (1828-1888). Goya decorated the dome. Casa de Lope de Vega, the home of the 17th-cent. poet, is open to visitors.

Parque del Retiro was once a royal garden. Now it is a beautiful park with a large lake. Concerts, art exhibitions, motor racing. Bull fighting in the Arena las Ventas. Modern buildings in the Ciudad Universitaria (University City). Casa del Campo, with amusement park.

SEVILLA (Seville, 675 000)
Capital of Andalusia, once capital of the Roman province of Baetica. From 712 an important Moorish city. Capital of a Moorish kingdom until it was reconquered by Christian forces in 1248. With the discovery of America in 1492, Seville flourished again. Magellan and Amerigo Vespucci left on their great journeys from this city. Now Seville is a large industrial city and inland port. University.

The *cathedral* is the world's largest Gothic church. It was built 1386-1506. The greater part of the façade was built during the 19th cent. The richly adorned interior is 130 m long, 76 m wide and 40-56 m high. 90 stained-glass windows. Tomb of Columbus. Capilla Real (Chapel Royal) with the remains of Ferdinand III in a silver and gold casket.

The *Giralda*, the cathedral's tower and the symbol of Seville, is 96 m high. It was originally a minaret, built during the 12th cent. for Emir Abu-Jakub. It was inspired by minarets in Rabat and Marrakech. Fine view from the 70 m high observation platform. Many splendid palaces. The Casa de Pilatos (1540) in the Mudéjar style (a combination of Spanish and Moorish styles) is a reproduction of the Roman palace of Pilate. Richly ornamented Ayuntamiento (town hall). *Museo de Bellas Artes* (Spanish art) in a former monastery. Barrio de Santa Cruz is a picturesque old part of the town with narrow streets, flower-adorned houses and lavishly ornamented façades.

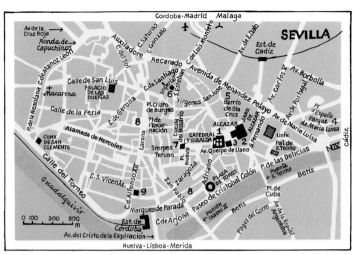

1 Cathedral. Giralda Tower (viewpoint).
2 Alcazar.
3 General Archives of the Indies.
4 María Luisa Park.
5 Santa Cruz (old quarters).
6 House of Pilate.
7 Town hall.
8 Markets.
9 Museum of fine arts.

It was once the Jewish Quarter. *Plaza Santa Cruz* with the wrought-iron Cerrajería Cross, is the centre of this section of the city. Lovely parks. Foremost among them is the *Parque de María Luisa* (19th cent.), designed by Forestier, a Frenchman.

The *Alcázar.* Palace in the Mudéjar style, designed by Christian architects, under Moorish influence. The greater part was built in the 14th cent. for Pedro the Cruel. Magnificent interior. Ferdinand and Isabella and Charles Quint also resided here. Huge celebrations during Holy Week. "Feria" April 20-25 and May 20.

TOLEDO (41 000)
One of Spain's oldest and most beautiful towns. Visigoth capital until 711. During the 16th cent., in the reign of Charles Quint, it became the capital of Spain. Madrid became capital in 1561. Toledo is the seat of the Archbishop of Spain. From the ring road, the *Carre-tera de Circunvalación*, on the opposite side of the Tajo Canyon (which surrounds the city on three sides), the traveller is greeted with a magnificent view over the tangle of houses that climb the steep slopes up to the *Alcázar,* a mighty fortress, originally built for El Cid. Lovely arcaded courtyards. The fortress was completely destroyed during the Civil War. The River Tajo protects three sides of the town. The fourth side is marked by a stout wall, with partially Moorish origins. Stately Puerta del Sol with sections from the 12th cent. The Puente San Martín bridge, protected by walls, is also part of early fortifications. Interesting maze of streets and alleys. Moorish Zocodover Square. The *cathedral,* one of the most impressive Gothic churches in Europe, was, in the main, created by the architect, Pedro Pérez. 90 m high clock tower crowned by a stylized crown of thorns. 750 stained-glass

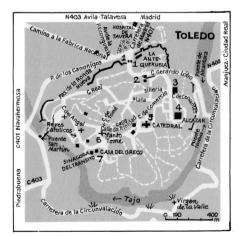

1 Puerta de Bisagra (town gate).
2 Puerta del Sol (town gate).
3 Museum of Santa Cruz.
4 Alcazar.
5 Cathedral.
6 Church of Santo Tomé.
7 House of El Greco.
Sinagoga del Tránsito.

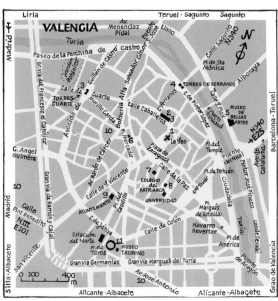

1 Cathedral. 2 Palacio de la Generalidad. 3 Torres Cuarte. 4 Torres de Serrano. 5 Museum of fine arts. 6 Lonja de la Seda (Silk Exchange). 7 Ceramics museum. 8 Colegio del Patriarca. 9 Town hall. 10 Markets. 11 Bull ring. Museo Taurino (bullfighting museum).

windows, ornate decorations, splendid High Altar, 22 chapels. Capilla Mozárabe with daily services held in the ancient Moorish and Visigoth manner. The treasure includes a 3 m high monstrance, adorned with 260 figures. It was made from gold that Columbus brought back from America. (A monstrance is a vessel in which the consecrated Host is exposed to the congregation.)

Works by El Greco, Van Dyck, Goya, Rubens and Titian in the sacristy. Santo Tomé Church with El Greco's famous painting of the burial of Count Orgaz.

Casa y Museo del Greco, on the site of the house where El Greco lived 1586-1614. (The present structure is a reproduction.) El Greco's studio with over twenty paintings. Museo de Santa Cruz (archaeology and art, including El Greco's "Anunciación". Although the artist's name reflects his Greek birth, he was a thoroughly Spanish artist, who studied in Venice. *Santa María la Blanca*, originally a synagogue, in the Mudéjar style, became a Christian church in 1405. The *El Tránsito Synagogue* is also interesting.

VALENCIA (750 000)

Spain's third largest city was founded by the Greeks. The Moors conquered it in 714. El Cid recovered it in 1094 and was proclaimed Duke of Valencia. He died here in 1099, and was buried in Burgos. Valencia is the centre of a fertile agricultural area, "la huerta". Large industries and harbour, from which fruit, e.g. Valencia oranges, are exported.

Old Town with narrow streets. Lonja (the Stock Exchange) is a splendid Gothic structure. *Museo Nacional de*

Cerámica, a ceramics museum, in a former nobleman's palace. *The Almudín* is an old merchant's house that now houses a paleographic museum (fossils of plants and animals). *Art museum* with self-portrait of Velásquez. *Corpus Christi abbey church* with the Museo del Patriarca (art). The high altar of the abbey church is adorned with Ribera's "Last Supper".

The greater part of the *cathedral* was built 1269-1389, but its Baroque façade dates from 1703. Tall Miguelete clock tower. The stone of the Apostle Portal is very weathered. A chapel contains the legendary Holy Grail.

"Fallas" celebrations March 12-19. Giant-sized papier-maché figures are paraded through the streets. On the final night, they are burned. "War of the Flowers" fiesta July 7-31.

Baleares

(The Balearic Islands)

The Balearic Islands are made up of Mallorca (Majorca), Menorca (Minorca), Ibiza and Formentera.

MAJORCA

Area: 3 660 km² (1 352 sq. miles).

Population: 420 000.

Palma de Mallorca (235 000) is the chief town and the amount of resort hotels around the Palma Bay testify to the importance tourism has on the island. And this is a fairly recent phenomenon: charter flights to Majorca only started in the 1950's.

Lonja, splendid stock exchange down by the harbour. Lovely Gothic cathedral and beautiful palaces. Palma's university was founded in 1967.

The little town of *Alcudia* has become a major tourist resort as have *Pollensa, Cala Millor* and a few more. *Cabo de Formentor*, a 189 m high rock with a 20 m high light-house. Scenic route from Puerto Pollensa. *Valldemosa*, an abbey in a lovely setting. Small museum with reminders of Chopin who spent the winter of 1838—1839 here with George Sand (Aurore Dupin).

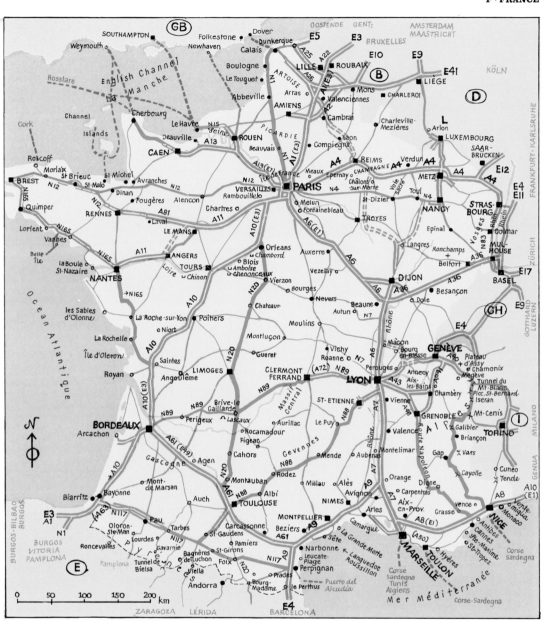

F · France

F·France

Area: 551 600 km² (210 038 sq. miles)

Population: 54.1 million. Although French is spoken by all inhabitants, some areas have their own languages or dialects: German, Flemish, Provencal, Catalan, Breton, Corsican and Basque. The majority of the population are Roman Catholics, with about 800 000 Protestants (Calvinists), about 500 000 Jews and a few hundred thousand Moslems. State and church were officially separated in 1905.

Major cities (figures in parentheses indicate total population including suburbs): Paris 2.6 million (9.2 million), Marseille 915 000 (1 million), Lyon 470 000 (1.2 million), Toulouse 385 000 (495 000), Nice 438 000 (390 000), Nantes 260 000 (460 000), Bordeaux 230 000 (620 000), Lille 190 000 (1 milj.).

Government: The Fifth Republic is a combination of presidential rule and parliamentarism. There are two houses of parliament: the Senate and the Chamber of Deputies. France is divided into 96 departments, each headed by a government-appointed Prefect (civil governor). Since 1977 Paris has had its own popularly elected mayor. The 22 provinces, roughly corresponding to counties, reflect an earlier administrative division of the country.

History

58-51 B.C. Romans under Caesar conquer Gaul.

A.D. 418 – about 500 Visigoth kingdom with capital at Toulouse.

400-800 The Merovingian dynasty rules the country. The Merovingian king, Clovis, becomes France's first Christian king (496).

732 Charles Martel defeats the Moors at the Battle of Poitiers.

800 Charlemagne, King of the Franks, is crowned Emperor of the Holy Roman Empire.

857 The Vikings raid Paris. In 911 they are pacified and given a province of their own – Normandy.

1066 The ruler of Normandy, William, invades England.

1137 The struggle begins against the English kings who own a large part of French territory.

1339-1453 The "Hundred Years' War" against England.

1429 Troops, led by Jeanne d'Arc, force the English to lift the siege of Orléans. She is executed 1431.

1453 The English are expelled from most of France. Calais remains in English possession.

1572 The Huguenot Wars culminate in the St. Bartholomew's Day Massacre.

1643-1715 Reign of Louis XIV.

1789 July 14, the French Revolution begins with the storming of the Bastille.

1792 France becomes a republic.

1799-1814 Napoleonic era. Napoleon becomes Emperor in 1804. All his enemies are defeated except England. The war against Russia leads to final disaster.

1814 Napoleon in exile on Elba. In 1815 he returns in triumph to Paris (the "Hundred Days"). Napoleon is finally defeated at the Battle of Waterloo. King Louis XVIII returns to the throne.

1830 July Revolution. Charles X forced into exile.

1848 February Revolution. Second Republic.

1870-1871 Franco-Prussian War. Germany defeats France. The Third Republic is proclaimed. Rebellion of the Paris Communes in 1871.

1914-1918 First World War. Paris threatened by a German drive, halted by the Battle of the Marne. Battle of Verdun (1916). Armistice at Compiègne (1918). Treaty of Versailles (1919).

1939-1945 Second World War. Germans enter Paris and occupy northern France. French occupation government, headed by Marshal Pétain, established in Vichy. Provisional government in exile established by General de Gaulle.

1942 Germans occupy all of France.

1944 Invasion of Normandy. Paris liberated. De Gaulle proclaims the Fourth Republic.

1958 Military coup in Algeria. De Gaulle establishes the Fifth Republic.

1962 Algeria granted independence. France leaves NATO.

1968 May Revolution in Paris.

1969 De Gaulle resigns.

1981 The Socialist Party win the election. Mittérand president.

Currency: French francs (FRF).
1 franc (F) = 100 centimes

Business hours: Banks 9.00 a.m.-12.00 noon and 2.30-4.00 or 5.00 p.m. In the country some banks are open on Saturdays but closed on Mondays. Post offices are usually open 8.00 a.m.-7.00 p.m. Saturdays 8.00 a.m.-12.00 noon. (Stamps may also be bought where the "Tabac" (tabacco) sign is displayed.) Shops 9.00 a.m.-12.00 noon and 2.00-6.00 p.m., but there are variations. In general there is no lunchtime closing in Paris, but foodshops may be closed between 1.00 and 4.00 p.m. Department stores usually have one late evening opening a week. Supermarkets are often open from 10.00 a.m. until late in the evening. In northern France lunchtime closing is 12.00 noon-2.00 p.m., in the east 12.30-3.00 p.m. and in southern France 1.00-4.00 p.m. During these hours the roads are almost free of traffic.

Holidays: New Year's Day, Easter Sunday, Easter Monday, May 1, Ascension Day, Whit Sunday, Whit Monday, July 14 (National holiday), August 15 (Assumption Day), Novem-

---

Routes described:

A 1   Lille – Paris

A 2   Mons – Valenciennes – Peronne

A 4   Strasbourg – Metz – Reims – Paris

A 6   Paris – Beaune – Lyon

A 7   Lyon – Marseille

A 8   Menton – Nice – Aix-en-Provence

A 9   Orange – Montpellier – Le Perthus

A 10   Paris – Orléans – Bordeaux

A 11   Paris – Le Mans – Nantes

A 13   Caen – Rouen – Paris

A 25   Dunkerque – Lille, see N 1

A 26   Calais – Arras see N I.

A 36   Mulhouse – Belfort – Besançon – Beaune

A 40   Genève – The Mont-Blanc Tunnel

A 41   Genève – Grenoble

A 42   Genève – Lyon

A 43   Chambéry – Lyon

A 48   Lyon – Grenoble

A 62   Bordeaux – Toulouse – Narbonne

N 1   Calais – Abbeville – Paris

N 4   Strasbourg – Nancy – Paris, see A 4

N 10   Bordeaux – Irún, see A 10

N 12   Brest – Rennes

N 13   Cherbourg – Caen – Paris

N 15   Le Havre – Rouen, see A 13

N 20   Orléans – Toulouse – Andorra

N 83   Strasbourg – Colmar – Belfort

N 85   Grenoble – Cannes (Route Napoleon)

N 88   Lyon – Le Puy – Toulouse

N 89   Lyon – Bordeaux

N 90   Col du Petit St-Bernard – Albertville – Chambéry see D 902

N 92   Grenoble – Valence, see A 42 and A 7

N 98   Nice – Toulon, see A 8

N 117   Biarritz – Toulouse

N 137   Nantes – Bordeaux

N 165   Brest – Nantes

D 117   St-Gaudens – Perpignan, see N 117

D 902   Thonon – Briançon – Nice (Route des Grandes Alpes)

Special map: Corse/Corsica

Town plans: Lyon, Marseille, Monaco, Nice, Paris, Strasbourg

ber 1 (All Saints' Day), November 11 (Armistice Day, 1918) and December 25.

Hotels

La Direction du Tourisme has given each hotel in France a rating of from one to four stars, or in special cases, an "L" (de luxe) classification. A blue sign with a large H followed by the rating should be posted at the hotel entrance. In Paris, breakfast (coffee with hot milk, a roll or croissant, butter and marmalade) is usually included in the price of the room. This is not always the case in the country. Paris hotel prices far exceed those in the provinces. Recently, several modern one and two-star hotels have been built in Paris.

Several hotel chains:
**** – de luxe Relais et Châteaux (castle hotels)
** – **** Relais du Silence (good family hotels)
* – *** France Accueil (family hotels)
* – ** Petits Nids de France (PFN) (simple family hotels)
* – ** Logis de France (inns)
** Asmotec (Ass. des Motels et Hôtels Economiques) and new chains such as Ibis, Arcade, Campanile
*** Novotel (modern motels maintaining high standards)
Hotels in the cities and business hotels:
** – *** Inter-Hôtels
*** – **** Mapotel
**** – de luxe Frantel
**** PLM
**** Concorde
**** – de luxe Sofitel

Logis de France is a state-supported chain of about 4000 small one- or two-star hotels that have signed an agreement. With the exception of the Paris area, they are often situated near the major roads. They are highly recommended for the traveller who wants to

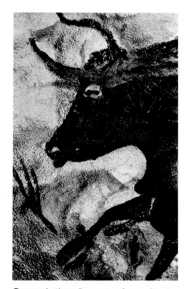

Cave painting, Lascaux, from about 18000 B.C.

Mont St-Michel

experience rural French traditions. Auberges Rurals (country inns) are even simpler, but often quite cosy.
Gîtes de France, self-catering accommodation in over 4 000 flats and small houses (often on farms), are controlled by a central organization, Féderation National de Gîtes de France, 34, rue Godot-de-Mauroy, Paris 9e. Booklets for different parts of the country.
Relais Routier is a sign often glimpsed along the major roads, sometimes half-obscured by rows of parked juggernauts. The sign indicates a restaurant that serves hearty meals at reasonable prices. Overnight accommodation is often available.
Syndicat d'Initiative is the name of the local tourist authorities (S d'I) and their tourist offices. Acceuil de France has a nation-wide telex booking service that can provide rooms in 35 cities. But reservations must be made in person and not more than seven days in advance.

Camping. There are 4 700 camping sites of different standard. Local tourist offices can give detailed information. There are 35 "castels et camping-caravanning" sites in castle grounds.

Youth hostels
Some of the youth hostels have special rooms for families.

Food and drink
Food and drink are serious matters in France. Many hotels like guests to have dinner in their restaurants. This is almost always a several-course repast, well worth the price. Even lunches are taken seriously. Count on at least three courses and over one hour. If you want to eat simple, quickly prepared lunches or snacks, it is best to seek out the town's cafés and brasseries, where snacks as well as complete meals are available. Most

restaurants display a sign reading "Repas à prix fixe" (price-fixed meal) in the window. These are often good buys.
Many restaurants and hotels adhere strictly to established meal-times: lunch about 12-2, dinner about 7-9. It is impossible to describe French cuisine fully. It would need a separate, very thick, book to do justice to the topic. Here are just a few of the local specialities to give you an idea of the culinary possibilities of France:
(The capital of each region is shown in parentheses).
Ile-de-France (Paris): pastries, chololate truffles, Brie cheese, mushrooms. *Loire:* asparagus, pears, apples, vinegar, sparkling wines, Muscadet, Cointreau. *Burgundy* (Dijon): mustard, snails, beef, fine wines, Crème de Cassis and Kir. *Auvergne* (Clermont- Ferrand): cheese, charcuterie (preserved meats, often pork), mushrooms, sweets, marmalade, Vichy water. *Limousin* (Limoges): foie-gras (goose liver), truffles, walnuts, chestnuts. *Poitou-Charentes* (Poitiers): oysters, butter, cognac. *Brittany* (Rennes): Belon oysters, shellfish, pâtés, fowl, crêpes (pancakes), biscuits, artichokes, onions, cider, apple juice. *Normandy* (Caen and Rouen): oysters, tripe, Camembert, calvados (apple brandy), cider, Benedictine liqueur. *Nord-Pas-de-Calais* (Lille): peppermint rock (bêtises de Cambrai), sugared almonds, fried pigs' trotters, turkey, beer. *Champagne* (Chalons-sur-Marne): champagne. *Lorraine* (Metz): quiche Lorraine, Eau de Vittel (mineral water), fruit brandy. *Alsace* (Strasbourg): choucroute (sauerkraut), pâté de foie gras, charcuterie, honey, white wine, beer. *Franche-Comté:* Gruyère cheese, bilberry

preserves and bilberry tart, white brandy. *Savoie* (Rhône – Alpes, Savoie, Grenoble): charcuterie, fondue, Chartreuse liqueur, Eau d'Evian (mineral water). *Provence-Alpes-Côte d'Azur* (Marseille and Nice): tomatoes, olives, garlic, fruit, vegetables, bouillabaisse (fish soup), ratatouille (vegetable stew, served hot or cold), pissaladière (pizza), salad Niçoise, citrus fruits, rosé wines. *Languedoc-Roussillon* (Montpellier): Roquefort cheese, early fruits and vegetables, light and fortified wines. *Midi-Pyrénées:* cassoulet (meat stew), plums, Cahors wines.

So perhaps a picnic is the best lunch alternative. French food shops are enticing. When choosing a cheese, remember the words of de Gaulle, "How can one govern a country that has 400 cheeses?"

Shopping

Porcelain (Limoges, Sèvres), earthenware, lace (Brittany, Le Puy), pottery (Normandy, Provence), perfume from Grasse, high fashion from Paris.

Speed limits. Traffic regulations.

Toll motorways 130 kmh, toll-free motorways and dual carriageways 110 kmh, other roads 90 kmh, built-up areas 60 kmh.

In conditions of rain, snow or sleet these limits are reduced to 110 kmh on motorways, 100 kmh on toll-free motorways and dual carriageways and 80 kmh on other roads.

Drivers who have been in possession of a driving licence for less than one year, and this includes non-French nationals, are not allowed to exceed 90 kmh.

Children under the age of ten are not allowed to travel in the front seat. If your car is fitted with seat belts it is compulsary to use them.

It is compulsory for all motorists to carry a replacement set of light bulbs. The right of way for vehicles coming from the right is strictly enforced, which is why the heavy traffic round the Arc de Triomphe functions as well as it does. The rule does not apply to roundabouts (new roundabout regulations from 1 May 1984). The French have their own symbol to designate major roads. It is a blue arrow on a yellow triangle. Signs reading "Passage protégé" indicate that the road you are on has priority over traffic coming in from the right. Signs with "Priorité à droite" indicate that traffic coming in from the right has priority. Pedestrians have right of way on non-signal-regulated pedestrian crossings, but take care. Motorcyclists are required to have their headlights on in daylight.

Parking

Many cities have a "Zone bleue" where parking discs must be used. These can be bought at police stations, but as a rule they are available, without cost, at tourist offices and major petrol stations. In these blue zones, parking is generally permitted, for one hour, 9.00 a.m.-12.30 p.m. and 2.30-7 p.m. Grey zones are equipped with parking meters. In Paris there is a green zone

Puy-en-Velay

where caravans are forbidden 2 p.m.-8.30 p.m., except Sundays. Large caravans are forbidden 8 a.m.-8.30 p.m. In almost all of Paris the parking of caravans is forbidden, as is the parking of private cars for more than 24 hours. Occasionally one comes upon a parking system based on the days of the month. 1-15 of every month it is permitted to park in front of odd-numbered buildings, 16-31 in front of even-numbered buildings. On dark streets parking lights must be left on.

Roads

The French road network was built up and expanded during the Napoleonic era. The road posts on the major roads were painted red, while those on rural roads were yellow. This is the reason why red is used to signify major roads on most of the world's road maps.

Routes Nationales are the national roads, indicated by an N before the number. D indicates Routes Départementaux (roughly, provincial roads). The road network has undergone great changes in the last few years and road maps (even the ones in this book) may not correspond to the actual situation in every respect. In general, the changes have meant that less important N roads have become D roads, often retaining their old number preceded by a 9. Most motorways, "autoroutes", are toll roads. Fees vary. Some examples of 1984 tolls (for private cars not towing caravans):
Paris – Lille 213 km, 36.50 F
Paris – Strasbourg 470 km, 127 F
Paris – Lyon 456 km, 87 F
Lyon – Aix-en-Prov. 295 km, 66.50 F
Aix-en-Prov.-Ventimiglia 218 km, 68 F
Paris – Bordeaux 585 km, 151 F
Paris – Caen 225 km, 39.50 F
Mt Blanc tolls are determined by axle

width: under 2.30 m the fee is 47 F, up to 2.63 m, 73 F.

French tourist offices can give you up-to-date information about prices. Itinéraires de Délestage are alternative roads that avoid towns and cities. They are indicated by blue signs with yellow arrows. Itinéraires Emeraudes indicate alternative routes avoiding heavy traffic. Green arrows on white signs indicate roads from Paris. Green and white arrows on a white background indicate roads going towards Paris. Even if these roads are not faster than more popular routes, they do provide good alternatives. Petrol stations displaying the Bison Futé symbol (the head of an Indian chief) provide free maps. On days when traffic is traditionally intense about 80 of these stations have hostesses who give information.

Road patrols

It is possible to request aid from the police. Major cities have a special police department that handle these requests (Police-Secours). On motorways, emergency telephones are about 2 km apart. They are directly connected to police lines from which calls are transferred to a Dépanneur (towing company).

Police and ambulance, tel. 17, fire brigade, tel. 18. After a motor accident, a Constat à l'amiable (a standard European printed form) must be filled out. If all of the participants in the accident cannot agree, then a Constat d'huissier must be obtained.

AFA Association Français des Automobiles, 9 rue Anatole-de-la-Forge, 75017 Paris. Tel. (1) 227 82 00. French Government Tourist Office, 178 Piccadilly, London W1V 0AL. Tel. (01) 491 76 22.

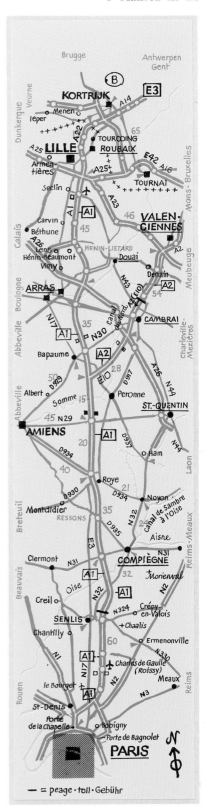

A1. Lille – Paris. *Autoroute du Nord*

Mouscron. Belgian border. E 3 comes from Helsinki – Stockholm – Århus – Hamburg – Ruhr – Antwerpen – Gent.

Roubaix (110 000). Industrial city. Chapelle d'Hem has exquisite stained-glass windows. 15th-cent. town hall in the Flemish style.

LILLE (120 000). Centre of a vast industrial area with 800 000 inhabitants. Hard-hit textile industry. Chemical industry. Several splendid buildings (Flemish Renaissance) such as the Ancienne Bourse (Old Stock Exchange) in the older districts of the city. Musée des Beaux-Arts displays Flemish, Dutch and French art. Many beautiful churches. Porte de Paris (15th cent.), Louis XIV's triumphal arch. Vauban citadel.

Douai (50 000). Industrial town. Museum with French, Flemish, Italian and antique art. Church of St-Pierre (1750). Splendid buildings and two town gates.

ARRAS (50 000). The town flourished during the 17th and 18th cent. Severely damaged during both World Wars, but the handsome buildings on the Grand-Place and the Rue de la Taillerie have been preserved. This street leads to the Petite-Place. Imposing town hall with beautiful belfry. *The Abbey Church of St-Vaast*, a museum, has displays of French art, medieval sculpture and porcelain.

500 workers, employed by the British and Commonwealth War Graves Commission, care for the 900 cemeteries from the First World War. The cemetery at *Notre Dame-de-Lorette* has 34 000 graves. Vimy Memorial Park has a monument dedicated to 64 000 Canadians. Beamont-Hamel Memorial Park. 40 000 Germans are buried at Neuville-St-Vaast. Here the crosses are black.

A 26. Calais – Amiens, see N 1.

Road N 44 to *St-Quentin* (70 000). Hôtel de Ville (town hall, 1509) with handsome façade. Musée Lécuyer with pastels by a local artist. Church with the tomb of St. Quentin. *Laon* (30 000). During the Middle Ages a bishop's seat and residence of the last Carolingian king. The town, surrounded by a wall, is high on a promontory. Early-Gothic *Notre Dame Cathedral* (1235). The West Front has three magnificent portals and two beautiful towers.

Soissons (30 000). In 511 Soissons became the capital of the kingdom of the West Franks. The 13th-cent. *cathedral* was severely damaged during the First World War. Altar painting, "The Adoration of the Shepherds", by Rubens.

Compiègne (40 000). Charles V had a castle here that was replaced in the 18th cent. by the present large palace. Napoleon III held court here as did several previous monarchs. The palace now houses the *Musée de la Voiture et du Tourisme* which displays carriages, motor cars and bicycles. Second Empire museum with 18th- and 19th-cent. art and furniture. 16th-cent. town hall and Musée Vivenel with Greek vases. Compiègne Forest is one of the largest and most beautiful in the country. In *Clairière de l'Armistice* is the Wagon-Lit carriage (reconstruction) in which the Germans capitulated to the French in 1918 and the French to the Germans in 1940. The French have reconstructed the former event. Even Marshal Foch's embalmed cigar end is in the ash tray. Statue of Foch and a few memorial stones.

Senlis with lovely old streets and fine view from the fortification walls. Old castle. Roman walls and amphitheatre. Chaalis with famous monastery. Chantilly. World-famous cheese. Two châteaux encircled by a moat. The châteaux contain the Musée Condé of French, Italian and Flemish art. Large library. Beautiful park. Écouen with 16th-cent. château. Renaissance museum with paintings, furniture and textiles.

PARIS, see town plans. Entrance through the Porte de la Chapelle.

A 2. Mons – Valenciennes – Peronne

Valenciennes (43 000). Famous for its lace. Industrial town in a coal mining district around the River Escaut (Schelde). Art museum. Birthplace of Jean-Antoine Watteau (1684). Notre Dame-du-St-Cordon pilgrimage church.

Cambrai (40 000) has given its name to cambric, a fine linen or cotton cloth that has been woven here since the 15th cent. Centre of the town is the Place Aristide Briand with handsome 19th-cent. town hall, restored after First World War damage. St-Géry Church with 76 m high belfry. Monument dedicated to Blériot's 1909 cross-Channel flight.

A 4. Strasbourg – Metz – Reims – Paris. *Autoroute de l'Est*

STRASBOURG, see town plans.
Haguenau (25 000). Old town with the Church of St-Nicolas.

Saverne. Little town with lovely houses. Beautifully situated at the foot of the Vosges. Bishop's palace (18th cent.) with museum (archaeology and sculpture). **Haut-Barr,** ruined castle. Marmoutier. Huge abbey church (11th–14th cent.) built of two-coloured sandstone. Two octagonal towers. Organ by Silbermann (1710).

METZ (120 000). Founded by the Romans. Seat of the Merovingian kings. Chief town of the dep. of Moselle. During the 17th cent. Vauban, the military engineer, expanded and strengthened the old fortress. The city was ceded to Germany by the Treaty of Frankfurt (May 1871) and remained a part of Germany until the end of the First World War. *Old Town* with narrow streets and splendid squares, e.g. the arcaded Place St-Louis. In the Place d'Armes is the *Cathedral of St-Étienne.* Construction lasted from the 13th to the 16th cent. 42 m high nave, original stained-glass windows. Newer stained-glass windows by Chagall, etc. The cathedral incorporates an older church, Notre Dame-de-la Ronde. The St-Pierre-aux-Nonains abbey church (10th cent.) contains the remains of France's oldest church.

Thionville. Old fortress with lovely square. Arcades and 16th-cent. belfry. Near by is what is left of the Maginot Line, built in 1934 for André Maginot, then Minister of War. One of history's mightiest fortifications systems, but the Germans by-passed it, and large sections of it were dynamited after the collapse of France. **Hagondange,** steel mill.

Verdun (27 000). Many battles have been fought for the possession of this important stronghold on the Meuse. The most ferocious was in 1916 when 5 million soldiers fought here. Although half a million died, the French front held. Now stillness reigns over the beautiful mountains and forests. *Fort de Vaux* and *Fort de Douaumont* are open for inspection. At *Tranchée des Baionettes,* bayonets stick out from trenches that were filled in during artillery bombardments. Large cemetery with *ossuaire* (charnel house). Enormous monument to the battle of 1916 in Verdun's High Street. Notre-Dame Cathedral (1083).

Voie Sacrée, the "Blessed Way", goes from Verdun to Bar-le- Duc (D34). This was the only road that was out of range of German artillery during the First World War. It was crowded with vehicles bearing supplies, reinforcements and the wounded. The road's milestones are crowned with soldiers' helmets. Large memorial at the start of the road in Verdun.

Châlons-sur-Marne. Wine trade. Place du Maréchal Foch with town hall. The 13th-cent. Cathedral of St-Étienne has a 1634 façade.

REIMS (RHEIMS, 184 000), where the French kings were crowned. The High-Gothic **cathedral,** built in the 13th cent., was the coronation cathedral. Severely damaged during the First World War. The West Front is one of the most magnificent examples of the Gothic style. Enormous 12 m rose window. The famous laughing angel is in the west porch. The cathedral is 138 m long. 11th-cent. Basilica of St-Rémi. *Musée des Beaux-Arts* contains French art from the 15th cent. up until the present time. Reims is an old established wine centre. Tours of the underground, several kilometres long wine cellars belonging to the Pommery champagne company. *Epernay* is the home of one of the best-known champagne producers, Moët & Chandon.

Château-Thierry has a splendid 12th-cent. castle and the Church of St-Crépin. **Meaux** has the 13th-cent. Cathedral of St-Étienne.

PARIS, see town plans.

N 4. Strasbourg – Nancy – Paris

STRASBOURG, see town plans.

NANCY (112 000) is distinguished by the buildings and works of art that came into being during the middle of the 18th cent. when Stanislaus Leszczyński, once King of Poland, resided here as the Duke of Lorraine. His magnificent monument in the *Place Stanislas,* surrounded by palaces, is one of the most splendid in the country. Extremely beautiful Old Town. Triumphal arch in honour of Louis XV. Place de la Carrière with 18th-cent. palaces. *The Duke's palace* (16th cent.) Zoological museum and botanical gardens.

Toul. Once a fortified town. Splendid Renaissance buildings. Cathedral (15th cent.). **Void.** Monument to the inventor Cugnot, born here in 1725. He constructed one of the first steam-driven carriages (4 kmh).

St-Dizier (40 000). Industrial town. Bar-le-Duc (20 000) with charming streets and houses. Castle, now a museum. Church of St-Étienne (1318).

A 6. Paris – Beaune – Lyon. *Autoroute du Soleil*

PARIS, see town plans. Exit between the Ports d'Orléans and the Porte d'Italie. Either drive on the monotonous motorway, or take N 6 all the way or part of the way. Another alternative is N 7 via Nevers.

Rungis has enormous markets, moved here from the famous "Halles". *Orly.* The largest airport in France. Impressive array of restaurants, super-markets and shops.

Créteil (65 000). Chief town of the dep. of Val-de-Marne. University. *Melun* (30 000). Renaissance Château de Vaux le Vicomte, built in 1661.

Fontainebleau. French kings since the 16th cent. have made additions to the medieval château, creating one of the most magnificent royal residences in France. Incredibly lavish decorations. A favourite of Louis XV and Napoleon who bade farewell to his Old Guard in the Cour des Adieux courtyard in 1814. The *Forest of Fontainebleau* (17 000 hectares) is beautiful and hilly. Many venerable oaks have been named after famous men: Voltaire, Lafayette, Washington. *Barbizon,* where many famous artists have worked. The studio of Millet is preserved. *Nemours.* Old streets and châteaux. Musée de Préhistoire de l'Ile de France.

Sens-sur-Yonne. The Gothic Cathedral of St-Étienne (12th cent.) may have been the model for the cathedral at Canterbury. Magnificent stained-glass windows and sculpture. One of the largest church treasures in France. Archaeological museum. *Joigny* has remains of a 12th-cent. town wall and castle. Lovely 18th-cent. wooden houses in the Grande-Rue.

Road N 77 to *TROYES* (80 000). Chief town of Champagne and the dep. of Seine. *Cathedral of St-Pierre et St-Paul* (13th–17th cent.). Splendid portals and rose windows. Exquisite stained-glass windows in the Church of Ste-Madeleine. Gothic Basilica of St-Urbain (13th cent.). Delightful Old Town with charming streets. Wooden houses in the *Rue des Chats.*

Auxerre (40 000). *The Cathedral of St-Étienne* (13th–16th cent.) is one of the most beautiful Gothic churches in France. Splendid West Front adorned with sculptures. The Church of St-Germain dates from the same period but has a 9th-cent. crypt decorated with 9th- and 10th-cent. wall paintings. Romanesque belfry. Beautiful bishop's palace.

Tonnerre. Old town in a wine district. A hospital founded in 1293 is the oldest building. Church of Notre Dame (13th cent.).

Tanlay has a splendid château. Notre-Dame Church (14th cent.) in *Semur-en-Auxois.* Beautiful north portal and stained-glass windows, which show craftsmen at work.

Vézelay. Little town, situated high up with 2 km long town wall. One of the most important places of pilgrimage during the Middle Ages. A stopping place on the road to Santiago de Compostela in Spain.

Saulieu. Little town on a hill, dominated by the 12th-cent. abbey church.

Autun (25 000) was an important Roman town. Ruins of a temple and an amphitheatre. The Cathedral of St-Lazare, erected in the 12th cent., was rebuilt in the Gothic style in the 15th cent. but the superb Romanesque carvings by the sculptor Gislebertus survive. Painting by Ingres. Musée Rolin (15th cent.). Bishop's palace with the Tour St-Léger. *Le Creusot* (35 000). Centre of a coal and iron district. Large industries.

Chagny. Small industrial town surrounded by vineyards.

Beaune (20 000). The Duke of Burgundy's old town, surrounded by a 16th-cent. town wall which now serves as wine cellars. Wine tasting. Handsome 17th-cent. houses in the Rue des Tonneliers. Well-preserved Hôtel Dieu, a 15th-cent. hospital that was in use up to 1971. Flemish Gothic. 72 m long ward, kitchen and pharmacy. *Musée du Vin de Bourgogne* in the Hôtel des Ducs de Bourgogne. Hôtel de Ville in a 17th-cent. convent with a museum (art and handicraft). To the west La Rochepot Castle (12th–15th cent.).

Châlon-sur-Saône. Inland port. Vineyards. Musée Denon (archaeology).

DIJON (160 000). The old capital of Burgundy, renowned for its mustard, is at the foot of the Côte d'Or. University. Beautiful old section of the city round the colonnaded Place de la Libération. Two of the loveliest streets are the Rue des Forges and the Rue Verrière. Part of the Baroque Palais des Ducs de Bourgogne remains. Once it was the palace of the Dukes of Burgundy, now it is the *Musée des Beaux-Arts.* Tomb of Philip the Bold. Works by Rubens, Frans Hals, etc. 13th-cent. Church of Notre-Dame with clock tower and an 11th-cent. Black Madonna. The Cathedral of St-Bénigne (1325) was once an abbey church. Archaeological museum. Some remnants of the Chartreuse de Champmol monastery, destroyed during the French Revolution.

Tournus. Church of St-Philibert (11th cent.) with sections of an earlier 9th-cent. church. The saint's reliquary. Musée Greuze.

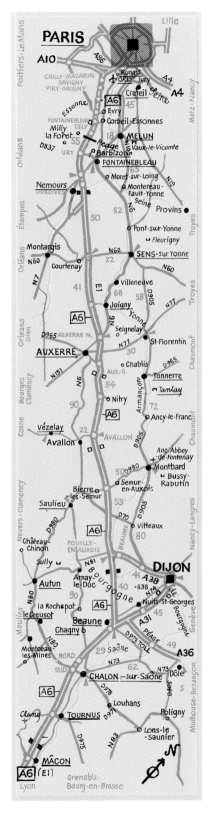

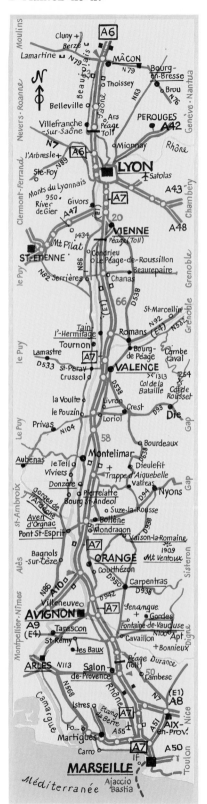

Mâcon (40 000). Centre of a wine district. Splendid *Hôtel Dieu*. The poet and politician Lamartine was born in Mâcon in 1790. Cluny. During the 11th cent. the famous abbey was the centre of Christendom. 2000 monasteries all over Europe were governed from here. The greater part of the *abbey* was destroyed during the French Revolution. Five of the original fifteen towers remain. The part of the abbey with the octagonal tower and the "Holy Water Tower" give an idea of its previous splendour. During the 12th cent. it was reputedly the world's largest church. Lovely streets in the little town of **Cluny**. Musée Ochier (weavings and paintings).

Bourg-en-Bresse (45 000) with the handsome Brou abbey church (1532). Tombs and ebony choir stalls. *Musée de l'Ain* (folklore museum).

LYON, see town plans.

A7. Lyon – Avignon – Marseille. *Autoroute du Soleil*

Vienne (30 000) was an important Roman town. *Temple d'Auguste et de Livie* was named in honour of Caesar Augustus and his queen, Livia. During the French Revolution it was used as a "Temple of Reason", but it has also served as a Christian church. Enormous *Roman amphitheatre*. *Cathedral of St-Maurice* and other interesting churches. The Church of St-Pierre, one of the oldest churches in France (6th–10th cent.), contains the Musée Lapidaire. La Pyramide stands on the site of the Roman town.

Tain-l'Hermitage. Little town near a vineyard slope. A monument on the Pont de l'Isère marks the 45th parallel. *Crussol* castle ruins. **Tournon** with two medieval towers and old bridges.

VALENCE (70 000). Chief town of the dep. of Drôme. The Cathedral of St-Apollinaire has a monument to Pope Pius VI who died here in 1799. Museum in the bishop's palace.

Livron. Castle ruins. Montélimar (30 000), famed for its production of nougat. Fine view from the Pic de Chenavari. Charming streets and houses in **Aubenas. Marcoule.** Nuclear power plant and research station in **Pierrelatte. Donzère-Mondragon** is Europe's largest power plant.

N 86 (formerly E 4) crosses the Rhône at **Bollène,** a pleasant little town. Beautiful *Pont St-Esprit* bridge. 1 km long and built during the 13th–14th cent., it carried E 4 traffic up until the 1970s. *Gorges de l'Ardèche* with impressive rock formations and the enormous *Aven d'Orgnac* stalactite and stalagmite caves.

Orange (25 000) has relics of the Roman era. Triumphal arch in memory of Caesar's victory in 49 B.C. *Amphitheatre* seating 7 000. The stage building is 100 m wide and 40 m long. Splendid view from the St-Eutrope Park. The Dutch royal family has its roots in Orange.

East of Orange there is a fine view from Mt-Ventoux. At **Vaison-la-Romaine** the excavations are comparable to the ones at Pompeii. 2nd-cent. theatre. Museum.

Fontaine-de-Vaucluse. An underground river that surfaces in a mighty limestone cliff landscape. Praises of the spring have been sung by Petrarch, the Italian poet and scholar who lived here during the 14th cent. **Gordes** small, typically Provençal, town. Cistercian Sénanque abbey. 16th-cent. château with works by Vasarély.

Carpentras. Remains of 13th-cent. fortifications and a Roman triumphal arch. Gothic *Cathedral of St-Siffrain*. Exquisite south portal with sculptures. 18th-cent. hospital with well-preserved pharmacy. Handsome Palais de Justice.

AVIGNON, see A9.

St-Rémy-de-Provence. Excavations in Glanum of a Greco-Roman town from the 2nd cent. B.C. Roman baths, covered markets and a triumphal arch. The finds are exhibited in the Renaissance Hôtel de Sade in the town. Van Gogh spent a few months in the St-Paul-de-Mausolée abbey (17th cent.) which still serves as a mental hospital.

Les Baux-de-Provence. Ruins of a large medieval town, destroyed in 1632 because Louis XIV thought it a gathering place for Huguenots. Several beautiful Renaissance buildings remain, but the town has only a few hundred inhabitants. The location is lovely as is the view from the remains of the castle.

Nîmes, Arles, Tarascon and the **Camargue,** see A 9.

MARSEILLE, see town plans.

A 8. Menton – Aix-en-Provence. *Autoroute la Provençale*

Vintemille/Ventimiglia, Italian border.

Menton (25 000). Long-established resort with many hotels. Beaches and picturesque old quarter. Flower market. Musée Jean Cocteau in the fortifications near the harbour. He also decorated the wedding hall in the town hall. The town museum has a collection of paintings. Biennial art exhibition. Chamber music festival.

MONACO, and *NICE,* see town plans.

Between Monte Carlo and Nice three lovely "corniche" roads run on shelves along the coast: the Grande, or Upper, Corniche; the Moyenne, or Middle, Corniche; the Inférieure, or Lower Corniche.

The mountains north and west of Nice are filled with delightful places. *Cagnes.* Winding streets round the château. *St-Paul.* Lovely old quarter and the remains of the town's fortifications. 13th-cent. church. *Fondation Maeght,* large art gallery. *Vence.* Beautiful old quarter round the cathedral. *Chapelle du Rosaire* (Chapel of the Rosary) decorated by Matisse. *Biot.* Idyllic town with artists and glass-blowing exhibitions. Biot glass comes in six colours. *Fernand Léger Museum,* both the interior and the exterior are well worth seeing.

Grasse and *Cannes,* see N 85.

The lovely coast road from Nice to Cannes is punctuated with towns and traffic jams. *Antibes* is one of the most elegant resorts on the Riviera. *Grimaldi Museum* with Picasso collection. *Meilland's Rose Garden* with 80 000 rose bushes and a fine view. Near by is *Sophia Antipolis,* "the City of Wisdom". Antipolis was what the ancient Greeks called Antibes. A complete town, built in the 1970s, it is a combination of university, research and industrial facilities that will concentrate on the problems of today and tomorrow: the search for oil, solar energy, computer techniques, telecommunications, and nuclear waste. The main street is named after Albert Einstein. Near the open-air theatre stands an apple tree, an offshoot of the tree that is said to have helped Sir Isaac Newton discover his inverse square law of gravity.

Juan-les-Pins, a youthful resort for the international jet set. *Vallauris* has hundreds of potteries. Picasso once worked here.

St-Raphaël (20 000). Port, resort, casino. Église des Templiers (Church of the Knights Templar), with a watch-tower from which pirates could be detected. *Fréjus* (30 000). Once a Roman port, now a few kilometres from the sea. Roman town gate and paving stones. The amphitheatre (3rd cent. B.C.) accommodates 9 000. The 12th-cent. cathedral has been built over the remains of a 5th-cent. church. Portal with two exquisitely carved 16th-cent. doors. The beautiful baptismal chapel is a part of the original church. *Ste-Maxime* and *St-Tropez.* Two large resorts. The *Chapelle de l'Annonciade* in St-Tropez is an art museum displaying the works of contemporary artists who worked in the area: Matisse, Braque, Bonnard, Rouault, etc. Citadel with marine museum.

N 98 continues up into the mountains. The *Corniche des Maures* coast road is lovely. The two roads meet again near the large resort of *Le Lavandou.* *Hyères* (40 000) is the oldest spa on the French Riviera.

TOULON (185 000). France's largest naval base (Mediterranean fleet). Lively Quai Stalingrad with view over the harbour and pavement cafés. Behind this are the narrow streets of the old part of the town.

At *Aubagne,* the road passes close to the barracks of the French Foreign Legion, "La Légion étrangère" which originated in Algeria in 1831. It is led by French officers, and the soldiers recruited are foreigners.

Compared with the coast road, the motorway is uneventful. However, it does provide motorists with beautiful mountain views on both sides of the road. The old section of *Draguignan* is lovely. *Le Thoronet* is a 12th- cent. Cistercian monastery of simple beauty. *Brignoles.* Old town, known for its bauxite mining. *Tourvres* has a ruined castle. Beautiful basilica in *Ste-Maximin-la-Ste-Baume.*

AIX-EN-PROVENCE (114 000). Spa, founded by the Romans. Its period of greatness was during the 17th and 18th cent. when many magnificent palaces were built. Folklore museum in the Hotel d'Estienne. Quatre-Dauphins and other lovely fountains give the town its distinctive atmosphere. 17th-cent. Hôtel de Ville (town hall) with the Méjanes Library that contains manuscripts and incunabula. The *Cathedral of St-Sauveur* is marked by many building styles – not surprisingly as it was under construction from the 11th to the 17th cent. The baptismal chapel was built in the 6th cent. *Musée des Tapisseries* in the archbishop's palace. Wall hangings from Beauvais. The *Musée Granet,* housed in an old building once owned by the Knights of Malta, contains collections of archaeological finds and sculptures. The Knights also founded the Church of St-Jean-de-Malte. *Musée Arbaud.* Provençal art. Music festival in June.

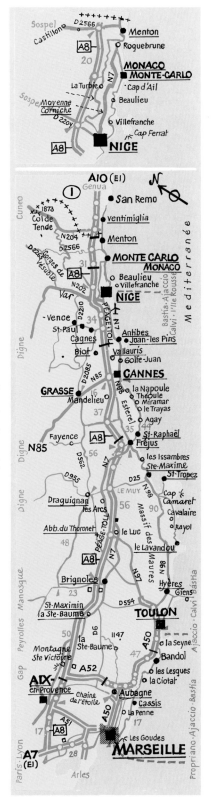

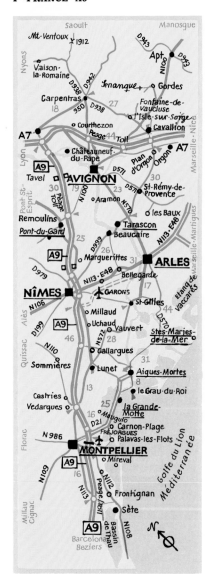

A 9. Orange – Montpellier – Le Perthus.
Autoroute la Languedocienne – la Catalane

Orange, St Rémy-de-Provence and *Les Baux-de-Provence,* see A 7.

AVIGNON (93 000). Roman city that became the residence (1309-1417) of the popes during their "Babylonian Captivity". Avignon was ruled by the papacy until the French Revolution. A 5 km long town wall with eight gates and 39 towers encloses the winding streets of this ancient town. The centre of Avignon is the Place de l'Horloge. *Palais des Papes.* The massive, fortified, papal palace with six towers and 4 m thick walls built for Benedict XII, a thoughtful pontiff. The new palace was built for Clement VI, who appreciated elegance and grandeur. The large hall for papal audiences is 52 m long and contains the "Fresco of the Prophets" by Giovanetti of Siena. The 15th-cent. Petit Palais, the archbishop's palace, is now a museum exhibiting Italian art. The famous bridge of the song ("Sur le pont d'Avignon") is *Pont St-Bénézet,* completed in 1185. Only four of its original arches remain. The *Promenade du Rocher des Doms* is a splendid place for an evening stroll. The 12th-cent. Cathedral of Notre Dame-des-Doms contains a bishop's throne and the tomb of Pope John XXII. Musée Calvet (archaeology, antique art) and Musée Lapidaire with Roman sculpture.

Tarascon. Little town made famous by Alphonse Daudet's comic character, Tartarin de Tarascon. Castle dating from 1450 and Condamin Porte from the 14th cent. *Daudet's windmill* in Fontvieille. *Beaucaire,* with views from the ruined castle. *Baux* and *St-Rémy,* see A 7.

ARLES (50 000). Splendid Roman and medieval buildings. Enormous 2nd-cent. arena, a 136 m long *amphitheatre* seating 25 000 spectators. Three medieval towers. *The ancient theatre* could accommodate 10 000, but most of it has been destroyed. *Les Aliscampes* is a Roman necropolis. Remains of Roman baths. *Cathedral of St- Trophime* (12th cent.). Portal with beautiful sculptures. *Museum of antiquities, Museon Arlaton* (folklore museum), *Musée Réattu* (paintings and tapestries). The most distinguished hotel in Arles is the Jules-César in a former 17th-cent. Carmelite abbey. The Pont-de-Langlois, subject of van Gogh's famous painting, is near Arles.

The *Camargue,* a huge marshy alluvial plain in the Rhône delta, is one of Europe's most peculiar natural phenomena. Here are wild horses, black bulls and pink flamingoes. The shepherds live in white, thatched houses, "cabanes". Rice fields.

Saintes-Maries-de-la-Mer with views out over the sea. Legend has it that the Virgin Mary's sister, Mary Jacobé, Mary Salomé and Mary Magdalene are buried here together with their servant girl, Sara. The town has been a pilgrimage place since the 6th cent., especially for gipsies who pray to their patron saint, Sara, whose reliquary is in the 12th-cent. *Church of Notre-Dame-de-la-mer.* The church is fortified and could withstand pirate attacks. Pilgrimages May 24-25 and Saturday-Sunday after October 21.

Uzès. Little town with old houses and the Duché château which used to belong to the Dukes of Uzès. Beautiful Renaissance façade. 17th- cent. St-Théodorit Church with the 12th-cent. *Tour Fenestrelle.* Its circular shape is unique in France.

The *Pont-du-Gard* aqueduct is one of the best-preserved Roman structures in the world. Erected in 19 B.C. for Agrippa, son-in-law of Caesar Augustus, the aqueduct has three levels. The road is on the lowest of these. If you do not suffer from vertigo, you can walk on the uppermost level, next to the conduit. 275 m long; it is 48 m above the river. The Pont-du-Gard carried water on its way from springs in Uzès to Nimes.

NÎMES (130 000). Chief town of the dep. of Gard. Silk industry. Wine trade. The French city with the greatest number of antique monuments. Before it became a Roman town in 121 B.C. it was a Celtic capital. Particularly during the reign of Caesar Augustus (63 B.C. – A.D. 14) several magnificent structures were erected here. *Arènes* (Amphitheatre) 135 × 105 m with 124 entrances and seating more than 20 000 spectators. Summer performances. *Maison Carrée,* a well-preserved temple built before the birth of Christ, was one of the most beautiful Roman temples. Now it is a museum of antiquities. *Jardin de la Fontaine.* Splendid park with canals, bridges and sculptures. It was created during the Roman era. The greatest part of the present park dates from the 18th cent. Roman temple of Diana. Tour Magne, a 30 m high octagonal Roman tower on Mt-Cavalier (about 100 m high). Roman town gates Porte d'Arles and Porte d'Auguste. Archaeological museum and art museum (old masters).

Villeneuve-les-Magelonnes. The 12th-cent. Cathedral of St.Pierre is all that remains of a once important town.

Aigues-Mortes is a marshland, "dead water". The town wall (13th cent.) is more than 1 600 m long. With its 20 towers and 10 gates it encircles the entire picturesque old town. *Tour de Constance,* a residential defence tower with a diameter of 22 m. The town was founded by St. Louis as an embarkation port for the Crusades to Palestine.

Not far from this old town lies **La Grande Motte,** the most modern holiday centre imaginable. Pyramid-shaped blocks of flats, built to provide sunlight to every flat while assuring perfect privacy. Large marina.

Here begins the **Languedoc – Roussillon Riviera,** which stretches 180 km south towards the Spanish border. Construction began in 1963 in what was then a desert-like landscape with stagnant lagoons and insufferable swarms of mosquitoes. Now the coast consists of a long row of hyper-modern resorts. The head architect, Georges Candilis, has worked with le Corbusier. If the result is frightful or fabulous – well, it's a matter of taste.

MONTPELLIER (196 000). University city. Chief town of the dep. of Hérault. Fine view from the lofty Peyrou Park, site of a triumphal arch built in honour of Louis XIV. The 800 m long aqueduct looks like the Pont-du-Gard but was built in the 17th cent. Exotic plants in the *Jardin des Plantes* (1593), the oldest botanical garden in France. The cathedral was rebuilt after the religious wars when Montpellier was a Huguenot stronghold. Magnificent palaces (17th–18th cent.). *Musée Fabre* with art and sculpture.

Sète (45 000). Old wine trading town with lovely canals. Large port. **Agde.** Old port town. Cathedral of St. Étienne. The new seaside resort of **Cap d'Agde** attempts to recreate the atmosphere of an old town. Arcades in the harbour district.

Pézenas, where the Prince of Conti and the Abbé Roquette lived. Molière had them in mind when he created Don Juan and Tartuffe. The playwright visited the town several times. Tapestry museum.

BEZIERS (85 000). Centre for the wine trade. Art museum. Bull ring. Cathedral of St-Nazaire.

NARBONNE (40 000). Roman town. Once a port on the Golfe du Lion, it is now connected with the sea by the 25 km long Canal de la Robine. The *Cathedral of St-Just* (13th cent.) was never completed but its 40 m high choir is impressive. Archbishop's palace (13th cent.) with museum of art and archaeology. *Carcassonne,* see A61.

Port Leucate-Port Barcarès. Large seaside resort on a 20 km long peninsula. Experimental architecture inspired by Greek and North African villages. The amusement centre is the 20 000 ton vessel "Lydia" in Port Barcarès. It was transported here in a canal that was subsequently filled in. 2 km long cable transport for water skiers.

Salses. Famous for its white wine. Innumerable vineyards offer wine tasting.

PERPIGNAN (110 000). Chief town of the dep. of Pyrénées- Orientales. Fruit, wine and vegetable trade. Its closeness to Spain is reflected in its architecture and atmosphere. *Palais des Rois de Majorque* (14th cent.), once the palace of the Kings of Majorca. Splendid views from the tower. The yellow-brick Porte Castille (1367) houses a folklore museum. The centre of the Old Town is the Place de la Loge. *Loge de Mer* (14th cent.) is now a part of the town hall. The St-Jean-Baptiste Cathedral was built during the 14th–16th cent. Chapelle du Christ with famous modern crucifix. Promenade des Platanes Park.

Canet-Plage is a giant modern development. The Côte Vermeille, the "Purple Coast", with its dark red granite cliffs, is a bit of the Mediterranean coast that has, as yet, eluded concrete and skyscrapers. **Collioure, Port-Vendres** and **Banyuls** are still idyllic fishing villages where the major catches are anchovies, mussels and oysters.

St-Martin-du-Canigou. Holy mountain of the Catalonians with a fortress-like monastery on a cliff ledge high above a wild river gorge. N 116 to **Prades,** well-known for its chamber music festival. The cellist Pablo Casals lived here for many years.

ANDORRA, see N 20.

Le Perthus, Spanish border.

E 4 continues to Barcelona – Madrid – Lisboa.

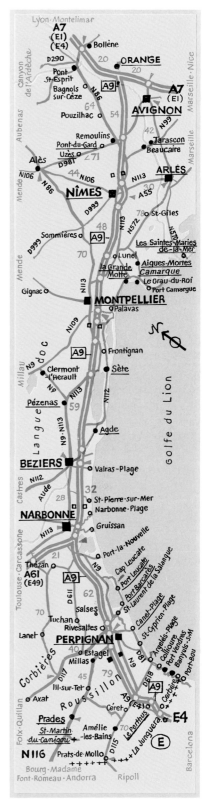

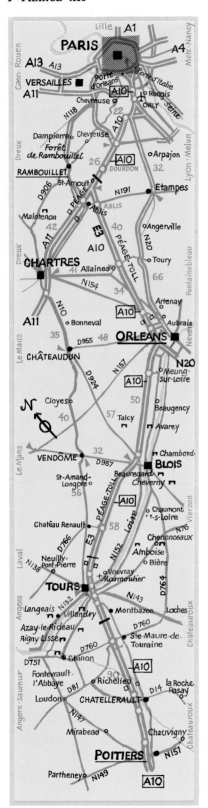

A10. Paris – Orléans – Bordeaux. *L'Aquitaine*

PARIS and *Versailles,* see town plans. *Orly* and *Rungis,* see A 6.

Maintenon, Rambouillet and *Chartres,* see A 11.

Étampes (17 000) with the 12th-cent. Church of Notre-Dame- du-Fort. Splendid views from the Tour Guinette.

ORLÉANS (100 000) with memories of Jeanne d'Arc, "The Maid of Orléans", who successfully defended the city agains the English. In 1431 she was tried for heresy and sorcery by an ecclesiastical court at Rouen, condemned and burnt at the stake. The *Cathedral of Ste-Croix* was started in 1278, destroyed during the 16th cent. and rebuilt during the 17th–19th cent. Historical and art museums. St-Benoit-sur-Loire. Romanesque basilica.

BLOIS (50 000). Full of handsome old patrician houses and churches. Cathedral of St-Louis (18th cent.). The tower and West Front are remnants from an earlier church, destroyed during a storm. 10th-cent. crypt. Notre-Dame-de-la-Trinité from 1939. The *château* consists of three buildings, dating from 1498, 1524 and 1638. They were used as residences by several French kings – Henri III and Catherine de Medici were just two of the many royal residents.

The châteaux of the Loire are exceptionally numerous and beautiful. From the 12th cent. up until the 18th cent. 120 châteaux and large manor houses were built in the Valley of the Loire from Orléans to Angers. A brief summary of those most popular with tourists:

Chambord (1519-1550) is one of the largest and most beautiful, but its interior is almost bare. The magnificent apartments of Louis XIV remain. This was also once the residence of Stanislaus Leszczyński, exiled King of Poland.

Cour-Cheverny (17th cent.) has beautiful interiors. *Montrésor,* fortified 16th-cent. château. *Chaumont-sur-Loire* with beautiful furniture. Catherine de Medici lived here.

Chenonceaux (1520). The oldest sections were built in mid-river, but were later connected to the bank by a structure that rests on five arches or vaults. Splendid interior with paintings and tapestries.

Amboise (about 1498), one of the most beautiful of all the châteaux. Sturdy walls and fortification towers that horses and riders could mount. Highest up is the Salle des États (Hall of State). St-Hubert's Chapel. Leonardo da Vinci lived in a separate building, Manoir de Clos- Luce, from 1516 until his death in 1519. Some copies of his mechanical inventions are on display. Pagode de Chanteloup (1778), palace in the Chinese manner in the form of a 40 m high tower. The little town has a gate with a beautiful clock.

TOURS (145 000). Chief city of the Loire Valley. Silks and wine. Lovely buildings on the Place Plumereau, the Place Foire le Roi and the Place des Carmes. Picturesque *old streets,* e.g. Rue de la Paix, Rue Paul-Louis Courier, Rue Dorée and Rue du Grand-Marché. *Musée des Beaux-Arts* (art museum) in the former archbishop's palace. Only one tower remains of the 11th-cent. Basilica of St. Martin. A new basilica was built at the turn of the century. Cathedral of St-Gatien.

Villandry. Renaissance château. Beautiful interiors and lovely park. *Azay-le-Rideau.* One of the most splendid Renaissance châteaux. Renaissance museum. St-Symphorien Church. *Langeais.* Fortress-like 15th-cent. château with interesting interior.

Chinon. Lovely old town. Handsome houses in Rue Voltaire and Rue J.J. Rousseau. Half-timbered houses on the Grand Carroi. The town is dominated by the ruined castle. Jeanne d'Arc came here in 1429 and a museum has an exhibition devoted to the life of the saint. The splendid *Fontevrault-l'abbey,* see A 11.

Montbazon. Little town with ruined castle.

Ste-Maure-de-Touraine. Romanesque church. Old houses. Town hall with museum. The Church of St-Jean-l'Évangéliste has a bell donated by Czar Nicholas II.

Châtellerault (40 000). Lovely houses in the old part of town. One of them belonged to the philosopher René Descartes. Called to the court of Queen Christina in Stockholm, he died in Sweden in 1650, probably of a cold. Pont Henri-IV, a 16th-cent. bridge with two towers. Castle (15th cent.), now a museum, displaying weapons and faience.

POITIERS (85 000). Chief town of the dep. Vienne. Important Roman town and historical capital of Poitou. University founded in 1432. The town is situated on a 50 m high promontory and its older sections are extremely beautiful. 12th-cent. Palais de Justice. Musée Ste-Croix (art and archaeology). 12th-cent. Notre-Dame-la-Grande is a beautiful Romanesque church with a façade lavishly adorned with sculptures. The baptismal chapel of St-Jean is probably the most ancient Christian structure in France. The *Cathedral of St-Pierre* (1166-1271) with beautiful stained glass. Saint Radegonde, patron saint of Poitiers, is buried in this church, which was consecrated in 1099. The Church of St-Hilaire-le-Grand has splendidly decorated portals. In 732 soldiers under Charles Martel repulsed the Moslem invasion of Europe at the Battle of Poitiers.

Chauvigny. Extremely lovely old town surrounded by rocky heights. Five ruined castles. Beautiful churches. *St-Savin.* Famous frescoes in the 11th-cent. St-Savin-et-St-Cyprien Church.

Montmorillon. Church of Notre-Dame. 13th-cent. wall paintings. Maison Dieu (hospital) with church and charnel house. *Civray* with lovely old houses. *Niort.* Two old fortification towers and an ethnographical museum. The Church of Notre-Dame has a tall belfry. Interesting old part of town. Art museum.

ANGOULÊME (50 000). Chief city of the dep. of Charente, high on a promontory. The views from its encircling walls are delightful. Cathedral of St-Pierre with splendid façade. Built in the 12th cent., it was restored during the 19th cent. when the dome was added. Picturesque old quarter.

Perigueux, see N 89.

BORDEAUX (226 000). Chief city of the dep. of Gironde. Centre of the wine trade and viticulture. Large port. Older sections south of the Place de la Comédie, the city's centre. The enormous Esplanade des Quinconces and Place de la Bourse are down by the river. Fountain of the Three Graces and maritime museum Art museum. The 846 m long *Pont de Pierre* crosses the Garonne on 17 arches. Grand-Théâtre in the classic style. The *Palais Rohan,* once an archbishop's palace, now serves as town hall. *Musée d'Aquitaine* (folklore) and Musée des Beaux-Arts (art) with works by Botticelli, Rubens, etc. in the palace's wings. *Cathedral of St-André,* completed in the 16th cent. with sculpture on the Porte Royale and the Pey-Berland bell tower crowned with a golden madonna. Romanesque *St-Sevrin Church.* The saint's marble sarcophagus (6th cent.) is in the 11th-cent. crypt. Two 15th-cent. town gates.

N10. Bordeaux – Irún

To the west the large wine producing areas of *Médoc, Margaux* and *Mouton-Rothschild. Côte d'Argent,* the "Silver Coast", 240 km long, between the Garonne and the Adour. Sand dunes and the Les Landes pine woods. Large seaside resorts. *Arcachon* is one of the largest. Casino. Dune du Pilat at 114 m is the highest sand dune in Europe.

Dax (20 000). Large spa. The springs (64° C) were known as early as the Roman era. Remains of a 9th-cent. town wall. Roman mosaic in the Church of St-Vincent de-Xaintes. Road to *Mont-de-Marsan* which preserves the buildings and atmosphere of the 14th and 15th cent. Remains of fortifications.

BAYONNE (45 000). Picturesque old streets and houses round the 15th-cent. castle. Fortress by Vauban, the military engineer. Ste-Marie, a Gothic cathedral with 19th-cent. tower and High Altar. *Musée Basque* in a lovely 16th-cent. building. One of the major industries is the production of Basque berets.

Biarritz (30 000). One of the most distinguished seaside resorts in France. Its traditions date from the time when the crowned heads of Europe gathered here. Casino. *Oceanographic museum* with aquarium. Sandy beaches and cliffs. *St-Jean-de-Luz,* Large, modern resort. Fishing port.

Spanish border. E 3 continues to Irún – San Sebastián – Valladolid – Lisboa.

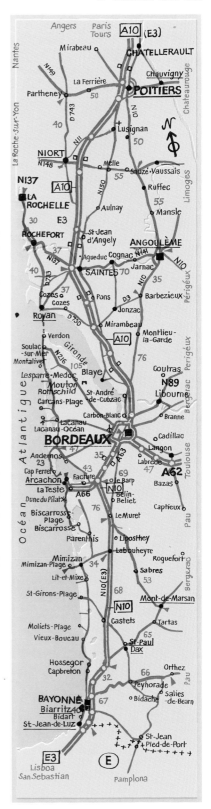

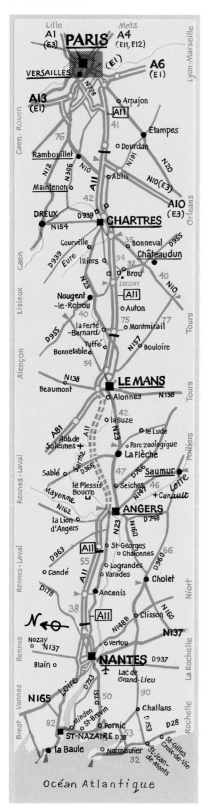

A11. Paris – Le Mans – Nantes. *Autoroute L'Oceane*

PARIS with **Versailles,** see town plans. Exit between the Porte d'Orléans and the Porte d'Italie together with A 6 and A 10. Paris – Ablis, see A 10. As an alternative, motorists can take route A 13 at the Porte St-Cloud and A 12/N 10 through the lovely Rambouillet Forest – or N 10 through Versailles.

Rambouillet. 18th- cent. château, a favourite of Napoleon. Lovely Rambouillet Forest rich in game and wild life. **Maintenon.** 17th-cent. château with a tower from a 12th-cent. fortress. The château was once the residence of Madame de Maintenon, mistress of Louis XIV. Beautiful park with incomplete aqueduct by Vauban, the military engineer.

CHARTRES (45 000). Chief town of the dep. of Eure-et-Loire. Famous for its **Cathedral of Notre-Dame,** the most glorious in France. Only St. Paul's in Rome and Canterbury Cathedral exceed it in size. Although it was consecrated in 1260, its three western doorways and their sculpture were originally a part of an earlier church and date from the mid 12th cent. The right tower is Gothic, while the spire on the left tower was added in 1510. The crypt, the largest in France, dates from the 11th cent. Lavish decorations. Exquisite stained-glass windows. The cathedral is 130 m long, 30-45 m wide and 36 m high. The tallest tower is 103 m. *Musée des Beaux-Arts* in the old bishop's palace. Flemish weavings, enamels and paintings. Handsome 15th- and 16th-cent. houses in the old section of the town.

N 10 to Châteaudun with old patrician houses. Stately castle (12th–16th cent.). Beautiful interiors and chapel.

LE MANS (155 000). Chief city of the dep. of Sarthe. *Le Vieux Mans,* the oldest part of the city, has lovely houses. Maison d'Adam et d'Eve, a beautiful Renaissance house on the Grande Rue. Folklore and ceramics museum in the Maison de la Reine Bérengère. Queen Berengaria was the widow of Richard the Lionheart, King of England. Her tomb is in the cathedral. Hôtel du Grabatoire (1530) is a bishop's residence. Remains of a Roman town wall with ten towers. Musée de Tessé contains art and the famous enamel plaque from the tomb of the royal English Plantagenet dynasty. The Cathedral of St-Julien is part Romanesque and part Gothic. Beautiful sculptures around the south portal (12th cent.). Famous stained glass.

Circuit automobile de la Sarthe, famed motor racing circuit (13.5 km) and *Circuit Bugatti* (4.5 km), a training and testing circuit. The average speed on the larger circuit is about 220 kmh, but speeds up to 350 kmh have been achieved (Porsche). The 24-hour rally is held in June. Race night is lively: fun fair, divine services and striptease. Motor car museum.

No motorway Le Mans – Angers. Follow N 23.

ANGERS (145 000). Chief town of the dep. of Maine-et-Loire and the old wine, flower- and fruit-producing province of Anjou. Splendid venerable houses in the Cité between the castle and the cathedral. Place de la Laiterie and Rue Beaurepaire. Hôtel Pince from 1530. Logis Barrault (15th cent.), houses an art museum displaying French paintings and works of the sculptor David d'Angers. The Hôpital St-Jean (1210) is a Gothic building. The large ward is now a museum displaying archaeological remains and examples of the goldsmith's art. Wine museum in the cellar. *Cathedral of St-Maurice* (13th cent.) has exquisite stained-glass windows. An imposing castle with 17 towers (1240) and pointed roofs stands on a 32 m high promontory above the River Maine and access is via a drawbridge. *Museum* with wall hangings and tapestries, most important of which is the 168 m long and 5 m high "Tenture de l'Apocalypse" depicting the Last Judgement.

Road to **Saumur** (36 000). 14th-cent. castle with four corner towers. One museum of decorative art, and one, *Musée du Cheval,* devoted to horses. Beautiful old section of the town. **Fontevrault,** south of Saumur, has 12th-cent. monastery and abbey church. Tombs of the members of the Plantagenet dynasty which became the royal family of England. Châteaux of the Loire, see A 10.

NANTES (265 000). Chief town of the dep. of Loire-Atlantique. Major port and industrial city. Largest city in the old province of Brittany. Handsome 18th-cent. buildings on the Cours Cambronne and Place Royale. A few 15th-cent. buildings near the *Château Ducal* (16th cent.), now a museum (Breton handicrafts and cultural history, maritime museum). In 1598, Henri IV signed the Edict of Nantes, which granted the Protestants of France freedom of worship. It was revoked by Louis XIV in 1685. The Gothic *Cathedral of St-Pierre-et-St-Paul* was begun in 1434 and finally completed in 1893. It is 102 m long and its vaults are 37 m high. Tomb of François II. He was the last Duke of Brittany and it was for him that the château was built. *Musée des Beaux-Arts* is one of the finest art museums in France. Interesting collections of local art and history in the Palais Dobrée. A modern section of the city, *Cité Radieuse,* was designed by Le Corbusier.

St-Nazaire, la Baule and **Noirmoutier,** see N 165 and N 137.

A13. Caen – Rouen – Paris. *Autoroute de Normandie*

N13. Cherbourg – Caen – Paris

CHERBOURG (35 000). Naval base, previously major port for North Atlantic passenger liners. Views from Fort du Roule. Museum devoted to the town's history and the June 6, 1944 "D Day" invasion. *Landing Museum* displays realistic models and interesting films. Beach monuments. Several large resorts along the coast. On "D-Day" June 6, 1944, Allied troops landed on Utah Beach and Omaha Beach.

Bayeux. Little town and bishop's seat since 360. Famous for its lace and porcelain. Lovely houses in the old part of town. The tourist office is in one of the oldest. Norman-Gothic Cathedral of Notre-Dame with 11th-cent. crypt. The famous *Bayeux Tapestry* (Tapisserie de la Reine Mathilde) is on display in the Musée de la Reine Mathilde. Embroidered on a band of linen in wools of eight colours, it depicts the conquest of England by William the Conquerer in 1066.

CAEN (123 000). Chief town of the dep. of Calvados. Large port and modern university. Most of the town was destroyed during the 1944 invasion, but the streets and buildings near the Place St-Sauveur and Rue St-Pierre survived and have retained their original charm. The 75 m high belfry of the 14th-cent. Church of St-Pierre has served as a model for several similar towers in Normandy and Brittany. The castle high above the town was built by order of William the Conquerer. Its handsome halls contain a folklore museum with one of the largest art collections in France (Middle Ages – 19th cent.). *Abbaye aux Dames* (Ladies' Abbey) and La Trinité abbey church where Queen Mathilde is buried. *Abbaye aux Hommes* (Men's Abbey) with the Church of St-Étienne. Two 80 m high towers.

N 13 goes to *Lisieux,* a place of pilgrimage. Reliquary of Saint Teresa of Lisieux in the Carmelite convent. 13th-cent. Cathedral of St- Pierre. The beautiful old town was almost completely demolished in 1944.
Several large resorts along the Côte Fleurie that extends from Cabourg to Honfleur. Cliffs and sandy beaches.

Trouville, an old fishing port that has become a part of *Deauville-les-Bains,* one of the best-known and most elegant resorts in France.

Honfleur. Splendid old town with picturesque houses clustered about the harbour in the town's centre. *Church of Ste-Catherine,* a large, wooden Gothic structure, was erected in the 15th cent. by shipbuilders. Folklore museum in the former Church of St-Étienne. *Musée Boudin* contains Impressionist works. The suspension bridge that crosses the mouth of the Seine at *Tancarville* is 1 400 m long and 48 m above the water.

ROUEN (118 000). One of the largest river ports in France. Handsome town with splendid buildings. 16th-cent. Palais de Justice with richly adorned façade. Hotel de Bourgtheroulde. *Gros-Horloge* (the Great Clock) built into an arch that spans a busy street. Rouen will always be associated with the trial of Jeanne d'Arc, Maid of Orleans in 1431. She was tortured and condemned to death in the Tour Jeanne d'Arc (1205) and burnt at the stake in the Place du Vieux-Marché. *Musée des Beaux-Arts* contains one of the most extensive collections of art in France. Particularly wide range of French and Italian works. Ceramics. The Cathedral of *Notre-Dame* (13th cent.) with 16th-cent. façade. Exquisite stained glass. Tomb containing the heart of Richard the Lionheart. On the south side, the Tour de Beurre (Butter Tower). 14th-cent. St-Ouen Church. Tour Couronnée (Crowned Tower). Lavish interior, large organ. Beautiful 16th- cent. half-timbered houses in the old artisans' street, the Rue Eau-de-Robec. Interesting old half-timbered houses near the Church of St-Maclou served as charnel houses up until the 18th cent. *Elbeuf.* Old centre of the textile industry.

Evreux (50 000). Bishop's palace (museum of antiquities), cathedral and botanical garden.

Les Andelys. Little town ringed by high chalk cliffs. Ruins of the Château Gillard, once the castle of Richard the Lionheart (1196). Fine view.

St-Germain-en-Laye. 16th-cent. château, once summer residence of the French kings. Musée des Antiquités Nationales.

PARIS, see town plans.

N15. Le Havre – Rouen

LE HAVRE (216 000) The largest French Atlantic port. Boat tours. Modern city with broad avenues. Art museum (1951). Beautiful stained glass in the modern Church of St. Joseph.

Road N 20 to *Étretat,* a seaside resort situated at the foot of 90 m high, fantastically shaped, chalk cliffs. *Fécamp,* where 16th-cent. monks invented Benedictine liqueur. Museum in the distillery.

St-Wandrille and **Jumièges.** Abbey ruins. **Yvetot.** The round Church of St-Pierre. Prior to the French Revolution, Yvetot was a separate kingdom. It was founded by Rollo, a Danish Viking chieftain.

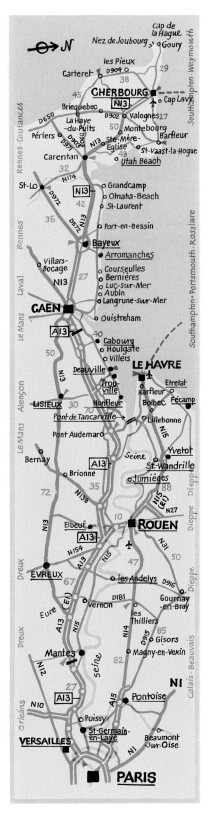

A 36. Mulhouse – Belfort – Besançon – Beaune

MULHOUSE (Mulhausen, 130 000; with suburbs, 200 000). The second largest city in Alsace. It has changed nationality from Swiss to German to French several times. The first French period started in 1798, the last one in 1918. Of the medieval city wall, the Tour du Diable (Devil's Tower) and the Nesle Tower remain. Now a large modern city with industries and port. Peugeot's motor car factories in Mulhouse and Sochaux. The Europa Tower on Place d'Europe is 31 storeys high and features a rotating restaurant. Many beautiful old buildings. Renaissance Hôtel de Ville (town hall, 1552) with painted façade and a covered entrance stairway. Neo-Gothic *Church of St- Étienne* with splendid stained-glass windows. *Musée de l'Impression sur Étoffes* is a museum of printed fabrics. Historical museum. The *Schlump Brothers' motor car museum* (periodically closed) has, among other exhibits, a large collection of Bugattis. *French Railway Museum.*

Altkirch. Beautiful old houses, Romanesque church.

Grand Ballon (Grosser Belchen). 1 423 m. Highest point in the Vosges. Views towards the Alps. Site of prehistoric sacrifices to the Sun God. Winter sports. Memorial dedicated to battles during the First World War. Opposite the monument is the *Musée d'Explosifs*, devoted to bombs, booby-traps and weapons.

Thann. Half-timbered town. Witch Tower and Stork Tower. *Alsace Museum* in a 16th-cent. house. The large, Gothic Church of St-Thiébaut.

BELFORT (60 000). Major fortress-town in the "Burgundian Gap" that separates the Vosges and Jura ranges. Built in 1687 by the military engineer Vauban. Famous in military history for sieges in 1813-1814, 1815 and 1870-1871. In memory of the last siege, the sculptor Bartholdi created the "Lion of Belfort", a 22 m long and 11 m high relief, carved in the sandstone rock adjoining the citadel's observation terrace (admission free). The same sculptor also created the Monument des Trois Sièges (Monument of the Three Sieges) on the Place de la République. His greatest work is the Statue of Liberty in New York.

Pilgrimage church in **Ronchamp** named Notre-Dame-du-Haut, on a 150 m high hill, was completed in 1955. Designed by Le Corbusier, it looms like a fortress or like a ship with a billowing sail. Although the interior is simple and rather dark, cascades of light stream down over the wall surfaces around the baptismal font. The little madonna over the altar is also visible from the outside when open-air church services are held. *Vesoul.* Chief town of the dep. of Haute-Saône. 18th-cent. St-Georges Church. At **Port-sur-Saône**, the river is spanned by a narrow 18th-cent. stone bridge.

Montbéliard (35 000). For 400 years the town was owned by the German Counts of Württemberg. As a result of this, many of its inhabitants are Protestants. The castle was built in the 15th cent. for the Württemberg's. Museum with room dedicated to the little-known inventor Étienne Oemichen, who invented the helicopter. The Peugeot factories in **Montbéliard-Sochaux** have been producing motor cars since 1889. **Audincourt.** Industrial town with *modern church* (1951) designed by Novarina. Stained-glass windows by Léger.

Baume-les-Dames. Convent for women of high birth, founded in the 7th cent. Baume-les-Messieurs. Monastery, founded in the 6th cent. by St. Columba, the Irish monk. Monks from here founded Cluny in 910. 3 km S cliffs at the Cirque de Baume.

BESANÇON (130 000). Chief town of the dep. of Daubs, previously the capital of the old province of Franche-Comté. University. Watchmaking industry. The *Musée des Beaux-Arts,* in a modern building, is one of the most splendid art museums in France. *Porte Noire* from the Roman period (2nd cent.). You can stroll on parts of the ramparts designed by Vauban. *Palais Granvelle* (16th cent.) contains watches, weavings and paintings. The *Cathedral of St-Jean* is part Romanesque and part Gothic. Clock tower with astronomical clock (1860). The citadel was restored in the 17th cent. by Vauban. Folklore museum. *Apothica* (pharmaceutical museum) in the Hôpital St-Jacques. Pharmacy donated to the town in 1640.

Dole (30 000). Lovely old quarter. Museum in the house where Louis Pasteur was born. He moved to Arbois when he was five years old. Museum in what was once the chapel of a Jesuit school (archaeology and 17th-cent. paintings). The Church of Notre-Dame (1574) contains many beautiful objects. 74 m high belfry.

Road south to **Poligny**. The beautiful buildings on the Grande Rue are famous for their carved doors. Louis Pasteur grew up in **Arbois**. His childhood home is open to visitors. Wine museum.

DIJON, se A 6.

Beaune, see A 6.

Jura mountains form a natural boundary between Switzerland and France. The roads often pass through narrow wooded gorges, but there are also farming villages, vineyards and over 70 lakes. Observation points are rare. *Colombey de Gex* above Col de Faucille, on the road to Geneva, and *Grand Colombier* (1 531 m) are two of the highest points.

A 41. Genève – Grenoble (part of E 4)
A 40. Genève – The Mont Blanc Tunnel (E 21)

GENÈVE, see Switzerland, town plans.

Annemasse (20 000) is just 8 km from Geneva. You abruptly leave Switzerland and find yourself in French villages if you drive the winding roads up the Salève, Geneva's own mountain. Lovely views.

A 40 *(Autoroute Blanche)* goes to Chamonix and the Mont Blanc tunnel, see Route des Grandes Alpes.

From Geneva to Annecy, the shortest route is N 201, west of Salève. *Col-du-Mont-du-Sion,* 798 m offers fine views out over the Jura mountains. The road was built in the 12th cent. by Carthusian monks from Pamiers.

ANNECY (60 000). Chief town of the dep. of Haute-Savoie. Extremely beautiful setting. Resort. *Old Town* with winding streets. Rue Ste- Claire with arcades. The oldest parts of the castle were built in the 12th- 16th cent. Cathedral of St-Pierre. Beautiful views from the Jardin Public. Sightseeing by boat. A trip around the lovely *Lac d'Annecy* (about 40 km) goes through the little town of *Duingt.*

Aix-les-Bains (20 000). One of the most elegant resorts in France, the town has hundreds of hotels and two casinos. The hot sulphuric springs (45° C) were well-known as early as the Roman era. Remains of *Roman baths.* The 9 m high Campanus triumphal arch, built by the Romans, still stands in the Square du Temple-de-Diane.

CHAMBÉRY (60 000). Chief town of the dep. of Savoie. The Dukes of Savoy ruled the independent Duchy of Savoy from the castle (14th–16th cent.) until the 16th cent. 15th-cent. Sainte-Chapelle. Beautiful paintings. Arcades in the Old Town. Art museum. Boat trip round the beautiful *Lac du Bourget* (about 50 km). This is the largest lake in France, 18 km long and 2-3 km wide. The *Abbaye de Hautecombe* was once a monastery.

La Grande-Chartreuse, a mighty building (17th cent.), 961 m above sea level, in a lovely forested valley at the foot of the Grand Som. The abbey belongs to the Carthusians, and was founded in 1085 by St. Bruno. The world-famous Chartreuse liqueur is produced in Voiron, but the abbey contains the world's largest liqueur cellars, 164 m long.

GRENOBLE (170 000). Chief town of the dep. of Isère. Beautifully situated between high mountains. Industry (gloves) and university. Lovely Old Town. The Palais de Justice (16th cent.) is one of the most beautiful buildings. Cathedral of Notre-Dame (12th cent.). Views from the 86 m high Tour Perret. The *Musée de Peinture et de Sculpture* is one of the most distinguished art museums in France. It exhibits both the works of old masters and modern art. Musée Dauphinois and Musée Hébert. Natural history museum. Museum in the town hall, dedicated to the writer Stendhal, whose works include "The Red and The Black" (1830) and "The Charterhouse of Parma" (1839). His real name was Henri Beyle (1783-1842) and he was born in Grenoble. Many lovely parks. Funicular to the *Fort de la Bastille* with splendid views. The Winter Olympic Games of 1968 created a surge in building. The Olympia Stadium accommodates 70 000 spectators.

SW of Grenoble is the *Vercors region.* Fantastic *Combe Laval* mountain road (completed in 1897) with stupendous views. Neither driver nor passengers should be susceptible to vertigo. From a distance the road looks more dangerous than it is. *Gorges de la Bourne* with caves. *Grands Goulets* with galleries and tunnels between the high cliffs. *Villard-de-Lans* is the major winter sports resort of the region.

A 42. Genève – Lyon *Autoroute Verte*

Impressive cliffs at *Fort l'Ecluse.* Power station at *Génissiat.* The lake is 23 km long, the dam 104 m high.
The little town of *Bellegarde* has an 18th-cent. palace and a church with a beautiful façade. Scenic route through the Valserine Valley to Col de la Faucille. Views from *Cret de Chalame,* 1 545 m. 30 minutes on foot.

Nantua. Small town in a beautiful setting on the shores of a little lake. Crayfish are a local speciality. The old Benedictine abbey was destroyed during the Revolution. The Church of St-Michel (12th cent.) has a handsome portal and contains a painting by Delacroix.

Pérouges. Little town (about 500 inhabitants) that flourished during the Middle Ages and has preserved its medieval character. Most of the buildings date from the 15th and 16th cent. Well-preserved town hall.

Bourg-en-Bresse, see A 5.

A 43. Lyon – Chambéry A 48. Lyon – Grenoble

LYON, see town plans.

Tour-du-Pin was an important town during the Middle Ages. Statue of the Madonna set high above the town. Views. Modern Church of Sacré-Coeur.

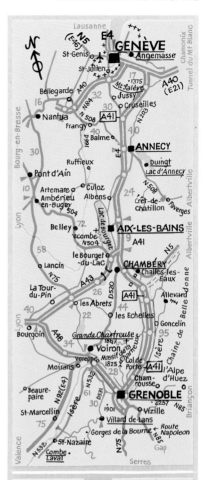

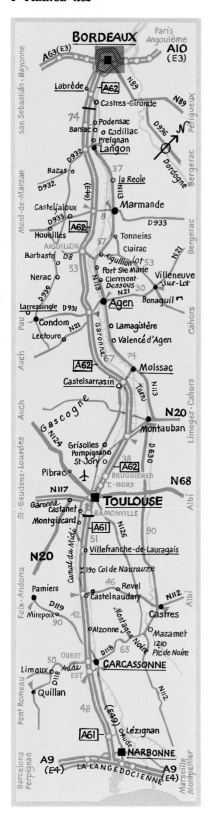

A 62. Bordeaux – Narbonne. *Autoroute des Deux Mers*

BORDEAUX, see A 10.

Labrède. Château, birthplace (1689) of the philosopher and writer Montesquieu. His greatest work, "De l'Esprit des Lois" (1748) had a great influence on later political thinking. 14th-cent. walls and moat.

Langon. Little town with Gothic church and Roquetaillade Château. St-Macaire. Lovely medieval buildings and atmosphere. Arcaded Place du Mareadieu. Town wall (13th–15th cent.) with three town gates. 14th- cent. paintings in the Church of St-Sauveur.

La Réole. Beautifully set on a hill. Abbey church of St-Pierre, castle and town hall date from the 12th and 13th cent. The Church of Notre-Dame contains a fine Entombment. Port-Ste-Marie. Venerable streets and houses.

Agen (36 000). Bishop's seat on the Garonne. Handsome canal bridge and charming old town centre. Arcades and covered galleries in the Rue des Cornières. Town hall (1666) on the square. *Museum* (antiquities, furniture, art by Goya, Tiepolo, etc.) situated in three lovely houses. Cathedral of St-Caprais consecrated in the 16th cent., took 400 years to build. The Chapel of the Holy Innocents (12th cent.) has a splendid portal. Road south to **Larressingle,** an interesting partially preserved, fortified village (13th–15th cent.).

Moissac. Little town with the famous *abbey church of St-Pierre* (12th-15th cent.). Richly sculpted south portal. Splendid cloister. **Castelsarrasin.** Churches of St-Sauveur (13th–15th cent.) and St-Jean (15th cent.).

TOULOUSE (380 000). Chief city in the dep. of Haute-Garonne. One of the holy cities of the Gauls, capital of the Visigoths. Major industrial city where Aérospatiale construct the Airbus. Parts for this aircraft are delivered from six separate countries and assembled here. University with origins in the 13th cent. *St-Sernin,* the largest Romanesque basilica in France, was consecrated in 1096 as one of the churches on the pilgrimage route to Santiago de Compostela in Spain. Lavish fittings. Augustinian abbey (museum with sculptures). 14th-cent. Jacobin church. St-Raymond Museum (Gallo-Roman finds), Paul-Dupuy Museum (handicrafts), Georges-Labit Museum (Egyptian and Oriental art), museum of natural history. Centre of the town is the Place du Capitole, site of the 120 m long 18th-cent. Capitol, which houses the town hall and a theatre. The Hôtel d'Assezat is one of the many Renaissance buildings in the city.

Villefranche-de-Lauragais. 14th-cent. church with fortified belfry. *Col de Naurauze,* highest point on the Canal du Midi that connects the Atlantic with the Mediterranean. Memorial obelisk.

CARCASSONNE (50 000). Chief town in the dep. of Aude. The old upper town, **La Cité,** is one of the best-preserved medieval towns in Europe. It is encircled by a stout 13th-cent. fortified wall. The oldest parts of Carcassonne date from the Visigoth era (about 5th cent.) and remained undamaged through the French Revolution. Only two gates: Porte d'Aude and Porte Narbonnaise. Comtal Castle (12th cent.), the Tour de Poudre (Powder Tower) and an *archaeological museum,* are all part of the wall. Church of St-Nazaire (11th–14th cent.). The lower town, *Ville Basse,* is built on a chessboard pattern. Churches of St-Vincent and St-Michel. *Art museum.*

Roads go from Toulouse and Carcassonne to **Albi,** site of one of the most interesting cathedrals in France, see N 88.

NARBONNE, see A 9.

A 25. Dunkerque – Lille

DUNKERQUE (Dunkirk, Dünkirchen, 28 000). Northernmost town in France. Shipyards, steel industry and large port. Views from the Leughenar ("Liar") lighthouse. The structure was given its Flemish nickname after a false alarm. The name of the town is also Flemish: Church in the Dunes. In 1940 345 000 allied soldiers were evacuated from its beach. Memorial stone. The sandy beach extends all the way to the large seaside resort of *Malo-les-Bains*.

Bailleul. Small industrial town, destroyed in 1918 and completely reconstructed in the Flemish Renaissance style. Lace. Annual carnival.

Armentières (30 000). Famous for its linen weaving mills. The town was founded by the Romans.

LILLE, see A 1.

A 26. Calais – Arras

St-Omer, is the centre of "Les Watringues", a lovely area marked by small rivers, canals and gardens. The town is set on the banks of the River Aa. Impressive art museum. The Church of Notre-Dame (13th–15th cent.) has a beautiful south portal. Modern town hall.

Arras, see A 1.

N1. Calais – Boulogne – Amiens – Beauvais – Paris

CALAIS (80 000). Port, particularly for ferries to England. Seaside resort with casino. Rodin's sculpture "The Burghers of Calais", dedicated to the memory of the men who, at the start of the Hundred Years' War, turned themselves over to the English and saved the town.

Wissant and *Wimereux,* seaside resorts. Views from the lighthouse on Cape Griz-Nez to the English coast 33 km away.

BOULOGNE-sur-Mer (50 000). Harbour and fishing port. The Colonne de la Grande Armée brings to mind the large Napoleonic army that gathered here to invade England. Needless to say, they never crossed the Channel. "Ville Haute", the old town with walled castle.

Etaples. Little town with picturesque fishing harbour. *Le-Touquet-Paris-Plage* and *Berck-Plage* are two large coastal resorts. *Abbeville.* 15th-cent. Church of St.Vulfran. Musée Boucher-de-Perthes (archaeology, art and 16th-cent. woodcarvings).

Road D 925 to Dieppe. *Le Tréport.* Idyllic port and seaside resort. Lovely views from the Calvaire des Terasses (cable car). German fortifications (from the Second World War) in the cliffs. The large palace in Eu was once the residence of Louis-Philippe.

Dieppe (26 000). Port. France's first seaside resort. 2 km long pebble beach. Old quarter and fishing harbour. A 15th-cent. castle, now containing a museum.

AMIENS (136 000). Old city with charming streets and houses. Old-established textile industry: silk and velvet. The *Cathedral of Notre-Dame* (1268) is the largest in France. West Front adorned with the statues of 22 kings. Three richly adorned high-arched portals. Elaborate woodcarvings with many exquisite details in the choir. 3 650 figures. *Musée de Picardie.* Archaeology and art. The Battle of the River Somme from July to November 1916 was the bloodiest combat in history. More than a million were killed.

BEAUVAIS (57 000). *Cathedral of St-Pierre.* Construction began in the 13th cent. and was stopped in 1578. But the transepts, completed in 1500, and the choir, make this one of the most remarkable churches in France. The choir vault, 48 m high, is thought to be the highest in the world. 19th-cent. astronomical clock. The Palace of Justice is now a museum.

Pontoise. The picturesque narrow streets of the old quarter lead up to the newer parts of the town. Beautiful Gothic Church of St-Maclou.

ST-DENIS (100 000). Industrial town. King Dagobert founded a monastery in the 7th cent. on the site of the final resting place of St. Denis (Dionysius). The saint had been beheaded on Montmartre but legend has it that he took his head in his hands and walked here. The *cathedral* that was erected here in the 12th cent. served as a model for many large churches. Many kings were buried here but their graves were plundered and the cathedral destroyed during the Revolution. The building has since been restored.

PARIS, see town plans.

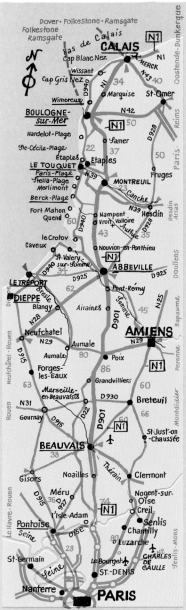

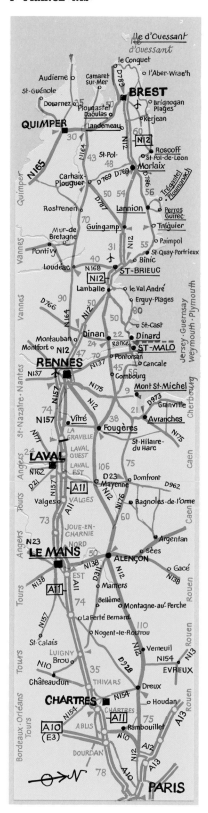

N 12. Brest – Rennes – Paris

BREST, Ile d'Ouessant, Landerneau and **Plougastel-Daoulas,** see N 165.

Morlaix (22 000) on a narrow, fjord-like bay. Old houses on the Grande Rue. 16th-cent. Church of St-Melaine with woodcarvings. Crisp, typically Breton, pancakes are a specialty of Morlaix.

NW of Morlaix is **Roscoff**. Port, seaside watering place and spa. University of Paris' marine biological station. Coast Guard control station since 1978, when the Amoco Cadiz foundered here, releasing 200 000 tons of crude oil on a 20 km stretch of the coast.

Lannion. Fishing port. Handsome houses on the Place Général-Leclerc. Church of la Trinité dates from the 12th cent. **Trégastel**, large seaside resort. **Perros-Guirec**. Little seaside resort. Red cliffs at **Ploumanach**, the "Côte de Granit Rose". **Tréguier**. Old bishop's seat. St-Tugdual Cathedral.

Guingamp. The Basilica of *Notre-Dame-de-Bon-Secours* (14th–16th cent.) is one of the most important places of pilgrimage in Brittany. **St-Brieuc** (55 000) with old houses in the Rue Fardel. Fortress- like Cathedral of St-Étienne (14th cent.). **Dinan**. Interesting old town. 14th-cent. town wall with the du Guichet gate. Handsome Place des Cordeliers. Splendid views from the castle and the Jardin Anglais.

Dinard is one of the smartest coastal resorts in Brittany. La Grande Plage is only about 500 m long and easily becomes crowded. *Musée de la Mer* with aquarium. The bit of coastline that stretches to **St-Brieuc** is known as the "Côte d'Emeraude", the "Emerald Coast".

ST-MALO (47 000). A port that has preserved its original character. During the Middle Ages it was an island fortress. Now it is a part of the mainland. The town is encircled by a 14th-cent. wall, which can be reached from steps that lead up from the town gates. A stroll along the wall can take up to an hour, but it is an exhilarating experience and the views out over the sea (particularly interesting at high and low tides) and the maze of alleys and houses are magnificent. In 1944, during the Second World War, the historic old town was almost completely destroyed, but it has been painstakingly restored. At the entrance to the town is the Place Châteaubriand, and the imposing 15th-cent. castle with four sturdy corner towers. The *town museum* is in one of its wings. Housed in the Quic-en-Groigne Tower are waxwork tableaux relating the history of St-Malo. *Aquarium*. The Malouinère de la Chipaudière (18th cent.), a mansion once owned by a ship-owner, has an interesting interior. Boat tours on the River Rance to Dinan past the "Usine marémotrice de la Rance", a unique power station that utilizes the river's enormous tidal energy.

Mont-St-Michel (110). One of the major sights of Europe. A rock island, the streets of the little town climb upward to the summit and the abbey church, founded in 966. The monastery was closed during the French Revolution and for a time the buildings served as a prison. Impressive cloisters and 28 m long Salle des Chevaliers (Knight's Hall). Abbey church with observation terrace 120 m above the sea. The tower is 87.5 m high and the statue of St- Michel (the archangel Michael) extends 155.5 m above sea level. An almost 2 km long causeway connects the island to the mainland. When the tide is out, it is possible to stroll on the sand round the island, but during high tide, the island is surrounded by water and parts of the car park may be flooded.

Avranches was an important town and a bishop's seat. The cathedral was destroyed during the French Revolution.

RENNES (200 000). Archbishop's seat, university. Chief city of the dep. of Ille-et-Vilaine. Next to the Cathedral of St-Pierre are a few handsome houses in charming old streets such as the Rue des Dames and the Rue du Chapitre. Most of old Rennes was destroyed during a week-long fire in 1720, and during the Second World War. Two surviving old buildings are the Palais de Justice (1654), once the seat of the Breton parliament, and the Palais des Musées, which houses the **Breton Museum** (archaeology, handicrafts, art) and an impressive art museum.

Fougères. Once a fortress on the border between Brittany and France. Town wall and mighty castle with 13 towers.

Vitré. Lovely half-timbered houses round the castle with its massive, circular fortification tower of St-Laurent. Its origins are in the 9th cent., but it was given its present appearance in the 15th cent. Town museum. Lovely Rue Beaudrairie. Château des Rochers, splendid manor house with memories of the letter-writer Madame de Sévigné.

From Rennes road F to Le Mans and A 11 is the fastest route to Paris.

Laval (55 000). Lovely old streets and houses, and an impressive château, now a museum.

LE MANS, see A 11.

N 20. Orléans – Limoges – Toulouse – Andorra

ORLÉANS, see A 10.

Blois and the châteaux of the Loire, see A 10.

BOURGES (80 000). The Gallic town was occupied by the Romans in 52 B.C. It became the capital of Aquitaine. University (1463) where Calvin studied. Beautiful Old Town with many splendid palaces, e.g. the Hôtel Lallemant (museum with furniture and domestic objects) and the Hôtel Cujas (1515) which houses the *Musée Berry* (archaeology and folklore). Most magnificent is the Palais Jacques-Coeur (1450). Cathedral of St- Étienne (13th cent.). Four imposing portals. Beautiful stained glass.

Châteauroux (56 000). Chief town of the dep. of Indre. Porte de la Vieille-Prison (16th cent.) in the old part of the town. *Musée Bertrand* in an 18th-cent. house. Napoleonic memorabilia and art. The old Franciscan monastery is now an art school. Lovely streets and houses in *Argenton-sur-Creuse. Gargilesse-Dampierre* with the Church of Notre Dame. 18th-cent. château. House of the writer George Sand.

LIMOGES (150 000). Chief town of the dep. of Haute-Vienne and formerly the capital of the old province of Limousin. Examples of the famous Limoges porcelain can be studied in the *Musée National Adrien-Dubouché* ceramics museum. Examples of the equally renowned Limoges enamel can be observed in the *Musée Municipal,* the city museum. Enamel studio in the Rue des Tanneries. Picturesque houses in the Rue de la Boucherie (Butchers' Street). The handsome St-Étienne and St-Martial bridges both date from the 13th cent. Work began on the *Cathedral of St-Étienne* in 1273. It was finally completed in 1876. 76 m high bell tower. Imposing railway station.

Oradour-sur-Glane. In 1944 the Germans destroyed the village and murdered all of its inhabitants. The ruins remain as a monument. Near by a new village with the same name has been erected.

Château *Pompadour* (15th cent.) was given to Antoinette Poisson (Madame de Pompadour) by her royal lover, Louis XV. He also established a stud farm which can be visited.

Uzerche. Lovely little town. Views from the Esplanade de la Lunade. Romanesque Cathedral of St-Pierre with clock tower. *Tulle* became a bishop's seat in 1317 and has many handsome 15th- and 16th-cent. houses. The 12th-cent. Cathedral of Notre-Dame was severely damaged during the French Revolution. Little museum (archaeology, weapons, ceramics).

BRIVE-la-Gaillarde (50 000). The name of the town brings to mind the courage that its inhabitants showed during the many sieges. Hôtel de Labenche (16th cent.) and other splendid palaces. Town history and medieval art in the *Musée Ernest Rupin.*

Périgueux, see N 89.

The *Vézère Valley* is pocked with many prehistoric caves which sheltered Cro-Magnon inhabitants 10 000-50 000 years ago. This long-skulled race of people more closely resembled modern man than the ape-like Neanderthals. The *Grotte de Lascaux* was discovered in 1940. It is no longer open to tourists, but films about the cave and its unique art are shown at an information centre.

Les Eyzies-de-Tayac is the centre of an area rich in prehistoric finds. *Grotte du Grand Roc.* Several caves with paintings and carvings of animals. Displays of prehistoric artifacts in the museum in the castle.

Sarlat-la-Canéda. The old part of the town is one of the most beautiful in all of France. Splendid 16th- and 17th-cent. bourgeois and nobles' houses. Among these the Hôtel de Maleville and Hôtel Plamon are notable. 16th-cent. Cathedral of St-Sacerdos with 12th-cent. tower. Lanterne des Morts (Lantern of the Dead) is a 12th-cent. burial chapel.

Souillac. Impressive Church of Ste-Marie (beginning of the 12th cent.).

Rocamadour in a gorge swarms with tourists and pilgrims during high season. A body, discovered in the 11th cent., was said to be that of the publican Zaccheus, who became St-Amadour. Pilgrims flock to the town and pray to the Black Madonna, a wooden 12th-cent. statue. Imposing 14th-cent. castle.

Padirac. A 75 m deep hole in the limestone plateau leads down to a labyrinth of stalactite and stalagmite caves and subterranean lakes. Legend has it that it is a descent into hell. Nowadays a lift makes the trip easier. 1.5 km by foot, 1 km by boat. Underground cathedral, ceiling height: 90 m.

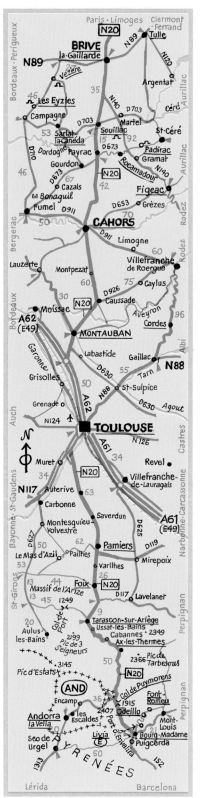

Cahors (20 000). During the Middle Ages this was an important trading centre and university town. Maison de Roaldès and other handsome houses in the lovely Old Town. Pont Valentré bridge with six arches and three defence towers. Remains of town wall and towers. *Cathedral of St-Étienne* (1090-1125) with splendid north doorway and cloisters. Memorial on the Place A. Briand to Louis Gambetta who was born here in 1838. The town hall also contains exhibits about this statesman. Truffles are found around Cahors. This delicacy, an essential ingredient in pâté de foie gras, is a subterranean fungus, usually rooted out by trained dogs or pigs. Before the First World War, 300 tons a year were found – now the annual amount yielded has dropped to about 50 tons. But attempts at truffle cultivation have been successful.

East of N 20 is *Figeac,* a charming old town. Town museum in the Hôtel de la Monnaie. Jean-François Champollion, the Orientalist who deciphered the Egyptian hieroglyphics on the Rosetta Stone, was born here in 1790.

Montauban (50 000). Musée Ingres (drawings) in the former bishop's palace. Arcaded Place Nationale. Fine view from the fortified Tarn bridge (1338).

TOULOUSE, see A 61.

Pamiers. Little town with the 17th-cent. Cathedral of St-Antonin and Church of Notre-Dame-du-Camp. Road to Le-Mas-d'Azil. The caves were Stone-Age dwellings. Rock paintings.

Foix. Beautifully situated at the foot of the Pyrenees. The three- towered château was once the residence of the Dukes of Comté. Church of St-Volusien (12th-15th cent.). Several half-timbered houses. 6 km north, the subterranean River *Labouiche* with stalactite and stalagmite caves. Boat trips.

Tarascon-sur-Ariège. Little town with handsome Gothic church and 14th-cent. tower of St-Michel. 4 km SW the *Grotte de Niaux* with prehistoric animal paintings. *Ax-les-Thermes.* Spa. More than 80 sulphur and natron springs with temperatures varying between 18° and 78° C. They were known as far back as the Roman era. During the Middle Ages, lepers were treated here. Cable car to the new winter resorts, Ax 1400 and Ax 2300.

Col de Puymorens. Rather narrow and winding road with a 10% gradient, but suitable for cars towing caravans. Its surface can be poor in a few places. Avoid night-time driving. Auto-rail Ax-les-Thermes – Latour de Carol.

Font-Romeu, 1 800 m above sea level. Elegant spa and winter sports resort. Forested area. *Hermitage.* Chapel and miracle-working Madonna. (Pilgrimages third Sunday after Whitsun, August 15 and September 8.) Fine views from Belvédère 2000.

Odeillo. Solar energy power station with enormous mirror (actually consisting of 9 000 small mirrors), against which the sunlight is reflected by 63 adjustable mirrors. The solar energy is thus concentrated on an area of 30-40 cm in diameter, where the temperature can reach up to 3 500° C. The heat is then transformed into energy. As yet, this is an extremely expensive method.

Bourg-Madame. Spanish border. Route 152 goes to Vich and Barcelona.

Livia has remained a Spanish enclave since 1659 when a confused peace treaty was signed. 6 km long road from Puigcerdá in Spain to Livia. 2 km of this road are on French soil. Medieval atmosphere. Europe's oldest pharmacy.

From Col de Puymorens another road leads to the independent republic of **ANDORRA**. Area: 462 km². Population: 33 000. Since 1278 it has been an independent republic under the protection of the Bishop of Urgel and the Counts of Foix (the Presidents of France have since assumed this right). The national language is Catalan, but Spanish and French are spoken by all the inhabitants. No taxation laws. Income is derived from Radio Andorra and the export of electrical energy. This is enough to pay for such items as ammunition for the country's cannon. Internal post is without charge. Cheap goods. Very low customs duties. The capital, **Andorra la Vella,** is filled with shops and tall buildings. The government meets in the Casa de la Vall (1400). Los Escaldes spa. Cable car to Lac d'Engolasters (1 850 m).

N 83. Strasbourg – Colmar – Mulhouse

STRASBOURG, see town plans.

N 83 is a fast-flowing, dual carriageway in the Rhine Valley with views towards the Vosges. *The Vosges,* a mountain ridge about 170 km long and 20 km wide, is almost completely covered with spruce forests. The most beautiful road is the *Routes des Crêtes* (the Mountain Ridge Road) from Ribeauville to Thann.

Molsheim. Remains of the town wall and the Schmiedtor. *Strutthof,* 5 km south of Schirmeck. Museum on the site of the former German concentration camp. Monument and cemetery. *Donon* (1 009 m), a holy mountain of the Celts. Roman temple, now a museum. Splendid view. Jupiter Column (replica) at the highest point of the pass (727 m).

Obernai. Delightful town with half-timbered houses, storks' nests, remains of town wall, splendid town hall and the beautiful Sechseimer Fountain from 1597. These, and other interesting sights, are clustered about the handsome square. *Barr, Andlau* and *Benfeld* are picturesque towns with many half-timbered houses. *Abbey of Ste-Odile* (9th cent.) high up in the mountains, is a pilgrimage place and tourist attraction. *Le Hohwald* (Champ du Feu). Climatic winter sports resort.

Sélestat. Little industrial town. During the 16th cent. the cultural centre of the Oberrhein. Beautiful old Churches of Ste-Foy and St-Georges. Picturesque narrow streets. Remains of town walls with towers.

West of Sélestat is *Haut-Kœnigsbourg,* a mighty medieval knight's castle burnt in the 17th cent. Restored in 1909. Fine views toward the Schwarzwald (Black Forest).

Ste-Marie-aux-Mines. Silver mines that have been in operation since the Middle Ages. Visitors can inspect the St-Barthélemy mine. Jousting matches and carnival first Sunday after Shrove Sunday.

Ribeauville. Small wine town dominated by three ruined castles: St-Ulrich, Hoh-Rappoltstein and Giersberg, a couple of hundred metres above the town. Charming streets and houses. The Maison des Ménetriers (Pipers' House) in the Grande Rue recalls the Count of Rappoltstein (one of those ruined castles belonged to him) who was king of all of the pipers, musicians and singers in the Oberrhein. "Pipers' Day", first Sunday in September when wine flows out of the fountain in the square.

Beautiful roads west to *St-Dié* where there is a splendid cathedral, and *Épinal,* a lovely old town, with particularly delightful streets and houses near the Place des Vosges. Interesting *old printing shop* that once created picture books. *Gérardmer* lies in a district of lakes. *Hohneck,* at 1 362 m, is one of the highest points in the Vosges. Winter sports.

Riquewihr. Perhaps the most beautiful of the wine towns, popular with tourists. The symbol of the town is the *Dolder Tower* (1291). Town gate and folklore museum. The medieval town wall and tower are well preserved.

Kaysersberg with delightful old buildings. 16th-cent. town hall. Museum in the house where Albert Schweitzer (1875-1965) was born. Castle from 1632. Church of Ste-Croix (1518) with a magnificent High Altar where Hans of Colmar depicted the suffering and death of Jesus Christ. *Turckheim* has half-timbered buildings. Place Turenne with fountain in the square. 14th-cent. town wall with three gates.

COLMAR (65 000). Chief town of the dep. of Haut-Rhin. Textile industry, market gardens. Rhine port. Splendid city with handsome buildings, e.g. the Maison des Têtes (1690) and the Maison Pfister (1537), at the corner of Rue Mercière and Rue des Marchands. The Schwendi Fountain in the Place du Marché aux Fruits (Fruit Market Square) near the Ancienne Douane (Old Customs House) is in memory of Col. Schwendi, a 16th-cent. warrior who fought the Turks. He introduced Tokay grapevines to Alsace. Near by is the *Quartier des Tanneurs* (Tanners' Quarter) where half-timbered houses have been restored and are now artisans' workshops. Rebmännlein Fountain near the market hall. Idyllic bridges over the River Lauch to the picturesque *Quartier de la Krutenau* (Vegetable Quarter) and *Petite Venise* (Little Venice) where charming houses line the canals.
Musée d'Unterlinden is housed in a 13th-cent. monastery with lovely red sandstone cloisters. Furniture, faience, examples of the goldsmith's art, etc. *The Isenheim Altarpiece* by Matthias Grünewald is an enormous work of art with glowing colours. The Church of St-Martin (13th– 14th cent.) has exquisite stained-glass windows and the famous "Virgin and the Rosebush" (Viêrge au buisson de roses) by Martin Schongauer. The house where he lived has been preserved. The former house of the sculptor Bartholdi (1834-1904) now contains a museum.

Besançon, see A 36. *Mulhouse, Ballon d'Alsace* and *Thann,* see A 36.

N 422 and A 35 lead to Basel, Switzerland.

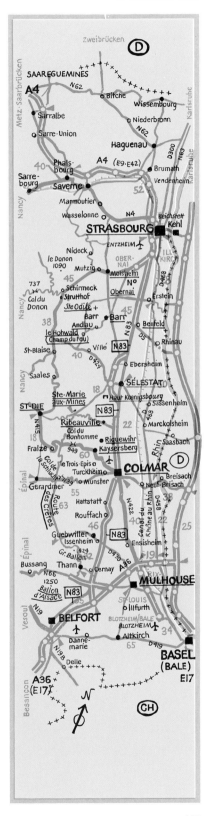

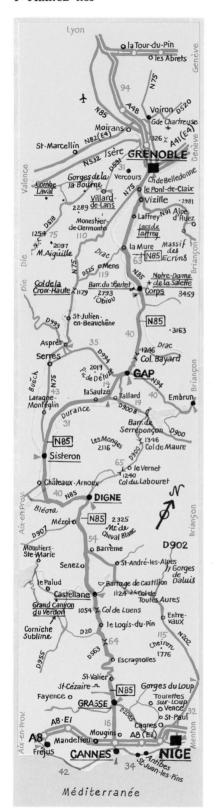

N 85. Grenoble – Cannes. *Route Napoleon*

GRENOBLE, see A 41.

The Route Napoléon follows the way that Napoleon took in March 1815 after he had stepped ashore at the Golfe St-Juan on his way from exile on Elba to Paris, at the start of the "Hundred Days". The milestones are topped with Imperial eagles. Six small shelters, "réfuges Napoléon", were built, at the highest elevations of the passes. Three remain, at Col de Vars, Col d'Izoard and Col de Lanse. The road goes through the old province of Dauphiné, between the Rhône and the Italian frontier. From 1349 this was the dependency of the Dauphin, as the French crown prince was known.

Le Pont-de-Claix. Delightful 17th-cent. bridge. *Vizille.* Little town with 17th-cent. château. Beautiful park. Monument du Centenaire commemorates a meeting held on July 21, 1788 when the townspeople refused to pay taxes. That event is said to have marked the beginning of the French Revolution.

Lacs de Laffrey. Five lakes on a high plateau. Monument on the *Prairie de la Rencontre* dedicated to the dramatic happenings when Napoleon met troops sent out to stop him. They joined his forces after he had walked towards them with chest bared defying them to shoot.

Corps. Little town. Starting point for the road to the *Sautet dam,* one of the world's highest, and the *Notre-Dame-de-la-Salette pilgrimage church,* at 1770 m above sea level, in a stupendous Alpine setting. 100 000 pilgrims come here annually. In 1851 two children saw the apparition of a weeping Virgin Mary.

Gap (30 000). Chief town of the dep. of Hautes-Alpes. Musée Départemental. Château de Charance with lovely park. Huge Serre-Ponçon hydroelectric power station.

Sisteron. Little town, beautifully situated in a gorge. Fine views from the citadel. 11th-cent. cathedral. Old houses in the La Baume quarter. *Digne.* Chief town of the dep. of Alpes-de-Haute-Provence. Notre-Dame-du-Bourg Church with 14th-cent. frescoes.

Between Grenoble and Sisteron it is possible to choose the route that goes via *Col-de-la-Croix-Haute,* travelling along the border between two climatic zones, showing pronounced differences between Alpine and Mediterranean vegetations.

Castellane. Beautiful town dominated by a 184 m high limestone rock crowned with the Notre-Dame-du-Roc Chapel.

Gorges du Verdon are the European equivalent of the Grand Canyon. Magnificent cliffs rise 700 m above the river that is marked by turbulent whirlpools. The area is about 30 km long and the valley is 200-1 500 wide. Views from the Balcon de la Mescia, the Corniche Point Sublime and the Belvédère de la Maline. The lovely little town of *Moustiers Ste-Marie* is famous for its ceramics.

Grasse (35 000). Its protected position and mild climate have enticed many, including the Rothschilds, to settle here. Grasse is the centre of the perfume industry. 12 tons of roses are required for just one litre of essence. Some of the scent factories welcome visitors. Beautiful views from the Cours Honoré-Cresp, site of the casino. Old quarter with the former Cathedral of Notre-Dame and bishop's palace. *Musée d'Art et d'Histoire de Provence* (town history, furniture, ceramics). *Musée Fragonard.*

Tourettes-sur-Loup. Picturesque village with many craftsmen. For the major tourist attractions near Nice, see A 8.

CANNES (70 000). One of the most elegant resorts on the Riviera. The Boulevard de la Croisette follows the sandy beach. Palms, flowers, large hotels and restaurants. Three casinos. The harbour is filled with small boats, luxury yachts and cruise ships. Old quarter in the western part of the town. Church of Notre-Dame-d'Espérance and Tour du Mt-Chevalier, a 22 m high tower, 67 m above sea level. It was built in the 12th cent. as a defensive watchtower against pirates. Musée Castre, next to the tower (antiquities). Superb views from the Observatoire-de-Super-Cannes. On the island of St. Honorat, 2 km off the coast, are a château and an abbey, founded in the 5th cent.

N 88. Lyon – Le Puy – Toulouse.

LYON, see town plans.

ST-ÉTIENNE (230 000). Industrial town. Palais des Arts with modern paintings, weapons and art. Beautiful view from Guizay, 10 km W.

LE PUY (30 000). Chief town of the dep. of Haute-Loire. This remarkable town is dominated by the peaks and cones of extinct volcanoes. On top of the 755 m high *Rocher Corneille* is a 16 m high statue of Notre-Dame-de-France, made from cannon captured during the Battle of Sevastopol. At the edge of the *Rocher St-Michel* is the St-Michel d'Aiguilhe Chapel (10th-11th cent.) with wall paintings from the same period. Cathedral of Notre- Dame (12th cent.). Façade of dark and light stone, six domes and a belfry. The Black Madonna that St. Louis brought back from Egypt after his Crusade in the 13th cent. on the High Altar has been an object of pilgrimage for centuries. Le Puy was also a stop for pilgrims on their way to Santiago de Compostela in Spain. The Theodolph Bible dating from 795 is on display in the sacristy. *Museum of ecclesiastical art. Musée Crozatier* has exhibits of folklore, local history and examples of the famous Le Puy lacemaking which started in the Middle Ages. Lovely buildings in the old quarter. 40 km to the north is the splendid *la Chaise Dieu abbey church.* 16th-cent. tapestries from Brussels and Arras. Painting of the "Danse Macabre" in the chancel. 5 km south of Le Puy is the *Lac du Bouchet* crater lake.

St-Flour on a 100 m high basalt cliff. Many interesting statues in the Cathedral of St-Pierre-et-St-Flour (15th cent.). The bishop's palace contains museums displaying ecclesiastical art, furniture, weavings.

Mende (11 000) lies 731 m above sea level. The Notre-Dame Bridge over the Lot was built in the 14th cent. The Cathedral of St-Pierre has two bell towers. Under the organ is the 2.15 m long clapper for a church bell said to have weighed 25 tons and to have been the largest in Christendom. It was destroyed during the War of Religion in the 16th cent.

Gorges du Tarn, south of Merde, a mighty 80 km long canyon formed a million years ago. The River *Tarn* has forced its way through the limestone plateau of "Les Causses". Some of the cliffs reach a height of 500 m. The Gorges du Tarn continue into the *Gorges de la Jonte.*

Ste-Enimie. Little town with old buildings that line steep, narrow streets.

Aven Armand. Caves with 30 m high stalagmites. A 200 m long tunnel leads to a 100 m long and 40 m high cave. *La Malène.* Flat bottom boats to the "Détroits" (the Straits), where the cliffs on either side of the river seem to meet. *Cirque des Baumes* is one of the most impressive places. Point Sublime, 400 m above the river. Marvellous sunsets. Occasional concerts of classical music. The audience sit in boats, listen, and gaze at the illuminated cliffs on both sides of the river.

Grotte de Dargilan. 1 600 m deep cave with impressive stalactites.

Millau (24 000), famed for its glovemaking. 18 km to the rocky maze of Montpellier-le-Vieux where the rock formations resemble a city in ruins. *Roquefort,* world-famous for its cheese which is aged in caves. In Combalou Mountain there are Stone-Age caves.

To the west is *Gorges du Lot,* a rocky landscape that can be compared with the Gorges du Tarn. The walls of the cliffs are as high as 300 m. The River Lot is a favourite of canoeists. The Viaduc de Garabit is a massive railway bridge, designed by Eiffel. Espalion, Estaing and Entragues-sur- Truyère are lovely little towns with old bridges over the Lot (13th-15th cent.). Entragues is a particularly beautiful town.

Conques, a little town with venerable buildings, one of France's project cities during the European Architectural Heritage Year 1975. Medieval streets, three town gates. This was a stop on the pilgrimage route to Santiago de Compostela in Spain. 15th-cent. Château d'Humière. *Ste-Foy Church,* mainly from the 12th cent., is famous for its sculpted West Front and its rich ecclesiastical treasures.

Rodez (30 000). Chief town of the dep. of Aveyron. The Cathedral of Notre-Dame, with its fortress-like façade is in the old quarter. *Musée Fenaille* with menhirs (prehistoric stone monuments).

ALBI (50 000). Massive Cathedral of Ste-Cécile, one of the most beautiful Gothic structures in France. Construction began in 1282. It was consecrated in 1480. Built of red brick, it is 100 m long, 20 m wide, 30 m high and enclosed by a 40 m high wall. Palais de la Berbie (13th-14th cent.) housing the *Musée Toulouse-Lautrec.* Paintings, drawings and lithographs by the town's most famous son (1864-1901) and his contemporaries. Splendid views from the Pont du 22 août and the Pont Vieux.

Cordes. Walled town. Beautiful 14th-cent. houses. Covered market from 1352.

Gaillac. Wine centre. Wine cellars with wine tasting.

TOULOUSE, see A 61.

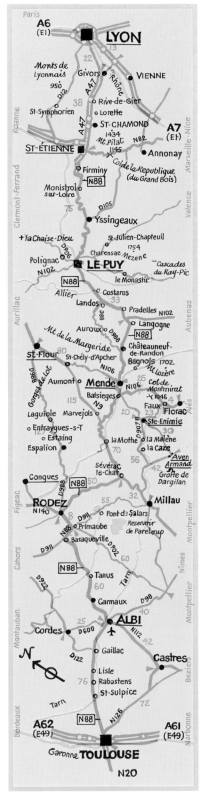

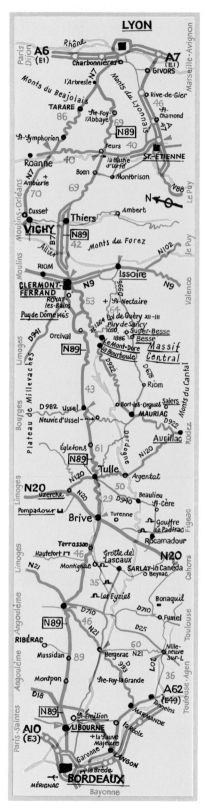

N 89. Lyon – Bordeaux

LYON, see town plans. **St-Etienne**, see N 88

Thiers (20 000). Beautifully situated. Lovely view from the ramparts. Handsome half-timbered houses in the old quarter. Church of St- Genès with remains of 11th-cent. mosaics.

Vichy (35 000). Famous spa. Even the early Romans were familiar with its hot springs (16°-43° C). Now Vichy is a large resort with over 300 hotels. Lovely Parc des Sources. *Pump room*. After paying a nominal admission fee one can taste the "Vichy Waters" that come from different springs: Chomel, Grande Grille, Célestins and Lucas. The salt content varies, up to 4%. Old quarter. 15th-cent. clock tower. *Maison du Bailliage* (16th cent.) with folklore museum. After the Germans had occupied northern France in June 1940, Vichy became the seat of the government of Marshal Pétain. It remained as such until August, 1944.

CLERMONT-FERRAND (160 000). Capital of the old province of Auvergne and chief town of the dep. of Puy-de-Dôme. University. Major industries including Michelin rubber tyre factories. Old quarter with handsome streets, e.g. the Rue des Gras. The Gothic *Cathedral of Notre Dame* was built during the 13th and 14th cent. of black lava rock. Exquisite stained-glass windows. Romanesque Basilica of *Notre-Dame-du-Port* (13th cent.). *Musée du Ranquet* with displays of medieval art and local history. Special exhibition concerning the mathematician and philosopher Blaise Pascal (1623-1662) who was born here. Thermal baths in the suburb of **Royat-les-Bains**. Circuit Automobile d'Auvergne motor racing circuit.

Puy-de-Dôme, 1 465 m above sea level, is the highest peak in the Mont Dômes region. The surrounding summits are about 1 000 m high. Volcanic cone with magnificent view. Observatory and the remains of a Roman Temple of Mercury. Toll road (12% gradient) leads to a car park at 1 465 m. Footpath. Puy means volcanic cone. There are over sixty in the district.

South of Clermont-Ferrand is **Issoire** with the Church of St- Austremoine. The magnificent Romanesque church in St-Nectaire was built in the 12th cent. Its impressive treasury contains enamels from Limoges. **Besse**, in the Massif Central. Lovely little town with half-timbered houses and old market hall. Remains of the town wall and the du Meze town gate. Church of St-André. The town is situated 1 050 m above sea level. **Super-Besse** at 1 350 m. Winter sports. Cable car and ski-lifts. **Riom**. Many lovely houses, including the Hôtel Guimoneau with fine staircase. The Church of Notre-Dame-du-Marthuret contains the famous *"Virgin of the Bird"*. The Palais de Justice has beautiful stained-glass windows in the Ste-Chapelle.

Le Mont-Doré is the major resort in Auvergne, an area that as yet has not been over-exploited by tourism. Spa. Casino. Cable car to *Puy de Sancy*, 1 886 m, the highest summit in the Massif Central. **La Bourboule**. Large spa with hot springs. Casino. Beautiful Parc Fenêstre. **Ussel**. Lovely little old town. Resort. A bit to the south *Monts du Cantal* with the 1 858 m high *Plomb du Cantal*. The chief town of this area is **Aurillac**, a lovely old town. Houses with carved doors. *Folklore museum* in the Hôtel des Delzons. Church of Notre-Dame-des-Neiges with a Black Madonna. **Salers** (950 m), picturesque old walled town.

Tulle (22 000). Chief town of the dep. of Corrèze. Important town since the Middle Ages, often ravaged by war. As late as 1944 it was the scene of violence. Beautiful old quarter round the 12th-cent. *Cathedral of Notre-Dame*. The belfry was damaged by lightning in 1645, and fire during the French Revolution. Treasury with famous copper, enamel and a silver casket. Museum in the cloister (antiquities, medieval sculpture and faience).

Uzerche, Brive, Pompadour and the caves of *Périgord*, see N 20.

Périgueux (40 000). Chief town of the dep. of Dordogne. Important town during the Gallic and Romans eras. The Tour de Vésone was once part of a Roman temple. Remains of an arena for 20 000 spectators. The Tour Mataguerre remains of the 15th-cent. town wall. *St-Front Cathedral* (12th cent.) was restored in the 19th cent. With its five Romanesque domes to which 17 small towers have been added (by the architect Abadie) it resembles a mosque.

Libourne (25 000). Industrial town. Arcaded Place Surchamp. 14th- cent. town hall. The bell tower at Isle remains of the town fortifications. **St-Émilion**. Beautiful old town with venerable streets and squares. Fine view from the Château du Roi (13th cent.). The church (11th-12th cent.) has been hewn out of the cliffs.

BORDEAUX, see A 10.

N117. Biarritz – Pau – Toulouse
D117. St-Gaudens – Perpignan

Biarritz, Bayonne and *St-Jean-de-Luz,* see N 10.

Cambo-les-Bains. Spa. The Cas-Cambo quarter has a typically Basque appearance. The dramatist Edmond Rostand, creator of Cyrano de Bergerac, lived here. His house is now a museum.

Peyrehorade is dominated by the ruins of Aspremont Castle. At Lacq ▮rè huge reserves of natural gas. L'Hôpital St-Blaise. Church in the Mudéjar style, a combination of Moorish and Spanish styles.

Orthez. Splendid old buildings. The Hôtel de la Lune was used by the Counts of Foix as a guest house. Pont Vieux, a 13th-cent. bridge with fortified tower.

PAU (60 000). Chief town in the dep. of Pyrénées-Atlantiques and capital of the old province of Béarn. Spa and resort. The Counts of Béarn resided in the château (built during the 12th–15th cent.) and Henri IV was born here in 1553. The *Boulevard des Pyrénées,* built by order of Napoleon, leads from the château. Splendid views. Beautiful tapestries and a museum (local history). Casino and climatic research institute in the Parc Beaumont. The *Musée des Beaux-Arts* is a splendid art museum. The Musée Bernadotte, 5 Rue Bernadotte, is dedicated to Jean-Baptiste Bernadotte, son of a Pau lawyer and founder of the present Swedish royal dynasty.

Road to *Oleron-Ste-Marie.* Little town that preserves its medieval character. Cathedral (14th cent.) with famous portal and church treasure. Road 134 goes on to Col du Somport, 1 632 m. 10% gradient. Rather easy driving but several narrow sections close to the Spanish border.

TARBES (65 000). Chief town of the dep. of Hautes-Pyrénées. Jardin Massey, a lovely garden with observation tower. Domed Basilica of Notre-Dame-de-la- Sède (13th cent.). Road to Lourdes.

Lourdes (18 000). One of the largest Roman Catholic pilgrimage places, filled with reminders of the shepherdess Bernadette Soubirous, who had a vision of the Virgin in the *Massabielle Grotto* in 1858. The grotto is 12 m wide and 10 m deep. Marble statue of the Virgin as Bernadette described her. This is also the site of the spring, said to have miraculous waters. The Roman Catholic church recognizes fifty miracles that have taken place here. Every day at 4.30 a procession begins here. It ends at the Place du Rosaire on the Esplanade des Processions. Every evening between April and October a torchlight procession follows the same route. The week after August 15 is the peak celebration period. Large churches at the grotto and at the Place du Rosaire. The underground *Basilica of Pope Pius X,* built in 1958, can accommodate a congregation of 20 000, seated round the altar in the centre of the church.
The town is dominated by the *Château* (13th–17th cent.) on a 80 m high promontory. *Musée Pyrénéen.* Fine view. The house where Bernadette was born is at the base of the rock. *Musée de Notre-Dame-de-Lourdes* displays testaments to the miracles. *Musée Bernadette* relates the life of the saint.

Road continues to *Cauterets* (930 m). Spa and winter sports. Casino. Cable car lines. *Pont d'Espagne* with waterfall. *Grottes de Bétharram* with subterranean river and large caverns.

Road N 21 continues to *Gavarnie* (1 357 m). One hour on foot to the *Cirque de Gavarnie,* a rocky ravine. The *Grande Cascade* is 422 m high – making it the highest waterfall in Europe.

Bagnères-de-Bigorre (D 935 from Tarbes) (550 m). Resort and spa, known as early as the Roman era. 36 springs containing sulphur and calcium. Beautiful old quarter. *Musée Salies,* art and folklore museum. *Grotte de Médous,* lovely stalactite and stalagmite cave with subterranean river.

La Mongie (1 800 m). Large winter sports resort at *Col du Tourmalet,* 2 115 m.

D 929 goes from *Arreau* to Spain via the *Bielsa Tunnel,* 3 080 m long. The road over the pass reaches altitudes of up to 2 465 m.

St-Bertrand-de-Comminges now has 300 inhabitants but is believed to have had 60 000 during the Roman era. Remains of Roman temples, baths, etc. The Church of Notre-Dame (14th cent.) has beautiful woodcarvings. Antique statues in the former Benedictine abbey.

Bagnères-de-Luchon. Large spa, known to the Romans, visited by Cardinal Richelieu. Casino. Winter sports in Superbagnères at an altitude of 2 000 m. *St-Gaudens* has lovely views from the Boulevard Jean-Bepmale.

Foix, Pamiers and *Andorra,* see N 20.

Prades. Little town famed for its music festival and the cellist Pablo Casals. Gothic church of St-Pierre. Serrabone and St-Michel-de-Cuxa abbeys in Molitg-les-Bains, a spa.

PERPIGNAN, see A 9.

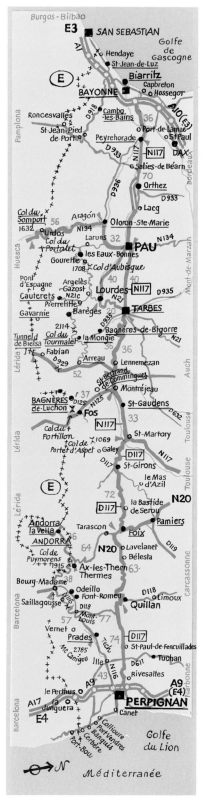

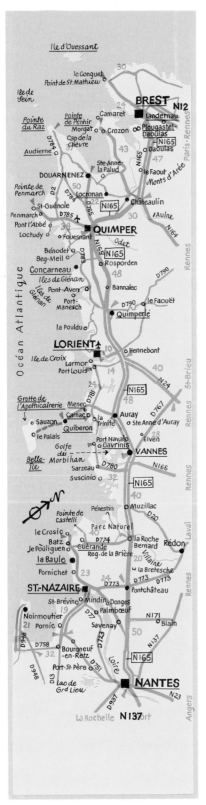

N165. Brest – Nantes

BREST (170 000). Second largest naval base in France. (Toulon is larger.) Major port. Visitors may inspect the arsenal. Two high bridges lead to the city. Views from the Cour Dajot. Harbour tours by boat. See also Roscoff, N 12.

Ile d'Ouessant, 7 km long and 4 km wide, lies in the Atlantic, west of the mainland. High cliffs and interesting bird life. Ruins of an 11th-cent. abbey on the Pointe de St-Mathieu. **Le Conquet.** Little town, lobster fishing port. Splendid views from the Trénanzan castle ruins.

Landerneau. Medieval bridge over the Elorn. Calvaire (chapel for Lenten divine services) from 1585 in Guimiliau.

Plougastel-Daoulas. Calvaire (1602), several Lenten chapels on a hill. **Crozon** has dramatic sea and cliff scenery. **Locronan.** Typical Breton town. Square with handsome Renaissance buildings and the Church of St-Renan. de Pénity Chapel (16th cent.) with grave of St. Renan. Canning industry. fj4Pointe de Penhir, 70 m high cliff.

Pointe du Raz. Westernmost point of France where even on the calmest days, breakers thunder against the 70 m high, grotesquely formed cliffs.

Audierne. Little fishing port. Large catches of spiny lobsters and sardines.

Quimper (60 000). Chief town of the dep. of Finistère, "the End of the World". Famous for its lace and faience. Typical Breton town. Handsome buildings in the Rue Keréon. *Musée breton* in the bishop's palace. *Musée des Beaux-Arts* with Flemish, Dutch and French art. The *St-Corentin Cathedral* was built during two periods, 13th–14th cent., and 19th cent. Splendid portals and stained glass. Two towers, 76 m high. Lovely churches on the Penmarch peninsula. 63 m high lighthouse (1897). In the little town of Pont l'Abbé fo¹k costumes are often worn and are traditional Sunday dress.

Concarneau. Little town with large fishing port (tuna) and canning industry. Boites à sardines (sardine tin) museum. Fine sandy beaches. Ville close (the closed town) on an island in the harbour. Old city fortress. Granite walls and towers (14th cent.) and narrow alleys. Lovely view from the Pont du Moros. Fête des Filets Bleus on the third Sunday of August. Boat to the *Glénau Islands.*

Quimperlé. Little town with beautiful old buildings in the Rue Brémond-d'Ars and near the Dom-Morice. Church of St-Croix (11th cent.) with rotunda. Church of St-Michel (15th cent.) in the upper town.

LORIENT (65 000). Naval base and fishing port. Keroman U-boat base, built by the Germans during the war, near the modern fishing port.

Carnac. Heath landscape with megaliths, here called "menhirs". Fine view from **Menec** (a few km NW) out over an area with more than 1000 menhirs. Also at Menec, "dolmen" tombs, probably erected by sun worshippers 5 000-6 000 years ago. Museum of archaeological finds.

Quiberon at the tip of a narrow peninsula. Spa, seaside resort, sardine fishing. Passenger ship service to *Belle-Ile* (1 hour), 17 km long and 5-10 km wide, Brittany's largest offshore island. Sandy beaches south of little Le Palais, chief town of the island. To the NW, the "Côte Sauvage", with the *"l'Apothicairerie"* (the Apothecary's Grotto), where birds nests on the rock ledges resemble the wares on a chemist's shelves.

VANNES (45 000). Lovely old quarter near the harbour. Remains of the town wall with the Tour du Connétable (14th cent.). Archaeological museum in the Château Gaillard (15th cent.). The town is situated on the *Golfe du Morbihan*, one of the loveliest areas in Brittany. *At Gavrinis* is a round tumulus, 18 m high and 100 m in diameter, containing a Neolithic burial chamber. Its walls were decorated 4 000 years ago.

Guérande has retained its medieval atmosphere. The town wall with ten towers has only four gates. **La Baule.** Large seaside resort. **St-Nazaire** (70 000). The World War II U-boat base here was the object of the first large-scale Allied attack on German – occupied Europe. Shipyards. Menhir and dolmen near the Place Marceau.

La Jonelière with motor car museum. The bridge over the Loire from St-Nazaire to St-Brévin is 2 636 m long, 61 m above the river's water.

NANTES, see A 11.

N137. Nantes – Bordeaux

NANTES, see A 11.

Pornic on the coast. 17th-cent. covered market. 14th-cent. château. Druidic stones. *Ile de Noirmoutier,* a 19 km long peninsula reached during low tide by the "Passage du Gois" road. At high tide, the road is covered by 4 m of water. It is best to check when the road is open, and to make certain that your car is not subject to breakdowns. Fine swimming and lovely walks. Château with sturdy walls. The Church of St-Philibert, originally an abbey church, has an 11th-cent. crypt.

Les Sables d'Olonne. Extremely fine sandy beach more than 2 km long. Large fishing port. Marine zoo with aquarium.

Fontenay-le-Comte with the Church of Notre-Dame and handsome château. *Niort* (50 000). Lovely old town. Venerable buildings in the Rue St-Jean. Château with two towers (12th–13th cent.), now an ethnographical museum.

Luçon. Magnificent bishop's palace, once residence of Richelieu and Colbert. Notre-Dame Cathedral dates from 1317.

LA ROCHELLE (80 000). Chief town of the dep. of Charente-Maritime. The old harbour fortifications and arcaded houses bring to mind the wars of Religion during the 16th and 17th cent. when the town was a Protestant (Huguenot) stronghold. The old harbour has two towers. To the east, the Tour St-Nicolas (1384), to the west, the Tour de la Chaîne, the Chain Tower. The chain still exists, see below. The Tour de la Lanterne was once a lighthouse. The Porte de la Grosse Horloge (13th cent. altered 1594) leads into the town which has several splendid Renaissance buildings. One of these, the town hall (1606), is enclosed by fortifications, 100 years older than the building. St-Louis Cathedral (1762). *Musée d'Orbigny,* local history, ceramics, Far Eastern art. In the courtyard is the chain which once connected the Tour St-Louis and Tour de la Chaîne. It used to be stretched across the harbour to close it to shipping. Art museum. The town's new port of *La Pallice* was completed in 1890. 15 minute car ferry trip to the island of *Ré* (25 km long, 5-7 km wide), where wine and salt are produced. Oyster beds. *St-Martin-de-Ré,* a lovely little port with narrow streets and walls designed by Vauban.

Rochefort (35 000). Harbour, built by order of Colbert in 1666. Town museum. Maritime museum.

Ile d'Oleron. France's second largest offshore island (Corsica is larger.). 3 km long bridge from the mainland. Oyster beds.

Saintes (30 000). Once a great Roman city. Arena with places for 20 000 spectators. Triumphal arch of Germanicus. Archaeological museum. Lovely old quarter with 17th- and 18th- cent. houses. Church of St-Eutrope (1096) has a 15th-cent. bell tower and a large crypt. Pilgrimage church partially demolished during the French Revolution. *Ste-Marie-aux-Dames Church,* founded in 1047 and restored in 1937. Beautiful portal. The town's most famous son was Dr. Guillotin. His invention for beheading people was in use from the time of the French Revolution until 1977. Capital punishment was abolished in France in 1981.

Royan. Large resort. Modern town. Almost all of the old town was destroyed in 1945 – only a little of it remains in the Pontaillac quarter. Notre-Dame Church built 1955-1958.

BORDEAUX and *Medóc.* see A 10.

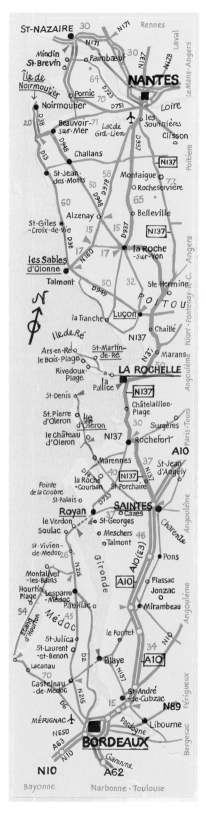

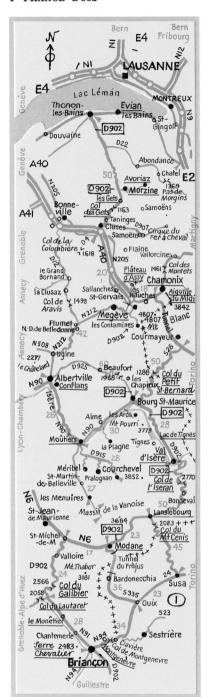

D 902. Route des Grandes Alpes

565 km from Lake Geneva to the Mediterranean. A fantastic road through unbelievable scenery. Driving the entire length of this road can be exhausting and can give a surfeit of impressions. Some of the passes should be avoided if you are not a trained Alpine driver, but there are many alternative roads. Some of the passes are obstructed by snow Oct.–May or June.

Thonon-les-Bains (30 000). Spa. Lovely views over Lake Geneva from Belvédères. Ripaille Château, residence of Amadeus VIII, Duke of Savoy. In 1439 he became Pope Felix V but did not have the strength to continue for more than ten years. After that he retired to the worldly pleasures of Thonon.

East of Thonon lies **Evian-les-Bains,** a resort on the shores of Lake Geneva. Famous mineral water.

Col des Gets with large resorts. **Les Gets** and **Morzine-Avoriaz** (24 000 beds). Interesting architecture in Avoriaz. Car park in Morzine and then by cable car to Lac de Montriond (1 049 m).

Sallanches. Little town, large resort. View towards Mont Blanc. Chapelle de Medonnet. *Plan-du-Lac.* Lovely little lake enclosed in a horseshoe of chalk cliffs (Cirque-du-Fer-à-Cheval), 1 100 m above sea level. **Plateau d'Assy** with **Notre-Dame-de-Toute-Grace** mountain church. Designed by Novarina and completed in 1945, it has been decorated by Matisse, Braque, Léger, Bonnard, Chagall and many more.

Chamonix (9 000), 1 035 m above sea level. Famous winter sports resort in the long valley. 25 000 hotel beds. Many rack railways and cable cars. One of them goes to Montenvers (1 913 m), a 20 minute ride. Views out over the **Mer de Glace,** a 7 km long and 1-2 km wide glacier. Cable car down to one of its caves where each year a "sitting room" is carved out of the ice.

The most fantastic cable car line goes to **Aiguille du Midi,** 3 842 m, with views of Mont Blanc. The route has roomy cars and the 5 km long trip takes 20 minutes. It is possible to continue on another line to Rifugio Torino (3 322 m). Italian passport inspection at Pointe Helbronner. Then the cable car line down to Entrèves/Courmayeur. The entire journey is 15 km long and takes 1 1/2 hours.

Mont Blanc/Monte Bianco, 4 810 m – the highest mountain in Europe. First climbed in 1786. The 11.6 km long Mont Blanc tunnel was opened in 1965. Overtaking and stopping are forbidden. Recommended speed: 60 kmh. Vehicles should be at least 100 m apart. TV cameras observe the traffic. **Entrèves** and **Courmayeur,** see Italy, A 5.

From Sallanches N 212 leads to **Megève,** one of the largest winter sports resorts with a permanent population of 5 000, and accommodation for 22 000 tourists. **St-Gervais-les-Bains.** Spa and winter sports resort.

Albertville with **Conflans,** a completely preserved medieval fortified village, high above the valley. Tour Ramus (15th cent.). Maison Rouge (14th cent.) with folklore museum (furniture, woodcarvings, etc.)

Road to **Moûtiers.** Splendid cathedral. Onward to the major winter sports resorts of **Méribel, Courchevel, Pralognan** and **Les Menuires** at altitudes of 1 600-2 900 m. Together these towns are known as **Les Trois Vallées,** a winter sports area with 40 000 beds and hundreds of ski-lifts. Cable car to **Sommet de Saulire.** Concrete underground supermarkets, skyscrapers, luxury hotels, discotheques – all in all a highly effective machine for holiday living.

Aime, one of the oldest towns in Savoy. The Romanesque Basilica of St-Martin has 13th-cent. frescoes and a 5th-cent. crypt. Old town. Resort.

Col du Petit St-Bernard. Relatively easy pass, suitable for small caravans. 5% gradient up to the pass height (2 188 m), then 8% gradient descent.

From **Bourg St-Maurice** an 8% gradient up to Col de l'Iseran. Good road but not quite suitable for caravans. A few dark tunnels.

Lac de Tignes, where the waters of the mighty artificial lake have inundated the old village. Tignes and Val d'Isère (connected by a cable car line) are two winter sports resorts with over 20 000 hotel beds and almost 100 ski-lifts. Views from Rocher de Bellevarde and Tête du Solaise.

Col de l'Iseran, 2 769 m. The second highest pass in the Alps. 8% gradient from Bourg St-Maurice, 11% from Lanslebourg. Magnificent views of Mt-Blanc and Gran Paradiso.

Lanslevillard (1 479 m). Winter sports. Frescoes in the 15th- cent. Chapel of St-Sébastien. **Lanslebourg-Mont-Cenis.** Winter sports. Important road junction. Napoleon had the road built 1803-1810. The chapels and crosses along the road bring to mind the pilgrimage route to Rome. 10% gradient up to Col du Mt-Cenis, 2 084 m. 12% gradient descending into Italy and Turin. Well constructed, rather easy road. Heavy traffic now travels the tunnelled route from Modane. Mt-Cenis was once one of the major Alpine pass routes. A railway tunnel was completed in 1872, before the openings of the Gotthard and Simplon tunnels.

Modane. Road to the 12.8 km long Fréjus tunnel (open 1980). The western entrance is at an altitude of 1 228 m, the eastern entrance at 1 297 m.

From **Valloire,** the road rises with a 12% gradient up to one of the most impressive Alpine passes, the **Col du Galibier.** The road is not for the faint-hearted: unprotected precipices on either side. Cyclists in the Tour de France rally must follow this route. Memorial plaque to H. Desgranges who founded the race.

Then 7% gradient down to the fields at **Lautaret** which, from June until August, are filled with flowers. Alpine botanical garden, owned by the University of Grenoble. Monument to the polar explorer Scott, who tested motorized sledges here in 1908, before his doomed expedition to the South Pole. (His rival, the Norwegian Amundsen, put his faith in sledges drawn by Arctic dogs, and was the first to reach the Pole.)

Serre-Chevalier, Le Monnetière and Montgenèvre. Winter sports resorts.

Briançon (10 500, 1 320 m above sea level), one of the loftiest towns in Europe. The old fortified town enclosed by double walls rises above the modern sections. The fortress, built in the 17th cent., was designed by Vauban. In 1815, it withstood an Austrian siege. In 1940 an Italian fort opened fire on Briançon, but the old French fort returned the fire and subdued the Italians on the other side of the frontier. This at a ripe old age when most forts have become museums. Emile Bourdelle's statue "La France". 55 m long Pont d'Asfeld over the Durance. To the west are the Alpine meadows of the Vallouise Valley. Allefroide, a resort 1 500 m above sea level, and the *Pelvoux National Park,* a part of the Des Ecrins National Park.

Col d'Izoard. Rather narrow, winding road. 10% gradient on the northern slope, 12% gradient on the southern slope. Beautiful views. Perceptible change in climate. **Château Queyras,** high on a mighty cliff. In 218 B.C. Hannibal with his army of 100 000 men and 37 elephants passed this way. They came from Cartagena in Spain. It took 15 days to cross the Alps, and the entire march took five months. 36 000 men were lost. During the Punic Wars the Carthaginians defeated the Romans at Cannae but never conquered Rome. Carthage was sacked by Scipio Aemilianus in 146 B.C.

Guillestre (1 000 m above sea level). Resort. Rocky landscape at Casse Déserte. Col de Vars, 2 111 m. 10% gradient. Rather easy road, suitable for smaller caravans.

From here three alternative routes: Col d'Allos, Col de la Cayolle and Col de la Bonette (Restefond).

Col d'Allos, 2 240 m. Narrow, winding road. 10% gradient. On through the Gorges du Verdon, a deep gorge lined with 600 m high cliff walls. Castellane, see below. Col de la Bonette, see below.

Col de la Cayolle, 2 327 m. Extremely narrow and twisting road on the north slope, but a beautiful Alpine meadow. 10% gradient. At the summit of the pass you can feel the warm Mediterranean wind.

Valberg, 1 669 m. Large resort. The road goes through the Gorges de Daluis, a six km gorge between 400 m high red, and occasionally green-flecked slate walls.

Annot. Resort. 17th-cent. church. Little Veireville Chapel stands between two enormous blocks of stone.

Entrevaux, 515 m above sea level. The road adjoins the little fortified town with town gate. The cathedral and moated castle were designed by Vauban.

Puget-Théniers. Little town with ruined castle. Portrait of the Madonna from 1525 in the Romanesque church.

Gorges du Cians is an impressive rocky landscape. Road from **Col de la Bonette** (Restefond) 2 802 m. This is the highest pass road in Europe. (The road to Obersolden in the Tyrol is 50 m higher but it is not a through-road.) Extremely winding and narrow. 11% gradient. It is closed early Oct–late June.

NICE, see town plans. The Riviera, see A8.

TOWN PLANS

LYON (470 000)

Chief town of the dep. of Rhône. France's third city. Greater Lyon with a population of 1.2 million is the second largest city in the country. Remains of a Roman theatre on the 294 m high *La Fourvière* granite hill. Museum displaying archaeological finds, and historical artifacts from Lyon. 19th-cent. Basilica of Notre-Dame. Views extend out over Lyon as far as Mont Blanc, 160 km away.

Le Vieux Lyon (Old Lyon) is well preserved and animated, with shopping streets, restaurants and handsome buildings. Gothic Cathedral of St- Jean (12th–15th cent.). Exquisite stained glass and an astronomical clock (16th cent.) that strikes at noon.

Woodcarvings.

The heart of the city lies on a narrow peninsula between the Rhône and the Saône. Large *Place Bellecour* with equestrian statue of Louis XIV. To the north, the Rue de la République, a shopping street, goes to the Hôtel de Ville (17th cent.) and the Grand-Théâtre. To the south, the pedestrianised Rue Victor-Hugo leads to the Gare de Perrache. This oldfashioned little railway station was opened by Napoleon III. It is now connected by glass-enclosed pedestrian walks and escalators to the startling architecture of the new railway station that resembles a futuristic lunar space station.

The new *Part-Dieu* section of Lyon is also hypermodern. Hundreds of shops and department stores. Artificial four-storey waterfalls, cultural centre and large concert hall. The Crédit Lyonnais Bank has a 42-storey building.

You can travel to it on the new Metro. Parc de la Tête d'Or with zoo and botanical garden.

The *Textile Museum* (Musée historique des Tissus) is unique. Exhibits concerning the city's famed silk-weaving industry. Jacquard, inventor of a loom for weaving patterned fabrics, was one of its pioneers. *Handicrafts museum. Pharmacy museum* in the Hôtel Dieu, a 17th–18th-cent. hospital with a 325 m long façade overlooking the Rhône. *Art museum* in the Palais St-Pierre. *Doll museum, natural history museum* with aquarium. Printing and banking museums, sewing machine museum, fire brigade museum and many more.

On the Quai St-Antoine, a speciality of Lyon: the *Puppet Theatre.* Marionette museum in the Hôtel de Ville. Music festival June 15-July 15. Berlioz Festival in the middle of September. Large university. Centre for cancer

Corsica
(Corse)

France's largest island, 8 722 km², 183 km long and about 85 km wide. 280 000 inhabitants. The island is 170 km from the Riviera, 80 km from Italy and 10 km from Sardinia. From the 14th cent. until the middle of the 18th cent., Corsica was ruled by the Genoese. In 1755, Pascal Paoli proclaimed an independent Corsican republic, which lasted for 14 years. In 1768, the Genoese sold Corsica to France and the following year the French supressed a Corsican uprising.

Rocky landscape with lush vegetation and vineyards. The highest point on the island is *Monte Cinto*, 2 707 m. Another observation point is *Mont l'Incudine*, 2 136 m. Excursions on mule back start from Zicavo. The roads are often narrow and winding. About 10 km inland the traveller enters an untamed mountainous region, e.g. from Solenzara to Col de Bavella, rising to 1 243 m above sea level.

Many curious folk traditions, particularly during Holy Week. On Good Friday many towns have candle-lit night-time processions of hooded penitents going through the streets. They march in complicated spiral patterns "La Gratinola". Corsica's folk music is marked by sorrow, "lamenti", by its outlaws, "ballate", and by mourning women exhorting their men to bloody revenge in the notorious Corsican feuds ("Vendetta" is a Corsican word). Up in the mountains you may hear "paghiella songs", an old three-part harmony style of male singing.

Some Corsican towns:

AJACCIO (50 000). Chief town of the dep. of Ajaccio. Splendid gulf and a background of mountains that are snow-clad until the early summer. The old quarter of the town is a veritable maze of animated streets. Napoleon was born in Ajaccio and the town's High Street has been named after him. In 1811 he made his birthplace the

capital of Corsica, a position previously occupied by Bastia. *Napoleon Museum* in the town hall. *Musée Fesch* with Italian art and Napoleonic memorabilia. Souvenirs of Napoleon also in the 16th-cent. *Notre-Dame Cathedral.* Tour de la Parata with fine views. Excursions by boat to the *Sanguinaires Islands.* A narrow-gauge railway that crosses awe- inspiring gorges connects Ajaccio with Bastia.

BASTIA (52 000) received its name from the bastion that was built by the Genoese in 1380. Old quarter with maze of narrow streets and buildings as much as nine storeys high. 17th-cent. cathedral. Citadel, originally built in 1378. *Military museum. Ethnological museum* (Musée Ethnographique Corse). The northern tip of the island, as far as *Cap Crose*, offers marvellous opportunities for excursions to picturesque villages and magnificent views. Passenger ship service to Elba.

Bonifacio. Fortress-town built on a 64 m high limestone cliff on the little more than 11 km wide sound that separates Corsica from Sardinia. Medieval streets and churches. All the restaurants serve the town's speciality, langouste (spiny lobster).

Calanche de Piana has fantastically shaped cliffs, as much as 300 m high. **Calvi** (3 000). Little town and resort, partially built as a fortress on a peninsula. Citadel and cathedral (both with origins in the 13th cent.). Excursions by boat to Girolata, a little village ringed by cliffs and almost impossible to reach by land. *Ile-Rousse,* large resort. Its name refers to its red cliffs. **Corte** (6 000) in the centre of the island. Seat of Pascal Paoli's Corsican republic. *Musée d'Historie Corse* in the Palais National. Exhibits concerning the island's history and independence. "Columbus' birthplace" (one of many – there are others in Spain and Italy).

Porto Vecchio (7 000) on a lovely bay. Remains of the town wall. 16th-cent.

citadel. Seaside resort.

Propriano. Seaside resort. Several hotels on both sides of the Valinco bay with its fine beaches.

Sartene (6 000). Medieval atmosphere. Narrow streets and dark granite buildings. Site of one of the most fascinating Holy Week processions on the island. The penitents enact Jesus' journey to Golgotha. The man who takes the part of Jesus acts with a veil over his face, only the parish priest knows his identity.

Many "menhirs" (megalithic stones) similar to the ones in Brittany, in the area. They were erected by prehistoric sun worshippers. Even more of these in Fillitosa at Sollecaro.

190

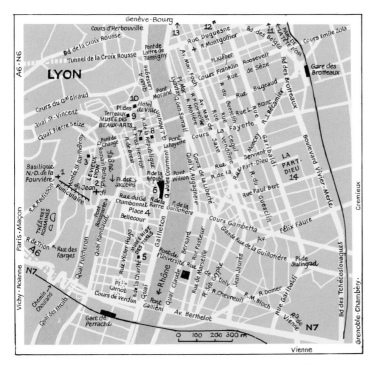

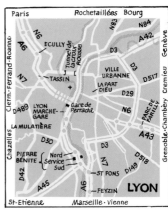

1 Fourvière Hill. Basilica of Notre-
   Dame. Roman theatres.
2 Old Lyons. Cathedral.
3 City museum. Puppet museum.
4 Place Bellecour.
5 Historical museum of textiles.
   Museum of decorative arts.
6 Hôtel-Dieu. Hospital museum.
7 Museum of printing and banking.
8 Stock exchange.
9 Museum of fine arts.
10 Town hall.
11 Zoo and botanical gardens.
12 Natural science museum.
13 La Part-Dieu.
14 Motor car museum.

research.
Motor car museum. *Musée de l'Auto-
mobile Henri Malartre* in Château
Rochetaillée, 11 km north of Lyon.
One of the foremost of its kind in
Europe. The Berliet factories, produc-
ing heavy vehicles, are the largest in
Lyon.

MARSEILLE
(915 000, Greater Marseille 1 million)
The second largest city of France.
Chief town of the dep. of Bouches-du-
Rhône and the region of Provence-Côte
d'Azur. Perhaps this is the country's
oldest city. It was founded in the 8th
cent. B.C. by the Phoenicians.

La Canabière is Marseille's famous
and lively main street. Its name comes
from the word cannabis (hemp) and
can be loosely translated as The Rope
Walk. It goes down to the *Vieux Port*
(Old Port) which even served the ancient Greeks. Now it is thronged with
fishing boats, excursion boats and private yachts. The Quai des Belges and
the Quai de la Rive Neuve are lined
with countless restaurants, all serving the city's speciality, the famous,
hearty bouillabaisse. The harbour
entrance is bordered by two 17th-cent.
forts. Boat trips to the *Château d'If*, the
old prison where Alexandre Dumas
Senior's Count of Monte Cristo once

languished. The Port Moderne (New
Port) is the largest in France. 25 km of
docks. Separate railway station, Gare
Maritime. Ships and car ferries to
Mediterranean and Black Sea ports.
On holidays you can stroll on the 5 km
long breakwater. The Basilica of
Notre-Dame-de-la-Garde (1864) on a
160 m high limestone cliff. Its bell
tower with a gilded statue of the
Virgin is the symbol of Marseille.
Views from the terrace. Fine views
also from the long Corniche Président
J.F. Kennedy. *Palais Longchamps*, art
museum and natural history museum. Large coin collection. *Musée
Grobet-Labadie. Musée du Vieux Mar-
seille* (city history). *Museum* with
fragments of ancient Greek and
Roman docks.

NICE (320 000)
Chief town of the dep. of Alpes-Mariti-
mes and the centre of the Riviera.
Founded by the Greeks about 350 B.C.
The city once belonged to Savoy. From
1812 until 1860 it was part of the
Kingdom of Sardinia which ceded it to
France in 1860. University since 1966.
Large resorts with rows of hotels. The
best known is the venerable Negresco,
situated on the long and distinguished *Promenade des Anglais* that follows the *Baie des Anges*. Hotels, restaurants, cafés, palm trees and long
pebbled beach. Famous casinos.
The heart of the city is the Place
Masséna with arcaded terra-cotta coloured buildings. *Vieille Ville* (Old
Town) with flower market (1 p.m. – 4

Place des Terreaux, Lyon

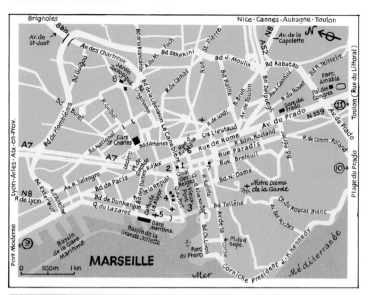

1 *La Canebière. Maritime museum.*
2 *Excavations.*
3 *Old Port. Boat to the island of If.*
4 *City museum. Museum of the Roman Harbour.*
5 *Cathedral.*
6 *Market.*
7 *Musée Cantini.*
8 *Palais Longchamps. Natural history museum. Zoo. Musée Grobet-Labadie.*
9 *Port Moderne.*
10 *Beach. Parc Borely. Archeological museum.*
11 *La Cité Radieuse.*

p.m.). Jardin du Roi Albert I, a delightful park. The 92 m high hill is still referred to as "The Château", although the castle on the site was destroyed in 1706. The Bellanda Tower is one of its remnants. Fine views. *Chagall museum* with the ponderous name Musée National Message Biblique Marc Chagall. *Musée Matisse, Musée Cheret* (the city's art collection). *The Musée Masséna* has medieval paintings and works of the Impressionists. The suburb of *Cimiez* is the site of remains of a Roman amphitheatre (6 000 spectators), and baths. Little museum.
11-day pre-Lenten carnival.

PARIS
(2.6 million, with suburbs 9.2 million) The capital of France was founded during the Roman era when it was known as Lutetia. It retained its medieval character until the second half of the 19th cent., when the city planner Haussmann created splendid boulevards that replaced the tangle of medieval streets and buildings. His broad avenues now give Paris its distinctive appearance. In 1973 the tremendous Boulevard de la Périphérique ring road was completed. It connects all of the major entry roads, the nine "Portes" of Paris. A road with fast-moving motor traffic follows the quays on the north bank of the Seine.

ILE DE LA CITÉ
This island in the Seine is the oldest part of Paris. This was where the ancient Parisii, a Celtic tribe, had a settlement and this is the site of the Gauls' and Romans' Lutetia. *Notre-Dame Cathedral* (12th–14th cent.). Magnificent façade with sculptures and three portals. The rose window is almost 10 m in diameter. Galleries and statues familiar to readers of Victor Hugo's "Hunchbank of Notre- Dame". The Bourdon-de-Notre-Dame bell, once ridden by Hugo's hunchback, weighs

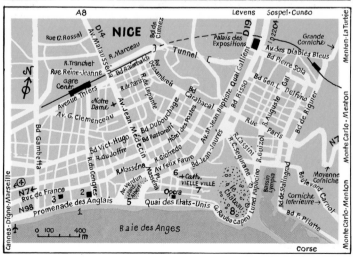

1 *Promenade des Anglais.*
2 *Palais de la Mediterranée.*
3 *Musée Masséna.*
4 *Musée Chéret.*
5 *Jardin Albert I. Casino Municipal.*
6 *Ste-Réparate Cathedral.*
7 *Old Town. Flower market.*
8 *Château. Park. Viewpoint.*
9 *Musée Marc Chagall.*
10 *Musée Matisse.*

15 000 kg and is situated in the south tower. Both of the uncompleted towers are 59 m high. It is possible to climb the north tower (376 steps). The interior of the cathedral is 130 m long, 48 m wide and 35 m high. Rich treasury. The Church of **Sainte-Chapelle**, a lovely 13th-cent. Gothic chapel with tall and beautiful stained-glass windows. Magnificent Palais de Justice on the site of the old Royal Palace.

RIVE DROITE, the Right Bank
The **Arc de Triomphe,** 50 m high, was erected in 1836 to commemorate Napoleon's victories. Eternal flame on the tomb of the Unknown Soldier. Splendid views out over Paris from the observation terrace above the arch. The arch is at the centre of the **Place Charles de Gaulle** (formerly Place de l'Étoile), where twelve streets and boulevards converge.
The **Champs-Elysées** is one of the most famous thoroughfares in the world. Restaurants, boutiques, exhibitions halls, cinemas, cafés and a constant stream of people and cars. Motor-car show-rooms – Renault's has a restaurant with a vintage car motif. **Place de la Concorde.** Traffic swirls around the 23 m high obelisk from Luxor (13th cent. B.C.). The elegant, arcaded Rue de Rivoli, a distinguished shopping street, goes east. The short

Rue Royale passes Maxim's restaurant and continues to the neo-classical façade of the Church of La Madelaine (19th cent.). This is where the **Grands Boulevards** begin. Under different names they lead to the Place de la République, a fascinating section of Paris with shops, cinemas, cafés, streams of heavy traffic and neon lights.
The *Opera* (1875) is an impressive Second-Empire building designed by Charles Garnier. It accommodates an audience of 2 167. Ceiling by Chagall. Famous staircase.
Near by are the large Louvre, Printemps, and Galeries Lafayettes department stores and the haute couture houses of Dior, Chanel and Patou. The Rue de la Paix is an elegant shopping street. Place Vendôme has uniform buildings and a 43 m high copy of Trajan's Column in Rome.
The Grands Boulevards continue east to the Place de la République, past the triumphal arches at the Porte St-Denis and Porte St-Martin and on to the *Place de la Bastille* where the French Revolution started. The storming of the Bastille took place on July 14, 1789. The 47 m high Colonne de Juillet commemorates those who fell during the uprising of July 1830.
Place des Vosges, one of the most

beautiful and symmetrical squares in Paris. Its harmoniously designed buildings reflect their 17th-cent. origins. *Le Marais* (the Marsh) still retains its aristocratic 16th-, 17th- and 18th-cent. "hôtels particuliers", noblemen's town residences. The famous food markets of Les Halles have been moved to Rungis, near Orly airport. They have been replaced with underground galleries of shops at the *Forum des Halles,* where the Metro underground railway and RER (Réseau Express Régional) trains have a station.
The Rue du Faubourg Montmartre leaves the Grands Boulevards and goes up the hill of **La Butte Montmartre,** 101 m above the Seine. A little funicular goes up to the *Church of Sacré-Cœur,* designed by Abadie (who had a predilection for churches that resembled mosques) and completed in 1914. The glistening white church can be seen from miles around. Fine views from the terrace and the dome. Next to it is the old Church of St-Pierre-de-Montmartre.
Place du Tertre, once an artist's hangout, is now filled with tourists and the type of restaurant that caters to them. Boulevard de Clichy and Boulevard de Rochechouart have strip clubs, pornographic book shops and other such entertainments. Place Pigalle and Place Blanche are famous for the Moulin Rouge.
La Défense, an area on the west side of Paris. Its over twenty skyscrapers have drastically altered the skyline of Paris. 20 000 people live and 40 000 work in this newly constructed district. Ingenious architects and city planners have either constructed a true city of the future or an awful nightmare – depending on your point of view. In any case, La Défense is eerily and totally deserted at night. But R.E.R. express trains take you to the Arc de Triomphe in only 10 minutes.

RIVE GAUCHE, The Left Bank
The vibrant *Boulevard St-Michel* goes through the Quartier Latin (Latin Quarter), an area famous for its artists and students. The Sorbonne, originally a college of theology, was founded in 1203. The Sorbonne Church contains the tomb of Cardinal Richelieu. *The Panthéon,* a church situated at the highest point in this part of Paris, 60 m above sea level, is 117 m high. It was opened in 1791 as a Panthéon for famous Frenchmen. Voltaire, Zola and Victor Hugo, among others, are buried here.
The 60 m high hill of *Montparnasse* is now the site of the 56-storey Tour Maine-Montparnasse. Modern railway station (trains to Brittany and the southwest). Bookstalls line the quays that face Notre-Dame Cathedral. Some restaurant-lined streets are redolent with the atmosphere of Algeria, packed with people and kiosks selling exotic fare. *Boulevard St-Germain* (3 km) goes west past the Church of St-Germain-des-Prés (11th cent.), the oldest church in Paris.

MC · Monaco

Area: 1.5 km² (8 sq. miles).

Population: 25 000
Principality, partner in a customs union with France. The population consists of 1 500 Monégasques, and large numbers of French and Italians. The capital is **Monaco-Ville** which has now spread out into Monte Carlo and Condamine. Monaco-Ville, high on a cliff, with its 16th- to 17th-cent. palace, gives a charming old-world impression. The large open square in front of the palace is beautiful and busy. Open-air theatre in the summer. *Oceanographic museum* with models.

Monte Carlo is one of the Riviera's major resorts. The town is bursting with luxury hotels, and its harbour is packed with luxurious yachts. The renowned casino was designed by Charles Garnier (architect of the Paris Opera).
The *Musée National de Monaco* has a large doll collection from the 18th and 19th cent.
The Monte Carlo Rally, an annual event with starting points in different places in Europe, finishes in the streets of Monte Carlo. The 3.15 km stretch has remained the same since 1929.

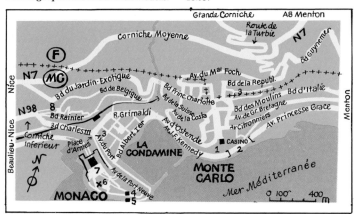

1 *Casino.*
2 *Congress Centre.*
3 *Markets.*
4 *Museum (Egypt and the antiquity).*
5 *Oceanographic museum.*
6 *Cathedral.*
7 *Palace.*
8 *Jardin exotique.*

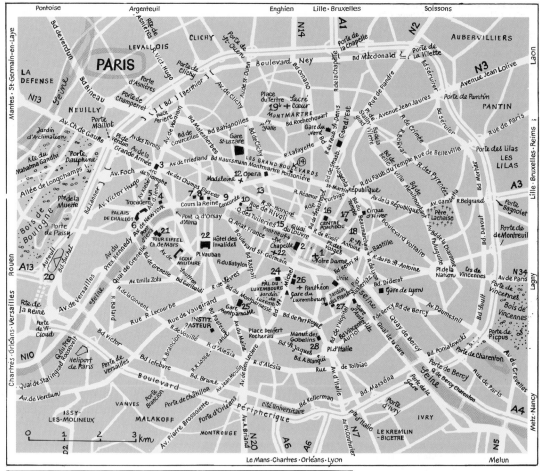

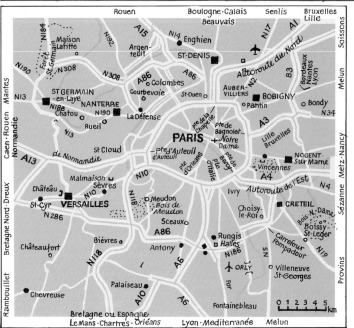

1 Notre-Dame Cathedral.
2 Palais de Justice (Law Courts). Sainte-Chapelle. Musée de la Conciergerie.
3 Arc de Triomphe.
4 Museum of modern art.
5 Musée Guimet.
6 Palais Chaillot.
7 Palais de la Decouverte.
8 Grand Palais and Petit Palais.
9 Place de la Concorde.
10 Musée du Jeu de Paume.
11 Jardin des Tuileries.
12 Church of La Madeleine.
13 Place Vendôme.
14 Musée Grévin.
15 Le Louvre.
16 Centre Pompidou.
17 Musée Carnavalet.
18 Place des Vosges.
19 Montmartre. Place du Tertre and Sacré-Cœur.
20 Jardin de Fleuriste de Paris.
21 Tour Eiffel.
22 Hôtel des Invalides.
23 St-Germain-des-Prés.
24 Jardin du Luxembourg.
25 Maine-Montparnasse.
26 Musée de Cluny. Sorbonne.
27 Jardin des Plantes. Museum of natural history.
28 Tapistry workshops.

Palais Bourbon, headquarters of the Legion of Honour. Quai d'Orsay, often the term used for the French Foreign Office.

Hôtel des Invalides (17th cent.) with 210 m long façade, built to accommodate old and disabled soldiers. *Dôme des Invalides with Napoleon's tomb. École Militaire, famous military academy (1774)* with *Champ-de-Mars* parade ground. The **Tour Eiffel** is the most famous symbol of Paris. Erected for the World Fair of 1889, it was considered a monstrosity that desecrated the Parisian skyline. Its total height is 318 m. The first platform is at about 60 m, the second at 116 m and the third at 276 m. Long queues for the lift are to be expected. About 1 million visitors annually. Ciné Musée on the first floor. Lift machinery from 1899 is on view one flight down. Restaurant and conference hall on the first étage.

MUSEUMS

The **Louvre,** opened in 1793, is one of the foremost museums in Europe. Greco-Roman section with the Venus de Milo, the Winged Victory of Samothrace and the Parthenon frieze. Finds from Egypt, Babylon and Assyria. Magnificent collection of paintings, including the Mona Lisa ("La Joconde") by Leonardo da Vinci. *Hotel de Cluny.* Medieval crafts. Remains of Roman baths.

Centre Georges Pompidou. commonly known as the Centre Beaubourg. Modern art and culture in a fantastic ultra-modern building supported by external steel girders. Many gnashed their teeth when the centre opened in 1977, but now it is one of the major tourist attractions of Paris.

Musée de l'Homme (ethnological museum) in the Palais de Chaillot. The *Musée Carnavalet* exhibits Parisian history. *Musée des Téchniques,* an enormous technical museum, similar to the one in Munich. *Musée Guimet,* Far Eastern exhibits. *Palais de la Découverte,* museum of inventions with Planetarium. *Army museum* in the Hôtel des Invalides. *Musée Grevin,* waxworks. *Musée du Jeu de Paume,* French Impressionists. *Picasso museum.* There is an Armenian museum, a museum of the Legion of Honour and museums of Jewish art, Polish history, postal services, the police, astronomy, hunting, printing, mining, medicine and many, many more. Most museums are closed on Tuesdays. Circus, both touring and permanent (Cirque d'Hiver).

PARKS

The **Bois de Boulogne** became a park during the 19th cent. Criss-crossed by motor roads and walks for strolling. Large waterfall and seven lakes. *Auteuil* and *Longchamps* race tracks. Little Bagatelle Palace (1777) with rose garden. Jardin d'Acclimatation, zoo and amusement park. Musée des Arts et Traditions Populaires (folklore, agricultural tools and equipment, etc.). *Bois de Vincennes,* east of Paris. Gardening exhibitions, lakes, zoo, race track.

Notre-Dame Cathedral, Paris

Le Jardin du Luxembourg, adjoining the Latin Quarter. Beautiful Renaissance park. *Le Jardin de Tuileries,* created by Le Nôtre in 1664 as a royal park, has remained relatively unchanged since then. The palace was demolished during the period of the Paris Commune, 1871. *Le Jardin Fleuriste* de la ville de Paris at the Porte d'Auteuil, supplier of flowers to the city of Paris. Large hot house. Azaleas in April and chrysanthemums in October. *Père-Lachaise Cemetery* with 100-year-old lindens and acacias. 97 sections, one for generals, one for rich Jews, one for poor Russians, etc. A thousand who were executed during the Paris Commune lie buried close to the wall where they were shot. Graves of Molière, Chopin, Delacroix, Balzac, Héloise and Abélard, Oscar Wilde, Edit Piaf, Sarah Bernhardt, etc. Many visitors to the grave of Allan Kardec, the founder of spiritualism. Many original and unique tombstones.

RESTAURANTS

There is not enough space in this book to try to mention all of the worthwhile restaurants in Paris. Among the best known are the Tour d'Argent with its famous numbered ducks, La Coupole

in the Boulevard Montparnasse, the Grand Véfour in the Rue Beaujolais, Prunier in the Rue Duphot, Fouget's in the Champs-Elysées, Maxim's in the Rue Royale, the Café de la Paix near the Opera and Chez la Mère Catherine at Montmartre.

Most of the above-mentioned are in the First Class cathegory and are expensive. If you are interested in dining in one of Paris's countless smaller and cheaper restaurants, it is best to refer to a specialized guidebook or to Michelin's Red Guide.

The Guide des Restaurant de Paris is available at the Paris Tourist Office.

The railway stations of Paris are impressive structures, built during the great age of European express trains. Six terminal stations, i.e. the trains must back in or out. The *Gare de Lyon* with its characteristic clock tower was once the starting point of the Istanbul-bound Orient Express. Now it handles the fast TGV (Trains Grande Vitesse) trains that travel to Lyon at speeds up to 260 kmh. The restaurant of the Gare de Lyon is a sight worth seeing, a landmark of Belle-Epoque décor. The theme of the restaurant is the famous "Train Bleu", Paris to Riviera express. The *Gare du Nord* is one of the most impressive railway stations. Trains including the Nord Express leave it for Scandinavia, the north Channel ports, Lille, Brussels, Amsterdam, etc. Fast turbo trains leave the *Gare St-Lazare* for Normandy. Other major stations are the *Gare de l'Est* (Strasbourg, Switzerland, etc.), the *Gare d'Austerlitz* (Bordeaux, Madrid, Lisbon) and the *Gare Montparnasse* (Brittany).

Airports: The *Charles de Gaulle* airport in Roissy-en-France is one of the most modern in Europe. Numerous shops and restaurants. Circular main building. *Le Bourget*, the old airport, is no longer used for international air traffic. Its big day was May 21, 1927, when Charles Lindbergh landed with his Spirit of St.Louis after the first single-handed trans-Atlantic flight. Large aviation museum. The collections in Meudon were moved here in 1981. Near by are large fields of tulips (April-May) and gladioli (August-September). *Orly*, see A 6.

The *Metro* (Metropolitan), the Paris underground railway, is often the fastest means of transport. Frequent services. Red carriages for first class passengers, green carriages for second class. The R.E.R is an express, two-lined Metro system. Both lines meet at Les Halles.

Versailles. The palace of Versailles was built in 1661 for Louis XIV by the architect Louis le Vau. All of the monarchs of Europe became envious and almost all tried to recreate the splendour of the palace and its gardens. The façade facing the park is 580 m long. An incredible treasury of halls and works of art. The Treaty of Versailles (1919) was signed in the famous "Galerie des Glaces" (Hall of Mirrors). The garden is a creation of André Le Nôtre. Hundreds of statues and foun-

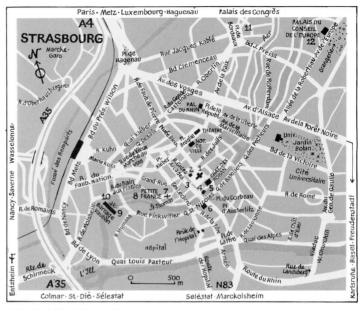

Strasbourg. Part of the Old Town and the cathedral

1 *Cathedral.* 2 *Maison Kammerzell.* 3 *Place Gutenberg and Rue du Vieux-Marché-aux-Poissons.* 4 *Musée Œvre-Notre-Dame.* 5 *Château des Rohan.* 6 *Musée Alsacien.* 7 *Church of St-Thomas.* 8 *Petite France ("Little France").* 9 *Barrage Vauban.* 10 *Market.* 11 *Art Museum.* 12 *Council of Europe Palace.*

tains. Grand Trianon and Petit Trianon pleasure palaces. The city of Versailles (100 000) is completely dominated by the palace and the broad avenues that extend from the Place d'Armes, the palace square.

STRASBOURG (260 000)

Chief town of the dep. of Bas-Rhin and capital of the old province of Alsace. Strasbourg can also be called the capital of Europe as it is the seat of both the Council of Europe and the European Parliament. The old German town was ceded to France in 1681. From 1870 until 1919 it was again German and capital of Elsass-Lothringen (Alsace-Lorraine). Major roads, railway lines and canals meet here. Large harbour, the second largest Rhine port after Duisburg.

The *cathedral* is one of the most magnificent in Europe. 142 m high tower. 12th-cent. foundation walls, chancel and transept. West Front with 13th- and 14th-cent. sculptures. Badly damaged during the French Revolution. Beautiful sculptures on the south portal (1230). Its interior is marked by the building's unusual width (103 m long, 41 m wide, 31 m high). Beautiful stained glass. Organ by Silbermann. 16th-cent. astronomical clock. Next to the cathedral, the *Musée l'Œvre-Notre-Dame* with Alsatian art and displays concerning the construction of the cathedral.

The *old quarter* near the cathedral

has many fascinating buildings, e.g. the half-timbered *Kammerzell* (15th–16th cent.), now a restaurant and the *Pharmacie du Cerf* (Hirschapotheke, the "Deer House"). The Cardinal-Bishops resided in the **Château de Rohan** (1742). The library, engraving room and chapel have been preserved. Archaeological museum, art museum, and handicrafts (ceramics and porcelain). Museum of modern art in the old customs house. Place du Corbeau (Rabenplatz, Raven Square) with post station where post coaches stopped from the 16th cent. until the 18th cent. *Musée Alsacien* with furniture, household equipment, folk costumes and art, etc. from Alsace.

Petite-France. Old Quartier des Tanneurs (Tanners' Quarter) with splendid half-timbered houses and canals. Four covered bridges and remains of the Barrage Vauban fortifications. Lovely view.

Miniature sightseeing trains go from the cathedral to Petite-France.

The heart of the modern city is the Place Kléber. To the east, the long Place Broglie with imposing buildings, among them the Opéra du Rhin. On this site, in 1792, "the Marseillaise" by Rouget de Lisle was first sung. University (1885). International conference centre with concert hall. Large exhibition grounds. Orangerie, a large park opposite the huge *Palais de l'Europe*, 105 m long. Outside fly the flags of all the member nations.

GB · Great Britain

GB·The United Kingdom of Great Britain and Northern Ireland

Area: 244 000 km² (94 500 sq. miles)

Population: 56 million. 74 % of the population are Protestants and belong to the Anglican Church of England and the Presbyterian Church of Scotland and Northern Ireland. 15 % of the population are Roman Catholics. The official language is English, but Welsh is spoken in Wales and Gaelic is spoken in Northern Ireland.

Major cities: London 6,7 million, Birmingham 920 000, Glasgow 762 000, Liverpool 510 000, Manchester 449 000.

Government: Constitutional monarchy. Parliament consists of the House of Lords and the House of Commons.

History

55 B.C. Troops of Julius Caesar land on Great Britain which is inhabited by Celtic tribes.

40 B.C. The Romans conquer England and Wales.

5th cent. Fall of the Roman Empire. Angles and Saxons establish small kingdoms that are united in 829.

1013 The Danish king, Sven Forkbeard, becomes ruler of England.

1066 The Anglo-Saxon king, Harold Godwinson, defeats the Normands at Stamford Bridge but he is later defeated at the Battle of Hastings. William the Conqueror, Duke of Normandy, becomes King of England.

1215 The barons force King John to sign the Magna Carta.

14th-15th cent. Civil war and war with France.

1587 Mary Queen of Scots is executed in England.

1588 The Spanish "Invincible Armada" is defeated.

1642 Civil war between supporters of the king and supporters of the parliament.

1649 King Charles I is executed, a republic is declared.

1653 Oliver Cromwell becomes dictator.

1660 "The Restoration". Charles II returns from exile and is proclaimed king.

18th cent. Parliament gains ever increasing power.

1707 England and Scotland are united into one kingdom.

1746 Dreams of an independent Scotland are finally crushed at the Battle of Culloden.

1776 The 13 North American colonies are lost as a result of the American Revolutionary War.

1815 The Napoleonic Wars are ended by the Battle of Waterloo.

19th cent. Industrialization. The British Empire becomes the world's greatest power. Reign of Queen Victoria 1837-1901.

1914-1918 First World War. The Allies defeat Germany and the other Central Powers.

1921 The Irish Free State (Eire) is established. Northern Ireland (Ulster) becomes a part of the United Kingdom of Great Britain and Northern Ireland in 1920.

1939-1945 Second World War. Led by Churchill the United Kingdom, almost alone, defies Hitler's Germany until the USA and the USSR enter the war. Germany is defeated.

During the post-war period, many of the colonies, once a part of the British Empire, achieve independence but become member states of the British Commonwealth of Nations.

1973 The United Kingdom enters the European Economic Community.

Currency: Pound (GBP).

1 pound (£) = 100 pence (p).

Business hours: Banks 9.30 a.m.-3.30 p.m. Lunchtime closings in Scotland and Northern Ireland. Post offices 9.00 a.m.-5.30 p.m. Saturdays 9.00 a.m.-1.00 p.m. Many shops close at 1.00 p.m. one day a week.

Holidays: New Year's Day, Good Friday, Easter Sunday, Easter Monday, the first Monday in May, the last Monday in May, the last Monday in August, December 25 and 26.

In Scotland January 3 is a holiday but not Easter Monday. Late Summer Holiday falls on the first Monday of August (bank holiday only). In Northern Ireland: March 17 (St. Patrick's Day), July 12 (Orangeman's Holiday, Battle of the Boyne).

Hotels

No official classifications but the AA and RAC have a hotel classification system of one to five stars. In general, the price of the room includes breakfast. The traditional English breakfast is slowly being replaced by the less filling "continental"breakfast. This is particularly true in the larger hotels

Routes described:

M 1	Leeds – London
M 2	(A2) London – Canterbury – Dover
M 3	London – Basingstoke – Southampton (see also A 30, A 31 and A 35)
M 4	London – Swansea (see also A 40 and A 48)
M 5	Birmingham – Bristol – Exeter (see also A 39)
M 6	Carlisle – Preston – Birmingham – Rugby
A 1	Edinburgh – Newcastle – Grantham – London (see also A 68)
A 5	Holyhead – Shrewsbury – Cannock
A 9	John O'Groats – Edinburgh
A 10	King's Lynn – London
A 11	Norwich – London
A 12	Great Yarmouth – London
A 20	London – Folkestone – Dover, (see also M 2)
A 27	Pevensey – Brighton – Southampton
A 30	London – Basingstoke – Exeter – Land's End
A 31	35 Southampton – Dorchester – Exeter
A 39	Bridgwater – Barnstaple – Falmouth
A 40	London – Fishguard, see M 4
A 48	Swansea – Carmarthen
A 68	Edinburgh – Galashiels – Newcastle
A 74	(M 74) Glasgow – Carlisle
A 75	Stranraer – Gretna Green, see A 74
A 77	Glasgow – Stranraer, see A 74
A 82	Inverness – Glasgow
A 259	Folkestone – Pevensey

Northern Ireland

A 1	Belfast – Newry (– Dublin)
A 2	Londonderry – Belfast – Portaferry – Newry
A 4	A 28 Belcoo – Clogher – Armagh – Newry

Special maps: Channel Islands, Isle of Man

Town plans: Belfast, Edinburgh, Glasgow, Liverpool, London, Manchester, Oxford

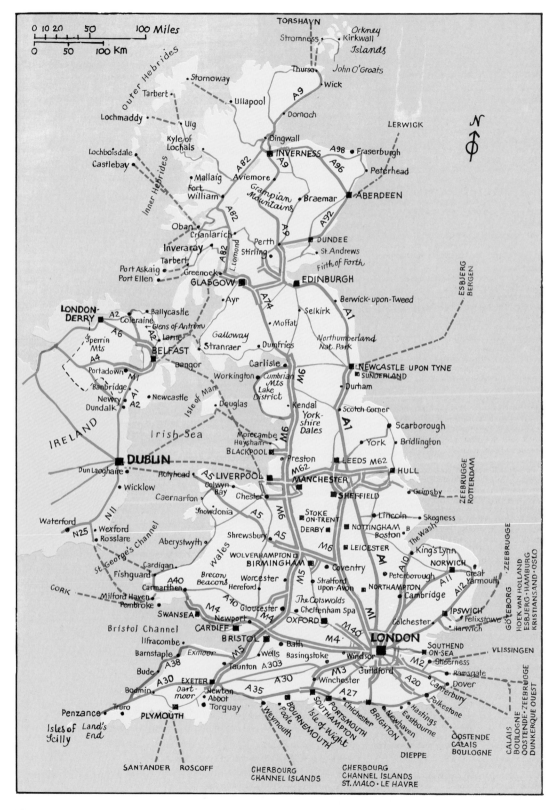

Loch Shiel near Glenfinnan in northwestern Scotland.

in the major cities. Many motels, usually offering a high standard of accommodation and charging rather high prices. Several hotel chains with central booking offices, e.g. Trust Houses Forte.

Local Tourist Information Centres displaying a special sign with a bed and "Tourist Accommodation Service" can assist personal callers in need of local accommodation. Several of them can also book rooms in other areas for the same day.

"Bed-and-Breakfast" accommodation, usually in private homes, are a British speciality. Aside from being inexpensive they provide the traveller with the opportunity to come in contact with the British. The AA has a special guide to Guest Houses, Farms and Inns, establishments that offer pleasant accomodation at prices that are usually lower than those charged by hotels.

Camping

Countless well-equipped camping sites. The AA's Guide to Camping and Caravanning in Britain lists thousands of approved camping sites.

Youth hostels

Although youth hostels accept travellers arriving by car, preference is given to hikers and cyclists.

Food and drink

The traditional British breakfast consists of fruit juice, cereals with milk, eggs with bacon or sausage, toast, butter, marmalade and coffee or tea. Kippers (smoked herring) are another popular breakfast dish.

Some traditional British dishes: Roast beef with Yorkshire pudding, potatoes and a vegetable. Steak and kidney pie. Fish and chips, deep-fried fish and potatoes. Available to take away from Fish and Chip shops and served in most cafés, this is one of the least ex-

pensive meals available in Britain today. Irish stew, mutton, onions and potatoes. Salmon is a Scottish speciality that is served hot, cold, or smoked. Arbroath smokies, smoked Scottish haddock. Cock-a-leekie soup, Scottish soup containing chicken and potatoes. Welsh rarebit, hot cheese sandwich flavoured with mustard. In restaurants sweets are often placed on a trolley and the diners can choose from a large variety of pastries, pies, gateaux and puddings. Instead of, or after, the sweet it is usually possible to choose one of the typical and famous English cheeses, e.g. Cheddar, Cheshire, Stilton and Wensleydale.

Beer, cider, wine or tea are the most usual mealtime beverages.

Good and reasonably priced lunches are available in most pubs. They usually serve simple and traditional British dishes – sandwiches, pies, sausages and hot dishes. In general pubs are open from 11 a.m. – 2 pm and 5.30 pm until 10.30 p.m. Monday to Thursday, and until 11.00 p.m. on Fridays and Saturdays. On Sundays they have shorter opening hours. In Northern Ireland and parts of Wales they are closed on Sunday. Customers under the age of 18 may not be served alcoholic beverages at the bar but young people between the ages of 16 and 18 may enter a pub if it has a special section where food is served.

In the country and in smaller towns, afternoon tea, accompanied by sandwiches or pastries is served in hotel lounges or tea shops. In London and other major cities it is not always easy to find such quiet oases. High tea, a speciality of Scotland, often takes the place of dinner.

Shopping

Material and yarn, sweaters, glass and pottery, porcelain, antiques,

silver and pewter, sports equipment, cosmetics, tea, marmalade and other foodstuffs.

Petrol

Although petrol is now measured in litres, gallons have by no means disappeared. One gallon = c. 4.5 litres. Octane content is indicated with a one to four star system.

Speed limits. Traffic regulations

Motorways and dual carriageways 70 mph (113 kmh), other roads 60 mph (96 kmh), built-up areas 30 mph (46 kmh). Cars towing caravans or trailers, maximum 50 mph (80 kmh). Traffic travels on the left-hand side of the road. A complete listing of rules

The Shambles, a street in York.

and regulations can be found in the booklet "The Highway Code", available at British Tourist Authority offices in Britain and abroad. Although the famous courtesy of the British drivers may not be as widespread as it once was, in general driving in Britain is not as nerve-wracking as it can be in some other European countries and the tempo of traffic in London is surprisingly relaxed considering that it is such an enormous city. Pedestrians have the right of way when they are crossing over a black and white-striped "zebra crossing". (Motorists are forbidden to park or wait on these crossings at any time.) If your car is fitted with seat belts it is compulsory to wear then.

Parking

Although parking can be a problem, car parks are usually easy to find. Kerb markings indicate that parking is forbidden at other than those times indicated on the information signs.
One yellow line signifies that parking is not allowed during working days; double yellow lines during any working day. "No waiting" means that although you may load or unload your vehicle, you are not allowed to park.

Roads

Although some roads may be narrow and twisting, with visibility limited by hedgerows, most are good. Motorways usually have three lanes going in either direction. Direction signs on motorways are blue, on primary routes green and on non-primary routes white.

Road patrol

The Automobile Association (AA), with 5.3 million members, is the world's largest motoring organization. It has pioneered road patrol service. Their yellow patrol cars and AA centres can be found all over Britain. In Greater London, their emergency centre can be contacted by dialling 01-

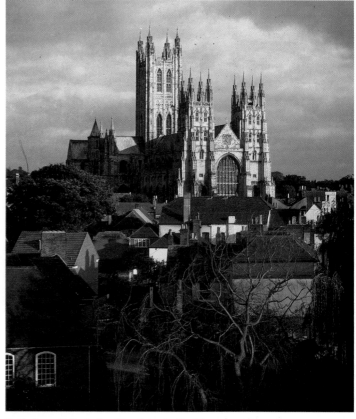

Canterbury Cathedral, with origins in the 7th cent.

954 73 73. It is open 24 hours a day. The Royal Automobile Club (RAC) provides similar services for their members. Their patrol cars are white.
The motorways are equipped with

emergency telephones. The nationwide emergency telephone number is 999. By dialling it you can come in contact with the police, fire brigade and medical services.

AA, The Automobile Association, Fanum House, Basingstoke. Tel. (0256) 20 123. Shop and information office in London: Fanum House, 5 New Coventry Street, close to Leicester Square.
British Tourist Authority, 64 St James's Street, London SW1A 1NF. Tel. 01-499 9325.
English Tourist Board, 4 Grosvenor Gardens, London, SW1W ODU (written enquiries only).
Scottish Tourist Board, 23 Ravelston Terrace, Edinburgh EH4 3EU. Tel. 031-332 2433 (written & telephone enquiries only).
Wales Tourist Board, 3 Castle Street, Cardiff CF1 2RE, Cardiff 27281.
Northern Ireland Tourist Board, River House, 48 High Street, Belfast, BT1 2DS. Tel. Belfast 231221.

The village of Selworthy in Somerset.

M1. Leeds – London

LEEDS, see A 1.

SHEFFIELD (477 000). Industrial city famed for its cutlery. Examples of the cutlers' craft can be seen in the *City Museum.* Cathedral. Art galleries. University. *Chatsworth House* (1707), 15 miles from Sheffield. Lovely interiors and gardens. The large fountain is the tallest in Great Britain.

Chesterfield (70 000). Industries and mines. All Saints' Church with famous twisted spire. The oldest sections of *Haddon Hall* (12 miles away) date from the 12th cent. 17th-cent. interiors include a splendid oak and walnut long gallery. Fine gardens.

Matlock. Spa town. Riber with the resort of Matlock Bath situated at the spot where the River Derwent flows through a beautiful gorge. Although *Riber Castle* looks as if it had been built in the Middle Ages, it was constructed in 1862 for John Smedley, the man who established the town as a spa. Now the centre of an animal reserve that specializes in the breeding and raising of British wildlife. Lynx colony.

The Tramway Museum, Crich, located in an abandoned limestone quarry, utilizes the tracks that were once a part of a factory managed by George Stephenson. 40 trams from different parts of the world. Some of them are in service along reconstructed streets.

NOTTINGHAM (271 000). Industrial city noted for cycles, lace and tobacco. Statue of Robin Hood and his men near the castle. He and his men lived in the nearby *Sherwood Forest.* His large oak still stands at *Edwinstowe* (Ollerton). The castle contains a museum and art gallery. Legend has it that the Crusaders quenched their thirsts before travelling to the Holy Land at The Trip to Jerusalem, a venerable inn and pub in the castle hill. The Salutation Inn is another famous establishment. It was once a favoured haunt of the highwayman Dick Turpin. However, Nottingham is not only known for its outlaws. William Booth, founder of the Salvation Army, was born in the city. The famous *Goose Fair,* held in October, has traditions that date back to the Middle Ages. *Newstead Abbey* (11 miles away) with a museum devoted to Lord Byron. *Wollaton Hall,* natural history museum.

DERBY (216 000). Rolls-Royce factories. Railway workshops. Crown Derby porcelain. 16th-cent. cathedral. *Kedleston Hall* (18th cent.) was rebuilt to the designs of Robert Adam. 12th-cent. church. Museum with displays of weapons, silver and ivory.

LEICESTER (280 000). Industrial city. Roman Jewry Wall and Museum. 14th- cent. *Newarke Houses* (local history museum). *Belgrave Hall,* furnished Queen Anne house and gardens.

NORTHAMPTON (145 000). Shoe factories. The *Central Museum* has a special section devoted to the history of footwear. *St. Sepulchre's Church* is one of the four remaining round churches in England. *Cromwell's House* (Hazelrigg Mansion) was built 1662.

Bedford with *Cecil Higgins' Art Gallery.* Graphic art, sculpture (some works by Epstein and Moore), glass, porcelain and handicrafts.

Towcester. Little town with old churches and a coaching inn. Originally the Roman town of Lactodorum, it was on the old Roman road that went from Dover to Chester. Near by are the *Waterway Museum* and *Silverstone,* a World War II military airfield that now serves as a motor-racing circuit . George Washington's ancestors lived in *Sulgrave Manor* until 1656. Contains relics relating to George Washington.

Woburn Abbey (18th cent.) has become one of England's major tourist atttractions since the Duke of Bedford opened it to the public in 1955. Impressive interiors with splendid ceilings and furniture. Chinese porcelain. The works of art include paintings by Rembrandt, Van Dyck, Frans Hals and Gainsborough. 45 shops in the Woburn Abbey Antiques Centre. *The zoo,* called the Wild Animal Kingdom, is one of the largest in Europe – tigers, lions, elephants, giraffes, bears, etc. Safari buses and cable cars.

LUTON (164 000). Car factories. *Luton Hoo* with art collections (Titian and Rembrandt) and English porcelain. Beautiful park.

Whipsnade Park Zoo on the slopes of the Chiltern Hills is a branch of the London Zoo. When it was opened in 1931, primarily as a resting place for sick animals, it was considered revolutionary.

St. Albans (51 000), named after Alban, a Roman soldier who was the first Christian martyr in England. Site of the Roman town of Verulamium. Remains of the town wall. England's sole *Roman theatre. Museum* with mosaics and and hypocaust. The red bricks in the tower of the *cathedral* (1115) were originally parts of buildings in the old Roman town. Church of St. Michael. *City museum. Organ Museum.* Ye Old Fighting Cocks on Abbey Mill Lane is one of the oldest inns in England. French mercenary soldiers were quartered in the French Row in 1216. *Gorhambury House* with handsome interiors was once the home of Francis Bacon, the statesman, philosopher and essayist. Vast rose gardens that belong to the National Rose Society. *Hatfield House* and *Stevenage,* see A 1.

Hendon. Royal Air Force Museum on former Hendon airfield.

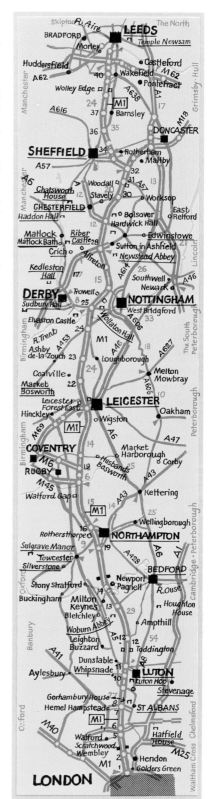

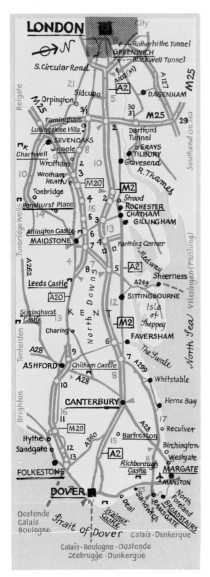

M 2 (A 2). London – Canterbury – Dover

A 2 and M 2 from London Bridge to Dover is also Europe Road 2 to Brindisi in Italy and Europe Road 5 to Istanbul. However, in Great Britain the European Road numbers are not signposted. They should be, for the Dover Road was a part of the very first European road system 2 000 years ago. This was the road followed by Roman legionaries and administrators and later by pilgrims from all of Europe on their way to Canterbury.

LONDON and *Greenwich,* see town plans.

Rochester (52 500). Old town. Sections of the Roman wall remain. The *cathedral* was constructed in the 11th cent. for Bishop Gundulf. Impressive west portal and high tower. Ruins of an enormous castle from the same period. The Guildhall (1687) is now a museum. Charles Dickens, who grew up in Rochester, mentioned the Royal Victoria and Bull Hotel in "The Pickwick Papers". Dickens Museum in Eastgate House.

Canterbury (35 000). Since the 7th cent. the centre of English Christianity. The Gothic *cathedral* was started in 1070. Thomas Becket, an archbishop, was murdered in the cathedral by four knights in 1170. Beautiful stained-glass windows depict the miracles that occurred after his death. The casket containing his remains became the goal for pilgrims from all of Europe. Chaucer's "Canterbury Tales" is about one group that made the journey to the shrine. The casket and the shrine were destroyed in 1538 on the orders of Henry VIII, but it is still possible to see exactly where the reliquary was placed. Tomb of Prince Edward (The Black Prince, d. 1367) behind the High Altar. 14th-cent. *West Gate.* Handsome half-timbered houses. The old part of the town is partially restored after World War II damage. Although Canterbury is the archiepiscopal seat of the Primate of All England, the Archbishop has his residence in London. *Chilham Castle* is one of the most beautiful villages in Kent. *Barfreston* with charming little village church dating from 1180.

Dover (33 000). The Romans settled here about AD 125. Recent street excavations revealed Roman pavements. Large car ferry port. The town lies in a gap in the famous white cliffs. *Dover Castle* (12th-13th cent.) is situated high above the town. Roman lighthouse within its walls. Numerous tunnels in the chalk cliffs under the castle. Stones in the grass mark the spot where Louis Blériot landed after his pioneering cross-Channel flight in 1909. Museum in the town hall. *Crabble Watermill* with museum. The mill was built to provide flour for the great numbers of soldiers who had assembled here to defend England against an expected invasion during the Napoleonic Wars.

Margate (53 300). Large seaside resort and fun fair. Long sandy beaches. *Broadstairs.* Seaside resort situated between the chalk cliffs. *Bleak House,* where Charles Dickens wrote the greater part of "David Copperfield", is now a museum devoted to the author. The Dickens House Museum is on the seafront near by. Annual Dickens festival in the middle of June.

Richborough. The Romans landed here in 43 B.C. and built the Rutupiae coastal fortifications. Roman Museum with examples of coins, vases and archaeological finds. Castle built for Henry VIII in *Deal.*

A 20. London – Folkestone – Dover

LONDON, see town plans. *Lullingstone Villa.* Excavations of a Roman villa. *Lullingston Castle.* A mainly 18th- cent. house with fine 15th- cent. gate tower.

Knole was begun in 1456 for the Archbishop of Canterbury. An enormous structure with seven courtyards, 12 entrances, 52 staircases and 365 rooms. Magnificent interiors with the original furniture and works of art. *Chartwell,* owned by Winston Churchill from 1922 until his death in 1965. Now Churchill Memorial with many relics of the famous statesman.

Penshurst Place, seat of the Viscount De L'Isle. The Great Hall is of particular interest. Toy museum. Beautiful park. *Tunbridge Wells* (45 000). Spa. The Pantiles is a delightful colonnaded street with uniform buildings.

MAIDSTONE (72 000). Chief town of Kent, a beautiful county famous for its lovely scenery, picturesque villages and half-timbered houses. *Allington Castle,* with origins that date back to the 13th cent., now belongs to the Carmelites who use it as a "Christian Centre".

Leeds Castle, named after Led, one of the ministers of the kingdom of Kent during the 9th cent. The stone castle was erected on two islands in the lake in 1119. Catherine of Aragon, Henry VIII's first wife, was one of the many queens who lived here. Henry VIII's banqueting hall.

Sissinghurst Castle Garden (16th cent.) was once the home of the writer Vita Sackville-West. Beautiful gardens, among them the "White Garden" planted with white flowers only.

Folkestone (44 000). Car ferry port and resort. Port and fish market. Pebble beach. The Leas, a fine promenade on the chalk cliffs.

M3 and A33. London – Basingstoke – Southampton

LONDON, Windsor and *Eton,* see town plans.

Kew Gardens (18th cent.). One of the world's largest botanical gardens. Palm house. George III lived in Kew Palace.

Richmond-upon -Thames (158 000), a beautiful town with fine views out over the River Thames. Handsome 17th- and 18th-cent. houses on Richmond Green. *Ham House* and *Syon House,* two stately homes with beautiful interiors.

Kingston-upon-Thames, an old market town with excellent shopping facilities that can be a good alternative to the crowded shops and department stores in central London. The Anglo-Saxon kings were crowned on the coronation stone that is near the Guildhall. Large areas of undisturbed parklands in *Richmond Park,* once the hunting preserve of Charles I. Fine views of the Thames from Richmond Hill.

Hampton Court. An enormous royal palace originally built for Cardinal Wolsey. In 1526 he gave it to Henry VIII. His generosity did not prevent the king from imprisoning the cardinal the following year. Parts of the palace are unchanged since the year of its completion, other sections were added in the 17th cent. by Sir Christopher Wren. Five of Henry VIII's wives lived here. Large parks and gardens.

Runnymede. A beautiful meadow on the banks of the Thames where King John was forced by the barons to sign the Magna Carta in 1215. On the other side of the road, monuments to the Royal Air Force and to John F. Kennedy.

Staines (54 000), *Chertsey* (43 000), *Egham* (28 000). Market towns and suburbs of London. *Ascot.* Race cource. The Queen is in attendance during the fashionable Ascot Week in June.

Thorpe Park. A gravel pit has been transformed into a park with open-air museum. Dwellings typical of different English historical periods have been reproduced: Celtic farm house, Norman castle, etc. Roman galley, Viking ship.

Guildford (57 000). Chief town of Surrey. Beautiful and steep High Street. Guildford was an important stop on the old coach routes and the old coaching inn remains. Famous 16th-cent. clock. 17th-cent. Abbot's Hospital. Art museum in Guildford House (1660). Ruins of a 12th-cent. castle. *Town Museum* with a section devoted to Lewis Carroll, author of "Alice in Wonderland". He died in 1898 and is buried in Mount Cemetery. The beautiful *cathedral on Stag Hill* was consecrated in 1961. The modern Yvonne Arnaud Theatre is set near the bank of the River Wey.

Sandhurst, site of the Royal Military Academy. *Farnborough.* British military aviation research institute. *St. Michael's Abbey Church* with the mausoleum of Emperor Napoleon III, Empress Eugenie and their son, the Prince Imperial. Military schools and museums in *Aldershot.*

Farnham with beautiful old houses in Castle Street and West Street. Delightful Bush Hotel. The castle was once the residence of the bishops of Winchester and Guildford. St. Joan of Arc, an interesting modern church.

Basingstoke (67 500). Commercial and industrial town. Head offices of the AA, the Automobile Association. Founded in 1905, with 5.4 million members, this is one of the oldest, and the largest organization of its type in the world. Its yellow patrol vehicles, service centres and telephone boxes are seen on roads all over Britain. *The Vyne* (16th cent.) is a splendid Tudor mansion with lovely interiors.

Winchester (30 500). Roman town that became the capital of England during the Anglo-Saxon and Danish periods. The Gothic *cathedral,* 170 m long, is the longest cathedral in Europe. Construction began in 1079 on a site that had been occupied by a 7th-cent. church. Pilgrim's Hall, a resting place for pilgrims on their way to Canterbury. Famous black marble baptismal font. Tombs of King Canute, Jane Austen and Izaak Walton, author of "The Compleat Angler". Ruins of Wolvesey Castle, once a bishop's residence. *Episcopal Palace* designed by Sir Christopher Wren. *Winchester College* was founded in 1382 for poor scholars. By the 19th cent. it had become the first public school in England. Several interesting buildings. The oldest is about 600 years old. *Castle Hall,* often used for royal banquets and even as a court of law. Sir Walter Raleigh received his death sentence here. A round table top, said to be King Arthur's legendary Round Table, hangs here. *Westgate Museum* with armour, weapons, etc. St. Cross Hospital, founded in the 12th cent, still serves as an old people's home. The pensioners of this former almshouse wear traditional black or purple cloaks. Visitors are still given the traditional "Wayfarer's Dole" – bread and ale. *Royal Hussars' Museum,* a regimental museum. *Marwell Zoo,* opened in 1972, is one of the most modern in the country. *Broadlands,* at Romsey, former residence of Earl Mountbatten. Exhibition.

SOUTHAMPTON, see A 27.

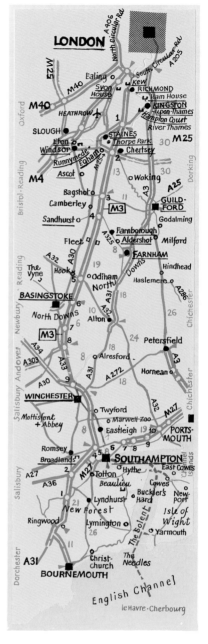

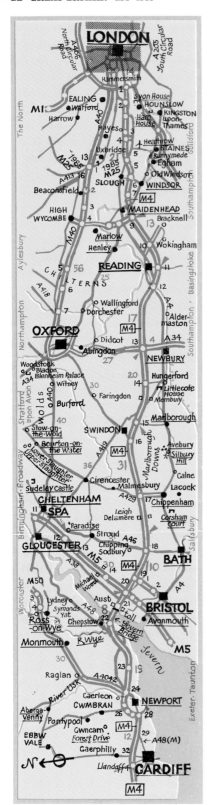

M 4 (A 40). London – Bristol – Cardiff – Swansea

LONDON and *Windsor,* see town plans.

Heathrow, Europe's largest airport. *Ham House* and *Syon House,* two stately homes with beautiful interiors.

Maidenhead (49 000). Boat trips on the Thames, an idyllic river all the way down to London. Pleasure boats and banks lined with lush vegetation and restaurants, inns and hotels. Many locks, e.g. Boulter's Lock. Jerome K. Jerome's "Three Men in a Boat" can be recommended as a guidebook to the river.

Marlow and *Henley,* two lovely little communities on the river. Royal regatta the first week in July at Henley. *Grey's Court,* near Henley, 16th-cent. house with the Carlisle Collection, a dolls' house museum.

Osterely Park (1780). Stately home by Robert Adam. Splendid interiors.

READING (124 000). Chief town of the county of Berkshire. *Museum of English Rural Life,* a folklore museum. *Municipal museum* with finds from the excavations of the Roman town of Silchester. The Abbey where Henry I was buried in 1136 is now in ruins. University.

Oxford, see town plans.

Newbury (26 500). The Cloth Hall, now a museum, is a reminder of the town's former importance as a textile manufacturing town. *Littlecote House* with Henry VIII's and Jane Seymour's initials on a window in the hall. Wild West Park.

Marlborough. Small town situated beside the River Kennet. The wide *High Street* is one of the most beautiful in the country. The nearby Ailesbury Column was erected in memory of George III's recovery from mental illness.

Avebury with a prehistoric stone circle, 6 m high, over 400 m in diameter. Circle with upright stones, the largest weighing over 40 tons. *Alexander Keiller Museum* with finds from excavations at Avebury and Windmill Hill *Silbury Hill,* thought to be a Bronze-Age burial mound. The Roman Bath Road, from Oxford Street in London via Notting Hill, Staines, Reading to Bath, went past here. The 18th-cent. London-Bath post coaches covered the distance of 180 km in 16 hours. In 1829 the first steam-driven cart passed Silbury Hill. It covered the distance in nine hours and 20 minutes. The new trains travel from London to Bath in one hour and ten minutes. *Avebury Manor* with tropical gardens.

Chippenham. Market town. A curious sight is Maud Heath's Causeway, a paved road (7 km) which a market woman had built from her home to the market place. *Lacock,* a pretty village with a 13th-cent. abbey converted into a house in 1540. *Corsham Court,* manor house (1585) built by Robert Adam. Splendid gardens. *Malmesbury* with 12th-cent. abbey church.

BATH (80 000). England's only hot springs, known to the Romans who founded the town of Aquae Sulis here. The beautiful *Roman Baths* are well preserved. The Pump Room (1796) is a suitable place for afternoon tea (with music). Abbey (founded 1140) with beautiful vaults. Many memorial tablets. One is dedicated to Beau Nash, who led Bath's fashionable society in the 18th cent. Elegant Regency houses along the Royal Crescent, Queen Square and the Circus. *Pulteney Bridge,* by Robert Adam, has shops on both sides. It is a copy of the Ponte Vecchio in Florence. The Assembly Rooms with the *Museum of Costume. Victoria Art Museum. Burrow Toy Museum. Carriage Museum.*

Cheltenham and *Gloucester,* see M 5.

The Cotswolds, to the east of Cheltenham, is one of England's most beautiful areas. Undulating landscape with hills reaching 200-300 m above sea level. Idyllic villages in the valleys. The narrow roads wind through the villages with their honey-coloured houses. *Broadway* is perhaps the best-known of the villages. The Lygon Arms and other hotels and inns along the High Street. Other fine villages: *Stow-on-the-Wold, Bourton-on-the-Water, Lower and Upper Slaughter* and *Chipping Campden.* The local pub in the village of *Paradise* is, of course, named the Adam and Eve. *Snowshill Manor,* near Broadway, built of the typical yellow Cotswold stone. Its last owner, Charles Wade, was an avid collector. Nautical instruments, musical instruments, bicycles and carriages. *Sudeley Castle,* near Winchcombe, was restored in the 19th cent. Large art collection. The chapel contains the tomb of Catherine Parr, sixth wife of Henry VIII, whom she outlived.

BRISTOL (388 000). Port linked to the sea by 11 km of the River Avon on the Bristol Channel. Aeronautic industry (British Aerospace). University . John Cabot sailed from Bristol in 1497 and discovered North America. Cabot Tower on Brandon Hill has been erected in his honour. Bristol's prosperity was largely a result of its involvement in the slave trade. Llandoger Trow, a tavern in King Street, was once the haunt of pirates. The Theatre Royal across the street, is the oldest (1766) of England's playhouses. It belongs to the Bristol Old Vic Company.

12th-cent. cathedral. *St. Mary Radcliffe* is one of the country's largest churches. A slender spire was added to the 13th-cent. tower in the 19th cent. *The Exchange* with the four "nails", bronze columns which were used by the brokers outside in Corn Street. *Municipal museum* in St. Nicholas Church. *Museum and Art Gallery* with archaeology, natural history and transport. *Red Lodge,* a beautiful 16th-cent. house. *Bristol Industrial Museum* in the harbour. Vehicles, aeroplanes, railway history and industrial machines. The *S.S. Great Britain,* launched in 1843, was the largest propeller-driven ship of its time. It was designed by Isambard Kingdom Brunel, who also built the *Clifton Suspension Bridge* (completed in 1834), 74 m above the gorge of the River Avon. *Bristol Zoo.*

Cheddar and *Wookey Hole,* see M 5.

Avonmouth. A port of Bristol built round the mouth of the River Avon. Highly mechanized docks. Oil basin.

Severn Bridge, built in 1966, is 988 m long. Tolls. Welsh border.

Chepstow. Old market town with narrow, steep streets. *Chepstow Castle,* a massive fortress on the limestone cliffs above the River Wye.

The Wye Valley is extremely lovely and there are several sign-posted hiking trails. Fine views from Wyndcliff and Symond's Yat. *Ross-on-Wye.* Small market town, one of the most beautiful in the Wye Valley. *Goodrich* is a splendid ruined castle. *Tintern Abbey,* a Cistercian monastery founded 1131. *Raglan Castle* was built in the 14th cent. The splendid Yellow Tower offers fine views.

Monmouth. Beautiful market town. Town gate (13th cent.) erected on a bridge across the Monmow. It served as watch tower and customs house. The castle was built in the 11th cent. and was destroyed in the 17th cent. *Museum of local history* with relics of C.S. Rolls (one of the founders of the Rolls-Royce Company). He was born in the nearby village of Rockfield and his statue stands in Agincourt Square. Nelson Collection with displays about Lord Nelson and Lady Hamilton.

NEWPORT (105 500). Third largest city in Wales. Seaport and steelworks. Interesting ruined castle and cathedral. Isca, a Roman legionary fortress at Caerleon, is supposed to have had a garrison of over 5 000 soldiers. Barracks and ramparts have been excavated, as has an amphitheatre seating 6 000 spectators. The fortress is also associated with the legend of King Arthur and the Knights of the Round Table.

Abergavenny. 12th-cent. castle with museum of rural life.

Cwmcarn Scenic Forest Drive is a 12 km long stretch of the road through the lovely Forest of Machen. Observation points and footpaths.

Caerphilly Castle, built in the 13th cent., is an enormous structure surrounded by moats and other defence works. The second largest castle in England (after Windsor). Partly in ruins.

CARDIFF (260 500). Capital city of Wales. Industrial centre and seaport. University. The 12th-cent. castle was built on the remains of a Roman fortress. Its military importance diminished in the 15th cent. and new buildings were added. Large parts of Cardiff are marked by the 19th-cent. predilection for exotic styles. *National Museum of Wales* is one of the largest museums in Great Britain. *Welsh Industrial and Maritime Museum* is situated near the harbour. *Welsh Folk Museum* is housed in St. Fagan's Castle. Enormous collections relating to the fascinating Welsh culture. Several old buildings round the museum. The castle is also an interesting sight. *Llandaff Cathedral* was built in the 12th cent. Epstein's aluminium sculpture of Christ in Majesty.

Coal mining district round the towns of *Ebbw Vale* (30 000), *Merthyr Tydfil* (54 000) with large steelworks, *Aberdare* (36 500). The little village of *Aberfan* was the scene of the 1966 tragedy when a slag heap collapsed and buried the school house. 142 people perished, most of them children.

Bridgend. Market town. *Margam,*country park, has been transformed into a recreation area with numerous attractions in the beautiful 840 acre park.

SWANSEA (168 000). Second large city in Wales. Seaport and industrial town. University. Maritime and industrial museum. *Glynn Vivian Art Gallery. Mumbles* and other resorts on the beautiful *Gower Peninsula.*

A 48 and A 40. Swansea – Fishguard

Kidwelly with the ruins of a large castle, built in 1130. Maes Gwenllian, is a battlefield named after the female general who fell at the head of the Welsh army during their fight with the Normans.

Carmarthen. Market town. One of the oldest town in Wales.

Pembroke with Monkton Priory Church, a Norman monastery. Pembroke Castle. *Pembrokeshire Coast National Park* with steep cliffs and numerous sea birds. *Pembroke Dock.* Naval base. Vintage and veteran cars and motorcycles in the Garrison Theatre. *Milford Haven,* fishing port. *Haverfordwest* in "Little England Beyond Wales", an area with English place names, populated by English-speaking inhabitants.

Fishguard. Lovely little port among the cliffs. Pebble beaches.

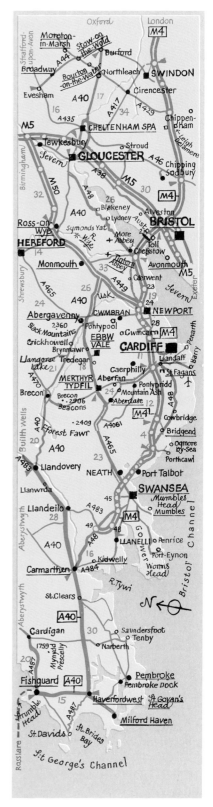

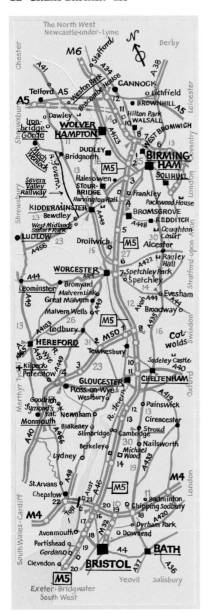

M 5. Birmingham – Bristol – Exeter

BIRMINGHAM, see town plans.

WOLVERHAMPTON (252 500). Industrial town. *St. John's Church* with the famous Renatus Harris organ. Art gallery, Moseley Old Hall. *Severn Valley Railway* (standard gauge), 21 km long, operates through the beautiful valley from Bridgnorth to Bewdley . About 30 steam engines are on display. *West Midlands Safari Park* with amusement park at Bewdley.

Much Wenlock. Small town with beautiful half-timbered houses and an inn. **Ironbridge Gorge Museum,** a large iron foundry museum. The Ironbridge was the first great bridge built of iron. The use of coke for the smelting of iron was first introduced here and eventually led to the great upsurge of the iron industry. The entire valley is full of interesting buildings. Blist Hill open-air museum. Coalport porcelain factory, now moved to Staffordshire.

Weston Park, an elegant manor house with art and tapestries. Large park designed by "Capability" Brown. Children's playground and aquarium.

WORCESTER (74 000). A bishopric was founded here in 680. The oldest parts of the *cathedral* date from about 1080. Tomb of King John. Prince Arthur's Chantry dates from the 16th cent. Beautiful gardens and buildings around the cathedral. The Commandery was founded as a hospital in 1085 by Bishop Wulston. Splendid hall, headquarters of Charles II in 1651. From the tower he watched as his armies were being defeated by the troops of Cromwell. Later he hid in what is now called King Charles House. Tudor House and Guildhall. *Municipal Museum,* art, archaeology, natural history and regimental history. The famous Royal Worcester porcelain factory was founded in 1751. Open to visitors by appointment. *Dyson Perrin's Museum,* near by, has a fine collection of Worcester porcelain.

Ludlow. Small town with old-world atmosphere in *the Marches,* the frontier country between Wales and England. Several black-and-white houses. Angel Hotel is an old coaching inn. 16th-cent. Feathers Hotel. Reader's House (13th cent.). Municipal museum in Butter Cross (18th cent.). *Broad Street,* one of England's most beautiful streets, leads from the old Ludford Bridge up to Broadgate, the only medieval gateway that remains in the town wall. Ruined castle.

Leominster, once an important wool trading town. Many black-and-white timbered houses. Grange Court dates from 1633. Eye Manor, a lovely 17th-cent. house. Collection of mannequins.

Hereford (47 500). Beautiful market town famous for the reddish- brown cattle bred in the surrounding area. Hereford cider is also famed. The light red sandstone **cathedral** was consecrated in 1070 but the town was a bishopric from 676. A chained library contains the famous *Mappa Mundi,* a map of the world from 1290. *The Old House,* a half-timbered house with beautiful interiors. *Bulmers Railway Centre* with steam engines. Bulmers is the world's largest manufacturer of cider. Cider museum.

Kilpeck with a small, interesting church, built in the middle of the 12th cent. Finely decorated southern doorway. The ornaments on the western doorway are identical to the ones on the cathedral of Santiago de Compostela in Spain.

The Cotswolds, see M 4.

CHELTENHAM SPA (73 000). One of the most beautiful Regency towns in England. Lansdowne Terrace, the Pittville Pump Room, Suffolk Place, Queen's Hotel and the Rotunda–modelled on the Pantheon in Rome–are all of note. Also the Promenade with the Neptune Fountain (1825). The mineral spring was discovered in 1715. Museum with exhibitions of handicrafts. Museum in the house where the composer Gustav Holst was born.

GLOUCESTER (92 000) Roman fortification on the military road crossing the Severn to Wales. Finds in the *Gloucester Museum.* The *cathedral* was begun in 1089. The largest stained-glass window in Britain window commemorates the victory at the battle of Crecy in 1346. Beautiful cloisters.

Chepstow and **Ross-on-Wye,** see M 4.

Stroud. Beautiful Cotswold town, once known for its cloth-making. *Slimbridge Wildfowl Trust* with a large collection of birds in a beautiful park, with bird watching towers and hidden observation points. Flamingoes, swans, geese and ducks. Tropical birds. Westonbirt Arboretum. *Berkeley Castle.*

BRISTOL, BATH, see M 4.

Cheddar. The shops in this pretty little town sell the famous cheese of the area. Stalagmite and stalactite caves in the Cheddar Gorge. Gough's Cave is the largest cave. The skeleton of the Cheddar Man, who lived 10 000 years ago, was found in 1903 and is now in the local museum. Motor car museum. **Wookey Hole.** Large caves with the subterranean River Axe. Hyena Den is thought to have served as a human dwelling 35 000 - 25 000 years B.C. Mill and paper mill, which may be visited. Some rooms contain amusing tableaux of carved figures from different periods. Warehouses belonging to Madame Tussaud's Waxworks Museum in London.

Wells. England's smallest city at the foot of the *Mendip Hills.* 13th-cent. **cathedral** with about 100 statues on the West Front. Medieval clock. The area round the cathedral is well preserved. The Bishop's Palace is surrounded by a moat, where the swans ring a bell to be fed. (The tradition is partially disturbed by tourists.)

Glastonbury. Old town associated with different legends. According to one, Joseph of Arimathea is supposed to have come here in the year A.D. 60 carrying with him the Holy Grail which he is supposed to have buried in Chalice Well. Another legend claims that King Arthur and Queen Guinevere are buried in the cathedral. St. Patrick is said to have been one of the first abbots. The cathedral is now in ruins. In the 12th cent. it was one of England's most important cathedrals. St. Mary's Chapel, the abbey church, and the Abbot's Kitchen have been preserved. Small museum in the lodge house. The cathedral was destroyed in 1538 and the last abbot was beheaded on Glastonbury Tor, a cone-shaped, grass-covered hill. *Somerset Rural Life Museum,* folklore museum in the abbey barn.

Taunton (35 500). Capital of Somerset. Market town. Cider-making. The 12th-cent. castle was built as a fortress – the walls are 4 m thick. *Somerset County Museum* with prehistoric finds from the area and a Roman mosaic. It also includes Somerset Military Museum. **Wellington.** Small market town. A monument to the Duke of Wellington and his victory over Napoleon's armies stands on the *Blackdown Hills.* **Tiverton** with ruined castle and museum. Grammar school, mentioned in "Lorna Doone" by R.D. Blackmore.

Killerton House (Hational Trust). Costume museum. Beautiful park.

EXETER, see A 30.

A 39. Bridgwater - Barnstaple - Falmouth

Running close to the beautiful coast in places, in parts narrow and winding.

Cleeve Abbey was founded in 1198 and several buildings remain on the banks of the River Washford. They have been reconstructed.

Dunster has a beautiful square, *Yarn Market,* with a splendid fountain house dating from the 17th cent. when the village was an important centre of trade. The Luttrell Arms Hotel is a fine building. The Luttrell family lived in the castle, which dominates the village.

Minehead. Seaside resort with long sandy beach. The modern section of the town has wide streets. The older sections contain fishermen's cottages and fishermen's chapel.

The road runs over the **Exmoor National Park,** beautiful valley and heather-covered moors rising to a height of 500 m above sea level. The setting for R.D. Blackmore's novel, "Lorna Doone". Fine views from Porlock Hill. Steep descent to the little village of **Lynmouth.** If you arrive in the evening the first thing you see are the many lights from "The Rising Sun", an inn down on the quayside. Cliff-railway up to **Lynton,** another large tourist resort, perched on the cliff above Lynmouth village. The railway is a real energy saver. The water tanks of the carriage are filled on top of the hill. On the way down the train pulls up the other train, with empty tanks.

Arlington Court, now owned by the National Trust. Miss Rosalie Chichester, the last owner, collected all sorts of things: ships' models, costumes, tin figures, porcelain and horse-drawn carriages.

Barnstaple, beautiful market town in the Taw Valley. 13th-cent. bridge with 16 arches.

Ilfracombe. Tourist resort with a pretty harbour.

Bideford. Small tourist resort. Bridge with 24 arches. Salmon fishing. Bathing at Westward Ho! named after the novel by Charles Kingsley. Kipling has written about it. Clovelly, lovely, historic village with narrow, steep street leading down to the little harbour. No cars allowed. Large car park above the village. Hobby Drive, a 6 km long toll road from Buck's Cross to Clovelly.

Boscastle. Small fishing village with a natural harbour, surrounded by cliffs. **Tintagel.** Tourist resort. Ruins of a castle where King Arthur held court. The castle was built 600 years after King Arthur's time, but the legend thrives. Old Post Office in a 14th-cent. house. Museum of witchcraft and black magic.

Newquay. The largest tourist resort in Cornwall, famous for its good surfing. Once a pirates' haunt. Zoo.

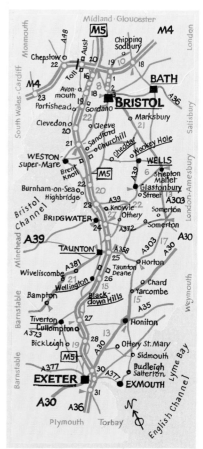

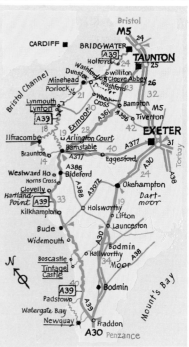

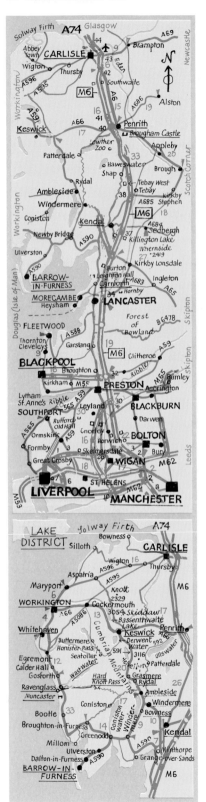

M 6. Carlisle – Preston – Birmingham – Rugby

CARLISLE (71 500). Roman fortress just south of Hadrian's Wall (see A 1). William II (Rufus) had the **castle** built as a stronghold against the Scots and many battles have been fought here between the Scots and the English. Bonnie Prince Charlie proclaimed his father King of Scotland here in 1745. Large parts of the castle and the town wall are well preserved. Regimental museum in Queen Mary's Tower. Museum and art gallery in Tullie House. Mary Queen of Scots was a prisoner here in 1568.

Penrith. Market town. Castle ruins. *Brougham Castle*, partly from the 12th cent. *Dalemain House* (1679). Museum with displays about the border fights. Agricultural museum.

The Lake District, a national park, is one of England's most beautiful areas, 150 km long and 40 km wide including the highest mountains in England and 16 lakes – the largest is *Windermere*. The others include *Ullswater, Bassenthwaite Lake* and *Derwentwater*. The latter is considered the most beautiful. Much of the Lake District is owned by the National Trust. Most of the area is mountainous. *Hard Knott Pass* is difficult to master even for an experienced Alpine motorist – the gradient is 1 in 3, i.e. 33%. *Kirkstone Pass* has one of England's loftiest pubs.

Large tourist resorts in the Lake District are **Keswick,** a stone town, centre for mountain-climbing. Narrow streets, beautiful square. Fitz Park Museum with a model of the Lake District. **Cockermouth,** where the poet of the Lake District, William Wordsworth, was born. His birthplace, Wordsworth House, is now a museum. He lived and worked in **Grasmere,** where his *Dove Cottage* is now a museum. In his later years he lived in **Rydal** where he died in 1850. His house is now a museum. *Dora's Field* is named after his daughter. It is famous for its many daffodils. Grasmere Sports in August (wrestling, etc.). Sheep dog competitions at about the same time.

Windermere has the Lake District National Park Centre. *Steamboat Museum* with unique collection of Victorian and Edwardian steamboats. **Ambleside,** which has a National Trust Information Centre, and **Bowness-on-Windermere.** Boats to **Belle Isle** in the middle of the lake can be hired at the dock near the Old England Hotel.

The coastal road passes the port towns of **Workington** and **Whitehaven** (coal). **Ravenglass.** Fishing port. *Ravenglass and Eskdale Railway* (15 inch gauge, 28 km long) runs through beautiful countryside. Small railway museum. *Muncaster Castle.* Beautiful castle and gardens. Bird Garden with exotic birds and Himalayan bears. Muncaster Mill. **Barrow-in-Furness** (62 000). Industrial town. Beaches. Ruins of Furness Abbey, founded 1123.

The motorway offers beautiful views of the hilly countryside. **Kendal,** market town with the ruins of the castle where Catharine Parr, last of Henry VIII's wives, was born. Art and furniture in Abbott Hall. *Sizergh Castle* with beautiful interiors and gardens. *Leighton Hall* is also interesting. *Steamtown Railway Museum* in **Carnforth.** About 30 steam locomotives, some from Germany and France. The most impressive exhibit is the locomotive that pulled the "Flying Scotsman" between London and Edinburgh.

Lancaster (46 500). The 12th-cent. castle has long been used as a prison. Beautiful church, St Mary's, originally an abbey church from the 11th cent. *City Museum* (local archaeology, history and local regiment).

Morecambe, large seaside resort with a pier and a vast range of holiday attractions. Aquarium and dolphins. *Heysham Head Animal Walk* is especially designed for children. **Leyland** (26 500). Lorry and bus factories.

BLACKPOOL (148 000). The most British of all British seaside resorts, an enormous holiday machine along the 10 km long promenade. Three piers with large amusement arcades. About eight million visitors come to Blackpool every summer. The famous tower, 150 m high, is the symbol of the town. An observation platform, The Space Tower, has been added in recent times. The famous "illuminations", when the promenade is lit up by hundreds of thousands of coloured lamps and figures, take place in September and October. The trams (the last in Britain) are dressed up to look like brightly coloured trains, ships, moon rockets, etc.

PRESTON (144 000). Former port and industrial town. Hoghton Tower and Astley Hall. *Rufford Old Hall*, a medieval half-timbered house with woodcarvings. Folklore museum.

LIVERPOOL and **MANCHESTER,** see town plans.

CHESTER (58 500). An important seaport in the 12th- 14th cent. The mouth of the River *Dee* silted up and the ships went instead to Liverpool. It is possible to walk 3 km along the *Roman walls*. Fine views of the town and its surroundings. The western and southern parts of the walls have been built since the Roman era. Four main streets lead from the town gates into the Cross. Eastgate has a beautiful wrought-iron clock tower (1897). *The Rows*, arcaded shops. There are also shops on the first floor and the "pavements" offer a good view of the bustling street below. A medieval pedestrian precinct which still functions well. The Rows are found along Bridge Street, Watergate and Eastgate Streets. The cathedral was completely remodelled in the 19th cent. Beautiful woodcarvings from the 13th cent. remain. *Heritage Centres. Regimental museum. Grosvenor Museum* (collection of Roman remains).

Jodrell Bank with two large radio telescopes used for research purposes. The Concourse Building with exhibitions about astronomy and space research.

The Peak District, a region of outstanding natural beauty between Manchester and Sheffield. Moorland in the north, valleys in the south. England's first national park. The centre of the area is *Buxton,* spa and tourist resort with the beautiful *Pavilion Gardens.* Opera and concert festival at the end of July and beginning of August.

Congleton with textile mills. *Little Moreton Hall,* a beautiful half-timbered house (1580) with fine woodcarvings and furniture. ***STOKE-ON-TRENT*** (257 000), six towns joined into one. Centre of the Potteries, an area with porcelain and ceramics factories. ***NEWCASTLE- UNDER-LYME*** (73 000). Industrial town. **Barlaston** with the museum of the famous *Wedgwood factory,* founded in 1769. *Trentham Gardens,* large gardens with a lake, children's playground, etc.

Lichfield. Small town with beautiful Tudor houses around the square. The house where Dr Samuel Johnson was born (1709) is now a museum. This original and learned man has become known through the writings of James Boswell, who recorded his thoughts and statements. *Cathedral* with three spires. The West Front has 113 figures. The interior contains many sculptures, from Chantry (1817) to Epstein. *Tamworth Castle Museum.* Exhibits concerning the history of the castle and beautiful interiors. *Drayton Manor Park* has been transformed into a Disneyland-like amusement park with boat trips through the jungle and a Zoo. Cable car above the park.

WOLVERHAMPTON, see M5, **BIRMINGHAM,** see town plans.

COVENTRY (314 000). Centre of the motor car industry. *Museum of British Road Transport.* November 14, 1940, Coventry was the victim of a German air-raid which destroyed large parts of the town and killed 400 of its inhabitants. It was the first great air-raid against a British town. The ruined shell of the old cathedral stands beside the modern cathedral. A cross made of burned beams from the roof on the site of the altar. A text reads: Father forgive. The new *cathedral* (1962) has a simple exterior. The interior is decorated by some of Britain's finest artists and craftsmen, among them Jacob Epstein, whose bronze sculpture depicts St. Michael with the defeated devil. Extremely beautiful colours in the baptismal chapel where the light streams in through 200 windows.
St Mary's Guild Hall, a merchants' house dating from 1360. Remains of a medieval wall and gateways. Half-timbered houses. Statue of *Lady Godiva,* who, according to the legend, rode naked through the town as a protest against her husband's, King Leofric's, oppression. The inhabitants showed their gratitude by staying indoors and not looking on – all except Peeping Tom. The figures can be seen in the carillon at Broadgate.

South of Coventry:

Warwick. Famous medieval castle, still inhabited. Weapons and armoury, art and furniture. Beautiful gardens. The Church of St. Mary with a 12th-cent. crypt. Several half-timbered houses. *Oken's House* with dolls' museum.

Leamington Spa, with Royal Pump Room. Concerts in the beautiful park. Regency buildings. **Kenilworth,** impressive ruins of a castle, founded in 1122.

Stratford-upon-Avon (21 000). Shakespeare's town. Many beautiful half-timbered houses in Church Street, High Street and Wood Street. Statue of Shakespeare. His birthplace in Henley Street is now a *museum.* Hundreds of thousands of tourists come to Stratford every year. *Anne Hathaway's Cottage* in the village of Shottery is a beautiful, thatched, half-timbered house. Shakespeare married Anne in 1582. The large *Royal Shakespeare Theatre* (1932). Theatre museum. Hall's Croft, a doctor's house. John Hall was Shakespeare's son-in-law. Nash's House is also associated with Shakespeare. *Church of the Holy Trinity* with Shakespeare's tomb. *Harvard House,* a half-timbered structure, was the home of the mother of John Harvard, who went on to found Harvard University in the U.S.A. Motor museum and model car museum.

Rugby (60 000), site of the public school where the game of Rugby was introduced in 1823.

Rugby-London, see M 1.

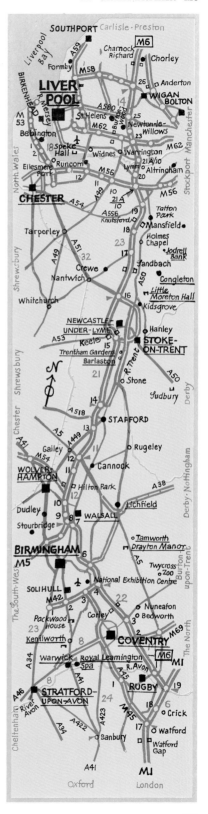

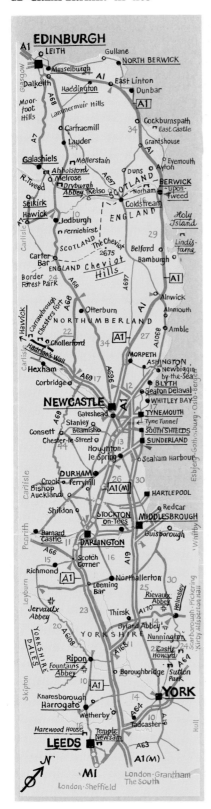

A1. Edinburgh – Newcastle – Grantham – London

EDINBURGH, see town plans

Musselburgh. Old town, now a suburb of Edinburgh. Annual autumn Walks of Thanksgiving ceremony when mussels are collected. **North Berwick.** Seaside resort with extensive sandy beaches and large fishing port. *Bass Rock,* a breeding ground for countless seabirds, rises 100 m from the sea. The world's oldest golf club, the Honourable Company of Edinburgh Golfers, plays on *Muirfield. Dirleton* and *Lennoxlove Castles.* **Haddington.** 15th-cent. abbey church. The Mercat Cross is topped with the figure of a goat. 16th-cent. Mungate Bridge. Haddington is the birthplace of the religious reformer John Knox.

Berwick-upon-Tweed. This old border town, founded in 870, has been the scene of many battles between the English and the Scots. It was conquered 13 times. 3 m thick town wall dating from 1565. The Berwick Bridge, built of pink sandstone in 1634, has 15 arches. The Royal Border Bridge from 1850 was designed by Robert Stephenson. The *River Tweed* has given its name to a famous fabric. Fine salmon fishing.

Coldstream, an old fording place (its name indicates that it was not a particularly pleasant place for wading) with a bridge that was completed in 1766. The toll house was the scene of many marriages in the simple Scottish tradition. The Coldstream Guards is one of the most famous British regiments. *Kelso,* see below.

Holy Island. During low tide it is possible to drive from Beale to the island. The road is closed during the six hours of high tide. Holy Island was the site of *Lindisfarne Priory,* one of the first strongholds of Christianity in Britain. St. Aidan and St. Cuthbert served here during the 7th cent. In 793 it was attacked by Norwegian Vikings, an introduction to the Viking raids on Great Britain. The ruins of the priory remain. Near by the monks produce mead and there is a little 15th-cent. castle that was restored by Lutyens as a private dwelling during the present century.

Alnwick Castle, an impressive border fortification. Museum with Italian-inspired interior. Art by such masters as Titian, Tintoretto, Canaletto and Van Dyck, weapons collection, antiques, porcelain.

Blyth. Industrial town and port. Seaside resort with sandy beaches and dunes that extend all the way to the little fishing port called **Seaton Sluice.** Baroque *Seaton Delaval Hall* (1728) by John Vanbrugh. Furniture, portraits, pottery. Large park.

A 68. Edinburgh – Galashiels – Newcastle

Galashiels. Little town famous for its tweed and wool. The "Braw Lads Gathering", a large war monument. A "Gathering" in the early summer celebrates the granting of the town's charter in 1599. Sir Walter Scott (1771-1832) wrote several novels while living in *Abbotsford House.* Ruins of *Dryburgh Abbey* on the site of an ancient Druid holy place. Remains of an abbey often attacked by English armies. Tombs of Sir Walter Scott, his biographer J.G. Lockhart and First World War Field Marshal Haig. *Melrose Abbey,* twice ravaged by war, was consecrated in 1136. The heart of Robert Bruce is entombed under the High Altar.

Selkirk and **Hawick** are famed for their tweeds. Over 20 knitting mills in the immediate area. The local sheep graze on the slopes of the *Cheviot Hills* which have given their name to a popular tweed. In addition to the wool from native, Scottish sheep, the mills also weave imported wool from Kashmiri goats to create cashmere products. *Bowhill* in Selkirk was the border home of the Scots of Buccleuch for many years.

From Hawick A 7 goes to Carlisle on M 6.

Hadrian's Wall, begun in A.D. 122, took seven years to complete. It was constructed on the orders of Emperor Hadrian and its purpose was to keep the Scots out of Roman Britain. From **Hexham** it is not far to Chesters Fort and Museum, Carrawbrough Fort, Housesteads Fort and Museum and Chesterholm. Large segments of the wall remain. Ruins and museum to the east of **South Shields.** Roman port. Splendid cathedral and ruins of a 7th-cent. church in Hexham.

NEWCASTLE UPON TYNE (192 500). Capital of England's North-East. Centre of the enormous Tyneside industrial area. The New Castle, built in 1080, was replaced by the present structure in 1177. Black Gate (1247) with Roman artifacts. The city' s most famous structure is the *Tyne Bridge.* Impressive Regency buildings in Grey Street. St. Nicholas Cathedral with a tower known as "The Scottish Crown". Antiques museum. Bagpipe museum.

Tynemouth (60 000) has an 11th-cent. priory. An earilier priory on this site was destroyed by Danish Vikings in 865. The 14th-cent. castle was built to defend the priory. Fine views. Seaside resort.

SOUTH SHIELDS (87 000). Industrial town. Seaside resort. Roman Park with museums and ruins of Hadrian's Wall.

SUNDERLAND (196 000). Large industrial town. Shipyards. Seaside resort. Lambton Pleasure Park. Amusements, safari park and zoo.

North of England Open Air Museum at **Beamish** with preserved steam railway. Reconstructed railway station and a replica of the world's first locomotive, built by Stephenson in 1825. Farmhouses, vintage-cars, school rooms, pharmacy, toys, etc.

Durham (26 500). The old town centre is on a little peninsula that extends out into a bend of the River Wear. Seven bridges. The *cathedral* is considered to be one of the most beautiful Romanesque cathedrals in Europe. Construction began in 1093 and large sections of the original building remains. Richly adorned tomb of St. Cuthbert. Tomb of the Venerable Bede (d. 735), England's first chronicler. Famed Sanctuary knocker. *Gulbenkian Oriental Museum* with examples of Far Eastern handicrafts.

DARLINGTON (85 500). The locomotive that hauled the first passenger train from Shildon to *Stockton-on-Tees* in 1825 is on display in the *railway museum* in the old North Road Station (1842). Memorial tablet on a building near Bridge Road Station, Stockton marks the spot where the world's first railway passenger ticket was sold in 1825.

TEES-SIDE is the name of the entire industrial area that stretches from Stockton to the coast.

MIDDLESBROUGH (150 000). Large industrial city. *Captain Cook's Birthplace Museum.*

Scotch Corner. Once famous crossroads.

Barnard Castle. This little town with old buildings is named after its ruined medieval castle. *Bowes Museum.* Impressive art museum with works of great European masters, porcelain, handicrafts, watches, snuff boxes, toys, etc.

Rievaulx Abbey. Beautiful ruins of a Cistercian abbey founded in 1131 by monks from Clairvaux in France. Henry VIII had the abbey closed in 1539. **Nunnington.** Charmingly Victorian Ryedale Lodge Restaurant in a converted railway station. Traditional Black Swan Inn in **Helmsley.** To the south, *Sutton Park,* a national park containing a stately home of the same name. Collections of clocks, enamels, and porcelain. Displays of 16th-19th-cent. farm life in the *Ryedale Folk Museum.* **Hutton-le-Hole** is a delightful little village. *Castle Howard* with splendid garden.

Pickering. Old commercial town with coaching inn. Exhibits concerning local farm life in the Beck Isle Museum. Castle ruins. North Yorks Moors National Park with a preserved steam railway that goes from Pickering to Grosmont through the lovely Newton Dale. Kirby Misperton Hall has become a large recreation area: Flamingo Land, zoo, fun fair, farmhouses, pottery, etc. Model railway.

Scarborough (43 000). A spa as early as the 17th cent., Scarborough is now a large, lively and noisy seaside resort with extensive sandy beaches. Zoo and Marine Land. Fisherman's Craft Centre. Museum of history, museum of art. Rotunda Museum with archaeological finds. *Scarborough Castle.*

Road north to the large resort and fishing port of **Whitby** where Captain Cook lived. A statue of the town's most famous son is on the quay at West Cliff and a room of the local museum is dedicated to him. To the south, Sewerby Hall (18th cent.) with park and zoo. Room dedicated to Amy Johnson, the pioneer aviator.

Jervaulx Abbey. Ruins of a medieval Cistercian abbey. Lovely surroundings.

Ripon. Little town with large square. The Wakeman stands at the obelisk every evening at 9 and sounds the horn. Little museum in the half-timbered Wakeman's House. Cathedral with impressive woodcarvings. Fountains Abbey, the most beautiful ruined abbey in the country. It was founded in 1132 by the Cistercians. Stately vaults and an impressive chapel remain. Studley Royal, a delightful park.

Harrogate (66 500). Large resort and spa with many mineral springs. Lovely parks and gardens. Annual Hallé Music Festival. New conference centre.

LEEDS (448 500). Textile industry and engineering. University and technical college. *Abbey House Museum* housed in a 12th- cent. abbey. Reconstructions of streets of old Leeds. Musical instruments and toys. *Industrial Museum.* Art and handicrafts in the City Art Gallery. Impressive town hall (1859). *City Variety Theatre* famed from the "Good Old Days" television programme. Fish and chips is best eaten under the crystal chandeliers of Harry Ramseden's Restaurant at Guiseley, an establishment that only serves this British national dish.

Harewood House, 8 miles north of Leeds, completed in 1771, was designed by John Carr and Robert Adam. Its park was created by "Capability" Brown. Beautiful interiors, furniture and porcelain. Bird park with exotic species. **Tudor Temple Newsam House,** 5 miles outside Leeds. Furniture, art, silver, etc. Park by "Capability" Brown. Wakefield. Wool industry. Stately cathedral.

Road west to **Bolton Abbey.** The parish church remains from a 12th- cent. abbey. *Skipton* on the Leeds-Liverpool Canal. Many beautiful old houses. *Craven Museum* in the municipal museum and *George Leatt Museum* in an old mill. Folklore and exhibits concerning the lead mines. *Skipton Castle.*

Yorkshire Dales, beautiful moorland scenery. **Haworth,** old village with stone houses and narrow streets. *Museum* in the vicarage which was once the home of the Brontë family. Emily Brontë wrote "Wuthering Heights".

York (100 000). During the Middle Ages this was England's second most important city and, with a total of 40 churches, it was one of the centres of European culture. It was a Roman town from 71 B.C. until A.D. 410. The Danes conquered it in 876 and the Normans put it to the torch in 1069. The four major roads that lead into the town still pass through the four medieval town gates. A stroll along the old *town wall* that encircles York can take as long as two hours. **The Shambles** is the most famous of the many narrow medieval streets that are lined with old shops and venerable inns. The **Minster,** a stately English Gothic cathedral, was under construction from 1220 until 1470. 130 large and beautiful stained-glass windows. The **Castle Museum,** housed in the old women's prison, is devoted to the history of York. Reconstructions of old street scenes with cobbled paving, old shops, and houses. Many interesting period interiors. Weapons, armour, old clothing and toys are on display in the nearby Debtors' Prison. *Yorkshire Museum and Gardens* with displays of Roman finds. Fossils and other geological finds in the guest house of the abbey. Fine botanical garden. The **National Railway Museum** is situated in an old locomotive shed. The Merchant Adventurers' Hall is a splendid medieval guildhall.

Road east to **Hull** (268 500). Port and fishing port founded in the 12th cent. Guildhall. Holy Trinity Church and Wilberforce House. *Ferens Art Museum* has works of old masters and contemporary sculptors. *Town Docks Museum*

A suspension bridge, with the world's longest span, 1 410 m, over the wide mouth of the Humber was completed in 1981. (Tolls.) On the south shore are the fishing ports and towns of **Grimsby** and **Cleethorpes.**

Doncaster (81 500). Industrial town. To the east lies *Burton Constable Hall,* a stately Elizabethan mansion. The park was created by "Capability" Brown. Playground, model railway, boat excursions on the lake, a collection of old agricultural machines and much, much more. Doll collection in the main house.

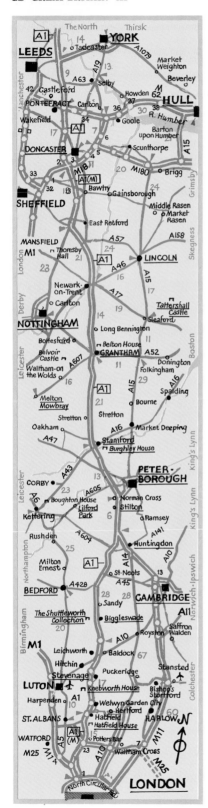

Lincoln (76 500). The Gothic *cathedral* is one of the finest in England. Although most of the structure was built during the 12th cent., there are sections that date from an earlier period. Impressive collection of gold and silver in the treasury. The best preserved of the four existing copies of the Magna Carta and a document signed by William the Conquerer granting permission for the construction of the church are on display in the cathedral. Ruins of the castle that was built on the site of a Roman fortress in 1068.

Lincoln was the final stop on the *Fosse Way*, a Roman army road that started at Axmouth on the English Channel and continued through Bath and Cirencester to Leicester. The Newport Arch, a Roman structure, still spans the road. Medieval High Bridge with half-timbered houses. The Cardinal's Hat, an interesting house on the High Street.

The House of Aaron the Jew (12th cent.) is said to be one of the oldest inhabited dwellings in England. Watches, porcelain and works of art in the *Usher Gallery*.

To the east on the coast is **Skegness,** a large seaside resort with *Nature Land Marine Zoo* and many amusements.

Boston (26 500), during the Middle Ages, was one of the most important ports in Britain. It was the departure port for the "Pilgrim Fathers" in 1620 and they gave its name to Boston in Massachusetts. The construction of the *Church of St. Botolph,* one of Britain's largest provincial churches, was started in 1310 and lasted several centuries. Its 88 m tall tower, "The Boston Stump", is a famous landmark. 15th-cent. Guildhall contains a museum and 18th-cent. Fydell House.

Tattershall, one of England's first brick castles.

NOTTINGHAM, see M 1.

Grantham. King John held court in 1212 in the Angel and Royal Hotel. In 1483 Richard III signed the Duke of Buckingham's death warrant in the same building. The hotel, still in use, has a magnificent dining hall. Beautiful St. Wulfram's Church. Belton House (1685), designed by Sir Christopher Wren, contains an art collection which includes a portrait by Leonardo da Vinci which resembles his Mona Lisa. An underground railway beneath the courtyard links the old kitchen with the dining room. Pleasant promenades, children's playground, horse museum, etc. *Belvoir Castle* has a large art collection and military museum.

Melton Mowbray, famous for meat pies and Stilton cheese. **Stamford.** Little market town with handsome stone buildings. Brewery museum. The George of Stamford is an old coaching inn. Browne's Hospital was founded in the 15th cent. Elizabethan *Burghley House,* England's greatest Elizabethan house, (1587) has splendid interiors and an art collection.

PETERBOROUGH (115 500). The imposing Norman *cathedral* (1118) was erected on the site of a previous church that had been sacked by the Danes. The Hedda Stone, behind the altar, tells of the Abbot, Hedda, who was murdered by Norwegian Vikings in 870. Beautiful Gothic West Front. Longthorpe Tower, a medieval building with interesting wall paintings. Steam and diesel locomotives draw the trains of the *Nene Valley Railway* that runs between Wansford and Orton Mere, Peterborough. *Lilford Park* with beautiful gardens and aviaries containing exotic birds. Flamingoes and childrens' playground. Exhibitions of handicrafts and antiques. The main house is not open to the public.

Stilton. Little village. The famous cheese of the same name was served to coach passengers who stopped at the Bell Inn. Despite its name, the cheese was actually made in Leicestershire.

Huntingdon, where both Oliver Cromwell and Samuel Pepys went to school.

CAMBRIDGE, see A 10.

BEDFORD (74 000). Chief town of Bedfordshire. Beautiful parks along the banks of the River Ouse. *Bunyan Museum. Cecil Higgins Art Gallery.*

Elstow, a village containing a museum in the house called *Moot Hall* where John Bunyan was born. *The Shuttleworth Collection* at Old Wardon Aerodrome with vintage aircraft, cars and bicycles. The collection includes a Blériot aircraft of the same model that was used for the pioneer cross-Channel flight. Several examples of aircraft from both World Wars. A nearby town has the fitting name of Biggleswade.

Stevenage (74 500). Once an Anglo-Saxon village, Stevenage became a "New Town", a satellite town of London, during the 1950s. *Knebworth House,* an impressive mansion that was built in 1492 and completely remodelled in the 19th cent. Magnificent interiors and splendid park. Children's railway. The restaurant is housed in a 16th-cent. barn.

Hatfield House was built in the 17th cent. for Robert Cecil, Earl of Salisbury. The Cecil family still own the enormous house which contains beautiful furniture and woodcarvings.

A 5. Holyhead – Shrewsbury – Cannock

Holyhead. Boats to Ireland. Beautiful views from Holyhead Mountain. On a clear day it is possible to see Ireland, the Isle of Man and Snowdonia.

Llanfairpwllgwyngyllgogerychwyrndrobwllllantysiliogogogoch is the name of a little railway station and village. It means The church of St. Mary in the valley of the hazel groves at the whirl pool and church of St. Tysilio. Llanfair P.G. is the shorter, most commonly used, name of the village. Tourist centre with exhibitions about the unique geography, fauna and flora of the island of *Anglesey.* **Beaumaris.** Tourist resort.

Menai Bridge, built by Telford. *Britannia Tubular Bridge,* the railway bridge, was designed by Robert Stephenson and was completed in 1850 and rebuilt 1970–80. *Museum of Childhood* in the litte town of **Menai Bridge.**

Bangor. 16th-cent. cathedral, built after the earlier structure had been destroyed during the Welsh War of Independence. University. *Penrhyn Castle* (1840), built for the owner of the Penrhyn quarries. Art collection, museum of industrial railways and dolls' museum.

Road north to **Conwy** with town wall and an enormous castle, built 1283–89. *Plas Mawr* contains an art museum.

Llandudno (19 000). Large seaside resort, beautifully situated on the bay between the limestone headlands of *Little Orme and Great Orme.* Rack-and-pinion railway up to Great Orme's Head and cable car line from Happy Valley. Panoramic view from the summit. Remains of Roman copper mines. *Marine Drive* (a toll road) is a beautiful road around the mountain of Great Orme. Dolls' museum and model railway. Folklore and art museum in *Rapallo House.* To the south are the beautiful *Bodnant Gardens.*

Caernarfon, to the south of Bangor, has massive town walls and an enormous castle. Construction was started in 1283 on the order of Edward I. Edward II was born here and was the first heir to the throne to be given the title of Prince of Wales. Excavations of the Roman fortress of Segontium.

Snowdonia. National park round several peaks in the Cambrian Mountains. The park extends all the way out to the coast. An idyllic railway goes from Llanberis up to the top of *Mount Snowdon,* 1 085 m, the highest mountain in Wales and England. Each train consists of one locomotive and one carriage. The speed is 8 kmh and the trip takes one hour. Six sign-posted hiking trails lead up to the summit, where there is a restaurant and a bar. There are many other fine narrow-gauge railways in Wales, the so-called *"Great little trains of Wales".* Festiniog Railway offers fine views. *Railway museum* in **Porthmadog,** a lovely little seaside resort. **Port-meirion** is a unique holiday resort, a romantic Italianate village built to the designs of the architect Clough William-Ellis. Gwyllt Gardens. Large tourist attraction. Fine views. *Harlech* is a beautiful resort town.

Dolgellau. Market town and tourist resort. The narrow-gauge *Talyllyn Railway* with museum at Tywyn.

Betws-y-Coed. "The Chapel in the Forest", beautifully situated with many lovely houses. Forests, hills, valleys and rivers. Sign- posted hiking trail along the *Swallows Falls.* Road A 5 goes on Telford's *Waterloo Bridge* (1815). *Railway museum.*

Llangollen with a beautiful 14th-cent. bridge over the River *Dee. The Eisteddfod,* an international folk music festival, is held here in the second week of July. Folk dancing and choir singing. **Plas Newydd,** a beautiful half-timbered house, home of the eccentric "Ladies of Llangollen". *Chirk Castle,* like many other castles in Wales, was built by Edward I.

Road north to **Wrexham** (40 000). 15th-cent. *church* with a beautiful spire and the tomb of Eilu Yale, the founder of Yale University in the U.S.A.

Oswestry. Lovely market town with many half-timbered houses. Griddle Gate dates from the 17th cent. Iron-Age fortifications.

Welshpool. Market town and agricultural centre. Some narrow streets with half-timbered houses have been preserved. *Powis Castle* (1260) is now owned by the National Trust. Relics of Clive of India. The gardens were designed by "Capability" Brown. *Powysland Museum* is a folklore museum. The *Welshpool and Llanfair Light Railway* was closed down in 1956 but is now a preserved steam railway. *Trelydan Hall.* Beautiful Tudor home.

SHREWSBURY (60 000). Capital of the county of Shropshire. England' s most beautiful Tudor town with narrow streets and half-timbered houses. Sometimes they lean so much that they almost touch across the street. Grope Lane and Butcher's Row are two of the picturesque houses. The Bear Steps is a row of lovely old houses. Castle, originally from the Norman period. Many fine churches. *Clive House* Museum, where Clive of India lived in 1762 when he was Mayor of Shrewsbury. Porcelain, silver, regimental museum. Charles Darwin was born in *The Mount* in 1809. *The Lion,* a famous inn, whose guests have included Charles Darwin, Jenny Lind, the Swedish singer, and the violinist Paganini. *Rowley's Museum* with finds from the Roman town of Wroxeter (8 km southeast). The Roman Forum has been excavated. Museum

WOLVERHAMPTON, see M5, *BIRMINGHAM,* see town plans.

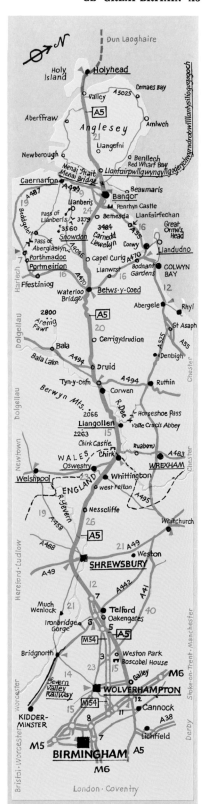

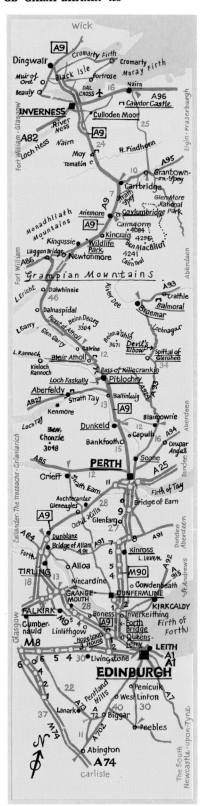

A9. John O'Groats – Edinburgh

John O'Groats – Inverness, see map page 223

John O'Groats near the northernmost tip of Scotland. View out over the stormy *Pentland Firth*, 10 km wide. The place is named after a Dutchman who lived here in the 16th cent.

The Orkney Islands. About 70 islands, 28 of which are inhabited. 17 000 people live here. The highest point, 477 m, is on the island of Hoy. Windy and rainy climate. From the 9th cent. until 1468 the island belonged to Norway (Trondheim bishopric), and up until the 17th cent. Norwegian was spoken here. *Kirkwall* is the chief town. Scapa Flow served as a British naval base in both Worlds Wars. In 1918 the German navy was scuttled here by its own crew. In 1939 a German u-boat managed to get close to the islands and to sink the Royal Oak, a battle-cruiser.

Thurso. Fishing port. Nuclear power plant at *Dounreay. Bettyhill,* small tourist resort. Museum. *Wick,* a town with stone houses. Fishing port. Ruins of Sinclair Castle and Grinigoe Castle, destroyed during 17th- cent. clan wars.

Dunrobin Castle (1275) has fine 19th-cent. interiors. *Dornoch.* Former county town. Now port of Highland region. Beaches and fishing. Tain has a famous golf course overlooking the Dornoch Firth. *Invergordon,* tourist resort.

Inverness (37 500). Chief town of The Highlands. Cromwell had a fort erected here in 1657. It was destroyed when Charles II became king but the clock tower remains. The new castle was built in 1834. Statue of Flora MacDonald who aided Prince Charles after his defeat in 1746. "Stone of the tubs" (Clach-na-Cudainn) near the town hall. It is said that women rested their heavy wash tubs on this stone when they were returning from the *River Ness.* Exhibits of Highland history and crafts in the *Abertariff House* (1593) in Church Street. Museum also in the *Castle Wynd.* Workshops where tartans and tweeds are woven. *Loch Ness* and the Loch Ness Monster, see A 82.

Culloden Moor, where the troops of Bonnie Prince Charlie (Charles Edward Stuart) were soundly defeated by English troops under the command of the Duke of Cumberland. After he had ordered the execution of prisoners and all those seeking to flee, he was known as "The Butcher". 1 200 Scots were killed. Graves of the Clans and Well of the Dead where wounded Highlanders in search of water were cut down. The Duke is said to have led the battle from the Cumberland Stone.

Aviemore. Scotland's enormous winter sports centre with new hotels, shopping centres, chalets, ice skating rink, cinemas and theatre. Hotels also in *Coylumbridge.* Glen More Forest park in the northern part of the Cairngorm Nature Reserve. Large desolate areas suitable for the 100- head herd of reindeer that has become a tourist attraction. The original herd was brought to Scotland in the 1950s by Mikel Utsi, a Swedish Lapp. *Highland Wildlife Park at Kincraig* with examples of local wildlife and animals that once existed in the area.

Blair Atholl. Little village with Blair Castle, still inhabited by the Duke of Atholl. Large sections of the castle are open to the public. Handsome interiors with impressive collections of furniture, weapons, porcelain and toys.

Pitlochry. Large resort famous for tweed and whisky. Annual Theatre in the Hills summer festival and Highland Games in September. A Pict fort existed here 2 000 years ago. The Dunfallandy Stone, a few km S is another reminder of the Picts. *Loch Faskally,* an artifical lake. Long salmon ladder at Pitlochry Dam. Faskally Wayside Centre, on the shores of the loch, a recreation area with children's playground and hiking paths. *Pass of Killiecrankie,* site of a battle in 1689.

Aberfeldy. Resort. The General Wade Bridge spans the River Tay. Castle of the Menzies Clan.

Dunkeld. Little town with ruins of a cathedral.

Scone. Until 843 the capital of the Kingdom of the Picts. When Scotland was united by Kenneth MacAlpine "The Stone of Destiny" was brought to Scone. It became the royal Scottish coronation stone, and as such was used for 400 years. It was eventually taken south and now lies under the coronation throne in Westminster Abbey in London. A special type of bread, "scones" were baked for the Scottish coronation festivities. *Scone Palace,* with origins in the 16th cent., was expanded in 1803. Fine examples of furniture, porcelain and works of art. Beautiful park with stately trees.

Perth (42 000) was capital of Scotland until the 15th cent. (now Tayside). Chief town of Perthshire. You can see splendid examples of the famous Angus bulls at the cattle market. *Balhousie Castle* with museum dedicated to the famed Black Watch Regiment. Art museum. *The Fair Maid's House* was described in Sir Walter Scott's novel, "The Fair Maid of Perth". *St. John's Church* was consecrated in 1243, but the greater part of the structure dates from the 15th cent. In 1559 John Knox, the Scottish religious reformer, preached a sermon in the church that was to be of great importance to the Scottish reformation movement. Splendid views from Kinncull Hill.

Kinross. Old town on the shores of Loch Leven. Boat service to *Loch Leven Castle.* **Dunfermline** (52 000). Ruins of the royal palace where Charles I was born. Tomb of Robert the Bruce in the abbey. He was a Scottish king. Until the new bridge over *the Forth* was opened, motor traffic was forced to take a detour via route A 9 or the ferry at Queensferry. A railway bridge, 1 740 m long, spanning the Forth was inaugurated as early as 1890. It is still an impressive example of engineering.

The A 9 continues via Stirling. **Dunblane.** Little town with 13th-cent. Gothic cathedral **Callander,** a large resort and the usual starting place for tours of *the Trossachs* (see A 82). Many lovely lakes near by.

Stirling (38 000), "Gateway to the Highlands", is an old town that has been the focal point of many battles. The *Auld Brig* (Old Bridge), completed in 1415, is now a pedestrian bridge. The *castle* (14th cent.) looms above the town. It was once a royal residence. Regiment Museum devoted to the Argyll and Sutherland Highlanders. Interesting audio- visual presentation of the history of Stirling in the Landmark Visitor Centre. The Wallace Monument, set on a nearby hill, was erected in memory of Sir William Wallace whose troops defeated the English at the Battle of Stirling Bridge in 1297. Mary Queen of Scots was crowned in the Church of the Holy Rood.

Falkirk (37 000). Industrial town. Steel mills. **Grangemouth,** port town. *Rough Castle,* Roman military site.

Hopetoun House *hear South Queensferry.* Perhaps the greatest work of William Adam, it was completed by his sons Robert and John in 1748. Long, elegant façade. Large collection of art.

EDINBURGH, see town plans.

It is also possible, as an alternative, to drive the coastal route, A96, A98, A92. **Nairn,** fishing port, resort. Fine golf course. *Cawdor Castle* (16th cent.). Handsome interiors. Perhaps this is where Shakespeare's Duncan was murdered. It is certain, however, that Macbeth met the witches in Harmuir Woods.

Elgin. Chief town of Morayshire. Beautiful ruins of the cathedral that was consecrated in 1224. **Banff.** Port and resort. The castle was built in 1750. *Duff House* (1735) is a beautiful example of the work of William Adam. Lovely park. **Fraserburgh.** Fishing port and seaside resort.

Peterhead. Scotland's easternmost town and biggest fishing ports. Base for North Sea oil industry. Excellent facilities for golf and tennis. Interesting rock formations.

ABERDEEN (190 000). Silver-grey granite buildings dominate the city. *The harbour* is filled with fishing trawlers. Large early morning fish market. Centre for North Sea oil. University. Seaside resort. Old Aberdeen, the university quarter, is the site of King's College and St. Machar's Cathedral which was named after one of the disciples of St. Columba of Iona. Town House and restored buildings on the High Street. Mercat Cross (1686) in Castlegate. Folklore museum in the 16th-cent. *Provost Skene's House.* Marischal College with anthropological museum. *James Dun's House* with exhibits of natural history, history and toys, all arranged especially for children. Near by *Crathes Castle* (14th-16th cent.), famed for the spectre of the Green Lady.

Stonehaven. Picturesque fishing port with lovely old houses. **Arbroath.** The abbey, founded in 1178, was the meeting place, 200 years later, for the first Scottish parliament. Large seaside resort famed for its "Arbroath smokies" (smoked haddock).

Glamis Castle was given its present appearance during the 17th cent., but sections of its massive tower date from an earlier period. If we are to believe Shakespeare's "Macbeth", Duncan met his fate in Duncan Hall. Childhood home of Queen Elizabeth and birthplace of Princess Margaret. *Angus Folk Museum* in *Kirk Wydd.*

DUNDEE (175 000). Large industrial city with old city centre. Dundee is famous for marmalade and Dundee cake. New bridge over *the Tay.*

St. Andrews. University town and old port. Ruins of a cathedral and a 13th-cent. castle. Golf has been played here for 500 years, "Home of Golf". Superb and world-famous *golf courses:* Old Course, Eden, Jubilee.

Kirkcaldy. Industrial town, birthplace of the architect Robert Adam and the economist Adam Smith.

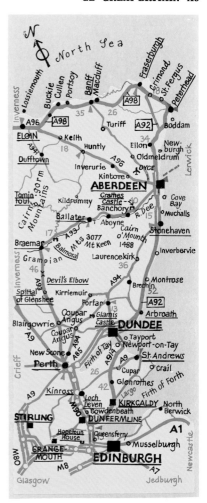

A third alternative to the road between Inverness and Edinburgh goes via Braemar through the wild Grampian Mountains. **Dufftown** in the Glen of Rothes is the centre of a whisky-producing area. Visitors are welcome to tour many local distilleries. The most famous in the area is probably Glenfiddich (Grants). The road continues through a dramatic mountainscape to **Tomintoul,** one of the most lofty villages in Scotland.

Ballater, chief town of "The Royal Deeside", famed for its magnificent scenery, superb salmon fishing and the royal **castle of Balmoral.** Prince Albert bought the castle in 1852 and the royal family usually resides here during August and September. The gardens are open to the public when the royal family is not in residence.

Braemar. Large resort. Highland Gathering with traditional Scottish dances, sports and music (bagpipes) in September. Braemar Castle and ruins of Kindrochit Castle.

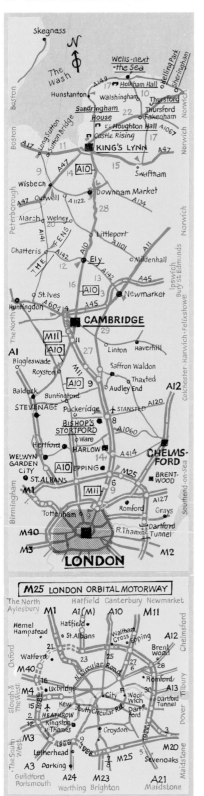

A10. King's Lynn – London

King's Lynn (33 500). The old name of the town was Bishop's Lynn. During the Middle Ages a trading partner with Bergen in Norway and other members of the Hanseatic League. Numerous historic buildings (14th-19th cent.). Merchant Princes' Houses in and around Nelson Street. *Lynn Museum* in Old Market Street. *Museum of Social History* in King Street, porcelain, glass, toys, costumes, etc. The *Wedgwood Glass Factory* is open to visitors. Saturday Market Place and Tuesday Market Place are still in use.

Sandringham House, home of the royal family, was bought by Queen Victoria for the Prince of Wales. Beautiful gardens. The Royal Waiting Room at Wolferton Station is of particular interest to the railway buff. *Houghton Hall* (once the home of Sir Robert Walpole) and *Holkham* Hall with a fine art collection. *Wells-next-the Sea,* seaside resort with a picturesque small harbour.

The Thursford Collection, Kelling Park and the North Norfolk Railway, see A11.

Welney Wildfowl Refuge in the marshland round the River Ouse attracts thousands of swans during the winter months.

The Fens. A flat and fertile area with reed-lined streams. The drainage work was started by the Romans. The extensive flower fields are at their most beautiful in the spring.

Ely. Small town with half-timbered houses. Waterside is a beautiful street. The impressive cathedral with a stained-glass museum was begun in 1083. The central octagon with the timber lantern was built after the original tower collapsed in 1322.

CAMBRIDGE (90 500). University city with many famous and beautiful university buildings. The first college was built in 1284. *King's College* with its beautiful chapel is perhaps the best-known structure. *Queens' College* with the Mathematical Bridge over the River Cam. (The name refers to the design – it is said to have been built without bolts, resting on mathematical principles only.) Christ Church, Trinity College and St. John's College with the Bridge of Sighs, patterned on the bridge in Venice. *The Backs,* beautiful garden along the River Cam. Many small boats on the river. The Church of the Holy Sepulchre (1104) is the oldest of the four round Crusader churches in England. Fine views from Great St. Mary's Church. Fitzwilliam Museum, antiques and art. Cambridge and County Folk Museum. Scott Polar Research Institute. University botanic garden.

Cambridge – London, see A11.

A11. Norwich – London

NORWICH (122 000). A fascinating 1 000-year-old city with a splendid cathedral and 32 medieval churches. Old quarter with half-timbered houses and narrow streets. Elm Hill is the centre of the antiques trade. Pull's Ferry is a beautiful old house near the river. Edward VI Grammar School from 1553. One of its pupils was Lord Nelson, who was born at Burnham Thorpe. *Stranger's Hall* with some parts dating from 1320, a former merchants' house, now a folklore museum. The name refers to the Flemish weavers who were called in during the 16th cent. St. Andrew's Hall is now a banqueting and concert hall. *Bridewell Museum,* merchant's house, jail, now an industrial museum. *The castle* (12th cent.) is now a large museum of art, geology, archaeology, coins, stamps, glass, weapons, etc. Church art (and Russian icons) in the medieval St. Peter Hungate Church. Norwich is known for its mustard and The Mustard Shop is unique in Europe.

Many interesting places north of Norwich. *Norfolk Wildlife Park,* Lenwade is supposed to contain the world's largest collection of European animals. Large collection of pheasants. The *Thursford Collection* with the improbable combination of steam engines and organs, mostly from amusement parks. A Wurlitzer cinema organ with 1 399 pipes. In summer concerts Tuesday afternoons. Gigantic merry-go-round. Steam-driven farm vehicles. Narrow-gauge railway. Children's playground. *Kelling Park* with European and exotic birds. *North Norfolk Railway,* a 5 km long preserved steam railway from **Sheringham.** Sheringham Hall, Regency mansion and park.

Cromer, large seaside resort. *Blickling Hall* with fine interiors and gardens.

Thetford. Old market town, capital of the Saxon kingdom of East Anglia. Remains of a monastery. Museum in the Ancient House. *Thetford Castle. Kilverstone* with a wildlife park. Falabellas, ponies from Argentina. *Bressingham Hall* with large gardens. Live Steam Museum with steam engines and steam locomotives. Miniature railway.

Bury St. Edmunds (29 000). Market town. Abbey, founded in 1020 by King Canute. In 1214 the barons gathered here and swore that they would force King John to seal Magna Carta. The town is named after King Edmund, the last King of the East Angles, who was killed by the Danes in 870. The remains of the abbey include a fine garden. A Norman tower is now the clock tower for St. Mary's Church (15th cent.). Municipal museum in 12th-cent. *Moyses Hall.* The Angel Hotel is mentioned in Dickens' "The Pickwick Papers". Art museum in Market Cross. *Ickworth House,* a circular building with an art collection.

To the south lies the pretty little town of **Lavenham** with beautiful half-timbered bouses. In the 15th cent. a centre of the wool trade. The old Wool Hall is now part of the Swan Hotel. The Angel Hotel has 14th-cent. wall paintings. Guildhall (1529). **Long Melford,** another beautiful town with a fine High Street. The splendid Holy Trinity Church. *Melford Hall* and *Kentwell Hall,* two elegant manor houses.

Bishop's Stortford. Museum in Netteswell House, birthplace of Cecil Rhodes. He founded Rhodesia, present-day Zimbabwe and Zambia. *Harlow* (79 500), one of the new satellite towns around London.

LONDON, see town plans.

A12. Great Yarmouth – London

Great Yarmouth (48 500). Large seaside resort with "Marine Parade" (seaside promenade), and long sandy beaches. Harbour with old merchants' houses. *The Rows,* alleys with small 17th-cent. houses. Museum in the *Old Merchant's House* and in the *Tollhouse. Elizabethan House Museum* with fine interiors, toys and porcelain. *Maritime Museum.* Two piers. Waxworks collection and the Merivale miniature town.

The Norfolk Broads, an area of marshland, lakes and waterways, has become a boating paradise. Rowing boats and motorboats can be hired in many places. The total length of the waterways is 160 km. No locks. The tidal forces are very weak. Rich bird life. Windmills. The Norfolk Broads came into being about 1 000 years ago when the Saxon inhabitants dug up the peat.

Lowestoft. Fishing port and seaside resort. *Somerleyton Hall* (1846), a splendidly adorned building. Garden with nature trail and miniature railway. *Suffolk Wildlife and Country Park.* The Otter Trust near the little town of Bungay is devoted to saving the otter. *Heveningham Hall* with fine 18th-cent. interiors and park. *Framlingham Castle* was a strong fortress in the days of King John. Massive walls. The interior is, for the most part, destroyed. *Easton Farm Park,* agricultural museum with cattle. Transport and maritime museums.

IPSWICH (120 500). Capital of the county of Suffolk. Important seaport and wool trading centre in the Middle Ages. The Ancient House, a decorated plastered house from 1567. *Christchurch Mansion* from 1548 is now a museum. *Old Custom House* from 1840. Museum with archaeological finds. **Felixstowe,** a large port which is also a seaside resort. **East Bergholt,** where John Constable was born in 1776. Along the *River Stour* is the beautiful countryside dotted with small idyllic villages which he loved to paint. The area is known as *"Constable's Country".*

COLCHESTER (82 000). Englands oldest town. Fortified long before the arrival of the Romans in 43 B.C. They called the town Camulodunum. 11 years later the town was conquered by Queen Bodiacea. The oldest parts of Colchester lie within the Roman walls with a westerly gate, Balkerne Gate. The *castle* contains a museum with Roman finds. This was the site of Emperor Claudius' temple. Near by is the Dutch Quarter where Flemish weavers lived. Several museums. *The Minories,* dating from 1776, houses an art museum. Bourne Mill from the 16th cent. Siege House with musket bullets in the walls, a souvenir from the Civil War in 1648. *Clacton-on-Sea,* large seaside resort.

Chelmsford (58 000). Capital of the county of Essex.

SOUTHEND-ON-SEA (156 600). Large seaside resort with a 10 km long beach. The pier is one mile long. **Thorpe Bay, Westcliff** and **Leigh** are seaside resorts, each with its own personal charm, although they now belong to Southend.

LONDON, see town plans.

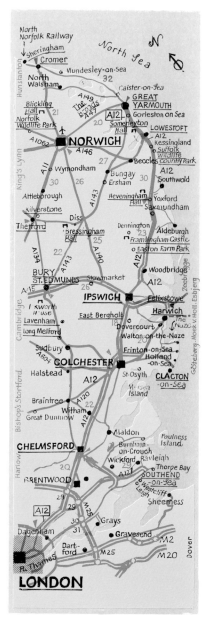

A 27. Pevensey – Brighton – Chichester – Southampton
A 259. Folkestone – Pevensey

Folkestone, see A 20.

Hythe. Seaside resort. Handsome old houses round the 12th-cent. church. Hythe was one of the ancient "Cinque Ports", or five ports, which were established during the reign of Edward the Confessor as a maritime defence for the south coast of England. The original five were Hythe, Dover, Sandwich, Romney and Hastings. Sir Winston Churchill was the Lord Warden of the Cinque Ports from 1941 until 1965. The nearly 40 km long canal that extends to Rye was built as a defence against invasion during the Napoleonic Wars.

Miniature railway at **Romney** runs 13 1/2 miles from Hythe, through Romney to **Dungeness.** Lympne. Castle and fragments of a Roman fort. West of the village is the *Port Lympne Zoo Park and Gardens* with wolves, leopards, tigers, bison, etc.

Rye. Picturesque old town. *Mermaid Street* is one of the many delightful, narrow, cobbled streets. 15th-cent. Mermaid Inn, once a smugglers' haunt. Several charming half-timbered houses. Baddings Tower, a medieval watchtower, was sold to John de Ypres in 1430 and since then it has been called the Ypres Tower.

Hastings (75 000). Seaside resort (with *St. Leonards*). Narrow streets and beautiful Tudor houses. *Hastings Castle* was the first Norman castle to be built on English soil after the Conquest. The famous Battle of Hastings, fought on October 14, 1066, was actually waged at the site of the nearby town of Battle. The defeat of the English forces under the command of King Harold decided the fate of England. *Battle Abbey* was founded on Senlac Hill on the spot where King Harold fell. William the Conqueror was crowned king in Westminster on Christmas Day. *Fishermen's Museum. St Clement's Caves.*

14th-cent. *Bodiam Castle*, moated, is one of the most beautiful and romantic medieval buildings in England. Its interior is almost bare. *Batemans*, Rudyard Kipling's home.

EASTBOURNE (77 500). Large and lively town with all of the amusements that are traditionally offered in a British seaside resort. Golf, tennis, fishing from the pier.

Herstmonceux. Herstmonceux Castle, a fortified and moated mansion, completed in 1440. The Royal Observatory moved to the castle from Greenwich in 1948. *Royal Tunbridge Wells,* see A 20.

Alfriston. Charming old Sussex village. The enormous 14th-cent. church is known as *"The Cathedral of the Downs".* Beautiful old buildings and inns. The Clergy House was built in 1350. Children can play with the domestic animals in Drusilla's Zoo. Playground and miniature railway.

Glyndebourne. The famous annual *opera festival* held on the grounds of a private estate was established in 1934 by John Christie and his wife. They were considered quite eccentric, but the Glyndebourne season attracts some of the world's most famous opera stars and a discerning audience. During the long intervals many members of the audience have picnics on the spacious and beautiful lawns. *Lewes.* Handsome High Street lined with Georgian buildings. 12th-cent. fortress with the "Barbican", a fortification tower. Museum of archaeology in *Barbican House.* Folklore museum in *Anne of Cleves' House.* She retired to this house after her divorce from Henry VIII.

BRIGHTON (146 000). One of the largest and most fashionable seaside resorts in Britain. University. Europe's largest *marina*, mooring more than 2 000 boats. Countless hotels and many facilities for entertainment and amusement. Only Brighton and Blackpool are large enough to accommodate the conferences of the major political parties. Palace Pier, 600 m long, has many places of amusement. West Pier, 385 m long, was damaged by fire and has not re-opened. Large Aquarium and Dolphinarium. Volks Electrical Railway, the first in England (1883), goes past the Peter Pan Fun Fair to Black Rock. *The Lanes,* old streets lined with antique shops and pubs. *The Royal Pavilion,* designed by John Nash for the Prince Regent, George IV, and completed in 1817. One of the most fantastic buildings in Britain, it resembles an Indian palace with Turkish minarets and Russian onion-shaped domes. Chinese-inspired interior. Art museum. *Booth Museum* of Natural History.

HOVE (66 500) has beautiful Regency buildings facing the sea. Seaside resort. Art museum. British Engineerium.

WORTHING (91 500). Large seaside resort with pier and many amusements. *Arundel.* Delightful little town with picturesque old buildings near the steep High Street. The castle was once the residence of Alfred the Great, King Harold, William the Conquerer and Henry I. For the last 500 years it has been the seat of the Dukes of Norfolk. Large and impressive art collection. To the north is a large wildfowl trust.

Bignor. Excavations of a Roman villa with interesting mosaic floor. *Weald* and *Downland Open-Air Museum* with reconstructed historic buildings including farm buildings and workshops.

Chichester. Old Roman town. Remains of the town wall. The cathedral was founded in 1080. Its slender tower collapsed in 1861 but was rebuilt soon after. The ornate 16th-cent. Market Cross is situated at the spot where the four old main streets of the town intersect. Cattle market every Wednesday. Roman antiquities in the Guildhall Museum. Town museum. The Festival Theatre (1962) is the scene of an annual drama festival. Near by large harbour and marina for pleasure craft. *Goodwood House* (1800), seat of the Duke of Richmond, contains impressive collections of art and Sèvres china. Excavations of a Roman palace and museum in *Fishbourne.*

Bognor Regis. Large seaside resort.

PORTSMOUTH and *Southsea* (180 500). England's great naval base with many reminders of its impressive past. *H.M.S. Victory,* Nelson's flagship, is now a museum. The Tudor *Mary Rose* is now being restored. Displays devoted to the Battle of Trafalgar, ships' models and figureheads in the Royal Navy Museum. The castle has been used as a fortress since the Roman era. *Dickens Museum* in the house where the famous author was born in 1812. *Southsea* is a large seaside resort.

South of *Petersfield,* on the A3, is the *Queen Elizabeth Country Park* with marked hiking trails that wind through beautiful, varied landscape. *Butser Ancient Farm* with reconstructions of Stone-Age dwellings and exhibitions which depict farming methods and stock raising.

Isle of Wight (118 000), 381 km². About 36 km long and 20 km wide. Mild climate and beautiful vegetation. The Isle of Wight is one of the largest and most popular tourists areas in Britain. Large seaside resorts and picturesque little villages. Osborne House near *Cowes,* once the residence of Queen Victoria, is now a museum. The Royal Yacht Squadron has its headquarters in Cowes. *Ryde* is a large seaside resort with many amusements. *Sandown* and *Shanklin,* merge to form the largest holiday resort. *Ventnor* has a large botanical garden and a museum devoted to the history of smuggling. Blackgang Chine Theme Park. *Newport* is the chief town on the island.

SOUTHAMPTON (210 000). England's most important port for trans-Atlantic liners until they were displaced by jet aircraft. Although the great age of the passenger ships has long been over, there are still some regular sailings from Southampthon to New York on the Queen Elizabeth II. A monument to the "Pilgrim Fathers", who sailed to America in 1620, is on the West Quay. Another monument in East Park is dedicated to the crew of the Titanic. The Tower of Holy Rood, a church bombed in 1940, has been preserved as a memorial to the men of the merchant navy. *Tudor House,* a historical museum. Town museum in *Bargate,* originally the nothern entrance to the medieval town. The *Maritime Museum,* housed in a 14th-cent. warehouse that was built to contain wool. *Art museum. Spitfire Museum* with interesting aviation exhibits. *Southampton Zoo.*

A 31 and A 35. Southampton – Dorchester – Exeter

SOUTHAMPTON, see A 27. Romsey with convent and church from the 10th cent. King John's hunting lodge from 1230. Broadlands, once the residence of Earl Mountbatten. Exhibitions. *New Forest,* once a royal hunting preserve. About half of the area is open heath. Wild ponies and many species of deer are guarded by "Agisters", mounted foresters wearing green uniforms. Abudant bird life. Several small and pleasant market towns. The *Rufus Stone* marks the place where William II was accidentally killed by an arrow on August 2, 1100.

Beaulieu with the *National Motor Museum.* Over 250 vehicles. Extensive gardens. Monorail to Palace House, a 14th-cent. structure that was originally the gatehouse of a Cistercian abbey. Now it is the residence of Lord Montague who created the motor museum. Down near the water is *Bucklers Hard,* an old shipyard with 18th cent cottages. Maritime museum. Inn in the shipyard's office building, Master Builders' House.

Christchurch. Ruined castle and Norman house. Priory church (12th cent.). Folklore museum in The Red House.

Tucktonia, a miniature town. Over 200 miniature reproductions of famous buildings, railways, roads, canals, Scottish castle, Cornish fishing village, etc. Fun fair.

Bournemouth (145 000). One of the largest seaside resorts in England, Bournemouth became popular in the 19th cent. A favoured retreat for British old age pensioners. Numerous hotels, guest houses and bed and breakfast estabilishments. Several language schools. Long seaside promenade below the cliffs. Pier. The famous Bournemouth Symphony Orchestra performs in the Winter Garden. *The Upper, Central and Lower Gardens* with magnificent displays of flowers among pines trees. *Rothesay Museum* with examples of Italian art, English furniture and porcelain, armour and typewriters. The *Russel-Cotes Art Museum* contains beautiful furniture, an aquarium and a theatrical museum. *Big Four Railway Museum. Compton Acres Garden.* Splendid gardens with marble statues.

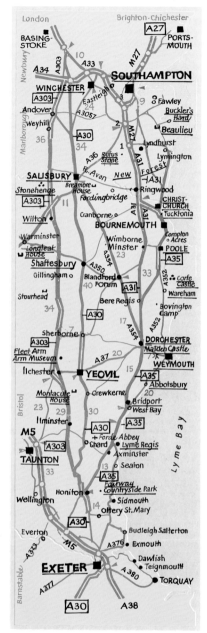

POOLE (119 000). Largest town in Dorset. Handsome buildings centred around the *old port*. Extensive sandy beaches. Poole Park with zoo and fun fair. Boats to a nearby nature reserve of Brownsea Island.

Wareham. Little town with the remains of a Roman town wall. T.E. Lawrence lived in Clouds Hill. Royal Armoured Corps *Tank Museum* in Bovington Camp. Ruins of *Corfe Castle* where Edward II was murdered in 978. Little picturesque square with lovely old houses and a beautiful church.

Dorchester. Little town on the site of the Roman Durnovaria. Remains of the Maumbury Rings, a Roman amphitheatre that accommodated 10 000 spectators. *Dorset County Museum* with exhibits of local history and a section devoted to Thomas Hardy who lived in the town. He was born in nearby Higher Bockhampton and is buried in Westminster Abbey. His heart is in the churchyard at Stinsford. Military Museum. The Old Crown Court is associated with a famous court trial in 1834. The defendants, the "Tolpuddle Martyrs" where forerunners of the trade union movement. Judge Jeffreys stayed in Judge Jeffrey's Lodging during the "Bloody Assize" of 1685. He sentenced 74 rebels to the gallows. *Maiden Castle*, a prehistoric earthwork completed about 2 000 B.C.

Weymouth (41 000). Port and seaside resort.

Portland. Little town built on an island. Famous for its cement and building stones. St Paul's Cathedral in London, as well as the majority of houses in the centre of Dorchester, are built of Portland stone. Naval base. *Portland Castle.*

Abbotsbury, where monks established a "swannery", a breeding place for hundreds of swans, almost 600 years ago. Sub-tropical gardens. **Bridport** is noted for the production of rope and nets. **West Bay**, a little seaside resort. **Lyme Regis** is a little picturesque town with a steep High Street. Impressive cliffs and fine sandy beaches Museum. *Farway Countryside Park* with examples of English domestic animals, children's zoo and nature paths.

EXETER, see A 30

A 30. London – Basingstoke – Exeter – Land's End

A 30 London – Winchester, see M 3.

New Forest and Bournemouth, see A 31.

SALISBURY (35 000). Chief town of Wiltshire. The old town of Old Sarum lies 2 miles to the north and is the site of an Iron-Age fort and the Roman town of Sorbiodunum. The Gothic **cathedral** is unique in England. Work was started on the structure in 1220 and it was completed only 38 years later. As a result of the brief building time, the cathedral has a uniform appearance and style. Richly sculptured west façade and 123 m high spire, the tallest in England. England's oldest clock (1386) strikes the hour but has no hands. Beautiful Close. The library contains one of the four surviving originals of the Magna Carta (1215). Stately tomb of William Longespere in the cathedral. He was one of the witnesses to the signing of the historic document. Town museum. Market on Tuesday and Saturday.

Wilton House (17th cent.) with many sections created by Inigo Jones. Beautiful furniture. Collection of 7 000 model soldiers. Lovely park with a bridge that resembles a Chinese temple. The little town of **Wilton** is famous for its carpets.

Stonehenge. Prehistoric monument. Originally (c. 2 500 B.C.) it consisted of a circular, 2 m high, earthen rampart, 100 m in diameter. At the NE opening a 35 ton monolith, the Heelstone. At a later date 82 blocks of stone, "Bluestones", each weighing at least two tons, were transported to the site from Wales, 250 km away. The temple stone stands in the centre of the ring. Some believe that Stonehenge was a holy place for sun worshippers, others have argued that it was used as an observatory and that the stones are arranged to predict solar and lunar eclipses.

Shaftesbury. Old hill-top town. Steep Gold Hill, lined with venerable houses, is one of the most picturesque streets in England. Folklore museum. *Stourhead House* with one of the most beautiful gardens in England. Temples and grottoes. Abbey ruins and museum.

Longleat House (1580), a stately Elizabethan country house, home of the 6th Marquess of Bath. Magnificent interiors and priceless works of art. Large garden created by "Capability" Brown who designed countless parks and gardens over all England. He was called "Capability" because he always said that a site was "capable of improvement". *Safari Park* with many exotic animals including about 50 lions. It is possible to drive through the Safari Park in your own car or in special safari buses.

Sherborne. 15th-cent. abbey church with sections that were once part of the original church on the site that was completed in 750. Ruins of a fortress built in 1139. Adjoining it is a castle built in 1594 for Sir Walter Raleigh. Garden by "Capability"Brown.

Yeovil (27 000) in an idyllic setting. Surrounded by delightful little villages, orchards and farms. Aircraft industries. Glove- and leather-making centre. **Yeovilton**, site of the *Fleet Air Arms Museum*, with military and civilian aircraft, including a British built prototype of the "Concorde".

Montacute House, a lovely Elizabethan mansion. Impressive art collection and lovely garden.

EXETER (95 500). Chief town of Devon. Old commercial town. Many of the old buildings were destroyed during a bombing raid in 1942. Tucker's Hall, a guildhouse for cloth workers, was completed in 1471. Guildhall from 1330 and many other old and historic buildings. *Cathedral* with two towers (12th-14th cent.). *Rougemont House Museum* with prehistoric and Roman artifacts. Lovely gardens. Displays of handicrafts in the *Royal Albert Memorial Museum*. Maritime Museum with a large collection of boats. *Devonshire Regiment Museum.*

Dartmoor National Park, extensive open countryside with deep valleys and moors. The hills are often topped with weathered granite blocks called "tors". The most impressive of these is *Haytor*. Narrow roads (sometimes exceedingly narrow when they pass between stone walls) lead to small villages and towns distinguished by houses built of stone.

Moretonhampstead has an enormous and distinguished hotel. Ruined castle in **Okehampton. Princetown**, site of the infamous Dartmoor Prison.

Widecombe-in-the-Moor, situated high up in Dartmoor. A stone outside the church has carvings that depict eight skeletons astride a skeletal horse. They represent the figures in a well-known song about Tom Cobley and his friends who lost their way while riding to the Widecombe Fair (an annual event held on the second Tuesday in September). A sunny day on Dartmoor can be soothingly tranquil, but at the same time it may make the traveller uneasy. When the rains and mists come sweeping over the heath it is easy to recall the eerie atmosphere that was the background of Conan Doyle's tale of "The Hound of the Baskervilles".

It is not far from the heath to the coast and **Torbay**, the collective name for the large seaside resorts of Torquay, Paignton and Brixham. **Torquay** is the major resort with numerous hotels and several bathing beaches. Beautiful roads with views out over the sea. When the town was laid out during the 19th cent. it was based on seaside resorts on the French Riviera. *Babbacombe* with a model railway set in a miniature landscape. *Natural history museum* with finds from Kent's Cavern where the bones of prehistoric humans, bears and sabre-toothed tigers, probably dating from the Late Ice Age, have been discovered.

Paignton has a pier, zoo with botanical garden, Festival Hall and lovely gardens on Goodrington Cliff. Trains drawn by steam locomotives from Paignton to Kingswear belong to the private Torbay and Dartmouth Railway. Torbay Aircraft Museum. Oldway House, built for the sewing machine magnate Isaac Singer, was inspired by Versailles and the Paris Opera House. **Brixham**. Picturesque fishing port with houses seemingly clinging to the sides of the cliffs. Steep and winding streets. Statue of William of Orange on the quay. He landed here in 1688 and subsequently became King William III. Maritime museum.

PLYMOUTH (265 000). Historic port and naval base. In 1580 Sir Francis Drake returned to the port after a round-the-world journey. The Pilgrim Fathers sailed from Plymouth in the Mayflower in 1620. Superb views out over the city and the sea from *the Hoe*. Here Drake was playing bowls when he was told of the approach of the Spanish Armada. He finished his game and went off to defeat the invaders. Drake statue. The Citadel was built in the 18th cent. The old *Barbican quarter*, with picturesque harbour and Elizabethan buildings, escaped destruction during the air raids of 1941. *City Museum and Art Gallery* with the works of local artists, particularly Sir Joshua Reynolds. Porcelain and silver. Museum in the Merchant's House. Boat to *Drake's Island*, a fort at the entrance to Plymouth Sound. The Hoe is also the location of the famous Eddystone Lighthouse that was built to the design of John Smeaton in 1759. In 1882 a new lighthouse was constructed and the old lighthouse was dismantled and rebuilt in its present position overlooking Plymouth Sound. *Saltram House*, a handsome 17th-cent. house in a lovely park.

St. Austell. Centre of the Cornish china clay industry.

Truro. Market town. 19th-cent cathedral. Folklore museum, art museum. Delightful houses in Lemon Street and Walsingham Place.

Come-to-Good, little village, once a centre for Quakers. Extremely beautiful *Trelissick Gardens*.

Falmouth. Built on a peninsula, the town is a port and seaside resort. Large marina. The great China Tea clippers including the Cutty Sark, sailed from Falmouth, which was also an important port for the old packet ships. Steep, narrow streets wind up the sides of the cliff. *Pendennis Castle* (1540) which now houses an armour and weapons museum, and *St. Mawes Castle* on the other side of the inlet were both constructed for Henry VIII. **Penjerrick Gardens,** 3 miles southwest. Beautiful sub-tropical flora.

St. Ives. One of the most picturesque seaside resorts in Britain. A labyrinth of delightful stone houses and narrow, twistling streets. Many artists and craftsmen. Fishing port. Sandy beaches and imposing cliffs. At *Lelant*, there is a model village with reproductions of Cornish buildings. Museum devoted to tin mining. Cornwall was famous for its tin as early as the Roman period.

Penzance (19 500). Resort, famous for its early spring flowers. Fishing port with opportunities for shark-fishing excursions. Charming houses in Chapel Street. Sub-tropical flora in the *Morrab Gardens* and *Trengwainton Gardens*. The last on the Isles of Scilly. St. Michael's Mount, originally the site of a Benedictine chapel, is a spectacular castle on a rock and dates from the 14th cent. It closely resembles Mont St. Michel in France. At high tide, the rock is completely surrounded by water. During the 17th cent. it was transformed into a citadel and later it became a private dwelling. Splendid interiors. **Mousehole** and **Newlyn** are picturesque fishing villages. Boat and helicopter service to the **Scilly Islands,** famous for early spring flowers and a mild climate. Here, "there are only two seasons – spring and summer." Tresco Abbey Gardens.

Land's End, the westernmost point of England, a huge beautiful granite promontory that juts out into the Atlantic.

The Channel Islands

The Channel Islands are closer to France than to Britain. Mild climate and lovely scenery have made them popular with tourists.

Jersey has an area of 72 km². Chief town is St. Helier. Gardens and a zoo. Mont Orgeuil Castle contains a museum. A subterranean hospital and a bunker remain from the German occupation of the island during the Second World War.

Guernsey. St. Peter Port is the chief town. Cobble-stone streets and Castle Cornet. **St. Andrews** with the small Chapel of Los Vauxbelets, adorned with china shards and shells. **Alderney** has old fortifications.

Cars are not allowed on the islands of **Sark** and **Herm.** Herm is only 2 400 m long and 800 m wide.

The Isle of Man

The Isle of Man is situated in the Irish Sea, 120 km from the mainland. Area: 360 km².

The chief town, **Douglas,** is the site of the island's parliament, the "House of Keys". The island has its own laws, coins and flag. Horse-drawn trams. 3 km long beach. International motor races in June. Museums with reminders of the kingdom that the vikings founded here 1000 years ago.

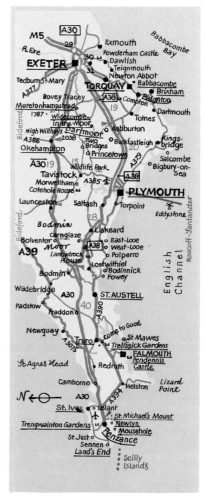

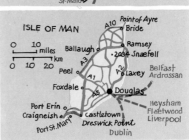

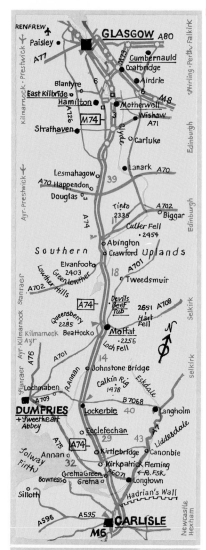

M74 and A74. Glasgow – Carlisle

EDINBURGH and *GLASGOW,* see town plans.
Glasgow is surrounded by several "new towns", attempts at creating independent satellite towns with housing, places of work and culture. *Irvine, Livingston, East Kilbride* and *Cumbernauld* are all "new towns".

Clydebank (51 500), west of Glasgow, has been seriously affected by the ship building crisis. *Greenock* (57 500). Shipyards. Statue of James Watt, inventor of the steam engine, born here in 1736.

Motherwell (30 500) and *Hamilton* (51 500), centre of the former coal mining area. *Blantyre,* birthplace of the explorer David Livingstone (1813-1873). Livingstone Memorial Church.

Moffat, centre of *Annandale.* The Colvin Fountain, crowned by a statue of a ram, is a reminder of the importance of sheep breeding in this area. *Devil's Beef Tub,* a natural amphitheatre among the hills. It was once used as a gathering place for stolen sheep, before they were driven across the border. *Lockerbie,* market town. *Ecclefechan,* birthplace of Thomas Carlyle, the author (1795-1881). Arched House, where he was born, is now a museum.

Gretna Green. Between 1825 and 1885 1 000 marriages were contracted in the Smithy in Gretna Green or in the *Sark Toll Bar House,* the "first house in Scotland". They were English couples who had not got the consent of their parents. In Scotland only a simple declaration before witnesses was needed in order to get married.

Hadrian's Wall, see A 68.
CARLISLE, see M 6.

Alternatively it is possible to drive via Ayr and Stranraer.
Kilmarnock (52 000), where Scotland's national poet, Robert Burns, lived, and, in 1786, published his first poems. *Burns' Museum.* Dick Institute, folklore museum with art, weapons and armoury. The town is also famous for the Johnnie Walker whisky which is produced here. *Dean Castle* with armour, musical instruments and fine gardens.

Ayr (49 500). Large tourist resort with fine beaches and a lovely fishing harbour. Robert Burns was born near Alloway. *Museum* next to Robert Burns' Cottage. Monument. *Museum* also in the former inn, Tam O'Shanter, in the High Street. Memorial procession in June. St. John's Tower and Wallace Tower. Auld Kirk from 1654. The churchyard contains the graves of the "Covenanters", Scottish rebels who were defeated at Bothwell Brig in 1679. The Twa Brigs, the two bridges over the River Ayr. Auld Bridge (now a pedestrian bridge), was built in the 13th cent. and was the only bridge across the river until 1788. International airport at *Prestwick.*

Ardrossan. Boats to the *Isle of Arran,* a Scotland in miniature with wild scenery. The island is 40 km long and 15 km wide.

Culzean Castle, a splendid manor house built in 1780 by Robert Adam for the Kennedy family. Collection of family portraits. Memorial room dedicated to General Eisenhower. Beautiful Country Park. *Galloway Forest Park,* a large, mountainous area. Rivers and lakes teeming with fish. Several beautiful sign-posted hiking trails and small roads. Memorial stones dedicated to Robert the Bruce, who defeated the English in 1307.

Stranraer. Tourist resort with car ferries to Ireland.

Newton Stewart, tourist resort. *Gatehouse-of-Fleet,* associated with Robert Burns and Sir Walter Scott.

Dumfries (32 000). *Burns' House,* where Robert Burns lived from 1791 until his death in 1796. He is buried in St. Michael's Churchyard along with his wife and five sons. The centre of the town is dominated by the 18th-cent buildings of Midsteeple, *Dumfries Museum* and *Old Bridge House Museum.* The medieval bridge has six arches.

A 82. Inverness – Glasgow

Inverness, see A 9. A 835 goes through an impressive mountain landscape to *Ullapool,* tourist resort and fishing port. Car ferry to Stornoway on the *Hebrides.*

Loch Ness is over 200 m deep and never freezes over. Famous home of the Loch Ness Monster. Memorial to John Cobb, the racing driver who died here in an attempt at breaking the world record in 1952. Ruins of *Urquhart Castle,* which was blown up in 1692 by its own defenders.

Fort Augustus, an important and often fought-over stronghold, built by General Wade and named after the Duke of Cumberland, the "Butcher" of Culloden. Now tourist centre. *Great Glen Exhibition,* folklore museum. General George Wade was ordered to pacify the Scots at the beginning of the 18th cent. He made his soldiers build roads on which troops could be moved quickly.

Invergarry. The *Castle* was put to the torch by the Duke of Cumberland, after Bonnie Prince Charlie had stayed here both before and after the Battle at Culloden.

A 87 to *Kyle of Lochalsh* with car ferries to the island of Skye and on to the Outer Hebrides, a fantastic island world. *Skye,* "often mistshrouded ", is a wild landscape with red granite rocks and lakes. *Portree,* the chief town. *Armadale Castle* was built by the MacDonalds in the 19th cent. *Dunvegan Castle* used to belong to the Macleod family. Folklore museums in *Kilmuir* and *Colbost.*

Spean Bridge with a monument dedicated to the Second World War commandoes who were trained here.

Fort William. Large tourist resort at the foot of *Ben Nevis,* the highest mountain on the British Isles (1 343 m). General Monk established a military base here in 1655. In 1690 a stronger fort was built, named after William III. *West Highland Museum* in the High Street with relics of Bonnie Prince Charlie. *Inverlochy Castle.*

A 830 goes west to *Mallaig.* At *Glenfinnan* a monument on the site where Bonnie Prince Charlie started his rebellion in 1745. He had arrived at Lochailort on board a French ship.

A 82 continues through *Glencoe,* "the Pass of Tears", one of the most magnificent of the passes in Scotland. Memorial dedicated to the massacre in 1692 when the Campbell clan, on the order of William III, slaughtered men, women and children of the MacDonald clan. Some escaped but eventually froze to death. *Glencoe and North Lorn Folk Museum.* National Trust Visitor Centre. Winter sports facilities.

From Fort William it is also possible to drive south to *Oban,* large tourist resort with boats and car ferries that leave for Mull and the Hebrides. Fish auctions at Railway Pier. The structure that looks like the Coliseum in Rome, on top of the mountain, is *McCaig's Folly,* erected by a 19th-cent. banker. Local manufacturing of tweed, glass and whisky. Visitors welcome. The Argyllshire Highland Gathering takes place in August. The bagpipes of the Oban Pipe Band can be heard throughout the summer.

Mull is a wild and mountainous island. *Aros Castle,* haunt of the legendary Lords of the Isles. *Isle of Iona.* St. Columba, apostle of the Scots, landed here in 563 and founded a monastery. 11th-cent. St. Oran Chapel. The churchyard is said to contain the graves of many Scottish kings, among them Macbeth and Fingal, as well as four Irish and eight Norwegian kings. The uninhabited island of *Staffa* is the site of *Fingal's Cave,* 68 m deep and 20 m high. The acoustics of the cave magnify the sound of the waves. Mendelssohn was inspired by this setting.

Beautiful road, A85, past *Loch Awe,* one of Scotland's loveliest lakes with the ruins of *Kilchurn Castle* from the 15th cent. *Inveraray* has one of the castles of the Campbell clan in splendid neo-Gothic style. Large collection of weapons and beautiful interiors. Cannon from the Florencia, one of the ships of the Great Armada which sank off the coast of Mull. Bell Tower with ten bells. Festival at the end of July.

Argyll Forest Park with fine sign-posted hiking trails. Botanical garden and Arboretum. from Inveraray road A 83 goes over a pass with the beautiful name of *Rest and Be Thankful* to Tarbet on the A 82.

Arrochar and *Tarbet.* Small tourist resorts. *Loch Lomond,* romantic and beautiful, is the largest lake in Great Britain, about 40 km long and with a maximum width of 8 km. 30 islands. Ruins of *Lennox Castle* on the island of Inchmurrin. Steamer from *Balloch.* Bathing and fine park at *Rossdhu House. Callander,* see A 9.

Cameron House with fine interiors. A collection of whisky bottles in the Whisky Galore Room. Wildlife park with Himalayan bears, brown bears and water fowl.

Road to *The Trossachs,* one of Scotland's largest tourist areas. Boat trips on the narrow *Loch Katrine* which has steep banks.

Dumbarton with shipyards and castle.

GLASGOW, see town plans.

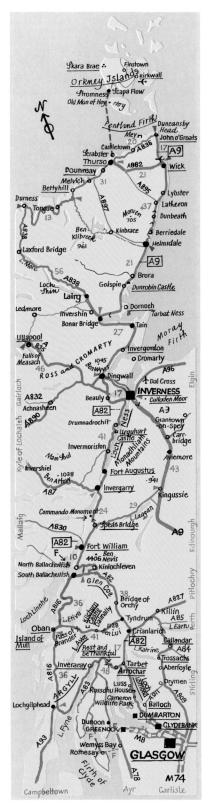

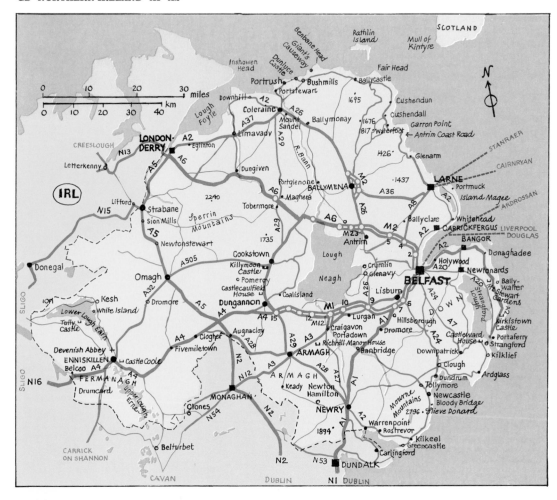

M1. Dungannon – Belfast, see A4.
A1. Belfast – Newry (– Dublin)

BELFAST, see town plans

Dunmurry with "barn"church.

Lisburn, industrial town. Cathedral with impressive spire.

Hillsborough. A nice little town with 18th-cent. houses.

Banbridge. Small market town. Famous linen centre.

Newry. Industrial town and port. *Narrow Water*, a narrow canal, leads to **Carlingford Lough.** Many lovely houses. The town hall has been built over the river. Ruins of an abbey from 1140. St. Patrick's Church (1578) was the first Protestant church to be built in Ireland.

A2. Londonderry – Belfast – Portaferry – Newry

LONDONDERRY (DERRY, 51 500) was founded in 546 by St. Columba. Northern Ireland's second largest city. The old parts of the town are still encircled by the walls that withstood a 105-day English siege 1688-1689. Bishop's Gate, a memorial to the siege in the shape of a triumphal arch. Boom Hall House, built 1770, has been named after the boom that the English placed across the *River Foyle*. St. Columba's Cathedral and a Protestant cathedral, both from the 17th cent. Guildhall. Bushmill's whisky.

Limavady in the *Roe Valley*. Fine mountain views towards the north and south-east. Thackaray's poem, "Peg of Limavady". *Rough Fort*, a prehistoric fortress. *Downhill Castle* with the remains of a bishop's palace. *Mount Sandel*, prehistoric fortification.

Portrush and **Portstewart.** Large seaside resorts with rocks and sandy beaches. Five golf courses. Boats to the Skerries where it is sometimes possible to see seals. *Dunluce Castle*, high on the cliffs, was built about the year 1300. Part of the servants' quarters collapsed into the sea in 1639 and many of the servants perished. *Chimney Point*, a nearby rock formation, looks so much like a castle that the Great Armada fired shots at it.

The Giant's Causeway consists of 400 000 basalt pillars, created when a volcano erupted. The regular, five and six-sided columns are a reddish colour. They stand within an area that is 275 m long and 50 m wide. According to legend it was built by the giant Finn McCoul.

Ballycastle. Market town and tourist resort. Fine beach and golf course. Sea fishing. The 200 m high *Fairhead Cliffs* where Marconi demonstrated wireless telegraphy for the first time. Uul Lammas Fair on the last Monday and Tuesday of August. Boats to *Rathlin Island* with the cave where Robert the Bruce hid after the defeat at Perth in 1306.

Cushendun and **Cushendall.** Small coastal villages with beaches. Starting point of the 40 km long **Antrim Coast Road** to Larne. It is one of the most beautiful coastal roads in Europe and an impressive engineering feat, especially considering that it was built as early as 1830- 1840. The road skirts the sea and is sometimes hewn out of the limestone and basalt cliffs. An old shoreline, 8 m above the present one, has been used. At *Garron Point* Scotland (Mull of Kintyre) comes into view, 30 km away. The **Glens of Antrim,** further inland, is a beautiful area with mountains and valleys.

Whitehead. Seaside resort at the mouth of Belfast Lough. Preserved steam railway, run by the Railway Preservation Society.

Carrickfergus. Old town, once an important port. More important than Belfast up until the 18th cent. The castle dates from 1205. Beach.

A 6 is the direct route from Londonderry to Belfast. It skirts the northern tip of *Lough Neagh,* the largest lake on the British Isles. According to legend the giant Finn McCoul pulled up a large piece from the ground with the intention of throwing it at a rival giant in Scotland. However, he did not throw hard enough. The piece of land became the Isle of Man. The shape is quite similar to Lough Neagh.

Antrim. Tourist resort. One of the best-preserved circular fortresses in Northern Ireland, built in the 10th cent. The walls are more than 1 m thick. Ireland's only steam-driven miniature railway. Pleasure craft harbour here and at Oxford Island on the south coast. To the west of the lake, *Cookstown,* see A 4.

BELFAST, see town plans.

Bangor (35 000). Northern Ireland's largest seaside resort with fine beaches and numerous attractions. Several golf courses. Long seaside promenade. *Mount Stewart* on the narrow Ard Peninsula. Large beautiful gardens. *Kirkistown Castle,* built in 1622.

Portaferry. Picturesque village at the mouth of Strangford Lough where rays weighing up to 80 kgs have been caught. *Portaferry House* from 1790. Marine Biology Station, open to the public.

Strangford. Lovely village, ancient Viking settlement. *Castle Ward House* was built in 1780 for the first Lord of Bangor. The southern part is in the classical style and the northern part in the Gothic style, lasting monuments to the different opinions of Lord and Lady Bangor. Fine 18th-cent. furnishings. Large gardens and forests. **Kilclief,** a 15th-cent. house, built for the Bishop of Down.

Ballynoe. A prehistoric stone circle, about 30 m in diameter. Inner stones laid out in a horse-shoe shape. Burial mound. **Ardglass.** Fishing village, during the Middle Ages an important town with five fortresses. Museum in *Jordan's Castle.*

Dundrum Castle, ruins on a high cliff. The strong 13th-cent. castle has been the object of many battles. It was finally destroyed in 1652 on the order of Cromwell.

Newcastle. Fine seaside resort. Royal Country Down golf course. **Mourne Mountains,** one of Northern Ireland's most beautiful mountain regions. Many hiking trails. Brandy Pad goes from Bloody Bridge to the sea. Here the smugglers transported brandy up to the Rocks, a pub. Beautiful minerals can be found at Diamond Rocks. *Tollymore Forest Park.* Ruins of Tollymore House.

Kilkeel. Main fishing port of N. Ireland.

Warrenpoint. On the border of the Republic of Ireland. **Newry,** see A 1.

A 4. A 28. Belcoo – Clogher – Armagh – Newry

Belcoo. Republic of Ireland border.

Enniskillen. Old town between the Upper and Lower Loughs. 17th-cent. cathedral. *Maguire Castle.* Tourist resort with boat excurions, fishing, beautiful roads. *Devenish Island* with abbey ruins and a well-preserved round tower, associated with St. Molaise. *Castlecoole.* A beautiful house, reconstructed in the 18th cent. after a fire.

Fivemiletown. Small, beautiful village with golf course.

Clogher with St. Macartan's Cathedral, built for Bishop John Stearne in 1745 at his own expense. *Knockmany,* a Bronze-Age tomb.

Omagh, to the north, is the capital of County Tyrone. Tourist resort known for its trout fishing. *Ulster-American Folk Park,* a large new open-air museum with Old and New World settlement reconstructions. Museum of the Royal Inniskilling Fusiliers.

Cookstown. Textile manufacturing town. *Tullaghoge Hill* was the coronation place of the Kings of Ulster. *Killymone Castle,* built by John Nash in 1803.

Dungannon. Market town. Once capital of the kings of Ulster. Linen centre. Ruins of Castlecaulfield House.

Armagh (12 500). Northern Ireland's spiritual centre, according to legend founded by St. Patrick. Seat of two archbishoprics. The Protestant cathedral bears the stamp of a 19th-cent. reconstruction, but stands on the site where St. Patrick founded his first church. The churchyard contains the grave of Brain Buru who repelled the Norwegians in the 11th cent. *Vicar's Hill* with beautiful 18th-cent. houses and library from the same period. Several lovely Georgian houses. Catholic cathedral (1873). Bishop Richard Robinson (Lord Rokeby) was very influential in the 18th cent. He founded the observatory in 1788. Now a large *astronomical centre* with planetarium and telescope. Open to the public. *Armagh Friary* (adjucent to town), ruined church of Franciscan Friary Founded 1264.

Newry, see A1.

TOWN PLANS

BELFAST (359 000)
Capital of Northern Ireland since
1912. Large harbour and shipyards.
The centre of the city is dominated by
several large 18th- and 19th-cent.
buildings. Up until the 18th cent.
Belfast was a small, unimportant
town. Carrickfergus was the major
city. City Hall, the Parliament Buildings at Stormont, and Royal Courts of
Justice. *The Custom House* (1857) is
one of the most beautiful houses in
Belfast. *Ulster Museum and Art Gallery* in the Botanical gardens. Irish
treasures from prehistoric times,
among them gold from the Bronze
Age. Geology, natural history, art,
glass, ceramics and a section devoted
to technology. Queen's University,
founded in 1845. The Grand Opera
House was re-opened 1980. *Ulster Folk
and Transport Museum* 9 km NE.
St. Malachy's Catholic Church (1848)
with a richly adorned interior. St.
Anne's Protestant Cathedral was
begun in 1898 and construction is still
in progress. Thirsty tourists are
recommended a visit to Kelly's Wine
Vaults or the elegant Victorian Crown
Liquor Saloon opposite the Great
Northern Station. Fine views out over
the city from *Cave Hill*. It is possible to
see as far as the Scottish coast. Giant's
Ring in *Lagan Park*, a prehistoric
cemetery, 250 m in diameter.

BIRMINGHAM (920 500).
Britain's second largest city. Two
cathedrals. Industrial centre. The
Town Hall is the home of the famous
symphony orchestra. *City Museum
and Art Gallery* with English art,
ceramics and silver. *Museum of
Science and Industry. Aston Hall,*
splendid 17th-cent. house with
museum. The Bull Ring is a modern
shopping centre. *National Exhibition
Centre,* a gigantic exhibition area
where the Motor Show, which used to
be held at Earl's Court in London, is
now held every two years. *Solihull*
with motor car factories.

EDINBURGH (419 000)
Capital of Scotland.
Princes Street is one of Europe's most
famous streets. The northern side is
lined with hotels, restaurants, clubs
and shops, where Scottish tartans and
plaids as well as Edinburgh's specialities, shortbread and Edinburgh rock
may be bought. On the southern side
of the street are the *Princes Street Gardens* and the low buildings in the
Greek style housing the Royal Institution and the Royal Scottish Academy.
National Gallery with a fine collection
of paintings. In Princes Street stands
the *Walter Scott Monument,* a 60 m
high black tower built over the white
marble statue of Scotland's great poet
and his dog Maida. 287 steps to the top
of the monument. Beyond the gardens
is High Rock, site of the Old Town and
the castle.

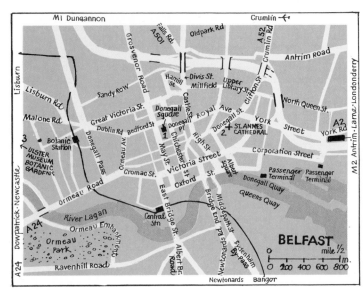

1 Town hall
2 St. Anne's Cathedral
3 University, Ulster museum, Botanical gardens

Edinburgh Castle was originally
built in the 11th cent., but the present
structure is a result of several centuries of additions and reconstructions. Mary Queen of Scots gave birth
to her son, James, in the Royal Apartments. He went on to become James VI
of Scotland and James I of England.
The Great Hall with weapons and armour. Scotland's Royal regalia. The
Esplanade, which leads up to the castle, is the scene of the annual summertime military tattoo, the highlight of
the Edinburgh Festival. The historic

Royal Mile leads from the castle to
Holyrood House, the official residence
of the Queen when she is in Edinburgh. Parts of the palace are open to
the public, among them the room
where Darnly, husband of Mary
Queen of Scots, and his conspirators,
murdered Rizzio, the queen's secretary. Darnley was killed a year later
when a house at the corner of Drum-
mond Street and South Bridge was
blown up. Mary and her new husband,
Bothwell, were suspected of having arranged the deed. Many interesting

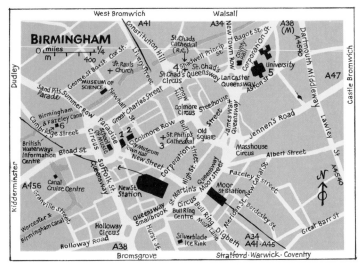

1 Town hall
2 City museum
3 St. Philip's Cathedral
4 St. Chad's Cathedral (Roman
  Catholic)

5 University
6 British Waterways Information
  Centre
7 Canal Cruise Centre

sights along the Royal Mile, among them the *house of John Knox*, the religious reformer, and the large Church of St. Giles, where Knox preached. The Mercat Cross stands outside the church. *Canongate Tolbooth* with a museum containing, among other exhibits, Highland costumes and tartans. *Museum of Childhood* with toys, dolls, books, etc. *St. Giles Cathedral*, mainly from the 14th and 15th cent.

Beautiful views from *Arthur's Seat* and *Carlton Hill*. The copy of the Parthenon, on Carlton Hill, was intended as a national monument. A statue of a dog, Greyfriars' Bobby, who for 14 years sat on his master's grave in the nearby churchyard, stands on George IV Bridge.

GLASGOW (762 500).

Scotland's largest city and the third largest city in Britain. Industries, port, shipyards. The city and its extensive suburbs can seem depressingly overpopulated, smoky and hectic but it is an exceptionally good centre for touring. The beautiful Highlands and the scenic coastal areas are less than two hours away from the city. Over 60 lovely parks provide green areas: *Queen's Park* with football stadium, *Hampden Park*. Nelson Obelisk in the Glasgow Green. University buildings in Kelvingrove Park. Botanical garden. Prince Charles was proclaimed Regent of Scotland at the old Glasgow Cross in 1745.

12th-cent. *cathedral* dedicated to St. Mungo who founded the city in the 6th cent. St. Andrew's Church (1756). Italian Renaissance City Chambers. City Art Gallery (Kelvingrove). The university's *Hunterian Museum* with archaeological, ethnographical and art collections.

Edinburgh Castle is over a thousand years old.

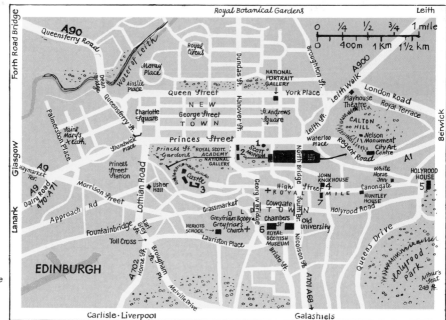

1 Walter Scott Monument
2 Royal Scottish Academy, National Gallery
3 Castle
4 John Knox House
5 Holyrood House
6 Royal Scottish Museum
7 Museum of Childhood

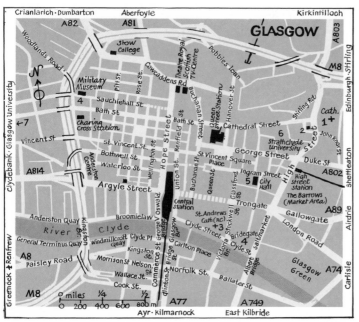

1 St. Mungo's Cathedral
2 Provand's Lordship House
3 St Andrew's Cathedral
4 Merchant's Hall
5 Town hall
6 Strathclyde University
7 Glasgow University, Kelvin Hall
   (exhibition hall)

Saint Mungo, Glasgow's cathedral, was under construction from the 13th to the 15th cent.

LIVERPOOL (510 500)

Second largest port in England with 10 km of docks and 48 km of quays. The compact city centre is dominated by huge office blocks, e.g. the Royal Liver Building (17 floors) and the Cunard Building. The Roman Catholic **Metropolitan Cathedral of Christ the King** was consecrated in 1967. The architect, Frederich Gibberd, has created a "cathedral for the Space Age". Enormous stained-glass and steel tower. The altar is situated in the centre of the circular structure which accommodates a congregation of 2 000. Work on the Anglican *cathedral* at the other end of Hope Street was started in 1904.

St. George's Hall with law courts and a concert hall. *Walker Art Gallery. County Museum* with pottery, silver, musical instruments, primitive art and ancient artifacts. Philharmonic Hall, which accommodates 2 000, is the home of the famous Liverpool Philharmonic Society. Liverpool perhaps received its greatest fame from the Beatles who began their career in The Cavern in Mathew Street. It has since been demolished. The 5 km long Mersey Tunnel connects the city with **Birkenhead**. New tunnel to **Wallasey**. *Speke Hall,* a beautiful, half-timbered 16th-cent. building.

Aintree, site of the Grand National Steeplechase, an annual sporting

event held in March. **St. Helens** (10 500) has *Pilkington's Glass Museum.*

LONDON (6 700 000)

The capital of the United Kingdom of Great Britain and Northern Ireland was founded by the Romans. "If you are tired of London, you are tired of life", said Dr. Johnson and the city does have more variety and more to offer the visitor than almost any other capital in the world. Even if London is no longer the largest city in the world, it is probably the world's most popular tourist attraction. Millions visit it every year. There is an abundance of excellent guidebooks and tourist brochures that can give more detailed information that the following brief summary of some of the most popular places of interest.

Principal streets and sights:
Piccadilly Circus with the statue of Eros is at the very heart of London. Nelson's Column and swarms of pigeons in *Trafalgar Square.* The broad thoroughfare of Whitehall begins beside the Admiralty Arch. The street is lined with administrative Government offices and in its centre is The Cenotaph, a memorial to the men who fell in the First and Second World Wars. The little and far from impressive Downing Street is world famous. The Prime Minister's residence at number 10 is usually guarded by one lone policeman. Near by, the Horse Guards where the colourful changing of the guards (daily) usually attracts hordes of camera-bearing tourists. *"Trooping the Colour",* an impressive military ceremony, takes place on the Queen's official birthday.
Piccadilly Circus is the starting place for Piccadilly, a broad street lined with distinguished hotels and elegant shops, e.g. Fortnum & Mason, where assistants in morning coats help customers choose pricey groceries. The shop also contains a fine tea shop. Interesting clock over the main entrance on Piccadilly. Many specialist shops in the streets south of Piccadilly. St. James Street with Paxton's (cheese), Lobb (bespoke men's shoes), Dunhill (tobacco and pipes), etc. St. James's Palace was a royal residence as late as the 19th cent.
The distinguished area of *Mayfair* is north of Piccadilly. *Burlington Arcade,* lined with luxury shops, begins at Piccadilly. Uniformed "beadles" act as watchmen. *New Bond Street* is one of the most elegant shopping streets in London. Aspreys and Cartier's exclusive shops. Sotheby's with famous auction rooms. Christie's is in King Street. Saville Row, home of several renowned tailoring establishments.

1 Town hall
2 Liver Building
3 Cunard Building
4 St. George's Hall
5 Walker Art Gallery
6 University
7 Philharmonic Hall

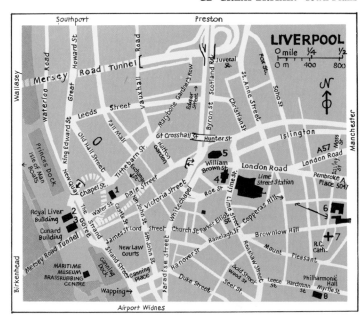

Berkeley Square where the wrought-iron fences are adorned with cone-like receptacles designed to hold torches. In the centre of Mayfair, *Shepherd's Market,* an old market square that seems as if it has been transported from a small town. The largest department store in Europe, Harrod's is not far from Hyde Park Corner. Near by is the charming *Beauchamp Place* with antique shops, luxury boutiques and restaurants. Many hotels in the adjoining area of Kensington. Knightbridge and Kensington High Street are two of London's major shopping streets. *Albert Hall,* an enormous auditorium that seats 8000, famous for its "Proms" concerts. To the south, *Chelsea* with many interesting boutiques in *the King's Road.* Victoria Street, starting from the enormous Victoria Station (trains to the continent) leads back to Parliament Square. The *Bayswater* area, north of Hyde Park, is filled with hotels, many of them centred about Paddington Station. Luxury hotels in the elegant Park Lane that stretches from Hyde Park Corner to Marble Arch. *"Speakers' Corner"* at Marble Arch. Oxford Street, which starts at Marble Arch, is a popular shopping street usually packed with shoppers. Baker Street, to the north, was the home of Sherlock Holmes. Regent Street curves from Oxford Circus to Piccadilly Circus. *Carnaby Street* (pedestrians only) where "Swinging London" was born in the 1960s. Now somewhat less fashionable, but still popular with tourists. The amusement area of *Soho* with shady nightclubs and elegant restaurants, many of which specialize in Indian and Chinese cuisine. Shaftesbury Avenue cuts through London's "theatreland." *Leicester Square* with cinemas and restaurants. Statue of Charles Chaplin. Kiosk where tickets for the same night's theatre performances can be bought at low prices. The Strand runs from Trafalgar Square to the Aldwych and on to *Fleet Street,* the newspaper street. Temple Bar, a monument crowned by a griffin, stands in the middle of the street. It marks the border between the City of Westminster and the City of London, which is a town of its own (5600 inhabitants) around St. Paul's Cathedral with the Bank of England and the Stock Exchange. To the north, the Barbican residential area with a giant conference and arts centre. Further along is Liverpool Street Station and Middlesex Street, known for its Sunday market, *Petticoat Lane.* The Dirty Dick, a pub, is on the corner. To the east lie the endless and depressing suburban areas around

Whitechapel Road and Commercial Road
Further north, Marylebone Road, Euston Road, modern Euston Station and the Victorian King's Cross and St. Pancras Stations.
The *Victoria Embankment* runs along the Thames and has Cleopatra's Needle, an obelisk.
Tower Bridge is the most famous of the bridges over the Thames. The first *London Bridge* was destroyed by the Danes in 805. The second burned in 1136. A stone bridge, the structure known from "London Bridge is falling down", was built in 1174 and until 1749 it was London's only bridge across the Thames. It was lined with shops and houses. A new London Bridge was completed in 1831. In 1973 it was dismantled and reconstructed in Lake Havasu City in Arizona, U.S.A. The present bridge across the Thames was opened in the same year. To the south of the Thames are grey and mostly less interesting parts of the city, seldom visited by tourists. Elephant & Castle, with its shopping centre, is the centre of the area. Waterloo Station is London's largest railway station. The *National Theatre* (the Old Vic) is near by. *Royal Festival Hall* (1951) with places for 3000 spectators. *National Film Theatre.* The charming 16th-cent. George Inn.
Museums and other sights:
British Museum with the Rosetta Stone, the gold finds from Sutton Hoo, a copy of the Magna Carta, the Elgin Marbles from Athens and Egyptian mummies. **Buckingham Palace.** The changing of the guards, usually at 11.30. Large crowds, get there early. The Queen's Gallery with the Royal Collections of art, etc. Royal Mews with carriages and horses.
Covent Garden. London's famous opera house. The flower and vegetable

market was moved to Nine Elms in 1974 and the old market buildings were transformed into shops, restaurants and bars. Site of the **London Transport Museum.** Tours in open, double-decker buses. **Houses of Parliament,** built in the 19th cent. Dominated by Big Ben, the clock tower.
Madame Tussaud's, waxworks museum, opened in 1835. The battle of Trafalgar and the Battle of London with sound and lighting effects. Chamber of Horrors, **Planetarium.**
National Gallery. Large collections of European art. Art also in the Tate Gallery. Wallace Collection and Courtauld Institute Galleries.
St. Paul's Cathedral (17th cent.), designed by Sir Christopher Wren. The crypt with the tombs of Lord Nelson and the Duke of Wellington. Whispering Gallery, Stone Gallery and Golden Gallery.
The Museum of London was opened in 1976 in the modern Barbican complex. It depicts the fire of London in 1666 when the City of London was almost laid waste. *Imperial War Museum* with exhibits related to the two World Wars. *Maritime Trust's Museum* in St. Katherine's Dock has a fine collection of ships, i.e. "Discovery", the ship of Scott, explorer of the Antarctic.
The Tower of London. The central White Tower was built for William the Conqueror in the 11th cent. The large fortress has grown up around it. It is guarded by the picturesque Beefeaters and by the ravens which have their home in the former execution grounds. Armour, dungeons and the Crown Jewels are brought in through the Traitor's Gate.
Victoria and Albert Museum contains an extraordinary collection of objects of artistic or curiosity value.

The Tower of London has been used as a palace, a treasury and a prison.

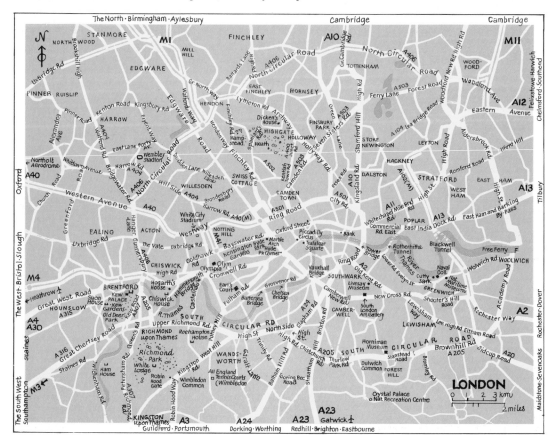

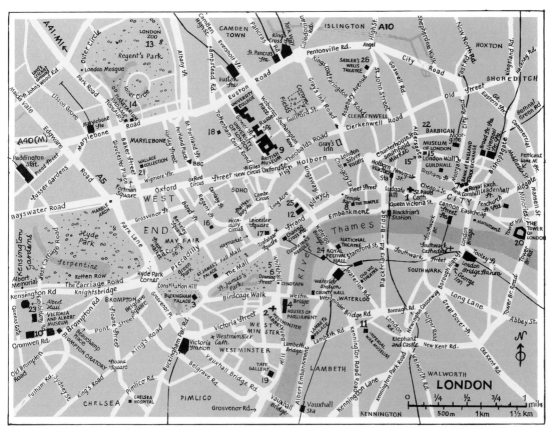

1 St. Paul's Cathedral
2 Westminster Abbey
3 Buckingham Palace
4 Houses of Parlament
5 Horse Guards
6 Downing Street
7 Bank of England. Stock Exchange.
   Royal Exchange
8 The Temple
9 British Museum

10 British Museum (Natural History). Science Museum, Victoria and
   Albert Museum
11 Imperial War Museum
12 London Transport Museum
13 London Zoo
14 Madame Tussaud's. Planetarium
15 Museum of London
16 Museum of Mankind
17 National Gallery

18 Pollock's Toy Museum
19 Tate Gallery
20 Tower of London. Tower Bridge
21 Wallace Collection
22 Barbican Centre
23 Royal Albert Hall
24 Royal Festival Hall
25 Covent Garden Opera House
26 Sadler's Wells

The Geological Museum is near by. **Westminster Abbey.** Coronation and burial church of nearly all of the monarchs since 1066. The coronation throne with the Stone of Scone, which used to be the coronation stone of Scotland. Henry VII's Chapel was added in the 16th cent. Poet's Corner with memorial tablets dedicated to authors and poets. Tomb of the Unknown Soldier. Memorial stone to Winston Churchill. Other museums are: *Geological Museum, National Army Museum, Science Museum* and *Tate Gallery* (art).
Street markets: Portobello Road Market, New Caledonian Market, Bermondsey Square, Petticoat Lane Market. Other (more expensive) places are the Chelsea Antique Market, the Design Centre and London's Silver Vaults.
Parks: Hyde Park, London's largest park, with the Serpentine Lake, and the statue of Peter Pan. *Kensington*

Gardens with the Albert Memorial (the book he is reading is the exhibition catalogue from 1851). *Kensington Palace,* where Queen Victoria and Queen Mary were born (open to public). *St. James's Park,* small but beautiful. Lake with pelicans. *Green Park* with straight paths. *Regent's Park* with London's large zoo. *Hampstead Heath* (north of Central London) with enormous grass expanses and views. *Keat's House* and *Kenwood Iveagh Bequest.* Spaniard's Inn and the Old Bull and Bush. Hampstead is an elegant residential area with beautiful houses and a long High Street.
Greenwich. The famous Old Royal Observatory (designed by Sir Christopher Wren) is now a museum. The observatory has been moved to Herstmonceux near Hastings. The world standard time, GMT = Greenwich mean time, is indicated by the meridian which runs through Green-

wich (a couple of metres north of the door to the observatory). The *National Maritime Museum* is housed in Queen's House, designed by Inigo Jones. *Royal Naval College* with a beautiful hall.
Cutty Sark, a famous clipper, is now in a dry dock. She was once one of the fastest sailing ships in the world. She won the "Great Tea Race" in 99 days, with a speed of 17 knots. *Gipsy Moth IV,* used by Sir Francis Chichester when he sailed around the world (1966 – 1967).
Richmond, Kew Gardens and *Hampton Court,* see M 3. **Windsor Castle,** which is the largest inhabited castle in the world and the homes of British kings and queens for nearly 900 years. Founded in the 11th cent. by William the Conquerer. The ramparts were added in the 13th cent. and the castle underwent many changes and additions until it achieved its present

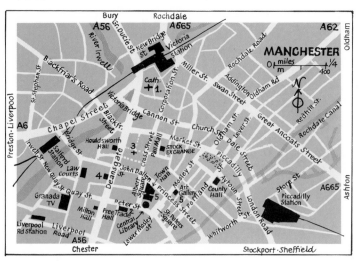

1 Cathedral
2 Free Trade Halls

3 St. Ann's Church
4 John Ryland Library

5 Town hall
6 Opera house

Canal (1893) links the city with Liverpool. It developed into a large city at the beginning of the Industrial Revolution (early 19th cent.). Manchester Liberalism was born in the local Chamber of Commerce. Manchester Guardian, one of England's foremost papers, was founded in 1821. *John Ryland University Library,* one of the most valuable in the world. Royal College of Music. *City Art Gallery* with large collection of art. Porcelain, glass, silver. Whitworth Art Gallery belongs to the university. English and French art, textile collection. 15th-cent. cathedral. Wythenshawe Hall, a 15th-cent. half-timbered house. Zoo.

OXFORD (98 500)
A Saxon town grew up where the ox carts crossed the River Thames and was named Oxenford. As early as the 13th cent. several colleges had been built, among them University College (1249) and Merton College (1264). Magdalen College was founded in 1458. The summer is greeted with singing from its tower on the first of May. Christ Church College with Great Tom, the big bell which tolls 101 times every evening at five minutes past nine. *Ashmolean Museum* of art and archaeology was founded in 1687 and is England's oldest museum. *Bodleian Library* is one of the world's largest (more than three million volumes). The circular *Radcliffe Camera* (1748) now serves as a reading hall. *Sheldonian Theatre* (1669), designed by Sir Christopher Wren. *Blenheim Palace,* to the north at Woodstock, was designed by Sir John Vanbrugh for the Duke of Marlborough. Sir Winston Churchill (1874-1965) was born here. His simple grave is in the churchyard of nearby *Bladon.*

appearance in the 19th cent. Enormous collections of art, furniture, porcelain. St. George's Chapel (16th cent.) with beautiful vaults and the banners of the Knights of the Garter. Charles I, Henry VIII and eight other kings are buried here, as is Henry VIII's wife Anne Seymour. Queen Mary's Doll's House, which she was given in 1924. It is built to the scale of 1:20 (an inch to a foot). In Home Park stands *Frogmore House* and *Mausoleum,* last resting place of Queen Victoria and her Consort, Prince Albert.
Windsor Great Park is a huge area of gardens, meadows, and woods. The Long Walk is 5 km long. The town of *Windsor* has fine old streets with 17th- and 18th-cent. houses. *Nell*

Gwynne's House in St. Alban's Street. She was the mistress of Charles II. *Guildhall* (1689) with town museum. *Household Cavalry Museum,* a museum dedicated to the Royal Life Guards.
Fine walks along the *River Thames.* *Eton College,* on the opposite banks of the river, was founded by Henry VI in 1440. England's most famous public school nurtures its traditions. The school boys still wear their black jackets or their morning coats with striped trousers.

MANCHESTER (449 000, Greater Manchester 3 million)
Port centre for the cotton industry. Coal. The 57 km long Manchester Ship

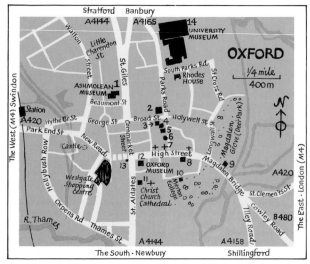

1 Ashmolean Museum. 2 New Bodleighan Library. 3 Museum of the History of Science. 4 Sheldonian Theatre. 5 Bodleighan Library. 6 Radcliffe Camera. 7 St. Mary's Church. 8 University College. 9 Magdalen College. 10 Merton College. 11 Christ Church College. 12 Oxford Museum. 13 Carfax Tower. 14 University Museum. Photo: The Bridge of Sighs in Oxford

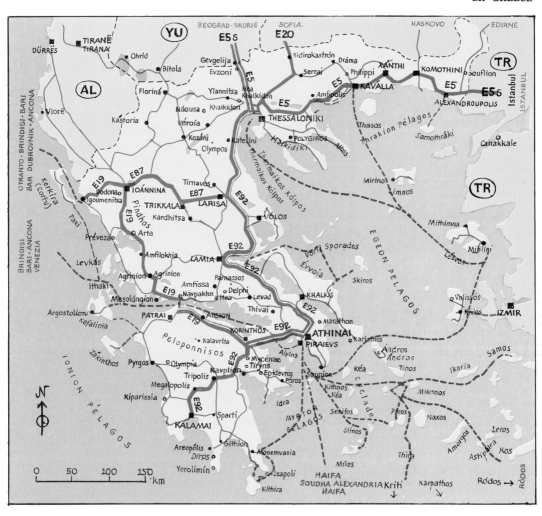

GR · Greece

GR·Hellas

Area: 132 000 km² (50 960 sq. miles)

Population: 9.5 million. 1.4 million live on the islands. 160 inhabited islands, 1 000 uninhabited.

Major cities: Athinai (Athens) including Piraeus 3 million, Thessaloniki (Salonica) 800 000, Patrai (Patras) 140 000. Rhodes has 70 000 inhabitants, Crete 456 000, Corfu 130 000. The national language is Modern Greek. The written language resembles Ancient Greek. 96 % of the population belong to the Greek Orthodox Church, which is headed by the Archbishop, who resides in Athens. The remaining 4 % are Roman Catholics, Moslems and Jews.

Government: Parliamentary republic.

History

1500-500 B.C. Prehistoric period until Athens emerges as a political power.

500-146 B.C. Numerous wars against Persia.
431-403 B.C. Peloponnesian War. With Persian assistance, Sparta defeats Athens.
336-323 B.C. Alexander the Great of Macedonia ruthlessly suppresses a Greek uprising in Thebes and defeats Persia.
194 B.C.-330 A.D. Period of Roman domination.
549-1453 The Byzantine era.
1456-1831 Greece under Turkish rule.
1831 Greece achieves independence. Until the First World War, it is involved in continuous Balkan wars, and wars against Turkey.
1914-1918 First World War. Greece on the side of the Allies (United Kingdom, France, Russia, etc.)

Routes described:

E 5S   Skopje – Thessaloníki – Alexandroúpolis

E 19   Igoumenitsa – Pátrai – Kórinthos

E 20   Sofia – Thessaloníki

E 87   Ioánnina – Lárisa

E 92   Thessaloniki – Lárisa – Athínai – Kórinthos – Kalámai
         Thessaloníki – Kozáni – Ioannina

Special maps: Kriti, Rhodos

Town plans: Athinai Thessaloniki

1924 The monarchy is abolished, but is re-established in 1935.
1941 The Germans occupy Greece during the Second World War. Armed resistance against Germans and Bulgarians.
1944 Liberation of Greece. Civil war breaks out. The Communists are defeated.
1967 The Colonels "junta" takes power. King Constantine goes into exile.
1974 Junta overthrown. Return to parliamentary democracy.

Currency: Drachmai
1 drachma = 100 lepta

Business hours: Banks 8.00 a.m.-1.00 p.m. Closed Saturdays. Post offices 8.00 a.m.-2.00 p.m. and 5.00 p.m.-7.30 p.m. Saturdays 8.00 a.m.-2.00 p.m. Shops 8.30 a.m.-1.00 p.m. and 5.00 p.m.-8 p.m. In some areas shops are only open half day on some days of the week, but the days and hours vary from place to place. Foodshops are open on Saturdays.

Holidays: New Year's Day, January 6 (Epiphany), March 25 (Greek Revolution Memorial Day), Good Friday, Easter Sunday, Easter Monday, May 1, Whitsun Monday, August 15 (Assumption Day), October 28 (Oxi Day), December 25 and 26.

Hotels
There are four hotel classes: deluxe, I, II and III. The government has built several "Xenia" hotels and motels. These are either operated by the state or by private companies under state supervision. They maintain high standards and charge reasonable prices.

Camping
There are 90 camping sites operated by the National Tourist Organization of Greece (NTOG), the auto clubs and a few private owners. In general, campers in possession of the AIT camping carnet are given a 10 % discount.

Food and drink
Fassolada, bean soup. Kalamarakia, deep-fried squid. Barbounia, marides, fish. Dolmádes, mince wrapped in vine leaves. Keftedes, meatballs with garlic and mint. Moussaka, mince

The amphitheatre at Epidhavros on the Peloponnesus

with aubergine and potatoes in layers topped with bechamel sauce. Souvlaki, pieces of meat grilled on a skewer. Styphado, hare or rabbit stew. Salata koriatiki ("Greek salad"), mixed salad with cheese made from sheep's milk. Feta, white cheese made of goat's milk. Shish kebab, meat grilled on a skewer. Ntolmas, mince wrapped in vine leaves with rice, onion and egg sauce.
Ouzo, anise-flavoured spirit. Metaxa, brandy.
White wines: Demestica, Kamba, Santa Elena, Santa Laura.
Red wines: Demestica, Chevalier Rhodes, Boutari.
Dessert wines: Samos, Mavrodaphni.
Beer: Fix, Alpha, Mamo.

Shopping
Traditional handicrafts, handwoven textiles, blouses, ceramics, earthenware, silver and copper articles, furs, leather goods.

Speed limits. Traffic regulations.
Motorways 100 kmh, other roads 80 kmh, built-up areas 50 kmh. No special speed limits for cars towing

caravans. The speed limits for motorcycles are 70 and 40 kmh.
Children under the age of 10 are not allowed to travel in the front seat.
The police are authorized to impose on-the-spot-fines. The fine is paid at a local government office. Ask for a receipt!
The police in Athens are empowered to confiscate and retain number plates from illegally parked cars. When you have paid the fine you will receive the plates in return. Remember: it is illegal to drive a vehicle without number plates.

Roads
Some stretches of the motorways are toll roads. Fees:
Athens – Corinth 30 Dr, Athens – Lamía 40 Dr, Corinth – Patras 35 Dr, Lamía – Lárisa 30 Dr, Lárisa – Kateríni 40 Dr. Motorists with cars towing caravans or trailers must pay double the above prices. By the time you read this, prices almost certainly will have increased.
Major roads are posted with signs written in the Latin as well as the Greek alphabet. In small communities and even in Athens it is a good idea to have a map with place names in both alphabets.

Road patrols
The Automobile and Touring Club of Greece (ELPA) has yellow patrol cars that bear signs reading "Assistance Routière, ELPA". Major roads are patrolled from 7 a.m. until 10 p.m. For assistance, telephone 104. Major roads are equipped with emergency telephones. In Athens, Piraeus, Patras and Salonica, the police telephone number is 100.

ELPA (Automobile and Touring Club of Greece), 2-4 Messogion, Athens 610. Tel 77 91 61 5.
National Tourist Organisation of Greece, 195/197 Regent Street, London W1R 8DL. Tel. 01-734 5997.

Fortress at Návplion

E 5 S. Skopje – Thessaloníki – Alexandroupolis

Evzoni. Yugoslavian border. E 5 comes from London – Bruxelles – Frankfurt – Wien – Budapest – Beograd – Gevgelija. Beograd – Gevgelija.

Pélla. Birthplace of Alexander the Great. Capital of Macedonia 5th-2nd cent. B.C. The ancient city was rediscovered in the 1950s. Ruins of buildings and streets give an idea of the city's enormous size. Mosaics. Museum with mosaics and architectural fragments. Some of the finds have been moved to Salonica.

East of Salonica is the *Halkidikí Peninsula* with three promontories: *Kassandra, Sithonia* and *Athos. Athos* is a semi-autonomous theocratic republic, inhabited by monks. 20 monasteries, including Vatopediou, Lavras and Khiliandarion (10th-12th cent.) A ruling dating from 1060 – still strictly adhered to – bans all women and female animals from the Holy Mountain of Athos. Men over 21 years of age can get permission to visit the monasteries – this is granted either in Salonica or in Athens if the traveller has a letter of introduction from his consulate or embassy.

The route out onto the peninsula passes the site where Xerxes, the Persian king, had a canal built.

Ólynthos. Demosthenes' town. Excavations. Rentina, narrow gorge. Near by are the remains of the school of Aristotle where Alexander the Great studied.

Amfipolis. Ruins of an ancient city: temples, tombs and the Lion of Amfipolis.

Dráma. Ruins of the ramparts and a beautiful little Byzantine church.

Philippi was founded by Philip of Macedonia in the 4th cent. B.C. There was gold here then. Famous battle in 42 B.C. when troops of Octavian and Mark Antony defeated the forces of Brutus and Cassius, two of the murderers of Julius Caesar. The apostle Paul founded the first Christian congregation in Europe and christened St. Lydia. The Direkler Basilica (direkler = pillar, in Turkish) was never completed. Several other 5th- and 6th-cent. basilicas. Remains of a Roman square and a magnificent Roman privy with 50 places. Forum and remains of several 2nd-cent. buildings.

Kaválla (50 000). Ancient town with remains of temples, often hidden under newer buildings. St. Paul preached here. Turks occupied the town until 1913. Byzantine fortress. Museum of archaeology. The "Roman aqueduct" was built in the 16th cent. The island of *Thassos* has fine sandy beaches. Foundations of an ancient town that existed when marble was quarried here. Little museum near the harbour.

Alexandroúpolis (22 000). Modern town, founded in 1860. Large port. Ship service to the island of *Samothráki* with remains of an ancient city. Temple of Aphrodite and theatre. In 1836, the "Nike of Samothrace", a famous statue of the winged Goddess of Victory, was discovered here. It is now in the Louvre in Paris. Beautiful views from Fengari, 1 586 m.

Kipi. Turkish frontier. E 5 continues to Istanbul – Ankara – Antakya.

E 20. Sofia – Thessaloníki

Kulata. Bulgarian frontier. E 20 comes from Cernovcy – Bucureşti – Sofia.

Serrai (Sérres). Ruins of a castle that played an important role in the defence of this part of the Byzantine Empire against the Bulgarians. In Turkish possession 1368-1913.

THESSALONÍKI, see town plans.

E 19. Igoumenitsa – Patrai – Kórinthos

Igoumenitsa. Beautifully situated port. Car ferries from Italy and Corfu.

Corfu (Kérkira) is a popular goal for tourists – sandy beaches, mild climate and lush vegetation with olive and cypress trees. Traditionally Corfu has had close contact with western Europe, and this relationship has effected its atmosphere and architecture. The island did not become Greek until 1864. The harbour is dominated by the Venetian fortress. *Achilléion Palace,* in the Italian Renaissance style, was built for Empress Elizabeth of Austria. It was later bought by Kaiser Wilhelm II of Germany. Museum with Corinthian pottery and sepulchral monuments. *Agios Spyridon* is a cathedral-like church dating from 1589.

Palaiokastritsa, resort famed for its lobsters. Abbey and ruined castle.

Ioánnina. Capital of Epirus, founded in the 4th cent. Beautifully situated by a lake surrounded by mountain peaks. The town retains much of the charm of its heyday, during the early 19th cent., when Ali Pasha had achieved independence from the sultan for himself and the town. At that

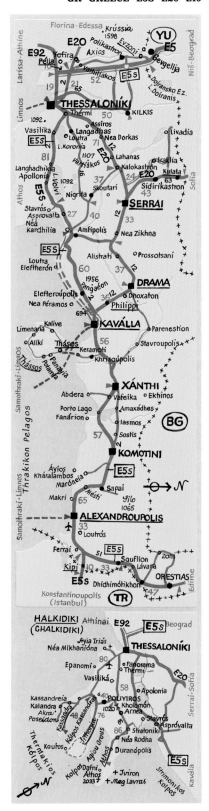

time there were 35 000 inhabitants. *Ágios Nikólos Spános* monastery (13th cent.) with frescoes from 1660. Ali Pasha was executed in the Penteleimon monastery in 1822. Four abbeys with beautiful wall paintings on the little island in the lake. The mosque of Aslan Bey, situated within the castle walls, is now a museum.

Dhodhóni. A temple of Zeus and his wife Dione/Naia (Hera was not mentioned) was built close to a sacred oak in the 4th cent. B.C. Later King Pyrrhos had an even larger temple erected, but not much of it remains. The theatre was restored in 1963 and ancient Greek tragedies are performed in August. Dhodhoni was known for its oracle who was almost as famous as the one in Delphi.

Arta. During the 6th cent. B.C. this was the site of Ambrakia, a Corinthian colony, but no ruins remain. However, there are several beautiful Byzantine churches, dating from the 13th-15th cent. when the town flourished. The church of *Panagía Parigorítissa* (1295) has four corner domes and a central dome. Mosaics and frescoes. 140 m long bridge (17th cent.).

Road to the port town of **Préveza,** situated on a peninsula. Venetian fort and ramparts. **Actium** where the fleets of Octavian in 81 B.C. defeated the fleet of Antony and Cleopatra. Nikópolis, the "Town of Victory", was built the following year on the orders of Octavian, who later became Caesar Augustus. Remains of a temple of Poseidon, a stadium and a theatre. Four large basilicas, the oldest dating from the year 500. Beautiful mosaic floors. 2 km long town wall.

Agrínion. Centre of a fertile agricultural area. Tobacco fields. **Mesólongion.** Famous as the site of heroic Greek resistance against the Turks 1825-1826. Museum and remains of the fortifications. Lord Byron, active in the cause of Greek independence, died here in 1824.

Frequent ferry service connecting Antirion with Rion. 20 min. journey.

PÁTRAI (Patras, 112 000), the largest port city on the Peloponnesus, was completely destroyed in 1821 during the struggle for Greek independence. Many conquerors have passed through the town. Beautiful views from the site of the former acropolis. One Venetian and one Turkish fort. Odeion, Roman theatre. Museum of archaeology.

Ferry to the island of **Kefallinía** where there are some remains of walls and Mycenaean tombs (15th-13th cent. B.C.). Museum with ancient artifacts. Museum of archaeology.The medieval capital is now in ruins. The most recent earthquake occured in 1953.

Itháki (Ithaca), where, according to Homer, Odysseus was king. Stavrós was probably his capital. Now the capital is called **Vathi.**

The motorway from Patras to Corinth offers fine views out over the *Bay of Corinth.* The old road that follows the coastline is beautiful but it is rather narrow and passes through many small towns.

Aiyion. Little port and town built on terraces. Ancient cave dwellings. Car ferries make the four-hour journey to Itea several times a day. Remains of the town wall. It was from here that Agamemnon sailed to Troy. Up in the mountains the Megaspileon monastery is perched high on a cliff. Visitors can reach it by cable cars that cross over a gorge. The Agía Lávra abbey was founded about the year 1000 and is considered a national shrine. This is where, in 1821, the War of Independence against the Turks began. Museum with manuscripts.

Sikyon. This old town flourished during the 6th cent. B.C. Remains of a temple. Museum in the restored Roman baths.

Up in the mountains is Lake Stymphalos where Hercules completed one of his labours by killing the man-eating Stymphalos birds.

KÓRINTHOS (Corinth, 27 000), with its two harbours, was an important commercial centre as early as the 8th cent. B.C. In the 10th cent. B.C. a town existed on Mount Akrokórinthos. Parts of the ancient fortress remain, but most was built much later by Venetians and Turks. Magnificent views.

The **temple of Apollo** was built in the 6th cent. B.C. Seven enormous columns remain. Originally there were 38, but the others were destroyed by earthquakes. Large market place, 255×127 m, with shops and a row of temples. The *Béma,* a monumental Roman rostrum, remains. St. Paul spoke from it in A.D. 52, *Amphitheatre* with places for 18 000 spectators. The ancient port is now under water. Ruins of a 5th-cent. basilica. *Museum* with sculptures, mosaics and coins. Here you can also study the famous Corinthian vases that were exported as early as the 7th cent. B.C.

E 87. Ioánnina – Lárisa

Ioánnina, see E 19.

Métsovon. Beautiful mountain town with old buildings. Church of St. Dimitrios. *Panaghia monastery. Tositsa,* an elegant home with exquisite furniture and interesting decorations from the 17th, 18th and 19th cent. The narrow and winding road that goes through the *Katara Pass* is usually closed from October/November until April/May.

Kalabáka. Little town at the foot of the steep Metéora rocks. The *Church of Our Lady* was built in the 14th cent. The mosaics come from a previous basilica. Green marble pulpit. 11th-cent. frescoes.

Metéora. 16th-cent. monastic buildings, beautifully set on top of a towering cliff. Large library, frescoes from 1438, portrait of Athanasios, a Serbian monk who founded the first monastery in this area in 1360. During the next 100 years a total of 23 monasteries were erected here. They were only accessible by ladders or primitive basket lifts, a form of protection against bandits. Nowadays they can be reached by road. *Agios Stéphanos monastery* with magnificent church dating from 1798.

Trikkala is dominated by two hills, one topped by a Byzantine fortress, the other by a church. Ruins of a temple of Asclepios. During antiquity this was a place of pilgrimage for the ill. Production of "flokates" rugs. Remains of a castle and town wall. Bazaar.

Kardhitsa. Mountain town. On Wednesday, market day, you can see many folk costumes and buy traditional local handicrafts such as "flokates" and

---

Thessaloníki (Salonica) – Kozáni – Ioánnina

Véria. Church of Agios Chrístos with 4th-cent. wall paintings. Museum with antique finds. Fragments of antique and Byzantine walls.

The road goes up in the *Vermion Mountains* to the *Kastanea Pass* (1 360 m). Views of Olympus to the south. *Kozáni.* Market town. Museum. Library. During the 17th cent. this was a centre for the preservation of Greek culture during the Turkish occupation. The road continues through the *Katara Pass* (1 706 m).

Ioánnina, see E 19.

From Kozáni a road goes to Bitola in Yugoslavia and Tiranë in Albania. At present it is not possible to make the journey in private vehicles.

Kastoria. Beautifully set on a peninsula that extends into Lake Orestias. Agamemnon, King of Mycenae, who led the Greek armies during the Trojan War, was murdered by his wife Clytemnestra and avenged by his son Orestes. All of this is described in Aeschylus' tragedies. Over 60 small churches, some of them unchanged since their construction (9th-16th cent.). Nearly all are adorned with frescoes, often the works of Serbian artists. Mavrotissa monastery on an island in the lake.

E 92. Thessaloníki – Lárisa – Athinai – Kórinthos – Kalámai

THESSALONÍKI (Salonica), see town plans.

Road to *Véria.* Church of *Agios Chrístos* with 4th-cent. wall paintings. Museum with antique artifacts. *Naoussa,* situated high above the plain. Wine centre. *Seli.* Winter sports resort on top of Mount Vermion.

Vergina with several tombs from the Macedonian period (4th cent. B.C.). One of them is believed to be that of Philip II. Discovered in 1977 it is completely intact. The finds are in the museum in Salonica. Perhaps this is the site of Aigai, Philip's capital, previously thought to be situated at Edessa.

Olympus. Highest mountain in Greece (2 917 m above sea level). The peak, often obscured by clouds, is covered with snow for about ten months of the year. Zeus and the other Greek gods are said to have lived on this mountain. *Katerini* is the starting point for climbs.

Lárisa (73 000). During antiquity this was an important city. Remains of a temple and a theatre. Museum of archaeology in an old mosque.

Road to *Vólos* (51 000). Large port and industries. Beautifully situated at the foot of Mount Pelion. *Museum* with antique finds. In 1956 two Mycenaean palaces (1500-1300 B.C.) were discovered here. Demétrias-Pagásai was founded in the 4th-3rd cent. B.C. Remains of a large building, a royal palace or a covered market. 8 km long remains of the town wall. *Néa Anchíalos.* Remains of four basilicas. Mosaics.

Lamía. Remains of a medieval castle built over the antique acropolis.

Thermopylae. Large memorial with bronze statue of Leonidas, King of Sparta. Here, in 480 B.C., he and a few hundred troops defended the pass

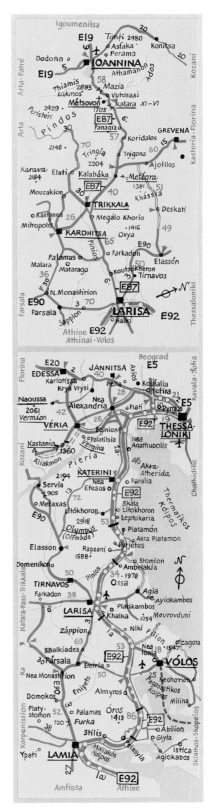

against the enormous army of the Persian king, Xerxes the Great. All of the Spartans were killed. The memorial bears the words: "Tell them at Lacedaemon, passer-by, that here obedient to their laws we lie.".

Ámfissa. Fortress from the 6th cent. B.C., destroyed by Philip II in 346 B.C. Medieval fortress built during the Fourth Crusade (13th cent.).

Delphi. Holy place of antiquity, "navel" of the world, where the oracle, dazed by the steam from a hot spring, prophesied the future of the world. Delphi is beautifully situated on the slope of *Mount Parnassos,* which was where Gaia, the Earth-Goddess, was worshipped. In about 1000 B.C. she was replaced by the god Apollo. The name of the town comes from the legend that relates that Apollo came here in the guise of a dolphin (delphos). Remains of an enormous *temple of Apollo,* built in th 6th cent. B.C. on the site of an earlier temple that had been destroyed by earthquake and fire. This is where the female oracle Pythia, obscured by clouds of steam, gave counsel to pilgrims who had first cleansed themselves in the spring. Stadium with places for 7 000 spectators (4th cent. B.C.). 177.5 m long running track. An inscription tells us that the spectators were forbidden to bring wine into the area – it would seem that drunk and unruly sports enthusiasts were a problem even then. *Marmariá,* an area with many marble ruins. Site of a temple of Athena. Tholos, a circular marble structure. Theatre that accommodates 5 000. Large museum.

Ósios Loukas. Abbey church, built in 1030 over the tomb of St. Luke. Magnificent floor and mosaics.

Cherónia. In a battle in 338 B.C. Macedonian armies, led by Philip II, defeated the armies of Athens and Thebes. This was the end of the Greek states. A marble lion was erected over the graves. Orchomenós has an abbey church dating from 874 and a domed tomb 14 m in diameter.

Levádhia was an important town during the Byzantine and Turkish periods. Castle (13th cent.) high on the cliffs. The place where the oracle Trophonios prophesied the future, lies at the summit. Pilgrims had to drink from the Spring of Memory and the Spring of Forgetfulness. Both still exist.

Ptoion. Ptoios, an ancient hero, was worshipped here. Seat of an oracle. Extensive temple ruins.

Thivai (Thebes) was one of the foremost cities of antiquity. Legendary birthplace of Heracles and domain of King Oedipus. Now it is a modern town and very little of its former glory remains. Fragments of Mycenaean ramparts (15th cent. B.C.). Large museum of archaeology.

The large island of *Évvoia* is separated from the mainland by the narrow Euripos Channel. Interesting phenomenon: the current in the Sound changes direction every sixth hour. *Khalkís* with museum displaying antique finds. Hot sulphur springs in the northern part of the island. At the end of the 1920s a magnificent statue of Zeus was discovered here. It is now in the National Archaeological Museum in Athens. Ruins of a temple of Artemis. South of Khalki is the ancient *Erétria* with ruins of temples, theatre, gymnasium, town gate, etc.

Amphiareion (Oropos). Remains of a temple from the 4th cent. B.C. Site of an ancient spa with a sacred spring in which pilgrims cleansed themselves. Theatre with well-preserved proscenium. Four marble thrones for the most honoured guests.

Rhamnous. Old town with remaining section of the town wall. 5th cent. B.C. temple of Nemesis, and other temples on an artifical terrace overlooking the town.

Marathón. Burial mound over the Athenians who fell during the Battle of Marathon, 490 B.C. 10 000 Greeks led by Miltiades defeated a 100 000- man strong Persian army. The first marathon runner raced to Athens. He announced the victory, then died of exhaustion.

ATHINAI (Athens), see town plans.

South of Athens, at the extreme tip of the peninsula, is *Sounion,* with a beautiful ruined Doric temple of Poseidon, high above the Mediterranean. It is particularly beautiful at sunset.

Salamis. Island with naval base. Olive groves and vineyards. Monastery. In 480 B.C. the scene of a great naval battle. Greeks under Themistocles destroyed the fleet of the Persian king, Xerxes. Remains of a 5th- cent. fortress. Faneroméni monastery (17th cent.). The beautiful island of *Egina,* off the coast of Salamis, has impressive temple ruins and excavations of 4000-year-old fortifications. Museum.

It is also possible to take road 3 via Thivai (Thebes)

Elevsis. Modern industrial town, famous during antiquity for its Eleusian Mysteries, cult rites of unknown significance. Only the initiated (myste) could take part. Remains of the 4th-cent. B.C. temple. The temple of Hades was thought to be the entrance to the underworld. *Museum* with ceramics and statues, among them the statue of a woman from the 21st cent. B.C.

Propylaia, the gates, are reminiscent of the Propylaia in Athens.

Daphni. During the 12th cent. an abbey church was built on the site of the former temple of Apollo. Beautiful mosaics. The church also served as a monastery. Frontier fortifications also at Pili (Phyle).

The **Corinth Canal**, 6 km long, 23 m wide and 8 m deep. Even the Emperor Nero entertained serious plans for a canal at this site, but it did not become a reality until 1893. (Photography forbidden.) As early as several centuries B.C. there was a stone-paved road over the isthmus along which boats were dragged.

KÓRINTHOS, see E 19.

Nemea with remains of a 4th-cent. B.C. temple of Zeus. Three upright columns and other temple ruins – some covered by a 7th-cent. basilica.

Mikínai (Mycenae). As early as 3 000 B.C. this was an important centre of culture that gave its name to a whole civilization. Th Mycenaean Civilization flourished during the 16th cent. B.C. Impressive ruins remain. Famous **Lion Gate** (1250 B.C), a 3.25 m high gateway. The lions' heads have disappeared. The wall, a few hundred years older, is 6 m thick. Many tombs near by. The Atreus, the largest, has a 13 m high dome. At one time it was thought to be the tomb of Agamemnon. The rich finds taken from the tombs, including gold face masks, are for the most part in the National Museum in Athens.

Árgos. Little remains of what was an influential town during antiquity. The large theatre (400 B.C.) accommodated an audience of 20 000. The antique castle has been rebuilt and extended several times – by Franks and Venetians, by Turks and Crusaders. Remains of Roman baths. Impressive museum with mosaics and ceramics.

Tirins (Tiryns). Excavations of a huge 14th-cent. B.C. Mycenaean fortress. The wall is composed of enormous blocks of stone, 7-10 m thick. Legend has it that the giant Cyclops built the fortress. *Agía Moní*, convent founded in the 2nd cent. Church dating from 1150. *Asini* with Mycenaean fortress built in the 11th cent. B.C. and excavated in 1926.

Epidhavros (Epidaurus). Religious centre devoted to the cult of Asclepius who was the son of Apollo and god of healing. His symbol, a snake coiled around a staff, is still used as a symbol for the medical profession. His daughter was Hygeieia – her name lives on in the word "hygiene". In the 4th cent. B.C. this was a large spa with hospitals and sanatoria. The holy spring can still be seen, as can ruins of many buildings: baths, dormitories, gymnasiums and temples. Handsome amphitheatre which accommodates 12 000. Performances of ancient plays. Museum with inscriptions of thanks for miraculous cures, and Roman medical instruments.

NÁVPLION (Nauplia, 9 000). Lovely town with 19th-cent. buildings. Fortress from the Venetian and Turkish periods. Museum with Mycenaean artifacts, including weapons and pottery.

Trípolis. Capital of Arcadia. Founded in the 14th cent. Interesting bazaar. The Athena Alea Temple in Tegea was adorned in the 4th cent. B.C. by the sculptor Skopas.

Megalópolis. An important city during antiquity. Large amphitheatre. Remains of a temple of Zeus. – *Messene*. Some remains of buildings from the independent city, among them a theatre and a stadium.

Kalámai (39 000). The second most important commercial town on the Peloponnesus, after Patras. Harbour and industry. 13th-cent. fortress.

Further south on the Peloponnesian Peninsula is *Spartí* (Sparta), one of the most important city republics in ancient Greece, known for its military ideals and the Spartan life style. Not much is left from that period. The modern city has partially been built on top of the old one. Some remains of temples, tombs, palaces. *Pantánassa*, a convent (1428) with a beautiful church in the Byzantine style. Lovely frescoes. Museum. Archaeological museum.

Monemvasia. Old town which Franks, Venetians and Turks have fought over. 14th-cent. *Agía Sophia* domed church. The lower town was built later and contains some beautiful 17th- and 18th-cent. houses.

On the western side of the peninsula is *Olympia,* a holy place named after Zeus, the Lord of Olympus. The temple of Zeus was erected in 456 B.C. This was the site of the famous Zeus statue, 12 m high, covered with gold and ivory. It was one of the seven wonders of the ancient world. The temple caved in during an earthquake in A.D. 6.

The Olympic Games were arranged here every fourth year from 776 B.C. until A.D. 394. Theodosius, the Christian king, forbade the heathen games. Earthquakes, floods and Visigoths destroyed what was left. Excavations started in 1875. Remains of several temples, baths, sports grounds and administrative buildings. **Archaeological museum** with the famous statue of Hermes of Praxiteles and Roman portrait sculptures. *Olympic museum* and monument to Baron Pierre de Coubertin who revived the Olympic Games in 1896. From here the Olympic fire is sent to the Olympic Games.

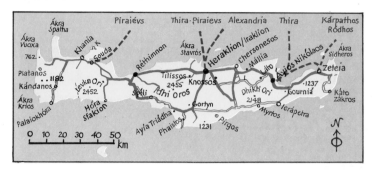

Kriti

(Crete, 460 000)

Area: 8 380 km² (3 235 sq. miles)

Crete is the largest and southernmost of the Greek islands. It is 260 km long and 60 km wide. The Minoan civilization flourished here 2800–1400 B.C. It was named after Minos, the legendary king, son of Zeus and Europa, a royal daughter. Arabs, Venetians and Turks have ruled the island. In 1912 it was annexed to Greece.

Irakleion (Iráklion, Heraklion) is the chief town. 5 km long city walls, for the most part built by the Venetians in the 17th cent. The Morosini Fountain (with four lions) dates from 1628 and the Bembo Fountain from 1558. Museum of archaeology with finds from the Minoan civilization. Museum of history with sculptures and frescoes from the Venetian period. Ikon museum in the Church of St. Catherine.

Knossós (5 km to the south). Excavations of the huge palace, once the centre of King Minos' empire. Four floors and a maze of rooms, stairs, and corridors. 22 storage rooms for beer, wine, and grain. The first palace was destroyed in an earthquake around 1800 B.C. Some altars and a paved courtyard remain from the second palace. The third, built around the 16th cent. B.C., has been excavated and the ruins have been reconstructed.

Other interesting sights on Crete—from west to east:

Khania (Canea). Administrative centre. Excursions to the *Gorge of Samaria,* Europe's largest canyon. Réthimnon has a Venetian fortress and a Turkish mosque.

Idhi Oros (2 432 m) is the highest mountain on the island. It was here, on Mount Ida, that Prince Paris was judge in the beauty contest between three goddesses. He gave the apple to Aphrodite which led to the Trojan Wars.

Ayia Triádha has remains of a palace, possibly a summer palace. *Phaistos* was the site of a huge palace on a 70 m high cliff overlooking the Messara plains. Extensive excavations but no reconstructions.

Mállia has remains of a palace. *Lato.* Remains of an antique city (7th cent. B.C.). *Ayios Nikólaos* is a large tourist resort. A sweet water lake surrounded by hotels and small fishermen's houses is connected to the sea by a 20 m long canal. Museum of archaeology.

Gourniá is the only town from the Minoan period, but there are few remains from that period.

Káto Zákros has remains of a palace, destroyed in an earthquake in 1450 B.C. *Ierápetra,* new tourist resort.

Rhodos

(Rhodes, 67 000)

Area: 1 400 km² (538 sq. miles).

Rhodes is the largest of the Dodecanese Islands (Twelve Islands). Up until 100 B.C. Rhodes was one of the most important seafaring nations in the Mediterranean. After that the Byzantine Empire, Venice and Genoa fought over the island. In 1309 it fell into the hands of the Crusaders, the Knights Hospitallers. In 1523 the island was conquered by Turkey (the Ottoman Empire). Italy ruled from 1911. Since 1945 Rhodes has belonged to Greece.

Rhodos (Rhodes) is the most important town and a large tourist resort. 4 km long medieval walls around the ancient town of the Knights Hospitallers. Palace of the Grand Master, hospital of the knights, now museum of archaeology, and the knights' street with hostels for the different nations. Turkish quarter with the mosque of Suleiman, the conqueror of Rhodes. Acropolis with the remains of antique structures. However, there is no trace of the Colossus, one of the Seven Wonders of the World, a giant statue of Helios, the Sun God, which stood at the entrance to the harbour. It was erected in 290 B.C. but destroyed in an earthquake in 224 B.C.

Lindhos is a well-preserved Turkish town. Acropolis with a lovely view. Tourists reach the summit on donkeyback. *Butterfly Valley* (Petalondes) is full of butterflies June–September.

The ruined city of Mycenae prospered 1550–1125 B.C.

TOWN PLANS

ATHÍNAI (Athens, 800 000)
Greater Athens, including Piraeus, has 3 million inhabitants.
Capital of Greece, centre of culture during antiquity, one of the most influential cities in the history of western civilization. The Agora, main square, of the ancient city at the base of the Acropolis, existed as early as the 7th cent. B.C. Remains of several interesting structures. One of the best-preserved is the temple of Hephaistos and Athena (445 B.C.) with sculptures by Alkamenes. Agora Museum in King Attalos II's "stoa", a building completed in the 2nd cent. B.C.

1 Acropolis
2 Acropolis Museum
3 Market square
4 Museum
5 Roman market square
6 Hadrian's Library
7 Cathedral
8 Hadrian's Arch and Olympieion
9 Russian Church
10 Syntagma (Constitution Square)
11 Parliament and Tomb of the
   Unknown Soldier
12 Exhibition halls
13 Castle
14 Byzantine Museum
15 National Museum (art)
16 Benaki Museum
17 University
18 Town hall
19 Archeological Museum
20 Railway station

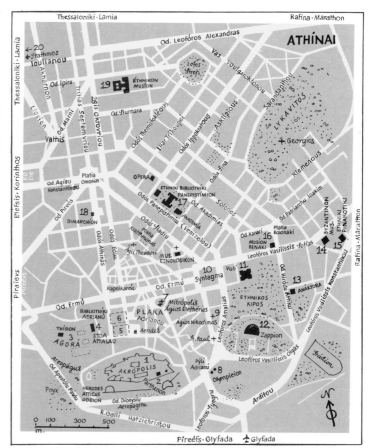

Acropolis,
Athens

The **Acropolis,** a 156 m high limestone elevation, had 10 m high ramparts as early as the 14th cent. B.C. Some sections remain. During the 7th cent. B.C. the Acropolis became a centre of worship of the goddess Athena. Several temples were built. In 479 B.C. they were put to the torch by the Persians. In 432 the Propylaia were built. 10 m high entrance hall with splendid ceiling. The large staircase that leads up to it dates from the Roman period. The **Parthenon** (438 B.C.). The Doric marble temple, the masterpiece of ancient architecture, is now threatened by air pollution, vibration caused by traffic and the assault of countless waves of tourists. This frequently photographed ruin is 72×34 m in size and has 17 columns on the N and S sides and 8 on the E and W sides. The Parthenon frieze is one of the best-known works of art of antiquity. Some of these sculptural decorations were the work of Phidas. The western part remains. Other sections are in the Acropolis Museum and the British Museum. The Parthenon once contained a famous and magnificent statue of the goddess Athena. In the 6th cent. the temple became a Christian church. In 1466 it was transformed into a mosque. In 1687 gunpowder stored in the Parthenon exploded and the building was transformed again – into a ruin. Large Erechtheion temple and the beautiful little temple of Nike. Museum with finds from the Acropolis.

The Aeropagus, a court of law where St. Paul preached in A.D. 50. Temple of Asclepios with health-restoring spring. The Theatre of Dionysos from 534 B.C., is the oldest in the world. Places for an audience of 17000 including special seats of honour for priests, governors and Emperor Hadrian. Several more antique temples and palaces. The largest is **Olympieion.** Construction (for the dictator Pesistros) started in the 6th cent. B.C. The building was finally completed for Emperor Hadrian in A.D.132. Originally it had 104 columns, 17 m high. 15 remain standing, one lies on the ground. The **National Museum** is the largest museum in Greece. Magnificent collection of prehistoric and ancient art. Particularly interesting are the artifacts discovered at excavations at Mycenae. Benaki Museum (private) with antique art. Byzantine museum. *Ethnographical museum. Historical museum.*

In 1864, once the Greeks had achieved freedom from the Turks, Athens became the capital of the new country. It was quickly transformed into a large modern city with a centre between the *Omonias* (Harmony Square) and *Syntagma* (Constitution Square). *Plaka,* a picturesque quarter with narrow alleys, taverns and a lively bazaar. University (1837) by the Dane, H.C. Hansen. Parliament, once the Royal Palace (1838), guarded by the Evzones wearing picturesque uniforms. Tomb of the Unknown Soldier.

View of Thessaloniki

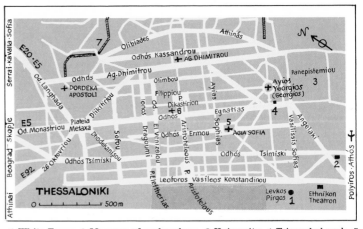

1 White Tower. 2 Museum of archaeology. 3 University. 4 Triumphal arch. 5 Church of St. Sophia. 6 Church of Panaghion Khalkeon. 7 Ramparts.

In 1984 private cars were banned from a part of the city centre in an attempt to reduce air pollution in the area.

PIRAEUS (Piraiévs, 200000). Port of Athens, largest port in Greece, built and fortified in the 5th cent. Many popular and lively seaside resorts line the Saronic Gulf (Saronikos Kolpos). They extend all the way out to Cape Sounion, site of a beautiful Doric temple, situated high above the sea. Beautiful sunsets.

THESSALONÍKI
(Salonica, 500000).
Second largest port and city in Greece. Founded in 300 B.C. by Kassander who was married to Thessalonikeia, half-sister of Alexander the Great. Important commercial centre on the major trade route that linked Rome with Constantinople. Outpost of the Roman Empire. In 904 it was conquered by the Saracens. From 1430 until 1912 it was under Turkish rule.
After a devastating fire in 1917 the city was rebuilt. About 3 km remain of the ramparts, parts of which date from the 4th cent. The Bloody Tower, also known as the White Tower (Lefkós Pirgos), once part of the ramparts, was built in the 15th cent. and later served as a prison. Part of the Arch of Galerius (A.D. 303) survives.

Agios Geórgios (Rotunda of St. George), a circular church mausoleum of the Emperor Galerius. Built in the 4th cent. with 5th-cent. mosaics and 10th-cent. frescoes. Now a museum of Byzantine art. *Agia Sophía* was founded in the 8th cent. Its mosaics and frescoes survived the city's devastating fires because the Turks had covered them with lime. *The Panaghiaton Halkeon* church of The Virgin of the Coppersmiths, founded in 1028, is another interesting ecclesiastical structure.
Fine views from the ramparts in the northern part of the city. The lovely panorama includes small abbeys, the sea, the city, and on clear days, Mount Olympus.

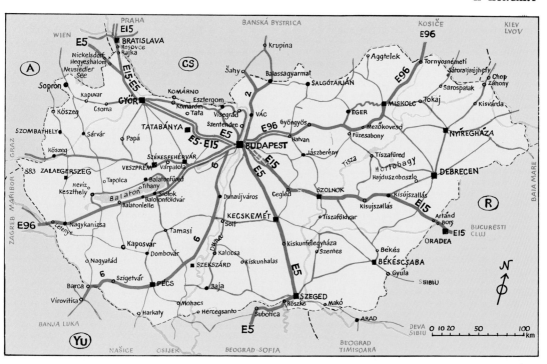

H · Hungary

H· Magyarorszag

Area: 93 000 km² (35 912 sq. miles)

Population: 10.7 million. The national language is Magyar (Hungarian). Serbian, German, Croatian, Slovakian and other minorities.

Major cities: Budapest 2.1 million, Miskolc 209 000, Debrecen 195 000, Szeged 175 000.

Government: People's republic with a National Assembly.

History
9th-10th cent. Magyar tribes (Hungarians), under their chief, Árpád, conquer what is now Hungary.
1000 St. Stephen christianizes and unifies the country. He is crowned King of Hungary by the pope.
1342-1382 During the reign of Louis the Great, Hungary flourishes and expands.
1458-1490 Hungary prospers during the reign of Mátyás I. His armies occupy Vienna in 1485. Art and science blossom at the court of Mátyás.
1514 Peasants' rebellion suppressed. The "Peasant King" György Dózsa is burned alive on a red-hot iron throne.
1526 Battle of Mohács. Hungary falls to the Turks who occupy all but the areas around Pressburg (present-day Bratislava) and Transylvania.
1699 Treaty of Karlowitz. The Turks withdraw from Hungary which comes under the control of the Habsburg Emperor Leopold I of Austria.
1703-1711 Hungarian uprising led by Prince Ferenc Rákóczi II.

1848-1849 Hungarian uprising led by Lajos Kossuth.
1914-1918 First World War. Austria-Hungary and Germany are defeated. The Kaiser abdicates.
1919 Brief Communist rule under Béla Kun, followed by a Conservative régime under the regency of Admiral Horthy.
1940 Hungary allies with Germany.
1944 German troops occupy Hungary.
1945 Soviet troops occupy Hungary. Heavy fighting.
1946 Republican constitution adopted. Hungary becomes a People's Republic.
1956 Internal disturbances, particularly in Budapest. Kádár reorganizes the Communist Party and a quiet period of development begins, which results in one of the most stable economic situations in Eastern Europe.

Currency: Forints (HUF).
1 forint = 100 fillérs
A limited amount of Hungarian currency may be imported. There are no restrictions on the amount of foreign currency imported, but it must be declared. Currency exchange is only allowed at officially recognized banks and exchange offices.

Business hours: Banks 9.00 a.m.-1.00 p.m. Saturdays 9.00-11.00 a.m. Post offices 8.00 a.m.-6.00 or 8.00 p.m. Saturdays 8.00 a.m.-4.00 p.m. Shops 10.00 a.m.-6.00 p.m. Saturdays 10.00 a.m.-2.00 p.m. In smaller towns lunchtime closings are not unusual. Foodshops 7.00 a.m.-7.00 p.m. Saturdays 7.00 a.m.-4.00 p.m.

Holidays: New Year's Day, April 4 (Liberation Day), Easter Sunday, May 1, August 20 (National Holiday), November 7 (Revolution Remembrance Day), December 25 and 26.

Hotels
Hotels are classified with stars:
***** = deluxe, **** = first class, *** = good tourist class, ** = simple tourist class, * = very simple tourist class. They are operated by different state-owned chains: Hungarhotels, Pannonia and Danubius. Advance book-

---

Routes described:

E 5   Wien – Budapest – Szeged – Beograd

E 15 Bratislava – Budapest – Oradea

E 96 Košice – Budapest – Balaton – Zagreb

2 and 6 Balassagyarmat – Budapest – Pécs – Barcs

Town plan: Budapest

The puszta, the plains of eastern Hungary

ing is advisable, particularly in Budapest. IBUSZ, the state-owned travel agency, has many offices and their staff can help you obtain a hotel room. Other travel agency chains include Express, Cooptourist, Budapest Tourist, Volántourist and Malév Airtours. Hungary has an abundance of hot springs. There are 373 spas.

Camping
Hungary has over 70 camping sites. In general they are open May-September. As a rule, holders of an International Camping Carnet (FICC, AIT, FIA) are given a discount. Self-catering cottages are available at major sites.

Food and drink
Hungarian cuisine is among the finest in Europe. It has been greatly influenced by the country's geographical position and has adopted dishes and cooking methods of many different cultures. Here are some of the dishes that the visitor should try while staying in Hungary.

Gulyás, goulash, pepper-spiced strips of beef or mutton with potatoes, onions and vegetables. There are many variations. Paprikás csirke, chicken with cream sauce, paprika and noodles, Fatányéros, mixed grill on skewers. Rántott szelet is Wiener Schnitzel. Rántott csirke, grilled chicken. Rácponty is a hotly spiced fish dish (carp). Halászlé is a soup containing large pieces of fish, onion, and paprika, a speciality of Lake Balaton towns. Hal pörkölt is a sort of fish stew. Several varieties of sausage, among them: salami, gyulai and csabai kolbász.

The national drink is the native Hungarian wine made from grapes grown in unique soil and climate conditions. Balaton wines from the vineyards north of the lake, Egri Bikavér (Bulls's Blood from Eger) and Tokay. The export of Tokay was important as far back as the 15th cent. when it financed the expensive wars and court of King Mátyás. Apricot brandy. Many different sorts of delicious pastry. Rétes resemble strudel. The famous Dobos Torta is made of thin layers of sponge cake filled with chocolate and covered with a layer of caramelized sugar.

Shopping
Handicrafts, ceramics, wood carvings, embroidery, and other needlework. Porcelain from Herend. Gramophone records and musical instruments. Wine and Cuban cigars. "Intertourist" shops (generally to be found in major hotels) only accept payment in foreign convertible currency.

Speed limits. Traffic regulations.
Motorways 100 kmh, other roads 80 kmh, built-up areas 60 kmh. Cars towing caravans, and motorcycles, 80, 70, 50 kmh.
Children under the age of six are not allowed to travel in the front seat.
If your car is fitted with seat belts it is compulsory to wear them.
All accidents, even the most minor ones, should be reported to the police and a statement obtained from them which must be produced at the frontier when leaving the country. They will certify that the cost of the damage has been settled. Otherwise it can be difficult taking the car out of Hungary. Repairs on foreign-registered vehicles cannot be carried out without a police certificate.
Diesel fuel can only be bought with special coupons that are sold at frontier currency exchange offices and at IBUSZ offices. Payment must be made in foreign currency.

Road patrols
The Hungarian Automobile Club (MAK) has patrol cars on the major roads from 7 a.m. until 7 p.m. On summer weekends this service is extended to 10 p.m. These cars have "bases" placed 30-50 km apart on the major roads. The MAK Breakdown Service can be called from 7.00 a.m. to 9.00 p.m. Tel. Budapest 152–040. On the M7 motorway, Budapest – Balaton, there are emergency telephones set up at every other kilometre along the road. Information can be obtained from MAK, tel. Budapest 666 404.

Police telephone: in Budapest, Debrecen, Miskolc, Pécs 07, other major cities 007. There are telephones in post offices that can be used free of charge in case of accident.

MAK, Magyar Autoklubb, 4, Rómer Flóris utca 4-6, 1277 Budapest Pf 1, tel. 15 20 40.
Danube Travel Agents, 6 Conduit Street, London W1R 9TG. Tel. 01-4930263.
Tourinform is a data bank, that provides tourist information in Hungarian, English, French and German. Tel. 179–800.

The Széchenyi Baths, Budapest

E 5. Wien – Budapest – Szeged – Beograd

E 5 comes from London – Bruxelles – Frankfurt – Nürnberg – Wien

Hegyeshalom. Austrian frontier.

Mosommagyaróvár is dominated by a castle with 2 m thick walls.

GYÖR (Raab, 75 000). Industrial town where railway coaches and locomotives are manufactured. Charming streets with Baroque houses. Castle and bishop's palace.

Tata (25 000). Old spa with hot springs. Beautifully situated between the Gerecse and Vértes Mountains. Roman finds in the *Domokos-Kuny Museum*. In the 10th cent., Tata became the seat of the Hungarian kings of the Árpád dynasty. Its first abbey and church were built in the 11th cent. During the resistance against the Turks, both castle and town were destroyed. Part of the castle of King Sigismund adjoins the lake.
During the 18th cent. Tata was given its Baroque charm and atmosphere by Jacob Fellner who designed the palace for the Eszterházy family. Beautiful park with fountains. Fellner also completed the church that had been started by Anton Pilgram. Statue of Fellner in front of the church. He also designed the unique watch and clock tower on the square and the lovely chapel on *Kalvária Hill*. Agostyan Arboretum, a collection of cypress and cedar trees. *Remeteség puszta* with wildlife park.

At **Vértesszölös** the jawbone of a man who lived 500 000 years ago has been found. He was a contemporary of the Peking and Java men.

Tatabánya (70 000). Industrial town with mines.

Esztergom. One of the oldest towns in Hungary, royal residence during the Middle Ages. The large *palace* is being restored. Visitors can inspect the chapel and the throne room. The 19th-cent. *cathedral* on the castle hill is the largest church in Hungary, 100 m high dome. The altar painting, 13 m high, is said to be the largest canvas painting in the world. It is a copy of a painting by Titian. The treasury of the cathedral has superb examples of the goldsmith's art. Museum of ecclesiastical art, Christian museum with a famous collection of medieval Italian art, Flemish tapestries and Hungarian religious art. Esztergom has a lovely old quarter with houses from the 17th and 18th cent.

Visegrád. Little town on the "Danube Bend". In the 13th cent., King Mátyás gathered to his court the leading scientists and artists of Europe. The *palace*, completed in the 15th cent., had 350 rooms, making it one of the largest in Europe. It was destroyed by the Turks, but interesting sections of it have been restored. The *Solomon Tower*, a 32 m high residential tower, now contains a museum of archaeology. The palace is set on a 300 m high hill and the views out over the Danube are delightful.

Szentendre is one of the most beautiful small towns in Hungary. Winding, sloping streets and houses that are a mixture of Balkan architecture and Baroque. Greek Orthodox cathedral with exquisite rococo wrought-iron gates. Serbian Museum of Religious History. An extremely lovely museum is devoted to the works of the artist *Margit Kovács*. Amusing sculptures and handsome utility goods.

BUDAPEST, see town plans.

It is also possible to drive from Vienna via Sopron to Györ.

SOPRON (50 000). The Roman Scarbantia at the crossing of major roads connecting north and south Europe, between Vienna and Istanbul. Sopron lies like a peninsula in Austria. As the result of a referendum in 1920, Sopron became Hungarian, but a distinctive Austrian atmosphere remains. The Franz Liszt Palace of Culture is not far from the Boulevard Lenin. The nine-year-old Franz Liszt had his first public performance in Sopron in 1820. In 1775 Haydn played here. Mozart's Magic Flute was performed in 1795. The town within the walls retains its old charm. Many Renaissance and Baroque houses, among them *Storno House* with lovely interiors and works of art. Sopron was Hungary's project city during the European Architectural Heritage Year 1975. *Franz Liszt Museum* with archaeology, cultural history and art.

Fertórakos is a charming little resort. Limestone quarry with open-air theatre. June Drama Festival featuring performances of ancient Greek tragedies.

A quarter of *Lake Fertö* belongs to Hungary. The Austrians call it Neusiedler See.

KECSKEMÉT (75 000). Centre of a district filled with orchards and vineyards. "Barack" apricot brandy. Old cultural centre. Artists' colony. Folk music festival every other year (odd-numbered years). Like the Kodály Collage it has been named after the music pedagogue Zoltán Kodály who was born here. The music institution that bears his name is in a Franciscan monastery. Many splendid Baroque buildings, e.g. Cifra Palace. The Bugac puszta in the **Kiskunság National Park** is one of the most remarkable

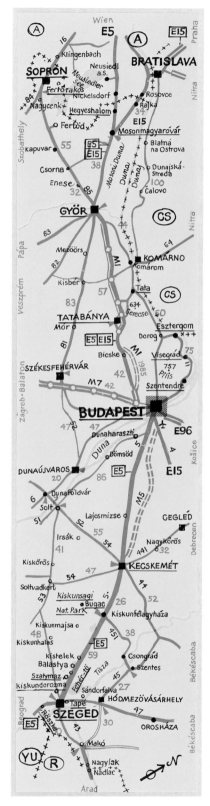

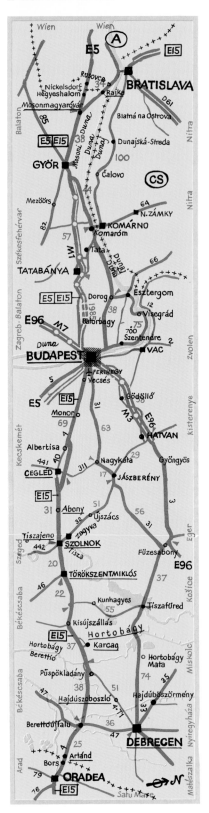

areas in Hungary. Abundant vegetation and wildlife. Visitors can learn about the lives of nomadic cattle-drivers in the *Shepherd's Museum*. Restored nearby farm houses open to visitors demonstrate modern cattle farming. At the inn in *Bugac*, the "Bugacer Csárda ", you can eat authentic goulash, whole ox that has been turned on a spit, and other Hungarian dishes. Riding exhibitions are arranged for tourists.

Szatymas. Little town with the Postakocsi Csárda (Post Coach Inn) on the site where the old post coaches once stopped. *Fehér-tó*, the "White Lake", a swampy area rich in bird-life. Over 200 species.

SZEGED (172 000). Economic and cultural centre of extensive plains. The history of the city dates back to the time of the founding of the Hungarian nation (10th cent.). During the 1848 War of Independence, it was briefly the capital of Hungary. The leader of the revolution, Lajos Kossuth, had the Kárász House built. Lovely arcaded courtyard. The National Assembly convened in Zsótér House at Széchenyi tér, the centre of the city. Most of the buildings here were erected after a flood in 1879. A bronze memorial plaque reads "River Tisza, bestowing blessings and destruction". Ornately adorned Serbian church. Large Romanesque Votiv Church with famous organ. *Music festival* of operas and concerts performed in the large square in front of the cathedral (July-August). Places for 7 000 spectators. *Ferenc-Móra Museum* (art). University with botanical garden.

Tápé, village or district of the city, on the outskirts of Szeged, famed for its folk costumes. *Kiskundorozsma* with windmills. *Röszke*. Old pepper-growing town and frontier station for Yugoslavia.

E 5 continues to Beograd – Sofia – Istanbul – Ankara – Syrian frontier.

E 15. Bratislava – Budapest – Oradea

Rajka. Czech frontier. E 15 comes from Hamburg – Berlin – Dresden – Praha.

Mosonmagyaróvár – Budapest, together with E 5.

BUDAPEST, see town plans.

Monor. (16 000). Little town with a couple of fine "csárdas" (inns). *Cegléd* (40 000). Typical rural Hungarian town that has grown up out of a large village. The sandy soil in the area produces a pleasant light local wine. *Abony*. Little town with a surprising number of classical buildings.

SZOLNOK (65 000). Spa. Baroque Franciscan church (18th cent.). Artists' colony on a spit of land between the Zagyva and Tisza Rivers. Art exhibitions. *Tiszajenö* has 17 springs. This is the source of the popular Mira mineral water.

Törökszentmiklós (24 000). Riding school in Almássy Palace. Riding exhibitions. *Karcag*. Museum (archaeology and folklore). *Zador Bridge* with five arches and an old windmill.

Ártánd. Roumanian frontier. E 15 continues to Oradea – Cluj – Bucureşti – Constanţa on the Black Sea.

Road 4 continues from Püspökladány to Debrecen.

Hajdúszoboszló (22 000). Spa with mineral spring (68- 74°C). The waters in the baths are 36-38°C. Park and lake.

Hortobágy. Centre of the 1 150 km^2 large *Hajdúság* (Heyduck Land) area, more popularly known as the puszta. A romantic plain famed for its courageous riders and fiery Gypsy musicians. Most of the old atmosphere remains as a sort of romantic stage set for tourists, for the 20th cent. has brought modern farming methods to the puszta. The shepherds have become farm labourers working with modern equipment. But the unique sight of endless fields of grass swaying in the breeze remains, and you can still see "Fata morgana", mirages, on a hot summer day. This is the only place in Europe where the phenomenon occurs. The famous inn, built in 1669, was once a meeting place for Hungarians who were fighting to rid themselves of Habsburg rule. They were called Hajdús or Heyducks. Hajdusági (Heyduck) Museum with local history and flora and fauna of the area.

DEBRECEN (195 000). Hungary's third city. Old university. Cultural centre. Large cathedral and university – both were centres of the Calvinist movement. Debrecen was once called "Calvinist Rome". Large coin collection in the library. Deri Museum (art).

E 96. Košice – Budapest – Balaton – Zagreb

Tornyosnémeti. Czech frontier. E 96 comes from Košice.

MISKOLC (209 000). Hungary's second city. Heavy industries. University. Several handsome Baroque churches and one Gothic Protestant church. Ruins of the 15th-cent. fortress. TV tower with expansive views from the top of Avas Hill. *Miskolctapolca*, in the southern part of the city, is a well-known spa with baths in natural grottoes. To the west, **Lillafüred**, a spa in a lovely valley touching the shores of Lake Hámori. Stalagmite and stalactite caves and the *Szeleta Cave* with prehistoric finds.

Another route from Czechoslovakia goes via the frontier post at Sátoraljaúhely. This road passes **Sárospatak**, a little town with lovely 17th- and 18th-cent. buildings. Beautifully situated at the foot of the *Zempléni Mountains*. Rákóczi Castle with *Tokay Wine Museum*.

Tokaj is the centre of the famous wine district. Folk costumes and festivals take place during the grape harvest.

NW of Miskolc are the **Aggtelek Caves.** The largest is *Baradla*, 22 km long with beautiful stalagmites and stalactites. The largest grotto is used as a concert hall. The climate of the caves is beneficial for those suffering from asthma. Subterranean *Vörös Tó*, the "Red Lake". Its waters have been coloured by red clay.

Mezökövesd (18 000) in the Matyó area. Famed for its folk traditions and handicrafts. Exhibits in the *Matyó Museum.* Zsori, a spa with hot springs.

From Miskolc, it is also possible to drive the beautiful but twisting road along the *Bükk Mountains,* the largest limestone mountains in Hungary. Dense forests, ravines and fantastic rock formations.

Eger (45 000) is famous for its red wine, Egri bikavér (Bull's Blood from Eger). Many wine taverns and cellars. Lovely town with several Baroque buildings. *Cathedral* with statues by the Venetian, Marco Casagrande. *Fortress*, where 2 000 Hungarians withstood a 150 000-man Turkish attack. Fortress museum with several kilometres of subterranean tunnels. 35 m high Turkish minaret.

North of Eger is **Szilvásvárad** with a famous stud farm. *Lippizaner Museum* is dedicated to the farm's history. Museum in the beautiful nearby *Szalajka Valley,* with displays of forestry in the *Bükk Mountains.*

Parád. Spa. Splendid carriages once owned by the aristocracy and the archbishops are on display in a *carriage museum* housed in what were the marble stables of the Károlyi Counts. **Mátraszentistván,** where you can eat superb trout at the Vidroczky csárda.

Kekestetö, Hungary's loftiest mountain peak, 1 015 m above sea level. **The Mátra Mountains** have rich deposits of metals and lignite. **Mátraháza.** Spa and winter sports resort, 715 m above sea level.

Gyöngyös (35 000). Gateway to the Mátra Mountains. Centre of a wine district. **Hatvan.** Old castle, now a hospital. **Gödöllö.** Grassalkovich Palace, in the Hungarian Baroque style (18th cent.).

BUDAPEST, see town plans.

Martonvásár. *Beethoven Museum* in the palace where the composer often stayed as guest of the Brunswick family. Here he composed the Moonlight Sonata. Concerts in the palace park. **Pakozd,** fishing village on *Lake Velencei* which is only 1-2 m deep.

SZÉKESFEHÉRVÁR (75 000). The first Hungarian kings (Árpád Dynasty) resided here. Excavations of the Royal Cathedral (11th cent.) where they were consecrated and buried . Rococo pharmacy from 1758, still in use. Ruins of the Roman settlement of Gorsium in Tác. Museum.

Polgárdi with arboretum.

Lake Balaton (German: Plattensee). Largest lake in Central Europe, 77 km long, up to 14 km wide, 3-4 m deep. During the summer, water temperatures can be as high as 28°C but the warmth is offset by the breezes from the *Bakony Mountains.* Lovely shifting of colour in the lake's waters. The Balaton is sometimes dangerous and the tranquil lake can quickly turn into a seething cauldron of windlashed waves. When red and white rockets are shot up as a warning, you should return to land as quickly as possible. Large resorts line the lake shore. It is estimated that about 2 million tourists visit it annually.

Siófok. Modern resort and large port. Harbour esplanade, rose garden, outdoor cinema. **Balatonföldvár,** resort, harbour, water sports. **Balatonszemes.** Resort. 15th-cent. Gothic church. *Post museum.*

Fonyód with lovely views from the castle hill. *Présház-czarda,* famous inn.

Nagykanizsa (40 000). Franciscan church and Church of the Holy Trinity, both Baroque, and neo-classical synagogue with impressive treasury.

Letenye. Yugoslavian frontier. E 96 continues to Zagreb and Rijeka.

North shore of Lake Balaton:

Veszprém (35 000). Chief town of the Bakony region. Centre of the chemi-

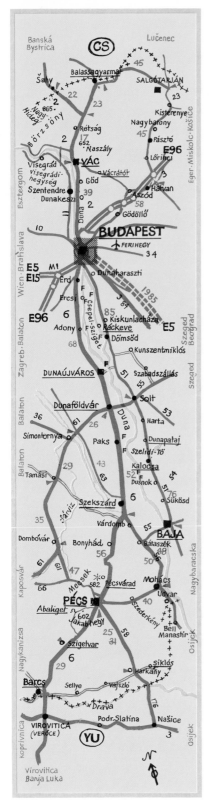

cal industry. University. Handsome town with many Baroque buildings and lovely views. Small, old houses and watermills line the twisting River *Séd*. 11th-cent. cathedral. Beautiful *Gizella-Kápolna* (chapel) with angel frescoes (13th cent.). The town is dominated by the mighty *fortress*, built in the 10th cent., enlarged in the 15th cent., destroyed by the Austrians in 1702 and rebuilt during the 18th cent. Splendid views from the terrace of the fortress which is adorned with statues of Stephen and Gizella.

Herend to the west. Famous for its production of exquisite porcelain. *Porcelain museum.*

Balatonfüred. One of the largest seaside resorts. Hotel Marin has 800 beds. Theatre Week at the beginning of June. Spa.

Tihany on a 6 km long, 2-3 km wide, peninsula. Some of its hills are 100 m high. Hundreds of dried-up geyser craters. National park. The Benedictine monastery with royal tomb was founded in 1055. Concerts in the Baroque church. Museum devoted to the boat traffic on the lake. *"Skanzen"* (the name has been taken from its Stockholm model) is an open-air museum which, among other things, has interesting displays of ceramics and fishing. Tihany also has a famous stud farm and riding school. Riding also at *Kinizsi Castle* (15th cent.). Jousting tournaments.

Badacsonytomai produces a well-known wine. The vineyards are on the slopes of an extinct volcano. *Museum* with works by the Balaton painter, Egri Jószef.

Tapolca. Boat trips into a 340 m deep grotto. *Szigliget* has remains of a 13th-cent. castle.

Keszthely. *Festetich Castle* with an enormous library. Summer concerts in the park. *Balaton Museum* with exhibits of geography, folklore, folk art, flora and fauna. Antique history and tourist history.

Héviz. Resort and spa. Imposing Thermal Hotel with lovely park and open-air theatre. Large *lake of mineral water*, the largest in Europe. A spring in the middle of the lake renews the water within 24 hours. Summer lake temperature: 32-35° C. Winter temperature: 28° C. Delightful old wooden bath house.

Kis-Balaton (Little Balaton), the westernmost section of the lake, south of Keszthely. This is Central Europe's largest nesting area for birds – in particular herons and flamingoes.

2 and 6. Balassagyarmat – Budapest – Pécs – Barcs

Balassagyarmat. Czech frontier. *Museum Palóc* and adjoining "Skanzen" open-air museum. Roman Catholic church from 1740.

Vác (30 000). Maria Theresia's Baroque triumphal arch was erected in 1754. The Holy Trinity statue and Franciscan church are also in the Baroque style. Cathedral (18th cent.). Facilities for Danube swimming and water sports. Ferry to *Szentendre Island*, site of the Pokol Czárda, "Inn of Hell". *Vácrátót* with arboretum.

BUDAPEST, see town plans.

Dunaújváros (45 000). New industrial town and Danube port. 25 to 30 m high river banks with fine places for fishing.

Dunaföldvár. The Turkish Tower remains from a medieval fortress. *Fadd*, little resort on the banks of the old river bed of the Danube, 7 km long and 400 m wide.

Szekszárd. Wine centre, site of the Roman town of Alisca. King Béla founded a Benedictine abbey here in 1061. Now a mixture of old and modern buildings. Town museum with art and archaeological artifacts.

Pécsvárad. 11th-cent. abbey church. Fortress with archaeological museum, and a tourist hotel in the cannon tower.

PÉCS (140 000). The German name for this town was Fünfkirchen. Large industrial city with an exceptionally well-preserved city centre. Lovely buildings and narrow streets. Ghazi Khassum Pasha had the enormous mosque ("djami") erected. It is the largest building in Hungary from the period of the Turkish occupation. It is now a Roman Catholic church. Large cathedral with four towers. *Janus Pannonius Museum* displays ceramics from Zsolnay. Museum dedicated to the works of the painters Csontváry and Vasarely ("op art").

South of Pécs is *Siklós* with a handsome fortress (14th-16th cent.). Chapel with frescoes. Museum with art and weapons.

Abaliget in the *Mecsek Mountains*. Stalactite caves. Lake with beach.

Szigetvár. Island fortress. Beautiful frescoes in the church that was once a mosque. *Barcs.* Yugoslavian frontier.

The road on the east side of the Danube passes a Baroque palace in *Ráckeve* and a salt lake in *Dunapataj*, Szelidi-tó, 2-3 m deep. Summer water temperatures 20-27° C. *Kalosca.* Famous for pepper and painted houses.

Baja (34 000), with Baroque church and palace. Observatory and planetarium. Large market town.

TOWN PLANS

BUDAPEST (2.1 million)
The capital of Hungary is beautifully situated on the Danube. The Romans built the city of Aquincum in the area that is now known as Óbuda (Old Buda). Remains of Roman fortifications, amphitheatre and baths.
The Magyars (Hungarians) arrived in the 10th cent. and Buda became a major centre of trade. It lost its commercial importance during the Turkish

1 *Matthias Church.*
2 *Fishermen's Bastion.*
3 *Buda Castle. Museum of Fine Arts.*
4 *Liberation Monument. Citadel.*
5 *Rudas Baths.*
6 *Gellért, hotel and baths.*
7 *Chain Bridge.*
8 *Lukacs Baths.*
9 *Parliament House.*
10 *Cathedral of St. István (St. Stephen).*
11 *Opera house.*
12 *City Church.*
13 *National Museum.*
14 *Museum of Applied Arts.*
15 *Market hall.*
16 *Botanical gardens.*
17 *Museum of Ethnography.*
18 *Kossuth Mausoleum.*
19 *Heroes' Square. Museum of Fine Arts.*
20 *Városliget Park. Castle of Vajda-hunyad.*
21 *Zoo and Luna Park.*
22 *Széchenyi Baths.*
23 *Museum of Transport.*

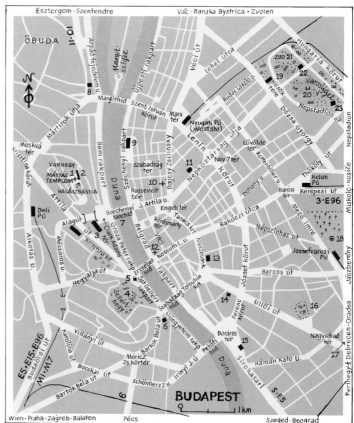

Matthias Church, the new Hilton Hotel and the Fishermen's Bastion, Budapest

occupation (1541-1686). The city of Pest grew up on the opposite bank of the river. The two cities were united in 1873 and became Budapest. At this point the Danube is 260- 500 m wide. The most famous of Budapest's bridges is the *Lánchid* (Chain Bridge), by the Scot, Clark Adam. The square at the western bridge-abutment bears his name (complemented with the necessary – for Hungarians – accent marks). This is also the site of a milestone bearing the inscription "O". All distances in Hungary are measured from this point.

The lovely *Margitsziget,* Margaret Island, lies in the Danube between Buda and Pest. Roman ruins, esplanades, sports facilities, cafés, swimming. In 1979, the Thermal Hotel Margitsziget, a luxury hotel, opened near the thermal springs. There are 123 hot springs in Budapest. Their waters have been piped to a large number of thermal baths and Budapest has become a spa and watering place.

Szechenyi Baths, the outdoor swimming-pool in the city park, is a unique installation for a major city. The 100-year-old *Lukács Baths* are particularly well-known for its impressive facilities for the treatment of rheumatism. Lovely garden. The *Rudas Baths* were built as long ago as 1560 for Sokoli Mustafa Pasha. Perhaps the most magnificent of these establishments are the facilities in the marble-halls in the ground floor of the distinguished *Gellért Hotel.*

Buda has several places where you can enjoy splendid views. *Gelért-hegy,* with an enormous monument dedicated to the Soviet Army's victory in 1945. It is possible to reach *Szabadsághegy* either by rack railway or the "Pioneer Railway" whose personnel (with the exception of the engine drivers) are all under 14. Cable cars to *János Mountain. Várhegy* (Castle Hill) with old quarter. Many Baroque houses. The huge *Royal Palace,* built in the 18th cent., was destroyed by fire in 1944. It is being restored and it

Vajdahunyad Castle in the Budapest City Park

already houses several museums. This was the site of a 13th-cent. castle that was damaged and ultimately destroyed during the war against the Turks. The oldest section of the *Mátyástemplom* (Matthias Church) dates from about 1255. Royal coronation and wedding church. The **Fishermen's Bastion** got its name from the Fishermen's Guild, one of the guilds responsible for the defence of the city during the Turkish wars. The romantic towers, ramparts and galleries were built in 1903. Wonderful views. Statue of St. Stephen, Hungary's first Christian king. The Fishermen's Bastion has recently gained an incongruous neighbour in the massive shape of the controversial Hilton Hotel. This modern addition to the Budapest skyline was built on the ruins of a Dominican abbey. Parts of the remains of the abbey are visible from the hotel foyer. Near by is Ruszwurm, Budapest's oldest pastry shop. The building dates from 1696, but a bakery was opened on this site in about 1500. It consists of two small rooms, a few tables and a cabinet with pastry shop museum.

Pest. The modern part of the city. Bustling, much city activity. New enormous luxury hotels and huge *Parliament* (268 m long, 123 m wide, 96 m high) near the quays. *Hösök tere* (Heroes' Place), a spacious square with monuments to the great men of Hungary. They were raised in 1896, to mark the foundation of Hungary, 1000 years earlier. *Art gallery* and *art museum* with impressive collections. Near by, on an island in a little lake, is a copy of *Vajdahunyad Castle* in Transylvania (now Hunedoara in Roumania). Architectural history, agri-

cultural museum, forestry museum. *Városliget,* the City Park, with zoo, botanical garden, amusement park and the *Szechenyi Baths* which has water piped in from mineral springs. *Népstadion* (People's Stadium) accommodates 100 000 spectators.

Museums

Hungarian National Museum. Historical museum with the royal Hungarian regalia – coronation robe, sword and orb. In a particularly well-guarded room is the **Crown of St. Stephen,** with its distinctive crooked cross. In 1978, after 30 years in the U.S.A., it was returned to Hungary.

The former Royal Palace in Buda houses the *National Gallery* (art), a museum of the workers movement, and an historical museum. The *Aquincum Museum* with Roman finds. *Museum of Applied and Decorative Art. Museum of Ethnography, Semmelweiss Medical History Museum, Museum of Transport, commerce and hotel museum, stamp museum, foundry museum,* and many more. The *Underground Railway Museum* is a reminder of the fact that the underground in Budapest is the oldest in Europe.

A few of Budapest's 10 000 eating-places: Mátyás Pince, cellar restaurant, opened in 1904 on a site near the Erzsébet Bridge, where inns have existed since the 15th cent. Not far away, the pleasant Karpatia and Apostolok. Gundel (close to the zoo), modern but with traditions that date back to the 19th cent. Hungaria with flamboyant décor, a literary café and restaurant. The décor of the Vörösmarty pastry shop is well worth a visit. Large rooms, marble, mirrors and an enormous pastry counter.

Statue of St. Stephen, Budapest

I · Italy

I·Italia

Area: 801 000 km² (110 280 sq.miles)

Population: 57 million. The official religion is Roman Catholicism, but state and church are separate and independent entities. The majority of the population speaks Italian, a Romance language that has developed from Latin. Some linguistic minority groups: German is spoken in Trentino-Alto Adige, French in Valle d'Aosta, Rhaeto-Romanic in the Dolomites and Slovene in Friuli-Venezia-Giulia.

Major cities: Roma (Rome) 3 million, Milano (Milan) 2 million, Napoli (Naples) 2 million, Torino (Turin) 1.2 million, Genova (Genoa) 813 000, Palermo 693 000, Bologna 500 000, Firenze (Florence) 462 000, Venezia (Venice) 355 000.

Government: Republic with a president and two houses of parliament (Senate and Chamber of Deputies). The president heads the government. Italy has 20 regions, 95 provinces and 8 000 local districts.

Rome is also the capital of another state: The Vatican City State, where the Pope has absolute legislative, executive and judicial powers. Population: 1 000. Area: 400 000 m². The world's smallest nation.

History

6th cent. B.C. Etruscan culture in the north. Greek culture in the south.

5th cent. B.C. Rome dominates the peninsula.

218-201 B.C. Second Punic War. Hannibal crosses the Alps.

58-51 B.C. Caesar conquers Gaul.

49 B.C. Caesar becomes dictator and strengthens the power of Rome. He is murdered by Brutus in 44 B.C.

30 B.C.- A.D. 14 Augustus emperor.

4th cent. Constantine the Great moves his capital to Byzantium (Constantinople).

476 Fall of the Roman Empire.

800 Charlemagne proclaimed Emperor of Rome.

11th cent. The struggle begins between the papal and imperial powers. During the Middle Ages Italy is under the rule of German emperors.

1271 The Venetian, Marco Polo, begins his journey to China.

13th-16th-cent. Despite internal struggles between warring city-states and princely houses, culture and trade flourish.

1300-1378 The popes, in exile from Rome, take up residence in Avignon, France.

1381 Venice defeats Genoa.

16th-17th cent. The French and then the Spaniards rule Italy.

1713 Austria occupies Milan, Naples and Sicily.

1796 Napoleon conquers Savoy, Piedmont and Lombardy.

1815 The Congress of Vienna restores the small Italian states. Austria controls the north of Italy.

1860 Italian uprising led by Garibaldi.

1861 Victor Emanuel of Sardinia is proclaimed king of a united Italy. Turin is made capital.

1864 The capital is moved to Florence.

1870 Rome becomes part of Italy and is made capital.

1911-1912 War with Turkey.

1914-1918 First World War. Italy sides with the Allies (1915) and gains South Tirol, Trieste, and other Austrian territories.

1922 Mussolini's "March on Rome". Fascist era begins.

1936 Italian occupation of Abyssinia (Ethiopia).

1939 Italian occupation of Albania.

1940 Italy enters the Second World War on the side of Germany.

1943 Fall of Mussolini. He is executed in 1945. Armistice with the Allies who have landed on Sicily and in southern Italy.

1946 Italy is proclaimed a republic.

1949 Italy joins NATO.

1954 Trieste is returned to Italy.

Currency: Lira (ITL).
The import and export of Italian currency is restricted to 200 000 lire in cash. Visitors to Italy who expect to take out more than 200 000 lire worth of foreign currency when leaving the country, must declare the total value of the money they bring on entering the country.

Business hours: Banks 8.30 a.m.-1.30 p.m. Closed Saturdays. Post offices 8.00 a.m.-2.00 p.m. In some places closed Saturdays, otherwise, the above opening times apply. The main post offices in the larger cities are often open until 9.00 p.m. on weekends and on Sunday mornings. (Stamps may be bought from tobacconists.) Shops 8.30 a.m.-1.00 p.m. and 3.00-7.00 p.m.

Holidays: New Year's Day, Easter Sunday and Easter Monday, April 25 (Anniversary of the 1945 liberation), May 1, August 15 (Ferragosto), November 1 (All Saints' Day), December 8 (Immaculate Conception), December 25 and 26.

Local holidays in honour of local patron saints: April 25, Venezia

Routes described:

The roads have been arranged according to national road numbers as E- numbers are not posted in Italy.

A 1	Milano – Bologna – Roma
A 2	Roma – Napoli
A 3	Napoli – Reggio di Calabria
A 4	Trieste – Venezia – Milano – Torino
A 5	Aosta – Torino
A 6	Torino – Savona
A 7	Milano – Genova
A 8 and SS 33	Simplon – Milano
A 9	Lugano – Como – Milano
A 10	Menton – Genova
A 11	Firenze – Lucca
A 12	Genova – Livorno – Roma
A 13	Padova – Bologna
A 14	Bologna – Ancona – Brindisi
A 16	Napoli – Canosa di Puglia
A 18	Messina – Catania
A 19	Palermo – Caltanisetta – Catania
A 22	Brennero – Bolzano – Verona – Bologna
A 24	Roma – L'Aquila – S. Benedetto
A 25	Roma – Arezzano – Pescara
A 29	Palermo – Trapani
SS 1	Livorno – Tarquinia, see A 12
SS 2	Firenze – Siena – Roma, see A 1
SS 3	Fano – Assisi – Roma
SS 114	Catania – Siracusa
SS 115	Trapani – Agrigento – Siracusa

Special map: Sardegna

Town plans: Bologna Firenze Milano Napoli Roma Torino Venezia Verona

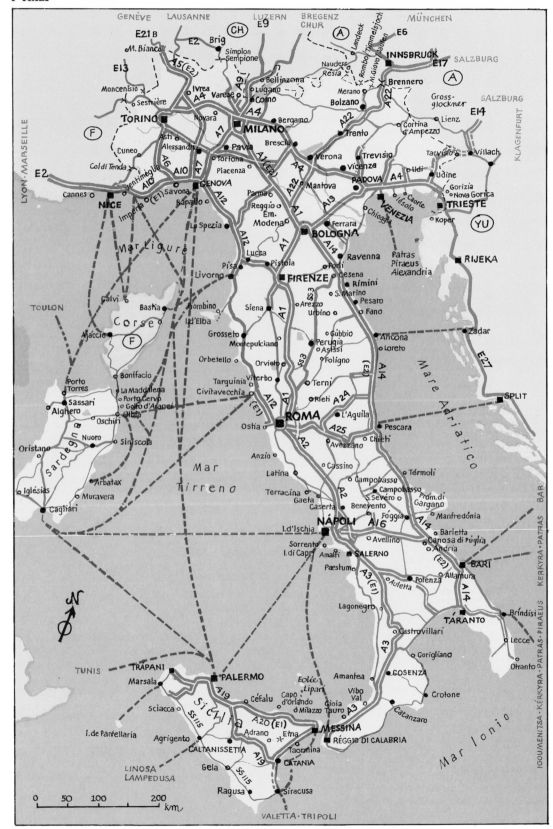

Bellagio on Lake Como

(Venice) S. Marco; June 24, Firenze (Florence), Genova (Genoa), Torino (Turin) S. Giovanni Battista; September 19, Napoli (Naples) S. Gennaro; October 4, Bologna S. Petronio; December 7, Milano (Milan) S. Ambrogio.

Hotels

Hotels are classified in five categories, from 4, to de Luxe. There are three categories of guest house. Category 1 is equivalent to hotel category 2.

An annual publication listing hotels and guest houses, with appropriate categories, the "Annuario Alberghi", is issued by ENIT, the Italian State Tourist Authority. There are almost 200 spas in Italy.

Camping

All camping sites are well guarded. TCI (Touring Club Italiano) publish a book called "Campeggi in Italia" (which also includes youth hostels) with Italian, French and English texts. A practical map is also issued by ENIT, the Italian State Tourist Authority. Further information from the Italian Camping Organization (Federcampeggio), Casella Postale 23, Firenze. The head office is at Exit 19 (Prato-Calenzano) on the Autostrada del Sole. The organization is a member of AIT.

Restaurants

Remember always to get a numbered receipt or an itemized bill that includes the VAT charge. The receipt, "ricevute fiscale", must be in your possession when you leave the restaurant. There are occasional official patrols waiting outside restaurants, and if customers cannot show the "ricevute fiscale", both they and the restaurant owner risk being fined.

Food and drink

Even the most superficial résumé of Italian food and drink would require far more space than this book can allow. Meals are tasty, large, and carefully prepared. Enormous pasta dishes that, outside of Italy, would be considered a meal in themselves are here just the beginning of a lunch or dinner. Local specialities:

Piemonte (Piedmont): Bagna cauda fondua, melted cheese dishes.

Lombardia (Lombardy): Risotto alla milanese, rice with saffron. Osso buco alla milanese, veal in tomato sauce, Minestrone, thick vegetable soup. Risotto alla Pilora, a rice-based speciality of Mantova (Mantua). Cotoletta alla milanese, breaded veal cutlet. Polenta e uccelli, polenta, a form of porridge made with maize, served with small birds. Bel paese, unspiced cheese.

Veneto: Risi e bisi, rice and peas. Risi e

Messina on Sicily and the Messina Straits

scampi, rice with prawns. Jota, vegetable soup.

Trentino-Alto Adige. Sausage, dumplings. Lasagne col pesto, green lasagne with a basil sauce.

Emilia-Romagna: Lasagna verdi. Capalletti, pasta filled with minced meat. Zuppa di pesce, fish soup. Pesce alla griglia, grilled fish.

Toscana (Tuscany): Bistecca alla fiorentina, grilled steak. Triglie alla livornese, red mullet with onion and tomato sauce. Arosto arrosto, roast pork.

Umbria: Porchetta, whole roast suckling pig. Tartofi neri, black truffles.

Lazio (Latium): Spaghetti alla carbonara, spaghetti with ham in a rich creamy sauce. Gnocchi alla romana, tiny potato and flour dumplings with meat or tomato sauce. Abbacchio, roast lamb.

Campania: Maccheroni al pomodoro, macaroni with tomato sauce. Calamari e triglie, squid and deep-fried fish. Carne alla pizzaiola, beef in marjoram-flavoured tomato sauce. Pizza napolitana.

Calabria: Arrosto di maiale, roast pork. Melanzane al funghetto, aubergines stuffed with mushrooms. Trote arrostite, fried trout.

Sicilia (Sicily): Pasta con le sarde, macaroni with sardines. Caponata, aubergines in tomato sauce. Cassate, cake or icecream with candied fruit.

Sardegna (Sardinia): Su schidoni, pork or lamb roasted on a spit.

Italian wines are world-famous. Some of the best-known table wines are: Barolo, Barbera, Barbaresco, Valtellina, Riesling, Vin Santo, Terlano, Soave, Valpolicella, Lambrusco, Malvisia, Trebbiano, Chianti, Verdicchio, Orvieto, Frascati, Est, Lacrimae Christi, Moscato, Ciró, Corco, Marsala, Vernaccia, Nuragus, Giró.

Aperitifs: Vermouth, Marsala, Cinzano, Malvasia, Martini, Campari, Punt e Mes.

Liqueurs: Strega, Sambucca.

Shopping

Lace from Burano, ceramics from Faenza, glass from Venice (Murano), leather goods from Florence, marble from Carrara, alabaster from Volterra, woodcarvings from Ortisei, terracotta figures from Sicily, silver and gold, gloves, hats, shoes.

Petrol

Although the sight of so many petrol stations is comforting, it is always best to buy petrol at the first opportunity, as they often close early in the evening and long lunchtime closings are the rule rather than the exception. Most petrol stations (about 75%) are closed on Sundays and holidays. Very few are open at night.

A package of petrol coupons giving a saving on the pump price can be purchased from the AA or at main ports and border crossings.

It is forbidden to carry petrol in cans in a vehicle.

Drivers of diesel-driven vehicles must, at frontier stations, declare the exact amount of diesel fuel they are importing in the tank (form V2). When leav-

The Organ Fountain in Villa d'Este, Tivoli

ing Italy, you may not take out more diesel fuel than you brought in.

Speed limits. Traffic regulations.

Speed limits are graded according to the volume of the vehicle's cylinders. Groupings are as follows: under 600 cc, under 900 cc, under 1300 cc, and over 1300 cc. Each group has its own speed limits. Speed limits for cars over 1300 cc are: Motorways 140 kmh, other roads 110 kmh, built-up areas 50 kmh. For cars in the under 1300 cc category the speed limits are:

Motorways 130 kmh, other roads 100 kmh, built-up areas 50 kmh.

Cars in the under 900 cc category 10 kmh less, cars in the under 600 cc category 20 kmh less on motorways and other roads.

Cars towing caravans are never allowed to drive faster than 100 kmh.

For motorcycles in the 150 cc and over category, the speed limits are 130 kmh on motorways and 100 kmh on other roads. Under 150 cc 10 kmh less, under 99 cc 20 kmh less.

These speed limits are a general guideline, but the regulations may change at any time. Fines for speeding can be quite expensive, and prison sentences are not unknown.

Italian drivers often use their horns to signal, but this is not allowed in built-up areas (except in cases of emergency). Children under 3 are not permitted to travel in the front seats.

It it compulsory to used dipped headlights at all times in tunnels.

It is recommended that motoristst carry a set of replacement light bulbs and have a rear-view mirror on the left external side of the vehicle.

Parking

It is advisable always to leave your car in a guarded car park. Parking discs are required in "Zona disco" areas, where parking in usually allowed from 8.00 a.m. to 8.00 p.m. In "Zona verde", green zones, parking is forbidden 8.00-9.30 a.m and 2.30-4.00 p.m.

Roads

The motorways, "autostrade", are generally toll roads. Drivers collect a card when entering the motorway. Often the booths are unmanned, and you must press a yellow button that releases the card. If you neglect to do this, then you must pay for the whole length of the motorway. Payment at motorway exits. New cards are required every time you join a motorway. Some motorway routes, Milano-Laghi, Firenze-Mare, Roma-Civitavecchia, and a few more, are "open" motorways, where you pay at toll booths – no cards are required.

Road patrols

The Italian Automobile Club, ACI (Automobile Club Italia), have "Soccorso ACI" patrol cars. Nationwide tel. 116. Information (ACI) tel.116.

Police and ambulance, nationwide, tel. 113.

ACI, Automobile Club, Via Marsala 8, 00185 Roma, tel. (06) 49981.
TCI, Touring Club Italiano, Corso Italia 10, Milano, tel. (02) 8526-1.
ENIT, Italian State Tourist Authority, Via Marghera 2, Roma tel. 497 11.
Italian State Tourist Office (ENIT), 1 Princes Street, London W1A 7RA. Tel. 01-408 12 54.

A1. Milano – Bologna – Roma. *Autostrada del Sole*

The *Autostrada del Sole* in itself is an impressive sight. One of the most beautiful roads in Europe – daring engineering with exciting bridges and tunnels. Shady rest-stops are non-existent. Sun-baked car parks, enormous service areas, supermarkets and crowded restaurants are the rule. But there are many excellent possibilities for combining fast motorway travel with side trips on pleasant secondary roads to interesting places.

MILANO (Milan), see town plans.

Lodi (32 000). 15th-cent. Incoronata Church. **Crema.** Beautiful Church of S. Maria delle Croce (15th cent.), circular exterior, octagonal interior. Magnificent Romanesque-Gothic cathedral.

PIACENZA (106 000). Founded 218 B.C. Renaissance town where brick is the predominant building material. Well-preserved ramparts (6.5 km long) and Renaissance palaces. Piazza dei Cavalli with town hall, "il Gotico", a remarkable medieval (1280) structure. *Duomo* (cathedral, 13th cent.) with lovely frescoes.

CREMONA (80 000). Made famous by its violin makers, Stradivarius, Amati, and Guarneri. The most famous, Stradivarius (1644-1737), is the subject of a museum in the *Palazzo dell'Arte.* Several handsome palaces. *Duomo* (cathedral), a mixture of Gothic and Romanesque, a typical Lombard style. *Torrazzo*, a 111 m high campanile, the tallest in Italy. *Loggia dei Militi* (1292) to the left of the Palazzo Comunale. Fidenza. Splendid 13th-cent. Romanesque cathedral. Beautiful façade.

PARMA (174 000), famous for its Parma ham and Parmesan cheese. Impressive 11th-cent. **cathedral** in the Lombard Romanesque style. Beautiful frescoes. *Battistero* (Baptistry), one of the most beautiful in Italy. Enormous brick Palazzo della Pilotta with National Gallery, museum of antiquities and Teatro Farnese.

REGGIO NELL'EMILIA (128 000). Baroque Church of Mad. della Ghiara. Galleria Parmeggiani (art museum).

MODENA (171 000). Elegant town with wide streets, tree-lined avenues and arcades. Local culinary specialities include zamponi (pigs' trotters) and the red Lambrusco wine. Maserati and Ferrari motor car factories. Romanesque *duomo* (cathedral) with beautiful bas-reliefs and doorways. *Ghirlandina*, an 87 m high leaning bell tower.

BOLOGNA, see town plans.

The road through the *Passo di Raticosa* and *Passo di Futa* is very beautiful. *Firenzuola.* Lovely little mountain town.

PRATO (143 000). Large textile centre. Several splendid buildings reflect the town's long history that was marked by its battles with Florence. Medieval town wall with five gates. Castello dell'Imperatore is part of the fortifications. Richly decorated Romanesque *cathedral* (12th-14th cent.). Pulpit with the Holy Girdle, given, according to legend, to St. Thomas by the Virgin Mary.

Autostrada A 11 goes to Lucca.

PISTOIA (93 000) has a beautiful square, Piazza del Duomo. Romanesque-Gothic basilica with a Madonna from 1485 and a famous silver altar begun in the early 13th cent., and finally completed in the middle of the 15th cent. The campanile, a 12th-cent. fortification tower. The Battistero (Baptistry) has a handsome portal. Museo Civico (art) in the Palazzo del Commune. Ospedale del Ceppo with famous terracotta frieze by the della Robbia family.

To the north, *Abetone,* winter sports resort in magnificent surroundings. To the west, *Montecatini Terme,* one of the most elegant spas in Italy. Cable car (10 min.) to *Montecatini Alto,* beautifully situated. Splendid panorama.

FIRENZE (Florence), including *Fiesole,* see town plans.

Vallombrosa. Abbey in Baroque and Renaissance styles.

AREZZO (87 000). Old Etruscan town. *Church of S. Francesco* with exquisite 15th-cent. frescoes. *Duomo* (cathedral) with fine stained-glass windows. *Piazza Grande,* surrounded by handsome palaces and the Church of S. Maria della Pieve. Birthplace of the poet Petrarca (Petrarch).

Cortona. Little town, unchanged since the Renaissance. Medieval ramparts and Palazzo Pretorio, site of the *Museo dell'Accademia Etrusca* with Etruscan and Roman exhibits and Italian art. 15th-cent. cathedral. *Museo Diocesano,* with art collections in the Church of Il Gesù.

PERUGIA and *Assisi,* see SS 3 Fano – Roma.

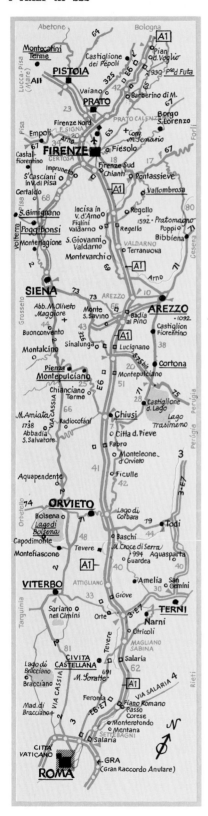

The SS 2 (Via Cassia) runs parallel to the Autostrada del Sole.

Poggibonsi. Old fortress with abbey.

San Gimignano. From a distance you can see 15 mighty towers rising above the city wall. Once there were 72. During the Middle Ages, the Italian city-states were caught up in the political struggles between the Guelphs and the Ghibellines. In addition to this, they were plagued by local disturbances and the violence of native tyrants. It was best to have a castle of one's own, and, for the sake of prestige, the castle should be more massive and higher than all the others. Medieval atmosphere and winding streets. La Collegiata Cathedral (12th cent.) on the beautiful *Piazza del Duomo.* Piazza della Cisterna with a cistern from 1273.

Volterra. Medieval walled town. Beautifully situated. Splendid palaces line *Piazza dei Priori.* Large art collection in the Palazzo dei Priori. Cathedral rebuilt in the 13th cent. Beautiful frescoes. Museo Etrusco Guarnacci.

SIENA (65 000). The chief town of Tuscany, with its turrets and towers, is set on three hills. Fascinating medieval atmosphere. On *Piazza del Campo,* at the heart of the town, is the Palazzo Pubblico with the Torre del Mangia, a 102 m high tower. Art gallery (Sienese School) in the palace. Countless picturesque streets, e.g. the winding Via di Città and Via Banchi di Sopra, a busy shopping street. Gothic *cathedral* with red, white and black marble façade and splendid floor. Renaissance Palazzo Piccolomini with library. *Pinacoteca,* art by painters of the Sienese School. *Museo dell'Opera del Duomo* with exhibits concerning the construction of the cathedral, an enormous task that was begun in 1339 but was interrupted in 1348 when the Black Plague ravaged Siena. 16th-cent. castle. Fine views, and Italy's Permanent Wine Exhibit.
Palio di Siena. Horse race held on July 2 and August 16 in Piazza del Campo. It begins with a procession of horses and knights in magnificent 15th-cent. costumes. They represent 17 "contradas", sections of the city, that compete against each other. The race is over after a couple of minutes. Tradition since 1656.
From Siena a good road goes to Grosseto. Other roads, e.g. via Massa Marittima or Roccastrada, are in some sections twisting mountain roads and take longer to drive, but they are interesting and provide lovely views.

Montepulciano. Lovely medieval town with Renaissance palaces. *Museo Civico* with terracottas by Andrea della Robbia. Renaissance Church of S. Biagio (1534). The 17th-cent. *cathedral* resembles S. Lorenzo in Florence.

Pienza. Small, almost wholly Renaissance town. Palazzo Piccolomini and other handsome Renaissance buildings on *Piazza Pio II.* A member of the Piccolomini family became pope in 1458 under the name of Pius (Pio) II, and the town was named after him. Museum.

Chiusi. Beautifully situated in olive groves. *Etruscan museum.* The entire area is filled with relics of the Etruscan period.

Orvieto (25 000). A medieval town high on a rock, this is one of the most beautiful places in Italy. Old quarter with twisting streets. *Cathedral* in the Romanesque-Gothic style. Famous façade, adorned with marble and mosaics. Its side walls are of light and dark stone. Beautiful frescoes, begun in 1447 by Fra Angelico and completed in 1504 by Signorelli. Reliquary containing the cloth in which the bleeding host was covered during the Miracle of Bolsena. (1263)

SS 2 goes to *Lago di Bolsena.* Former volcano crater, now beautiful lake. 14 km long, 146 m deep. 11th-cent. Church of S. Christina.

VITERBO (54 000). A town of medieval character. The *Piazza S. Pellegrino* is one of the most beautiful squares in Italy. Romanesque Church of S. Pellegrino and picturesque Via S. Pellegrino. *Fontana Grande* (13th cent.) is perhaps the most beautiful of the town's many fountains. *The Papal Palace* on Piazza S. Lorenzo, residence of 13th-cent. popes, is now an episcopal palace. Beautiful Gothic loggia. Splendid frescoes in the Convento S. Maria della Verità. *Museo Civico.* Etruscan and Roman exhibits, terracotta sculptures by della Robbia. Popes Adrian V and Clement IV are buried in the Gothic Church of S. Francesco.

Civita Castellana on a pumice-stone plateau. Site of the ancient city of Falerii Veteres, destroyed in A.D. 241. Romanesque *cathedral* with handsome portico. Palace, once residence of Cesare Borgia. Falerii Novi, built by the Romans after the destruction of Falerii Veteres. Extensive ruins and 2 km long town wall with 50 towers and nine gates.

ROMA (Rome), see town plans.

A2. Roma – Napoli

ROMA (Rome), see town plans.

Frascati with lovely parks and splendid palaces. The oldest is Villa Falconieri, built in 1548 for Cardinal Ruffini.

Albano Laziale. Roman amphitheatre for 15 000 spectators. Swimming baths constructed in the 3rd cent. for Roman legionaries.

Genzano di Roma. Little town on a lofty site. Palazzo Cesarini has beautiful gardens on a hillside that slopes down to the lake.

Palestrina. Medieval atmosphere. The enormous *Tempio della Fortuna* (Temple of Fortuna) built in the 8th cent. B.C, destroyed 82 B.C., but rebuilt. *Palazzo Barberini* with archaeological museum. 12th-cent. cathedral. Birthplace of the composer P. Palestrina (1525-1594).

Velletri (38 000). The Palazzo Ginetti has a Baroque staircase.

Cori. One of the oldest towns in the land. 2 km long remains of the *town wall.* Remains of a temple of Hercules (90 B.C.).

Segni. Little town. 2 km long town wall (5th cent. B.C.) Interesting *Porta Saracena.* Church of S. Pietro on the Acropolis. *Anagni.* During the Middle Ages often a residence of the popes. Cathedral of S. Maria (11th cent.). Mosaic floor.

Ferentino. Well-preserved town wall. Porta Sanguinaria to the south and Porta S. Maria to the east. Episcopal palace and *cathedral* with mosaic floor at the highest point of the town. *Fossanova.* Oldest Cistercian monastery in Italy (12th cent.). St. Thomas Aquinas died here in 1274.

Alatri. Medieval quarter. Abbazia di Casamari, Cistercian abbey. Legend says that the grave of Cicero is near the road. He was murdered in 43 B.C.

Montecassino. St. Benedict founded the famous abbey in 529. During the Second World War the Germans made it a part of the fortifications of the Gustav Line and from it were able to repel Allied forces attempting to liberate Rome. During a massive aerial bombardment on February 15, 1944, the abbey and most of its centuries-old treasures were destroyed, and the ruins made the struggle for the strategic point even more difficult. On May 18, Montecassino was taken by a Polish regiment under the command of the legendary General Anders. He was buried here in 1970. A large part of the library was rescued by two German officers. Earlier the abbey had been destroyed during wars in 581 and the 9th cent., and by an earthquake in 1349. Reconstruction work, following old plans, started in 1944.

Teano. Beautiful 12th-cent. cathedral. Remains of the once important ancient town of *Teanum.*

Capua (15 000). Archbishop's seat, founded in the 8th cent. after the destruction of the ancient town of Capua. *Museo Campano* (archaeology).

Santa Maria Capua Vetere. Enormous *amphitheatre* (170 × 140 m), largest in Italy before the construction of the Coliseum in Rome. Subterranean meeting place of followers of the Persian Mithras cult (2nd cent.).

Caserta (55 000). Provincial capital. The huge **Royal Palace** was built in the 18th cent. to outshine Versailles. 1 200 rooms. Site of the German capitulation in 1945. Beautiful park with fountains and a waterfall. English garden with exotic plants. **Caserta Vecchia** has ancient streets and a cathedral.

NAPOLI (Naples), see town plans.

Coastal towns:

Anzio. Villa of Emperor Nero. The Allies landed here in 1944.

Sabaudia. Modern town on Lake Sabaudia. Water sports centre. The entire area round San Felice Circeo is now a national park. Many caves.

Terracina. Seaside resort. Splendid Piazza del Municipio. Cathedral of S. Cesario. Views from the Temple of Jupiter.

Sperlonga. Fishing village and seaside resort. It is said that Emperor Tiberius held banquets in the *Grotta di Tiberio.* In 1957 statues were recovered here.

Gaeta. Important town during the Roman period. 12th-cent. cathedral. Lombard castle (8th cent.). Views from the Torre di Orlando (Roland's Tower).

Formia. Seaside resort. **Minturnae.** Ruins of a Roman town. The *Garigliano* River, natural boundary between Latium and Campania.

Villagio Coppola – Pinetamare. Large, newly built resort with seven large hotels on the beach. Pine forest. Beautiful modern church of Sta. Maria del Mare. **Cuma.** Ruins and excavations of the oldest Greek colony in Italy (800 B.C.).

Pozzuoli (60 000). Industrial town. Thermal baths. Cathedral. Amphitheatre. Tourist resort on the shores of *Lago d'Averno.* **Campi Flegrei,** volcanic area with the 770 m wide la *Solfatara* crater. **Baia** and **Miseno.** Ancient ruins.

A 3. Napoli – Reggio di Calabria

ISCHIA (33 000). Island with volcanic origins. Major tourist attraction. Greeks settled here in the 7th cent. B.C. Large fortress (1438), built to withstand pirate attacks. *Chiesa (Church) dell'Asunta* in the mountains. Archaeology museum. Forio, a spa.

CAPRI (11 000). This island is a major resort and tourist attraction. Towns of *Capri* and *Anacapri* with white houses and picturesque streets. Beautiful Piazza with campanile. Some of the noteworthy sights: The *Blue Grotto* (Grotta Azzura, 50 × 30 m), *Villa Jovis*, once the palace of Emperor Tiberius, *San Michele,* villa built for the Swedish doctor and writer Axel Munthe (1857-1949) who wrote about the island in "The Story of San Michele". Lovely park with avenue of cypress trees. Large art collection which includes a head of Medusa, recovered after 2 000 years from the sea bed just off San Michele.

Vesuvio, Ercolane and **Pompei,** see Napoli, town plans.

Torre del Greco (90 000) has been destroyed many times by earthquakes.

Castellamare di Stabia (80 000). Built on the site of the ancient town of Stabiae which was destroyed in A.D. 79. Museum of antiquities. A fine Roman villa was destroyed in the 1980 earthquake.

Sorrento (15 000). Countless songs have been written about this famous tourist resort, situated on a lovely gulf renowned for its sunsets.

Positano. Elegant spa and seaside resort. **Praiano.** Fishing town with the famous *Grotta di Smeraldo* which can be reached by boat. **Amalfi.** Resort. During the Middle Ages an independent republic. Church of *S. Andrea* (13th cent.) with Arabian influences. Colourful façade and bronze doors made in Constantinople in 1066.

Minori. Picturesque fishing town and resort.

Ravello. Old hill town. During the 13th cent. it boasted 13 abbeys and many churches and palaces. Splendid *cathedral.* Narrow stepped streets and medieval atmosphere. Romanesque Church of S. Giovanni del Toro.

Vietri sul Mare, famous for its ceramics.

SALERNO (155 000), industrial city. Beautifully situated. A large part of Salerno retains its medieval character. Cathedral with ancient columns from Paestrum and bronze doors made in Constantinople in the 11th cent. Via Mercanti, a picturesque old shopping street. Impressive Lungomare Trieste, a seaside esplanade. *Eboli* (20 000). Palace.

PAESTUM. Ruins of a 6th-cent. Greek colonial town founded in the 6th cent. B.C. Remains of a Temple of Poseidon (Tempio di Nettuno) and Temple of Hera (Tempio di Juno). Superb museum.

Auletta. Little town. Beautiful stalactite and stalagmite cave, Grotta di Pertosa, with several kilometres of tunnels.

Vallo di Lucania is dominated by Monte Sacre with the Santuario della Madonna di Velia. **Sapri.** Old trading town. Stalactite and stalagmite cave at Maratea. **Castrovillari** is dominated by an old castle. Views from the Church of Madonna del Castello. **Spezzano Albanese.** The inhabitants are Albanians who maintain their old traditions.

COSENZA (102 000). Provincial capital and archbishop's seat. Cathedral with tomb of Isabella of Aragon (d. 1271).

La Sila. Beautiful, rather deserted range with peaks between 1 000 and 1 900 m. Highest is Mt Botte Donato, 1 928 m. Forests, green mountain lakes, snow as late as June. The Strada della Sila is extremely beautiful. Impressive views. Chief towns are S. *Giovanni in Fiore* and *Rossano.* The isolation is now being broken by a new series of resorts, built as a part of the government's plan to improve economic conditions in southern Italy.

Rogliano. Little town. Beautiful views out over the fertile countryside, Monte Coruzzo and the surrounding mountains.

East to **Catanzaro** (45 000). Founded in the 10th cent. Capital of Calabria since 1971. Cathedral and beautiful Chiesa (Church) del Rosario.

Crotone. Memorial pillar dedicated to Pythagoras who is said to have been born here. **Tropea.** Seaside town built on a cliff. Cathedral (12th cent.).

Vibo Valentia (31 000). Beautifully situated remains of a Greek ring-wall, built in the 4th cent.

Gioia Tauro. Little town in olive-growing district. **Bagnara Calabra.** Resort. Swordfish fishing. **Scilla.** Fishing port and resort.

Locri. Museum of antiquities. Splendid cathedral.

REGGIO DI CALABRIA (165 000). Port. Devastated by earthquakes in 1783 and 1908 (when 12 000 people were killed). The *Lungomare* along the shoreline is one of the loveliest promenades in Italy. Modern buildings. The major street is the Corso Garibaldi. *Museo Nazionale* with archaeological exhibits and large coin collection. The beautiful *Aspromonte Massif.*

A 4. Trieste – Venezia – Verona – Milano – Torino

Trieste (270 000). Most important port on the Adriatic Sea. Shipyards, metal-working industry, university. From the 14th-cent. until 1920, Trieste belonged to Austria. From 1920 until 1944 it belonged to Italy. Under international control from 1944 until 1954, then returned to Italy. *Piazza dell'Unità d'Italia* with harbour view. Large palaces and cafés. In the old part of town are the citadel and the Basilica di S. Giusto (14th cent.) *Museo del Mare* has displays related to ports, navigation and fishing.

Splendid coastal road that passes *Miramare Palace* (1871) with collection of Venetian art. Lovely park.

Gorizia (45 000). Modern town, scene of fierce battles during the First World War. Corso Roosevelt is the busiest street. Venetian castle with bastions above Piazza della Vittoria. Baroque Church of Sant'Ignazio. *Museo di Storia Patria* (handicrafts, etc.).

Aquileia was an important Roman town. Cathedral of S. Maria (11th cent.), rebuilt in the Gothic style. 4th-cent. mosaic floor. Museum of archaeology. Forum Romanum.

Grado, large seaside resort, once port for ancient Anquileia. Picturesque old town. Basilica of S. Eufemia, consecrated in 579. Mosaic floor and magnificent pulpit supported by six pillars.

Long row of seaside resorts along the Golfo di Venezia: *Grado, Lignano, Caorle* and *Lido di Jesolo.* Higher percentage of Italian guests than on the better known Rivieras but the number of foreign visitors is increasing. *Bibione,* for example, is popular with Germans.

Portogruaro lies in a wine district. The museum has objects found during the excavations of the Roman town of Concordia Sagittaria. *Pordenone.* Beautiful cathedral and campanile. Collection of art in the Palazzo Comunale.

Mestre. Suburb of Venice. Heavily industrialized. Massive Torre dell'Orologio (clock tower, 1808). It can be advantageous to stay in Mestre rather than in the often booked-up city. Frequent and convenient train and bus service to Venice.

VENEZIA (Venice), see town plans.

TREVISO (91 000). Old trading town, a part of the Venetian Republic since 1389. Beautiful old quarter, reminiscent of Venice – River Sile and canals. A daily fish market is held on an island in the Botteniga Canal. Calmaggiore, an arcaded street from the cathedral to the beautiful *Piazza dei Signori.*

Bassano del Grappa (30 000), west of Treviso, is famed for its ceramics. The Ponte Coperto, a remarkable covered wooden bridge over the Brenta, was originally constructed in 1209, but it has been rebuilt several times, most recently in 1945. *Museo Civico* has a large art collection. Road up to Monte Grappa (1 775 m). Magnificent panorama. Fierce battles 1917-1918 when Italian troops defended the summit against Austrian attacks.

PADOVA (Padua, 230 000). University founded 1222. Pilgrimages to the tomb of St. Anthony of Padua in the *Basilica del Santo.* Donatello's bronze statue of Venetian general Gattamelata outside the church, Scuola di Sant'-Antonio with famous paintings by Titian. Splendid frescoes in the Cappella di San Giorgio. More remarkable frescoes in the *Capella degli Scrovegni.* Palazzo della Ragione with a 79 m long and 27 m high grand hall. Law courts, now a concert hall. Picturesque *Piazza della Frutta* and *Piazza della Erbe.* Museo Civico (art). Europe's oldest botanical gardens (1545) with lovely views. Passenger ship service to Venice via the Brenta Canal.

VICENZA (115 000). Chief town of the Veneto. Elegant and beautiful town with many buildings by the Renaissance master, Andrea Palladio (1519-1580). He was a simple stone mason who caught the eye of a rich property owner who gave him the name Palladio (descendent of Pallas Athena). His task was to restore the wisdom and art of Ancient Greece to Italy. He became one of the most influential architects of Italy and his ideas and innovations spread throughout all of Europe. The English, in particular, responded to his classical style of architecture. Vicenza's most important street is called the Via Palladio.

Two of his buildings are in *Piazza dei Signori*: the Loggia del Capitano and the large basilica. The double-storeyed galleries are a typical example of Palladio's art. The large metal roof is a post-war addition. Torre di Piazza with 12th-cent. clock tower. *The Teatro Olimpico,* inspired by the theatres of antiquity, is one of the works of the school of Palladio. It was created by his student Scamozzi. Thought to be the world's oldest covered theatre, it seats 1 200 spectators and is still in use. *Palazzo Chiericati* (by Palladio) with Museo Civico. Large collection of art. Lombard section, coins and stamps. Outside the town is Villa *Rotunda* (Villa Capri), one of the most famous of Palladio's creations. Frescoes by Tiepolo in Villa Valmarana. *Monte Berico* with lovely views and pilgrimage church (17th cent.).

Marostica. Handsome square where a chess match with living figures is held every year in September.

VERONA, see town plans. *MANTOVA,* see A 22.

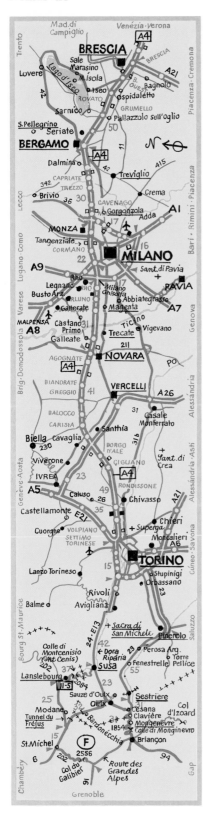

Lago di Garda (Lake Garda). Italy's largest lake, 370 km², 52 km long, 4-17 km wide. Maximum depth, 346 m. In the mild climate semi- tropical and Alpine flora flourish. Several resorts, see A 22.

Peschiera. Fishing port with Austrian fort. **Sirmione,** one of the largest resorts on Lake Garda. Spa with sulphur springs. Lovely old town with pleasant harbour. 13th-cent. Scaliger Castle. At the furthest tip of the spit are the Roman ruins of Grotta di Catulla, thought to have been baths.

BRESCIA (180 000). Industrial and commercial town. The heart of the city is *Piazza della Loggia*. The Loggia, a Renaissance building from 1550, was rebuilt after wartime damage. Now it serves as town hall. 11th-cent. Rotunda, also known as *Duomo Vecchio* (Old Cathedral). The *Duomo* (Cathedral) is a white marble Renaissance building with an 82 m high dome. *Broletto*, a medieval palace. *Pinacoteca Martinengo*, art gallery. Museum of medieval religious art, weapons, coins, etc. Tempio Capitolino, built for Emperor Vespasian. Museum of Roman antiquities with, among other displays, the Nike of Brescia. *Mount Maddalena* with splendid views out over the plains of the Po and Lake Garda towards the Alps.

Lago d'Iseo. Lovely little lake with large Monte Isola island. Pilgrimage church 400 m above the lake waters.

BERGAMO (120 000), consists of two towns. *Città Alta* (High Town), is the old town. Below it, *Città Bassa (Low Town), the modern city. Città Alta.* Important town during the Roman period, then a member of the Longobard (Lombard) League of Cities. It withstood a siege by the troops of Emperor Barbarossa. Venice had the fortress and ramparts built in the 14th cent. Heart of the town is the *Piazza Vecchia*, surrounded by handsome buildings: *Palazzo della Ragione* (16th cent.) with the Venetian Lion of St. Mark on the façade and impressive views from the tower, Romanesque Church of *S. Maria Maggiore* with paintings and tapestries (tomb of the composer Donizetti) and *Cappella Colleoni*, a richly adorned Renaissance building erected in 1476 as a mausoleum for the Venetian general, Bartolomeo Colleoni. Frescoes by Tiepolo. Its architect, Amadeo, also designed the Certosa di Pavia. Splendid 16th-cent. palaces and churches. *Città Bassa.* Busy, industrial town, with Piazza Matteotti at its heart. Accademia Carrara is one of the foremost art museums in northern Italy.

From Bergamo, a beautiful road goes through the Val Brembana to the distinguished spa of **San Pellegrino.**

Treviglio. Church of S. Martino. **Gorgonzola,** famous for its cheese. Most Gorgonzola cheese is actually produced in the province of the same name.

MILANO (Milan), see town plans. **Monza.** Site of a world-famous Autodrom, motor racing circuit. The time-saving motorway ring road that encircles Milan is now complete. But one must have nerves of steel when approaching the labyrinth of exit roads. Instead of signs for Novara, Torino, Bergamo, Brescia or Verona, there are sometimes signs reading "Tangenziale". This word, from the Latin "tangere" ("to touch"), means "the ring road", in this case A 4.

Magenta. Industrial town. Memorial plaque dedicated to the Battle of Magenta in 1859, a French and Sardinian victory which resulted in Milan gaining independence from the Austrians.

NOVARA (80 000). Industrial and agricultural centre. Gorgonzola cheese is produced here. Ramparts ring the old part of the town. 19th-cent. *cathedral* with 15th-cent. baptismal chapel. *Broletto* with Museo Civico (art gallery). Church of S. Gaudenzio with 120 m high dome.

Vercelli (50 000). Centre of a rice-producing area and the most important rice market in Italy. Picturesque buildings and streets between Piazza Cavour and the cathedral (16th cent.). *Borgogna art museum.*

TORINO (Turin) with the Basilica di Superga, see town plans.

Sacra di San Michele. The abbey was founded in 966 atop the summit of Monte Pirchiriano (962 m). Space was limited so tall pillars and supporting walls play an important role in the building's architecture. The apse hangs suspended over the valley. 16th-cent. frescoes.

Pinerolo. In the fortress the "Man in the Iron Mask" was imprisoned for 19 years. Some say that he was an Italian nobleman opposed to Louis XIV. Alexandre Dumas held that he was the king's twin brother and Voltaire claimed that the mysterious man was the true king and that Louis XIV was the son of Cardinal Mazarin.

Susa. 11th-cent. cathedral with beautiful campanile. Arco di Augusto, Roman triumphal arch (8 B.C.). Starting point of a lovely road via *Monceniso* (Mont-Cenis) to *Lanslebourg.* This was once one of the major Alpine passes and a traditional route for invaders. Rather easy road, suitable for cars towing caravans. 12% gradient up to the pass level, 2 083 m, then 10% gradient descent.

The new road through the **Fréjus Tunnel** is 12.8 km long.

Sestrière, 2 035 m, has become a large winter sports resort. The road via **Monginevro** is easy and suitable for cars towing caravans. 7% gradient to the pass level, 1 854 m, and descent with a 9% gradient.

A 5. Aosta – Torino

Roads from Genève (Ginevra/Geneva) and Lausanne (Losanna) meet in Aosta.

Monte Bianco (Mont Blanc) and tunnel, see France. **Courmayeur,** 1 228 m above sea level, has become a large winter sports resort. **Entrèves,** resort with cable cars to *Colle del Gigante* and on to **Aiguille du Midi** and **Chamonix.**

Colle di Gran S. Bernardo, see Switzerland. Well constructed road from the tunnel to Aosta. 5.8 km long tunnel (tolls) and 14 km galleries.
The road through the pass is narrow, and caravans are prohibited. Near the summit, at 2 469 m, are an observatory and the famous hospice of 1700. Kennels for St. Bernard dogs, used for Alpine rescues. Plan de Jupiter with statue of St. Bernard.

Aosta (36 000). Founded by the Romans in 24 B.C. Triumphal arch raised in honour of Caesar Augustus. Roman bridge, until as late as the 13th cent. the only access to the town. Porta Praetoria, on the site of a military encampment. Roman theatre that could accommodate 4 000 spectators. *Collegiata di San Orso,* abbey church with 8th-cent. crypt and 11th-cent. frescoes. Façade of terracotta. Museum of archaeology. *Cathedral* with façade of 1848. Stained- glass windows and mosaic floor. The heart of the city is the handsome *Piazza Chanoux.*

The Aosta Valley, virtually untouched by mass tourism until the opening of the Mont Blanc Tunnel, is now thronged with tourists. But the valley is very beautiful and the new motorway is a masterpiece of engineering. 38 bridges and four tunnels. 1 km long tunnel at Montjovet. Several bridges and some galleries have heated road surfaces to prevent the formation of ice.

To the south in the **Gran Paradiso** National Park can be found ibexes, chamois, roedeer, foxes, martens, golden eagles and lemmings.

Completed trans-Alpine road at **Borgofranco d'Ivréa.** The valley is filled with castles. **Cogne,** resort. **Fenis.** 14th-cent. citadel.

Valtournanche. Resort. **Breuil-Cervinia,** resort 2 024 m above sea level, surrounded by lofty peaks. Ski lifts, cable cars to *Plateau Rosa* (3 480 m above sea level) and *Cresta della Forca* (3 492 m).

St-Vincent. Spa. **Verrès.** Industrial town, castle. **Issogne Castle** (15th cent.). **Pont St-Martin,** Roman bridge where the Aosta Valley joins the *Lys Valley.* The road to **Gressoney-la-Trinité** passes a series of resorts.

Ivrea. Old town with modern buildings. Manufacture of office machines (Olivetti).

TORINO (Turin), see town plans.

A 6. Torino – Savona

Moncalieri. Little town with large 15th-cent. castle. Beautiful courtyard, marble staircase and galleries. Gino, artificial grotto with stalactites and lake.

Stupinigi. *Palazzina Stupinigi,* hunting lodge of Victor Amadeus II of Savoy, designed by Juvara. Beautiful park. Art and furniture museum.

Alba (21 000). Wine and grape commerce. School of oenology (study of wines and winemaking). Medieval buildings, churches and taverns.

Trinità. 11th-cent. Trinità della Cava, Benedictine abbey. Painting of "The Last Judgement" in the crypt.

Mondovi. Large cathedral. 17th-cent. Church of Gesù.Lovely views of the Alps from the Belvedere of the Torre dei Bressani. Santuario di Vicoforte, begun in the 16th cent., completed in the 19th cent. Dome with frescoes.

SAVONA (79 000). Major port and industrial town. Church of S. Giovanni Battista with Baroque façade. Leon Pancaldo Tower (16th cent.) commemorates one of Magellan's captains. Museo Civico. Renaissance palaces in the old quarter. Via Paleocapa with shops in the arcades. The Good Friday procession is a 500-year-old tradition.

Road SS 20 goes to Ventimiglia on the Mediterranean by way of the tunnel at *Tende* and the town of **Cuneo.**

Cuneo. (45 000). At the foot of the northern limits of the French Alpes Maritimes. Beautiful views from the fortress. Piazza Duccio Galimberti. Church of S. Croce (1715), oval form and concave façade.

Colle di Tenda. One of the oldest of the Alpine tunnels (short stretch), now an expanded modern road with hairpin bends. Suitable for cars towing caravans, but not during the winter. 9% gradient.

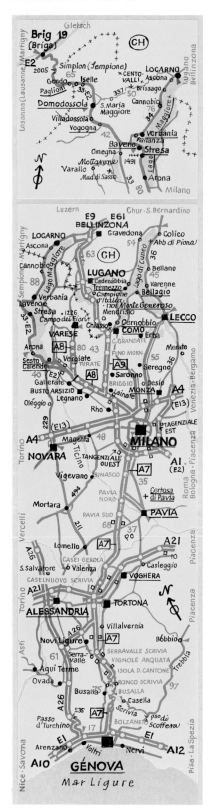

A 7. Milano – Genova

MILANO (Milan), see town plans.

Certosa di Pavia. This Carthusian monastery, founded in 1396 and completed in the 16th cent., is one of the foremost architectural wonders of Italy. Ornately adorned Renaissance marble façade. Tombs and magnificent altar. Chiostro Grande, cloisters with 125 arcades. Courtyard 125 × 102 m. Liqueur made by the monks is sold in the forecourt.

PAVIA (70 000). Capital of the province of Ticino. The Roman town on this site became the capital (6th-8th cent.). of the Longobards (Lombards). Old town centre. The *Broletto* (town hall, 12th cent.). Loggia from the 16th cent. *Palazzo della Pilotta* with art museum, antiquities museum and the famous *Teatro Farnese. Ponte Coperto,* reconstruction of a covered medieval wooden bridge. *San Michele,* in the Lombard-Romanesque style, was a coronation church. This is where Frederick Barbarossa was crowned. Beautiful façade. Church of *S. Pietro in Cielo d'Oro* (1132). Cielo d'Oro means "golden heaven" and it refers to the gilded ceiling that Dante mentions in his Divina Commedia. Tomb of St. Augustine (1370) with 95 statues.

Voghera (30 000). Medieval town centre round *Piazza Vittorio Emanuele II.* Cathedral of S. *Lorenzo* (1605). *Tortona* (20 000) at the foot of the Ligurian Apennines. 12th-cent. Church of S.Maria dei Canali. Museo Civico in the *Palazzo Guidobono.* The Santuario Madonna della Guardia has a 70 m high tower with statue of the Madonna.

ALESSANDRIA (70 000). Once an important fortress, now an industrial town whose best known products are Borsalino hats. *Piazza della Libertà* is the centre of the town. *Palazzo Municipale* (1826) with three beautiful tower clocks.

The Autostrada winds through valleys and goes over enormous viaducts. Although the gradient is only 7%, it is noticeable on the high-speed motorway. Sharp curves. At times the road skirts precipices several hundred metres deep. Holiday motorists often drive heavily loaded cars, and the heavy lorry traffic does not help at all, so drive carefully. 905 m long *Giove Tunnel.*

GENOVA (Genoa), see A 10.

A 8 and SS 33. Simplon Pass – Milano

Swiss border. Sempione (Simplon), see Switzerland, road E 2.

Paglioni. Italian customs station during the summer. Iselle – Villagio. Italian customs station during the winter.

Domodossola. (20 000). Chief town of the Valle d'Ossola. Picturesque Piazza del Mercato. 17th-cent. Palazzo Silva.

Vogogna. Village, beautifully situated high on a promontory. Two ruined castles. Beautiful but twisting road from Gravellona to Ascona and Lugano in Switzerland.

Lago Maggiore. One of the most beautiful lakes in Italy. 60 km long, maximum depth 372 m. Many resorts. *Verbania,* a town of winding streets. Beautiful rhododendron garden. *Baveno.* Spa with splendid lakeside esplanade.

Stresa. Spa and elegant resort. Mountain railway to Monte Mottarone. Excursions by boat to *Isola dei Pescatori* (Fishermen's Island) and *Isola Bella* which is almost completely covered by the Palazzo Borrameo. Construction was begun in 1632 and finally concluded in 1958. Splendid Baroque garden. Statues and fountains on 10 terraces down to the lake.

MILANO (Milan), see town plans.

A 9. Como – Milano

Both A 8 and A 9 going north from Milano are sometimes posted with signs reading "Laghi" (Lakes).

COMO (85 000). Beautifully set on the shores of the lake of the same name. The Milanese destroyed the town in 1127. Emperor Frederick Barbarossa had it built up again. Handsome old quarter. The Tempio Voltiano was built in the 19th cent. in honour of the physicist Volta, born here in 1745.

Bellagio. Arguably the most beautiful of all of Lago di Como's lakeside resorts. *Villa Serbelloni* with magnificent garden. *Tremezzo* with the beautiful *Villa Carlotta.* Splendid garden and handsome interiors. *Cernobbio* with the Villa d'Este, now a luxury hotel.

Monte Generoso has extraordinary panoramic views. Railway from Capolago.

Lecco. Industrial town. *MONZA* (110 000). Industrial town. The 13th-cent. cathedral contains the Longobard (Lombard) coronation crown. The famous iron crown was used for Napoleon's coronation in 1805. *Villa Reale* with beautiful park. Famous motor racing circuit in the former royal park.

MILANO (Milan), see town plans.

A10. Menton – Genova

Italian border.

Ventimiglia (25 000). Beautiful old quarter. Remains of a 12th- cent. town wall and excavations of a Roman town. Caves in the *Balzi-Rossi* area. *Pigna.* Lovely little town in the Valle della Nervia.

Bordighera. Seaside resort famed for its gardens and beautiful palm trees. A particularly beautiful grove, the Palme di Scheffel, adjoins the road to Ospedaletti.

SAN REMO (65 000). Famous resort and watering place. Chief town of the *Riviera dei Fiori*, centre of the flower trade. Large ***flower market,*** busiest in the early morning. Picturesque old quarter with fishing port. Casino and large hotels. 13th- to 14-cent. cathedral of S. Siro. Madonna della Costa pilgrimage church. Lovely views from the Corso Inglesi. Casino. Race track. Cable car up to *Monte Bignone*, 1 299 m, with beautiful view. Delightful mountain excursions to Ceriana and Baiardo.

Taggia. Little town with noblemen's palaces and churches. Violet market.
Arma di Taggia. Seaside resort. Excursions to *Bussana Vecchia*, a ruined town where many artists and craftsmen have studios and workshops.

Imperia (40 000). Surrounded by olive groves. The town plan reflects its Roman origins. Straight streets and harmonious façades.

Diano Marina. Beautiful little seaside resort with open-air cafés under the palm trees. ***Cervo***. Picturesque little town with steep streets.

Alassio. One of the largest and oldest seaside resorts. An esplanade follows the 4 km long sandy beach.

Albenga. Port since the Roman period. Lovely streets and buildings near the 13th-cent. cathedral with Baroque portal. 6th-cent. mosaics in the baptismal chapel.

SAVONA (79 000). Major port and industrial town with steel mills. Baroque façade on the 16th-cent. Church of S. Giovanni Battista. Museo Civico. The Leon Pancaldo Tower at the port is in memory of one of Magellan's captains.

Albisola Marina. Known for peaches and ceramics. ***Varazze***, picturesque resort and town. Olive groves, and semi-tropical fruits.

GENOVA (Genoa, 842 000). Capital of Liguria. Largest port in Italy, it competes with Marseille as the largest Mediterranean sea port. However, during the Middle Ages, when it was ruled by Andrea Doria, the powerful prince, it was the greatest port in Europe. Picturesque old quarter above the old port. Medieval street plan, a tangle of lively "carungi" (alleys). The *Piazza dei Ferrari* is the heart of Genoa. Large opera house (1828) and building owned by the "Italia" shipping concern. Near by the lovely little Piazza S. Matteo with the *Doge's Palace*. Tomb and sword of Andrea Doria in the Church of S. Matteo. Cathedral of *S. Lorenzo* with a façade of chequered black and white marble blocks. Birthplace of Columbus (but it should be noted that several others towns and cities claim the explorer as their native son) in the Via Dante.

But Genoa also has sections with broad streets, splendid palaces and spacious squares. The most important streets are the Via Balbi and the Via Garibaldi. *Palazzo Bianco* (White Palace), 16th cent., and *Palazzo Rosso* (Red Palace), 17th cent. Both serve as art museums, as do the *Palazzo Spinola* and the *Palazzo Reale*, a 17th-cent. former royal palace. Both Rubens and van Dyck worked in Genoa. *Palazzo Doria* on the Piazza del Principe contains interesting frescoes. Lovely garden. Andrea Doria's villa in the suburb of ***Pegli***.

Many passenger and car ferries use the old port of Genoa as the terminus for their Mediterranean services. Some Atlantic liners may still be seen berthed here. New harbour with 5 km long breakwater. Genoa's old lighthouse, the 76 m high Lanterna, was completed in 1544.

Cable car to *Monte Righi*, 302 m. Splendid views out over the city, the coast and the sea. *Campo Santo* is one of the most original and interesting cemeteries in Italy.

A12 and SS 1. Genova – Livorno – Roma

GENOVA (Genoa), see A 10.

Nervi. Oldest winter health resort on the Riviera di Levante. Major seaside resort and lovely little town. Parco Municipale and art museum in the *Villa Serra.* Lovely views from the Passeggiata Anita Garibaldi.

Portofino. Rocky peninsula with Monte Portofino, 1610 m. Lovely views from the roads and observation points. The harbour of the picturesque town of **Portofino,** filled with fishing boats – and luxury yachts. **Camogli** and **Santa Margherita,** two lovely small ports.

Rapallo (26 000). Elegant seaside resort with the beautiful *Lungomare Vittorio Veneto* seaside promenade. Cable car (7 min.) to *Madonna di Montallegro.* Glorious views.

Sestri Levante. One of the most beautiful seaside resorts in Italy. Lovely mountain road up to *Castelnuovo* where there is an old fortress.

Levanto. Resort. The Loggia del Parlamento recalls the town's 13th- cent. greatness. Remains of the medieval town wall. Church of S. Andrea.

LA SPEZIA (128 000). Naval base, industries and shipyards. *Maritime museum.* The 14th-cent. *cathedral* was partially destroyed during the war. Terracottas by della Robbia. The museum of archaeology contains finds from Luni. Twisting road to *Portovenere.* Beautiful old town with splendid views. 12th-cent. castle. Medieval town gate. Church of S. Pietro at the tip of the promontory. Modern landscape paintings with local themes. Island of *Palmaria* with famous bridge and a beautiful grotto.

Sarzana. Old town that played an important role during the struggles between Genoa and Pisa. 13th-cent. cathedral with famous crucifix. Remains of a citadel and remparts.

CARRARA (65 000). World-famous for its white marble that is shipped from the Marina di Carrara. The town is also a seaside resort.

Pietrasanta with beautiful cathedral. **Viareggio** (55 000). Seaside resort with famous carnival. Torre del Lago Puccini where Puccini (1858-1924) wrote several operas. His grave is near the lake.

LUCCA (90 000). Etruscan town. Handsome buildings, streets and squares in the old quarter. The 17th-cent. town wall is 12 m high and several metres thick. *Piazza dell'Amfiteatro Romano* is situated inside a Roman amphitheatre. 13th-cent. cathedral. Statue of St. Martin in the entrance hall. Inside, Tintoretto's "Last Supper". *Museo Nazionale* with Etruscan and Roman finds, etc. Lavish collections of art in the *Pinacoteca Nazionale.* The Church of *S. Frediano* (1147) is built over a 7th-cent. basilica.

PISA (103 000), once an important city state with large port, was finally defeated by Genoa and Florence. University dating from 1343. The historical centre of Pisa is *Piazza dei Cavalieri,* lined with handsome buildings but it is the **Leaning Tower** (1350) which has made Pisa famous. It is a 55 m high campanile (bell tower) 5.2 m off the perpendicular. It has probably leaned from the very beginning. Some experts claim that it leans as a result of a fault in the foundations, others claim that it is the fault of the subsoil. Whatever the cause, when you climb the 294 steps to the top of the tower, you can feel that it leans. The tower played a role in one of Galileo's experiments. (Acceleration of a falling body does not depend on its mass.) The entire building complex comprising **cathedral, baptistery and bell tower,** are all in shimmering white marble in the Pisan style: Romanesque architecture with classical and Oriental influences. *Campo Santo Cemetery* (1278) has four long galleries decorated with frescoes. Interesting sculpture and tombstones. Church of *S. Maria della Spina,* with a part of Jesus' crown of thorns. *Museo Nazionale* in an old Benedectine monastery. Art of the Pisan School.

LIVORNO (Leghorn, 177 000). Small fishing port, in the 16th cent. a major port. 15 km long canal to the River Arno. Viale Italia, with the Naval Academy of Italy and long beach. Cathedral on Piazza Grande. The Venezia and S. Marco quarter were built in the 16th cent. It is marked by canals used to transport goods to warehouses.

Montenero. Pilgrimage church with Oriental portrait of the Madonna, donated by seamen.

Volterra. Etruscan Porta all'Arco. Remains of a 7 km long, Etruscan ring wall. *Museo Etrusco Guarnacci* contains ceramics and objects made of alabaster. Medieval town wall and splendid palaces on *Piazza dei Priori.* Beautiful *Viale dei Ponte* promenade beneath a medieval fortress. Cathedral with octagonal baptismal chapel dating from 1283.

Populonia. Etruscan port with the remains of a 2 km long town wall. Medieval castle. Priombino. Port with iron industry (iron from Elba). Beautiful views out to Elba from the Portovecchio harbour.

Isola d'Elba (30 000). Major tourist attraction. Lovely mountainous landscape and luxuriant vegetation. In the 6th cent. B.C. the Etruscans discovered the rich iron deposits. The capital is **Portoferrario** and the highest point is **Monte Capanne** (1 019 m). Mementoes of Napoleon in *Villa* *dei Mulini.* Following his abdication he was granted the newly formed principality of Elba, and he remained here from May 3, 1814, until February 26, 1815. Then he returned to France for the brief rule known as the "Hundred Days". His villa in *San Martino* is a tourist attraction.

Close to Elba is the island of **Monte Christo.** Its name is known to all who have read Alexandre Dumas' novel.

Massa Marittima. Small old town. Imposing cathedral on the lovely Piazza Garibaldi. Wild and rather desolate mountain scenery.

Castiglione della Pescaia. Picturesque fishing town with winding stepped streets and alleys. **Vetulonia.** Site of an Etruscan burial ground.

Grosseto (40 000). Provincial capital. The old quarter is encircled by a wall built in the 16th cent. for the princes of the Medici family. Handsome cathedral (13th cent.). Etruscan and Roman finds in the Museum of Archaeology.

Tarquinia. Medieval town with 25 towers built by rival noble families. Beautiful Church of S. Maria de Castello. *Palazzo Vitelleschi,* a museum on Piazza Cavour, contains examples of Etruscan art. Many of the artifacts (6th-2nd cent. B.C.) were discovered in the Etruscan burial grounds a few km E of the town. Frescoes depict scenes from Etruscan life.

Tuscania. Etruscan town with medieval walls. The town was badly damaged by an earthquake in 1971, but it has been restored. The churches of S. Pietro and S. Maria Maggiore have their origins in the 8th cent.

Viterbo, see A 1.

Civitavecchia was one of the Romans' most important ports. The mighty fortress, planned by Bramante, was completed by Michelangelo in 1557. Etruscan and Roman finds in the Museo Civico.

Cerveteri was an important Etruscan port. Remains of Roman and medieval walls. Large Etruscan necropolis (burial ground).

ROMA (Rome), see town plans.

A13. Padova – Bologna

PADOVA (Padua), see A 4.

Monselice. Beautiful *Piazza Mazzini* with the Torre Civica (City Tower). Castle (13th cent.), now a museum. The conical **Colli Euganei** are of volcanic origin. Highest summit, 602 m. Beautiful and interesting area for motor touring. Hot springs and spas, e.g. **Montegrotto Terme, Abano Terme** and **Battaglia Terme.** Views from the Eremo di Rua. The great Renaissance poet, Petrarch, spent the last four years of his life in the little house at Arquà Petrarca. He died on his 70th birthday in 1374 and was buried here.

Este. Original home town of the Este family that ruled Ferrara. Beautiful palace. *Cathedral* with altar painting by Tiepolo, "St. Thecla delivering Este from the plague" (1759). *Museo Nazionale Atestino* with artifacts from the area's long history. Valsanzibio. *Villa Barbarigo* with splendid park: terraces, grottoes, statues, a maze.

Montagnana with an almost 2 km long 13th-cent. town wall. Gothic cathedral with splendid interior.

FERRARA (154 000). Famous university. Major centre of culture during the Middle Ages and Renaissance. The Dukes of the Este family ruled from the Castello Estense (1385), a castle with four corner towers and a drawbridge. The interior has been partially destroyed. *Palazzo Schifonoia* (15th cent.), now a museum with frescoes, ceramics, etc. *Palazzo dei Diamanti* (art museum). Cathedral of *S. Giorgio* in the Lombard style. Several more handsome palaces. Medieval atmosphere in the Via della Volta. *Archaeological museum* with Etruscan and Greek artifacts in the Palazzo di Ludovico il Moro.

Chioggia (50 000), on the coast resembles Venice. Canals and houses built on an island. The 800 m long Ponte Lungo leads to the long *Sottomarina* beach. Road continues past the *Pomposa abbey* with beautiful and interesting interiors. Famous frescoes. It was founded by Benedictine monks in the 6th cent. The impressive campanile was built in 1063.

Comacchio on the shores of the lagoon has a unique appearance: fishermen's houses, canals and bridges. Trepponti, three bridges built in 1634. Several seaside resorts out along the coast.

RAVENNA, see A 14. *BOLOGNA,* see town plans.

A14. Bologna – Ancona – Brindisi. *Autostrada Adriatica*

Faenza (53 000), encircled by 15th-cent. ramparts. Extremely beautiful old quarters around Piazza Libertà and Piazza del Popolo. Since the 12th cent., Faenza has been famous for its glazed earthenware – the term "faience" comes from the name of this town. Enormous collection of ceramics from all over the world in the *Museo delle Ceramiche. Museo Civico* (art). Unfinished cathedral (15th cent.).

RAVENNA (132 000) was the capital of the Roman Empire during the 5th cent. It became the Ostrogoth capital and residence of governors appointed by the Byzantine Emperors. The exquisite mosaics, for which Ravenna is famous, date from that period. Noteworthy mosaics in the octagonal Church of *S. Vitale*, completed in 547 during the reign of Emperor Theodoric "The Great", and in the *Basilica di S. Appolinare Nuovo* and the Mausoleo di Galla Placidia. Theodoric's domed mausoleum with a circumference of 34 m, hewn out of a single rock and known as the *Rotonda*, was built in 524, but the king is not buried here. An eternal flame burns on Dante's grave, which is also to be found here. The creator of the "Divina Commedia" (Divine Comedy) died here in 1321.

S. Appolinare in Classe. Beautiful Byzantine basilica, begun in the 6th cent. Remarkably fine mosaics.

CESENA (86 000). The town lies at the foot of a hill with Malatestiana Castle. Famed library. *Cesenatico.* Large seaside resort with beautiful old quarter.

Near by is the little River **Rubicon,** famed in Latin history. When Caesar crossed the Rubicon with his army in defiance of the Roman Senate, he had taken a decisive step. Hence the expression "to cross the Rubicon" – to take a step from which there is no turning back. Caesar is said to have uttered the words "alea jacta est", meaning "the die is cast" as he crossed the river.

Sant' Arcangelo di Romagna. Little town with castle and triumphal arch raised in honour of Pope Clement XIV.

RIMINI (119 000). Enormous resort on the Adriatic Sea. One of the largest holiday centres in Europe. Wide, shallow sandy beach packed with holiday-makers. German is heard more often than Italian. Hectic nightlife. And yet Rimini is just the centre of a long row of Adriatic resorts that are marked by mile after mile of hotels. A wide street separates the beach from the town. Fishing port. The centre of Rimini is *Piazza Cavour,* site of the Palazzo dell' Arengo from 1204. *Arco d'Augusto,* Augustus' triumphal arch, erected in 27 B.C. Pinacoteca (art museum). Ponte di Tiberio, a Roman bridge.

San Marino is the world's oldest and smallest republic, 60 km², 17 000 inhabitants, of which 4 300 live in the town. Of all Italy's city states only San Marino and the Vatican have miraculously managed to survive. San Marino was founded in 301 by a stone mason who had escaped from persecution in Dalmatia. Major industries are agriculture, tourism and postage stamps. Twice annually, on April 1 and October 3, two members of the Great and General Council are appointed to act as regents. On the National Holiday, September 3, colourful national costumes and picturesque uniforms are to be seen throughout the land. Piazza della Libertà with Government Building. Lovely views from **Monte Titano,** 739 m.

Riccione (28 000). Popular and lively seaside resort. 6 km long, shallow sandy beach. **Cattolica** (15 000). Large resort. Gradara Castle and Panoramica esplanade.

Pesaro (84 000). One of the chief towns of the region of Marche. Seaside resort with 4 km long sandy beach. Famous ceramics. *Museum of ceramics* in the Musei Civici, which also have art exhibits. The Palazzo Ducale, on Piazza del Popolo, was built for the Sforza family in the 15th cent. Near by is the birthplace of the composer Rossini (1792-1868).

To the west is the Baroque town of **Urbino** with old streets and splendid palaces. Beautiful views towards Monte Titano from *Piazza Roma.* During the 15th cent. the Duke of Montefeltro established Urbino as a centre of culture. His palace, the Palazzo Ducale, is magnificent. Site of the distinguished *Galleria Nazionale delle Marche* with large collections of art. Beautiful frescoes in the *Oratorio di San Giovanni.* The painter Raphael was born in Casa Di Raffaello in 1483. One of Italy's greatest architects, Donato Bramante, was also born in Urbino. Beautiful views from the Strada Panoramica.

Fano. Large seaside resort. Festival in August. Roman colony with the Arco di Augusto, a triumphal arch that marks the end of the Via Flaminia that starts in Rome. The upper section was damaged by a 15th-cent. cannon ball. The Duke of Montefeltro was the culprit. A relief on the nearby Church of S. Michele shows the arch as it originally appeared. The *Fontana della Fortuna,* a fountain that is the symbol of the town, is in Piazza 20 Settembre. S. Maria Nuova Church (18th cent.). Handsome palace. Mighty Rocca Malatestiana Castle.

ANCONA (108 000). The city was founded in the 4th cent. by Greeks. Car ferries to Yugoslavia and Greece. Industries. Large accordion factory.

Merchants' Loggia (Loggia dei Mercanti) with Venetian-Gothic façade. The *cathedral,* with Byzantine influences, was completed in the 13th cent. A Temple of Venus once occupied its site. *Arco di Traiano* (Trajan's Arch) was erected in 115. *Francesco Podesti Art Museum. Museo Nazionale delle Marche* contains archaeological finds, including beautiful Greek vases from the cemetery at Numana. The 11th-cent. Church of S. Maria di Portonovo, in a beautiful setting by the sea.

Loreto. Large pilgrimage place. The major pilgrimages take place on March 25, August 15, September 8 and December 10. Pilgrims flock to the white marble *Santuario della Santa Casa,* a vast 15th-cent. church, created by the foremost architects and artists in Italy. Beneath the dome is the *Casa Santa,* the House of Mary, said to have been brought by angels in the 13th cent. when the Muslims conquered the Holy Land and Nazareth.

Fermo. Beautifully set on a hilltop. Picturesque town with ramparts, which in part date from the Etruscan period. Fine view from *Piazza del Duomo.* The *cathedral,* built in 1227, replaced an earlier church that had been destroyed by fire on order of Frederick Barbarossa. Beautiful façade. *Piazza del Popolo* with handsome palaces and arcades. *S. Benedetto del Tronto.* Modern seaside resort on the Riviera Picena. Church of S. Benedetto in the picturesque old quarter. Beautiful marine promenade.

Ascoli Piceno (55 000). Beautiful old quarter with picturesque streets, e.g. Via delle Torri and Via Solesta. The *Torre Ercolani* (40 m) is the tallest of the towers that were built by noble families. Roman *Ponte di Solesta* with a single arch more than 25 m long, spans the River Tronto. Beautiful Piazza del Popolo and Corso Mazzina. Most of the *cathedral* dates from the 15th cent. Baptismal chapel from the 12th cent. Pinacoteca (art museum).

PESCARA (122 000). Chief town of the Abruzzi, and largest resort on the Riviera degli Abruzzi. Long seaside promenade with pine woods. *Montesilvano Beach* is 6 km from the city. Roman town, then important stronghold against the Austrians and the Turks. The newer parts of the city are centred around Piazza Duca d'Aosta. Modern town hall and museum of fisheries. Old quarter with *Casa di d'Annunzio* where the poet and patriot Gabriele d'Annunzio (1863-1938) was born. Museum.

Chieti. Resort surrounded by olive groves. Splendid parks and views. The most important street is the Corso Marrucino. Roman temple discovered in 1935. *Museo Nazionale della Antichità* with Greek, Roman and Etruscan finds, including the famous Warrior of Capestrano (6th cent.).

Vasto. Old town set in olive groves. 18th-cent. Church of S. Maria Maggiore. *Térmoli.* Old town on a peninsula. Medieval town wall.

FOGGIA (141 000). Chief town of Apulia. Founded during the Middle Ages. The town has often been ravaged by earthquakes – the one in 1731 was particularly violent – so modern buildings predominate. The *cathedral,* built in the 12th cent., was rebuilt in the Baroque style in 1731. Emperor Frederick II of Hohenstaufen resided here and in nearby *Lucera,* site of a magnificent 14th-cent. cathedral. *Museo Civico* with terracottas and coins.

Promontorio del Gargano on the spur of the boot of Italy, is a wild and partially inaccessible area of great beauty, quite unlike the nearby mainland. Beautiful views from the mountains and mountain roads. *Manfredonia,* the chief port, was founded in the 13th cent. On the summit of **Monte S. Angelo** is the *San Michele* pilgrimage church (13th cent.). Bronze doors made in Constantinople (1076). The church is built above the cave where St. Michael (the Archangel Michael) is said to have appeared. The legend closely resembles a similar one about Mont St. Michel in Normandy. Crusaders visited the shrine before setting sail from the port of Manfredonia.

Barletta. Port and resort. Ecclesiastical treasures in the 13th-cent. Church of S. Sepolcro. In front of the church, the *Colosso,* a 5 m high 4th-cent. bronze statue. It is possible that is portrays the Emperor Valentinian. In one hand the figure holds a globe, in the other a cross. Impressive cathedral. The castle was once owned by the Hohenstaufens.

Canosa di Puglia with 12th-cent. Romanesque cathedral. *Museo Civico* with Roman frescoes. *Cannae,* between Barletta and Puglia, with some ruins and a little museum with exhibits concerning one of history's most famous battles, in 216 B.C. when Hannibal's troops defeated a 90 000 strong Roman army.

Castel del Monte. Mighty octagonal castle that Frederick II of Hohenstaufen had built in 1250 on a hilltop. It was used as a hunting lodge.

Trani (40 000). Port, seaside resort, vineyards. Antique port with old buildings. 12th-cent. cathedral with splendid bronze doors. *Molfetta* (60 000). Cathedral with three domes, built between the 12th and the 13th cent. *Ándria* (77 000) was one of Frederick II's favourite towns.

Bitonto with well-preserved ramparts and cathedral.

BARI (357 000). Chief town of Puglia (Apulia). Second largest city in southern Italy (Naples is larger). Ancient city that flourished during the Middle Ages. Still a major port with important trade connections with the Orient. University. Fiera del Levante, annual September fair. *Old quarter*

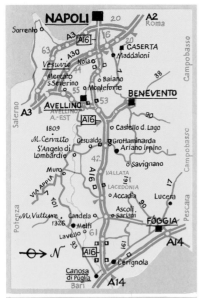

on the tongue of land between Porto Vecchio and the new Gran Porto. Several picturesque places: Piazza San Pietro, Strada del Carmine and Portico del Pellegrino. Beautiful views from the *Lungomare Nazario Sauro* seaside promenade. The fortress with massive bastions was built in 1233 on order of Frederick II. *Museum of archaeology* and *art museum.* 11th-cent *basilica* with bishop's throne and the tomb of St. Nicholas. He was Bishop of Myra in the Near East and on May 8 the Festa del Mare procession is held in his honour. In northern lands, he is still thought of as Father Christmas. 13th-cent. S. Sabino Cathedral. One of the two towers collapsed in 1613.

Altamura. Beautiful town encircled by a town wall. Cathedral from 1232, rebuilt after a 14th-cent. earthquake.

Matera (44 000) in a strange rocky landscape at the edge of a deep ravine. The Strada dei Sassi follows the edge of the cliff and provides views of the *Sassi quarter* of the town with caves that were once inhabited. The S. Maria di Idris and S. Barbara Churches have been hewn out of the rock. Frescoes dating from the 13th-15th cent. Beautiful views from the *Piazza Pascoli*. 13th-cent. cathedral rebuilt in the Baroque style. Museo *Nazionale Ridola* with archaeological finds from nearby burial grounds. Local handicrafts.

TARANTO (227 000), port and naval base, founded by the Spartans 708 B.C., destroyed by the Saracens in 927. Beautiful old quarter on an island at the harbour's entrance. Bridges connect it with the other parts of the city. Beautiful views from the palm-lined *Lungomare Vittorio Emanuele*, site of the Prefectural Palace, and from the *Giardini Comunali*, a city park with luxuriant vegetation. S. Cataldo Cathedral (11th cent.).

SS 16 and SS 379. Bari – Brindisi – Lecce

Monopoli. Fishing port with Hohenstaufen castle. Medieval quarter but modern buildings predominate. Excavations of the antique port of Egnazia.

Zona dei Trulli. "Trulli" are unique white stone structures with conical or domed roofs. There are over 1 000 of these small buildings in the area, whose chief town is *Alberobello*. Even the Church of S. Antonio has been constructed in this style. *Grotte di Castellana*, extremely beautiful stalacite and stalagmite caves.

BRINDISI (82 000). One of the chief towns of Apulia. Since the Roman era this has been an important town for trade and transport to Greece, Africa and the Orient. Beautiful views from the *Lungomare Regina Margherita*. At the port a 20 m high pillar, the end of the *Via Appia*, queen of roads.

A 16. Napoli – Canosa di Puglia. *Autostrada Dei Due Mare*

NAPOLI (Naples), **Vesuvio** (Vesuvius) and **Pompei**, see town plans.

Avellino (52 000). Provincial capital. Modern buildings. The town has been ravaged by earthquakes, the latest in 1930. Museo Irpino, archaeology.

Benevento (52 000). Provincial capital. Arco di Traiano (A.D. 114). Restored Roman theatre. Benevento is famed for its nougat and liqueur (Strega). At the Battle of Benevento (A.D. 275), the Romans defeated the troops of Pyrrhos, the Greek king.

To the north **Campobasso** (41 000) with the 16th-cent. *Montforte Castle*. Museum of archaeology with silver and gold collections.

Canosa di Puglia, see A 14.

A 18. Messina – Catania

Sicily covers an area of 25 700 km² population of nearly 5 million.

MESSINA (270 000). Modern city built on a grid plan after being several times destroyed by earthquakes. The worst one was in 1908 when 60 000 people perished and 90% of the town was laid in ruins. At the heart of the city are Piazza Carioli and *Piazza del Duomo* with the 16th-cent. Orion Fountain. The cathedral is a copy of the old one which was destroyed in the 1908 earthquake. Astronomical clock. Mosaic created in 1933. *Museo Nazionale* (archaeology and art). In August the large Fiera di Messina fair.

Ali Terme. Spa with sulphur springs. Splendid views from a road that has been hewn out of the rocks.

Taormina. One of Sicily's most beautiful towns, 206 m above sea level. Large resort. Fine views from *Piazza 9 Aprile*. *Teatro Greco* (Greek Theatre), 109 m in diameter, renovated by the Romans in the 2nd cent. The beautiful *Giardino Pubblico* park. Remains of a castle on top of *Mount Tauro*, 390 m. The mountain town of **Castel Mola**, castle and ramparts.

Acireale (45 000). Spa with hot springs. Corso Vitt. Emanuele with the Baroque Church of S. Sebastiano. *Aci Castello* with ruined castle on a rock.

Etna (3 370 m). Europe's largest volcano. Still active. Its most violent eruption, in 1669, devastated Catania. The peak is covered with snow most of the year. Motor road to the Refugio Sapienza (1 915 m). Cable car to observatory at 2 953 m.

CATANIA, see A 19.

SS 114. Catania – Siracusa

Lentini. The Baroque Church of *S. Nicola* is the largest on Sicily. Excavations of the Greek burial ground of Leontinoi. Museum. *Palazzo Acreide* with remains of a Greek town. *Augusta.* Port on a rocky island.

Castello Eurialo. Greek fortress. From this point, on the advice of Archimedes, the defending troops, with mirrors and lenses, set fire to an attacking Roman fleet.

SIRACUSA, see SS 115.

A 19. Palermo – Caltanisetta – Catania

PALERMO (690 000). Capital of Sicily and the island's largest port. Founded by the Phoenicians, the city was subsequently ruled by Carthaginians, Romans, Normans, Germans, Saracens and Spaniards. Palermo flourished culturally during the reign of Frederick II of Hohenstaufen. The "Sicilian Vespers" was a bloody 1282 uprising against the French.

Quattro Canti is a bustling square where the Via Marqueda, Corso Vitt. Emanuele, Via della Libertà and Piazza Castelnuovo meet. Pleasant outdoor cafés where you can taste authentic Sicilian cassata, ice-cream with candied fruit.

Old quarter with Piazza Pretoria and Piazza Bellini, site of the *Martorana* (Church of S. Maria dell'Ammiraglio), built in the Arab-Norman style in 1143. Beautiful mosaics. Church of *S. Giovanni* degli Eremiti from the same period and in the same style. Five pale-red Arabian domes. Gothic-Renaissance *S. Maria della Catena*. Its name means "of the chain" and refers to a chain that once closed off the old port. The *cathedral*, founded in the 12th cent., is a mixture of Norman and Catalonian Gothic styles. Beautifully decorated 14th-cent. West Front. Frederick II and Henry VI of Hohenstaufen are buried here.

Museo Nazionale with prehistoric, Greek, Etruscan and Roman collections. Finds from the temple in Selinunte. A macabre "sight" are the 8 000 well-preserved corpses in the Capuchin catacombs.

Palazzo dei Normanni. Some parts of the 9th-cent. palace show its Arabian origins. Façade from the 16th-18th cent. Magnificent interior. Interesting mosaics in the Capella Palatina (about 1140).

The *Opera dei Pupi*, a puppet theatre in the old quarter, is a unique institution. Splendid figures perform plays about "The French Knights". Morning and evening performances that delight a demanding local audience.

The *cathedral* in **Monreale**, south-west of Palermo, built in 1174, resembles a fortress. Constructed in the Norman style of light-coloured limestone and dark lava. Burial church of its founder, William II. The interior is covered with gold mosaics. Exquisite cloisters in the adjoining Benedictine abbey. Views out over the fertile Conca d'Oro plain.

Piana degli Albanesi. Beautiful little town south of Palermo founded by colonists from Albania in 1488. They have preserved their language, folk costumes, traditions and colourful holiday celebrations.

Solunto (Soluntum) on the Capo *Zaffarano.* Phoenician colony. Excavations of a Roman town. *Bagheria* with beautiful Baroque buildings. *Termini Imerese.* Spa with hot springs.

Caltanisetta with the Mazzarino, Falconara and Mussomeli castles. Enna. Mountain town situated at 1 000 m. Medieval castle with impressive panoramic view. Lovely walks with views towards the ancient village of *Calascibetta.* Baroque cathedral. A Temple of Ceres once stood near the little *Lago di Pergusa.*

Piazza Armerina has the Roman *Villa Casale* that probably belonged to Emperor Mexentius. The mosaics tell the tale of the Labours of Hercules. Hunting scenes. *Paterno* (43 000) with 11th-cent. Norman castle.

CATANIA (400 000). Founded by the Greeks in the 8th cent. B.C. it was conquered by the Romans in 263 B.C. A Greek theatre restored by the Romans and a Roman amphitheatre, remain. The university was founded in 1434. Some of the old buildings have survived earthquakes and eruptions of Mt. Etna. Lovely views of the volcano from the important *Via Etnea,* a shopping street. Piazza del Duomo with handsome buildings by Vaccarini, an 18th-cent. architect. The *Fontana dell'Elefante,* symbol of the city, is a fountain distinguished by a statue of an elephant bearing an obelisk on its back (as in Elephant and Castle in London). Beautiful Giardino Bellini. *Bellini Museum.* The composer was born in Catania in 1801. 12th-cent. *cathedral* rebuilt after an earthquake in 1693. The 18th-cent. façade is a work of Vaccarini. Tomb of St. Agatha. *Castello Ursino* with 30 m high circular corner towers. Built in the 13th cent. for Frederick II, it now houses the Museo Comunale.

A 29. Palermo – Trapani

PALERMO, Monreale and Piana d. Albanesi, see A 19.

Segesta. Ruins of a once influential town, destroyed about the year 1 000. Remains of a temple with 36 Doric columns and a theatre. The ancient town of Erice (cable car from Trapani) has been levelled, but the site is lovely. Norman castle. Chiesa (Church) Matrice (Mother of God) dates from the 14th cent.

TRAPANI (61 000). Cube-shaped white houses give this town an African appearance. Cathedral built in 1635. Villa Margherita park.

SS 115. Trapani – Agrigento – Siracusa

Marsala (Marsah el Allah – Port of Allah). Famous wine. Cathedral of S. Tomaso. Roman baths. Large seaside resort. Mazara del Vallo with many towers and domes. Beautiful Piazza Repubblica.

Selinunte. Ruins of a Greek town (650 B.C.) that was destroyed by Carthaginians and earthquakes. *Acropolis* with eight large temples, only one with upright columns. Manicalunga Necropolis (burial ground).

Agrigento (49 000). Spa. Beautiful medieval buildings round *Piazza Roma. Vallata dei Templi* (Valley of the Temples) with temples from Agrigento's period of greatness. The Doric Temple of Concord (Tempio della Concordia) is the most beautiful and best preserved. The Temple of Jupiter (Tempio di Giove) was never completed. 38 figures of Atlas supported it. A 7.5 m long reproduction of one of these figures lies on the floor of the temple.

Caltanisetta, see A 19.

Gela (67 000). Seaside resort. Greek colony 688 B.C. Destroyed by Carthaginians 405 B.C., rebuilt by Frederick II in 1233. Remains of 8 m high and 12 km long town wall. *The archaeological museum* has splendid displays. American troops landed here in 1943.

Ragusa (62 000) has an interesting old quarter. Museum of archaeology. The town is dominated by an important chemical industry. *Marina di Ragusa,* a seaside resort.

Noto (24 000). Lovely Corso. The town was destroyed during an earthquake in 1693.

SIRACUSA (Syracuse, 124 000). Along with Rome, Carthage and Athens, this was one of the great cities of antiquity. Founded by the Greeks in 734, as early as the 4th cent. B.C. it boasted a population of 300 000. When the Romans conquered the city they killed its most illustrious inhabitant, Archimedes. Syracuse's days of glory ended in the 9th cent. when the Saracens destroyed the city.

Città Vecchia, the old quarter, is clustered on an island. The cathedral bears the stamp of the 18th cent. but its oldest pillars were once a part of a Temple of Athene that was transformed in the 7th cent. into a Christian church. Fonte Aretusa (Arethusa Fountain), with fresh water, is next to the sea. Fine views.

The ancient quarter covers a large area. Fine views of this part of the city, the sea and the newer sections from the *Viale Rizzo. Greek Theatre* (5th cent. B.C.), 134 m in diameter. Roman *amphitheatre* hewn out of a cliff. *Latonia del Paradiso.* Large, ancient quarry, now a park. Ear of Denys, an artificial grotto, 65 m deep, in the shape of an ear-lobe. Remarkable acoustics that allowed the Tyrant Denys (4th cent.) to hear his prisoners' conversations. It was this Denys who had a sword suspended on a horse-hair over the head of one of his critics, Damocles. The term "sword of Damocles" has come to mean impending danger. Enormous *Museo Nazionale Archeologico* has particularly fine ancient Greek exhibits. Sculpture and art in Bellomo, a Hohenstaufen castle.

Santa Lucia church, abbey and catacombs.

A 22. Brennero/Brenner – Bolzano – Verona – Modena.
Autostrada del Brennero

Passo di Brennero (Brenner Pass), 1 371 m. Austrian border. Terme di Brennero, spa. Colle Isarco. Beautiful church and old buildings. Between Mules and Fortezza the road passes through the narrow Sachsen Gorge.

Vipiteno (Sterzing). Little town at 948 m. Austrian appearance with gaily painted Tyrolean houses and arcades. Medieval atmosphere. Gothic church with famous High Altar (1458) by Hans Multscher of Ulm. Multscher Museum in the school house.

Alternative roads:

Vipiteno – Sarentino – Bolzano

Beautiful narrow, partially gravelled, road. *Passo di Pennes*, 2 214 m.

Vipiteno – Merano – Bolzano

Passo di Monte Giovo/Jaufen-Pass, 2 094 m. Gradients 12% and 9%. Well constructed hairpin bends. No caravans allowed.

Merano (Meran, 30 000). Beautiful surroundings. Spa with lovely walks. Old quarter around the Via dei Portici/Laubengasse with handsome buildings and arcades. One Bishop's Castle and one Prince's Castle.

Imst – Timmelsjoch – Vipiteno

Passo di Rombo (Timmelsjoch). Passo di Rombo, 2 491 m at the Italian-Austrian border. Gradient on the Austrian side 14%, on the Italian 12%. Toll. Caravans, trailers and buses prohibited. (Several narrow tunnels).

Landeck – Passo di Resia – Merano – Bolzano

Landeck, see Austria, E 17. *Reschenpass/Passo di Resia,* good road, suitable for caravans. 10% gradient. Sample distances: Augsburg – Resia – Bolzano 355 km; Augsburg – Brennero – Bolzano 355 km.

Parco Nazionale dello Stelvio (Stilfer-Joch), one of Italy's four national parks, established to protect rare species – deer, chamois, lemmings, roe deer, pheasants.

Bressanone (Brixen). The oldest town in the South Tyrol has escaped wartime damage, so different building styles from many eras can still be seen. 13th-cent. cathedral, rebuilt in Baroque. Prince-Bishop's Castle with three- storey arcaded courtyard. Beautiful road to ***Brunico*** (Bruneck), a lovely little town with the large *Plan de Corones* (Kronplatz), winter sports recreation area at the height of 2 275 m.

The ***Dolomites,*** a large mountain range of great and unique beauty. Composed of limestone and formed into fantastic shapes and peaks by erosion – the changing light makes them seem particularly magnificent. Several resorts. *Cortina d'Ampezzo,* 1 210 m, internationally famous, is the largest. Lovely church with campanile. School of woodcarving.

Ortisei (St. Ulrich) in the lovely *Val Gardena* (Grödnertal). The local language, Ladin, is a variant of Rhaeto-Romanic. *Chesa de Ladins,* folklore museum. Cable car to *Alpe di Siusi* (Seiser-Alm).

BOLZANO (Bozen, 106 000). Capital of Trentino-Alto Adige (Oberetsch) and chief town of the German-speaking South Tyrol, ceded to Italy in 1919. In principle, both German and Italian are recognized but the German speakers feel that they are being subject to an unwanted Italianization. Resistance, at times violent, has been the result.
Lovely old quarter. *Via dei Portici* (Laubenstrasse) with arcades. Gothic cathedral. Dominican and Franciscan churches. Palazzo Mercantile with arcades and magnificent Kaisersaal. Castel *Roncolo* (Schloss Runkelstein), an authentic knight's castle, rises above the river. Cable car to the *Renon* high plateau (1 200 m) with fine views of the Dolomites.

Salorno. German-Italian language boundary.

TRENTO (Trent, 91 000). One of the chief towns of Trentino – Alto Adige (Oberetsch). Pleasant blend of Tyrolean peasant and noble Venetian architectural styles. The palaces on the Via Belenzani are Venetian. Via Manci is Baroque. Lombard basilica with later additions. Baroque *dome.* Romanesque interior. Bishops' tombs. 15th-cent. wooden crucifix. Neptune Fountain (1769). Beautiful *Piazza del Duomo,* site of the medieval Palazzo Pretorio with the Torre Civica, tower clock, and *Museo Diocesano* (Archbishop's Museum). Buildings with arcades and façade paintings. Castello del Buon Consiglio, 13th-cent. residence of the Prince-Bishops. Large castle containing the *Museo Nazionale Trentino* (archaeology, art, coins). Trento has become a major winter sports centre as a result of new facilities on *Monte Bondone,* only 14 km away from the town. The highest summit is *Cima Palon,* 2 096 m.

Beautiful road with fine views goes east from Bolzano through the Dolomites over several Alpine passes to ***Cortina d'Ampezzo.***

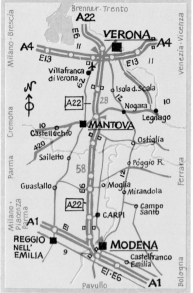

Rovereto (23 000). Dominated by a 14th-cent. castle that once figured in many battles and now serves as a war history museum, *Museo Storico della Guerra*. The large memorial bell tolls every evening at 9 in memory of the fallen. 12 000 graves from the First World War at Ossario di Castel Dante. *Museo Civico* with archaeology and geology exhibits.

Lago di Garda (Lake Garda). Italy's largest lake, 52 km long, maximum depth 346 m. The lake, famous for its beauty, attracts many tourists. After the heights and ice of the Alps, it provides a sudden and pleasant introduction to the delights of Italy. And for Italians, and travellers from the south, the lake provides cool and fresh relief. Unique blend of Alpine and semi-tropical vegetation. Roads around the lake are lovely but winding. On the western side, the road between Riva and Salo has 70 tunnels and galleries within a distance of 42 km. But they are interrupted by beautiful views from 50 bridges. Tourist steamships and hydrofoils.

Some of the major resorts: Old and beautiful *Limone*, with lemons, figs and honey, *Gardone Riviera*, surrounded by olive and cypress groves. Museum in *Vittoriale* where the poet and patriot Gabriele d'Annunzio (1863-1938) lived. On the eastern side *Malcesine*, beautifully set on a peninsula below *Monte Baldo*. *Garda*. Lovely old port that gave its name to the lake. *Lazise*. Large zoo. *Sirmione*, see A 4.

VERONA, see town plans.

MANTOVA (Mantua, 66 000). Beautifully set near three small lakes, formed by the River Mincio. Old cultural centre. The Roman poet Publius Vergilius Maro (Virgil) was born here in 70 B.C. At the heart of the town, *Piazza Mantegna* and the arcaded *Piazza del Erbe*. Renaissance Church of S. Andrea with frescoes by Mantegna. Large *Piazza Sordello* with the *Palazzo Ducale*, former residence of the Gonzagas, Mantua's ruling family. About 500 rooms with art collections.

MODENA, see A 1.

A 24. Roma – L'Aquila – S. Benedetto
A 25. Roma – Avezzano – Pescara

ROMA, see town plans.

Tivoli. Little town on a hill overlooking a plain. Beautiful buildings in a lovely setting. *Villa d'Este* with magnificent garden, sculpture and fountains. Via delle Cascatelle, road passing the famous Little Cascades of Tivoli. The Tempio di Vesta is one of the few remaining Roman buildings – Tivoli was a summer resort for rich Romans. Emperor Hadrian resided in Villa Adriani.

Palestrina, see A 2.

Subiaco. Medieval town with Roman origins. Here St. Benedict founded the Benedictine Order's first 12 monasteries. S. Scolastica and S. Benedetto may be visited. Hermit's grotto where the saint lived. Remains of Nero's villa. Pius VI's triumphal arch from 1789.

L'AQUILA (60 000). Chief town of Abruzzi. The town was founded in 1240 by Frederick II. *Fontana delle 99 Canelle*, a fountain with 99 faces that spout water. Constructed in the 13th cent., it commemorates the 99 villages that joined to form the town. 99 was a cabalistic number and it was believed that the town would survive as long as the number was respected. For this reason there were 99 churches, 99 fountains, 99 squares, etc. Old beliefs live on and every evening, two hours after Angelus, you can hear the bell in the Law Courts toll 99 times. Church of *S. Maria di Collemaggio* (1287). 15th-cent. façade of pink and white stone. The huge 16th-cent. castle houses the *Museo Nazionale d'Abruzzo*: archaeology, sculpture and ecclesiastical art.

The Abruzzi. Beautiful mountain range, a part of the Apennines, separates central Italy and southern Italy. The highest part is the *Gran Sasso d'Italia* with the peak of Corno Grande, 2 914 m. *Parco Nazionale degli Abruzzi* covers almost 30 000 hectares. Wolves, foxes, chamois, otters, martens, boars and Italy's last bears.

PESCARA, see A 14.

SS 3. Fano – Assisi – Roma. *Via Flaminia*

Fano and *Urbino,* see A 14.

Gubbio (31 000). One of the most beautiful cities in Italy. Medieval *Città Vecchia* (Old Town) around *Piazza della Signora*. 14th-cent. *Palazzo Comunale* and *Palazzo dei Consoli* (designed by Angelo of Orvieto), museum and art collection. 13th-cent. Gothic cathedral. Gubbio is famed for its beautiful ceramics. Corsa dei Ceri, race held on May 15. Last Sunday in May, archery competition against the town of Sansepolcro.

Assisi (25 000). Medieval town with art treasures. Birthplace of St. Francis (1182). Pilgrimage place. *S. Francesco Basilica* over his grave. Frescoes by Giotto in the upper of the two churches. You can view the corpse of St. Clara in a glass coffin in the Church of S. Chiara. Basilica of *S. Maria degli Angeli* on the site where St. Francis and his disciples built their simple dwellings. He died here in 1226. Statue of the saint by della Robbia. *S. Rufino Cathedral* (1140) with handsome façade. Fine views from the medieval fortress *Rocca Medievale*. Impressive, medieval street of S. Francesco.

PERUGIA (129 000). Capital of Umbria. Ancient town with art treasures and remains from the Etruscan period. Piazza 4 Novembre is the centre of the old quarter. Its fountain, the *Fontana Maggiore* (1278), by the brothers Pisano, is one of the most impressive in the country. *Palazzo dei Priori* (Palazzo Comunale) from the 13th-14th cent. Beautiful *Collegio della Mercanzia* (Merchants' Chamber) is completely covered with colourful woodcarvings. Art museum *Galleria Nazionale dell'Umbria*. 15th-cent. *Collegio del Cambio* (Exchange Building) with splendid woodcarvings and frescoes, some created by Perugino and his pupils (one of them was Raphael). Gothic cathedral with Baroque doorway. The museum explains the story of the construction of the cathedral. Near by the remarkable *Via delle Volte della Pace*, a covered medieval street. The elongated Piazza Matteotti leads to the picturesque, medieval Via Baglioni. Archaeological museum in the Church of *S. Dominico*, which contains Etruscan relics. Etruscan gates in the town wall. Near by *Ipogeo dei Volumni*, an Etruscan family grave.

Montefalco. Encircled by a 14th-cent. wall. Extensive views from the terraces of this little town, called "The Balcony of Umbria". Views also from the Torre Comunale.

Foligno (50 000). The cathedral (1133) and the *Palazzo Trinci* (14th cent.) with its art and archaeological museum are on the Piazza della Repubblica. *Abbazia di Sassovivo*. Beautiful cloisters in the Benedictine abbey.

Spoleto (36 000) was an important town when it was destroyed by Emperor Frederick Barbarossa. Its ramparts had withstood an attack led by Hannibal in 217 B.C. The old *Rocca Fortress* (1367) is joined to the 14th-cent. *Ponte delle Torri*, 230 m long, 80 m high with ten Gothic arches. It is built over a Roman aqueduct. Picturesque old streets. Flower market in the *Piazza del Mercato. Piazza del Duomo* with beautiful palaces. The Church of S. Eufemia and the cathedral (1198). Frescoes. 4th-cent. Basilica of S. Salvatore and the Church of S. Gregorio Maggiore. The Arco di Druso was erected in A.D. 23.

TERNI (106 000). Industrial centre. Piazza del Popolo is the heart of the old quarter. Musei Civici, art and archaeology. Ruins of a Roman amphitheatre. The artificial cascade, *"Cascata della Marmore"*, 106 m high and built by the Romans, operates only on Sundays.

Narni. Beautifully situated little medieval town. Splendid 14th-cent. *Loggia dei Priori* on Piazza dei Priori. 13th-cent. *Palazzo del Podesta* with art museum. Romanesque cathedral. Fortress and town gate. Fountain inspired by Perugia. Remains of the Ponte d'Augusto, a Roman bridge.

Autostrada del Sole (A 1) to Roma (Rome).

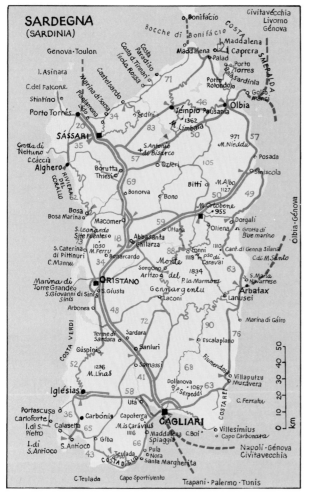

Sardegna

(Sardinia, 1.6 million)

Area: 24 089 km² (9 302 sq. miles).

The capital is Cagliari. The inhabitants, Sardinians, have their own language which resembles Latin. Sardinia is an autonomous region. In 1297 the island was granted to Spain, in 1713 to Austria and in 1720 to the Dukes of Savoy who proclaimed the Kingdom of Sardinia. The capital of the kingdom was Torino (Turin). In 1861, King Victor Emanuel of Sardinia became king of a united Italy.

Mountainous terrain. The highest point on the island is Punta la Marmora, 1 834 m.

Some Sardinian towns (in alphabetical order):

Alghero (22 000). The beautiful little resort has a certain Spanish flavour, but the alleys in the old quarter are typically Italian.

Arbatax. Picturesque little port town. Lovely roads to *Dorgali. Castelsardo* with splendid Gothic cathedral. Famous Madonna.

Borutta, with Church of S. Pietro di Sorres (1190), the oldest church on the island.

CAGLIARI (173 000). Capital of Sardinia. Old quarter surrounded by the modern city. Beautiful views from the *Terrazza Umberto I* (Piazza Costituzione). 14th-cent. *cathedral,* rebuilt in the Baroque style. Impressive ecclesiastical treasures. *Museum of archaeology* (weapons, sculpture, paintings). Roman amphitheatre. Fortification towers. Beautiful botanical garden.

Iglesias. Mountain town with mines (several minerals). *Museum of mining.* Cathedral dating from 1288.

Nora. Phoenician port. Excavations. Roman temple and baths.

Nuoro. Beautiful town in the mountains in an area with many prehistoric tombs, "nuraghi". There are 7 000 remains of a civilization that existed 1400-400 B.C. spread about the island. They served as fortifications and refuge castles. Nuoro is the site of the *Museo Regionale de Custumo,* in the form of a Sardinian village. Vast panoramas from Monto *Ortobene.* Pleasant restaurants.

Oristano. Centre of an agricultural area. Piazza Roma with Christoforus Tower (1291). 13th-cent. cathedral. Museum of archaeology. Ruins of Tharros, a town with Carthaginian origins (10th cent.B.C.). *Marina di Torre Grande,* a seaside resort.

SASSARI (76 000). Centre of a wine district. Modern town built around the medieval town centre. *Cathedral* of S. Nicola (13th cent.) with Spanish Baroque façade. *Museo Nazionale G. A. Sanna* with artifacts from the "nuraghi", art, coins, ethnographic exhibits. Churches of S. Maria di Betlem and Santissima Trinità di Saccargia (16 km S).

Arbatax on the Sardinian east coast

TOWN PLANS

BOLOGNA (500 000)

Capital of Emilia-Romagna, at the edge of the Po Plain and at the foot of the Apennines. Bologna is "la dotta" and "la grassa" – "the learned" and "the fat". Site of Europe's oldest university (1119), it is also one of the culinary centres of Italy. Spaghetti bolognese, tagliatelle, lasagne, are among the local specialities. Bologna is also an industrial centre and the first major city in Italy to have a Communist city government.

Long arcaded streets, countless palaces and churches. Piazza Maggiore and Piazza Nettuno (with fountain of Neptune, 1566) are in the heart of the city. Palazzo Comunale and Palazzo del Podestà with the Torre dell'Arenge (1212). *Basilica of S. Petronio*, begun in 1390 and still unfinished. Its entire length is 217 m and the height of its dome is 152 m. Charles V was crowned Emperor here by the pope in 1530. Famous doorway from 1438.

The symbol of the city, two 12th-cent. towers, *Due Torri*, stand at Piazza di Porta Ravegnana. Leaning towards the west is the *Asinelli tower*, 98 m high and 2.23 m off the perpendicular. Leaning towards the northeast is the *Garisenda Tower*, 48 m high, 3.22 m off the perpendicular. Many other aristocratic families erected towers but they were better built and never became famous. *Piazza della Mercanzia* with the elegant Loggia dei Mercanti.

Museo Civico (archaeology, Etruscan finds, medieval art, ceramics). Pinacoteca (art). Teatro Comunale with magnificent large interior.

Cable cars travel up 211 m (6 min.) to the 13th-cent. Church of *S. Luca*. Fine views. Pontecchio Marconi with the *Villa Grifone* where Guglielmo Marconi made the experiments that resulted in wireless telegraphy. He is buried here.

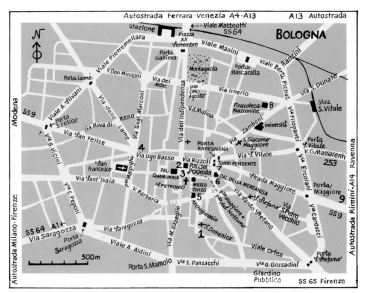

1 *Cathedral.*
2 *Piazza Nettuno.*
3 *Piazza Maggiore and Palazzo del Podestà.*
4 *Market square.*
5 *Municipal Museum.*
6 *Palazzo della Mercanzia.*
7 *The towers of Asinelli and Garisenda.*
8 *Museum of fine arts.*

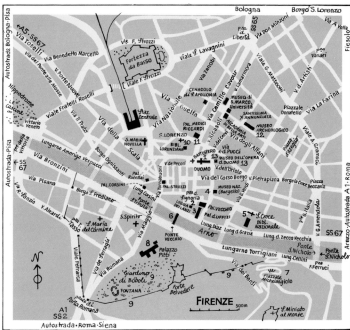

1 *Piazza del Duomo. Cathedral and battistero.*
2 *Piazza della Signoria and Palazzo Vecchio.*
3 *Uffizi Gallery.*
4 *Bargello (museum).*
5 *Church of Santa Croce.*
6 *Ponte Vecchio.*
7 *Piazzale Michelangelo (viewpoint).*
8 *Palazzo Pitti (museum of modern art).*
9 *Boboli Gardens.*
10 *Church of San Lorenzo.*
11 *Medici Palace.*
12 *Archaeological museum.*
13 *Sculpture museum.*

The Nettuno Fountain in Bologna

Galleria degli Uffizi in Florence

Aerial view of Milan

FIRENZE (Florence, 462 000).
Capital of Toscana (Tuscany) and one of the world's foremost centres of culture. A major tourist attraction. During the 15th, 16th and 17th cent. the city was ruled by the art-loving Medici family.
Cathedral of S. Maria del Fiore is a masterpiece of Italian Gothic. Construction began in 1296. In 1436 Filippo Brunelleschi created the magnificent 91 m high dome that rises above the 169 m long and 104 m high church. Among the cathedral's treasures are della Robbia's "Ascension", Michelangelo's "Pietà" (Madonna with the dead Jesus) and Donatello's "Maddalena".
The free-standing **campanile**, 82 m high, was created by Giotto and Pisano. **Battistero** (baptistery) (11th-13th cent.) with famous doors. The bronze ones on the south side are by Pisano, the others by Ghiberti. The best known are on the east side – Michelangelo called them "The Gateway to Paradise". The cathedral and Battistero have black and white marble façades. The façade of the campanile is more colourful.
The **Piazza della Signoria,** at the heart of the city, is dominated by the **Palazzo Vecchio** (1314), the town hall, which has a slender 94 m high tower. **Loggia dei Lanzi** (Loggia della Signoria) with works by Grambologna and Cellini. Bronze group of Judith and Holophernes by Donatello. Neptune Fountain by Ammanati.
Galleria degli Uffizi in a palace, built in the 16th cent. by Vasari. Here the Medici family founded one of the finest art collections in the world. Paintings from Italy, Holland, Germany and Spain. Antique statues.
Ponte Vecchio, a 14th-cent. bridge, lined on both sides by shops – silversmiths, leather goods, high fashion and souvenir shops. A unique, almost Oriental atmosphere.
Palazzo Pitti (the Pitti Palace). Vast royal palace, now an art museum (Galleria Palatina), handicraft exhibits.
Galleria dell'Academica. Sculptures. Michelangelo's David "il Gigante". Medici Museum in the *Palazzo Medici-Ricardi, Museo di S. Marco,* once a Dominican abbey. Frescoes by Fra Angelico. Last supper by Ghirlandaio.
Bargello in fortress-like Palazzo del Podestà. National museum of sculpture, arms, coins, silver, majolica. *Museum of archaeology* contains Etruscan finds. Ethnological museum in *Palazzo Strossi.* **Casa Buonarotti,** Michelangelo's home and museum.
The Church of *S. Croce* (1443) has frescoes by Giotti and tombs of Michelangelo, Dante, Gallilei, Machiavelli. *S. Lorenzo,* where the first church was built 393. The present church was built in the 15th cent. by Brunelleschi. The church is adorned with impressive works of art. Capelle Medici with imposing tombs. Statues by Michelangelo. Beautiful view of the city from the **Giardini di Boboli** (Boboli Gardens).

1 *Piazza del Duomo.*
2 *Galleria Vitt. Emanuele II.*
3 *Teatro alla Scala (opera house).*
4 *Pinacoteca di Brera (art museum).*
5 *Museum of natural history.*
6 *Castello Sforzesco.*
7 *Church of S. Maria delle Grazie.*
8 *Museum of Science and Technology.*
9 *Ambrosiana (library, art gallery).*

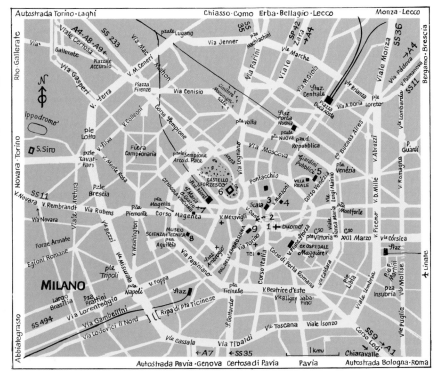

S of Firenze is the abbey church of *S. Minato al Monte* with a marble façade.

MILANO (Milan, 1.7 million).
Second largest city in Italy. Capital of Lombardy and centre of Italian commercial activity. 40% of the country's industry is in the Milan area. Impressively modern centre, bustling during the day and deserted at night. The fantastic *cathedral,* built 1386-1522 with a façade that dates from 1805 and main portal from 1908, accommodates 40 000. It is adorned with 135 towers and spires and about 2 000 roof-top statues. You can go up and get a closer look at them. *Piazza del Duomo* with the Palazzo Reale which houses the Museum of Cathedral Works. *Galleria Vitt. Emanuele II,* covered pedestrian galleries with restaurants, shops and cafés. It leads to Piazza della Scala, site of the world-famous Teatro alla *Scala Opera House,* designed by G. Piermarini and completed in 1778. Destroyed during the Second World War it was restored and seats an audience of 2 800. *Theatre museum.* The Piccola Scala, a smaller theatre, is in the Via Filodrammatici.
Castello Sforzesco (Castle of the Sforzas), facing the Sempiene Park, was built in the 15th cent. and underwent extensive renovations at the turn of the century. Now serves as an art museum. *Pinacoteca di Brera* is one of the greatest art museums in Italy. Renaissance Church of *S. Maria delle Grazie* with dome by Bramante. In the former monastery refectory Leonardo

da Vinci's *"Last Supper".* New methods of restoration have brought out its original colours. The Basilica of S. *Ambrogio* was the coronation church of the Lombard (Longobard) kings and the German emperors. The iron coronation crown is in Monza, directly north of Milan. 8 km outside the city is *Chiaravalle abbey,* founded in 1435 by Bernard of Clairvaux (= light valley = Chiaravalle). Art collection in the Ambrosiana Library and the *Poldi-Pazzoli Museum. Leonardo da Vinci Museum of Science and Technology* with sections devoted to railways, transport and agriculture. Museum of *natural history, aquarium, maritime museum.* The enormous and imposing Stazione Centrale (central railway station) is a sight worth seeing. Near by is the Pirelli skyscraper. Major shopping streets: Via Manzoni, Via Montenapoleone, Corso Matteotti and galleries and the streets near the cathedral. Milan is now a centre of high fashion and hypermodern furniture. Simpler purchases can be made at the flea market in the Mercato di Senegallia.

NAPOLI (Naples, 1.3 million).
Italy's third largest city and second most important port, Naples was founded by the Greeks and became Roman in the 4th cent. B.C. Beautiful setting. Splendid buildings, historical monuments, picturesque old quarters and bustling streets have all made the city a major tourist attraction. It fans out around the Gulf of Naples, and the

horizon is dominated by the silhouette of Vesuvius. The massive *Castel Nuovo* (1228) looms over the busy harbour. Triumphal arch in honour of Alfonso of Aragon. Bronze doors with reliefs. *Quartiere Vecchi di Spacca-Napoli* (the Old Spacca Quarter) with Piazza del Gesù and Piazza Miraglia. Narrow streets, beautiful churches and lively streets. Old quarter also near the harbour, where it is almost impossible to see the sky for all of the colourful, freshly washed clothes, hung out to dry on lines that bridge the streets. West of the harbour is *Santa Lucia,* a fishermen's quarter that has become a tourist attraction. Fine views from the quay, *Via Sauro.*
The city itself is distinguished by its long, straight streets. Corso Umberto I, the main street, leads to the large Piazza Garibaldi. *Galleria Umberto,* a shopping arcade with high glass ceilings and a 60 m high glass dome in the centre. Beautiful *Piazza d. Plebiscito,* site of the Palazzo Reale (Royal Palace, 17th cent.). Art collections. The largest museum in Naples is the *Museo Nazionale,* one of the world's greatest classical museums. Many finds from Herculaneum and Pompeii and a particularly fine display of mosaics. *Galleria di Capodimonte,* a former royal palace. Art, porcelain, weapons. Beautiful hill-top park. Historical museum with additional sections for art and architecture in the *Certosa di S. Martino* abbey church, built 1325 and rebuilt in the Baroque style. Beautiful view. Above the church and the vast monastery, the

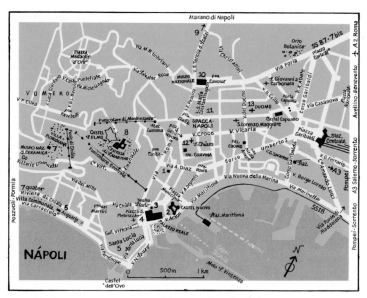

NÁPOLI

1 *Town hall.*
2 *Castel Nuovo.*
3 *Teatro S. Carlo (opera house).*
4 *Piazza d. Plebiscito. Palazzo Reale.*
5 *Santa Lucia.*
6 *Aquarium.*
7 *Villa Floridiana. Museum of ceramics.*
8 *Castel Elmo. Abbey church of S. Marino.*
9 *Capodimonte Museum.*
10 *National Museum.*
11 *Spacca-Napoli (old quarter).*
12 *Cathedral of S. Gennaro.*
13 *Church of S. Chiara (museum).*

notorious *Castel S. Elmo*, long used as a prison.
The Gothic *Cathedral of S. Gennaro* has a 19th-cent. façade. The previous cathedral was destroyed by an earthquake in 1456. The church has been built onto the 4th-cent. Basilica of S. Restituta. *Santa Chiara* (1328), burial church of the Anjou dynasty, restored after the war. Extremely beautiful views from *Cape Posillipo*, site of the Parco Rimembranza (Garden of Remembrance).

Hadrian's Column and remains of Foro Romano

Vesuvio (Vesuvius). The only active volcano on the European mainland. Since the great eruption in 1631 when 3000 people were killed, there have been frequent minor eruptions.

Ercolane (Herculaneum). The "City of Hercules", destroyed when Vesuvius erupted in A.D. 79. Its buildings were covered and filled with lava which preserved them. Excavations began in 1920. Several well-preserved buildings with mosaics and wall paintings. Baths.

Pompei. The town was destroyed and covered by ashes and pumice after an eruption of Vesuvius in A.D. 79. Ex-

cavations of Pompei have been going on since the 18th cent., providing fascinating insights into urban life 2000 years ago. Temple of Apollo, basilica and shops adjoining the Forum. Baths and amphitheatre. The earthquake in 1980 caused some damage.

ROMA (Rome, 3 million).
Capital of the Italian Republic. Site of the Vatican City State, capital of Roman Catholicism. Legend has it that Rome was founded by Romulus in 753 B.C. Built on seven hills – the smallest but historically most important of these is the Capitolium (Capitol).
A brief selection of some of the major tourist attractions:

THE VATICAN CITY STATE.
Autonomous state with 1000 inhabitants, of which 200 are diplomats. The Vatican has its own mint, post, telegraph, radio station and newspaper (L'Osservatore Romano). This is the spiritual capital of the world's 700 million Roman Catholics, and as such

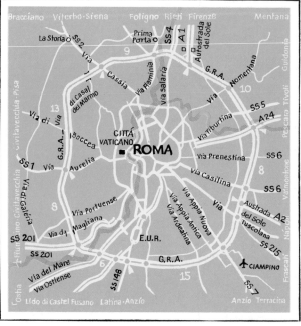

it is a major political power. The Vatican City State, by tradition, is defended by the colourfully uniformed Swiss Guard. Although their uniforms were designed by Michelangelo, they carry modern equipment (including tear gas in the halberds).

St. Peter's Square is an enormous oval square (340 × 240 m), created by Lorenzo Bernini. In its centre, an obelisk from the circus of Nero. Colonnades, fountains, and statues. Crowds gather here to be blessed by the Pope.

St. Peter's Church (San Pietro in Vaticano), Christendom's largest church, designed by Michelangelo, has a 186 m long interior. The 132 m high dome was erected over the tomb of St. Peter. The first stage of construction started in 1452 and was concluded in 1506. Bramante Bernini created the altar tabernacle (1633), a baldaquin supported by contorted bronze pillars. Bronze statue of St. Peter in the nave. Its foot has been worn smooth by the kisses of the faithful. Enormous burial monuments and tombs of early popes. Later popes have been buried in the Vatican Grottoes under the church. Sepulchral tablet of Queen Christina of Sweden in a side aisle to the right.

The Vatican Museum, in a section of the Vatican Palace. Antique sculpture – the Apollo Belvedere, the Laocoön group, Belvedere Torso, etc. Egyptian museum, Etruscan museum. Pinacoteca Vaticana, an enormous art museum. Frescoes by Raphael.

The Sistine Chapel (Cappella Sistina), built in 1484 as the chapel for the Papal Palace, is used for the Conclaves. Michelangelo's enormous ceiling paintings with *"The Creation"* in the centre, and *"The Last Judgment"* on the west wall. On other walls, frescoes by Botticelli, Ghirlandaio, Perugino and many more. *The Lateran Palace* in southeast Rome is a Vatican enclave. Papal residence until 1308. Museum of Religious and Missionary History. The Baroque Cathedral of *S. Giovanni* is the Pope's own cathedral in his capacity as Bishop of Rome. Opposite the palace, the *Scala Santa* (Holy Staircase), crowded daily with pilgrims who ascend it on their knees.

ANCIENT ROME

The Capitol, the holy mountain of Rome where the temples once stood and where the cries of the sacred geese of Juno warned the people of a force of invading Gauls. Michelangelo created the present square, the Piazza del Campidoglio, which is surrounded by palaces and museums.

Foro Romano, the Roman Forum, was the centre of ancient Rome and the Roman Empire that at its peak, stretched from southern Scotland to the Sahara, and from Portugal to Persia. Remains of several buildings including the Senate (Curia). The oldest buildings date from the 5th cent. B.C. *Triumphal arch of Septimius Servus* (A.D. 203). *Temple of Castor and Pollux. The Arch of Titus* (A.D. 81) was erected in memory of the destruction of Jerusalem. The Basilica di Massenzio was a law court and commercial building. The Via Sacra cuts through the area. Fine views from the pine-clad 40 m high *Palatino* (Palatine) Hill. *Casa di Livia,* named for the wife of Augustus. Frescoes.

On the other side of the Via dei Fori lies the **Fori Imperiali** (Imperial Forum) with the remains of buildings constructed in honour of Augustus and Trajan. 30 m high *Trajan's Column* adorned with reliefs. The *Pantheon,* a Roman temple erected 27

1 St. Peter's Square and St. Peter's Church.
2 The Vatican Museum and the Sistine Chapel.
3 Castel Sant'Angelo (mausoleum of Emperor Hadrian)
4 The Church of S. Maria in Trastevere.
5 Piazza Navona. Pantheon.
6 Piazza Colonna.
7 Piazza Venezia.
8 The Capitol, Foro Romano and Palatino Hill.
9 Imperial Forum.
10 Colosseo and Arch of Constantine.
11 The Church of S. Maria in Cosmedin.
12 Baths of Caracalla.
13 Church of S. Paulo fuori le Mura.
14 Lateran Palace.
15 Church of S. Pietro in Vincoli.
16 Church of S. Maria Maggiore.
17 The Quirinal.
18 Fontana di Trevi.
19 Via Vittorio Veneto.
20 National Museum and Baths of Diocletian.
21 Scala di Spagna (the Spanish Steps).
22 Mausoleum of Emperor Augustus.
23 Villa Medici.
24 Galleria Borghese (art museum).
25 Villa Giulia (Etruscan museum).

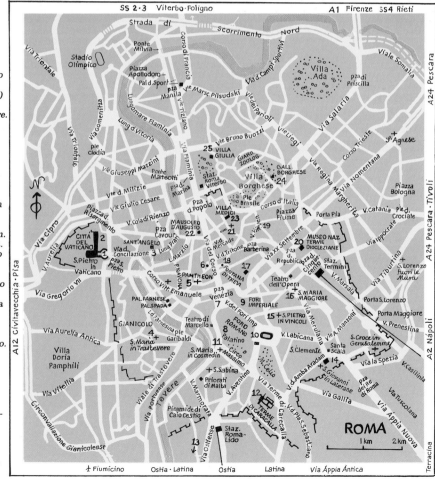

Construction on St. Peter's, the principal church of the Roman-Catholic world, began in 1506.

B.C. and transformed into a Christian church in 609. Magnificent dome. Seven chapels containing the tombs of the kings of Italy and the painter Raphael.

The **Coliseum** (Colosseo), the Roman amphitheatre which seated 50 000 spectators, was completed in A.D. 80. Its spectacles included gladiatorial combats. Large sections were destroyed by earthquakes during the Middle Ages and some of its building materials were removed and used for later structures. Next to the Coliseum is the *Arch of Constantine* (Arco di Constantino, A.D. 312), a well-preserved triumphal arch, erected in honour of Emperor Constantine. *Via Appia Antica* (312 B.C.), the earliest of the great Roman roads, begins at Porta Capena and ends at Brindisi. Some of the original stone paving remains. At its start it is lined with tombs. This is the site of the enormous *Catacombs*, subterranean cemeteries. *Column of Marcus Aurelius*, 30 m high, built of blocks of marble. The *Baths of Caracalla* (Terme di Caracalla, A.D. 223), ancient Rome's largest baths, could accommodate 1500 bathers.

MUSEUMS AND PALACES
Vatican Museum and Lateran Museum, see above. *Galleria Borghese* (1616). Large art museum in a beautiful park. **Museo Nazionale Romano** in the ruins of the Baths of Diocletian (A.D. 306), **Museo Nazionale Etrusco**. Etruscan museum in Villa Giulia, built for a pope in 1550. *Palazzo Venezia*, Renaissance palace

(1445). Art and ceramics. Once residence of Mussolini, who used to harangue the crowds from its balcony. *Palazzo Farnese*, splendid Renaissance palace (1546), now the French Embassy. *The Palazzo Barberini* and *Palazzo Doria* are art museums.

CHURCHES
St. Peter's and S. Giovanni in Laterano, see above. *S. Giovanni in Fonte*, a 5th-cent. octagonal church, is one of the oldest in Christendom. *S. Maria Maggiore*, built in 431, has mosaics from the same period. *S. Paolo fuori le Mura*, with origins in the 4th cent. and built over the tomb of St. Paul, is the second largest church in Rome. (Only St. Peter's is larger.) Mosaics, 80 columns. *San Pietro in Vincoli* (St. Peter in Chains) was built in 439 to contain the fetters of the Apostle. Michelangelo's "Moses" and his uncompleted tomb of Pope Julius II.

STREETS AND SQUARES
Piazza Venezia is dominated by the enormous white marble *Vitt. Emanuele II Monument*, erected in 1911 to celebrate the unification of Italy. Tomb of the Unknown Soldier. The shape of *Piazza Navona* originates from the racecourse of the Emperor Dominitian. Large fountains by Bernini. Colourful street life, restaurants and café terraces. **Fontana di Trevi**, enormous Baroque fountain with figures of Neptune and his retinue. Tradition has it that you should turn your back on the fountain and then throw two coins into it: the first coin to assure your return to Rome, the second to make

certain that your wish will come true. **Scala di Spagna** (the Spanish Steps). A picturesque staircase with 136 steps leading up from the Flower Market (Piazza di Spagna) to the Church of Trinità dei Monte.
Piazza del Popolo with the north city gate. Near by is the Pincio Hill. Lovely view. *Via del Corso* is the classic major street of Rome. Churches and Baroque palaces. The Via del Tritone and Via dei Condotti (which goes to the Spanish Steps) are busy shopping streets. The Antico Caffé del Greco, first opened in 1760, has had many distinguished guests. *Via Vittorio Veneto*, with luxurious hotels, restaurants, night clubs and shops is, if we are to believe Fellini's film, the centre of the sweet life (la dolce vita).
Trastevere, an interesting old quarter with narrow streets, countless restaurants and colourful street life. *Gianicolo Hill* with fine views from the Piazzale Garibaldi. Flea market every Sunday at the *Porta Portese*.
Stazione Termini is one of the most modern and beautiful railway stations in Europe. The Zona *EUR* in the south of Rome, built for the 1942 World's Fair (which was cancelled by the Second World War), is now an administrative centre with monumental buildings. Modern residential area with parks and private gardens. Sports grounds and facilities, originally built for the Olympic Games of 1960. *Lido di Ostia* (Lido di Roma) on the sea coast, 40 minutes by underground. *Ostia Antica*, excavations of a large port town that once had 100 000 inhabitants.

1 *Via Roma.*
2 *Palazzo Madama.*
3 *Cathedral.*
4 *Palazzo dell'Accademia della Scienze (museums).*
5 *Royal Armoury.*
6 *Palazzo Carignani.*
7 *Automobile museum.*
8 *Basilica di Superga.*
9 *Market squares.*

TORINO (Turin, 1.2 million).
Capital of Piemonte (Piedmont) and
one of the most important industrial
centres of Italy. Its Baroque buildings
and atmosphere were created during
the rule of the House of Savoy. Impressive period of expansion at the turn of
the century. The network of streets
and roads established in the 17th and
18th cent. was actually based on the
original Roman plans. However, Turin
seems closer in atmosphere and
architecture to Lyons than to Rome.
The *Via Roma*, a magnificent avenue
with arcades and elegant shops, goes
from the Stazione di Porta Nuova
(central railway station) to the large
Piazza San Carlo and on to Piazza
Castello, site of the *Palazzo Madama*.
18th- cent. façade and tower from the
Roman Porta Decumana. *Museo
Civico di Arte Antica.* The *Palazzo
dell'Accademia della Scienze* houses
several museums: Egyptian museum,
Museo d'Antichità (archaeological
museum with Etruscan and Roman
finds), Galleria Sabauda with the impressive collections of the House of
Savoy.
Renaissance white marble cathedral
of *S. Giovanni. Cappella della Sindone,*
with 60 m high dome by Guarini.
Here, in an urn, is the Holy Shroud in
which Jesus was wrapped after the
descent from the cross. The outline of

a man's crucified body is imprinted on
the cloth. Roman Porta Palatino.
Palazzo Reale (1660) with the L'Ar-
meria Reale and its famous collection
of weapons. Park created by the
Frenchman André le Nôtre. Palazzo
Carignano, by Guarini, houses the
Museo Nazionale del Risorgimento,
with exhibits related to the unification
of Italy. Museum of modern art,
museum of films, artillery museum,
etc. Large *Parco Valentino* with a
reproduction of a medieval castle.
Enormous exhibition halls. Annual
motor show.

*Museo dell'Automobile Carlo Bis-
caretti di Ruffia* is one of the foremost
motor car museums in Europe. Turin
is the home of FIAT which produce
2 000 cars daily and has a work-force
of 60 000. The automated Mirafiori
factory is one of the most advanced in
the world.
Just outside town is the beautiful
Basilica di Superga (1731) by Juvara.
Tombs of the kings of Sardinia and the
princes of Savoy in the crypt. Beautiful panorama of Turin, the plains of
the Po and the Alps.

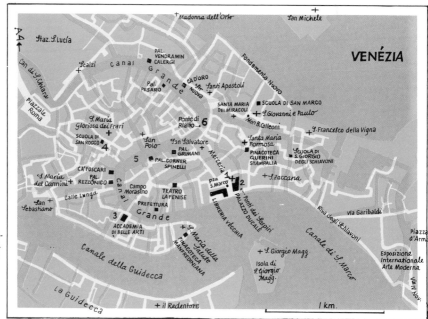

1 *Piazza S. Marco. Ca-
  thedral of S. Marco.*
2 *Palazzo Ducale and
  The Bridge of
  Sighs.*
3 *Art museum.*
4 *Scuola di S. Rocco.*
5 *Canal Grande.*
6 *Rialto Bridge.*

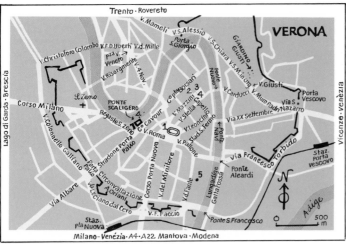

1 Piazza Bra. Arena.   2 Piazza delle Erbe.   3 Piazza dei Signori.   4 Juliet's house.   5 Juliet's tomb.
6 Castel Vecchio and Scaligero Bridge.   7 Church of S. Zeno.   Photo: The amphitheatre in Verona

VENEZIA (Venice, 355 000)
One of the most beautiful cities in the world, and a justifiably popular goal for generations of tourists. This venerable city, with houses built on wooden pillars sunk into the canals, criss-crossed by 150 canals, punctuated by narrow, winding streets, accessible only to pedestrians, has over 400 bridges. Traffic is limited to gondolas, motor boats, vaporetti (small steam-driven water buses) and traghetti, small ferries that take passengers across the Grand Canal. Cars are left on the mainland or in the garage on the Piazzale Roma. A 4 km long railway and motor car bridge connects Venice to the mainland.
St. Mark's Square (Piazza San Marco), one of the most beautiful squares in the world, is surrounded by magnificent buildings. The Cathedral **S. Marco** contains famous Byzantine mosaics. The *Torre dell'Orologio*, on the north side of the square, has two gigantic bronze figures which have tolled the hours for over 500 years. On the other side, the 96.8 m high campanile, a reconstruction of the one that collapsed in 1902. The bronze horses of St. Mark, originally Greek or Roman were taken from Constantinople in 1204. The square is filled with people and pigeons that take wing when the figures toll the hour. The famous *Café Quadri* and *Café Florian*. *Libreria Vecchia* by Sansovani and the *column* that bears the winged lion, symbol of Venice, are also in the square. **Palazzo Ducale** was under construction from 1309 until 1442. It was the residence of the Doges, who governed the autonomous Republic of Venice. During the 15th cent., this was the most important centre of trade on the Mediterranean. The palace contains, among other works of art, Tintoretto's "Paradise", 22 m wide and 7 m high. The pink and white marble façade of the palazzo is one of the most distinctive elements in this unique

city. The Danieli, a luxury hotel on the Canal S. Marco, first opened in 1822. The *Grand Canal* (Canal Grande) is 3 800 m long and 30-70 m wide. It is lined with countless palazzi of varying splendour. Each building has its own landing stage. Among them is the *Ca d'Oro* with the Galleria Franchetti. The *Rialto* (16th cent.), a bridge lined with shops. The *Bridge of Sighs* (Ponte dei Sospiri) is another famous bridge. It leads from the Doge's Palace to the city prison.
Museums: *Gallerie dell'Accademia, Museo Correr, Scuola di S. Rocco* (Tintoretto), *Scuola di San Giorgio degli Schiavoni, Palazzo Pasaro* (Galleria d'Arte Moderna). Maritime museum in the huge *Arsenal*. Examples of Cubism, Dadaism and Surrealism in the *Collezione Peggy Guggenheim*.
Churches: S. Marco, see above. *S. Maria Gloriosa* dei Frari (15th cent.) with the grave of Titian. *S. Maria della Saluta* (17th cent.), Baroque church. *S. Giovanni e Paolo* in the Italian Gothic style. *Madonna dell'Orto* with the tomb of Tintoretto. In general, all of the hundred churches of Venice contain exceptional works of art.
The island of **Murano**, in the lagoon, is a glassworks centre. *Glass museum* (Museo dell'Arte Vetraria). *Burano*, on another nearby island (9 km from Venice), is famous for its lace. *Torcelli* with village and imposing cathedral, is 10 km from Venice. University, shipyards and foodstuffs industry in **Mestre**. Many hotels, with lower prices than those in Venice. It can be a good idea to stay here. Good and frequent train and bus service to Venice. On the tongue of land that separates the lagoon from the sea, is the **Lido di Venezia**, a fashionable seaside resort, known for its annual film festival.

VERONA (270 000)
A beautiful city, rich in art treasures and splendid buildings. The centre of the city is the large **Piazza Bra** with

open-air cafés. It overlooks the **Roman arena**. 152 × 128 m and 30 m high, this structure is second only to Rome's Coliseum in size. It was even larger until destroyed in 1183 by an earthquake. Site of an opera festival, July-August, the arena seats 22 000.
The narrow and busy Via Mazzini cuts through the old quarter to **Piazza delle Erbe**, once the ancient Forum, and one of the most beautiful squares in Italy. The buildings that line it date from the Middle Ages to the Baroque. *Torre del Gardello* (14th cent.) with tower clock. The *Madonna Verona Fountain*. Umbrella-like roofs cover the fruit and vegetable market in the square. *Piazza dei Signori* contains a statue of Dante. Numerous magnificent palaces, e.g. the Renaissance Loggia del Consiglio. Near by, at Via Capello 23, is Juliet's balcony. Romeo Montecchi and Giulietta Capuleti fell in love in about the year 1300. Shakespeare immortalized their tragedy in "Romeo and Juliet". The *tomb of Juliet* is in an abbey near Adige.
During the Middle Ages, Verona was ruled by the Scaligeri family. Their palazzo is on Piazza dei Signori, their tombs adorned with the statues of knights are at the Arche Scaligere. Their bridge, the *Ponte Scaligero* (1354) with three arches of varying length spans the River Adige. It was blown up by retreating Germans in 1945 and restored with period building material. It leads to the Scaligeri's enormous old castle, the *Castelvecchio*, now an art museum. Cathedral of *S. Maria Matricole* (1187). Beautiful, red marble transept, Roman mosaics from a previous basilica. Titian's painting of the Assumption of the Virgin. S. Zeno Maggiore, beautiful Romanesque church (1138). Magnificent bronze doors, crypt with relics, frescoes, etc. Verona was one of Italy's project cities during the European Architectural Heritage Year 1975.

IRL · Ireland

IRL·Republik of Ireland

Area: 70 000 km² (26 600 sq. miles)

Population: 3.4 million. 95 % of the population are Roman Catholics. Two languages: Gaelic and English.

Major cities: Dublin 860 000, Cork 135 000, Dun Laoghaire 98 000, Limerick 63 000.

Government: Republic. Parliament (Dáil Éireann). The president holds office for seven years.

History

400 B.C. Celts settle in Ireland.

432 Christianity introduced by St. Patrick who becomes the Patron Saint of Ireland.

800-1000 Ireland invaded and subdued by Norwegian and Danish Vikings who are defeated at Clontarf in 1014.

1172 Armies of Henry II land in Ireland and establish British rule.

1594-1603 Bloody uprising suppressed by the British.

1649 Cromwell and his armies ravage Ireland. Catholics expelled from northern Ireland and replaced with English and Scottish settlers. This provides the origins of the present troubles in Northern Ireland.

1690 Protestant armies of William of Orange defeat Catholic armies at the Battle of the Boyne. July 12 is still marked by parades and riots in Northern Ireland.

1845-1847 The potato harvest fails and causes the Great Famine. Vast areas become uninhabited as a result of deaths and emigration. More than 2 million Irish flee to America.

The *18th and 19th cent.* are marked by struggles between the native Irish and the British. The conflicts culminate in unrest during the first decades of the 20th cent. The resistance is led by the Sinn Fein party.

1916 Easter Uprising in Dublin. The battles are centred around the General Post Office. The British execute the leaders of the uprising.

1921 Establishment of the Irish Free State. Northern Ireland (Ulster, or the 'six counties') is granted a parliament.

1937 New constitution introduced. The Autonomous Republic of Eire is established. This remains the name of the republic until 1949. Gaelic is proclaimed the primary national language. English becomes the second language.

1939-1945 Eire remains neutral during the Second World War. Eamon de Valera, premier 1937-1948, 1951-1954 and 1957-1959. President of the Irish Republic in 1959.

1948 Eire leaves the British Commonwealth.

1973 The Irish Republic joins the Common Market.

Currency: Irish Pound (or "punt")
I pound = 100 pence
British currency is accepted.

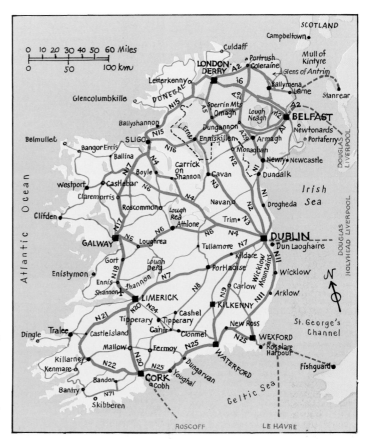

Business hours: Banks 10.00 a.m.-12.30 p.m. and 1.30-3.00 p.m. Open Thursdays until 5.00 p.m. in Dublin. Post offices 9.00 a.m.-6.00 p.m. Saturdays 9.00 a.m.-1.00 p.m. or closed. Shops 9.00 a.m.-5.00 or 6.00 p.m. Half- day closing once a week, usually Wednesday or Saturday. Lunchtime

Routes described:

N 1 Belfast – Dundalk – Dublin

N 3 Enniskillen – Kells – Dublin

N 4 Sligo – Boyle – Dublin

N 6 Galway – Athlone – Dublin

N 7 N 8 Dublin – Cork

N 9 Dublin – Kilkenny – Waterford

N 11 Dublin – Wexford

N 15 Londonderry – Sligo

N 17 Sligo – Galway

N 18 Galway – Limerick

N 20 Limerick – Cork

N 21 Limerick – Tralee

N 22 Tralee – Killarney

N 25 Rosslare Harbour – Wexford – Waterford – Cork

N 70, N 71 Killarney – Bantry – Cork

Town plan: Dublin

Killarney

closings are not unusual. Shopping centres are usually open until 8.00 or 9.00 p.m. on Thursdays and Fridays.

Holidays: New Year's Day, March 17 (St. Patrick's Day), Easter Sunday, Easter Monday, Whit Sunday, Whit Monday, December 25 and 26. Bank holidays on the first Mondays of June and August and the last Monday of August.

Hotels
Hotels are placed into DeLuxe, 1st class, 2nd class and 3rd class categories.

Food and drink
Irish cuisine closely resembles its English counterpart. Mutton, fish and shellfish often appear on Irish menus. Some specialities: Irish stew, a combination of mutton, potatoes and onion. Cottage pie, minced mutton, browned onion gravy. Lordly steaks, slices of beef up to 6 cm thick. Smoked salmon. Galway oysters. Dublin Bay prawns. Beer is a popular drink and of the many varieties available, the dark, strong Guinness stout can be considered the Irish national beverage. There are also other dark "stouts". The Harp Lager is also popular. Cider and Irish whiskey. Irish Mist (liqueur) and Irish Coffee (coffee, whiskey, whipped cream and sugar).
"Licensing hours": weekdays 10.30 a.m.-11.30 p.m. in summer, 11.00 p.m.

in winter. Pubs in Dublin and Cork closed 2.30-3.30 p.m. All pubs are open on Sundays 12.30-2.00 and 4.00-10.00 p.m. Wine is served with meals in restaurants until midnight.

Shopping
Lace from Carrickmacross and Limerick. Crystal from Waterford and Galway, towels, linens, tweeds, antiques, pottery, knitted woollens from Aran and Donegal.

Petrol
Petrol is sold in three grades: Top grade, approx. 98/99 octane, Middle Grade, approx. 94/95 and Lower Grade, approx. 90 octane.

Speed limits. Traffic regulations
Outside built-up areas 55 mph (88 kmh) or 40/50 mph (64/80 kmh) as signposted, built-up areas 30 mph (40 kmh). Maximum speed limit for cars towing caravans or trailers 35 mph (56 kmh).
Traffic travels on the left-hand side of the road.
If your car is fitted with seat belts, it is recommended that they be used.

Roads
All "T" (Trunk) and "L" (Link) routes are being renumbered as "N" (National Primary or National Secondary). There are still many old signs. Direction signs are in both Irish and English.

Road patrol
AA road patrols. For towing assistance in Dublin, dial 77 94 81, in Cork 50 51 55. Emergency number in case of personal injury 999.

The Automobile Association, 23 Suffolk Street, Dublin. Irish Tourist Office, Ireland House, 150 New Bond Street, London W1Y 0AQ. Tel. 01-493 3201.

The harbour at Dunquin, Dingle Peninsula.

N1. Belfast – Dundalk – Dublin

Northern Ireland border.

Dundalk. Little market town. Cathedral of St. Patrick.

Ardee, where the legendary Cuchallain, Knight of Ulster, fought with Ferdia, the warrior of Connaught. Supposedly they were really great friends who duelled during the day and tended each other's wounds at night.

Monasterboice. Remains of a 5th-cent. abbey. Three crosses, typical of early Irish ecclesiastical art. Some crosses of this type are ornamented, some are inscribed and some depict religious scenes. Muiredach's Cross close to the entrance is the most splendid of the three.

Mellifont Abbey. Ireland's first Cistercian abbey. King William's Glen where William III was slightly wounded before the Battle of the Boyne, which took place near by. His Protestant army defeated the forces of King James II and ended the Catholic king's hopes of regaining the throne of England. Brugh-na-Boinne (on the Boyne). Three Bronze-Age burial cairns (2 000 B.C.). The largest is *Newgrange,* 90 m in diameter, 12 m high. They contain tunnels and stone sepulchral chambers, some with ornamental carvings.

Drogheda. One of the oldest towns in Ireland. Of the town gates only St. Laurence's Gate is left. Ruins of the Abbey of St. Mary d'Urso. Magdalen Steeple, a tower from an 11th-cent. convent.

Skerries. Bathing beach. The Church of *Lusk* has a "round tower".

N 3. Enniskillen – Kells – Dublin

Northern Ireland border.

Cavan and *Monaghan.* Amateur fishing.

Virginia, a little resort beautifully situated on the 8 km long Lough Ramor. Swimming and fishing. Swift wrote "Gulliver's Travels" while staying at nearby Cuilcagh House.

Kells, a little, idyllic town. The famous "Book of Kells", a beautifully illustrated 8th-cent. Latin manuscript of the Gospels, now in Trinity College, Dublin, was created in the monastery here. House of St. Columba who founded the abbey c. 550. Beautiful market cross, one of five High Crosses at Kells. A "round tower". Horse-racing in Navan.

Slane. Village with remains of a Franciscan abbey.

Trim was one of the most important English strongholds in Ireland. Large castle. Tower of a 14th-cent. Augustinian abbey.

Tara was at one time the religious and cultural capital of Ireland. Important as early as the Bronze Age it flourished in the 3rd-6th cent. Only a few mounds and building fragments remain of what was once the royal palace. The kings were buried at Brugh-na-Boinne.

DUBLIN, see town plans.

N 4. Sligo – Boyle – Dublin

Ballinafad in the Curlew Hills. *Northern Moytura* where a legendary battle took place between the Tuatha de Danaan and the Firbolg in 1330 B.C. Beautiful ruins of 12th-cent. *Boyle Abbey* with Cistercian abbey church.

Carrick on Shannon. Centre for amateur fishing. Lough Ree where the waters of the River Shannon have formed a 20 km long and up to 9 km wide lake. Several islands, some of them with ruined churches. To the west *Roscommon,* with a Dominican abbey and enormous ruined castle, both built in the 13th cent.

Longford. St. Mel's Cathedral (17th cent.). *Ballymahon* in the area associated with the writer Oliver Goldsmith, born near by in 1728. *Mullingar.* Market town. Cattle breeding. *Castlepollard* with Tullynally Castle, the home of the Earls of Longford.

DUBLIN, see town plans.

N 6. Galway – Athlone – Dublin

GALWAY, see N 17.

Loughrea. Diocesan Museum in the town gate. Examples of modern Irish ecclesiastical art in the Catholic cathedral which was remodelled in 1903. Ruins of a Carmelite abbey (1300). The Turoe Stone, a richly ornamented Late Iron-Age work.

Kilconnell Friary. Beautiful ruins of a 15th-cent. Franciscan abbey that suffered damage and eventual destruction during a late 16th-cent. uprising and Cromwell's warfare in 1651. 13th-cent. Clonfert Cathedral (St. Brendan's). The famous doorway gracing its west façade is 100 years older than the main building.

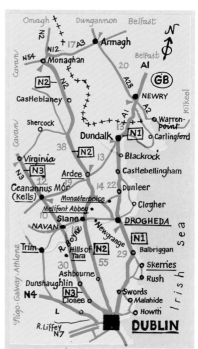

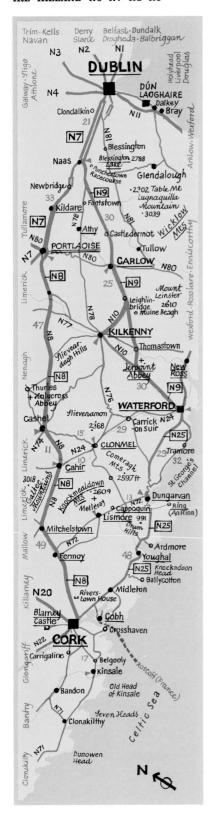

Athlone. Capital of "the Midlands". 16th-cent. town wall and large castle with origins in the 13th cent. Abbey ruin (1241). Boat trips on the Shannon and Lough Ree. Modern Church of St. Peter and St. Paul. Lough Ree has 52 islands. Boat excursions. Boher. Church with relics of St. Manchan. The casket containing the saint's remains is a superb example of Irish craftsmanship.

Clonmacnois was an important monastic city, founded in 548 by St. Cirian. Remains from the 8th and 9th cent. The cathedral was originally founded in 904. O'Rourkes Tower (10th-12th cent.), a refuge tower. The monks of Clonmacnoise wrote "The Book of the Dun Cow", now in the Bodleian Library at Oxford. The Vikings raided Clonmacnoise and there have been many raids since. Deserted in 1522. Pilgrimages every year on September 9.

N 62 from Athlone south to **Birr,** a beautiful town that has preserved its 18th-cent. buildings and atmosphere. 17th-cent. Birr Castle with lovely gardens. **Roscrea** where St. Cronan founded an abbey in the 7th cent. Ruins of an enormous 12th-cent. abbey.

DUBLIN, see town plans.

N 7 and N 8. Dublin – Cork

N 7 from Dublin to **Kildare,** a centre for horse breeding, "The National Stud". Japanese Gardens. 12th-cent. cathedral. Beautiful 32 m high "round tower".

Holy Cross Abbey, 12th-cent. church. Exquisite woodcarvings.

Portlaoise. N 7 proceeds to Limerick. N 8 goes to Cork. **Stradbally** with a steam engine museum.

Cashel. One of the most historic places in Ireland. Remains of 4th- to 12th-cent. cathedral and castle on the 60 m high rock. Cashel was the capital of the kingdom of Munster. St. Patrick's Cross, an 11th-cent. stone cross once used as a coronation throne. 10th-cent. "round tower".

Road to **Tipperary,** a village that was made famous during the First World War in the song "It's a long way to Tipperary".

Clonmel is the chief town of the County of Tipperary. Only the turreted West Gate remains of the town's four original gates. Art museum.

Cahir. Mightiest medieval castle in Ireland, now restored. Sturdy walls and towers. Large banqueting hall with enormous fireplace. Ruins of Athassel Priory (13th cent.). Beautiful church and cloister.

The beautiful **Galtee (Galty) Mountains.** A white, 5 m high statue of Christ the King overlooks the Glen of Aherlow.

Mitchelstown Caves. Beautiful stalactite and stalagmite formations (2.5 km deep caves). Burncott House, an Elizabethan mansion.

Fermoy. Once a British garrison town. Angling centre.

CORK (134 000). The republic's second largest city. Winding streets near the steep banks of the River Lee. Large port for the export of agricultural products. An abbey was founded here in the 7th cent. by St. Finbarr (Finn Barre) and the Protestant cathedral, completed in 1964, bears his name. The Eight "Bells of Shandon", famous carillon in the Church of St. Anne. Several other interesting churches. Art museum. Cork's Municipal Museum in Fitzgerald Park. Open-air market in Cornmarket Street. University founded in the 9th cent. Modern 17 storey high County Hall.

Blarney Castle. 15th-cent. ruined castle, site of the famous Blarney Stone which is now a part of the 25 m high tower. If you kiss the stone you will be granted the gift of eloquence. At the same time, you may run the risk of lumbago for to kiss the stone you must bend backwards and then put your head through a hole in the wall. A guard holds your feet.

N 9. Dublin – Kilkenny – Waterford

DUBLIN, see town plans.

Wicklow Mountains, Blessington Lakes, and **Glendalough,** see N 11.

Athy with a fine Dominican church. *Carlow.* Small industrial town. During the 1798 uprising the English won a victory here. Memorial cross.

Kilkenny (11 000) founded in the 6th cent. by St. Canice. The cathedral (1286) is named after the saint. The castle, where several parliaments have been held, was rebuilt in 1826. Three of the towers remain from the 13th cent. Kilkenny is well known for its handicraft. Kilkenny Design Workshops in old stables. Many fine old buildings, e.g. Shee's Almshouse built in 1594. The nearby Dunmore Caves have beautiful stalactites and stalagmites. Jerpoint Abbey Church with lovely cloister has its origins in the late 12th cent.

Waterford, see N 25.

N 25. Rosslare Harbour – Wexford – Waterford – Cork

Rosslare Harbour and *Wexford*, see N 11.

New Ross, where St. Abban founded an abbey in the 4th cent. Dunganstown where President J.F. Kennedy's great-grandfather was born. Memorial park in the form of an arboretum.

WATERFORD (30 000). Port town. Exceptional views from Cromwell's Rock. Medieval atmosphere, buildings and narrow alleys in the old quarter. Reginald's Tower (1003), constructed for a Danish prince, is one of the 11th-cent. fortifications that remain. Art museum. It is possible to visit the famous glass factories. The Protestant Christ Church Cathedral was completed in 1779. The Catholic Cathedral dates from the same period. The French Church (a Franciscan church) dates from 1240. Dominican abbey.

Dungarvan. Ruins of a 15th-cent. castle and the town wall. An Ring, southeast of Dungarvan, is an Irish-speaking area. N 72 to *Cappoquin* with the strange Dromana Gateway, which could be described as "Brighton Pavilion Architecture".

Lismore. Cathedral and large castle, mainly from the 18th cent. but with older parts. The Castle Gardens can be visited.

The Knockmealdown Mountains are beautiful. The Vee, a mountain gap, offers a fine view. *Mitchelstown* and *Fermoy,* see N 8.

Youghal. 13th-cent. Church of St. Mary. Clock gate tower, a part of the old town wall. It is a reconstruction of the old gate and contains a museum, handicraft centre and tourist information office. The pottery industry is said to have traditions from Phoenician days, 200 years B.C. Myrtle Grove, an Elizabethan building, where the mayor, Sir Walter Raleigh, introduced potatoes and tobacco to Ireland.

Cobh. Old harbour and naval station. Centre for deep-sea angling. The impressive St. Colman's Cathedral was built 1868-1919. Lusitania Memorial commemorates the sinking of the British liner "Lusitania", which was torpedoed off Kinsale in 1915. 1198 people, died among them 124 Americans. Many are buried in the Clonmel cemetery.

CORK, see N 8.

N 11. Dublin – Wexford

DUBLIN, see town plans.

Dún Laoghaire (98 000). Industrial town, port and seaside resort. At the end of the Promenade a Joyce museum in a Martello tower. James Joyce, the writer, lived here and the opening scene in "Ulysses" takes place here. Martello towers were built to resist a Napoleonic invasion.

Dalkey and *Bray,* seaside resorts.

Enniskerry, one of the most beautiful villages in Ireland. Powerscourt House was destroyed by fire in 1974, but has beautiful 16th- to 19th-cent. gardens. Terraces follow the banks of the river. 130 m high waterfall.

The Wicklow Mountains. Beautiful area with dramatic rock formations. Gorges and waterfalls at Pollaphuca. The "Military Road", built after the uprising in 1798, allowed the English to reach the rebels' strongholds. The Blessington Lakes, part of the Pollaphuca hydro-electric scheme.

Glendalough, "Glen of the Two Lakes", a delightful place where St. Kevin built a complete monastic town in the late 6th and early 7th cent. It became a renowned centre of culture and one of the period's great European centres of Christianity. The abbey was in operation until the 16th cent. and this was a place of pilgrimage until the mid 19th cent. 30 m high "round tower", one of the best preserved in Ireland. Its entrance doorway, a few metres above ground level, indicates that it was used as a place of refuge during attacks. Its pointed roof is typical of the style. Such structures can be found all over Ireland. St. Kevin's Church, built of granite, is only 3.3 m high. Cathedral and three other churches.

Russborough House has a large art collection, donated in 1976 by the industrialist Sir Alfred Beit.

Wicklow and *Arklow,* seaside resorts. The water temperature is, however, seldom enticing. Perhaps as a result of this, amusement areas of the traditional British type have been constructed. Arklow is also known for its pottery and for its *maritime museum,* opened in 1976. Botanical gardens at Ashford (open only on Sundays).

Ferns. Castle ruins. The oratory is in a good state of preservation. The Gothic cathedral and Augustinian abbey are surprisingly impressive buildings in so small a town, but during the 12th cent. Ferns was the capital of the kingdom of Leinster. After the Viking Age, Ireland was independent but made up of several small kingdoms. Its kings and princes were constantly involved in bloody internal wars. The king of Leinster requested English assistance.

Enniscorthy. Market town and port on the River Slaney. Castle.

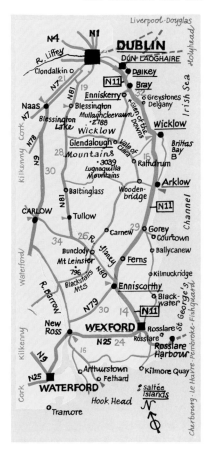

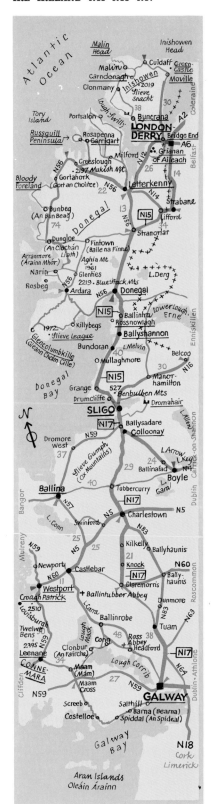

Wexford was founded by the Vikings. Narrow streets and medieval town gate. 14th-cent. ruined castle and medieval Westgate Tower. Selskar Abbey. A surprising structure is the bull-fighting arena, built during the Norman period. The bulls were not killed. Annual autumn opera festival. Large ferry port at Rosslare.

Saltee Islands is the largest bird sanctuary in Ireland.

N 15. Londonderry – Sligo

LONDONDERRY (DERRY), see Northern Ireland, Great Britain.

Bridge End. Northern Ireland border.

The Granian of Aileach, a concentric fort. A 5 m high, 4 m thick stone and earth wall, 25 m in diameter, protected the settlement. In Ireland such fortifications are called "cahir", "lisses", or "raths". There are said to be as many of 30 000 of these forts in Ireland.

Inishowen. A peninsula. Fine views from *Malin Head,* northernmost point of Ireland. **Buncrana** and **Moville,** seaside resorts. **Greencastle.** Castle ruins. **Gardonagh,** site of the stone Donagh Cross (St. Patrick's Cross), probably the oldest in Ireland.

Donegal is a beautiful, wild landscape. The coast is just as romantic. Modern cathedral in **Letterkenny,** chief town of the area. **Carricart,** beautifully set on **the Atlantic Drive** that circles the little Russguill Peninsula. **Bloody Foreland,** a promontory, gets its name from the magnificent sunsets in the Atlantic that give it a dark red hue. **Ardara.** Cotton industry and manufacture of embroidery, tweeds and lace. Beautifully situated in a valley.

The walls of the *Slieve League* rise 601 m out of the sea. Most climbing expeditions use Carrick as a starting point.

Glencolumbkille, where St. Columba and his disciples had their retreats. Now a place of pilgrimage. St. Columba founded the abbey at Kells.

Donegal. Market town which was the centre of feuds and warfare between families and lords. Donegal Abbey. To the east, on the border, *Lough Derg.* St. Patrick is said to have fasted on an island in the lake in the 5th cent. It is now a place of pilgrimage from June 1 until August 15.

Rossnowlagh. Little resort with fine beach. **Ballyshannon.** Power station. **Bundoran.** One of Ireland's largest seaside resorts.

Drumcliff, next to the steep Ben Bulben Mountain. Grave of William Butler Yeats (1865-1939) in the churchyard. He led the Irish cultural Renaissance at the turn of the century. His plays and poems are often set in this region which has come to be known as Yeats Country. He was awarded the Nobel Prize in 1923.

Cooladrummon, near by, was the scene, in 561, of the "Battle of the Books" between the followers of St. Columba and the followers of St. Finian of Movilla. The conflict was fought over a copy of a psalter made by St. Columba.

Sligo. Little town, beautifully situated. Ruins of the Franciscan Sligo Abbey. St. John's Church and the Catholic cathedral are also interesting. *Lough Gill* is a lovely lake with small islands and very old ruined churches. Yeats has written about "Lake Isle of Innisfree". He spent his childhood in Sligo. Dromahair Castle. Collooney. Pretty village with castle ruins.

N 17. Sligo – Galway

The direct road is neither as scenic nor as interesting as the roads close to the coast. **Knock.** Pilgrimage place every Sunday from May until October. The Virgin Mary is said to have appeared here in 1879.

N 59 more or less follows the coast and passes many interesting places:

Dromore Castle has been transformed into a luxurious hotel especially popular with American tourists who can afford its prices. It is extremely picturesque. Waterfall.

Ballina. Fishing centre. 6th-cent "dolmen", a prehistoric burial place. Five large ruined churches close to the town.

Achill Island. Ireland's largest island. Splendid scenery. Resorts. The cliffs on the western shores of the island rise dramatically 600 m out of the Atlantic. Sharks are caught in the spring at Dooagh on Keem Bay.

Westport. Chief town of the area. Westport House (1703) is well worth a visit. Beautiful interior, displays of silver, glass and works of art. To the east, Ballintubber Abbey, now a picturesque ruin.

Croagh Patrick, Ireland's holy mountain where St. Patrick prayed and fasted. In addition to this, he rid Ireland of snakes and loathsome beasts. Every time the saint rang his bell he hurled it into the sea. Each time it was followed by toads, serpents and reptiles. As often as he threw the bell it was returned to him by helpful spirits. Thousands of people gather for the great

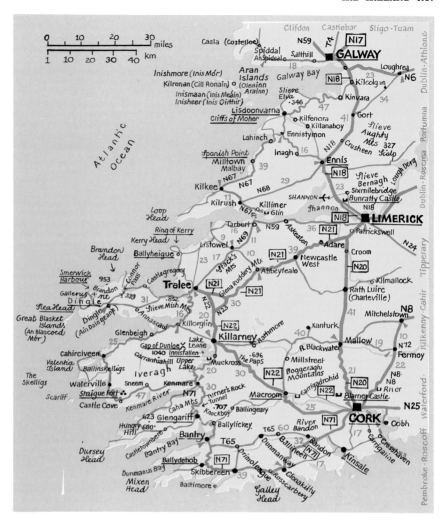

annual pilgrimage held on the last Sunday in July. The ascent can be difficult. In the evening the mountain is illuminated with torches. The pubs in Louisburgh extend their opening hours.

Leenane. Centre for amateur fishing. Cong. Beautiful area between the lakes. John Ford filmed "The Quiet Man" with John Wayne and Maureen O'Hara here.

Connemara. One of the most dramatic and magnificent landscapes in Ireland. Rocky coast and Twelve Bens mountains.

GALWAY (25 000). Some of the older buildings reflect the commercial and cultural links that the city had with Spain prior to the 17th cent. The Spanish Arch remains of the old town wall. Some medieval buildings have also been preserved. The centre of Galway is Eyre Square. Salmon fishing from the *Salmon Weir Bridge.* Legend has it that Columbus prayed in the Church of St. Nicholas before sailing to America. University College with extensive library. Centre of Gaelic studies. The old language is widely spoken in this part of Ireland. Salt Hill, suburb and seaside resort.

Boats to the **Aran Islands.** The inhabitants of these islands are famed for their preservation of old traditions and customs. Robert J. Flaherty, the documentary film maker, made a film about the islanders and their ways ("Man of Aran", 1934). The dramatist Synge set "Riders to the Sea" on one of the islands (Inishman). There are three islands that can easily be visited: **Inishmore** with the venerable Dunaengus Castle, perched high above the sea. Several churches also dating from the 9th cent; **Inishman** with an even older castle, Dun Conor; **Inisheer** with old churches.

N18. Galway – Limerick

To the west, County Clare with a beautiful coastline. *Lisdoonvarna.* Most distinguished spa in Ireland. Many caves, some with fascinating stalactites and stalagmites. The *Polnagullum Grotto,* deepest in the country, is open to tourists. Several ships of the Great Armada foundered at **Spanish Point** in 1588.

The Cliffs of Moher, an 8 km long stretch of steep rock formations with interesting bird colonies, is perhaps the most dramatic section.

Ennis is a lovely little town with twisting narrow streets. During the Middle Ages it was a centre of culture, and it is said that at its peak 300 monks lived and worked in the abbey which is now in ruins. Ruins of *Quin Abbey,* an old church used as a fortress during the 13th cent.

Shannon Airport was of great importance during the early post-war years when trans-Atlantic aircraft required an airport in the extreme west of Europe. Dublin's airport was too far from the ocean. Large power station.

Bunratty Castle (15th cent.), completely restored with furnishings faithful to its original period. Medieval banquets are arranged here throughout the year. *Open-air museum* with farm houses, fishermen's houses and workshops.

LIMERICK (63 000). Ireland's third largest city with large port and industries. Although it is the oldest town in Ireland, most of the buildings are modern. *O'Connell Street,* the beautiful High Street of the town, is 1.6 km long. *The Newton Pery* (English Town) district is a typical 18th-cent. fortified town with streets laid out at right angles. The Irish Town district has a more medieval character. King John's Castle (13th cent.) and sections of the old town wall remain. St. Mary's Cathedral was founded in 1172. Neo-Gothic St. John's Cathedral. The town is famous for its guipure lace that is made in the Convent of the Good Shepherd. But the town's main claim to fame stems from "limericks", nonsense verses. Although their origins are unknown, they were introduced in a book published in 1884 and their popularity spread throughout the world. Now they exist in hundreds of languages. Example:
There was an old fellow of Lyme
Who lived with three wives at a time.
When asked, "Why the third?"
He replied, "One is absurd,
And bigamy, Sir, is a crime."

N20. Limerick – Cork

The direct road has not as much to offer as the N21 – N22 route via Killarney.

Mallow Castle has a museum which includes some relics from Stanley's African expeditions. *Blarney Castle,* see N8.

N21. Limerick – Tralee

Adare. Beautiful village with half-timbered houses and Adare Manor set in lovely gardens. *Askeaton,* ruins of Desmond Castle (1199). Delightful road that follows the banks of the Shannon Estuary. *Ballyheigue.* Little seaside resort.

Tralee. Small town with handsome Court House in the classic style, a creation of the architect Morrison. Dominican church. Day Place, a street lined with beautiful Georgian houses.

West of Tralee, *Dingle Peninsula,* marked by high mountains that extend out to *Slea Head* where it is possible to drive on a "corniche" road that has been hewn out of Mount Eagle. Several archaeological excavations. Near by are the small *Blasket Islands.*

Dingle is a picturesque little town where old traditions are maintained and the everyday language is Gaelic. Scenic route through the *Connor Pass.*

Tranquil, little **Smerwick Harbour** where 600 Spaniards and Irishmen surrendered to the English in 1580. Lord Grey had them duly slaughtered.

Anascaul, with the South Pole Inn. This was the home town of Thomas Crean who died with Scott at the South Pole.

N22 Tralee – Killarney

Killarney (7 000) is set in a particularly beautiful area. One of the great tourist attractions of Ireland. The three *Lakes of Killarney* are dominated by the country's highest mountain, Carrantuohill, 1 041 m (Macgillycuddy's Reeks). Excursions to the *Gap of Dunloe* and *Innisfallen Island* by boat, pony or jaunting cart (two-wheeled carts drawn by ponies).

Ross Castle (15th cent.) is a beautiful structure. *Muckross Abbey,* constructed in the 15th cent., was destroyed in 1632. *Muckross House* (1843) with *Folk Museum,* handicraft, and hand-carved furniture. Beautiful gardens. In the churchyard is the grave of German writer R.E. Raspe (died 1794). He is rather unknown, but he created a famous character, Baron Münchhausen.

Macroom. Old market town where the inhabitants are said to speak the most ancient form of Gaelic. Ruins of a 15th-cent. castle. Birthplace of William Penn, the founder of Pennsylvania.

CORK, see N8.

N70 and N71. Killarney – Bantry – Cork

The road that circles the *Iveragh* Peninsula is known as the *Ring of Kerry* (170 km). It is one of the most beautiful tourist routes in Europe. *Killorglin.* Fishing centre where a mountain goat is "king" for three days during the annual August Puck Fair. *Glenbeigh* with a fine beach. *Valentia Island* and *Waterville* are Europe's foremost centres for deep sea fishing. *Staigue Fort* (2nd cent. B.C.), a concentric fort, 34 m in diameter with 4 m high walls.

From Kenmare to *Glengarriff* via the Tunnel Road or through the Healy Pass. *Glengarriff* is a lovely town set in a wild landscape. Wooded mountains frame the bay and provide protection for the semi-tropic vegetation. Over a hundred islands. Excursions to the *Garinish Islands,* site of a Japanese garden. *Bantry,* beautifully situated on a bay. *Ballydehob* with views out over an archipelago.

Skibbereen and *Lough Ine,* a salt-water lake with Marine-Biology Institute. Baltimore on the tip of the peninsula.

Kinsale. Venerable old town with beautiful houses. Narrow and steep streets. A yachting and angling centre, once an important naval base and shipbuilding town. Its history can be seen in the interesting museum in Market House (17th cent.). The Battle of Kinsale took place on Christmas Eve 1601, when the British defeated a combined Irish and Spanish army. *Old Head of Kinsale.* Viewpoint. A fort with three rings (7th cent.). *Carrigaline* with famous pottery.

CORK, see N8.

TOWN PLANS

DUBLIN (Baile Atha Cliath, 860 000)
Beautifully situated between the mountains and the Irish sea. Large parts of the city have a charming 18th-cent. atmosphere. Dublin was founded by Danish Vikings who gained rule in 825. Their power was crushed at the Battle of Clontarf in 1014. The English captured the city in the 12th cent. Capital of the Irish Free State in 1922. The General Post Office played a role in the last stages of the struggle for independence. It was occupied during Easter 1916 by Irish volunteers and severely damaged during the fighting that followed (since restored). The loveliest parts of Dublin are Georgian, and of all the sections of the city built during that period, perhaps the most beautiful is *Merrion Square* (1762), created by the architect John Ensor.
Trinity College, Dublin's university, has a library with 800 000 volumes and 3 000 manuscripts. Its best known possession, the most valuable book in Europe, is the 8th-cent. *"Book of Kells",* an "illuminated" (illustrated) Latin manuscript of the Gospels. *The National Museum* has a splendid collection of gold artifacts from the Bronze Age. *The National Gallery* and the *Municipal Gallery of Art* are distinguished museums of art. *Christ Church Cathedral* was founded by the Danes in 1038. 12th-cent. *St. Patrick's Cathedral,* the largest church in Ireland, contains the tomb of Jonathan Swift, the author of "Gulliver's Travels", who was Dean of the cathedral until 1745. St. Audoen's Church, the oldest parish church, has six bells. St. Audoen's Arch is the only remaining city gate.
The *Abbey Theatre* was a centre for Irish cultural independence. The original theatre was destroyed by fire in 1951, but a new theatre was constructed in Lower Marlborough Street.
Leinster House (1745), seat of the Irish Parliament. The building provided inspiration for the White House in Washington.
The Custom House is a splendid example of Irish Georgian architecture. Museum of Heraldry in *Dublin Castle.* The Wardrobe (or Record) Tower remains of the 13th-cent. castle. Chapel Royal (1814) with exceptional woodcarvings, plaster work and stained-glass windows. Race course in the vast and beautiful *Phoenix Park.* The large obelisk commemorates the first Duke of Wellington, who was born 1769 in Dublin. There is a flower garden in the park. The president of the republic has his residence here. Fine *Zoological Garden,* famous for the breeding of lions.
St. Stephen's Green is a beautiful park or square with an artifical lake. It is surrounded by fine buildings, among them the famous Shelbourne Hotel. University College buildings near by. A fashionable shopping street, Grafton Street, leads to College Green, one of the main streets.
Botanical gardens in Glasnevin. *St. Anne's rose garden* at Clontarf, a beautiful site by the sea.
Guinness, Ireland's foremost producer of stout, allows visitors to inspect the breweries.
The Dublin Tourist Trail is a specially signposted walking tour through the city. An illustrated booklet is available from the Tourist Information Offices at 14 Upr. O'Connell Street and 51 Dawson Street.

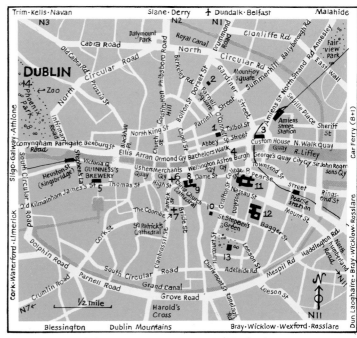

1 *General Post Office.*
2 *Municipal Gallery of Modern Art.*
3 *Custom's House.*
4 *O'Connell Bridge.*
5 *Guinness Brewery.*
6 *Christ Church Cathedral.*
7 *St. Patrick's Cathedral.*
8 *City Hall.*
9 *Dublin Castle.*
10 *Civic Museum.*
11 *Trinity College.*
12 *Leinster House. National Library, National Museum.*
13 *University College.*
14 *Zoo.*

O'Connell Street in Dublin

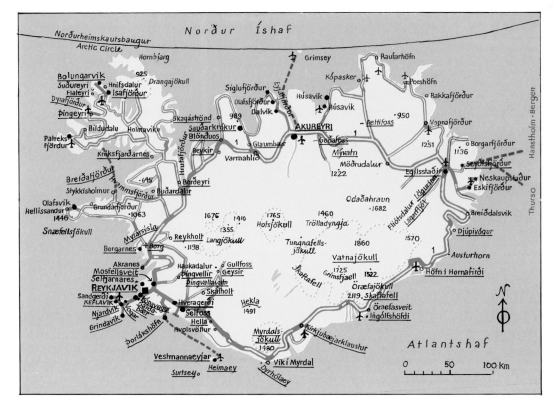

IS · Iceland

IS · Ísland

Area: 103 000 km² (39 600 sq. miles)

Population: 232 000. 93% of the population are Lutherans. The language is Icelandic.

Major cities: Reykjavík 85 000 (with suburbs 118 000), Kopavágur 14 000, Akureyri 13 000, Hafnarfjördur 12 000.

Government: Republic, The Althing (parliament) has two chambers.

History

870—930 Norwegians settle on Iceland.

930 The Althing meets for the first time; it is the world's oldest functioning parliament. 999/1000 Christianity becomes the official religion.

13th cent. Feudal disputes.

1264—1814 Iceland ruled by Norway; together with Norway in a personal union with Denmark from 1380.

1783 Eruption of Lakis, a volcano, lays waste large areas of Iceland.

1814 Iceland ceded to Denmark at the Treaty of Kiel.

1874 Iceland is granted a constitution.

1903 Iceland gets its own government.

1918 Independence in a personal union with Denmark.

1944 Proclamation of the Icelandic republic.

1972 The "Cod War" against Britain after an extension of the coastal fisheries to 500 km.

1980 Vigdis Finnbogadóttir is elected president of Iceland. (The world's first woman president.)

Currency: Króna.
1 króna = 100 aurar.

Business hours: Banks 9.15 a.m.—16.00 p.m. Thursdays also 5.00—6.00 p.m. Post offices 9.00—5.00 p.m. Closed Saturdays. Shops 9.00 a.m.—6.00 p.m. Saturdays 9.00—10.00 p.m. or 9.00 a.m.—12.00 noon. Many shops are closed on Saturdays. All shops and offices are closed on the first Monday in August.

Holidays: Christmas and Easter as in Norway, May 1, June 17 (National Holiday).

Hotels

Plenty of hotels all over the country, but few luxury hotels. Most hotels are small and simple, but all are clean. Some hotels accept guests who bring their own sleeping bags.

Camping

There are several camping sites. Camping gear can be rented in Reykjavik and a few other places.

Youth hostels

There are youth hostels in Reykjavik, Akureyri, Seyðisfjörður, Vestmannaeyjar, Höfn, Berunes, Leirubakki and Fljótsdalur.

Food and drink

Icelandic cooking is dominated by fish and mutton prepared in many different ways.

Fish and shellfish: trout, salmon, lobster. Dried fish, especially haddock. Hakarl (håkjerring), cured shark meat with a characteristic odour which one does best to overlook.

Meat: Hangikjöt, smoked lamb. This is a popular speciality much eaten during holidays. Svid, pig's head. Skyr is a yoghurt-like national dish made from skimmed milk.

Brennivin, Icelandic aquavit.

Shopping

Woollens, especially pullovers; furs, handicrafts.

Speed limits and traffic

70 kmh, built-up areas 45 kmh. Outside of towns and villages only a couple of hundred kilometres of roads are paved. Use dipped headlights. There is plenty of dust on the roads, so keep a good distance from the car ahead. Many roads have loose verges.

Ambulance: Reykjavik tel. 11100, *police:* tel. 11166, *emergency medical assistance:* tel. 22411.

The Icelandic motor organization Felag Islendska Bifrei aeigenda, tel. 29999, Reykjavik.

1. Reykjavík – Akureyri – Vík – Reykjavík
The Ring Road

REYKJAVÍK (85 000, Greater Reykjavik 118 000) Iceland's capital, largest city and most historic place. It was here, in the "smoking bay" (which is what Reykjavik means) where Ingolffur Arnarson, the first Norwegian settler, built his farm. The smoke came from the hot springs at Laugardal. Until about 1700 Reykjavik was nothing but a large farm. In 1786 it had grown into a small village with 170 inhabitants. It was not until after 1900 that the town began to grow.

The town consists of both small houses and blocks of flats. Most buildings are heated with water from the hot springs. In the centre is an open square with the **cathedral** and the **Althing building.** The government buildings. The National Theatre and the National Library are situated right where the first farm was built. The university, Háskola Islands, is on Lake Tjörnin in the centre of town. This is also the location of the **National Museum.** On a hill is a monument to Leif Eiriksson, who discovered America.

Nordens Hus (a cultural centre), was inaugurated in 1968. **Árbæjarsafn,** an open-air museum, was opened in 1957. Peat-covered houses, a church with a peat-covered roof. Several buildings, the oldest dating from 1820. The museum is open June—August.

Large open-air swimming pools with water from the hot springs are open all year round.

The president lives at Bessastadir, west of Reykjavik/Kopavagur.

Mosfellssveit (3 000). Modern community. Hot springs. Ferry or road to **Akranes** (5 200) on a peninsula of the same name. One of Iceland's largest fishing harbours. Industries, among them the state-owned concrete factory. New bridge across the Borgarfjörður to **Borgarnes.** Through Myrarsýsla, Lovely surroundings. Egil Skallagrimsson lived at Borg.

Eastwards to **Þingvallavatn,** Iceland's largest lake, site of Þingvellir (50 km east of Reykjavík). The world's oldest existing parliament, the Althing, held its first meeting here in 930 and this was Iceland's most important place until 1800. Lögberg. The chief legistator stood here while the other members stood on the slope below. Old church and national cemetary.

The national road continues northeastwards. Road to **Reykholt.** Snorre Sturlason's farm. Snorre was killed here in 1241. Snorralaug, Snorre's swimming pool made out of rock, is still intact. Gustav Vigeland's statue of Snorre. Folk high school built in 1931.

Northwest to **Buðardalur** (430) in Hvammsfjörður, a branch of the beautiful Breidafjörður. North to **Króksfjardarnes** (91) and **Þingeyri** (450) with the waters of the lovely Dyrafjörður surrounded by beautiful mountains covered with brush-wood. **Flateyri** (450). Fishery industry and harbour.

Isafjörður (3 400) with high mountains to the east and west. The town is situated on a large sandy plain. The oldest farm is Eyri which dates from the time when Iceland was first settled. Interesting church from 1863. **Bolungarvík** (1 300), one of Iceland's oldest and largest fishing ports.

Borðeyri (39), one of Iceland's smallest villages. Old trading centre. **Reykir** on Hrutafjörður, one of the country's longest fjords (36 km). Hot springs. **Blönðuos** (1 000). Commercial centre. Fishing, farming, industry.

Instead of driving the national road to Akureyri, you can take the Skagaströnd road to **Höfdakaupstaður** (Skagaströnd) (650) at the foot of the Spákonufell mountain. It looks like an old woman sitting with her knitting in her lap. Onwards to **Sanðarkrókur** (2 200). Its oldest buildings date from 1871. Lovely view towards the islands of Drangey and Málmey. Boats to Drangey every weekend (half-day trips).

South to Varmahlið, past **Glaumbaer,** a farm with peat-covered roofs. Museum.

Varmahlið (300) where you meet the national road if you come from Sandarkrokur. Westwards through Oxnadalur to Akureyri,

Geyser

AKUREYRI (13 000). Northern Iceland's chief town in a lovely setting on Eyjafjörður is a centre of trade, industry and education. The town is situated on Oddeyri, a sand bank created by the River Glerá. Iceland's most industrialized town. **Lystigarðurinn,** a park with several species of trees and over 400 Icelandic flowers. Museum of Icelandic poets: Nonnahús (Jon Sveinsson), Sigurhæðir (Matthias Jochumsson) and the houses that used to belong to Dávid frá Fagraskógi and Friðbjörn Steinsson.

Vaglaskogur with Iceland's most popular birch forest. The beautiful waterfalls of **Goðafoss** and the 44 m high **Dettifoss.** It is possible to get close to both falls by car. **Myvatn,** Iceland's fourth largest lake. Lovely lava scenery and an eldorado for bird-watchers. There are more species of ducks here than anywhere else in the world.

Eastwards to **Egilsstaðir** (1161), a modern community, centre of transport in eastern Iceland. Leaving the national road you can drive out to the coast at **Seyðisfjörður** (989) with one of the country's best harbours and ferries to Norway, the Faroe Islands and Scotland.

From Egilsstaðir across Lagarfljót, Iceland's longest river which also creates Iceland's third largest lake, Lögurinn. According to legend, the lake contains a sea monster.

Djúpivogur (400). Good harbour. Fish industries. The oldest houses were built by Danish tradesmen 1788—1920.

Routes described:

1. Reykjavík –Akureyri – Vík – Reykjavík (the Ring Road)
2. Reykjavík – Grindavík – Keflavík

Reykjavík

Höfn í Hornafirði (1 500). One of Iceland's youngest villages.

On the southeast coast, below Europe's largest glacier, Vatnajökull, is one of Iceland's three national parks, **Skaftafell** (500 km²). Several marked trails in the beautiful landscape. Restaurant and shop open June 15—August 25. **Öræfasveit** (120) south of Öræfajökull was completely cut off until the national road round Iceland was completed in 1974. Volcanic area.

To the west along the south coast past the **Ingolfshöfdi**. A rock near the water in the sandy landscape where Iceland's first settler, Ingolfur Arnarson, spent his first winter. Across the sandy plains to **Kirkjubæjarklaustur** (270) where Irish monks are supposed to have lived before the Norwegian settlers arrived. Kirkjúholar with remains of an abbey founded in 1186. In 1783 Jón Sigurdsson held his "fire sermon" during a volcanic eruption; the lava stream changed its course and left the church unharmed. Chapel in memory of the abbey was constructed in 1974. **Kirkjugólf** is a peculiar, cobblestone-like basalt formation in the grassy slope.

Vík í Myrdal (500). Iceland's southernmost community below the Mýrdalsjökull glacier. Fishing used to be the main source of income, but now farming has become more important. **Dyrhólaey.** 120 m high rock with a mountain wall facing the sea; fine views. When the sea is calm boats can travel right through a large hole in the rock.

Vestmannaeyjar are situated off the coast, a bit further west. 15 islands and 30 skerries. Several bird rocks. **Surtsey,** furthest out, emerged from the sea as a result of a volcanic eruption in 1963. It continued to grow up until 1966. **Heimaey** (4 700) has Iceland's largest fishing port and fish industries. In January 1973 the inhabitants had to be evacuated in just a couple of hours because of a volcanic eruption that eventually buried half the town under lava. The harbour was unharmed and the inhabitants moved back. Airport with daily connections with Reykjavík. Daily ferries to **Þorlákshöfn,** (extra sailings in July).

The national road continues to the villages of **Hvolsvöllur** (700) and **Hella** (600) in a flat, green landscape with mountains as a backgrop.

Selfoss (3 400), about 15 km from the sea. Industry, trade and farming. Dairy. Sports facilities. **Hveragerði** (1 200). Hot springs and hot houses, 35 000 km² under glass. The Grýta geysir erupts regularly every two hours. School of agriculture.

Sideroad to **Skálholt,** southern Iceland's old bishop's residence (1056–1796), and once the country's chief site of learning. New church from 1963. Excavations in 1954 uncovered the grave of Bishop Páll Jónsson (who died 1211). His stone sargophagus and bishop's staff were found. **Geysir** with hot springs that erupt out of the ground. **Gullfoss** in Hvitá is an important tourist attraction. The 32 m high waterfall is Iceland's most famous.

To the west is **Hekla** (1 491 m), a volcano that has had 20 eruptions since 1140. Particularly violent were the ones in 1300, 1766 and 1947. The most recent eruption took place in 1980. In the Middle Ages people both in Iceland and in the rest of Europe were convinced that Hekla's crater was the entrance to hell.

Þjórsárdalur. Lovely valley with water falls and shrubbery. It was deserted during Hekla's eruption in 1104. At that time there were nearly 30 farms in the areas. One of them, **Stöng,** has been excavated and reconstructed. Open to the public. Now there are only two farms in the valley. The road continues westwards to Reykjavík.

2. Reykjavík – Grindavík – Keflavík

REYKJAVÍK, see road 1.

KOPAVÁGUR (14 000), southeast of Reykjavik, is Iceland's second largest town. Modern housing, mostly built after 1936. The bridge across the Gjá connects the eastern and western parts of the town. The centre is the geographic centre of Greater Reykjavik.

Garðabær (5000). Shipyards and industries. Around the turn of the century the town had only 374 inhabitants. The oldest house dates from 1803.

Vogar (600). Fishing port. Directly south of Vogar is Vogastapi, a 80 m high rock with shelves rich in fish, Gullkista, just outside. The church in Kálfatjörn is one of the largest in Iceland.

To *Grindavík* (1 900) on the south coast. Fishing port and fish industries. The number of inhabitants has increased dramatically during the last decade.

Njardvík (2 000). Good harbour. Fish industries.

Keflavik (6 700). Commercial centre; the town has Iceland's second largest exporting harbour. Cross-shaped church from 1915; lovely stained-glass windows. The international airport is west of the town and 30 km southwest of Reykjavik.

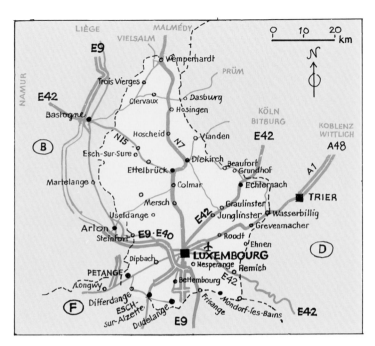

L · Luxembourg

L·Luxembourg/Lezebuurg

Area: 2 587 km² (1 705 sq. miles)

Population: 360 000. The majority of the population are Roman Catholics. Most tourists to Luxembourg will find the native language, "letzeburgesch", difficult to fathom, but both French and German are spoken by almost everyone, and English is widely understood.

Major cities: Luxembourg 100 000, Esch 27 000, Differdange 20 000, Dudelange 15 000.

Government: Monarchy. The Grand Duke acts as regent. Parliament.

History

900 The area that is present-day Luxembourg and the present Belgian Luxembourg form an earldom.

1308 The Count of Luxembourg becomes King Henry VII.

1477 Luxembourg is brought under the rule of the House of Habsburg.

1839 A part of Luxembourg is incorporated into Belgium. The remainder, what is now the Grand Duchy, becomes an independent neutral state.

1890 The Duke of Nassau becomes Grand Duke of Luxembourg. The House of Nassau still rules.

1914 German occupation.

1940 The Germans incorporate Luxembourg into the Third Reich.

1945 Luxembourg is liberated after the last German offensives in the Ardennes.

Currency: The Luxembourg franc (LUF).

1 franc = 100 centimes.

Belgian francs are accepted in Luxembourg. A word of advice: Luxembourg francs can be difficult to exchange abroad, so it is a good idea to change them before leaving the country.

Business hours: Banks 8.30 a.m.-12.00 noon and 1.30-4.30 p.m. In some areas the after-lunch opening hours are 2.00-5.00 p.m. Closed Saturdays. Post offices 9.00 a.m.-12.00 noon and 2.00-6.00 p.m. Closed Saturdays. Shops 8.00 a.m.-12.00 noon and 2.00-6.00 p.m. Occasionally shops are closed on Monday mornings. Supermarkets are often open until 8.00 p.m.

Holidays: New Year's Day, Easter Sunday, Easter Monday, May 1, Ascension Day, Whit Sunday, Whit Monday, June 23 (National Holiday), August 15 (Assumption Day), November 1 (All Saints' Day), December 25 and 26. Shops, banks and offices are also closed on February 23 (Carnival Monday) and November 2 (All Souls' Day).

Food and drink

Some of the national specialities are triepen, black pudding served with mashed potatoes and radishes, judd mat gardebohn'en, smoked pork and green beans in white sauce, Liéwekniddelen (quenelles), calf liver served with boiled potatoes and sauerkraut, fierkelsgelli, suckling pig in aspic, Ardennes ham, served in raw, paper-thin slices, and Kachkés, a boiled cheese that is unique to Luxembourg.

Beer is popular. In addition to the domestic brands, beers from Belgium, France and Germany are available everywhere. Wines of the Mosel Valley, Moselle, Riesling, Rivaner, Pinot, Ruländer and Traminer are popular. Visitors can inspect, taste and buy the products at the cooperative vineyards in Grieveldange, Grevenmacher and Wormeldange.

Shopping

Lace, leather, wine, stoneware and crafts.

Speed limits. Traffic regulations

Motorways 120 kmh, other roads 90 kmh, built-up areas 60 kmh.

Children under the age of ten are not allowed to travel in the front seat. If your car is fitted with seat belts it is compulsory to wear them.

Road patrols

The patrol cars of ACL are yellow and carry the sign "Automobile Club, Service Routier". There is also a commercial road patrol, Secours Automobile Luxembourg, which charges a fee for its services.

Emergency telephones: 012 for fire brigade, police and ambulance.

Road assistance: dial 31 10 31 to ACL. An AIT assistance booklet should be shown.

ACL, Automobile Club du Grand Duché de Luxembourg, 13 Route de Longwy, Helfenterbruck/Bertrange, Luxembourg, tel. 31 10 31.

Luxembourg National Tourist and Trade Office, 36-37 Piccadilly, London W1V 9PA. Tel. 01-434 2800.

The oldest part of the city of Luxembourg.

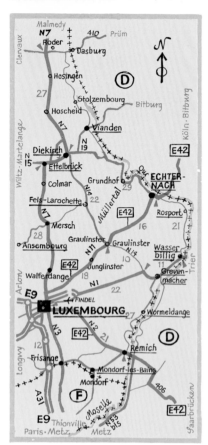

E42. Echternach – Luxembourg

E42 comes from Köln.

Echternach is situated on the Sauer, the frontier river. One of Luxembourg's major resorts. Picturesque medieval town with winding streets and alleys. The 15th-cent. town hall is on the Marktplatz. In 698, St. Willibrord, who brought Christianity to the Frisians, founded a Benedictine abbey here, but the settlement had been known as early as the Roman period. Roman columns still bear the weight of the bridge over the Sauer. The Romanesque *St. Willibrord's Basilica* (11th-13th cent.) is decorated with 12th-cent. frescoes. The crypt containing St. Willibrord's white marble sarcophagus was excavated after the Second World War. The altarpiece had been found after the First World War in the neighbouring town of **Rosport**, but at the time its place of origin was unknown. This 8th-cent. stone relief is now in the Luxembourg National Museum. Echternach is well-known for its Penitents' Procession which takes place at 9 a.m. on Whit Tuesday. The participants hop three steps forward and two steps backward. To the west is the charming area known as the "Luxembourg Switzerland". The scenery is both idyllic and wild. 16th-cent. castle at **Befort/Beaufort**. The beautiful little town of **Fels/Larochette** nestling between high cliffs, contains the ruins of two medieval castles.

LUXEMBOURG, see town plan.

From Echternach it is possible to follow the scenic route along the **Moselle: Rosport** with enormous hydro-electric works, **Wasserbillig**, with a modern church built in the Baroque style, **Grevenmacher**, an old town with narrow streets and **Wormeldange**, with a large cooperative wine factory open to the public.

Remich. Wine centre. Resort with a lovely promenade along the Moselle. Enormous wine cellars which may be visited. **Mondorf-les-Bains,** see E9.

E42 continues to Saarbrücken.

From Bitburg in West Germany another delightful road enters Luxembourg at Vianden.

Vianden, a resort in one of the country's most exquisite settings, is dominated by a mighty castle on the cliff. The town is situated at a bend in the river and its ramparts and tower are well preserved. A chair lift takes the visitor up to the *castle* which dates from the 13th cent. and ultimately became one of Europe's largest feudal fortified buildings. Superb views. The church was completed in 1248. There is a museum in the Victor Hugo house where the famed writer lived during his exile. Folklore museum with collection of antique furniture. Chair lift to impressive observation point 440 m above sea level.

Huge pumping station at the River *Our*. Inspections can be made at Lohmühle and at the dams at Mont St-Nicolas.

Diekirch. Luxembourg's oldest tourist resort. Famous for its beer. 8th-cent. church. The *museum* houses Roman mosaics, discovered during street repair work 1926-1950. Among the motifs is a large head of Medusa (with two faces).

Ettelbrück. Road and railway junction where three valleys meet. Resort. Museum and monument dedicated to the American general, Patton.

Ansemburg with a 12th-cent. castle and a château which was completed in 1639. Castle *Hollenfels* is now a youth hostel. **Abbey Marienthal** with *African Museum*.

LUXEMBOURG, see town plans.

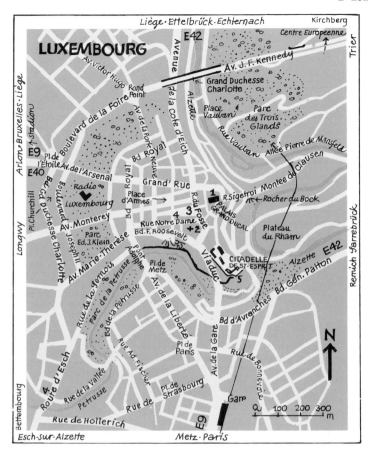

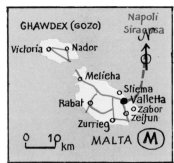

M · Malta

M · Malta

Area: 315 km² (122 sq. miles).

Population: 370 000.

Malta is situated 93 km south of Sicily. The island was inhabited as early as 4000 B.C. Carthaginians, Romans, Saracens, Normans (the Kingdom of Sicily), Knights Hospitallers and Britons ruled up until the island became an independent republic in 1974. Official languages are English and Maltese.

Valletta (14 000), the capital, has a strong British flavour. It is situated on a peninsula between the two harbours, Grand Harbour and Marsamxett. The town was named after Jean de Lavalette, the Grand Knight of the Knights Hospitallers. He broke the Turkish blockade in 1565. After this the order was known as the Knights of Malta. *The Grand Master's Palace* (1574) has splendid rooms and a weapons collection. *The Cathedral of St. John* (1577) contains famous paintings by Caravaggio. Cathedral museum with tapestries. *The Manoel Theatre* from 1731 is one of Europe's oldest. Views from the Baracca Gardens.

Madina. Fortified medieval town, once the chief town of the island. Museum of natural history and cathedral museum. *Mosta* has a church with a huge dome.

Several remains of Stone-Age temples and burial grounds from the 21st cent. B.C.

1 Grand ducal palace and national
museums
2 Cathedral Place Guillaume (flower market)
3 Town Hall

5 Citadel and city wall
6 Casemates
7 European Parliament and European Court of Justice

LUXEMBOURG (100 000)

Capital of the Grand Duchy. Seat of the Parliament of Europe's General Secretariat. University. The city was founded in the 10th cent. and during the following centuries its fortifications were expanded until they were the mightiest in Europe. They were largely dismantled at the end of the 19th cent. The casemates are open to the public. One of the ramparts was transformed into the present city park.

The modern city is situated on the lower level and spreads out around the railway station. The older city lies higher up and a fine view of the valley can be obtained from its *Corniche promenade*. The great differences in height are traversed by 91 bridges. The *Adolphe Bridge* is 46 m high and the five viaducts are about the same height. The new Grand Duchess Charlotte Bridge is 355 m long. It leads to the airport and passes the *Kirchberg European Centre*.

The *cathedral* has a beautiful Renaissance portal. Crypt with the tombs of the Grand Dukes. The *palace* is an imposing Renaissance structure. The 14th-cent. *St. Quidrin Church* is partially built into a cliff.

Staatsmuseum with many impressive collections: mineralogy, zoology, archaeology, sculpture and paintings. The Echternacher stone relief (see Echternach, E 42) now rests here. American military cemetery in *Hamm* with 5 100 American graves, among them that of General Patton. *Schleifhof*, a German military cemetery with 11 000 graves.

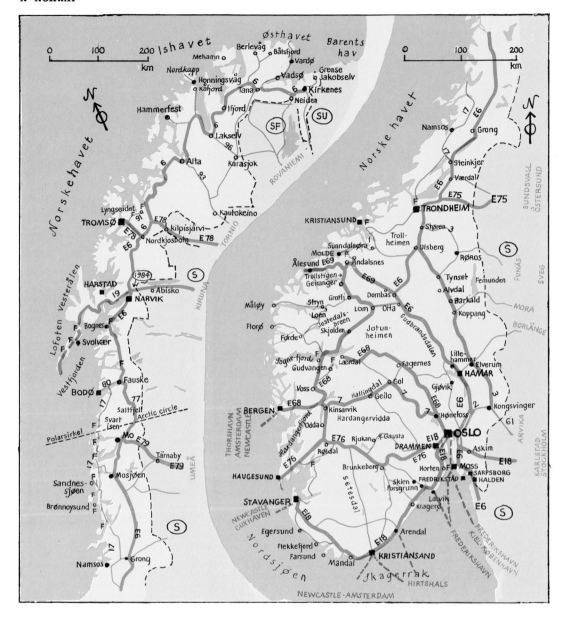

N · Norway

N·Norge

Area: 324 000 km² (125 064 sq. miles). Overseas territories: Svalbard (Spitsbergen), Jan Mayen Island, Queen Maud Land (in the Antarctic).

Population: 4 million. Language: Norwegian. Small Lapp minority. The majority of the population belong to the Evangelical Lutheran State Church. Small Roman Catholic and other religious minorities.

Major cities: Oslo 470 000, Bergen 215 000, Trondheim 140 000, Stavanger 90 000.

Government: Constitutional monarchy. One-chamber "storting" (parliament).

History

9th cent. Harald I unites Norway into one kingdom.

995 Olaf Tryggvason (Olaf I) begins the conversion of the Norwegians to Christianity.

1030 The Battle of Stiklestad. Olaf Haraldsson (St. Olaf) is killed and pilgrimages begin to the Nidaros Cathedral (Trondheim).

1349-1350 More then one-third of the population dies during a Black Plague epidemic.

1450 Union with Denmark.

1645 Jämtland and Härjedalen are lost to Sweden.

1658 Bohuslän is lost to Sweden.

1716-1718 Swedish attack against Norway ends with the death of the Swedish king, Charles XII, at

Fredrikshald.

1814 Norway is ceded to Sweden by the Peace of Kiel. Norway declares its independence and a brief war results in a union of Sweden and Norway.

1905 The union is dissolved. Norway becomes an autonomous kingdom.

1940 Germans occupy Norway. Government in exile, headed by King Haakon, established in London.

1945 Norway is liberated. Towns and villages in the northern parts of the country are razed to the ground by retreating Germans.

1970s Enormous deposits of oil are discovered in the North Sea, off the Norwegian coast.

Currency: Norwegian kroner (NOK). 1 krona = 100 øre

Business hours: Banks 8.30 a.m.- 3.00 p.m.; during the winter months also Thursdays 5.00-6.00 p.m. Closed Saturdays. Post offices 9.00- a.m.- 5.00 p.m. Saturdays 9.00 a.m.-1.00 p.m. Shops 8.30 or 9.00 a.m.-5.00 p.m. Saturdays open until 1.00 or 2.00 p.m.

Holidays: New Year's Day, May 1, May 17 (National Holiday), Maundy Thursday, Good Friday, Easter Eve, Easter Sunday, Easter Monday, Ascension Day, Whit Sunday, Whit Monday, December 25 and 26, New Year's Day.

Hotels

The term "hotel" is protected by law in Norway. Both buildings and management must conform to established standards. No official classifications but there are regulations for different types of hotels: mountain hotel (høyfjellshotel), fjord hotel, tourist hotel. But simpler establishments, known as pensjonat (guest house), seter (mountain guest house), gård (farm accepting paying guests), etc., have high standards and offer good value. Over 1 000 establishments are listed in the official hotel guide available free of charge from the Norwegian Tourist Authority. Some hotel chains: Inter-Nor (superior hotels), F-Hotel (popular hotels), Kilde-hotel (superior hotels), Carotel, Norske Fjord- og Fjellhotell, Narvesens hoteller, Kompasshotell, Økonomihoteller. Information about special low-cost holiday accommodation can be obtained from the Norwegian Tourist Authority. Many hotels have advantageous full or half board prices for visitors who stay 3-5 days.

The Norwegian breakfasts, often served buffet-style on an enormous table, frequently consist of large selections of cold cuts, fish dishes, salads, cheese, porridge, etc. and unlimited amounts of juice, milk, tea or coffee. The lunchtime buffet is twice as large and complimented by a large selection of main courses. Larger hotels in the major cities provide less lavish breakfast and lunchtime buffets.

Camping

There are more than 1 300 camping sites, each classified with from one to three stars. Most camping sites have cottage accommodations. About 600

Hammerfest, the world's northernmost town

are affiliated with the NAF (Norges Automobil-Forbund, the Norwegian Auto Club). In northern Norway, particularly in the Lofoten area, there are "rorbuer", fishermen's cottages that are used by their owners during the winter fishing season and rented out during the summer.

Youth hostels

Ungdomsherberger are Norwegian youth hostels, run by NUH. As in all of Scandinavia, there are no age limits and guests are usually of all ages. Many hostels provide private rooms for families. Most people staying at hostels travel by car.

Food and drink

A few of the Norwegian specialities: Karbonade, large meatballs. Rømmegrøt, a porridge made with sour cream. Rakørret, trout marinated in salt and sugar in a wooden bowl and

---

Routes described:

E 6 Kirkenes – Narvik – Trondheim – Oslo – Göteborg

E 18 Karlstad – Oslo – Kristiansand – Stavanger

E 68 Bergen – Gudvangen – Lærdal – Oslo

E 69 Ålesund – Åndalsnes – Dombås

E 75 Trondheim – Storlien, see E 6

E 76 Haugesund – Haukeli – Drammen – Oslo

E 78 Tromsø – Karesuvanto, see E 6

3   Ulsberg – Tynset – Elverum – Kongsvinger, see E 6

7   Kinsarvik – Geilo – Oslo, see E 68

19   Narvik – Svolvær – Å, see E 6

37   Haukeli – Rjukan – Kongsberg, see E 76

47   Kinsarvik – Haukeli, see E 76

80   Fauske – Bodø, see E 6

93   Alta – Kautokeino, 94 Skaídí – Hammerfest, see E 6

95   Olderfjord – North Cape, 96 Lakselv – Karigasniemi, see E 6

98   Varangerbotn – Vardø see E 6

Åndalsnes – Geiranger – Lom – Voss (roads 63, 15, 55, 5, 13)

Town plans: Bergen, Oslo, Trondheim

served with scrambled eggs or mustard sauce. Dravle, milk boiled so that it separates. Pinnekjøtt, mutton spare-ribs steamed on skewers. Spekekjøtt, salted, dried and often smoked mutton.

Spirits are not served on Sundays or holidays, except in specially selected tourist and mountain hotels.

Shopping

Knitted woollen sweaters, "lusekofter", pewter, silver and enamels, reindeer skins, goat's milk cheese and other cheeses.

Speed limits. Traffic regulations.

Maximum speed limit 80 kmh. On some short motorway stretches 90 kmh (if sign posted). Private cars towing caravans or trailers 80 kmh if the towed vehicle has breaks, otherwise 60 kmh. Built-up areas 50 kmh. Children under 12 are not permitted to travel in the front seat of a car. If your car is fitted with seat belts it is compulsory to use them.

In the daylight hours motorcyclists must drive with dipped headlights. It is recommended that all motorists carry a set of replacement light bulbs. Many roads are unsuitable for caravans. Special maps can be obtained from the Norwegian tourist offices. Please note that caravans must not exceed a width of 2.20 m. Exemptions should be sought in advance from Vegdirektoratet, Postboks 8109 DEP, Oslo 1, Norway. The Norwegian police are very effective when on the lookout for traffic offenders.

Roads

The roads are usually good but sometimes they can be narrow and twisting. Do not count on high average speeds. Often one must drive with the greatest of care for long distances, 50-60 kmh being the most suitable speed. If you want to get the most out of a scenic journey, plan on driving no more than 200 km a day. The roads that follow the fjords, in particular, are beautiful but usually require careful driving. In the eastern parts of the country, it is possible to cover longer distances in a day. Some mountain roads are blocked by snow the greater part of the year. In general, they are open from about June 1.

Road patrols

NAF (Norges Automobil-Forbund) has road patrols on selected major roads and mountain passes during the summer months. Emergency telephone in Oslo 02-42 94 80 (24-hour-service). In case of emergency and personal injury, refer to the first page of the local telephone directory.

NAF, Norges Automobil-Forbund, Storgata 2, Oslo. Tel 02-42 94 00.
Norwegian Tourist Board, 20 Pall Mall. (entrance St James's Square), London SW1Y 5NE. Tel. 01- 839 6255.

E 6. Kirkenes – Narvik – Trondheim – Oslo – Göteborg

The total length of the Norwegian section of E 6 is 2 650 km. From Kirkenes to Nordkjosbotn (the road forks to Tromsø) the road number is simply "6". Driving through green valleys and an unspoiled Arctic landscape is an exhilarating experience. Day-long summer sunlight has created lush vegetation. The nearness of the Gulf Stream provide an unusually mild climate for this latitude.

Kirkenes (5 000). Ore port for mines in Bjørnevatn. Kirkenes was laid waste by the Germans in the Second World War, and was liberated by the Russians in 1945. Monument. Kirkenes is the northern terminus of the *Hurtigruten*, a passenger and freight service that links it with Bergen. Five day journey. Daily sailings. The line provides an essential service for the local population and is also an extremely popular tourist route. Peak season summer passages are usually fully booked six months in advance. One of the longest bus routes in Europe (North Norway Bus) covers the 1 307 km distance from Kirkenes to Fauske in 3-4 days (overnight stops). The *"Iron Curtain"*, the Soviet frontier, here rather discreet and peaceful. This is one of the two places in Europe (the other is Turkey) where the Soviet Union borders directly on a NATO country. Signpost at a crossroads in Storskog points towards the Soviet Union and a Soviet watch tower can be seen a few hundred metres away. North of the road is the conference house (used by the frontier marshall), equipped with a telephone that links it to the Russian side. *Boris Gleb*, old chapel on Soviet territory. *Jakobselv*. On the other side, about 15 m from the Norwegian road, you will suddenly see red and green Soviet mileposts – Norwegian mileposts are yellow. A bit further on, a tall Russian watch tower comes into view. Suppress any urge to photograph it. *Oscar II's Chapel*, an granite church (1869). View out over the Barents Sea. The Soviet Union has an enormous military force concentrated in the Murmansk area. Symbolic Norwegian strength is concentrated in some mountain chalets.

From Kirkenes south through the lush Pasvik Valley. View towards the Soviet town of *Nikel* (18 000) from "Hill 96". Military watch tower.

Neiden. St. George's Chapel, a very small and simple structure, is the only Greek Orthodox chapel in Norway. It was built in the 16th cent. by St. Trifon, a monk who preached to the Skolts, a local Lapp tribe. Once-a-year church services. Salmon fishing. A narrow, twisting but negotiable 160 km long road goes to Inari in Finland. The road to Inari via Skipagurra and Utsjoki is 290 km long.

Many traces of Stone Age habitation (2 000-3 000 years old) along the coast. Remnants of an 8 000-year-old "Komsa Civilization" settlement at *Karlebotn*. It was built on the coast, but is now, as a result of intensive land elevation, 80 m above sea level.

Varanger Peninsula (Varanger halvøya). Fantastic scenery. Road 98 goes from Varangerbotn, site of a little private museum devoted to Lapp folklore and history, past countless camouflaged trenches that once served as wild-animal traps. There are about 3 000 of these on the road to Vadsø. *Nesseby* with remains of a 9 000-year-old settlement (Komsa Civilization). *Mortensnes* with Iron Age memorial stone, used as a place of sacrifice by the Lapps.

Vadsø. Fishing industry. Capelan (small, herring-like salmon) fishing. Town museum. Vadsø Church (1958). A unique sight is a dirigible *mooring mast* that was used by polar explorers Amundsen (in 1926 for the airship "Norge") and Nobile (in 1928 for the airship "Italia").

Stone Age settlements and graves. Fishing hamlets, bird-cliffs, remains of German (World War II) fortifications. Views towards the USSR. The countryside becomes increasingly wild as the road approaches its summit. The "Cathedral", a rock where witches used to gather. Although this is the highest section of the road it is only 127 m above sea level.

Vardø (3 800). The road tunnel was completed in 1982. Easternmost town in Norway – further east than Istanbul and the rest of Europe, excluding the Soviet Union. *Vardøhus Fortress*, completed in 1302, but later destroyed, was replaced in 1738 by the present octagonal, star-shaped structure. Although the fortress was never used in wartime, the greater part of the town was destroyed during the Second World War.

Skipagurra where once ships were dragged overland between Tana and Varangerfjord. Road over the mountain to the fishing villages of *Berlevåg* and *Båtsfjord*. Bird-cliffs. The final stretch of the road to Berlevåg passes through an unbelievable landscape marked by twisted and grotesque rock formations. *Tana Bridge* (Tana bru), 180 m long, rebuilt after the war. Beautiful new church (1964).

Road 92 and 96 Tana – Karasjok – Lakselv is about the same distance as road 6 but faster and open all year.

The road over *Ifjord Mountain*, 370 m, is closed during the winter months. Lapp chapel. From *Ifjord* road and car ferry to *Mehamn* and *Gamvik*. This is as far north as you can get in continental Europe.

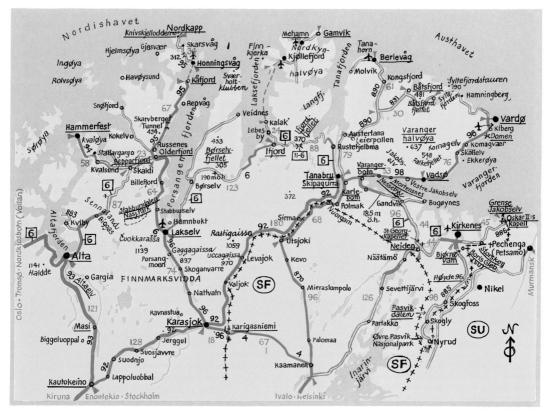

Børselvfjellet. Summit 190 m. Lapp chapel. Shorelines that show the water level at the end of the Ice Age, 14 000 years ago. It was 62 m higher than now!

Lakselv. Little town. Northernmost airport (70° 04' Latitude North), served by SAS (Scandinavian Airlines System).

96. Lakselv – Karasjok – Karigasniemi

Karasjok. Lapp centre with Lapp folk high school and **Lapp museum** with exhibits of Lapp hunting techniques and equipment and examples of Lapp dwellings. Library with the world's largest collection of Lapp books. The old church from 1807 escaped wartime damage. New church (1974). River boat tours. Sport fishing. One of the coldest and warmest places in Norway. Winter temperatures drop to –50° C and summer temperatures rise to +30° C. **Karigasniemi.** Finnish border.

Stabburdalen National Park, with the world's northernmost pine forest. **Olderfjord.** Crossroads.

95. Olderfjord – Honningsvåg – Nordkapp

Every summer, this last stretch of the road leading to the North Cape is used by thousands of motorists from all over Europe. The journey is still something of an adventure.

Dark, 3 040 m long tunnel. **Kåfjord.** Ferry terminus. Car ferries to Honningsvåg (45 min. journey).

Honningsvåg (4 500). Important fishing port. Fish processing and fish freezing industries. Fisheries trade school. The Germans razed the town to the ground in 1944 and colourful postwar buildings have replaced the previous structures. Bus to the North Cape (4 hours). 1-2 daily round-trips. The road over the **Arctic tundra** provides views of enormous, eroded mountain formations.

Nordkapp (the North Cape), at 71° 10' 21" Latitude North. The 307 m high cliffs rise up from the Arctic Ocean, 2 080 km from the North Pole. Midnight sun May 17 – July 30. It

is often cold, windy and cloudy, but still an unforgettable experience. August is often the best month of the year to visit the North Cape. Then the weather tends to be more reliable and the shifting colours of the sea and mountains are particularly beautiful. Monument on the North Cape plateau commemorating a visit made by King Oscar of Sweden-Norway in 1873. Bust of Louis-Philippe of Orléans (later King of France), who came here in 1795. Statue of Madonna and Child, placed here by an Italian donor. **Nordkapphallen,** a stone structure with large plate-glass windows facing north. Café and souvenir shop. Many hundreds of tourists every night during the summer.

94. Skaídi – Hammerfest

Repparfjord. Former copper mines. Rock carvings at Leirbukt. 525 m long suspension bridge over the Kvalsundet. Toll. **Akkanjarg-stabba,** a Lapp sacrificial stone.

Hammerfest (7 500). The world's northernmost town – 70° 40'. Midnight sun May 15 – July 28. Complete winter darkness November 21 – January 21. Considering the latitude, Hammerfest has a remarkably mild climate. The average January temperature is -4° C. Town charter 1789. Plundered by the British in 1809, severely damaged by fire in 1890, the town was occupied by the Germans in 1940 and used as a naval base. Razed to the ground by its occupiers in 1944. **Hammerfest Church,** with large stained-glass windows, is extremely modern. The mortuary chapel in the churchyard was the only structure left standing after the German capitulation. St. Michael's Church (Roman Catholic), built by German volunteers in 1958.

"Meridianstøtten", with bronze globe, is a reminder of a 19th-cent. cartographer's exercise. The other "støtte" (pole) is in the town of Ismail on the Black Sea, along the same longitude.

Road with extensive views out over the **Sennaland** mountain plateau. Lapp encampment and reindeer pasture land. Lapp chapel. The road is built on an embankment so that the winter winds blow away the snow.

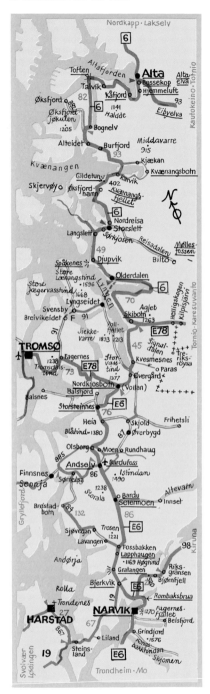

Alta (8 000) with the old Bossekop trading place. Education centre. Slate quarries. Alta slate is exported all over the world. The Komsa Mountains (Komsafjell) have given their name to the Komsa Civilization, a late Stone Age culture that existed in the area 5 000-9 000 years ago.

Altaelva. One of the world's finest rivers for salmon fishing. Fishing rights are let but the price charged is discouragingly high. Fishing licences valid for the *Eibyelva,* a tributary of the Altaelva, are far less costly. During 1980, and 1981, the Altaelva was prominently mentioned in news reports. Protesters tried to stop the construction of a dam and hydro-electric power station.

---

93. Alta – Kautokeino – Finnish frontier
The fastest route from the North Cape to Stockholm in Sweden. Very good road follows the banks of the Kautokeino River. *Masi.* Lapp settlement. River boat tours. Chapel from 1965.
Kautokeino (1 600 inhabitants, about 50 000 reindeer). Famous Easter festivities with reindeer racing (100-150 reindeer-drawn sleighs). Scandinavian Lapp Institute and Lapp schools.
Finnish frontier. Road to E 78 between Tromsø and Tornio and road to Gällivare in Sweden.

Hjemmeluft with remains of a Stone Age settlement and rock carvings.
Kåfjord with abandoned copper mines. Extensive fishing. In 1943 the 40 000 ton German battleship Tirpitz was attacked here by three British mini-submarines and severely damaged. One of the submarines was sunk. Remains of German fortifications at *Toften.* Stone Age settlement.

Kvænangsbotn. Large power station. The *Sørstraumen* is an extremely strong tidal current. Road ascends to Kvænang Mountain. Large Lapp settlement. Fine *views* out over the fjord and the Øksfjord Glacier from the inn at *Gildetun.*

Beautiful *Reisa Valley* with luxuriant vegetation. River boats to Møllesfossen, a 269 m high waterfall.

Djupvik. Plateau at Spåkenes with German fortifications and impressive panorama out over the **Lyngen mountain range.**

Olderdalen. Car ferry to Lyngseidet on the route to Tromsø. The road on the west side of the fjord is 50 km shorter than the new E 6.

The new road that skirts the eastern shore of the *Lyngenfjord* passes through an untamed and dramatic landscape. Unlit 500 m long tunnel.
Skibotn. Important trading centre that attracted Lapps and trappers from northern Sweden and Finland. A few market stalls remain. E 78 goes to Tornio in Finland.

Oteren. The beautiful Signal Valley with luxuriant summer vegetation is surrounded by high mountains.
Nordkjosbotn (Vollan). Centre of the area. Starting point of E 6 that ends in Piazza del Popolo in Rome. Vollan has a pleasant gjestestue (inn). Just north of the little community is a large stone covered with the names of generations of passers-by. E 78 to Tromsø.

TROMSØ (30 000). Situated on the low island of Tromsøya. A 1 036 m long **bridge** from the mainland spans the sound. The town got its charter in 1794, but the first church here had been built as early as 1250. Old wooden houses.
The **Polar Museum** in a warehouse in the harbour. Exhibits related to the many Arctic expeditions which have started out from the town (Nansen, Andrée, Amundsen). In 1928 Amundsen set out to assist a group headed by Nobile that had disappeared in the Arctic in an airship. Amundsen never returned from the journey. His statue is down by the harbour. *Tromsø* **bymuseum** (town museum) with interesting interiors.
The *Tromsø Museum* is part of the university (the world's northernmost). Folklore, fauna and flora of northern Norway. Tromsø folkemuseum (an open-air museum) and Tromsø Aquarium. Fisheries college and many other schools. *Tromsdal Church* (the Arctic Cathedral) is an impressive wooden structure (1965) with an enormous stained-glass window. The *cathedral* (1861), a large wooden church. *Elverhøj* Church. Catholic church. **Fjellheisen** (a lift) to Storsteinen, 420 m above sea level. Sandnes bridge, 1 220 m long, leads to **Kvaløya.** 4 000-year-old rock carvings. *Hella* with old Tromsø houses.

Storsteinnes. Dairy producing goat's-milk cheese, a Norwegian speciality. Rock carvings near **Balsfjord** church. **Andselv** (Bardufoss). Military air base, also used for civilian traffic. The Bardu Valley is surrounded by beautiful mountains. **Setermoen** (Bardu). Bardu Church is an octagonal wooden structure from 1829.

Lapphaugen and **Gratangen.** Mountain inns with beautiful views.
Bjerkvik. Church from 1955. Memorial dedicated to French soldiers.
Lofoten, see route 19.

19. Narvik – Melbu – Svolvær – Å

Narvik – Bjerkvik, see E 6.

Tjeldsund-Bridge, 1 005 m long. Road 83 to **Harstad.** Lovely setting. The midnight sun can be viewed from Nupen Mountain from May 23 to July 22. Gothic **Trondenes Church,** a stone structure (1250). Large altarpiece with carved figures. Frescoes. The wall enclosing the churchyard, 5 m high and 3 m thick, once served as a fortification wall.

Lødingen. Pilot station. Car ferry to Bognes (E 6). 10 daily trips (60 min.). *Sortlandsbrua,* a 961 m long toll bridge. *Stokmarknes* airport.

Hadselbrua, 1 020 m long toll bridge. High frequency sound barriers here (which should not disturb humans) are meant to prevent foxes from crossing over to Hadsel Island. *Stokmarknes* village. Hadsel Church, completed in 1824, contains a 16th-cent. altarpiece, once in an earlier church on this site. Pulpit with sculptures depicting St. Olaf and the Evangelists. *Skipshausthaug,* a 35 m high Viking mound.

Melbu. Fishing industry. Folklore museum. Car ferry to Fiskebøl (30 min., 10 daily sailings).

Svolvær (4 500). Lofoten's largest fishing town and port. Fish industries. Magnificent scenery. Artists' House with studios used by selected Swedish and Norwegians artists. Car ferry to Skutvik, close to E 6 (2 hours, 6-8 daily sailings). *Vågan Church* (1898), the "Lofoten Cathedral", a wooden church seating a congregation of 1 200.

Kabelvåg. Fishing village. *Aquarium.* **Storvågan.** Old trading town. *Lofoten Museum.*

Henningsvær, one of the best-known fishing villages, is spread out over a number of small islands. *Nusfjord,* well-preserved fishing village. (Project city during the European Architectural Heritage Year 1975). *Reine.* Fishing village with magnificent mountain background. *Å.* End of the road. The boat to Værøy and Røst, two islands with impressive bird-cliffs, passes the Moskenesstraum, the notorious "maelstrom", immortalized by Jules Verne and Edgar Allan Poe.

Lofoten is justifiably famous for its beautiful scenery and quaint fishing villages. Many fishing villages offer holiday accommodation in "rorbu", fishermen's cottages, usually perched over the water. Some are quite simple, many are newly equipped especially for tourists.

Rombaksbrua, a 765 m long bridge that permits the passage of vessels under 41 m high. Views of the Rombaksfjord where four German and one English destroyer either sunk or were beached during a 1940 battle. A primitive road on the north side of the fjord leads to the Swedish border. It is estimated that a new road to Kiruna in Sweden will be opened in 1984.

NARVIK (20 000). Chief town of Nordland fylke (province). Beautifully situated on a peninsula that separates the fjords. To the south, "Den Sovende Dronning" (the Sleeping Queen), a famous rock formation. A railway connecting the Swedish iron mines with the port of Narvik was opened in 1902 and created the town's growth and prosperity. The fully automated ore port is one of the largest of its kind in the world. Fierce battles in 1940. Norwegian, English, French, Polish and German war graves. Beautiful Peace Chapel. War museum. Park with rock carvings. **Fjellheisen** (a lift) up to the Fagernesfjell, 700 m above sea level, (13 min.). Superb views and beautiful mountain scenery. Lift services until 2 a.m. in the summer. The local tourist office arranges fjord and fishing excursions. Lofoten tours. 375 m long bridge to **Fagernes.**

Memorial stone in **Beisfjord** dedicated to 1 500 Yugoslavians who died in German captivity. Road from **Grindfjord** up to **Skjomen.** Power station. Hiking trail to Lake Sitasjaure in Sweden. Skjomen Bridge, 709 m long with 100 m high towers.

Ferry over the **Tysfjord,** one of the deepest and most storm-prone fjords in the country. Frequent ferry service. 24 daily trips during the peak season. (25 min. journey). Norway's narrowest point is in the fjord – it is only 6 km to the Swedish border.

Tømmernes with numerous 4 000-5 000-year-old rock carvings. Many depict reindeer. Memorial stone dedicated to Soviet soldiers. The Norwegian Nobel-prize-winning writer Knut Hamsun lived and wrote for a time at Kråkmo gård.

Car ferry **Bonnåsjøen – Sommarset** (15 min.). Frequent service, 7.15 a.m. – midnight. Long queues are not unusual. The ferry is to be replaced by a bridge. Several tunnels. The Kalvik Tunnel is 2.7 km long.

Fauske (4 000). Centre of the area. Starting point for the North Norway bus line to Kirkenes. The length of this line is 1 307 km, and including overnight stops the journey takes 3-4 days.

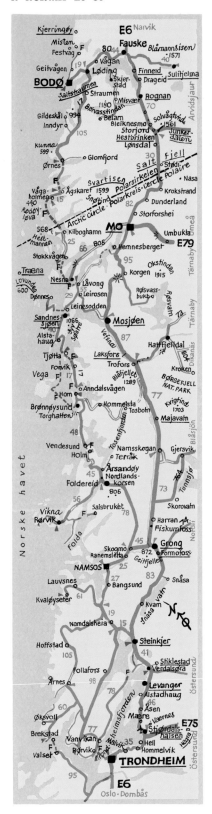

80. Fauske – Bodø

Saltstraumen (13 km from route 80). Four times a day fierce tidal waters force their way through the 150 m wide sound. Their speed and violence are most dramatic at full and half moon. Tidal schedules available from the tourist office in Bodø. *Bodin*. 13th-cent. stone church, Baroque altar painting.

BODØ (32 000). Chief town of Nordland fylke (province) and military headquarters of the North Norway district. Northern terminus of the Norwegian State Railway. (Narvik, to the north, has rail connections only with Sweden.). *Cathedral* (1956). Nordland fylkemuseum. Open-air museum with 15 buildings at *Kjerringøy*, an old trading centre. Ferry (15 min.) six times daily to Festvåg. Helicopter service to *Væerøy* and *Røst*, fishing village and bird colony out in the Atlantic.

Finneid. Road to *Sulitjelma mines*. Little town with 1 000 inhabitants. Four tunnels, 9 km.

Rognan. Centre of the area. War cemetery with the graves of 1 500 Yugoslavians and 2 700 Germans. At Hestbrinken road 77 enters the wild and beautiful *Junker Valley* and continues on to Sweden (Arjeplog)

Saltfjell with extensive mountain views. Highest point on the road, 707 m. *Arctic Circle*, 6° 3' Latitude North. From here it is 3 330 km to the North Pole and 6 660 km to the Equator. Little café. Memorial stone dedicated to Yugoslavian prisoners of war who died while being forced to build the Nordland Railway. The road then twists through the Dunderland Valley.

Mo i Rana (10 000). Old trading centre. The Meyergården Hotel was named for the Meyer family of merchants. Large state-owned iron works. Open-air museum. Lovely views, particularly at sunset, towards the *Svartisen* (Black Ice) glacier. The local tourist office arranges excursions to the glacier and to Grønli Grotto, one of about 120 grottoes in the area. Beautiful stalagmite and stalactite formations.

Road 805 Mo – Nesna is an extremely beautiful route. From the heights above *Nesna* you will be rewarded with a magnificent view out over the sea and the islands of *Lovunden* and *Træna*.

Korgen. Fine views out over the Okstindan mountains on the Swedish border. Church with exquisite wood carvings.

Mosjøen (3 000). Large aluminium processing plant. Octagonal Dolstad Church with lovely 18th-cent. interior. *Vefsn Museum* (folklore). Large town with 19th-cent. wooden buildings near the River Vefsna.

Road 810 to *Sandnessjøen*, built on cliff ledges in the mountains passes through several tunnels. Route 17 is a time-consuming alternative to the E 6, but an exhilerating scenic and motoring experience.

Laksfoss, 17 m high waterfall and rapids with a 200 m long salmon ladder. Popular fishing place. In former days most of the fishermen were English.

Majavatn. In the minds of Norwegians this place is associated with the resistance movement during the Second World War. Memorial stone dedicated to 24 Norwegians who were executed by the Germans here. By-roads to Stora Blåsjön in Sweden (shortcut to Östersund). *Fiskumfoss*. Large hydro-electric power station. 32 m high cascade. Long salmon ladder. *Grong*. Centre of the area.

Formofoss, 30 m high waterfall with salmon ladder.

Steinkjer (10 000). Beautiful church (1965) and chapel. Museum.

Stiklestad, where St. Olaf fell in 1030. Memorial stone. The church was built 100 years after his death. After the saint's body was taken to Nidaros (Trondheim) and miracles occurred at his tomb, Nidaros became the most important place of pilgrimage in northern Europe. *Mære Church*. 12th-cent. stone church with a pagan place of sacrifice. *Værdalsøra*. Large port. Construction of oil platforms.

Levanger (6 000). Old trading centre, and starting point for the old road to Sweden. 30 burial mounds (4th-5th cent.) *Alstahaug Church*, a stone structure completed in 1250. Medieval paintings.

Værnes and *Stjørdalshalsen*. The road goes through a tunnel under the military airport, which also serves commercial traffic to and from Trondheim. Medieval stone church and folklore museum. *Hegra Fortress* withstood a 27-day German siege before it finally surrendered in 1946.

E 75 goes to Sweden. Many *rock carvings* in the Leirfall area. *Meråker*, resort. *Kopperå*, large foundry. E 75 continues to Östersund and Sundsvall in Sweden.

TRONDHEIM, see town plans.

The road ascends providing a magnificent view out over Trondheim – the same view that greeted pilgrims on their way to the shrine of St. Olaf in Nidaros. Many had a long journey and were forced to spend the winter along the way.

Støren. Octagonal church dating from 1817.

Oppdal. Resort. Narrow *Driva Valley* to **Kongsvoll,** 887 m above sea level. Higher up the old "Royal Road" or "Spring Path" that was travelled by horsedrawn carts in the 18th cent. despite the fact that the gradient is sometimes as much as 40%. Now a hiking trail. Kongsvoll fjellstue (mountain cottage) was founded in the 12th cent. Kongsvoll kro (inn) with old furnishings. Little botanical garden at the station with examples of the mountain flora typical of this area.

The road passes above the timber line. Highest elevation 1 026 m.

Hjerkinn, 956 m above sea level. Driest place in Norway, average annual rainfall 217 mm. 12th-cent. mountain cottage. Eystein Church (1969), erected in memory of King Eystein who had the first mountain cottage built here. Army gunnery school. Large ironpyrite mine.

Dovregubben's hall. Café, wood carvings, weavings. The Dovregubben was a legendary troll. *Fokstumyra.* Nature reserve with abundant bird life that can be studied from a marked trail (very wet).

Dombås, 659 m above sea level. Road and railway junctions.

Dovre, south of the Dovre Massif at the northern edge of the Gudbrandsdalen Valley. *Dovre Church,* timber church from 1740. Toll road from Selsverket to Mysuseter passes *Kvitskriuprestinn,* 6 m high earth pyramids that resemble priestesses (steep footpath). **Mysuseter,** mountain village with mountain hotel. Starting point for hiking trips to Rondvassbu and Rondane National Park.

Otta. Centre of the area. Steep and twisting motor road up to Pillargurikampen. Splendid views. Legend has it that a maiden named Pillarguri saw an approaching army of Scottish mercenaries from this point, and warned the local population. The Scots were defeated at **Kringen.** "Sinclairstøtten", a memorial stone near the E 6. Another memorial stone at **Kvam.** Wooden church (1952). Memorial park dedicated to British soldiers who fell in the Second World War.

---

3. Ulsberg – Tynset – Elverum – Kongsvinger
30. Støren – Røros – Tynset

Kvikne. Church from 1654. **Bjørgan.** Birthplace of dramatist, novelist and poet Bjørnstjerne Bjørnson (1832-1910).

Tynset. Folklore museum and church from 1793.

Støren, see E 6.

RØROS (3 500), set in the middle of a great mountain expanse, 628 m above sea level. The town was founded in 1644 in conjunction with the inauguration of the Røros copper works. The town was put to the torch by the Swedes in 1678, 1679 and 1718. Well-preserved streets and houses, particularly in Den gamle bergstad (the Old Mining Town), which contains 250- year-old miners' cottages. Enormous slag heaps. Tours into the copper mines. *Olavsgruva* has been transformed into a museum. Interesting collections in Røros Museum and Røros Kobberverk. The octagonal Røros Church, the only stone structure in the town, was built in 1784.

The road follows the banks of the River Glomma through the **Østerdalen** (East valley) where unique buildings and venerable folk traditions have been preserved.

Os. Large resort. *Kopparleden,* "the Copper Trail", goes over the mountains to the large Femunden Lake and to Mora and Falun in Sweden.

Alvdal with *folklore museum.* Mount **Tron,** 666 m. Fine views. Steep toll road.

Barkald. Twisting, 2 km long road to Jutulhogget Canyon, 100-200 m deep and over 2 km long.

Koppang. Koppangtunet, a folklore museum with several houses.

Elverum (9 000). Over 30 buildings in **Glomdal Museum,** one of the largest open-air museums in Norway. Norwegian **Museum of Forestry,** with exhibits devoted to forestry, hunting, fishing, fauna and ornithology. Aquarium. A bridge over the falls connects the museums. Wooden church from 1738.

Kongsvinger (17 000). Bridge over the River Glomman. The fort, built in 1682, was closed down in 1823. Although it was never attacked, the area around Kongsvinger was the site of many battles with the Swedes.

Road 2 east to Magnor, a popular shopping centre for Swedes. Swedish border and Peace Monument at Eda. Route 2 west following the Glomma as far as Kløfta, just north of Oslo where it meets the E 6.

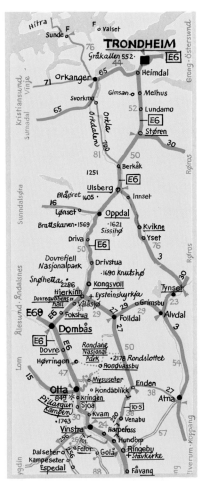

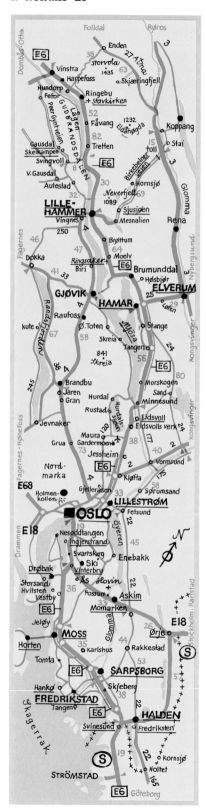

Vinstra. Centre of the area. *Sødorp.* Timber church (1752), with memorial stone dedicated to Peer Gynt, leading character in Ibsen's play. **Peer Gyntveien** (the Peer Gynt road), goes on the west side of the Gudbrand Valley. It is extremely beautiful and leads to large tourist hotels: Fefor, Golå, Wadahl, Skeikampen, Gausdal, Austlid. A bit to the west, a beautiful road goes through the Espedalen Valley.

Ringebu Church, 13th cent. stave church, expanded in the 17th cent. and restored in 1981. Stave churches are built of vertical planks (staves). Handsome interior and fine views from the steep little churchyard. *Tretten Church* from 1728. **Hunderfossen.** Power station with 16 m high dam, artificial lake and fish farms.

LILLEHAMMER (14 000). Centre of a popular tourist area. *Maihaugen* (De Sandvigske Samlinger), the life's work of dentist A. Sandvig (1862-1950). Large open-air museum with over 100 buildings in typical Gudbrandsdalen Valley style. *Garmo Church,* (13th-cent. stave church), shepherds' huts, workshops, and farm buildings. Fine arts museum.

Road 216, *"Birkebeinerveien"*, goes to **Sjusjøen**, a popular tourist area with several hotels and chalets. The Birkebeiner Stone marks the highest point of the road (1 090 m above sea level). The Birkebeiners supported the king during 12th cent. civil wars. An annual skiing competition is held in their honour.

Ringsaker Church, 12th-cent. stone basilica, enlarged in the 13th cent. Splendid altarpiece (1520), carved in Antwerp. Tower from 1694.

HAMAR (16 000). During the Middle Ages this became a centre of trade and education. On *Domkirkeodden*, the ruins of a 12th-cent. cathedral that was put to the torch by Swedes in 1557. *Hedmark Provincial Museum* and open-air museum. The *Railway Museum* of the NSB (Norges Statsbaner = Norwegian State Railway), displays the old locomotive "Tertitten". Hamar *Cathedral*, in the square, was completed in 1866 and restored in 1954. Altar painting by Henrik Sørensen.

Mjøsa, Norway's largest lake, 100 km long, maximum depth 449 m. Area: 366 km². Akersvika Nature Preserve with abundant bird life. The S.S. *Skibladner*, oldest operating paddle steamer in the world (built 1856) still has regularly scheduled sailings on the lake. *Minnesund*, 600 m long bridge over Vorma.

Eidsvollbygningen (the Eidsvoll building), where the constitution was formulated on May 17, 1814. After a brief war Norway entered a union with Sweden. This was dissolved in 1905 and Norway achieved autonomy. May 17 is the Norwegian national holiday. The room where the constitution was drawn up still has its original early 19th-cent. furnishings.

Lillestrøm (12 000). Industrial surburb.

OSLO, see town plans.

Ingjerstrand open-air swimming baths and *Uranienborg*, Polar explorer Roald Amundsen's home in *Svartskog*. Zoo with miniature railway. **Ås,** Norwegian College of Agriculture. West to **Drøbak**, little idyllic town and resort, popular with artists. Views towards the old Oscarsborg Fort. On April 9, 1940, cannons from this venerable old structure managed to sink the German cruiser Blücher, which was carrying officers and troops to Oslo.

Moss (25 000). Konventionsgården, a beautiful old house (privately owned) was the site of the ratification of the union between Norway and Sweden in 1814. Car ferry from Moss to Horten (40 min.), every 20 min.

Hankø. Holiday resort, famous for its international sailing regattas.

Sarpsborg (13 000). Legend has it that the town was founded by St. Olaf in 1016. Fortification walls, St. Olafs Voll, are almost 1000 years old. Large lumber industry and port. Borregaard's large factories at the Sarpsfoss rapids. The River *Glomma* is the longest in Norway (587 km). Borregaard Monument at the bridge. Many interesting buildings, placed about the ruins of the 12th-cent. Nikolas Church.

FREDRIKSTAD (30 000). Modern industrial town with an 824 m long and 40 m high bridge to **"Gamlebyen"** (the Old Town), a fortified town with streets placed at right angles and French Empire-style buildings, 18th-cent. church and town hall.

Oldtidsveien, road 110 between Fredrikstad and Skjeborg. Concentration of various prehistoric finds: rock carvings, burial mounds, remains of Stone Age dwellings.

HALDEN (27 000). Fredriksten frontier fortress (late 17th cent.). Three times it resisted fierce attacks. In 1719 the Swedish king, Charles XII, was shot and killed during a siege. Memorial stone. Military museum and folklore museum. Lovely view. Baroque theatre in Rød manor house. Atomic Energy Institute.

Svinesund Bridge (1946), 420 m long, 60 m high.

Swedish border. E 6 continues to Göteborg – Malmö – Berlin – Munich – Firenze – Roma. The distance from Kirkenes to Svinesund is 2 650 km, from Svinesund to Rome 2 600 km.

E18. Karlstad – Oslo – Kristiansand – Stavanger

Ørje – Drøbak, see map E 6,

Ørje. Swedish border. E 18 comes from Stockholm – Västerås – Karlstad.

Momarken. Race course. Old market place. The present August market, sponsored by the Red Cross, usually attracts about 100 000 people and world-famous stars perform. *Mysen.* Folklore museum with old buildings. 12 burial mounds.

Askim. Large tyre factory. Folklore museum. Fossum Bridge over the Glomma, Norway's longest river. *Hovin.* Wooden church, rebuilt 1720-21. Once pilgrimages were made to the Michael Spring. *Ås.* Norwegian College of Agriculture.

Vinterbru. Zoo with miniature railway and model trains. *Ingierstrand* open-air swimming baths. *Uranienborg,* home of Polar explorer Roald Amundsen.

Drøbak, see E 6.

OSLO, see town plans. Henie-Onstad Museum of Art, see Oslo.

Skaugum, residence of the Crown Prince. Magnificent views out over the Lier Valley during the descent to Drammen.

DRAMMEN (51 000). Port for paper and lumber exports. The town is stretched out along both banks of the River Drammen. Fine views from the Bragernes Ridge. You drive up on the *Spiral,* a toll road with tunnels and six loops. Town *museum* in an 18th-cent. building. The neo-Gothic Bragernes Church dominates the square. The 2 km long motorway bridge (toll) is the longest in Norway.

Holmestrand. Little town. *Museum* with exhibits relating to the town's history, shipping and art. Y-shaped church from 1674.

Horten. Old naval base, now the site of a *maritime museum* devoted to maritime and naval history. The *Preus Museum* is the only museum of photography in Norway. *Borre Church,* built in the 12th cent. in memory of St. Olaf. Renaissance and Baroque interior. Churchyard with royal graves from the Viking Age. Ferry Horten – Moss (40 min.) every 20 minutes.

Åsgårdsstrand. Idyllic little community, previously an artists' colony. Edvard Munch's house is now a memorial museum. *Slagen,* where the Oseberg Ship from 850 (now in Oslo) was found.

Tønsberg. Oldest town in Norway, founded about 870. Traditional whaling and shipping port. Vestfolds fylkesmuseum (folklore) with open-air exhibits. *Klåstadskipet,* a 9th-cent. Viking ship, is partly reconstructed in one of the museum's buildings. Ruins of Tunsbergshus, a castle built for Håkon Håkonsson. Slottsfjellet, medieval church ruins. *Sem.* Medieval church. *Jarlsberg.* Norway's largest farm. Road to *Tjøme* and *Hvasser,* popular seaside resorts. Furthest out "Verdens ende" (the End of the World).

Sandefjord. Hvalfangstmuseet with exhibits that recall the brief but intensive period when the town was deeply involved in Antarctic whaling. 21 m long model of a blue whale. A large, rotating whaling monument by Knut Steen beside the harbour. Maritime museum in a handsome old patrician house (1792). Modern town hall with theatre. Gokstadhaugen, 2 km E, where the Gokstad Ship was discovered.

Larvik. Port. Town museum in the 1673 Herregården, once residence of the Danish governors of Norway. Maritime museum in the old customs house. Church (1677) with a painting by Lucas Cranach the Elder. Bekeskogen, nature preserve. Iron industry museum.

Stavern, idyllic little town, earlier a naval base. *Fredriksvern,* created in 1756 as the major base of the Norwegian fleet. Citadelløya with naval base from 1677. Memorial hall dedicated to Norwegian seamen killed in the World Wars. Stavern Church (1756). The old Empire-style fountain is the symbol of Stavern.

Porsgrunn. Export harbour. Famous Porsgrund Porcelain Factory, (1887). Tours. Two churches with Baroque interiors. Town museum with beautiful houses.

SKIEN (30 000). Lumber export. Telemark Museum with Ibsen collection. *Venstøp,* where Henrik Ibsen (1828-1905) grew up. Canal boat to Ulefoss on the Telemark Canal. The *Brevik Bridge* over the Breviksstrøm is 677 m long and 47 m high. Home town of naval hero Cort Adeler who fought for both the Netherlands and Venice. *Heistad.* Limestone quarries with cable car line up to the large cement factory.

Several small idyllic towns with white Empire-style houses line the coast. Many have long maritime traditions. Now pleasant summer resorts. *Langesund, Kragerø, Risør* and *Tvedestrand* are all worth detours from E 18.

Arendal. Oldest town in Sørlandet. Important port in the days of sailing ships. Beautiful old houses on Tyholmen. Large Church of the Holy Trinity (1888). *Merdøy* with old skipper's house.

Grimstad. Town museum in the old pharmacy, where Henrik Ibsen was once employed. Several market gardens.

Nørholm. Knut Hamsun's home, where the Nobel-prize-winning writer lived until his death in 1952. Now a museum. **Lillesand.** Idyllic town with lovely houses. Zoo with a particularly fine collection of Scandinavian animals. Children's zoo. *Varodd Bridge*, 618 m long, 32 m high.

KRISTIANSAND (60 000). Capital of Sørlandet. Falconbridge Nickel Factory. The town was founded in 1641 as a military garrison that complimented the fortifications on Flekkerøy. Christianholm Fort now serves as an exhibition hall. *Vest-Agder Museum* with many old buildings. *Oddernes*, medieval church.

The Setesdal railway, a 5 km long steam railway operates on Sundays.

Mandal. Southernmost town in Norway. A typical Sørlandet idyll. Among the many white Empire-style houses is Andorsengården (1801), now the *town museum* with works of art and maritime exhibits. Skrivergården (1766) now serves as town hall.

Lindesnes. Southernmost point of Norway, 2 518 km from the North Cape. The present lighthouse was built in 1915. The first lighthouse on this site was completed in 1655. Restored charcoal-fuelled lighthouse from 1822. Vernal and autumnal flights of birds. Beautiful roads wind between the sea and the mountains.

Listalandet. Several species of migrating birds. **Farsund.** Small town, important for shipping. Museum in an old skipper's house. Lista Museum, folklore and sculpture. Lista Lighthouse.

Kvineshela. Highest point on the road (326 m above sea level). Fantastic views out over the *Kvines Valley*. Centre of the area. Centre of Pentecostal missionary activity. Iron mill.

Flekkefjord. Old wooden houses, fishermen's huts and picturesque streets in Hollenderbyen (the Dutch village). Octagonal wooden church from 1833. Town museum in a patrician house built in 1720.

Moi. Station for satellite communications to oil platforms in the North Sea. The antenna reflector has a 13 m diameter. Remains of Iron Age farms at *Storsheia* and *Homslandsvatnet*.

Road 44 is in parts more narrow and twisting than the newer E 18, but scenically it is much more rewarding.

Hidra, with picturesque, small fishing hamlets. The car ferry has transformed the island into a popular tourist attraction. The museum in the Rasvåg school is devoted to sailing ships and emigration.

The road's highest point, 275 m above sea level, is slightly to the west of Åna-Sira. After a short, 6 km long drive, you come to *Jøssingfjord* and the sea. Then 2 km ascent to 185 m above sea level. The best views are west of the fjord. 14 twists and turns. Jøssingfjord became world-famous in 1940, when the German ship, Altmark, was stopped and boarded in neutral Norwegian waters by the crew of the British destroyer, Cossack. The British freed British prisoners of war who were being transported on the German vessel. Memorial stone. Now the port handles titanium ore.

Egersund. Small town. Dalane folkemuseum (folklore).

The Atlantic comes into view at Brusand. The *Jaeren Plain*, with many prehistoric remains, is Norway's most fertile farming district.

Sandnes. Industrial town with bicycle factory. Fine areas for swimming at **Viste** and **Sola**. Petroleum industry at **Tananger**. Road 13 to *Jøssang* and **Prekestolshytta**. 2 hours on foot to *Prekestolen,* one of Norway's best-known and most photographed look-out points. The promontory rises 600 m above the *Lyse Fjord.*

STAVANGER (88 000). Old shipping and industrial town, now capital of Norwegian North Sea oil activity. The oil boom has left a noticeable mark on Stavanger. World's largest concentration of canning industry. Canning trade school. Statue of Alexander Kielland, the Norwegian writer, beside the fishing harbour. Charming old business area around Kirkegata. Fine views from Valbergtårnet, an old fire-watcher's tower. The stone Romanesque **Cathedral of St. Svithun** is one of the most impressive and best-preserved medieval ecclesiastical structures in Norway. Construction was begun in 1125 while Bishop Reinald from Winchester was in residence in Stavanger. A new Gothic choir was constructed after a fire in 1272. *Stavanger Museum*, archaeology, folklore, natural history and shipping. Museum of art. School museum.

Old Stavanger, an entire town quarter complete with 150 small white-painted wooden houses, cobbled streets and gas lights. *Ledaal* manor house (1800), childhood home of Alexander Kielland.

Boat and bus to the island of *Mosterøy*, site of the 13th cent. Augustinian *Utstein* monastery. Church with splendid portals and windows.

E 68. Bergen – Gudvangen – Lærdal – Oslo

BERGEN, see town plans.

Mongstad. Largest refinery in Scandinavia and petro-chemical factories. Route 560 via Ytre Arna is a few km shorter than E 68. In parts twisting and narrow.

Kvamskogen. Mountain plateau covered with thousands of chalets. Recreation area for the inhabitants of Bergen. Two tunnels, 630 and 420 m long.

Tokagjelet. Impressive example of road engineering. Four tunnels, 339, 680, 403 and 332 m long. 7% gradient. Prior to the 1950s the road hugged the mountain side. Fine views from the summit and at the entrance to the lowest tunnel.

Steindalsfossen (Øysthusfossen), where you can walk under the falls.

Norheimsund and **Øystese,** on the shore of the fjord. *Ingebrigt Vik Museum* (sculpture) and folklore museum in Øystese. *Fyksesund Bridge,* a 344 m long suspension bridge.

Kvanndal. Large ferry terminus. Frequent peak season services to Kinsarvik (35 min.). To Utne (20 min.) about 15 daily trips. Although the usual route to Oslo is via route 7 (Kinsarvik – Gol – Oslo), travellers can experience more dramatic scenery if they choose route 47 to Odda and then E 68 via Haukeli to Oslo.

Granvin. Resort with Mæland's Hotel, an establishment rich in tradition. Folklore museum. Granvin Church (1720). *Ulvik,* a beautiful resort. Gardeners' college. Church (1858).

Skjervet, a 3 km long twisting stretch of road that ascends to a look-out point (232 m). The road's highest point (262 m) is reached after an additional 4 km drive.

Voss, 57 m above sea level. Large resort, particularly popular during the winter. The Hangursbane (cable cars) makes the 550 m long journey up to a look-out point in four minutes. Several ski lifts. *Voss Church,* completed in 1270, was decorated in the 17th cent. *Mølstertunet.* Folklore museum with 16 buildings on their original sites.

Vinje. Road 13 to Vik and Vangsnes passes over *Vika Mountain.* The highest point on the road is at 986 m. Magnificent views out over the Sogne Fjord. See route 55.

Stalheim, 372 m. One of the most incredible panoramas in Norway. The hotel is perched on an abyss over the Nerøy Valley, 550 m below. *Stalheimfossen* with a 126 m high vertical waterfall. The panorama is dominated by the sugar-loaf shaped Jordalsnuten. The road below Stalheimskleiva is steep, in some sections the gradient is 20%. 13 curves. The new road has two tunnels.

7. Kinsarvik – Geilo – Oslo

Kinsarvik. Car ferry (35 min.) to Kvanndal.

Utne, (20 min., 12 daily sailings). Viking ships were drawn up at Skiparstod, close to the quay where the ferries dock.

Måbø Valley. Five curves and several tunnels. 9% gradient.

Vøringfossen, 182 m high. One of the most magnificent waterfalls in Norway. It can also be viewed from its base, 20 min. on foot from the road.

Hardangervidda, enormous 5 750 km² mountain plateau, 1 000-1 300 m above sea level. Innumerable lakes and bogs. Wild reindeer. From the highest point of the road (1 250 m above sea level) you can see the Hardangerjøkulen Glacier to the north. Several tourist hotels. Chalets at *Dyranut. Tinnhølen* attracts ornithologists.

Ustaoset, resort with large holiday chalet village. Station on the Bergen Railway. This 100 km long section of the Oslo – Bergen railway line is the longest trans-mountain rail route in Europe.

Geilo. Large resort. *Fekjo* with 9th- to 10th-cent. burial mounds. *Hol Museum* (folklore). Annual Hol Festival first Sunday in August.

Ål. Folklore museum. Folk music festival in June. *Torpo.* 12th-cent. stave church. Its choir was dismantled in 1880. Ceiling paintings (13th cent.).

Gol. Large resort equipped for winter sports. Open-air museum. *Nesbyen.* Hallingdal folkemuseum (folklore).

Hønefoss – Oslo, see E 69.

Gudvangen. Long popular with tourists. Before the advent of the motor car, as many as 500 chair-carts were lined up to take tourists (mostly British) from cruise ships to Stalheim. *Kjelsfossen,* a waterfall also known as Brudesløret (the Bridal Veil).

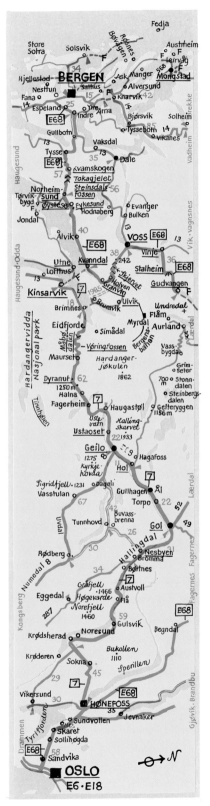

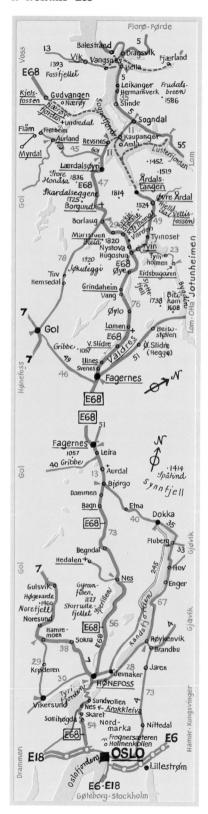

Ferries to Revsnes (2 hours, 15 min.) five times daily, to Aurland (1 hour, 30 min.) three times daily, and to Kaupanger (2 hours, 15 min.) five times daily. The **Nerøy Fjord,** an arm of the Sogne Fjord, is one of the most dramatic and beautiful in Norway. It is 500 m wide and cliffs that rise from it reach up to 1 200 m.

Revsnes. Ferry terminus. 25 daily sailings to Kaupanger (15 min.) and five daily sailings to Gudvangen (2 hours, 15 min.).

Lærdalsøra. Centre of the area and resort. The town is well-known for its fishing flies and goat's-milk cheese.

The **Aurland Road** links Lærdal with Aurland and Flåm. Highest point 1 306 m above sea level. High walls of snow line the road until mid July. Twists and bends down to Aurland.

Flåm, 2 m above sea level. Flåmbanen trains make the 20 km trip up to **Myrdal** (867 m above sea level) and connect with the Oslo–Bergen railway line (55% gradient). A road to Gudvangen is in the planning stage. It would allow for a ferry-free road link between Oslo and Bergen.

The road skirts the **Lærdalselva,** a river famous for its great number of salmon. Sections of the valley are very narrow. **Sjurhaugsfossen.** Salmon ladder in a 140 m long tunnel that goes through the mountain. The oldest road, the "Sverrestig", is said to have been used by King Sverre in 1177. A postal service between Christiania (Oslo) and Bergen via Fillefjell was inaugurated in 1647. The first road was opened in 1793.

Borgund. The stave church, built in 1150, is one of the best-preserved in Norway. Stave churches are built of vertical planks (staves). Splendid exterior. Roof on six levels adorned with dragons' heads. The new church dates from 1868.

Maristuen (850 m above sea level). Resort. The mountain cottage, first mentioned in 1358, was named for Margaret, Queen of Scandinavia. The "new" Margarethestuen was built in 1791.

Kyrkjestølen. The Church of St. Thomas that once existed on this spot was dismantled in 1808 in an attempt to abolish an annual religious festival held on July 2. The festival was the occasion for a popular market that was notorious for drunkenness, fighting and illicit sexual activity. The beautiful, modern Church of St. Thomas, consecrated in 1971, has bells from the original church.

Varden. Highest point on the road, 1 013 m above sea level. *Nystuen* and *Hugostua,* resorts.

Route 53 to **Tyin,** resort. Up to the highest point of the road, 1 117 m, and then down to the fjord. The old road had 42 curves.

Øvre Årdal, site of the largest aluminium factory in Europe. *Ytre Moa,* a Viking Age farm. **Vettisfossen,** one of the highest cascades in Europe, waterfalls of a total of 370 m. Through five tunnels (they total a distance of 2 700 m, one-fourth of the road's length) to **Årdalstangen.** Shipping port.

Road 252 skirts the shore of *Lake Tyin.* Magnificent views of the highest mountain range in Norway, **Jotunheimen,** to *Eidsbugaren* Mountain Hotel, overlooking **Lake Bygdin.** Motorboats to the eastern shores of the lake. See map at E 68 and E 69.

Grindaheim near Vangsmjøsa, resort (464 m above sea level). Rune stone with pictures and inscription carved in about the year 1000.

Stave churches in *Hurum* and *Lomen.* **Slidre,** centre of the beautiful *Valdres* area. Church completed in 1170. Medieval paintings. *Garberg* with 600 burial mounds from the Viking Age. The *Einang Stone,* a 4th-cent. rune stone. Ulnes. Medieval stone church decorated by local artists. Lovely road to Hemsedal.

Fagernes. Centre of the Valdres area. Large tourist resort. **Valdres Museum** (folklore) consists of over 70 interesting buildings. Mountain museum. **Bagn.** Hydro-electric power station. Wooden church from 1735. **Nes** i Ådal with little octagonal wooden church from 1860. 12th-cent. stave church in *Hedalen.*

Hønefoss (12 000). Timber industry. Military schools. Ringerike Museum with Riddersgården (the Knight's House). Norderhov kirke, a medieval church. The twisting road via *Krokkleiva* with splendid views out over the *Tyri Fjord.*

OSLO, see town plans.

E 69. Ålesund – Åndalsnes – Dombås

ÅLESUND (40 000) is built on three islands. Export harbour. Fishing town. *Aquarium.* After a devastating fire in 1904, the town received its present uniform appearance. Some buildings such as *Aspøy Church*, are in the Art Nouveau style. Splendid views from Aksla (189 m), reached by motor road or a staircase with 418 steps. The oldest sections of *Borgund Church* date from the 13th cent. New decorations in the old style. *Sunnmøre Museum* next to the church contains many old houses and some reconstructed ships. SW of the town are the *Runde* bird- cliffs. Hundreds of thousands of seabirds.

Åndalsnes. Beautifully set on the shores of the fjord. The peak of the *Romsdalshorn*, 1 550 m, is a popular goal for mountain climbers.

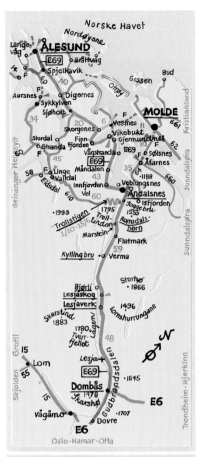

Road north to *Molde* (21 000). Modern streets and buildings have replaced the idyllic town that was destroyed in a 1940 air attack, but Molde still justifies its old title, "Rosernes by", the Town of the Roses. Lush vegetation. The *Molde panorama:* view towards 87 snow- capped mountain peaks. Fine views from *Varden*, 407 m. *Romsdal Museum.* Fisheries Museum on Hjertøya. Modern church. Fishing excursions. Annual August jazz festival.

Further north is *Kristiansund* (18 600) with colourful, modern buildings. Church (1864) with original exterior and exquisite stained-glass windows. Nordmøre Museum. Boat excursions to **Grip,** once a fishing village. Interesting little stave church.

Trollstigen, see Åndalsnes – Geiranger

The road follows the *Trolltindene,* an area of tall, eroded rock formations. *Marstein,* surrounded by high mountains. To the west, Mannen Mountain, 1 515 m. Five months of the year it obscures the sun. *Kors* Church (1910), with carved altarpiece from 1769. *Kylling bru,* a remarkable railway bridge 50 m above Rauman. *Bjorli.* Resort. **Lesjaskog,** 615 m above sea level, 17th cent. church. Here the dramatic mountains of the Romsdal subside into a forest area with more gentle contours.

Dombås, see E 6.

E 76. Haugesund – Haukeli – Drammen – Oslo

Map on next page.

HAUGESUND (27 000). Young town in a long-settled area. Fishing, shipping, shipyards, canning industry. *Haraldshaugen,* where King Harald I (Harald Fairhair) is said to be buried. Granite obelisk and 29 smaller monuments that represent each of the 29 parts of Norway that became Harald's kingdom. *Museum* in the town hall. Exhibits devoted to fishing and shipping. Art gallery.

The 50 m high *Karmsund Bridge* over the busy boat traffic on the sound leads to Karmøy. **Skudeneshavn.** Old fishing and trading town with beautiful white Empire-style buildings. *Avaldsnes Church,* built about 1250 for Håkon Håkonsson. This was the site of Harald Fairhair's royal manor. Next to the wall of the church "Virgin Mary's Needle", a memorial stone. Legend has it that if the stone topples and touches the church, the end of the world is near. For the sake of mankind the upper part of the stone was hacked off in 1840. *Regehaugene* with six mounds, a large Bronze Age cemetery.

Gjerde Church, a wooden structure from 1675. *Sæbøtunet,* a typical Vestlandet farm. The road continues along a ledge in the mountain side. 12 tunnels and 24 bridges. Langfoss Bridge over *Langfossen,* a cascade that falls 600-700 m. Untamed scenery at Rullestadsjuvet.

Steinaberg Bridge. The provincial road to Seljestad (old E 76) provides magnificent views from the curves. The new E 76 goes from Jøsendal.

Seljestad. Resort in a magnificent setting. The old road up through *Seljestadsjuvet* with six bends. Maximum gradient 8%. Highest point: 1 067 m. 13 km to Røldal, 373 m.

New road open year-round through the 1 240 m long *Seljestad Tunnel* and the 4 671 m long *Røldal Tunnel.* Highest point, 876 m, in the Røldal Tunnel, almost 200 m below the old road.

Røldal, 373 m, at Røldalsvatn, surrounded by high mountains. **Church** (13th cent.) with 17th-cent. paintings. The medieval crucifix was said to have miraculous powers. At Midsummer Røldal was an important pilgrimage place. Religious services for the sick were held here on Midsummer Eve until 1835.

The road ascends. Lovely views out over Røldal and Røldalsvatn. The 70 m high hydro-electric dam is one of the tallest in Europe.

Austmannlien. The road, distinguished by impressive engineering, was completed in 1880. Seven bends, 8% gradient. 1 058 m long *Svandalsflona*

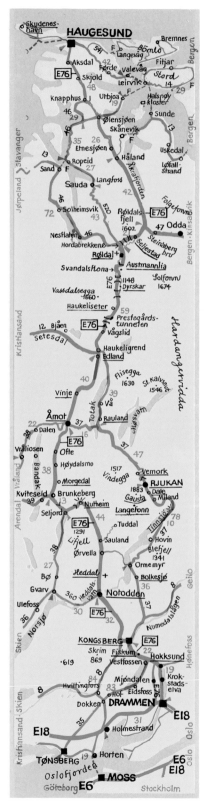

Tunnel. The highest point of the road is 1 085 m above sea level. Starting point of the 5 700 m long *Haukeli Tunnel.* The highest point of the old road is at **Dyrskar** (1 148 m). Here great walls of snow line the road until mid or late summer.

Haukeliseter was opened in 1870. Pleasant cafeteria.

The *Prestegård Tunnel,* 1 600 m. Watch out for the clusters of sheep that usually lie on the road at the tunnel entrance. The road descends. End of the dramatic mountain pass route. It is difficult to decide which is more impressive, the modern road with its remarkable series of tunnels, or the fascinating, twisting, old road, an astounding example of 19th-cent. engineering. *Edland.* Dairy where you can buy any of a wide variety of Norwegian cheese.

Vinje. Wooden church built in 1796. Beautiful modern decorations. Vinjestoga where the poet A. O. Vinje spent his childhood. Tomb of the writer Tarjei Vesaas.

Åmot, centre of the area. Near by *Ravnejuvet* with remarkable air currents. If you throw a piece of paper or a handkerchief into the abyss, it will float back up to you. It is said that you can perform the same trick with banknotes. However the author of this book takes no responsibility for the results of the experiment.

Morgedal. Resort and the centre of Telemark's "Cradle of Skiing" where modern ski-bindings were introduced in 1866. *Brunkeberg Church* (1790) with primitive paintings and sculptures. *Nutheim.* Magnificent views out over Flatdal. The old inn on the highest bend of the road contains antique furnishings and works of art.

Heddal Church. The largest stave church in Norway, 24 × 14 m. Consecrated in 1241, but the oldest part dates from the 12th cent. 12 large and six small "staves" support the structure. Life-size paintings of the 12 apostles in the choir. Heddal *bygdemuseum* (folklore museum) with works by "the Rose Painter", Ola Hansson.

Notodden (13 000). Power station and iron foundry. Lavishly decorated church (1938).

Saggrenda, site of the old *Kongsberg silver mines,* closed down in 1957. A miniature train takes visitors on a 2 km long trip to Kongens grube, 342 m beneath the surface of the mountain. The deepest mine shafts extend 1 000 m below the surface (or 450 m below sea level). During the 18th cent. 4 000 men were employed in the mines. Mountain chair lift.

KONGSBERG (20 000). Mountain town spread round the three Numedalslågen rapids. Kongsberg was founded after the discovery of silver in 1624. During the 18th cent. it was Norway's second city (Bergen was larger). The *church* (1761) is one of the largest in the country. Splendid Baroque interior. Places for a congregation of 2 000. Mining museum in the old workshop. *Lågendal Museum* (folklore). "Kronene i Håvet", a mountain wall where the monograms of all of the kings of Norway have been carved into the rock.

---

37. Åmot – Rjukan – Kongsberg

Rauland Mountain Hotel and the large *Møsvanns dammen.* Many hydroelectric power stations. *Vemork.* Closed-down hydro-electric power station with conduits. The present power station is hidden deep in the mountain. In a since demolished factory Germans produced "heavy water" as part of a World War II nuclear bomb project. The factory was blown up by nine Norwegian saboteurs who had been sent out from England.

Rjukan (5 000), 303 m above sea level, huddled between the mountains. Mount Gausta hides the sun from October 1 to March 5. *Krossobanen* (cable cars, 5 min.) to Gvepseborg, 890 m above sea level.

Dale Church (1750). Mår power station in the mountain is open to visitors. The longest wooden flight of steps in the world: 1 270 m, 3880 steps. If you are fast, you can make it in two hours (Guinness Book of Records). Road to Langefonn, 1 065 m above sea level. From here a 2-3 hour walk to the top of *Gausta,* 1 883 m. From this height you can see one-sixth of Norway's total area.

Views out over Lake Tinn, 460 m deep. (In Europe only Hornindalsvatnet is deeper). Although situated at an altitude of 191 m above sea level the bed of the lake actually lies below sea level. 37 km long. A ferry transporting "heavy water" was sunk by Norwegian saboteurs in 1944 (this action was depicted in the American film, "Heroes of Telemark").

Bolkesjø. Resort with old traditions.

Fiskum. Medieval stone church, dedicated to St. Olaf. This is one of the smallest churches in Norway. Fiskumvatnet nature reserve.

Hokksund. Industrial town. Drammen – Oslo, see E 18.

Åndalsnes – Geiranger – Lom – Sogndal – Voss

This route is made up of a few roads of special interest to tourists. *Åndalsnes*, see E 69.

Trollstigen. The most fantastic example of Norwegian road engineering. 11 curves ascend up the side of the mountain. Maximum gradient 8%. 30 m long stone bridge over the almost 180 m high Stigfoss waterfall. Trollstigheimen, at the highest point of the road, 850 m above sea level.
Valldal. Beautifully set on the shores of the Norddal Fjord.

Geiranger Fjord is one of the most beautiful in Norway, and the view from *Ørnesvingen* is famous. On the north side of the fjord *De syv søstre* (the Seven Sisters) waterfall and on the south side, *Prekestolen* (the Pulpit), a remarkable rock formation. After an almost 9 km long drive on a 10% gradient with 11 curves, you are down at sea level again.

Geiranger. Large resort. Boat excursions on the fjord. Octagonal church completed in 1842. 20 hairpin bends (8% gradient) up to *Flydalsjuvet,* 1 038 m. Magnificent view. 5 km long *Nibbeveien* toll road to *Dalsnibba* (1 494 m). Stupendous view. 12% gradient.

Langevatnet. In 1977 an all-year road to Stryn was completed. One- fourth of the 40 km long road consists of tunnels. The old road from Grotli to Stryn passes over a 1 139 m high mountain plateau. At *Videseter,* a marvellous *panorama.* Summer skiing. Strynsrennet, annual slalom competitions held on the last weekend in June. 19 curves, 9% gradient descent to the lovely resorts of *Loen* and *Olden.* The road continues to Måløy and Florø.

Grotli, 870 m above sea level. *Pollfossen,* an 81 m high waterfall.

Lom, 362 m above sea level, adjoins the remarkable 2 068 m high Lomseggi. Lom's medieval *church* (12th cent.) was expanded into a cruciform church during the 17th cent. Ceiling paintings. Ornamented West Front.

Route 15 goes to *Otta* via Vågåmo, a resort.

Jetta. Toll road to Blahø, 1 618 m above sea level. An extremely scenic road goes from Vågåmo, through *Jotunheimen,* the loftiest mountains in Norway, past the resorts of *Bessheim, Gjendesheim* and *Beitostolen* to *Fagernes* (E 68). Hiking paths from Gjendesheim and Bessheim up to *Besseggen,* a narrow mountain crest where Peer Gynt rode on an enormous he-goat. Regularly scheduled boat services on the Gjende and the Bygdin.

Røysheim. Private toll road to *Spiterstulen* and the *Svellnosbreen* Glacier. *Galdesand,* centre of the Bøver Valley. Toll road to *Juvasshytta.* The road is steep. Rather than attempting it in your own car, it is advisable to travel in one of the specially constructed coaches that regularly make the journey.

Galdhøpiggen, 2 469 m, Norway's highest mountain.

Elveseter (700 m above sea level). The old farm has been in the possession of the Elveseter family for five generations. Now a modern tourist hotel with new and old wings grouped about the old farm yard. *Bøvertun* and *Krossbu* (1 267 m), mountain hotels. *Sognefjell* tourist cottage at the highest point of the road (1 440 m). *Turtagrø* Tourist Hotel is a popular starting point for mountain climbers. Views of *Skagastølstindene.*

10 curves in the 11 km section of the road as it descends to Fortum, 25 m above sea level. 10% gradient. *Skjolden* and *Luster,* lovely resorts. *Feigumfossen,* a waterfall on the opposite side of the fjord, 218 m. Extremely scenic road from *Gaupne* into the *Jostedalen Valley.* Beautiful waterfalls, church from 1660 and the Nigardsbreen Glacier.

Solvorn. Boats to **Urnes Church,** the oldest stave church in Norway (12th cent.). Stave churches are built of vertical planks (staves). Exquisitely carved portal. Viking Age ornamentation featuring Romanesque creepers. This "Urnes Style" is closely related to traditional Irish art.

Årøyelva, one of the world's best salmon-fishing rivers. *Sogndal,* centre of the area. A few old houses and a rune stone. *Rune stones* and *burial mounds.* Route 5 goes to Kaupanger. De **Heibergske Samlinger,** folklore museum. *Stave church* from 1180.

Sogne Fjord is the longest in Norway, 183 km. 5 km wide, maximum depth 1 240 m. Particularly beautiful road during the late spring. Large orchards near Hermansverk and Leikanger. **Leikanger,** site of a medieval church.

Balestrand is the major resort in the Sogn area. Kviknes Hotel is an enormous wooden structure. 9th-cent. burial mounds.

Vangsnes. Ferry terminus. Fridtjof Torsteinsson, made famous by the Icelandic sagas, lived here. The 12 m high statue of the Viking, on a 14 m high pedestal, was donated in 1913 by Kaiser Wilhelm II of Germany. It might have looked better on the banks of the Rhine.

Vik. Centre of the area. *Hopperstad.* Stave church (1150). A series of curves up to *Svingen.* Glorious panorama out over Sogne Fjord and the *Jostedalsbreen* Glacier. Highest point of the road at Skjelingsvatn, 986 m.

Vinje and *Voss,* see E 68.

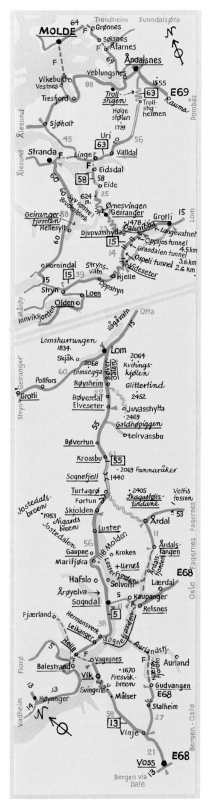

TOWN PLANS

BERGEN (213 000)
Norway's second largest city, founded in 1070 by Olav Kyrre. Up until the end of the 19th cent. Norway's largest city. The old parts of the town around Vågen, the inner harbour, bear witness to Bergen's former glory. Here is *Bryggen,* the old merchants' houses with pointed gables and small courtyards. Rebuilt after a fire in 1702, but since then twice again ravaged by fire. Many craftsmen. Hanseatic museum in Finnegården. Bergen was a member of the Hanseatic League from 1350 until the mid 1500s. Schøtstuene, halls where the medieval merchants gathered.
Bergenhus Fortress with the Royal Ceremonial Hall, *Håkonshallen* (1261), in the Gothic style. It has been reconstructed after being damaged by an explosion in 1944. The Rosenkrantz Tower (1560) served as a residential tower as well as a watch-tower. The lively *Fish Market* at Vågen is part of the splendid *Torgalmenningen,* the square that is the centre of the town. C Sundt's Street is a pleasant shopping street (pedestrian precinct). Several fine 19th cent. wooden houses in narrow, steep alleys, "smug". About 30 old houses have been gathered together to form a little town of their own, *Old Bergen.*
Seven mountains surround the city. *Fløibanen* to Fløifjellet (320 m above sea level) with a splendid view of the sea and the entrance to the Bergen harbour. Cable car to *Ulriken,* an observation point. *Mariakirken,* a 12th- to 13th-cent. church, is Bergen's oldest building. Baroque pulpit, altarpiece by Bernt Notke of Lübeck. The oldest parts of the cathedral date from the 12th cent.

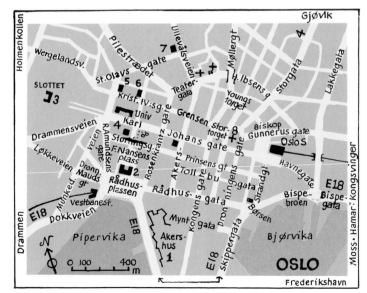

1 Bergenhus.
2 Schøtstuene. St Mary's Church.
3 Bryggen with museum.
4 Flower Market. Fish Market.
5 Fløyen (viewpoint).
6 Town gate.
7 Leprosy museum.

8 Rasmus Meyer's Art Collection.
9 Vestland Museum.
10 Art gallery. Fisheries museum.
11 Museums of Bergen University.
12 Maritime museum.
13 Aquarium.

The *Vestland Museum* of Industrial Arts. Examples of the goldsmith's and silversmith's arts, furniture, porcelain from Copenhagen, Meissen and China. The University Collections. Museum of history and natural science. The *Bryggen Museum* (at Mariakirken) illustrates life in medieval Bergen. *Fisheries museum* and northern Europe's largest and most modern *aquarium. Maritime museum.* Art galleries. Leprosy museum (devoted to the struggle against leprosy) in a medieval hospital.
The *Grieg Hall,* modern concert hall, centre of an annual music festival (end of May – beginning of June).
Troldhaugen (8 km S) where Edvard Grieg, the composer, and his wife Nina, lived. He is buried here. Near by is the *Fantoft stave church* (probably from 1150), moved here from Sogn in 1883. Further south is the medieval *Fana Church* with a silver cross that is supposed to have miraculous powers. Fana Mountain (131 m) with a beautiful view out over the *Folgefonna* Glacier.
Vestlandske setermuseet, an open-air museum devoted to farming in the mountains. *Lysekloster,* ruins of a Cistercian monastery, founded in 1146 by monks from Fountain's Abbey in Yorkshire.

OSLO (462 000)
Capital of Norway, founded in 1050 by Harald III (Harald Hardrada). Following a devastating fire in 1624, the town was renamed Christiania, after

1 Akershus Castle. Home Front Museum.
2 Town hall.
3 Royal Palace.
4 Karl Johans gate with National Theatre and university.
5 Historical museum.
6 National Gallery.
7 Museum of industrial arts.
8 Cathedral.

the Danish King Christian IV. The old name was re-adopted in 1925.

Karl Johans gate (gate=street) is the main thoroughfare. It runs from the central railway station to the Royal Palace. Between *Stortinget* (the Parliament, 1866) and *Nationaltheatret* (the National Theatre) is *Studenterlunden*, a park with summer cafés. Near by are two restaurants rich in traditions, Grands Café and Theatercaféen. The ***town hall*** with two massive towers was designed by A. Arneberg and M. Poulsson. In the central hall there is a monumental painting by Henrik Sørensen and under it is the glass façade through which the lively Oslo harbour and the Oslo Fjord can be seen. The Per Krogh Room, depicting life in old Christiania, is one of the richly adorned rooms.

Anne Grimdalen's relief of Harald III is on the west façade. The entrance façade is adorned with wooden sculptures by Dagfin Werenskiold. ***Akershus,*** castle and fortress, was originally built for Håkon V (1300). Christian IV had a Renaissance palace and a fortress built (17th cent.). Now used for official receptions. Hjemmefrontsmuseet (the Home Front Museum) is devoted to the Second World War Resistance Movement.

Vigelandsanlegget in the Frogner Park (always open) with 191 sculptures, grouped around the monolith and the fountain, Gustav Vigeland's impressive description of the life of mankind. *Vigeland Museum.* The ***Munch Museum*** (1963) with paintings, drawings and graphics by Norwegian artist Edvard Munch.

The *National Gallery,* mainly Norwegian art and modern European art. Russian icons. Museum of industrial arts. Historical museum. Geological

Oslo's main artery, Karl Johans gate, leads to the royal palace.

9 Bygdøy with museums.
10 Henie-Onstad Art Centre.
11 Vigeland Museum.
12 Oslo City Museum.
13 Vigelandsanlegget.
14 Holmenkollen. Skiing museum.
15 Botanical gardens.
16 Munch Museum.
17 Museum of technology.

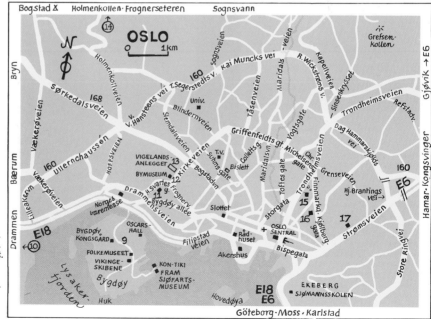

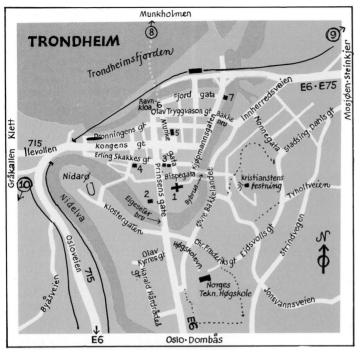

TRONDHEIM

Munkholmen

Trondheimsfjorden

E6 · E75

Mosjøen-steinkjer

Fjord gata

Ravnkloa
Olav Tryggvason gt
Bakke bru

Innherredsveien

Nonnegata
Stadsing Dahls gt

Dronningens gt

Kongens gt

Erling Skakkes gt

Gråkallen Klett

715
Ilevollen

Nidarø

Munke gata

Prinsens gate

Bispegata

kristianstens
festning

Tyholtveien

Strindvegen

Eigeseter bru

Klostergaten

Bybrua
Kjøpmannsgaten
Øvre Bakkelandet

Chr. Frederiks gt
Eidsvolls gt

Jonsvannsveien

Nidelva

Osloveien

715

Bysiveien

Olav Kyrres gt

Høgskoleivn

Harald Hårdrådes gt

Norges Tekn. Høgskole

E6

E6
Oslo · Dombås

1 *Nidaros Cathedral.*
2 *Archbishop's House. Home Front Museum.*
3 *Museum of Industrial Arts.*
4 *Museum of natural science.*
5 *Stiftsgården.*
6 *Ravnkloa (fish-market).*
7 *Maritime museum.*
8 *Munkholmen ("Monk's Island")*
9 *Ringve Museum of Musical History.*
10 *Trøndelag Folk Museum.*

Trondheim's cathedral is Scandinavia's largest religious building.

museum. Post museum. Museum of technology with automobile museum. Zoological museum. City museum. Bogstad gård, a house with beautiful 18th- to 19th cent. interiors.
On **Bygdøy** there are several sights. The **Viking ships** from Gokstad, Oseberg and Tune, all found around the Oslo Fjord. **Maritime museum** (shipping, fishing). Polar exploring and whaling. The **Fram House** with Fram, the ship (built 1892) which was used by Nansen, Svedrup and Amundsen. **Gjøa,** the ship that carried Amundsen on his way through the North West Passage, is outside the house.

Norsk folkemuseum with 150 timber houses. Gol stave church. Ibsen's workroom. Ecclesiastical art, toys and much more. The **Kon-Tiki Museum** with Thor Heyerdahl's balsa raft which crossed the Pacific Ocean. *Ra II,* the papyrus boat that was used in the South Atlantic in 1970. A 9 m high reproduction of a statue from Easter Island. **Henie-Onstad Kunstsenter,** a donation by ice skater Sonja Henie and her husband, is on the E 18 going towards Drammen, 15 km SW. Five large concrete buildings (1968). Modern art. Theatre, films, concerts. Oslo is surrounded by mountains and large forests and recreation areas are

to be found within the city's boundaries. The Holmenkollen railway line goes up to **Holmenkollen,** the famous ski jump. *Skiing museum* with the 2500-year-old Øverbo ski. Restaurant and convention hotel. *Tryvann Tower* with fine views.

TRONDHEIM (136 000)
The city was founded by Olaf Tryggvason in 997. Up until the 13th cent. it was known as Nidaros and was the residence of the king. Archbishopric since 1152. University and university of technology. Wide streets and low houses, built after a fire in 1681. Old seamen's houses near the Nidelva River. Bustling fish market at *Ravnkloa,* a part of the harbour. The square with a *statue of Olaf Tryggvason,* on a high column, is the heart of the city. It brings to mind the statue of Lord Nelson in Trafalgar Square. There are other things that remind the visitor of England. The cathedral looks like an English cathedral, and afternoon tea is served in the Palmehaven (Palm Garden) in the venerable Britannia Hotel.
Nidaros Cathedral, Scandinavia's most impressive medieval structure, is 102 m long and 50m wide. Construction of the central tower started in the 12th cent. and was not completed until about 1320. Six fires have ravaged the church. The restoration, which started in 1869, is still in progress. Coronation church and royal burial church. Splendid western façade with 54 stone figures. Richly adorned interior. The church was built over the *grave of St. Olaf,* who fell in the Battle of Stiklestad in 1030. Soon after he had been buried, miracles started to occur at his grave. For 500 years, innumerable pilgrims came to Nidaros. Most of them came through Sweden, following the Klarälven Valley. Present-day tourists throw coins into the Olav Fountain in one of the chapels of the cathedral.
Erkebispegården (the Archbishop's House), a medieval stone structure, next to the cathedral. Armoury with collection of weapons. Museum with exhibits relating to the Resistance Movement during the Second World War.
Folkemuseet, an open-air museum, with fishermen's houses and farm buildings. *Haltdalen stave church.* The ruins of Sion, King Sverre's castle (1180s). Tavern, an inn from 1739. The **Nordenfjeld Museum of Industrial Art** contains, among other things, tapestries by Hannah Ryggen. Museum of municipal history. **Museum of musical history** in Ringve. Musical instruments in period interiors. Museum of natural science (the town's history, ecclesiastical art, the history of the Vikings). *Stiftsgården,* a large wooden rococo building with splendid interiors. Used for royal visitors. Boat service to *Munkholmen,* a fortified island. Tram to *Gråkallen,* 554 m above sea level. Fine views.

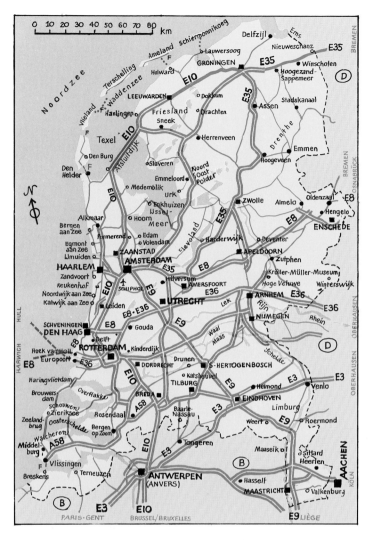

NL · Netherlands

NL·Nederland

Area: 41 000 km² (15 785 sq. miles)

Population: 14 million (414 inh. per km²). 31 % of the population are Protestants (Lutherans or Dutch Reformed Church), 40 % are Roman Catholics and 5 % belong to other faiths. 24 % do not belong to any religious group. The national language is Dutch. The correct name of the country is The Netherlands. Holland, as it is more commonly known, reflects the former importance of the provinces of North and South Holland. Frisian, a dialect, is spoken in the province of Friesland.

Major cities: Amsterdam 960 000, Rotterdam 1 million, den Haag (the Hague) 670 000, Utrecht 240 000.

Government: Constitutional mon-

archy with a two-chambered parliament. Amsterdam is the capital and the Hague is the seat of government. The country is divided into eleven provinces (the provincial capitals are in parentheses): Groningen (Groningen), Friesland (Leeuwarden), Drenthe (Assen), Gelderland (Arnhem), Overijssel (Zwolle), Noord-Holland (Haarlem), Zuid-Holland (the Hague), Utrecht (Utrecht), Zeeland (Middelburg), Noord-Brabant (den Bosch), Limburg (Maastricht). A twelfth province is being created through the drainage and recovery of a 2 220 km² area. Its capital is Lelystad.

History

100 B.C. Frisians and other Germanic tribes invade the area.

A.D. 402 The Romans retreat.

768-814 Charlemagne incorporates

the area into his empire and introduces Christianity.

1515 Reign of Charles Quint.

1521 The first Protestants, regarded as heretics, are punished. The Duke of Alba leads an Inquisition in an attempt to quell the resistance.

1648 The 80 Years' War with Spain is terminated with the signing of the Treaty of Westphalia.

1652-1784 Wars with England, France and Spain weaken the country.

1795 Troops of the French Revolutionary armies invade the Netherlands which in 1810 is incorporated into France.

1813 The French leave the country. The Netherlands becomes a monarchy and in 1814 is united with Belgium and Luxembourg.

1830 The Belgians revolt. Belgian independence is recognized in 1839.

1890-1948 Reign of Queen Wilhelmina.

1914 First World War begins. Holland is neutral.

1940-1945 Holland is occupied by the Germans. 100 000 Jews are deported.

1949 Indonesia achieves independence.

1954 Belgium, the Netherlands and Luxembourg join in the Benelux economic union.

1948-1980 Reign of Queen Juliana.

Currency: Florins (Gulden) (NLG). 1 florin = 100 cents

Business hours: Banks 9.00 a.m.-3.00 p.m. Closed Saturdays. There are currency exchange offices in the major railway stations. Post offices 9.00 a.m.-3.00 p.m. Closed Saturdays. Shops 9.00 a.m.-5.30 p.m. or 9.00 a.m.-6.00 p.m. Half-day closing once a week. In Amsterdam shops are usually closed on Monday mornings.

Holidays: New Year's Day, Good Friday, Easter Sunday, Easter Monday, 30 April (Queen's Birthday), 5 May (Liberation Day), Ascension Day, Whit Sunday, Whit Monday, December 25 and 26.

Hotels

The Netherlands has a unique central booking bureau (NCR) with nationwide coverage. The services are free of charge. Address: P.O. Box 3387, 1001 Amsterdam, tel. 02021 1211. Bookings should be made well in advance. Once in the Netherlands, tourists can receive assistance from the local tourist offices which are identified by a VVV sign. These offices charge a nominal fee when booking hotel accommodation.

In Amsterdam hotel rooms are always in short supply.

Breakfast, included in the room price in all but luxury hotels and motels, is usually a hearty meal consisting of bread, cheese, ham and eggs.

Food and drink

Koffietafel is a typical lunch. It is similar to Dutch breakfasts but much more elaborate. It often includes, in addition to coldcuts, bread and cheese, a salad and an omelette or some other small hot dish. At lunchtime it is also possible to go into a "broodjeswinkels" (sandwich shop) and buy sandwiches with a great variety of fillings. Sandwiches are called "broodjes".

Uitsmijter is an open-face sandwich with roast beef or ham topped by a fried egg.

Erwtensöep, the thick Dutch pea soup, usually contains small bits of sausage. Another favourite dish is Boerenkool met Rookworst–kale, potatoes, and smoked sausage. Indonesian dishes, a reminder of the Netherlands' colonial past, are quite evident. An Indonesian rijsttafel is rice which is served with several accompaniments.

Dutch pancakes are thin, delicate and come in many different varieties. Often they are enormous and require special plates.

Maatjes herring is young, fresh herring without roe or milt. Salted herring can be bought at the many street stalls. Dutch beer is world famous, the best known brands being Amstel and Heineken. Genever, the Dutch gin, is often drunk as an aperitif. It should be served ice cold. The visitor should also taste Rode Bessen, a red-currant-flavoured Genever.

The River Vlist. Below, Dutch tulip fields

Shopping

Porcelain from Delft, wooden shoes, antiques, cheese, art reproductions and diamonds.

Speed limits. Traffic regulations

Motorways 100 kmh, other roads 80 kmh, built-up areas 50 kmh. Cars towing caravans 80 kmh. Vehicles equipped with studded tyres 80 kmh. (Studded tyres are only allowed on foreign-registered vehicles which come from countries that permit their use.)

Children under the age of 12 are not allowed to travel in the front seat.

Be particularly cautious with the heavy bicycle traffic. When turning remember that cyclists who are going straight on have the right of way. Unfortunately we cannot advise you how to make a right turn during the rush-

hour when the stream of cyclists seems endless and impenetrable.

The sign reading Woonerven (in residential areas) warns of bumps built into the road to prevent speeding.

Roads

Dutch roads are excellent. They are well signposted with clear and large direction signs put up by the ANWB (the Dutch automobile club). But remember that the motorways, in the Netherlands called Autowege, often become ordinary four-laned roads with level crossings and merging traffic. Try to use the idyllic by-roads instead. Peacefully driving along by the side of a Dutch canal is one of the great pleasures of motoring. *Toll bridges:* Zeelandbrug and Prins Willem-Alexander Brug, Tiel. The Kil Tunnel linking 's-Gravendeel and Dordrecht is also a toll route.

Police and ambulance: Amsterdam and the Hague 22 22 22. Rotterdam 14 14 14. Fire brigades in Amsterdam 21 21 21, the Hague 22 23 33, Rotterdam 29 29 29. Refer to local telephone directories for the nearest emergency alarm centre. There is a national police telephone number, 03438-14321, but it is always advisable to try the local number first.

ANWB (Koninklijke Nederlandse Toeristenbond) with 2 million members is, in relation to the population, the world's largest automobile club – even cyclists, canoeists, etc. belong to this organization. The head office is at Wassenaarseweg 220, The Hague, tel. 070-26 44 26. The same telephone number is used when requesting the aid of an ANWB patrol car, called Wegenwacht.

Netherlands National Tourist Office, Savory & Moore House, 2nd floor, 143 New Bond Street, London W1Y OQS. Tel. 01-499 9367/9.

Routes described:

E 3   Venlo – Eindhoven – Antwerpen – Gent – Lille, see E 9

E 8   Oldenzaal – Utrecht – den Haag – Hoek van Holland

E 9   Amsterdam – Eindhoven – Liège – Luxembourg

E 10 Groningen – Afsluitdijk – Amsterdam – den Haag – Rotterdam – Antwerpen

E 35 Bremen – Groningen – Zwolle – Amsterdam

E 36 Hoek van Holland – Arnhem – Oberhausen

E 37 Utrecht – Breda, see E 9 and E 10

E 38 Eindhoven – Breda, see E 9 and E 10

A 58 Breda – Vlissingen – Breskens

Town plans: Amsterdam, den Haag, Rotterdam

E8. Oldenzaal – Utrecht – den Haag – Hoek van Holland

E8 comes from Moscow – Warszawa – Berlin – Hannover – Osnabrück.

E72 comes from Bremen – Cloppenburg – Lingen – Nordhorn – Oldenzaal.

Oldenzaal (27 000) and *HENGELO* (75 000) are industrial towns.

ENSCHEDE (343 000). Textile industry and textile museum. There is a collection of paintings by Dutch masters in the *Rijksmuseum Twente*. Technical university. The open-air swimming pool in *Boekelo* in the middle of the heath has both salt water and waves.

ALMELO (63 000). Textile industry. The town is beautifully situated in the Twente woods. There is a horse market in *Delden. Twickel Castle* (14th cent). *Holten* at Holtenberg. Woods and fine view. Museum of natural history. Canadian war cemetery.

DEVENTER (65 000). Hanseatic town. The large Grote Kerk, completed in 1338, has an 11th-cent. crypt. De Drie Haringen is a beautiful house from 1575. The town hall dates from the 17th cent.

Zutphen (30 000) Hanseatic town, once a major fortified town. There are three large open squares: Groenmarkt, Houtmarkt and Zaadmarkt. Sint Walburg Church has a famous library.

APELDOORN (135 000). To a large extent this is a garden city. The Royal Palace, *Het Loo*, was built in 1688. The Queen now resides in the Hague. The lovely, hilly Berg en Bos Park is well worth visiting.

Arnhem and the *Kröller-Müller Museum*, see E36.

AMERSFOORT (90 000). Industrial town. Three town gates and the fortified Muurhuizen houses are all that remain of the mighty fortifications. They have been replaced by canals that circle the centre of the town in two rings. A puppet theatre in the *Koppelpoort* performs plays about the former battles. On Saturday mornings in the summer the Amersfoort town trumpeters march through the streets. The Dierenpark is a zoo.

Spakenburg. A picturesque fishing village, where many of the inhabitants still wear their traditional folk costumes.

De Bilt is the site of the Netherlands Meteorological Institute.

UTRECHT, see E36.

Woerden has retained its original town walls. Stone bridge and castle. Antiques museum. Cheese market every Wednesday morning.

Oudewater. Little town with famous witches' scale. If the suspect weighed too little in relation to the width of her waist, then she was a witch. If her weight proved to be satisfactory, then she had to take a further test: she was flung into the River Ijssel. If she sank, she was innocent. Occasionally a proven innocent was recovered alive and told the good news.

There is a cheese market in *Bodegraven. Alphen aan de Rijn* (46 000) with the large *Avifauna bird park*. Many exotic species. Tulip park. *Boskoop*. Flower exhibitions and tree nurseries. Home of the Belle de Boskoop apples.

GOUDA (60 000) is world famous for its cheese. Near the old *Weigh House* (1688), now the tourist office and a cheese warehouse, the *cheese market* is held every Thursday morning from May until September. One of the country's most beautiful town halls. Carillon with figures that appear every half-hour. The 16th-cent. St. Janskerk has beautiful stained-glass windows.

The *De Moriaan pipe museum* is in an old tobacco shop. There are beautiful interiors in the town's museum. Het Catarina Gasthuis (1655).

DELFT, see route E10. *Den Haag*, see town plans. *Hoek van Holland* (Hook of Holland). Car and train ferries to Harwich.

E8 continues to London.

It is faster to drive the slightly longer E36 (A20) to the Hook of Holland.

ROTTERDAM, see town plans.

Schiedam (70 000). Industries, shipyards, harbour. Zakkendragershuis from 1725. Four windmills: The *Walvisch* (The Whale) at 33 m is said to be the tallest in the world. *Liqueur museum*. Dutch gin (Genever) is produced here.

Vlardingen (80 000). Fishing port. The State *Fisheries' Museum* is in the Reederhuis.

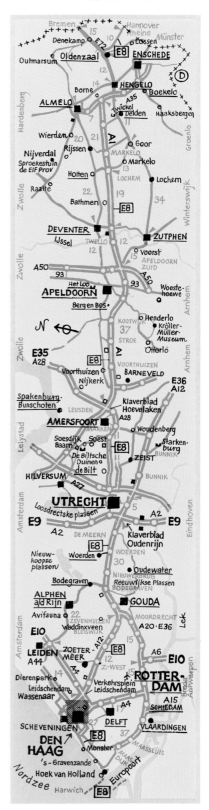

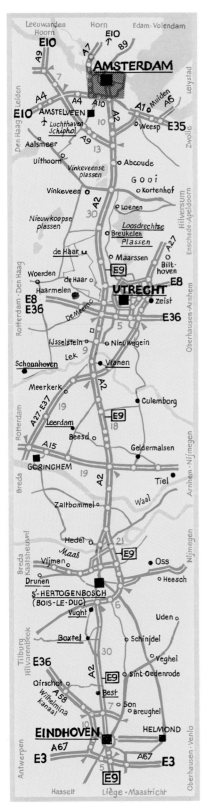

E 9. Amsterdam – Eindhoven – Liège

AMSTERDAM and *Schiphol*, see town plans.

Hilversum (94 000). Headquarters of Dutch radio and television. Modern (1928) town hall.

Loosdrechtse Plassen and Gooi. Lakes in a sylvan setting, canals, recreation areas, yacht harbours. Sightseeing by boat on the lakes. Woods near Gooi. *Haren Castle* is in a lovely park.

Breukelen. The 15th-cent. church has covered pews. 17th-cent. town hall. 17th-cent. emigrants gave their town's name to what is now a New York borough, Brooklyn.
The de Haar château in Haarzuilens was built around 1900 on 12th-cent. ruins. Splendid furniture, tapestries, carpets and works of art.

UTRECHT, see E 36.

Vianen. The Lekpoort and Hofpoort town gates are from the 16th cent.
Schoonhoven, to the west, has many small workshops. Fine silverware. Glass can be bought directly from the glass works in **Leerdam.**

E 37 goes from Vianen to Breda on E 10. Large dune area.

'S-HERTOGENBOSCH (87 000). Capital of Noord-Brabant. It is more commonly known as den Bosch. The Duke, Godefry de Brabant, had his hunting grounds here – 's-Hertogenbosch means "The Duke's Woods". The 15th-cent. *St. Jans Cathedral* was restored 1860-1955. Splendidly decorated façade and beautiful copper baptismal font. Bishop's Museum with ecclesiastical art. Beautiful square with statue of the painter, Hieronymus Bosch (born 1450). The Stadshuis (Town Hall) has a façade dating from 1640. Carillon with the figures of knights. Cattle market on Wednesdays.

Drunen has a car museum, *Lips Autotron*, with 300 vehicles. Horse-drawn tram. Films. Children's motor-racing circuit. Café and restaurant.

The little town of **Katsheuvel** is the location of the fairy-tale park of *de Efteling*, where you can meet Hansel and Gretl, Red Riding Hood and the wolf, and many others. Steam-driven carousel, steam train, playground. And best of all for harassed parents, the price of admission includes all rides and amusements.

E 38 goes from Eindhoven to Breda on E 10.

TILBURG (160 000). Industrial city. The *Volkenkunde Museum* (Ethnographical Museum) has collections from Africa, Asia and Indonesia.

Beekse Bergen Safari Park at *Hilvarenbeek* has many wild animals: elephants, giraffes, antelopes, lions, monkeys, rhinoceroses etc. Lake with beach. Train rides, cable car, miniature golf, watercycles, pony farm etc. Everything is included in the price of admission, except the cable car and the use of the sailboats. Café, restaurant, camping.

Vught (24 000) has an imposing town hall which was once William III's castle. Maurick Castle is now a first class hotel and restaurant.

Boxtel. Textile industry. *Stapellen Castle, Best.* Dutch wooden shoes are made here.

EINDHOVEN, see E 3.

Weert (38 000) has a lovely square and the Gothic St. Martinskerk. Ruins of Count van Hoorn's castle. Lovely surroundings (Limburg province).

ROERMOND (38 000). Roman Catholic bishopric. Limburg is one of the Roman Catholic strongholds in the Netherlands. *Munsterkerk* from 1218 and the beautiful gabled *De Stenen Treppen* house from 1666. Redemptorist chapel-shrine.

From here it is possible to make a short excursion into Belgium to **Maaseik,** a little town with beautiful buildings along the Grote Markt, among them Belgium's oldest pharmacy. A culinary speciality is Maseiker Knapkoek, a delicious pastry. To the south lies Limburger Maastreek, a beautiful valley dotted with lakes, woods and heaths. Fishing. Numerous hotels. There is a splendid, modern church in **Eisden. Susteren** has a two-towered Romanesque basilica.

Sittard (35 000) has preserved its town walls. 13th-cent. St. Pieterskerk. A church-shrine on the Kollenberg.

Geleen (37 000). Industrial town. **Beek.** 18th-cent. Gebroek château. **Meerssen.** Site of a 14th-cent. abbey church.

MAASTRICHT (112 000). A fortified Roman bridge built over the River Maas provided the beginnings of the city. Industrial town. Capital of Limburg.

The main sections of the *St. Servaaskerk* date from the 10th-12th cent. There is a treasury in the neighbouring monastery. *The Onze Lieve Vrouwkerk* basilica with a treasury. **Bonnefantenmuseum** (Musée des Bons enfants) is an art and antiques museum. Carillon concerts from the town hall.

Belgian border at *Vise*. E 9 continues to Liège – Luxembourg – Basel – Milano – Genova.

E 3. Venlo – Eindhoven – Antwerpen – Gent – Lille

E 3 comes from Leningrad – Helsinki – Turku – Stockholm – Göteborg – Fredrikshavn – Hamburg – Bremen – Oberhausen.

VENLO (63 000). Hanseatic town with beautiful 17th-cent. town hall and gabled houses. Venlo is said to have been founded by Valuse, whose effigy often appears in carnivals and processions.

Asten. Natural history and carillon museums. Helmond (60 000). The medieval castle now serves as town hall.

EINDHOVEN (196 000). At the turn of the century this thriving city was a small town with only 5 000 inhabitants. Philips, which has 35 000 employees, is Eindhoven's leading industry. There is also a Volvo automobile factory (previously DAF). *The Evoluon* is a unique Philips exhibition of modern technology. It is housed in a 30 m high and 80 m wide "flying saucer". The exhibit gives fascinating glimpses of the present and the future: laser beams, space flights, colour television, the population explosion, the world food shortage, the problems of the developing countries. The *Stedelijk van Abbe Museum* of modern art.

Belgian border. E 3 continues to Antwerpen – Gent – Lille – Paris – Bordeaux – Madrid – Lisboa.

E10. Groningen – Afsluitdijk – Amsterdam – den Haag – Rotterdam – Antwerpen

GRONINGEN (160 000). The major city of north-east Holland and a meeting-place of water and road networks. Hanseatic town. The university was founded in 1614. *Grote Markt* and adjoining fish market, the *Vismarkt*, in the centre of the city. Market Tuesdays. The town hall was built in 1810. The Renaissance *Goudkantoor* (Gold Office) houses a maritime museum. The Martinikerk has an imposing 96 m high tower and lovely frescoes. The *Museum voor Stad en Lande* has displays of art and ceramics, and a section devoted to the history and development of the city.

Menkemaburg is a charming castle in Uithuizen. The present three buildings date from the 14th cent. Museum with furniture, porcelain and arms. Large beautiful park with maze.

Dokkum. This small and very old town was once a major port. In the church are holy relics of Bonifacius (Winifred), the German saint who was murdered by Frisian heathens in 754. There is a chapel dedicated to him.

LEEUWARDEN (85 000). Capital of Friesland, a fertile area where the blond, blue-eyed Frisians have lived since the 5th cent. B.C. The university preserves the Frisian traditions and language. The **Fries Museum** is devoted to native history, art, furniture and local ceramics (Majolica). Rembrandt's portrait of Saskia. *Het Princessehof* (17th cent.) has displays of ceramics, porcelain, mosaics, and Indonesian arts and crafts. Extremely fine Weigh House (1598). The Kanselarij is a splendid 16th-cent. Renaissance house. Lovely buildings, canals and parks on the site of the old fortifications. Friday livestock market.

Marssum with the seats of the Frisian nobility: Heringa-Staat, Popta-Slot and Popta-Spital.

Franeker. Little town with old university. Picturesque Voorstraat. Renaissance town hall. Weigh House from 1632. The *planetarium* (designed by Eise Eisinga) was built in 1781.

Harlingen (15 000). Port with charming old streets. Picturesque 17th-cent. façades near the harbour. Monument to the Spanish governor, Robles, "the Stone Man", who, in 1573, had the mighty breakwater constructed. An earlier town on the same site was flooded and destroyed in 1134. Ferry to **Terschelling,** one of the **West Frisian islands,** famous for its great numbers of aquatic birds.

The new A 7 motorway that goes via Herrenveen is equally long in mileage, but it is the quicker route. It passes Heerenveen and **Sneek** (28 000). Sneek, or "Snits" in Frisian, is in the centre of a lake district. Water sports. Boat trips on the town's canals. Maritime museum.

Afsluitdijk is the 30 km long and 90 m wide dike which has transformed the IJsselmeer (Zuiderzee) into an inland lake. There is a statue of Lely, the dike's creator, at den Oever. He died in 1929, just three years before the completion of the dike. The capital of the province that has been created on the polder is called **Lelystad** (see E 35). Fine views from the tower.

Medemblik. A little town, once an important trading centre. 17th-cent. Weigh House. The first castle on the site of the Kasteel Radboud was built in the 8th cent. for the Frisian king, Radboud. This is the beginning of the Wieringermeer polders. Lely pumping station.

Enkhuizen (15 000). Fishing industry. There are three herrings on the town's coat of arms. Numerous houses of great beauty on Westerstraat. Drommedaris defence tower (1540). Lovely town hall. *Zuiderzee Museum* and *Waagmuseum.* The new road atop the dike leads to Lelystad.

Hoorn (40 000). One of the major ports that "died" when the Zuiderzee became an inland lake. Wilhelm Schouten, who came from Hoorn, named Cape Horn after the town of his birth. Another native of the town, Abel Tasman, gave his name to Tasmania. The **West Fries Museum** is in a Baroque house from 1632, on the Roode Sten, the town's main square. Statue of J. P. Coen who founded the Dutch Empire in Indonesia. Defence tower and many beautiful houses, especially near the harbour.

Edam (22 000) has given its name to the famous round, red-coated cheese. Beautiful and picturesque streets and squares. There are lovely stained-glass windows in the 14th-cent. Grote Kerk. Weigh House from 1778. The Speeltoren is a tower with carillon.

Volendam (15 000). Old port and fishing town, nowadays swarming with tourists. The natives wear their traditional folk costumes (as they do in nearby Marken, which was once an island, but has been joined to the mainland since 1957). Here boys and girls are dressed alike until they reach the age of five.

Monnickendam. The Speeltoren is a tower with carillon and mechanical figures of knights. The *Stuttenburgh restaurant* has a unique collection of music boxes in a charmingly old-fashioned setting.

Purmerend (32 000). The centre of the three polders that were drained as early as the 17th cent. Cheese and butter markets on Tuesdays. *Zaandijk* with the *Zaandlandse Oudheimkamer,* an antiques museum.

Zaandam (70 000). Industrial town. Once the home of several large shipyards where Czar Peter the Great worked, incognito, in 1697. It was here that he was inspired to modernize Russia. The little wooden house where he lived still exists, enclosed in a larger structure, just like his little house in present-day Leningrad. *Zaanse Schans,* open-air museum. Four windmills – Zaandam once had 700. *Windmill museum* (the Molen-museum).

AMSTERDAM, see town plans.

Alternatively you can choose the west road with sidetrips to the coast.

Den Helder (60 000). Chief Dutch naval base. *Marine Museum.* Ferries to **Texel Island,** famous for its extensive dunes and enormous colonies of sea-birds. *Natuur Recreatic Centrum* is a museum of natural history.

Callantsoog is the location of the *Het Zwanenwater* bird sanctuary.

Alkmaar (70 000). The famous cheese market is held on Fridays from May until September. The cheese porters are dressed in white, and their hats are ornamented with long, colourful ribbons. Lovely *Weigh House.* One of the oldest Baroque organs in Europe is in the *Sint Lauritzkerk.* The windmill, built in 1769, is still in operation.

Bergen aan Zee, Egmord aan Zee and **Wijk aan Zee** are seaside resorts situated among the dunes. They were once old harbours and fishing ports.

HAARLEM (160 000). Picturesque city. The beautiful town hall and the Grote Kerk are on the *Grote Markt.* In the church is a splendid organ which has been played by Mozart and Handel. The *Frans Hals Museum* is in the house where the famous painter died in 1666. Exhibitions in the Vleeshal and the Vieshal. There is ecclesiastical art in the Bishop's Museum. The Museum Croquius, drainage techniques and the building of dikes.

Zandvoort. Large seaside resort. The *Circuit de Zandvoort* is a famous motor-racing circuit, used for the Netherlands Grand Prix and other races. *Dolfirama* with performances by trained dolphins.

The Swedish botanist, Carolus Linnaeus (Carl von Linné), worked in what is now the *Linnaeushof* in Bennebroek. Recreation area with bulbfields, playgrounds, exhibitions of sculpture, etc. Tulip show.

Keukenhof is the centre of the flower-growing area between Haarlem and Leiden. Tulips have been grown here since the 17th cent. The export of tulips, hyacinths, narcissi, etc. is now one of the largest industries in the Netherlands. The extensive fields are at their most beautiful in April. On April 23 a large flower parade goes between Haarlem and Sassenheim. The *Flower show* in Keukenhof is held from March until the end of May.

Noordwijk aan Zee (24 000). Large seaside resort and spa. Start and finish of the Tulip Rally.

Katwijk aan Zee (39 000). Seaside resort. Parade of flowers in the middle of August. At the end of August there is a military tattoo.

Schiphol, see Amsterdam, town plans. **Aalsmeer** (22 000). Centre of the flower export industry. A flower auction is held in the enormous halls Mondays –Fridays about 8-11 a.m.

LEIDEN (105 000). The famous university, Holland's first, was founded in 1575. During the 17th cent. many famous artists, among them Rembrandt, worked here. Beautiful old streets and houses near the Oude Rijn, and Vismarkt (Fish Market) at Nieuwe Rijn. The Rapenburg Canal is particularly lovely. Gen. Hoefer arms museum. Pieterskerk (1679).

De Lakenhaal (Stedelijk Museum) is the old guildhall of the cloth merchants. Its displays include items of local interest and Dutch art. In 1574 Spaniards laid siege to Leiden. The end of the siege is remembered every October 3, when there is a festival and parade, and loaves of bread, and herring are distributed.

The *Rijksmuseum voor Volkenkunde* is housed in the old university hospital. Collections of art from Indonesia, Japan, China and Central America. The *Rijksmuseum van Oudheden* has a rich collection of antiquities. Other museums include the Rijksmuseum van Geologie en Mineralogie and the National Museum of Military History (Koninklijk Nederlands Leger-en-Wapen- museum). A 9th-cent. fortification, the Burcht, is on a man-made hill in the centre of the town.

Wassenaar (30 000). An elegant suburb of the Hague. Large zoo. Playground. Restaurant. Duinrell is a recreation area on the dunes.

Den HAAG and **Scheveningen,** see town plans.

DELFT (90 000). A typical old Dutch town. The canals are lined with trees and spanned by graceful bridges. There are many lovely façades. Those near the *Koornmarkt* are particularly beautiful. The Oude Delft Canal passes the 13th-cent. Oude (Old) Kerk. Its interior has works of art from different periods and beautiful contemporary stained- glass windows. *Nieuwe (New) Kerk* was built in the 15th cent. William the Silent's sarcophagus. 108 m high tower (276 steps) with fine views. Carillon. The town hall has a splendid façade that faces onto the square.

Prinsenhof was once the residence of William the Silent. In 1584 he was assassinated on its steps by a Catholic fanatic. The marks left by the bullets can still be seen. Museum with paintings, sculpture and porcelain.

Ethnographical museum and the beautifully furnished 19th-cent. Huis Lambert van Meerten.

Delft is world-famous for its blue and white porcelain. The 300-year-old *De Porcelyne Fles* porcelain factory has a permanent exhibition as does De Blauwe Pauw. University of technology and nuclear reactor.

ROTTERDAM, see town plans. The *Hoek van Holland* (Hook of Holland), **Schiedam, Vlardingen,** see E 8/E 36.

To the west are several islands and peninsulas that offer an interesting alternative to the motorist travelling from Rotterdam to Ghent/Ostend. You drive over the 5 km long **Zeeland Bridge** which is the second longest in Europe. Toll bridge. Ferry between Vlissingen and Breskens.

Kinderdijk has a famous view of seventeen windmills. They are usually put into operation in August.

DORDRECHT (105 000). A cosy old Dutch town, less known to tourists than its more famous neighbours. Its large river port handles primarily freight traffic. Yachting centre. This is one of the oldest towns in the Netherlands. In 1572 the first Dutch independent national assembly was held here and Wilhelm of Orange became the leader of the insurgents.

The Grote Kerk (14th-15th cent.) has a leaning tower. Carillon with 48 chimes. The church is on one of the lovely canals. Many fine houses along Voorstraat and the Greenmarkt. Groothoofdspoort, the north city gate, is well preserved.

BREDA, see A 58.

Belgian border. E 10 continues to Antwerpen – Bruxelles – Paris.

A 58. Breda – Vlissingen – Breskens

BREDA (120 000). This has been one of the most important cities in the Netherlands ever since the Middle Ages. William the Silent lived here until the 1567 uprising against the Spaniards. Many battles took place near Breda. A painting by Velásquez depicts the city's capitulation to the Spaniards in 1625. On the *Grote Markt* are the town hall, the *Grote Kerk* with a 97 m high tower and the old slaughter-house, which is now the Museum of the City of Breda. The *Volkenkundig Museum* Justines von Nassau has collections from exotic lands. The Begijnhof (Almshouse), built in 1270, has been moved to the lovely *Valkenburg* Park. The pretty little houses are still occupied. A few kilometres to the south, in a beautiful park, is the 17th-cent. Bouvigne Castle. The road to Rotterdam, via Zevenbergen (for the most part motorway A 29). At the *Hollandsch Diep* lies **Willemstad** with a well-preserved fortress built in 1583 for William the Silent. The *Herwormd Kerk* is an octagonal brick church (1607) surrounded by canals. An interesting road leads from Willemstad out to the island of *Schouwen-Duiveland.* Charming **Zierikzee** is its major town. The town hall from 1554, and three town gates, Nobelpoort, Zuidhavenpoort and Noordhavenpoort, from the 14th-16th cent.

Goes. Tuesday market. Fruit and vegetables are grown on the Wilhelmina Polder. The area is particularly lovely during April and May.

Veere. During the Middle Ages this was an important centre of trade. Its former glory can be seen in the large town hall (1474) which has a magnificent façade and carillon. A museum contains the Maximilian chalice from 1511. The *Schotse Huizen* (Scottish Houses) were built for the Guild of Scottish Merchants during the 16th cent. The incomplete Grote Kerk.

Middelburg (40 000). The provincial capital of Zeeland. It was a thriving trading centre during the Middle Ages. The *Abbey,* founded in the 12th cent., was restored after the Second World War. The *town hall* (Stadshuis) is one of the most magnificent in the Netherlands. It was built during the 15th and 16th cent. by members of the Kelder family of builders. The façade is adorned with 25 statues of the Counts and Countesses of Zeeland. The 55 m high centre tower has been nicknamed "Lange Jan" (Long John). The building was damaged by fire caused by an air raid in 1940, but it has been restored. Thursday market. Picturesque Kuhtor (Cow Gate) and many beautiful houses. In a park is the *Walcheren Miniatuur,* a model of the island of Walcheren that covers an area of 7 000 m². The scale is 1:20.

Vlissingen (Flushing). Car ferries to England and Breskens.

E 35. Bremen – Groningen – Zwolle – Amsterdam

Winschoten (20 000). Trading town and church from the 14th cent. Renaissance town hall. Windmills. Delfzijl (24 000). Fishing port. A canal links it with Groningen. Petro-chemical industry. The "Adam" windmill. Statue of Inspector Maigret. Simenon wrote his first book here in 1929.

Menkemaburg. Original castle at Uithuizen. The present three buildings date from the 14th cent. Museum with furniture, porcelain, weapons. Large, beautiful park with maze.**Hoogezand** (35 000). Industrial town.

GRONINGEN, see E 10.

Assen (45 000). Capital of Drenthe. Contemporary architecture. 13th-cent. abbey church. Archaeological museum. **Slagharen**. Shetland pony park.

From Winschoten you can also take a southerly route towards Zwolle – this eliminates driving by way of Groningen. You travel through a part of the Netherlands that is unknown to most tourists. **Veendam** (27 000). **Stadskanaal** (35 000) is an elongated town that follows the canal. **EMMEN** (90 000). Industrial town. Friday market.

Around the towns of Borger and Emmen are numerous **"hunebedden"**, megalithic tombs (about 2700-1800 B.C.) The moraine ridge here marks the southern boundary of the glacier that covered Scandinavia during the ice age. There is a **Hunebudden Museum** in **Borger**.

Meppel. Industrial town and the centre of an agricultural district. At the Thursday market you can usually see natives of nearby **Staphorst** dressed in their traditional folk costumes. Boys and girls up to the age of three are dressed in identical clothing. **Steenwijk** (21 000). Gothic church with tall tower.

Giethoorn. A village without streets. All transport must be carried out by boat. But there are some winding paths and bridges. Wedding parties and funeral processions must travel by boat.

ZWOLLE (80 000). Old Hanseatic town. The lovely town centre is girded by a star-shaped moat. The Grote Kerk dates from the 17th cent. The 500- year-old Schepenzaal (Aldermen's Room) is in the town hall. The red-brick Sassenpoort town gate dates from the 15th cent.

Kampen (30 000) was an important fishing port during the Midddle Ages. Hanseatic town. The centre of the town is a well-preserved bit of the 13th cent. St. Nicolaaskerk and Onze Lieve Vrouwekerk. Bovenkerk has a 70 m high tower and a famous organ (1741). There are three old town gates: Broederpoort, Cellebroederpoort and Koornmarktpoort. Splendid interiors in the Oude Raadhuis (Old Town Hall).

Harderwijk (30 000). Hanseatic town. The Swedish botanist, Carolus Linnaeus (Carl von Linné) visited the university. One of the church towers is named after him. **Dolphinarium** with performances by dolphins and sea lions. It seats 2 500 spectators. Underwater panorama. Bathing beach at Veluwestrand. Playground. Boat tours to the *Flevo polders.* There is a market every Wednesday in Putten.

Bunschoten-Spakenburg. Well-preserved fishing community where people still wear their traditional folk costumes. On the Sabbath the natives are dressed in magnificent Sunday clothing.

AMERSFOORT, see E 8.

HILVERSUM (94 000). Town hall from 1928. Radio and television stations. The town is situated in the lovely Gooi, a woodland area and nature reserve. To the south the **Loosdrechte Plassen** lake district, see E 9.

Naarden is an old fortified town that was totally destroyed in 1552 by the Spaniards who killed all of the town's inhabitants. The present star- shaped fortifications were constructed in the 17th cent.

Alternatively, it is possible to drive from Groningen on the new A 7 motorway which passes **Heerenveen** (35 000), and then continue along routes A 50 and A 6 through the Noord-Oost Polder and Flevoland. The **Noord-Oost Polder** is the second large land area that has been reclaimed from what was once the Zuiderzee. It was first walled off from the sea by the construction, in 1932, of the Afsluitdijk. In 1942 farming began and **Emmeloord,** the major town of the area, was built. There is a harbour at **Urk.** The **IJsselmeer Polder Museum** is in old church and some farm buildings at **Schokland. Flevoland** is the third stage of the draining that was carried out in 1957. The southern sections were completed in 1967. The capital, **Lelystad** (40 000) is named in honour of the engineer, Lely, who outlined the work as early as 1891 and led the construction until his death in 1929. Lelystad has been built in accordance with contemporary city-planning ideas: motor traffic and pedestrians are segregated. The result is rather sterile. The road leading south from Lelystad is unique – the view out over IJsselmeer and the future *Markerwaard Polder* is memorable. Do not drive too fast: great clouds of birds can hover over the road.

Ketelhaven. Marine archaeological museum. *Flevohof* is a recreation area with an interesting agricultural exhibition. There is a special village and playgrounds for children.

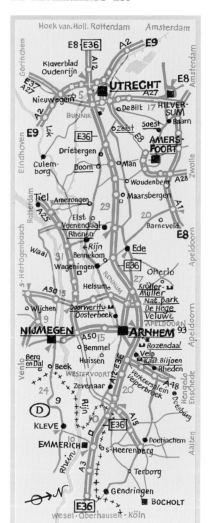

E 36. Hoek van Holland – Arnhem – Oberhausen

Hoek van Holland – Utrecht, see E 8.

UTRECHT (240 000). Fourth largest city in the Netherlands. One of the country's oldest communities, it has been a bishopric since 695. The Union of Utrecht in 1579 initiated the Dutch struggle for freedom against the Spaniards. The War of the Spanish Succession was concluded by the Peace of Utrecht in 1713.

The Gothic *cathedral* was built between 1254 and 1517. The nave collapsed during a storm in 1674. Of the original building, the choir, the transept and the tower remain. The cathedral tower (Domtoren, 1382) is 112 m high and has 465 steps. Fine views. There is a famous crypt in the 12th-cent. Romanesque *Pieterskerk*. Many lovely streets and places: Vredenburg, the Oudegracht (Old Canal), the monastery. As a contrast to the lovely old buildings you can pay a visit to the attractive, modern Hoog Catharijne shopping complex adjacent to the central railway station.

The ***Centraal-Museum*** is actually three museums: the City Museum, the Archbishop's Museum (with art and ecclesiastical treasures), and the Nederlands goud-, zilver- en klokkenmuseum (examples of the goldsmith's art and clocks. The *Spoorwegmuseum* (Railway Museum).

Zeist (60 000). 17th-cent. castle. Hussites, followers of the teachings of the Bohemian religious reformer, Jan Hus (John Huss) live in collectives in this town. **Soest** has the *Vogelflora* flower and bird park. **Soestdijk**. Royal palace. ***Amersfoort***, see E 8. ***Doorn***. Castle and lovely park. Tomb and monument of Kaiser Wilhelm II who resided in exile here from 1920 until his death in 1941. ***Amerongen*** with a 17th-cent. château.

Veenendaal with Ritmeester cigar factory.

Rhenen with the *Ouweland zoo*. Tigers, elephants, monkeys. Aquarium. Playground. Ede (80 000). Industrial town situated at the edge of the Hoge Veluwe national park.

ARNHEM (130 000). Provincial capital of Gelderland. The city was largely destroyed during the battles of 1944 when 10 000 British paratroops were landed to secure the Rhine bridges. The operation failed – 2 000 men were killed and 5 000 wounded. There is a monument at the bridge and a museum in Doorwerth Castle.

The ***Gemeentemuseum*** (City Museum) has collections of art, glazed pottery-ware, postage stamps, etc. The Duivelhuis (Devil's House) is a beautiful Renaissance house with bizarre, sculptured devils. Lovely fountains in the Sonsbeek Park.

The ***Openluchtmuseum*** is an open-air museum. Among its exhibits are over 70 farmhouses, windmills and old Dutch houses. There is a display of folk costumes. Herb garden.

The ***Burgers Zoo en Safaripark*** adjoining the open-air museum covers a 50 acre area. Lions, giraffes, zebras, ostriches. Zoo with 2 500 animals. Boat tours on the Rhine, the Waal and the IJssel.

Doorwerth Castle contains the *Airborne Museum* and has exhibits that depict the battles of 1944. Nederlands Jachtmuseum.

Park de Hoge Veluwe, covering 22 square miles, is a lovely national park that contains the famous ***Kröller-Müller Museum*** with works of art from many different periods. There is a particularly interesting and extensive collection of late 19th- and early 20th-cent. art. Over 300 works by Vincent van Gogh. Right next to the museum is the unique *Beeldenpark* sculpture park with works by Henry Moore, etc. Hunting museum in St. Hubertus Castle (groups only). The founder of the museum, Mrs. Kröller-Müller, resided here until her death in 1939. International Castle Museum in Castle *Rozendaal*. Photographs, models and paintings of several European castles. Concealed fountains (Bedriegertjes) in the 17th-cent. park. **Velp**. Handsome interiors in *Castle Biljoen* (1531).

NIJMEGEN (150 000). Celtic and Roman origins. Hanseatic town. *Castle Valkhof,* built for Charlemagne in 768, was demolished as early as the 11th cent. Rebuilt and again destroyed in the 18th cent. The octagonal Niklaus Chapel, with probable 11th-cent. origins, remains. 13th-cent. *Grote Kerk* (Sint Stevens). Imposing 16th-cent. Stadhuis (town hall). Weigh House completed in 1612. City museum with collection of furniture and paintings. Museum of archaeology. *Museum of the Holy Land*, an open-air museum dedicated to the life of Christ. Annual four-day march held the third week of July. When this tradition began in 1908 it was a military exercise. Now between 15 000 and 17 000 marchers gather from many countries.

Berg en Dal. Africa Museum with reconstructed native village.

E 36 continues to Emmerich – Oberhausen – Köln.

TOWN PLANS

AMSTERDAM (960 000)
Situated at the point where the River Amstel flows into the IJ, the city is joined by 400 bridges that span the "grachten", canals that are lined with old merchants' and patrician houses (all built on stout piles). Amsterdam is truly a city with its very own unique charm. Sight-seeing boats tour the canals and then travel out to the harbours (the second largest in Holland). Ocean harbour and Rhine harbour.
The city was founded in the 13th cent. and had its first great period of prosperity when the Dutch East India Company was founded in 1602. It has been the capital of the Netherlands since 1814. The seat of government is the Hague. Amsterdam is one of the world's most important centres of business and finance. Many of the famous diamond cutting workshops welcome visitors.
The Dam is the city's centre. It is the location of the *Koninklijk Paleis*, the Royal Palace. Built in 1665 and resting on 13 659 piles, it has a 51 m high clock tower. Damrak and Rokin are the major shopping streets. Nieuwendijk and Kalverstraat are pedestrian precincts. There is a flower market at Singel. You can find bargains, particularly on a windy day, at the Wednesday and Saturday postage stamp market at N.Z. Voorburgwaal. Finding a bargain in the flea market, held on the Waterlooplein, is not quite so easy. Leidserstraat leads to the *Leidseplein* which is an amusement centre and the location of the Staatsschouburg (City Theatre). Another amusement and nightlife centre is the *Rembrandtplein*.
There are restaurants that can satisfy every possible taste. Amsterdam's Indonesian restaurants are especially interesting. There are many old, famous restaurants such as the expensive Vijf Vliegen (Five Flies) which first opened in 1627; De Groene lanteerne (Green Lantern) which is the narrowest restaurant in the world – the restaurant itself is just 6 m wide and its façade a mere 1.28 m; Die Port van Cleve is famous for its soups and its loud waiters.
The *Rijksmuseum* contains many Dutch masterpieces, including Rembrandt's *"The Night Watch"*. Rembrandt's house, where the artist lived from 1639 until 1658, has examples of his graphic art. Newer art, by Picasso and others, is exhibited in the Stedelijk Museum. The *Rijksmuseum Vincent van Gogh,* opened in 1973, contains 200 paintings, 500 drawings and 700 letters by the artist. The *Tropenmuseum* (Tropical Museum) reflects the great Dutch colonial period. Maritime Museum. Toneel Theatre Museum. Netherlands Press Museum. Biblical Museum. Jewish Museum. The *Artis Zoo* is one of the oldest in Europe. Bird houses.

1 Royal Palace. Nieuwe Kerk (New Church). 2 Kalverstraat. 3 Crafts centre. 4 Town Hall. 5 Oude Kerk (Old Church). 6 City Museum. 7 Rembrandt's House. 8 Botanical Gardens. 9 Maritime Museum. 10 Rembrandtplein. 11 Rijksmuseum (National Gallery). 12 Van Gogh Museum. 13 Stedelijk Museum. 14 Leidseplein and Theatre. 15 Westerkerk and House of Anne Frank. 16 Zoo.

Westerkerk, Amsterdam

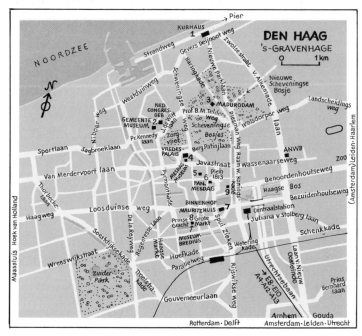

1 Kurhaus
2 Gemeentemuseum (City museum) and Congress Hall
3 Madurodam
4 Peace Palace and Mesdag Museum
5 Postal Museum
6 Panorama Mesdag
7 Mauritzhuis and Binnenhof
8 Bredius Museum (art)
9 Museum Meermanno (books)

Aquarium. Nocturnal animals are housed in buildings that are illuminated with special lighting so that they are awake during visiting hours. Anne Frank wrote her famous diary in the **Anne-Frank-Huis** which is now a museum. She was 16 when she died in the Bergen-Belsen concentration camp. During the Second World War 60 000 Jews were deported from Amsterdam.

The *Oude Kerk* (Old Church) is the oldest in Amsterdam. It was built about 1300 in honour of St. Nicholas. The present church dates from the 15th cent. Beautiful stained-glass windows. The *Nieuwe Kerk* (New Church) was reconstructed after a fire in 1645. de Ruyter, the Dutch admiral, is buried here. *Westerkerk* (1638) is the largest Renaissance church in the Netherlands. Rembrandt's tomb (1669). Dutch crafts can be seen at Holland's Arts and Crafts Centre, Nieuwendijk 16. Opposite the entrance to the Crafts Centre you can see the "Holland Happening", a giant slide-show about the Netherlands and the Dutch that provides the visitor with a half-hour sightseeing tour of the country.

Amsterdam is divided into nine districts (postal numbers) and each district is divided into nine"wijken". A ring road encircles the city. It is posted with A10 or N10 road signs (A for motorway). The "wijken" and the districts are joined by roads that are numbered from S101 to S108. When you drive on one of these roads you will be informed by the sign which district you are in and which district you are driving towards. When you come to the right district you look for the right "wijk". Does this seem complicated? In reality it is even worse, but fortunately all of Amsterdam is so charming that it does not really matter where you end up.

Schiphol is one of the largest airports in Europe. Well worth visiting, it can be reached in 15 minutes by train from Amsterdam Zuid or by airport bus from the Central Railway Station. In the mid 80's trains will connect Schiphol to central Amsterdam. Sightseeing trains and observation terrace. Aviodome is a museum of aviation and space travel. *Shipside* is Europe's sole car supermarket for tax-free cars. The prices are attractively low and deliveries are prompt, but remember that you may have to face stiff custom duties, taxes and insurance costs when you take the car home.

den HAAG (the Hague) (670 000)
Seat of the Dutch government. The capital of the country is Amsterdam. Sometimes the city is called 's-Gravenhage (The Count's Enclosed Wooded Pasture). At the beginning of the 13th cent., the Counts of Holland had their hunting lodge here. William II built a castle here and in the 16th cent., the Hague became the seat of government.

The Royal Palace is situated in the centre of the **Binnenhof** on the site of the Count's original wooded pasture. Parliament is opened in the Knights' Hall which has stained-glass windows with the coats of arms of the provinces. The many beautiful façades around the Binnenhof date mainly from the 17th and 18th cent.

Mauritshuis, one of the most beautiful Baroque buildings in the country, is the home of the royal collection of paintings. It is one of the world's great art museums. Holbein, Vermeer, Rembrandt and many others. Many government buildings in Buitenhof. The largest carillon in the Netherlands is in the 14th-cent. *Grote Kerk.* There are 51 chimes in a 96 m high tower. Beautiful stained-glass windows and a carved 16th-cent. pulpit. *Nieuwe Kerk* (New Church) from the 17th cent. with the grave of Spinoza (d. 1670) in the churchyard. *Gemeentemuseum* (City Museum) has handicrafts sections with glass, ceramics, musical instruments, art and exhibits related to the city's history. The Royal Library contains manuscripts and coins. International Press Museum and Netherland Post Museum. The *Mesdag Panorama,* an enormous (14×120 m) circular painting that depicts Scheveningen in 1881. Huis ten Bosch is the palace where the Queen resides. It is situated in a little wood just outside the town. The *Vredespaleis* (Peace Palace) was built in 1913 by the Carnegie Foundation. It still serves as the seat of the International Court of Justice.

Although the Hague has the hustle and bustle of a large modern city, it retains a Dutch small town atmosphere. Many parks. There is a Rosarium in Westbrockpark. The unique miniature town of *Madurodam* is near by. Here you can see examples of typical Dutch buildings, bridges and canals – all reduced to a scale of 1/25 life size. Beautiful evening illumination. Madurodam was built in memory of G. Maduro, a student from Surinam, who was killed in the war. There is a zoo in *Wassenaar.*
Scheveningen. Old fishing village, now a part of the Hague. It is a large seaside resort with a 381 m long pleasure pier. Aquarium. Numerous restaurants line the long beach. The newly restored Kurhaus Hotel has an indoor swimming pool with artificial waves, casino and a large hall.

ROTTERDAM (1 000 000)

Rotterdam's harbour (including Europoort), with over 50 km of piers, is the largest in the world. Over 30 000 vessels arrive yearly. Major oil port. The so-called spot market regulates the price of all oil sold outside the long-term contracts. Boat tours of the harbour and down the River Maas and the completed Delta project.

The centre of Rotterdam was totally destroyed during a bombing raid on May 14, 1940. It is now primarily modern even if the planners have attempted to give back to the *Lijnbaan* some of its former glory. It was once a sailors' amusement area and is now a shopping centre. *Grote Kerk,* a 16th

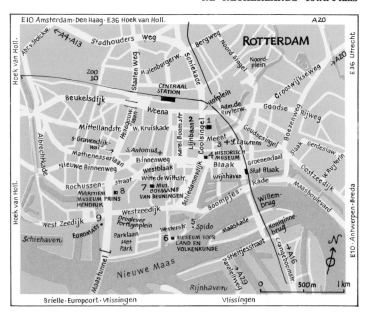

1 Town Hall
2 Lijnbaan (shopping street)
3 St. Laurent Church
4 Historical museum
5 Harbour tours
6 Ethnological Museum
7 Boymans van Beuningen Museum
8 Maritime Museum
9 Euromast (observation tower)
10 Zoo

cent. Gothic church, has been recontructed. 64 m high tower.
Boymans-van Beuningen Museum has a rich collection of art that includes not only works of Dutch painters but also Chagall, Picasso, etc. There are also displays of porcelain, silver, lace and furniture. *Prins Hendrik Maritime Museum* has more than 650 ships' models and maritime exhibits. The *Ethnological Museum* displays art, textiles and coins from the former overseas possessions of the Netherlands. The *Euromast* is a 96 m high observation tower with restaurants. *Blijdorp,* the most modern zoo in the Netherlands. Extensive grounds.

Rotterdam harbour

P · Portugal

P·Portugal

Area: 92 000 km² (34 821 sq. miles), including Madeira and the Azores.

Population: 10 million. 90 % of the population are Roman Catholics. The national language is Portuguese but Spanish is widely understood.

Major cities: Lisboa (Lisbon) 812 000, Porto (Oporto) 330 000, Aveiro 29 000, Setúbal 77 000, Coimbra 72 000.

Government: Republic since 1910. Parliamentary form of goverment since 1976.
2nd cent. Portugal becomes the Roman province of Lusitania. During the 5th cent. Visigoths overrun the country.
712 The Moors conquer Portugal.
11th cent. Christian reconquest begins.
1128 Afonso Henriques establishes a little kingdom north of Oporto.
1147 Lisbon reconquered.
1270 The Moors are driven from the Algarve, their last foothold in Portugal.
1498 Vasco da Gama discovers the sea route to India.
1500 Discovery of Brazil. With a large overseas empire, Portugal prospers.
1570 King Sebastião is defeated in Africa during an attempt to establish Christianity there. King Philip II of Spain seizes the throne of Portugal in 1581. 60-year-long Spanish occupation.
1755 Earthquake in Lisbon kills 32 000.
1910 Republic proclaimed – 40 changes of goverment in 16 years.
1928 Military coup. Salazar becomes Prime Minister and dictator.
1974 The dictatorship falls after a bloodless military coup.

Currency: Escudos (PTE).
1 escudo = 100 centavos

Business hours: Banks 9.00 a.m.-11.45 noon, 1.00-2.45 p.m. Closed Saturdays. Post offices 7.00 a.m.-7.00 p.m. Closed Saturdays. Shops 9.00 a.m.-7.00 p.m. Lunchtime closing 1.00-3.00 p.m. are not unusual. Shopping centres 10.00 a.m.-midnight.

Holidays: New Year's Day, Good Friday, April 25 (Liberation Day), May 1, Corpus Christi, June 10 (National Holiday), June 13 (only in Lisbon), June 24 (only in Oporto, Faro and Braga), August 15 (Assumption Day), October 5 (Republic Day), November 1 (All Saints' Day), December 8 (Feast of the Immaculate Conception), December 24, 25 and 26.

Hotels
Hotels are placed in the following categories: De Luxe A, De Luxe B, 1, 1A, 1B, 2 and 3. Pousadas are modern, state-owned roadside inns for tourists. They are often near popular tourist areas and in general, stays are limited to a maximum of five days.

Estalagens are small, well-equipped, privately owned inns under the supervision of the Ministry of Tourism (Direcção Geral do Tourismo). It is extremely difficult to obtain rooms in pousadas and estalagens during the high season. Lists of pousadas and estalagens can be obtained from local tourist offices.

Camping
Several excellent camping sites near the major cities.

Youth hostels
Youth hostels, here known as Pousadas de Juventude, have a minimum age limit of 7 years. Some youth hostels accept only female or only male guests.

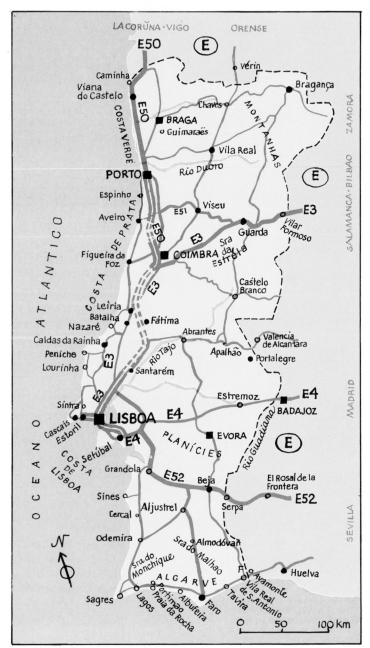

Food and drink
Fish and shellfish often appear on Portuguese menus. Some specialities: Bacalhau, dried cod. Caldeiradas, stew containing several varieties of fish, onions, tomatoes, etc. Linguado, sole with shrimps, potatoes, and cheese. Lulas guisadas, squid ragout. Sopa de lagosta, lobster soup. Sopa de peixe, delicious fish soup with onions and tomatoes. Sopa de mariscos, soup with several types of fish and shellfish. Guisado de carneiro, mutton with rice and potatoes. Canja de galinha, a delicious chicken dish. Caldo verde, kale soup with sausages. Sopa de sebola, onion soup. Cheeses, e.g. Queijo da Serra.

Portugal is the home of Madeira and Port but there are also several good red, white and "green" (young) wines-known as "vinho verde", a perfect accompaniment to fish and shellfish. The best red wines come from the Dão region.

Shopping
Gold and silver filigree, leather goods, baskets, pottery, wrought-iron and copperware, embroidery.

Speed limits. Traffic regulations
Motorways 120 kmh. Private cars towing caravans or trailers 70 kmh. Minimum speed is 40 kmh. Other roads 90 kmh. Private cars towing caravans or trailers 70 kmh. Built-up areas 60 kmh and 50 khm. Often there are no signs indicating the end of a stretch with speed limits. Drivers should be on the lookout for speed limits posted in the opposite direction. Motorists who have held a driving licence for less than a year must not drive faster than 90 kmh. They are also required to fit a sign with the figures "90" on the back of their cars. These signs can be obtained at frontier stations.

It is recommended that children do not travel in the front seat. If your car is fitted with seat belts it is compulsory to wear them.

Daytime use of horns is allowed and usually put into effect when visibility is limited and when overtaking. At night lights are used for signalling.

It is forbidden to carry petrol in cans in a vehicle.

Road patrols
The ACP has towing service in all of the major cities. Telephone in Lisbon 77 54 75, in Oporto 29 21 7. In case of accident resulting in personal injuries, assistance can be reached by dialling the nation-wide emergency number, 115.

ACP, Automóvel Club de Portugal, 24-26 Rua Rosa Araújo, Lisbon. Tel. 56 39 31. ACP publish an annual up-to-date road map.

Direcção-Geral do Tourismo, Av. Antonio Augusto de Aguiar 86, 1000 Lisboa. Information office: Praça dos Restauradores.

The Portuguese National Tourist Office, 1-5 New Bond Street, London W1Y ONP. Tel. 01-493 38 73.

Abbey of S. Maria de Vitoria, Batalha

Nazaré, a fishing port

Routes described:

E 3   Salamanca – Coimbra – Lisboa

E 4   Badajoz – Lisboa

E 50 Vigo – Porto – Coimbra

E 52 Lisboa – Beja – Sevilla

N 120 Grandola – Lagos, see E 52

N 125 Sagres – Lagos – Faro, see E 52

Town plan: Lisboa

E 3. Salamanca – Coimbra – Lisboa

Vilar Formoso. Spanish frontier. E 3 comes from Helsinki – Stockholm – Hamburg – Antwerpen – Paris – Bordeaux – San Sebastián – Salamanca.

Almeida has well-preserved, star-shaped, fortifications.

Guarda, Portugal's (and probably Europe's) most highly situated city (1 056 m above sea level). Now a spa. The medieval castle and walls, together with the city's name, illustrate their original purpose: protection against Castilian attacks. King Sancho I founded Guarda in 1199. His statue is in the steep, arcaded Praça Camões. The 14th-cent. granite cathedral is on the square. Beautiful Misericordia Church.

Belmonte. Ruins of 13th- to 14th-cent. fortifications. The Romanesque Church of S. Lago is situated at the highest point of the city. Nossa Senhora da Esperanza (Our Lady of Esperance), a Gothic statue, was aboard the ship when Cabral (born in Belmonte) discovered Brazil in 1500.

Lousa with Matriz Church, founded 912. A mixture of Romanesque and Moorish styles. *Viseu* and *COIMBRA,* see E 50.

Conimbriga. An excavated Roman city from the time of the province of Lusitania. Remains of houses, baths, graves, mosaics and a city wall.

Pombal. Hill fortress, founded 1171.

Leiria. Historic city, dominated by a castle which Afonso Henriques reconquered from the Moors. King Dinis lived here with his wife Isabel. She became Portugal's patron saint. Lovely garden with fine view, and magnificent palace. Bishop's palace with museum. Road to Ourém, a massive but elegant fortress, dating from the 15th cent., continuing to *Tomar,* a beautiful old city, founded by the Portuguese branch of the Order of the Knights Templar, the Knights of Christ. Their headquarters were in the Convento de Christo. Henry the Navigator was one of the Knights. Reconstructed several times. Lovely gardens beside the river.

Batalha. The Gothic abbey of *S. Maria de Vitoria* is one of Portugal's most magnificent structures. It was founded as an expression of gratitude for the Portuguese victory over the Castilians in 1385. (Annual festival, August 14-17.) The victor, King João I, and his consort, Dona Felipa, are buried in the church, as is Henry the Navigator. There is a lovely little church on the battlefield near the village of *Aljubarrota.*

Fátima. Annual goal for thousands of pilgrims. The Holy Virgin appeared before some shepherds in 1917. Shrine church. Pilgrimages take place on the 13th of each summer month and on May 12 and October 12.

Nazaré is one of Portugal's most picturesque fishing ports. Large painted fishing boats. Nossa Senhora de Nazaré is a 17th-cent. pilgrimage church.

Alcobaça. Large Cistercian abbey, *Real de S. Maria,* founded in 1178 by Afonso Henriques in gratitude for the victory over the Moors. Splendid tombs of Pedro I and his consort. Several other royal tombs. Lovely cloisters. Vineyards and orchards. Famous for its pottery.

Caldas da Rainha, "The Queen's Baths", founded by Queen Leonor in 1484 at the hot springs. Pottery. *José Malhoa Museum* with works by Malhoa and other 18th-cent. artists. *Nossa Senhora do Populo Church,* founded by Queen Leonor. Manueline style (a 16th-cent. mixture of late-Gothic and Renaissance). The name comes from Immanuel (Manuel) I. *Obidos.* Well-preserved castle, now containing a Pousada (state-run inn). Picturesque medieval buildings within the city walls. *S. Maria Church* with an altar painting by Josefa de Obidos, a native of the town (d. 1684).

Lourinhã. Misericordia Church with beautiful paintings. *Torres Vedras.* da Graça abbey and lovely Chafariz dos Canos fountain. Colega with Matriz Church in the Manueline style. Splendid portal. Alpiarca. *Casa dos Patudos* (1905), a magnificent private residence, now open to visitors. Beautiful interiors graced with art, furniture, tapestries and ceramics.

Santarem has a 1 km bridge over the Tejo, high above the fertile plains of the province of Ribatejo. Pedro I lived here. *Cabral,* the discoverer of Brazil, is buried in the Nossa Senhora da Graça Church. S. João d'Alporão is now an archaeological museum.

Vila Franca de Xira, centre of an area where bulls are bred.

LISBOA (Lisbon), see town plans.

Many places worth seeing N and W of Lisbon.

Odivelas with the Dinis E.S. Bernardo abbey. In the chancel of the abbey church is the tomb of Dinis I (from 1325). A statue of his wife, Isabel, stands in front of the abbey. Most of the abbey was destroyed by an earthquake in 1755 and rebuilt in the Baroque style.

Mafra. Enormous square abbey, with a 220 m long façade, and an immense dome. The structure is even larger than the Escorial outside Madrid. It also served as palace for the Bragança dynasty. 88 m long library and hospital with furnishings and equipment from the 18th cent. The abbey was built 1717-1730 by Ludovice (the German master-builder, J.F. Ludwig).

Sintra. Beautiful old town with lovely surroundings. *Paço Real*, previously the royal family's summer residence, completed for Immanuel (Manuel) I in the early 16th cent. Splendid, flamboyant interiors, e.g. 27 swan sculptures in "The Swan Room ", a gift from Charles V to his brother- in-law. *Palacio Nacional de la Pena* (1850) was also a royal residence.

The Sintra Mountains are an 11 km long volcanic mountain range which ends at *Cabo da Roca*, the European continent's westernmost point. *The Boca do Inferno* (Mouth of Hell) Grotto, where the water rushes in and out with great force.

Cascais and *Estoril*, large, elegant seaside resorts. In Cascais, the *Castro Guimarães museum* (art) and the Nossa Senhora da Assunção Church (18th cent.). Sacristy with pictures of fishing. **Queluz** with a magnificent palace and a French park with sculptures, fountains, and grottoes.

E 4. Badajoz – Lisboa

Punto de Caya. Spanish frontier. E 4 comes from Helsinki – Stockholm – København – Hamburg – Basel – Genève – Barcelona – Madrid.

Elvas. Small fortified town on the slopes of a mountain. Baroque Church of S. Domingo. Borba. Two-storey cloister in the Servas abbey.

Estremoz. Hilltop castle of the Burgundian kings. Portugal's patron saint, Queen Isabel, died here in 1336. The room where she died has been transformed into a chapel.
A beautiful part of the town, with Gothic and Baroque buildings, surrounds the castle. Well-preserved town walls with handsome town gates. Potteries. Loggia of King Dinis (Isabel's husband). Museu Municipal (art). Many splendid palaces.

Vila Vicosa. Small town with a large palace, which once belonged to the Dukes of Bragança (1602). Now a museum.

Évora (24 000). One of Portugal's most beautiful towns with old picturesque buildings, narrow streets and lovely parks. The town was founded by the Romans. Temple of Diana with 14 Corinthian columns. Parts of the town walls are also Roman, parts are Moorish. *Sé Cathedral* (12th-13th cent.) is Portugal's largest Gothic church. Museum of ecclesiastical art. *S. Francisco Church* (1481) is considered to be one of the loveliest in the country. Many other beautiful churches and palaces. *Provincial museum* with Flemish art. Casa dos Ossos (House of Bones). Chapel with walls covered with skulls and skeletons. Many other fine churches and palaces.

Arraiolos with the Quita dos Loios abbey, including a lovely cloister. *Montemor-o-Novo* with castle. Old part of the city with S. Lago Church. In the lower part of the town, Misericordia Church, founded by Immanuel (Manuel) I.

SETÚBAL (50 000). Large harbour and fishing port with fish market. Canning industry. 15th-cent. church, Igreja de Jesus, built 1491 in the Manueline style. *Oceanographic museum*. Most of the old buildings were destroyed by the earthquake of 1755.

Sesimbra. Fishing village and seaside resort. 17th-cent. castle. The fortress of Teodosio with lighthouse. Church of Misericordia.

The 28 m high *Christo Rei statue* marks the entrance to Lisbon. It was erected as an expression of gratitude for Portugal's being spared involvement in the Second World War. A lift goes up the 100 m high cliff.

E 4 runs into Lisbon over the *April 25 Bridge*, about 2 km long – Europe's longest suspension bridge when completed in 1966. Then it was called the Ponte Salazar. Ships up to 70 m high can pass under it. The towers are 190 m high.

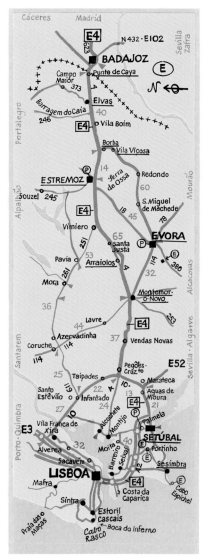

From Zamora in Spain it is also possible to drive to Bragança.

Bragança. Roman town. Lovely buildings and atmosphere. Portugal's oldest town hall, Domus Municipalis. Medieval chapel with wall. The Dukes of Bragança became the Portuguese royal dynasty. Extraordinary *cathedral*. .

From Santiago de Compostela in Spain (E 50) road N 525 leads to **Chaves**. Spa, known to the Romans, who built a bridge. Beautiful churches.

Road N 2 goes to Vila Real and Coimbra.

Vila Real. Old mountain town surrounded by vineyards. Gothic cathedral (15th cent.), formerly a Dominican church. The house of Diego Cão is now a museum. He explored the Congo. Old bishop's town built on the slopes of Mount Penude. The bishop's palace is now the *Museu Regional*. *Sé Cathedral* (12th and 16th cent.) with three Gothic doorways. 450 steps lead up to *Nossa Senhora dos Remedios*, a pilgrimage church. Pictures describing the Passion of Jesus.

COIMBRA, see E 50.

E50. Vigo – Porto – Coimbra

Spanish frontier. E50 comes from San Sebastián – Bilbao – La Coruña.

Valença. Fortified village. Romanesque church. City wall.

Caminha. Small town on a peninsula created by the Minho and Coura Rivers. Beautiful square, old houses, Gothic church with exquisitely carved ceiling and belfry.

Viana do Castelo. Small, lovely town with large fish market, magnificent town wall and Romanesque church. Casa da Câmara, previously the town hall, is on the *Praça da Republica*. Splendid façade. Arcades on Casa da Misericordia (1589). At the harbour is Nossa Senhora da Agonia, a Baroque church. Mount Luzia offers fine views.

Barcelos. Historic town with magnificent palaces. Pinheiros, a fortress-like palace with two towers. *Torre de Menagem* is a ruin of the town fortifications. *Church do Terco* (18th cent.). Beautifully carved pulpit and blue and white tile walls. To the east lies the former abbey church, *Vilar de Fradres* (national monument). Barcelos is known for hand-painted carthenware cocks. Pottery-fair every Thursday.

BRAGA (50 000) was founded by the Romans. Sé Cathedral, consecrated in the 11th cent. The present church, built in 1530, has a Baroque interior. Ecclesiastical museum. 5 km to the east lies **Bom Jesus do Monte,** a Baroque pilgrimage church. An attractive, high stairway leads up to it.

Guimarães (25 000), founded in 980. Medieval buildings and atmosphere. Portugal's first capital, birthplace of Portugal's first king, Afonso Henriques. After the victory over the Moors, he founded the Nossa Senhora da Oliveira Church (Colegiada). Many other beautiful churches. *Paço Ducal* (1442), the splendid palace of the Dukes of Bragança, is now a museum with elegant furnishings and tapestries. *Museu Regional de Alberto Sampaio* with a Madonna that King João I is said to have brought back from the Battle of Aljubarrota.

Povoa de Varzim, fishing port and seaside resort. Casino and race track.
Vila do Condo, dominated by ruins of the S. Clara abbey. Aqueduct with 99 arches. Famed for its lace.

PORTO (Oporto, 306 000). Portugal's second largest city and most important port. Built on the right bank of the Douro River, 5 km from the estuary (Foz do Douro). Three bridges cross over the river, including the railway bridge, Dona Maria Pia, designed by Eiffel. University. Factories producing textiles, ceramics and examples of the goldsmith's art. Oporto's most famous product is the port which comes from vineyards along the Douro further inland, where hot summers and cold winters provide the right climate. Once transported in sailing boats the wine now arrives by lorry or train. It is stored in Nova de Gauia, a suburb.
Oporto has many magnificent churches and palaces. Palácio da Bolsa (the Stock Exchange) has a beautiful Moorish Hall, copied from Alhambra. *Cathedral* (15th cent.) founded in the 12th cent. *S.Clara Church* with splendid Baroque interiors. Everything is gilded, even the original Gothic vaults in the chancel. *Church of S. Francisco* is now a museum. *Clérigos church* with a 75 m high tower, the landmark of Oporto. Carrancas Palace with the *Museu Nacional. Soares des Reis* (medieval sculpture, art, china and examples of the goldsmith's art). Ethnographic museum. Museum in the house in which Henry the Navigator was born. The Festival of St. John the Baptist is held on June 23.

Along the coast there are several small fishing villages and seaside resorts.

Espinho. Fishing village and seaside resort. Casino. **Aveiro** is an old town on a lagoon. Canals and beautiful churches.

To the east lies **Viseu,** a museum town with picturesque streets, churches and palaces. Pottery, basket weaving, lace. Sé Cathedral (12th cent.) with a Renaissance façade. Splendid vaults. *Church of S. Miguel de Fetal.* Granite sarcophagus of the last Visigoth king, Roderick, killed in a battle with the Moors at Jerez de la Frontera in 712. *Museu Grão Vasco* in the former bishop's palace. Named after the painter, who was born here in 1480.

COIMBRA (57 000). One of the oldest universities in Europe (1290). The large university building was originally a royal palace. It was given to the university by João III, in 1540. Porta Ferrea, an iron door. Cabra, the clock tower. Baroque library and lovely palace church. Traditionally the students are dressed in black capes. *S. Creus abbey church* (originally from 1131) with a Baroque façade. Tomb of Afonso Henriques, the first king of Portugal. Charming cloisters. Carved pulpit which depicts the adventures of Vasco de Gama, the explorer.
Sé Velha Cathedral is the country's most extraordinary Romanesque building. Flemish altar. In the former bishop's palace is the *Machado de Castro*, a museum (art, furniture, and pottery). Remains of Aeminium, the Roman town, are under the museum.

Montemor-a-Velho. The abbey of Nossa Senhora dos Anjos. Castle with town wall.

Figueira da Foz. Picturesque fishing village and large holiday resort.

E 52. Lisboa – Beja – Sevilla

LISBOA (Lisbon), see town plans. *Setúbal* and *Sesimbra,* see E 4.

Alcacer do Sal has lovely churches and the abbey of S. Antonio.

Beja. Historic town on the Alentejos plains. Roman origins. Beautiful buildings. White houses decorated with black wrought-iron. Citadel with a fine view. Torre de Menagem, a watch tower in the town wall, is the symbol of the city. Museum of art and archaeology. Well-preserved abbey church with cloisters (formerly the abbey of Nossa Senhora da Conceição).

Serpa with town wall, medieval gates and castle ruins. S. Anton abbey. Ruined castle at *Barrancos. Pulo de Lobo* waterfall, 25 m high, and 100 m wide.

Vila Verde de Ficalho. Spanish frontier. E 52 continues to Sevilla.

N 120. Grandola – Lagos
N 125. Sagres – Lagos – Faro

Sines. Small fishing village and holiday resort. Nossa Senhora das Salas Chapel. The explorer Vasco da Gama (1460-1524) was born in Sines. He discovered the sea route to India. Statue.

The Algarve Coast, the sun-drenched, exotic south coast, is reminiscent of Morocco and brings to mind the long Moorish occupation. It is 180 km long. Certain areas have been heavily exploited, but compared with other Mediterranean coasts, it is on the whole untouched. Most of the sandy beaches are surrounded by high, jagged cliffs. North of the Algarve are the Monchique Mountains.

Sagres, a fishing village at the foot of the cliff where Henry the Navigator's navigation school was built. *Silves* is situated high up in the Monchique Mountains, surrounded by orange groves. Once the capital of the Moorish kingdom of Al-Gharb. The large castle remains. To the east is *Atle,* with a beautiful church.

Portimão. Large fishing harbour and canning industry. Necropole, burial ground next to Mexilhoeira Grande and the Roman ruins at Abicada.

Albufeira. A fishing village which has become Algarve's tourist capital with large hotels and holiday apartment blocks. Hectic nightlife. Praia da Oura and Armacão are smaller and quieter seaside resorts.

Loulé is a small lovely town. Matriz Church (14 cent.).

Faro. Fishing port and capital of Algarve. Seaside resort. Airport, important for charter flights. Beautiful old section of the town and particularly lovely harbour. Most of the town was destroyed by an earthquake in 1755. A tower and a chapel in the cathedral escaped damage, but other sections were rebuilt in the Renaissance style. Church of S. Pedro with a splendid relief of the Last Supper. Nossa Senhora da Assunção abbey. *Ethnographic, maritime and archaeological museums.* Ruins of a Roman town.

Tavita. Roman bridge spans the River Ségua. Ruined castle.

TOWN PLANS

LISBOA (Lisbon, 1.6 million)
The city is beautifully situated on hills and terraces that rise 100-200 m above the fjord-like estuary of the Tejo River. Splendid views over the river and Lisbon's tangle of houses.
Alfama is the old part of the city with narrow alleys and stairs. It is a remnant of the old Lisbon that existed before the earthquake on All Saints' Day, 1755, an event that left a deep impression on all of Europe. 32 000 people were killed within one minute. In Alfama is *S. Jorge Citadel* (originally Moorish). A remnant of the castle of King Dinis (14th cent.). Lovely views. Romanesque *Cathedral of Sé Patriarcal* with royal tombs. In Alfama there are many restaurants, where you can hear the "fado", the typical Portuguese sentimental song, accompanied by guitar.
Baixa with its centre, the Praça de Dom Pedro IV, commonly called Rossio. Shopping streets Rua Augusta and Rua Aurea continue to the large *Praça do Comercio* (Terreiro de Paço), Lisbon's most lovely square with arcades and Baroque houses. The royal palace stood here before the earthquake. Equestrian statue of João I, and view over the river. *Avenida da Libertade* is one of Europe's great streets. It is 1.5 km long, and 90 m wide. Eduardo VII Park, named after the English king. Very fine view. *S. Roque Church* (1566) with a richly adorned baptismal chapel, created by the Italian, Luigi Vanvitelli (who designed the Italian royal palace, Caserta). The church contains the Misericórdia museum for sacred art.
Museu Nacional de Arte Antiga, one of Europe's finest museums of art, silver and examples of the goldsmith's art, pottery, carpets, etc. **Museu Gulbenkian** in a palace in Oeiras, west of Lisbon, contains a collection of art from different periods and countries. It is named after the world's richest man, the Armenian oil tycoon Gulbenkian, who died in 1955.
Several other **museums**: *Archaeological museum*, in the remains of the Carmo abbey. *Museu da Artilharia*, military museum. *City museum, in Mitra palace*. Museum of modern Portuguese art. *Ethnological museum*. *Industrial arts museum*. Coins and medals in *Casa de Moeda*.

Belém (Bethlehem) is situated west of the bridge. It was from this old port that the Portuguese explorers sailed out on their voyages, and it was here that they were welcomed home in triumph. Large *Explorers' monument*. **Belém Tower** is one of Lisbon's best known buildings – fortification tower and lighthouse combined (1521). Enormous **Mosteiro dos Jerónimos** (Abbey of St. Jerome), consecrated in 1496 by Manuel I. Large abbey church with his tomb as well as

Barrío Alto, Lisbon

those of many other kings and queens. Vasco da Gama's tomb. In Belém, the *Museu de Arte Popular* (handicrafts, costumes, musical instruments). *Museu Nacional dos Coches* with magnificent carriages and coaches in the former Royal Riding Academy. *Museu de Marinha*, maritime museum, with ships' models and the small seaplane that crossed the Atlantic in 1922 (Coutinho and Cabral). *Aquarium*.
The April 25 Bridge over the Tejo, about 2 km long, is Europe's longest suspension bridge (previously known as the Salazar Bridge). Toll for southbound traffic.

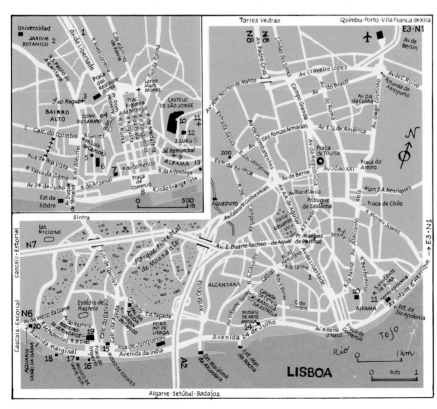

1 *Avenida da Libertade.*
2 *Botanical gardens.*
3 *São Roque Church. Misericordia Museum (religious art).*
4 *Archeological museum.*
5 *Don Carlos Opera house.*
6 *Museum of contemporary art.*
7 *Town hall.*
8 *Praça do Comercio.*
9 *Alfama.*
10 *Cathedral of Sé Patriarcal.*
11 *São Jorge Citadel.*
12 *Industrial arts museum.*
13 *Museu da Artilharia (military museum).*
14 *Museu Nacional de Arte Antiga.*
15 *Museu Nacional dos Coches.*
16 *Explorers' monument.*
17 *Museu de Arte Popular*
18 *Belém Tower.*
19 *Mosteiro dos Jerónimos*
20 *Aquarium*

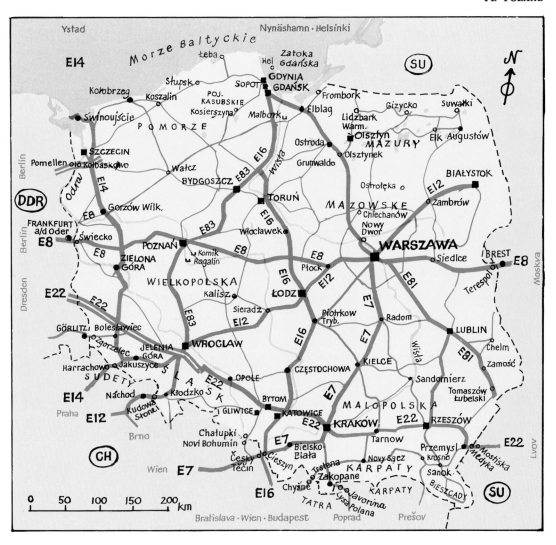

PL · Poland

PL·Polska

Area: 312 500 km² (120 733 sq. miles)

Population: 35 million. 98% of the population are Poles. Minute Ukranian, White Russian and Jewish minorities. Language: Polish, a Slavic language. 95% of the population are Roman Catholics.

Major cities: Warszawa (Warsaw) 1.5 million, Łódź 830 000, Kraków 706 000, Wrocław 609 000, Poznań 545 000, Gdańsk 450 000, Szczecin 388 000, Katowice 351 000.

Government: People's democracy. The authority of government is held by the Sejm which elects a Council of State. The country is divided into 49 voivodships (wojewodztwo).

History
1025 Boleslaw Chrobry is proclaimed king.
1226 Teutonic Knights occupy Poland.
1300-1400 Poland is divided.
1320 Wladyslaw Lokietek unites Poland.
1386 Lithuania united with Poland.
1410 Teutonic Knights defeated at the

Routes described:

E 7   Warszawa – Kraków – Praha

E 8   Brest – Warszawa – Frankfurt a/d Oder

E 12 Białystok – Warszawa – Wrocław – Praha

E 14 Szczecin – Jelenia Góra

E 16 Gdańsk – Toruń – Łódź – Katowice – Cieszyn – Žilina

E 22 Berlin – Wrocław – Kraków – Przemysl – Lvov

E 81 Gdynia – Warszawa – Lvov

E 83 Gdynia – Jelenia Góra

Town plans: Gdańsk, Kraków, Warszawa

Warsaw's Old Town has been reconstructed after the Second World War.

cabbage. Kaczka zjablkami, grilled duck served with apples. Pierozki, a ravioli-like concoction filled with meat, cabbage, plums and cottage cheese. Sarna Pieczona, saddle of vension.

Popular desserts include fruit pudding and mazurek pastries. Beer from Gdansk, Kraków and Żywiec is good even if it has a rather special character. Wines are usually imported products from nearby Hungary. Polish vodka is popular as are liqueurs and sliwowica (plum brandy).

Shopping

Handwoven cloth, embroidery, lace, pottery, silverware from Zakopane, amber from the Baltic coast. Prints and engravings, boxes with wood and metal inlays from Krakow and Zakopane. Special shops for foreigners that accept only hard (western) currancy: Pewex, Baltona, Cepelia.

Petrol

Foreign motorists are allowed to buy petrol only with ORBIS petrol exchange coupons that can be purchased with western currency at frontier stations, hotels and travel offices. It is possible to buy limited złoty petrol coupons.

Strictly obey all regulations. On departure from Poland you must be able to present properly stamped petrol coupons that have been used during your stay in the country.

Speed limits. Traffic regulations.

Maximum speeds: Motorways and similar roads 110 kmh. Outside built-up areas 90 kmh for private cars. Cars towing caravans and motorcycles 70 kmh. Built-up areas 60 kmh.

Children under 10 are not allowed to travel in the front seat. If your car is fitted with seat belts it is compulsory to wear them.

You are advised to carry a set of replacement light bulbs.

Avoid driving after dark. Horse-drawn carts and riders seldom have warning lights.

Roads

In general, major roads are good and usually paved. Secondary roads vary in quality.

Road patrols

PZM (Polski Zwiazek Motorowy), the Polish Automobile Club, can be contacted through their emergency telephone number, in Warsaw (address: ul. Krucza 6/14, Warsaw), tel. 29 35 41, 29 04 67, or at local provincial offices.

PZM, Polski Zwiazek Motorowy, Ul. Kasimierzowska 66, 02-518 Warsaw, tel. (22) 49 93 61. Tourist office at Aleje Jerozolimskie 63, 00-697 Warsaw, tel. 28 62 51.

Polorbis Travel Ltd 82 Mortimer Street, London W1N 7DE. Tel 01-580 8028.

Battle of Tannenberg.
1500-1600 Golden Age of Poland.
1683 John II defeats the Turks at Vienna.
1772-1793 Prussia, Austria and Russia divide Poland.
1794 Unsuccessful uprising.
1795 Third partition of Poland.
1918 Poland achieves independence.
1939 The Second World War begins with the German invasion of Poland and the bombardment of the free city of Danzig (present-day Gdansk).
1945 Poland is liberated and becomes a people's democracy.
1971 Unrest in Gdansk.
1981 Establishment of Solidarity, an independent trade union. The formation of Solidarity leads to a confrontation with the Communist party. A military government is formed.

Currency: Złoty (PLZ).
1 złoty = 100 groszy
The import and export of Polish currency is prohibited. Currency exchange is only permitted at authorized banks and exchange offices. Visitors from non-Socialist countries are required to have visas and to exchange a certain amount of Western currency daily. For complete details, enquire at your local travel bureau or the Polish Tourist Authority.

Business hours: Banks 8.00-11.30 a.m. Saturdays 8.00 a.m.-10.00 noon.

Post offices 8.00 a.m.-6 p.m. Saturdays 8.00 a.m.-2 p.m. or closed. Major shops 11.00 a.m.-7.00 p.m.

Holidays: New Year's Day, Easter Monday, May 1, Corpus Christi, July 22, November 1, December 25 and 26.

Hotels

The state-owned ORBIS Travel Bureau operates a large number of hotels, guest houses and restaurants. Local offices in all major cities. Hotel rooms can and should be booked in advance through Orbis. There are several other hotel chains. Many spas.

Camping

There are about 200 camping sites divided into three categories. In addition, there are 350 simpler sites, for tents only.

Food and drink

Traditional Polish cuisine offers the visitor many original dishes. Mushrooms are especially popular and they are served in many ways: boiled, marinated, salted, fried and served with gravy, butter-fried, etc. Cucumber is perhaps the most popular vegetable. Often it is served raw accompanied by white pepper or honey. Sometimes it is served sliced with cream. "Mizeria" (sour cream or yoghurt) accompanies roast chicken. Polish inns often serve sauerkraut soup, and beetroot soup. Bigos is smoked meat with ham and sauerkraut. Golabki, meat, rice and

E 7. Warszawa – Kraków – Praha

WARSZAWA (Warsaw), see town plans.

RADOM (145 000). Chief town of the district. Industries. Known for its fortress as early as the 12th cent. Two Gothic churches. Museum.

Szydlowiec with sandstone quarries. Beautiful town hall in the Renaissance style. 17th-cent. castle with museum. *Skartysko-Kamienna,* industrial town. *Wachock.* Iron works. Romanesque church.

Bodzentyn. Ruins of a castle which used to belong to the bishops of Krakow. Beautiful Gothic church with an altar which once stood in a church in Krakow. *Święta Katarzyna.* Tourist resort near *Lysica* (611 m above sea level), the highest point in the *Swietokrzyskie Mountains.* Gothic abbey (12th cent.) at the summit. Fine hiking trails. National park. *Bartkow* with famous oak, 1 200 years old.

KIELCE (100 000). Seat of the Voivod (governor). Important cultural centre between the 14th and 16th cent. Industries. Baroque cathedral and 17th-cent. bishop's palace in the Renaissance style. Now residence of the Voivod. The *Swietokrzyskie Museum* (archaeology, ethnography and natural history). Stefan Zermonski Museum.

Szydłów with ruined abbey, churches and fortification wall with the Krakow Gate (14th cent.).

Busko Zdrój. Spa with springs. Park and pump room. The *Skororice Nature Reserve* is near by (steppe vegetation, grottoes, subterranean rivers). *Wiślica.* An important town during the Middle Ages. Excavations in the church have revealed a church from the 10th cent. *Pińczów* with many churches was in the 16th cent. an important religious centre ("arianism").

Chęciny. Ruined fortress (14th cent.) on a hill. Marble from Checiny has been used for the Sigismund Column in Warsaw. *Jedrzejów.* 14th- cent. Cistercian abbey and church, rebuilt in the Baroque style. Museum with sundials. *Kslaż Wielki* with beautiful churches. *Mirow,* a Renaissance palace.

The *Woiski Forest,* recreation area. Ojkow and the Pradnik Valley together form the *Ojców National Park* with deep valleys and fantastically shaped limestone cliffs.

KRAKÓW, see town plans.

Wieliczka with 1 000-year-old salt mines. 13 km long tunnels, 3 km of them open to visitors. 55 m long, 12 m high hall, used as a church, with salt reliefs and chandeliers made of rock-crystal. Chapel with saints' figures. Mining museum and tennis court 135 m below the earth's surface. The 42 m high Staszik Hall housed a German aeroplane factory during the Second World War.

Oświęcim (Auschwitz). Over four million people from 29 nations perished in the concentration camp here. The sign above the entrance reads "Arbeit macht frei" (Work liberates). The museum is an unbelievable – for many intolerable – memorial to the evil of mankind.

Kalwaria-Zebrzydowska. Baroque church and Bernardine abbey.

Bielsko-Biala (90 000). Industrial town. Textile industries. Road to *Zywiec* with well-known brewery.

Cieszyn. Old town with beautiful houses round the square. Museum in *Larischow Palace.* Baroque churches. The Polish-Czechoslovakian frontier divides the town into two.

E 7 continues to Wien – Klagenfurt – Venezia – Bologna – Roma.

The Kraków – Zakopane road goes through the *Bedskid Mountains* with many tourist resorts. *Rabka.* Small spa. Museum with folk sculptures in a small wooden church (1609). *Chabówka.* Hairpin bends up the Obidowa Ridge. (810). Wooden church (1759). Tourist resort.

Nowy Targ (20 000), chief town of Podhale, an area with interesting old traditions and architecture. Tuesday is market day.

Road through *Dębno* with beautiful wooden church to Czorsztyn, starting point for 3 to 4 hour long trips on rafts, through rapids to *Charny Dunajec.* There are about 100 rafts which transport 20 000 tourists a year.

Poronin. Tourist resort. Lenin Museum in the house where he lived 1913-1914. House of poet Jan Kasprowicz. The road to Bukowina Tatrzańska and Morskie Oko is very beautiful.

Zakopane (30 000), 1 000 m above sea level. The country's largest tourist resort. Winter sports facilities and many hotels. *Tatra Museum.* Swimming pool (18°C water from a warm spring).

Gubalówka (1 123 m) with panoramic views out over the *Tatra Mountains,* Poland's loveliest mountain range (national park) with Poland's highest peak, *Rysy,* 2 499 m. *Gerlach,* 2 663 m, is in Czechoslovakia. *Morskie Oko,* a lovely mountain lake, is surrounded by steep cliffs.

Zybryca Gorna. Interesting open-air museum.

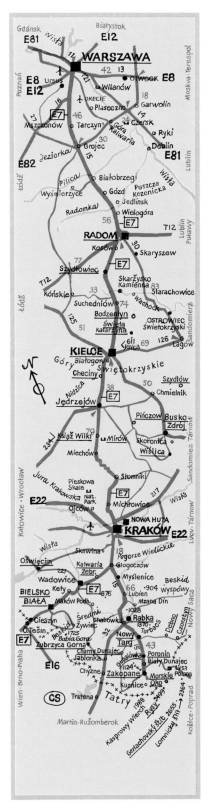

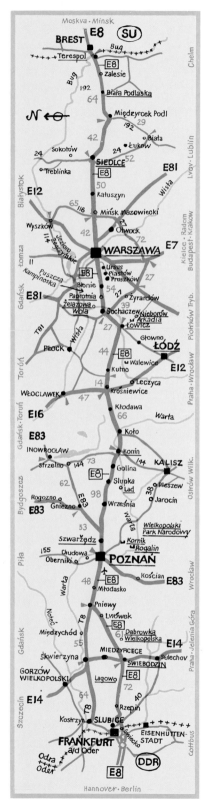

E 8. Brest – Warszawa – Frankfurt a/d Oder

E 8 comes from Moscow. (The Soviet Union does not use European road numbers).

Soviet frontier at **Terespol**. Bridge across the River *Bug*.

Biała Podlaska (25 000) with remains of a Radziwill castle. **Siedlce** (40 000). Industries. 17th-cent. château.

WARSZAWA (Warsaw), see town plans.

Kampinos Forest, see E 81. **Paprotnia** with the wellknown inn "The forge of Napoleon" (Kuźnia Napoleońska).

Zelazowa Wola, birthplace of Frédéric Chopin. Museum. Concerts on Sundays in the summer.

Łowicz (20 000). Former capital of a principality. Old folk traditions are kept alive. Folklore festival in July. Beautiful square with 17th-cent. church. Bishops' tombs. Łowicz Museum with folk art and crafts. The museum has a Baroque chapel with fine frescoes.

Arkadia. Romantic park created in 1773 for Princess Helen Radziwill. Pavillons, temple of Diana. **Nieborów.** Baroque palace with beautiful paintings and furnishings. A branch of the National Museum of Warsaw. Work centre for writers.

Walewice. 18th-cent. palace which once belonged to Marie Walewska, Napoleon's mistress. Their son, Aleksandr Walewski, who became French Foreign Minister, was born here.

ŁODŹ, see E 12.

Konin. Industrial town, centre of a coal mining district. **Lad** with famous abbey, founded by Cistercians in 1175. Gothic frescoes and Baroque church.

Gniezno, see E 83.

KALISZ (100 000). Probably Poland's oldest town, mentioned by the geographer Ptolemy in A.D. 145. Trading centre on the Amber Route from southern Europe to the Baltic Sea. *Sw. Mikolaja,* the oldest church, is from the 13th cent. "The Descent from the Cross" by the School of Rubens.

Schwarzędz with an unique collection of bee-hives.

POZNAŃ (500 000). Main town in Wielkopolska (Greater Poland). Seat of the Voivod (governor). Important centre with one of Europe's major industrial trade fairs. Seat of the first bishop of Poland (968). Even before the 13th cent. Poznań had served as Poland's capital. *Stary Rynek* (Old Square). The impressive town hall has a beautiful eastern façade with arcades and a loggia. Rebuilt in the 16th cent. in the Renaissance style. Reconstructed after the Second World War. Historical museum. The watchtower in the square is now a revolutionary museum. *The Museum of Musical Instruments* with one of the largest collections in the world. Wielkoposka Military Museum and and Art Gallery are also near by. National Museum (medieval art etc.). Archaeological museum. The Palace of Culture was built at the beginning of the 20th cent. as a residence for Kaiser Wilhelm II. Adam Mickiewicz University is near by. Statue of the poet.

The **cathedral,** situated in *Ostrów Tumski,* the oldest part of the town, was consecrated in the 10th cent. Destroyed and rebuilt several times (last in 1945). Reconstructed in the shape of a Gothic basilica. Several other interesting churches.

Cytadela (the Citadel). Remains of the fortress. This was the last German stronghold in Poland in 1945. Heroes' Cemetary with Soviet, Polish, French and British Commonwealth graves (The French are from 1981). Rose garden. In the Eastern part of Poznań is the zoo, the largest in Poland.

Wielkopolski National Park. Large wooded area with many beautiful lakes. **Kornik.** 16th-cent. castle, rebuilt in the 19th cent. in English neo-Gothic style. Museum with collections of art, weapons, furniture, hunting trophies, etc. Fine park. **Rogalin.** Baroque palace from the 18th cent., now part of the National Museum of Poznań.

Swiebodzin. Old town with remains of fortification walls. **Dabrowka Wielkopolska,** known for its beautiful folk costumes and for the "kozły", a kind of bag-pipe. **Lagow** with medieval castle and town walls. Beautifully set between lakes.

Swiecko. Polish frontier station at Odra. DDR (GDR) border.

E 8 continues to Frankfurt an der Oder – Berliner Ring – Hannover – Osnabrück – den Haag – London.

E 12. Białystok – Warszawa – Łódź – Wrocław – Praha

Kuźnica. Soviet frontier, closed for foreigners. E 12 was intended to provide a direct link with Leningrad.

BIAŁYSTOK (165 000). Seat of the Voivod (governor). 75 per cent of the city was destroyed during the Second World War and more than half of its inhabitants perished. Folklore museum in the town hall. The Baroque *Branicki Palace* has been restored after a severe 1944 fire. *Kruszyniany,* 50 km E, has an 18th-cent. wooden mosque. The inhabitants of the village are Muslim Tartars. More than half the total area of the *Białowieska Forest* (1 290 sq. km.) is on Soviet territory. Part of the forest is a national park. Forestry and natural history museum (special section devoted to apiculture). Many European bison.

To the north, *Augustów.* Beautiful lakes and Poland's largest continuous forest.

Masurian Lake District, see E 81.

Zambrów. Monument dedicated to over 12 000 Soviet prisoners of war who were murdered in a concentration camp. *Treblinka,* a slave-labour camp where 10 000 Poles perished. *Treblinka II,* an extermination camp where 700 000 died. Monument on the site of the gas chambers.

The road goes through the extensive Puszcza Biala (White Forest).

WARSZAWA (Warsaw), see town plans.

Warszawa – Łowicz, see E 8.

ŁÓDŹ (800 000) Poland's second city. Centre of the Polish textile industry. At the beginning of the 19th cent., Łódź was a small community. University. The Schiller School, an institute of higher learning specializing in film and theatre studies. Film studios. Art, textile, and several other museums.

Pabianice (62 000) and *Zdúnska Wola.* Textile industry. In the 13th cent., *Sieradz* was the capital of a principality. Agricultural district famed for its handicrafts. The village of *Monice* is well-known for its distinctive textiles and paper cut-outs.

Oleśnica. Renaissance palace. Wrocław Gate in the remains of the town wall.

WROCŁAW (570 000). Capital of Lower Silesia (Śląsk). University. Heavy industry. Seat of the Voivod (governor). The city was known as early as the 9th-cent. Important stop on the Amber Route that linked the Baltic with the Mediterranean. Until 1945 the city, known as Breslau, was in what was then Germany. 70% of Wrocław was destroyed during the war but the 13th- and 14th-cent. buildings in the Old Town have been painstakingly restored. The handsome town hall contains an historical museum. Baroque university buildings and Ossiliński Library. The imposing 14th-cent. *cathedral* and *Church of the Holy Cross,* both in the Gothic style, are in Ostrów Tumski, the oldest part of the city, which boasts many Baroque buildings. *The Church of Our Lady on the Sands,* a Gothic structure, is situated on an island in the Odra. Several islands. 84 bridges. Silesian museum. Medal museum. Post and telegraph museum, etc.

Niemcza on the slopes of the Sudety (Sudentan) Mountains. Excavations of a fort destroyed in 1017. Castle and town walls. *Ząbkowice Śląskie* has an old church. The bell tower leans 1.5 m off the perpendicular.

Kłodzko in a geographic basin. A mighty fortress as early as the 10th cent. The present town dates from the 17th cent. Renaissance town hall. The stone bridge (1390), adorned with statues, resembles the Charles Bridge in Prague. Beautiful Baroque buildings on the square.

Polanica Zdrój. Modern spa. *Duszniki Zdrój.* Spa. Theatre where Chopin gave a concert in 1826 when he was 16 years old. Annual Chopin festival in August. Paper mill with machinery from 1605, now a museum. *Kudowa Zdrój.* Large spa. Excursions to the beautiful Stolowe Mountains.

The Polish Gate (Polskie Wrota, 670 m) with ruins of 11th- cent. Homole Castle. A very beautiful mountain road goes through *Bystrzyce Mountains* to Spalona and *Bystrzyca Kłodsko.*

Kudowa Zdrój. Large spa. Excursions to Stolowe Mountains. Fantastic rock labyrinth at Szczeliniec Wielki.

E 12 continues to Praha – Nürnberg – Metz – Paris.

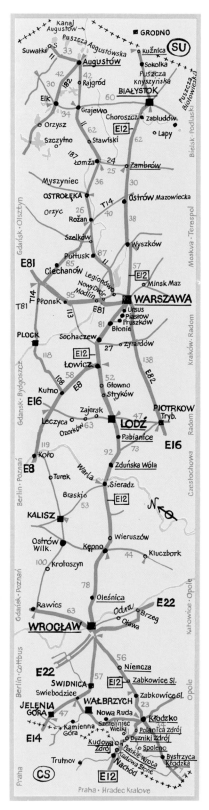

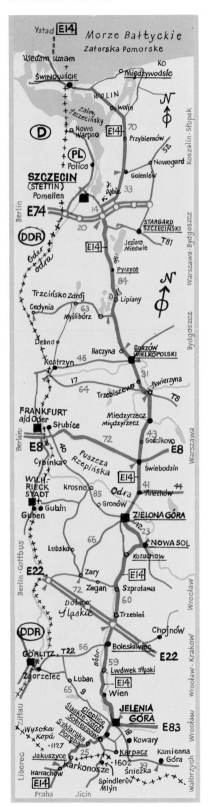

E 14. Szczecin – Jelenia Góra

E 14 comes from Malmö – Ystad. Ferry to Swinoujscie twice daily (6 hours).

Świnoujście (22 000). Fishing port. *Międzywodzie.* Seaside resort at the foot of the wooded hills of the Wolin National Park.

SZCZECIN (Stettin, 400 000). Poland's major Baltic port. Shipyards. Provincial capital and financial and cultural centre of western Pomerania. The *Old Town* was completed destroyed during the Second World War but has been rebuilt. Beautiful churches and a 13th-cent. town hall. Renaissance palace that once belonged to the Duke of Pomerania. Museum. Beautiful surroundings–forests and lakes. Miedwie, 13 km long and 2 km wide, is one of the largest lakes of the area.

Stargard Szczeciński (40 000). Beautiful churches, town hall and impressive town wall with town gates.

Pyrzyce. Centre of a fertile agricultural area. Most of the town was destroyed in the war, but the fortification wall with towers and gates survived.

Gorzów Wielkopolski (70 000). Textile industry. Gothic cathedral. Museum.

Zielona Góra (100 000). Provincial capital. Many 15th- and 18-cent. buildings. Museum with a section dealing with wine. Vineyard-covered slope with a pleasant café in a green-house. Wine festival in October.

Nowa Sol. Industrial town and river port.

Kózuchow with medieval fortification walls. Castle. *Szprotawa* with fortifications.

Bolesławiec (30 000). Old town, now site of copper mining and chemical industries. Remains of fortifications. Kutuzov Museum in memory of the Russian Field Marshal who died here in 1813 during the Napoleonic Wars.

Lwówek Śląski. Beautiful old town with remains of medieval fortification walls. Renaissance and Baroque houses.

JELENIA GÓRA (60 000). Old trading centre. Beautiful square. Baroque houses with arcades. Wojnowska Tower at St. Anne's Chapel. A relief map of the Karkonosze Mountains can be found on Wzgorze Hill (412 m).

Cieplice Śląskie Zdrój. Holiday resort and spa with warm springs. Museum of ornithology. Butterfly collection. *Sobieszów* with ruins of Chojnik Castle on a promontory. The house where Gerhard Hauptmann, the German writer, lived (and died, 1946) is in *Jagniatkow.* Museum of the National Park. *Piechowice* with glass works.

Szklarska Poręba (500-800 m above sea level). Winter sports resort. Glass works. *Swieradów Zdrój.* Large spa.

Karkonosze Mountains is the highest part of the Sudet Mountains. Highest peak: *Sniéžka,* 1602 m, on the Czech border. Chapel, observatory, hostels. *Karpacz,* holiday resort and winter sport centre. The stave church (wooden church from the 13th cent.) was brought here from Wang in Norway (see road E 68).

Jakuszyce. Czechoslovakian border.
E 14 continues to Praha – Salzburg – Villach – Trieste.

E 16. Gdańsk – Toruń – Łódź – Katowice – Cieszyn

The three cities of *Gdańsk, Gdynia* and *Sopot* along the Gdańsk Bay, together form an urban area with about half a million inhabitants. It is called Trójmiasto (Tri-City).

North of these cities is the *Hel Peninsula,* 35 km long and 300 m to 3 km wide. Many resorts. The fishing village of *Hel* (boat from Gdańsk) with fisheries museum in a Gothic church. *Puck,* once a naval base, now a fishing port with old houses. The *Amber Coast* (Krynica Morska) is a part of the Baltic coast where amber is often found. This was the starting point of the Amber Route which went south to Prague and Vienna. Several seaside resorts and fishing ports. Museum in the concentration camp *Stutthof* (Sztutowo).

GDYNIA (170 000). The city was built in 1924-39 on the site of an old fishing village. Now Poland's second largest port (Szczecin is larger). Shipyards. Naval base. Museum in the old battleship *Blyskwica.* Splendid views from the Kamienna Góra hills. Naval museum. Outside Lenin shipyards is a monument to the workers who were killed here in 1970.

Sopot (50 000). Seaside resort and spa with a broad sandy beach. Open-air theatre and summer festivals. Pier (512 m) with boats to Hel, Gdynia and Gdańsk. Orbis-Grand is worth a visit – it is an elegant old-fashioned hotel.

GDAŃSK, see town plans.

Łeba. One of the largest resorts on the Baltic coast. Large sand banks, wandering dunes. Remains of Hitler's V1 and V2 rockets which were fired against London.

Malbork (30 000). The enormous castle, (German name: Marienburg) was built in the 13th to 14th cent. by the Teutonic Knights who reigned over large parts of Poland. Złota Gate was part of a 13th-cent. church which was razed in 1945. Amber museum.

Elbląg and *Frombork,* see E 81.

Sztum. A 14th- to 15th-cent. castle, built by the Teutonic Knights, on an isthmus between the lakes.

The Kashubian Lake District, see E 83.

Pelplin with lovely Gothic cathedral. *Gniew.* Beautifully situated on a hill in the Vistula Valley. Teutonic Knight castle. Remains of fortification wall and beautiful old houses.

Kwidzyn. Splendid castle and beautiful Gothic cathedral.

Grudziadz (75 000). Churches, abbey buildings and museum.

Chełmno. Beautifully set. Fortification wall with 17 towers. Splendid town hall in the Renaissance style (16th cent.). Beautiful churches.

Piaseczo with beautiful church. *Świecie.* Ruins of a Teutonic Knight castle and fortification walls.

TORUŃ (150 000). University (founded 1945) named after Nicolaus Copernicus (1473-1543), who was born here. *Old Town Square* (Rynek Staromiejski) is the centre of one of Europe's finest medieval quarters. Gothic town hall, rebuilt in the Dutch Renaissance style. A memorial to Copernicus is to be found in front of the town hall.
Church of St. John (Sw. Jana) from the 13th to 14th cent., has beautiful Gothic frescoes. The Church of Our Lady (N.P. Marii). Gothic Church of St. James (Sw. Jakuba) on the New Square.
The town is known for its honey biscuits and its gingerbread, famous as early as the Middle Ages.

BYDGOSZCZ and WROCŁAW, see E 83.

Ciechocinek. Spa. *Włocławek* (70 000). Industrial town and port. Gothic *cathedral* with a sepulchral monument by Wit Stwocz. Museum of ethnography.

Łęczyca. Iron mines. Once one of Poland's oldest fortresses.

ŁÓDŹ (800 000). Poland's second largest city, which developed as a textile town in the 19th cent. Centre of science and culture. The main thoroughfare is the 5 km long Ulica Kosciuszko. Museum of archaeology and ethnography. Revolution museum. Art gallery. *Textile museum.* Monument at the former concentration camp of *Radogosszcz.*

Piotrków Trybunalski (60 000) was once an important town, where parliaments and synods met. Old Quarter with medieval houses, surrounded by walls. Renaissance *castle*, now museum, built in the 16th cent. (reconstructed). Many churches. Glass and textile industry.

CZĘSTOCHOWA (200 000). Pilgrimage place, especially in August, when believers flock to the *Jasna Góra* abbey and church. The famous *Black Madonna* is said to have averted a Swedish attack in 1655. It was taken out and carried in a procession through Warsaw during the disturbances in March 1981. When marshal laws were proclaimed in December 1981 the archbishop went to the Black Madonna. Museum and cemetery with 7th-cent. graves.

Siewierz. Ruins of the palace of the Krakow bishops. *Bedzin* with castle (museum) from the 14th cent. *Sosnowiec* (140 000). Industries and mines. Mining museum.

BYTOM (192 000). Mining town as early as the 12th cent. Coal mines since the 19th-cent? Silesian museum and opera house.

KATOWICE (320 000). Centre of Silesia. Large industries. Mines. Modern city centre and a new cathedral. Large "Palace of Youth". In the Park of Culture are a planetarium, an observatory, and a stadium seating 100 000. Water sports centre. Zoo.

Cieszyn is separated from the Czechoslovakian town of Český Těčín by the River Olza. Beautiful churches. Museum in Larischow Palace.

E 16 continues to Zilina and Bratislava.

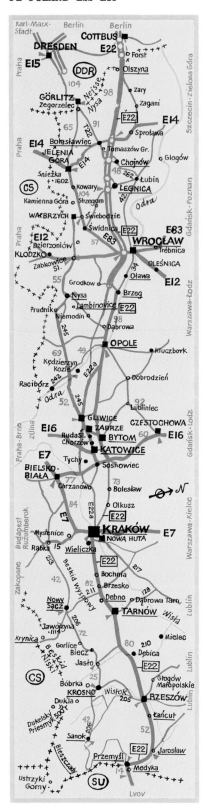

E 22. Berlin – Wrocław – Kraków – Przemysl – Lvov.

Olszyna. East German (DDR) frontier. E 22 comes from Berlin – Cottbus. The road from Dresden joins E 22 at Zgorzelec. *Bolesławiec,* see E 14.

Chojnów. 15th-cent. Gothic church. Castle museum. Remains of a 14th-cent. town wall with Weavers' Tower.

LEGNICA (76 000). From 1248 until 1675 this was the capital of a principality ruled by the Piast dynasty. Their castle, with origins in the 13th cent., was destroyed by fire in 1945. Partially restored. Splendid town gates. Town hall and the *Church of Saints Peter and Paul* on the square. Mausoleum of the Piast dynasty in the *Church of St. John.* Copper works and museum devoted to copper mining. *Legnickie Pole,* where the Tartars were repelled in 1241. Museum. Benedictine abbey with splendid Baroque abbey church (1731), designed by I. Dientzenhofer.

Through one of the most fertile areas of Poland to *WROCŁAW,* see E 12.

Oława. Princes' palace with origins in the 14th cent. *Brzeg.* Renaissance castle (1570), now a museum. Castle chapel (1371). Lovely square lined with several lovely Baroque and Renaissance buildings and the town hall. Road south to *Nysa* (30 000), historic old town. St. James Cathedral, (1430). Many beautiful buildings, most of them are reconstructions after 80 per cent war destruction.

OPOLE (87 000). Recognized town as early as the 8th cent. Handsome Baroque buildings line the square. The tower of the town hall is a copy of the tower of the Palazzo Vecchio in Florence. 16th-cent. *Cathedral of the Holy Cross. Archaeological excavations* of a Slav settlement. Piast Tower (14th cent.), all that remains of a castle that the Germans dynamited in 1941. Folklore museum. Annual June festival.

Łambinowice, site of a World War II prison camp where 100 000 died. *Gora Sw. Anny.* Monument dedicated to the Polish uprising of 1921. The amphitheatre seats 70 000 spectators.

Upper Silesia is a vast industrial area pocked with coal mines. *BYTOM* and *KATOWICE,* see E 16. *Oswięcim,* see E 7.

KRAKÓW and *WIELICZKA,* see town plans.

Dębno is famed for its ceramic ware.

TARNÓW (90 000). 15th- to 16th-cent. town hall and cathedral. Ecclesiastical museum. Remains of the original town wall.

Road south to the magnificent *Beskidy Mountains* and *Nowy Sącz* (40 000), site of a folklore museum with impressive examples of the works of Nikofor, a primitivist. Raft excursions on the River Dunajac go through a national park. *Krynica.* Large spa and winter sports resort. Zuber mineral water. Cable cars to Góra Parkowa, 714 m.

Road from Nowy Sasz east to *Biecz,* an old town with lovely buildings that date from the time when the town flourished (14th to 18th cent.). *Krosno* is the centre of the Carpathian oil district. Open-air museum devoted to oil drilling in *Bobrka.* The Castle in *Sanok* has the largest collection of ikons in Poland. Open-air museum in the *Olchowce Forest.*

Bieszcady, a sparsely-populated and very beautiful mountain area. The circular Bieszczady route from Sanok is 130 km.

RZESZÓW (82 000). The Baroque abbey (1642) houses an interesting museum (folklore, woodcarving, ceramics, archaeology, art). Restored synagogues. *Łańcut.* Enormous Baroque palace that once belonged to the Patocki dynasty. Museum. 300 rooms. Splendid park. Orangery. Museum with over 50 horse-drawn vehicles.

Jaroslaw. Town named after its founder, the 11th-cent. Prince of Kiev. Several historically important buildings in the centre of the town. The many-storeyed cellars are open for inspection.

Przemyśl (50 000). One of Poland's most venerable towns. In 1873 the Austrians constructed a mighty fortress here. Lovely views from the castle hill.

Medyka. Soviet frontier station (open 7.00 a.m. - 9.00 p.m.).

E 22 continues to Lvov.

E 81. Gdynia – Warszawa – Lvov

Gdynia, see E 16. *GDAŃSK,* see town plans.

Elbląg (85 000). Industrial town, once important port and naval base. Splendid church and 14th- to 15th-cent. Targowa Gate. Museum of modern art in the ruined Dominican church. The old town centre was destroyed during the Second World War. Folklore museum and House of Culture.

Frombork (30 km), where Nicolaus Frombork (Copernicus), the astronomer, worked from 1510 until his death in 1543. The tower where he worked (Wiege Kopernika) is still standing. View of the Baltic Sea. *Museum.* Splendid 14th-cent. Gothic *cathedral* surrounded by medieval ramparts. The tomb of Copernicus, in the church, was destroyed in the 17th cent. *Malbork,* see E 16.

Pasłęk. The town was founded in the 13th cent. by Dutch immigrants. Medieval town wall and a few old houses remain.

Ostróda. Tourist resort. Water sports centre in a network of rivers, lakes and canals. Steam boat to Elblag (10 hours), where the boat is dragged across the isthmus between the lakes.

Olsztynek. Remains of 14th-cent. town wall. *Open-air museum* with beautiful old wooden houses.

Olsztyn (75 000). Centre of Masuria and Warmia. *Wysoka Brama* is a gate in the old fortification wall. The old part of the town has been rebuilt since the war. Baroque town hall. 15th-cent. Gothic cathedral. 14th- cent. castle with *Masurian Museum.*

The Masurian Lakes, east of Olsztyn – forests, lakes and rivers, joined by canals. Many interesting little towns: *Swieta Lipka* with splendid Baroque church and Jesuit monastery. *Lidzbark Warminski* with splendid Gothic *castle* (14th cent.), which used to belong to the Bishops of Warmia. Fine courtyard with arcades. *Gizycko.* Water sports centre. Near by is *Mamry,* the second largest lake in Poland. Passenger boat services. *Gierloz* (German name: Rastenburg) with remains of Hitler's headquarters, his "Wolf's Lair". In 1944 Colonel von Stauffenberg tried to kill him, but the attempt failed and the conspirators were executed. *Ruciane* and *Mikolajki.* Large tourist resorts.

Grunwald, where Polish King Wladyslaw Jagiello defeated the Teutonic Knights in 1410. A modern monument with high pillars has been erected after the Second World War, and a new museum has been built. An inscription in the museum reads: Grunwald 1410 Berlin 1945. The battle outside the nearby village of Stebark is not mentioned. This was where the Germans under Hindenburg defeated the Russians in 1914. The German name of the place is Tannenberg. Hindenburg was buried here in 1934 but his sepulchral monument was destroyed during the Second World War.

Nidzica. Teutonic Knight castle, now House of Culture with hotel and café.

Modlin. *The Fortress,* built on the order of Napoleon, withstood a long siege in September 1939.

Palmiry. Churchyard with monument to 2 000 victims of the Nazis.

Puszcza Kampinoska (Kampinos Forest). National park. Forest, bogs and 30 m high sand dunes and marshes. 150 miles of marked paths.

WARSZAWA (Warsaw), see town plans.

Czersk, 13th-cent. castle ruins.

Puławy. Agricultural college. Beautiful 18th-cent. château with park.

Kazimierz Dolny. Beautiful little town with Renaissance houses. Splendid views from the ruined castle, built in the 14th cent. for Casimir the Great. Another ruined castle on the opposite bank of the Vistula, in *Janowiec.*

Nalezców. Tourist resort and spa. Beautiful park with 18th-cent. palace, museum devoted to Boleslaw Prus, the author.

LUBLIN (300 000). Seat of the Voivod. Old centre of science and culture. Beautiful *Old Town* in the centre. Renaissance houses on the square. Krakow Gate (16th cent.) at Krakowskie Przedmiescie, the main thoroughfare. Grodska Gate at the splendid 14th-cent. palace, rebuilt in the 19th cent. Museum and beautiful chapel with frescoes. *Radziwill Palace* now belongs to the university, named after Marie Curie-Sklodowska. There is also a Catholic university. Obelisk in memory of the Union of Lublin in 1569 between Poland and Lithuania. *Majdanek,* a former concentration camp, now a museum, is 4 km from the centre of Lublin. Half a million people perished here. About 300 000 were executed in the forest at *Kasimierzówka,* where a monument has been erected.

Road to *Sandomierz,* one of the oldest towns in Poland. Many fine buildings. Castle. *Cathedral* (1382) with Baroque facade and Bysantine frescoes. Diocesan museum. Romanesque church of St. James with fine portal. Glass factory. **Tarnobreg.** Chemical industri enormns sulphur deposits. **Chelm.** Old town with museums and churches.

Zamość (30 000) has retained its Renaissance atmosphere. The city was built in the 16th cent. to the plans of Morando, an Italian architect.

Tomaszów Lubelski with Baroque church built of larch wood.

No frontier crossing on the E 81. Traffic continues via Jaroslaw.

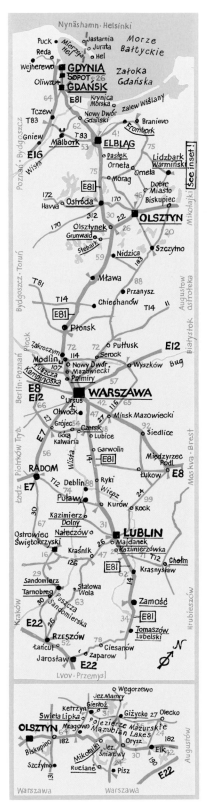

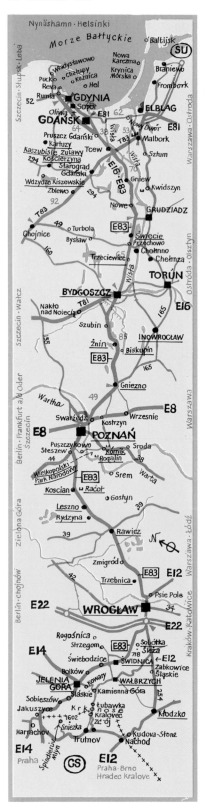

E 83. Gdynia – Jelenia Góra

Gdynia – Świecie together with E 16.

The Kashubian Lake District (Pojezierze Kaszubskie) is a very beautiful area around **Kościerzyna**. Hills, forest and lakes. Its interesting folk art can be studied in the museum and inn in **Kartuzy** and in the open-air museum in **Wdzydze Kiszewskie**.

Świecie. Ruins of a Teutonic Knight castle (14th cent.) and remains of fortifications. **Trzeciewiec** with Poland's tallest TV mast (317 m).

BYDGOSZCZ (250 000). Trading and industrial town. River port. The 15th- to 16th-cent. parish church is the city's oldest structure. *Old Square* (Stary Rynek), where the Germans executed civilians on "bloody Sunday" in 1939. Museum of archaeology and art.

Żnin. Beautiful 15th-cent. houses. *Gasawa* with 17th-cent. wooden church.

Biskupin. A 2 000-year-old Slav settlement, partially reconstructed. Museum. Finds also in the archaeological museum in Poznań.

INOWROCŁAW (50 000), industrial town and spa (saline springs).

Gniezno (50 000). According to legend this town became Poland's first capital when the chieftain Lech found a white eagle here – it is now part of Poland's coat of arms. Splendid *cathedral* (14th-15th cent.) with chapel, rebuilt after wartime destruction. 12th-cent. bronze door with pictures from the life of St. Adalbert. His silver sarcophagus (15th cent.). Wit Stwosz has created a marble sepulchral monument over the grave of a 15th-cent. cardinal. Museum of archaeology.

POZNAŃ, see E 8.

Wielkopolskie National Park. Beautiful hilly woodlands. *Kórnik*. Castle. Art and handicraft museum. *Rogalin*. Raczyński Palace (1782). Art museum. Fine park with the largest oaks in Europe (800 years).

Kościan with beautiful Gothic church. *Racot*. Palace, park, horse stud farm.

Leszno (30 000). Cultural centre since the 16th cent. A refuge for Protestants from Bohemia. The city bears the stamp of the Italian Baroque. Splendid town hall.

Rydzyna. Square with Baroque buildings. Town hall from 1752. *Pałac Leszczyński*, one of Poland's finest Baroque structures, destroyed in 1945 but reconstructed. Large park.

Rawicz. Baroque town hall in the market square. Promenades on former fortifications. Barycz River Valley, bird sanctuary.

Trzebnica. Small town. Large Romanesque-Gothic basilica (13th cent.). Former *abbey* of the Cistercian nuns. St. Hedwig's sarcophagus, adorned with Polish eagles. Fine views from Mount Farna.

WROCŁAW, see E 12.

Sobótka, at the foot of **Ślęża**, a beautiful mountain (718 m), with small church and splendid views. Folklore festival the last ten days in June. Archaeological excavations at an old cult place.

ŚWIDNICA (50 000). One of the oldest towns in Poland, capital of the Silesian Piast dukes. Fine market square. Gothic church with 103 m high tower.

Kłodzko, mentioned as a fortress as early as the 10th cent. The stone bridge across the River *Nysa* was built in 1390. Beautiful Renaissance houses.

Wałbrzych (125 000). Coal mines, gas, chemical industries. Valley with porphyry rocks, surrounded by the *Wałbrzyskie Mountains*.

Jelenia Góra, see E 14.

TOWN PLANS

GDAŃSK (400 000)

Formerly called Danzig, situated on one of the arms of the estuary of the River Vistula. Large port and industrial town. Important shipyards. Gdańsk is devided in three parts: The Old Town (Stare Miasto), the Main Town (Glowne Miasto) and the Old Suburb (Stare Przedmiescie). The **Old Town** (Glowne Miasto) with town walls and the beautiful and impressive **Long Market** (Dlugi Targ). All of the beautiful buildings have been reconstructed after being razed to the ground in 1945. Zielona Brama, a Renaissance palace. The Golden House (Zlota Kamienica), number 14, has a beautifully ornamented Renaissance façade. *Neptune Fountain* (17th cent.). Several town gates. Archaeological museum and Stutthof Museum at the Mariacka Gate. Near by is the medieval harbour crane building, *Stary Zuraw* (14th cent.) destroyed in 1945, but reconstructed. Maritime museum.

The **Church of the Virgin Mary** is one of the largest churches in Europe (105 m long, 66 m wide, height of the tower: 78 m). Originally built 1343-1502, but severely damaged in 1945. Beautiful Madonna. Royal Chapel (1681), built for John III Sobieski. Church of the Holy Trinity (Sw. Trojcy) in the Old Suburb (Stare Przedmiescie). **National Museum** with sculpture, handicrafts and paintings, among them "The Last Judgement" by the Flemish master Memling.

Westerplatte, where the Second World War started September 1, 1939, with a German attack on the 182-man-strong Polish garrison. They fought for 7 days. Ruins of barracks. Graves. Exhibition. Enormous monument. Large Lenin shipyards. Monument to the 28 who were killed in the disturbances of 1970: Three crosses with an anchor.

KRAKÓW, (670 000)

According to a legend the city was founded by Prince Krak in the 9th cent. Capital of Poland until 1596, when Sigismund moved to Warsaw. Ravaged by Tartars in the 13th cent. and by Swedes in the 17th cent., the city suffered little destruction during both World Wars. The **Old Town** is surrounded by a green belt, laid out on the site of the old ramparts and moats. A few fortification towers remain. *Brama Florianska* city gate and the Barbakan fortification tower.

Rynek Glowny, the main square, is the centre of the city and retains its 14th-cent. atmosphere. In the middle of the square is the 120 m long Cloth Hall, **Sukiennice** (14th cent.). Souvenir shops on the ground floor. Exhibits of Polish art, a section of the National Gallery, on the first floor.

Church of the Virgin Mary (13th cent.), with two spires. Every hour on

Gdańsk, view of the Old Town

1 Long Market.
2 Town Hall in the Main Town.
3 Church of the Virgin Mary
4 Zielona (Green) Gate.
5 Mariacka (St. Mary's Gate).
6 Stary Zuraw. Maritime museum.
7 Great Mill.
8 Town Hall in the Old Town.
9 Armoury.
10 Zlota (Golden) Gate. Prison Tower.
11 Wyżynna (Upland) Gate.
12 Pomeranian Museum.

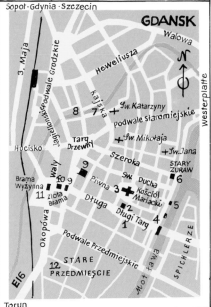

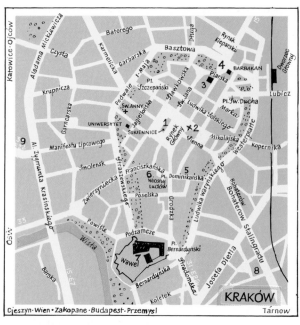

1 Sukiennice (Cloth Hall). 2 Church of the Virgin Mary (Mariacki). 3 Czartoryski Museum. 4 Floriańska Gate. 5 Dominican Church and Monastery. 6 Franciscan Church and Monastery. 7 Wavel. Castle and Cathedral. 8 Old Synagogue. 9 Art Gallery. Photo: Kraków. The main square with Sukiennice, the Cloth Hall

the hour a bugle call is heard from the highest of the spires (81 m). The bugle call ends on a sudden high note – in memory of the original trumpeter who, according to legend, had his throat pierced by a Tartar arrow.

The Gothic *polyptych* (13 m high, 11 m wide) was carved by Wit Stwosz (15th cent.). There is also a stone crucifix by Wit Stwosz. Stained-glass window (19th cent.) by Jan Matejko. One of the many lovely houses on the square is *Wierzynek,* a wine tavern and coffee house, which has been here since the Middle Ages. A painting shows kings who have visited the tavern.

Czartoryski Museum with works by Leonardo da Vinci and Rembrandt. The Jagiellonian University was founded in 1364. Its old main building, *Collegium Maius,* is now a museum. Its exhibits include the famous Jagiellonian Globe (c. 1510), the first globe on which the American continent was shown. It is the work of Nicolaus Copernicus (1473-1543) who studied here.

Several other fine museums, among them an ethnographical museum. Splendid churches.

Wavel Castle, on a limestone cliff high above the Vistula, is surrounded by beautiful buildings. The arcaded *courtyard* is one of the most splendid of its kind in Europe. Museum with tapestries, weapons, the crown jewels and a collection of Oriental art.

Wavel Cathedral (14th cent.) was the Polish coronation church. The main part of the structure is in the Gothic style. 18 chapels in the Baroque and Renaissance styles. Sigismund Cha-

pel, Zygmuntowska, Holy Cross Chapel. In the centre of the cathedral stands the silver casket of St. Stanislaus, Poland's patron saint. Treasury. Tombs of kings and national heroes. The Zygmunt Bell (1520), in the bell tower, weighs 8 tons. Impressive collection of Renaissance tapestries, specially made in Belgium for King Sigismund. Below the wall is the entrance to the Dragon's den, part of a local legend about Krak. Statue of the dragon spitting fire.

Kasimierz (the southern part of the town). Old Jewish quarter with interesting buildings. The *synagogue,* Poland's oldest, was destroyed by the Germans, but has been reconstructed and is now a museum.

Nowa Huta (130000 inhabitants) is Krakow's new industrial area. Steel works. On Midsummer Eve the River Vistula is decorated with floating flower garlands. Juvenalia, a student festival, in the middle of May. *Wieliczka* with 1 000-year-old salt mines. 13 km long tunnels. 3 km of them open to visitors. 55 m long, 12 m high hall, used as a church, with salt reliefs and chandeliers made of rockcrystal. Chapel with saints' figures. Mining museum and tennis court 135 m below the earth's surface. The 42 m high Staszik Hall housed a German aeroplane factory during the Second World War.

WARSZAWA (Warsaw, 1.4 million)
The Polish capital was built on the site where the trading caravans from Rome and Greece crossed the Weichsel/Vistula on their way to the Baltic coast. The legend tells of a mer-

maid who ordered Wars and Zawa, two fishermen, to found a city. Sigismund Vasa moved the capital from Krakow to Warsaw in 1596. By the end of the Second World War, 85% of the buildings had been razed to the ground and 800000 of the city's 1.3 million inhabitants were dead. But Warsaw rose again.

The *Old Town* (Stare Miasto) was almost totally destroyed in 1944 but has been painstakingly reconstructed. The houses dated from the 17th-18th cent. and the fortification walls from the 14th-16th cent. *Barbaken,* a fortification tower and town gate. *Old Town Square* (Rynek Starego Miasta) is lined with beautiful Renaissance and Baroque houses. The *Historical Museum* gives fascinating glimpses of the city's history and its reconstruction. Many cafés and restaurants: Fukier's 300-year-old wine tavern, Pod Krokodylem, a restaurant with dancing, and Kamienne Schodki (the Stone Stairs) where duck with apples is served.

The *New Town* (Nowe Miasto) was built in the 15th cent. The Church of the *Holy Sacrament* (17th cent.), built in memory of the victory over the Turks, is on *New Town Square* (Rynek Nowego Miasta).

The typical Vasa-style *Royal Castle* was destroyed during the Second World War. As late as 1971 it was still in ruins, but now it has been reconstructed. In front of the castle is the Sigismund Column, erected 1644, destroyed 1944, reconstructed in 1949. (King Sigismund Vasa made Warsaw his capital in 1596.)

Krakowskie Przedmiescie is the first

1 Royal Castle and Column of King Sigismund III Vasa.
2 St. John's Cathedral (Sw. Jana)
3 St. Martin's Church (Sw. Marcina)
4 Old Town Square. Warsaw Historical Museum.
5 Barbakan (Barbican)
6 The Maria Skladowska-Curie Museum.
7 Monument to the Heroes of the Ghetto
8 Pawiak Prison. Museum
9 Grand Opera and Ballet Theatre. Theatre Museum
10 Tomb of the Unknown Soldier
11 Palace of Culture. Museum of Technology
12 Railway Museum
13 Church of St. Anne and Carmelite Church
14 Church of the Holy Cross (Sw. Krzyża)
15 Mermaid Statue
16 National Museum and Polish Army Museum
17 The White Cottage
18 Łazienkowski Palace (The Palace on the Water)
19 Różycki Market

of the three streets which make up the "Royal Route", a 4 km long road leading south. This is one of Warsaw's most beautiful streets, lined with palaces and churches. St. Anne Church, originally from the 15th cent., but with an 18th-cent. façade. Carmelite church (Kar Kosciol) with a beautiful altar, escaped wartime destruction. Near by, the Radziwill Palace and the Potocki Palace (both from the 18th cent.), where Napoleon once danced with Marie Walewska. Now used as government buildings. A monument to Copernicus, by the Danish sculptor Thorvaldsen (1830), stands in front of the Staszic Palace. Frédéric Chopin's heart is immured in a pillar in the Holy Cross Church (Św. Krzyża). His body is buried in the Père Lachaise Cemetery in Paris. The street now changes name to Nowy Swiat (the New World). Beautiful, uniform, early 19th-cent. houses. Ostrogski Palace with the Chopin Institute and museum. Ul. Tamka leads down to the Vistula and a lovely view of the statue of the militant mermaid, the symbol of Warsaw.
The National Museum with paintings, graphics and coins. Ceramics by

Picasso. Museum of the Polish Army in one of the museum wings. Lazienki Park with the famous Chopin Monument, rebuilt in 1958. Open-air piano concerts throughout the summer. The Lazienki Palace, the Palace on Water, was the residence of the last Polish king, Stanislaw August Poniatowski (18th cent.). Neo-classical building with beautiful interiors. Reconstructed after wartime destruction. The Theatre on the Island, also in the park, is an open-air theatre. The White House (Bialy Domek), where Louis XVIII lived in exile. Beautiful orangery with a fine 18th-cent. theatre. The Royal Route ends at the Belvedere Palace (1820), the presidential palace. Warsaw's great shopping street and major thoroughfare is Marszalkowska, with the department stores of Wars and Zawa and the 30-storey Forum Hotel. This is the site of the new shopping district and the wedding-cake-like Palace of Culture and Science, a gift from the Soviet Union. The structure is 234 m tall and has 3 288 rooms. Academy of science, exhibition halls, cinemas, theatres, conference halls and museum of technology.

Tomb of the Unknown Soldier with changing of the guard every hour on the hour. The arcade remains from the former General Staff Headquarters. The Victoria, a luxury hotel, is on the square. Ghetto Monument on the site of the former Jewish Ghetto. Fighting started here in 1943 and led to the final destruction of the ghetto in 1944. The shape of the monument brings to mind the Wailing Wall in Jerusalem. This was where German Chancellor Willy Brandt knelt on the first official German state visit after the war. Some prison cells and death cells have been preserved in the Pawiak prison.
Warsaw has more than 20 theatres and 26 museums, among them the Maria Sklodowska-Curie Museum. The stadium seats 100 000 spectators. A new, modern, central stadium has been built.
The Wilanow Palace and Park is situated 7 km from the centre of Warsaw. The palace was built in the 17th cent. as a summer residence for Jan Sobieski (who defeated the Turks at Vienna). Polish Portrait Gallery. Poster Museum in the park (one of the first of its kind in Europe).

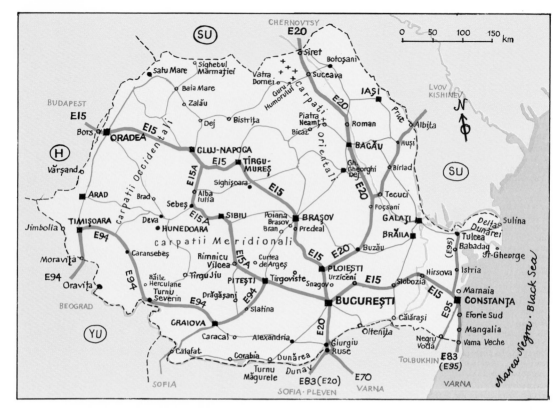

R · Roumania

R· România

Area: 237 500 km² (91 700 sq. miles)

Population: 22 million. The majority of the population (80 %) are Greek Orthodox, but there are Roman Catholic (16 %), Calvinist (5 %), Lutheran (2 %) and other minorities. The national language is Roumanian. There are Hungarian, German, Ukranian, Gypsy, Yugoslav and Russian minorities.

Major cities: Bucureşti (Bucharest) 2.0 million, Braşov 300 000, Timişoara 290 000, Constanţa 290 000, Cluj-Napoca 275, Isaşi 260 000.

Government: Socialist republic, 39 judetje (counties) and the capital.

History
106-271 Dacia is a Roman province.

4th-7th cent. Period of the great migrations. The area is consecutively invaded by Goths, Huns, Slavs, Longobards, Avars and Bulgarians.

13th cent. Establishment of the kingdoms of Moldavia and Wallachia.

1460-1513 Moldavia and Wallachia become vassal states of the Ottoman (Turkish) Empire. The following centuries are marked by armed resistance against the Turks.

1856 Peace after the Crimean War. Wallachia and Moldavia become sovereign states but formally recognize Turkish supremacy.

1877 The independent state of Romania is proclaimed. Roumanian and Russian armies defeat the Turks.

1881 Romania becomes a kingdom with Carol I as head of state.

1913 Romania gains South Dobruja from Bulgaria after the Second Balkan War.

1916 War against Austria-Hungary and Germany. As late as May 1918, the Germans are strong enough to force Romania to accept harsh terms.

1919 After the First World War, Transylvania, Bukovina, Banat and Bessarabia are ceded to Romania.

1930 King Carol II is reinstated with the help of the Agrarian Party.

1938 Royal dictatorship. The fascist "Iron Guard" gains considerable influence.

1940 King Carol II is deposed, his son Michael becomes king. General Antonescu becomes dictator. Romania supports the Axis in the Second World War.

1944 Romania forms an alliance with the Allies. Bessarabia is lost to the Soviet Union and South Dobruja is returned to Bulgaria.

1947 King Michael abdicates. Romania is proclaimed a people's republic.

1965 Nicolae Ceauşescu becomes first leader of the Communist party, then president. Particularly within the sphere of foreign policy, Romania has shown considerable independence compared with other Warsaw Pact nations.

Routes described:

E 15 Oradea – Cluj – Braşov – Bucureşti – Constanţa

E 15 A Cluj – Sibiu – Piteşti – Bucureşti

E 20 Cernovcy – Bacău – Bucureşti – Giorgiu

E 94 Beograd – Timişoara – Piteşti – Bucureşti

E 95 Tulcea – Constanţa – Varna

Town plan: Bucureşti

Currency: Leu (plural Lei)
1 leu = 100 bani
It is forbidden to import or export Romanian currency. Visitors to Romania are required to exchange a certain amount of currency, the amount varying according to age, length of stay and if pre-paid vouchers have been purchased with western currency outside the country. For complete information please contact your local travel agency or the Romanian Tourist Office.

Business hours: Banks 8 a.m.-3.00 p.m., Saturdays 8.00 a.m-12 noon. In the major tourist centres, Bucharest, Constanţa, Mamaia and Poiana Braşov, currency exchange offices have extended opening hours. Post offices, Monday-Saturday 7.00 a.m.-8.00 p.m. Shops Monday-Saturday 8.00 a.m.-7/8.00 p.m. Lunchtime closings are not unusual. Some foodshops and department stores are also open on Sunday morning.

Holidays: January 1-2, May 1-2, August 23-24 (National Holiday), 30 December (Republic Day). Religious holy days are celebrated but are not official holidays.

Hotels
Hotels are placed in one of three categories: Deluxe, 1st and 2nd class. Complete listings are compiled by Carpati, the official state-owned tourist organization.

Camping
About 100 camping sites, some of which include chalets sleeping 2-4.

Food and drink
A few specialities: Mititei, spiced sausage served with bread. Mititei, charcoal-broiled, coarsely minced beef. Sarmale, mince and rice wrapped in cabbage or vine leaves and served with sour cream. Musaca, mince and vegetable pie. Ciorba de pui, chicken soup. Ciorba de burta, delicious soup based on offal. Ciorba de legume, vegetable soup, often accompanied by sour cream. Mamaliga, a maize porridge, similar to the Italian polenta, is served instead of potatoes. A popular dessert is papansi, hot cheese pancakes topped with cream.
Several exceptionally good domestic wines: Aligoté, Feteasca and Tîrnave (white), Pinot Negra and Nicoresti Băbeasca (red), and Cotnari and Murfatlar (dessert wines). The Romanian version of plum brandy is known as Tuica.
After the grape harvest in the autumn, small outdoor restaurants are erected. Fresh grape juice is served with spiced sausages, salt, charcoal-broiled goat and mutton and the popular mamaliga (maize porridge).

Shopping
Gramophone records with traditional folk music, rugs, hand- embroidered blouses and jackets, pottery and wood carvings. Tourists are entitled to a 20% discount in Comtourist shops when they pay in western currency.

Petrol
Distances between petrol stations

Bicaz in the eastern Carpathians

(PECO) are about 50 km on the main roads. They are usually open 6.00-a.m.-10.00 p.m. Petrol must be paid for with coupons, bought in a tourist office or from ACR (the motoring club) with western currency.

Speed limits. Traffic regulations
Maximum speed on country roads for private cars (including those with trailers or caravans in tow) with a maximum cylinder volume of 1 100 cc. 70 kmh, 1 101 cc-1 800 cc 80 kmh, over 1 800 cc. 90 kmh. Built-up areas 50 kmh. Motorcycles 40 kmh.
If your car is fitted with seat belts it is compulsory to wear them. Children under 12 are not allowed to travel in the front seat.
In built-up-areas horns must not be used between 10.00 p.m. and 6.00 a.m. It is illegal to drive a dirty or badly corroded car. Do not move your vehicle after an accident until the police (militia) arrives. Police should also be summoned when an accident has caused only vehicle damage. Garages can refuse repairs if there is no police

report and there will be problems at the frontier when leaving the country.

Roads
Many roads lead through villages where it is advisable to be extremely cautious and drive slower than the speed-limit. Most major roads are good, but secondary roads can be bad and traffic can be held up by horse- and ox-drawn carts.

Road patrols
ACR operate patrol cars on all of the major roads from June 1 until September 15, between 9 a.m. and 9 p.m.

ACR, Automobil Clubul Român, 27, rue Beloianis, Bucharest. Tel. 59 50 80. Branches in all major cities and tourist resorts.
CARPATI, the National Tourist Office, 7, Boulevard Magheru, Bucharest, Tel. 14 51 60
Roumanian National Tourist Office, 77–81 Gloucester Place, London WIH 3PG. Tel. 01-935 8590.

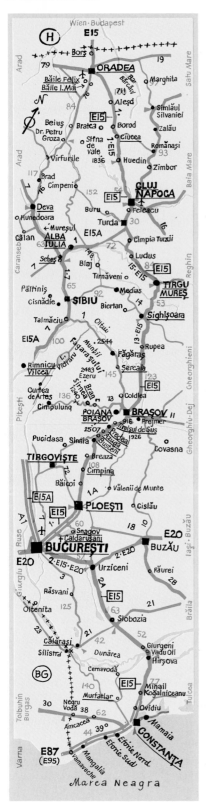

E15. Oradea – Cluj – Braşov – Bucureşti – Constanţa

Bors. Hungarian frontier. E15 comes from Hamburg – Berlin – Praha – Bratislava – Budapest.

ORADEA (150 000). Industrial city. Star-shaped citadel. *Baroque palace* (1779), the largest in the country. 365 windows, one for each day of the year. Orthodox church with the "Moon Clock" which also shows the phases of the moon. Museums and large zoo.

Baile Felix and **Baile 1 Mai,** spas with radioactive springs, well-known even in Roman times. *Padurea Neagrâ,* known for its glass blowers. The road goes through the western Carpathians. Castle at *Ciucea.* Wooden church from 1575 with icons on glass. Many towns famous for handicrafts.

CLUJ-NAPOCA (275 000, at 345 m above sea level), beautifully situated on terraces. Important city in the Dacian kingdom. Chief town of Transylvania. The earlier name of the town was Klausenburg. Attractive Baroque houses in the old quarter. The Transylvanian *Ethnographical Museum* in the large 19th-cent. "Reduta" (Redoubt), an Empire-style building. Museum of art in the Baroque *Banffy Palace.* Pharmaceutical museum in a *pharmacy* from 1573. Large botanical garden. Open-air museum in *Hoia Forest.*

North of Cluj is **BAIA MARE** (70 000), a modern town with remarkably mild climate and lush vegetation. Ruins of old fortress walls. Wooden church , typical of the region. Baia Mare is the chief town of Maramures, a beautiful area off the beaten tourist track. Unique wooden architecture in the village churches, e.g. Plopiş, Dragomireşti and Surdeşti (with a slender, 54 m high belfry).

ARAD (145 000). Palace of Culture in the Renaissance style. Cathedral from 1698. Serbian-Orthodox Church (17th cent.). From Cluj to Bucharest, you can also take route E15 A via Sibiu – Piteşti.

TIRGU MUREŞ (150 000). University. Beautiful Piaţa Trandafirilor (Square of the Roses), Apollo Palace (1820), Palace of Culture (1913). Several churches and museums.

Sighişoara (30 000, 412 m). Attractively situated. Beautiful buildings and charming atmosphere. Medieval alleys round the 12th-cent. castle distinguished by its turrets and towers. *Clock tower* (14th cent.) with historical museum (the House with the Deer). The house where Prince Vlad Dracula "Tepeş" was born in 1431. He was a Wallachian patriot, but also a cruel lord (even a little more than was usual in those days). He enjoyed impaling people on stakes, hence the name Tepeş (the Stake). He inspired the Irish novelist Bram Stoker to write his books about the vampire, Count Dracula.

Road to the village of **Sercaia** in *Narcissus Valley.* Mountain slopes and meadows are covered with narcissi in bloom at the end of May. Road on to the Fâgâraş Mountains, see E15 A.

BRAŞOV (200 000, 571 m). Winter sports centre. Many medieval streets and houses, e.g. the Schei Quarter. Here you feel as if you are in a German or Austrian town – the city was earlier known as Kronstadt. *Black Church* (Biserica Neagrâ), built 1384-1477. 15th-cent. wall paintings, and a large collection of Oriental carpets. Roumania's largest church bell. Organ with 4 000 pipes. The church has room for a congregation of 3 000. *Town hall* (13th-14th cent.), now museum of history and art. A merchant's house (1545) contains the Cerbul Carpatin restaurant. Fine view from Mount Timpa (950 m, cable car). Sports museum. Large industrial city (tractors and furniture).

Poiana Braşov (1 020 m). Winter sports resort with many hotels and restaurants. Ski lifts and artificial lake.

The road continues to **Bran Castle** (1378), one of Count Dracula's castles, now an open-air museum. Jules Verne has written about Bran. Here you are in the midst of the dramatic Carpathians, a vampire lair, according to legend. Garlic protects you from people who are actually vampires – but also repels those who are not.

Predeal, Azuga, Buşteni, Timişul de Sus, tourist resorts with beautiful views.

Sinaia (800 m), tourist resort. Famous mineral water. Cable car line (2 100 m long) to the tourist hotel at 1 400 m. *Peleş Museum,* formerly a royal palace. Mount *Caraiman,* with a cross at the summit erected to "protect the souls of mountain-climbers". East of the road stands a monument dedicated to one of the pioneers of aviation. Roumanians gained prominence at an early date in aviation.

Cimpina, large oil city.

PLOIEŞTI (170 000, 160 m). Centre of Roumanian petroleum industry. The country is one of Europe's largest oil producers. Old buildings, modern tower blocks and many oil rigs, a unique mixture by European standards. The Republic's Museum of Oil. Oilworkers' Day is celebrated on the first Sunday of October. *Palace of Culture* with a unique collection of clocks and watches. *Hagi Prodan,* a Roumanian 18th-cent. building. Most of the old houses were destroyed in bombing raids during the Second World War. The planes came from bases in Africa. War cemetery for American and British pilots who were shot down during the raids.

Snagov, lovely lake, camping site. According to tradition, Count Dracula's tomb is in the vicinity. It has been opened and found to be empty. Beautiful park on a peninsula in the lake.

BUCUREȘTI, see town plans.

The road runs across Roumania's largest plain, *Bărăgan*, a rather monotonous stretch of road. No particular places of interest here. To the south lies *Călărași* with large new steel works. **Vadu Oii Giurgeni**, formerly reached by car ferry, now accessible by way of a 1 500 m long bridge (1970).

CONSTANȚA and **Murfatlar,** see E 95.

E 15 A. Cluj – Sibiu – Pitești – București

CLUJ, see E 15.

Alba Iulia (30 000). Founded 25 B.C. Capital (1600) for a short time, of Moldavia, Wallachia and Transylvania. Transylvania's incorporation into Roumania was proclaimed here (1918). Ruins of a Roman town and encampment. 18th-cent. fortress.

Sebes. Road west to *Deva* (50 000), beautifully situated on the banks of the Mures. *Magna Curia Castle*, now a museum of history and natural science. Statue of Decebal, famous Dacian chieftain. Sarmisegetuza, with remains of the Roman capital of Dacia. Ruins of amphitheatre, town walls, Forum and palace.

SIBIU (130 000). Formerly called Hermannstadt. Old quarter with medieval buildings and atmosphere. 15th-cent. town hall. Medieval towers and city wall. **Brukenthal Museum**, one of Europe's oldest, in a Baroque palace (1785). Art and history. Hunting museum. Bishop's palace with icons on glass. Open-air museum. Zoo. Jazz festival in May.

Păltiniș with gorges and waterfall. **Șelimbăr** with a monument commemorating the victory of Michael the Brave (1599). Graves of 3 000 soldiers. *Cisnădie*, famous for its beautiful carpets and rugs. Fortress church. The road leads through the southern Carpathians. **Turnu Roșu Pass** (360 m), a narrow passage at the Olt River.

Călimanești-Căciulata, spa with mineral springs. The monastery of *Cozia* (1388).

Rimnicu Vilcea (40 000, 440 m). One of the oldest towns in Wallachia. Once the site of a salt mine. 16th-cent. bishop's palace, where Prince Constantin Brincoveanu started a printing office in the 17th cent. *Museum* with sections devoted to history, archaeology, art, etc. The road winds over the Negru Hills. Passability often hindered by landslides. You can also take the magnificent Alpine route from Sibiu to Pitești, which passes the *Vidraru* hydro-electric power station and artificial lake, and continues to **Curtea de Arges**, 14th-cent. capital of Wallachia. Beautiful 16th-cent. church with interestingly shaped tower.

PITEȘTI (90 000) at the beginning of a plain. Industrial city with car factories (Dacia). *Museum* (history, natural science, art). Lovely churches. Trivale National Park (27 hectares).

Tirgoviște (40 000). Capital of Wallachia in the 14th-16th cent. Chindia Tower (15th cent.) with *Vlad Tepeș Museum*. Prince's palace with museum. The first Roumanian books can be seen at the Printing Press Museum.

BUCUREȘTI (Bucharest), see town plans.

E 20. Cernovcy – Bacău – București – Giurgiu

Siret. Soviet frontier. The road goes through the lovely Bukovina, the northernmost part of Moldavia.

The churches and monasteries of **Moldavia** are famous. Their outer walls were painted in the 15th-16th cent. with colourful frescoes that have resisted the attacks of wind and weather for hundreds of years. The frescoes, which completely cover the church walls, mostly depict biblical scenes. Beautiful landscape with wooded heights and blossoming meadows.

Sucevița (1580) is surrounded by monastic buildings. Splendid altar. **Arbore** (1503), built for Luca Arbore, one of Stephen the Great's generals. Scenes from the lives of the saints. *Voronet* (1488) with elegant roof and tower. The paintings were completed during the reign of Petru Rareș, Stephen's son. "The Last Judgement", a magnificent composition, covers the west wall. The devil is wearing a Turkish hat. **Humor** (1530) with one wall devoted to the Virgin Mary. Great enmity towards the Turks is felt both here and in Sucevița. **Moldovita** (decorated 1537) with a colourful painting

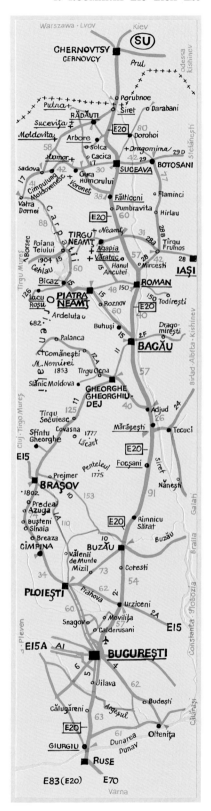

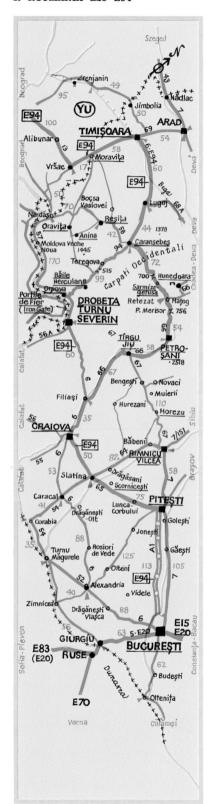

relating the story of the destruction of Constantinople – it was only a pious hope, of course. **Rădăuti** with a museum of ethnography. Stephen the Great was buried in the monastery of **Putna**.

SUCEAVA (75 000), residence of the Moldavian princes. Stephen the Great's capital. Many beautiful churches, e.g. **Mirăuti** (1390). Ruins of castle and fortress (15th-16th cent.). Museums. **Fălticeni** (20 000). House of Mihail Sadoveanu. The writer lived here 1891-1961. Hunting museum.

IAŞI (Jassy, 210 000). Capital of Moldavia for 300 years. Roumania's first university (1860). The Palace of Culture in neo-Gothic style (1927) contains several museums. Trei-Ierarhi Church (1639).

The eastern Carpathians is one of the most beautiful tourist areas in Roumania. Monasteries in Văratec, Bistriţa and Neamt. The monastery of Agapia contains icons painted by Nicolae Grigorescu and famous, hand-woven carpets.

Bicaz with the Ceahlău artificial lake. The dam measures 127×435 m . **Borsec,** spa with mud, mineral springs and grottoes. **Lacul Roşu.** Climatic health and tourist resort on a lake, formed by an earthquake in 1837. Nature preserve, hiking trails, mountaineering. **Mount Ceahlău,** 1 904 m. Annual festival with ancient traditions held on August 6.

PIATRA NEAMT (65 000), beautifully situated in the Bistriţa Valley. Ruins of a 15th-cent. castle. St. Loan's Church with belfry. Museum of the Carpathians (natural science) and other museums.

Roman (50 000). Industrial town with many historical monuments and a beautiful park. Mărăşesti with a large mausoleum containing the remains of 6 000 Roumanians killed in the First World War.

Focşani. Museum in the building where the Roumanian state came into being as a result of an agreement between Moldavia and Wallachia.

Brasov – Ploiesti, see E15.

BUCUREŞTI (Bucharest), see town plans.

The road goes through the large agricultural area of Burnaz towards **Giurgiu,** an important port on the Danube. "The Friendship Bridge", a combination railway and motor bridge, spans the Danube to Bulgaria.

E20 continues to Pleven – Sofia – Thessaloniki.

E 94. Beograd – Timişoara –Piteşti – Bucureşti

Moraviţa. Yugoslavian frontier.

TIMIŞOARA (290 000) on the Banat plain. University, opera house, three theatres, one with performances in Roumanian, one in German and one in Hungarian. Performances also in the Serbian language. **Hunedoara Castle** (1318) contains a museum. Old town hall (1734). Roman Catholic cathedral and Serbian Orthodox cathedral, both dating from the 18th cent. Cathedral from the beginning of the 20th cent. Open-air museum.

Caransebeş with Muntele Mic, a winter sports centre at 1 540 m. **Sarmizegetusa,** capital of the Roman province of Dacia. **Reşita,** iron and steel works at the foot of the Semenic Mountains. Hydro-electric power stations and dams. Near by, remains of a Roman gold mine.

Winding road through the mountains to **Orşova.** You can save 100 km when driving from the frontier to Orşova by taking the route through **Oraviţa,** a small town where the first Roumanian theatre was built in 1817. There is an intersting mountain railway line (built 1854) to **Anina,** a mining town (30 km, 14 tunnels, 16 viaducts).

Băile Herculane, radioactive mineral springs, known as early as the Roman period. Statue of Hercules.

Orşova (12 000), a town which was relocated when the hydro-electric power station and locks were built.

The Iron Gate (Porţile de Fier). The Danube's last narrow gorge before the river's approach to the Black Sea is 130 km long. The Iron Gate is the narrowest point, 100 m. Giant hydro-electric complex. Djerdap 1 was completed in 1972, Djerdap 2 is under construction. Jointly built by Yugoslavia and Roumania. Between the power stations are Europe's largest locks, on two 310 m levels that admit vessels of up to 5 000 tons. They are a link in the Europa Canal: the Rhine – Danube – Black Sea.

DROBETA-TURNU SEVERIN (65 000). Danube port, shipyards, industries. Ruins of a **Roman bridge** built in A.D.105 by Apollodorus of Damascus. It is depicted on the Trajan Column in Rom. It was built to allow the transport of troops who would fight the Dacians. Ruins of Roman baths. Severin Castle (13th cent.). **Iron Gate Museum** (archaeology, ethnography, natural science). **Simian.** Open-air museum showing a typical village from Oltenia.

TIRGU JIU (90 000). Centre of a mining district. Palace of Culture (1913) with art museum. Fortress. Park with sculptures by Constantin Brancusi (1876-1957), who was active in Paris. He was born in the village of **Hobiţa.**

Narrow and winding, but very pretty road to **Petroşani**. From Tîrgu Jiu road to **Rîmnicu Vîlcea** past several beautiful monasteries. **Horezu**, a beautiful white building in the "Brancovan" style. Horezu is known for its pottery and its pleasant inn. Interesting monasteries also in Bistriţa, Arnota, Govora, Surpatele and Dintr-un Lemn.

CRAIOVA (200 000). Chief town in the region of Oltenia, in the 15th-cent. a "banat", i.e. a frontier province. The ruler was called "ban", the closest equivalent being margrave. His residence, the city's oldest building, is now a museum of ethnography. Art museum with several works by Brancusi. Museums, parks. *Trivale National Park* (27 hectares) with the Trivale monastery (17th cent.).

Scorniceşti, birthplace of President Nicolae Ceauşescu.

PITEŞTI, see E15 A.

E 95. Tulcea – Constanţa – Varna

Tulcea. Old town built on seven hills. Boats leave here for the Danube Delta.

The Danube Delta, a huge area surrounding the three arms of the Danube. The flora varies from reed-filled marshland to dense forests. One of Europe's largest breeding places for about 300 different species of aquatic birds. Many are rare, such as pelicans, flamingoes and swans. Extensive fishing – over 60 species of fish. Sturgeon is caught for the production of black caviar. A sturgeon can reach a length of 8 m. The large channels are frequented by paddle steamers. If you want to venture into the smaller channels, you need the help of locals who are able to find the way through the ocean of reeds. Water buffaloes are used on the farms.

The Danube's source is at Donaueschingen in Germany (route E 70) and it flows through Regensburg, Passau, Linz, Bratislava, Budapest and Belgrade. With its 3 000 km, it is the second longest river in Europe (the longest is the Volga).

GALATI (200 000). Large river port where the Siret and Prut Rivers flow into the Danube. The big shipyard constructs vessels of up to 55 000 tons. Larger ships cannot pass through the Sulina Canal. Roumania's largest steel factory. Seaside esplanade. Museums. **Braila.** Paper is made from the reed of the Danube Delta. A large new port is under construction at **Agigea**. Reloading between ocean-going ships and river vessels from Regensburg (in 1985, perhaps from as far away as Rotterdam).

Babadag with folklore museum and the Ala-Gazi Pasha Mosque (18th cent.). Istria, founded by Greek colonists in the 4th cent. B.C. Ruins of a temple of Aphrodite. The town was abandoned in about the 7th cent A.D.

Mamaia. Large, modern seaside resort with an 8 km long sandy beach, 100-150 m wide. Over 50 hotels on an isthmus between Lake Siutghiol and the Black Sea.

CONSTANŢA (280 000). Roumania's largest port. The Greek port town, Tomis, was founded here in the 5th cent. B.C. Archaeological museum and excavations with Roman mosaics from the ancient market place. Mosque with 50 m high minaret. Statue of Ovid, who was banished here after Augustus Caesar had been offended by some of the poet's verse. Seaside esplanade with casino and large aquarium. Extensive vineyards and wine cellars in Murfatlar. Wine tasting.

A row of seaside resorts south of Constanţa. **Eforie Nord**, situated between the Black Sea and Lake Techirghiol. Sandy beaches and a promontory. Modern architecture. Medical treatments. Mudbaths on Lake Tekirghiol, a salt lake. **Neptune, Venus** and **Jupiter**, modern seaside resorts.

Mangalia. Roumania's southernmost seaside resort, also has facilities for medical treatments. Long beach and swimming pool with heated sea water. Esmahan Sultan Mosque (1540) is now a museum.

Vama Veche. Bulgarian frontier. E 95 continues to Varna, Burgas and Istanbul.

The road that follows the shore is very busy during the peak season and because it goes through the seaside resorts, passing between the beaches and hotels, congestion is not unusual. The fastest route between Constanţa and Varna goes via the Negru Voda and Tolbuhin frontier stations.

TOWN PLANS

Ateneul (Atheneum), the concert hall in Bucharest

BUCUREŞTI (Bucharest, 2 million)
The capital of Roumania and the country's most important industrial city was founded in the 15th cent. Centre of a fertile agricultural area on the Wallachian plain. The city is distinguished by broad boulevards and modern buildings. The Intercontinental Hotel and the National Theatre dominate the Bulevardul Bălcescu. The *Piaţa Victoriei*, location of a monument dedicated to Soviet heroes, is the site of the Museum of Natural History, the Museum of the Revolution and government buildings. The broad Calea Victoriei, a shopping street, leads south. The *Palace of the Republic*, formerly the royal palace, now an art museum, is on *Piaţa Gheorghiu-Dej*, as are the Ateneul Concert Hall, the modern Conference Hall and the little Cretulescu Church (1722). Beautiful Cişmigiu Park. The 16th-cent. *Curtea Veche Church* was once a part of the city's oldest castle. Stavropoleus Church (1724). Lively market square and an old quarter. Hanul Manuc Restaurant with walled-in garden. Other establishments are the Caro Cu Bere and Bucur.
The wide *Sosea Kiseleff*, marked by a triumphal arch from the First World War (a copy of the triumphal arch in Paris), leads north from the Piaţa Victoriei. The *Park of Culture*, close to Lake Herăstrău, is a charming recreation area. **The Roumanian Village Museum** exhibits over 50 reconstructed farmhouses, wooden churches and windmills. Enormous Casa Scinteii: newspaper, publishing house, printing office. Large hotels in parks. *Liberty Park* with zoo in the southern part of the city. 23rd of August Park with stadium, seating 80 000, and open-air theatre. Fire brigade and music museums.
Deer park and several restaurants in the *Baneasa Woods. Mogasoaiai Palace* (14 km from Bucharest) in a beautiful setting on the shore of a lake. Built in 1702 it is a lovely example of the Brincoveanu Style.

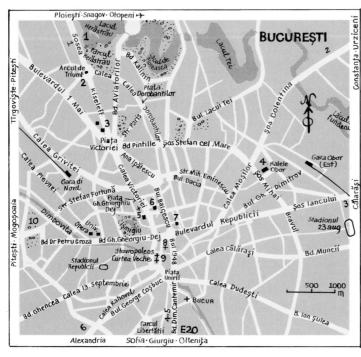

1 *Herăstrău Park and Roumanian Village Museum*
2 *Triumphal Arch*
3 *Museum of the Revolution Museum of National History*
4 *Indoor market*
5 *Palace of the Republic (art museum). Cretulescu Church*
6 *Ateneul Concert Hall*
7 *National Theatre*
8 *Russian Church*
9 *Stavropoleous Church and Curtea Veche Church*
10 *Botanical Gardens*

S · Sweden

S·Sverige

Area: 449 600 km² (173 600 sq. miles)

Population: 8.2 million. People and language Swedish, small Finnish and Lapp minorities. 95 % of the population belong to the Evangelical Lutheran state church. English is widely understood.

Government: Constitutional monarchy. One-chamber "Riksdag" (Parliament).

History

800-1050 The Viking period. The Svear kingdom centred in Gamla (Old) Uppsala gains power.

829 Ansgar introduces Christianity to Sweden.

11th cent. Christianity is accepted. Sweden is united into one kingdom.

1250 Stockholm becomes capital of Sweden.

1389-1521 Margaret, elected Queen of Sweden, unites Sweden with Denmark and Norway in the Union of Kalmar.

1523 Gustav Vasa is elected King of Sweden.

1527 Lutheranism becomes the state religion as a result of the decision of the Västerås Riksdag.

1630 Gustavus Adolphus (Gustav II Adolf) intervenes in the Thirty Years' War. Sweden becomes a Great Power. Swedish armies in Russia, Poland, Austria and Germany.

1658 Peace of Roskilde. Denmark loses the provinces of Scania (Skåne), Blekinge, Halland and Bohuslän to Sweden.

1718 Charles XII falls at Fredrikshald during the Northern War. Sweden's period as a Great Power is over. The German possessions are lost.

1772-1792 Reign of Gustavus (Gustav) III, a despotic king. He is murdered at a masked ball in the Stockholm Opera House.

1808-1809 War against Russia whose fleets raid the Swedish Baltic coast. Finland is ceded to Russia.

1810 Marshal Jean Baptiste Bernadotte, hero of the French Revolutionary Wars, becomes heir apparent to the Swedish throne.

1814 Union of Norway and Sweden.

1818 Jean Baptiste Bernadotte accedes to the throne, becomes King Charles XIV and founds the present royal dynasty.

1814-1905 Sweden and Norway are joined in a personal union.

20th cent. Compared with other countries Sweden has experienced tranquil development, politically, socially and economically. The country maintained a policy of strict neutrality during both World Wars and has achieved a high standard of living.

Currency: Swedish kronor (SEK). 1 krona = 100 öre

Business hours: Banks 9.30 a.m.-3.00 p.m., often 4.30-6.00 p.m. one or two days a week. Post offices 9 a.m.- 6 p.m. Saturdays 9 a.m.-1 p.m. Shops have widely varying opening hours. The most usual are 9.00 a.m.-6.00 p.m. Saturdays 9.00 a.m.-2.00 p.m. Foodshops are often open even later and "jour" shops, usually specializing in foodstuffs, can be open until 9.00 or 10.00 p.m. Some foodshops and major department stores are open on Sundays from 12.00 noon until 4 p.m.

Holidays: New Year's Day, January 6 (Epiphany), Good Friday, Easter Sunday, Easter Monday, May 1, Ascension Day, Whit Sunday, Whit Monday, Midsummer Day (Saturday closest to the summer solstice), Saturday closest to All Saints' Day, December 25 and 26.

Hotels

Several hotel chains, among them SARA, Reso, Scandic, OK, Inter S Sweden. Hotel prices in Sweden are rather steep, but family rooms during the summer can be quite reasonable. Hotel cheques are available.

Camping

About 800 camping sites, 500 of which are officially recognized and classified with one, two or three stars. Of these about half offer chalets, sleeping 2-4 people.

Smögen, one of the beautiful tourist resorts on the west coast

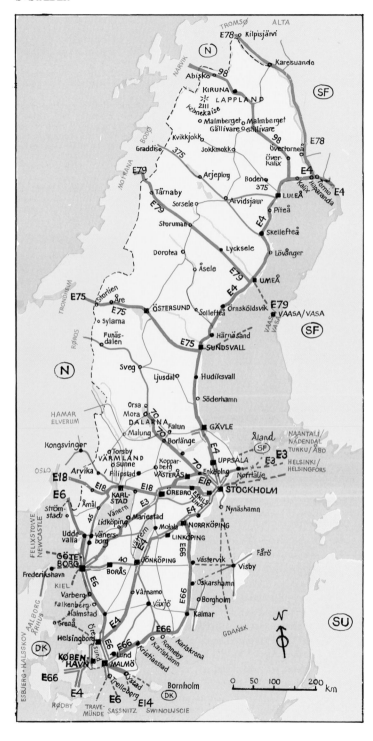

Youth hostels

Swedish youth hostels, like their counterparts in the other Scandinavian countries, have developed into establishments that cater more for family trade than for individual, young travellers. Most of the country's 230 hostels have rooms for families and self-catering facilities. The Swedish guests usually arrive by car. Swedish youth hostels are managed by the Svenska Turistföreningen (Swedish Touring Club), Vasagatan 48, 101 20 Stockholm.

"Everyman's right"

According to Swedish law everyone has the right to move about freely in the countryside, both on public and privately-owned land. However, it is obvious that one should not disturb the local residents or damage the land or private property. You are not permitted to enter the private land on which a house is built. Special regulations apply for nature reserves, bird sanctuaries and restricted military areas.

You are allowed to camp for one night without asking the land owner's permission, but you must not damage his land, and the tent must not be pitched too close to his dwelling or garden. If possible, it is always advisable to ask the land owner's permission first.

You are allowed to pick wild berries, most flowers and mushrooms on public and privately-owned land. You may not enter newly planted woodland, or fields of growing crops. You may only light a fire where there is no danger of forest fire. (Some districts have a special period of the year when it is unlawful to light fires in the countryside.) You should not fish without first finding out about the local regulations – and buying a fishing card.

Food and drink

Some specialities: Inlagd sill, raw salted herring marinated in vinegar, sugar, onion and spices. Jansons frestelse, oven-baken anchovies, onion, potatoes and cream. Stekt strömming och potatismos, fried Baltic herring and mashed potatoes. Surströmming, salted and fermented Baltic herring – a speciality of northern Sweden, and a culinary experience for the adventurous. Biff à la Lindström, mince combined with chopped beetroot and capers, fried and served with onions and potatoes. Gravlax med senapssås, marinated salmon served with sweet mustard sauce. Reindeer meat in various forms. The famous Swedish smörgåsbord, usually a lunchtime buffet, with many cheese, meat and fish and hot and cold dishes both, is often available at roadside country inns and hotels. Knäckebröd, crisp bread, comes in many shapes and forms, as does the unleavened tunnbröd, a favourite in the northern parts of Sweden. Three types of beer are available: lättöl (very low alcoholic content – an ideal beverage for motorists), folköl (2.8 % alcohol) and exportöl (strongest). Several domestic types of brännvin

The town wall, Visby

(closely related to vodka), liqueurs and Swedish punsch.

Shopping
Glass and crystal (Orrefors, Boda, Kosta, Lindshammar, Reijmyre), wood carvings, ceramics and porcelain, handwoven towels and other handicrafts, Lapp handicrafts in the northern parts of Sweden, wooden Dala Horses.

Speed limits. Traffic regulations
Motorways 110 kmh, other roads 70, 90 or 110 kmh, depending on sign postings. Built-up areas 50 kmh. Maximum speed limits are always displayed. Private cars with trailers or caravans in tow 70 kmh on country roads.

It is recommended that children do not ride in the front seat. Drivers and front seat passengers are required by law to wear seat belts. Studded tyres, almost a necessity for winter driving, are not permitted between May 1 and November 1.

Motorists must always have their headlights illuminated. During daylight hours dipped headlights are the rule.

Roads
Major roads are usually of high standard, and almost always paved. Secondary roads may be paved with gravel. The severe Swedish winters have their effect on the roads and it is best not to expect the even surfaces common in southern countries.

No steep gradients. Roads are kept open during the winter. Good roads and, at least in the province of Norrland, sparse traffic, makes driving hundreds of miles a day an attractive possibility. But be on the lookout for deer, and especially elk, on the roads.

Elk are large animals and every year they cause severe and sometimes deadly traffic accidents.

Road patrol
Car towing is provided by Larmtjänst (owned by insurance companies). Local emergency numbers in telephone directories. Stockholm 08-24 10 00, Göteborg 031-42 71 00, Malmö 040-10 000. The emergency number, 90 000, puts you into contact with police, ambulance and fire brigade assistance.

M, Motormännens riksförbund (National Motorists' Association), Sture-gatan 32, 102 40 Stockholm. Tel. 08-782 38 00. Over 20 nationwide offices. KAK (the Royal Automobile Club) is now administered by M.

Svenska Turistföreningen (Swedish Touring Club), Stockholm. Tel. 08-22 72 00.

Offices in Göteborg and Malmö.

Sveriges Turistråd (Swedish Tourist Council), Sverigehuset, Hamngatan 27, 103 82 Stockholm. Tel. 08-789 20 00.

Swedish National Tourist Office, 3 Cork Street, London W1X 1HA, tel. 01-437 58 16.

Old wooden buildings, Arboga

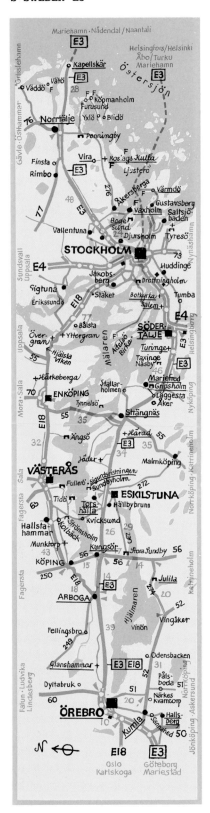

E3. Kapellskär – Stockholm – Eskilstuna – Göteborg

E3 comes from the Soviet frontier at Vaalimaa – Helsinki/Helsingfors – Turku/Åbo.

Norrtälje (13 000). Idyllic little town centred around a stream and Lilla torget (the Little Square). Roslagen Museum in an old rifle factory. This section of the coast is called Roslagen, and Vikings from the area were known as "Rus". They colonized an area near Novgorod and are still remembered in the name Russia. During the Viking Age there was a water passage to Lake Mälaren. For this reason, the entire area has a profusion of rune stones and other Viking remains. 20 rune stones in the *Husby-Sjuhundra* churchyard. St. Birgitta was born at *Finsta* in 1302. She prayed in the grotto in the park and eventually founded the Birgittine Order in Vadstena.

Route 276 past **Roslags-Kulla** which has a wooden church (1706) with an onion-shaped dome. *Vira bruk*, once a major Swedish armaments factory, has been restored. Now a historic monument. Idyllic scenery.

Route 274 to **Vaxholm,** a lovely little town with many picturesque wooden buildings. Vaxholm Fortress (1838) with museum on an island is linked to the town by a little ferry. The route via the car ferry to Värmdö and on to the southern part of Stockholm makes it possible to take a sightseeing tour through the Stockholm archipelago (skärgård), an area with 25 000 islands and skerries covering about 140 km from north to south and up to 80 km from east to west. Vaxholm is one of the centres for passenger ship service to the archipelago.

STOCKHOLM, see town plans.

E18 (signposted Oslo) goes via Västerås to Örebro. E3 (signposted Göteborg) goes via Eskilstuna to Örebro. Both routes are about equally long. E3 and E4 come together on Essingeleden motor road complex, which provides excellent views of Stockholm.

Midsommarkransen with the Ericsson factories (telephones). *Botkyrka Church,* consecrated in 1176 by Stefan, Sweden's first archbishop. *Salem Church* (12th cent.).

SÖDERTÄLJE, see E4.

Turinge Church (19th cent.). Field Marshal Eric Dahlberg's tomb and chapel. He dared to march the Swedish armies across the ice-covered straits against Denmark. His careful representational drawings have given us an idea of how Sweden looked in the 17th cent.

Mariefred. Idyllic town with 18th-cent. buildings. The Pax Mariae (Marie fred) abbey existed here as early as the 10th cent., and a Carthusian abbey was founded in 1493. *Gripsholm Castle* (16th cent.), a royal residence until 1840. Beautiful interiors. Duke Johan (eventually King of Sweden 1568-1592, under the name of John III) and his wife, Catherine Jagellonica, were prisoners here. Their son, Sigismund, who went on to become King of Poland, was born here. The castle and the nearby Gripsholm Folk High School contain the collections of the *Swedish National Portrait Gallery* (2 600 portraits). *Östra Södermanlands järnväg,* a 4 km long, 600 mm gauge preserved steam railway, runs from the steamboat quay past Mariefred station to Läggesta, on the Stockholm – Eskilstuna railway line.

Strängnäs, founded in the 12th cent., was once one of Sweden's most important towns. *Roggeborgen,* a 15th-cent. bishop's palace. Gustav Vasa was proclaimed King of Sweden here, on June 6, 1521. The **cathedral,** a Gothic brick structure, was consecrated in 1291. Paintings from the 14th-15th cent. Tomb of Charles IX (d. 1611). Several idyllic small-town streets and a windmill.

Härad Church, one of the smallest in Sweden (12th cent.). *Jäder Church,* in the Dutch Renaissance style. The *Kjula Ridge* with many burial mounds and tomb stones. *Sundbyholm Castle* in Eskilstuna's recreation area. **Sigurdsristningen** (11th cent.), a 5 m long rune stone with an inscription and carved scenes depicting Sigurd (Siegfried) killing the dragon, Fafner. This story is also included in the German Nibelungen epic, a source of inspiration for Wagner.

ESKILSTUNA (65 000). Industrial town famous for its knives, scissors and precision instruments. The **Rademacher smithies,** workshops in a unique 17th cent. setting. The *Factory Museum* is in a rifle factory from 1840. Weapons museum and technical museum. Museum of art. The large *People's Park* includes Eskilstuna Park, one of Sweden's finest zoos. *Torshälla,* a delightful little town, is now part of Eskilstuna.

Bogsten, a large prehistoric fortified settlement. **Kungsör.** Small community with many industries. *King Charles' Church* is a splendid Baroque structure.

Arboga was Sweden's most prominent town in the Middle Ages. The first Swedish parliament (Riksdag) met here in 1435, and elected Engelbrekt as guardian of the realm. His statue is in front of the church, which contains a fine altarpiece depicting St. Birgitta. Museum. Picturesque old houses.

Glanshammar Church (13th cent.) with frescoes.

ÖREBRO (90 000). Town charter 1265. Massive castle on an island in the River Svartån. The old houses have been moved to *Wadköping*, a museum town. Wadköping was the name given to Örebro by Hjalmar Bergman, a well-known Swedish novelist who grew up here. Provincial museum and technical museum. Theatre (1976). At the northern approach to the city stands *Svampen* (the Mushroom), a water tower with a café and fine views out over the fertile Närke plain.

Kumla. The shoe industry has closed down as a result of foreign competition, and the name Kumla is now associated with Sweden's largest prison. Shoemaking museum. *Sannahed,* old army drill-ground. Officers' mess hall with museum.

Hallsberg. Sweden's largest railway station. Prehistoric cemetery at Norrby: about 50 grave stones from the 5th-7th cent.

Ramundeboda. Remains of a 15th-cent. abbey, intended as a shelter for travellers passing through the large and dangerous *Tiveden* forest. ***Finnerödja,*** known for its extensive strawberry fields. ***Södra Råda Church*** (14th cent.), a wooden church with colourful 14th-15th cent. paintings.

Mariestad. Founded in 1583 by Duke Karl (later King Charles IX) and named after his wife Maria of Pfalz. Paper industry.

Kinnekulle (307 m). Lovely views, interesting flora and many beautiful old churches. Next to *Husaby Church* is the spring where the first Christian king of Sweden is said to have been baptized by Sigfrid, an English missionary. Memorial stone. Tombs where according to legend, Olof Skötkonung and his queen, Estrid, are buried. Restored fortress.

Lidköping. The old *town hall* on the main square was once a hunting lodge. Long-established porcelain industry (Rörstrand). *Porcelain museum.*

Road to ***Läckö Castle*** at the tip of a peninsula in Lake Vänern. The castle was built in the 17th cent. for the de la Gardie family. Later in that century all the noble families' were confiscated and the castle's furnishings were carried away. Now renovated. Annual exhibitions.

Skara. Traditional centre of learning with a splendid Gothic ***cathedral*** (12th cent.). The beautiful fountain in front of the cathedral is decorated with scenes from the history of the town. Museum and botanical gardens.

Sparlösa. Famous rune stone (with pictures) in the churchyard. *Levene* with Sweden's tallest rune stone, 5 m.

Alingsås. The textile industry was founded in the 18th cent. by Jonas Alströmer, the man who introduced the potato to Sweden. His statue can be seen in the square, and the museum is housed in his former warehouse. Beautiful manor with park.

Road south to ***Hedared*** with Sweden's only stave church (13th cent.). Compared to the Norwegian churches, this is a very simple structure built of tarred oak. 7 by 5 m, with a choir of 3 by 3 m. The altar painting has been painted direct on the wall.

North of Alingsås lie the ruins of ***Gräfsnäs Castle*** within a beautiful park and recreation area. Preserved ***steam railway*** between Anten and Gräfsnäs.

Beautiful road through a countryside marked by hills and lakes. *Nääs Manor* (18th cent.) once a famous arts and crafts school. 19th-cent. interiors, open to visitors. Elaborate Midsummer celebrations.

GÖTEBORG (Gothenburg), see town plans.

E 3 continues by car ferry to Fredrikshavn. From there to Århus – Hamburg – Antwerpen – Paris – Bordeaux – Lisboa.

Alternative routes 50 and 49 Hallsberg – Askersund – Skövde – Skara.

Tiveden. The Tivedsleden goes along a narrow gravel road. Signposted hiking trails. Some are short, like those to Trollkyrka and Stenkälla (blocks of primary rocks). Tivedstorp is run by IM, a charitable organization specializing in aid to refugees. Pleasant café, chapel, shop selling handicrafts from many different countries. *Skaga Chapel,* reconstructed stave church on the site of an 11th-cent. sacrificial altar.

Karlsborg Fortress (19th cent.), a so-called central fortress for the defence of Sweden. You can drive through the fortress town and view Lake Vättern from the ramparts.

Skövde (30 000). Industrial town. Oden, a House of Culture, with library, theatre, art gallery. ***Billingen,*** a 23 km long mountain range on the plains. Orchards on the slopes. The top of the ridge is a desolate, wooded area. Billingehus, a large conference hotel.

Varnhem abbey and church were founded by monks from Clairvaux in the 13th cent. The abbey is now a ruin. The church was restored in 1674.

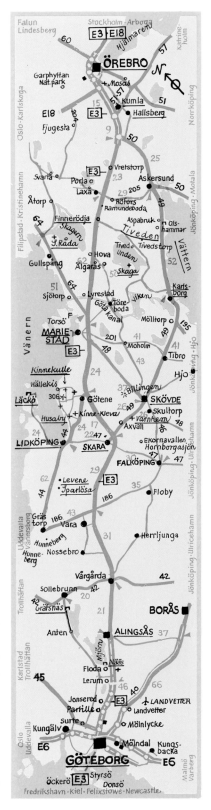

E 4. Haparanda – Sundsvall – Stockholm – Helsingborg

Finnish border. E 4 comes from Helsinki/Helsingfors – Lathi – Jyväskylä – Oulu (Uleåborg) – Tornio (Torneå).

Haparanda. Sweden's easternmost town, situated at 24° E, at about the same longitude as Sofia and Athens. The town was founded after Sweden had lost Finland to Russia in 1809. Modern church (1967).

Routes 99 and 400 north through the *Torne Valley,* see Finland, route 78. The *Kukkola Rapids* are well worth an excursion from Haparanda. Whitefish are caught from "pata", a 150 m long pier, and served in a variety of interesting forms in the nearby restaurant. Annual whitefish festival last Sunday in July. 19th cent. mills. Holiday cottage village.

500 m long bridge to *Seskarö* in the archipelago. *Kalix* with wood-processing industry. *Gammelstad* with Kyrkstad (Church Town), 450 cottages that were once used by churchgoers from all over the north of Sweden during high holy days. Lovely paintings and furnishings in the 15th cent.

LULEÅ (45 000). Chief town of Norrbotten, a province that takes up one-fifth of Sweden but is home for only 3% of the country's population. Founded 1649. State-owned Norrbotten Iron Works. Large exporting harbour with a 450 m long quay for the landing of iron ore from Gällivare and Kiruna. Huge town hall. The Luleå shopping centre, an indoor complex, was one of the first of its type in Europe (1950). *Norrbotten Museum* has impressive exhibits devoted to the Lapps.

Boden. Railway junction and Sweden's mightiest military stronghold. The fortifications are concealed in the mountains near the town. Överluleå Church (1831) with church town. *Garrison museum* with uniforms. Power station with aquarium. Trotting races. *Piteå.* Centre of forestry industry. Pite Beach "Norrland's Riviera". Fine sandy beaches, elegant hotel (open all year). The long hours of sunlight during the summer make up for the invigorating water temperature. A particularly popular resort for the inhabitants of northern Norway. (It is "only" 900 km away from Tromsö.)

The *Archaeologist's trail* at *Byske* is a signposted hiking trail that leads through a prehistoric cemetery. A stone dolmen was erected on the shore 3 000 years ago. Land elevation has been quite exceptional here, 1 m per 100 years. The mound is now 30 m higher that it was originally.

Skellefteå (26 000). Port and centre of industry based on forest products. Boliden AB in Rönnskär. Gold, silver, copper etc. Museum in Nordanå Park. Church village for worshippers from outlying districts. *Lövånger.* Large church village, converted into a hotel.

UMEÅ (50 000). Chief town in the province of Västerbotten. University town. The town is famous for the birch trees that line the streets. *Gammlia.* Open-air museum and provincial museum.

Örnsköldsvik. Site of the Hägglund factories (buses, carriages for the Stockholm underground, etc.).

Skuleberget, 293 m, with fine views. Cable car to the summit. *Kungsgrottan,* a cave inhabited during the Stone Age. Originally it was near the seashore, but land elevation has raised it to near the summit of the mountain. Luxuriant vegetation with interesting examples of Arctic flora. *Slåttdalsskrevan,* a 40 m deep and several hundred metres long ravine. The mountains extend all the way to the sea, and the area is known as "the High Coast", *Höga kusten* (Nordingrå). A beautiful area, well worth a detour. Several fishing villages that produce a local delicacy, "surströmming", Baltic herring which has been allowed to ferment. It has an interesting taste and an extraordinary aroma. A culinary "must" for the adventurous.

The *Sandö Bridge,* 2 km long and 45 m above the surface of the water. Monument on Sandö dedicated to the composer Frans Berwald who was manager of the Sandö Glassworks during the 1850s. The *Ångermanälven River,* 450 km long, is one of the longest and most important rivers in Sweden. Large hydro-electric power stations. The *Ådalen Valley,* an industrial area, stretches to the south passing Sollefteå and Kramfors.

Härnösand (20 000). Old centre of learning and bishopric. Neo-classic cathedral (1846) and town hall. Picturesque wooden houses in Östanbäcksgatan. *Murberget* is one of Sweden's foremost open-air museums. Panorama from *Vårdkaseberget* (175 m) out over the hills and the sea.

Bergeforsen hydro-electric power station and salmon farms are open to visitors. Industries line the road as far as *Njurunda,* south of Sundsvall. Over 40 early-20th cent. sawmills have been abandoned, and the still-operating industries are dominated by SCA (Svenska Cellulosa AB). Interesting geology and flora on the island of *Alnö.* Sales of examples of minerals, as souvenirs. Prehistoric remains. It is estimated that the area was inhabited 40 000 years ago.

SUNDSVALL (55 000, Greater Sundsvall 110 000). Beautifully set between two mountains. Lovely views of the sea. Folklore museum on the northern mountain. Sundsvall is a centre for industries related to forestry and is the headquarters for SCA (Svenska Cellulosa AB). Special section with forestry displays in Sundsvall's Museum.

Prehistoric remains at *Njurunda*. *Lörudden*. Fishing village.

Hudiksvall. Lumber industry. Old quays and fishermen's sheds at Strömmingssundet. "Fiskarstaden", an area with preserved wooden structures. Museum. *Hornslandet*, recreation area managed by the Board of Crown Forests and Lands. Beautiful road (84) past the Dellen Lakes to *Ljusdal*.

Järvsö with the remarkable Järvsö klack, a 390 m high rock formation at Ljusnan. *Stenegården*, handicrafts centre. *Järvsö Church* is one of the largest in Sweden. *Karlsgården*, a folklore museum in a large 19th-cent. farm house. Routes 84 and 81 are lovely and fast routes to Östersund. Njutånger Church and Enånger Old Church are well-preserved medieval churches with works of Haaken Gulleson, a local 16th cent. artist.

Trönö Old Church, a 13th-cent. granite structure, is northern Sweden's best-preserved medieval church. Altarpiece by Haaken Gulleson. *Söderblomsgården*, next to the church, is the birthplace of Nathan Söderblom (1866-1931). He went on to become archbishop and pioneered ecumenical work. Söderblom was awarded the Nobel Peace Prize in 1930.

Söderhamn. Forestry industries. Museum in the former rifle factory. *Söderala*. Granite church.

Mårdängssjön with large rest stop and bird sanctuary. *Bönan* and *Utvalsnäs*, fishing villages where "böckling", smoked Baltic herring, is sold. Museum in the old lighthouse (1840).

GÄVLE (67 000). Port and large forestry industries. *Gamla Gefle* (Old Gävle), a collection of preserved wooden houses. *Silvanum*, modern forestry museum. *Gävle Museum* with porcelain etc. *Railway museum* (Swedish State Railways) with a large collection of locomotives and carriages.

Road 80 to *Sandviken*, with one of Sweden's largest iron works. Museum. Picturesque 17th-cent. workers' dwellings at *Högbo*. Wooden church (1622).

The old road goes past *Furuvik Park* (recreation area, amusement park, zoo). *Älvkarleby* with power station (1915). Open to visitors during the summer months. Water works laboratory with models of hydro-electric power plants and waterways where logs are floated. Salmon-fishing in the River Dalälven has centuries-old traditions. Exhibition hall with aquariums. The water in the falls is allowed to take its old course during one day in June, the "Day of the Falls". Charles XIII's bridge, built 1816, reconstructed 1965.

Österbybruk, picturesque old iron working village with manor house, church, workers' dwellings, park. Walloons from what is now Belgium emigrated to Sweden in the 17th cent.

Söderfors. Modern industrial town in a traditional setting. **Vendel Church** (1310) with beautiful decorations. The finds from graves in the area (the "Vendel Civilization", 7th-10th cent.) are on display in the Historical Museum in Stockholm.

UPPSALA (100 000)

Chief town of the province of Uppland, the original heart of the old Swedish kingdom. The archbishop moved here in the 13th cent. from Old Uppsala. The university was founded in 1477. *Heliga Trefaldighetskyrkan* (Holy Trinity Church) from the 12th cent. The **cathedral**, Sweden's largest, was consecrated in 1435. Heavily restored after a fire in 1702. Two towers, 119 m high. The church is 119 m long. King Gustav Vasa (d. 1560) and his son, John III, are buried here. Casket with the relics of St. Eric. Tomb of Emanuel Swedenborg (1688-1772), Swedish scientist and mystic thinker. His teachings are kept alive by the Swedenborg Society in Blomsbury in London. University library with the *Silver Bible* (Codex Argenteus) by Bishop Wulfila, brought here from Prague during the Thirty Years' War. The old university building, *Gustavianum* (1623) with museums. The *castle*, high on top of the ridge, is now used as an administration building. This is the site of the symbol of the town, *Gunilla's bell,* which strikes the hours at 6 a.m. and 9 p.m. every day. *Uppland Museum* in a restored mill near the Mill Rapids on the banks of the Fyris Stream. *Linnaean Gardens and Museum.*

Old Uppsala, 5 km northeast of Uppsala, was the seat of the kings during the heathen period. The three burial mounds are from the 6th cent. The little **church** dates originally from 1164. It was the archiepiscopal church of Sweden until the 13th cent. It is believed that the church was built on the site of a pagan temple in order to mark the victory of Christianity. Odinsborg, an old timber-built inn, where visitors can drink "mjöd" (mead) out of huge bulls' horns just as the Vikings used to do.

Linné's Hammarby where the botanist, Carl von Linné (Carolus Linnaeus, 1707-1778) spent the summers during the 1760s and 1770s. Museum and small botanical garden. The *Mora Stones*, where the Swedish kings were elected during the Middle Ages. The Great Stone has disappeared but some of the smaller stones are preserved in a little building at the side of the road.

Märsta, with **Arlanda**, Stockholm's international airport.

Sigtuna. Sweden's oldest town, founded in the 11th cent. An idyllic little town with square and diminutive town hall (1744). *Stora Gatan*, the High

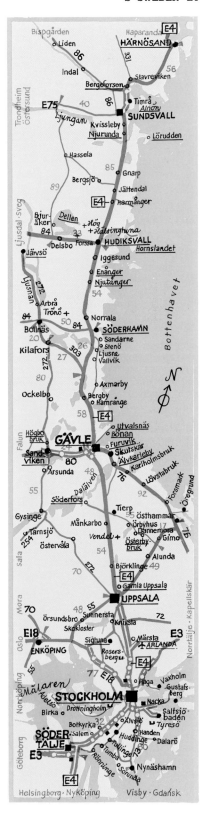

Street, follows the same route as its medieval predecessor. Excavations have revealed several streets that were laid out along the same route. *Maria Church,* a brick structure with wall paintings, was completed in 1250.

STOCKHOLM, see town plans. Stockholm – Södertälje, see E 3.

SÖDERTÄLJE (60 000). One of the oldest towns in Sweden, now a major industrial centre. Saab-Scania factories. *Torekällberget,* open-air museum with photography museum, electricity museum, fire-fighting museum.

Tullgarn (1720). Royal summer residence, open to visitors. Interiors reflect different 18th- and 19th-cent. styles. Pleasant inn. Lovely park.

Trosa was once a spa. Idyllic small town with picturesque wooden houses and lovely gardens on both banks of the Trosa Stream. *Garvaregården,* a museum of handicrafts.

Nyköping (30 000). Idyllic town centre. *Nyköpingshus,* built in the 13th cent. as a royal castle, is associated with dramatic events, some of which are portrayed during the annual July theatre festival. Folklore museum.

The road continues through the *Kolmården Forest,* once notorious for its bandits and highwaymen. Kolmården Zoo, opened in 1965, is one of the foremost of its type in Europe. Safari park which can be toured in your own car or the park's buses. Typical Swedish farm. Dolphinarium. Cable cars link the park's many sections. Road to *Reijmyre glass works,* with shop. Red glass is the company's speciality.

NORRKÖPING (85 000). Industrial town. *Holmen* paper mill. Art museum, municipal museum, dye-works museum.

LINKÖPING (42 000). Residence of the governor of the province of Östergötland. Old trading town that became a bishop's see in 1060 and was granted a cathedral school in 1260. The *cathedral* was built 1230-1500. The architect was Gerlach of Cologne. 105 m high tower (18th cent.). The interior reflects the long construction period. Its columns, no two alike, are unique in Europe. Old altar painting by Maerten van Heemskerck that hung in a church in Alkmaar until 1581. New altar painting by Norwegian artist Henrik Sørensen. *Folkunga Fountain* by Carl Milles in the square. The Folkungas were a local royal dynasty that eventually ruled Sweden. *Gamla Linköping,* preserved old houses from the 18th and 19th cent. Workshops, shops, herb gardens. SAAB factories.

Mjölby. Railway junction and industries. *Vadstena,* where the Birgittine Order was founded. The Birgittine Church (the "blue" church) from the 14th cent. is very beautiful. The convent is now a charming hotel. Castle from 1545. *Alvastra* with ruins of a 12th cent. monastery. *Omberg.* Fine view and beautiful surroundings. The *Rök Stone* (9th cent.), one of the most remarkable rune stones in Sweden. The inscription has proved difficult to decipher. *Heda Church* with famous madonna.

Splendid views out over *Lake Vättern,* Sweden's second largest and Europe's fifth largest lake. It is 136 km long and 30 km wide. Maximum depth 128 m. It is famous for the beautiful shifting colours of its water. Lovely views from the rest stop at *Brahehus.* Count Per Brahe had a castle erected here in 1640. It was destroyed by fire in 1708.

Gränna. Little, well-preserved town with delightful wooden houses. Unlike most Swedish towns, Gränna has never been ravaged by fire. Orchards (Gränna pears). Red and white "polkagrisar" (peppermint rock) are a local speciality. Fine views from Gränna Mountain. *Museum* with finds from S.A. Andrée's ill-fated balloon journey to the North Pole (1897). *Vättern Museum.* Boat to *Visingsö* with many memories of the Brahe family that once ruled here. *Brahe Church. Kumlaby Church* has a spire that was partially dismantled so that Tycho Brahe, the famous astronomer, could carry out his astronomical investigations. Special excursions on Visingsö in "remmalag", horse-drawn carts.

Close to the road is "The runners", a statue by Carl Eldh. The *Gyllene Uttern* Hotel looks like an old German knight's castle, but it was built in 1936.

Huskvarna. Armaments factory. The old *factory workers' cottages* are now inhabited by artists and craftsmen. *Museum* in the old powder house.

JÖNKÖPING (80 000). Largest town in the province of Småland. Museum (1955), iron foundries, local art, pottery and missionary activity (Jönköping is the centre of the non-conformist religious sects). Match museum.

Riddersberg, workshop of sculptor Calle Örnemark. The sculpture "The rope trick", 103 m high, and the ship Bounty with 200 seamen.

Taberg, 323 m, with fine views. Previously the site of iron mines. *Store Mosse.* Unspoiled landscape with abundant bird life. *Hillerstorp.* Site of the High Chaparral Wild West amusement park.

Värnamo (16 000). Old market town. Swed-Expo, a permanent exhibition of art and industrial products from Småland. Road to the ruins of *Nydalakloster,* Sweden's first monastery, founded in the 12th cent. by Cistercian monks from Clairvaux in France.

Ljungby. Charming buildings around the old square. Centre of an area famous for its handicrafts and small industries.

Silver Hill, large Rolls Royce collection. Children's amusement park. Horse-show (Lippizaner).

HELSINGBORG (80 000). Large port and industries. The centre of the town still reflects its Danish origins. Scania (Skåne) became a Swedish province in 1658. Long square between the ferry terminus and *Kärnan,* a 34 m high tower, all that remains of a 14th cent castle. Neo-Gothic town hall (1897). Municipal museum. Vikingberg Museum of Art. *Fredriksdal* open-air museum. Beautiful parks and beech woods. View out over Öresund, the busy strait that separates Sweden and Denmark. *Ramlösa,* spa with famous mineral water. *Råå,* fishing village with small maritime museum.

Sofiero (1865), former summer residence of the Swedish royal family. Large park with roses and rhododendrons.

Car ferries to Helsingør in Denmark. Two ferry lines: SJ/DSB and SFL Ferries. Ferries sail every 10-15 minutes. The journey takes 25 minutes.

E 4 continues to Helsingør – København – Hamburg – Basel – Genève – Barcelona – Madrid – Lisboa.

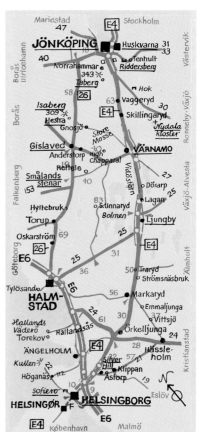

Alternative route: 26 Jönköping – Halmstad ("Nissastigen" – "The trail along the Nissan"). E 6 Halmstad – Helsingborg.

Driving time is about the same as on E 4. The road passes through extensive forests. Winter sports area at *Hestra,* site of Mount Isaberg. *Gislaved.* Rubber tyre factory and highly developed small industries. *Smålandsstenar.* Viking Age stones placed in a circular pattern.

---

30. Jönköping – Växjö – Ronneby

JÖNKÖPING and *Taberg,* see E 4.

Nydalakloster was founded in the 12th cent. by monks from Clairvaux in France. Remains of the monastery make up part of the church that was built in 1688.

Alvesta. Railway junction. Agricultural museum.

VÄXJÖ (40 000). Sigfrid, an English missionary, built the first church here in the 12th cent. The *cathedral* dates from the 16th cent. but has been ravaged by fire and lightning several times since then. It was rebuilt in 1960. Beautiful stained-glass windows. Statue of Esaias Tegnér, poet and bishop. *Museum of Småland* with glass and forestry exhibitions. The *House of the Emigrants* (Utvandrarnas hus) is devoted to the emigrations at the end of the 19th cent. when more than 200 000 people from the province of Småland left their homes for America. North of the town, *Evedal,* an idyllic little spa, and *Kronoberg,* a ruined castle.

The *glass works* of Småland are situated east of Växjö. The oldest is *Kosta* (1743). Old Kosta Museum. *Orrefors,* where the glass blowers can be watched from a special balcony. *Boda* is another well- known glass works. *Lessebo,* paper mill specializing in stationery. The manual production may be watched.

Dädesjö with an old church, famous for 13th cent. paintings that have been painted directly on the ceilings. They depict scenes from the Bible. No pews.

Korrö (route 122), idyllic artisans' village. Youth hostel. Nature reserve. *Blomstergården,* a large garden in Eriksboda.

Ronneby, see E 66.

Route 23: Växjö to Malmö.

Stenbrohult. Statue of Carolus Linnaeus, the 18th cent. botanist who grew up in the vicarage. He was born in 1707 in the nearby village of Södra Råshult.

Älmhult with IKEA, furniture manufacturers with huge warehouse furniture shops throughout Europe and even on other continents.

Hässleholm (17 000). Göinge Park and folklore museum. The statue of the "Snapphane" brings to mind the 17th-cent. Danish guerillas, the "Snapphanar", who fought the Swedish occupation force. *Vätteryd.* One of Sweden's largest prehistoric cemeteries, has 375 upright stones.

Frostavallen. Recreation area. *Skåne Zoo,* large park with Scandinavian animals.

Bosjökloster castle on an isthmus between the Ringsjö Lakes. A Benedictine convent was founded here in 1080. The 18th- and 19th cent. buildings have been restored. Tours. Exhibitions, beautiful park and restaurant.

Rolsberga – Malmö, see E 66.

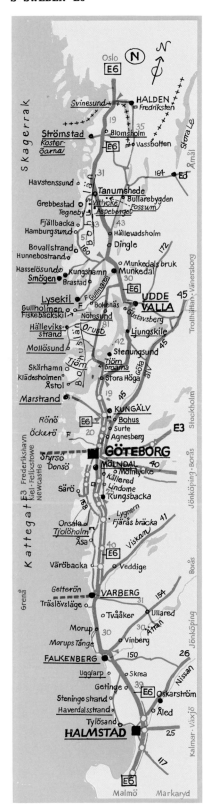

E 6. Svinesund – Göteborg – Malmö – Trelleborg

Svinesund Bridge, 65 m high. *Norwegian border.* Shops. E 6 comes from northern Norway – Narvik – Trondheim – Oslo.

Blomsholmsskeppet, a 42 m "ship setting", a prehistoric representation of a ship, and a "judge's ring", stones placed in a 33 m wide ring.

Strömstad. Little town, long a seaside resort. Boats to the *Koster Islands* which have interesting scenery and a charming atmosphere.

Tanum. An area with several large rock carvings, 2 500-3 000 years old. **Vitlycke** with 100 inscribed figures and symbols. **Rock Carving Museum.**

Road 163 skirts the coast of the province of **Bohuslän** passing several picturesque fishing villages and seaside resorts nestled on the rocky shoreline. **Smögen,** one of the best-known towns in the province. Pleasant walks along the 1 km long wooden quay that is lined with old warehouses. The fishing fleet sails from the harbour every morning. In the evening the boats return with catches of shrimp that are duly and immediately auctioned off.

Brofjorden. Oil refinery. **Lysekil.** Fishing port. Canning industry. Ferry to **Fiskebäckskil,** picturesque fishing village.

Gullmarsfjorden. Sweden's only true fjord, 125 m deep but with a mouth only 35 m wide. Interesting for marine-biologists. Several research stations.

UDDEVALLA (33 000). State-owned shipyard with one of the largest docks in the world, close to the road. Statues of King Charles X Gustav and Eric Dahlbergh in the square. They succeeded in wresting the area from Denmark in 1658. *Bäckebankarna* at Kuröd. Enormous remains of salt water shellfish that lived in the bay that existed here 10 000 years ago. Finds in Uddevalla Museum.

The road goes along a shelf that has been hewn out of the cliffs overlooking the fjord. **Gustavsberg** and **Ljungskile,** traditional seaside resorts. **Stenungsund,** old seaside resort, now dominated by a petro- chemical complex and an oil-fired steam power station.

Alternative route: 180 Uddevalla – Orust – Stenungsund

Orust. Sweden's third largest island after Gotland and Öland. Magnificent views at *Nötesund.* Roads to the idyllic fishing villages of **Gullholmen,** **Hälleviksstrand** and **Mollösund.** The *Tjörn Bridges,* with fine views over the skerries. Three bridges with a total length of over 1 km. The centre bridge collapsed when a ship crashed into it on a January night in 1980. Eight people died, when they drove over the edge in the darkness. Its replacement was completed in December 1981.

Kungälv was founded in 959. The medieval Kungahälla, on this site, was one of the largest towns in Norway. The province of Bohuslän and the town were ceded to Sweden 1658. The nearby *Bohus Fortress* was no longer of any use and eventually became a ruin. Sculpture on Nya Torget (the New Square) commemorates the brotherhood of the three Scandinavian countries.

Road to **Marstrand,** an old seaside resort. The Societetshus is a particularly fine example of the charming turn-of-the-century architecture that marks the town. Narrow streets and pleasant parks. Large *Karlsten Fortress* (1697) became a notorious prison in the 18th and 19th cent. Car park on the island of Koön. A little ferry connects it with Marstrand which is almost free of motor traffic.

GÖTEBORG, see town plans.

Mölndal. Åby race course. **Särö,** a traditional seaside resort on the Onsala Peninsula. Fine restaurant in the old railway station. **Råö.** Observatory. *Onsala Church* has a splendid Baroque interior. **Kungsbacka.** Idyllic little town. **Fjärås bräcka,** an enormous gravel ridge left when the Ice Age glacier that covered this area retreated 12 000 years ago. Prehistoric cemetery.

Tjolöholm. Splendid early-20th cent. mansion in the English Tudor style, originally built for a Gothenburg merchant, now owned by the city of Gothenburg. Tours. Carriage museum. Café in the former stables. Beautiful park. Swimming facilities.

Ringhals. Nuclear power station. *Morups tånge.* Bird sanctuary.

Varberg (20 000). Industrial town and seaside resort. The 13th cent. **fortress** houses a museum whose most famed exhibit is the 14th cent. Bocksten Man. His well-preserved corpse was found in a nearby peat bog.

Falkenberg. Resort with fine beaches. Famed pottery. **Ugglarp.** Beach. Svedino's *Automobile Museum* with over 70 cars, motorcycles and early flying machines. **Haverdalsstrand,** seaside resort with Sweden's highest dune, 36 m. Tylösand, seaside resort. The sandy beach stretches several kilometers. *Miniland,* Sweden in miniature. The model town is built on a scale of 1:25.

HALMSTAD (45 000). Chief town of the province of Halland. Modern town hall on Stora Torget (the Great Square) next to a picturesque half-timbered building that was once a hospital but now serves as a coffee shop. The sculpture group *"Europa and the Bull"*, in the square, is by Carl Milles. 14th-cent. St. Nikolai Church in the Dutch Baroque style. Norre Port, a town gate.

Laholm. Little town near the ruins of the medieval Danish Lagaholm Castle. The annual drama festival has financed a great number of works by Stig Blomberg and other Swedish sculptors.

Lugnarohögen. Bronze Age burial mound. It can be reached by an underground tunnel. *Båstad,* to the west. Large seaside resort, swarming with tourists. Several craftsmen. International tennis competitions. Fine folklore museum. *Norrviken Botanical Gardens* were laid out in 1907. *Torekov,* fishing village and seaside resort. Boats to the island of *Hallands Väderö,* a nature reserve.

E 6 goes over the Halland Ridge, 40 km long and 5-10 km wide, the natural boundary between the provinces of Halland and Scania (Skåne). *Margretetorp* inn with traditions dating back to the 1600s.

Ängelholm. Idyllic town. Large seaside resorts along the sandy coast. **Kullaberg.** Rocky coastline with lovely views. Prehistoric remains and rich vegetation. Footpaths. Be careful on the heights – unnecessary accidents occur every year. Kullen's lighthouse, 68 m above sea level. At **Skäret,** "Flickorna Lundgren", a well-known, exceptionally good, café. *Krapperup Castle* (1570) with beautiful park. *Höganäs,* famous for its ceramics, both factory-made and hand-made. Mining museum.

HELSINGBORG with **Ramlösa** and **Råå,** see E 4.

Glumslövs backar (the Glumslöv Slopes), service area with fine views out over Öresund and the island of Ven.

Landskrona (30 000). 16th cent. *citadel* with three moats. Lovely park. *Museum* with industrial and folklore exhibits. Special section devoted to Sweden's first aircraft factory, founded here in 1910. Boats to the island of **Ven** (25 min.) where there is interesting vegetation. Saint Ibb's Church. Remains of *Uranienborg* Castle and Stjärneborg Observatory. Ven was the residence of the astronomer Tycho Brahe, famed for his false golden nose (the original nose was lost in a duel). He was not popular with either the natives of Ven or the king, and eventually moved to Prague where he died in 1601.

Barsebäck, a nuclear power station, can be seen to the west. Many, not least Danes, protest its location which is right in the middle of a densely populated area.

MALMÖ (235 000). Sweden's third largest city. Handsome buildings around *Stortorget* (the Great Square). Residence of the provincial governor since 1720. Town hall from 1546. 14th cent. St. *Petri Church* with ornately carved interior and verdigris green spire. *Lilla Torg* (Little Square) with delightful 17th- and 18th-cent. buildings. Charlotte Weibull's house contains handicrafts, dolls and an exceptional pastry shop. *The market hall* has old-fashioned shops and stalls.

Malmöhus slott, a 16th cent. castle that now houses a large museum (history, archaeology, natural history and handicrafts). Technical museum with motor cars, trams, fire extinguishers and the history of flying. Carriage museum. Art gallery. Impressive municipal theatre (1944). Many fine parks and large People's Park (dances, entertainments, etc.). Ribersborg Swimming Baths on Öresund, not far from the city centre. Jägersro, race cource.

Skanör with **Falsterbo.** Idyllic small towns on a peninsula. Fine inn at Skanör. Outside, picturesque flocks of geese waddle along the street. *Falsterbohus.* Castle ruin.

Trelleborg (22 000). Industrial town and car ferry port. Ebbehallen with works by Axel Ebbe, a local sculptor.

Route 10 along the south coast. The **Ale Stones,** Sweden's largest "ship setting". 58 stones have been placed in the shape of a ship measuring 67 m long and 19 m wide. The position of the stones, arranged so that they seem to form an astronomical calender, a "Swedish Stonehenge". The stones are on a promontory overlooking the Baltic. Fine sea views.

Backåkra. Farm (open to visitors) that once belonged to Dag Hammarskjöld, Secretary General of the U.N. 1953-1961.

Glimmingehus. Well-preserved medieval castle with stepped gables (1499). Four floors, 26 m high, thick walls.

Simrishamn. Charming little town that has retained traces of its Danish origins. Situated in a lovely undulating area known as Österlen.

Route 10 continues to Kristianstad, see E 66.

E18. Oslo – Karlstad – Västerås – Stockholm

Hån. Norwegian border. E18 comes from Stavanger – Oslo – Askim.

Årjäng. Trotting races. The symbol of the town, a large troll, is in the main square. Canoeing centre in Risviken. Lakes and canals offer unlimited possibilities for canoeists. *Dalsland's Canal*, see route 45. The *Gla Forest*, large area with hiking trails.

Large industrial area along Lake Vänern. *Sörmon*, a gravel ridge, left when the Ice Age glacier retreated.

KARLSTAD (50 000). Chief town of the province of Värmland, built on an island in the Klarälven River delta. Town charter 1584. KMW, manufacturers of turbines, propellers, power stations. *Stora Torget* (the Great Square) with the Peace Goddess, erected in memory of the peaceful dissolution of the union with Norway in 1905. *Almen*, a part of the town with old houses that survived the fire of 1865. Cathedral (1730). The *East Bridge* (1770) with 12 arches is Sweden's oldest stone bridge. *Värmland's Museum* has sections devoted to the Finnish immigrants in Värmland. *Marieberg Forest*, open-air museum and zoo.

Skoghall. Billerud-Uddeholm wood pulp and paper mills. Hammarö *Church* (1748) with beautiful paintings.

Alternative route from Olso via Kongsvinger: 61 Eda – Karlstad.
Eda with border shops. *Peace monument,* erected 1914 in memory of the 100-year-long peace between Norway and Sweden.

Arvika (14 000). Built on the slopes that extend down to the almost circular Kyrkviken (Church Bay), a part of Lake Glafsfjorden. Centre for local art and handicraft. Many shops and exhibitions. *Oppstuhage,* museum devoted to the sculptor Christian Eriksson. *Sågudden,* open-air museum. **Brunskog** where *"Gammelvala"* (the Old World) is celebrated annually. Old trades and traditions are brought to life for one week in summer.

Fryksdalen, the area around Lake Fryken, is north of Karlstad. It was made famous by Selma Lagerlöf, author of "Gösta Berling's Saga". Centre of the area is **Sunne** with **Mårbacka,** Selma Lagerlöf's home (open to visitors). **Rottneros,** the "Ekeby" of her book. Large, beautiful park with about 100 sculptures.

The River **Klarälven** is one of Scandinavia's longest (270 km in Sweden and 230 km in Norway, where it is called Trysilelva). The road that follows the river (routes 61 and 235) is now called the *Pilgrim's Route* in memory of the pilgrimages to the cathedral of Trondheim (Nidaros). *Alster manor house,* where Gustaf Fröding, the poet, was born in 1860. Memorial museum and exhibition devoted to the iron-works of Värmland.

Kristinehamn (21 000). Industrial town and port. Idyllic town centre around the stream and the square. Beautiful archipelago. Sculpture by *Picasso,* a stylized head of an Indian, 15 m high.

Degerfors, industrial town. *Sveafallen,* large canyons. 310 000 years ago this was the site of waterfalls, 1 km wide. Signposted hiking trails.

Karlskoga (37 000). Red, shingled church from 1580. Art museum. AB Bofors produce anti-aircraft cannons, missiles and tanks, as well as such less lethal products as toothpaste.

E18 goes over the Kilsbergen Mountains with *Garphytte National Park* down to the Närke Plains around the town of Örebro.
Örebro – Arboga, see E3.

Köping (20 000). Large industries. A statue of the local apothecary C.W. von Scheele (d. 1786) who discovered oxygen and chlorine. *Ströbohög,* a burial mound, at the town's northern exit.

The Strömsholm Canal, built in the 18th cent. for the iron-works, now a beautiful tourist route, goes north to Ludvika (107 km). **Strömsholm Castle** (1654). Riding academy. Beautiful park.

Tidö Castle, built in 1645 for Chancellor Axel Oxenstierna. Art collection and toy museum. A part of the medieval castle remains in the park. *Fullerö,* a wooden manor house, built in 1656.

VÄSTERÅS (100 000). Chief town of the province of Västmanland. In 1623 the country's first "gymnasium" (upper secondary school) was established here. Some of the houses around *Kyrkbacken* survived a fire in 1714. The *cathedral* (originally from the 13th cent.) contains the tomb of Eric XIV. Modern town hall with 65 m high campanile. *Vallby open-air museum.* The largest of the town's many industries is Asea.

Badelundaåsen, a ridge, contains many Stone Age graves. *Anundshögen,* a 5th- to 9th-cent. burial mound, is 60 m in diameter. *Ångsö* manor house (1740) with beautiful interiors. Church with 14th cent. paintings. Beautiful park and nature reserve.

Enköping (18 000). Idyllic town. The Church of Our Lady (Vårfrukyrkan), with origins in the 12th cent. **Härkeberga Church** (14th cent.) contains beautiful and lively wall paintings by 15th-cent. master Albertus Pictor. The *Kaplan House* has an early-19th-cent. interior. *Hjälstaviken* with interesting bird life.

Skokloster, castle built in the 17th cent. for Field Marshal K.G. Wrangel. Splendid interiors and furnishings. The armoury still houses all the weapons that were there in 1660. 14th-cent. church with crypt that contains the tombs of the Wrangel family. Skokloster Automobile Museum with cars, motorcycles and fire engines.

STOCKHOLM, see town plans.

E 66. Norrköping – Kalmar – Karlskrona – Malmö

NORRKÖPING, see E 4.

Söderköping. Important town during the Middle Ages. Spa since the 18th cent. Idyllic small town.

St. Anna archipelago is in a beautiful area with mountains and narrow valleys. *Gusum,* brass works since 1661, now specializing in zip fasteners. **Valdemarsvik,** port. The Tjust archipelago is beautiful and varied.

Västervik. Port town. Museum with a section devoted to maritime exhibits. St. Gertrude Church in the Baroque style.

Oskarshamn. Old quarter with seamen's houses and gardens. View out over the harbour from a 72 m long bench. The *House of Culture* contains a museum dedicated to Axel Petersson from Döderhult who carved sharp-featured men and women.

Pataholm, shipping town with well-preserved old houses. *Kläckeberga* Church, a fortified church from the 12th-cent. The communion vessels are war booty from Poland.

The *Öland Bridge* (1972) is Europe's longest bridge, 6 km. The highest point on the bridge is 40.6 m. Car park, view and tourist information on Svinö (on the west side). The bridge is often buffeted by strong winds. *Öland,* 137 km long. Maximum width, 16 km. Tourist island. Interesting flora and fauna. *Stora Alvaret,* on the southern part of the island, is a grassy heath. At the extreme north of the island, *Böda kronopark.*

Borgholm, situated beneath the 40 m high "citadel", the coastal ridge. **Solliden,** the royal summer residence, has a beautiful park. *Borgholm Castle Ruin,* an enormous 17th-cent. structure.

Two large fortified settlements from the 5th-6th cent. One is **Ismanstorp** which has a 400 m long perimeter, 9 gates and 88 house foundations.

Himmelsberga. Folklore museum consisting of a whole farm with fine interiors. Seven windmills in a row at *Lerkaka.* Rune stone.

Eketorp. A reconstructed fortified settlement which gives a good idea of the original appearance of the structure. Guided tours. The first citadel was built in the 4th cent. and served as a sanctuary. A farming settlement developed during the 5th cent. The community existed until the Middle Ages.

Bird sanctuary at the southern tip of Öland. *Bird museum* and a bird marking station. Fine views from *Långe Jan,* a 42 m high lighthouse (1785).

Kalmar (32 000). One of Sweden's oldest towns. The Union of Kalmar (1397) joined the three Scandinavian countries under Eric of Pomerania. It was dissolved in 1521. The centre of Kalmar is *Kvarnholmen* where new houses were built after the fire of 1647. Several well-preserved old houses and streets. Ramparts. *Kavaljeren* is the most beautiful of the town gates. The **cathedral** is a large Baroque structure (1682) built to the designs of Tessin the Elder. **Kalmar Castle,** separated from the mainland by a moat. Renaissance castle (16th cent.). Five towers. Beautiful fountain in the courtyard. The castle now houses a museum.

Glass works of Småland, see route 30.

Brömsebro with a memorial stone dedicated to the peace treaty with Denmark in 1645. *Kristianopel* with ramparts, remainders of a fortress.

Karlskrona (33 000). Since 1680 Sweden's most important naval base. Shipyards. One of the barracks contains a *maritime museum* with ships' models, figure heads, weapons, etc. The Admiralty Church (1685) with Rosenbom, a carved wooden almsbox in the shape of a boatswain. Splendid *Stortorget* (the Great Square) with two churches and a magnificent town hall. Blekinge Museum. *Vämö Park,* open-air museum.

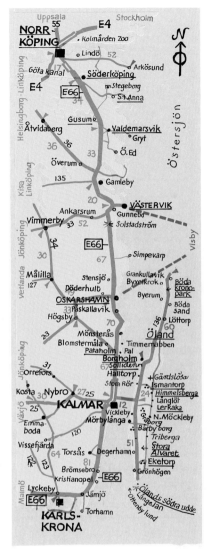

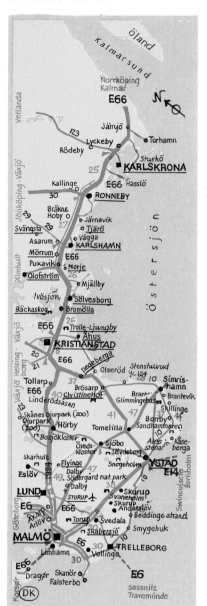

The province of Blekinge is known as "the Garden of Sweden". Many small roads lead out to the archipelago. Oak and beech woods. *Tjärö.* Tourist village run by the Swedish Touring Club. *Eriksberg,* a nature reserve, contains different species of deer. Guided tours.

Ronneby, see 30 (E 4).

Karlshamn. Fishing port. Some beautiful houses remain from the 18th cent. During the end of the 19th cent. Karlshamn was the major port of departure for emigration to America. Emigrant monument. Beautiful *Vägga Park.*

Svängsta, well-known for the production of fishing gear for amateur fishermen. *Mörrum,* site of salmon fishing (April-September). Aquarium. Recreation area at Norje.

Sölvesborg. Small town with the idyllic Stortorget (the Great Square). Carillon. Ruined castle. Glass works.

Bäckaskog. 17th-cent. castle built on the ruins of a medieval monastery. Now open to tourists. Rose garden, monastery garden and English park. *Trolle-Ljungby Castle* (17th cent.). Private.

Kristianstad (30000). Founded in 1614 by the Danes as a frontier stronghold against the Swedes. *Trinity Church* (Trefaldighetskyrkan) was completed in 1628. Museum devoted to military history. *Film museum.*

Route 10 along the east and south coast of Scania (Skåne).

Åhus. Small town with many reminders from the Middle Ages when Åhus was an important town. Eel fishing. Private residence. Beautiful garden. **Degeberga** with the Forsakar Waterfall. Castle *Christinehof* (1740), now open to visitors. Guided tours. Inn.

Simrishamn – Ystad, see E 14.

The *Linderöd* Ridge has beautiful beech woods.

Flyinge. State-owned stud farm with 250 fullblooded stallions. The stables and the park are open to visitors. *Eslöv.* Industrial town and railway junction.

LUND (42 000). Bishop's see since 1060 and archbishop's see for the whole of Scandinavia in 1103. In the 14th cent. the town had 28 churches and monasteries. The university was established in 1688. The *cathedral* is Scandinavia's foremost example of the Romanesque style. Construction started in 1080. Master builders from Lombardy directed the work during the 12th cent. In the 16th cent. Adam of Düren was the architect. Triptych from 1398. *Astronomical clock* (14th cent.). One of the pillars in the crypt has been carved in the shape of a giant (perhaps Samson). *Kulturen.* One of the country's largest folklore museums, housed in a number of old buildings. Fine collection of pottery. Historical museum, museum of the cathedral, antiques museum, art museum, etc. *Lundagård* with the university buildings.

MALMÖ, see E 6.

E 14. Malmö – Ystad

MALMÖ, see E 6.

Skabersjö, 18th-cent. manor house (private). *Torup Castle* (16th cent.), owned by the city of Malmö. Open to the public in the summer. Beautiful park. *Sturup,* modern airport.

Svaneholm Castle (16th cent.). Folklore museum. Beautiful interiors, costumes, weapons, coins, toys. Monument to MacLean, a Scotsman who introduced modern agricultural techniques to Sweden in the 1790s.

Ystad (14 000) with about 300 well-preserved half-timbered houses. Charles XII's House is one of the finest. *Maria Church* (13th-15th cent.) has the country's only tower watchman.He blows his horn every night. *Grey Friar Monastery* (13th cent.). Museum area with half-timbered houses, patrician homes, art, military museum, etc.

E 14 continues by car ferry to Poland (Swinoujscie) and onwards to Praha – Salzburg – Trieste.

E 6 Continues to Berlin – München – Roma.

E 75. Storlien – Östersund – Sundsvall

Norwegian border. E 75 comes from Trondheim.

Storlien (592 m above sea level). Large mountain hotel. Brudslöjan (the Bridal Veil), a 24 m high waterfall in Norway. *Handöl*. Village with a chapel. Soap-stone for stoves has been quarried here since the 16th cent. Monument to the soldiers of Charles XII who, around New Year 1718-1719, started the march back from Norway, where their king had been shot. 4 000 froze to death. Survivors straggled down to Handöl and other places in the area. Suspension foot-bridge below the beautiful Handöl Rapids. Total height 120 m. Beautiful road onwards to *Storulvån*, site of a mountain hotel run by the Swedish Touring Club (730 m above sea level). On foot to *Sylarna*, the highest mountain in the province of Jämtland (1 762 m).

Ånn Lake with bird life and remains of Stone Age habitations. Rock carvings at *Landverk*. *Tännforsen* (the Tänn Waterwall) one of the most beautiful in Sweden, is 60 m wide and 27 m high. Fantastic ice formations in the winter. The old road from Levander via Skalstugan is winding but scenic.

Duved and *Åre* are Jämtland's largest tourist resorts. Cable car (1 250 m long) up to 750 m above sea level at Mullfjället, Duved. Long ski slope. Memorial to the soldiers of King Charles XII. New church in Åre. Cable car to Åreskutan, at an altitude of 1 274 m above sea level. The summit is 1 420 m above sea level. Old *church* (13th cent.) with 17th-cent. interior. The Danish coat of arms is still on the wall. Sculpture of St. Olof wearing a Carolingian hat instead of the crown which has been lost. *Vålådalen*, mountain hotel and sports college. *Undersåker* with Ristafallet, an impressive waterfall, 14 m high.

Järpen and *Mörsil*, with redoubts from the 17th cent., also used during the 1808-1809 war. Rock carvings at *Glösabäcken*. Lake *Storsjön*, Sweden's fifth largest lake.

ÖSTERSUND (40 000). Chief town in the province of Jämtland, founded in 1786. Views of the mountains from the sloping *square*. Impressive *town hall* (1912). *Jämtland's Museum* (provincial museum). *Jamtli* open-air museum. Bridge to *Frösön*, the old centre of Jämtland. *Frösö Church* with splendid view of the mountains. *Sommarhagen*, residence of the composer Peterson-Berger. His musical drama, "Arnljot", is presented here every summer. *Frösö Zoo. Thomée*, a steamboat, built in 1875, is in regular traffic on Lake Storsjön during the summer. The Storsjö Monster is just as shy as its Loch Ness counterpart. A specially constructed trap is displayed in the museum in Östersund.

Brunflo. Road 81 goes south through extensive forests to Sveg and Mora. Beautiful views out over Storsjön.

Hackås Church, with an aspe from the 11th cent., is the oldest church in northern Sweden. Paintings and furnishings by local artists. Hoverberget on the opposite shore of the lake has an 81 m deep and 25 m high cave. Old church at Ålvros. Beautiful interior. Another fine road goes over the Klövsjö Mountains to the large tourist resort of Vemdalen.

Pilgrimstad ("Pilgrims' town"). The name brings to mind the old pilgrimage route which went from the Gulf of Bothnia to the grave of St. Olof in Trondheim (Nidaros). *Borgsjö Church* (1768) resembles a rococo manor house.

SUNDSVALL, see E 4.

E 79. Mo – Storuman – Umeå. *The Blue Route*

The Norwegian border is situated high above the timber line. E 79 comes from Mo i Rana. Beautiful views towards Mount *Okstindan.*

Tärnaby. Old church village, tourist resort, customs station. Home of skiing champion Ingemar Stenmark.

From Slussfors road to Dikanäs on the *"Saga Road"*, a beautiful road that goes past Kittelfjäll to Hattfjelldal in Norway and on to Mosjøen.

Numerous power stations on the Ume River. *Lycksele* (9 000). Folklore museum. Lycksele *Zoo* with Scandinavian animals.

Pengsjö Pioneer Museum, an interesting private folklore museum. *Stornorrfors*, one of Sweden's largest hydro-electric power plants. Tours. Salmon breeding. The water is allowed to follow its natural course one Sunday in the middle of June. *Brännland* with four soldiers' homes and other old houses that have been turned into a folklore museum. Power station museum in *Klabböle*.

UMEÅ, see E 4.

E 79 continues by car ferry to Vaasa – Tampere – Helsinki.

375. Bodø – Arvidsjaur – Luleå, see p. 374.

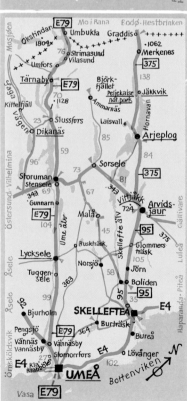

40. Göteborg–Jönköping

GÖTEBORG (Gothenburg), see town plans.

Hindås is beautifully situated. Recreation area. Winter sports. Stave church at *Hedared*, see E 3.

Ulricehamn. Well-preserved wooden houses around the square.

Komosse, an almost 7 km wide bog with a lake which is a refuge for wildfowl. *Bottnaryd Church.* Timber church with colourful paintings on the ceiling and walls (17th cent.). They depict the Last Judgement and Jerusalem.

JÖNKÖPING, see E 4.

Roads north to the Västgöta Plains with ranges of hills where the Stone Age farmers erected their burial monuments 4000 years ago. Passage tombs, rune stones and medieval churches – this area was densely populated.

Falköping. There are seven passage tombs in the town. Museum. St. Olof's Church, originally from the 12th cent. *Mösseberg.* Old hotel and observation tower. *Ålleberg* is another plateau mountain, especially popular with glider enthusiasts.

45. Karlstad – Vänersborg – Göteborg

Karlstad – Segmon, see E 18.

Säffle. Head offices of Billerud, one of Sweden's largest industrial concerns. Säffle Canal connects Lake Vänern with Lake Glafsfjorden. The Trätälja Mound, a 6th-cent. burial mound. *Västra Smedbyn*, see E 18.

Åmål. Idyllic town with old houses along the stream.

Beautiful route through an area marked by lakes and mountains to Strömstad on E 6. *Baldersnäs,* manor house with café. Large park with grottoes, ponds and gazebos. Museum of handicrafts. *Steneby* has a handicraft school.

Ed. Splendid views out over Stora Le, an almost 100 km long, narrow lake. Reminders of Charles XII's last war with Norway.

Route 45 across the wide Dalbo Plain with mountains in the background. Bridge across the *Dalsland Canal,* built in 1868 for the transport of iron ore. Now a beautiful tourist route. The actual canal consists of short stretches (a total of 100 km) between the lakes. The water route to Årjäng on E 18 is 250 km long and has 28 locks. The *aqueduct* at *Håverud* was designed by Nils Ericsson, railway engineer and brother of John Ericsson, the inventor. It is a 32 m long steel tube across the rapids, now dry, which are also crossed by a railway bridge and a road bridge.

Kroppefjäll, mountain plateau and wooded area, about 50 km long and 10 km wide. The "Carolingian Route", a hiking trail, named in memory of Charles XII's last campaign.

Vänersborg (20000). High bridge across the Trollhätte Canal which connects Lake Vänern with the sea. Ships of up to 13500 tons can use this waterway. Vänersborg is associated with Birger Sjöberg, a poet who is remembered for his songs set in this idyllic town and its environs.

Halleberg and *Hunneberg.* Wooded hills (155 m) separated by a 500 m wide valley. The area teems with elk. "Elk safaris" are arranged from Vänersborg.

Trollhättan (42000). Industry (SAAB). Construction on the power station started in 1910. Tours. The water is allowed to follow its natural course once a year on the "Day of the Falls", in July. 20000 ships pass through the six locks annually.

The River *Götaälv* is lined with communities and industries especially south of Bohus and Kungälv, where the narrow valley has room for two roads, a railway line and the intensive canal traffic. The clay banks are insecure – many landslides have occurred here.

Bohus Fortress, see E 6. *GÖTEBORG* (Gothenburg), see town plans.

The Härjedalen Mountains – Dalarna – Stockholm

Fjällnäs and *Tänndalen.* Tourist resorts. Mount Hamra with rich vegetation. *Funäsdalen.* Cable car to the summit of Mount Funäsdal, 981 m. Tourist centres of *Bruksvallarna* and *Ramundberget.* Hiking trail to the summit of *Mittåkläppen* with views towards the Sylarna mountains in the province of Jämtland. Road over *Flatruet*, a mountain plateau, 975 m above sea level. *Ljungdalen.* Mountain village. Hiking trail to Helags.

Tännäs is Sweden's loftiest church village, 648 m above sea level. Views out over the extensive forested landscape.

Vemdalen, Vemdalsskalet and *Björnrike,* tourist resorts. *Sånfjället National Park,* mainly wooded foothills.

Sveg. Road 81 from here through wooded areas to Mora. *Fågelsjö,* ancient village which is now almost deserted. *Los* with a monument to A.F. Cronstedt who discovered nickel in the 18th cent. *Storstupet* and *Helvetesfallet,* two waterfalls. *Orsa.* Small industries. *Fryksåsen* with old farmhouses that have been turned into a hotel.

Våmhus, known for the traditional "jewellery" made from human hair.

Mora. The popular "Vasaloppet" skiing race, 85 km from Sälen to Mora, takes place on the first Sunday in March. In the last ten years over 10 000 skiers have participated in each race. It is held in memory of Gustav Vasa who skied the same route in 1521. He became King of Sweden (1523-1560).

Studio and home of artist Anders Zorn (1860-1920). *Zorn Museum* and an open-air museum. *Church* (15th cent.) with furnishings from the 17th and 18th cent. Nusnäs, where the wooden horses typical of the province of Dalarna are made. The large factory can be visited.

Road 295 to the mountains of northern Dalarna around *Grövelsjön* and Mount *Idrefjäll.* 17th-cent. church in Särna. *Älvdalen* with large forests, fishing, hiking trails and mountain huts.

Rättvik. Tourist centre. The church received its present appearance in the 18th cent. 90 stables, once used for the churchgoers' horses. Pottery in *Nittsjö.* Observation tower on Lerdalshöjden, 325 m above sea level.

Tällberg. Tourist resort with several hotels. Idyllic roads and fine views. *Holen,* a folklore museum. Tin figure museum in *Hjortnäs.* 20 000 figures.

Leksand. Tourist resort. Tens of thousands of people take part in the annual Midsummer celebrations. Performances of *Himlaspelet* (the "Road to Heaven") every summer. The simple religious faith of the characters in the play is an attempt at recreating the atmosphere of the naive religious paintings typical of the province. Music festival in July. Leksand *Church,* originally from the 13th cent. The onion dome was added in the 18th cent. Baroque furnishings. Fine views from *Käringberget,* where witches were burnt during the 17th cent. Cable car to *Åsledsberget.*

Siljan. Sweden's seventh largest lake, 161 m above sea level. 36 km long, about 25 km wide. Maximum dept 133 m. The area around the lake is one of Sweden's major tourist areas. Boat excursions. *Mount Gesundaberget,* 501 m, dominates the area. Cable car. Fine views. *Sollerön,* a fertile island, has been inhabited since prehistoric times. Artisans' village. The making of church boats has been resumed. These boats are used at Midsummer and for the annual church boat race on the first Sunday in July.

Gagnef. Österdalälven (the East Dal River) and *Västerdalälven* (the West Dal River) join here to form the *Dalälven,* Sweden's longest river, 520 km.

BORLÄNGE (40 000). Stora Kopparberg iron works and Kvarnsveden paper mill. The local museum has souvenirs of J.O. Wallin, hymn writer, and Jussi Björling, opera singer. *Ornässtugan,* Sweden's oldest timber building (1450), on a peninsula in Lake Runn. Associated with Gustav Vasa.

Road 60 goes to *Falun,* the chief town of the province of Dalecarlia (Dalarna). Mining started in the copper mine here in the 11th cent. The mine caved in in 1687 and the *"Stora stöten"* was formed. Now the main products of the town are chemicals and Falu Red Paint (made from iron oxide), which gives the houses and farm buildings of the Swedish countryside their typical red colour. Mining museum. Tours of the old mine, 55 m below the surface. Dalarna's Museum.

Stora Tuna Church (15th cent.). One of Sweden's largest country churches.

Hedemora. Town charter 1446. The main square is the site of a pharmacy from 1779 and a hotel from 1860. Folklore museum. The old theatre (1820) is used during the summer. *Husbyringen* is the name of a 60 km long tour of the area. It includes several beautiful and interesting places, among them *Stjärnsund,* where the 18th-cent. inventor Christopher Polhem constructed machines and clocks. *Långshyttan* with steel industry.

Sala. Picturesque small town. The *silver mine* was worked from the 15th cent. until the beginning of the 20th cent. The deepest shaft goes down to 318 m. Mining museum. Carriage and artisans' museum at *Väsby Kungsgård,* (1730). Museum with the works of artist Ivan Aguéli.

Härkeberga Church and *Enköping,* see E 18.

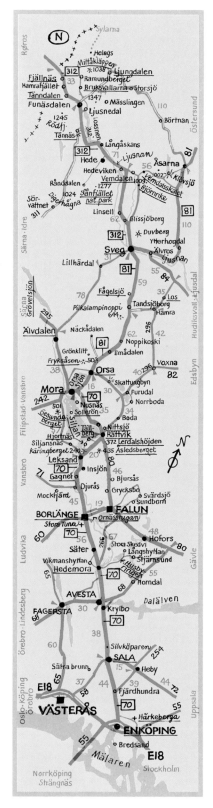

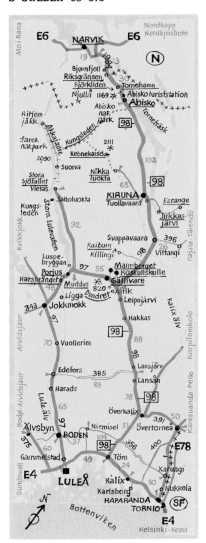

98. Narvik – Luleå

Norwegian border. The road via Björnfjell to Rombak Bridge and Narvik will be opened in 1984.

Riksgränsen. Tourist resort. The annual rainfall figure, 1169 mm, is the greatest in Sweden. Abisko, a bit to the east, has 300 mm, the least in Sweden.

Tornehamn with a cemetery for the navvies who built the Riksgränsen railway line, at the turn of the century. Peaceful and idyllic little churchyard with views out over Lake Torneträsk. The road follows the steep sides of Mount Njulla along Lake Torneträsk. Beware of avalanches!

Björkliden. Tourist hotel. *Abisko* with the Swedish Touring Club's largest hotel. Chair lift, almost 2 km long, to the summit of *Mount Njulla.* Midnight sun from May 31 until July 16. *Kungsleden* Hiking Trail to Kebnekaise and Saltoluokta is Sweden's most famous hiking trail. Abisko *National Park. Torneträsk,* a 70 km long and 9 km wide lake. Maximum depth 168 m.

KIRUNA (25 000). Mount Kirunavaara, with the world's richest iron ore deposits. Modern town, 200 km north of the Arctic Circle. In 1890 the only structure in the area was a peat hut. Church (1912), resembling a Lapp hut, with a lavishly adorned interior. Town hall with a high bell tower. Bus tours into the *mines* include a visit to a mine 370 m under the surface.

Road to *Nikkaluokta.* 19 km on foot to *Kebnekaise,* Sweden's highest mountain, 2 111 m. Mountain hotel (STF).

Jukkasjärvi Church has a wooden relief by Bror Hjort which depicts Laestadius, a Revivalist preacher. *Folklore museum* with Lapp museum. *Esrange,* space research station.

Road 395 to Karesuando, Sweden's northernmost church village. For the route to the North Cape, see Finland, E 78 and Norway, E 6.

Kaitum. Memorial chapel dedicated to Dag Hammarskjöld, Secretary General of the U.N.

Gällivare-Malmberget (19000) has rich iron ore deposits. Mining museum and exhibitions. 250 km of underground galleries. *Church* with an altar made out of a piece of iron ore.

Dundret, 823 m, large recreation area with tourist cottages and Björnfällan (the Beartrap) inn. Winter sports.

Muddus National Park. Road to *Stora Sjöfallet,* once one of Sweden's major attractions, now an almost dry waterfall, due to the power stations which have been built here. Power stations in Porjus and Harsprånget. *Jokkmokk,* famous for its large Lapp market in February. Museum and old church.

The Aitik mine annually produces 37 000 tons of copper, 40 tons of silver and 1 ton of gold.

The *Arctic Circle.* Northerly latitude 66° 33'. From here it is 3 330 km to the North Pole and 6 660 km to the Equator. Elsewhere in the world, the Arctic Circle runs through desolate areas, often covered with snow and ice, but in Scandinavia, thanks to the Gulf Stream, it is possible to drive on good roads to communities with large populations far north of the Circle.

Töre – Luleå, see E 4.

Road 400 Karesuando – Övertorneå and road 99 Övertorneå – Haparanda, see Finland, E 78.

375. Bodø – Arvidsjaur – Luleå, see map p. 369.

Norwegian border high above the timber line. The "Silver Route" comes from Bodø – Fauske – Hestbrinken. See E 6, Norwey.

The road passes through an impressive mountain landscape and along mountain lakes. *Peljekaise National Park.* Jäkkvik Chapel (1977) with special celebrations the Sunday before Midsummer and around September 20.

Arjeplog is beautifully situated on an isthmus between two lakes. Population density 1/3 inhabitant per km². In the 17th and 18th cent. silver ore from the mines in Nasafjäll on the Norwegian border was transported here. (Hence the name, the"Silver Route".) The *Silver Museum* with extraordinary collection of Lapp silver.

Arvidsjaur. 4 000 inhabitants, a large community for the area. Founded in 1605 during the campaign to convert the Lapps to Christianity. *Kyrkstan* (Lappstan), an open-air museum with Lapp huts and other local structures. Recreation area and winter sports centre at *Vittjåkk* mountain.

LULEÅ, see E 4.

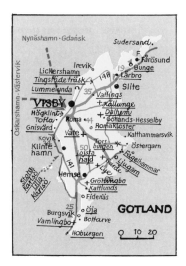

Gotland

(55 300). Area: 1 342 km².
With its rugged coastline, its lush vegetation and its many reminders of its illustrious past, Gotland has a unique standing among the provinces of Sweden.
The island has been inhabited since the Stone Age. Finds of Roman coins and of coins and artifacts from other countries testify to Gotland's importance as a trading centre. Over 90 churches, all but one built before 1350. The anonymous stone masons who worked on the churches have been given names such as Byzantios, Majestatis, Egypticus, etc.
Visby (20 000), one of Europe's most important towns during the Middle Ages, member of the Hanseatic League. Its period of greatness ended in 1361 when Valdemar Atterdag, the Danish king, defeated the Gotland peasant army and occupied Visby, which was sacked.
The town wall is the most impressive in northern Europe, 3.5 km long and 12 m high, 45 towers. Many preserved medieval houses. Visby was one of Sweden's project cities during the European Architectural Heritage Year 1975.
St. Mary's Cathedral (the church of the German merchants) is the only preserved medieval church. *St. Catherine* (a Franciscan abbey church). The ruins of the Dominican abbey church, *St. Nicholas*, is the site of annual summertime performances of the opera "Petrus de Dacia".
Gotlands fornsal, a museum with exhibits of rune stones, finds from the Viking Age, medieval art, the history of the Hanseatic League, etc. Skeletons, skulls and armour found in the mass grave from the battle against the Danes in 1361 bear witness to the ferocity of the fighting.
Lovely parks. Beautiful views from the slopes north of the town, outside the town wall.

North of Visby:
Fårö is 20 km long and 2–8 km wide. Moors with pine forests. Sandy soil. Thatched houses and sheep. "Raukar"– strange rock formations created by the sea.
Bunge Museum, an open-air museum with about 50 houses from the 16th to 18th cent. *Lärbro* Church with octagonal tower. *Tingstäde träsk,* a shallow lake with remains of a fortified Iron-Age settlement in the middle of the lake. *Vatlings,* a 13th- cent. farm.
Lickershamn, a fishing harbour on the coast route, has a large rock, Jungfrun (the Virgin), down by the water. *Lummelunda Caves* (open to visitors).
East of Visby:
Romakloster, founded in 1164 by Cistercian monks. Remains of the monastery are immured in the manor house. *Dalhem.* Small preserved railway and museum.
Väte Church with beautiful stone reliefs. *Lojsta* heath, a large area where semi-wild ponies, "rus", roam freely. Once they were found all over Gotland. *Lojstahallen,* a reconstruction of a 6th-cent. structure.
Ljugarn, old seaside resort. Youth hostel in the former home and office of the local customs inspector. Customs museum. *Fågelhammar* with strange rock formations. *Torsburgen,* a fortified iron settlement on a 58 m high limestone cliff.
South of Visby:
Högklint, a 45 m high limestone cliff with fine views. Vintage car museum. *Gnisvärd,* old fishing village. "Ship setting", Viking Age monument consisting of stones arranged in the shape of a ship. Fishing museum in *Kovik.*
Stora Karlsö and *Lilla Karlsö.* Sweden's only bird cliffs. Interesting vegetation. Meadows covered with orchids on Stora Karlsö. "Stora förvar", a cave, was a Stone-Age dwelling. Sheep pastures on Lilla Karlsö. Nature reserve which can only be visited with guided tours. Boats from Klintehamn.
Uggarde rojr, a 7 m high Bronze-Age mound. *Grötlingbo* Church, one of Gotland's largest. *Kattlund's* Farm, with some parts dating from the 12th cent. *Öja Church* has a large Triumphal Cross.
Vamlingbo Church. The cross was hit by lightning in 1350. Large painting depicting Emperor Henri II being weighed on the scales of the Archangel Michael.
Hoburgen. Interesting rock formations on the southern tip of Gotland. Hoburgsgubben, "The Hoburg Man", is the most famous rock. Restaurant.

TOWN PLANS

GÖTEBORG (Gothenburg 470 000)
Sweden's second largest city and largest port. Founded in 1621 by Gustavus Adolphus, it was laid out in the Dutch manner (several canals). Headquarters of shipping lines. Shipyards. Volvo car factories.
Town hall (1672), designed by Tessin the Elder. Residenset, residence of the provincial governor. Östra Hamngatan and Kungsportsavenyn lead from Gustav Adolfs torg, site of the stock exchange, to the wide *Götaplatsen,* distinguished by Carl Milles' statue of Poseidon. At the end of the square are the Art Museum, the City Museum and the Concert Hall.
Lovely parks: Trädgårdsföreningen, Slottsskogen, and the Botanical Gardens. Liseberg, Sweden's foremost amusement park, has a fun fair set in beautiful gardens.
Museums: The *Art Museum* displays 19th- and 20th- cent. Scandinavian, French and Dutch art. Historical, ethnological and archaeological displays in *Ostindiska Huset,* a 1750 office building. *Kronhuset* (1653), Gothenburg's oldest building, now serves as the *City Museum.* Examples of handicrafts in Kronohusbodarna. *Ship Museum. Maritime Museum* with aquarium and Maritime Tower erected in memory of sailors who perished during the First World War. Röhsska Museum of Industrial Art. Military Museum in the *Kronan* fortifications. Boats to the *Elfsborg Fortress* (1670), situated on an island at the harbour entrance.
Fine views from the *Masthugget Church.* Old *Örgryte Church,* with origins in the 11th cent., was given its present appearance in the 18th cent. Interesting ceiling paintings.
Scandinavium, an indoor arena that accommodates 14 000 spectators (seating 11 000). Ullevi, with space for 52 000, is Sweden's largest sports arena.
Impressive traffic arteries span the Göta River. Götaälv Bridge, 927 m long, 22 m above the water. The Älvsborg Bridge, 933 m long. The Tingstad Tunnel, 454 m long.

STOCKHOLM (650 000),
Greater Stockholm 1.3 million)
Capital of Sweden, founded in 1254 on an island at the entrance to Lake Mälaren. *Gamla stan* (the Old Town) is northern Europe's best preserved medieval town. *Stortorget* (the Great Square) where the Danish king, Christian II, had 82 people beheaded in 1520, "Stockholm's Blood Bath". *Storkyrkan* (the Great Church) with St. George and the Dragon, a famous sculpture by Bernt Notke of Lübeck. A copy of the statue stands in Köpmanbrinken. The restaurant Den Gyldene Freden is owned by the Swedish Academy. Splendid row of merchants' houses along Skeppsbron.

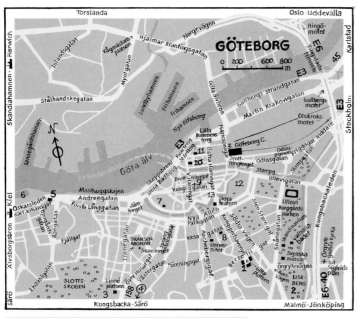

GÖTEBORG

0   200   600   800
m

Götaplatsen

1 Art Museum,
   Concert Hall, Mu-
   nicipal Theatre
2 Liseberg Amuse-
   ment Park
3 Slottsskogen (na-
   ture reserve).
   Museum of Natu-
   ral History
4 Botanical Gar-
   dens
5 Maritime Mu-
   seum. Aquarium
6 Fishing Harbour
7 Market hall (fish)
8 Röhsska Museum
   (arts and crafts)
9 Cathedral
10 East India House.
11 Kronhuset (city
   museum). Work-
   shops. Shops
   from the turn of
   the century
12 Trädgårdsföre-
   ningen
13 Kungsportsplat-
   sen. Sight-seeing
   boats

park with ice-skating rink in the winter and concerts and performances of
other kinds in the summer. Flower
shows.
The **Town Hall** (1923), designed by
Ragnar Östberg, is an impressive
brick building with arcades facing
Lake Mälaren and a campanile with
the three golden crowns of the
Swedish coat of arms 106 m above the
water. Observation terrace at 76 m.
The Blue Hall (which is red) and the
Golden Hall (with mosaics) are the two
most famous rooms.
The island of **Djurgården** contains
many sights: **Skansen,** one of the
world's first open-air museums with
about 100 buildings from different
parts of Sweden. Zoo specializing in
Scandinavian animals. Aquarium.
Terrarium. Gröna Lund, an amusement park, is also situated on
Djurgården as is the **Wasa**, a 50 m
long war ship from the 17th cent. She
foundered on her maiden voyage in
1628. After 333 years at the bottom of
the Stockholm harbour the Wasa was
lifted up in 1961 and placed in a
museum building. The restoration
work is still in progress. *Finn-
grundet,* a lighthouse ship, is moored
near by. *Waldemarsudde,* home of
Prince Eugen. Art collection. *Thiel's
Gallery,* also art collection.
Millesgården, on Lidingö, sculpture
park with the works of Carl Milles
(1875-1955).
The *Nordic Museum,* folklore, crafts,
furniture, costumes. The *National
Museum,* art. The *Museum of Modern
Art* includes a photography museum.
Natural history museum, maritime
museum, museum of architecture,
museum of Mediterranean civilizations, museum in the Royal Palace,
tram museum, municipal museum,
Strindberg museum, toy museum,
museum of technology, Far Eastern
museum, ethnographical museum.
Many of the new stations of the
Stockholm **underground** have been
decorated by artists and are architecturally interesting.
Drottningholm Palace (1662), a
Swedish Versailles, is situated 12 km
west of the centre of Stockholm. Built
by Tessin, father and son. Baroque
palace and gardens and an English
park. Home of the Swedish royal
family since 1981. Some rooms are
open to the public. The **Drottningholm Court Theatre** (1766) is one of
the world's best preserved 18th-cent.
theatres. Performances during the
summer months. Theatre museum.
China Palace, a folly in the Chinese
style. Boats to Drottningholm from
the Town Hall. **Birka,** Sweden's most
important trading centre in the 9th to
10th cent. can also be reached by boat.
Earth ramparts and graves. The
Stockholm archipelago, an area 80
km wide and 140 km long, has about
7 000 islands. Boats from Nybroviken.
One popular goal is the little town of
Vaxholm. Another is the porcelain factory in *Gustavsberg.*

Västerlånggatan is the main shopping street in the Old Town
(pedestrian precinct). The **Royal
Palace** is an impressive Italian Baroque structure (18th cent.) designed by
Tessin, father and son, and Carl Hårle-
man. Several museums. The changing
of the guards once a day is a popular
tourist event. The royal family now
lives in Drottningholm Palace, outside
Stockholm. The *German Church* (St.
Gertrude), the church of the German
merchants. Carillon.
Riddarhuset (the Knights' House,
1674), where the nobility met. Dutch
Baroque. *Riddarholmskyrkan* (the

Riddarholmen Church), with royal
tombs. The House of the Swedish
Parliament (1905) on Helgeandshol-
men. Sergels torg, Kungsgatan and
Hamngatan are the main shopping
streets. NK and other big department
stores. *Hötorget,* a lively market
square in front of the *Concert Hall*
(1926), where the Nobel Prizes are annually awarded on December 10.
"Orpheus", fountain by Carl Milles,
stands at the entrance. *Sergels torg*
with a 37 m high glass sculpture.
Kulturhuset (the Culture House) with
library and exhibition halls. Modern
buildings. Kungsträdgården, a lovely

1 The Old Town.
  Royal Palace.
  Cathedral
2 Riddarholm
  Church
3 Town Hall
4 City Museum
5 National Museum
  of Art
6 Museum of Mo-
  dern Art
7 Museum of Musi-
  cal History
8 Historical Museum
9 Nordic Museum
10 Skansen (open-air
   museum)
11 Royal Warship
   Wasa
12 Waldemarsudde
   and Thiel's Gallery
   (art collections)
13 Technical Museum
   and Ethnographi-
   cal Museum. Mari-
   time Museum
14 Kaknäs Tower
15 National Museum
   of Natural History
16 Drottningholm
   Palace
17 Millesgården

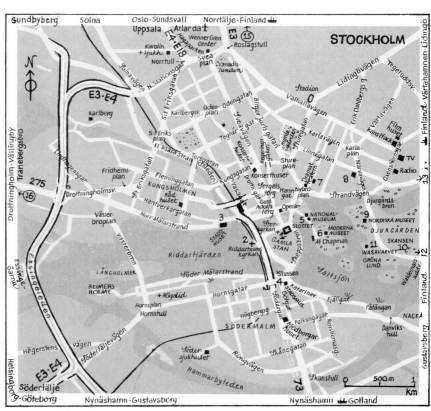

Stockholm. City Hall
and the Old Town

SF · Finland

SF·Suomi/Finland

Area: 337 000 km² (130 160 sq. miles) including the Åland Islands.

Population: 4.8 million. The official languages are Finnish (a Finno-Ugric language) and Swedish, but the Swedish-speaking minority now comprises a mere 6.5 % of the population. About 2 000 of Finland's inhabitants speak Lapp, another Finno-Ugric language. 91 % of the population are Lutheran and 1.2 % belong to the Russian Orthodox church.

Major cities: Helsinki/Helsingfors 880 000, Tampere/Tammerfors 170 000, Turku/Åbo 165 000, Espoo/Esbo 137 000, Vanda/Vantaa 132 000, Lahti/Lahtis 100 000, Oulu/Uleåborg 95 000, Pori/Björneborg 80 000.

Government: Parliamentary republic. One-chamber parliament.

History

1323 Finno-Swedish frontier established. The north-eastern section of Finland is ceded to Russia, the remainder of Finland becomes a province of Sweden.

1617 Peace of Stolbova after eight years of war with Russia. Karelia is ceded to Finland.

1741-1743 War with Russia. Large sections of south-eastern Finland lost.

1808-1809 War with Russia. As a result of the Peace of Fredrikshamn Finland becomes an autonomous grand duchy in the Russian Empire.

1899 The czar abolishes Finland's autonomy. Russianization policies are introduced.

1917 Finland proclaims its independence.

1918 Civil war between "White Guards" and "Red Guards". "Red" revolutionaries hold Helsinki, Tampere and Viborg, but after a few months of bloody and brutal fighting, they are ousted by "White" troops under the command of General Mannerheim.

1919 Finland becomes a republic.

1939-1940 Winter War. Finland is invaded by the Soviet Union and loses the Karelian Isthmus, Viborg, Hangö and eastern sections of the country.

1941-1944 War against the Soviet Union. Finland is allied with the Axis powers.

1947 Peace treaty signed in Paris.

1956 The Soviet Union returns the military base of Porkkala to Finland.

Post- war period: Relations with the Soviet Union improve, as a result of efforts of Finnish Presidents Mannerheim, Paasakivi and Kekkonen.

Currency: Finnish marks (FIM). 1 mark = 100 penni

Business hours: Banks 9.15 a.m.-4.15 p.m. Closed Saturdays. Post offices 9.00 a.m.-5.00 p.m. Closed Saturdays. Shops 8.30 or 9.00 a.m.-5.00 p.m. During the winter until 6.00 p.m.

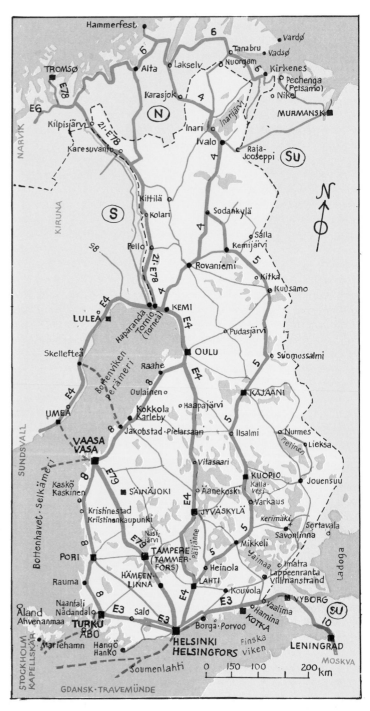

Holidays: New Year's Day, Saturday closest to the Feast of the Epiphany, Good Friday, Easter Sunday, Easter Monday, May 1, Saturday closest to Ascension Day, Whit Sunday, Whit Monday, Saturday closest to Midsummer Day, Saturday closest to All Saints' Day, December 6 (Independence Day), December 25 and 26.

Hotels

No official classifications. Several hotels chains that maintain high standards: Cumulus, Point Hotels, Polar Hotels, Rantasipi, Scanhotels, SOKOS. Unique to Finland are the numerous large, up-to-date, first-class country hotels that are almost always set in beautiful countryside. Many are owned by the Rantasipi chain.

Camping

There are about 300 camping sites of varying standards scattered about the country. Most of them have self-catering chalets. Camping and tenting away from the official sites is possible, but permission from the land-owner is mandatory.

Youth hostels

There are about 100 youth hostels. All of them accept guests of all ages, and motorists. 30 of the best-equipped are open year-round, and many have family rooms. In general there are no cafeterias or meal services.

Food and drink

Finnish cuisine has been influenced by Russian and West European (especially Swedish and French) cooking traditions. In Finland, as in neighbouring Sweden, meat, fish, potatoes, milk, butter and crispbread are the main ingredients.

Some specialities: Savustetta siika, smoked white-fish with scrambled eggs. Kalakukko (a speciality of Kuopio), rye-bread filled with bits of sausage and whitefish – best when served hot and accompanied by melted butter. Karjalan piirakka, pastries served hot with butter and eggs. Karjalan paisti, mixed beef, mutton and pork. Poronkieli, reindeer tongue. Poronpaisti, roast reindeer. Reindeer heart is an exclusive delicacy. Russian specialities often appear on Finnish menues: shashlik, borshch, smetana. The season for crayfish (ragu) begins on July 21.

Cloudberries and cranberries often accompany ice cream. It is not unusual for coffee to replace dessert.

Excellent beers and liqueurs: Mesimarja (Arctic brambleberry liqueur), Lakka and Soumuurain (cloudberry liqueur), Polar (cranberry liqueur). Of all of the many varieties of domestic vodka, Koskenkorva is the best known.

Shopping

Handicrafts, glass, porcelain, textiles, costume jewellery (Kalevala jewellery is based on centuries-old patterns), fishing equipment, knives (puokko), furs, women's leather boots.

Speed limits. Traffic regulations

The speed limits are 60, 100 and 120. They are always posted. Private cars

Saimaa, the scenic system of lakes in south-eastern Finland

Routes described:

E 3   Vaalima – Helsinki/Helsingfors – Turku/Åbo

E 4   Tornio – Jyväskylä – Helsinki/Helsingfors

E 78   Tromsø – Tornio

E 79   Vaasa/Vasa – Tampere – Helsinki/Helsingfors

4   Karigasniemi – Ivalo – Rovaniemi – Kemi

5   Kemijärvi – Kaajani – Kuopio – Mikkeli – Lahti – Helsinki

8   Oulu – Jakobstad/Pietarsaari – Vaasa/Vasa – Pori – Turku/Åbo

Special map: Åland

Town plans: Helsinki/Helsingfors, Turku/Åbo

Porvoo (Borgå), one of Finland's best-preserved 18th-century towns

towing caravans or trailers must not exceed 80 kmh. Built-up areas 50 kmh.

If your car is fitted with seat belts it is compulsory to wear them.

All vehicles must have dipped headlights during the daylight hours outside built-up areas.

Roads

Direction signs indicate the language spoken in the areas: If the overwhelming majority of the local population is Finnish-speaking, then the signs are only in Finnish. If the local population is Swedish-speaking, then the signs are in Swedish. In areas where both languages are used, the language spoken by the majority of the local population is given the topmost position on road signs. We have followed the same system in this book. If the Swedish name for a town is in parentheses, this indicates that officially the Finnish name is the accepted one.

Road patrols

Towing assistance can be obtained from the nearest service station, garage or by contacting the police. The Autolitto Auto Club has only volunteer-staffed cars that do not patrol set routes. By dialling 90-694 04 96, you will reach Autoliito, and they will give advice and tell you where you can get assistance.

In case of personal injury, the emergency number in Helsinki is 000. For emergency numbers in other cities and towns, please refer to the local telephone directory.

Autolitto/Automobilförbundet (Finnish Automobile Association), Kansakoulukatu 10, Helsinki. Tel. 694 00 22.

Finnish Tourist Board, Greener House, 2nd floor, 66-68 Haymarket, London SW1 4RF. Tel. 01-839 4048.

Lappland, Finland's northernmost province

E 3. Vaalimaa – Helsinki/Helsingfors – Turku/Åbo

Vaalimaa. Soviet frontier.

Hamina (Fredrikshamn). Founded in 1653 as a fortress. The octagonal square and the town hall (1789) is the starting point for eight streets, connected by two ring roads. Museum and ramparts. Church by Engel. Exporting harbour.

KOTKA (62 000). Finland's largest exporting harbour. Centre of wood-processing industries and wood export. The town was founded in 1878 by Czar Alexander II, on the site of Routsensalmi (Svensksund), a naval base. The Russian fleet was defeated by the Swedes in a battle off the coast in 1790. An *open-air museum* on one of the fortified islands (Varissari) depicts the battle. The fortifications were destroyed by the British navy during the Crimean War 1855. The Greek Orthodox church from 1795 was spared. Lutheran church from 1898. *Sibelius Park* with "The Eagles", a sculpture by Jussi Mäntynen. (Kotka means eagle.) The beautiful island of *Kaunissari.*

Glass works with museum in *Karhula.* Near the Sunila Cellulose Factory is a residential area designed by Alvar Aalto, the famous architect. *Langinkoski* is the site of an imperial fishing cottage, built in 1889 for Czar Alexander II, who liked to fish and chop wood – to the horror of the Russian court. The little cottage is now an interesting museum. Beautiful scenery with rapids. National park.

Road 15 to *Kouvola* (30 000). Modern town and railway junction. *Poulakka* open-air museum. Factories at the *Myllykoski* rapids. *Kuusankoski.* Fine sculptures. Archives of religious music.
Anjala with folklore museum. Souvenirs of the "Anjala Association", a conspiracy of officers who wanted to achieve peace with Russia.

Lappenranta and *Imatra,* see road 5.

Pyhtää/Pyttis. Medieval church with murals from the 1320s. *Ahvenkoski.* Power station. Site of the Russian frontier 1743-1809. *Ruotsinpyhtää/ Strömfors.* Small 18th-cent. factory town.

Lovisa/Loviisa. Founded in 1745. Degerby gård (1680) is probably Finland's oldest wooden structure. The oldest section of the town is made up of well-preserved wooden houses. The House of *Sibelius,* where the famous composer spent his summers. Remains of fortifications. *Museum* in the House of the Commandant. Nuclear power plant. *Pernå/Pernaja.* 15th-cent. church. Statue of Bishop Agricola (1508-1557), who brought the Reformation to Finland.

Porvoo/Borgå (20 000). Founded in 1346, set to the torch by the Danes in 1508. Borgbacken, remains of a 13th-cent. stronghold. Cathedral (1418). Well-preserved Old Town. The town is a Finnish cultural centre. Johan Ludvig Runeberg, Finland's national poet, lived here. His home is now a *museum.* He is buried in the old churchyard. Art museum (Albert Edelfelt, Ville Vallgren). Hunting museum and museum of natural science. *Haikko gård,* a manor house, is now a hotel. Albert Edelfelt Museum.

HELSINKI/HELSINGFORS, see town plans.

Espoo/Esbo (133 000), a suburb of Helsinki. Finnish national artist Akseli Gallen-Kallela is best known for his pictures illustrating the Finnish national epic saga, the Kalevala. In 1913 he built *Tarvaspää,* now a museum. A rather bizarre structure with a church-like studio and another building with arcades. A bridge connects them.

Lohja (Lojo). Modern town. 15th-cent. *St. Laurentius Church* is one of the country's largest and most beautiful medieval churches. Frescoes – over 160 groups of pictures. Folklore museum.

Salo is a town in the apple-growing Salojoki valley. Signs of Stone Age settlement.

Pargas/Parainen. Tourist resort. *Grey stone church* from the 14th cent. The sacristy is even older. Frescoes from 1486. Folklore museum. *Kirjala House,* where Lenin spent the night during his flight to the West in 1909. *Qvidja.* Medieval granite castle.

TURKU/ÅBO, see town plans. E 3 continues by ferry to Stockholm or from Naantali (Nådendal) to Kapellskär, north of Stockholm. E 3 continues on to Stockholm – Göteborg – Hamburg – Paris – Lisboa.

Alternative route via Ekenäs and Hangö.

Kyrkslätt/Kirkkonummi and the area all the way out to Porkkala Peninsula were leased to the Soviet Union for a number of years after the Second World War.

Hvitträsk, a castle-like studio built in 1902 by architects Saarinen, Gesellius and Lindgren. Museum, handicrafts exhibitions. Recreation area with swimming baths.

Ingå/Inkoo. Small, old manufacturing town. Fagervik Iron Works was founded in 1646. The manor house and the church were built in the 18th cent., the High Street in the 19th cent.

Ekenäs/Tammisaari. Splendid wooden houses. Granite church from 1674. Folklore museum. Knipan, an inn built on pillars in the water. *Raseborg,* a ruined 14th-cent. castle. Open-air theatre with performances in Swedish.

Hangö/Hanko. Industries and harbour. Resort with 7 km of sandy beaches. Sailing sports centre. Regatta in mid July. Museum in the old fortress. The *Hangö Peninsula* is Finland's southernmost point. This was one of the stops on the Vikings' journey from Sweden to Russia. According to Adam of Bremen, the old chronicler, it took five days for the Swedish Vikings to reach Russia. They probably dragged their ships across the sandy peninsula. The rock carvings at *Gäddtarmen Harbour,* however, were made by the crews of trading ships and naval vessels in the 16th and 17th cent. who used this port as a refuge during bad weather.

E 4. Tornio – Jyväskylä – Helsinki/Helsingfors

The bridge between Haparanda and Tornio marks the Swedish-Finnish border. E 4 comes from Luleå – Stockholm – København – Hamburg – Basel – Barcelona – Madrid – Lisboa.

Tornio (Torneå, 22 000). The old *wooden church* (1686) has a six-cornered clock tower, shingle roof and slender spire. Beautiful painted ceiling and wood carvings.

Kemi (28 000). Large wood-processing industries and exporting harbour. Town hall with museum and observation platform. Isohara Power Station at the estuary of the *Kemi River,* Finland's longest river, 512 km.

OULU (Uleåborg, 95 000). Chief town of the province of Uleåborg. Industries. Wood processing. University. Modern buildings. Cathedral and the old school by C.A. Engel. Remains of fortifications on the island of *Linnansaari* (Borgholmen). Oulu was once known for its export of tar, which was brought down the river in long boats. Some of these are on display in the museum in *Ainola Park.* Charcoal-kiln in Turkansaar. Tar burning week in June.

Road to **Kajaani** (Kajani, 34 000). Ruins of Kajani Castle, built 1604, destroyed 1716 in the Russo-Swedish war.

Pyhäjärvi. Beautiful lake. *Pyhäjärvi Ridge.* **Viitasaari** with observation tower. War graves at Haapasaari.

Beautiful road to **Saarijärvi.** Monument to Paavo, a peasant who is a hero of one of Runeberg's famous poems. Study of the national poet in *Kolkonlahti,* open to visitors. *Pyhähäkki National Park* with 500-year-old forest.

JYVÄSKYLÄ (863 000). University. The first institutions of higher learning to use Finnish as the teaching language were founded here. *Alvar Aalto museum. Museum of Central Finland,* with handicrafts museum. *Laajavuori,* winter sports centre. The Thousand Lakes Auto Rally takes place in this area in August every year.

Säynätsalo on an island in Lake Päijänne. Town hall by Aalto. **Korpilahti** in a beautiful setting. Folklore museum. *Vaaravuori Nature Reserve.*

Padasjoki. *Vesijako Nature Reserve.* Monument commemorating the "War of Clubs", a peasant uprising against the Swedish governor (1597).

LAHTI (100 000). Industrial town, founded 1905, which has rapidly developed into Finland's fourth largest city. Wood processing and other industries. Radio station and radio museum. Ethnographical museum. Art museum. Town hall by Saarinen. Skiing stadium. *Salpausselkä* is made up of two ridges, formed when the Ice Age Glacier retreated.

At the road east of **Päijänne,** Luhanka open-air *museum* in Tammijärvi village. Fish farms. **Juotsa** with ecclesiastical museum in the bell tower. **Heinola,** a former spa. *Heinola Ridge* with observation tower. *Vierumäki* with college of athletics.

Järvenpää. Ainola, the *home of Jean Sibelius,* the composer, may be visited. Sibelius lived here from 1904 until his death in 1957. He is buried here. Statue in the city park. *Vanhakylä manor house* (1634), where Aleksis Kivi, the writer, died. *Tuusula* folklore museum. Town museum. Anti-aircraft defence museum.

Kerava. Industries. Town museum in Heikkilälä House. *Paasikivi museum,* with the president's study. Statue.

HELSINKI/HELSINGFORS, see town plans.

E 78. Tromsø – Tornio

Helligskogen. Norwegian border. E 78 comes from Tromsø.

Kilpisjärvi, 20 km long mountain lake at 423 m above sea level. Mountain hotel. Shops. Boat service to *Treriksröset,* where the borders of Sweden, Norway and Finland meet. *Haltia,* 1 328 m, is Finland's highest mountain.

The road goes through a deserted landscape. It is known as the "Road of the Four Winds" after the name of the hats the local Lapps wear – the "Hat of the Four Winds" (it has four corners). On the opposite bank of the river is Sweden. The northernmost farm, *Kummavuopio,* cannot be reached by road on the Swedish side. *Markkina,* old trading place. Monument on the site of the 17th-cent. church that was dismantled in 1826. The timber from the church was floated down the river to Palojoensuu, where the church was erected again.

Karesuvanto, Lapp settlement. Bridge to *Karesuando* on the Swedish side. Traditionally a site of ferry crossings.

Palejoensuu with the church which was moved here from Markiina. Road to *Enontekiö,* a church village with mountain hotel, and onwards to *Kautokeino* and *Alta* on the Arctic Ocean. This is the fastest route from Sweden to the North Cape.

Muonio, church village with fishermen's hut in Kemiönniemi. *Åkeslompolo,* winter sports area. *Pallastunturi,* mountain hotel.

The Arctic Circle (Naapapiiri), 6 660 km to the Equator, 3 330 km to the North Pole. Midnight sun June 5 – July 5. Rapids between Pello and Turtola.

Ylitornio (Övertorneå). *Aavasaksa,* a mountain which once attracted visitors from the south who wanted to see the Midnight Sun. Maupertius, the French astronomer, was here in 1737. Midsummer night festival. *Karunki,* church village with wooden church from 1815.

The *Kukkola Rapids* (Kukkolankoski), over 8 km long, total height 22 m. Whitefish and salmon fishing, using old methods. Bag-net fishing from a 150 m long pier. Whitefish festival end of July to beginning of August.

Kemi, see E 4. *Rovaniemi,* see E 4.

TORNIO (Torneå), see E 4.

Roads on the Swedish side:
400. Karesuando – Övertorneå
99. Övertorneå – Haparanda

Karesuando is Sweden's northernmost church village. Large wooden church (1905) seating 600. Only a few hundred people live in Karesuando. Reminders of the great 19th-cent. religious revival, led by Laestadius.

Pajala. Associated with Laestadius. *Juoksengi,* Sweden's northernmost market garden. Grapes and cucumbers grow at an extraordinary rate, due to the long and intensive summer sunlight.

Hietaniemi, beautiful 17th-cent. chapel. *Övertorneå.* Enormous *wooden church* with bell tower. Famous Madonna.

Luppio with a mountain from which the Midnight Sun is traditionally observed. According to legend, this is the home of Father Christmas. Fine views, but the actual sun is obscured by mountains. *Armasjärvi.* Memorial to 44 soldiers who drowned in a ferry accident 1940.

The *Kukkola Rapids,* see above. A restaurant on the Swedish side serves whitefish cooked in many different ways.

Haparanda, see Sweden, E 4

E 79. Vaasa/Vasa – Tampere – Helsinki/Helsingfors

VAASA/VASA (54 000). Founded 1060. Ravaged by fire 1852. The new town was rebuilt closer to the coast. Large square with a statue dedicated to Finnish independence. *Österbotten Museum.* Brage open-air museum has a section devoted to seal hunting. Art museums. Summer festival.

Stundars Artisans' Village with numerous old buildings. Every summer a wedding party is held according to old traditions. Barley porridge and other local specialities are served.

Ilmajoki. Folklore museum with coin collection. **Seinäjoki** with a cultural and administrative town centre, designed by Alvar Aalto. Part of this is Lakeuden Risti, the *"Church on the Plain"*, built in the form of a 65 m high cross, visible from miles away. Folklore museum, open-air museum, agricultural museum, gunpowder museum. Music festival in June.

Jurva. Furniture industries and permanent furniture exhibitions. **Jalasjärvi.** Museum in a former army warehouse. **Parkano** with folklore museum. Scenic route between the lakes.

Ikaalinen. Large spa. Wooden church (1799). Folk music festival in June. **Nokia.** Church by Engel (1837). Memorial to the "War of Clubs" (1596). Rubber-tyre factory.

Road to **Virrat** on the beautiful lakes. From here passenger boat service, "Poet's Way", to Tampere. **Ruovesi.** The *studio of Akseli Gallen-Kallela* (1865-1931) is now a museum. Kallela, a Finnish national artist, was particularly interested in the East Karelian culture, the "Kalevala Culture".

TAMPERE (Tammerfors, 170 000). Finland's second largest city. Industries. Founded 1779 on the isthmus between Lakes Näsijärvi and Pyhäjärvi. 180 smaller lakes within the city boundaries. University. Hämeenkatu, the main throughfare, includes a fine bridge over *Tammerkoski* (The Tammer Rapids) with four statues by Wäinö Aaltonen. The *cathedral* is a stone structure in the National Romantic style (Art Nouveau), built 1907. Designed by Lars Sonck. Frescoes by Hugo Simberg: "Wounded Angel" (being carried home by Finnish peasant boys) and "Garden of Death". Magnus Enckell's fresco, "The Resurrection". *Kalevala Church* is a modern structure (1966). *Messukylä Church* (15th cent.) is one of the oldest buildings in Tampere. *Pyynikki open-air theatre* with revolving auditorium seating 1 000 spectators. One of the plays performed here is Väinö Linna's "Unknown Soldier" with realistic battle scenes. Tampere Summer Theatre with extensive programmes. *Häme Museum,* folklore museum with handicrafts. *Tampere City Museum,* Finnish school museum, museum of technology, museum of natural history (cars and aeroplanes). Dolls' museum in *Haihara* manor house. Art museum. Athletics museum.

Särkänniemi Park (amusement park and children's zoo). *Näsinneula* observation tower has a revolving restaurant. Scandinavia's only public *planetarium* with 6 000 stars that can be discerned by the human eye. *Aquarium* with 150 different species. Seal pond.

Winter sports centres at *Lamminpää* and *Mustavuori.* 45 km to the west, on the road to Vammala, is *Ellivuori* skiing centre and hotel.

Two famous passenger boat lines start here: *"Poet's Way"* to Virrat and *"Silver Line"* to Hämeenlinna.

Kangasala. Poet Zacharias Topelius lived at Franssila manor house in 1833. Memorial there and on the Harala Ridge, 171 m.

Valkeakoski (23 000). Large factories on the canal between the lakes. *Kauppilanmäki,* open-air museum describing living conditions of industrial workers 1870-1914. *Visavuori.* Museum in the studio and home of sculptor Emil Wikström.

Ittala. Glassworks. Shop and *glass museum.* **Parola** with *museum* devoted to armoured vehicles and monument (Aaltonen-Puustinen).

Hattula Old Church (1350), a red-brick structure. 16th-cent. paintings on walls and ceiling. New church from 1867. Wood carvings. Church wall with four gates. Wooden tower from 1813.

HÄMEENLINNA (Tavastehus, 42 000). Starting point of the "Silver Line". *Castle* (1260), partially stone, partially brick. Town museum. Automobile museum. Birthplace of Jean Sibelius, the composer. Art museum. *Aulanko.* National park with beautiful paths and fine tourist hotel. Observation tower.

Rihimäki (24 000). Railway junction. Wood-processing industry. Glassworks and *glass museum* (Lasimuseo). Town museum. Työväentalomuseo, museum of the workers' movement. Trotting races.

HYVINKÄÄ (37 000). Railway museum. Railway navvy monument by Wäinö Aaltonen.

4. Karigasniemi – Ivalo – Rovaniemi – Kemi

Karigasniemi. Norwegian border. Road from Lakselv on E 4 via Karasjok. Through desolate landscape past Kaamasmukka Lapp village to *Kaamanen* crossroads.

From Tana Bridge in Norway on E 6 a good road comes from the broad *Tenijoki* (Tana River) across the border at **Nuorgam** to the little village of **Utsjoki,** the northernmost village in Finland. Most of its inhabitants are Lapps. The 200 km long road to Inari is almost uninterrupted wilderness.

From **Kaamanen** a narrow, twisting, and in some parts, poor road leads to **Neiden** in Norway on E 6, via **Sevettijärvi.** That route to Kirkenes is 130 km shorter than the route via Utsjoki. Sevettijärvi is inhabited by Skolts, a Lapp tribe that moved here when Finland lost Petsamo to the Soviet Union.

Inari (Enare). Church village on the shores of Finland's largest lake, Inari. Rapids at Juutanjoki. **Lapp museum,** an open-air museum with Lapp dwellings, hunting equipment, costumes, etc. A simple, but interesting, museum. A 7 km long path leads to *Pielpajärvi Church* (1760). Road to *Lemmenjoki,* a beautiful national park. Hiking trail along the river, the "Golden Path", to *Morgam-Mara.* Gold panning. 4 km south of Inari, a path (300 m) leads east to *Karhunpesäkivi* (the Bear's Den), a strangely shaped rock with a cavity.

Ivalo, church village. First settled in the 1760s. Modern community, rebuilt since the war. Modern church (1966). Airport, the northernmost served by Finnair's domestic lines.

Kaunispää. Motor road up to the top of the mountain, 438 m. Radio station. Resort with hotels, cottages, restaurant. *Laanila.* Hotel and forestry research station.

Tankavaara. Gold-panning centre. Pans and other equipment can be hired and good advice can be had from the staff. And there is gold! But the profits per hour are not impressive. The annual gold-panning championship started in 1977.

Sompio Nature Park. **Vuotso,** the southernmost Lapp village. Large artifical lakes.

Sodankylä. Large church village. Wooden church from 1689. Open-air museum. Several hotels. *Luosto,* winter sports resort. *Vikajärvi* crossroads. Road to Kemijärvi, see road 5.

The Arctic Circle with Arctic Circle Hut, shop and café. Road to the *German war cemetery* and chapel at lovely Lake Norvajärvi.

ROVANIEMI (30 000). Chief town of the province of Lapland. The whole town was ravaged by fire in 1944. The new town was designed by Altar Aalto. The streets have been laid out in the shape of a reindeer horn. Aalto also designed the library, *Lappia House,* which also contains a collection of birds and minerals. Log-floating competitions at Midsummer. Rovaniemi *Church* (1950) is the fourth on this site. Folklore museum. Forestry museum. *Ounasvaara,* Midnight Sun mountain with views out over the endless forests. Winter sports competitions. The Rovaniemi nightlife is surprisingly hectic, even though the Klondyke atmosphere of the 1950s has vanished by now. The Finnish predilection for tango can be studied on the dance floor. The local beer is called Lapin Kulta ("Lapland's Gold").

Artificial lakes at *Isohaara* hydro-electric power station. *Kemi Old Church* contains the mummy of the Reverend Rungius, who died in 1629. He once said in a sermon that as a proof of the truth of faith his body would be preserved. It has been preserved for 400 years without being embalmed.

KEMI, see E 4.

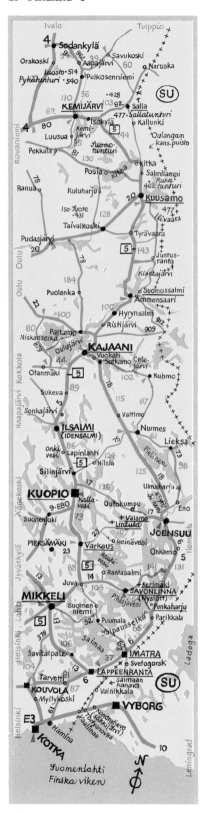

5. Kemijärvi – Kajaani – Kuopio – Lahti – Helsinki/Helsingfors

Kemijärvi. Modern town (1973). Folklore museum. *Salla.* Site of a great Finnish victory during the Winter War 1940. The battlefield at *Paikanselkä* has been preserved with memorials and "korsun" (trenches). The old church village is now situated on Soviet territory.

Kuusamo (18 000). Tourist resort with the *"Bear Round"*, a signposted hiking-trail. *Kiutaköngäs,* 600 m, 14 m high waterfall. *Taivalkoski,* skiing centre.

Suomussalmi. Monument commemorating the fighting in the winter of 1940 when Finnish skiing soldiers annihilated large Russian units.

KAJAANI (30 000). Ruins of a castle from 1604, destroyed 1716. The town was founded 1651 below the fortress. *Paltaniemi,* site of a wooden church (1726) with rococo paintings.

Ilsalmi (Idensalmi, 22 000). Wooden church from 1770. Museum devoted to writer Juhani Aho.

KUOPIO (75 000). University. Cathedral from 1815. The Greek Orthodox cathedral contains the only *Greek-Orthodox museum* in Europe. Bustling market square where kalakukko, a local speciality, can be bought. It is a fish and sausage pie. Karelian pastries have many different fillings. The Market Hall is a fantastic palace. *Puijo* with observation tower. Fine views and rotating restaurant. Winter sports centre.

Boat service from Kuopio to *New Valamo Monastery.* The old monastery was founded on an island in Ladoga in 1329. According to some sources it existed as early as the 10th cent., and was founded by monks from Mount Athos in Greece. When the whole of Ladoga became a part of the Soviet Union in 1940, the 200 monks left the monastery. New Valamo is housed in an old mansion on an island in Lake Heinävesi. A bridge connects it with the mainland. Only a few of the monks remain. A new church was inaugurated in 1977. Most of Valamo's treasures can be seen at Kuopio's Greek Orthodox Museum. *Lintula* is a convent.

Varkaus (28 000). Industries on the Ämmenkoski Rapids. Europe's largest machine for the production of newspaper paper.

MIKKELI (29 000). Marshal Mannerheim had his headquarters here. Provincial museum. Several war monuments and cemeteries. Art museum.

Heinola and *Lahti,* see E 4.

Alternatively it is possible to take road 18 to Joensuu and road 6 to Helsinki.

Nurmes with agricultural museum. *Lieksa* with *Pielinen open-air museum,* one of the largest in Finland. Log-floating festival in July.

JOENSUU (45 000). Chief town of Northern Karelia. *Karelia House* with a museum devoted to Karelian culture. Art museums. Town hall by E. Saarinen. *Sirmakka,* Karelian music festival in June.

Kerimäki Church is the largest wooden church in the world. Seating a congregation of 3 300 and with standing room for an additional 1 700 it is 45 m long and 24 m wide and has a 24 m high dome. According to legend, the master-builder misunderstood the scale of the drawing.

SAVONLINNA (Nyslott, 28 000). *Olavinlinna* (Olofsborg) *Castle* on Saimen was built in 1475 to safeguard the eastern frontier of Sweden- Finland. Opera performances during the summer. Music Days in July and August.

Punkaharju on *Salpausselkä,* the long boulder-ridge that traverses Finland and ends in the Baltic Sea with the Hangö Peninsula.

IMATRA (36 000) on the Soviet frontier. Once the site of one of Europe's mightiest waterfalls, now dammed up into an artifical lake. Every summer Sunday, for one hour, the water is let out. The beautiful old hotel was built at the time when the waterfalls were a major attraction. *Church of the Three Crosses* by Alvar Aalto. Open-air museum.

LAPPEENRANTA (Villmanstrand, 54 000). Founded 1649. *Provincial museum* and cavalry museum in the fortress. Art museum. The Church of the Virgin Mary in the fortress is Finland's oldest. Greek Orthodox church (1785). *Lauritsala Church* (1969). Restaurant and café in Princess Amaada, an old boat. "Humppa" festival, around-the-clock folk music.

8. Oulu – Jakobstad/Pietarsaari – Vaasa/Vasa – Pori – Turku/Åbo

OULU, see E 4.

Raahe (Brahestad, 16 000). Founded as a port in 1649. Destroyed by fire in 1810. Fine views from the tower of the town hall. Town museum. Large ironworks.

Kalajoki. Resort with 2.5 km of sandy beaches and dunes. Fishing museum. Fishermen's church and fishermen's huts.

KOKKOLA/KARLEBY (33 000). Founded 1620 as a port. Due to the land elevation the town is now 5 km from the harbour, where a deep harbour and an oil harbour have been built. Large chemical industries. An area with *old wooden houses* has been preserved in the centre of the town. 15th-cent. stone church. Folklore museum. In the English Park is a small building which houses an English pinnacle, captured here during the time of the Crimean War. The British officer and seamen who were killed in the skirmish off the coast are buried in the Maaria Cemetery.

Jakobstad/Pietarsaari (20 000). Industries. The Strengberg tobacco factory was founded in the 18th cent. Viexpo is a permanent export exhibition. Town museum. The School Park is a botanical garden. The school which Johan Ludvig Runeberg, Finland's national poet, attended is preserved as a *museum.* The poet was born in Jakobstad in 1804.

Nykarleby/Uusikaarlepyy. Once a port. Birthplace of poet Zacharias Topelius in Kuddnäs. Open-air theatre at the *Juthbacka* tourist centre. Memorial to an 1808 battle.

VAASA/VASA, see E 79.

Österbotten (Pohjanmaa) is the name of the coastal area along the Finnish side of the Gulf of Bothnia. Flat landscape with vast plains and bogs. Mainly Swedish-speaking.

Korsholm. Administrative centre before the foundation of Vaasa (Old Vaasa). *Korsholm Church* once housed the Swedish law courts. The old royal castle has been turned into an agricultural college. Wooden churches in *Solf* and *Kvevlax.* *Stundars Artisans' Village, Solf* with fine old houses and artisans' workshops. Festival in the summer in the form of a traditional wedding. Barley porridge and other local specialities are served.

Jurva with large furniture industries and permanent furniture exhibitions. *Närpes.* Museum area. Open-air theatre with revolving stands for the audience. *Kaskinen/Kaskö.* Idyllic wooden town and harbour. Fishermen's cottages. Museum in old windmill.

Kristinestad/Kristiinankaupunki is an idyllic little town. Narrow streets with low red and yellow wooden houses set among trees. The Ulrika Eleonora Church (1700) is a wooden structure. Customs sheds (17th cent.). Windmill on *Myllymäki* (Mill Hill). Museum in *Lebell House,* a merchant's home (1760s).

Merikarvia with large wooden church, the second largest in the country. *Villa Mairea,* a house built in 1937 by Alvar Aalto with furniture by his wife Aino. A unique private home, part of which is open to the public in the summer. Impressive art collection: Toulouse-Lautrec, Picasso, Léger.

PORI (Björneborg, 80 000). Founded 1558. Important harbour (20 km from the centre of the town). Chief town in the Satakunta area. Ravaged by fire in 1852. *Town hall* (1895), which brings to mind palaces in Florence or Venice. *Satakunta Museum. Kirjuinluoto* (Writers' Island), park and open-air theatre with annual summer jazz festival. The Juselius Mausoleum in Käpperä Cemetery contains frescoes by Akseli Gallen-Kallela. Church (1863) in the neo-Gothic style. *Reposaari* (Räfsö), island and fishing village 30 km from the town centre. Church in "Norwegian" style. *Yteri* (Ytterö), resort.

RAUMA (Raumo, 31 000). The town was founded in 1442, but in 1550 its inhabitants were forced to move to Helsinki, which had just been founded. The town flourished in the era of the sailing ships. Exporting harbour. *Vahakapunki,* the old quarter, has well-preserved wooden houses. The *Church of the Holy Cross* (Pyhän Risi Kirkko) was built in 1446 as part of a Franciscan monastery. 16th-cent. frescoes. *Ecclesiastical museum* in the bell tower. Municipal museum in the town hall. Rauma is known for its strange dialect and for its lace. Lace Week end of July – beginning of August.

Uusikaupunki (Nystad). Idyllic town. Saab-Valmet car factories. Shipyards. Museum of cultural history. Old church (1629).

Naantali (Nådendal). A church remains of a Birgittine abbey, founded 1443, "Vallis gratiae" (Valley of Grace, in Swedish "Nådendal"). Fine wooden houses round the beautiful yacht harbour. Car ferries to Åland and Sweden.

TURKU/ÅBO, see town plans.

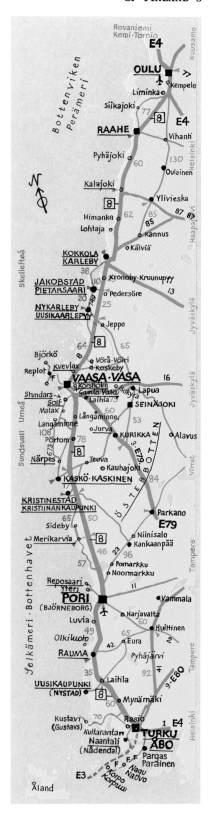

TOWN PLANS

HELSINKI/HELSINGFORS (500 000, with suburbs 750 000)
Finland's capital was founded in 1550 by Swedish King Gustav Vasa, at the mouth of the River Vantaa. In 1640 it was moved to its present situation. After a fire in 1807 the town aquired its present appearance, thanks to architects Carl Ludvig Engel and Johan Albert Ehrenström. In 1812 Helsinki was proclaimed capital of Finland. At the time it had a mere 4 000 inhabitants.
Senate Square became the new centre of the town. It is surrounded by harmonious Empire-style buildings designed by Engel, the cathedral, the university and the State Council Building. A splendid staircase leads up to the *cathedral,* which has four corner towers around a cupola. A statue of Czar Alexander II is in the square.
Market Square with colourful stalls selling flowers, fruit, berries, fish, handicrafts, etc. from 7.00 a.m. Near by is the Market Hall.
President's Palace and City Hall. Katajanokka (Skatudden) with the Greek Orthodox *Uspensky Cathedral* (1868) with golden onion-shaped domes. Esplanadinkatu leads from the Market Square to Erottaja, a traffic

junction. *Havis Amanda* by Ville Vallgren is Helsinki's most famous statue. *Kapellet,* an old wooden building, is a restaurant and coffee-shop. Finnish shops of interest to the tourist line Esplanadikatu (Espan): Arabia, Pentik, Marimekko. The Academic Book Shop (Scandinavia's largest). Statue of J.L. Runeberg. Stockmann's department store and Metsovaara in Aleksanterinkatu. Mannerheimintie, a broad avenue, goes past the massive

Parliament Building (J.S. Sirén, 1931), built of Finnish granite. Alvar Aalto's impressive *Finlandia Hall,* white marble and grey granite. The concert hall accommodates an audience of 1 718 and the conference hall an audience of 1 300.
The *Church at the Temple Square* (Timo and Tuomo Suomalainen) is built inside a rock. Granite walls and copper dome. It looks like a flying saucer that has landed in the middle of

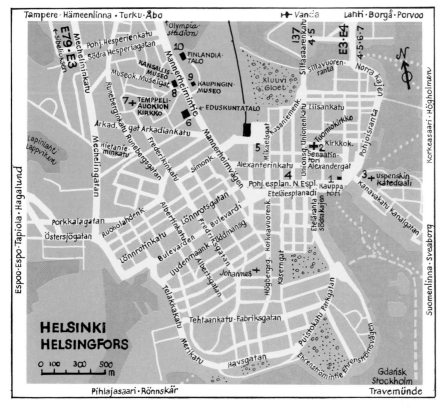

1 Market Square.
  President's Palace
2 Senate Square.
  Cathedral.
3 Uspensky
  Cathedral.
4 Esplanadinkatu
5 Art Museum of
  the Ateneum.
6 Parliament
  Building.
7 Church at the
  Temple Square.
8 National
  Museum.
9 City Museum.
10 Finlandia Hall.
11 Hietaniemi. War
   Cemetery
12 Sibelius
   Monument.
13 Olympic
   Stadium.
14 Linnanmäki
   Amusement
   Park.
15 Seurasaari Open-
   Air Museum.
16 Gallen-Kallela
   Museum.
17 Tapiola.
18 Technical
   Museum
19 Korkeassari Zoo.
20 Sveaborg
   Fortress.

*Helsinki. The south-
ern harbour with
the cathedral in the
background*

the town.
The **Sibelius Monument** (1967), a
wind organ by Eila Hiltunen in the
Sibelius Park. The *railway station*
(1916) is an impressive structure by E.
Saarinen. *Hakkaniementori* (Hagnäs-
torget), a square with open-air market
and market hall.
Museums: The *National Museum* in
the National Romantic style (archaeology, history and ethnography).
Helsinki *City Museum*, a charming
little museum in the Villa Hakasalmi
(Hagasund, 1848). Interiors of homes,
glass, porcelain, silver, jewellery, costumes, toys. A model of Helsinki 1870.
Domarby manor house (1790) is also a
section of the Helsinki City Museum.
Open-air museum on *Seurasaari* Island. Folk dancing and folk music.
Ateneum is the largest art museum in
the country. Several other art
museums. *Gallen-Kallela Museum*
and *Hvitträsk*, see E 3.
Hertonäs with manor house museum.
Mejlan manor house with art and exhibitions. Bank museum, war museum, anti-aircraft defence museum,
agricultural museum. Mannerheim
Museum, medicine museum, geological museum, mission museum, post
and telecommunications museum,
theatre museum, Stockman's Museum, museum of technology, customs
museum, clock museum, zoological
museum.
Suomenlinna (Sveaborg). Boat service from the Market Square to the
fortress, now a museum. Recreation
grounds and writers' flats (scholar-
ships to Scandinavian writers). Summer restaurant. Augustin Ehren-
svärd, the architect of Suomenlinna,
is buried on the island. The fortress
was considered to be impregnable but
surrendered to the Russians in 1808.
During the Crimean War it was under
bombardment from an Anglo-French
fleet. *Korkeasaari* (Högholmen) zoo.

Linnanmäki (Borgbacken) amusement park. The *Olympic Stadium*,
built for the Olympic games of 1952.
72 m high, slender tower, with fine
views. Wäinö Aaltonen's statue of
Paavo Nurmi, the long-distance runner. Interesting *sports museum*. Nurmi's gilded shoe is preserved as a relic.
Hietaniemi (Sandudd). Beautiful war
cemetery. Mannerheim's tomb.
Tapiola (Hagalund), is a modern
suburb, built as a garden city. Café
terrace on the top of the 13-storey
Keskustorni. Helsinki's restaurants
include some that specialize in Russian food. Fazer's pastry shop and café
in Kluuvikatu (Glogatan) is well
worth a visit.

TURKU/ÅBO (165 000)

Finland's third largest city was founded about the year 1300. Bishopric
since 1279. Large port and industries.
Shipyards. Two universities. *Turku
Castle*. Construction was started
about 1280. The castle has been
destroyed and gutted by fire many
times, but there are parts of it left from
both the Middle Ages and the 16th
cent. 14 kings have stayed here. Its
most important period was at the end
of the 16th cent. when Johan III of
Sweden lived here with a staff of over
600. The castle houses the *Historical
Museum*. Banqueting halls and castle
church.
The **cathedral** is Finland's national

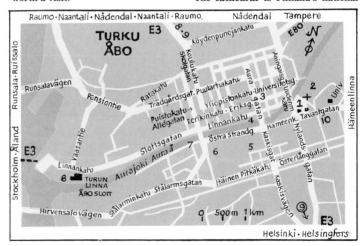

1 *Cathedral. Turku Academy.*
2 *Sibelius Museum.*
3 *Market Square.*
4 *Pharmacy Museum*
5 *Klosterbacken (open-air museum)*
6 *Aaltonen Museum.*

7 *"Sigyn" (museum ship)*
  *"Suomen Juotsen". (sail training
  ship)*
8 *Turku Castle.*
9 *Chapel of the Resurrection.*

shrine. Construction started in the 14th cent. and parts have been added during the centuries that followed. Idyllic 19th-cent. houses around the cathedral and along the banks of the Aura River. Nothing remains of medieval Turku. *Klosterbacken* (Luostarinmäki) is an open-air museum with 18th-cent. houses and a handicraft museum in a part of the town that escaped an 1827 fire.

Large *Market Square* with stalls selling vegetables, fruit, handicrafts, etc. The old *Market Hall*, interesting architecture and excellent stalls. Quensel House with *pharmacy museum*. Sibelius museum. Museum devoted to Wäinö Aaltonen, the sculptor. Handicraft museum. Biological museum. *"Sigyn of Wårdö"*, a 500-ton schooner, was built 1887. Next to it is the sail training ship *"Suomen Joutsen"* ("the Swan of Finland"). The modern Chapel of the Resurrection is very beautiful. *Ruissalo/Runsala* has the country's largest oak woods. Fine sandy beaches. Large hotel. Botanical gardens. A myriad of islands in the archipelago beetween Turku and the Åland islands.

Turku (Åbo) Castle, built in 1280, contains the city museum. Below, a view of the Finnish archipelago

Åland

(Ahvenanmaa)

Åland, consisting of 6 500 islands and skerries, has a total area of 1 450 km², scattered over 10 000 km². As early as the 7th cent. A.D. Åland was one of Scandinavia's most densely populated areas. Graves and finds from the Viking Age. Finland's oldest churches (12th cent.). The 22 000 inhabitants are Swedish-speaking. Åland's enjoys autonomy and has its own flag. According to a League of Nations decision of 1921 Åland belongs to Finland and is permanently neutral.

Mariehamn (9 500) was founded in 1861 by Czar Alexander II. Every day hundreds of Swedes arrive on ferries to shop in Mariehamn. Idyllic garden town with linden avenues. *Maritime museum* with the "Pommern", a bark that sailed with grain from Australia to England. *Åland's Museum* with the history of the province. Art museum.

The southern parts of Åland are green and fertile, while the northern parts are rocky and barren. *Eckerö*. St. Laurentius' Church (13th cent.) looks like a fortress. *Post museum* in the Storby post and customs house, designed by C.L. Engel. *Finström*. The 14th-cent. *church* is one of the country's most beautiful churches. Frescoes and wood carvings. Altar casket and statue of a saint (1740).

Jomala Church, dedicated to St. Olof. 13th-cent. frescoes. Madonna statues from Lübeck and Visby. Frescoes. *Lemland, Saltvik* and *Sund* also have beautiful old churches. Ruins of *Lemböte Chapel* (12th cent.)

Bomarsund. The Russians started to build this fortress in 1830 intending to create a Gibraltar of the North. But construction was halted in 1858 when an Anglo-French fleet attacked the fortress. *Kastelholm Castle* was built in the 14th cent. by Bo Jonsson Grip, a Swedish nobleman. Several times gutted by fire. A restored part of the castle contains *Åland's Folklore Museum.* Near by is the *Jan Karlsgården* open-air museum.

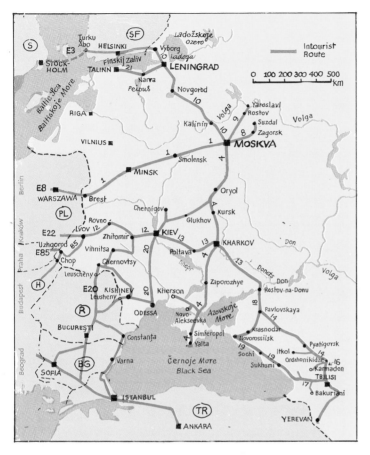

2.1 million, Tashkent 1.8 million, Baku 1.6 million, Kharkov 1.4 million, Gorky 1.4 million, Novosibirsk 1.3 million, Minsk 1.3 million.

Government: Union of Soviet Socialist Republics. 15 constituent republics. Eight autonomous regions and four autonomous republics. The only legal political party is the Communist Party. A Soviet (council) is elected in every republic and region.
The Supreme Soviet, which convenes in Moscow, is the parliament of the Soviet Union. The Council of Ministers is the highest executive and administrative organization.

History
9th cent. Swedish Vikings, "rus", establish a kingdom, first with Novgorod, later with Kiev, as the capital.
1237 The Mongol "Golden Horde" conquer Russia.
1480 Ivan III, Prince of Moscow, defeats the Mongols.
1533-1584 Ivan the Terrible centralizes the powers of the czar despite resistance from the boyars, a group of nobles.
1598-1613 The "Time of Troubles".
1689-1725 Peter the Great modernizes Russia along western lines. The Swedes are defeated at Poltava. St. Petersburg (present-day Leningrad), founded in 1703, becomes the capital.
1812 The armies of Napoleon occupy Moscow. Two-thirds of the city is destroyed by fire. The Grand Army is forced to evacuate the city and begin a disastrous retreat.
1867 Russia sells Alaska to the USA for 7.2 million dollars.
1904 Russo-Japanese War. The Russian fleet sails from the Baltic to a humiliating end at the Battle of Tsushima.
1905 "Bloody Sunday", January 9. Cossack troops fire into crowds of protesters in St. Petersburg. Many are killed.
1914 First World War. Heavy losses and defeat caused by German armies at the Battle of Tannenberg.
1917 February Revolution. The czar is forced to abdicate. Lenin returns from Switzerland. Bolsheviks gain power after the October Revolution and proclaim a Socialist state.
1924 Lenin dies. Stalin takes power.
1941 The Germans attack the Soviet

SU · Union of Soviet Socialist Republics

SU·Soyuz Sovyetskikh Sotsialist-icheskikh Respublik (SSSR)
Area: 22.4 million km² (8.65 million sq. miles).

Population: 267 million. Third largest in the world. (Only China and India have larger populations.) One quarter of the nation and three-quarters of the population are in Europe. Hundreds of ethnic groups – among them 137 million Russians, 42 million Ukrainians, 12 million Uzbeks, 9 million White Russians.
The administrative language is Russian. Every nationality has its own language. State and religion are separate but there is a Council for Religious Affairs that maintains relations between the government and the many faiths. Despite anti-religious propaganda there are many actively religious Soviet citizens and the Russian Orthodox Church is represented at the Ecumenical World Council of Churches. Unofficial estimates indicate that about 50 million Soviet citizens are members of the Russian Orthodox Church, about 3 million are Roman Catholics and about 30 million Muslims.

Major cities: Moskva (Moscow) 8 million, Leningrad 4.6 million. Kiev

Routes described:

1 Moskva – Minsk – Brest (E 8)

4 Moskva – Kharkov – Yalta

8 Moskva – Zagorsk – Suzdal, see road 1

9 Moskva – Yaroslavl, see road 1

10 Vyborg – Leningrad – Novgorod – Moskva

12 and 13 Kharkov – Kiev – Lvov

20 Kiev – Odessa

21 Leningrad – Narva – Tallinn, see road 10

The Great Caucasian Circular Route: Kharkov – Rostov-na-Donu – Krasnodar – Sochi – Tblisi – Ordzhonikidze – Kharkov

Town plans: Leningrad, Moskva

Lake Ritsa in Georgia, situated 950 m above sea level, is a famous tourist resort

Union and advance to Moscow. The Battle of Stalingrad changes the course of the war in Europe. In 1945 Russian troops occupy Berlin.

1953 Stalin dies. Khrushchev becomes Secretary of the Communist Party and the Premier of the Soviet Union.

1964 Brezhnev becomes Secretary of the Communist Party, and, in 1977, President of the Presidium of the Supreme Soviet and Premier of the Soviet Union.

1982–84 Yuri Andropov becomes Secretary of the Communist party. He is succeeded in 1984 by Konstantin Tchernenko.

Currency: Rubel (SUR).
1 rubel = 100 kopek
It is forbidden to either import or export Soviet currency. Although unlimited amounts of foreign currency may be imported into the USSR, it must be declared on entry. It is forbidden to take out more foreign currency than you have brought in. Foreign currency may only be exchanged at authorized banks and exchange offices and travellers must keep receipts of all currency transactions.

Visas: Itineraries must be carefully planned in advance and submitted to Intourist for approval. Once this has been given, visas, free of charge, are issued.

Business hours: Banks 10.00 a.m.-4.00 p.m. Hotel currency exchange offices 9.00 a.m.-8.00 p.m. Shops 11.00 a.m.-2.00 p.m. and 3.00 p.m.- 7.00 p.m. Department stores 8.00 a.m.-8.00 p.m. Foodshops open at 7.00 a.m.

Holidays: New Year's Day, March 8, May 1-2, May 9, October 7 (October Revolution Holiday), November 7-8.

Hotels
Hotels are divided into two classes. Usually travellers may not choose their hotels. Instead Intourist, the official travel association, assigns rooms in a hotel of the desired class. Advance payment in Western (hard) currency is mandatory.

Camping
Places in camping sites must be booked and paid for in advance in Western (hard) currency.

Food and drink
Soups are the pride of the hearty Russian cuisine and they are well worth experiencing. Borsch (beetroot soup), shchi (cabbage soup), rasolnik (salt cucumber soup), solyanka (fish or meat soup with smetana – sour cream) and akroshka (chilled vegetable and meat soup, served with ryebread) are among the most popular. Beef Stroganoff is an internationally famous meat dish. Chicken à la Kiev, almost as well known, is breast of chicken containing a knob of butter. Boroshonok, suckling pig. Shashlyk, mutton grilled on a skewer and Tabaka chicken, a highly spiced chicken dish, both with origins in Georgia. Pelmeni, similar to ravioli, has a filling of mince and is served with sour cream. Piroghi (pirozhki), pastry, often filled with mushrooms and mince. Sturgeon is the most popular fish. Osetrina Shrenom is boiled sturgeon and horse radish. Blini, small pancakes with sour cream and caviar or preserves. Caviars.

Beach in Jalta on the Crimea

Popular mealtime drinks are mineral water, apple flavoured soft drinks and beer. Between meals, tea is the most popular beverage. Although vodka is the traditional Russian alcoholic drink, there are several good wines, sparkling wines, cognac and liqueurs.

Shopping

Berjozka shops, to be found in major tourist hotels, railway stations and airports, have a wide range of merchandise but accept only western (hard) currency. In these shops you can buy wood carvings, paintings, table cloths, lacquer work from the villages of Palech and Fedoskino, gold and silver clocks and watches, amber, costume jewellery, toys, balalaikas, gramophone records, perfume, furs.

Petrol

Petrol stations and garages are few and far between. Always travel with a filled reserve tank. Foreign motor car parts can be difficult if not impossible, to obtain. It is best to have spare parts with you. Coupons, purchased from Intourist, are usually required as payment at petrol stations. In general they have, at the most, 93 octane – and often lower. Petrol stations lack accessories, oil and toilets.

Speed limits. Traffic regulations.

In the country 90 kmh. Motorists in possession of driving licences for less than two years 70 kmh. Built-up areas 60 kmh.

If your car is fitted with seat belts it is compulsory to wear them.

All motorists must carry a first aid kit and a fire extinguisher. It is illegal to drive a dirty car. It is recommended that children do not travel in the front seat and that spare bulbs for the vehicle are carried.

Roads

Tourists are only permitted to drive on roads that are included in the Intourist list of approved routes, and must follow the itinerary stated on the travel documents that they have purchased abroad. It is forbidden to drive more than 500 km per day.

Major roads can vary in quality. Surfaces are often uneven. Verges are often covered with loose gravel. Few stopping places. No kiosks or shops. Have food supplies with you. In towns, watch out for tram tracks. Avoid night-time driving. Street lighting is often inadequate and Soviet drivers wait until the last moment before turning on their headlights. In towns and cities, parking lights are used when driving at night.

Repairs

Car repairs are difficult. Most foreign insurance is invalid in the Soviet Union. Foreign automobile associations are usually agents for the Ingosstrakh organization. In any case motorists must have an Ingosstrakh policy when driving in the USSR.

Intourist, Prospekt Marksa 16, SU-10 30 09 Moskva. Tel. 203-69-62.

Intourist Moscow Ltd, 292 Regent Street, London W1R 7PO. Tel. 01-6311252.

Kalinin Avenue, Moscow

Moscow underground station

1. Moskva – Minsk – Brest

MOSKVA (Moscow), see town plans.

A monument on the exit road marks the furthest point of the German advance during their attack on Moscow in late 1941. A statue in the village of Petrishchevo is of an 18-year-old girl Partisan who was executed by the Germans. A bit east of Mozhajsk, the silhouette of Moscow University can still be seen.

Mozhajsk, centre of a large agricultural area. Road to **Borodino** where, in 1812, Napoleon's Grand Army defeated the Russian army led by Kutuzov. Museum.

The town formerly known as Gzhatsk has been renamed after its most famous son, **Gagarin,** the first cosmonaut.

Vjazma, founded in the 9th–10th cent., has large industries but it is best known for its gingerbread.

SMOLENSK (275 000), founded in 863 by Swedish Vikings. The city has often suffered destruction from invading armies on their way to Moscow. Napoleon's Grand Army attacked Smolensk in 1812 as did Hitler's army in 1941. 13th-cent. churches. Uspensky Sobor, cathedral (1679). Peter and Paul Church (1146). Exhibition of Economic Achievements. Fortress. University. 130 km east of Smolensk the road leaves the Russian Republic and enters the White Russian Republic. At the town of **Borisov** the road crosses the River Berezina where Napoleon lost a large part of his Grand Army on the retreat from Moscow.

MINSK (1.3 million). Large industries. Capital of White Russia, first mentioned in documents from 1067. The city has been involved in battles with Tartars, Swedish armies, Napoleon's Grand Army, and the armies of Hitler. University and Academy of Agriculture with large botanical gardens. Museum, opera house, ballet. Handicrafts. Exhibition of Economic Achievements of the White Russian Republic. Museum dedicated to the "Great Patriotic War" (the Second World War). Minsk has been awarded the title "Heroic City." Victory Square with tall obelisk. Lenin Prospekt, the main thoroughfare, is 9 km long and 50 to 70 m wide.

Chatyn. Village which was burned by the Germans in 1943. Its 149 inhabitants, 76 of them children, perished. The sooty chimneys still stand and bells ring continuously. Glory Hill, on the main road, is a monument dedicated to the victory of the battle of 1944.

Dzerzhinsk. Famous for its diamond industry. **Stolbtsy** on the River Niemen. **Baranovichi.** Industrial town. Memorial to 3 000 Czechs who were killed by the Nazis. The village of **Zaosie** where the Polish poet Adam Mickiewicz was born in 1798.

Kobrin, founded in the 11th cent. Museum devoted to Suvorov, the field marshal who fought against Napoleon.

BREST (180 000). Industrial and administrative centre. The town was built in the 11th cent. around an enormous fortress. It withstood a month-long German siege in 1941. *The Hero Fortress* was built in 1971 in memory of this event. New buildings and sculptures in the Old Fortress. The central sculpture is a 100 m high bayonet.

Polish frontier. E8 continues to Warszawa – Poznań – Frankfurt an der Oder – Berliner Ring – Hannover – den Haag – London.

8. Moskva – Zagorsk – Suzdal

Vladimir. One of the oldest cities in Russia (12th cent.). The Golden Gates are the main entrance through the old town wall. The Uspensky Sobor was once the most important church in Russia. Cathedral of St. Demetrius. Both churches contain beautiful works of art created by Andrey Rublyev. Beautiful *Tserkov Pokrov,* a 12th-cent. church in the village of *Bogolyubovo.*

Suzdal, founded in the 10th–11th cent., one of the oldest towns in Russia. Interesting museums and several splendid cathedrals and monasteries. Rozjdestvensky Cathedral (12th cent)

9. Moskva – Yaroslavl

Abramtsevo. Manor house museum housing works of art by Ilya Repin. He and many other Russian artists, writers and actors have worked and stayed here.

ZAGORSK (100 000), previously known as Sergiev. The mighty **Troitse-Sergiev Monastery** (1337) has played an important role in Russia's religious and political history. Several buildings now compose a vast museum containing ikons, frescoes and handicrafts. Zagorsk is the headquarters of the Russian Orthodox Church. Theological schools. Toy industry. Toy museum.

Pereslavl-Zalesky with 12th-cent. cathedral and the Church of Metropolitan Peter. Earth ramparts constructed in the 12th cent. for Prince Yuri Dolgaruky, the founder of Moscow.

Rostov. The **Kremlin** is a collection of buildings that formerly belonged to the Metropolitan. Incredible number of domes. 17th-cent. belfry with carillon. The largest of the bells, the "Sysol Bell", weighs 32 tons.

Yaroslavl. Industrial town with old fortress. Many churches have beautiful wall paintings, among them the Church of St. John the Baptist. Fortifications around the Kremlin that was founded by Yaroslav the Wise (1036- 1054).

4. Moskva – Kharkov – Yalta

MOSKVA (Moscow), see town plans.

PODOLSK (200 000) *Lenin museum* in the house where the Ulyanov family lived 1898-1901. **Melikhovo** where the writer Anton Chekhov spent six years of his life. His former home now houses a Chekhov museum.

TULA. Large mechanical industries. Metal handicrafts, weapons, samovars. Weapons museum. Peter the Great ordered an armaments factory built here. Tula kremlin, a fortress.

Yasnaya Polyana, once the estate of Leo Tolstoy, now a museum. The writer lived here for 70 years and is buried in the park. The park's avenue of lindens is described in "War and Peace", a novel which, like "Anna Karenina", he wrote at Yasnaya Polyana.

Spasskoe-Lutovinovo, once the estate of the Turgenev family. Museum devoted to the writer Ivan Turgenev.

ORÉL (300 000) was founded in the 16th cent. as a frontier fortification against the Crimea Tartars. **KURSK** (375 000). Centre of an iron-mining area. War museum. Three 17th cent churches. In 1943 the German armies launched a pincer offensive from Belgorod and Orël against the city. The battle that followed, one of the most decisive of the Second World War, was extremely bloody. A large area on the eastern side of the road near **Belgorod** has been preserved, so that it appears just as it did when the Battle of Kursk was over. Trenches, guns, etc. One of the tanks that took part in the battle is mounted on a high pedestal. Border of the Ukraine, second largest Soviet Republic.

KHARKOV (1.4 million). Second largest city in the Ukrainian Soviet Republic. Centre of a large industrial area. The city was founded in 1650 and has been rebuilt after severe World War II damage. Several industries and colleges. *Dzerzhinsky Square,* with a monument to Lenin and the Building of Industry, is at the heart of the city. Very rich art museum. Two 17th-cent. cathedrals. Pokrov Monastery (1689).

POLTAVA (270 000). Industrial city and centre of an agricultural district. Monument in Alexandrovsky Square in memory of a battle held on June 28, 1709, when Swedish troops under the command of King Charles XII were defeated by the armies of Peter the Great. Museum and restored fortifications on the battle field. A few days later the Swedish invaders capitulated at Perevolochna.

The Dnepropetrovsk area with large cities and enormous power stations. Extensive iron mines in the Krivoy-Rog district. The city of **Dnepropetrovsk** (not on the Intourist route) with almost a million inhabitants is situated on the 2 285 km long River Dnieper – the third longest river in Europe. The Dnieper flows into the Black Sea and during the Viking Age it was the main route for Swedish Vikings on their way to "Miklagård"(Constantinople in Byzantium). They hauled their boats past mighty rapids, now the site of the impressive Dneprogres hydro- electric power station, and usually rested up on the shores of Lake Khortitsa.

ZAPOROZHYE (500 000). Enormous Lenin statue in front of the Dneproges power station.

The road continues over the seemingly endless steppes.

MELITOPOL (150 000), centre of a fruit-producing area, is famous for its melons. Large canning factories. The battle for the Crimean Peninsula began in this area in 1920. The peninsula was held by "White"troops. They advanced as far as Melitopol but were defeated by an army led by the Soviet Marshal Michail Frunze. (The capital of the Central Asian Soviet Republic of Kirghizstan, and a famous military academy in Moscow, among others, have been named after this Soviet hero.) Close to Melitopol are Scythian graves that date from the 5th cent. B.C. The Scythians were a nomadic Indo-European people. Extensive finds of gold ornaments.

Novoalekseyevka. Starting point for an Intourist route to Kherson, Lake Kakhovka and the mouth of the Dnieper. Wild horses, antelopes, zebras and stags on the steppe near **Askania-Nova. Novaya Kakhovka** with the Kachovsk power station.

Kherson with remains of a fortress. Arsenal. Church of St. Catherine.

The long *Chongarsk Bridge* leads to the **Crimea.** A narrow sound connects the Sivash Lagoon, 2 600 km², with the *Sea of Azov.* The waters of the lagoon evaporate quickly leaving thick layers of salt that are collected and put to practical use. The mud from the lagoon is used for medical treatments. **Perekop** with a prehistoric fortification wall built to protect the northern tip of the Crimean Peninsula.

The Crimea has a total area of 26 000 km². Its population is about 1.2 million. The northern part of the peninsula is a steppe, the mountainous southern part is rimmed with seaside resorts. The vegetation of the Crimea is similar to that of the Mediterranean.

SIMFEROPOL (300 000). Cultural and scientific centre of the Crimea. Art museum. An 86 km long trolley-bus line connects the city with Yalta.

The Angarsky Pass, 762 m. The Kutuzov Fountain, dedicated to a 1774 battle against the Turks. Kutuzov, who took part in the battle, later became Napoleon's fiercest adversary.

Alushta. Resort with several rest homes and guest houses. Tobacco farms. Vineyards. **Gurzuf,** site of Sputnik, a youth camp, and Artek, a camp for young Pioneers (the Soviet equivalent of Boy Scouts and Girl Guides). Curious *Aju Dag* (Bear Mountain), a 565 m high rock formation that resembles a crouched bear.

Nikitsky Botanical Gardens, founded in 1812, is one of the largest of its type in the Soviet Union. 7 000 species collected from all over the world.

Yalta. The best-known Soviet health resort, set in lush, semi-tropical vegetation and bordered by the Black Sea, offers a warm climate suitable for warm-water swimming from May until October. The coastline has over 100 seaside resorts and "sanatoria". Although the majority of the "sanatoria" – rest homes, are reserved for Soviet workers, some accept foreign visitors. Anton Chekhov, the writer, lived in Yalta 1899-1904. During that time he created such classics as "The Cherry Orchard" and "Lady with a Lap Dog". His former home is now a *museum.*

Livadia, once a residence of the last two emperors, was built in 1848 for Prince Voronstov. The building is an incredible mixture of the Moorish and Tudor styles. Impressive stone staircase adorned with marble lions. In 1945 this was the site of the Yalta Conference when Stalin, Churchill and Roosevelt decided the fate of post-war Europe. *Swallow's Nest* (Lastochkino gnezdo), a little palace on a picturesque mountain ledge. **Miskhor.** Seaside resort. **Alupka,** seaside resort and spa. The 19th-cent. mansion now serves as a museum. The steep slopes of *Mount Aj-Petri* (1 223 m) rise behind the town.

SEVASTOPOL (290 000). (Closed to non-Soviet nationals.) Shipyards, naval base and port. Originally a Greek colony founded in the 5th cent., Sevastopol became an important Tartar city. Conquered by the Russians in 1784, its fortress became world famous when it at first withstood then fell to a combined British, French, Turkish and Italian siege during the Crimean War. The city was occupied by the Germans during both World Wars.

Balaklava (not on Intourist Route), where the "Light Brigade" met its doom.

i0. Vyborg – Leningrad – Novgorod – Moskva

Finnish border. E 3 comes from Stockholm and Helsinki. Torfyanovka border station.

VYBORG (Viborg, Viipuri, 80 000). Industrial town. The castle was founded by Swedes in the 13th cent. as a fortress against the Russians. From 1721 until 1811 Vyborg was in Russia. It was part of Finland from 1811 until 1940. During the early 1940s most of the Finnish population fled to Finland. St. Anna Fortress (1740).

Zelenogorsk (Terijoki). Seaside resort and spa. *Repino.* Spa. The artist Ilya Repin lived near by.

LENINGRAD, with *Pushkin* and *Pavlov,* see town plans.

NOVGOROD (82 000). One of the oldest towns in Russia. According to The Chronicle of Past Days by Nestor, a Kiev monk, it was founded in 862 by the Swede, Rurik. The Swedes were called Rus – this is perhaps the background of the word Russia. Novgorod became an important commercial town on the trade route between Scandinavia and the Orient. From 1236 until 1263 it was ruled by Prince Alexander Nevsky. He was able to successfully defend the town against attacks from Lithuanians, Teutonic Knights and Swedes, and became a national hero and saint. Novgorod also has a *Kremlin,* a city ringed by ramparts. Russia – 1 000 years (1882), a monument with hundreds of figures that portray historically important Russians. During the Second World War the Germans defaced the monument and dismantled it, but they did not carry away or destroy the fragments. No other city in Russia has preserved so many 12th- to 18th-cent. churches and works of religious art. The oldest church is the *Sophia Cathedral* (1050). The middle of its five cupolas is gilded. Cathedral of the *Nativity of the Virgin* (1119) in the monastery of St. Anthony. *The Church of St. Theodore Stratilates* (1360) and the *Znamensky Cathedral* (1374) contain frescoes attributed to Theophanes the Greek, a master of Byzantine art. *Yuri Monastery* with the *Church of St. George* (1119). Several more churches from different periods.

Opposite the Kremlin on the other side of the River Volkhov is the *Yaroslav Palace.* Beaches, fishing and water sports. There is a legend about a Novgorod merchant named Sadko who fell in love with the Queen of the River Volkhov. This legend inspired Rimsky-Korsakov to the opera "Sadko".

Vishniy Volochek, where boats were once dragged across land during the journey from the Baltic to the Volga. Site of Russia's first canal. *Torzhok,* famous for its gold embroidery.

KALININ (previously Tver, 400 000). Important trading town, founded in the 12th cent. Folklore museum in old buildings. *Palace of Catherine II* (Catherine the Great) by architects Kazakov and Rossi. Belaya Troitska Church (1564). Splendid monument dedicated to Afanasy Nikitin, the first Russian merchant who travelled to India (15th cent.)

Bridge over the River *Volga,* the longest river in Europe (3 690 km). It rises in the Valday Plateau, south-west of Kalinin, flows through Lake Rybinsk, the city of Gorky and to the Caspian Sea. Navigable from Kalinin.

Klin. Large industrial town. The estate of the composer Peter Tchaikovsky is now a museum. His piano is on display here. Annual concerts held on May 7 (Tchaikovsky's birthday) and November 6 (day of his death).

ZELENOGRAD (120 000). Suburb of Moscow.

War cemetery and memorial 40 km from Moscow. A memorial 23 km from the capital marks the point of the furthest German advance in 1942.

MOSKVA (Moscow), see town plans.

21. Leningrad – Narva – Tallinn

Krasnoe Selo. Peter the Great had Russia's first paper-mill constructed here. General Suvorov, the poet Lermontov and the artist Ilya Repin, have all lived here. *Kingisepp* was founded in 1384. The Catherine Cathedral (18th cent.) was created by Rinaldi. *Ivangorod* with 17th-cent. fortress. *Narva* is on the other side of the river that forms the natural boundary between the Russian and the Estonian Soviet Republics.

TALLINN (320 000). Capital of the Estonian Soviet Republic. Well-preserved medieval city centre with narrow streets, towers and gabled houses. The 12th-cent. town wall was built by Germans, Swedes and Danes. The large castle, *Toompea,* completed in 1219, was built for the Danish king, Valdemar Atterdag. The *town hall* is one of the oldest in Europe. *Old Toomas* weather-vane is something of a symbol of the city. *Oleviste Church* is mentioned in documents from the 13th cent. Many craftsmen, small shops and cafés. One of the oldest *pharmacies* in Europe. The modern sections of Tallinn have broad streets and handsome squares. Major industrial city. Intourist arranges excursions from Tallinn to Riga, capital of the Latvian Soviet Republic.

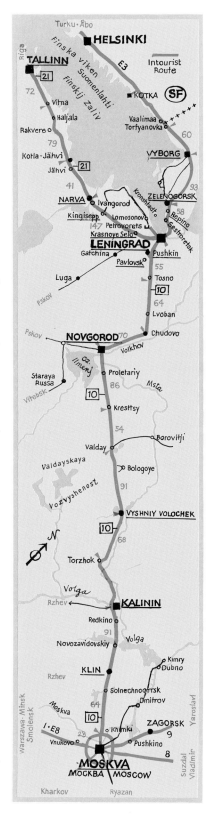

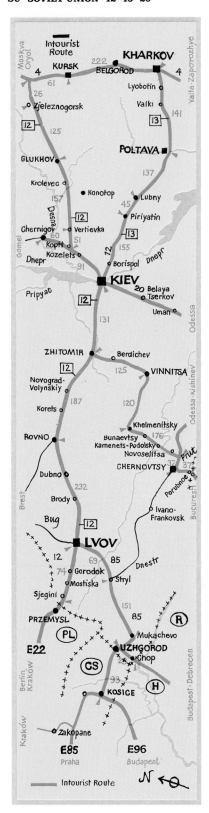

12 and 13. Kharkov – Kiev – Lvov

KHARKOV, and *Poltava* see route 4.

KIEV (2.1 million). Capital of the Soviet Republic of the Ukraine. Third largest city in the Soviet Union. The Swedish chieftain Rurik founded Novgorod and Oleg founded the Kingdom of Kiev (Old Russia) in 882. It lasted until 1125. Kiev is a beautiful city with many historic buildings and monuments. *Sophia Cathedral* (11th cent.) with Byzantine mosaics. Outside the cathedral is an equestrian statue of Bogdan Khmelnitsky, a popular hero who united the Ukraine with the Russian states at the end of the 17th cent. Blue and white Church of St. Andrew (18th cent.). *Pecherskaya Lavra,* a monastery where Yuri Dolgoruky, founder of Moscow, is buried. The famous Kreshchatik is the city's most important street. The River Dnieper flows through Kiev. It is the third longest river in Europe (2285 km). Only the Volga and the Danube are longer. Kiev has become one of the Soviet Union's major industrial cities. University (1834) and several other institutes of higher learning. Permanent exhibition dedicated to Ukrainian economic achievements. Fertile "Black Soil" agricultural area. Scene of fierce World War II battles. Kiev is a "Heroic City".

Rovno. During the Second World War a centre of resistance activity. Bridge over the frequently turbulent River **Bug** where log floating is carried out in the traditional manner.

LVOV (500000). Beautiful old city with Renaissance and Baroque buildings. Founded in the 13th cent. in lovely, undulating countryside. The *Church of St. Nicholas* is the oldest structure in the city. Powder tower and arsenal from the 16th cent. Museums of art, handicrafts and popular architecture (wooden buildings). Handsome Rynok (square). The *Kony Kornyakt* House with historical museum and house where Peter I lived. University and colleges. Many industries. Park of Culture and Rest with children's miniature railway.

Shaginya. Polish frontier. E22 goes to Krakow, Wrocław and Berlin.

A transit road from Lvov passes through the foothills of the Carpathian Mountains to the Hungarian and Czechoslovakian frontier at *Chop,* and then continues to Budapest. Small villages with picturesque one-storey houses with large windows and beautifully ornamented outer walls. Several spas.

Uzhgorod. The imposing castle with origins in the 11th cent. now serves as a folklore museum.

An Intourist route goes from Zhitomir to the old town of **Vinnitsa** with old fortress and 18th cent. wooden churches. **Khmelnitsky,** previously known as Proskurov, was given its new name in conjunction with the celebration of the Ukraine's 300-year-long unification with Russia. One of the men who played a major role in this was Bogdan Khmelnitsky. **Kamenets- Podolsky** with 14th-cent. fortress.

Chernovtsy. The university was once the residence of the Metropolitan of Bukovina. The greater part of the region of Bukovina is now in Roumania.

Porubnoe. Roumanian frontier. E20 continues to Bucureşti – Sofia – Thessaloniki.

20. Kiev – Odessa

The road passes through the enormous, fertile steppes of the Ukraine. South of Uman there are hills and oak groves.

ODESSA (1.1 million). The ancient Greeks founded a colony they called Odessos on this site, but the city of Odessa was not founded until 1794. Largest port on the Black Sea. Regular passenger and freight ship service to Marseilles. Theatre for performances of opera and ballet. Severely damaged during the Second World War, it was granted the title "Heroic City". Broad boulevards, splendid palaces. Deribasov Street is the city's busiest thoroughfare. The Potemkin Steps became world famous through Eisenstein's film "The Battleship Potemkin".

An Intourist route connects Odessa with Kishenev. *Tiraspol,* centre of an agricultural area, has lush semi-tropical vegetation.

KISHINEV (270000). Capital of the Moldavian Soviet Republic. 19th-cent. cathedral. *Pushkin Museum* (the poet Alexander Pushkin once lived in the city). University and Academy of Science. Moldavia has a mild climate and 20 % of all of the Soviet vineyards are situated in this area. Tobacco, canned goods and cooking oil are all typical products of the republic.

Road to the frontier station at Leusheny and the neighbouring Roumanian town of *Iasi.*

The Great Caucasian Circular Route

Kharkov – Rostov na Donu – Krasnodar – Sochi – Tbilisi – Ordzhonikidze – Kharkov

KHARKOV, see route 4.

Chuguev. Birthplace (1844) of Ilya Repin, the artist. The road goes over the plains. In the *Donets* region they are replaced by a landscape dotted with hills and mining towns. One of them is even named *Bokovo-Antracit.* Pyramid-shaped slag heaps. Coal mines and industry. *DONETSK* (800 000) is the centre of the area (it is a few score kilometres off the approved road).

NOVOCHERKASSK (120 000). Industrial town. Large *Hetman's Palace* (a hetman was the supreme commander of Cossack troops) and a triumphal arch are reminders of the period when the city was the capital of the Don Cossacks. *Cossack museum.*

ROSTOV NA DONU (Rostov on the Don, 700 000). Industrial town and major port on the broad River *Don* where it is linked by a canal with the Volga and Volgograd.

The road goes west through a fertile area. Enormous fields of wheat, sunflowers, maize. Vineyards and orchards. Foreign visitors may tour the *Kuban Kolkhoz* (cooperative farm). *Krasnodar* is the chief town of the area. Through the Volchi Vorota (Wolf Gate) Pass to *NOVOROSSIISK* (160 000). Major port and "Heroic City", Eternal flame in Heroes' Square. "The bells of Novorossiisk" by Dmitry Shostakovich is played once an hour. *Gelendzhik.* Spa.

SOCHI (100 000). Largest and most modern health resort in the Soviet Union. Centre of a 145 km long coastal area lined with seaside resorts and spas. Mild climate. Semi-tropical vegetation. Beautiful views from Mount Akhun. Sulphur springs in *Matsesta* and *Khosta.* The River Psou is the natural boundary to Georgia and also the boundary of a new time zone (one hour ahead of Moscow). This part of Georgia is called *Abkhazia. Pitsunda* and other health resorts.

Lake *Ritsa,* at 925 m above sea level, is one of the most beautiful places in the entire Soviet Union. The road passes the *"Blue Lake"* (Goluboe Ozero), 25 m in diameter and 75 m deep. The bottom is covered with lazurite.

Sukhumi. Capital of the autonomous republic of Abkhazia. Spa. Botanical gardens and scientific institutions. Kutaisi was mentioned as long ago as the 3rd cent. B.C. *Bakuriani* is a winter sports resort. Botanical gardens with alpine flowers. *Gori* with 7th-cent. fortress. House where Stalin was born. Museum. *Uplistsiche,* cave dwellings from the 3rd-2nd cent. B.C.

TBILISI (800 000). Capital of the Georgian Soviet Socialist Republic (Gruzia). Known as early as the 4th cent. B.C. *Narikala,* a fortress. *Metekh,* a 12th-cent. castle. *Anshiskhati Church* (5th–6th cent.). Large industrial city. University. Museum. Theatre for performances of opera and ballet. Tea and wines. Views from *Mount Mtatsminda.* Gold and enamel handicrafts.

Mtskheta. Capital of Georgia prior to the 6th cent. Old churches. Ceramics.

Road to *YEREVAN* (610 000). Capital of the Armenian Soviet Socialist Republic, founded in the 8th cent. B.C. It is situated at about 1 000 m above sea level. Ruins of the 7th-cent. Zvartnots Church . University and many institutions established to preserve the Armenian culture and traditions. The library *Matenadaran,* a collection of 10 000 Armenian manuscripts. The earliest dates from the 5th cent.

The Georgian Military Highway (Gruzian Army Road) is one of the most beautiful roads through the Caucasus Mountains. It follows an ancient route once travelled by camel caravans. The early paths that went through the dramatic mountain passes were transformed into a road in the 19th cent. At some places it has been hewn out of the mountain sides of narrow passes, e.g. at *Chertov* (the Devil's) Pass. The road ascends from the *Kaishauri Valley* (640 m) in twists and turns up to the *Krestovy Pass* (2 388m).

The Caucasus, the highest mountain range in Europe, is 180 km wide and 1 500 km long. The climate and flora are similar to those found in the Alps.

Ordzhonikidze. Cultural and industrial centre. Old fortress. *Karmadon* and *Tsey,* two lovely spas. *Pyatigorsk,* with memories of the poet Lermontov. Museum. *Zheleznovodsk* with mineral springs and spas.

ROSTOV NA DONU (Rostov on the Don). The fantastic journey is now complete. The entire circular trip covered 2 250 km.
LENINGRAD (4.6 million)

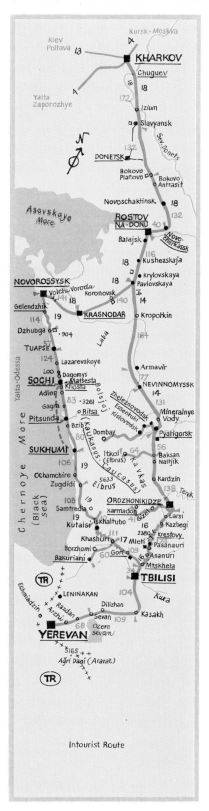

Intourist Route

TOWN PLANS

LENINGRAD (4.6 million)
A Swedish stronghold was established at the mouth of the River *Neva* in the 14th cent. It fell to the troops of Peter the Great in 1703, and he commanded his new capital built on the marshlands. In 1712, 40 000 forced-labourers had completed the first stages of the construction. Thousands of lives had been claimed. St. Petersburg, as it was originally called, was a modern western city that provided a striking contrast with the old Russian traditions and buildings of Moscow. During the First World War it was renamed Petrograd, and in 1924 it was given its present name.
The plan of the city is marked by enormous dimensions: wide streets, huge open places, great expanses of water. Architecturally, Leningrad is one of the most beautiful cities in the world. Many canals that follow the Dutch patterns and traditions. The delta of the River Neva has 100 islands connected by 700 bridges.
The **Admiralty** (by Zakharov) is in the heart of the city. Its slender 72 m high spire, topped with a little ship, can be seen from all of the streets that fan out from Admiralty Square. The most famous street is **Nevsky Prospekt**, the over 5 km long artery of Leningrad. Dom Knigi, a bookshop. Anichkov Bridge over the Fontanka River.
St. Isaac's Cathedral, an enormous structure that can accommodate 13 000 people. Designed by Montferrand, it was under construction from 1819 until 1858. 43 different types of stone have been built into the church. St. Isaac's is 102 m high and has a gilded dome. Beneath the dome hangs Foucault's pendulum, an instrument that records the rotation of the earth.
Kazan Cathedral has a magnificent half-circle of columns.
Decembrists' Square, distinguished by Falconet's famed equestrian *statue* of Peter the Great on a rearing horse. Falconet's 20-year-old pupil, Marie-Anne Collot, created the face. The Decembrists were a band of revolutionaries active in 1825. The group was brutally crushed.
The **Winter Palace** by Rastrelli, completed in 1762, and inspired by Versailles, was the residence of the czars. The storming of the Winter Palace in 1917 marked the beginning of the Russian Revolution. Round the palace are several magnificent buildings connected by a famous portal or triumphal arch. The chariot of the Goddess of Victory commemorates the 1812 defeat of Napoleon. The 47 m high Alexander Column.
The **Hermitage** in the Winter Palace is one of the world's foremost museums. A tour through all of its 300 halls would entail a 30 km walk. Archaeological artifacts, finds from the Far East, collections of antiques and 140 rooms of West European art.

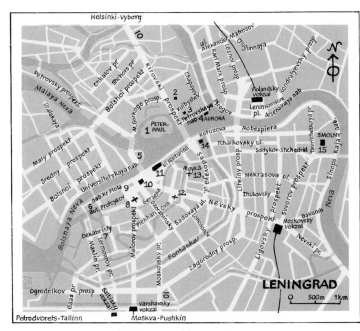

1 Peter-Paul Fortress. 2 Museum of the Revolution. 3 Peter the Great's Log Cabin. 4 Cruiser Aurora. 5 Naval museum. 6 Museum of the History of Leningrad. 7 Kirov Theatre. 8 St. Isaac Cathedral. 9 Decembrists' Square. The Bronze Rider. 10 The Admiralty Building. 11 Palace Square. The Winter Palace. The Hermitage Museum. 12 Nevsky Prospekt. The Kazan Cathedral. 13 The Russian Museum. (The Church on the Blood). 14 The Summer Palace. 15 Smolny.

Leningrad. The Winter Palace which contains the Hermitage, art museum

There are 40 works by Rubens alone. 19th- to 20th-cent. paintings by Picasso, Matisse, Renoir, Gauguin and many more. Magnificent collection of carriages and sleighs from the Czarist period. Wax figure of Peter the Great, who, in real life, was truly "great" – he was 2.04 m tall. The figure, grotesquely realistic, was modelled shortly after his death. The face is based on his death mask, and the hair is his own.

The cruiser **Aurora,** now a museum, has been preserved as a national monument. Shots fired at the Winter Palace from the warship in 1917 marked the start of the November Revolution. Near by is the little **log cabin** (1703) where Peter the Great resided during the construction of his new capital. The simple structure has been built into a sturdier building.

Peter-Paul Fortress, by the Swiss architect Trezzini, was completed in 1703. It became a notorious prison for revolutionaries. Now it serves as a museum. The 121 m high slender, gilded spire of the cathedral is visible from almost all of central Leningrad. Mausoleum church of the czars and czarinas. Tomb of Peter the Great. The magnificent, Baroque **Smolny Convent,** by Rastrelli, was completed in the middle of the 18th cent. Neoclassic Smolny Institute (1807). The buildings became the headquarters for Soviet political activity during the revolution and they still serve as a centre for the Communist Party. The new Soviet State was proclaimed by Lenin in the white-columned Great Hall in 1917. The *Tauride Palace* (1789) was given to Potemkin, a favourite of the czarina, by his imperial patroness, Catherine the Great. The **Russian Museum** (by Rossi) with Russian art. *Military Museum. Kirov Museum.* Kirov was the leader of the Communist Party in Leningrad from 1926 until 1934, the year of his assassination. *Lenin Museum.* There are many places and memorials dedicated to Lenin in the city where he lived, at times illegally.

Museum of the History of Leningrad. October Revolution Museum. Porcelain museum. Museum of industrial art. Sculpture museum. Theatre museum. Pushkin's flat, etc.

The Finland Station (Finlandsky Vokzal), the railway station where Lenin arrived in 1917. He had spent years in exile. During the First World War, the Germans permitted him to travel from Switzerland through Germany to neutral Sweden and then on to Finland and Petrograd. He proclaimed the World Revolution in the czar's waiting room. Large memorial.

Opera and Gorky Theatre. Pavlova, Nijinsky, Ulanova and many more famous dancers have performed at the Kirov Ballet Theatre. University and colleges. Industries and shipyards.

During the Second World War, Leningrad withstood a 28-month siege. The Germans almost ringed the city and only a precarious supply line

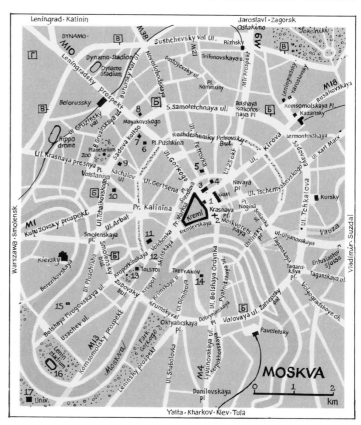

1 The Red Square. Kremlin. Lenin Mausoleum. Gum Department Store. 2 St. Basil's Cathedral. 3 Historical Museum. 4 Lenin Central Museum. 5 Bolshoi Theatre. 6 Museum of the Revolution. 7 Tchaikovsky Concert Hall. 8 Puppet Theatre. 9 Chekhov Museum. 10 Gorky Museum. 11 Pushkin Museum of Fine Arts. 12 Moscow Swimming Pool. 13 Tolstoy Museum. 14 Tretyakov Picture Gallery. 15 Novodevitchy Convent. 16 Moscow University.

routed over Lake Ladoga allowed its defenders to survive. The winter of 1941-1942 was brutally cold and at least 650 000 people in Leningrad died of starvation or froze to death.

Petrodvorets (Peterhof). Summer palace of Peter the Great, by Rastrelli. Completed in 1724 and expanded in 1730. Enormous park and gardens. More than 100 monumental fountains.

Pushkin, previously known as Tsarskoe Selo, was named after the poet Alexander Pushkin (1799-1837) who studied here. Summer residence of the czars (18th cent.). The Catherine Palace was designed by Rastrelli (1756). Lovely park. The Agate Pavilion has walls of agate.

Pavlovsk, 6 km east of Pushkin. Palace situated high on a hill. Summer residence of the czars, now a museum. Large park.

MOSKVA (Moscow, 8 million)
Capital of the Union of Soviet Socialist Republics. Moscow was first mentioned in documents from 1147. In 1156 Prince Yuri Dolgoruky had a

little wooden fort built here. The first Kremlin walls were erected in 1495. Moscow became the capital of Russia. In the beginning of the 18th cent., Peter the Great had the capital transferred to his new city, St. Petersburg. In March 1918, Moscow became the capital of the world's first Socialist nation.

The heart of Moscow are the Red Square and Kremlin, starting point for many wide streets that fan out over the city. Circular streets ring the inner city. Furthest out is a 109 km long ring road that marks the city's boundaries.

Red Square (Krasnaya Ploshchad) was given its name as early as the 17th cent. The Russian word "krasnaya" means both red and beautiful. Scene of enormous military and popular parades. The corpse of Lenin has been on view in the **Lenin Mausoleum** since 1924. Long queues to see the remains of the founder of the USSR. The changing of the guard outside the mausoleum takes place once an hour. Although it is a simple ceremony it attracts large crowds of

*The Kremlin
and St. Basil's
Cathedral,
Moscow*

spectators. The corpse of Stalin was placed in the mausoleum in 1953 but was moved to a grave near the Kremlin wall in 1961. The **Spasskye Tower** is one of the Kremlin's most beautiful towers. Its bells are heard every day on Radio Moscow. **St. Basil's Cathedral** with 12 colourful, shimmering domes was built for Ivan the Terrible in the 16th cent. The *Historical Museum*, a red brick building, is on the side of the square. Opposite the Kremlin is the large market-hall-like *GUM* department store.

The **Kremlin** is a medieval city within the city. It is the centre of Moscow and the Soviet Union. Three white cathedrals with interesting domes were built in 1479, 1489 and 1505: the **Uspensky Sobor** (Cathedral of the Assumption), the **Blagoveshchensky Sobor** (Cathedral of the Annunciation), where the czars were baptized and married, and the **Arkhangelsky Sobor** (Cathedral of the Archangel Michael) where many of the czars are buried. Cathedral of the Twelve Apostles and the Belfry of Ivan the Terrible (80 m high). *Czar Cannon* (1586) and the 200-ton *Czar Bell* (1735). The bell has never rung. A piece that fell from it lies to the side. The **Armoury** with an enormous collection of art, weapons, armour, gold, silver and precious stones. The Palace of Congress, a modern building completed in 1961, is constructed of aluminium, glass, and white marble from the Urals. The Great Hall, which accommodates 6 000, is the meeting place of the Supreme Soviet. The Council of Ministers meets in the Sverdlov Hall of the former senate. *Lenin's study* has been

preserved.

Moscow has 150 museums. The foremost art museum is the **Tretyakov Gallery** with an enormous collection of Russian art from different periods. Among the other museums are the Lenin Museum, Revolution Museum, Marx and Engels Museum, National History Museum, History of Moscow Museum, Pushkin Museum (art from many countries), Oriental Culture Museum and a museum with a panorama of the Battle of Borodino. Moscow is famous for its superb theatre and ballet performances. Of all of the city's theatres, the **Bolshoi** is the best known. There are frequent performances in the Palace of Congress. Two unique theatres are the Central Puppet Theatre and Romen, a Gipsy theatre. The symphony orchestra and the Red Army song and dance ensemble perform in the *Tchaikovsky Hall*. Annual festival of Russian opera, ballet and music at the beginning of May ("Stars of Moscow") and during the Christmas/New Year holiday ("Russian Winter"). The *circus*, housed in a modern building, is very popular. Its ring can be transformed into an ice rink.

The **Exhibition of Economic Achievements** spreads out over an enormous area in the park of Ostakins. 70 huge exhibition halls with displays related to the latest cultural and scientific developments. Atomic energy and space exploration exhibits. Theatres, concert halls, restaurants. Vast botanical gardens. *Lenin Stadium,* the largest sports complex of its type in Europe. The small stadium has places for 15 600 spectators, the large

stadium seats 103 000. The indoor arena seats 17 000 and the *Dynamo Stadium* 60 000. The Moscow *Swimming Pool*, one of the largest swimming pools in the world, can accommodate 2 000 swimmers at one time. Open year-round, on even the coldest days of the severe Moscow winter. The water is 27° C.

Trotting races at the Moscow *Hippodrome.* Half a million students are enrolled in Moscow's schools of higher learning. The city's skyline is dominated by the huge *Moscow University* building, 240 m high and with a 450 m long main façade. Founded in 1775 the university has been named after the scientist Lomonosov. Students from the developing countries attend Friendship University (sometimes referred to as Patrice Lumumba University).

Moscow's famous **underground** with its flamboyant marble and crystal adorned stations, is one of the major sights of the city.

Moscow is the centre of the Soviet Union's enormous network of air transport. The Soviet national airline, Aeroflot, is the largest in the world. Pravda, the newspaper of the Soviet Communist Party, is produced in Moscow. With a circulation of 9 million it is the most-read newspaper in the world. Izvestia is the official government newspaper. Tass is the Soviet news agency. Gosbank is the largest bank in the world. The Russia Hotel near Red Square has 6 000 beds. Intourist offices, found in all of the major tourist hotels, arrange theatre and circus tickets, restaurant bookings, car-hire and excursions.

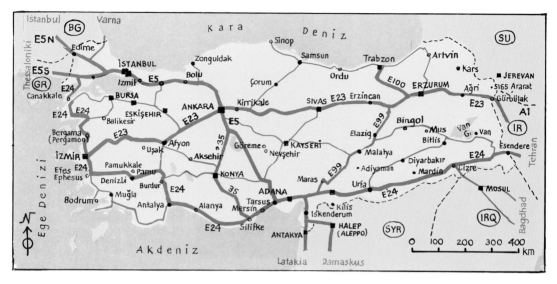

TR · Turkey

TR·Türkiye

Area: 780 576 km² (301 200 sq. miles) Trakky (Thrace), European Turkey: 24 000 km². Asian Turkey is known as Anatolia.

Population: 47 million. 1.5 million Kurds comprise the largest minority group. 95 % of the population is Muslim. The national language, Turkish, is a Finno-Ugric language written with the Latin alphabet.

Major cities: Istanbul 4.8 million, Ankara (capital) 2.5 million, Izmir 1.9 million.

Government: Constitutional republic. Legislative power is vested in the Grand National Assembly.

History
50 000 B.C. Traces of prehistoric dwellings in Anatolia.
6 500 B.C. Çatal Höyük, oldest known Stone-Age town.
3 000 B.C. Founding of Troy which is eventually destroyed in 1 200 B.C.
500 B.C. Period of greatness for the cities of Pergamon, Miletus and Priene.
c. 2 000 B.C.-c. 713 Rise and fall of the Hittite Empire. Other groups, Phrygians, Lydians, Assyrians, Persians and Greeks gain power.
133 B.C. Turkey becomes a Roman province.
1071 The Byzantine Empire is defeated by Seljuk Turk Prince Alp Arslan.
1326 Ottoman Turks occupy Bursa which becomes their capital. The Ottoman Empire lasts until 1923.
1453 Constantinople captured and proclaimed the capital of the Ottoman Empire under the name of Istanbul.
1520-1566 Reign of Suleiman the Magnificent. Turkey is at the height of its power. Hungary, the Balkans, Greece and large areas of Arabia are

conquered. Turkish fleets rule the Mediterranean.
1571 The Turks are defeated at the Battle of Lepanto and in 1683 at Vienna.
18th-19th cent. The Turkish Empire begins to disintegrate. Internal political reorganization.
1908 A revolutionary movement, the "Young Turks", takes power.
1911-1920 Turkey is involved in several wars. During the First World War, Turkey joins with Germany and Austria-Hungary against the Allies.
1920 Mustafa Kemal (Atatürk) becomes president and war begins with the Greeks who occupy western Anatolia. Greeks driven from Asia Minor. The present frontiers established in 1923 as a result of the Treaty of Lausanne.
1925-1935 Reform period: the Latin alphabet, Gregorian calendar and metric systems are put into effect as well as compulsory education and women's suffrage.
1938 Death of Atatürk.
1939-1945 Turkey is neutral during the Second World War.
1980 After political unrest marked by frequent outbursts of violence, a military council comes to power.
1983. General elections.

Currency: Turkish lira (TRL).
1 turkish lira = 100 kuruş

Business hours: Banks 8.30-12.00 a.m., 1.30-5.00 p.m. Saturdays closed. Post offices 9.00 a.m.-5.00 p.m. Some post offices are closed on Saturdays. Shops 8.00 a.m.-1.00 p.m., 2.00-7.00 p.m. On Saturdays lunchtime closings often 12.00 noon-1.00 p.m. Some shops stay open until 7.30 p.m. Smaller foodshops usually open earlier and stay open later.

Holidays: New Year's Day, April 23 (Independence Day), May 19 (Youth and Sport Day), October 29 (Republic Day). Muslim religious holidays are based on the lunar calendar. Seker Bayrami, three days, and Kurban Bayrami, four days.

Hotels and restaurants
In major cities in western Turkey and in the larger resorts, hotels maintain West European standards. Restaurant is "Restoran" or "Lokanta" in Turkish. Simpler eating places are known as Aş Evi, while establishments serving spirits are called Içkili Lokanta. Coffee shops are known as Kahvehane.

Camping
Many camping sites along the Black

Homes and churches hewn out of the volcanic rock. Cappadocia, near Kayseri

The beach at Antalya

spirits do exist. Raki, an anise-flavoured drink distilled from grapes, often diluted with water, is a popular accompaniment to lunch and dinner. When water is added, Raki becomes a cloudy white – Aslan sütü, "Lion's milk".

Shopping

Copper and brass work, costume jewellery (gold, silver, filigree), leather goods, handwoven rugs, pottery, embroidery. Leather jackets and coats. Ordinary shops have set prices. In bazaars, often after a cup or two of complimentary coffee or tea, you are expected to haggle.

Speed limits. Traffic regulations

Outside towns and cities 90 kmh, built-up areas 50 kmh. Private cars towing trailers, caravans, etc. 80 kmh, built-up areas 40 kmh. The maximum speed for motorcycles is 70 kmh.
If your car is fitted with seat belts it is compulsory to wear them.
All vehicles entering the Istanbul province must keep their interior lights on while moving at night.
You are required to carry two warning triangles.

Roads

The major roads are generally good, but they can also be narrow, twisting and filled with heavy lorry traffic. Flocks of animals, unheeding pedestrians and motorists without thought or regard to traffic regulations all help to make motoring in Turkey a bit of a challenge. Even if you manage to emerge unscathed from a motor accident, you will find that motor accidents in Turkey are serious occurrences. Contact with the police is mandatory, particularly if you seek compensation. Avoid night-time driving, as many vehicles are driven without lights.
Directional signs can be inadequate. Road signs are international but many signs are posted only in Turkish:
Azami park 1 saat = 1 hour parking
Capraz yol = crossing
Dur = stop
Durmak yasaktir = no stopping
Hastane = hospital
Yavas = reduce speed
Tamirat = road works
Dikkat = warning
Bozuk satih = uneven road
Nakil vasitasi giremez = motor vehicles prohibited
Park yapilmaz = no parking
Gümrük = customs

Road patrols

TTOK, The Turkish Tourist and Automobile Club has yellow cars that patrol the Edirne – Ankara road. Assistance can be obtained by dialling 46 70 90 in Istanbul, 18 65 78 in Ankara, 25 50 92 in Izmir, and Kapikule.

TTOK, Türkiye Turing ve Otomobil Kurumu, 364 Şişli Meydani, Istanbul. Tel. 011-46 70 90.
Turkish Tourism Information Office, 170–3 Piccadilly, London WIU 900. Tel. 01-734 8681.

Sea, west and south coasts and near the major cities. They are called "Mocamps".

Food and drink

Uncomplicated charcoal-broiled meat (often veal and lamb) and fish dishes are prominent on Turkish menus. Often they are accompanied by tomatoes, pepper and salads. Even though some dishes ar highly spiced, most seasoning is mild.
Some specialities: Dolma means "filled" and dolmasi have a great variety of fillings. Biber dolmasi are stuffed peppers, domates dolmasi, stuffed tomatoes, midye dolmasi, mussels stuffed with spiced rice. Pattican, fried or stuffed aubergine. Köfte, meatballs, often appear on menus. Adana Köfte is a popular and highly spiced version. Kadin Badu, "ladies' thighs", are oval-shaped meatballs grilled on skewers. Meze – an assortment of hors d'œuvre, usually including salads and often cheese. Imam bayildi ("the priest swooned") is a blending of aubergine, onions, tomatoes, served cold. Cherkez Tavugu, chicken with pepper and walnut sauce. Döner Kebab, thin slices of lamb that has been grilled on a rotating spit. Shish Kebab Tavuk, grilled chicken. Pilav, mutton or lamb rice stew. Fish is popular. Kalkan, turbot. Kiliç baglili, swordfish, skewer-grilled served with onions and pepper. Palamut, bonito. Barbunya, carp. Levrek, sea bass.
Sweets can be extremely sweet. Baklava, flaky pastry with nuts. Halva is a compressed sweet made of sugar and sesame seeds. Kadin Bobergi, "lady's navel", pastry with a little hole in the middle.
Yoghurt is popular and often served as sauce. When a pinch of salt and a little water is added, yoghurt goes under the name of Ayran. Turkish coffee is served hot, sweet and strong, in diminutive cups, that have a heavy coffee-ground ballast.
The most usual mealtime beverage is water, usually presented in sealed bottles, but excellent domestic wines and

E5. Plovdiv – Edirne – Istanbul – Ankara – Antakya

Kapikule. Bulgarian frontier. E5 comes from London – Bruxelles – Frankfurt – Wien – Beograd. From Skopje it has the E5N numbering. E5S follows the road's original routing through Greece.

Edirne. Earlier known as Hadrianopolis, founded by Emperor Hadrian in the 2nd cent. In the 5th cent. it was the residence of the first Turkish sultan. Edirne has often been ravaged by earthquakes and wars. The *Great Tower*, a wooden belfry, remains of Edirus Kalesi Castle. Beautiful Old Turkish town centre and handsome stone bridges. Narrow alleys, wooden houses, bazaars and mosques. *Selimiye Mosque* is a creation of the famed architect Sinan. Exquisite mosaics. Annual greased wrestling tournaments held in June on the island of Sarayici.

Babaeski. Cedit Ali Pasha Mosque, another work of Sinan. 17th-cent. bridge. *Çorlu* on *Via Egnatia*, an ancient road that originally linked the Bosphorus with the Adriatic Sea. Roman bridge. Several mosques.

E95. Burgas – Babaeski

Dereköy. Bulgarian frontier. E95 comes from Constanţa – Varna – Burgas.

Kirklareli. Beautifully situated on the western slopes of the Istranca Mountains. Settlement since prehistoric times. Hirzibey Mosque (1407) is the oldest of the town's eight mosques.

Silivri is one of several seaside resorts that line the Sea of Marmara. Long sandy beaches. E5S from Niš via Thessaloniki and Androupolis meets E5N here.

Malkara. Several mosques. **Tekirdag,** old town with important port. Mosques and covered market, *Bedesten.* Museum in a palace once owned by King Rákóczy, patriot and hero of the Hungarian struggle for independence. He died while in exile here, in 1734.

E5 becomes a part of the "Londra asfalti" road and enters the city through the Topkapi Gate. It is also possible to drive past Yesilköy airport and along the shore of the Sea of Marmara beneath the walls of the Seraglio around the peninsula. Suddenly, the Golden Horn, the Galata Bridge, the busy harbour and Istanbul's countless minarets appear before you. No other European city can offer such a beautiful and dramatic approach.

ISTANBUL, see town plans.

The **Bosphorus Bridge** links Europe with Asia. Completed in 1973, it is 1074 m long. The first bridge that joined two continents was a pontoon bridge built 2000 years ago for Darius, the Persian king. It was used by his soldiers on their way to Greece.

Gebze, in a lovely setting. The great architect Sinan designed the Mustafa Pasha Mosque. Tomb of the Carthaginian general, Hannibal. **Hereke.** Carpet factories.

IZMIT (130000). Important trading town on the old caravan route. Caravanserai (inn where caravans stopped) and mosque by Sinan. The old city walls date from the Hellenic period. Roman aqueduct.

Road to **BURSA** (280000) (not on map). Spa with thermal (sulphur and iron) springs. Covered bazaar. Inhabited as early as 1000 B.C., Bursa was the capital of the Ottoman Empire 1326-1453. Many buildings remain from that period. Yesil Camii (the Green Mosque) with exquisite blue and green tiles. Tombs of sultans and princes. Mausoleum of Mehmet I. Mosque of Murat I and baths in the suburb of Cekirge. On a hill the tombs of Osman and Orhan, founders of the Ottoman kingdom. Fine views of the city.

Road and cable car to *Ulu-Dag* (2543 m), large winter sports centre.

From Şile to Akçakoca there is an unbroken beach with small harbours and fishing villages.

Lake Sapanca. 16 km long, 5 km wide, beautifully situated in a countryside marked by hills and cherry and apple orchards.

Adapazari. Byzantine bridge, with eight arches, built in 561 for Emperor Justinian. It is landbound and its original purpose is not known.

Road to **Iznik** (the ancient Nicaea). Town wall. *Hagia Sophia* Church, where Emperor Constantine presided over an Ecumenical Council which condemned the Arian Heresy and established the Nicene Creed. 14th-cent. Green Mosque. Displays of the famous Iznik pottery in the museum. *Lake Abant,* 1400 m above sea level. A crater lake known for its trout. *Gerede.* Typical Anatolian town with picturesque wooden buildings.

ANKARA, see town plans.

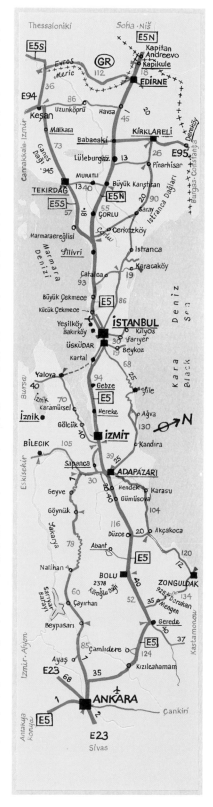

Tuz Gölü, "Salt Lake". Partially dried up during the summer when its bed is covered with thick layers of salt. Maximum depth 3 m. Salt content 32%.

Aksaray. 14th-cent. Karamanoglu Mosque. Ulukisla in the centre of the Taurus Mountains. 17th-cent. caravanserai. Sultanhani. Well-preserved caravanserai. These inns where caravans stopped for the night were placed a day's journey (about 30 km) apart along the old caravan routes.

Kirşehir. Cacabey Mosque and Observatory.

Road 73 to *Nevşehir.* Kurşunlu Mosque with lead-covered cupola.

Göreme Valley, a fantastic landscape of eroded pyramid-shaped rocks and deep ravines. The caves were inhabited as early as the Bronze Age. Early Christians secretly transformed them into churches, monasteries and dwellings. 8th- to 15th-cent. frescoes. Several other caves in the area, e.g. in Ortahisar. Some of the caves in Avanos are still inhabited.

Urgüp. Fantastic rock formations, created from eroded blocks of lava from the nearby Ercias-Dag, a volcano (3 990 m).

Gülek boğazi (1 050 m above sea level), known to the Romans as the Cilcian Gates. The River *Taurus* flows through a narrow, 20 m wide gorge that cuts through the Taurus Mountains. Twisting but well constructed road on the west side. The old road went eastern bank and had been used by Cyrus, Xenophon, Alexander the Great and scores of other conquerers on their way into inner Anatolia or the coast of the Mediterranean.

Tarsus. Birthplace of the Apostle Paul. The river where Cleopatra met Mark Antony.

ADANA (350 000). Fourth largest city in Turkey with predominantly modern buildings. Cotton and citrus fruit centre. *Great Mosque,* built of black and white marble. *Ramazanoglu Mosque.* Archaeological museum. *Roman bridge* over the River Ceyhan, built for Emperor Hadrian. 14 of the original 21 arches remain.

Karatepe was an important town during the time of the Hittite kingdom (2 000-700 B.C.) and large sections of the ancient city have been excavated. *Open-air museum.* Inscribed stones. One of these orthostates (from about 725 B.C.), near the town gate, is inscribed in two languages and has provided one of the keys to the deciphering of hieroglyphic Hittite.

ISKENDERUN (100 000). The city's ancient name was Alexandrette. Turkey's largest Mediterranean port. Modern buildings.

ANTAKYA (Antioch, 70 000) was founded 300 B.C. by Antiochus, one of the generals of Alexander the Great. It was a very early centre of Christian activity. St. Peter is said to have preached on the site of the Church of St. Peter (oldest Christian church in the world), which is situated in a cave. During the Hellenic and Roman eras Antioch was a major trading centre and by the 4th cent. about 300 000 people are believed to have lived here. In the 13th cent. the Egyptian Mamluks razed the city. Subsequent earthquakes have helped to destroy almost all of the remains, but a *Roman bridge,* part of an aqueduct, survives. *Museum of archaeology* with an outstanding collection of Roman mosaics. Medieval *Habib Neccar Mosque.*

Ylayadağı. Syrian frontier. The road continues to Latakia.

Alternative route: Ankara – Konya – Adana is 675 km long, E 4 is 495 km. See also maps for roads E 23 and E 24.

KONYA (the ancient Iconium, 250 000). Founded about 5 000 B.C. Hittites, Phrygians, Lydians, Persians and Romans have held power here. During the 11th, 12th and 13th cent. it was the capital of Turkey, i.e. the Kingdom of the Seljuks and the Rum sultanate. Many magnificent buildings. The Palace of *Sultan Ala-Eddin* (1220). The *Karatay madrasah* (Muslim theological school), completed in 1251, now houses a pottery museum. Tombs of the Sultan in the Ala-Eddin Mosque. Museum in the former *Mevlâna monastery* which also contains the tomb of Mevlâna Celal Addin-Rum. He was the founder of the Order of Mevlevi Dervishes. By spinning round at varying speeds for hours, the dervishes achieve a state of religious ecstasy. Atatürk dissolved the order in 1925. *Museum of Islamic art.* Carpets. *Ince minaret. Mosaics museum. Archaeological museum.*

Karaman. During the 12th and 13th cent. capital of the Karamanoğlu dynasty. Many buildings from that period. Ak Tekke Dervish monastery. Splendid Hatuniye madrasah (Muslim theological school). Tomb of the poet Yunus Emre (d. 1332) in the Emre Mosque. The area is known for its carpets. *Valley of Binbir Kilise* (the Thousand and One Churches) at the foot of Mount Karadağ. Hundreds of ruins of Byzantine churches, palaces and castles.

Uzuncaburç with extensive excavations of a 3rd- to 2nd-cent. B.C. city. 30 columns, once part of a temple of Zeus, theatre, town gates, etc.

Silifke – Adana, see E 24.

E 23. Gürbülak – Ankara – Izmir

Gürbülak. Iranian frontier. Asia Road 1 (A 1) continues to Teheran, Delhi and Ho-Chi-Minh-Ville, 10 870 km away.

The road passes over the high plains via the **Ağri Daği Massif**, best known for **Mount Ararat**. Many expeditions have climbed the mountain in search of remains of Noah's ark. **Dogoübayazit**, 14th-cent. fortress.

Erzurum (60 000). Largest town in Eastern Anatolia, close to the source of the Euphrates. Trading town on the old caravan route. 5th-cent. fortress. University. 13th-cent. Muslim theological schools. Hatun Mausoleum and handsome mosques.

E 100 goes to Trabzon on the Black Sea. **Gümüshane** in a narrow valley. 19th- cent. Süleimanye Mosque. **Macka** on the wooded heights of Mount Zigina.

Trabzon (Trapesunt), founded 400 B.C. Once the starting point for camel caravans on their way to Persia and Central Asia. After the Crusaders plundered Constantinople in 1204, Trabzon became the capital of an empire that lasted 250 years. *Church of St. Anne* (8th cent.), now a mosque. *Hagia Sophia* is now a museum.

Erzincan, at 1 400 m, was severely damaged by an earthquake in 1939. **Divriğe**. Magnificent Great Mosque and other splendid buildings.

SIVAS (52 000). Trading town on the important caravan route that went from the Persian Gulf to the Black Sea. "Kayseri" in the town is famous for its cotton cloth.

KAYSERI (130 000), see map road 2 E 23. During the Roman period this was the capital of Cappadocia. The citadel looms over the city. Near by is a large building that houses a museum, a mosque and the octagonal mausoleum (1237) of a Seljuk lord. *Covered market.* The beautiful 16th-cent. *Kurşunli Camii* (the Lead Mosque) is a creation of the famous architect Sinan. **Göreme, Nevşehir**, see E 5.

Route 45 to **Samsun** on the Black Sea.

Tokat with vineyards and market gardens. **Amasya**, beautifully situated in a narrow gorge. Capital of the Persian king, Mithradates. Turkish mosques.

Corum. Typical Turkish industrial and market town. *Ulu Camii* (the Great Mosque, 13th cent.). 19th-cent. clock tower. **Alacahöhük,** excavations of a town founded in the 4th cent. B.C.

Boğazkale with excavations of a Hittite city. The Hittites entered Anatolia from the north-east about 2 000 B.C. From about 1 400 B.C. until 1 200 B.C. theirs was the mightiest empire in Asia Minor.

ANKARA, see town plans.

Gordion. Excavations of Phrygian (8th cent. B.C.) and Persian gateways. Large tomb of King Gordius of Phrygia. Legend has it that he tied a knot which an oracle predicted could only be undone by the man destined to become the ruler of Asia. Alexander the Great severed it with the blade of his sword and fulfilled the prophesy.

Route 2 to **ESKIŞEHIR** (170 000). Modern city rebuilt after the War of Independence (1921).

Sivrihisar. Lovely little town at the foot of Mount Gal Daği. Ruins of a Byzantine church on the mountain top.

Afyon (38 000). High on a promontory. Large 13th-cent. castle. Ulu Camii (the Great Mosque , 1272) and several other mosques. Museum of archaeology in a former Muslim theological school. Museum of the War of Independence. Afyon is the centre of an opium producing area. Road to **Kütahya,** famed since the 16th cent. for its predominantly blue and white tiles and ceramics. The old patterns and traditions still survive. 15th-cent. *Ulu Camii.*

UŞAK. Modern town and railway junction. Carpet manufacturing. Near by ruins of the city of *Flaviopolis*. **Alaşehir.** Charming little town.

Sardes (Sart). When it was capital of Lydia, this was one of the richest cities of antiquity. A ruler during the 6th cent. B.C. was the famous King Croesus whose name is still associated with great wealth. An enormous *Temple of Artemis* was built during the time of Alexander the Great. Some parts of it survive. Christianity came early to Sardes and it became one of the Seven Churches of the Apocalypse mentioned in the Revelations of St. John.

MANISA, the Magnesia of antiquity. *Muradiye Mosque* is a creation of the great architect Sinan. Several other beautiful mosques. Wine centre. Annual Mesir festival April 18-26.

IZMIR, see E 24.

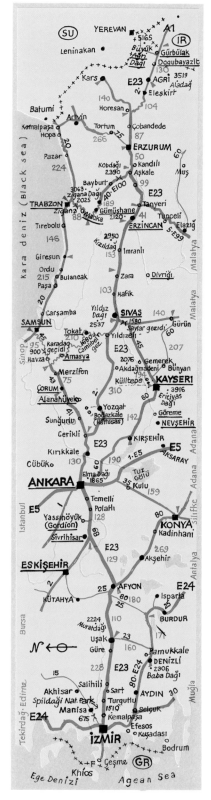

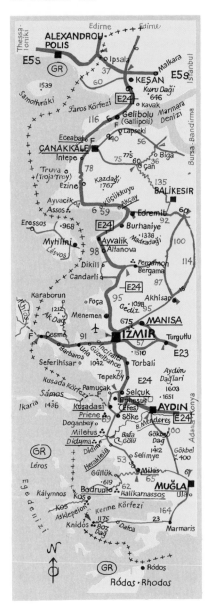

E 24. Keşan – Izmir – Antalya – Adana – Urfa – Esendere

Car ferry Eceabat – Canakkale (30 min.), services 6.30 a.m. – midnight.

Canakkale. Old town on the Dardanelles, the ancient Hellespont, a narrow strait named after the Trojan king Dardanus. Bolayir on the European shore with tombs of Suleiman Pasha and Namik Kemal, the Turkish poet. *Museum* with archaeological finds: pottery and other artifacts from the Hellenic and Roman periods.

Troy at the base of Mount Ida. The city's glory and fall have been immortalized by Homer in "The Iliad". The Trojan War lasted ten years. The Trojans were finally defeated by the cunning of Odysseus. He saw to it that a huge, wooden horse was brought into Troy. It was filled with Greek soldiers who proceeded to sack the city. Burial mounds of Achilles, Patroclus and Ajax on the north-western shore.

Akçay, a seaside resort, is the site of an annual festival. *Ören.* Little town and resort surrounded by olive and orange groves. *Ayvalik,* seaside resort and fishing port. Wonderful views from "The Devil's Table". The Greek island of Lesbos is not far from here. 15 min. by boat to the Alibey Islands, famous for their luxuriant vegetation, superb local wines and excellent fish restaurants. Annual July festival.

BERGAMA (Pergamon). Known to the Romans as Ascleipion, this was a "health centre" with sun and water treatments, salutory beverages, library, theatre and other amusements, which were all part of the treatment. The *theatre* (seating 4 500 spectators) is the site of an annual theatre festival (in May) when classical plays are performed. Museum of archaeology and ethnography. 14th-cent. *Ulu Mosque.* The slender minaret made of glazed, brightly coloured brick, is from the 14th cent. A 4 km long motor road leads up to the *Acropolis* with ruins of a palace. This was the site of a Zeus altar (188-160 B.C.) which is now, along with numerous other archaeological artifacts, in the Pergamon Museum in East Berlin. The upper part of the Acropolis, the large theatre and the gymnasium, are surrounded by a well-preserved, narrow town wall. Pergamon was the capital of a kingdom that existed during the 3rd cent. B.C., after the death of Alexander the Great. It subsequently became the Roman province of Asia.

Manisa, see E 23.

IZMIR. (Smyrna, 650 000). Turkey's third largest city, and major port, beautifully situated on a horseshoe-shaped gulf. Founded around 2 000 B.C., the city has been repeatedly destroyed by earthquakes. The worst earthquake was in A.D. 178, the last catastrophe was a fire in 1922. A few mosques and caravanserais remain from the old Smyrna. Hisar Mosque (1375). A few fragments are left from the ancient Roman square. *Saat Kulesi,* the clock tower, a beautifully ornamented monument to Sultan Abdülhamit. *Theatre* (A.D.54) with a stage in three tiers and places for 24 000 spectators. *Museum of archaeology. Atatürk museum.* Large covered *bazaar.*

To the west, the Greek island of *Chios,* birthplace of Homer.

Efes/Ephesus. Ruins of one of the richest and mightiest towns of antiquity. Capital of the Roman province of Asia. St. Paul lived here A.D. 55-58 and wrote the Epistle to the Ephesians.

Temple of Hadrian (2nd cent.), one of the finest of the remaining ancient buildings in the area. Theatre that accommodated 24 500. Superb acoustics. Reliefs depicting one of King Androcles' hunting parties. Emperor Claudius (A.D. 41-54) ordered the theatre enlarged, and the construction work was completed during the reign of Emperor Trajan (A.D. 98-117). St. Paul preached at this site. The 2nd-cent. *Church of the Virgin Mary* is the oldest basilica in Ephesus. In 431 this church was the meeting place of the Third Ecumenical Council that condemned the Nestorian Heresy and defined the articles of faith. Streets of marble. The main street is 530 m long.

Archaeological museum in the village of *Selçuk* with finds from Ephesus, including a statue of Artemis that once stood in the Temple of Artemis, one of the seven wonders of the ancient world. The temple was destroyed in a fire set by Herostiathós in 356 B.C. The act was his (successful) attempt for immortality.

Kuşadasi, "Bird Island", little harbour with clear water and sandy beaches. Several hotels. A caravanserai has been transformed into a hotel and an old Seljuk castle now serves as a discotheque.

Road south to the ruined city of *Priene* (4th cent. B.C.). Square, temple of Athena and theatre. *Milet* (Miletos) was an important port city in the 7th cent. B.C. and founded several colonies. Birthplace of the philosopher Thales of Miletos. The Roman theatre had places for 25 000 spectators. The town is situated near the River Menderes (Meander). Its winding course is remembered in the word "meander". *Didim* (Didyma). Dedicated to the god Apollo. Its famous temple, well-preserved, had a revered oracle.

Herakleia was an important port city. Preserved city wall from the Hellenic period, Roman theatre and Byzantine Endymion monastery. Silt from the

River Menderes has transformed the bay into a slightly salty, fish-filled lake that attracts thousands of aquatic birds at certain times of the year.

Milâs (Mylasa). Ancient town with remnants of many civilizations.

Bodrum (Halicarnassus). Little town and port, site of the ancient Halicarnassus, 375-353 B.C. capital of the kingdom of Caria. In 351 B.C. the reigning queen, Artemesia, had a tomb erected for her husband (he was also her brother), Mausolus. It became one of the seven wonders of the ancient world and has been remembered in the word "mausoleum". Severely damaged by an earthquake, its destruction was complete when Crusaders used the surviving stones for the construction of the enormous nearby fortress (15th cent.). Bodrum was the birthplace of the Greek historian Herodotos.

Muğla. Provincial capital. Bazaar. Ulu Camii (the Great Mosque, 1344). To the south, *Marmaris,* a beautiful port town. *Fethiye,* on a partially inadequate coast road, was known in antiquity as Telmessos. 4th-cent. B.C. tomb façades carved out of the rock. Beach. *Xanthos.* Capital of the kingdom of Lycia. Several tombs hollowed out of the rock (6th-4th-cent. B.C.).

Aydin. Industrial town. *Ciharzade Mosque* (18th cent.). 16-cent. *Ramazan Pasha Mosque.*

Pamukkale, the "Cotton Castle". Its name reflects the curious white limestone rock formations. The waters from nearby hot springs constantly seek new outlets. Not far away, *Hierapolis,* an important trading town during antiquity. Roman theatre, remains of a temple of Apollo, Roman baths and necropolis (cemetery). The town has been destroyed by countless earthquakes.

Burdur in an area that has been inhabited for more than 2 000 years. 21 mosques. 14th-cent. Ulu Mosque. Clock tower. Museum. *Isparta,* famous for its attar of roses, silk and carpets. Firdex Pasha's Mosque and Carsi Mosque (14th cent.). Large library with manuscripts. Museum of archaeology with interesting coin collection.

ANTALYA (120 000), founded in the 3rd cent. B.C. Two town walls – one protects the harbour, the other encircles the entire city. *Gate of Hadrian,* originally 8 m high, completed A.D. 130. *Kesik Minare Mosque* was originally a Christian church. Yivli Mosque. *The Yivli minaret,* covered with blue faience (glazed earthenware) tiles is the outstanding feature of Antalya's skyline. Museum of archaeology. Seaside resort with exceptional facilities for swimming, fishing and hunting. Extensive orchards. *Perge* with well-preserved town wall. Stadium and theatre with places for 12 000 spectators. Two Byzantine basilicas. St. Peter and St. Bartholomew both visited Perge. *Side.* During the Hellenic period an important town with a theatre that accommodated 2 000. Now it is a tranquil fishing village that is becoming a popular seaside resort. Town wall. The *Dalatas Caves* were discovered in 1948. Beautiful stalactites.

Alanya was originally a pirates' headquarters. The Romans constructed the town wall. It fell into a state of disrepair and was restored during the Byzantine period. During the same period the Roman acropolis was transformed into a Christian church. The Seljuks built a shipyard and a naval base. Aksebe- Sultan Mosque (1230) and Kale Mosque, a part of the palace. *Bedesten,* a covered market. Alara Palace was built by the Seljuks and originally served as a caravanserai.

Anamur. Medieval Crusaders' castle. Greek theatre and Ak Mosque. *Silifke* (Selucia), founded by Seleucus I in the 3rd cent. B.C. A tower remains of his castle. Ruins of a basilica erected on the place where St. Tecla achieved martyrdom. *Gösku River* where Emperor Frederick Barbarossa drowned in 1190. To the north, *Uzuncaburç* with extensive excavations of a 3rd - to 2nd-cent. B.C. city. 30 columns of a temple of Zeus, theatre, town gate and other remains. *Mut* (Claudiopolis). Ruins of a fortress and a little mosque. *Korykos.* Ruins of early Christian churches, two castles and a cemetery. *Kiz Kalesi,* the "Fort of the Virgin", island fortifications, dating from the 11th cent. The other structure was built in the 13th cent.

Mersin. Beautiful town with lovely white buildings set among orange and lemon groves. Major port. *Tarsus.* Birthplace of St. Paul.

ADANA, see E 5. *Karatepe,* see E 5.

Urfa. Ancient town, that brings the biblical Abraham to mind. Job's tomb. King Abgar was presented with the holy shroud. The Crusader Balduin of Bouillon founded a kingdom here. It lasted about 50 years. Legend has it that Abraham resided here and one of the tomb's mosques is dedicated to him (the Muslims call him Ibrahim).

Diyarbakir. Several interesting mosques. Museum housed in *Zincirli,* a Muslim theological school. Caravanserai. Town wall.

Lake Van, surrounded by mighty mountains. 250 m deep. Train ferries on the Istanbul-Teheran route. On the Turkish side, the rail lines ascend to a height of 1 670 m, on the Iranian side they reach 2 188 m. *Van.* Modern town founded in 1920. Lowest average temperature in Turkey. Ruins of *Vankale* and *Toprakkale* fortresses (8th cent.) and an old city on the lake shore. An aqueduct brought the water from the lake to the ancient city.

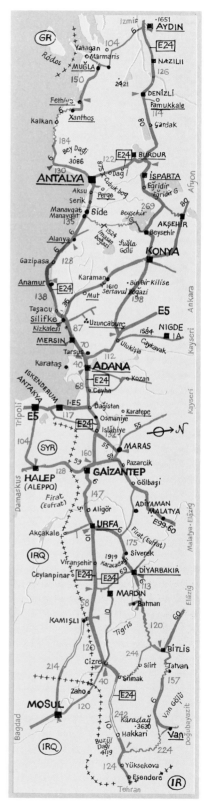

TOWN PLANS

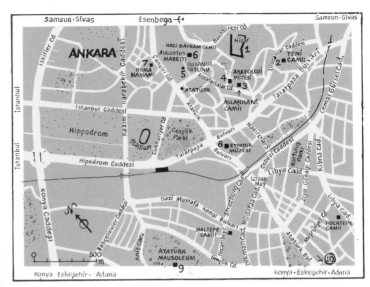

ANKARA (2.1 million)
Previously known as Angora.
Capital of Turkey since 1923 when it had a population of 30 000. A massive construction project began then, and now Ankara is a predominantly modern city set 900 m above sea level on a high plain. Views to the south and *Mount Elmadağ*, the "Mountain of Apples". The city was founded in the 8th cent. B.C. and has endured many occupations. It fell to the Crusaders in 1101. In 1402 the Cubuk Plain was the scene of a famous battle waged between the armies of Sultan Bayezit and the Mongol Prince Timour Leng (Tamerlane).
The *citadel* existed here before the Roman period. 20 towers. Built of Ankara stone (red porphyry). *Museum of archaeology* containing the world's largest collection of Hittite artifacts. The old quarters surround the citadel. Column of Julian the Apostate, 14 m high, assumed to date from the 4th cent. *Temple of Augustus* (2nd cent. B.C.), originally dedicated to the goddess Cybele. Ruins of Roman baths. Several interesting mosques. Largest is the *Aslahane Mosque* (1209) *Yeni Camii* is probably a work of Sinan.
Atatürk's Mausoleum, museum and house where he lived during the War of Independence. Atatürk's farm is 5 km south of Ankara. Parks, restaurants and zoo. Genclik Park (Park of Youth) with artificial lake and amusement park.
The area around the city is famed for angora goats, angora rabbits, angora cats and angora wool.

ISTANBUL (3 million)
Largest city in Turkey, beautifully situated on the Bosphorus, the strait that separates Europe from Asia. Founded by the Greeks in the 7th cent. B.C. During the 4th cent. A.D. capital

1 Citadel
2 Aslanhane Mosque
3 Yeni Camii (New Mosque)
4 Archaeological Museum
5 Julian Column

6 Temple of Augustus
7 Roman Baths
8 Ethnographic Museum
9 Atatürk's Mausoleum. Museum.
10 Atatürk's House. Presidential Palace.

of the Byzantine Empire. It was called Constantinople in honour of the first Christian emperor, Constantine the Great. In 1454 Constantinople fell to the Turks. It became their capital in 1458. After the War of Independence (1921) its name was changed to Istanbul.
The European section of the city is divided by the **Golden Horn,** a curved inlet. The **Galata Bridge,** swarming with pedestrians and motor traffic, is the best-known bridge in Istanbul. The harbour here is filled with floating restaurants (speciality: grilled fish), boats and ferries that link different parts of the city. Locomotive in front of the Sirkeci railway station, legendary eastern terminus of the Orient Express that once started from

London and Paris.
The **Great Bazaar,** also known as the Covered Bazaar (Kapali Çarşi). Bedesten, in the middle of the bazaar, is a section of the original 15th-cent. building. More than 4 000 shops in a tangle of streets. It is easy to lose one's way. The goldsmiths have their own street, as do the carpet-sellers.
The **Spice Bazaar** (Misir Carşisi), close to the Galata Bridge. The air is filled with exotic aromas. Snacks and barrels of Oriental spices, vegetables, fruit, cheese and honey.
Hagia Sophia, the Church of Divine Wisdom, built for Emperor Justinian, was consecrated in 538. The emperor had it adorned with gold mosaics and marble from all corners of his empire. Eight columns were brought from the Temple of Artemis in Ephesus and eight columns from the Temple of Jupiter at Baalbeck. After Constantinople fell to the Turks, the church was transformed into a mosque. In 1935 it became a museum. The **Blue Mosque** (Sultan Ahmet Camii, 1616) is so called because of the blue Iznik tiles that adorn its interior. 264 colourful stained-glass windows. The floor is covered with carpets. This is the only mosque in Turkey with six minarets.
Suleiman's Mosque (Süleymaniye Camii, 1557), one of the largest mosques in Istanbul, was designed by the architect Sinan. Four minarets with ten balconies. It is surrounded by several buildings: schools, hospital, caravanserai and Turkish baths. Several other interesting mosques. Of Istanbul's 900 mosques, 200 are designated as "djami" (great). Tomb of Suleiman and Roxelane, his favourite wife. Tomb of the architect Sinan.
Topkapi. Enormous palace of the sultans. Construction was started in

The Mevlana Mausoleum, Konya

1459 for Mehmed the Conquerer. The Church of St. Irene is preserved. The long kitchen building is now a museum of *Chinese porcelain*. The sultan's *harem* faces onto the same courtyard. Famous 17th-cent. *hall* with fountain. World's richest *treasury* with gold and precious stones, armour and weapons. In a special pavilion the Prophet Mohammed's mantle, a hair from his beard, and other relics. Museum of *archaeology* with Persian sarcophagi, classical sculpture, vases, etc. Oriental museum. Museum of *ceramics* in Cinili Kösk, built in 1472 for Mehmet the Conquerer.

On the other side of the Golden Horn, the *Dolmabahçe Palace,* sultan's residence completed in 1853. Lavish interior. Atatürk died here in 1938. Splendid gardens. Beautiful *Yildiz Park* where the porcelain factory founded by Sultan Abdülhamit is still in operation.

Small white *Kiz Kuleşi* (the Virgin Tower), also known as the Leander Tower. A legend tells of a princess who was hidden away here. But the prophesy that she would be killed by a snake came to pass. The reptile was delivered in a basket carried by doves. North of the Galata Bridge are modern shopping streets, theatres, cinemas and large tourist hotels. The heart of the area is *Taksim Square*. The *Galata Tower* (14th cent.) which has served as a fire-watcher's tower, is now a restaurant and nightclub. The city's "underground", a rail line connecting two stations under the Galata Hill, was completed in 1873.

A 1074 m long suspension *bridge,* completed in 1973, links the shores of the Bosphorus. Small passenger-carrying boats zig-zag along its banks. It is always possible to find a convenient sight-seeing tour as the excursions vary in length.

The entire round trip usually takes about four hours. On the European side, the mighty *Rumelihisar,* a fortress built in only tree months in 1454 for Mehmet the Conquerer. On the opposite shore, the *Anadoluhisar,* built in 1395. Boats to the *Prince Islands.* Of the nine islands in the group, four are inhabited. *Büyükada* with pine woods, idyllic villages, fine areas for swimming, hotels and restaurants. You can tour it in horse-drawn carriage or on donkeys.

1 Topkapi Palace. Archaeological Museum. Museum of Oriental Antiquities.
2 Hagia Sophia (Museum).
3 Sultan Ahmet Mosque (The Blue Mosque).
4 Grand Bazaar (Covered Bazaar).
5 Valens Aqueduct. Municipal Museum.
6 Suleiman's Mosque.
7 Spice Bazaar (Egyptian Bazaar).
8 Galata Bridge.
9 Galata Tower.
10 Dolmabahçe Palace.
11 The Europe-Asia Bridge.

The Sultanahmet Mosque, Istanbul

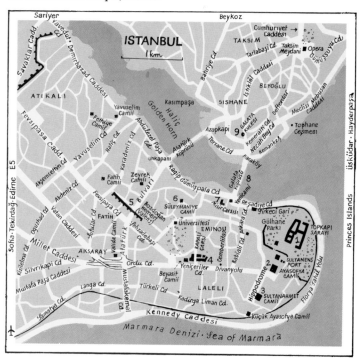

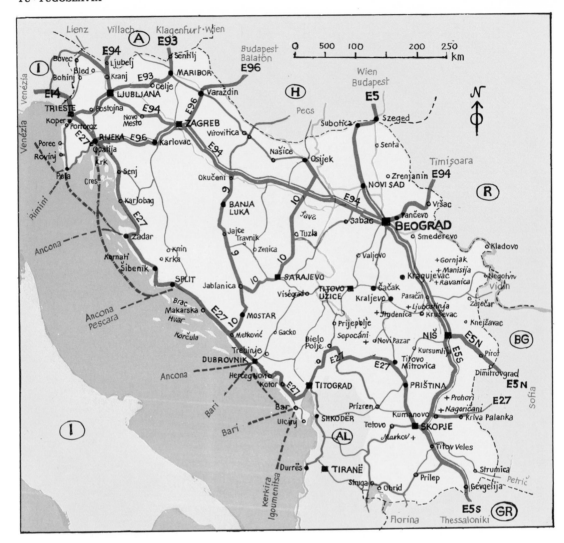

YU · Yugoslavia

YU·Jugoslavija

Area: 256 000 km² (98 725 sq. miles)

Population: 22.4 million. The population consists of 8.1 million Serbs, 4.4 Croatians, 1.7 million Slovenes, 1.3 million Macedonians, 0.5 million Montenegrins, 1.7 million Albanians, 0.5 million Hungarians, 200 000 Turks and 148 000 gipsies. There are further Slovakian, Roumanian, Bulgarian, Italian and other minorities. Several religions: Serbian Orthodox in Serbia and Montenegro, Macedonian Orthodox in Bosnia-Herzegovina, Kosovo and Macedonia, Roman Catholicism in Slovenia and Croatia. About 1 million of the inhabitants are Muslims.
Four official languages: Serbian, Croatian, Slovene and Macedonian.

"Serbo-Croatian" serves as a linguistic bridge for the population of this linguistically varied country. The Croats use the Latin alphabet and the Serbs (in the southeast) use the Cyrillic.

Major cities: Beograd (Belgrade) 1.2 million, Zagreb 700 000, Skopje 500 000, Sarajevo 400 000, Ljubljana 240 000.

Government: Socialist federal republic consisting of six republics: Bosnia-Herzegovina, Croatia, Macedonia, Montenegro, Serbia (including Vojvodina and Kosovo) and Slovenia. The republics and autonomous provinces have considerable rights of self-government. Two-chamber federal parliament.

History

2nd cent. B.C. Illyria, in what is now northwest Yugoslavia, becomes a Roman province.

6th cent. The Slavs (Avars) force their way into what is now Yugoslavia.

11th cent. Serbian and Croatian kingdoms are established. Both fall under Habsburg control. The coastal areas are dominated by Venice. The Kingdom of Serbia is proclaimed in 1217.

1389 The Turks are victorious at the Battle of Kosovo, north of Skopje. Within 100 years they are in possession of all of what is now Yugoslavia. Their rule lasts 500 years.

1717 The Austrians conquer Belgrade.

1878 Serbia and Montenegro become autonomous states.

Perast on the Bay of Kotor

1908 Bosnia-Herzegovina incorporated into the Austro-Hungarian Empire.
1914 Political tensions between Serbia and Austria-Hungary lead to the assassination of Archduke Franz Ferdinand and his wife in Sarajevo – the beginning of First World War.
1921 Alexander I, after a period as regent becomes King of Yugoslavia.
1934 Assassination of King Alexander I while he is in Marseilles.
1941 Yugolavia allies with Germany, but a government formed after a military coup annuls the agreement. Yugoslavia occupied by Axis troops of Germany, Italy, Hungary and Bulgaria. Armed resistance is brutally fought by the occupying Germans.
1945 Liberation of Yugoslavia. Josip Broz Tito forms a government.
1980 Death of Tito.

Currency: Dinar (YUD).
1 dinar = 100 para

Business hours: Banks 8.00-11.00 a.m., in major cities 7.00 a.m.-7.00 p.m. Saturdays closed. Exchange offices at frontier stations and in railway stations, hotels and local travel offices. Post offices 8.00 a.m.-2.00 p.m. and 4.00-6.00 p.m. Saturdays 8.00 a.m.-2.00 p.m. No lunchtime closing in the major cities. Shops 8.00 a.m.-12.00 noon and 4.00-8.00 p.m. Saturdays 8.00 a.m.-2.00 p.m.

Holidays: January 1-2, May 1, July 4, November 29-30. In addition to the above national holidays there are local holidays: July 7 (Serbia), July 13 (Montenegro), July 27 (Bosnia-Herzegovina and Croatia), August 2 and October 11 (Macedonia) and November 1 (Slovenia).

Hotels
Many new hotels in the major cities and popular tourist resorts. Modern motels on the major roads.

Camping
There are up-to-date camping sites near all the major cities and coastal resorts.

Food and drink
There are both national and regional specialities. Djuveč, meatballs containing chopped pepper, onions, potatoes and rice, oven-baked in clay bowls. Sarma, cabbage-wrapped mince. Purica s mlincia, turkey with noodles. Musaka, baked anbergines with of minced meat (usually lamb or mutton). Stajerski kostrun, roast beef with spices and onions. Sogan dolma, onions stuffed with mince, rice and pepper. Sirnica, pie with cheese and egg. Zeljanica, pie with filling of spinach, cheese, cream and eggs. Specialities of Zagreb: Zagrebacki odrezak, thin breaded slices of veal filled with cheese and ham. Teleca pisanica, filet of veal with tomato and mushroom sauce.

Routes described:

E 5   Szeged – Beograd – Niš

E 5 N Niš – Sofia

E 5 S Niš – Skopje – Thessaloníki

E 27 Trieste – Split – Dubrovnik – Titograd – Skopje – Sofia

E 93 Graz – Ljubljana – Trieste

E 94 Klagenfurt – Zagreb – Beograd

E 96 Budapest – Zagreb – Rijeka

9   Virovitica – Banja Luka – Jajce

10   Osijek – Sarajevo – Dubrovnik

Town plans: Beograd Savajevo Zagreb

Dubrovnik, "Pearl of the Adriatic", was founded in the 7th century

Predjamski, a castle near the Postojna Caves

Desserts: baklava, flaky pastry with nuts and honey. Kadif, thin slices of pie dough with melted sugar. Several domestric beers and wines. Dingac wine from Pelješac. Amber-coloured Grk Wine. Prosek, a dessert wine. Maraschino is a popular liqueur and Sljivovica is plum brandy.

Shopping
Leather goods, embroidery, lace, handwoven rugs (particularly those that can be used as wall hangings), wood carvings, pottery, silver and filigree.

Petrol
Visiting motorists cannot obtain fuel without petrol coupons which are available at the frontier.

Speed limits. Traffic regulations
Motorways 120 kmh, other roads 100 kmh or 80 kmh. Cars towing caravans and trailers 80 kmh (including motorways). Built-up areas 60 kmh.
Children under the age of 12 are not allowed to travel in the front seat.
All vehicles must be equipped with a first-aid kit and a replacement set of light bulbs. Any visible damage to a vehicle entering Yugoslavia must be certified by the authorities at the frontier and a certificate obtained. When leaving the country the certificate must be produced.

Road patrol
Patrol cars belonging to AMSJ bear a sign reading "Pomeć"- Informacije". They can be summoned anywhere by dialling 987. Ambulance, tel. 94.

AMSJ, Auto-Moto Savez Jugoslavije 18, Ruzveltova, Belgrade, tel. 401-699. Yugoslavian National Tourist Office, 143 Regent Street, London W1R 8AE. Tel. 01-734 5243/01-734 8714/ 01-439 0399.

E 5. Szeged – Beograd – Niš

Horgos. Hungarian frontier. E 5 comes from London – Bruxelles – Köln – Frankfurt – Nürnberg – Wien – Budapest.

SUBOTICA (97 000). Vineyards and orchards. Archaeological museum.

NOVI SAD (165 000). Capital of the autonomous province of Vojvodina. Cultural centre. *Matica Srpska,* library and art from the province of Vojvodina. The bishop's palace also contains an art collection. *Muzej Vojvodina* (1947). Many interesting churches containing icons and wood-carvings. The centre of the town is *Trg Slobode* with the old town hall (observation tower) and the Orthodox cathedral. *Petrovaradin* is one of Europe's largest fortresses. In its present form it dates from the 17th and 18th cent. Fine views out over the city and the valley. 16 km of underground passages. Restaurants. *Fruška Gora National Park.* Many interesting monasteries in the mountains.

Sremski Karlovci. Ancient town surrounded by vineyards. Castle, Baroque church and museum of archaeology. Site of the peace treaty of 1699 (the Peace of Karlowitz) between Austria, Poland, Turkey and Russia. Hungary, Croatia and Slovenia became part of Austria. The delegates of the four nations entered the house where the treaty was signed through four different entrances.

Zemun. Suburb of Belgrade. Up until 1918 this was a frontier post between Austria and Serbia.

BEOGRAD (Belgrade), see town plans.

Smederevo was built in 1430 by Prince Djordje Branković. It fell to the Turks in 1459. One of Europe's largest fortresses, 24 sturdy towers, 25 m tall, 5 m thick walls.

KRAGUEJVAC (50 000), industrial town, once the capital of Serbia. Memorial park commemorates the massacre 1941 of 1000 inhabitants.

The monastery of *Manisija* on a cliff above the River Resava. Church of the Holy Trinity (Sveti Trojica) with beautiful frescoes. One shows the founder, Prince Stefan Lazarević.

Ćuprija with a Turkish wooden bridge (17th cent.) over the River Morava. The name of the town is derived from the Turkish word for bridge (köpru). Road to the beautiful monastery of *Ravanica* (1381) with a lovely, red-and-white brick church. Frescoes and icons. Monastery of *Kalenič.*

KRUŠEVAC (60 000). Industrial town. Capital of Serbia in the 14th cent. *Lasarica* Church (1370) with sculptures on the façade. Monastery of Naupara.

Road past the monastery of *Ljubostinja* and *Trstenik* to *Kraljevo* (30 000). Modern town, rebuilt since the war. The monastery of *Žiča* (13th cent.) in Romanesque-Byzantine style without any decorations on its red walls. Frescoes. Monastery of *Kalenič* (1413). The monastery of *Studenica* is perhaps its most beautiful of all of the Serbian monasteries. Stefan I and Stefan II (of the Nemanjić dynasty) are buried here. Three churches. The main church is the white marble Sveti Bogorodica.

Priština, see E 27.

NIŠ (128 000) has a violent history and has been destroyed many times. The last time was during the Second World War. This was the site of Naissus, a Roman frontier fort. Roman Emperors Constantine and Justinian were both born in Niš. Remains of Mediana, Justinian's summer residence. In 1189 Frederick Barbarossa passed through the town on his way to Jerusalem. He made an alliance with the Serbs. By 1343 Dušan the Great had pushed back the Bulgars and was proclaimed Emperor of Serbs, Greeks and Romans (the East-Roman Empire). But in 1386 the Turks arrived. They stayed until 1877. *Čele Kula* (Tower of Skulls) is a monument to Serbs who fell in the war against the Turks (1809). Their skulls were immured in the tower, which can still be seen next to road E 5 going towards Sofia. It is now enclosed in a pavillon. About 60 of the skulls remain. Turkish fortress (17th cent.), now a park with open-air theatre and restaurant. Archaeological museum.

E 5 N. Niš – Sofia

Niška Banja. Spa with radioactive springs. Monastery of Sveti Petka. *Bela Palanka* next to the *Sicevo Gorge.* Tower from a Turkish fortress, built over the remains of a Byzantine and (earlier) Roman fortress. Beautiful *Nišava Valley. Pirot,* carpet-making centre. The town was a Byzantine caravanserai on the route to Constantinople.

Dimitrovgrad. Bulgarian frontier. E 5 continues to Sofia – Plovdiv – Istanbul – Ankara – Antakya – Syria.

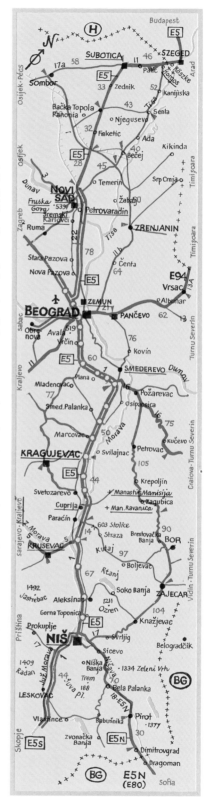

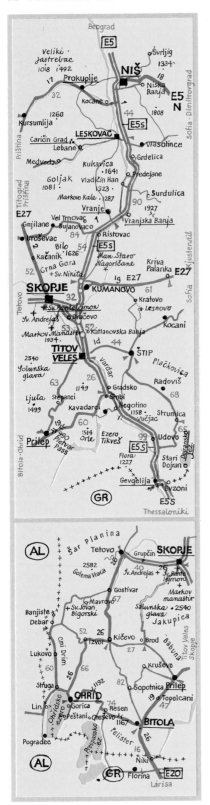

E 5 S. Niš – Skopje – Thessaloniki

Leskovac (45 000). Important textile industries. International textile fair in July. Old Serbian houses with wood carvings. Road to *Caričin grad*. Excavations of a Byzantine town, in the 5th cent. residence of Emperor Justinian. Remains of walls and towers, churches and streets. The town is said to have had 10 000 inhabitants. It was laid waste by the Slavs in the 7th cent.

Prokuplje, old town on the Roman trade route from the Adriatic coast to Constantinople. Castle ruins and church from the 10th cent. Archaeological excavations at *Pločnik*.

Vranje. Oriental atmosphere. *Pašin konak* (the House of the Pasha) was the residence of the Turkish pasha. Turkish bridge and baths.

Markovo Kale, a fortress. Vineyards, tobacco fields and hemp. **Vranjska Banja,** spa, surrounded by mountains. The springs, 65°- 95° C, are the hottest in the country. Serbian-Macedonian boundary.

SKOPJE (420 000). The clock on the railway station shows 16 minutes past five. It stopped in June 1963 and is a reminder of the great earthquake. Previous earthquakes 518 and 1535. Skopje is a modern town, but there are many reminders of the Turkish period (1392-1912) in the old parts of the town. The former caravanserai is now an *archaeological museum* with finds from the old "Skupi" which was an important town as early as the 3rd cent B.C. Beautiful courtyard with arcades. *Turkish bazaar.* 14th-cent. bridge with ten arches. Turkish baths (Daut Paša Hammam) with art and icons. *The Mustafa Paša Džamija,* a 15th-cent. mosque, has survived the earthquakes. Grave of the pasha in the courtyard. Beautiful minaret. One of the country's largest and most beautiful mosques. *Sveti Spa,* an Orthodox church with a beautiful 19th-cent. iconostasis. Ethnographical museum. *Skropsko Kale,* a fortress. The monastery of **Sveti Pantelejmon** (1164), near the village of Nerezi, is one of the most beautiful in Macedonia. Church with five cupolas. Unique frescoes.

Titov Veles (40 000). Known as early as the 3rd cent. B.C., under the name of Bylarzora. Important point on the caravan route during the Turkish period. Sveti Pantelejmon Church. Excavations of a Roman town in Stobi.

Dojransko jezero (Lake Dojran) is 40 km long, 10 m deep. There is plenty of fish in the lake and the method of catching them is unique: the fish are driven into nets by trained cormorants. Similar fishing methods are said to be used in China and Japan.

Gevgelija. Greek frontier. E5 S continues to Thessaloniki – Alexandroupolis – Istanbul.

From Gradsko a road leads west to Ohrid.

Prilep. Oriental atmosphere. Ruined castle and the monastery of Sveti Bogorodica-Treskavec (14th cent.).

BITOLA (70 000). Macedonia's second largest city. Predominantly modern town. Old market square in the centre. Mosques and the Turkish municipal tower with clock (Sahat kula). *Yeni Mosque* is now an art museum. Large Greek Orthodox Church of Sveti Dimitrije. *Heraclea,* excavations of a Roman town on the trade route, Via Egnatio, from the Adriatic Sea to Constantinople.

Ohrid (26 000). One of Yugoslavia's most beautiful towns. Its Old Town has narrow streets and typical Macedonian houses. *Samuilovgrad,* a 10th-cent. fortress on a cliff high above the lake. Ruins of the towers. Once the residence of Bulgarian-Macedonian Emperor Samuel. Open-air theatre during the *Ohrid Festival.* Splendid icons in the Church of Sveti Kliment (Sveti Bogorodica Peribleptos) from 1295. *Sveti Sofija* is Macedonia's most important church, built in the 11th cent., expanded in the 14th cent. Mosque during the Turkish period. Beautiful frescoes. Numerous other interesting churches, among them Sveti Jovan Kano (14th cent.), restored 1963. The Džamija-Ali-Pašina, a mosque, is still in use. *National museum* with archaeology, icons, folk costumes and the history of the Partisan Movement.

The modern part of the town, with hotels and parks, is down by the lake. **Lake Ohrid** (Ohridsko jezero) is 30 km long and up to 15 km wide. 286 m deep. The water is very clear – visibility down to 20 m. Rocky shores. *Mount Mokra* (1 525 m) to the west, *Mount Galičica* (2 255 m) to the east. The unique fauna of the lake is being investigated by a hydro-biological institute.

E 27. Trieste – Split – Dubrovnik – Titograd – Skopje – Sofia

TRIESTE, see Italy, E 14.

Novi Pazar with Oriental atmosphere. Alem Aitum Mosque (16th cent.). 8th-cent. *Petrova Crkva* (Church of St. Peter) is the oldest church in Serbia. Remains of a 15th-cent. town wall. The monastery of *Sopoćani* was founded in 1265 by King Uroš I. Interesting frescoes.

Postojna, Škocjanske jame and Lipica, see E 93.

The route Trieste – Pula – Opatija is 225 km long. The direct route (E 27) is 75 km long. Many resorts on the peninsula of *Istria,* especially on the western side and in the Bay of Trieste. Enormous purpose-built resorts, filled with foreign, mostly German, tourists. But many small Yugoslavian towns with Italian atmosphere are near by. Venice ruled Istria 1279-1797.

Koper. Splendid square with cathedral (Stolnica), loggia (loža) and palace (Pretorska palača). Town museum in the Belgramini-Tacco Palace. Roman mosaics on the floor. One of 12 town gates remains. Izola, lovely little town. Church with valuable paintings.

Piran. Medieval seaport with narrow alleys. Remains of town wall with towers. Baroque church (1637) with some parts from the 14th cent. Octagonal baptistry with a Roman sarcophagus used as baptismal font.

Portorož, important tourist centre. Spa. Casino. The peninsula of Seca with "Forma viva", an international sculpture exhibition (July and August).

Poreč. 2 500-year-old seaport on a peninsula. The *Eufrazijeva Basilica* (6th cent.) is one of Europe's oldest churches. It is built over an even older church and mosaics from the 4th cent. have been preserved. Dekumanova, lovely seaside promenade. Museum in the Sinčić Palace. Poreč has become Yugoslavia's largest resort. Hotels, guest houses and camping sites can accomodate 70 000 tourists.

Road to interesting places in the centre of the peninsula. *Beram* with the Marija na Skriljinama Church with 15th-cent. frescoes by Ivan of Kastav, e.g. a Dance of Death. *Motovun* (national monument). Town walls from the 13th-14th cent. Splendid tower with massive clock tower. The town hall is one of the oldest in the country. It was in use from the 13th until the 20th cent. Renaissance church by Palladio, with loggia. *Pazin,* small town with beautiful Renaissance and Baroque houses. The Romans called the town Castrum Pisini, the Austrians named it Mittenburg.

Rovinj. A fascinating old town on a peninsula. A maze of streets and stepped alleys. Piazza on the water, as in Venice. The campanile, too, resembles the one on the Piazza di San Marco. 60 m high statue of St. Euphemia.

PULA (50 000) with an enormous *Roman amphitheatre* (ellipse-shaped, 132×105 m), seating 25 000 spectators. The second largest, after the Coliseum. Three tiers, 72 arcades. Concerts, theatrical performances, film festival. Temple of Augustus, Porta Aurea (the triumphal arch of Sergius).

Labin. Historic little town on a 320 m high hill, which has been honeycombed by coal miners. Mining museum.

Opatija. Old spa on the "Kvarner Riviera". One of the most elegant seaside resorts. Casino. Emperor Franz Joseph used to move his court here during the winter months. Park with 100-year-old cedars, seaside promenade, sailing regattas and festivals. Beautifully situated on the broad bay. View out towards the islands of Krk and Cres.

RIJEKA (140 000). Yugoslavia's largest seaport. Second largest city in Croatia. Shipyards and industries. The Italian name of the town was Fiume – the town did not become part of Yugoslavia until 1945. It belonged to Austria in the 17th-19th cent. In 1919 it was the object of a much publicized conquest by Italian poet and politican Gabriele d'Annunzio. Beautiful old quarter, *Starigrad,* which is entered through the 15th-cent. Gradski Toranj, the municipal tower with Roman town gate (Rimski vrata).

The *Adriatic Magistral,* Jadranska Magistrala, all the way down to Dubrovnik through the beautiful province of Dalmatia. It is a well-built road, but it carries a lot of traffic – local traffic, holiday traffic, lorries and buses. Do not count on covering too many miles a day on this rather tiresome, meandering road.

Bakar. Historic town wtih 16th-cent. castle. Below it, the Baroque Church of Sveti Andrija. Town museum (art). Excavations of a Roman cemetery. *Kraljevica* with Uvala Scott, a modern purpose-built resort. Large shipyards.

Crikvenica with bridge to the island of *Krk* (20000), the largest of the Yugoslavian islands (408 km²). *Krk,* its chief town, remains from the Roman period. Medieval streets and houses.

Senj. Walls, palaces, splendid fortress and old quarter. The inhabitants of the surrounding area, the Uskoks, fled here from the Turks in the 16th cent. For 100 years the town resisted attacks from both Venice and the

Turks and was finally defeated in 1617. Open-air theatre with Uskok festival. Beautiful square, *Marka Balena*, with Baroque palace and fountain. Nehaj (1558), a fortress. Car ferry to the island of *Rab*, one of the most beautiful tourist islands. *Lopar* is one of the largest resorts. *Rab*, the chief town, is a spa with a lovely old section. Four bell towers dominate the skyline. The *Cathedral of Sveti Maria Velika*, "Gospa", a Romanesque basilica from the 12th cent. Renaissance doorway. Relics of St. Christopher. *Prince's Palace* (Knežev Dvor) and Loggia. *Varoš*, a suburb with beautiful palaces.

Starigrad-Paklenica. National park with a few deep canyons, divided by a high plateau. A 175 m deep cave.

Jablanac. Small fishing village in the long, narrow bay. *Karlobag* with ruined fortress. A side-trip up to the *Stara Vrata Pass* is well worth the effort. The view out over the coast is magnificent.

ZADAR (50 000). Old town, several times ravaged by war – most recently damaged by aerial bombardment during the Second World War. The town belonged to Italy up until 1944. Remains of a Roman forum. *Town gates* and *ramparts* round the old part of the town, situated on a peninsula. Ethnographical museum on Narodni Trg. *St. Donat's Church* (9th cent.), a Romanesque rotunda, is now museum. *Cathedral of St. Anastasia* (Sveti Stošija) from the 15th cent. The interior contains remains of a 9th-cent. church. Stone sarcophagus of St. Anastasia. 56 m high bell tower. The *Church of St. Simon* (Sv. Simun) contains the 14th cent. silver coffin of the saint. Museum with examples of the goldsmith's art. Bas-reliefs depicting scenes from the life of the saint and from the history of Croatia. Enormous purpose-built resort on the peninsula of Borik.

Off the coast at Zadar are the two islands of *Ugljan* and *Pašman* with small fishing villages and beaches. The *Kornat Islands,* to the south, consist of about 100 large and small islands, most of them uninhabited. Excellent waters for underwater fishing and skin-diving. National park.

Biograd. Small fishing town. During a short period in the 12th cent. this was the seat of the Croatian kings. Modern purpose-built resort of Crvena Luka. *Pakoštane*, a small seaport. *Vodice*, a small, picturesque fishing town with large hotels.

Šibenik (30 000), founded in the 10th cent., one of the Venetian strongholds in the fight against the Turks. Three 16th-cent. fortresses. The largest is Sveti Ana. Old quarter with stepped streets and alleys. The *cathedral*, Sveti Jakov, was started in the Gothic style in 1431 and completed in the Renaissance style 100 years later.

The *Krka Falls* between Knin and Šibenik. The river runs 70 km through narrow gorges and creates eight cataracts. The last waterfall is also the largest, 100 m wide and 45 m high. It is situated near Skradin. In the autumn there is not much water in the river, as the hydro-electric power plants utilize most of it. 15th-cent. Franciscan monastery on the island of *Visovac.* Near by is the Orthodox *monastery* of Sveti Arhandeo.

Primošten, small seaport and fishing town with beautiful old quarter on a peninsula, surrounded by a fortification wall. Purpose-built resorts.

Trogir, one of the oldest towns on the Adriatic coast. In the 13th cent. ruled by the Croatian kings, in the 15th-18th cent. by Venice, Trogir became an important seaport. Beautiful streets and houses. *Narodni Trg* (the square) is lined with beautiful buildings: the cathedral, the 15th cent. town hall, loggia, clock tower and the lovely Čipiko Palace.

Kaštel Stari, the largest of the tourist resorts on the Kaštel Riviera, the Riviera of the seven citadels. 13 citadels were built in the 15th cent. as protection against the Turks. Seven remain as ruins. *Solin* with remains of the Roman town of Salona, which is supposed to have had 60 000 inhabitants. They fled to Split, when the Slavs arrived in 615.

SPLIT (150 000). The country's second largest port (after Rijeka). *Diocletian's Palace*, built in the 3rd cent. is 250 m long, 175 m wide. It was intended as the Emperor's residence after his retirement, and as his mausoleum (he was born in Salona). When Salona was destroyed by the Slavs in 615 its inhabitants fled to the now empty palace and built the town of Spalato. 3 000 people still live within the walls of this old part of the town. Four gates lead into it: the Gold Gate, the Silver Gate, the Iron Gate and the Bronze Gate. Diocletian's mausoleum was transformed into a *cathedral* (Sveti Dujam) in the Middle Ages. Egyptian Sphinx from the 15th cent. B.C. Cindro Palace (Baroque, 17th cent.) and other beautiful palaces.

Mileši Palace with maritime museum. Ethnographical museum in the old town hall. Archaeological museum. *Meštrović Museum* with works of Ivan Meštrović (1883-1962). Sculptures also in the beautiful park. Summer festival in July-August.

Car ferry to *Brač.* Its famous quarries provided the marble for the Palace in Split. *Hvar* is one of the largest resort islands. *Hvar*, the chief town, has picturesque streets and houses. Many splendid palaces and fortifications. The Španjola Fortress is now a restaurant. *Starigrad* with remains of the Greek colony. A Roman mosaic. *Jelsa*, a fishing village.

The **Makarska Riviera** with a long line of seaside resorts at the foot of the rocky Bikovo Mountains. Like all the towns along the Adriatic coast, Makarska has a stormy past. The Roman settlement was destroyed by the Slavs (the Avars) in the 7th cent. Since then the rulers have succeeded each other: Croatians, Bosnians, Turks, Venetians, Frenchmen and Austrians. Franciscan monastery, which the Turks turned into a mosque. **Podgora.** Tourist resort. Memorial to the Partisans. **Zaostrog** with monastery.

The island of **Korčula** attracts a growing number of tourists. Mild climate, 2 700 hours of sun a year, rocky landscape, luxuriant vegetation, beautiful beaches. **Korčula,** the chief town, resembles Dubrovnik. Splendid town wall and town gates with towers (14th cent.). This is the site of annual performances of "Moreška", an open-air spectacle depicting the battles against the Turks. Beautiful old streets and houses. The *Cathedral* of Sveti Marko, a blend of different styles. Altar painting by Tintoretto. Art museum in the bishop's palace.

Metković. Mostar is only 50 km away. See route 10.

DUBROVNIK (Ragusa, 35 000), one of Europe's largest tourist resorts. Singularly beautiful and interesting. The town was founded in the 7th cent. and in the 10th cent. had risen to a mighty city republic and trading town with a fleet of 300 ships. The town later fell under the dominance of Venice for 160 years but did not lose its autonomy totally until 1808, when it was occupied by France.

The **town wall** was built in the 9th-17th cent. It is nearly 2 km long and up to 6 m thick. 15 defence towers. The largest is Minčeta, the symbol of Dubrovnik. The little fortress of Bokar, which marks the end of the wall, is the oldest casemate fortification in Europe. *Clock tower* (Zvonik) with astronomic clock from the 15th cent. and loggia. Orlando's Column (Orlandov stup), a symbol of the autonomy of the city republic. The *Rector's Palace* (Knežev dvor), the seat of the Council. Originally built in the 12th cent. it was destroyed by explosions in 1435 and 1463 and the earthquake of 1667. Rebuilt in the Renaissance style. Beautiful arcaded courtyard. Municipal museum. *Museum Rupe.* Archaeological and ethnographical museum with beautiful folk costumes. Baroque *cathedral* (Velika Gospa). Splendid treasury. Altar painting by Titian. 14th-cent. *Franciscan monastery* with large library and Europe's oldest pharmacy. Maritime museum, aquarium, ethnographical museum.

Outside the fortification wall, on a peninsula, stands the *Lovrijenac Fortress.* One of the open-air stages is used during the Dubrovnik Summer Festival (July-August). Cable car to Mount Srd, 412 m. Panoramic views from the fortress, built for Napoleon.

Modern resort on the peninsula of *Lapad.* The island of *Lorum* with subtropical vegetation. The castle once belonged to Archduke Maximilian, who became Emperor of Mexico and was executed in 1867.

Cavtat. Small fishing village with a palm-tree-lined seaside promenade. In front of the unusual Hotel Albatros, and 6 m below the surface of the sea, lies the Greek town of Epidurus, which sank into the sea 2 300 years ago. Land elevation is strong here and earthquakes are not unusual.

Herceg-Novi. Seaport and resort. *Spanjola,* a Turkish fortress, *Forte Mare,* a Venetian fortress and *Kanli kula,* a Turkish fortification tower. The old quarter of the town is Venetian with some Serbian and Byzantine features.

Kotor. Old seaport and large resort, beautifully situated at the foot of the Lovćen Mountains, at the innermost point of the fjord-like **Gulf of Kotor** (Boka Kotorska), where the sea water is comfortably warm. Beautiful old quarter, whose splendid palaces reflect the town's importance during the Middle Ages. 4 km long town wall, 10 m high with three town gates. *Cathedral of Sveti Tripun* (12th cent.), a Romanesque basilica with two Renaissance towers. Treasury with examples of the goldsmith's art, among them a casket with the head of St. Tryphon. Gradska kula, the city tower. Maritime museum in the *Grugina Palace* (18th cent.). Bokeljska nóc – "Fishermens's Nights"are celebrated in July.

The Lovćen Mountains offer some of the most beautiful scenery in Yugoslavia. National park. The *Lovćen Route* from Kotor to Cetinje is very beautiful. It was built at the end of the 19th cent. and goes in 32 hair-pin bends up to the pass level (1 212 m).

Cetinje, 672 m above sea level. Capital of Montenegro 1418-1918. Destroyed by the Turks in 1683, 1714, 1785. The *Vlaška Church* is surrounded by a fence of rifles, taken from the Turks. Monastery of *Sveti Petar* (1701) with icons and the first book printed in the Cyrillic alphabet (1493).

Budva. Small town, large tourist resort, on a peninsula. The picturesque old quarters were severely damaged by the 1979 earthquake. Many hotels, monasteries and the cathedral were damaged. 120 people perished. The massive town walls (15th cent.) survived the 1979 earthquake. Beautiful churches, archaeological museum. Monastery of Podostrog. The 1.5 km long *Slovene Beach* (Slovenska Plaža). *Zeta-Film,* film city, where many American westerns have been filmed. *Bécići,* a modern tourist resort. *Milocer,* once a royal summer palace, now a hotel in a beautiful park.

DUBROVNIK

Sveti Stefan, for 500 years a poor fishing village with houses squeezed together on a fortified island, now turned into a luxurious modern tourist resort. Churches and monasteries.

Petrovac. Kaštel Lastva, a former Venetian fortress, is now a restaurant. Remains of a mosaic in a Roman villa. The monasteries of *Gradište* and *Rezevići.* Beautiful churches with frescoes.

A road continues south to **Sutomore** with the church of Thekla, used for both Greek Orthodox and Roman Catholic services . Two altars and two churchyards.

Bar. The old quarter, *Stari Bar* (Old Bar), was founded in the 9th cent. Ruins of the higher, fortified, town which was destroyed in 1878. The lower town in parts has a Turkish character. *Novi Bar,* the newer quarters, with harbour and seaside resort. 3 km long sandy beach, unusual for Yugoslavia where most beaches have rocks or pebbles.

Ulcinj. Large resort with Oriental atmosphere. Long a pirate stronghold, ruled by Algerian and Turkish buccaneers. Conquered by the Montenegrins in 1878. Old quarter with a maze of narrow streets, mosques, fountains, and a bazaar. Friday is market day. 5 km from the town is the seaside resort of *Ulcinj-Lido* with a 12 km long sandy beach. Ulcinj collapsed in an earthquake in 1444. The ruins are visible in the sea.

The road continues to Albania. No frontier crossing for private motorists.

Skadarsko Jezero (Lake Skadar) is 43 km long. The largest lake in the Balkans, plenty of fish and rare birds. Churches and monasteries with lovely frescoes. Rocky islands in the lake.

TITOGRAD (60 000, formerly called Podgorica). Capital of Montenegro, mainly a modern town. The Turks ruled the town from 1474 until 1878, and most of the old part of the city reflects this. Mosques and the *Sahat kula,* a clock tower from the 18th cent. Excavations of the Roman capital of Dioclea. Remains of the Greek fortress of Medun.

The **monastery of Morača** in the beautiful, wild valley of the River Morača. The Church of the Assumption of Mary (13th cent.) has beautiful frescoes from different periods. Collection of icons, library.

Bijelo Polje. Small, modern town. Tourist resort at a major crossroads. *Sveti Petra,* monastery church from the 12th cent. 13th-cent. frescoes. Serbia's oldest book, Evangelium (now in the National Museum in Belgrade) was written in the monastery.

Titova Mitrovica (46 000) in the Ibar Valley. Earlier name: Kosovska Mitrovica. Folklore museum in a domed Turkish bath. Section devoted to mining.

PRIŠTINA (80 000). Capital of the autonomous region of Kosovo. Modern town with few reminders from its long history. The Imperial Mosque (Careva džamija) from the 15th cent. Clock tower (Sahat kula), Turkish baths (hamam). Museum. A battle between Serbs and Turks at Kosovo Polje (Amselfeld) in 1389 resulted in 500 years of Turkish rule and the end of the dream of a Serbian empire. It was reborn again in 1914 in Sarajevo.

Lipija. The site of the Roman city of Ulpiana, founded in the 2nd cent. by Emperor Trajan. Excavations. *Uroševac* with many mosques.

It is also possible to take the road from Ivangrad via Peć to Uroševac.

Peć (30 000). A bazaar, a clock tower and a mosque remain from the Turkish period. The **monastery of Peć,** the Patriarchate, was of great importance to Serbian culture during the Turkish period. Three churches with frescoes. Visoki Dečani monastery church (1335). Splendid basilica with a marble façade, 400 frescoes. The River Bistrica flows through Rugovo canyon.

Prizren (30 000). Ancient, oriental town. Capital of Serbia during the Middle Ages. Under Turkish rule 1455-1912. Sv. Bogorodica Ljeviška, built in 1307 by King Milutin, was transformed into a mosque by the Turks. The frescoes were covered with plaster but have now been restored. The church has five cupolas. Sinan-Paša Mosque (1615). Museum in the Turkish baths. Remains of Ribnik Fortress (11th cent.). Viségrad castle ruins. The River Beli Drim flows through a canyon. **Brezovica,** a winter sports resort.

SKOPJE and **Tetovo,** see E 5.

Kumanovo (38 000). Industries. Site of the Serbian victory over the Turks in 1912. The *monastery of Staro Nagoričane,* dedicated to Saint George (Sveti Djordje). Monastery church (1314) with frescoes, e.g. St. George and the Dragon. *Matejče monastery* (1356) with frescoes.

Kratovo. Roman settlement. Typical Macedonian houses. Five medieval watch-towers from the time when there was a mine in the crater of an extinct volcano. *Kriva Palanka,* frontier town. The monastery of Sveti Nikola and Sveti Jovan Osogovski.

E 27 continues to Sofia and Varna on the Black Sea.

E 93. Graz – Ljubljana – Trieste

Sentilj. Austrian border. The first road east of the Alps.

MARIBOR (120 000). Slovenia's second largest city. As early as the 12th cent., this was the seat of the Dukes of Carinthia (Marburg an der Drau). The old part of the town bears the stamp of the Austrian period and the Baroque style. Old town hall on the Glavni trg (Main Square).

Ptuj with beautiful old quarter (protected by law as a medieval national monument). Old trading town on the Amber Route from the Baltic Sea to the Adriatic Sea. The old Town Hall Square is lined with beautiful old buildings i.e. the Gothic church, the 54 m high city tower and a Roman tombstone (2nd cent.) with a bas-relief of Orpheus. *Ptujska Gora* with a fortified *church*, the most beautiful in Slovenia.

Rogaška Slatina, one of Yugoslavia's largest spas. Beautifully situated at the foot of the Boč mountain. *Veliki Tabor*, a Renaissance palace.

CELJE (60 000). Founded by the Celts. Site of the Roman town of Claudia Celeia. During the Middle Ages, seat of the Counts of Celje, who built a town wall and a castle. Archaeological museum in the *Counts' Castle* (Grofija) noted for its beautiful interiors and arcaded courtyard. *Sveti Daniel Church* from the 15th cent. *Sempeter,* Roman cemetery. Excavations started in 1950. *Kamnik*, small tourist resort with churches and monasteries.

Rimske Toplice, Roman baths.

LJUBLJANA, see E 94.

The *caves of Postojna* (Adelsberg caves), the largest in Europe with fantastic stalacite and stalagmite formations in large halls. Stalactites hang down from the ceiling, while stalagmites grow up from the floor. They are formed by calcarious water. The highest hall is 50 m from floor to ceiling. 25 km of tunnels are open to visitors. An open miniature train takes the visitors through the interesting halls.

Predjamski grad, a castle which is partially built into a cave. Archaeological museum. *Škocjanske jame.* Caves around the River Reka which goes underground for 30 km. Subterranean lakes and a 100 m deep chasm. Foot path from Matavun.

Lipica. Home of the beautiful Lippizaner horses. The stud farm was established here in 1580 when a few dozen Andalusian horses were brought here for the Spanish Riding School in Vienna. The colts graze in herds on the plains and are driven back to the stables in the evening, admired and photographed by hordes of tourists.

TRIESTE, see Italy, E 14.

E 94. Klagenfurt – Zagreb – Beograd

Ljubelj (Loiblpass). Traditionally much-used frontier station where long queues often occur. The old road over the *Karawanken* Pass was quite steep. Now the roads are well-built on both sides of the tunnel, which is 1.6 km long and is situated at 1 067 m. 12 % gradient on the Austrian side and 17 % descent on the Yugoslavian side. Not suitable for caravans.

Kranj (30 000, 385 m above sea level), in Slovenia, retains much of its Austrian charm. Beautifully set between Alp massifs. *Gorenskij muzej* (Oberkrainer museum).

Road 1a comes from Villach in Austria and Tarvisio in Italy (E 7 and E 14). The road via Tarvisio is recommended for caravans. Negligible gradients.

Wurzenpass, 1 073 m. Well-built, but with an 18 % gradient (no caravans), it is rather frightening for drivers who are not used to Alpine driving. (This section is very short, though.) Views out over Yugoslavia's highest mountain, Triglav, 2 863 m.

The *Karawanken Tunnel* (8 km) is scheduled for completion in 1985. It is planned as an extention of the Tauernautobahn from Salzburg. Now the cars travel by train Rosenback – Jesenice.

Kranjska gora, 810 m above sea level. Large resort and winter sports centre. Cable car to Vitranc, 1 590 m.

Bled. Idyllic tourist centre and spa that retains its Austrian character. The little lake is surrounded by 2 500 m high Alps. On a little island in the lake is the Baroque *pilgrimage church* of Sveta Maríya Božja (Saint Mary in the Lake), from the 17th cent. It is built over earlier churches on the site of a cult place from the 8th cent. B.C. Freestanding belfry, and frescoes. Now museum. *Blejski grad,* a castle high up on a cliff. Chapel, museum, restaurant, observation terrace.

From Völkermarkt in Austria it is also possible to take the route via Seeberg-Sattel 1 216 m. Gradients: 12 % and 10 % respectively. *Jezersko,* tourist resort in a beautiful valley. Artificial lake.

LJUBLJANA (290 000). Capital of the republic of Slovenia. From the 13th

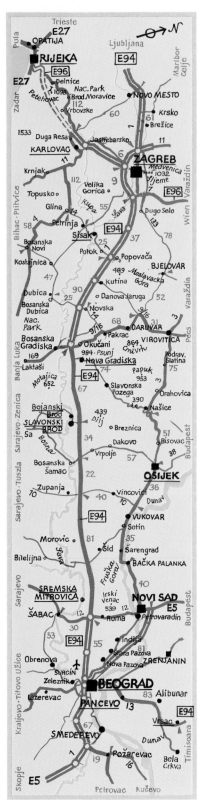

cent. until 1918 a part of the Habsburg empire. The old quarter is a typical Austrian town with beautiful Baroque houses, but the Italian influence is also noticeable. The old town hall (Rotovž) has an arcaded courtyard and the Robba Fountain (1751). The three dolphins symbolize the Rivers Sava, Krka and Ljubljanica. Baroque *cathedral*. The old church was put to the torch by the Turks in 1649. The old quarter is connected to the new town centre by Tromostovje (the Three Bridges), a motor car bridge and two pedestrian bridges. Enormous *Franciscan monastery* from 1660. Baroque altar by Robba. *Križanke*, a church of the Knights of the Cross and a *castle*, now museum of the town of Ljubljana, containing finds from the Roman town of Emona. *Ursuline Church*, national museum (archaeology, cultural history, ethnography, natural history). Slovene National Opera.

Novo Mesto in a beautiful, undulating landscape. The arcaded square has a distinct Austrian flavour. Museum with finds from local excavations. *Otočck*, medieval castle (now hotel) on an island in the River Krka. Fine park with rare trees.

Brežice. Small, historic town surrounded by vineyards. *Attems Castle* (15th cent.) was built as a defence against the Hungarians. Now Slovene folklore museum. Splendid Knight's Hall. *Kumrovec* with the house where Tito was born (1892). Museum.

Krapinske Toplice. Spa. Homo crapiensis, a Stone-Age man, contemporary with the Neanderthal Man, was found in the Hušnjakova Cave. Now in the provincial museum in Zagreb.

ZAGREB, see town plans.

Sisak. Industrial town. Historical and ethnographical museum in the old fortress. *Kostajnica,* on both sides of the River Una, the boundary between Croatia and Bosnia-Herzegovina. Picturesque town with mosques. *Zrin*, a 17th-cent. fortress.

Nova Gradiška, small industrial town with a Baroque church.

Road to *BANJA LUKA* (110 000) in Bosnia-Herzegovina with many reminders of the Turkish period. The *mosque of Fehad Paša* (16th cent.) has a slender, 42 m high, minaret. The pasha's grave in the courtyard. He also had the clock tower built. The inhabitants are for the most part Muslims, and the town has several mosques. *Ethnographical museum* in the medieval fortress. The greater part of the town is of a relatively recent date. *Trapista monastery* is famous for its cheeses. See map route 10.

Road further on to the beautiful waterfalls at *Jajce*, see route 10.

Slavonski Brod (38 000). Industrial town where railway carriages and locomotives are manufactured. Museums with finds from the Roman town of Marsonia. *Bosanski Brod* (30 000), with seven mosques, is on the opposite banks of the River Sava.

OSIJEK (80 000). Industrial town. Castle from 1712 with museum (coins). The first fortress on this site was built by Emperor Hadrian in 133.

Sremska Mitrovica (32 000), the Roman Sirmium, an important Roman encampment and town. Excavations of the Forum, streets, houses, baths and Imperial palace.

BEOGRAD (Belgrade), see town plans.

Pančevo (50 000). Industrial town. The Baroque monastery of *Hopovo*.

VRŠAC (60 000). Centre of a wine district. Mesić monastery with frescoes.

Vatin. Roumanian border.

E 94 continues to Timoşoara – Craiova – Bucureşti.

E 96. Budapest – Zagreb – Rijeka

Gorican – Zagreb, see map E 94 and E 27.

Gorican. Hungarian frontier. E 96 comes from Košice – Budapest – Balaton.

Varaždin (30 000) with numerous beautiful Baroque houses. Museum of cultural history in the 13th-cent. castle. Vineyards and old castles in the area around the town. *Varaždinske Toplice*. Spa with sulphuric hot springs, known as early as the 3rd cent. B.C.

ZAGREB, see town plans.

KARLOVAC (50 000). Beautiful old quarter in the Renaissance style. Remains of Karl Habsburg's strong fortress, built in the 16th cent. At that time the town was known as Karlstadt.

Road south to the *Plitvice lakes* (Plitvicka jezera). 8 km long row of waterfalls, interrupted by 16 large and small lakes. The difference in height between the beginning and the end of the system of lakes and waterfalls is 156 m. The last waterfall is 76 m high. The water shimmers in many colours and the vegetation is luxuriant.

RIJEKA, see E 27.

10. Osijek – Sarajevo – Dubrovnik

OSIJEK (80 000). Industrial town. Castle from 1712 with museum (coins). The first fortress on this site was built by Emperor Hadrian in 133.

Maglaj. Small Oriental town. The inhabitants are Muslims. *Kursumli Mosque* with lead cupola. 14th-cent. fortress.

TUZLA (80 000). Chemical industries. Coal and salt mines. Spa with hot springs.

Kladanj with Turkish baths (hamam). The spring still attracts large numbers of vistors, since the water is supposed to have salutary effects on several different body organs. In German the water is called "Männerwasser" and in Latin "aqua vita Casanova".

Zvornik with a strong Oriental flavour. Remains of a fortress.

SARAJEVO, see town plans.

Ilidza. Spa. Remains of Roman baths. *Konjic* with medieval section. The town is known for its wood carvings. Remains of a *Mithras temple.*

Jablanica, climatic health resort in the wild *Neretva Valley. Jablaničko jezero,* a 30 km long artificial lake with a 76 m high dam.

MOSTAR (65 000). Capital of Herzegovina and one of the largest tourist resorts of the country. A wooden bridge over the Neretva River existed here long ago, probably as early as the Roman era. The bridge-masters, "mostari", have given the town its name. *Stari Most* (the Old Bridge), a bold span 20 m above the river, was completed in 1566. It was built on the order of Sultan Suleiman II. The first attempt of master-builder Hajruddin failed. The bridge is 30 m long. Two 17th-cent. towers. The local boys dive from the pier to amuse the tourists. The area around the western bridge-abutment has an Oriental atmosphere with alleys full of workshops, silver and copper smiths, souvenir shops and cafés. Karadzoz Beg's mosque (1575) with a tall, slender minaret. *Biščeviča C Konak* (1635) and *Kajtaz Konak,* two Turkish residential houses. Tekija, an abandoned Dervish monastery (for Dervishes, see Turkey, E 5) a mosque. Near by are the ruins of *Stepan Grad* (15th cent.), a mosque.

Počitelj. Small town with an Oriental appearance. Major tourist resort. 16th-cent. walls. *Ibrahim Paša Mosque,* baths, Muslim theological school, clock tower, caravanserai. Radimlje. Cemetery with 133 tombstones, decorated with reliefs. They derive from the Bogomil sect, named after their high priest. Bird sanctuary in the swamps near *Hutovo Blato.*

5, 11 and 15. Beograd – Sarajevo

From the town of *Čačak* the road goes through the gorge of *Ovčarsko-Kablarska* with *Ovčar Banja,* a spa. Large power station. On the hills above the road there are eight medieval monastaries.

Titovo Užice, one of the oldest towns in Serbia, situated in a deep mountain valley. The road to Titograd and the coast passes the large holiday resort of Partizanske Vode on the Zlatibor mountain.

Visegrad, a small picturesque town, once an important place on the caravan road from Dubrovnik to Istanbul. The Turkish bridge, 170 m long, was constructed in the 15th cent. Its history is described by Nobel-prize winning author Ivo Andrić in his novel "A bridge on the Drina". From Visegrad (and Goradže) timber-raft excursions down the rapids.

9, 5. Okucani – Banja Luka – Sarajevo

Okucani and *Banja Luka,* see E 94.

Jajce. Bosnia's coronation town. In 1463, the last king, Stepan Tomašević, was defeated here by the Turks. In 1943 the Yugoslavian state was proclaimed here. Beautiful town with town wall and town gates. A few old Bosnian houses with shingle roofs remain. The 20 m high waterfalls in the River *Pliva* can be seen from the bridge near the town wall. Subterranean rock church from the 15th cent., *the "Catacombs".*

Travnik, for 200 years seat of the Turkish governor of Bosnia. The old section has a Turkish atmosphere, old residential houses and a beautiful town fountain under a linden. *Suleiman Mosque,* the "bright Mosque" (Sarena) with a Muslim theological school. Residence (Konak) and clock-tower (Sahat kula). Turkish tombs (Turben). *Fortress,* built by the Bosnian King Tvrtko (15th cent.). Ivo Andrić, the author, was born in Travnik. He was awarded the Nobel prize in 1961. Most of the town was rebuilt after a fire in 1903.

12. Novi Sad – Sarajevo

Šabac with ruined fortress. *Trži.* Memorial Museum, dedicated to Vuk Karadžić, the reformer of the Serbian language. *Banja Koviljača,* a large spa. *Zvornik.* Ruin of fortress. Large dam for the power station.

TOWN PLANS

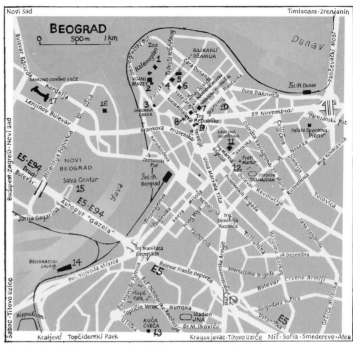

BEOGRAD (Belgrade, 1.5 million)
Capital of Yugoslavia and the republic of Serbia. Beautifully situated on the Rivers Sava and Dunav (Danube). Predominantly modern city. Terazije, the main shopping street. Knez Mihajlova is the major street of the old part of the town, round the fortress, **Kalemegdan.** The Hungarians, under the command of Huyadi, defended the fortress against the Turks in 1456, and it was not defeated until the 16th cent. The present fortress dates from the 18th cent. Belgrade was seized by Hungarians, Germans, and Austrians during the 18th-19th cent. The Turkish rule ended in 1867. Many souvenirs from the Turkish period in the fortress. Roman well. Army museum. Hunting and forestry museum. Ružica, the garrison church. Kalemegdan is now a recreation area with beautiful parks and viewpoints. Open-air café and zoo.
National Museum. Archaeology, history, art and coins. The gold treasure from the cemetery at Trebeniŝte (6th cent.). *Ethnographical Museum* with Yugoslavian folk art, costumes, jewellery, musical instruments. *Fresco Museum.* Museum of modern art in Novi Beograd.
Municipal museum. The parliament (1907), an enormous neo-classical structure. The entrance is decorated with sculptures by Rosandić.
The Orthodox *cathedral* (Saborna crkva) from 1845. Iconostasis and princes' tombs. *Bajrakli Mosque* (17th cent.), the only mosque in the city – there used to be more than 20. *Sveti Marko* with the graves of King Milan Obrenović and Queen Draga, assassinated by officers in 1903. *Topčider Park* with open-air theatre, restaurant, museum devoted to the first Serbian rebellion. The home of Marshal

1 Kalemgdan Fortress. 2 Military Museum. 3 Cathedral. 4 Fresco Museum. 5 Bajrakli Mosque. 6 Ethnographical Museum. 7 National Theatre and Opera. 8 National Museum. 9 Republic Square and Albania House. 10 Skadarlija. 11 Parliament House. 12 Church of St. Mark. 13 House and Tomb of Tito. 14 Belgrade Trade Fair. 15 Convention Centre. 16 Museum of Modern Art. 17 Government Building.

Tito and his grave in the Kúca cveca (Flower House).
Avala, 565 m high mountain with fine views. Excursion goal and winter sports centre. Monument to the Unknown Soldier (1938) by Meŝtrović. Six figures symbolize the Yugoslavian republics and autonomous regions. 200 m high TV-tower. *Alpinist museum* at Čarapićev Brest.

Hydrofoil excursions from Belgrade to the **Iron Gate** *(Ðerdap),* where the Danube is squeezed together by the Carpathians to a width of 400 m for a distance of 9 km. At **Kazan** (the Cauldron) the river is only 150 m wide. The cliffs rise to 780 m. At the end of the gorge is the *Tabula Traiana* (the Trajan tablet) that recounts the campaign in 103 when a road had been hewn into the cliff face. Stone Age settlements (6000 B.C.) were discovered during the construction of the dam. Large hydro-electric power stations. See also Roumania, E 94.

SARAJEVO (320 000).
Capital of the republic of Bosnia-Herzegovina. The town was built by the last Turkish Vizier (governor), Gazi Husref-Beg. Its name comes from the Turkish word seraj (residence). The town's skyline, marked by church towers, tower blocks and 78 minarets, is typical of this part of Europe where East and West meet. One-third of the inhabitants are Muslims, one-third Greek Orthodox.
Baŝčarŝija, the old Oriental quarter with market and workshops. Cizmidziluk is the street of the coppersmiths. **Gazi-Husref-Beg Mosque** (16th cent.) is one of the most beautiful mosques in the Balkans. The grave of the Vizier (d. 1541). Valuable carpets. The *clock tower* (Sahat kula) with a

The park near Kalemegdan, Belgrade's old fortress

Dobrinja, a modern suburb of Sarajevo

1 National Museum. 2 Ali Pasha Mosque. 3 Bašcarsija and Gazi Husref-Beg (Begova) Mosque. 4 City Museum. 5 Old Town Hall. 6 Princip's Bridge and Museum of Young Bosnia. 7 Exhibition Hall

clock which shows the lunar phases. It was calculated in the star observatory of Muvekithana. The small, old *Orthodox church*, a building of unknown date. Museum with a collection of icons. Synagogue (19th cent.), during the war a prison for Jews, now a Jewish museum. Neo-Gothic cathedral (1889). *Despića kuća*, Serbian home and Svrzina kuća, a Muslim home.

Town hall (Gradska Kuća), built 1896 in "Arabian"style.

National Museum with sections devoted to archaeology, ethnography and natural history (folk crafts, folk costumes, musical instruments, etc.). One of the four Hagadah books, a Jewish book of rituals.

Princip's Bridge, named after the student, Gavrilo Princip, the assassin of Franz Ferdinand, the successor to the Austrian throne. His foot prints are cemented into the pavement. Memorial tablet with words about the "shot for freedom". The fact that it sparked off the First World War is not mentioned. Cable railway to *Mt Trebenrić* for fine view. *Mt Jahrina* (32 km SE) is a large winter sport centre and was one of the arenas for the Winter Olympic Games 1984. *Tje Bridge over the Frina*. *Sarajevo* see town plans.

ZAGREB (700 000)

Capital of the republic of Croatia. Yugoslavia's second largest city. In 1094 Ladislaus, the Hungarian king, established a bishopric on the Kaptol hill. On the other hill, Gradex or Grić, was a fortress and town which King Bela IV proclaimed a free royal town in 1242. The two towns were enemies and 1527-1529 they even waged a war against each other. The bridge between them was named "Bloddy Bridge". In 1557 Zagreb (Agram) was made the capital of the kingdom of Croatia, a part of Hungary. The Turks never conquered it. The final joining of the upper town, Gornji Grad (on Kaptol) and the lower town, Donji Grad, took place in 1850. *Gornji grad* is a beautiful Baroque quarter encircled by a wall. The *Stone Gate*

(Kamenita vrata) is the most beautiful of the city gates. It contains a Chapel of Mary. Every day at noon, a cannon shot is fired from the lower fortification tower (kula lotšcak). Beautiful views. *Church of St Mark* (Sveti Marka, 13th cent). Many-coloured tile roof with the coats of arms of Croatia, Slavonia and Dalmatia and the emblem of the city of Zagreb. Originally from the 13th cent., the church was completely rebuilt at the end of the 19th cent. and in 1937 it received a new interior, designed by I Meštrović. The Baroque Church of St. Catherine.

The *Cathedral of St. Stephen* was originally built in the 11th cent. That church was destroyed by the Mongols. Rebuilt in the 13th cent. The Turks shot off the towers. The next set of towers caved in during the 1880 earth-quake.

Between Grić and Kaptol is the lively *market square*. **Dolac,** the largest in Yugoslavia.

Donji Grad (the lower city) modern Zagreb with the shopping streets. The National Theatre, in Baroque, is on Trg Maršala Tita. Fountain of Life by I Meštrović. University. *Ethnographical Museum* with folklore and folk costumes, folk crafts, jewellery, pottery, etc. *Archaeological* museum.

Opera house and rich music life. Folklore festival at the end of July. Film festival. Zagreb has over 700 restaurants, many of them excellent. *Novi Zagreb* on the banks of river Sava with modern town-planning and high buildings. In April and September large international trade fairs are held here.

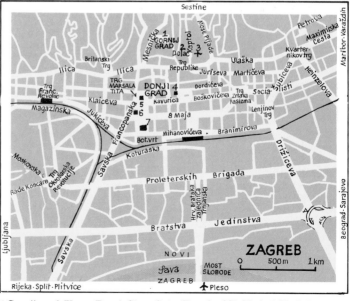

1 Gornij grad (Upper Town). Stone Gate. Church of St. Mark. 2 Market square. 3 Cathedral of St. Stephen. 4 Archaeological Museum. 5 Opera house. 6 Ethnographical Museum. 7 University Library.

Before starting out

Roadbook Europe is a personal travel guide based on the experiences and impressions that the author has gained from his many European motoring journeys.

The tourist organizations in the various countries have generously provided advice, assistance and colour illustrations.

Europe is full of impressions

This relatively small area is almost overflowing with places of interest, enormous cities and diminutive villages, high speed motorways, extensive plains and great forests, mighty rivers and high mountains, warm dark southern nights and the Midnight Sun over the continent's Arctic north.

A motoring holiday in Europe can entail a lot of hard work. You do have to put a bit of effort into the planning and preparation of your journey. It is not as easy as simply going to your local travel agent and buying a package tour.

Europe is best explored by car

Have you ever managed to emerge unscarred from the traffic madness of the Place de la Concorde and then driven along the Champs Elysées?

Have you ever driven over Dartmoor on a foggy day towards the sunshine in Torbay?

Have you ever experienced the exhilaration of a high-speed journey on the Autobahn?

Have you ever looked out over the Aegean from Sounion, or out over the Arctic Sea from the heights of the North Cape?

Have you ever driven through a small Dutch town when the carillon in the church was playing and where the buildings seemed like dolls' houses?

Have you ever driven over the longest bridge in Europe – to Öland?

Have you ever driven round the Coliseum and then continued past the Forum Romanum?

Have you ever driven along La Canebière, Piccadilly, Kurfürstendamm, Kungsportsavenyn, the Marszalkovska, the Damrak, the Avenida da Libertade or Nevsky Prospekt?

Congratulations! – But you still have a lot left to experience. In other words, you are going to have a full and memorable holiday, and you are going to experience infinitely more than those sun-seeking charter-package holidaymakers who merely fly over Europe's fascinating highways and byways.

Pack with care

What shall we pack for the journey? A difficult problem. Not too much, of course, but at the same time we do not want to be forced to buy essentials during the first day away from home.

A few weeks before you start out, write a list of things that you think you will need. This gives you time to think about, and add and subtract the items that you consider necessary. Smaller cases are better than large ones if you want to fill your boot efficiently. Soft items can be put into plastic carrier bags that can fill out empty spaces. But remember to knot the handles of the plastic bags securely – you do not want their contents to spill out the very first time you use the brake.

Before you start to pack, carry out all of your luggage to the car. Then you can see all of the pieces of the puzzle. At first it often seems impossible to fit everything in, but appearances can be deceptive; a little rearranging can work wonders.

A *roof-rack* creates greater wind resistance and the car's road-holding qualities suffer accordingly. Furthermore petrol consumption is increased. If, despite everything, you must have a roof-rack, make certain to use it for your lightest luggage.

And do not forget that you must carry all of your bags up to your hotel room *when you make an overnight stop.* Times were when it was possible to leave some items of luggage in the boot, but nowadays this is too risky. Do not even leave a single blanket in the car. Modern thieves are inclined to believe that blankets conceal valuables.

Re-read your car's book of instructions and check up on the vehicle's *maximum legal load.* If it is carrying a full complement of passengers, each one weighing an average of 75 kg, there may not be many kilogrammes left over for luggage. Occasionally the police make spot checks to see if cars are overloaded.

Plan ahead

To get the very most out of your precious days on the roads of Europe, you must be prepared to spend time and effort on advance preparation. Do not overestimate your capacity for long distance driving during a three or four week holiday. And remember that the countries that are closest have a lot to offer. After a few weeks of travelling it can be comforting to know that the road home is a relatively short one. Shorter itineraries also give you the opportunity to improvise and truly enjoy the freedom that motoring holidays can offer.

If your goal is a long distance from home you will have to keep to the fast roads and force yourself to avoid impromptu sightseeing. Now that the gaps in the network of European motorways have been filled, it is possible to drive directly from Continental Channel ports to Vienna or from the Baltic to Sicily without ever leaving a high-speed road.

Fast driving on the motorway system allows you to spend more time at your final destination. These modern roads avoid cities and towns, and if you have planned to make a stopover further along the route, try to resist the temptation to leave your original planned route for a short visit in an urban centre. This sort of detour will probably cost you far more hours than you had planned and it might ruin all your travel plans.

The road maps in this guide may tempt you to make brief *detours.* They need not take up too much of your travelling time, all that is required is a fair sense of direction. It can be therapeutic to exchange the frantic rush of motorway traffic for calming, idyllic and quiet country lanes for a short period.

Avoid long non-stop stretches of driving. Although you can travel at high speeds on the Autobahns, when traffic is heavy you can expect sudden decreases in speed, accelerations, frantic lane changing and even mile-long traffic jams. All of these can be exhausting or time consuming.

Get an early start. A difficult bit of advice for many – but you will be amazed at how much you can accomplish if you start your driving day in the early morning. Continental hotels often provide breakfast as early as 7 a.m.

Your day's drive should end at about 5 p.m. – perhaps even a little earlier. You will have a better chance of finding suitable hotel or camping accommodation. Of course it is tempting to keep on the road so that you can come closer to your final destination, but if this is the case, it is always advisable to book your lodgings for the night in advance. There are more pleasant travel experiences than searching for a hotel room late at night after a long day's drive.

In general it is better, and usually cheaper, to leave the motorways when night is approaching and you are looking for a place to stay. A little pension or Gasthaus in a picturesque village that neither you nor the writer of your guidebook have ever heard of, can provide you with delightful holiday memories.

Pre-paid package holidays

A package tour has its merits. Hotel and car ferry accommodation are booked for you – and the prices are usually lower than those for independent travellers. In any case, they allow you to have better control over your expenses for transport and lodgings. Some of the pure fun of spur-of-the moment improvisation is lost, but it is reassuring to know that you will always have a place to spend the night. A variation of the package tour is the "Go As You Please"-arrangement. In this, your first overnight hotel stay is booked, and then the hotel receptionist assists you in booking rooms for the following night in any one of a variety of hotels. This form of travel gives you a good combination of freedom and security.

The car ferry companies can provide worthwhile and interesting suggestions for package holidays, hotel bookings, and holiday houses and flats.

Car ferries

The English Channel, Mediterranean ports and Scandinavia are all served by a wide selection of car ferry lines. But during the high season it can be difficult to obtain accommodation. So, try to book well in advance. You may be able to save money by choosing a longer ferry route; you can cut petrol and hotel costs.

Car ferry routes are indicated on the general map together with travel times.

Motor-rail

Many drivers do not like tiring, long-distance Continental driving and this has lead to the increased popularity of the motor-rail system. Considering today's petrol costs, hotel prices and all of the other expenditure necessary for a long journey, motor-rail can provide a suitable, restful solution. In addition, it can be to your advantage to be, by the second or third day of your holiday, well on your way towards your final destination. If you drive on board in Hamburg in the evening, by the next morning you will be in Munich. Your car is stowed in a goods wagon and you can spend the night comfortably in a couchette or sleeping compartment.

Your travel agent can give you further information about trains and prices.

Hotels

The official tourist offices of the individual European countries provide hotel listings. You can find the addresses for these offices in the introductory section of each chapter in this guide.

The British Automobile Association publishes "Hotels and Restaurants in Britain" and "Guesthouses, Farmhouses and Inns in Britain". The latter lists 3,000 reasonably priced and comfortable establishments. The AA also publishes similar books covering Europe such as "Travellers Guide to Europe" and "Guesthouses, Farmhouses and Inns in Europe".

During your journey it is possible to obtain assistance from local tourist offices and from the accommodation bureau that are to be found in major railway stations. But remember, the earlier in the day you arrive, the easier it is to find suitable accommodation.

Camping

In general, the national tourist offices have listings of their country's camping sites, and detailed guidebooks about camping in Europe can be found in most bookshops. Although many campers seem to manage very well without an international camping carnet, it is a good idea to carry one. The carnet is an identity paper that can be deposited with the manager of the camping site if you do not wish to turn in your passport. It also contains third party liability insurance that covers all of the car's passengers (up to 5) but not the driver. Some camping sites give discounts to carnet holders. A carnet is available to members through the AA.

Youth hostels

Youth hostels were originally simple establishments where young hikers and cyclists could spend the night. Today, for the most part they also accept older, motoring travellers. In Scandinavia, where the majority of the hostel guests arrive by car, the youth hostels are usually equipped with special rooms for families. In mainland Europe however, many youth hostels retain their original character. The national

youth hostel organizations are joined together in the International Youth Hostel Federation (IYHF). In order to stay in a youth hostel, you must be a member of your country's organization.

Travel formalities

Passports. Each person travelling outside the British Isles must hold, or be named on an up-to-date passport valid for all the countries through which it is intended to travel. Passports should be carried at all times and, as an extra precaution, a separate note kept of the number, date and place of issue. There are various types of British passports including the standard or regular passport and the limited British Visitor's Passport.

Application forms are available from main post offices. A British Visitor's Passport obtainable from any main post office (in Northern Ireland only at the Passport Agency, Belfast) is acceptable for travel in Western Europe and West Berlin, but not for Yugoslavia. It cannot be used for a business trip or overland travel through the German Democratic Republic to West Berlin.

Visas. United Kingdom and Republic of Ireland passport holders need a visa for certain Eastern European countries. A visa is not normally required for Western European countries when visiting for periods of three months or less. However, if you hold a passport of any other nationality, a UK passport not issued in this country or are in any doubt at all about your position, you should check with the embassies or consulates of the countries you intend to visit.

Driving licence. It is recommended that you always carry your national driving licence with you when motoring abroad, even when an International Driving Permit is held (see also IDP requirements below). In many countries you can drive a temporarily imported car without formality for up to three months with a valid (not provisional) licence issued in the United Kingdom or Republic of Ireland but must be 18 or over, unless driving in Denmark, German Federal Republic, Iceland, Luxembourg, Norway, Portugal and Turkey where you can drive at 17. In Greece a UK licence holder can drive at 17, but Republic of Ireland licence holders must obtain an IDP. If you should wish to drive a hired or borrowed car in the country you are visiting make local enquiries about age requirements. In Italy your licence must be accompanied by a translation which can be supplied by the AA. In Austria a UK driving licence is legally valid and, although occasional difficulties may arise with local officials who are not conversant with the licence, this can generally be resolved by production of your passport. The Austrian motoring club (ÖAMTC) will supply a free translation of your licence into German, but this is only available from their head office in Vienna.

International Driving Permit. An internationally recognized document issued by the AA for a statutory fee to persons of 18 or over who hold a valid (not provisional) United Kingdom driving licence. It enables the holder to drive for a limited period in countries where their national licences are not recognized. The permit is compulsory in Algeria, Austria, Bulgaria, Greece, Hungary and Spain (unless a certified Spanish translation of driving licence is obtained, although this is more expensive than an IDP) and USSR. The permit is recommended when visiting the German Democratic Republic, Poland and Turkey.

Nationality plate. You must display a nationality plate of the approved design (oval with black letters on a white background) and size (GB at least 6.9 inches by 4.5 inches), at the rear of your vehicle (and caravan/trailer if you are towing one). Failure to comply with this regulation may be punishable by a fine.

Currency

There is no limit to the amount of sterling notes you may take abroad. However, it is best to carry only enough currency for immediate expenses.

As many countries have regulations controlling the import and export of currency, you are advised to consult your bank for full information before making final arrangements.

The greater part of the money for the journey should be in the form of travellers' cheques, made out in the currency of the country that you intend to visit. For extended trips, travellers' cheques made out in German marks, dollars or pounds are advisable. Be certain to have a little supply of local currency for every country that you will visit. They should be able to cover your first expenses. Do not forget that it can be difficult to exchange money at weekends.

The great advantage of travellers' cheques is that they are easily replaced if lost or stolen, if you report your loss *immediately*. Enquire at the bank where you buy your cheques about the standard procedures involved if you have to report the loss of travellers' cheques.

Money is usually exchanged in banks. Although it is possible to exchange money in hotels, they, like the currency exchange offices that are open after normal banking hours, inevitably give less favourable rates. Do not make illegal currency transactions. Even if the rumour that the hotel's hall porter or a man just round the corner gives double the official rate of exchange is perfectly true (as it can be in parts of eastern Europe) the risks are too high. The consequences can be disastrous.

Credit cards can be useful, particularly for unexpected expenses.

Try to protect yourself from the Continent's nimble pickpockets by distributing your travelling funds among the members of your party.

Insurance

Transit insurance. Make sure you are covered against damage in transit (e.g. on ferry or motorrail). Most comprehensive motor insurance policies provide adequate cover, but check with your insurer to be certain.

Vehicle insurance/Green Card. Motor vehicle insurance is compulsory in all countries mentioned in this guide except the USSR where it is strongly recommended. Insurance policies issued in the United Kingdom and the Republic of Ireland automatically provide minimum cover in the following EEC countries: United Kingdom, Republic of Ireland, Belgium, Denmark, France, German Federal Republic (West Germany), Italy, Luxembourg and the Netherlands. Austria, Czechoslovakia, German Democratic Republic, Finland, Hungary, Norway, Sweden and Switzerland, although not members of the EEC subscribe to this regulation. The overseas cover automatically provided by your home country policy will reduce to satisfy only the minimum legal requirement in the country in which you travel, and this varies from country to country, thus it is unlikely that you will enjoy the same measure of cover as you do at home.

Before taking your car abroad you should therefore contact your insurers for their advice and ensure that you are adequately covered to your satisfaction. Your UK policy cover can be extended to apply on the Continent and your insurers will issue an International Green Card of Insurance which is the usual evidence of insurance and is accepted in most European countries. Although not a legal requirement for those countries listed previously, *the Green Card is still required for Bulgaria, Greece*, Iceland, Poland, Portugal, Roumania, Spain, Turkey and Yugoslavia.* In any case you are recommended to carry the Green Card because it may prove more effective than a UK insurance certificate in establishing that the minimum insurance requirements operating in the country you are visiting have been met.

If you are towing a caravan or trailer it will need separate insurance, and to be mentioned on your Green Card.

Remember the cover on a caravan or trailer associated with a Green Card is normally limited to third party risks so a separate policy (such as AA Leisureplan) is advisable to cover accidental damage, fire and theft.

Bail Bonds. An accident in Spain can have serious conse-

quences, including the impounding of your car and property, and the detention of the driver pending trial. A Bail Bond can often facilitate the release of a person and his property. You can obtain one from the AA free of charge when you purchase AA 5-Star Service. An AA Bail Bond is a written guarantee that a cash deposit of up to £1,500 will be paid to the Spanish Court as surety for bail and for any fine which may be imposed; in such an event you will have to reimburse any amount paid on your behalf.

Medical treatment and health care

Urgently needed medical treatment can be obtained by most visitors, free of charge or at reduced cost, from the health care schemes of those countries with whom the UK has health care arrangements. Details are in leaflet SA30 available from local social security offices of the Department of Health and Social Security or from its Leaflets Unit at PO Box 21, Stanmore, Middlesex HA7 1AY. In some of these countries visitors can obtain urgently needed medical treatment by showing their UK passport but in some a NHS medical card must be produced and in most European Community countries a certificate of entitlement (E111) is necessary. A form to obtain this certificate is included in the DHSS leaflet. Applicants should allow at least one month for the form to be processed although in an emergency the E111 can be obtained over the counter of the local DHSS office (residents of the Republic of Ireland should apply to their Regional Health Board for the E111). The DHSS will also supply on request a leaflet SA35 giving advice on health precautions and information about vaccinations.

Breakdown

If your car breaks down, endeavour to move it to the side of the road or to a position where it will obstruct the traffic flow as little as possible. Place a warning triangle at the appropriate distance on the road behind the obstruction. Bear in mind road conditions and if near or on a bend the triangle should be placed where it is clearly visible to following traffic. If the car is fitted with hazard warning lights these may be switched on but they will only warn on the straight and will have no effect at bends or rises in the road. If the fault is electrical, the lights may not operate and it is for these reasons that they cannot take the place of a triangle. Having taken these first precautions, seek assistance if you cannot deal with the fault yourself.

Motorists are advised to purchase AA 5-Star Service which provides a wide range of services, insurance and credit vouchers which offer security and peace of mind when travelling in Europe. Cover may be purchased by all motorists. However, a small additional premium must be paid by non-members. Details and brochures may be obtained from travel agents and AA Centres, or by telephoning 021-550 7648.

Spares

The problem of which spares to carry is a difficult one; it depends on the vehicle and how long you are likely to be away. However, you should consider hiring an AA Spares Kit for your car; full information about this service is available from the AA.

Lights

For driving abroad headlights should be adjusted so that they do not dip to the left. This can be achieved by the use of beam deflectors which may be purchased from your nearest AA Centre. However, do not forget to remove the deflectors as soon as you return to the UK. Dipped headlights should be used in conditions of fog, snowfall, heavy rain and when passing through a tunnel. Headlight flashing is used only as a warning of approach or as a passing signal at night. In other circumstances it is accepted as a sign of irritation and should be used with caution lest it be misunderstood. In Finland (outside built-up areas only) and Sweden the use of dipped headlights during daylight hours is compulsory throughout the year. In many countries it is compulsory for motorcyclists to use dipped headlights during the day. In France a regulation requires all locally registered vehicles to be equipped with headlights which show a yellow

---

*Although it is now a member of the EEC a Green Card is, for the time being, still a compulsory requirement for entry and travel in Greece.

beam and, in the interests of courtesy and safety, visitors are advised to comply with this regulation. Amber lens converters may be used or alternatively the outer surface of the headlamp glass can be painted with yellow plastic paint which is removable with a solvent. The yellow headlamp paint may be purchased from your nearest AA Centre.

It is a wise precaution (compulsory in France, German Democratic Republic, Spain and Yugoslavia and recommended in Czechoslovakia, Italy, Norway, Poland and the USSR) to equip your vehicle with a set of replacement bulbs when motoring abroad. These form part of the AA Spares Kit.

Tyres

Inspect your tyres carefully; if you think they are likely to be more than three-quarters worn before you get back, it is better to replace them before you start out. Expert advice should be sought if you notice uneven wear, scuffed treads or damaged walls, on whether the tyres are suitable for further use. In some European countries, drivers can be fined if tyres are badly worn. The regulations in the UK governing tyres call for a minimum tread depth of 1mm across 75% of the width of the tyre. European regulations are tougher, requiring 1 mm or 1.6 mm across the whole width of the tyre.

When checking tyre pressures, remember that if the car is heavily loaded the recommended pressures may have to be raised a few pounds per square inch above normal. This should also be done for high-speed driving. Check the recommendations in your handbook but remember pressures can only be checked accurately when the tyres are cold and don't forget the spare tyre.

Petrol

Petrol price concessions in the form of petrol coupons may be purchased inside Czechoslovakia from the Czech State Bank and its branch offices; at the frontiers when entering Bulgaria, German Democratic Republic, Poland, Roumania, USSR and Yugoslavia. The coupons are necessary to obtain supplies of petrol in all the above named countries except Czechoslovakia and the German Democratic Republic.

When travelling by ferry you must ensure that your petrol tank is not so full as to create a possibility of spillage. Petrol cans must be empty and any gas cylinders securely affixed in accordance with the manufacturer's instructions with all taps turned *OFF* and sealed whilst the vehicle is in motion or on the ferry.

The use of a lockable filler cap to secure the petrol tank is always a wise precaution. If any petrol is carried in cans across country borders duty may be payable on the fuel. However, in Finland, Greece, Italy, Portugal and Yugoslavia it is forbidden to carry petrol in cans in a vehicle.

Further advice

Be certain that your warning triangle is always near at hand. Give each of your fellow passengers a reserve car key. Remember that heavy luggage in the boot can cause the headlamps to point upwards, thus dazzling oncoming drivers. If this is the case, see that they are readjusted.

Traffic

Laws regarding *safety belts* exist in most countries. Although there can be some variations, this is no reason for carelessness. Belt up! *Alcohol* and driving do not mix. Strict laws exist in most countries, so do not take needless risks.

Drive carefully

A traffic accident can be particularly unfortunate if it occurs in a foreign country. Even minor damage to the coachwork can develop into a prolonged incident.

● Remember that even an experienced driver is probably an inexperienced holiday driver. You drive longer stretches at higher speed than usual. Your car is probably carrying a heavier load than usual and its road-holding qualities are altered. It can react differently in a difficult situation. Perhaps you will be driving in a warmer climate than you are accustomed to.

● Do not forget to take regular breaks. You should not be at the wheel for more than two consecutive hours.

● Avoid night-time driving. It is both tiring and potentially dangerous. This is particularly true in southeast Europe where horse and donkey drawn carts, lacking any illumination are not unusual.

● *Driving on motorways* is fun, but demanding. It is easy to be carried away by the intense tempo. But give the speed-demons in the fast lanes the right of way. It will not be a disaster if you stay in a lane where the traffic moves along at 80–90 kmh. Be particularly careful when beginning to overtake on a slope. It may seem like an uncomplicated manoeuvre, but it can be a strain on your car. Make certain that the road ahead of you is clear—at high speeds you can come close to the car ahead of you. If, in addition, there is a risk of fog, be extra careful. A fog bank can approach with amazing speed and when that happens it is not unusual that several cars, all with screeching brakes, pile into each other. It is a sight you will never forget—if you survive. Motorways are even more dangerous when there has been an accident: people get out of their cars to inspect the damage, others remain in their cars. All can be run over by other motorists who do not have time to brake. If you must stop your car on a motorway, immediately set up your warning triangle at a proper distance from the vehicle. You might be safer to set up two triangles! Make certain that every passenger gets out of the car and goes to safety on the other side of the guard rail.

● Wet roads are always potentially dangerous and motorway driving can be hazardous when the road is in this condition.

By heeding the warnings, and by taking more than adequate rest-stops, you can see to it that your holiday does not end in disaster. Some final words of advice: always keep an eye on your mirror, and signal before and after overtaking. Running out of petrol on some motorways is regarded as a mortal sin. In Germany, the police fine offenders.

Driving on Alpine roads

Driving in the Alps is not as difficult as many imagine. Obviously one must take greater care and there are a few things to keep in mind:

● You should always change to a lower gear when driving up a steep incline. Your engine should not be overworked.

● If the engine seems as if it is going to boil over, stop immediately. Its temperature will sink faster if you let it idle a moment before switching it off. When the water has stopped boiling, slowly remove the radiator cap with a handkerchief or cloth and refill with small amounts of water at a time. A water can should be part of your emergency equipment.

● Keep to the same gear when going down a hill as when going up. Brake for short periods so that the break linings can cool and rest a bit.

● Change gear in good time when approaching a bend. You will have quite enough to do guiding the steering wheel and looking out for oncoming cars.

● Stay well to the right. Vehicles driving upwards on Alpine roads have the right of way. In Switzerland some of the roads are "Alpine Post Roads" where post buses have the right of way.

● If you must park on a slope, set the brake, engage a gear and see to it that the wheels are adequately chocked. You can also place a wedge or rock under the wheels as an extra safety measure.

Motoring Clubs in Europe

The Alliance Internationale de Tourisme (AIT) is the largest confederation of touring associations in the world and it is through this body that the AA is able to offer its members the widest possible touring information service. Its membership consists not of individuals, but of associations or groups of associations having an interest in touring.

Tourists visiting a country where there is an AIT club may avail themselves of its touring advisory services upon furnishing proof of membership of their home AIT club. AA members making overseas trips should, whenever possible, seek the advice of the AA before setting out and should only approach the overseas AIT clubs when necessary.

Motoring terms in five languages

Bonnet *Fr* capot, *Ger* Motorhaube, *It* cofano motore, *Sp* cubierto del motor, *Swed* motorhuv

Brake *Fr* frein, *Ger* Bremse, *It* freno, *Sp* freno, *Swed* broms

Brake fluid *Fr* huile de frein, *Ger* Bremsflussigkeit, *It* liquido per freni, *Sp* liquido de frenos, *Swed* bromsvätska

Bumper *Fr* pare-chocs, *Ger* Stosstange, *It* paraurti, *Sp* parachoques, *Swed* stötfångare

Carburettor *Fr* carburateur, *Ger* Vergaser, *It* carburatore, *Sp* carburador, *Swed* förgasare

Clutch *Fr* embrayage, *Ger* Kupplung, *It* frizone, *Sp* embrague, *Swed* koppling

Disc brake *Fr* frein à disque, *Ger* Scheibenbremse, *It* freno a disco, *Sp* freno de disco, *Swed* skivbroms

Distilled water *Fr* eau distillée, *Ger* destilliertes Wasser, *It* acqua distillata, *Sp* agua destilada, *Swed* destillerat vatten

Distributor *Fr* distributeur, *Ger* Verteiler, *It* distributore, *Sp* distribuidor, *Swed* strömfördelare

Dynamo *Fr* dynamo, *Ger* Lichtmaschine, *It* dinamo, *Sp* dinamo, *Swed* generator

Exhaust pipe *Fr* tuyan d'echappement, *Ger* Auspoffrohr, *It* tubo di scappamento, *Sp* tubo de escape, *Swed* avgasrör

Fan belt *Fr* Courroie de ventilateur, *Ger* Ventilatorriemen, *It* cinghia del ventilatore, *Sp* correa del ventilador, *Swed* fläktrem

Gasket *Fr* joint, *Ger* Dichtung, *It* guarnizione, *Sp* junta, *Swed* packning

Gear lever *Fr* levier de commande, *Ger* Schalthebel, *It* leva del cambia, *Sp* palanca del cambio, *Swed* växelspak

Gearbox *Fr* boite de vitesse, *Ger* Wechselgetriebe, *It* scatola cambio, *Sp* caja de velocidades, *Swed* växellåda

Handbrake *Fr* frein à main, *Ger* Handbremse, *It* freno a mano, *Sp* freno de mano, *Swed* handbroms

Headlamp *Fr* phare, *Ger* Scheinwerfer, *It* fanale, *Sp* faro, *Swed* strålkastare

Horn *Fr* klaxon, *Ger* Hupe, *It* klaxon, *Sp* bocina, *Swed* tuta

Ignition *Fr* allumage, *Ger* Zündanlage, *It* accensione, *Sp* encendido, *Swed* tändning

Jack *Fr* cric, *Ger* Wagenheber, *It* cricco, *Sp* gato, *Swed* domkraft

Key *Fr* clé, *Ger* Schlüssel, *It* chiave, *Sp* llave, *Swed* nyckel

Leak *Fr* fuite, *Ger* Undichtigkeit, *It* mancante di tenuta, *Sp* gutera, *Swed* läckage

Lock *Fr* serrure, *Ger* Schloss, *It* chinsura, *Sp* cerradura, *Swed* lås

Lubricate *Fr* grasser, *Ger* schmieren, *It* lubrificare, *Sp* engrasar, *Swed* smörja

Oil *Fr* huile, *Ger* Öl, *It* olio, *Sp* aceite, *Swed* olja

Petrol *Fr* essence, *Ger* Benzin, *It* benzina, *Sp* gasolina, *Swed* bensin

Petrol can *Fr* bidon d'essence, *Ger* Benzinkanister, *It* bidone di benzina, *Sp* bidón de gasolina, *Swed* bensindunk

Petrol pump *Fr* pompe à essence, *Ger* Brennstoffpumpe, *It* pompa della benzina, *Sp* bomba de la gasolina, *Swed* bränslepump

Piston ring *Fr* segment de piston, *Ger* Kolbenring, *It* fascia elastica del pistone, *Sp* aro de émbolo, *Swed* kolvring

Puncture *Fr* crevaison, *Ger* Reifendefekt, *It* bucatura di pneumatico, *Sp* pinchazo, *Swed* punktering

Radiator *Fr* radiateur, *Ger* Köhler, *It* radiatore, *Sp* radiador, *Swed* kylare

Repair shop *Fr* atelier, *Ger* Werkstatt, *It* officina di riparazioni, *Sp* taller de reparaciones, *Swed* verkstad

Reverse *Fr* faire marche arrière, *Ger* rückwerts fahren, *It* invertire il senso di marcia, *Sp* poner marcha atrás, *Swed* backa

Safety belt *Fr* ceinture de sécurité, *Ger* Gurt, *It* cintura di sicurezza, *Sp* cinturón de seguridad, *Swed* säkerhetsbälte

Shock absorber *Fr* amortisseur, *Ger* Stossdämpfer, *It* amortizzatore, *Sp* amortiguador, *Swed* stötdämpare

Snow chains *Fr* chaînes antidérapants, *Ger* Schneeketten, *It* catene antisducciolevoli, *Sp* cadenas para nieve, *Swed* snökedjor

Spare part *Fr* pièce de rechange, *Ger* Reservestücke, *It* pezzo di ricambio, *Sp* repuesto, *Swed* reservdel

Sparking plug *Fr* bougie, *Ger* Zündkerze, *It* candela, *Sp* bujia, *Swed* tändstift

Speedometer *Fr* indicateur de vitesse, *Ger* Geschwindigkeitmesser, *It* indicatore di velocità, *Sp* velocimetro, *Swed* hastighetsmätare

Starter *Fr* démarreur, *Ger* Anlassmotor, *It* messa in motor, *Sp* arranque, *Swed* startmotor

Steering wheel *Fr* volant de direction, *Ger* Lenkrad, *It* volante, *Sp* volante, *Swed* ratt

Tyre *Fr* pneu, *Ger* Reifen, *It* copertone, *Sp* neumático, *Swed* däck

Tow rope *Fr* corde de remorque, *Ger* Schlepptau, *It* corda da rimorchiare, *Sp* cable de remorque, *Swed* bogserlina

Wheel *Fr* roue, *Ger* Felge, *It* routa, *Sp* llanta, *Swed* fälg

Windscreen wiper *Fr* essuie-glace, *Ger* Scheibenwischer, *It* tergicristallo, *Sp* limpiaparabrisas, *Swed* vindrutetorkare

Tour tips

There are so many beautiful and interesting sights in Europe and so many touring possibilities that it is difficult to suggest any particularly rewarding motor tours.

The following tour tips include both long and short excursions. The maps provide hints for further touring alternatives. Detailed information about each stretch of road can be found in the sections devoted to particular countries.

Great Britain

London – Cambridge – York – Newcastle – Edinburgh – Inverness – Glasgow – Lake District – Liverpool – Chester – Birmingham – Cheltenham – London.
1235 miles (1 985 km).

Newcastle – Lake District – Carlisle – Glasgow – Fort William – Inverness – Aberdeen – Edinburgh – Newcastle.
657 miles (1060 km).

The Midlands and Southern England. Wales

London – Oxford – Stratford-upon-Avon – Coventry – Birmingham – Liverpool – Chester – Llandudno – Bangor – Snowdon – Shrewsbury – Hereford – Gloucester – Bristol – Bath – Barnstaple – Land's End – Plymouth – Torquay – Dartmoor – Exeter – Bournemouth – New Forest – Beaulieu – Southampton – Brighton – Dover – Canterbury – London.
1216 miles (1955 km).

London – Colchester – Ipswich – Great Yarmouth – Norwich – King's Lynn – Cambridge – London.
325 miles (520 km).

South of France – Spain – Portugal

Bordeaux – Toulouse – Andorra – Barcelona – Zaragoza – Madrid – Toledo – Badajoz – Lisboa – Estoril – Coimbra – Salamanca – Valladolid – Burgos – Pamplona – San Sebastián – Biarritz – Bayonne – Bordeaux.
3080 km.

San Sebastián – Burgos – Madrid – Toledo – Granada – Málaga – Algeciras (Gibraltar) – Cádiz – Jerez de la Frontera – Sevilla – Lisboa – Estoril – Sintra – Coimbra – Porto – Santiago de Compostela – La Coruña – Oviedo – Cuevas de Altamira – Bilbao – San Sebastián.
2960 km.

Barcelona – Tarragona – Valencia – Alicante – Granada – Córdoba – Toledo – Madrid – Zaragoza – Barcelona.
1920 km.

France

Paris – Dijon – Lyon – Nice – Cannes – Toulon – Marseille – Avignon – Nîmes – Camargue – Languedoc – Roussillon – Carcassonne – Toulouse – Biarritz – La Rochelle – the châteaux of the Loire – Orléans – Paris.
2620 km.

France

Calais – Amiens – Reims – Verdun – Metz – Nancy – Strasbourg – Colmar – Grand Ballon – Belfort – Ronchamp – Besançon – Grenoble – Lyon – St. Etienne – Le Puy – Gorges du Tarn – Cahors – Périgord – the châteaux of the Loire – Tours – Nantes – Brest – Mont-Saint-Michel – Arromanches (the Invasion Coast) – Bayeux – Caen – Rouen – Paris – Calais.
2840 km.

Netherlands – West Germany – Belgium

Oostende – Zeebrugge – Vlissingen – the Oosterschelde bridge – Rotterdam – Delft – den Haag (Hoek van Holland) – Groningen – Bremen – Hamburg – the Lüneburg heath – Hameln – Hannoversch Münden – Kassel – Marburg – Frankfurt – Rüdesheim – the Mosel valley – Trier – Luxembourg – Namur – Bruxelles – Gent – Brugge – *Oostende*. *1836 km.*

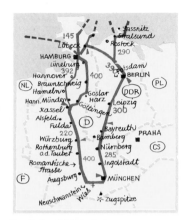

Deutsche Ferienstrasse

The distance between Puttgarden and Berchtesgaden is 1095 km. The Deutsche Ferienstrasse which runs between these two points is 1785 km long. It provides such an enormous amount of impressions that it is hardly advisable to travel the entire length of it. But it does offer possibilities for interesting side trips.

Germany. East and West

Hamburg – Lübeck – Berlin – Leipzig – Nürnberg – München – Neuschwanstein – Romantische Strasse – Würzburg – Fulda – Alsfeld – Kassel – Hannoversch Münden – Göttingen – Harz – Goslar – Braunschweig – Lüneburg – Lübeck/*Hamburg*. *1995 km.*

Puttgarden – the Baltic Coast – Lübeck – Lüneburg – Celle – Braunschweig – Goslar and Harz – Göttingen – Homberg – Vogelsberg – Miltenberg – Eberbach – Schwäbisch Hall – Dinkelsbühl – Eichstätt – Landshut – Chiemsee – *Berchtesgaden*. *1785 km.*

Southern Germany – Austria – Switzerland – France – Belgium

Bruxelles – Liège – Köln – the Rhine Valley, Koblenz and Rüdesheim – Frankfurt – Würzburg – Bamberg – Nürnberg – Regensburg – München – Garmisch – Innsbruck – Arlberg – Bregenz – Lindau – Schaffhausen – Schwarzwald (the Black Forest) – Strasbourg – Luxembourg – the Ardennes – *Bruxelles*. *2015 km.*

Switzerland

Basel – Zürich – Luzern – Gotthard – Lugano – Locarno – Verbania – Simplon – Brig – Martigny – Chamonix – Genève – Lausanne – Fribourg – Bern – Baltsthal – *Basel*. *885 km.*

Basel – Zürich – Schaffhausen with Rheinfall – Steim am Rhein – Konstanz – Mainau – Bregenz – Vaduz – Chur – San Bernardino – Lugano – St. Gotthard – Sustenpass – Ballenberg – Interlaken – Bern – *Basel*. *745 km.*

Southern Germany – Austria – Italy – France

Köln – the Rhine Valley – Frankfurt – Heidelberg – the Neckar Valley – Romantische Strasse – Neuschwanstein – Innsbruck – Verona – Firenze – Pisa – Genova – the Riviera – Monaco – Nice – Grenoble – Genève – Bern – Basel – Freiburg – Frankfurt – *Köln*. *3070 km.*

The Alps: Roads easily travelled by cars towing caravans.

Italy

Nice – Riviera dei Fiori – Genova – Pisa – Firenze – Siena – Roma – Napoli – Cosenza – Taranto – Bari – Pescara – Rimini – San Marino – Ravenna – Venezia – Bergamo – *Milano*.
2480 km.
Alternative route from Cosenza – Reggio di Calabria – Palermo – Messina – Trapani – Siracusa – Catania – Messina – *Cosenza* and onwards.
3755 km.
Bari by ferry to Dubrovnik – Mostar – Split – Trieste – Venezia – *Milano*.
2600 km.

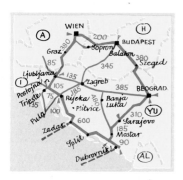

Austria – Hungary – Yugoslavia

Wien – Eisenstadt – Sopron – Györ – Budapest – Szeged – Beograd – Sarajevo – Mostar – Dubrovnik – Split – Zadar – Rijeka – Trieste – Postojna – Ljubljana – Graz – *Wien*.
2415 km.

Germany – Czechoslovakia – Hungary – Yugoslavia

Nürnberg – Plzeň – Praha – Karlštejn – Brno – Wien – Bratislava – Budapest – Zagreb – Ljubljana – Postojna – Villach – Grossglockner (alternatively Tauern or Felbertauern) – Salzburg – *München*.
1740 km.

Greece

Thessaloníki (excursion to Athos) – Lárisa – Delfi – Athinai – Kórinthos – Tripolis – Olympia – Pirgos – Patrai – (ferry to Brindisi) – Ioánnina – *Igoumenitsa*.
1330 km.

The Meteóra Monastery, an interesting sight, is 135 km from Ioánnina, 85 km from Lárisa.

Bulgaria

Sofia – the Rila Monastery – Borovets –
Plovdiv – Stara Zagora – Burgas – Ne-
sebŭr – Varna – Madara – Shumen –
Turgovishte – Veliko Turnovo – the
Dryanovo Monastery – Gabrovo – the
Shipka Pass – Kazanlŭk – the Valley of
Roses – *Sofia*.
1358 km.

Roumania

Arad – Sibiu – Piteşti – Bucureşti –
Constanţa – Tulcea – Ploieşti – Braşov –
Cluj – *Oradea*.
1670 km.
Oradea – Cluj – Braşov – Bucureşti –
Constanţa – Tulcea – Bacău – Suceava –
the Moldavian monasteries – Cluj –
Oradea.
1900 km.

DDR – Poland – Hungary – Austria – Czechoslovakia

Berlin – Szczecin – Gdynia – Gdańsk –
Frombork – Olsztyn – the Masurian
Lakes – Bialystok – Warszawa – Cze-
stochowa – Kraków – Wien – Praha –
Dresden – *Berlin*.
2582 km.

Alternative route from Kraków – Zakopane – Budapest – Wien – Praha –
Berlin.
2735 km.

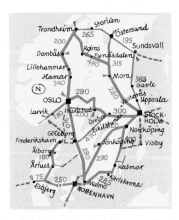

Southern and central Scandinavia

København – Malmö – Kalmar – Norrköping – Kolmården – Stockholm –
Mora – Funäsdalen – Røros – Trondheim – Lillehammer – Oslo – Göteborg
– Helsingborg – *København*.
2700 km.

Alternative route by car ferry Oslo –
København or Larvik – Frederiks-
havn.
København – Helsingborg – Jönkö-
ping – Kolmården – Stockholm –
Gripsholm – Eskilstuna – Örebro –
Karlstad – Sunne – Arvika – Oslo –
Drammen – Horten – Moss – Göteborg
– Frederikshavn – Ålborg – Århus –
Odense – *København*.
1850 km.

The fjords and mountains of Norway

Oslo – Fagernes – Jotunheimen –
Dombås – Åndalsnes – Trollstigen –
Geiranger – Sognefjord – Kinsarvik –
Haukelid – Rjukan – Drammen – *Oslo*.
1310 km.
Alternative route from Haukelid
through the Setes Valley to
Kristiansand.
1285 km.

Northern Sweden, Norway and Finland

Stockholm – Sundsvall – Umeå – Mo –
Saltfjell – Bodø – Narvik – Tromsø –
Hammerfest – the North Cape – Kauto-
keino – Ivalo – Rovaniemi – Jyväskylä
– Helsinki – ferry to *Stockholm* (or
Travemünde).
4000 km

Routes to the North Cape

Oslo – Trondheim – Narvik – *the North
Cape.*
2170 km.
Stockholm – Luleå – Karesuando –
Alta – *the North Cape.*
1840 km.
Helsinki – Oulu – Rovaniemi – Karasjok – *the North Cape.*
1530 km.
Turku – Oulu – *the North Cape*
1570 km.

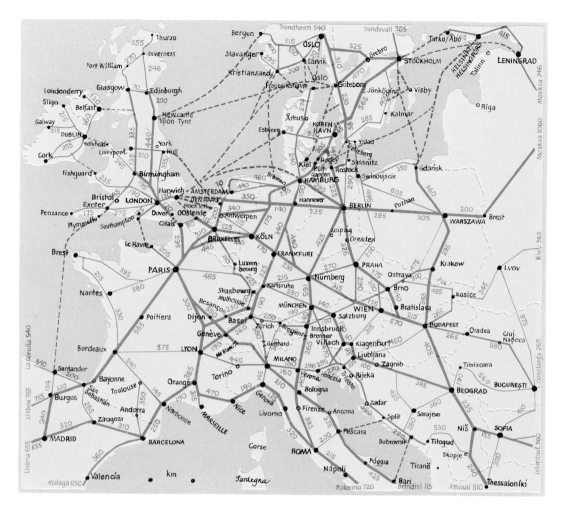

ROUTES THROUGH EUROPE

London – Dover 120 km – ferry to Calais – **Paris 415 km** (via motorway)

London – Dover 120 km – ferry to Boulogne – **Paris 360 km**

London – Folkestone 116 km – ferry to Boulogne – **Paris 354 km**

London – Southampton 125 km – ferry to Le Havre – **Paris 330 km**

London – Newhaven 100 km – ferry to Dieppe – **Paris 280 km**

London – Paris 415 km – Bordeaux 915 km – Burgos 1380 km – Madrid 1625 km – **Lisboa 2280 km**

London – Southampton 125 km – ferry to Cherbourg – Bordeaux 770 km – Burgos 1235 km – **Madrid 1480 km**

London – Plymouth 350 km – ferry to Santander – **Madrid 745 km**

London – Paris 415 km – Lyon 880 km – Nice 1350 km – Genova 1545 km – **Roma 2045 km**

London – Paris 415 km – Genève 965 km – Milano 1280 km – Firenze 1580 km – **Roma 1865 km**

London – Paris 415 km – Lyon 680 km – Torino 980 km – Milano 1120 km – Roma 1710 km – Napoli 1925 km – Cosenza 2240 km – Villa S.Giovanni 2242 km – ferry to Messina – **Palermo 2646 km**

London – Milano 1120 km – Bologna 1335 km – Ancona 1550 km – Pescara 1710 km – Foggia 1890 km – Bari 2019 km – **Brindisi 2135 km**

London – Milano 1120 km – Bologna 1335 km – Ancona 1550 km – ferry to Zadar – Split 1707 km – **Dubrovnik 1930 km**

London – Harwich 130 km – ferry to Oostende – Bruxelles 245 km – Köln 470 km – Frankfurt 640 km – München 1040 km – Trieste 1510 km – Split 1890 km – **Dubrovnik 2110 km**

London – Harwich 130 km – ferry to Oostende – Bruxelles 245 km – Köln 470 km – Frankfurt 640 km – Wien 1385 km – Budapest 1655 km – Beograd 2060 km – Sofia 2450 km – Istanbul 1310 km – **Ankara 3450 km**

London – Harwich 130 km – ferry to Esbjerg – København 415 km – Helsingør 460 km – ferry to Helsingborg – Stockhom 1025 km – ferry to Turku/Åbo – **Helsinki/Helsingfors 1190 km**

Roads to the North Cape, see Tour tips.

London – Harwich 130 km – ferry to Esbjerg – Frederikshavn 405 km – ferry to Oslo 405 km or Larvik 405 km – **Oslo 535 km**

London – Dover 120 km or Harwich 130 km – ferry to Oostende or Zeebrugge – Antwerpen 245 km – Hamburg 820 km – Puttgarden 155 km – ferry to Rødby – **København 1125 km**

London – Harwich 130 km – ferry to Göteborg

London – Harwich 130 km – ferry to Hoek van Holland – Hannover 600 km – Berliner Ring 835 km – Poznan 1130 km – Warszawa 1435 km – **Moskva 3000 km**

London – Harwich 130 km – ferry to Göteborg – Stockholm 585 km – ferry to Leningrad – **Moskva 1330 km**

DISTANCE CHART (KM)

	Amsterdam	Athinai	Basel	Beograd	Berlin	Bruxelles	Bucureşti	Budapest	Frankfurt	Genève	Hamburg	Helsingfors	Istanbul	København	Lisboa	London	Madrid	Malaga	Milano	München	Nice	Oslo	Paris	Praha	Roma	Sofia	Stockholm	Warszawa	Venezia	Wien
Amsterdam	–	2820	760	1800	690	200	2430	1490	460	1040	440	1520	2780	750	2270	350	1760	2340	1180	950	1440	950	510	910	1770	2190	1350	1220	1310	1130
Athinai	2820	–	2490	1180	2040	3030	1230	1640	2620	2700	2910	3990	1200	3220	2880	3220	4170	4470	2300	2230	2560	3420	3060	2210	1420	870	3820	2310	2030	1900
Basel	760	2490	–	1380	860	550	2000	1830	330	260	820	1900	2360	1130	2230	890	1640	2070	380	390	650	1330	580	730	970	1770	1730	1350	530	840
Beograd	1800	1180	1380	–	1050	1790	730	400	1380	1460	1790	2160	950	2090	3370	2070	2790	3230	1060	990	1350	2290	1820	970	1320	380	2690	1080	790	680
Berlin	690	2040	860	1050	–	790	1490	640	560	1140	290	1110	2260	370	2890	880	2360	2900	1110	590	1400	970	1130	330	1530	1440	940	580	1080	660
Bruxelles	200	3030	550	1790	790	–	2400	1400	410	820	620	1700	2730	930	2290	250	1560	2130	960	800	1240	1020	310	910	1550	2140	1530	1330	1230	1130
Bucureşti	2430	1230	2000	730	1490	2400	–	850	1800	1960	2220	4300	700	1860	4120	2580	3530	3710	1780	1700	1310	2730	2400	1470	2150	410	2430	1800	1500	1150
Budapest	1490	1640	1830	400	640	1400	850	–	990	1300	1370	2450	1340	1010	3280	1670	2710	3080	1010	690	1000	1880	1560	580	1350	780	1580	680	820	270
Frankfurt	460	2620	330	1380	560	410	1800	990	–	590	490	1570	2320	800	2240	640	1840	2400	800	395	1000	1020	580	500	1310	1740	1400	1100	860	730
Genève	1040	2700	260	1460	1140	820	1960	1300	590	–	1080	2160	2400	1390	1950	970	1420	1830	400	585	430	1590	550	1040	950	1720	1990	1550	680	1030
Hamburg	440	2910	820	1790	290	620	2220	1370	490	1080	–	1070	2730	310	2720	570	2230	2750	1200	780	1480	510	920	310	1790	2170	910	890	1260	1100
Helsingfors	1520	3990	1900	2160	1110	1700	4300	2450	1570	2160	1070	–	3810	770	3800	2230	3310	3820	2280	1860	2560	690	1990	1440	2870	2910	170	360	2340	2180
Istanbul	2780	1200	2360	950	2260	2730	700	1340	2320	2400	2730	3810	–	3040	4360	3040	3690	4120	2020	1930	2750	2840	2750	1890	2470	590	3650	1940	1730	1570
København	750	3220	1130	2090	370	930	1860	1010	800	1390	310	770	3040	–	3030	400	2540	3060	1510	1090	1790	590	1230	700	1840	2450	605	960	1570	1410
Lisboa	2270	2880	2230	3370	2890	2290	4120	3280	2240	1950	2720	3800	4360	3030	–	2280	660	630	1285	2540	1920	3230	1790	2910	1810	3750	3630	3630	2650	3000
London	350	3220	890	2070	880	250	2580	1670	640	970	570	2230	3040	400	2280	–	1625	2230	1120	1130	1350	1270	410	1310	1710	1750	1480	1440	1600	1380
Madrid	1760	4170	1640	2790	2360	1560	3530	2710	1840	1420	2230	3310	3690	2540	660	1625	–	580	1570	2000	1790	2740	1315	2290	2040	3070	3140	2930	2000	2420
Malaga	2340	4470	2070	3230	2900	2130	3710	3080	2400	1830	2750	3820	4120	3060	630	2230	580	–	2100	2570	1790	3260	1830	2930	2470	3530	3800	3510	2450	2920
Milano	1180	2300	380	1060	1110	960	1780	1010	800	400	1200	2280	2020	1510	1285	1120	1570	2100	–	570	320	1710	860	865	590	1440	2110	1510	280	820
München	950	2230	390	990	590	800	1700	690	395	585	780	1860	1930	1090	2540	1130	2000	2570	570	–	570	1290	850	320	960	1690	1690	990	470	440
Nice	1440	2560	650	1350	1400	1240	1310	1000	1000	430	1480	2560	2750	1790	1920	1350	1790	1790	320	570	–	1990	940	1230	690	1750	1280	1470	1770	1160
Oslo	950	3420	1330	2290	970	1020	2730	1880	1000	1590	510	690	2840	590	3230	1270	2740	3260	1710	1290	1990	–	1430	1260	2340	2680	530	960	1770	1170
Paris	510	3060	580	1820	1130	310	2400	1560	580	550	920	1990	2750	1230	1790	410	1315	1830	860	850	940	1430	–	1000	1400	2170	1830	1720	1130	1320
Praha	910	2210	730	970	330	910	1470	580	500	1040	310	1440	1890	700	2910	1310	2290	2930	865	320	1230	1260	1000	–	1290	1360	1280	1470	780	300
Roma	1770	1420	970	1320	1530	1550	2150	1350	1310	950	1790	2870	2470	1840	1810	1710	2040	2470	590	960	690	2340	1400	1290	–	1670	2700	1830	530	1140
Sofia	2190	870	1770	380	1440	2140	410	780	1740	1720	2170	2910	590	2450	3750	1750	3070	3530	1440	1690	1750	2680	2170	1360	1670	–	3080	1470	1170	1040
Stockholm	1350	3820	1730	2690	940	1530	2430	1580	1400	1990	910	170	3650	605	3630	1480	3140	3800	2110	1690	1280	530	1830	1280	2700	3080	–	420	1870	2010
Warszawa	1220	2310	1350	1080	580	1330	1800	680	1100	1550	890	360	1940	960	3630	1440	2930	3510	1510	990	1470	960	1720	1470	1830	1470	420	–	1330	690
Venezia	1310	2030	530	790	1080	1230	1500	820	860	680	1260	2340	1730	1570	2650	1600	2000	2450	280	470	1770	1770	1130	780	530	1170	1870	1330	–	860
Wien	1130	1900	840	680	660	1130	1150	270	730	1030	1100	2180	1570	1410	3000	1380	2420	2920	820	440	1160	1170	1320	300	1140	1040	2010	690	860	–

Index to place names

The index refers to the most important places mentioned the route descriptions on pp 8–425.

Comments about the distance chart on the opposite page.

To convert km to miles, delete the last number and multiply the remainder by 6.2.

Distances have been based on the most frequently used routes.

Distances from London to the Continent use the Calais, Oostende and Hook of Holland gateways. Distances from Britain to Scandinavia are based on the Harwich – Esbjerg route.

Distances from southeastern Europe to Scandinavia are via Hamburg; those from Prague and Berlin are via Sassnitz or Warnemünde, and from Warsaw to Stockholm and Helsinki via Gdańsk.

Distances from Oslo to the Continent are based on the route via Frederikshavn.

Distances from western Europe to Helsinki are via Stockholm. The Travemünde – Helsinki ferries shorten the distance by about 1000 km.

INDEX